CONCEPTUAL AND CONTEXTUAL PERSPECTIVES ON THE MODERN LAW OF TREATIES

In recent years there has been a flourishing body of work on the Law of Treaties, crucial for all fields within public international law. However, scholarship on modern treaty law falls into two distinct strands which have not previously been effectively synthesized. One concerns the investigation of concepts which are fundamental to or inherent in the law of treaties generally—such as consent, object and purpose, breach of obligation and provisional application—while the other focuses upon the application of treaties and of treaty law in particular substantive (e.g. human rights, international humanitarian law, investment protection, environmental regulation) or institutional contexts (including the Security Council, the World Health Organization, the International Labour Organization and the World Trade Organization). This volume represents the culmination of a series of collaborative explorations by leading experts into the operation, development and effectiveness of the modern law of treaties, as viewed through these contrasting perspectives.

MICHAEL BOWMAN is Associate Professor of Law and Director of the Treaty Centre at the University of Nottingham.

DINO KRITSIOTIS is Professor of Public International Law and Head of the International Humanitarian Law Unit in the Human Rights Law Centre at the University of Nottingham.

T0393885

CONCEPTUAL AND CONTEXTUAL PERSPECTIVES ON THE MODERN LAW OF TREATIES

Edited by

MICHAEL BOWMAN

University of Nottingham

DINO KRITSIOTIS

University of Nottingham

CAMBRIDGE
UNIVERSITY PRESS

CAMBRIDGE
UNIVERSITY PRESS

University Printing House, Cambridge CB2 8BS, United Kingdom

One Liberty Plaza, 20th Floor, New York, NY 10006, USA

477 Williamstown Road, Port Melbourne, VIC 3207, Australia

314-321, 3rd Floor, Plot 3, Splendor Forum, Jasola District Centre, New Delhi - 110025, India

79 Anson Road, #06-04/06, Singapore 079906

Cambridge University Press is part of the University of Cambridge.

It furthers the University's mission by disseminating knowledge in the pursuit of education, learning and research at the highest international levels of excellence.

www.cambridge.org
Information on this title: www.cambridge.org/9781108978521
DOI: 10.1017/9781316179031

© Cambridge University Press 2018

First published 2018
First paperback edition 2020

A catalogue record for this publication is available from the British Library

Library of Congress Cataloging in Publication data
Names: Bowman, Michael | Kritsiotis, Dino.
Title: Conceptual and contextual perspectives on the modern law of treaties /
edited by Michael Bowman, University of Nottingham; Dino Kritsiotis,
University of Nottingham.
Description: Cambridge, United Kingdom ; New York, NY, USA :
Cambridge University Press, 2018.
Identifiers: LCCN 2017024707 | ISBN 9781107100527
Subjects: LCSH: Treaties. | International organization. | International obligations.
Classification: LCC KZ1301 .C66 2017 | DDC 341.3/7–dc23
LC record available at https://lccn.loc.gov/2017024707

ISBN 978-1-107-10052-7 Hardback
ISBN 978-1-108-97852-1 Paperback

CONTENTS

v

CONTRIBUTORS

FRANK BERMAN KCMG QC Barrister and international arbitrator; formerly Legal Adviser, Foreign & Commonwealth Office, United Kingdom; Visiting Professor of International Law, University of Oxford and University of Cape Town; Member of the Permanent Court of Arbitration.

MICHAEL BOWMAN Associate Professor of Law, University of Nottingham; Director of the Treaty Centre, University of Nottingham.

CATHERINE BRÖLMANN Associate Professor of Law, Amsterdam Center for International Law, University of Amsterdam.

IRINA BUGA Associate in International Arbitration at De Brauw Blackstone Westbroek, Amsterdam.

CHRISTINE M. CHINKIN Emerita Professor of International Law and Director of the Centre on Women, Peace and Security, London School of Economics and Political Science.

MATTHEW CRAVEN Professor of International Law and Director of the Centre for the Study of Colonialism, Empire and International Law, School of African & Oriental Studies, University of London.

OLUFEMI ELIAS Legal Adviser and Director, Organization for the Prohibition of Chemical Weapons; Visiting Professor of Law, School of Law, Queen Mary University of London.

MALGOSIA FITZMAURICE Professor of Public International Law, School of Law, Queen Mary University of London.

DUNCAN FRENCH Professor of International Law and Head of Lincoln Law School, University of Lincoln.

RICHARD GARDINER Visiting Professor of Law, Faculty of Laws, University College London.

EGLE GRANZIERA Legal Officer, Governing Bodies and International Law, Office of the Legal Counsel, World Health Organization.

FRANÇOISE J. HAMPSON Professor Emerita, University of Essex.

JAN KLABBERS Academy Professor (Martti Ahtisaari Chair), University of Helsinki; Visiting Research Professor at Erasmus Law School, Rotterdam.

PANOS KOUTRAKOS Professor of European Union Law and Jean Monnet Professor of European Union Law, City University London.

DINO KRITSIOTIS Professor of Public International Law, University of Nottingham; Head of the International Humanitarian Law Unit, Human Rights Law Centre, University of Nottingham.

RANDALL LESAFFER Professor of Legal History, Tilburg University and University of Leuven.

DOROTA LOST-SIEMINSKA Head, Legal Affairs Office of the International Maritime Organization, London.

JEREMY MCBRIDE Barrister, Monckton Chambers, London; Visiting Professor, Central European University, Budapest.

BARBARA MILTNER Wydick Fellow, University of California Davis School of Law.

DANIEL MOECKLI Assistant Professor of Public International Law and Constitutional Law, University of Zurich.

JULIAN DAVIS MORTENSON Professor of Law, University of Michigan Law School.

DAVID M. ONG Professor of International and Environmental Law, Nottingham Law School, Nottingham Trent University.

JOOST PAUWELYN Professor of International Law, Graduate Institute of International and Development Studies, Geneva; Murase Visiting Professor of Law, Georgetown Law Center, Washington, DC.

ANNELIESE QUAST MERTSCH Associate Legal Officer at the United Nations Mechanism for International Criminal Tribunals (UNMICT), The Hague.

KAREN SCOTT Professor of Law and Head of the School of Law, University of Canterbury, New Zealand.

STEVEN A. SOLOMON Principal Legal Officer, Governing Bodies and International Law, Office of the Legal Counsel, World Health Organization.

LISA TABASSI Head of Legal Services, Organization for Security and Co-operation in Europe (OSCE); formerly Chief of Legal Services Section, Preparatory Commission for the Comprehensive Nuclear-Test-Ban Treaty Organization (CTBTO) and Legal Officer, Organization for the Prohibition of Chemical Weapons (OPCW).

CHRISTIAN J. TAMS Professor of International Law, School of Law, University of Glasgow; Academic Member of Matrix, London.

ANNE TREBILCOCK Former Legal Adviser of the International Labour Organization; Member of the Asian Development Bank Administrative Tribunal and of the Centre de Droit International, University of Paris Nanterre-La Défense.

ISABELLE VAN DAMME Référendaire, Chambers of Advocate General Sharpston, Court of Justice of the European Union; Visiting Lecturer, Université Catholique de Louvain.

MICHAEL WAIBEL University Senior Lecturer in International Law, Fellow of Jesus College and Deputy Director of the Lauterpacht Centre for International Law, University of Cambridge.

NIGEL D. WHITE Professor of Public International Law and Head of the School of Law, University of Nottingham.

ELIZABETH WILMSHURST CMG Distinguished Fellow of the Royal Institute of International Affairs, London; Visiting Professor, University College London.

SIR MICHAEL WOOD KCMG Barrister, 20 Essex Street, London; Member of the International Law Commission.

FOREWORD

Participants in the contemporary debate about the sources of international law will probably still agree that the international treaty appears as a resting pole in an environment marked by decomposition of established truths and loss of orientation. Just observe the current discussion on the theory and doctrine of customary international law: a dance-floor on which anything goes, few bother about traditional steps, wishful thinking reigns and I certainly don't envy the International Law Commission in its effort to have people fall again into the familiar foxtrot of the two elements ...

Compared to this disquieting picture, treaties and their law do strike us as solid, stable, orderly. Law-making by treaty may appear to the most progressive within our profession as 'medieval', but if that is so, it feels good to live in such a medieval world. As to practical relevance, it is the treaty that for a long time has enjoyed priority, and at least for the practitioner, this priority is here to stay. For many decades now, writers have witnessed a movement away from customary international law towards treaties. This movement has grown so strong that nowadays one needs to emphasise that international custom does still have a role to play. In the practical business of international legal relations, treaties still are the unchallenged backbone, workhorse, coalface, ('sadly overworked') instrument, to name just a few terms by which they are being appreciated in the literature. And, of course, the figures are truly staggering: more than 50,000 treaties having been registered with the United Nations and its predecessor.

On the other hand, recent doctrine has noted a marked increase in informal norm-setting, quite apart from the dilution of custom mentioned above, and thus another cause of 'thinning' international law. According to a growing stream of voices, also among practitioners, the difference between legally binding and 'soft' commitments is not as sharp as traditional international lawyers claim it to be. Against this, a call for a return to formalism is building up. I would suggest that this provides an element explaining the renaissance of interest in the law of treaties on the part of doctrine, witnessed by the present book: a certain defensive stature, a doctrinal trench dug to preserve the (relative) stability and formalism of the treaty.

Developments in the literature on the law of treaties in the wake of the adoption of the Vienna Convention on the Law of Treaties of 23 May 1969 appear to confirm this observation. There was a first wave, modest in quantity but laden with authenticity, stemming from veterans of the International Law Commission's and the Vienna Conferences' labours – above all the works of Paul Reuter, Shabtai Rosenne and Ian Sinclair. But what I find striking is that following that early reaction to the successful codification exercise, while, as could be expected, large numbers of articles and monographs on certain topical issues of the law of treaties were being published all along, for several decades no great comprehensive treatise appeared. This abstinence came to an end only in 2006, when Olivier Corten and Pierre Klein published the French two-volume edition of their commentary on the 1969 and 1986 Vienna Conventions, followed in 2011 by an English edition to which no fewer than eighty authors contributed. In 2009, Mark Villiger published his single-author commentary on the 1969 Convention, while the commentary edited by Oliver Dörr and Kirsten Schmalenbach and published in 2012 is the joint effort of twelve scholars. This sudden wave of commentaries, accompanied by the monograph on *Modern Treaty Law and Practice* by Anthony Aust for Cambridge University Press in 2000, was soon joined by a number of collective works, like *The Law of Treaties beyond the Vienna Convention*, a (beautifully) camouflaged *Festschrift* for Giorgio Gaja edited by Enzo Cannizzaro in 2011; *The Oxford Guide to Treaties* edited by Duncan Hollis, which appeared in 2012; and, most recently, in 2014, the *Research Handbook on the Law of Treaties* organised by Christian Tams, Antonios Tzanakopoulos and Andreas Zimmermann. The present anthology on *Conceptual and Contextual Perspectives on the Modern Law of Treaties* now completes – and, in a way to be explained later, tops – this impressive display of scholarship.

The reader will have noticed that among the works just cited, several titles put the emphasis on a 'modern' law of treaties. This is not just a coincidental use of smart adjectives. At a first, positive-law level, it is the recognition that the text of the Vienna Convention does not exhaust the law of treaties in its entirety, its 'infinite variety', and, of course, that this law has not remained frozen in the almost five decades since the Convention was adopted. We have to remember that, from the outset, the International Law Commission's project was designed to be modest and embrace only those issues that had a chance of success. This explains the limited scope of the Convention – see, for instance, its Article 73 – but also that the Commission left unanswered a number of important questions also within what everybody would regard as the core of the law of treaties. To give just one example: I find it no less than shocking that the Vienna Convention left open what was to happen with a reservation to a multilateral treaty clearly incompatible with that treaty's object and purpose and thus allowed a view to appear respectable according to which the Convention could outlaw certain reservations and then go on to subject such impermissible exceptions to precisely the same regime as harmless ones. It took decades until Alain Pellet's and the International Law Commission's low-profile 'Guidelines' came up with a reasonably satisfactory answer, without calling the spade a spade and the Convention's omission to regulate the fate of impermissible reservations a major loophole.

But the recent 'modern' works on the law of treaties intend to go further than just fill gaps. The ways in which they intend to go beyond the technical debate on how to make the law of treaties more complete and more smooth comes out beautifully in the very title of the present collection – the emphasis now is on conceptuality and contextuality: *conceptuality* in the sense of attempting to identify and explore concepts and mechanisms recurrently encountered, but straddling various law-of-treaties themes or extending beyond the scope of that law, in recognition of the inherent interdependence of the law of treaties and other branches of international law, like the law of State responsibility; and *contextuality* aiming at a depiction of treaty law as it operates in a variety of fields, like human rights, disarmament or protection of the environment.

It is to this second point – of contextuality – that the present work accomplishes a truly remarkable contribution. To my knowledge, nowhere else has the law of treaties been so thoroughly shown at work in the various branches of international legal regulation and in the context of major international organizations. The book devotes no fewer than fifteen chapters – about half of its content – to the task of demonstrating how the law of treaties applies or undergoes specific modifications, both in fields like human rights, international criminal or world trade law and in the functioning of international organizations. Two of these contributions caught my particular attention: Christine Chinkin's virtuous treatment of (a favourite subject of mine) the specificities of human rights treaties and Sir Michael Wood's case study on

Security Council Resolution 687 (1991) and the law of treaties, demonstrating the differences between treaty interpretation and the interpretation of Security Council resolutions and concluding that '[i]t was for the Security Council, not one or more members of the "coalition of the willing", to determine whether there was a material breach [of Resolution 687] ... '.

In conclusion, the present collection does fulfil the promise of uncovering the dynamics of the modern law of treaties and of determining how particular instruments function within that system. I am convinced that it will trigger further intra-disciplinary research and thus contribute to solidify that tower of strength, the international treaty.

Bruno Simma

PREFACE AND ACKNOWLEDGEMENTS

This project was formally inaugurated by the University of Nottingham Treaty Centre in the spring of 2011. It sought to bring together two distinct dimensions to the study and practice of the modern law of treaties – what were called respectively the 'conceptual' and 'contextual' perspectives – which are further explained in the Introduction to this work. However, at its heart, the project was a collaborative enterprise, not only providing an intellectual home of sorts for all of its authors but encouraging them to exchange ideas, anecdotes and interpretations – and to do so on a regular and ongoing basis. To this end, we were incredibly fortunate to benefit from the wonderful generosity of our then Head of School, Professor Stephen H. Bailey, to host two stimulating workshops for authors – the first of these was held at University Park, University of Nottingham, in September 2012, and, prompted by the immense success of that meeting, a second in January 2013 at Essex Court Chambers, in Lincoln's Inn Fields, London. We are most indebted to one of our contributors, Sir Frank Berman KCMG QC, for facilitating and hosting that second meeting, as we are to Gordon Pollock QC, then Head of Chambers, for kindly agreeing to the use of that venue.

The project could not have survived, and it certainly would not have seen the light of day, without the impressive and efficient assistance we received throughout from the secretarial team at the University of Nottingham. Particular mention should be made of Anne Crump, Ann Chudleigh, Jo Grabowksi, Kobie Neita, Vicky Spencer and Helen Wade, who stoically kept on top of a vast correspondence, ferried draft chapters back and forth and kept the work environment alive with good cheer when there were many other demands on their time.

We wish also to thank Cambridge University Press and, in particular, Elizabeth Spicer for expertly steering this project to its conclusion; she did so with enormous enthusiasm and commitment, and we are delighted that she shared in the vision of this ambitious work from the outset. And, with her characteristic professionalism and endless charm,

Finola O'Sullivan has overseen the entire project to its ultimate conclusion; her support has been invaluable to us, too, over these many years.

Our final expression of gratitude is to our authors, who produced a series of first-rate essays that, we are confident, will make its mark on the literature of treaties for a good while to come. They have also participated in a process that, we hope, will put front and centre the importance of a methodological commitment to the pursuit of research on the law of treaties that takes on both the conceptual and contextual perspectives explored in the chapters that follow. However, without exception, they have also shown an immense patience with the progress of publication, and that has meant much to us as editors of this work. The fact is that, while we kept to the structure of our original vision for the project, as it got under way, we gave in to various temptations to conscript new authors and chapters to the cause, and this resulted in various delays, but we believe the volume has been enriched immeasurably. And we took frequent advantage of the editorial prerogative to probe contributors for more detail on the themes and arguments being prepared for a wider readership; the publication of this volume must provide them considerable respite that they no longer stand at risk of receiving our voluminous and often very detailed prods and enquiries. That said, we were profoundly encouraged when one of our contributors was moved to remark at the London meeting of January 2013 that the extent of editorial engagement with contributors and their contributions really meant that this project had acquired a 'soul' of its own – that it stood apart from other similar projects of collective endeavour.

This has all meant that the project has taken a while longer to come to fruition, with chapters presented to us in their final form on a rolling basis from October 2013 onwards. Contributors were subsequently offered a chance to make limited updates to their chapters, but not all of them were able to avail themselves of this opportunity. The nature of the exercise has thus precluded us from setting a single deadline for the law and material contained in each contribution, and we would ask readers to bear this point in mind as they set to reading the chapters that we are delighted to include in this volume.

MJB & DK
Nottingham, December 2017

ABBREVIATIONS

AC	Appeal Cases
AFDI	Annuaire Français de Droit International
AJIL	American Journal of International Law
AJIL Supp.	Supplement of the American Journal of International Law
ALR	Australian Law Reports
African HRLJ	African Human Rights Law Journal
Am. Pol. Sci. Rev.	American Political Science Review
Am. Univ. Int'l L. Rev.	American University International Law Review
Ann. Digest	Annual Digest of Public International Law
Annual Rev. Earth & Planetary Sci.	Annual Review of Earth and Planetary Sciences
Asian J. WTO & Int'l. Health L. & Pol'y	Asian Journal of World Trade Organization and International Health Law and Policy
Asian YbIL	Asian Yearbook of International Law
Austrian Rev. Int'l & European L.	Austrian Review of International and European Law
BYbIL	British Yearbook of International Law
Boston Coll. Int'l & Comp. L. Rev.	Boston College International and Comparative Law Review
Brooklyn JIL	Brooklyn Journal of International Law
CETS	Council of Europe Treaty Series
CLR	Commonwealth Law Reports
CTS	Consolidated Treaty Series
CYbELS	Cambridge Yearbook of European Legal Studies
California WILJ	California Western International Law Journal

Cambridge JICL	Cambridge Journal of International and Comparative Law
Cambridge Law J.	Cambridge Law Journal
Canadian YbIL	Canadian Yearbook of International Law
Chicago JIL	Chicago Journal of International Law
China Oceans L. Rev.	China Oceans Law Review
Chinese JIL	Chinese Journal of International Law
Colorado J. Int'l Env. Law & Policy	Colorado Journal of International Environmental Law and Policy
Columbia JTL	Columbia Journal of Transnational Law
Columbia L. Rev.	Columbia Law Review
Common Market L. Rev.	Common Market Law Review
Comp. & Int'l L.J. Southern Africa	Comparative and International Law Journal of Southern Africa
Comp. Labor L. & Policy J.	Comparative Labor Law and Policy Journal
Connecticut JIL	Connecticut Journal of International Law
Const. Comment.	Constitutional Commentary
Cornell ILJ	Cornell International Law Journal
Cornell Law Q.	Cornell Law Quarterly
Dalhouise Law J.	Dalhouise Law Journal
Denver JILP	Denver Journal of International Law and Policy
Dept. of State Bull.	Department of State Bulletin
ECR	European Court Reports
EHRR	European Human Rights Reports
EJIL	European Journal of International Law
EJLS	European Journal of Legal Studies
ER	English Reports
ETS	European Treaty Series
EYB	European Yearbook
Ecology L. Quarterly	Ecology Law Quarterly
Emory ILR	Emory International Law Review
Encyclopaedia PIL	Encyclopaedia of Public International Law
European L. Rev.	European Law Review
European Rev. Private L.	European Review of Private Law
Finnish YbIL	Finnish Yearbook of International Law
Fordham ILJ	Fordham International Law Journal
Fordham L. Rev.	Fordham Law Review

Ga. J. Int'l & Comp. L.	Georgia Journal of International and Comparative Law
Georgetown JIL	Georgetown Journal of International Law
Georgetown Law J.	Georgetown Law Journal
George Wash. JIL & Econ.	George Washington Journal of International Law and Economics
German YbIL	German Yearbook of International Law
Goettingen JIL	Goettingen Journal of International Law
HRLR	Human Rights Law Review
Hague Recueil	Collected Courses of the Hague Academy of International Law
Hague YbIL	Hague Yearbook of International Law
Harvard ILJ	Harvard International Law Journal
Harvard L. Rev.	Harvard Law Review
ICJ Rep.	International Court of Justice Reports
ICLQ	International and Comparative Law Quarterly
ICLR	International Community Law Review
ICSID Review	Foreign Investment Law Journal
ILM	International Legal Materials
ILR	International Law Reports
ITLOS Rep.	International Tribunal on the Law of the Sea Reports
Indian JIL	Indian Journal of International Law
Industrial Law J.	Industrial Law Journal
Inter-Am. L. Rev.	Inter-American Law Review
Int'l Aff.	Journal of International Affairs
Int'l J. Comp. Labour L. & Industrial Relations	International Journal of Comparative Labour Law and Industrial Relations
Int'l J. of Marine & Coastal L.	International Journal of Marine and Coastal Law
Int'l Rev. Red Cross	International Review of the Red Cross
Int'l Negotiation	International Negotiation
International Labour Rev.	International Labour Review
Irish YbIL	Irish Yearbook of International Law
Israel L. Rev.	Israel Law Review
Italian YbIL	Italian Yearbook of International Law
JIWLP	Journal of International Wildlife Law and Policy
Japanese YbIL	Japanese Yearbook of International Law

J. Am. Med. Assoc.	Journal of the American Medical Association
J. Bio. Ed.	Journal of Biological Education
J. Conflict & Sec. L.	Journal of Conflict and Security Law
J. Env. L.	Journal of Environmental Law
J. History of Ideas	Journal of the History of Ideas
J. History Int'l L.	Journal of the History of International Law
J. Industrial Rel.	Journal of Industrial Relations
J. Inst. Theor. Econ.	Journal of the Institutional and Theoretical Economics
J. Int'l Crim. Just.	Journal of International Criminal Justice
J. Int'l Econ. L.	Journal of International Economic Law
J. Law, Medicine & Ethics	Journal of Law, Medicine and Ethics
J. Maritime L. & Comm.	Journal of Maritime Law and Commerce
J. Politics	Journal of Politics
J. World Trade	Journal of World Trade
Kobe J. Law	Kobe Journal of Law
LNOJ	League of Nations Official Journal
LNTS	League of Nations Treaty Series
LQR	Law Quarterly Review
LR	Law Reports
Law & Contemp. Prob.	Law and Contemporary Problems
Law & Practice Int'l Courts & Tribs.	Law and Practice of International Courts and Tribunals
Legal History Rev.	Legal History Review
Leiden JIL	Leiden Journal of International Law
Lloyd's Rep.	Lloyd's Law Reports
Maastricht JECL	Maastricht Journal of European and Comparative Law
Maine L. Rev.	Maine Law Review
Max Planck Yb. UN Law	Max Planck Yearbook of United Nations Law
Melbourne JIL	Melbourne Journal of International Law
Michigan JIL	Michigan Journal of International Law
Michigan L. Rev.	Michigan Law Review
Michigan State Int'l L. Rev.	Michigan State International Law Review
Modern L. Rev.	Modern Law Review
N.Y.U. J. Int'l L. & Pol.	New York University Journal of International Law and Politics
N.Y. Univ. L. Rev.	New York University Law Review

N.Z. J. Public & Int'l L.	New Zealand Journal of Public International Law
Netherlands ILR	Netherlands International Law Review
Netherlands YbIL	Netherlands Yearbook of International Law
Nonproliferation Rev.	Nonproliferation Review
Nordic JIL	Nordic Journal of International Law
NZLR	New Zealand Law Reports
OJ (OJEU)	Official Journal of the European Union
OJLS	Oxford Journal of Legal Studies
ÖZöR	Österreichische Zeitschrift für öffentliches Recht
Ocean Dev. & Int'l L.	Ocean Development and International Law
PAULTS	Pan-American Union Law and Treaty Series
Policy Studies J.	Policy Studies Journal
Proceedings ASIL	Proceedings of the American Society of International Law
Proc. Nat. Acad. Sci.	Proceedings of the National Academy of Sciences
Q. Rev. Biology	Quarterly Review of Biology
Quinnipiac L. Rev.	Quinnipiac Law Review
RIAA	Reports of International Arbitral Awards
RBDI	Revue belge de droit international
RGDIP	Revue Générale de droit international public
Revue de droit de l'ULB	Revue de droit de l'Université libre de Bruxelles
SUR Int'l J. on Hum. Rts.	SUR – International Journal on Human Rights
Santa Clara J. Int'l L.	Santa Clara Journal of International Law
Stanford L. Rev.	Stanford Law Review
Stat.	United States Statutes at Large
Sydney L. Rev.	Sydney Law Review
Syracuse J. Int'l L. & Comm.	Syracuse Journal of International Law and Commerce
TIAS	Treaties and Other International Acts Series (U.S. Dept. of State)
Texas ILJ	Texas International Law Journal
Texas L. Rev.	Texas Law Review

Transactions G. Soc.	Transactions of the Grotius Society
Tulane L. Rev.	Tulane Law Review
UC Davis JILP	University of Davis Journal of International Law and Policy
UKTS	United Kingdom Treaty Series
UNJYB	United Nations Juridical Yearbook
UNTS	United Nations Treaty Series
UST	United States Treaties and Other International Agreements
Univ. Cincinnati L. Rev.	University of Cincinnati Law Review
Univ. Tasmania L. Rev.	University of Tasmania Law Review
Vanderbilt JTL	Vanderbilt Journal of Transnational Law
Virginia JIL	Virginia Journal of International Law
W. Trade Rev.	World Trade Review
Wayne L. Rev.	Wayne Law Review
Wm. & Mary L. Rev.	William and Mary Law Review
Yale Hum. Rts. & Dev. Law J.	Yale Human Rights and Development Law Journal
Yale JIL	Yale Journal of International Law
Yale Law J.	Yale Law Journal
YbECHR	Yearbook of the European Convention on Human Rights
YbEL	Yearbook of European Law
YbIHL	Yearbook of International Humanitarian Law
YbILC	Yearbook of the International Law Commission
ZaöRV	Zeitschrift für ausländisches öffentliches Recht und Völkerrecht

Introduction: The Interplay of Concept, Context and Content in the Modern Law of Treaties

MICHAEL BOWMAN AND DINO KRITSIOTIS

According to Article 38(1) of the Statute of the International Court of Justice,[1] the Court is mandated to resolve all disputes that come before it by reference to certain well-established bodies of legal norms, most notably (i) international treaties or conventions, on the grounds that they generate rules which have been explicitly recognised by the parties; (ii) international custom, as evidenced by general practices which are accepted as legally binding and (iii) general principles of law recognised by the international community as a whole.[2] For the purposes of the international legal system generally, the proposition that custom and treaties represent the primary mechanisms for the creation of legal norms is unlikely to generate much controversy. By contrast, the question of whether either of these sources of legal norms and functions can be said to enjoy primacy *inter se* – and, if so, which – is liable to prove more contentious.

It is clear that the practice of treaty-making is one of considerable longevity, being commonly asserted to date back to the stone-inscribed boundary treaty concluded around 2100 BC between the ancient Mesopotamian kingdoms of Lagash and Umma.[3] Yet treaties of themselves cannot really be expected to produce meaningful normative effects in the absence of some pre-existing, or at least co-emergent, customary conception regarding their inherent capacity to bind the parties to them: to put it another way, pacts alone are of little service in the absence of

---

[1] The Statute is, of course, an integral part of the 1945 Charter of the United Nations: 1 UNTS 16.

[2] Academic writings and court decisions are, of course, also mentioned in the Statute as 'subsidiary means for the determination of rules of law'.

[3] See, e.g., M. N. Shaw, *International Law* (Cambridge: Cambridge University Press, 8th ed., 2017), p. 10.

concomitant recognition that *pacta sunt servanda*.[4] From that perspective, then, custom (from which this fundamental principle is ultimately derived) must perhaps be regarded as the *primordial* source of all international obligation. On the other hand, any discussion of custom itself is certain to turn before long to its rather crude and cumbersome nature and relative unsuitability to the needs of modern society, which typically require the crafting of technically complex and structurally detailed bodies of rules in written form in order to achieve the sophisticated mode of normativity that the situation is likely to demand. As a result, treaties have for most practical purposes come to secure pride of place within the global legal order, enhancing their claim currently to be regarded as the primary (or perhaps 'prime-ordinal') source of international rights and obligations.

Even here, however, the practical utility – indeed, the very viability in principle – of such instruments is ultimately dependent upon the co-existence of a supporting (though ideally no less detailed and highly elaborated) body of norms to regulate the conclusion, activation, application, interpretation, development, enforcement, duration and possible extinction of treaties themselves: it therefore comes as no surprise that such a body of rules is now long established, having been generated originally by customary means, before itself being progressively translated into treaty form, from the late 1960s onwards, under the aegis of the United Nations' International Law Commission.[5] Perhaps, then, treaties and custom should now be regarded as co-existing, of necessity, in a state of profound and permanent interaction and co-dependence. Whatever the truth of the matter, the absolutely central and critical role played by the law of treaties within the contemporary international legal order can scarcely be doubted.

Yet if treaties, and perhaps more importantly the body of legal norms by which they themselves are regulated, are to continue to serve the interests of the international community to maximum effect, it would seem essential that they be subject to continuous evaluation and appraisal of the most radical and rigorous kind. In the light of this consideration,

---

[4] That is to say, that treaty commitments are to be complied with, which constitutes the foundational principle of treaty law: see the second preambular recital of the 1969 Vienna Convention on the Law of Treaties, 1155 UNTS 331.

[5] For access to the entire product of the Commission's work on the law of treaties, see the *Analytical Guide to Work of the ILC* (http://legal.un.org/ilc/guide/gfra.htm), Topic 1. For an earlier, purely regional, attempt at codification, see the Pan-American Union's 1928 Havana Convention on Treaties, reproduced in *AJIL Supp.*, 29 (1935), 1205–1207.

the relative paucity of scholarly writing on the subject of the law of treaties, at least until very recently, must be regarded as somewhat surprising. As far as the English language was concerned, there was, to be sure, one renowned monograph on the old customary law of treaties,[6] and once the law came to be codified, this was supplemented by a couple of basic commentaries on the 1969 Vienna Convention of the Law of Treaties (VCLT) itself,[7] together with a handful of other works on specialised aspects of the subject.[8] Naturally, the law of treaties was also from time to time the subject of attention in the periodical literature.[9] Yet by comparison with other major substantive areas of international law, such as the law of territory and jurisdiction, human rights, the law of the sea, international humanitarian law and so forth – all of which are themselves to a considerable extent treaty-based – the depth and breadth of this body of legal scholarship seemed surprisingly modest, especially in light of the fact that the significance of treaty law is so deep and pervasive across the international legal order as a whole. The position has, however, been radically transformed in recent times by what can only be described as a veritable explosion of writing in this field, with works at every level of generality and specificity having been presented for our edification and enlightenment.[10] No longer can it be claimed, at least with any semblance of justification, that the field of treaty law has been unduly neglected.

***

It is perhaps not surprising that this dramatic proliferation of scholarly activity and attention should have generated some soul-searching of a rather fundamental kind. In particular, no less an authority than Vaughan Lowe, the erstwhile Chichele Professor of Public International

---

[6] A. D. McNair, *The Law of Treaties* (Oxford: Clarendon Press, 1961).

[7] R. D. Kearney and R. E. Dalton, 'The Treaty on Treaties', *AJIL*, 64 (1970), 495–561; T. O. Elias, *The Modern Law of Treaties* (Dobbs Ferry, NY: Oceana, 1974); I. Sinclair, *The Vienna Convention on the Law of Treaties* (Manchester: Manchester University Press, 2nd ed., 1984) and P. Reuter, *Introduction to the Law of Treaties* (London/New York, NY: Pinter Publishers, 2nd ed., 1989). See, further, S. Rosenne, *The Law of Treaties: A Guide to the Legislative History of the Vienna Convention* (Dobbs Ferry, NY: Oceana Publications, 1970).

[8] See, e.g., S. Rosenne, *Breach of Treaty* (Cambridge: Grotius Publications, 1985) and S. Rosenne, *Developments in the Law of Treaties 1945–86* (Cambridge: Cambridge University Press, 1989).

[9] For a selection of seminal articles, see S. Davidson (ed.), *The Law of Treaties* (Aldershot: Ashgate/Dartmouth, 2004).

[10] No attempt will be made here to catalogue these works in full. Invaluable bibliographies can, however, be found at the end of each chapter of D. B. Hollis (ed.), *The Oxford Guide to Treaties* (Oxford: Oxford University Press, 2012).

Law at the University of Oxford, has questioned, in a recent essay,[11] whether convincing justification can any longer be found for the proliferation, or even for the very existence, of works concerning the law of treaties, given that the subject matter to which they relate must now be regarded as a decidedly curious and questionable phenomenon. This judgement is based upon the perception that, while the long familiar body of norms that collectively comprise the law of treaties might be judged to convey 'the appearance of solidity and certainty',[12] it is in reality 'creaking under the weight of exceptions', being 'applied only formally and in a manner that sits awkwardly with the realities of the underlying situation', rendering it 'right to review the adequacy' of the analytical framework it provides.[13]

This mismatch is seen to stem primarily, it would seem, from the vast array of different types of instrument it has perforce to embrace, ranging (to take just a handful of examples) from 'dispositive' treaties declaring the course of international boundaries, through bilateral agreements for the disbursement of financial aid, then to multilateral, standard-setting arrangements concerning marine affairs, human rights or Antarctica, and ultimately to constitutional documents establishing such bodies as the United Nations, the European Union or the World Health Organization (which are all themselves agencies of fundamentally different political characters). Amongst the most striking and significant legal outcomes generated by this vast miscellany of accords, he observes, have been the creation of (i) objective regimes or forms of status intended to be valid for parties and non-parties alike; (ii) directly enforceable rights for individuals, who had not traditionally been regarded as subjects of international law at all and (iii) dispute settlement bodies which serve not merely in the capacity of a 'passive, neutral adjudicator' of controversies that might occasionally arise regarding the meaning of treaty terms but rather as 'key organs' of the regime of which they form part, charged with an 'active role to play in [its] progressive development'.[14] Treaties, accordingly, represent a class or category of instrument which is by no means 'homogenous',[15] a point which is explicitly recognised, he notes, by the regime itself, insofar as it both accepts and addresses the

---

[11] A. V. Lowe, 'The Law of Treaties; or, Should this Book Exist?' in C. J. Tams, A. Tzanakopoulos and A. Zimmermann (eds.), *Research Handbook on the Law of Treaties* (Cheltenham: Edward Elgar, 2014), pp. 3–15.

[12] *Ibid.*, at p. 3.   [13] *Ibid.*, at pp. 14–15.   [14] *Ibid.*, at p. 7.

[15] *Ibid.*, at p. 12. For further discussion of this particular epithet, see the contribution to this volume of Bowman at pp. 392–439 (Chapter 13).

need to make exceptional provision for some of these special cases.[16] If such special provision is necessary, he continues, it begs the question as to whether the divergent needs of these various sub-categories might not in fact be better served by the abandonment of any attempt to maintain the viability of a single, distinct and unified law of treaties.

In addition to questioning the internal coherence of the category of 'treaties' itself, he goes on to doubt the conviction with which one might seek to distinguish the treaty-making process from cognate modes of norm-creation, such as that which comprises formal commitments undertaken unilaterally, in the fashion that has been recognised as legally binding by the International Court of Justice in various cases.[17] He further highlights the point by referring to the ongoing studies that are currently being conducted by the International Law Commission concerning (i) the unilateral acts of States and (ii) the identification of customary international law[18] and concludes by asking whether the law of treaties might not be similarly ripe for fundamental reconsideration.[19] At first glance, it might be assumed from this that the author is about to advocate the initiation of some grand, over-arching synthesis or re-configuration of *all* the various mechanisms of international norm-creation, but closer inspection makes clear that this is not in fact his intention; indeed, he seems disposed to accept the existence of a significant and meaningful divide between obligations deriving from treaty and from custom respectively, on the grounds that the latter category of norm

> binds a State not because it has expressly assented to it but because State practice in general, in which the State may or may not have participated, has generated a rule from which the State has not excepted itself.[20]

It seems reasonable to suppose, however, that the distinction between these two venerable modes of norm-creation is actually significantly greater than this, in the sense that the generative processes involved in each case work primarily with raw materials of a very different kind. To be specific, a treaty can be seen as a network or system of inter-

---

[16] Within the VCLT, see, e.g., Arts. 5, 20(3), 60(5) and 62(2)(a).

[17] *Legal Status of Eastern Greenland*: Denmark v. Norway, 1933 PCIJ, Series A/B, No. 53; *Nuclear Tests Case*: Australia v. France (1974) ICJ Rep. 253, and *Nuclear Tests Case*: New Zealand v. France (1974) ICJ Rep. 457.

[18] For details of this work, see the 'Analytical Guide to the Work of the International Law Commission' (viewable at http://legal.un.org/ilc/guide/gfrashtml).

[19] Lowe, *supra* n. 11, at p. 15. [20] *Ibid.*, at pp. 13–14.

related commitments and entitlements which are essentially forged and fashioned in *language*, with conduct playing only an ancillary role in shedding light on the meaning of the words that have been used.[21] In the case of custom, by contrast, the basic fabric from which norms are constructed comprises *actions* rather than words, or, to be more precise, actions as coloured by the *attitudes* by which they are motivated, at least in formal terms.[22] Here again, it must no doubt be conceded that the alternative form of fabric, language, plays an important ancillary role: for example, if putative customary principles are to prove capable of bearing normative import at all, they must certainly be capable of eventual encapsulation and expression in verbal form.[23] In addition, the conduct from which they are ultimately derived is very likely to be questioned, explained, challenged and defended through verbal exchanges of one sort or another. Yet, for all that, it remains the case that the basic fabric of custom as a source of law typically comprises actions rather than words.[24]

This in turn suggests that not only the processes by which the respective types of norm are initially generated but those through which they are identified, investigated and evaluated are likely to differ very significantly. In the case of custom, the enquiry will focus on conduct and therefore be of an essentially behavioural and sociological nature, as it would be, for example, when investigating the unwritten customs of tribal communities, whereas the process whereby legislative or treaty-based norms are analysed will require an approach and expertise of a rather different – essentially linguistic

---

[21] See, e.g., Art. 31(3)(b) VCLT, which allows subsequent practice a role in the interpretation of legal norms: *supra* n. 4.

[22] Thus, the two essential ingredients of custom as a source of law are the behavioural element of State practice – usually described as requiring a 'constant and uniform usage' – and the mental element of *opinio iuris* – typically translated as a feeling of legal obligation (or, presumably, in the case of permissive rules, *entitlement*). For further discussion, see, e.g., A. A. D'Amato, *The Concept of Custom in International Law* (Ithaca, NY: Cornell University Press, 1971); M. Akehurst, 'Custom as a Source of International Law', *BYbIL*, 47 (1976), 1–53, and G. J. Postema, 'Custom in International Law: A Normative Practice Account' in A. Perreau-Saussine and J. B. Murphy (eds.), *The Nature of Customary Law: Legal, Historical and Philosophical Perspectives* (Cambridge: Cambridge University Press, 2007), pp. 279–306.

[23] This may, of course, eventually lead to formal codification, but any such development will be of a radically transformational character from a juridical point of view.

[24] Proverbially, of course, the former are regarded as having greater force and authenticity, but the maxim 'actions speak louder than words' was doubtless not conceived with States or governments in mind: in any event, much is likely to depend upon the precise context in which the words in question have been uttered or the conduct performed.

and semiotic – character.[25] Considerations such as these would seem to render any proposal for the simple amalgamation of the two processes an inherently unpromising project.

***

It is accordingly easy to understand why Lowe's tentative proposal for regulatory unification is instead targeted specifically at the rather different interface between obligations generated by treaty and those assumed purely unilaterally, of the kind already mentioned.[26] Here the gulf is admittedly significantly smaller, since each category entails commitments which are voluntarily assumed and both conceived and expressed in verbal form. Nevertheless, there would still seem to be a potentially important distinction between commitments which are framed, expressed and embraced on purely unilateral terms and those which, as in the case of treaties (whatever the exact nature of the process through which they were negotiated), depend for their very validity on the fact of their *plurilateral* assumption and ownership. In particular, it seems reasonable to suppose that a rather different legal regime might be required to govern the *formal creation, effectuation* and *interpretation* of the commitments in question,[27] not to mention their duration,

---

[25] For a wide variety of perspectives, see, e.g., C. K. Allen, *Law in the Making* (Oxford: Clarendon Press, 1964); J. Austin, *The Province of Jurisprudence Determined* (1832) (Cambridge: Cambridge University Press, 1965) (W. E. Rumble, ed.); H. Kelsen, *Pure Theory of Law* (Berkeley, CA/Los Angeles, CA: University of California Press, 2nd ed., 1970) (transl. by M. Knight); J. B. Murphy, 'Nature, Custom and Stipulation in Law and Jurisprudence', *The Review of Metaphysics*, 43 (1990), 751–790; H. P. Glenn, *Legal Traditions of the World* (Oxford: Oxford University Press, 2000); Perreau-Saussine and Murphy (eds.), *supra* n. 22, and D. J. Bederman, *Custom as a Source of Law* (Cambridge: Cambridge University Press, 2010).

[26] See, in particular, *supra* n. 17 and n. 18 (and accompanying text).

[27] With regard to the interpretation of unilateral commitments, for example, the significance to be attributed to *individual intentions* would seem potentially to be very different from (and, in particular, much more prominent than) that which applies to treaty-based undertakings: note in this context the observations of the ICJ in the following cases with regard to declarations accepting the jurisdiction of the Court under Art. 36(2) of its Statute: the *Anglo-Iranian Oil Co. Case*: United Kingdom v. Iran (Preliminary Objection) (1952) ICJ Rep. 93, at pp. 102–107 and especially at p. 105; *Fisheries Jurisdiction Case*: Spain v. Canada (Jurisdiction) (1998) ICJ Rep. 432, at p. 454 (paragraph 49) and *Whaling in the Antarctic*: Australia v. France; New Zealand intervening (2014) ICJ Rep. 226, at p. 244 (paragraph 36). These are admittedly unilateral declarations of a highly specialised kind, since they not only derive their very force and validity from a treaty-style source (i.e. the Statute itself) but also result in the creation of something resembling a network of additional, bilateral treaty commitments (i.e. to other states that have made similar declarations). Yet these features seem only to magnify one's sense of the distinctions which might potentially be required

modification and possible extinction. It is difficult to be sure, since there are so few instances of purely unilateral pronouncements having been formally recognised as producing decisive legal effects, and it is this very point which generates a second and independent source of scepticism regarding the seriousness of the challenge that such undertakings should be judged to pose to the established law of treaties: for it is currently far from clear that their practical significance is really such as to justify a radical overhaul of a regime which is so well-entrenched and supported.

Indeed, Lowe himself observes that the invitation that was offered to the International Court of Justice in the *Case Concerning the Frontier Dispute* of December 1986[28] to recognise and give effect to another alleged unilateral commitment was not merely declined but rejected in terms which 'distinguished almost out of existence' the statement of principle through which the Court had recognised the possibility of attributing legal significance to such undertakings in the first place.[29] It seems clear that the key authority relied upon for that purpose, the *Nuclear Tests* cases from the 1970s,[30] involved circumstances of a highly unusual kind, in the sense that France was evidently seeking a means to forestall the possibility of an unfavourable decision being reached – and a highly unwelcome court order being made against it – in international legal proceedings in which it had resolutely refused to participate from the outset; in addition, however, it will doubtless have been anxious to assuage the concerns of other States in the South Pacific region which had not actually initiated the litigation but were seeking to become involved.[31] As was pointed out by the Court in the later, 1986, case, the French government had very few practical means of achieving these goals 'without jeopardizing its contention that its conduct was lawful'.[32] If, moreover, it was truly on the point of completing its programme of atmospheric testing, it had rather little to lose by giving an undertaking not to conduct any more such operations in the future. The circumstances were accordingly such as to be unusually conducive to the inference that its intention was to undertake a binding legal commitment

---

between the respective regimes governing treaty-based norms and commitments of a purely unilateral and genuinely free-standing character.

[28] *Case Concerning the Frontier Dispute*: Burkina Faso v. Mali (1986) ICJ Rep. 554.

[29] Lowe, *supra* n. 11, at p. 14 (fn. 30) (referring to paragraphs 39–40 of the judgment).

[30] *Supra* n. 17.

[31] See the Orders of 12 July 1973 (New Zealand), 20 Aug. 1973 (Australia) and of 20 Dec. 1974 (both) concerning the application by Fiji to intervene in the two sets of proceedings.

[32] *Case Concerning the Frontier Dispute, supra* n. 28, at p. 574 (paragraph 40).

through the medium of a purely unilateral pronouncement. Although it would probably be unwise to assume that an *exactly* similar array of factual features would have to be demonstrated before an international court or tribunal could once again be persuaded to construe such an undertaking as legally binding, it does seem unlikely that any such finding would ever become anything other than wholly exceptional. Consequently, while it would doubtless be prudent to maintain a watching brief with regard to the potential impact of unilateral undertakings upon the on-going viability of the international law of treaties, calls for a fundamental overhaul of the existing law on this ground alone seem at this stage to be unconvincing.

These considerations point strongly to the conclusion that the principal question marks that hover over the modern law of treaties must stem from the doubts, if any, that must be entertained with regard to its *internal* coherence in the light of the vast array of different kinds of instrument for which it has to cater. Yet, here again, there is scope for questioning the extent to which the legal regime is actually undermined by this undeniable diversity. It is true that there are certain provisions of the Vienna Convention that are designed to secure exceptional treatment for particular categories of instrument, but the firm impression to be drawn from a preliminary survey of these provisions is surely how *few* of them there are rather than how many.[33] Furthermore, they share the tendency to provoke a degree of doubt as to whether the Vienna Convention is genuinely strengthened by their inclusion or whether they might not better have been drafted in modified form (or even, perhaps, excluded altogether).

In particular, it is open to question whether these exceptions were, or should rightly have been, intended to serve a genuinely *categorical and definitive* purpose or whether they are not rather of an essentially *indicative* or *illustrative* character. To take the most obvious example, Article 60(5) VCLT provides that the rules set out in the first three paragraphs of that article to govern the termination or suspension of treaties on account of breach

> do not apply to provisions relating to the protection of the human person contained in treaties of a humanitarian character, in particular to provisions prohibiting any form of reprisals against persons protected by such treaties.

---

[33] *Supra* n. 16.

Although it is commonplace to see this provision explained as one designed to provide a custom-fit and exclusive safeguard for the self-evidently unique category of human rights treaties,[34] it might be argued in response that neither the desirability nor the feasibility of applying the provision in that way is easily established. In the first place, there may be a considerable difficulty in determining where the precise boundary should be drawn between that particular category and cognate types of treaty designed for the protection of the human person, such as those more usually designated as international humanitarian law,[35] labour law or investment law.[36] There are, moreover, additional categories of treaty – environmental instruments come most readily to mind – which seek to protect an array of interests, including but not necessarily limited to those of humankind. Finally, there are still others, of which treaties for the protection of animal welfare represent an example, where the principal interests at stake are ostensibly not those of humans at all and yet very obviously not those of States either and where the exception provided by Article 60(5) VCLT might be judged to have at least a tenable claim for applicability.[37] Indeed, this provision seems in truth to encapsulate a rule that should arguably be applicable to *any* commitment that has been undertaken by States not in defence of their individual interests as key international actors with a material well-being of their own but rather as a form of 'trustee' for the fundamental moral needs and interests of some non-State entity or of the international community itself, conceived in its broadest sense. Since it is not drafted in terms which are *either* definitively exclusive or explicitly exemplary, it is presumably

---

[34] See, e.g., *Legal Consequences for States of the Continued Presence of South Africa in Namibia (South West Africa) Notwithstanding Security Council Resolution 276 (1970)* (Advisory Opinion) (1971) ICJ Rep. 16, at p. 47 (paragraph 96).

[35] Itself a term in contention: see the contribution to this volume of Hampson at pp. 538–577 (Chapter 17).

[36] For discussion of this issue, see the contribution to this volume of Chinkin at pp. 509–537 (Chapter 16).

[37] It should be acknowledged that some might seek to uphold a clear distinction of principle between human rights and these other areas of policy concern, on the grounds of there being a greater element of normative reciprocation in all the latter: that is to say, that while States cannot be expected to take on environmental or animal welfare commitments unless other States are prepared to do likewise (so as to avoid incurring a competitive disadvantage), human rights reflect absolute values and are therefore not 'tradable' in this way. Many others, however, would doubtless see all these matters as being fundamental moral imperatives and on that account reject the applicability of the competitive advantage argument in any of these cases.

open to deliberation exactly how it should be interpreted and applied in the future.

*

Considerations such as these appear to raise an important general question concerning the nature and role of the international legal order insofar as it impacts upon the regulation of international instruments negotiated and concluded amongst States in verbal form: this concerns specifically the extent to which the substantive *content* of the overarching regulatory regime should be determined primarily by *contextual* considerations or whether there are not rather certain features of a *conceptual* character which are sufficiently fundamental and pervasive to the process to be regarded as its principal driving force and as investing it with the necessary level of intellectual cohesion. One might, indeed, go so far as to suggest that it is virtually impossible to say anything significant about treaty law without reference to this triad of ideas – in Lowe's piece itself, for instance, it is noteworthy that one of them makes its first appearance in only the second line of the text and all three can be found together as early as the third paragraph. It is, however, relatively uncommon to find the relationship between them the subject of explicit or sustained exploration: thus, to take Lowe's account once again as an example, their joint appearance is seemingly no more than coincidental, and certainly no overt attempt is made to explore their precise inter-relationship.[38]

To the contrary, traditional treatments of treaty law issues have been inclined to focus principally on one particular pairing of the triad, as if the content of the law was to be dictated essentially by either context or concept alone. Thus, much of the literature traditionally produced by specialists in the law of treaties as such has tended to be of a rather arid, abstract and theoretical character, replete with reference to the fundamental concepts of treaty law but disappointingly thin and unenriched by insights and illustrations from the many substantive contexts in which it falls to be applied – instead, the application of particular rules tends to be demonstrated by the same few stock examples (very often those selected by the International Law Commission itself for the purposes of its commentary on the Vienna Convention).[39] Conversely, the output of

---

[38] The general thrust of the piece, however, must certainly be to suggest that contextual considerations have been undervalued in a regime that assumes a considerable degree of internal conceptual coherence and structures its contents accordingly.

[39] As to which, see *supra* n. 18.

specialists in the various recognised sub-disciplines of international law who chance across questions of treaty law in the course of their writings is prone to be characterised by an overemphasis upon the supposedly peculiar demands of the particular substantive context from which the treaties in question have emerged and a comparatively low level of awareness of the extent to which parallel problems have fallen for consideration elsewhere and of the underlying conceptual threads that might conceivably provide a unifying path to their solution.

This analytical shortfall seems as surprising as it is disappointing, since the inter-relation of content, concept and context – which is actually fundamental to the development of complex structures or artefacts generally, whether decorative, functional or normative in character – has been much better appreciated in other fields of intellectual endeavour. Within the discipline of fine art, for example, the relationship between these elements is considered so fundamental that they are sometimes referred to as the 'Three C's',[40] while architectural commentators have highlighted the 'complex and productive triangulation' which can be detected amongst them in every individually designed building.[41] The potential relevance of these disciplines to the present debate is, in fact, incidentally acknowledged, albeit perhaps inadvertently, by Lowe himself in his passing references to works of art (specifically, a tapestry) and buildings ('hammering into place the . . . great beams' that support the overall structure) as explicit analogies for the various aspects of the legal order with which he is concerned.[42]

With regard to constructions of the architectural kind, it is suggested that, although the factor that generates the most obvious and immediate impact of a building upon the layperson is likely to be its *content* – namely the shape, size, structure and materials that determine its appearance, together with what actually goes on there – to the more expert eye the other two elements will be regarded as no less significant. In this vein, it has been pointed out that there can in truth be no architecture at all without both *a concept* – the 'overriding idea that gives coherence and identity to a building' – and also *a context* – the historical, geographical and cultural backcloth against which that concept has been projected.[43]

---

[40] This was, for example, the title of a public lecture recently given by Professor Yves Larocque, of the Ottawa School of Art: for an overview, see http://walkthearts .wordpress.com/page/6/.

[41] See, e.g., B. Tschumi, *Event-Cities 3: Concept vs Context vs Content* (Cambridge, MA: MIT Press, 2005).

[42] Both references may be found in Lowe, *supra* n. 11, at p. 6.   [43] Tschumi, *supra* n. 41.

Yet there is no settled consensus, it would seem, regarding the precise relationship that exists, or should exist, between these various elements. Rather, the attitude has tended to vary over the course of time and in the judgments of different practitioners and critics.

Such questions have, for example, recently been explored in the work of the internationally renowned, yet controversial, architect Bernard Tschumi, whose particular perspective has been described in the following terms:

> Against the contextualist movement of the 1980s and 1990s, which called for architecture to blend in with its surroundings, Tschumi argues that buildings may or may not conform to their settings – but that the decision should always be strategic. Through documentation of [various] recent projects ... Tschumi examines different ways that concept, context and content relate to each other in his work ... Through provocative examples, Tschumi demonstrates that the relationship of concept, context and content may be one of indifference, reciprocity or conflict – all of which, he argues, are valid architectural approaches. Above all, he suggests that the activity of architecture is less about the making of forms than the investigation and materialization of concepts.[44]

Plainly, however, the tangible products of this approach have not commanded universal approval, one particular commentator having described a prominent example of Tschumi's work – namely, the New Acropolis Museum in Athens – as lacking any semblance of 'coherence, logic or architectural life' and his overtly 'deconstructivist' style as 'fundamentally nihilistic' and 'an architecture of aggression carried out by viral means'.[45] It is evident that these controversies are directly traceable to acute underlying differences of theoretical perspective concerning the precise relationship that should properly exist amongst these three elements of concept, content and context in the architectural field and that these differences are still very far from resolution.

*

Needless to say, even in the unlikely event that an appropriate consensus with regard to such matters could somehow be fashioned for the purposes of that particular discipline, it would by no means follow that it would necessarily be capable of direct translation into another field, and especially the realm of law: after all, the precise demands and constraints

---

[44] Bernard Tschumi Architects, 'Publications' at www.tschumi.com/publications/4/.

[45] N. A. Salingaros, 'Architectural Cannibalism in Athens', *Orthodoxy Today*, 20 Nov. 2007 (www.orthodoxytoday.org/articles7/SalingarosAthens.php).

imposed by society with regard to the tectonics of their normative structures cannot simply be assumed to be identical to those applicable in the case of their physical counterparts. Furthermore, there is one very obvious distinction to be found between the two disciplines in that, whereas in the field of architecture and building science the raw materials to be used in the construction process are of an unmistakably physical and (often quite literally) concrete character, in the legal field the equivalent components are themselves of a wholly abstract and purely verbal kind (mere literary concretions, if you will). Legal rules and principles, that is to say, are themselves inherently *conceptual* in nature, and their structuring and deployment into a coherent body of norms is itself a form of *contextualisation*, albeit of a rather narrowly circumscribed kind. It is accordingly to be expected that the exploration of conceptual and contextual perspectives upon the substantive content of legal subject matter might prove a rather more complex, multi-layered and recursive process, entailing that the concepts and contexts in question have themselves to be conceptualised and contextualised, and possibly in some freshly revised form. Yet the fundamental importance both of the three elements in themselves and of determining the optimal nature and form of their precise inter-relationship remains undeniable and seems if anything only to be magnified by these considerations. It was this realisation that prompted our original embarkation upon this project.

At the same time, this very recognition of an as yet unsatisfied need for further reflection upon the concepts and contexts that have shaped the content of treaty law suggests that the present study must necessarily assume a somewhat exploratory and provisional character and be understood as representing only the opening stages of a particular mode of enquiry rather than anything even approximating to the last word. Happily, however, it does not begin with a totally blank canvas, since a good deal of useful guidance is potentially available from the codification exercise itself, and in particular the explanatory and narrative elements of its component instruments. Thus, the preamble to the 1969 Vienna Convention identifies a number of fundamental and enduring objectives of the international legal order, including 'the maintenance of international peace and security, the development of friendly relations and the achievement of co-operation among nations'.[46] Of no less importance is the need for all international disputes to be 'settled by peaceful means and in conformity with the principles of justice and

---

[46] Seventh preambular recital: *supra* n. 4.

international law'.[47] Critical to the achievement of these goals, moreover, is the recognition of certain other key principles, including 'non-interference in the domestic affairs of States', 'the prohibition of the threat or use of force' and 'universal respect for, and observance of, human rights and fundamental freedoms of all'.[48] This is of itself extremely useful in identifying a range of key substantive contexts in which the law will have to operate and also as reflecting a certain assessment of functional priorities. There is also, however, a degree of open-endedness reflected in some of these ideas, in the sense that 'security', for example, should in the contemporary context sensibly be understood to incorporate economic and ecological dimensions, alongside the traditional concern for protection from the use of military force. Accordingly, many of the crucial areas of normative concern have already been made evident, and the role of treaties and treaty law in these various substantive contexts is extensively explored in Part II of this work.

***

The enduring relevance of these considerations is confirmed by the reiteration of many of them two decades later in the 1986 Vienna Convention on the Law of Treaties between States and International Organizations or between International Organizations,[49] which is also valuable in highlighting the important role of international inter-governmental organizations in the field of treaty-making,[50] whether as participant, progenitor or product.[51] Accordingly, the now extensive array of such institutions constitutes a further, and potentially distinctive, form of context in which treaty dispositions are realised, negotiated, adopted and applied. With that in mind, a number of the other chapters in Part II have been devoted to consideration of the role and significance of treaties and treaty law within such forums. In addition, attention is given to the application of certain particularly important principles (those of State responsibility) in the judicial forum specifically and to

---

[47] Fourth preambular recital: *supra* n. 4.   [48] Sixth preambular recital: *supra* n. 4.

[49] ILM, 25 (1986), 543–592. Note, in particular, the fifth, sixth and ninth preambular recitals.

[50] Note in particular the fifth, eighth, ninth and tenth preambular recitals: *ibid*. See also Art. 2(1)(i), which for its own purposes restricts the category of international organizations to those of the inter-governmental variety.

[51] Art. 5 captures all three capacities. Note also, respectively, the ninth and eleventh preambular recitals and Arts. 1, 2(1)(a-d, f-h); eleventh preambular recital and Art. 2(1)(e) and twelfth and thirteenth preambular recitals and Art. 2(1)(j): *ibid*.

the relevance of treaty law principles to an alternative, highly specialised mode of norm-creation, namely Security Council resolutions.

These various chapters serve as a useful testing-ground for the charge which is commonly levelled against the modern law of treaties, and especially in Lowe's analysis: namely, that its subject-matter is essentially too wide-ranging, multi-faceted and diverse for unitary treatment and that divergent, tailor-made rules may be required for particular types of treaty, such as constituent instruments, and/or for agreements addressing particular areas of policy concern, such as human rights. Prior to that, however, it seems appropriate to focus upon the essential nature and ethos of the instruments that are to be contextualised, as viewed particularly through the lens of conceptuality, as manifested in some of the more important general ideas by which they are infused and inspired. Here again, the Vienna Conventions are of assistance in shaping the discussion, with the focus placed once again upon their respective preambles.

Of particular note in this regard are the immediate acknowledgement of 'the ever-increasing importance of treaties as a source of international law and as a means of developing peaceful co-operation among nations' and the determination 'to establish conditions under which justice and respect for the obligations arising from treaties can be maintained'.[52] Their capacity in that regard must of course depend upon the existence of certain 'universally recognized' principles, namely those of 'free consent and of good faith and the *pacta sunt servanda* rule',[53] which through their inter-linkage would seem to underpin both the sanctity of solemn commitments and the means by which they may first be effectively assumed in a world of sovereign, independent States.[54] These pronouncements seem to draw clear attention to the inherent significance of such concepts as consent and intention and of the complex ways in which these ideas are reflected in treaties, including through such elusive and abstract notions as the 'object and purpose' and, more concretely, through direct preambular exposition. They also raise important questions concerning the application of treaties, whether in a personal, temporal or functional sense, as well as the essential nature of treaty obligations and the character and consequences of the concept of breach. Underlying all these issues is the ubiquitous issue of interpretation and the extent to which the

[52] Second and fifth preambular recitals of the VCLT: *supra* n. 4.
[53] Third preambular recital: *ibid.*
[54] This sovereignty and independence is also noted in the sixth recital as a key principle embodied in the Charter of the United Nations.

relevant principles may have been affected by emerging perceptions of the treaty as a 'living instrument'. This in turn highlights further issues concerning the way in which treaties are themselves to be conceptualised and categorised. Accordingly, matters of this kind constitute the subject of exploration in Part I of this work, which is devoted to conceptual perspectives.

***

Finally, it might be observed that, although the discussions and deliberations appearing within these covers have been elaborated by, and for the benefit of, lawyers specifically, law itself cannot feasibly exist entirely in the abstract but must be viewed against the broader backcloth of human affairs, as shaped by considerations of a political, philosophical and psychological character. Indeed, however much we may try to tell ourselves otherwise, human psychology must itself always remain constrained by certain principles which derive from the realms of biology, chemistry and, ultimately, physics. Needless to say, the present work does not offer any systematic or sophisticated exploration of these issues but aspires nonetheless not to overlook them altogether, especially where they appear to have some direct bearing upon the way in which lawyers are wont to conceptualise or contextualise their subject matter. With that in mind, one particular point of potential relevance to note at this preliminary stage is that the two broad perspectives upon substantive content which have been identified for the purposes of the present work – namely, the conceptual and the contextual – do appear to correspond, at least in a very general way, to the different modes of cognition that have respectively been associated with the two halves of the human brain.[55]

Early approaches to the identification of the functions handled by each hemisphere tended broadly to associate the right with emotion and

---

[55] See, especially, I. McGilchrist, *The Master and His Emissary: The Divided Brain and the Making of the Western World* (New Haven, CT: Yale University Press, 2012), p. 386, where it is noted that the 'right hemisphere delivers . . . experience of whatever it is that exists apart from ourselves – this is not the same as the world of concrete entities out there (it is certainly more than that), but it does encompass most of what we would think of as actually existing things, at least before we come to think of them at all, as opposed to the *concepts* of them, the abstractions and constructions we inevitably make from them, in conscious reflection, which forms the contribution of the left hemisphere' (emphasis added and replacing that given to the word 'same' in the original). Note also his earlier observation, at p. 49, that the right hemisphere not only takes in these externals but 'sees each thing in its *context*, as standing in a qualifying relationship with all that surrounds it, rather than taking it as single, isolated entity'.

impulse and the left with reason, logic and language.[56] However, a comprehensive and widely endorsed study that has recently been completed, by multi-disciplinarian Iain McGilchrist,[57] criticises this approach as being too crudely overdrawn, on the grounds that cognitive functions described at that level of generality cannot sensibly be located in such a precisely bicameral fashion, being in reality rather more widely distributed throughout the brain as a whole.[58] In his view, the true distinction lies not so much in which of these key cerebral functions is performed by each hemisphere but rather in the specific fashion in which each chamber influences their overall performance: in short, the question is subtly reformulated in terms of *how* rather than *what* these two structures respectively contribute. To be specific, the left half of the brain shapes our worldview predominantly through processes of abstraction, reduction, division, categorisation, definition and analysis, and with a view to manipulation and control, while the right approaches matters instead in terms of recognition, contextualisation, integration, synthesis and holistic awareness, so as to accommodate their raw complexity. As the author himself explains it, the latter permits the 'presentation' of

---

[56] For influential early expert works, see V. L. Deglin and M. Kinsbourne, 'Divergent Thinking Styles of the Hemispheres: How Syllogisms are Solved during Transitory Hemisphere Suppression', *Brain and Cognition*, 31 (1996), 285–307; M. Gazzaniga, 'The Split Brain Revisited', *Scientific American*, 297 (1998), 51–55, and for a recent overview of developments, McGilchrist, *ibid*. In truth, the drawing of overly sharp distinctions in this respect has been more characteristic of populist than of serious scientific accounts, which emphasise that the clear principal significance of brain lateralisation is that each hemisphere tends to control the opposite side of the body: on this point specifically, see C. McManus, *Right Hand, Left Hand: The Origins of Asymmetries in Brains, Bodies, Atoms and Cultures* (London: Phoenix/Orion, 2003), esp. at pp. 184–220. It is also true, however, that the brain regions known as Broca's area and Wernicke's area, which have been shown to play an important role in the production and comprehension of language respectively, are located in the left hemisphere. For a more detailed, but still readily accessible, consideration of lateralisation generally (yet one which still manages to avoid undue exaggeration or excess), see R. Carter, *Mapping the Mind* (London: Phoenix/Orion, 1998), pp. 47–80. For a debunking of the populist view (though only to replace it with an even less plausible approach, based on horizontal division of the brain), see J. McCrone, *The Myth of Irrationality: Science of the Mind from Plato to Star Trek* (London: Macmillan, 1993).

[57] *Supra* n. 55. Its author is a former consultant psychiatrist and clinical director at the Bethlem and Maudlsey Royal Hospital in London. He has also conducted research in neuro-imaging at John Hopkins University Hospital in Baltimore. Prior to that, he taught English at Oxford University as a Fellow of All Souls College, a distinction to which he was twice re-elected. For further details, see his website at www.iainmcgilchrist.com/index.asp #content.

[58] McGilchrist, *supra* n. 55, at pp. 16–31 and 32–93, especially at pp. 58–64.

the world around us, while the former is more concerned with its 're-presentation' in abstracted form.[59] While this modified portrayal undoubtedly preserves a reasonably clear element of distinction between the logical, analytical and mechanistic, on the one hand (specifically, the left brain), and the intuitive, synthetic and organic on the other (namely, the right), it does so in a fashion which seems less inclined to skate over the inconvenient complexities of experimental findings in psychology and neuroscience.

The overall thesis of McGilchrist's work is complex, multi-faceted and ambitious and extends into areas that lie far beyond the purview of our own project, so it will be preferable for current purposes to focus primarily upon his basic point that in order to obtain a reliable picture of the world it is necessary to achieve an appropriate balance between, and effective synthesis of, the contrasting perspectives that the bicameral brain offers us. This essentially reflects what the present volume aspires to achieve – or, at least, initiate. All the same, it can do no harm to advert briefly to one of his other key conclusions, which is that humankind has tended to struggle rather haplessly to achieve this desired balance, with one or other hemispheric perspective having successively gained the upper hand during different historical eras, at least where Western cultural traditions are concerned. Thus, the early developments in the philosophy of ancient Greece, the Renaissance and the era of Romanticism are judged to constitute manifestations of right-brain pre-dominance, while the Platonic era, the Reformation, the Enlightenment and the modern era exemplify the accession to supremacy of the left. In his view, the currently well-entrenched dominance of left-brain think-ing is very much to be deprecated, since its proper role is to function only as the 'emissary' of the more holistic, relational and contextualised perspective of the right hemisphere: it is simply that, after the fashion of Dirk Bogarde's character in Joseph Losey's acclaimed 1963 film *The Servant*,[60] the subordinate has somehow contrived over time to usurp the place of its master.[61]

---

[59] This distinction, introduced *ibid.*, at p. 50, represents a pervasive theme of the book.

[60] The film, scripted by Harold Pinter, is based on a 1948 novel of the same name by Robin Maugham.

[61] McGilchrist's own source for this idea – as explained at p. 14 of his work, *supra* n. 55 – is the story of the master and the emissary, recalled from 'somewhere' unspecified in Nietzsche. The distinction between 'master morality' and 'slave morality' and the notion of 'slave revolt' seems in fact to have been a recurrent theme in Nietzsche's work: see, e.g., the first essay in *On the Genealogy of Morality* (1887) (Cambridge: Cambridge University Press, 1997) (K. Ansell-Pearson ed., D. Ciethe trans.) and, more generally, *Beyond Good*

Needless to say, such conclusions cannot blithely be carried over from the physical into the normative realm – with which McGilchrist himself is not directly concerned at all – because in the latter case the very raw material of experience itself is intrinsically abstract and conceptual in character, with the result that the very parameters of the discussion are radically altered. On the other hand, many of the rhetorical devices that are commonly employed to elucidate the law of treaties itself – instruments, mechanisms, force, breach, severance, suspension, etc. – are taken directly from the physical context, and it may therefore be instructive to consider the extent, if any, to which the ascendancy of one or other hemispherical perspective at particular times might in some way have skewed the nature or orientation of legal discourse.

While these are matters to which it may be useful to return in due course, for the time being it is necessary to refocus our attention (essentially a left-brain function, it seems)[62] simply upon the tripartite relationship of content, concept and context. As noted above, this relationship does not seem to have been the subject of systematic or detailed attention in legal scholarship to date. Indeed, it is noticeable that the majority of the recent works referred to above are essentially driven by, focused upon, and structured around straightforward considerations of *content*. Thus, they are inclined to draw their structural inspiration from the basic instruments of treaty law itself, beginning perhaps with the rules regarding the nature and definition of treaties as such, and then addressing successively the functional rules regarding their conclusion, application, interpretation, inter-relation, validity, termination or suspension, and functional management.[63] While it would doubtless be excessive to assert that no light at all is shed upon the conceptual and contextual dimensions of the subject, it would probably be fair to conclude that whatever

---

and Evil: Prelude to A Philosophy of the Future (1886) (London: Penguin, 1973), and, for analysis, see W. Kaufmann, From Shakespeare to Existentialism (Princeton, NJ: Princeton University Press, 1980), pp. 207–218. It may be that the Losey film, *ibid.*, captures McGilchrist's point more vividly and effectively for many readers.

[62] Most forms of attention, including the exploratory kind, are handled by the right hemisphere, but the left takes over for the purpose of developing a detailed, focused grasp of particulars: McGilchrist, *supra* n. 55, at pp. 32–93.

[63] This is most clearly the case, naturally enough, in the various commentaries that elucidate the Vienna Conventions on an article-by-article basis, such as O. Corten and P. Klein (eds.), *The Vienna Conventions on the Law of Treaties: A Commentary* (Vols. I and II) (Oxford: Oxford University Press, 2011); O. Dörr and K. Schmalenbach (eds.), *Vienna Convention on the Law of Treaties: A Commentary* (Heidelberg: Springer Verlag, 2012) and M. E. Villiger, *Commentary on the 1969 Vienna Convention on the Law of Treaties* (Leiden: Martinus Nijhoff, 2009).

illumination may be provided in that regard is largely incidental. This is not in any way to cast doubt upon the value and utility of their approach, since it is clear that many of the works in question have contributed most extensively and impressively to the scholarly development of the subject. The contention here is only that the very considerable enlightenment that they offer can be enhanced still further by the adoption of a different and complementary approach – one that pays more overt and systematic attention to these alternative dimensions of concept and context and to their respective impacts upon the evolving content of treaty law.

It is to this particular task, accordingly, that the current work is dedicated. Taking a cue once again from the Vienna Convention itself, the very first consideration to which the preamble draws attention concerns 'the fundamental role of treaties in the history of international relations', and it is therefore with the relationship between history and modernity that it would seem appropriate to begin.

2

A 'Modern' Law of Treaties?

FRANK BERMAN

A work dealing with the modern Law of Treaties, examined both conceptually and contextually, calls for some prior investigation of the underlying object itself. What do we mean by 'the law of treaties', and what is it that we expect from a law of treaties? And what particular content would we give to the idea of a 'modern' law of treaties?

1 A 'Law of Treaties'? Some Antecedents

The phrase 'Law of Treaties' is commonly used – sometimes with capital letters and often without – but its import seldom analysed. In fact, to find any discussion of the question at all is hard. A good starting point is the work of the International Law Commission (ILC), since that eventuated in the Vienna Convention on the Law of Treaties (VCLT) of May 1969,[1] which by any account represents the foundation stone of the modern law.[2] James L. Brierly, who had been the Rapporteur of the Committee that drew up the Statute of the ILC and then became its first Special Rapporteur on the Law of Treaties,[3] had some years earlier expressed the firm view that the codification process 'should endeavour to find those subjects of international law which were of practical, not of theoretical, interest and, if possible, to choose questions which would, as a result of the Committee's work, be capable of settlement by international

---

[1] 1155 UNTS 331.

[2] It led also in due course to the 1986 Vienna Convention on the Law of Treaties between States and International Organizations or between International Organizations, ILM, 25 (1986), 543–592, though that is better regarded as an *arrière pensée* made necessary by a gap left consciously in the VCLT more for ideological than legal reasons.

[3] From 1949 to 1952; Brierly was succeeded in this position by Sir Hersch Lauterpacht (1952–1955), and he in turn by Sir Gerald Fitzmaurice (1955–1961) and ultimately Sir Humphrey Waldock (1962–1966). See, further, S. Rosenne, *The Law of Treaties: A Guide to the Legislative History of the Vienna Convention* (Leiden: A.W. Sijthoff, 1970), p. 29.

agreement'.[4] The first Report of the newly formed ILC on its inaugural Session in 1949,[5] which established the topic as one of the three priority items in its basic programme of work, simply uses the term as is, in the form 'Law of treaties', without further explanation of what the Commission had in mind by it. Nor is much more to be gleaned from the record of the discussion itself inside the Commission, where only seven contributions are recorded.[6] Brierly, proposing the inclusion of the topic, says, negatively, that the only possible objection to its inclusion was that it was 'a very wide question which might take up several meetings of the Commission' (sic!), and Georges Scelle, in support, agrees that it would be undoubtedly difficult to undertake the codification of 'the whole question of treaties'.[7] J. P. A. François is the only member of the Commission to delve a little more deeply by pointing out two aspects to the question, which he calls the unification of the drafting of treaties on the one hand and the unification of the fundamentals of treaties on the other, though he seems to be calling on the Commission to concentrate on the first, not the second.[8]

2   The 1949 Survey and Earlier Codification Efforts

In taking this unspecific approach, the Commission was however doing no more than following the Survey of International Law, the study produced by the UN Secretariat to serve as the basis for the Commission's discussion of its work programme.[9] Somewhat surprisingly, given its provenance, the Survey itself deals with the topic in an unsystematic way.

Although it begins the relevant chapter[10] with what appears to be a panoptic sense of a 'law of treaties' and refers in that context to the desirability of including 'the entire subject of treaties' within the orbit of codification, in the context that 'there is hardly a branch of the law of treaties which is free from doubt and, in some cases, from confusion',[11] when it comes to potential content, the Survey merely mentions earlier codification efforts.[12] The references are to the work within the Pan-

---

[4] The Committee in question being the League of Nations Committee of Experts in 1925; see the UN Secretariat Survey, *infra* n. 9, at p. 5.

[5] Doc. A/CN.4/13 & Corr. 1–3 (12 Apr. 1949).   [6] Doc. A/CN.4/SR.6 (20 Apr. 1949).

[7] *Ibid.*, at pp. 48–49.   [8] *Ibid.*

[9] Doc. A/CN.4/1/Rev.1 (10 Feb. 1949) (now known to have been the work of Lauterpacht).

[10] *Ibid.* (paragraph 90).   [11] *Ibid.* (paragraph 91).

[12] See, generally, O. J. Lissitzyn, 'Efforts to Codify or Restate the Law of Treaties', *Columbia L. Rev.*, 62 (1962), 1166–1205.

American Union in 1927–1928 and the Harvard Research of 1935, each
of which had led to a draft Convention,[13] and to the League of Nations
Committee of Experts, which, by contrast, had a much more limited and
piecemeal focus, confined to the possible codification of 'the procedure of
international conferences and the conclusion and drafting of treaties'.[14]
None of these precursors, however, nor the substantial differences
between them in scope and aim, is further discussed in detail. All that
the Survey does is to list an undifferentiated bundle of questions meriting
attention. The bundle includes (amongst a few others) terminology,
ratification, constitutional limitations on the treaty-making power, effect
on third parties, interpretation, the most-favoured-nation clause and the
doctrine of *rebus sic stantibus*. The assumption must be that these items
are singled out because they had caused difficulties in practice, not
because of any conceptual link between them – other than the fact that
they all relate to treaties.

A very similar pattern can be found in the academic literature. The first
edition of A. D. McNair's *Law of Treaties*, published in 1938,[15] was
plainly intended to consider both the content of the international law
on the subject and its practical application in a particular country.[16]
The authoritative and influential revised and much expanded edition
that appeared in 1961 begins with 'the essential character of a treaty' and
with the sentence: 'The user of a book entitled *The Law of Treaties* has
a right to know what the author means by the word "treaty"'.[17] But it
seems that the user was not similarly entitled, in the author's mind, to
know what the latter meant by 'the law of' treaties! One deeply regrets the
omission; it may be that McNair regarded the answer as so obvious as not
to be worth mention, but his reflections on the question would have been
of huge interest.[18] The same gap appears in the literature in other

---

[13] The Pan-American Convention, adopted by the Sixth International Conference of
American States at Havana in Feb. 1928, is reprinted in *AJIL Supp.*, 29 (1935),
1205–1207. The Draft Convention on Law of Treaties of the Harvard Research in
International Law appears in *AJIL Supp.*, 29 (1935), 653–1226.

[14] In the circumstances, it is not entirely surprising that the League Council decided not to
pursue the proposed codification, as being 'in no sense urgent': *supra* n. 9, at p. 52
(paragraph 91).

[15] As *The Law of Treaties: British Practice and Opinion* (New York, NY: Columbia
University Press, 1938).

[16] See the introductory note on the flyleaf of the 1961 edition: A. D. McNair, *The Law of
Treaties* (Oxford: Clarendon Press, 1961).

[17] *Ibid.*, at p. 3.

[18] See, also, *infra* n. 23. McNair's book, classic though it is, is nevertheless empirical through
and through in its selection of topics for treatment.

languages: Paul Reuter's classic *Introduction au droit des traités*, for example, simply launches into the definition of treaty without any prologue other than a discussion of the frontier between the international and the national legal orders.[19] A glance at the comprehensive bibliography prepared for the ILC by the UN Secretariat at its second session in 1950,[20] although itself carrying the title 'The Law of Treaties', shows that the majority of the works cited similarly plunge directly into particular questions arising in respect of treaties, with a small minority using a more general rubric, usually simply 'Treaties'.[21] Once again, one must assume that the Secretariat was following Sir Hersch Lauterpacht, in the Survey[22] and that Lauterpacht had simply been following the rubric adopted in the Harvard Research, without much consideration of its possible implications. This assumption is borne out by the subsequent work of the ILC, both at its inception and later, which will be discussed later.

3   The International Law Commission

We may continue a little longer with the terminology, not as a *jeu d'esprit* for its own sake but for whatever illumination it may throw on what the members of the ILC had in their minds. The title under which the topic was actually adopted was 'Law of treaties', this time with a capital 'L' but a small 't'. There is no sign, as indicated previously, of consideration having been given to what scope or range should be understood by 'Law of' – nor why the 'The' had been dropped from the formulation used in the Lauterpacht Survey. But then, nor did Lauterpacht himself explain his terminology – although the terminology he adopted here marched in parallel with his use of 'the law of' as the introductory rubric to a great many of the items on his list, so perhaps 'the law of' should simply be understood as purely neutral, as something equivalent to 'the area of'.[23] That would make sense against the historical background described

---

[19] First published in 1975, this work is now in its third edition prepared with the assistance of Philippe Cahier (Paris: Presses Universitaires de France, 1995).

[20] Doc. A/C.4/31 (27 June 1950).

[21] McNair, *supra* n. 16, at p. 744, has a wonderfully pungent phrase about 'the traditional rules as to the formation etc. of treaties which swell the bulk of our text-books, too often written in slavish imitation of their predecessors'!

[22] *Supra* n. 9.

[23] It is also more than a platitude to observe that certain subjects demand the insertion of a phrase like 'the law of' just because they have a natural content that goes beyond (sometimes far beyond) their specifically legal aspects; good examples are 'war' or 'armed conflict' or 'the sea'; whereas in other cases of legal regulation, where the regulation is being

previously, which seems to have regarded the treaties' rubric more as an assortment of individual questions under that heading that looked as if they could do with resolution on an agreed basis, in keeping with Brierly's insistence on topics of practical, rather than theoretical, interest, and that promised to be capable of settlement by international agreement.

That was, at all events, the way in which Brierly began, after his appointment as the first of a long chain of distinguished Special Rapporteurs. The draft Convention he put to the Commission at its Second Session consisted of eleven articles – two on definitions, three on treaty-making capacity and six on what we would now call consent to be bound and entry into force, including one on reservations, with the comment that it would be 'a matter for further consideration whether or not there ought to be also a chapter ... on what may be termed the obligation or effect of treaties'.[24] The scope and coverage slowly broadened in successive years, but it was not until Brierly had been succeeded by Lauterpacht and Lauterpacht by Sir Gerald Fitzmaurice[25] that the idea emerged of a comprehensive treatment of the subject of a kind that could properly claim to represent 'the law of treaties'. Fitzmaurice's First Report, of 1956, offered forty-two draft articles – on definitions, fundamental principles of treaty law and 'formal validity' (i.e. the framing, conclusion and entry into force of treaties) – and promised more to come on essential validity, termination, interpretation, operation and enforcement while still leaving a number of further matters to be dealt with after that.[26] But Fitzmaurice, it should be recalled, was not in favour of a Convention, preferring the idea of an expository code, carrying with it the advantage of 'rendering permissible the inclusion of a certain amount of declaratory and explanatory material in the body of the code, in a way that would not be possible if this had to be confined to a strict statement of obligation'.[27] Even at this point, though, all that Fitzmaurice has to say about the overall material scope of the work is that governments are generally familiar with the broad principles of treaty law

brought about by treaty, the *absence* of 'law' from the treaty's title is equally intuitive. Some cases, again, fall in between, an obvious example being 'human rights'. An interesting counterpoint is offered by the 1986 Vienna Convention – *supra* n. 2 and dealt with later – which, like its 1969 progenitor, calls itself a Convention on the 'law of treaties' between States and international organizations etc. where the inclusion of 'law' offers some bureaucratic consistency, but little else, and indeed offers the possibility of real and damaging confusion if *this* 'law of treaties' were thereby thought to stand in contrast to the other 'law of treaties'!

[24] Doc. A/CN.4/23 (14 Apr. 1950), p. 224.   [25] *Supra* n. 3.
[26] Doc. A/CN.4/101 (14 March 1956), p. 104.   [27] *Ibid.*, at p. 107 (paragraph 9).

and that a code ought therefore to deal with at any rate the more prominent of the 'more specialized, but all the same important points, [on which] they would welcome greater certainty and a more systematic treatment'.[28]

It was only three years later that the ILC for the first time began to give concentrated attention to Fitzmaurice's proposals. In its Report to the General Assembly for 1959, the Commission expresses itself as follows:

> It is obvious that the topic of the law of treaties, considered as a whole, is so extensive as to require a number of years for completion . . . Since, however, the topic of the law of treaties is subdivided into a number of well-defined branches [e.g. conclusion, termination, execution, interpretation, etc.] . . . and these branches, while interrelated in certain respects, are to a large extent self-contained, there is no reason why the Commission's work on each of them, as and when accomplished, should not be submitted to Governments . . . without awaiting the completion of the work of the remaining branches *or on the subject as a whole.* Nevertheless, because of the interrelationship of the different branches . . . it will be necessary for the Commission eventually to review its work on the different branches . . . so as to present the work in the form of a single co-ordinated Code.[29]

In other words, it was not until 1961, on the election of Sir Humphrey Waldock to succeed Fitzmaurice, that after a general discussion the Commission gave him a specific mandate to 'prepare draft articles on the law of treaties intended to serve as the basis for a convention', and to make its intentions plain, it issued him the specific instruction to 're-examine' the work done until then by his predecessors and by the Commission as a whole.[30]

The debate within the Commission on these 1961 decisions is not however particularly instructive on the question of the scope of 'the law of treaties'. For the most part, those members who spoke confined their contributions to the debate to the formal question whether the end product should take the form of a convention or a code. Only three members – Eduardo Jiménez de Aréchaga, Roberto Ago and Jaroslav Zourek – delve a little into the question of what organising principle should determine the *content* of the draft convention (or code), and in all

---

[28] *Ibid.*, at p. 106 (paragraph 4).

[29] Report of the Commission on the Work of its Eleventh Session: Doc. A/CN.4/122, p. 90 (paragraph 13) (emphasis added).

[30] Report of the Commission on the Work of its Thirteenth Session: Doc. A/CN.4/141, p. 128 (paragraph 39).

cases the burden of their remarks is the need for selectivity, which one of them defines in terms of the need for an instrument setting out 'the general principles governing the law of treaties'.[31] Others warn against theory. That should not, however, be understood as an aversion to theory as such, but rather a wish to concentrate on practicality and therefore achievability.[32] One can infer (though only by implication) a general feeling that an advantage of a convention was that it facilitated selectivity, by comparison with a code, and that to be comprehensive meant possibly to face unmanageability. Responding to the debate in his capacity as Special Rapporteur, Waldock confirms that his approach would be pragmatic not abstract; he would 'avoid entering into theoretical questions or into issues of detail and reduce the draft articles to those points which could be submitted to States with the expectation of their approval'.[33]

So far as the present author can ascertain, these two short debates were the closest the ILC came to giving an overall definition to the scope of the work contemplated by what was now to be a 'Convention on the Law of Treaties'. Waldock's marching orders, as captured in the Commission's decision at the end of the debate, were that he should begin with the question of the conclusion of treaties and then 'proceed with the remainder of the subject of the law of treaties', which, despite its apparently global reach, cannot in fact have been thought of as that extensive, given that Waldock was also requested at the same time to cover the whole subject in two years if possible![34] And the Commission then reports in identical terms to the General Assembly, without further elaboration of any kind.

From then onwards, the Commission proceeds incrementally, step by step, without further discussion of the principles underlying the delineation of the scope of the project – except to the extent that (as will be discussed further later) it reaches concrete decisions to omit this or that question from the coverage of the draft. When the Commission comes to present the final set of draft articles to the UN General Assembly in 1966, the section in its Report on the 'Scope of the draft articles' is given over entirely to listing these exclusions,[35] and in Article 1 of the draft articles

---

[31] Zourek, Summary Record of the 621st Meeting: Doc. A/CN.4/SR.621, p. 257 (paragraph 33).

[32] It should also never be lost sight of that the work was taking place against the background of strong ideological contradictions including in the field of international law, and 'theory' could well have been a polite code word for this.

[33] *Supra* n. 31, at p. 257 (paragraph 39).   [34] *Ibid.* (paragraph 37).

[35] Treaties between States and other subjects of international law, or between such other subjects of international law, treaties not in written form, the effect of the outbreak of hostilities, State succession in respect of treaties, international responsibility for failure to

themselves, the word 'scope' is given a more laconic meaning still.[36] As regards the articulation of the project as a whole, on the other hand, more or less all the Commission has to say in the final stages of the work appears in its Report on the Seventeenth Session in 1965: '[I]n addressing itself to the revision of the draft articles as a whole, the Commission concluded that the legal rules set out in the different parts are so far interrelated that it is desirable that they should be codified in a single convention. It considered that, while certain topics in the law of treaties may be susceptible of being dealt with separately, the proper coordination of the rules governing the several topics is likely to be achieved only by incorporating them in a single, closely integrated, set of articles'.[37] No attempt, in other words, to enunciate a positive defining principle.

4 Conclusions to Be Drawn from the ILC's Work

Is this to be understood as indicating that the whole idea of a 'law of treaties' lacks meaning (or significance)? Or is it merely an indication that its meaning and significance were so far taken for granted that no need was felt – nor has been felt since – for further exploration?

To pose these questions is not intended as in any sense a criticism of the ILC, and least of all in an area that is commonly regarded by academics, legal practitioners and courts alike as one of its greatest successes, which meets the fundamental requirement enunciated from Brierly through to Waldock as being to find operational solutions to practical problems, and in a form capable of achieving international agreement. Even though never given expression as such, it seems legitimate to draw out from the record the following general thoughts as underlying the lengthy consideration of the treaties topic by successive Commissions over so many years:

- That there does exist a general concept of 'the law of treaties' sufficient to validate the use of the term, but it consists of propositions of two

---

perform a treaty, most-favoured-nation clauses and treaties providing for obligations or rights for individuals: Report of the Commission on the Work of its Eighteenth Session, Doc. A/CN.4/191, pp. 176–177 (paragraphs 28–33).

[36] I.e. '[t]he present articles relate to treaties concluded between States'.

[37] Report of the Commission on the Work of the first part of its Seventeenth Session, Doc. A/CN.4/181, pp. 157–158 (paragraph 18).

kinds: rules of law (though these tend towards the abstract) and rules of
practice or conduct (though these can at the extreme tend so far
towards the workaday that they hardly qualify as 'law').

- That the subject as a whole is vast and overlaps with other semi-
  autonomous chapters of international law, to the point that it is most
  unlikely ever to prove possible to capture it all in one comprehensive
  'Code'.
- That neither of the preceding two elements, nor indeed the two of
  them in combination, stands in the way of selective problem-solving
  nor even selective codification, so long as it is borne in mind that each
  part may affect other parts and that all represent components of
  a larger whole.

This is very much the conclusion reached by Sir Ian Sinclair in his
authoritative commentary on the Vienna Convention as it ultimately
emerged from the two sessions of the Vienna Conference.[38] As Sinclair
puts it, in accounting for what he calls the Commission's uncertainty
about the scope of the law of treaties: 'Treaties are one of the primary
sources of international law in general; they are simultaneously technical instruments governed by a distinct set of rules relating to their
conclusion, entry into force, interpretation, application, amendment,
validity and termination. In the broader sense, the law of treaties
touches upon and interacts with every other branch of general international law'.[39] Sinclair does not make the connection directly, but his
assessment does seem to lie in a straight line from McNair's differentiation between the 'content' of international law and its 'practical application' or François's observation of the distinction between 'treaty
fundamentals' and on the other hand the rationalization of treaty
practice and the way treaties are formulated, and it fits snugly with
Brierly's original preference for topics of practical (rather than theoretical) interest on which agreement was likely to be possible. That other
acute observer of international treaties, Shabtai Rosenne, made a not
dissimilar retrospective assessment of the ILC's work in his 1984 Sir
Hersch Lauterpacht Memorial Lectures:

> By basing the codification of the law of treaties in this way on the
> instrument, itself an obligation-creating instrument, and thus not on the
> obligation created by that instrument, the International Law Commission

---

[38] At which the author had played a notable part: I. Sinclair, *The Vienna Convention on the
Law of Treaties* (Manchester: Manchester University Press, 2nd ed., 1984).
[39] *Ibid.*, at p. 244.

may have simplified to some extent its task of codifying the law of treaties and, in the long run, may also have simplified the task of those called upon to interpret and apply the codified law of treaties.[40]

5 An Alternative View

The eminent scholar/practitioner Vaughan Lowe seems in a recent book chapter to have gone for a different view with some iconoclastic vigour and has suggested that the 'law of treaties' is a concept that is 'ripe for reappraisal'.[41] The exact nature of his objection is, however, less clear. It diverges from the view expressed by the book's editors themselves in their preface.[42] From the context it would seem that Lowe is reverting to the classic question raised many years ago by McNair, whether one set of rules can be adequate to cater for the wide variety of purposes pursued by treaties of different kinds.[43] As posed by Lowe, the specific question is: 'Do all treaties have enough in common to warrant the creation[44] of a distinct law of treaties?'[45] This question raised, Lowe does not pursue the argument much further other than to draw a distinction between dispositive and 'relationship' treaties and to pose the more general enquiry whether the law of treaties is not just 'part of a broader body of law applicable to obligations to which a State explicitly commits itself, as distinct from the body of customary international law, which binds a State not because it has expressly assented to it but because State practice in general, in which the State may not have participated, has generated a rule from which the State has not excepted itself'.[46] If so, the objection, somewhat uncomfortably, faces both ways: it would defy the unifying process deliberately sought after in the work of the ILC, by breaking the law down into a series of rule-parcels, each applicable to one kind of treaty, but at the same time dilute the concept of the generation of rights and obligations by 'treaty' to a point of indistinguishability. In any

---

[40] S. Rosenne, *Breach of Treaty* (Cambridge: Grotius Publications, 1984), p. 5.

[41] A. V. Lowe, 'The Law of Treaties; or, Should This Book Exist?' in C. J. Tams, A. Tzanakopoulos and A. Zimmermann (eds.), *Research Handbook on the Law of Treaties* (Cheltenham: Edward Elgar, 2014), pp. 3–15, at p. 4.

[42] C. J. Tams, A. Tzanakopoulos and A. Zimmermann, 'Introduction' in *ibid.*, pp. x–xv, at p. xi ('[The] existence of *some framework* governing treaties is a practical necessity. Dominated by treaties, international law needs a law of treaties').

[43] A. D. McNair, 'The Functions and Differing Legal Character of Treaties', *BYbIL*, 11 (1930), 100–118. See, also, McNair, *supra* n. 16, at pp. 5–6.

[44] *Sic*, though it may be queried whether 'creation' is the right word or whether it corresponds at all to the process which the ILC conceived itself as undertaking.

[45] Lowe, *supra* note 41, at p. 12.   [46] *Ibid.*, at pp. 13–14.

case, as Lowe himself points out, and correctly so, in real life treaties do
not enclose themselves in homogeneous typological boxes: '[to] be more
precise, I should say that the differences lie between treaty provisions,
because provisions with different characteristics can and commonly do
co-exist in a single instrument'.[47] The statement is surely incontestable;
take, for example, the 1945 United Nations Charter,[48] the 1982 United
Nations Convention on the Law of the Sea[49] or the 1998 Statute of the
International Criminal Court.[50] The McNair question remains of course
a valid one (as we would expect) despite the rather archaic feel of his
classic article, written in 1930, and its typology of treaty cases.[51] But to
apply it to contemporary circumstances *via* the Lowe formula would
surely take us back to a state of nature, for example to the tangled mess of
maxims and presumptions that passed for the rules of treaty interpretation before the unifying hand of the Vienna Convention. Allied to the
widening field of judicial settlement of treaty-based disputes, the result is
more likely to be a ballooning field for arbitrary discretion than
a burgeoning corpus of judicial exegesis of common principles. But in
the end it seems that neither the deconstruction nor the dilution is quite
what Lowe has in mind, but rather, '[a] certain common core of principles relating to the validity of a State's assent, the withdrawal or termination of that consent, and so on, would exist; but beyond that core, many
other questions such as the approaches to treaty interpretation, the effects
of treaties on third States, the effects of reservation and the like would be
recognized as differing from one class of treaty or commitment and [*sic*]
another'.[52] And the Lowe formula itself, on close examination, begins to
yield a rather different intention, one that allows (compels, perhaps) it to
be read as an orthodox restatement of what a 'law of treaties' in reality
means. In other words, a 'law of treaties', properly understood, should be
endowed with the inherent flexibility to enable the application of common principles to the particular treaty, or even the particular treaty
clause, in the broader context of the nature of the treaty itself and of
the specific circumstances that call for its application. Inasmuch as the
main body of the material prompting Lowe's argument is the approaches
taken to particular treaties by judicial bodies entrusted with a dispute-
settlement function under them, it seems to the present writer that what
one sees happening (whether one agrees with the particular judicial

---

[47] *Ibid.*, at p. 5.   [48] 1 UNTS 16.   [49] 1833 UNTS 3.   [50] 2187 UNTS 90.
[51] See, further, the contribution to this volume of Brölmann at pp. 79–102 (Chapter 4).
[52] Lowe, *supra* n. 41, at p. 14.

decision or not) is precisely an illustration of the 'many other questions being recognized as differing from one class of treaty to another', but without detracting from the common framework provided by a 'law of treaties'.

6 The Content of a 'Law of Treaties'

This chapter will therefore essay a provisional attempt at giving content to our innate understanding of a 'Law of Treaties', describing what it should contain and what we expect it to do. It will thus incorporate both a descriptive dimension and also a qualitative one. That having been done, the next stage will be to offer a brief assessment of how far the Vienna Convention, following its title, did indeed set out to be 'a law of treaties' and, if so, how far the attempt succeeded. It will not, however, make any attempt to assess the customary law status of the Vienna Convention's provisions. That is a task justifying a study of its own and is in any event beside the point of the present exercise, though it does have some indirect relevance to the concept of a 'modern' law of treaties, which will be discussed later.

First, though, it is worth taking a moment to look at sources, in other words where we would go to find the component materials of a 'law of treaties'. The first and most obvious source is the VCLT itself,[53] taken together with its supplement of 1986 on treaties between States and international organizations or between international organizations,[54] as well as that further product of the ILC, the 1978 Vienna Convention on Succession of States in Respect of Treaties.[55] It is self-evident, though, that these Conventions could not be taken on their own without consideration, on the one hand, of the areas of conscious omission from their texts, and on the other of State practice in their implementation (so far as that can be ascertained). One particularly informative source of additional material is subsequent international debate, mediated through the UN General Assembly, on the subject of inadequacies or deficiencies in the regimes of these Conventions either on their own or as a collective corpus of treaty law, when that leads to further studies commissioned from the International Law Commission.

From that, we can move on to the question of what, from a conceptual point of view, we would expect to be dealt with in order to justify the description 'law of treaties'. What follows is an indicative list, drawn up

---

[53] *Supra* n. 1.   [54] *Supra* n. 2.   [55] 1946 UNTS 3.

on the footing of the general proposition that, given the central place and all-purpose function of treaties in the international system, a law of treaties would be expected to resolve, with a reasonable degree of certainty, or to point to the materials needed to resolve, all questions anticipated as likely to arise in the creation and operation of treaties:

I   the formal elements identifying what is a treaty and distinguishing it from similar instruments that are not treaties;

II treaty-making capacity and (as the case may be) its limits;

III the conditions defining how a treaty comes into being and how the parties become bound by it as well as how they may cease to be bound by it;

IV the general principles of law that delineate the nature and scope of the binding effect of a treaty and identify the mutual rights and obligations of the parties to it, including in relation to rights and obligations arising out of other treaties, out of custom or out of other sources of international law;

V   conditions of validity and invalidity, as well as voidability, of individual treaties; and

VI the legal effects of the failure, or alleged failure, by one or more of the parties, to give effect to their obligations under the treaty.[56]

Questions that are not, or arguably not, part of the – or *a* – law of treaties include:

i   the administrative arrangements for maintaining and preserving treaties and related instruments and facilitating communication between the parties or would-be parties;

ii special rules for the implementation of particular treaties or types of treaty; and

iii the settlement of disputes arising out of treaty relations.

Around the preceding list is a penumbra of topics that could, depending on one's viewpoint, be regarded either as forming part of the law of treaties or as falling elsewhere. This intermediate category might include

---

[56] This multiple criterion accords, coincidentally but happily, with the recent suggestion by Hugh Thirlway that '[t]he "law of treaties" ... is the body of law which regulates the operation of treaties, including their conclusion, coming into force, validity, interpretation, suspension and termination': ' Treaty Law and the Law of Treaties in Recent Case-law of the International Court' in M. Craven and M. Fitzmaurice (eds.), *Interrogating the Treaty: Essays in the Contemporary Law of Treaties* (Nijmegen: Wolf Legal Publishers, 2005), pp. 7–28, at p. 7.

succession to treaties, the effect of war on treaties and international responsibility for breach of treaty. In each case, the question of scope would seem to be open to a reasonable answer either way. To take one striking example, the questions that had exercised the ILC in the 1950s, 1960s and 1970s and led to the inclusion of Article 6 in the Vienna Conventions of 1969 and 1986[57] no longer seem of great relevance in a post-colonial era and one in which treaty-making by international organizations has lost whatever it formerly had in the way of legal controversy. In the present author's view, therefore, the question hardly seems part of a 'law of treaties', and certainly not part of a 'modern' law of treaties. For similar, though not identical, reasons, the international responsibility element of treaty breach seems to find its place more naturally under the international responsibility heading itself.[58] The two more doubtful topics are the effect of war and treaty succession, in both of which cases it could be said that the inclusion of the topic under the rubric 'law of treaties' would be as much for the practical convenience of the consumer as for any compelling logic in the coupling – which is not conversely to say that the coupling would lack logic.[59]

A law of treaties assembled along those lines would accordingly be composed of rules corresponding to:[60]

- the appropriate parts of Articles 1, 2 and 5 VCLT and the equivalent provisions of the 1986 Vienna Convention (I);
- Articles 6 and 53 VCLT and the equivalent provisions of the 1986 Vienna Convention (II);
- Articles 9–17, 19–22, 24, 25, 39–41, 44 and 54–60 VCLT and the equivalent provisions of the 1986 Vienna Convention and the substantive provisions of the 1978 Vienna Convention on Succession of States in Respect of Treaties as well as the rules governing the effect of war on treaties (III);

---

[57] *Supra* n. 1 and n. 2.

[58] As it does indeed in Art. 12 of the ILC's Articles on State Responsibility (cf. paragraph (4) of the Commentary to that article): GAOR 56th Sess., Supp. 10, Doc. A/56/10, 43.

[59] Treaty succession is now dealt with in the 1978 Vienna Convention, *supra* n. 55, also the product of an ILC project, though with markedly less success, in the sense of general approbation and adoption, than the two general Conventions. As this has more to do, however, with the solutions the Convention proposes to the problems identified than with the problems themselves, the detailed contents of the 1978 Convention will not be further analysed here.

[60] And in addition, it goes without saying, such additional material as may be necessary to cover treaty-making by entities other than States or international organizations.

- Articles 18, 26–38, 45–52 and 69–72 VCLT and the equivalent provisions of the 1986 Vienna Convention (IV);
- Articles 44, 45, 47, 53 and 61–64 VCLT and the equivalent provisions of the 1986 Vienna Convention (V); and
- Articles 60, 70 and 72 VCLT and the equivalent provisions of the 1986 Vienna Convention (VI).

but would not include material corresponding to Articles 3 or 4, 7, 8, 23, 42, 43, 60(5), 62(2)(a), 65–68, 73–75, 76–80 or 81–85 VCLT (or their equivalents in the other Conventions cited previously).

Inevitably, there is a degree of duplication in some of these listings, but limited and conscious. Inevitably, too, there is room for disagreement over their arrangement. Nevertheless they provide a sketch of the substantive content of 'the law of treaties', in a way which, one hopes, would meet even the anxieties of McNair or the scepticism of Lowe, subject to the important proviso that the material content of certain parts of the substantive rules was cast in terms flexible enough to cope with – or perhaps even to require – some adjustment of their application to individual cases so as to take account of the particular circumstances, including the nature and purpose of the treaty in question, or in some cases the nature and purpose of the individual provisions of the treaty that are in issue. That would apply particularly, one would imagine, to the material covered under IV and VI in the preceding list.

7   A Convention 'on the Law of Treaties': A Retrospective Assessment

Against that background, this chapter can now conclude with an attempt to answer the questions posed earlier: how far did the VCLT[61] indeed set out to be 'a law of treaties', and if so, how far did it succeed in doing so?

It is difficult to answer those questions in terms of the underlying purpose of the Convention itself or of the Conference that concluded it. The intentions were those of the International Law Commission, which were never seriously put in question, once the ILC's work had got into its stride, either in the General Assembly or later at the Conference itself. And the work of the ILC, as will have been seen from the condensed account earlier, was characterised throughout by the tension (even in the shaping minds of individual Special Rapporteurs) between the wish to be

---

[61] Supplemented of course by the 1978 and 1986 Vienna Conventions: *supra* n. 55 and n. 2 respectively.

coherent and the impossibility of being comprehensive, which had its effect on both the form and the substance of the ultimate product. Alongside that was the further tension between principles general enough to qualify as rules of law and techniques, practices and administrative arrangements that do not, even though the second might be essential to the effective operation of the first.[62] From this, one can conclude that the ILC never set itself the ambition of producing 'the' law of treaties, and certainly not in one single text. The title of the draft articles, as the raw material for a Convention 'on' the law of treaties, is accurate on its face.[63]

But there are other indications, too, and more overt ones, that the ILC's ambition was more realistically modest.

The first among them, and the most obvious, are the express exclusions that narrow down the scope of the instruments to which the Convention is to apply: written agreements only, agreements between States only. These are well known but are trivial for present purposes because, even in its very drafting, Article 3 VCLT hints heavily that the Convention rules are likely to be applicable in large measure to the excluded cases as well, and so it has proved in practice.[64]

Then come the express exclusions that delimit the material scope of the Convention's rules: State succession, the effect of war, severance of relations, aggressor States, grouped together in Part VI.[65] These are not so much limitations as delimitations; the drafting in all cases takes a 'without prejudice' form. Moreover, the Commission had by then on its work programme[66] a separate project on State succession in respect of treaties.[67]

And then there is the further exclusion arising out of Article 4 VCLT, with its elaborately expressed temporal application clause[68] that has had the *effect* – whether so intended or not – of making only a small minority of the treaty disputes adjudicated since the Convention entered into force into cases directly regulated by the Convention itself.[69]

---

[62] See *supra* n. 8 and n. 32.

[63] Thirlway, *supra* n. 56, reaches a similar conclusion: 'The 1969 Vienna Convention is thus properly entitled a convention on the "Law of Treaties"'.

[64] See the 1986 Convention on Treaties between States and International Organizations or between International Organizations: *supra* n. 2.

[65] Arts. 73, 74 and 75 VCLT: *supra* n. 1.

[66] Apart from the continuation of work toward the 1986 Convention: *supra* n. 2 and n. 23.

[67] Which eventuated in the 1978 Convention: *supra* n. 55.

[68] '... applies only to treaties which are concluded by States after the entry into force of the present Convention with regard to such States'.

[69] See also Sinclair, *supra* n. 38, at pp. 8–10.

The most interesting of these self-limitations, however, are the implicit ones that emerge out of structural features of the 1969 Convention itself. The most important amongst them is that the Convention is in its entirety based on the fundamental notion of freedom of contract. This is embodied in the simple and lapidary wording of Article 6 VCLT: 'Every State possesses capacity to conclude treaties'.[70] The form itself signals that this is an inherent quality. The only restriction on this inherent capacity is found in Article 53 VCLT, *via* the operation of *jus cogens*, but that remains a highly controversial issue, both as to the identification of 'norms' falling within it and the method of their formation and as to identifying the real scope of the practical applicability of the rule in the article.[71] So far as concerns the treaty-making of international organizations, the definition of capacity to be found in Articles 6 and 2 of the 1986 Convention is (as the drafting shows) less a restriction on freedom to contract than an identification of the source and scope of the capacity. It does not touch the fact that, once acting *within* its treaty-making capacity, an international organization has a similar freedom of contract to that possessed by a State.

The consequence of this fundamental freedom of contract – and it is an important one – is that the provisions of the Vienna Conventions are almost without exception no more than residual rules – residual, that is, in the sense that they only come into application if, and to the extent that, the negotiating Parties have not arrived at their own disposition on the particular subject, for the purposes of their treaty. Both 1969 and 1986 Conventions are shot through with phrases deferring to the terms of the actual treaty, along the lines of 'unless the treaty otherwise provides' or 'if the treaty so permits'.[72] In the VCLT, for instance, clauses to that effect can be found in Articles 10, 11, 12, 13, 14, 15, 16, 17, 19, 20, 22, 24, 25, 28, 29, 30, 33, 35, 36, 39, 40, 41, 44, 54, 55, 57, 58, 59, 60, 70, 72, 76, 77 and 78. More striking still is the prevalence of sub-clauses further extending the operation of the above to agreements reached outside of, or later than, the treaty text itself, by the addition of phrases such as 'or it is otherwise

---

[70] For the somewhat more elaborate original form, with its second paragraph dealing with the case of federal States (dropped by the negotiating Conference), see the ILC's Commentary on Art. 5 in the draft articles; see, also, Sinclair, *supra* n. 38, at p. 21.

[71] See, for example, the flat refusal of the International Court of Justice to allow it any extended effect: *Case Concerning Armed Activities on the Territory of the Congo (New Application: 2002)*: Democratic Republic of the Congo v. Rwanda (Judgment: Jurisdiction and Admissibility) (2006) ICJ Rep. 6, at p. 33 (paragraph 69).

[72] The clauses themselves are phrased in a wide variety of forms.

established' or 'unless the Parties otherwise agree'. Extensions of that nature appear in Articles 7, 10, 11, 12, 13, 14, 15, 17, 22, 24, 25, 28, 29, 31, 33, 35, 36, 37, 44, 54, 56, 57, 59, 70, 72, 76 and 79. Some of them are freestanding, i.e. not appendages to clauses of the first kind.

This technique is largely one of Waldock's devising.[73] It was the key that unlocked the door to the eventual completion of the draft articles and opened the way to the conclusion of the VCLT. Under its application, some problems, which until then had seemed insoluble, simply melted away.[74] It can be seen as the inspiration for and lineal predecessor of the distinction between primary and secondary rules that ultimately made possible thirty years later the completion of the ILC's subsequent major architectural project on State responsibility. The last and likewise ultimately successful Special Rapporteur on the latter has commented in relation to the former:

> Waldock had the insight to see the Vienna Convention on the Law of Treaties as strictly focussing on what could be achieved by consent: one might say, the treaty, the whole treaty, and nothing but the treaty. Accordingly, things are left out of the Vienna Convention which on a broader view might have been there, for example the question of the supersession of treaties by subsequent practice. It is not there – not because it cannot happen – but because it is not part of the law of treaties, it is part of the law of custom, which the Convention was not codifying.[75]

8 Conclusion

These remarks are self-evidently directed towards the conceptual scope and purpose of the provisions contained in the Vienna Convention, without regard to whether, as a matter of substantive law, the solutions contained in these provisions are accepted as accurately capturing the state of 'the law' as it then was. There would be no

---

[73] Though Fitzmaurice could be said to have prefigured it, in the wonderfully tart remark in his first Report: 'Nevertheless, even though it may be possible to summarize treaty law in the one sentence that anything can be done that the parties agree upon, it is still desirable to make clear what it is that will usually require specific agreement, and what is to be the position if there is none'. *Supra* n. 26 (paragraph 5).

[74] A good example, though incomprehensible to present-day eyes, is Art. 14 VCLT, which resolved the titanic struggle over the 'necessity' of ratification.

[75] J. Crawford, 'A Consensualist Interpretation of Article 31(3) of the Vienna Convention on the Law of Treaties' in G. Nolte (ed.), *Treaties and Subsequent Practice* (Oxford: Oxford University Press, 2013), pp. 29–33, at p. 29.

dissent from the assessment that there are some areas in which the
provisions contained in the Convention had an almost immediate success
in putting to rest seemingly endemic controversies (interpretation, the
'requirement' of ratification, the 'all States' clause, *rebus sic stantibus*),
some areas in which it has notably failed (reservations, denunciation)
and yet others where there has been only partial success (depositaries,
procedure in cases of invalidity etc., third parties). Leaving those issues
aside, however, we can draw from the above the conclusion that, at the
conceptual level, the VCLT, even as supplemented by the Vienna
Conventions of 1978 and 1986, does not represent 'the law of treaties',
both because it achieves too little and because it does too much.
It does too much by including a quite considerable corpus of
material (see earlier),[76] which, however useful, is too much administrative and practice-oriented to qualify as 'law'. It achieves too
little for the simple reason that, by definition, it could not achieve
a degree of comprehensiveness for which the ILC never strove.
Over and above the areas explicitly set aside in Part VI of the
VCLT ('Miscellaneous Provisions') for possible treatment
elsewhere,[77] there is no sign that, in areas such as territorial
application or denunciation, the Commission saw its work as offering more than a very broad and incomplete outline of the subject.
Much the same could be said for the area of breach, but there the
issue became subsumed into the continuing work on State
responsibility.[78]

Does this detract from the ILC's achievement, as measured by the
Vienna Convention on the Law of Treaties? The wise and balanced
answer is 'no', for three reasons. The first is the success of the ILC's
carefully pragmatic analytical process in sweeping out of the way what
had become some rather stale controversies, notably by the way it
found to balance the freedom of contract with residual rules and fixed
principles, in devising the treaty equivalent of the elusive, but nonetheless conceptually important, distinction between the primary and
the secondary. The second is for the Commission's skill in conceiv-
ing – if not in every case – codifying formulae that, if they do not
produce cut-and-dried answers to the multifarious questions thrown
up by the life of treaties, offer a common starting point for argument

---

[76] See *supra* pp. 35-36.   [77] See *supra* p. 37 (and n. 35).
[78] See the contributions to this volume of Tams and Fitzmaurice at pp. 440–467 (Chapter 14)
and 748–789 (Chapter 23) respectively.

and waymarks towards the achievement of case-specific answers through the application of legal reasoning. The third is in the very stimulus that this admittedly incomplete exercise has administered in the continuing search for a solid conceptual base for the law of treaties.

That leaves unanswered, all the same, the question of a 'modern' law of treaties, mentioned at the beginning of this chapter. The notion depends, obviously, on the existence, as the starting point, of a 'law of treaties' as such. Given that point of departure, the epithet 'modern' could have one of two meanings. It could be purely descriptive and indicate little more than 'contemporaneous'. The sense would not be wholly trivial since, as has already been pointed out, the problems preoccupying treaty-makers and students of treaty-making in the nineteenth century were not the same as those on which the ILC concentrated in the mid-twentieth century and in all probability will be different from those confronting their counterparts fifty or even twenty-five years from now. That would not, however, be a particularly satisfying or productive usage. It would focus in too strongly on the problem areas, and the problem areas might relate quite possibly to the periphery not the centre.

An alternative use of the epithet 'modern' could advert, in a rather more abstract way, to something less tangible but at the same time deeper, namely to a conception that is still in the process of formation, of the multifarious purposes that treaties serve in the international system, and in particular to the principles and rules that are required to make those purposes properly effective. Used that way, 'modern' could have a real meaning, and one of value. It would signify the continuing search for a solid, and theoretically satisfying, architectural framework, one that would allow us to make sense of the entire gamut of the uses of treaties, from the purely synallagmatic to the largely legislative, distilling the general and separating out the particular. That would not decry the achievement of a firm and invariant core of principles and rules that the dense and continuing practice of treaty-making and treaty application takes as its axiomatic basis. Quite the contrary, it should consolidate and enhance them. It would illuminate and validate the modest programmatic caution shown over the years by the ILC and its Special Rapporteurs. It would explain the difficulty in which Lauterpacht or McNair or Reuter may have found himself in any attempt at essaying a more thoroughgoing systemization at a period of enormous development in international law and international law-making. And as to the questions posed by – though perhaps one should say problems experienced in practice by – Lowe, it might provide the material to find answers to them. At all events, the questions are too important not to be pursued, and one may hope that the present book will be seen as a worthwhile step down that road.

3

Treaties within the History of International Law

RANDALL LESAFFER[*]

1 Introduction

The earliest traces of the use of treaties in international relations date back to the very beginnings of recorded history. The oldest 'international' agreement on record stems from Sumerian Mesopotamia from about the twenty-fourth century BC. It concerns the settlement of a border dispute between the cities of Lagash and Umma. Several other treaties have been recovered in Mesopotamia and Syria from the third millennium, as from all the great civilisations of the Ancient Near East.[1] Ever since, treaties have been a constant occurrence of international relations in all parts of the world.

Scholars have generally traced the history of current international law back to the emergence of the modern sovereign State, which they situate in late-medieval Europe. Many historians of international law from the nineteenth and early twentieth centuries have taken this State- and Eurocentric approach to its ultimate consequence by claiming that no international law existed during Antiquity or most of the Middle Ages. Over the last decades, a more relativist understanding of 'international law' has gained the upper hand, leading to the recognition of different types of international law throughout history.[2] Whereas few if any scholars would conceive of the history of international law from pre-

---

[*] The author would like to express his gratitude to Inge Van Hulle (Tilburg University) for her help with the research for this chapter.

[1] A. Altman, *Tracing the Earliest Recorded Concepts of International Law: The Ancient Near East (2500–330 BCE)* (Leiden: Martinus Nijhoff, 2012), pp. 20–22, 34–38, 67–75, 111–142 and 190–199.

[2] The German Roman lawyer Wolfgang Preiser has been instrumental in this: W. Preiser, 'Zum Völkerrecht der vorklassische Antike', *Archiv des Völkerrechts*, 4 (1954), 257–288, and 'Die Epochen der antiken Völkerrechtsgeschichte', *Juristenzeitung*, 11 (1956), 737–744. For an early example of the relativist approach: P. Vinogradoff, *Historical Types of International Law: Lectures Delivered in the University of Leiden* (Leiden: E.J. Brill, 1923). Also in W. E. Butler (ed.), *On the History of International Law and*

classical or classical Antiquity as the history of a single evolving system, there is a general recognition that there is continuity for some institutions or principles of international law.[3] Treaties are among those. In case of treaties, it has been established that a tradition runs from the Ancient Near East over the Greeks and the Romans to the Byzantine Empire and the Germanic vanquishers of the Western Roman Empire.[4] Through this and the mediating role of Roman and canon law in the Late Middle Ages, this tradition feeds into the international legal order as it started to develop in late-medieval and Renaissance Europe.[5]

This chapter highlights some aspects of the role of treaties as instruments of international law from Antiquity to the present. The discussion is limited to the line that flows from classical Antiquity over the European Middle Ages and the Early Modern Age to the treaty law of the nineteenth and twentieth centuries, which then found its codification in the Vienna Conventions of 1969[6] and 1986.[7] This is not to deny that the European encounter with the wider world during the Age of Colonisation had an impact on the development of modern treaty law. But within the limits of this chapter, focus is laid on the main line of tradition. Revision of Eurocentric historiography of international law is valuable and much needed, but one should be careful not to overstate the case of the impact of non-European cultures through the colonial encounter on the formation of the European classical law of nations, that is prior to the nineteenth century.[8] Certainly, the European imperialists of the sixteen to eighteen centuries in their dealings with particularly

International Organization. Collected Papers of Sir Paul Vinogradoff (Clark, NJ: Lawbook Exchange, 2009), pp. 69–143.

[3] For a discussion of this shift in historiography and a survey of literature: C. Focarelli, 'The Early Doctrine of International Law as a Bridge from Antiquity to Modernity and Diplomatic Inviolability in 16th- and 17th-Century Practice' in R. Lesaffer (ed.), *The Twelve Years Truce (1609): Peace, Truce, War and Law in the Low Countries at the Turn of the 17th Century* (Leiden: Koninklijke Brill NV, 2014), pp. 210–232.

[4] P. Karavites, *Promise-Giving and Treaty-Making: Homer and the Near East* (Leiden: E.J. Brill, 1992) and E. S. Gruen, *The Hellenistic World and Coming of Rome* (Berkeley, CA: University of California Press, 1984).

[5] R. Lesaffer, 'Roman Law and the Intellectual History of International Law' in A. Orford and F. Hoffmann (eds.), *The Oxford Handbook of the Theory of International Law* (Oxford: Oxford University Press, 2016), pp. 38–58.

[6] 1155 UNTS 331.   [7] ILM, 25 (1986), 543–592.

[8] The foremost representative of the revisionist historians of the 'Third World Approaches of International Law' is A. Anghie: see his *Imperialism, Sovereignty and the Making of International Law* (Cambridge: Cambridge University Press, 2005). See, further, M. Koskenniemi, 'Histories of International Law: Dealing with Eurocentrism', *Rechtsgeschichte*, 19 (2001), 152–176.

Asian but also African rulers were often not in a position to one-sidedly impose their legal institutions. Moreover, research under the lens of the colonial encounter may very well indicate instances of how non-European elements fed into the European law of nations, but this does not reach the point where one could with justice deny that the historical roots of modern treaty law are predominantly Mediterranean and European.[9] The backbones of the customary law of treaties which was codified in the Vienna Conventions – such as the doctrine of good faith, the many analogies from contract law, its State-centeredness, its various forms – were already present in the classical law of nations of Early Modern Europe. Its major roots lay in late-medieval and early-modern European practices as well as in doctrines taken from Roman (private) law and canon law.[10]

This chapter falls into two sections. In the first section, the evolving function of treaties in international law is discussed in general terms. The focus is on the question to what extent treaties, apart from creating specific obligations between the treaty parties, were also constitutive sources of international law and order.[11] This relates to but goes beyond the modern distinction between *traités-contrats* and *traités-lois*.[12] It also includes the function of treaties as 'social contracts' which constitute or reform the legal and political order to which they belong. In other words,

---

[9] On treaty relations between Europe and Asian and African polities in the Early Modern Age, see C. H. Alexandrowicz, 'Treaty and Diplomatic Relations between European and South Asian Powers in the Seventeenth and Eighteenth Centuries', *Hague Recueil*, 100 (1960–II), 203–321; see, also, C. H. Alexandrowicz, *An Introduction to the Law of Nations in the East Indies (16th, 17th and 18th Centuries)* (Oxford: Clarendon Press, 1967); C. H. Alexandrowicz, 'The Afro-Asian World and the Law of Nations (Historical Approach)', *Hague Recueil*, 123 (1968–I), 117–214, and C. H. Alexandrowicz, *The European-African Confrontation: A Study in Treaty Making* (Leiden: A.W. Sijthoff, 1973).

[10] R. Lesaffer, 'The Medieval Canon Law of Contract and Early Modern Treaty Law', *J. History Int'l L.*, 2 (2000), 178–198.

[11] A brief word on terminology as used throughout the chapter is necessary. Treaties are called 'informative sources' of international law to indicate the case in which they apply and thus render evidence of existing international law. They are called 'constitutive sources' of international law if they contribute to the creation of new international law. This encompasses several modes in which treaties contribute to the law-making process. The term 'formal source' is restricted to one of these modes, namely the case of treaties which directly introduce new generally binding rules between the parties on the basis of their agreement. 'Constitutional' refers to the formation or reformation of international organizations or polities through the use of treaties.

[12] On the origins of the distinction, see H. Lauterpacht, *Private Law Sources and Analogies of International Law (with Special Reference to International Arbitration)* (London: Longman, Green & Co., 1927), pp. 156–159.

a third category of *traités-constitutions* needs to be added. The first section also discusses the basis for the binding character of treaties as well as their form. The second section gives a survey of the main functions of treaties from the perspective of their content. An attempt is made to offer a functional classification of treaties throughout (Western) history.[13] The conclusion offers a brief reflection on the different historic functions of treaties as sources of international law.[14]

2   Treaties and the Formation of International Law

2.1   Antiquity (2500 BC–500 AD)

The question of the constitutional role of treaties for international order and law in classical Antiquity can be best approached from the debate about the function of *amicitia* (friendship). *Amicitia* is a qualification of peace. It goes beyond the mere absence of a state of war or armed conflict as it entails a general obligation to favour and not to harm one another. The obligation extends to the subjects and sometimes allies of the *amici* but is not necessarily concretised in any way.[15] The German historian Theodor Mommsen (1817–1903) cast a long shadow over this debate. Mommsen applied the Hobbesian doctrine of natural enmity to Roman international relations and law. According to Mommsen, the natural state of relations between the Romans and foreign peoples was one of permanent war. This state could only be terminated through a treaty of friendship.[16] Later historians, chiefly among them Alfred Heuß (1909–1995), have refuted Mommsen's theory on two major points.[17] According to Heuß and the vast majority of scholars after him, the natural or initial state of relations between foreign peoples was one not

---

[13] Attempts at classifications of treaties are to be found in A. D. McNair, 'The Functions and Differing Legal Character of Treaties', *BYbIL*, 11 (1930), 100–118, and A. Rapisardi-Mirabelli, 'La classification des traités internationaux. Aperçus de systématique', *Revue de droit international et de législation comparée*, 4 (1923), 653–667.

[14] See, further, the discussion in the contribution to this volume of Brölmann at pp. 79–102 (Chapter 4).

[15] R. Lesaffer, 'Amicitia in Renaissance Peace and Alliances Treaties', *J. History Int'l L.*, 4 (2002), 77–99, and B. Paradisi, 'L'amitié dans les phases critiques de son ancienne histoire', *Hague Recueil*, 78 (1951–I), 325–378.

[16] T. Mommsen, *Römisches Staatsrecht* (Vol. III.1) (Leipzig: Hirzel, 1887), pp. 590–592.

[17] L. C. Winkel defends the doctrine of natural enmity: 'Einige Bemerkungen über ius naturale und ius gentium' in M. J. Schermaier and Z. Végh (eds.), *Ars boni et aequi. Festschrift für Wolfgang Waldstein zum 65. Geburtstag* (Stuttgart: Steiner, 1993), pp. 443–449.

of enmity but of indifference. Moreover, whereas *amicitia* was indeed, as Mommsen suggested, the foundational and necessary precondition to the development of peaceful international order and law between polities – at least outside the bonds of ethnical and religion kinship – according to Heuß, there were no autonomous, constitutive treaties of *amicitia* and the relationship was established through less formal ways such as the exchange of emissaries and gifts.[18] Later research has sustained the theory of Heuß in general terms, but some scholars have discovered treaties of *amicitia* leading them to claim that treaties were not a necessary condition for *amicitia* but a possible form of it.[19] In any case, *amicitia* through treaty was exceptional. The vast majority of initial treaties between polities and peoples established a relation between polities which included but also went beyond *amicitia*, such as commerce, alliance, subjection or federation. Also, they stipulated more concrete obligations between the partners. So it can be said that already in Antiquity – as these findings are also confirmed for Greek international practice and by records on the Ancient Near East – treaties were first and foremost used to create specific obligations between peoples and polities.

From this, however, it cannot be concluded that treaties were not constitutive sources of international law. In many cases, treaty parties had relatively little pre-existing common international law to draw on and to apply in treaties. There are several instances of multi-party international systems – in the Ancient Near East between 1450 and 1200 BC, the Greek-Persian world (600–338 BC), the Roman-Hellenistic world (500–168 BC) and the Roman Empire (168 BC–500 AD)[20] – wherein relations were sufficiently intense and sustained for a common body of norms and institutions of international relations to develop. Treaties formed a constitutive source of this international law. Although the vast majority of treaties were bilateral, they were instrumental in the articulation of general rules and forms as in these systems, standard forms of treaty-making as well as standard material stipulations emerged.

---

[18] A. Heuß, 'Die völkerrechtliche Grundlagen der römischen Außenpolitik in republikanischer Zeit', *Klio, Beihefte*, 13 (1933), 1–59.

[19] F. de Martino, *Storia della costituzione romana* (Vol. II) (Naples: Jovene, 1973), pp. 26–29, and K.-H. Ziegler, 'Das Freundschaftsvertrag im Völkerrecht der römischen Antike' in *Pensamiento juridico y sociedad internacional. Estudios en honor Antonio Truyol y Serra* (Vol. II) (Madrid: Centro de estudios constitutionales–Universidad Complutense, 1986), pp. 1263–1271.

[20] Preiser, 'Die Epochen der antiken Völkerrechtsgeschichte', *supra* n. 2, and K.-H. Ziegler, *Völkerrecht. Ein Studienbuch* (Munich: Beck, 2nd ed., 2007), pp. 11–51.

Treaties were the most important sources for later treaties and were thus constitutive for the customary practice and even customary law of treaty-making, in relation both to form and to content.[21]

The emergence of organised international order found its reflection in the Greek stoic idea of common humanity and natural law. In Roman doctrine, natural law came to be associated to the *jus gentium*. Originally the body of law the Roman *praetor peregrinus* applied to cases involving foreigners, in the works of the orator Marcus Tullius Cicero (106–43 BC) and different lawyers from the imperial period, the *jus gentium* appeared as the common law of mankind and as an articulation of natural law. By the end of the Roman period, the term *jus gentium* was used both to refer to universal private law as well as to (public) international law.[22]

The commonality and continuity of ancient treaty practice are most obvious in relation to the forms of treaty-making. From the earliest treaties of the Ancient Near East to the treaty practice of the later Roman Empire, the standard form of treaty-making combined oral commitment with the swearing of an oath under the invocation of the gods or God. In remoter times, the oath-taking had often been accompanied by self-cursing and religious rituals such as sacrifices. Already in the Ancient Near East, treaties were also written down and published on tablets or pillars, and sometimes copies were preserved in temples. It was, however, the oral commitment and the oath, and not the recording, which were constitutive of the obligation. The records served as proof of the treaty and its content, for men as well as for the gods whose retribution for future violation was invoked under the oath.[23]

---

[21] C. Baldus, *Regelhafte Vertragsauslegung nach Parteirollen* (Frankfurt: Peter Lang, 1998); D. J. Bederman, *International Law in Antiquity* (Cambridge: Cambridge University Press, 2001), pp. 137–206; Gruen, *supra* n. 4, at pp. 13–53, and C. Phillipson, *The International Law and Custom of Ancient Greece and Rome* (Vol. II) (London: Macmillan, 1911), pp. 1–89.

[22] H. C. Baldry, *The Unity of Mankind in Greek Thought* (Cambridge: Cambridge University Press, 1965); M. C. Horowitz, 'The Stoic Synthesis of the Idea of Natural Law in Man', *J. History of Ideas*, 35 (1974), 3–16; T. Honoré, *Ulpian. Pioneer of Human Rights* (Oxford: Oxford University Press, 2nd ed., 2002), pp. 76–93; M. Kaser, *Ius gentium* (Köln/Weimar/Vienna: Böhlau, 1993); Lesaffer, *supra* n. 5; L. Winkel, 'The Peace Treaties of Westphalia as an Instance of the Reception of Roman Law' in R. Lesaffer (ed.), *Peace Treaties and International Law in European History: From the End of the Middle Ages to World War One* (Cambridge: Cambridge University Press, 2004), pp. 222–238, at pp. 225–229.

[23] A. Watson, *International Law in Archaic Rome: War and Religion* (Baltimore, MD: Johns Hopkins University Press, 1993), pp. 1–19 and 31–37, and K.-H. Ziegler, 'Conclusion and Publication of International Treaties in Antiquity', *Israel L. Rev.*, 29 (1995), 233–249.

The binding character of treaties was vested in the commitment of their faith by the treaty parties to the sanction of their respective gods. In the past, this has induced scholars to refute the very existence of international legal obligation, but over recent decades, scholars have come to accept religious obligation as just another form of normativity and as the ancients' form of international legal obligation.[24] In archaic Greece and Rome, the binding character of treaties was not so much based on mutual agreement as on the separate commitments by both parties. Of course, an agreement to make such commitments underlay this form and, over time, the idea of agreement started to surface. As one scholar recently elucidated, religious obligation came to be supplemented by a normativity founded, first, on social sanction coming from the fear of gods and, second, on intellectual sanction, coming from the fear of moral indignation and political isolation. While originally based on religion, the foundations for this were gradually secularised into a customary rule of the obligatory character of international agreements. As in domestic law, this found its doctrinal expression in the Greek and Roman concept of good faith (πιστις, bona fides).[25]

2.2   The Middle Ages (500–1500)

Many of the concepts, forms and institutions of ancient treaty law and practice survived into the Early Middle Ages, both in the Byzantine Empire as in the defunct Western Roman Empire. The Germanic peoples who conquered the West and founded new kingdoms there had at some point established treaty relations with the Roman emperors as their *foederati* (allies). During the Early Middle Ages, among the Germanic kingdoms, *amicitia* was an important institution of international relations and regained its meaning as the foundation to more elaborate legal relations. It was associated to the institution of 'sworn friendship', a personal relation with mutual obligations between equals. More than in Antiquity, treaties were used to establish friendship – and stipulate more specific obligations – just as personal sworn friendship was established through pacts.[26]

---

[24] For a survey of the discussion, see Bederman, *supra* n. 21, at pp. 1–15, and Focarelli, *supra* n. 3.

[25] Bederman, *supra* n. 21, at pp. 48–53.

[26] On the Early Middle Ages: G. Althoff, 'Amicitiae as Relationships between States and Peoples' in L. K. Little and B. H. Rowenstein (eds.), *Debating the Middle Ages: Issues and Readings* (Malden: Blackwell, 1998), pp. 191–210; B. Paradisi, *Storia del diritto*

After the revival of the Latin West in the so-called Renaissance of the Twelfth Century, a new international legal order emerged. On the one hand, this order was marked by the extreme fragmentation of public authority over a great variety of polities ranging from the Empire and the Church over great kingdoms, secular and ecclesiastical principalities, feudal fiefs, city-states to the smallest seigniories. These all stood in some kind of hierarchical relationship to one another but could also hold far-reaching autonomy. On the other hand, the Latin West was an integrated political order. This was based on the unity of faith and of the Church under the supreme authority of the Bishop of Rome and on the idea of the continuity of the Roman Empire (*renovatio/translatio imperii*). One has to think of the *respublica christiana* – as it was to be named during the Renaissance – as a hierarchical continuum of a myriad of polities which ultimately all fell under the supreme authority of the pope in spiritual matters, which was real, and of the emperor in temporal matters, which was at best theoretical but came to be rejected altogether under the doctrine of the division of empire.[27] Its unity found legal expression in the universal application of canon law and the commonality of the learned study of canon and Roman law.[28]

Within the confines of the legal space that was the *respublica christiana*, the divide between the 'inter-national' and 'intra-national' sphere faded. Moreover, the personal character of political relations of dependency which came with feudality as well as the Germanic patrimonial conception of kingship blurred the distinctions between private obligations and public authority, to the point of public law fading into private law, or rather the law at large. Treaty practice reflected this in the highly personal character of political treaties. These were rather compacts between persons than between polities. Medieval treaties were styled

---

internazionale nel Medio Evo (Milan: Giuffrè, 1940); H. Steiger, *Die Ordnung der Welt. Eine Völkerrechtsgeschichte des karolingischen Zeitalters (741 bis 840)* (Köln/Weimar/ Vienna: Böhlau, 2010) and K.-H. Ziegler, *Die Beziehungen zwischen Rom und dem Partenreich. Eine Beitrag zur Geschichte des Völkerrechts* (Wiesbaden: Steiner, 1964).

[27] Under the papal bull *Per venerabilem* of 1202: X. 1.6.34. See, also, J. Canning, *Ideas of Power in the Late Middle Ages 1296–1417* (Cambridge: Cambridge University Press, 2011) and K. Pennington, *The Prince and the Law 1200–1600. Sovereignty and Rights in the Western Legal Tradition* (Berkeley, CA: University of California Press, 1993).

[28] M. Bellomo, *The Common Legal Past of Europe 1000–1800* (Washington, DC: Catholic University of America Press, 1995); J. Brundage, *Medieval Canon Law* (London: Longman, 1995); R. Lesaffer, *European Legal History: A Cultural and Political Perspective* (Cambridge: Cambridge University Press, 2009), pp. 192–288, and P. Stein, *Roman Law in European History* (Cambridge: Cambridge University Press, 1999), pp. 38–103.

as contracts between princes who undertook personal obligations to one another and committed themselves to impose these onto their subjects, vassals and adherents. Until the very end of the Middle Ages, this found its expression in the wordings of preambles and treaty clauses, the express stipulations about the validity of treaties for the successors of the treaty principals or the system of co-ratification whereby powerful subjects were directly bound to the treaty of their prince. This implied that there was no autonomous doctrine of the law of nations. Nevertheless, within the learned law at large were found numerous rules which were applied to relations between polities and matters of war, peace, diplomacy and trade. To this, the learned lawyers would refer with the Roman term *jus gentium*, a term that encompassed – as it had done for later Roman jurists – both universal (private) law and inter-polity law.[29]

In the highly legalised sphere of late-medieval inter- and trans-polity political and personal relations, thick layers of legal doctrine and customs pertaining to matters of war, peace, diplomacy and trade were developed. Because there was no autonomous body or scholarship of the law of nations as yet, modern scholars have far and wide neglected this period and underestimated the impact of the Late Middle Ages on the formation of the modern law of nations. All this is also true for treaty law and practice. From the late eleventh century onwards, increasingly standardised as well as sophisticated treaty practices developed, as regards both material clauses and formalities. These did not develop in a relative juridical vacuum as in Antiquity but against the backdrop of a rich, pluralist and complex legal reality. Late-medieval treaty practice took inspiration from many sources. These included ancient and Germanic practices, feudal law, ecclesiastical arbitration and adjudication and above all the learned *jus commune* of canon and Roman law.[30] The blurring of the distinctions between the

---

[29] J. Canning, *The Political Thought of Baldus de Ubaldis* (Cambridge: Cambridge University Press, 1987), pp. 76–78; R. Lesaffer, 'Peace Treaties from Lodi to Westphalia' in Lesaffer (ed.), *supra* n. 22, pp. 9–41, at pp. 17–22; H. Mitteis, 'Politische Verträge des Mitterlalters' in H. Mitteis (ed.), *Die Rechtsidee in der Geschichte. Gesammelte Abhandlungen und Vorträge* (Weimar: Böhlau, 1957), pp. 567–611, at pp. 569–574. On the different meanings of *jus gentium*, see J. Waldron, *'Partly Laws Common to Mankind': Foreign Law in American Courts* (New Haven, CT: Yale University Press, 2012).

[30] The *jus commune* also encompassed some feudal law through the inclusion of the *Libri feudorum*, a compilation of feudal law, into the *Liber parvum*, the final part of the medieval collation of the Justinian codification.

'international' and the 'national' as well as between the private and public spheres allowed for the application of doctrines and concepts of private law to inter-polity relations. Thus the medieval civilians and canonists did not only take inspiration from the scarce references to Roman public international law in the Justinian collection for the formation of treaty doctrine. Much of what would become modern treaty law found its origins in the Roman law of contract and made its way into international treaty practice and doctrine thanks to the mediating role of the medieval *jus commune*.[31]

All this meant that medieval treaties played a lesser role in the constitution of international law and order. There were primarily, and often exclusively, instruments to settle particular disputes and create specific obligations between the treaty partners. They applied rather than created the *jus gentium*, although through standardised practice treaties remained a source for later treaties and thus, ultimately, for formal treaty law and material law of nations. All this explains why medieval treaties, regardless of the use of elaborate notarial forms with their repetitive language, were often short. Even one of the more extensive peace treaties, that of Brétigny between England and France of 8 May 1360, while being quite articulate on the details of the concrete undertakings of the parties, was relatively short as there was no need to explain the specific legal implications of the concepts and institutions referred to.[32]

Canon and civilian doctrine found its way into treaty practice through three main channels. Firstly, ecclesiastical courts played a significant role in the settlement of disputes about treaties. Because most treaties were confirmed by oath, disputes about the execution, interpretation and violation of treaties fell within the jurisdiction of the Church. Secondly, medieval rulers made use of notaries – who generally had been trained in Roman and/or canon law – to produce the written charters of treaties and their ratifications. Notarial practices played a significant role in the development of treaty practice and law. Some medieval notarial

---

[31] Mitteis, *supra* n. 29, at pp. 568–569; J. Muldoon, 'A Canonist Contribution to the Formation of International Law', *The Jurist*, 28 (1968), 265–279; J. Muldoon, 'The Contribution of Medieval Canon Lawyers to the Formation of International Law', *Traditio*, 28 (1972), 483–497; A. Wijffels, 'Early-Modern Scholarship on International Law' in A. Orakhelashvili (ed.), *Research Handbook on the Theory and History of International Law* (Chelthenham: Edward Elgar, 2011), pp. 23–60, at pp. 29–32, and K.-H. Ziegler, 'Die römische Grundlagen des europäischen Völkerrechts', *Ius Commune*, 4 (1972), 1–27.

[32] J. Dumont, *Corps universel diplomatique du droit des gens* (Vol. II.1) (Amsterdam/The Hague: Brunel/Husson & Levrier, 1726–1731), p. 7.

formularies include forms for specific kinds of treaties.[33] Thirdly, canonists as well as civilians were often asked for their legal advice on disputes of an international political nature. The collections of *consilia* of major commentators such as the fourteenth-century Italians Bartolus of Sassoferrato (1313/1314–1357) and Baldus de Ubaldis (1327–1400) or their fifteenth- and sixteenth-century successors such as Andrea Alciato (1492–1550) include several advices relevant to the law of treaties or general treaty practice.[34]

For the whole of the Middle Ages, confirmation by oath remained the primary formality in the conclusion of treaties. This was not limited to treaties among Christians. Oaths were also used for treaties with Muslim rulers or, later, during the Age of Discoveries, with rulers outside Europe and the Middle East.[35] Within the Latin West, the oath-taking brought treaty-making within the sphere of the Catholic Church. The oath-taking did not only entail the invocation of the name of God but was generally performed in church and accompanied by religious gestures such as the touching of the Gospel, the Holy Cross or relics. Moreover, the confirmation of a treaty – or any pact such as private contracts – brought it squarely under the jurisdiction of the Church and its courts, including the highest one, the papal court. Whereas any promise triggered the jurisdiction of the Church *ratione peccati* (because of sin) *in foro interno* – in conscience and in the court of God at the Last Judgment – perjury was also a sin considered to be actionable *in foro externo* – leading to ecclesiastical sanction in the here and now.[36]

From Carolingian times onwards, the written form of treaties gained in importance. This was, in part, consequential to the emergence of a new method of treaty-making. In the Early Middle Ages, most treaties were directly made by the principals of the treaties – kings or other

---

[33] E.g. in G. Durantis (c. 1237–1296), *Speculum iudiciale* (c. 1290), 4.1: *De treuga et pace*; see K.-H. Ziegler, 'The Influence of Medieval Roman Law on Peace Treaties' in Lesaffer (ed.), *supra* n. 22, pp. 147–161, at pp. 152–153.

[34] J. Mearns, 'A Consultation by Andrea Alciato on the Laws of War', *Legal History Rev.*, 90 (2014), 100–140.

[35] Alexandrowicz, 'Treaty and Diplomatic Relations', *supra* n. 9, at 294, and A. Nussbaum, 'Forms and Observance of Treaties in the Middle Ages and the Early Sixteenth Century' in G. A. Lipsky (ed.), *Law and Politics in the World Community: Essays on Hans Kelsen's Pure Theory and Related Problems in International Law* (Berkeley, CA: University of California Press, 1953), pp. 191–196, at p. 195.

[36] Papal decree *Ille novit* from Innocent III (1198–1216), X. 2.1.13. See, further, R. H. Helmholz, *The Spirit of Classical Canon Law* (Athens, GA: University of Georgia Press, 1996), pp. 162–163.

rulers – during a meeting. Oral commitment and confirmation by oath could thus take place on the spot, with the recording as the final outcome. Gradually, an alternative method – which had ancient precedents – emerged. By the end of the Middle Ages this superseded the old method and became the standard form of treaty-making. This new, composite method involved the negotiation of the treaties by representatives of the principals, followed by the confirmation or ratification by the principals through the taking of an oath. The latter was done separately by each of the treaty principals, generally in the presence of a representative of the treaty partner. This method implied the production of three sets of written charters: full powers, the treaty text concluded by the negotiators and the charters attesting the confirmation by oath of the treaty by each of the principals. These charters took the form of notarial instruments and were signed and sealed either by the principals, in the case of full powers and ratifications, or by the diplomatic representatives, in the case of the compromise text. It is hard to assess when and how the written instruments of ratification gained constitutive apart from evidentiary value, but it is safe to assess that by the twelfth or thirteenth century this was the case.[37] By consequence, written ratifications gained a dual function: on the one hand they offered evidence of the ratification by oath, while on the other hand they had constitutive value for the consent and commitment of the treaty parties.[38] During the Late Middle Ages, treaties were also made by princes upon their honour as king and knight. This made them binding under the code of chivalry.[39]

Historians of international law have questioned what made the treaty binding under the law of nations. The German international lawyer Heinhard Steiger has put forward the view that whereas the oath made it binding under canon law, the written form made it so under the law of nations. For the Middle Ages, this misses the point as it neglects the inherent pluralist character of the *jus gentium*. There was no *jus gentium* as a self-sufficient, autonomous body of law. Instead, there was a mass of practices and doctrines that were themselves derived from a plurality of

---

[37] Steiger considers this to be already the case for some Carolingian treaties: *supra* n. 26, at pp. 386–415.

[38] L. Bittner, *Die Lehre von den völkerrechtlichen Vertragsurkunden* (Stuttgart/Berlin/Leipzig: Deutsche Verlagsanstalt, 1924); A. Z. Hertz, 'Medieval Treaty Obligation', *Connecticut JIL*, 6 (1991), 425–443, and Nussbaum, *supra* n. 35.

[39] A. Z. Hertz, 'Honour's Role in the International States' System', *Denver JILP*, 31 (2002), 113–156.

practices and doctrines. The oath made the treaty enforceable before ecclesiastical courts, while the oral commitment and the written form made it binding under canon law, feudal law, Roman law and traditional treaty practice. All these sources combine to form the law and practice of treaties under the *jus gentium* of the Late Middle Ages.[40]

2.3   Early Modern Age (1500–1815)

The first half of the sixteenth century was marked by major upheavals that caused the transformation of the international legal order of Europe over the century to follow. In the decades *after* the Peace Treaties of Westphalia (1648), a new international order would emerge, that of the modern States system and the classical law of nations (1648–1815). The crisis of the international system during the sixteenth century had three causes. First, the Reformation caused half of Europe to reject the authority of the pope and of canon law and collapsed the very foundation of the unity of the Latin West and of its legal order. Second, the discoveries and conquests outside Europe challenged the relevance of canon and Roman law as authoritative sources for the law of nations. Third, powerful dynasties started a process of centralisation within what would become the sovereign States of Europe. It led to the final demise of the claims to universal authority in secular matters of pope and emperor and the gradual monopolisation of matters of war, peace and diplomacy by one type of polity to the exclusion of all others. Thus a sphere for a separate public international law was created.[41]

The crisis and transformation of the international legal order had its impact felt on treaty practice in three ways. Firstly, there was the monopolisation of treaties by the emerging sovereign States. This led to the emancipation of treaty law as part of the newly emerging law of nations from general contract law. This was, among others, reflected in the rapid disappearance of the last remnants of the personal character of medieval treaties such as personal co-ratification or the limitations of treaty

---

[40] Lesaffer, *supra* n. 29, at pp. 22–29; H. Steiger, 'Bemerkungen zum Friedensvertrag von Crépy en Laonnais vom 18. September 1544 zwischen Karl V. und Franz I', in U. Beyerlin, M. Bothe, R. Hofmann and E.-U. Petersmann (eds.), *Recht zwischen Umbruch und Bewahrung: Völkerrecht–Europarecht–Staatsrecht: Festschrift für Rudolf Bernhardt* (Berlin: Springer, 2nd ed., 1995), pp. 249–265, at pp. 256–260.

[41] R. Lesaffer, 'The Grotian Tradition Revisited: Change and Continuity in the History of International Law', BYbIL, 73 (2002), 103–139, and R. Lesaffer, 'The Classical Law of Nations (1500–1800)' in Orakhelashvili (ed.), *supra* n. 31, pp. 408–440.

duration to the life of the signatory princes. Although until the very end of the *Ancien Régime*, treaties would still mention the princes and not their polities as treaty partners, by the late seventeenth century it was clear that the princes acted as constitutional agents of their polities binding their subjects directly to the treaty. This shift found expression in the increasing use of titles rather than names of princes.[42] The emergence of an autonomous body of 'public' treaty law also allowed for treaty law to materially divert from general contract law. The debates, in doctrine and practice, about the application of the *clausula rebus sic stantibus* – which came from medieval theology and learned contract law – and the refusal to apply to public treaties the exception of duress (*vis metusve*) which was generally applied to contracts under Roman law are prime illustrations thereof.

Secondly, the Reformation collapsed the major pillars under the structure of the international order of the Middle Ages: canon law and ecclesiastical jurisdiction. This, together with the more gradual erosion of the universal authority of Roman law and of feudal law, threw the emerging States of Europe upon their own devices to develop and articulate international legal rules. Thus custom and treaties came once again to the fore as major constitutive sources of the law of nations to the detriment of doctrine. The backbones of the new political and legal order of Europe which emerged in the late seventeenth and eighteenth centuries were for a large part to be found in treaties, in particular treaties of peace, alliance and commerce. The great peace compacts made at important, often multi-party peace conferences, such as those of Westphalia (1648), Nijmegen (1678–1679), Ryswick (1697), Utrecht-Rastadt-Baden (1713–1715), Aachen (1748) or Paris-Hubertusburg (1763), laid out the basis for the peace ordering of Europe. While the compromises reached there were mainly of a political nature, they were also vested on a consent about the foundational principles and values which through the treaties gained normative value. The inscription of the principle of the 'balance of Europe' in some of the Utrecht peace treaties is a prime example thereof.[43] It must be noted that whereas most of these major peace compacts were negotiated at multilateral peace conferences ending

---

[42] W. G. Grewe, *The Epochs of International Law* (Berlin: De Gruyter, 2000), p. 361, and Lesaffer, *supra* n. 29, at pp. 22–29.

[43] Most clearly in the Peace Treaties of 13 July 1713 between Great Britain and Spain (Art. 2) as well as between Savoy and Spain (Art. 3): 28 CTS 269 and 28 CTS 295 respectively. See, further, F. Dhondt, 'From Contract to Treaty: the Legal Transformation of the Spanish Succession, 1659–1713', *J. History Int'l L.*, 13 (2011), 347–375, and A. Osiander, *The States*

wars which involved multiple belligerents and their auxiliaries, with the exception of the Aachen Peace Treaty of October 1748,[44] these peace settlements were actually laid down in bilateral treaties between the different belligerents. Nevertheless, the constitutional role of these treaties for the over-arching European political and legal order was materialised in different ways, such as through the inclusion of similar or literally the same material clauses, cross references between treaties made at the same conference or references to older peace settlements.[45]

But treaties were also material in the development of customary law of nations, both in the field of treaty law as of other material fields of law. Treaties were of particular importance for the laws of maritime commerce, neutrality and the *jus post bellum*, especially with regard to the treatment of private property, prisoners of war and surrendered territories. Between the sixteenth and early eighteenth centuries, treaties became increasingly elaborate legal documents, often fine-tuning the implications of the parties' concrete undertakings in great detail.

The main source of inspiration for the negotiators and drafters of early-modern treaties were, without any doubt, earlier treaties. Scholarship, albeit not without significance, came a distant second. This does not serve, however, to deny that the doctrinal concepts and institutions developed by late-medieval civilians and canonists, which had made their way into treaty practice before, survived in early-modern practice. Throughout the period which runs from the Late Middle Ages to the nineteenth century, one can see the gradual development of concepts, institutions and rules of law in the fields of the law of treaties, navigation, commerce, neutrality and peace-making through strings of consecutive treaties. These traditions follow a process whereby clauses first become more elaborate and detailed but are later standardised and abridged, whereby use is made of a more fixed terminology. The first phase, generally speaking, runs to the late seventeenth century; the second phase covers the eighteenth and nineteenth centuries.[46]

System of Europe 1640–1990: Peacemaking and the Conditions of International Stability (Oxford: Oxford University Press, 1994).

[44] 38 CTS 297.

[45] K. Marek, 'Contribution à l'étude de l'histoire du traité multilatéral' in E. Diez, J. Monnier, J. P. Müller *et al.* (eds.), *Festschrift für Rudolf Bindschedler: am 65. Geburtstag am 8. Juli 1980* (Bern: Stämpfli, 1980), pp. 17–39, and S. C. Neff, 'Peace and Prosperity: Commercial Aspects' in Lesaffer (ed.), *supra* n. 22, pp. 365–381, at pp. 367–370.

[46] J. Fisch, *Krieg und Frieden im Friedensvertrag. Eine universalgeschichtliche Studie über die Grundlagen und Formelemente des Friedensschlusses* (Stuttgart: Klett-Cotta, 1979),

One can dispute whether these traditional practices constitute customary law. From the perspective of a strict definition of customary law, for many cases the answer is in the negative as a clear indication of *opinio juris* is lacking. The emergence of customary practices in treaty-making did not necessarily lead to the creation of customary law. Their basis was ultimately their acceptance in each and every particular treaty. Treaty parties had the right to divert from tradition while its acceptance did not reflect upon third parties. In this sense, one should rather speak of customary practice, or the *mores* or lore of treaty-making, than of customary law. But, on the other side, there are instances whereby this *mores* or lore did lead to the creation of customary law. Some rules were so widely respected that one can say that they were considered binding. The clearest expression for this are the cases in which a rule came to be considered as simplified in a treaty, for example the concept of amnesty from peace treaties. Whereas during most of the Early Modern Age, it was customary to include a stipulation of amnesty for all the acts related to the war, by the nineteenth century it was generally accepted that this was silently implied in every peace treaty.[47]

Thirdly, between the early sixteenth and late seventeenth centuries, a major transformation in relation to the forms of treaty-making occurred: the disappearance of the oath. The Reformation and the end of the religious unity of the West did not spell an immediate end to the confirmation by oath, certainly not among Catholics and even not between princes of different religions. Nevertheless, the rejection by somewhat half of Christian Europe of ecclesiastical jurisdiction radically eroded its usefulness. As canon law could no longer serve as a source of authority for the law of nations and ecclesiastical courts were no longer of use to enforce treaties, the oath did not add much more to the safeguard of the binding character of a treaty than the written form. The gradual secularisation of international relations which followed the era of the wars of religion did the rest. Within a few decades from the beginning of the Reformation, all references to canon law or ecclesiastical jurisdiction and sanction which had been usual in older treaties disappeared from

pp. 536–537, and R. Lesaffer, 'Alberico Gentili's *ius post bellum* and Early Modern Treaties' in B. Kingsbury and B. Straumann (eds.), *The Roman Foundations of the Law of Nations: Alberico Gentili and the Justice of Empire* (Oxford: Oxford University Press, 2010), pp. 210–240, at pp. 212–213.

[47] R. Lesaffer, 'Peace Treaties and the Formation of International Law' in B. Fassbender and A. Peters (eds.), *The Oxford Handbook of the History of International Law* (Oxford: Oxford University Press, 2012), pp. 71–94, at pp. 80 and 89.

treaties, even among Catholics. By the late seventeenth century, the practice of oath-taking itself withered and stopped. The written form of ratification remained.[48]

The crisis of the international system during the sixteenth century triggered intense scholarly debate on the law of nations. Between the early sixteenth and the mid-seventeenth century, an autonomous jurisprudence of the law of nations with its own literature emerged. The emancipation of the law of nations from jurisprudence at large went hand in hand with the gradual monopolisation of international relations by the emerging sovereign States.[49] The demise of the *jus commune* as the ultimate frame of reference and source of authority for the *jus gentium* forced sixteenth- and seventeenth-century theologians and lawyers to indicate an alternative basis for the law of nations. This was to be natural law. In his *De jure belli ac pacis libri tres* of 1625, Hugo Grotius (1583–1645) crystallised earlier ideas into what was to be the mainstream theory of the law of nature and of nations of the later seventeenth and eighteenth centuries. Grotius distinguished two bodies of the law of nations: natural law as applied to relations between polities and the voluntary law of nations which was man-made and based on consent.[50] Later writers, such as Christian Wolff (1679–1754) and Emer de Vattel (1714–1767), would distinguish three categories of manmade law of nations. Firstly, there was conventional law based on express consent; secondly, customary law based on tacit consent; and thirdly, general voluntary law of nations based on presumed consent. Whereas the first two were particular law and only applied to those polities which had effectively given consent, the third was general. Wolff and Vattel retained a clear link between the voluntary law of nations and natural law. In their view, general consent could not be presumed for a rule which contravened natural law.[51]

---

[48] D. Gaurier, *Histoire du droit international: Auteurs, doctrines et développement de l'Antiquité à l'aube de la période contemporaine* (Rennes: Presses Universitaires de Rennes, 2005), pp. 334–337; R. Lesaffer, *Europa: een zoetocht naar vrede 1453-1763 en 1645-1997* (Leuven: Leuven University Press, 1999), pp. 406–414, and Lesaffer, *supra* n. 29, at p. 27.

[49] Wijffels, *supra* n. 31, at pp. 28–60.

[50] H. Grotius, *De jure belli ac pacis libri tres* (Vol. I) (1625) (Oxford: Clarendon Press, 1925) (F. W. Kelsey trans.), Prolegomena.

[51] C. Wolff, *Jus Gentium methodo scientifica pertractatum* (Vol. I) (1748) (Oxford: Clarendon Press, 1934) (J. H. Drake trans.), Prolegomena; E. de Vattel, *Le droit des gens*

Mainstream doctrine made consent into the very foundation of the positive law of nations. According to Grotius and others, its ultimate basis was to be found in the natural law maxim of the binding force of all promises.[52] The doctrine of the enforceability of all promises, including nude pacts, had been articulated by medieval canonists from the conjunction of Christian moral precepts with the Roman law of contract. It was recycled by the theologians and jurists of the sixteenth century and by the natural lawyers of the seventeenth century into the jurisprudence of the law of nature and of nations and forged into the modern doctrine of consent as the basis for manmade order and law. According to the mainstream writers of the law of nations since the later seventeenth century, consent was constitutive of the binding character of treaties, whatever their form. In reality, it was almost always expressed in the form of a written ratification by the principal.[53] Whereas most early-modern writers of the law of nations did underscore that treaties could only create law between treaty parties themselves, writers of the later eighteenth and nineteenth centuries expressly pointed out that customary treaty practice formed a source for the general law of nations as it gave evidence of customary law.[54]

The demise of the authority of the *jus commune* did not cause the demise of many of its concrete doctrines with relation to the law of nations in general or treaty law in particular. Natural law served as a conduit to recycle many of the doctrines of medieval *jus gentium* but also of medieval canon law and private Roman law which had not been applied to international relations before to be operated into this field

ou principes de la loi naturelle (1758) (Washington, DC: Carnegie Institution, 1916) (C. G. Fenwick trans.), Préface and Préliminaires; P.-M. Dupuy, 'Vattel et le droit des traités' in V. Chetail and P. Haggenmacher (eds.), *Vattel's International Law from a XXIst Century Perspective* (Leiden: Martinus Nijhoff, 2011), pp. 151–166; R. Lesaffer, 'A Schoolmaster Abolishing Homework? Vattel on Peacemaking and Peace Treaties' in Chetail and Haggenmacher (eds.), *ibid.*, pp. 353–386, at pp. 359–361, and S. C. Neff, 'A Short History of International Law' in M. D. Evans (ed.), *International Law* (Oxford University Press, 4th ed., 2014), pp. 3–28, at pp. 9–12.

[52] Grotius, *supra* n. 50, at Prol. 8.

[53] Wolff, *supra* n. 51, at 4.375–4.378 and 4.548–4.550; Vattel, *supra* n. 51, at 2.12.152–2.12.164 and 2.15.222–2.15.234; R. Hyland, '*Pacta Sunt Servanda*: A Meditation', *Virginia JIL*, 34 (1993–1994), 405–433; Lesaffer, *supra* n. 10, and H. Wehberg, '*Pacta Sunt Servanda*', *AJIL*, 53 (1959), 775–786.

[54] G. F. von Martens, *Summary of the Law of Nations Founded on Treaties and Customs of the Modern Nations of Europe* (Philadelphia, PA: T. Bradford, 1795) (W. Cobbett trans.), pp. 2–5; W. O. Manning, *Commentaries on the Law of Nations* (London: S. Sweet, 1839), p. 74, and H. Wheaton, *Elements of International Law with A Sketch of the History of Science* (Philadelphia, PA: Carey, Lea and Blanchard, 1836), pp. 40–42.

now. In the great treatises of the law of nations of the seventeenth and eighteenth centuries, an autonomous doctrine of treaty law, separate from or as a species of general contract law, was formed. In large part, it drew on older doctrines of treaties and contract.[55] Apart from formal treaty law, by far the most attention was given to peace treaties.[56]

2.4   Modern Age (1815–1969)

The gradual rise of legal positivism and the material extension of international relations following from the Industrial Revolution combined to enhance the role and function of treaties in the organization of international society and the creation of international law. The successful rebellion of the Northern and Southern American colonies around 1800, the inclusion of such powers as the Ottoman Empire, Japan and China in the international community and the processes of colonisation and decolonisation led to the gradual formation of one global order.[57] This process was achieved by the end of the 1960s, after the great wave of decolonisation and the articulation of the doctrine of peaceful co-existence by the Soviet-Union.

Apart from the enhanced functionality of treaties, the nineteenth and early twentieth centuries saw two major, interconnected, changes in treaty practice. Firstly, there was the emergence of multilateral conventions. Although multilateral treaties already occurred in Antiquity, the vast majority of historical treaties were bilateral. This was even the case for treaties emerging from general conferences such as the major peace settlements of the seventeenth and eighteenth centuries. This changed with the Vienna Peace Congress of 1814–1815, where the dictates of interest of the anti-Napoleonic coalition prompted the switch to multilateral peace agreements. Whereas opportunism would continue to rule the choice for bi- or multilateral treaties in major peace settlements – as with the Paris Peace Conference at the end of both World War I and II (1919–1920 and 1947) where multilaterism was only applied to the side of the winning coalition – the use of multilateral conventions expanded to other types of treaties. The creation of international organizations at the

---

[55] E.g. Grotius, *supra* n. 51, at 2.11–2.16.

[56] Lesaffer, *supra* n. 46, at pp. 210–220, and Wijffels, *supra* n. 31.

[57] H. Bull and A. Watson (eds.), *The Expansion of International Society* (Oxford: Clarendon Press, 1984) and Y. Onuma, 'When Was the Law of International Society Born? An Inquiry of the History of International Law from An Intercivilizational Perspective', *J. History Int'l L.*, 2 (2000), 1–66.

global and regional level in the twentieth century gave the multilateral conferences and conventions an institutional framework.[58]

Secondly, there was the emergence of law-creating treaties – *traités-lois* – in the form of multilateral conventions for the codification of customary law and/or the creation of new rules of international law. The Vienna Congress also formed the setting for the first multilateral *traités-lois*, more specifically in relation to the slave trade, the international status of rivers and diplomats. The multilateral character of these treaties, the involvement of a large number of States and the fact that these conventions often emerged in the context of the League of Nations or the United Nations have fostered the general acceptance of the doctrine that these treaties themselves render evidence of general customary international law, allowing them to transcend the rule of *pacta tertiis nec nocent nec prosunt*.[59] From the late nineteenth century onwards up to the 1969 Vienna Convention of the Law of Treaties, various substantive areas of international law have been codified, from traditional fields such as diplomatic law, trade law and the laws of war and treaty law itself to new fields such as transport, communications, private international law, labour and human rights.[60]

Lastly, one change in relation to the form of treaties from the twentieth century must be pointed out. Article 18 of the 1919 Covenant of the League of Nations stipulated the obligation for treaty parties to register every future treaty with the Secretariat of the League and made its binding character conditional upon fulfilment of this formality.[61] In this way, it was hoped to make an end to the practice of secret treaties.[62] The 1945 United Nations Charter, in its Article 102, watered down the effects of

---

[58] G. Fitzmaurice, 'The Juridical Clauses of the Peace Treaties', *Hague Recueil*, 73 (1948), 259–367; Marek, *supra* n. 45; Osiander, *supra* n. 43, at pp. 166–315, and H. Steiger, 'Peace Treaties from Paris to Versailles' in Lesaffer (ed.), *supra* n. 22, pp. 59–99.

[59] C. Chinkin, *Third Parties in International Law* (Oxford: Clarendon Press, 1993); E. David, 'Article 34 (1969)' in O. Corten and P. Klein (eds.), *The Vienna Conventions on the Law of Treaties: A Commentary* (Vol. II) (Oxford: Oxford University Press, 2011), pp. 887–896, and B. Simma, 'From Bilateralism to Community Interest in International Law', *Hague Recueil*, 250 (1994–VI), 217–384.

[60] 'The Progressive Development of International Law', *AJIL Supp.*, 41 (1947), 32–49; 'The Progressive Development of International Law by the League of Nations', *AJIL Supp.*, 41 (1947), 49–65; Grewe, *supra* n. 42, at pp. 606 and 663–665; F. Honig, 'Progress in the Codification of International Law', *Int'l Aff.*, 36 (1960), 62–72; M. O. Hudson, 'The Progressive Codification of International Law', *AJIL*, 20 (1926), 655–669, and M. O. Hudson, 'The Development of International Law Since the War', *AJIL*, 22 (1928), 330–350.

[61] 225 CTS 188.

[62] The banning of secret treaties featured in President Woodrow Wilson's Fourteen Points of Jan. 1918.

non-registration to the non-invocability before organs of the UN.[63] But this has not been consequentially applied.[64]

3   The Historic Functions of Treaties in International Law

This section offers a survey of the main historic functions of treaties through a classification of treaties by their content.[65]

3.1   Treaties Establishing Friendly Relations in General Terms

A fairly general consent among historians now reigns that treaties were never the exclusive or even foremost instrument for the peoples of Antiquity to establish initial relations. From the very beginnings of recorded history, treaties were mainly used to specify relations in terms of concrete obligations. Nevertheless, general treaties of friendship which only stipulate peace and friendship in the vaguest terms have existed since Antiquity and continue to exist. The concept of international friendship which emerges from these treaties shows a remarkable continuity. It implies a general commitment not to harm but to favour one another and one another's subjects. In many cases, general treaties of friendship include more specific consequences of 'friendship', such as the duty to include one another in future alliances, the recognition of each other's boundaries, the obligation to extend the protection of the law to each other's subjects or the concrete organization of cooperation in particular fields.[66]

3.2   Treaties Ending War and Settling Disputes

Treaties have been used as instruments to end war since the remotest times. The Treaty between Lagash and Umma from the twenty-fourth

---

[63] 1 UNTS 16.

[64] A. Aust, *Modern Treaty Law and Practice* (Cambridge: Cambridge University Press, 3rd ed., 2013), p. 303, and A. Hinojal-Oyarbide and A. Rosenboom, 'Managing the Process of Treaty Formation: Depositaries and Registration' in D. B. Hollis (ed.), *The Oxford Guide to Treaties* (Oxford: Oxford University Press, 2012), pp. 248–276.

[65] For a survey of collections of historical treaties: P. Macalister-Smith and J. Schwietzke, *Treaties, Treaty Collections and Documents on Foreign Affairs: From Sun King Suppilulima I to the Hague Peace Conferences of 1899 & 1907. An Annotated Bibliography* (Berlin/Munich: AjBD, 2002).

[66] The latter in the 1963 Treaty of Friendship between France and the Federal Republic of Germany: 821 UNTS 338; see, further, Lesaffer, *supra* n. 15, at p. 94, and Paradisi, *supra* n. 15.

century ended a military conflict. The first peace treaty between equal partners is the Egyptian-Hittite Treaty of Kadesh from the early thirteenth century BC.[67] Since then, peace treaties have been the common means to end wars in all regions of the world.

Already in classical times, a distinction was made between perpetual treaties and treaties which were limited in time. Among the Greek city-states, peace treaties were generally concluded for a limited number of years. Peace treaties between Islamic rulers and Christian rulers were also made for a set period of time, generally ten years, in respect of Islamic doctrine. From the eighteenth century, this practice was gradually disregarded and perpetual peace treaties were made.[68] In late-medieval and early-modern doctrine, the perpetual character of peace treaties gained specific juridical meaning. Rather than a vague and seemingly naïve undertaking by the treaty partners never to resort to war again, it only exhausted the right of the former belligerents to resort to force in the future over the disputes settled in the peace treaty. It does not infringe upon the rights of treaty partners to resort to war for other causes.[69] This doctrine has become obsolete under the present *jus contra bellum*.

Generally speaking, peace treaties have three functions and include three different sets of stipulations. A first set of clauses settles the claims and disputes between the belligerents or provides for peaceful means to settle them in the future. The second set of clauses puts an end to the state of war and deals with its consequences. These clauses relate to booty, confiscated property, prisoners of war, restitution of occupied territories and generally the lifting of wartime measures. The third set concerns the regulation of future peaceful relations between the treaty parties and their subjects. These clauses extend to matters of trade and the legal position of subjects. In this category fall the stipulations which serve to make the peace more sustainable and deal with the consequences of the violation of treaty clauses. During the Early-Modern Age, peace treaties among European powers became elaborate and detailed with regards

---

[67] Altman, *supra* n. 1, at pp. 123–134.

[68] M. Khadduri, *War and Peace in the Law of Islam* (Baltimore, MD: Johns Hopkins University Press, 1955); G. Vismara, 'Impium Foedus: Le origini della respublica christiana' in G. Vismara, *Scritti di storia giuridica* (Vol. VII) (Milan: Giuffrè, 1989), pp. 3–115, and K.-H. Ziegler, 'The Peace Treaties of the Ottoman Empire with European Christian Powers' in Lesaffer (ed.), *supra* n. 22, pp. 338–364.

[69] B. Klesmann, *Bellum solemne. Formen und Funktionen europäischer Kriegserklärungen des 17. Jahrhunderts* (Mainz: Zabern, 2007) and R. Lesaffer, E.-J. Broers and J. Waelkens, 'From Antwerp to Munster (1609/1648): Peace and Truce under the Law of Nations' in Lesaffer (ed.), *supra* n. 3, pp. 233–255.

the second and third sets of clauses. This change was consequential upon the fact that, during this period, wars became a far more encompassing state of affairs than before, involving the comprehensive disruption of normal relations between the belligerents. Peace treaties thus became crucial instruments spelling out the legal implications of ending the state of war and restoring the state of peace. By consequence, they are essential informative and constitutive sources for the laws of peace – in the sense of the laws regulating the state of peace – among former belligerents. Many peace treaties included detailed stipulations regarding commerce and navigation. From the seventeenth century onwards, it became customary to relegate these stipulations to separate treaties of friendship, commerce and navigation – the so-called FCN treaties – accompanying the proper peace treaty.[70]

Since the end of World War II, peace-making practice has undergone remarkable changes. Firstly, formal peace treaties no longer played the dominant role in the ending of inter-State armed conflicts. In some cases, as that of Germany after World War II, this was due to political circumstances. But in general terms, this is consequential to the emergence of the *jus contra bellum*. The outlawing of war in the 1928 Briand-Kellogg Pact[71] and of force in the Charter of the United Nations of 1945 has caused a sharp decline in the number of formally declared wars. In the Charter Era, the lines between the state of war and the state of peace have been blurred, and wars are again – as they were in the Middle Ages – perceived of in terms of separate acts of hostilities rather than of the complete disruption of the normal, peaceful relations. For this reason, the traditional peace treaty has fallen into relative disuse. But whereas this is often seen as the demise of peace treaty practice, it can as readily be considered part of a process of its transformation. Formal peace treaties marking the transit from state of war to state of peace may have become relatively rare but have not disappeared altogether.[72] As legal forms and concepts of inter-State armed conflict became more varied, legal forms and contents of agreements to end them likewise became more varied. Some conflicts ended with an armistice and/or a preliminary agreement whereby relations quickly or gradually regained a level of normalcy.[73]

---

[70] Lesaffer, *supra* n. 46, at pp. 210–214, and Neff, *supra* n. 45.   [71] 94 LNTS 57.

[72] Such as Art. 1 of the 1994 Treaty of Arava: ILM, 34 (1995), 46–66.

[73] Under current international law, an armistice 'denotes a termination of hostilities; even though it does not introduce peace in the full sense of that term'. See Y. Dinstein, *War, Aggression and Self-Defence* (Cambridge: Cambridge University Press, 6th ed., 2017), p. 44.

In other cases, treaties of friendship organising aspects of the relations between belligerents were used without a formal end to the war being expressly declared.

Secondly, the years since 1945 have been marked by a proliferation of intra-State armed conflicts, in which third powers were often involved. In this context, hundreds of peace agreements were made. These agreements take the form of international treaties but are mostly of a hybrid nature because they span inter- and intra-State affairs. More than being instruments of conflict resolution, current peace agreements are as much instruments of constitutional formation that break through the confines of domestic and international order.[74] They incorporate detailed regulations of constitutional (re-)formation at the State level.

Thirdly, next to State building, another important issue has come to expand the concern of peace-making – or peace building as it is now called – and widened the domain of the *jus post bellum*: the protection of human rights. This has started with the inclusion of stipulations on minority rights in the late nineteenth century.[75] By the late twentieth century, peace agreements incorporate stipulations on general human rights, including political and economic rights as well as on the prosecution of violations of international humanitarian law.[76]

Fourthly, peace-making turned into a drawn-out process of peace building, involving a series of agreements and documents. This was not completely new as even in the Early-Modern Age use was made of armistices and preliminary peace treaties in preparation of the peace treaty or of additional treaties detailing particular aspects of the peace process. But then, there had always been a formal peace treaty at the centre which marked the sudden reversion from war to peace. As war and peace have become relative concepts, so the notion of an abrupt change transit from war to peace has given way to that of a transition process.[77]

---

[74] There are historical precedents for this, the Peace Treaties of Westphalia of 24 Oct. 1648 actually being the most significant ones, although this has been completely overlooked by the framers of the Westphalian myth. R. Lesaffer, 'The Westphalian Peace Treaties and the Development of the Tradition of Great European Peace Settlements prior to 1648', *Grotiana*, 18 (1997), 71–95, and H. Steiger, 'Der Westfälische Frieden – Grundgesetz für Europa?' in H. Duchhardt (ed.), *Der Westfälische Frieden. Diplomatie, politische Zäsur, kulturelles Umfeld, Rezeptiongeschichte* (Munich: Oldenbourg, 1998), pp. 33–80.

[75] 1878 Treaty of San Stefano, 152 CTS 395, and 1878 Treaty of Berlin, 153 CTS 171.

[76] C. Bell, *Peace Agreements and Human Rights* (Oxford: Oxford University Press, 2000).

[77] C. Bell, *On the Law of Peace: Peace Agreements and the* Lex Pacificatoria (Oxford: Oxford University Press, 2008) and C. Stahn and J.K. Kleffner (eds.), Jus Post Bellum: *Towards a Law of Transition from Conflict to Peace* (The Hague: T.M.C. Asser Press, 2008).

Next to peace treaties, there are also treaties which settle legal claims and disputes between polities without them having resorted to war. This can be considered a separate category closely associated by its function to peace treaties.[78]

3.3   Treaties Regulating Warfare

Treaties between belligerents or non-belligerents to regulate the conduct of war are also a common occurrence in human history. Under this category fall proper treaties between the 'sovereign' rulers of polities as well as agreements between commanders in the field. Wartime treaties can be divided in five subgroups according to their content. These are (i) agreements concerning prisoners of war; (ii) capitulations of armies, towns and fortresses; (iii) agreements restricting violence against certain places and categories of persons, often including stipulations about garrison rights and financial contributions; (iv) agreements about the rights of third powers and their subjects, mainly concerning neutral trade and (v) armistices and truces. Agreements about the rights of neutral powers and non-belligerents could be made either between belligerents and non-belligerents or among non-belligerents as in the case of the armed neutralities of the late seventeenth and eighteenth centuries.[79] The distinction between truces and armistices roots back to ancient practice. It was first elucidated as a point of doctrine by the civilians of the Late Middle Ages. Whereas an armistice (*indutiae*) is a mere cessation of hostilities for a restricted period of time – from hours to a few years – and often limited to a certain theatre of war, a truce (*treuga*) is a peace treaty limited in time. It can stretch to the almost complete suspension of the state of war in all its practical consequences but reserves belligerents the right to resume war for the same causes after its expiration.[80]

---

[78] Fisch, *supra* n. 46; J. Fried (ed.), *Träger und Instrumentarien des Friedens im hohen und späten Mittelalter* (Sigmaringen: Jan Thorbecke Verlag, 1996); Lesaffer, *supra* n. 47; H. Steiger, 'Friede in der Rechtsgeschichte' in W. Augustyn (ed.), *PAX. Beiträge zu Idee und Darstellung des Friedens* (Munich: Scaneg, 2003), pp. 11–62, and K.-H. Ziegler, 'Friedensverträge im römischen Altertum', *Archiv des Völkerrechts*, 27 (1989), 45–62.

[79] S. C. Neff, *The Rights and Duties of Neutrals: A General History* (Manchester: Manchester University Press, 2000), pp. 39 and 71–74.

[80] M. H. Keen, *The Laws of War in the Late Middle Ages* (Aldershot: Routledge, 1965); J.-M. Mattéi, *Histoire du droit de la guerre (1700–1819): Introduction à l'histoire du droit international* (Aix-en-Provence: Presses Universitaires d'Aix-Marseille, 2006); J. F. Witt, *Lincoln's Code: The Laws of War in American History* (New York, NY: Free Press, 2012); J. Q. Whitman, *The Verdict of Battle: The Law of Victory and the Making of Modern War*

3.4   Treaties of Alliance

Treaties have been used to forge alliances between polities since pre-classical Antiquity. Their major historic function is to secure the treaty partner's support – military or otherwise – during an ongoing or future war. Alliance treaties form an important source of information about the *jus ad bellum* as it was accepted in the practice of a certain period or civilisation. The vast majority of alliance treaties are limited in time or directed at specific enemies. They can be general and stipulate the treaty parties' duty to aid one another in war in general terms – as the Greek and Roman formula of stating that the parties would be 'friends of friends and enemies of enemies' – or they can specify very concrete obligations in terms of the number of troops or amount of money an ally had to provide. A distinction can be made between offensive and defensive alliances. Most treaties do not stipulate a concrete *casus foederis*, but it is generally implied in the very notion of defensive alliance treaties that prior violence needs to have been used against the ally. In several periods of history, alliance treaties formed an essential part of the security management of great powers and were part of the foundations of international order, as in classical Greece, the Hellenistic world, the Roman Republic and Early Empire as well as in Europe for the whole period running from the Renaissance to the Cold War. In these times, alliances often became multilateral networks, at times even taking the form of multilateral treaties such as the Quadruple Alliance of 1718 or, more recently, the alliances of the Cold War. In some periods, as during and after the Cold War, alliances have taken on a more permanent character.[81] In the practice of Early Modern Europe, alliances did not always force treaty parties to resort to war but could also provide for aid as an auxiliary power. This implied that the ally would render aid to his treaty partner without declaring war. This aid could include arms deliveries, financial subsidies and even direct military support.[82]

(Cambridge, MA: Harvard University Press, 2012) and K.-H. Ziegler, 'Kriegsverträge im antiken römischen Altertum', *Zeitschrift der Savigny-Stiftung für Rechtsgeschichte, Romanistische Abteilung*, 102 (1985), 40–90.

[81] E.g. NATO which was made permanent in 1999, but also the bilateral alliances between the USA and Japan or South Korea.

[82] Gruen, *supra* n. 4, at pp. 13–53; Lesaffer, *supra* n. 48, at pp. 215–273, 443–485 and 551–595; S. Oeter, 'Neutrality and Alliances' in Chetail and Haggenmacher (eds.), *supra* n. 51, pp. 335–352; Steiger, *supra* n. 26, and K.-H. Ziegler, 'Das Völkerrecht der römischen Republik' in H. Temporini (ed.), *Von den Anfängen Roms bis zum Ausgang der Republik, Austieg und Niedergang der römischen Welt. Geschichte und Kultur Roms im*

3.5   Treaties of Subjection and Empire

From the earliest beginnings, treaties have been used to create or confirm relations of submission between polities. In fact, the very oldest treaty on record between Lagash and Umma was one of subordination. The Greeks and the Romans made common use of alliance treaties (ςυμμαχια, *foedus*) to submit other polities or people to their power. 'Unequal' treaties could stipulate the payment of tribute or one-sided duties of military aid and even, factually or legally, limit the right of the subject power to wage an independent foreign policy. A radical form of submission is the Roman *deditio*, whereby a foreign polity subjected itself to Roman power to the point of extinguishing its existence as a separate entity. The *deditio* was not properly a treaty as it did not create obligations between independent polities. In many cases, the *deditio* was often followed by a Roman decision – whether or not confirmed by treaty – to re-establish the polity as an ally and client State.[83] Until its legal consolidation around 200 AD, the Roman Empire was in fact and law a network of alliances centred on a hegemonic power and not a true empire. Its legal structure can rather be compared to the 1955 Warsaw Pact and the Soviet Bloc in the Cold War than to the European colonial empires of the nineteenth century.[84]

Particular use was made of treaties by European powers in the eras of colonisation and imperialism, although their relative importance as an instrument of territorial acquisition differed by period, region and colonial power.[85] The two major forms were treaties of cession, whereby the political government of territories and their inhabitants were passed over to the colonial power, and treaties of protectorate, whereby the indigenous ruler retained his power in internal affairs but relegated foreign policy to the imperial power. In practice, the lines between these two types of treaties were often blurred by the colonising powers, as were the

Spiegel der neueren Forschung (Berlin/New York, NY: De Gruyter, 1972), pp. 68–114, at pp. 90–94.

[83] D. Nörr, *Aspekte des römischen Völkerrechts. De Bronzetafel von Alcantara* (Munich: Bayerische Akademie der Wissenschaften, 1989) and Ziegler, *supra* n. 82, at pp. 94–96.

[84] P. J. Burton, *Friendship and Empire: Roman Diplomacy and Imperialism in the Middle Republic (353–146 BC)* (Cambridge: Cambridge University Press, 2011); R. Kallett-Marx, *Hegemony to Empire: The Development of the Roman Imperium in the East from 148 to 62 BC* (Berkeley, CA: University of California Press, 1995) and A. Lintott, *Imperium Romanum: Politics and Administration* (London: Routledge, 1993).

[85] J. Fisch, *Die europäische Expansion und das Völkerrecht. Die Auseinandersetzungen und dem Status der überseeischen Gebiete vom 15. Jahrhundert bis zur Gegenwart* (Stuttgart: Streiner, 1984) and P. Seed, *Ceremonies of Possession in Europe's Conquest of the New World, 1492–1640* (Cambridge: Cambridge University Press, 1995).

lines between concessions of private property and rights by indigenous rulers and treaties of cession of sovereignty. Also, in some cases the colonising power argued that the instrument of cession was not a treaty under international law or even a convention at all as the colonised power lacked international legal personality, thus eroding any rights the colonised could derive from the instrument.[86] Also within this category fall treaties of devolution whereby the colonial power grants autonomy or independence to the colony and future relations are regulated.[87] Whereas treaties had been known and used by all major civilisations throughout world history, there had been important differences in relation to their use and significance. It was particularly during the Age of New Imperialism (1870–1920) that the Western model and law of treaties was imposed and globalised.[88]

3.6   Constitutional Treaties

Early-modern theory of social contract projected consent and contract to the very centre of constitutional theory and practice.[89] Together with theories of popular sovereignty, it formed the intellectual backdrop to the written constitutions of the Revolutionary Era (1776–1848). It also had its impact felt in the domain of international law. For the great writers of the law of nations of the seventeenth and eighteenth centuries, consent became the constitutive source of the positive law of nations. Several of the leading international lawyers of the nineteenth century considered the free will of States the ultimate foundation of the international

[86] Alexandrowicz, 'Treaty and Diplomatic Relations', *supra* n. 9; see, also, Alexandrowicz, *Law of Nations in the East Indies*, *supra* n. 9; Alexandrowicz, 'The Afro-Asian World and the Law of Nations', *supra* n. 9; Alexandrowicz, *European-African Confrontation*, *supra* n. 9; Anghie, *supra* n. 8, at pp. 32–114; J. R. Crawford, *The Creation of States in International Law* (Oxford: Oxford University Press, 2nd ed., 2006), pp. 282–329; Fisch, *supra* n. 85; P. McHugh, *The Maori Magna Carta: New Zealand Law and the Treaty of Waitangi* (Oxford: Oxford University Press, 1991), pp. 145–238, and W. A. M. van der Linden, 'New Imperialism (1870–1914) and the European Legal Traditions: A (Dis)Integrative Episode', *Maastricht JECL*, 19 (2012), 281–299.

[87] M. Craven, *The Decolonization of International Law: State Succession and the Law of Treaties* (Oxford: Oxford University Press, 2007), pp. 120–128, and Crawford, *supra* n. 86, at pp. 329–448.

[88] Apart from the works by Alexandrowicz, cited at *supra* n. 9, see, also, M. R. Austin, *Negotiating with Imperialism: The Unequal Treaties and the Culture of Japanese Diplomacy* (Cambridge, MA: Harvard University Press, 2006).

[89] P. Riley, 'Social Contract Theory and its Critics' in M. Goldie and R. Wokler (eds.), *The Cambridge History of Eighteenth-Century Political Thought* (Cambridge: Cambridge University Press, 2006), pp. 347–375.

community. Although this latter theory remained just one position among several, treaties became the dominant instrument for the constitution of international organizations and institutions in the twentieth and twenty-first centuries.[90]

Consensualism has, however, far deeper roots in the Western constitutional tradition than early-modern social contract theory. Indeed, the early-modern writers themselves could draw on ideas and practices which went back to the Middle Ages. Four major instances of the use of contract as a basis for political organization can be quoted from the European Middle Ages. Firstly, the Germanic conception of kingship was based on consent between the king and his people. Secondly, under the feudal system, power relations were based on personal contracts between lords and vassals. This convolution of private legal relationships and public authority enhanced the role of consent between rulers and subjects.[91] Thirdly, many political entities of the Late Middle Ages, such as towns, were legally construed as communities of citizens who had taken an oath to uphold the peace and law of the community.[92] Fourthly, constitutional charters need to be mentioned. These were sworn compacts whereby the princes and the representatives of the people or the estates agreed an arrangement of their mutual constitutional rights and duties. The English Magna Carta of 1215 only serves as an example for this wide-spread practice.[93] In view of the civilian doctrine of *princeps legibus solutus* – which states the primacy of sovereign power over the law – contract was the indicated instrument of binding the prince to constitutional arrangements. Both civilian and canon law – conciliarism – developed a rich tradition of constitutional contract theory.[94]

In practice, the use of treaties as constitutional acts goes back to Antiquity. A conceptual distinction can be made between international

---

[90] Wehberg, *supra* n. 53, at pp. 778–784.

[91] F. L. Ganshof, *Feudalism* (London: Longman, 3rd ed., 1964); S. Reynolds, *Kingdoms and Communities in Western Europe* (Oxford: Oxford University Press, 1984) and S. Reynolds, *Fiefs and Vassals: The Medieval Experience Reinterpreted* (Oxford: Oxford University Press, 1994).

[92] R. Celli, *Pour l'histoire des origins du pouvoir populaire: l'expérience des villes italiennes (XIe–XIIe siècles)* (Louvain-la-Neuve: Université Catholique de Louvain, 1980) and L. Martines, *Power and Imagination: City-States in Renaissance Italy* (New York, NY: Alfred A. Knopf, 1979).

[93] J. C. Holt, *Magna Carta* (Cambridge: Cambridge University Press, 2nd ed., 1992).

[94] B. Tierney, *Foundations of the Conciliar Theory* (Cambridge: Cambridge University Press, 1955) and B. Tierney, *Religion, Law and the Growth of Constitutional Thought, 1150–1650* (Cambridge: Cambridge University Press, 1982).

and national constitutional treaties. The former serves to constitute or reform an international organization whereby the treaty partners retain their position as subjects of international law. The second constitute or reform a polity – a federation, confederation of empire – which absorbs or has absorbed the international legal personality of the treaty partners. For most periods of history, the distinction has an element of anachronism in it as it derives from the modern notion of Statehood. But allowing for a large grey zone in which polities surrender some of the international competences which normally pertain to independent polities and retain others, it is functional.

One of the earliest forms of international organization were the Greek multilateral leagues and amphictyonies. The former could either be an alliance between equal partners or be of a hegemonic nature, such as the Attic-Delian League of the fifth century BC. In the latter case, a set of bilateral treaties between the hegemonic power and the different tributary powers would form the legal framework to the league.[95] Before its further integration in the second and third centuries AD, the Roman Empire was legally speaking a complex alliance system of bilateral relations between Rome and its allies. Many of these were bound to Rome by a treaty of alliance (*foedus*), which may have been preceded by a *deditio*, but many were not.[96] From the European Middle Ages, leagues of cities and other polities, such as the Lombard League from the twelfth century or the Hanseatic League can be quoted.[97] In modern times, multilateral treaties have been the standard form for the constitution of international organizations.

Throughout history, there are different cases of multilateral alliances which with time led to federations or empires. The Roman Empire is undoubtedly the most significant example of this. For later times the Swiss Confederation and the Dutch Republic of the United Provinces, which was based on the Union of Utrecht of 29 January 1579, can be quoted.[98] From Early-Modern Europe, some peace treaties had constitutional significance. The most important examples thereof are undoubtedly the two Peace Treaties of Westphalia (Munster and Osnabruck) of 24 October 1648 which were at the same time bilateral peace treaties

---

[95] Bederman, *supra* n. 21, at pp. 165–171, and Phillipson, *supra* n. 21, at pp. 1–33.

[96] Gruen, *supra* n. 4, at pp. 54–95.

[97] H. Spruyt, *The Sovereign State and Its Competitors* (Princeton, NJ: Princeton University Press, 1994).

[98] J. K. Oudendijk, *Het contract in de wordingsgeschiedenis van de Republiek der Verenigde Nederlanden* (Leiden: A.W. Sijthoff, 1961).

between the Holy Roman Empire, on the one hand, and, on the other, France and Sweden respectively, as well as an 'imperial peace' and as such part of the constitution of the Empire.[99] In more modern times, the constitutional process in federal States sometimes took on characteristics of the process of the conclusion of treaties, as in the case of the Constitution of the United States.[100] The role of treaties in the constitution and devolution of colonial empires has already been remarked upon.

3.7   Treaties on Rights of Private Citizens (Including Matters of Trade, Transport and Navigations)

Among the very earliest treaties are compacts which provide for the protection under the law for foreign traders and their property. In Northern Syria, a treaty from around 2400–2250 BC has been found whereby the king of Ebla extends his jurisdiction and legal protection to the traders from his treaty partner.[101] The Greeks and Romans made use of public treaties of guestfriendship (çυμßολα, hospitium).[102] Ancient treaties also include clauses regulating different aspects of trade, such as taxation or currency issues. Commercial treaties have been made in all periods of history and are known from almost all civilisations. The relationship can be equal or of a tributary nature. In general, these treaties provide legal protection for foreign traders and their property. Commercial treaty relations became particularly elaborate in early-modern Europe. Many peace treaties from that period and region contained detailed stipulations in relation to trade, navigation and the legal protection of subjects. By the late seventeenth century, it became customary to refer these clauses to separate FCN treaties. Many peace settlements included stipulations to regulate the protection of foreign property in case of new war.[103] By the nineteenth century, industrialisation, technological evolutions and the ensuing globalisation of the economy and of travel had started to expand the variety of transnational contacts between persons which were covered in treaties. Numerous

---

[99] Par. 112 IPM = Art. 17.3 IPO; A. Oschmann (ed.), *Die Friedensverträge zwischen Frankreich und Schweden 1 Urkunden* (Munster: Aschendorff, 1998).

[100] For a radical interpretation of the US Constitution as a treaty regime, see F. F. Martin, *The Constitution as Treaty: The International Legal Constructionalist Approach to the U.S. Constitution* (Cambridge: Cambridge University Press, 2007).

[101] Altman, *supra* n. 1, at pp. 36–37.

[102] K.-H. Ziegler, 'Regeln für den Handelsverkehr in Staatsverträgen des Altertums', *Legal History Rev.*, 70 (2002), 55–67.

[103] Neff, *supra* n. 45.

treaties were and are made on international communication, transport, financial transactions, taxation, travel and many other occurrences of international life. In some cases, one can see a process whereby in a first phase networks of bilateral treaties are made until multilateralism takes over, as the GATT agreements and the World Trade Organization have done for general aspects of trade. A similar process has now commenced in the field of investment, after massive numbers of bilateral investment treaties were made in recent decades.[104]

3.8   Treaties on General Issues of International Law and Common Concerns of the International Community

Multilateral treaties dealing with general aspects of international law or common concerns of the international community are a recent phenomenon. The regulations with relation to the navigation of rivers, diplomatic practice and the slave trade from the Congress of Vienna are often quoted as the first instances of it. Over the nineteenth and particularly the twentieth century, multilateral conventions have gradually grown into one of the major law-making instruments of the globalised international community. Large parts of the traditional law of international relations have been codified so that now a great variety of major issues, from the *jus ad bellum* over the laws of war and the law of the sea to diplomatic law, the law of treaties and State responsibility are covered in multilateral conventions or authoritative draft conventions. Since World War I, treaties have become a much-used instrument to deal with common concerns of international life, ranging from minority protection and labour rights in the Interbellum over human rights and the use of space, the seabed and the polar regions to environmental protection today.

4   Conclusion

All through history, the primary function of treaties has been to constitute concrete obligations between polities. But treaties have also played

---

[104] F. Baetens, 'Preferential Trade and Investment Agreements and the Trade/Investment Divide: Is the Whole More Than the Sum of Its Parts?' in R. Hoffmann, S. W. Schill and C. J. Tams (eds.), *Preferential Trade and Investment Agreements: From Recalibration to Reintegration* (Baden: Nomos, 2013), pp. 91–128; K. Miles, *The Origins of International Investment Law: Empire, Environment and the Safeguarding of International Capital* (Cambridge: Cambridge University Press, 2013) and K. J. Vandenvelde, 'A Brief History of International Investment Agreements', *UC Davis JILP*, 12 (2005), 157–194.

an important role in the articulation and creation of international law, as they continue to do. Five different roles treaties play as informative or constitutive sources of international law can be distinguished.

Firstly, treaties are informative sources of international law. Since they apply rules of international law to create concrete obligations among parties, they render evidence of international law. To the historian of international law, they are an important source of knowledge about the concepts and doctrines of international law of a certain time or place. This includes treaty law as well as substantive areas of international law such as *jus in bello, jus post bellum,* trade and navigation.[105] Secondly, because treaty makers often use older treaties for inspiration, different traditions – referred to as lore or *mores* – of treaty practices have been formed throughout history. This does not extend to formal law creation as long as the treaty parties accept no legal obligation to sustain an existing practice. But, thirdly, in some cases, particular treaty traditions may become binding as they are accepted as an expression of customary law and *opinio juris* is attached to them. So the custom of extending amnesty for wartime actions in peace treaties was for a long time just a part of the *mores* of peace treaties, until amnesty came to be considered implied in peace treaties and was made part of the customary law of peace-making. Fourthly, treaties are used to codify customary international law. This only came to the fore during the nineteenth century with the emergence of multilateral conventions. Fifthly, treaties can create new rules of international law by agreement between the parties. In this role, treaties act as formal sources of international law. This is the category of so-called *traités-lois.* Whereas this form of law creation by treaties occurred in earlier times at the bilateral level – one can consider treaties of guest friendship, trade and navigation as such – it became particularly important through the use of multilateral conventions.[106]

---

[105] See the note on terminology at *supra* n. 11.

[106] For the role of law-making treaties in different fields of international law, see the chapters comprising Part II of this volume.

PART I

Conceptual Perspectives

4

Typologies and the 'Essential Juridical Character' of Treaties

CATHERINE BRÖLMANN

1 Introduction

Legal scholarship, doctrine and practice differentiate between treaties. References to 'peace treaties', 'environmental treaties', 'fundamental treaties', 'contract treaties', 'constitutional treaties' and 'self-executing treaties' are a received part of public international law discourse. In his dissenting opinion in the *South West Africa Cases* of July 1966, Judge Tanaka spoke of the League Mandates' 'characteristics similar to law-making treaties'.[1] In its judgment in the *Loizidou Case*, the European Court of Human Rights labelled the European Convention on Human Rights (ECHR)[2] as a 'law-making treaty', with matching competences for the 'Convention institutions'.[3]

Classifications of treaties are also not new. In his 1930 article for the *British Yearbook of International Law*, Lord Arnold McNair distinguished between the 'widely differing functions and legal character of the instruments which it is customary to comprise under the term "treaty"'.[4] Heinrich Triepel had earlier proposed a distinction between a *Vertrag* on the one hand and a *Vereinbarung* as

---

[1] Following Lassa Oppenheim, he defined this as 'concluded for the purpose of establishing new rules for the law of nations'; see *South West Africa Cases*: Ethiopia v. South Africa; Liberia v. South Africa (Second Phase) (1966) ICJ Rep. 6, at p. 266 (Dissenting Opinion of Judge Tanaka).

[2] 213 UNTS 221.

[3] *Loizidou v. Turkey* (Preliminary Objections), Judgment of 23 March 1995, Series A, No. 310, p. 25 (§84).

[4] A. D. McNair, 'The Functions and Differing Legal Character of Treaties', *BYbIL*, 11 (1930), 100–118.

a communal expression of identical wills on the other.[5] More recently, Joseph Weiler has pointed to 'differentiating factors of treaties', with accordingly differing hermeneutics.[6]

This chapter aims to trace the classifications of treaties prevalent in international affairs and to examine their significance within the framework of the law of treaties and of international law in general. The findings make no claim to exhaustiveness, but they do further our understanding of the variety of treaty typologies in use and their legal meaning, with concomitant implications for the politics of treaty making and application. A first aim is to explore – in line with the original project of which this chapter is a part – which typologies of treaties are reflected in the 1969 Vienna Convention on the Law of Treaties (VCLT).[7] As it turns out, the 1969 Vienna Convention, as is the case with the 1986 Vienna Convention on the Law of Treaties between States and International Organizations or between International Organizations,[8] differentiates between treaties only sparingly. This is somewhat different when we look at international law (doctrine) at large, or at broader discourses, such as those concerning justice and effectiveness.

The following sections consider the use of 'typology' (rather than 'taxonomy') as a tool – with form, normative effect and content as the main distinctive elements (Section 2). The chapter then addresses some typologies based on form (Section 3); on normative effect – with special attention for the 'law-making treaty'[9] as this typification has a prominent place in public international law discourse (Section 4) – and on content (Section 5).

---

[5] H. Triepel, *Völkerrecht und Landesrecht* (Leipzig: Verlag von C.L. Hirschfeld, 1899). The basis for the binding force of the Gemeinwillen, Triepel himself admitted, had to be found in an extra-legal context. Cf. A. Verdross, *Die Verfassung der Völkerrechtsgemeinschaft* (Vienna: J. Springer, 1926), p. 20 ('... als Grundlage des Völkerrechts'); see, also, P. Kooijmans, *The Doctrine of the Legal Equality of States* (Leiden: A.W. Sythoff, 1964), pp. 133–134.

[6] See J. H. H. Weiler, 'Prolegomena to a Meso-theory of Treaty Interpretation at the Turn of the Century', IILJ International Legal Theory Colloquium: Interpretation and Judgment in International Law (NYU Law School, 14 Feb. 2008), p. 6, and J. H. H. Weiler, 'The Interpretation of Treaties – A Re-examination', *EJIL*, 21 (2010), 507.

[7] 1155 UNTS 331.   [8] ILM, 25 (1986), 543–592.

[9] This chapter partly builds on earlier research: C. M. Brölmann, 'Law-Making Treaties: Form and Function in International Law', *Nordic JIL*, 74 (2005), 383–404, and C. M. Brölmann, 'Specialized Rules of Treaty Interpretation: International Organizations' in D. B. Hollis (ed.), *The Oxford Guide to Treaties* (Oxford: Oxford University Press, 2012), pp. 507–524.

2 Typologies, Taxonomies and the 'Essential Juridical Character' of Treaties

Treaty classifications have been frequently connected with propositions about fundamental differences in legal instruments. McNair famously recommended that 'we free ourselves from the traditional notion that the instrument known as the treaty is governed by a single set of rules',[10] although he did not elaborate. The presumption that all treaties are in a fundamental sense the same legal instrument had been a point of contestation before with, for example, Triepel's distinction and later that of Shabtai Rosenne, who considered constituent treaties of international organizations to be so different that 'it is deceptive to see in diplomatic and legal ... incidents concerning the constituent instruments "precedents" for the general law of treaties, and *vice versa*'.[11]

Such propositions are generally framed as *challenges* to the law of treaties – which brings out the underlying conception (confirmed during the forty years' codification process of the law of treaties) of the treaty as a single legal instrument governed by a unified set of rules; this conception was again under discussion in relation to the 'Vienna Plus' International Law Commission's (ILC) *Guide to Practice on Reservations to Treaties*,[12] but the theoretical debate is inconclusive. The current chapter does not aim to engage with that debate and does not deal with questions of the completeness or, indeed, of the fragmentation of international law.[13] It proceeds from the class of legal instruments generally taken to be governed by the 'law of treaties'.

For a discussion of prevailing treaty classifications, this chapter, as would be fitting in our discipline, takes as a starting point the work of the pre-eminent scholar on the law of treaties of the pre-VCLT era.[14] In his 1930 article, McNair tentatively distinguished between treaties 'having the character of conveyances'; contract treaties; lawmaking treaties (comprising both 'constitutional international law' and 'ordinary international law') and 'treaties akin to charters of incorporation', that is, constitutive

---

[10] McNair, *supra* n. 4, at 118.

[11] S. Rosenne, *Developments in the Law of Treaties 1945–1986* (Cambridge: Cambridge University Press, 1989), pp. 257–258.

[12] International Law Commission, Guide to Practice on Reservations to Treaties, Doc. A/66/10; see, e.g., the comments of M. Milanovic and L.-A. Sicilianos, 'Reservations to Treaties: An Introduction', *EJIL*, 24 (2013), 1055–1059. See, further, *infra* n. 72 and n. 73 (and accompanying text).

[13] For further development of these themes, consider M. Koskenniemi and P. Leino, 'Fragmentation of International Law? Postmodern Anxieties', *Leiden JIL*, 15 (2002), 553–579.

[14] McNair, *supra* n. 4.

treaties of international organizations. McNair related these differences to the 'fundamental juridical character' of treaties,[15] but it is uncertain to what extent he meant to make an ontological claim about different legal instruments. He did attach specific legal consequences to some of the treaties he singled out, such as treaties of cession, which (after execution) would not be affected by hostilities,[16] and the *rebus sic stantibus* doctrine, which would not be applicable to 'legislative treaties' in the same way as to 'contractual' treaties.[17]

McNair's distinctions combine criteria of form with those based on normative effect and internal-legal with external perspectives. His listing of various international agreements works as a single level *taxonomy*, creating a clear picture of variety that makes good support, for example, for a plea to relax the traditional unified view of treaties. The current chapter chooses a somewhat different approach by looking at *typologies* of treaties – this is relevant as a host of typifications is found in legal doctrine and debate today. The notion of typology[18] suggests a classification of concepts rather than empirical facts, and it points to a construct built around particular attributes or dimensions to which the actual objects of classification do not necessarily correspond fully nor exclusively. The rationale of a particular typology, moreover, depends partly on the context. Typologies do not necessarily last forever, as they hinge on particular questions to be answered and analyses to be made.

Along these lines, McNair's 'treaties of conveyance' – which comprised cession treaties and other arrangements dealing with recognition or transfer of title over territory, somewhat analogous to domestic property rights[19] – arguably would nowadays include also status treaties, such as a boundary treaty or, in late modern terms, treaties creating territorial *objective regimes*, such as the 1959 Antarctic Treaty.[20] For its part, the type of treaty creating objective regimes (conceptualised around the 1960s, even if actual examples can be found from the nineteenth century onwards)[21] initially was often used to include also *non-territorial*

---

[15] *Ibid.*, at 103.   [16] *Ibid.*   [17] *Ibid.*, at 110.

[18] Leaving aside the distinction between ideal-type, extreme-type and empirical-type: see, further, S. Kluge, 'Empirically Grounded Construction of Types and Typologies in Qualitative Social Research', *Forum Qualitative Sozialforschung*, Vol. 1 (http://nbn-resolving.de/urn:nbn:de:0114-fqs0001145).

[19] McNair, *supra* n. 4, at 101–103.   [20] 402 UNTS 71.

[21] M. Fitzmaurice, 'Third Parties and the Law of Treaties', *Max Planck Yb. UN Law*, 6 (2002), 37–137, and C. Fernández de Casadevante Romani, 'Objective Regime' in R. Wolfrum (ed.), *Max Planck Encyclopedia of Public International Law* (Vol. VII) (Oxford: Oxford University Press, 2012), pp. 912–915.

arrangements, notably constitutive treaties of international organizations (IOs).[22] In fact, constitutive treaties are a case in point for the relativeness of treaty typologies. McNair found that such treaties 'create[d] something organic and permanent and they seem[ed] therefore to demand recognition as falling into a special category of treaty'.[23] In the 1930s, international organizations were less ubiquitous in international affairs, their legal status was uncertain and to attribute separate legal personality to organizations was an exceptional and controversial proposition;[24] so it made sense not to include IO constitutive treaties in a larger category but to set them apart completely as a *sui generis* type of treaty 'akin to charters of incorporation'.[25] This was different once the taboo on legal personality for organizations had been lifted through the advisory opinion of the International Court of Justice (ICJ) in *Reparation for Injuries Suffered in the Service of the United Nations* in April 1949,[26] while the number of organizations started growing rapidly. Unsurprisingly, constitutive treaties of IOs were now frequently found in a category with other treaties that produce an effect for third parties – generally speaking, the treaty type creating objective regimes. In fact, the 'objective legal personality' of the United Nations as proclaimed by the ICJ in the *Reparation* opinion was often linked and likened to the 'objective effect' of a treaty.[27] More recently, this has changed again; with the advancement of international organization and phenomena of multilevel governance, organizations increasingly have come to stand out for their *institutional* dimension. The debate now has come to be focused on the organization's legal independence, its institutional or even 'constitutional' mechanisms, its autonomous development on the basis of *compétence de la compétence*, while the treaty by which all this was created has faded into the background. The typification of IO constituent treaties, changing from a separate class of 'treaties akin to charters of incorporation' to a sub-type of objective regime treaties, to a separate type of

---

[22] See P. Reuter, *Introduction to the Law of Treaties* (Geneva: Geneva Institute of International Studies, 2nd ed., 1995), pp. 124–125; see, also, the contributions to this volume of Waibel and Miltner at pp. 201–236 (Chapter 8) and 468–505 (Chapter 15) respectively.

[23] McNair, *supra* n. 4, at 117.

[24] C. M. Brölmann, *The Institutional Veil in Public International Law* (Oxford: Hart Publishing, 2007), pp. 54–64.

[25] McNair, *supra* n. 4, at 116.

[26] *Reparation for Injuries Suffered in the Service of the United Nations* (Advisory Opinion) (1949) ICJ Rep. 174.

[27] See Reuter, *supra* n. 22, at p. 121.

constitutive (and 'constitutional') treaties, is one example of how seemingly self-evident typologies may shift over time.

A typology, then, may be relevant because it can be connected to certain differentiations in the VCLT framework; for example, Article 60(2) VCLT sets out a special rule for the unilateral termination of a *multilateral* treaty commitment (while, incidentally, there is no special regime for reservations to multilateral treaties – unsurprisingly so, in view of the bilateralised concept of reservations in the VCLT). A typology can also point to implications in the general public international law framework; for example, 'lawmaking' treaties which create *erga omnes partes* obligations have implications for the definition of 'injured State' in the law of responsibility. Or a typology can bring out effects in a non-formal legal discourse such as that based on justice; for example, the category of 'unequal treaties' has weak legitimacy in the justice debate.

This chapter is concerned with treaty types identified in contemporary international law discourse. Treaties, as legal phenomena in general, often appear conceptualised and rubricated in binary oppositions,[28] especially within the formal legal framework. This means one-dimensional classifications (a rule is either 'of a general normative scope' or 'not of a general normative scope') rather than multidimensional ones. Moreover, as the treaty types in use are often not mutually exclusive,[29] as in the case of the 'lawmaking' and the 'multilateral' types, it means we are technically dealing with several typologies simultaneously, many of them of the single level kind that is built on two opposing ('polar') types.[30] Any treaty is thus likely to belong to more than one typology. For example, the 1982 United Nations Convention on the Law of the Sea[31] may be called a multilateral treaty (as opposed to a bilateral treaty, for example), or a lawmaking treaty (as opposed to a contract treaty, for example) or an environmental treaty (as opposed to an arms treaty, for example). The choice for a particular typology will depend on the discursive

---

[28] Classically, M. Koskenniemi, *The Politics of International Law* (Oxford: Hart Publishing, 2011), pp. 298–299. See, also, D. A. J. Telman, 'International Legal Positivism and Legal Realism' in J. Kammerhofer and J. d'Aspremont (eds.), *International Legal Positivism in a Post-Modern World* (Cambridge: Cambridge University Press, 2014), pp. 241–263, at pp. 261–262.

[29] K. B. Smith, 'Typologies, Taxonomies, and the Benefits of Policy Classification', *Policy Studies J.*, 20 (2002), 379–385, at 381.

[30] 'Community–society Continua' in *International Encyclopedia of the Social Sciences* (1968), in Encyclopedia.com (31 July 2014) (www.encyclopedia.com/doc/1G2-3045000227.html).

[31] 1833 UNTS 3.

context – which might be an activist agenda but also a courtroom procedure – and can be an element in legal framing.

I single out a number of typologies under three main headings: typologies based on form, typologies based on normative effect and typologies based on content. *Form typologies* include the ones based on laterality, on the participation to a treaty, on the nature of parties, on appearance of the treaty and on designation of the treaty. The *normative effect typologies* include the ones based on normative force, on normative completeness at the international level, on normative completeness at the national level and (most famously) on regulatory function. The *content typologies* hinge on substantive areas of international law and on (implicit) claims of hierarchy.

3 Typologies Based on Form

This category includes various typologies revolving around formal aspects of the treaty instrument. The most commonplace is the typology based on *laterality*; it comprises *bilateral treaties* and *multilateral treaties* as well as the occasionally mentioned *plurilateral treaties*, which may point to either bilateralised agreements, with more than two parties but two 'sides' to the agreement (with a treaty such as the 1975 Lomé Agreement as a typical example),[32] or to treaties open to a limited group of parties 'due to subject matter or geography'[33] or, in the context of the World Trade Organization (WTO), to treaties to which WTO members can choose to become a party[34] (as opposed to 'multilateral treaties' which by definition have all WTO Member States as a party). Into this typology might be fitted also *mixed agreements*; even if these treaties have other attributes that technically provide a better basis for typification – notably the additional normative layer of the internal order of the European Union – they seem to be discussed most often in terms of laterality.

The Vienna Convention recognises laterality as a factor in the somewhat unwieldy provision of Article 60, on termination or suspension of a treaty on the basis of material breach by another party.[35] The article

---

[32] ILM, 9 (1975), 595–640.

[33] K. Schmalenbach, 'Article 2' in O. Dörr and K. Schmalenbach (eds.), *Vienna Convention on the Law of Treaties: A Commentary* (Berlin: Springer, 2012), pp. 27–48, at p. 31.

[34] B. Hoekman and P. Mavroidis, 'Embracing Diversity: Plurilateral Agreements and the Trading System', CEPR Discussion Paper No. DP10204 (2014) (http://ssrn.com/abstract=2512732).

[35] On Art. 60 VCLT, see, e.g., J. Klabbers, 'Side-stepping Article 60: Material Breach of Treaty and Responses Thereto' in M. Tupamäki (ed.), *Finnish Branch of ILA 1946-1996: Essays on International Law* (Helsinki: Finnish ILA Branch, 1998), pp. 20–42, and

provides what would be a parallel to the *exceptio non adimpleti contractus* in domestic law of contract, but (logically) not without effort when it comes to multilateral treaty relations.[36] Thus, Article 60(2)(b) VCLT maintains strict reciprocity in the relation between the defaulting State and the State that is 'specially affected' by the breach, but in regard of other States parties the VCLT adds a requirement ('radically changed' positions) related to the normative effects of the treaty (see Section 4). In practice since the 1969 Vienna Convention, 'material breach' has rarely been explicitly invoked – with the *Gabcíkovo-Nagymaros Case* of September 1997 as a comparatively recent exception – and never successfully.[37]

The typology based on *participation* comprises 'open' and 'closed' treaties, which – if turning on geographic parameters – are generally dubbed 'universal' and 'regional' treaties. The aforementioned term 'plurilateral' is sometimes found as synonymous to 'closed' treaties, in that only specific States are allowed to become a party.[38] The Vienna Convention regime attaches some importance to such treaties through Article 20(2); the flexible formulation goes back to a strict unanimity rule in an earlier draft for the category of 'plurilateral treaties', which as such was temporarily under discussion in the ILC in the 1950s and 1960s.[39]

A typology which in the past had considerable legal relevance is the one based on the *nature of parties*. Since international law doctrine puts up a threshold for treaty-making capacity, in a positive law framework this boils down to three types of treaties: treaties between States, treaties

---

M. Fitzmaurice, 'Material Breach of Treaty: Some Legal Issues', *Austrian Rev. Int'l & European L.*, 6 (2001), 3–44.

[36] Cf. Art. 60(2) VCLT ('A material breach of a multilateral treaty by one of the parties entitles: . . . (b) a party specially affected by the breach to invoke it as a ground for suspending the operation of the treaty in whole or in part in the relations between itself and the defaulting State . . .'); *supra* n. 7.

[37] *Case Concerning Gabcíkovo-Nagymaros Project (Hungary/Slovakia)* (1997) ICJ Rep. 7 (on Art. 60 VCLT as invoked by Hungary, in particular at pp. 60–62 (paragraph 96) and pp. 65–66 (paragraphs 105–108)). See, further, the contribution to this volume of Fitzmaurice at pp. 748–789 (Chapter 23).

[38] A. Aust, *Modern Treaty Law and Practice* (Cambridge: Cambridge University Press, 3rd ed., 2013), pp. 15 and 125.

[39] Art. 20(2) VCLT ('When it appears from the limited number of the negotiating States and the object and purpose of a treaty that the application of the treaty in its entirety between all the parties is an essential condition of the consent of each one to be bound by the treaty, a reservation requires acceptance by all the parties'): *supra* n. 7. See, further, C. Walter, 'Article 20' in Dörr and Schmalenbach (eds.), *supra* n. 33, pp. 287–306, at p. 296.

between IOs and States and, finally, treaties between IOs. Initially, the emerging treaty-making practice of international organizations had been reconciled with the statist legal system by taking the position that agreements concluded by IOs were legally different instruments from agreements concluded by states.[40] Such had been the suggestion of the Permanent Court of International Justice when it said 'tout contrat qui n'est pas un contrat entre des états en tant que sujets du droit international a son fondement dans une loi nationale';[41] it was also the opinion of sole arbitrator René-Jean Dupuy in the 1978 *Texaco v. Libyan Arab Republic* award, who held that States alone can be parties to a treaty, whereas agreements between, for example, States and IOs would be 'instruments of another nature'.[42] This conception was likewise at the root of a proposal tabled in the ILC during the preparatory stages of the 1969 Vienna Convention to disregard treaties between organizations but to take into account treaties to which a State *and* an organization were parties.[43]

Although the terminological distinction between 'treaties' of States and 'agreements' of organizations persisted for quite some time and to some extent still does today,[44] the underlying concept was abandoned, essentially because it became untenable in the light of developing doctrine and practice. The crucial factor here was the prevailing vision of international law as a unified legal order in which different legal subjects interact by definition under one single set of rules. Moreover, the law of treaties operates from the principle of equality of parties; thus – in defiance of initial recommendations to the contrary – the system could not and did not make a legal distinction between treaties on the basis of parties. This was ultimately confirmed by the two Vienna Conventions, which turned out extremely similar.[45] There may come a time when other

---

[40] Brölmann, *supra* n. 24, at pp. 132–133.

[41] *Case Concerning the Payment of Various Serbian Loans Issued in France*: France v. Serb-Croat-Slovene State, 1929 PCIJ, Series A, No. 20, 41. A similar view is found in C. Parry, 'The Treaty-Making Power of the United Nations', BYbIL, 26 (1949), 108–150.

[42] *Texaco Overseas Petroleum Company/California Asiatic Oil Company v. Govt. of Libyan Arab Republic*, ILM, 17 (1978), 1–37, at 23 (paragraph 66).

[43] YbILC (1965–I), 10 (paragraph 7).

[44] If only because IO treaties can generally be set apart from treaties of States for their politically modest purport; see, also, H. G. Schermers and N. M. Blokker, *International Institutional Law: Unity with Diversity* (Leiden: Koninklijke Brill NV, 5th rev. ed., 2011), p. 1121 (§1744), who observe the distinction but without attaching (general) legal implications.

[45] Brölmann, *supra* n. 24.

actors, such as transnational corporations or non-governmental organizations, unstoppably enter international treaty-making practice, causing a party-based typology to gain new prominence.

Finally, there are typologies based on the *appearance* of the treaty instrument (which may consist of a number of component documents or two letters or a single piece of parchment or a paper napkin) and on the *designation* of the treaty. Possible legal implications of such typifications, which could be seen before the UN era,[46] have been neutralized *qua* distinctive features in the 1969 Vienna Convention regime (Article 2(1)(a) VCLT: 'whatever its particular form or designation').[47] Outside the VCLT framework, on the other hand, references to a particular type such as an 'MOU' can have considerable legal or political relevance, as negotiating parties who are like-minded States may use particular terms to express their intention for striking a non-binding political accord (thus the UK and the Netherlands make extensive use of gentleman's agreements, often named 'MOU',[48] but France does not, while the UN consistently uses the name 'MOU' for its many binding agreements with other organizations and States). The typology based on designation may otherwise point to the political context of treaties in a different sense. Even if the name does not determine the international juridical status, an unassuming title such as 'letter of intent' may have effects in domestic law: it may downplay the necessity for explicit approval of parliament, or it may increase the possibility of striking an accord in the form of an 'executive agreement' in constitutional systems such as those of the United States, France and Germany.[49]

These typologies are based on formal aspects of the treaty. This is true to the spirit of the Vienna Convention, which is famously focused on the instrument as such rather than on the obligations stemming from it.[50]

---

[46] Cf. A. M. Stuyt, *Formeel Tractatenrecht* (Den Haag: Staatsuitgeverij, 1966), p. 29.

[47] *Supra* n. 7. As far as form is concerned, this was e.g. confirmed in the *Aegean Sea Continental Shelf*: Greece v. Turkey (1978) ICJ Rep. 3, at p. 39 (paragraph 96).

[48] Aust, *supra* n. 38, at pp. 34–39.

[49] Cf. C. Davenport, 'Obama Pursuing Climate Accord in Lieu of Treaty', *N.Y. Times*, 27 Aug. 2014, A1.

[50] See S. Rosenne, *Breach of Treaty* (Cambridge: Grotius Publications, 1985) and S. Rosenne, 'Bilateralism and Community Interest in the Codified Law of Treaties' in W. Friedmann, L. Henkin and O. J. Lissitzyn (eds.), *Transnational Law in a Changing Society: Essays in Honor of Philip C. Jessup* (New York, NY: Columbia University Press, 1972), pp. 202–227, at p. 205. Cf. J. Klabbers, 'The Community Interest in the Law of Treaties: Ambivalent Conceptions' in U. Fastenrath, R. Geiger, D.-E. Khan, A. Paulus, S. von Schorlemer and C. Vedder (eds.), *From Bilateralism to Community Interest: Essays in Honour of Bruno Simma* (Oxford: Oxford University Press, 2011), pp. 768–780, at p. 770.

4   Typologies Based on Normative Effect

A next class of typologies hinges on what might be called the *normative effect* of treaties. These typologies seem to be the most prevalent in international law discourse – even though little trace of them can be found in the VCLT framework or even the law of treaties generally. In this category four appear especially prominent: the typology based on *normative force*, the typologies based on *normative comprehensiveness* in an international context and in a national context, respectively, and the typology based on *regulatory function*.

The *normative force* typology comprises two polar types, *viz.* treaties creating objective effects or an 'objective regime', on the one hand, and treaties creating a subjective regime on the other. The legal effect *vis-à-vis* non-parties of the former type of treaty is taken as one of scope and not one of content, as the typification of 'objective regime' revolves around normative *effect*. The typology is tried and tested among international lawyers. However, it falls outside the framework of the Vienna Convention, which through its Articles 34–37 rigorously adheres to the requirement of approval (or, in technical terms, 'consent', 'assent' and 'acceptance') on the part of third States for both rights and obligations.[51] The exception is Article 62(2)(a) VCLT, which explicitly singles out boundary treaties. It is a reflection of general international law doctrine, which has come to terms with the phenomenon by detaching the regime from the treaty by which it was created: the paradigmatic account is found in the judgment of the International Court of Justice in *Case Concerning the Territorial Dispute between Libya and Chad* in February 1994.[52]

The typology based on *normative completeness at international level* contrasts framework treaties with comprehensive treaties.[53] The VCLT framework shows no sensibility to this distinction, but the typology is a factor in international governance discourse, a notable example being the context of environmental protection. The typology also points to the composite character of a treaty regime as a whole and usually also to the continuous development of the treaty('s regime). This characteristic is very familiar and present in the public debate as a vehicle for policy-making and normative development in the issue area at hand; witness, for example, the public stature of the United Nations Framework Convention on Climate

---

[51] See, also, the contribution to this volume of Craven at pp. 103–135 (Chapter 5).

[52] *Case Concerning the Territorial Dispute*: Libyan Arab Jamahiriya v. Chad (1994) ICJ Rep. 6, at p. 37 (paragraph 73) ('[a] boundary established by treaty thus achieves a permanence which the treaty itself does not necessarily enjoy').

[53] To be distinguished from the treaty *regimes* which can be divided at least into composite types of regime (*traité cadre* plus, e.g., protocols), on the one hand, and singular types on the other.

Change and protocols,[54] tied together and dynamized by annual COPs and MOPs and ensuing 'decisions' which may themselves lead to new and prominent treaties, as in the case of the 2015 Paris Agreement.[55] The only reflection of this typology in the VCLT, one could argue, is the *ineptitude* of provisions operating with a temporal factor (the later in time principle and the earlier in time principle, in Article 30(3) and 30(4)(b) respectively) for governing this type of treaty which, for the dynamic aspect of the regime it creates, has been termed 'continuing treaty'.[56]

The typology based on *normative completeness at a national level* comprises the polar types of self-executing and non-self-executing treaties. Through the VCLT prism this typological distinction is, again, invisible; but in international law discourse it has an important role, as the linchpin for the connection between international and domestic law. In the context of domestic law it is a key typological distinction in the process of actual application and implementation of a treaty. Thus, in 2006, the Netherlands was reprimanded by the Committee of the International Covenant of Economic, Social and Cultural Rights 'to reassess the extent to which, the provisions of the Covenant might be considered to be directly applicable. It urges the State Party to ensure that the provisions of the Covenant are given effect by its domestic courts, as defined in the Committee's General Comment 3, and that it promotes the use of the Covenant as a domestic source of law'.[57]

The most prominent normative effect-based typology is the one focused on *regulatory function*. It comprises three types: constituent or constitutive treaties of international organizations; contract (or 'synallagmatic') treaties; and lawmaking ('non-synallagmatic' or – the slightly awkward – 'normative') treaties.

A constitutive treaty is a portal to the internal, institutional dimension of an organization.[58] This dimension sits uneasily with the horizontal set-up of international law, as becomes apparent, for example, in the problematic construction in the 2011 Articles on the Responsibility of

---

[54] 1771 UNTS 107.

[55] Entered into force on 4 Nov. 2016 (http://unfccc.int/paris_agreement/items/9444.php). See, also, the contribution to this volume of French and Scott at pp. 677–709 (Chapter 21).

[56] The term is taken from Joost Pauwelyn who conceptualises the WTO treaty, multilateral human rights treaties or environmental treaties as 'continuing treaties' which makes it, in his view, inappropriate to apply Art. 30 VCLT: J. Pauwelyn, 'The Role of Public International Law in the WTO: How Far Can We Go?', *AJIL*, 95 (2001), 535–578, at 546.

[57] UN Committee on Economic, Social and Cultural Rights, Concluding Observations on the Netherlands (24 Nov. 2006), U.N. Doc. E/C.12/NLD/CO/3, §19.

[58] Rosenne, *supra* n. 11, at pp. 246–248.

International Organizations for Internationally Wrongful Acts,[59] to take the 'rules of the organization' not as internal law but as *lex specialis*.[60] The 1969 and 1986 Vienna Conventions, on the other hand, do recognise the internal legal sphere of organizations in a general reservation clause contained in similar Articles 5.[61] Article 5 of the Vienna Conventions genuinely delimits the operation of international law and demarcates a boundary between the law of treaties and the institutional law of organizations. The provision is a 'without prejudice' clause expressly reserving the right of international organizations to maintain their own rules with regard to their constituent treaties and to the treaty-making process in their framework.[62] That the institutional order is thus construed as to some extent closed off from general international law is also reflected in the special role reserved for the 'competent organ of the organization' in Articles 20(3) (Reservations) and 77(2) (Depositary) of the 1986 Vienna Convention.[63]

That leaves 'contract treaties' and 'lawmaking treaties'.[64] McNair appears to have considered the distinction between these two types as one of the most 'fundamental'[65] and linked to the 'essential juridical

---

[59] GAOR 66th Sess., Supp. 10, Doc. A/66/10, 54.

[60] This is contestable for several reasons, for one because internal rules cannot have general normative force under general international law, and general 'internal law' by definition does not amount to a more specific rule 'on an identical subject'. See, also, J. d'Aspremont, 'A European Law of International Responsibility? The Articles on the Responsibility of International Organizations and the European Union' in V. Kosta, N. Skoutaris and V. Tzevelekos (eds.), *The EU Accession to the ECHR* (Oxford: Hart Publishing, 2014), pp. 75–86.

[61] K. Schmalenbach, 'Article 5' in Dörr and Schmalenbach (eds.), *supra* n. 33, pp. 89–99 ('Article 5 – *Treaties constituting international organizations and treaties adopted within an international organization* – The present Convention applies to any treaty between one or more States and one or more international organizations which is the constituent instrument of an international organization and to any treaty adopted within an international organization, without prejudice to any relevant rules of the organization').

[62] As to the 1986 Convention, in view of the – still – scant practice of organizations functioning in the framework of other organizations, the Special Rapporteur had considered '[i]t is obvious that there can be no article in the draft articles similar to Art. 5 of the 1969 Convention': Reuter, *YbILC* (1974–II) (Part One), 145. The Commission thought differently. On second reading, a parallel Art. 5 (*Treaties constituting international organizations and treaties adopted within an international organization*) was inserted in the draft ultimately to become part of the 1986 Vienna Convention; the provision is, however, not entirely symmetrical to its 1969 counterpart. It secures 'no prejudice' to 'any relevant rules of the organization' in case of constituent instruments only when these are treaties between States and organizations. Constituent treaties with exclusively organizations as parties were left out of account, with no further explanation on the part of the Commission: *YbILC* (1982) (Part Two), 23.

[63] *Supra* n. 8.   [64] Reuter, *supra* n. 22, at pp. 26–28.   [65] McNair, *supra* n. 4, at 106.

character' of the treaties.[66] Whereas the 'contract treaty' (with a normative content susceptible to reciprocity, matching the contractual form of the instrument) is generally taken to be the unmarked, prototypal form of treaty, the 'lawmaking treaty' is here a logical starting point. This treaty type has a long-standing position in legal discourse, and merits some elaboration,[67] all the more because it is an awkward notion. Firstly it is questionable whether treaties can create law at all, as Sir Gerald Fitzmaurice famously pointed out: 'Considered in themselves, and particularly in their inception, treaties are, formally, a source of obligation rather than a source of law'.[68] But regardless even of how 'law' is defined, 'lawmaking' has a received meaning in relation to treaties. It refers to treaty provisions with a general normative scope, with a statutory rather than a contractual function. This was what the International Court of Justice looked for when it examined whether a treaty provision was likely to have assumed force of customary law, *viz.* that 'the provision concerned should ... be of a fundamentally norm-creating character'.[69]

Of the four ILC Special Rapporteurs on the Law of Treaties, Fitzmaurice was the most sensitive to this typification.[70] Next to bilateral or multilateral treaties that are based on a reciprocal exchange of rights or benefits (as would be any classically contractual treaty, for instance establishing a customs union), he identified a category of 'lawmaking treaties (*traités-lois*) ... where the juridical force of the obligation is inherent, and not dependent on a corresponding performance by the

---

[66] *Ibid.*, at 103 and 106.

[67] Cf. the search for provisions of 'a generally norm-creating character' in the 1958 Geneva Convention on the Continental Shelf by the International Court of Justice in *North Sea Continental Shelf Cases*: FRG/Denmark; FRG/Netherlands (Judgment) (1969) ICJ Rep. 3, at pp. 41–42 (paragraph 72). Cf., also, the statement by Alain Pellet, as Special Rapporteur for the ILC on reservations to treaties, on how it is 'unusual for a treaty to be entirely normative or entirely synallagmatic': *YbILC* (1997-I), 176 (paragraph 79).

[68] G. G. Fitzmaurice, 'Some Problems Regarding the Formal Sources of International Law' in F. M. van Asbeck *et al.* (eds.), *Symbolae Verzijl: présentées au Professeur J.H.W. Verzijl à l'occasion de son LXX-ième anniversaire* (La Haye: M. Nijhoff, 1958), pp. 153–176, at p. 159.

[69] *North Sea Continental Shelf Cases*, *supra* n. 67, at pp. 41–42 (paragraph 72); the passage also points to the practical complication that many treaties contain a mixture of lawmaking and contractual norms, which would make it more helpful to apply the notion to individual norms rather than to treaties as a whole. This aspect is left out of account in the present chapter.

[70] This section relies partly on C. M. Brölmann, 'Law-Making Treaties: Form and Function in International Law', *Nordic JIL*, 74 (2005), 383–404.

other parties to the treaty'.[71] Fitzmaurice took a novel and rather technical approach which not only looked to the function of a treaty – up until then the main take on 'lawmaking treaties'[72] – but also to the legal relations resulting from it. Thus, in addition to contractual and lawmaking treaties,[73] he identified a class of 'interdependent treaties', for which the performance of one party is dependent on that of *all* the other parties (the standard example given by him was a disarmament treaty). The latter category, although analytically sound, never caught on and cannot count as a 'type' that was ever in use.

The essence of a lawmaking treaty is the absence of a bilateral, synallagmatic relation with other treaty parties (even if in the framework of a multilateral treaty). This means a lawmaking treaty is different from the grid of bilateralised relations envisaged for the purpose of the reservations regime by the International Court of Justice in its advisory opinion in *Reservations to the Convention on the Prevention and Punishment of the Crime of Genocide* in May 1951.[74] Rather, the construction is reminiscent of the 'consensual bond' which comes into being upon acceptance of the jurisdiction of the International Court of Justice under the optional clause in Article 36(2) of the ICJ Statute.[75] Indeed, Lea Brilmayer conceptualises the commitment to a non-synallagmatic treaty as a 'pledge,' in contrast to the commitment to a 'treaty' of the contract type.[76]

---

[71] G. G. Fitzmaurice, Second Report on the Law of Treaties, Doc. A/CN.4/107 (15 March 1957), p. 31.

[72] Cf. the position of Georges Scelle that '[lawmaking treaties] present an entirely different interest of stability and generality. They aim to establish a rule of law and are true legislative acts': *Le Pacte des Nations et sa liaison avec le Traité de Paix* (Paris: Recueil Sirey, 1919), p. 49 (translation quoted in A. D'Amato, 'Treaties as a Source of General Rules of International Law', *Harvard ILJ*, 3 (1962), 1–35, at 15).

[73] A distinction which he carried on from interbellum legal scholars, as is pointed out by J. Pauwelyn, *Conflict of Norms in Public International Law: How WTO Law Relates to Other Rules of International Law* (Cambridge: Cambridge University Press, 2003), pp. 56–57.

[74] *Reservations to the Convention on the Prevention and Punishment of the Crime of Genocide* (Advisory Opinion) (1951) ICJ Rep. 15; even though the Court took a synallagmatic approach to the question of the 1948 United Nations Convention on the Prevention and Punishment of the Crime of Genocide, the Court also shed light (at p. 32) on the overall nature of the Convention: '[i]n such a convention the contracting States do not have any interest of their own; they merely have, one and all, a common interest'. Cf. C. Focarelli, 'Common Article 1 of the 1949 Geneva Conventions: A Soap Bubble?', *EJIL*, 21 (2010), 125–171.

[75] Cf. *Case Concerning the Land and Maritime Boundary between Cameroon and Nigeria*: Cameroon v. Nigeria (Preliminary Objections) (1998) ICJ Rep. 275, at p. 291 (paragraph 25).

[76] L. Brilmayer, 'From "Contract" to "Pledge": The Structure of International Human Rights Agreements', *BYbIL*, 77 (2006), 163–202.

Lawmaking treaties elude the compliance pull of reciprocity – it is noteworthy that Fitzmaurice had proposed to extend the exception for 'treaties of a humanitarian character' in Article 60(5) VCLT (see Section 5) to all lawmaking treaties. Human rights treaties are the pre-eminent example of lawmaking treaties in this sense.[77] They are not only non-synallagmatic, they are what has been called essentially 'inward-turned'. This is how the Inter-American Court for Human Rights construed that '[i]n concluding these human rights treaties, the States can be deemed to submit themselves to a legal order within which they, for the common good, assume various obligations, not in relation to other States, but towards all individuals within their jurisdiction'.[78] The complexities arising when regular treaty mechanisms (and concomitant reciprocity dynamics) are applied to human rights treaties[79] fully came to light during the seventeen years of work in the ILC on reservations to treaties (see also Section 5). In 2011, the ILC adopted the Guide to Practice on Reservations to Treaties[80] as 'a soft law instrument mixing, however, hard rules with soft recommendations'.[81]

Lawmaking treaties are recognised only implicitly by the VCLT framework (in the wake of Fitzmaurice's distinctions, which, in Joost Pauwelyn's words, have left 'traces' in the Vienna Convention),[82] in the context of termination/suspension or modification by one or *some* of the parties. Articles 41(1)(b) VCLT (as confirmed by the reference in Article 30 VCLT) and 58(1)(b) VCLT stipulate that no *inter se* modification or suspension, respectively, is allowed if this changes the effectuation of rights and obligations for the other treaty parties (without, however, the sanction of invalidity proposed by Fitzmaurice).[83] Since this would

---

[77] See the contribution to this volume of Chinkin at pp. 509–537 (Chapter 16).

[78] *The Effect of Reservations on the Entry into Force of the American Convention on Human Rights (Arts. 74 and 75)*, Inter-American Court of Human Rights, Advisory Opinion OC-2/82, 24 Sept. 1982, §29.

[79] See, e.g., B. Simma and G. I. Hernández, 'Legal Consequences of an Impermissible Reservation to a Human Rights Treaty: Where Do We Stand?' in E. Cannizzaro (ed.), *The Law of Treaties Beyond the Vienna Convention* (Oxford: Oxford University Press, 2011), pp. 60–85, and L. Lijnzaad, *Reservations to UN Human Rights Treaties: Ratify and Ruin?* (Dordrecht/Boston, MA/London: Springer, 1995).

[80] Guide to Practice on Reservations to Treaties, *supra* n. 12, at p. 19 (paragraph 75).

[81] A. Pellet, 'The ILC Guide to Practice on Reservations to Treaties: A General Presentation by the Special Rapporteur', *EJIL*, 24 (2013), 1061–1097.

[82] J. Pauwelyn, 'A Typology of Multilateral Treaty Obligations: Are WTO Obligations Bilateral or Collective in Nature?', *EJIL*, 14 (2003), 907–951, at 912–915.

[83] G. G. Fitzmaurice, Third Report on the Law of Treaties, Doc. A/CN.4/115 (18 March 1958), p. 27 (Art. 19).

always be the case in a treaty with integral or interdependent obligations (which are, after all, *erga omnes partes*), lawmaking treaties are here set aside. Following on from Article 60(2)(b) VCLT,[84] paragraph (c) of Article 60 VCLT gives the right to invoke unilateral suspension of the treaty between itself and the breaching party if the treaty is of such nature (that is, containing integral or interdependent obligations) that the breach were to fundamentally change treaty performance by the other parties.[85] Treaties which set out *erga omnes partes* obligations – as arguably most lawmaking treaties do – have implications for the defini- tion of 'injured State' in the law of responsibility.[86]

Other than this, the VCLT framework shows no sensibility to the typological distinction between lawmaking and contract treaties. One likely reason is the tension between form and function apparent in this treaty type. The treaty instrument (and arguably the treaty concept as such) is based on a contractual notion and hinges on the precepts of freedom of contract and consent as the basis of obligation and reciprocity as the mechanism for performance – which is the reason for its historic success as a norm-creating tool in international affairs in the first place.

Meanwhile international law is increasingly expected to cater to com- munal values and communal needs, as transpires from the statement of the then president of the International Court of Justice *en marge de* the advisory opinion in *Legality of the Threat or Use of Nuclear Weapons* in July 1996:

> [t]he resolutely positivist, voluntarist approach of international law still current at the beginning of the century . . . has been replaced by . . . a law more readily seeking to reflect a collective juridical conscience and respond to the social necessities of States organized as a community.[87]

But for their contractual form, treaties are not *per se* the instrument for the creation of such communal international rules. In fact, 'treaties' have existed much longer than the notion of international law,[88] while 'inter- national law' existed long before it started to be written in treaties. That in

---

[84] On which, see Section 3 earlier in this chapter.
[85] On treaties conflicting with *jus cogens*, see Section 5 (*infra*).
[86] Art. 42(b) of the 2001 ILC Articles on the Responsibility of States for Internationally Wrongful Acts: GAOR 56th Sess., Supp. 10, Doc. A/56/10, 43.
[87] *Legality of The Threat or Use of Nuclear Weapons* (Advisory Opinion) (1996) ICJ Rep. 226, at pp. 270–271 (paragraph 13 of Declaration by President Bedjaoui).
[88] P. Allott, *The Health of Nations: Society and Law beyond the State* (Cambridge: Cambridge University Press, 2002), p. 304; see, also, the contribution to this volume of Lesaffer at pp. 43–75 (Chapter 3).

our time the central (inter-State) lawmaking role which has come to lie with the UN codification conventions is essentially due to a lack of alternative. States drafting the 1945 United Nations Charter[89] had strongly opposed conferring upon the Organization the power to enact binding international rules. Likewise, proposals to give the General Assembly powers to impose certain general conventions on States by some form of majority vote had been rejected.[90] That treaties have thus been taking care of both the contractual and the statutory function in international law lies at the root of the much-quoted statement by McNair that '[t]he treaty is the only and sadly overworked instrument with which international society is equipped for the purpose of carrying out its multifarious transactions'.[91]

While the idea of 'lawmaking treaties' goes back to the late nineteenth century, this treaty type, as the vehicle for codification, became a key element in the postwar narrative of a secure, fair and objective international law – and hence of the *international rule of law*, as can be seen from the fostering of multilateral treaty-making as part of declared 'rule of law' promotion by the United Nations today.[92]

In contemporary international law discourse, moreover, the lawmaking treaty type often appears to be linked to a public[93] aspect of international law, usually combined with the idea of a communal dimension of the international legal order. Such a dimension, sometimes in a particular issue area (be it the use of force, the care for transboundary watercourses or the protection of the individual), is part of a complex debate which addresses communal values, rules with a general normative content and a 'statutory' function and a decline in the importance of individual states' consent – sometimes in an intricate combination. The vision of an international community[94] then implicitly proceeds from the idea of

---

[89] 1 UNTS 16.   [90] Cf. introduction on the ILC website (www.un.org/law/ilc/).

[91] A. D. McNair, *The Law of Treaties* (Oxford: Clarendon Press, 1961), p. 739.

[92] See Fifth Annual Report of the Secretary-General on the Strengthening and Coordinating United Nations Rule of Law Activities: Doc. A/68/213/Add.1 (11 July 2014); and see, e.g., the strong lawmaking narrative in the United Nations codification project: *Treaty Event 2014: Towards Universal Participation and Implementation* (United Nations Headquarters: 23–25 Sept. 2014 and 30 Sept.–1 Oct. 2014).

[93] Cf. Hersch Lauterpacht, who early on set forth a reasoning that international law necessarily comprised both 'objective law' and consent-based rules stemming from treaties: *Private Law Sources and Analogies of International Law (with Special Reference to International Arbitration)* (London: Longmans, Green & Co., 1927), pp. 54–55.

[94] See, e.g., B. Simma & A. Paulus, 'The "International Community": Facing the Challenge of Globalization', *EJIL*, 9 (1998), 266–277; cf. the different contributions on this theme in the

a unified system of law (as becomes clear also from the concern over its 'fragmentation').[95]

5   Typologies Based on Content

Finally, two *content-based typologies* stand out: a typology based on issue area and – intricately connected – a typology based on hierarchy linked to the substance of the treaty.

The law of treaties is famously agnostic to the substance or the *negotium* of treaties. Rosenne held that 'as the law of treaties does not envisage a legal distinction between treaties on the basis of content, it is unsurprising that it has proven difficult to classify international agreements in a legally relevant manner'.[96] This is true depending on one's understanding of 'legally relevant'. The one type of treaty (provisions) set apart on the basis of content in the Vienna Conventions, in Article 60(5), is 'the protection of the human person contained in treaties of a humanitarian character' (for Article 62(2)(a) VCLT, which sets apart the objective effect of a boundary created by treaty as mentioned in Section 4). This exception to the rule of Article 60 VCLT (on the termination or suspension of the operation of a treaty as a consequence of its breach) was introduced in the text during the Diplomatic Conference in 1969 and served to save individuals from the 'entirely inappropriate negative application of the principle of reciprocity'.[97] From the *travaux préparatoires*, it can be gleaned the provision is to cover both human rights law and humanitarian law treaties.[98]

This said, there is commonly mention of 'human rights treaties' and 'humanitarian law treaties' in a wider context than termination/suspension and of 'environmental law treaties', 'trade law treaties' or any other rubric linked to an area of human activity and cooperation.[99] In these cases, aside

---

broad sense in Fastenrath, Geiger, Khan, Paulus, von Schorlemer and Vedder (eds.), *supra* n. 50.

[95] See the Report of the ILC on the Work of its Fifty-Sixth Session: Doc. Supp. No. 10 (A/59/10), pp. 281–304.

[96] Cf, Rosenne, *supra* n. 11, at pp. 190 *et passim*.

[97] T. Giegerich, 'Article 60' in Dörr and Schmalenbach (eds.), *supra* n. 33, pp. 1021–1050, at p. 1046.

[98] B. Simma and C.J. Tams, 'Article 60 (1969)' in O. Corten and P. Klein (eds.), *The Vienna Conventions on the Law of Treaties: A Commentary* (Vol. II) (Oxford: Oxford University Press, 2011), pp. 1351–1378, at pp. 1367–1368.

[99] Or linked to a long-standing area of legal study and classification: see the list of Multilateral Treaties Deposited with the Secretary-General of the United Nations

from actual normative content, the *genre* is so to speak a self-standing value. This can be seen in a division of policy areas (take, for instance, the division of policy areas in domestic governments and concomitant mandates for treaty negotiations) or in a form of 'legal modelling' of treaty arrangements on certain subjects (take, for example, the contested argument that customary investment law may be created through a quantity of uniform bilateral investment treaties).[100]

Different epistemic communities may use different typologies. Most international organizations employ a typology for internal categorisation purposes. For example, in the International Labour Organization, a distinction is employed between the 'fundamental' Conventions, the 'governance' (or 'priority') Conventions and the 'technical' Conventions, with consequences in terms of reporting duties for the Member States (regular reports on implementation are requested at shorter intervals for the first two types).[101]

Related to the content typology based on issue area, is the typology which makes a (sometimes implicit) claim of hierarchical order,[102] or 'relative normativity' to use an older term, among treaties or treaty provisions. In this category we find among others a 'fundamental rights treaty', a 'codification treaty', a 'constitutional treaty' or on the other hand a 'treaty with subsidiary rules' – to name a few typifications frequently used. Three in particular come to the fore.

The first is human rights discourse, which oftentimes relies on an intricate combination of hierarchy typology and issue-area typology, for example by the use of the word 'fundamental' (which, unlike *jus cogens*, does not denote a formal legal category). Even though the VCLT framework does not recognise human rights treaties outside the context of Article 60, the typification of human rights treaties or 'fundamental rights' treaties does appear as a persuasive authority both outside and within the framework of positive international law, the latter in processes of interpretation (Article 31 VCLT) and conflict of treaties

---

(https://treaties.un.org/pages/ParticipationStatus.aspx) including the types of 'obscene publications' and 'maintenance obligations'.

[100] A. Al Faruque, 'Creating Customary International Law through Bilateral Investment Treaties: A Critical Appraisal', *Indian JIL*, 44 (2004), 292–318.

[101] I am indebted to Anne Trebilcock for information on the ILO; see, further, that author's contribution to this volume at pp. 848–880 (Chapter 26), and, otherwise, Brölmann, *supra* n. 24, at pp. 128–132 on the typologies used by OECD, FAO, UN and EU.

[102] Cf. J. Vidmar, 'Norm Conflicts and Hierarchy in International Law: Towards a Vertical International Legal System?' in E. de Wet and J. Vidmar (eds.), *Hierarchy in International Law: The Place of Human Rights* (Oxford: Oxford University Press, 2012), pp. 13–41.

(Article 30 VCLT). See in this respect for instance the 1991 *Short Case,* in which the Dutch Supreme Court gave priority to Article 2 ECHR (which in conjunction with the 'Soering doctrine' prohibited extradition of the American officer to the United States) over the Status of Forces Agreement with NATO (which prescribed extradition).[103] Moreover, human rights treaties seem eligible for interpretation through a variant of the *living instrument doctrine,*[104] whereas an appeal for evolutionary interpretation of certain conventional treaties is less likely to be honoured (note for instance the refusal of the ICJ to extend the prohibitive rule regarding chemical weapons in the 1925 Geneva Gas Protocol[105] to the later developed nuclear weapons).[106] Otherwise, differentiation in the context of reservations to treaties in public international law doctrine at large has received something of a push from the work of the ILC on reservations to human rights treaties.[107] On the attempts to adjust the legal regime on reservations to these 'inward-turned' rules, see Section 4 earlier in the chapter.

Second is the 'constitutional treaty' type that was singled out by McNair. He identified two kinds of lawmaking treaties: 'Treaties creating Constitutional International Law' (such as Hague Convention I for the Pacific Settlement of International Disputes[108] and the 1919 Covenant of the League of Nations)[109] and 'Treaties creating or declaring ordinary International Law' or 'pure lawmaking treaties' (such as 'most of The Hague Conventions of 1899 and 1907, [which] contain rules governing the conduct of war').[110] In our time, the constitutional treaty (not to be confused with treaties constituting an international organization) does not have a place in the VCLT framework. It is, however, a *topos* in international law and policy[111] – one reflection of which are the efforts to construe the United Nations Charter as the world's constitution.[112] Otherwise, this typification too may be taken as persuasive authority in the context of treaty interpretation. Compare the approach of the Court of Justice of the European Union in the first *Kadi* decisions; in 2005, the

---

[103] *Short v. Kingdom of The Netherlands,* ILM, 29 (1990), 1375–1389.

[104] See, further, the contribution to this volume of Moeckli and White at pp. 136–171 (Chapter 6).

[105] 94 LNTS 65.

[106] *Legality of the Threat or Use of Nuclear Weapons, supra* n. 87, at p. 248 (paragraphs 54–56).

[107] Simma and Hernández, *supra* n. 79.   [108] 187 CTS 410.   [109] 225 CTS 195.

[110] McNair, *supra* n. 4, at 112.

[111] J. Klabbers, A. Peters and G. Ulfstein, *The Constitutionalization of International Law* (Oxford: Oxford University Press, 2009).

[112] B. Fassbender, 'The United Nations Charter as Constitution of the International Community', *Columbia JTL,* 36 (1998), 529–619.

Court of First Instance had reasoned in a classic international law framework, in line with which the United Nations Charter took precedence over the EU treaty *ex* Article 103 of the Charter. In 2008, the Court took the EU treaty as a constitutional treaty, setting out concomitant 'fundamental values'; it thus bypassed altogether the traditional 'conflict of treaties' position.[113]

A third type of treaty that creates normative hierarchy based on its content is the treaty which conflicts with *jus cogens*. This type is actually addressed by the VCLT, and the relevant treaty is rendered void by Articles 53 and 64 (Fitzmaurice originally had proposed this sanction for treaties conflicting with any lawmaking treaty or 'integral obligation').[114] This is a strong feature of the Vienna Convention framework. However, as the category of *jus cogens* is essentially contested, and agreement exists about few norms other than the prohibition of slavery and the prohibition of genocide, there is room for considerations of justice and morality outside the VCLT. This is difficult in contemporary international law discourse. McNair held that 'a treaty is null and void if its object is either illegal or immoral',[115] but international law these days is uneasy in addressing such questions (think of the phenomenon of 'unequal treaties'), with dimensions of fairness and justice relegated to other disciplines.

6   Concluding: Multiple Typologies and Multiple International Law Discourses

This chapter has outlined a number of treaty typologies *en vogue* in international law discourse today, rubricated under the headings of form, normative effect and content. Going back to the starting point of this chapter, from our cursory overview it appears the Vienna Conventions offer few flexibilities to particular types of treaties. The typology based on laterality, for example, plays a role in that Article 60 VCLT sets out a variant of the *exceptio non adimpleti contractus*, with special rules for multilateral treaties. Otherwise, the Vienna Conventions recognise IO constitutive treaties by way of a general reservation clause in their (almost) identical Articles 5. As for content, only Article 60(5) VCLT explicitly singles out treaties of a 'humanitarian character'. Thus, apart from a few traces described in this chapter, the

---

[113] Case T-306/01 *Kadi and Al Barakaat Foundation v. Council and Commission*, p. II-3533, ECJ (CFI), 21 Sept. 2005; Judgment on appeal in Joint Cases C-402/05 P and C-415/05 P, ECJ (GC), 3 Sept. 2008.

[114] Fitzmaurice, *supra* n. 83.   [115] McNair, *supra* n. 4, at 108.

Vienna regime has special rules only for one form-type (multilateral treaties), two normative effect-types (boundary treaties and constitutive treaties), and one content-type ('treaties of a humanitarian character'). Treaties concluded by IOs then are set apart by the 1969 Vienna Convention to the extent that they are excluded from its scope and dealt with in the 1986 Vienna Convention (which, however, is so similar that it is difficult to speak of 'differentiation'). While McNair wrote a plea for legal awareness of the differing 'legal character' of treaties and of the need to develop different rules accordingly,[116] this was not to become a trend during or after the codification process of the law of treaties that started in the late 1940s.

Meanwhile, it seems typologies of treaties abound among lawyers and policy-makers. In the category of normative effect typologies, the most prominent typological distinction is the one between 'lawmaking' and 'contractual' treaties. The lawmaking treaty type has been an object of discussion since the late nineteenth century and is still today a frequently used analytical tool in treaty practice, doctrine and international relations. It has also been a key element in the postwar narrative of an 'international rule of law'. With the exception of Article 60(3) VCLT, the VCLT framework is however famously unreceptive to the special characteristics of 'non-synallagmatic treaties'. Surely this is partly due to the fact that lawmaking treaties suffer from a gap between form and function.[117] After all, in form the treaty instrument is very much geared to contractual, reciprocal relations, based as it is on the freedom of contract and 'the general principle of consensualism which constitutes the basis of any treaty commitment [and which] necessarily entails the legal equality of the parties'.[118]

A prominent treaty type defined by content is the 'human rights' or 'fundamental rights' treaty. This typification has considerable persuasive power, but its relevance lies outside the VCLT framework, even if

---

[116] *Ibid.*, at 118.

[117] Even if in practice issues are partly captured by the VCLT's special rule for multilateral treaties in Art. 60: *supra* n. 7.

[118] P. Reuter, Tenth Report on the Question of Treaties Concluded between States and International Organizations or between Two or More International Organizations, *YbILC* (1981–II), 46; this looks to concrete traits of the treaty instrument and not to the fair doubts as to whether the contractual analogy as such is the most helpful in the conceptualisation of treaties. On this issue, see A. Rasulov, 'Theorizing Treaties: The Consequences of the Contractual Analogy' in C. J. Tams, A. Tzanakopoulos and A. Zimmermann (eds.), *Research Handbook on the Law of Treaties* (Cheltenham: Edward Elgar, 2014), pp. 74–122.

partly *within* the law of treaties paradigm, related to application and interpretation.

A single chapter cannot do justice to the variety of treaty typologies and the ways in which these are put to use in international law, especially outside the scope of the Vienna Conventions. Moreover, the relevance of typologies, and hence their existence, is partly defined by the context, such as a legitimacy or fairness discourse or – in a positivist framework – the circumstance of an 'armed conflict'. The fact that this latter context is expressly excluded from the VCLT regime (Article 73) does not preclude the possibility that, as suggested by McNair and the recent work of the ILC,[119] the occurrence of hostilities may give relevance to particular typological distinctions among treaties. In this sense, a treaty typification may indeed point to the 'essential juridical character' of a particular type (McNair also used the term 'type'), as specific 'legal consequences ... seem ... to follow' from that classification.[120] But issues of context and choice of typology remain, with further questions to be answered and trends to be discerned: Is there a hierarchy among treaty typologies? What are the politics of treaty typologies? What this chapter does show is how the treaty has moved beyond its role of a content-neutral, formal instrument to gain relevance as a context-dependent body of normative authority.

---

[119] McNair, *supra* n. 4, at 103 ('the real reason why a treaty of cession ... is not, once it has been carried out, affected by a subsequent state of war between the parties is surely that the treaty has, like a conveyance, produced its effect and has ceased to have vitality; ... it creases no outstanding obligations'). See, also, 2011 Draft Articles on the Effects of Armed Conflicts on Treaties: *YbILC* (2011–II).

[120] McNair, *supra* n. 4, at 103.

5

The Ends of Consent

MATTHEW CRAVEN

1 Introduction

In the preamble to the Vienna Convention on the Law of Treaties (VCLT) it is 'noted' that 'the principles of free consent and of good faith and the *pacta sunt servanda* rule are universally recognized'.[1] What is to be made of this prefatory affirmation, however, is less clear. On the one hand, and as was consistently reiterated through the drafting of the Convention at the hands of various Special Rapporteurs in the International Law Commission, the idea of free consent appears to be an indispensable ingredient in any understanding of the law of treaties. As Sir Gerald Fitzmaurice was to put it, the 'mutual consent of the parties, and the reality of consent on the part of each party, is an essential condition of the validity of any treaty'.[2] On the other hand, however, the very ubiquity of consent as an analytic – governing everything from the underpinnings of treaty obligation (*pacta sunt servanda* and good faith), to processural dimensions (competence, signature, ratification, accession and approval), conditions of validity (capacity, error, fraud, mistake, coercion), interpretation (*travaux préparatoires*) and effect (*pacta tertiis* etc.) – is such as to make it very much more difficult to isolate what consent actually means in this context.[3] Whether, for example, it is to be understood as the instantiation of a practice of autonomy (self-rule),[4] as a processural trigger providing for

---

[1] 1155 UNTS 331. See, also, the preamble of the 1978 Vienna Convention on Succession of States in Respect of Treaties: 1946 UNTS 3.

[2] G.G. Fitzmaurice, Third Report on the Law of Treaties, Doc. A/CN.4/115 and Corr. 1 (18 March 1958), p. 25 (paragraph 7).

[3] For a discussion of the 'different kinds of consent', see S. Rosenne, '"Consent" and Related Words in the Codified Law of Treaties' in S. Rosenne (ed.), *An International Law Miscellany* (Dordrecht: Martinus Nijhoff, 1993), pp. 357–377.

[4] See, e.g., G. Jellinek, *Die rechtliche Natur der Staatenverträge: ein Beintrag zur juristischen* (Vienna: Alfred Hölder, 1880). In the field of contract law, see C. Fried, *Contract as Promise* (Cambridge, MA: Harvard University Press, 1980).

the imposition of certain obligations[5] or as a convergence of wills (a meeting of minds)[6] may depend upon where one starts, or which aspects of treaty law one takes as fundamental. In that sense, the most significant or, perhaps, elucidatory features of the law of treaties (if one understands it as a systemically coherent enterprise) might be thought to be found in the places in which consent appears to be either entirely absent (duress, succession, objective agreements) or where its effects are systematically constrained by other factors (*rebus sic stantibus*, necessity, *force majeure* and *jus cogens*). Only, it might be argued, by looking at the limits of freedom of contract may one discern what it is that such freedom seems to imply or entail.

This itself may immediately put a number of questions in the frame: To what extent is consent indispensable for the assumption of obligations under treaties? May conventional obligations be assumed/imposed absent consent? What is required by way of consent? What is its practical content? In what contexts is consent sufficient/insufficient, effective/ineffective? At what moments may it be left aside? If, in method, I am attracted to the idea that the positive content (if any) of the idea of consent is to be discerned through the medium of its potential displacement (the point at which it 'ends'), there is also another sense of its 'ends' to which I also want to draw attention – that which concerns what it enables or produces as a discursive practice. My hypothesis, here, is that the idea of consent is more than simply an instrumental medium by which other things are to be achieved (as a vehicle for social transactions of one kind or another) but operates as a way of producing that to which it seeks to give effect: namely, a legal world configured around the idea that it is the systematic outcome of acts of collective free will rather than of coercion. Consent, in other words, takes itself as its own end.

Lying behind this general hypothesis are two related theoretical or methodological intuitions. The first is that consent, as an idea, operates as a way of linking domestic and international authority by seeking to secure the validity of international transactions by reference to the

---

[5] G. G. Fitzmaurice, Second Report on the Law of Treaties, Doc. A/CN.4/107 (15 March 1957), p. 42, n. 33 ('Consent is only a method ... by which obligations arise or come into force; but it is not the foundation of the binding force of the obligation once it has come into force. It is not consent that makes consent binding, for if it depended on that it would be necessary to provide yet another principle in order to give it juridical force to the consent that made consent binding'). See, further, G. G. Fitzmaurice, 'The Foundations of the Authority of International Law and the Problem of Enforcement', *Modern L. Rev.*, 19 (1956), 1–13, at 8.

[6] Cf. Arts. 31 and 32 VCLT: *supra* n. 1.

conditioning grounds of (territorial) sovereignty. This is not to say, however, that its content has remained entirely stable over time. Indeed, despite the adoption of a position of ostensible neutrality towards the operative conditions of domestic political arrangements, one may note a general shift from a conception of consent premised upon the keeping of the sovereigns' promises to a modern, popular, perhaps democratic, notion of consent as 'self-rule'.[7] Whether or not there be a right to democratic government or to popular control over the exercise of foreign policy, the practice of consent (by which I mean both the performance of formalities by which a State engages itself internationally and the rhetoric that underpins it) is such as to keep those agendas alive.

The second, related, intuition is that that if consent is to operate as a category of evaluation against which one might test the validity of international transactions, it does so not because it is intuited that the necessary conditions are already in place but because (in part at least) it seeks to operationalize those conditions and bring them into fruition. Consent, in these terms, is better understood as a practice concerned with the 'production' of both domestic and international authority through the performance of a range of largely formal, and symbolic, acts the purpose of which is to demonstrate the existence of a pre-existent right to govern but yet on grounds that are constantly in the process of being established. As such, one is left with the almost impossible formulation: 'the practice of consent is concerned with the production of consent as desire'.

In the course of this chapter, I will attempt to elucidate these ideas in three stages: first through a discussion of the place of consent, more generally, in international law outlining its productive characteristics; secondly through a brief account of its emergence in international legal history; and finally through an account of its 'limits' that brings to the fore the problem of producing an idea of consent that is 'authentic' under conditions of social constraint.

2   Consent and Will

If consent appears, most visibly, as a structuring feature of treaty law, it may nevertheless be said to reflect a more general condition of international law. As the Permanent Court of International Justice suggested in

---

[7] On which, see P. Allott, 'Power Sharing in the Law of the Sea', *AJIL*, 77 (1983), 1–30, at 24–25.

the *Lotus Case*, consent was to be understood as a fundamental legitimating condition: 'the rules of law binding upon States' are only those that 'emanate from their own free will'.[8] This was to emphasise at least two (somewhat contrasting) ideas. In the first place, it was to identify a common ground for both custom and treaty law.[9] Rather than imagine treaties as being merely formal, 'private' arrangements concluded under cover of general law (the law of treaties), it was to provide a rationality that enabled one to link the substantive content of treaties to the emergence of general international law (in which both formal and tacit consent is registered). As Sir Hersch Lauterpacht was to put it, consent could thus be understood as a 'formal source' which 'finds its partial materialization in custom and treaty which sit in relation to it as material sources'.[10] Treaties, on this score, are not merely formalised through consent (to obligation) but are also evidence of consent (to law). In the second place, if the Permanent Court was overtly to assert a broadly 'empirico-positivist' conception of law here (one whose sources were confined to the material practices of States), it was also to situate this within a broader legal environment in which States were presumed to enjoy an otherwise untrammeled freedom of action. Treaty-making, on such an analysis, takes the character of a restriction on the sovereignty of States assumed in virtue of an act of self-limitation in which the demonstrable characteristics of 'consent' are the key. Thus, as the Permanent Court was to suggest in the *Wimbledon Case*, a treaty engagement might

---

[8] *The Case of the S.S. 'Lotus'* (Judgment), 1927 PCIJ, Series A, No. 10, 18.

[9] Rasulov suggests that this commonality is no longer apparent in 'modern doctrinal consciousness' in which the 'processes of customary norm-production must ultimately be grounded in the logic of *belief* and *perception* . . . rather than any kind of *tacit consent* or *deliberate choice*'. See A. Rasulov, 'The Doctrine of Sources in the Discourse of the Permanent Court of International Justice' in C. J. Tams and M. Fitzmaurice (eds.), *Legacies of the Permanent Court of International Justice* (Leiden: Martinus Nijhoff, 2013), pp. 271–318, at p. 276. For an early critique of the mythic character of consent, see J. L. Brierly, *The Law of Nations* (H. Waldock ed.) (Oxford: Clarendon Press, 1963), pp. 52–53 ('The truth is that states do not regard their international legal relations as resulting from consent except where the consent is express, and that the theory of implied consent is a fiction invented by the theorist').

[10] See H. Lauterpacht, 'Decisions of Municipal Courts as a Source of International Law', *BYbIL*, 10 (1929), 65–95, at 81. For an early statement, see G. F. de Martens, *Précis du Droit des Gens Moderne de L'Europe* (Vol. I) (Paris: Guillaume & Co., 1838), Ch. ii, s. 46 (in which he distinguishes between three categories of 'volonté' – express, tacit or presumed – that give rise to three sources of law – 'conventions expresses', 'conventions tacites' and 'l'observance ou l'usage'). For a review of the late-nineteenth- and early-twentieth-century literature, see P. E. Corbett, 'The Consent of States and the Sources of the Law of Nations', *BYbIL*, 6 (1925), 20–30.

be said to consist of a 'restriction upon the exercise of sovereign rights of the State' enacted in consequence of an exercise of sovereignty.[11]

This idea of consent as an act of 'self-limitation' has its obvious limits. It is evident, to begin with, that within the context of treaty law, consent is clearly not an unregulated phenomenon. Not only is consent in some cases ineffective or insufficient (governed by considerations of process, validity and subsequent change), but consent is also occasionally unnecessary (e.g. in case of succession to treaties).[12] Consent is also hemmed in by rules relating to duress and the subsequent interpretation of agreements. If self-limitation remains a viable descriptive category, in that sense, it is an act of limitation capable of being performed only under terms already largely determined in advance. And this is to draw attention to the way in which the Vienna Convention itself both performs and subverts its own content. On the one hand, as a treaty, it is conditioned by the effectiveness of the rules it elaborates (the rules contained within the Convention stipulating the effect of its own ratification); on the other hand, it also purports to establish rules whose application necessarily exceed the limits of its own form (these are general rules, not simply rules for the contracting parties).[13]

In the second place, there is a question as to whether the generic standpoint articulated in the *Lotus Case* is analytically coherent as a way of understanding the effect of consent in treaties. To some degree, this is a question that goes to the different implications of the two terms in operation here: 'will' and 'consent'. An act of 'will' has distinctively active connotations suggestive of a power or a capacity to create law. Consent, by contrast, seems to evoke a passive idea of acceptance or of a dutiful concession. Each speaks in a particular way to the text of a treaty: one as the desire to impose obligations on others, the other as an

---

[11] *Case of the S.S. 'Wimbledon'*: France, Italy, Japan and United Kingdom v. Germany (Judgment), 1923 PCIJ, Series A, No. 1, 20, at p. 25. To the same effect, see *Case Concerning Military and Paramilitary Activities in and against Nicaragua*: Nicaragua v. United States of America (Merits) (1986) ICJ Rep. 14, at p. 131 (paragraph 259) ('A State ... is sovereign for the purpose of accepting a limitation of its sovereignty [by way of treaty]'). Rasulov adds a suggestive gloss to this: 'the more effectively the given state finds its hands tied by international law, the more convincingly it thus reaffirms its sovereignty': Rasulov, *supra* n. 9, at p. 279.

[12] See pp. 122–126.

[13] See I. Sinclair, *The Vienna Convention on the Law of Treaties* (Manchester: Manchester University Press, 2nd ed., 1984), pp. 3–5. It was for such reasons that Fitzmaurice had moved towards the drafting of an expository code. See G. G. Fitzmaurice, First Report on the Law of Treaties, Doc. A/CN.4/101 (14 March 1956), p. 106 (paragraph 4).

agreement to have obligations imposed upon oneself. Each also conceptualises the relationship between law and power in particular ways – one (will) as conjunctive or accumulative, the other (consent) as negative or subtractive.

That the Vienna Convention speaks of consent rather than will is, in that sense, to draw attention to the general idea that treaties are primarily vehicles for the assumption of obligations or for the limitation of authority rather than instruments that confer power and legal authority. This is reinforced, in part, by the occasional substitution of the word 'consent' by that of 'assent' (Article 36 VCLT) and 'acquiescence' (Article 45(b) VCLT), both of which maintain the metaphorical stance of subordination, even if their purpose may be to signal the legal relevance of actions or omissions beyond the formalities laid down in Articles 11 to 15 VCLT for purposes of determining the validity of obligations in relations between different States.[14]

Nevertheless, even if 'consent' carries with it a notion of subordination (with its associated metaphorical allusion to 'bondage'), there are at least four different ways in which one may understand consent as plausibly extending, as opposed to merely limiting, authority. In the first place, it may be seen to be a function of the standard synallagmatic correlation that has long been recognised in juridical thought[15] – in each case a State assumes an obligation under an international agreement, so also does it create certain rights for other parties to ensure the fulfilment of that obligation (the parameters of which, in case of breach, being determined by principles of State responsibility).[16] In the second place, and beyond the rights of enforcement, it is not infrequently the case that treaties may endow a State with authority to take certain measures that would not otherwise be available to it (e.g. to allow the exercise of immigration

---

[14] Rosenne differentiates between the 'comprehensive' conception of consent (consent to be bound) that is associated with the performance of the formalities outlined in Arts. 11 to 15 and that which he calls 'consent *simpliciter*' that is found in Art. 9 (relating to the adoption of the text); Art. 22 (concerning objections to, or withdrawal of reservations); Arts. 34, 36 and 37 (relating to the establishment, revocation or modification of rights of third States); Art. 54 (relating to termination or withdrawal) and Art. 57 (relating to suspension) of the Vienna Convention: *supra* n. 3, at pp. 259–260.

[15] W. N. Hohfeld, 'Some Fundamental Legal Conceptions as Applied in Judicial Reasoning', *Yale Law J.*, 23 (1913), 16–59.

[16] See, e.g., *Questions Relating to the Obligation to Prosecute or Extradite*: Belgium v. Senegal (Judgment) (2012) ICJ Rep. 422, at p. 449.

powers in the territory of other States[17] or provide for the overflight of civilian or military aircraft).[18] Both of these first two categories, however, operate within the standard framework of consent in the patrimonial sense of rights being 'transferred' from one party to another under conditions of exchange.[19]

In other cases, however, the conception that consent invariably involves the 'conferral' or 'transfer' of legal authority through the medium of an exchange is somewhat more difficult to sustain. In the case of powers assumed by members of the UN Security Council under Chapter VII of the 1945 United Nations Charter,[20] for example, it is only with some difficulty that one might imagine such authority being 'transferred' from individual members of the United Nations given that no individual State possessed parallel authority prior to the creation of the United Nations.[21] In a similar sense, treaties providing for the exercise of universal jurisdiction (such as over pirates on the high seas)[22] can only be

---

[17] See, e.g., 2007 Italy-Libya Bilateral Cooperation Agreement to Combat Clandestine Immigration, cited in *Hirsi Jamaa and Others v. Italy*, European Court of Human Rights (Grand Chamber), Judgment, 23 Feb. 2012.

[18] See, e.g., 1944 Chicago Convention on International Civil Aviation, 15 UNTS 295 (which first establishes that 'every State has complete and exclusive sovereignty over the airspace above its territory' (Art. 1) and then continues by establishing, under certain conditions, rights of entry and overflight).

[19] *North Sea Continental Shelf Cases*: FRG/Denmark; FRG/Netherlands (Judgment) (1969) ICJ Rep. 3, at pp. 25–26 (paragraph 28): 'if . . . a State which, though entitled to do so, had not ratified or acceded, attempted to claim rights under the convention, on the basis of a declared willingness to be bound by it, or of conduct evincing acceptance of the conventional régime, it would simply be told that, not having become a party to the convention it could not claim any rights under it until the professed willingness and acceptance had been manifested in the prescribed form'. For a critique of the contractual model as a way of understanding human rights agreements (and the proposal that they should be treated as straightforward 'pledges'), see L. Brilmayer, 'From "Contract" to "Pledge": the Structure of International Human Rights Agreements', BYbIL, 77 (2006), 163–202.

[20] 1 UNTS 16.

[21] It is true that Art. 24(1) of the United Nations Charter, *ibid.*, speaks of member States 'conferring' on the Security Council primary responsibility for the maintenance of international peace and security and that in discharging its duties it 'acts on their behalf', but it is equally clear that this is intelligible only so far as it is framed as a collective endeavor operating within an institutional setting in which the UN has certain designated 'functions' or 'responsibilities'. It is notable that even those who support the contention that UN authority is premised upon its transfer from member States are forced to admit that this provides little basis for the assertion of 'implied powers'. See D. Sarooshi, *International Organizations and Their Exercise of Sovereign Power* (Oxford: Oxford University Press, 2005).

[22] Art. 105 of the 1982 United Nations Convention on the Law of the Sea: 1833 UNTS 3.

squared with a patrimonial conception of exchange if one assumes from the outset that individual States possessed an intrinsic capacity to take such action.[23] The rubric established in the *Lotus Case*, of course, was one that encouraged precisely this idea: that every conventional arrangement operated as a form of limit upon a legally protected privilege of sovereignty,[24] so what was to be exchanged would always be part of a pre-existent legal 'patrimony', or authority, that inhered in the mere fact of a State's existence. Yet even leaving aside the fact that this almost entirely obscured the conditions under which that background authority was to be produced or justified in the first place,[25] it had the distinctly ideological function of allowing every novel claim to authority to assume the guise of a limitation.

Finally, one may also note that by conspicuously agreeing *not* to do something there is a sense also in which States may, at the same time, be asserting for themselves the authority to do that act absent agreement otherwise. Thus, whilst the prohibition on torture or slavery found in treaties might seem to be directed towards the elimination of a practice already regarded as illegal, the very conventional character of its prohibition is only such as to strengthen the argument that, absent the agreement itself, it would not be prohibited (or, at least, not prohibited in all circumstances). Of course, as was pointed out at some length in the *Nicaragua Case*,[26] the argument is always available that the treaty in question merely 'codifies' customary international law or causes it to 'crystallize'.[27] And this has certainly been the position adopted in the case of torture.[28] But even so, all this does is to bring into prominence

---

[23] See, further, Allott, *supra* n. 7, at 26–27.

[24] *Lotus Case, supra* n. 8, at p. 19: 'Far from laying down a general prohibition to the effect that States may not extend the applicability of their laws and the jurisdiction of their courts to persons, property and acts outside their territory, it leaves them in this respect a wide measure of discretion which is only limited in certain cases by prohibitive rules; as regards other cases, every State remains free to adopt the principles which it regards as best and most suitable'.

[25] See, e.g., H. Lauterpacht, *The Function of Law in the International Community* (Oxford: Clarendon Press, 1933), pp. 94–96.

[26] *Case Concerning Military and Paramilitary Activities in and against Nicaragua, supra* n. 11, at pp. 93–97 (paragraphs 174–182).

[27] *Ibid.*, at pp. 94–95 (paragraph 177).

[28] See, e.g., *Questions Relating to the Obligation to Prosecute or Extradite, supra* n. 16, at p. 457 (paragraph 99): 'the prohibition of torture is part of customary international law and it has become a peremptory norm (*jus cogens*)'. The Court added, however, *ibid.*, at p. 457 (paragraph 100), that 'the obligation to prosecute the alleged perpetrators of acts of torture under the Convention applies only to facts having occurred after its entry into

not merely the fact that processes of negotiation and contracting always take place against a background architecture of distributed legal author- ity (bargaining, as it is often said, in the 'shadow of the law') but that the visibility of that background (or, perhaps, its status) may only become apparent through the medium of agreements that seek to 'limit' that self-same authority. The act of limiting, in other words, will often be characterised by a double movement: in one direction towards the assertion of a (historic) claim to authority or dispensation to act; in another towards the recognition of a will to subordinate that authority to law.[29]

If this is to suggest that the formative place assumed by 'consent' in the law of treaties may in some ways disguise the operations of authority that are brought into play as a consequence of their purported 'limitation', that is all the more evident when one reflects upon its phenomenology. The language of consent invites us to think about the State, in organic terms, as a morally autonomous agent capable of pursuing 'the dictates of its own will' and rationally promoting or defending its own 'interests' through the medium of international agreements.[30] This idea, however, has always been mediated through a conception of formal agency – exemplified by the requirement that delegates possess 'full powers', that treaties be subject to 'ratification', and by the insistence that the validity of treaty obligations is unaffected by the severance of diplomatic rela- tions – in which the State is situated as a legitimating force behind the exercise of governmental authority but never immediately there in its own right. The State never consents, one may say, only the agents of government acting on its behalf. Consent, in that sense, brings into play two different operations: in one direction it serves as a simplifying metaphor, bracketing the internal political struggles attendant to the definition of those interests, the formulation of State policy or the capacity of the government to speak in the name of the State. In the other, however, it also operates as a way of giving visibility or meaning to the idea of the State itself – not merely as a pre-supposition of legitimate governmental activity but

---

force'. In other words, whilst the prohibition on torture was customary, the obligation to criminalise was exclusively conventional.

[29] One may note the same structure being followed in case of the Chicago Convention: *supra* n. 18.

[30] For an early statement, see, e.g., W. E. Hall, *A Treatise on International Law* (Oxford: Clarendon Press, 4th ed., 1895), p. 339.

as a 'structural effect' that is produced through, amongst other things, the treaty making activity undertaken in its name.[31]

3   History

It has been suggested, at least in the Anglo-American legal traditions, that the modern law of contract is fundamentally a creature of the nineteenth century, the time at which judges finally rejected the long-standing belief that the justification of contractual obligation was to be derived from the inherent fairness of an exchange and substituted in its place the idea that the source of obligation was to be found in a convergence of the wills of the contacting parties.[32] It was a shift, in other words, from a substantive evaluation of the contract in terms of justice and equity to an evaluation governed purely in terms of a 'meeting of minds'. Behind this, of course, was an abandonment of a pre-physiocratic notion of the 'just price'[33] (or the idea that there might be some external measure by which the content of an exchange might be evaluated) and a corresponding adhesion to the idea that the exercise of individual will through the medium of the contract not only constituted a vital expression of individual autonomy but also contributed to the general social utility.[34] It was only in the nineteenth century, on this account, that consent, and consent alone, became the measure of contractual obligation – the story from there being that of the ensuing encroachment of social legislation upon the principle of contractual autonomy[35] and the displacement of a concern for actual intentions in favour of an attentiveness to the 'empirical' character of the agreement that is produced.[36]

---

[31] See T. Mitchell, 'The Limits of the State: Beyond Statist Approaches and Their Critics', *Am. Pol. Sc. Rev.*, 85 (1991), 77–96.

[32] M. J. Horowicz, 'The Historical Foundations of Modern Contract Law', *Harvard L. Rev.*, 87 (1974), 917–956, and R. Kreitner, *Calculating Promises: The Emergence of Modern American Contract Doctrine* (Stanford, CA: Stanford University Press, 2007).

[33] See E. Bonnnot de Condillac, *Commerce and Government* (1776) (trans. W. Eltis) (Cheltenham: Edward Elgar, 1997).

[34] See M. R. Cohen, 'The Basis of Contract', *Harvard L. Rev.*, 46 (1933), 553–592, at 558–562.

[35] P. S. Atiyah, *The Rise and Fall of Freedom of Contract* (Oxford: Clarendon Press, 1979).

[36] O. W. Holmes, 'The Path of the Law', *Harvard L. Rev.*, 10 (1897), 457–468, at 464 ('no one will understand the true theory of contract or be able even to discuss some fundamental questions intelligently until he has understood that all contracts are formal, that the making of a contract depends not on the agreement of two minds in one intention, but on the agreement of two sets of external signs – not on the parties' having *meant* the same thing but on their having *said* the same thing').

The trajectory of treaty law partly follows, and partly departs from, this account.[37] It is certainly clear that up until the nineteenth century, both humanist and scholastic teachings had encouraged the idea that the obligation to abide by treaties was a matter of individual virtue and good faith (*pacta sunt servanda*) and would be guided by principles of equity and justice (*ex aequo et bono*). Strict adherence to what was promised would not always be recommended, particularly if considerations of necessity or survival were at stake. In the same sense, however, it was recognised that the forms of equality that underpinned the validity of individual contracts (equality of knowledge, bargaining power and substance)[38] were not uniformly evident in case of treaties. Treaties, as Hugo Grotius was to explain, could be equal or unequal, could assume the form of an equivalent exchange or could result in the diminution of sovereignty of the other party.[39] Treaties of peace were invariably at the forefront of analysis.[40] If justice, equity and good faith were still the primary conditions, they did not automatically deny the validity of agreements substantially unequal in character – indeed, if anything, that was the exception.[41]

By the end of the eighteenth century, however, treaties started to acquire the marks of an autonomous source of law, and, as such, emphasis was placed upon the meeting of minds or upon the expression of a 'mutual will' through reciprocal consent to the terms of the agreement. This had several consequences. In the first place it became apparent that, since the value of an exchange had no external measure,[42] it was

---

[37] See, generally, the contribution to this volume of Lesaffer at pp. 43–75 (Chapter 3). See, also, D. W. Bowett, Review of Evangelos Raftopoulos, *Inadequacy of the Contractual Analogy in the Law of Treaties* (1990), BYbIL, 64 (1993), 439.

[38] H. Grotius, *De Jure Belli ac Pacis* (trans. F. W. Kelsey) (Washington, DC: Carnegie Endowment for International Peace, 1925), Bk. II, Ch. xii, pp. 346–350.

[39] *Ibid.*, at pp. 394–397.

[40] See R. Lesaffer (ed.), *Peace Treaties and International Law in European History: From the Late Middle Ages to World War One* (Cambridge: Cambridge University Press, 2008).

[41] See E. de Vattel, *The Law of Nations or the Principles of Natural Law* (trans. C. G. Fenwick) (Washington, DC: Carnegie Endowment for International Peace, 1916), Bk. II, Ch. xii, pp. 161 and 164. Various exceptions were recognised, however: treaties 'disastrous to the state' are void (p. 161) as are treaties conflicting with the duty of the nation to itself (p. 164).

[42] See J. L. Klüber, *Droit des Gens Moderne de L'Europe* (Stuttgart: J.G. Cotta, 1819), p. 226, and de Martens, *supra* n. 10, at pp. 168–169 and 185. One may relate this to Hume's reformulation of the idea of 'free will' in which, he argued, it was to be construed as acting in accordance with one's will as opposed to having the freedom to have acted otherwise: D. Hume, *A Treatise of Human Nature* (Oxford: Clarendon Press, 1739), pp. 399–412.

impossible to determine in any abstract way what interest States might have in the bargain. Thus, as Georg Friedrich de Martens was to maintain:

> The injury . . . that a nation may sustain from a treaty, is not a justifiable reason for such nation to refuse complying with its conditions. It is the business of every nation to weigh and consult its own interests; and, as nothing hinders a nation from acquiring a right in its favour by a covenant with another, and it being impossible for any one to determine the degree of injury requisite to set a treaty aside, or to judge, in any obligatory manner, of the injury sustained, the security and welfare of all nations require, that an exception should not be admitted which would sap the foundations of all treaties whatever.[43]

Consent, thus, when mediated through the abstract idea of the 'interest' a State may have in coming to agreement with another,[44] was incapable of being rationalised in any kind of material balance. The equality of the agreement understood in terms of the value of what was exchanged – a material or substantive reciprocity – was excluded from the outset.[45]

In the second place, if the abstract notion of a meeting of wills was to deny, in principle, any means of evaluating the equivalence of an exchange, it was nevertheless premised upon the idea that an exchange had indeed taken place. Yet this was by no means always obvious. The Ottoman capitulations[46] (and, to a lesser extent, the regimes of consular jurisdiction in China and Japan)[47] were particularly problematic in this respect. As one commentator was to observe, the word 'capitulation' (letter of privilege) had historically been used to 'indicate that these were not stipulations between two contracting parties, entered into for their reciprocal good, but only grants of privileges and immunities that the Porte made, out of its generosity, to the nations with whom

---

[43] G. F. von Martens, *Summary of the Law of Nations, Founded on the Treaties and Customs of the Modern Nations of Europe* (trans. W. Cobbett) (Philadelphia, PA: Thomas Bradford, 1795), ii, p. 52.

[44] For an account of the role of 'interest' in the thought of Kelsen, in particular, see M. Garcia-Salmones, *The Project of Positivism in International Law* (Oxford: Oxford University Press, 2013).

[45] See, e.g., H. Wheaton, *Elements of International Law* (Boston, MA: Little, Brown & Co., 8th ed., 1866) (R. H. Dana ed.), p. 44.

[46] E. A. Van Dyck, *Capitulations of the Ottoman Empire* (Washington, DC: U.S. Govt. Printing Office, 1881) and T. Kayaoglu, *Legal Imperialism: Sovereignty and Extraterritoriality in Japan, the Ottoman Empire and China* (Cambridge: Cambridge University Press, 2010), pp. 104–148.

[47] See, e.g., F. E. Hinckley, *American Consular Jurisdiction in the Orient* (Washington, DC: W.H. Lowdermilk & Co., 1906) and Kayaoglu, *supra* n. 46, at pp. 66–103 and 149–190.

it dealt'.[48] That they appeared to represent gratuitous concessions rather than reciprocal engagements, in fact, was subsequently taken by Turkey to be a ground to justify their unilateral denunciation (or, perhaps better, their 'withdrawal').[49] The Turkish claim, here, was not unique. A similar argument had also been advanced by the Tsar of Russia who abolished the status of Batoum as a 'free port' (as so designated under Article 59 of the 1878 Treaty of Berlin),[50] on the basis that such a status was essentially a 'privilege' rather than an entitlement guaranteed as part of a contractual 'exchange'.[51] In both cases, however, the response was to deny the necessity of any substantive exchange for purposes of conditioning the opposability of the obligations: no unilateral right of denunciation thus existed outside the terms specified within the agreements themselves.[52] This, of course, was to not deny the importance of reciprocity but made clear that its content was a purely formal one: linking the obligations of one party to rights of performance on the part of another.

Lying behind the problem of substantive reciprocity, however, was a broader problem that concerned the effect of coercion upon the validity or otherwise of treaties – this being a problem, in particular, in the context of treaties of peace. In the first place, whilst jurists were increasingly concerned with emphasising the importance of freedom of consent for purposes of establishing the validity of treaty obligations, they nevertheless continued to be swayed by Grotius's intuition that since war could be held just on both sides, the absence of coercion was incapable of standing as an absolute condition of validity. De Martens, for example, came to the conclusion that 'in default of a superior judge, and in default of a right to judge in their own cause', violence must be treated as just and hence cannot be opposed to the validity of a treaty unless its injustice is so

---

[48] Van Dyck, *supra* n. 46, at p. 24. See, also, U. Özsu, 'Ottoman Empire' in B. Fassbender and A. Peters (eds.), *The Oxford Handbook of the History of International Law* (Oxford: Oxford University Press, 2012), pp. 429–448, at pp. 430–431 ('For the Ottoman sultans … the capitulations were at root imperial decrees – unilaterally granted and unilaterally revocable pledges to non-Muslim sovereigns with which political alliances or trading partnerships had been struck … These privileges were not to be confused with permanent rights. And the Ottoman State was not to be seen as engaged with a non-Muslim entity on terms of strict formal equality').

[49] See, generally, L. E. Thayer, 'The Capitulations of the Ottoman Empire and the Question of their Abrogation as it Affects the United States', *AJIL*, 17 (1923), 207–233, at 224–225.

[50] 153 CTS 171.

[51] A. D. McNair, *The Law of Treaties* (Oxford: Clarendon Press, 1961), p. 498.

[52] See, generally, McNair, *ibid.*, at pp. 498–499, and Thayer, *supra* n. 49, at 225–226.

manifest 'as not to leave the least doubt'.[53] In this context, jurists were ultimately only able to maintain their commitment to consent by introducing into their accounts new 'safety clauses' or by subtly changing the content of consent itself. In one direction, thus, jurists such as Paul Pradier Fodéré were to seek to obviate the possibility of 'consensual slavery' by adducing, in emergency, a right of unilateral denunciation:

> Cases must necessarily be admitted in which the State must be able to declare itself freed from any engagement, even when it has not expressly reserved this right by a clause of the treaty. Respect for engagements contracted should not, for example, be pushed to a suicidal extent. Though a State may be required to execute burdensome engagements contracted by it, it cannot be asked to sacrifice its development and its existence to the execution of the treaty.[54]

The limits of consent, in other words, found their expression in the fundamental social conditions of a State's existence. It could not be used as an argument for suicide.[55]

In a different direction, however, the value of autonomy to which consent appeared to give expression was often re-framed in social terms. Henry Wheaton, for example, was to suggest that:

---

[53] See, e.g., de Martens, *supra* n. 10, at p. 51. For a similar statement, see Hall, *supra* n. 30, at pp. 341–342.

[54] P. L. E. Pradier Fodéré, *Traité de Droit International Public Européen et Américain* (Vol. II) (Paris: Pedone, 1911), p. 264. See, also, Oppenheim who maintained that:

> When the existence or the vital development of a state stands in unavoidable conflict with its treaty obligations, the latter must give way, for self-preservation and development, in accordance with the growth and the vital requirements of the nation, are the primary duties of every state.
>
> No state would consent to any such treaty as would hinder it in the fulfilment of these primary duties. The consent of a state to a treaty presupposes a conviction that it is not fraught with danger to its existence and vital development. For this reason every treaty implies a condition that if by an unforeseen change of circumstances an obligation stipulated in the treaty should imperil the existence or vital development of one of the parties, it should have a right to demand to be released from the obligation concerned.

L. Oppenheim, *International Law: A Treatise* (Vol. I) (London: Longmans & Co., 4th ed., 1926) (A. D. McNair ed.), p. 748.

[55] Woolsey refers, in similar sense, to the non-binding character of treaties in which the government 'flagitiously sacrifices the interests of the nation which it represents. In this case the treacherous act of the government cannot be justly regarded as the act of the nation': T. S. Woolsey, *Introduction to the Study of International Law* (New York, NY: Charles Scribner's Sons, 1883), p. 168.

> By the general principles of private jurisprudence, recognised by most, if
> not all, civilised countries, a contract obtained by violence is void.
> Freedom of consent is essential to the validity of every agreement, and
> contracts obtained under duress are void, because the general welfare of
> society requires that they should be so.[56]

While he was to insist, like many others, upon the importance of 'freedom of consent' to the validity of every agreement, Wheaton carefully
reshapes, here, the justificatory discourse underpinning it: the virtue of
consent lying less in the expression it gave to the idea of sovereign
autonomy, than in what it appeared to contribute to the 'general welfare'
of society. In socializing consent in this way, Wheaton was able to
circumvent what otherwise appeared to be a fundamental tension
between upholding the value of consent but yet admitting the possibility
of coercion or duress:

> On the other hand, the welfare of society requires that the engagements
> entered into by a nation under such duress as is implied by the defeat of its
> military forces, the distress of its people, and the occupation of its terri-
> tories by an enemy, should be held binding; for if they were not, wars
> could only be terminated by the utter subjugation and ruin of the weaker
> party.[57]

For Wheaton, then, the value of consent was to become subordinated to
the more general social utility of maintaining the peace: the meaning and
effect of any agreement being governed, ultimately, not by resort to the
principle of free consent but by reference to the broader social purposes
which the agreement appeared to advance.

Wheaton's concern to bring to the forefront the social conditions upon
which an agreement might be thought to rest was one widely shared,
particularly in respect of peace agreements given their putative role in the
preservation of 'peace and good order' or the 'balance of power'.[58] Yet the
more this tendency to 'contextualise' consent, or subordinate it to higher
social imperatives, the more contingent its function was to become.
It quickly became vulnerable, as a result, to arguments in favour of the
termination of agreements when the circumstances upon which it was
premised appeared to change. The doctrine *rebus sic stantibus* would thus
emerge as a plausible ground for denunciation of putatively permanent
agreements even if, in practice, it was frequently resisted. As Lord Arnold

---

[56] Wheaton, *supra* n. 45, at p. 340.   [57] *Ibid.*

[58] *Ibid.*, at p. 39. In similar vein, see A. Rivier, *Principes du Droit des Gens* (Vol. II) (Paris:
Arthur Rousseau, 1896), pp. 35–36.

McNair notes, the doctrine was (inferentially) relied upon by Russia in its repudiation of the Black Sea clauses (Articles 11, 12 and 13) of the 1856 Treaty of Paris[59] and by Austria-Hungary following its annexation of Bosnia-Herzegovina in 1907.[60] Whilst the 1871 London Protocol seemed to deny the possibility of fundamental change in its insistence upon the 'sanctity of treaties' and the requirement that treaty engagements might only be terminated with the consent of other parties,[61] this was not to prevent it becoming a durable theme acquiring more specificity in the course of the twentieth century.

Thus, at the end of the nineteenth century, one was to find a conception of treaty law that was built, by analogy, upon the idea of individual consent to contractual obligation but in which two movements were perceptible. In one direction it was to become increasingly formal in the sense that it was emptied of any substantive evaluation of exchange and in which the condition of mutuality was sustained only so far as signature or ratification was required. In another direction, however, it was also to become increasingly 'social' in the sense that the validity and effect of consent were ever more closely linked to the political context in which it was located. No one, it seems, was willing to treat the absence of coercion as an absolute condition of validity. But at the same time no one was to rule out the possibility of denunciation if the 'political circumstances' so required.

On the face of it, these might appear to have been entirely contradictory tendencies. The more attention given to the social and political

---

[59] 114 CTS 409. See McNair, *supra* n. 51, at pp. 494–497 and 682.

[60] The annexation was inconsistent with Art. 25 of the 1878 Treaty of Berlin, *supra* n. 50, in which European Powers had agreed to the occupation and administration of the Turkish provinces of Bosnia and Herzegovina by Austria-Hungary.

[61] The 1871 London Protocol, 143 CTS 99, provided that:

> It is an essential principle of the Law of Nations that no Power can liberate itself from the engagements of a Treaty, nor modify the stipulations thereof, unless with the consent of the Contracting Parties by means of an amicable arrangement.

See, further, D. J. Bederman, 'The 1871 London Declaration, Rebus Sic Stantibus and a Primitivist View of the Law of Nations', *AJIL*, 82 (1988), 1–40, at 15; G. Distefano, 'Le Protocole de Londres du 17 Janvier 1871: Miroir du Droit International', *J. Hist. Int'l L.*, 6 (2004), 79–142, and L. H. Woolsey, 'The Unilateral Termination of Treaties', *AJIL*, 20 (1926), 346–353, at 349 ('This declaration ... would seem to amount to no more than a declaration that a treaty cannot be annulled by one of the parties without the consent of the other in circumstances which involve no change in the fundamental conditions on which the treaty is based and which show no violation of the treaty by the other party').

setting in which treaties were located, the more it might seem that the content of treaties would have to become central to an evaluation of their validity. Consent could surely not be made both more formal and more social simultaneously. Yet one may also understand these movements to be entirely consonant with one another: to produce the idea of autonomous consent as a consistent marker of treaty validity required the removal of its social or material content. And this was achieved not by its total elimination but by shifting it from the inside to the outside – it was to become the 'context' within which the exchange was to take place rather than something that impinged upon the question whether consent itself had been given. A purely juridical conception of consent, in other words, was to be produced through the simultaneous construction of an autonomous external 'political' or 'social' environment within which it was embedded. The formalisation of consent, in other words, was intimately related to its embedding in a social environment.

4   The Conditions of Effective Consent

At the beginning of this modern period, as de Martens was to suggest, five things appeared 'necessarily supposed' for a treaty to be obligatory: '1. that the parties have power to consent; 2. that they have consented; 3. that they have consented freely; 4. that the consent is mutual; and 5. that the execution is possible'.[62] All five of these 'conditions of authenticity' continue to be reflected in one form or another in the Vienna Convention. The question of authority to consent is addressed in Articles 6 to 8[63] dealing with the initial question of capacity, the validation of full powers and the subsequent 'adoption' of unauthorised agreements (sponsions).[64] The fact of consent – or rather the process by which consent might be evidenced – is addressed in Articles 11 to 15 dealing with signature, ratification, exchange of instruments, acceptance, approval and accession, supplemented by the provisions in Articles 34 to 38 governing the means by which third States may 'assume' rights or obligations in relation to an agreement to which (by definition) they are not party.[65] The question of freedom of consent understood as 'the

[62] De Martens (Vol. II), *supra* n. 10, at p. 48.

[63] See, also, *Case Concerning the Land and Maritime Boundary between Cameroon and Nigeria*: Cameroon v. Nigeria (Judgment) (2002) ICJ Rep. 303, at p. 430 (paragraph 265).

[64] See, also, Art. 47 VCLT: *supra* n. 1.

[65] See, further, *North Sea Continental Shelf Cases, supra* n. 19, at pp. 25–26 (paragraphs 27–28).

absence of coercion' is addressed in Articles 51 and 52. Of relevance, here, are also the questions of error (Article 48), fraud (Article 49) and corruption (Article 50) which seek to engage with the conditions of knowledge and communication under which consent may be discerned to be fully free. Mutuality of consent is ensured through provisions relating to entry into force and termination following breach, and the final condition relating to execution finds expression in Article 61 governing supervening impossibility of performance.

If one takes the Vienna Convention, broadly speaking, as an attempt to institute a regime of law directed towards enabling or facilitating a system of 'mutual self-rule' through free consent, the most problematic features would seem to be those that appear to describe its limits – that dispense with consent, militate against it being 'free' or condition its effects by reference to the social or political environment. Each provides a slightly different account of the phenomenon called 'consent' that is being ushered into existence.

4.1   The Necessity of Consent

The Vienna Convention is overtly rigorous about the necessity of consent for purposes of the assumption of obligations under treaty. Whilst it makes no claims as to the broader significance of consent in relation to customary international law, so far as treaties are concerned, obligation follows consent (rather than the other way round).[66] Yet the Convention clearly also provides certain stipulations that describe what meaning is to be attributed to consent. A simple example here is the move initiated by Lauterpacht amongst others away from the 'principle' of unanimous consent in the context of multilateral agreements. In admitting that there was no right of 'accession',[67] he was to encourage the view that if a multilateral agreement provided for the possibility of accession, the formal act of consent also implied tacit consent to the participation of any other party that subsequently undertakes the requisite formalities. No additional act of 'consent' should be required unless specified by

---

[66] See, here, *International Status of South-West Africa* (Advisory Opinion) (1950) ICJ Rep. 128, at p. 139 (an obligation to conclude an agreement is a contradiction in terms: 'An "agreement" implies consent of the parties concerned ... The parties must be free to accept or reject the terms of the contemplated agreement. No party can impose its terms on the other party').

[67] See, e.g., *Case Concerning Certain German Interests in Polish Upper Silesia*: Germany v. Poland (Merits), 1926 PCIJ, Series A, No. 7, 19, at pp. 28–29.

the terms of the agreement.[68] Of course, in a sense, this goes to the content of consent itself, and it is obviously arguable that if the treaty allows for the participation of other States, consent to the agreement also necessarily implies consent to the participation by all, or any, other States. But it is equally clear that in setting such matters out in general provisions, a formalized distance is thus erected between actual and imputed intentions: tacit consent being less concerned with the actual content of the original agreement (as might be discerned, for example, through expressed intentions) than with the imputation of certain rational intentions to the author.

This kind of regulatory architecture is carried throughout the Vienna Convention: interpretation is not governed by the actual intentions of the authors but by the 'ordinary meaning' that may be given to its terms (although the *travaux préparatoires* may be resorted to as a supplementary means of interpretation);[69] error may vitiate consent only if it formed an essential basis for participation and was not otherwise a consequence of the negligence of the party concerned (Article 48); fraud is relevant only so far as it may be evidenced and attributed to another negotiating party (Article 49). That the Convention regulates consent in this way is wholly unsurprising in the sense that were it not to do so, the principle of *pacta sunt servanda* would be virtually emptied of content by a practice of self-judgment. But the point that consent, here, is separated from the putatively psychological conditions of intentionality and motive[70] or that States may be treated as having consented even in circumstances in which they might think they have not is nevertheless revealing: the concern being not so much to mirror social life as to provide an idealised account of it.

Even if the Vienna Convention is largely structured around the operationalization of the idea of consent, there are several circumstances in which the necessity of consent is attenuated. Reservations do not always

---

[68] See, e.g., Art. 4 of 1899 Hague Convention (II) With Respect to the Laws and Customs of War and Its Annex, 187 CTS 429, and Art. 6 of 1907 Hague Convention (IV) With Respect to Laws and Customs of War on Land, 205 CTS 277. See, also, Art. 10 of 1949 North Atlantic Treaty, 243 UNTS 34 (accession by invitation).

[69] Art. 31 VCLT: *supra* n. 1. Reuter comments, in this regard, that 'law cannot take into consideration anything that remains buried away in the minds of the parties'. 'Will' he suggests must be 'spelled out': P. Reuter, *Introduction to the Law of Treaties* (Geneva: Geneva Institute of International Studies, 2nd ed., 1995), p. 30.

[70] Fitzmaurice comments, in this vein, that a treaty is both a text and a legal transaction: 'In the latter sense, the treaty evidences but does not constitute the agreement'. See Fitzmaurice, First Report on the Law of Treaties, *supra* n. 13, at p. 110.

require acceptance by other parties,[71] rights in favour of third parties might be established or withdrawn without express consent,[72] and two or more parties may 'modify' the terms of the agreement *inter se* without the consent of other parties.[73] The one field in which the necessity of consent is most problematic, however, is that which was explicitly left outside the terms of the 1969 Vienna Convention – State succession.[74]

On the face of it, the term 'succession' implies a regulated process by which rights and obligations assumed by one legal person are 'inherited' by another. In the context of treaty law, thus, it brings to mind a process by which a 'successor' might assume such rights and obligations as might arise from a treaty signed and/or ratified by its historic forbear as a consequence of the operation of certain general rules, as opposed to through the medium of a separate act of consent. To use the terminology of the 1978 Vienna Convention on the Succession of States in Respect of Treaties (VCSSRT),[75] the successor may be seen to 'replace' the 'predecessor' State in its responsibility for treaty relations of a specified territory – stepping into its legal shoes, so to speak, by reason of rules of inheritance rather than by act of will.

Behind this superficial gloss are two very different ideas. The first relates to the tacit or implied effects of the original act of consent. It is ordinarily imagined that if a government ratifies an international agreement, it (or rather the 'State') will continue to be bound by that agreement for the future until such a juncture as the treaty ceases to have effect in accordance with the terms of the agreement or under the terms of general international law. Such consent, it is supposed, is not to be vitiated by incidental changes in the local environment such as a change in government or a change in the identity of those responsible for concluding international agreements.[76] Only, as far as the Vienna Convention is concerned, would a 'fundamental change of circumstances' warrant the termination of the agreement (which of course implies the continuity of the agreement until the moment at which that idea is invoked). Seen in such terms, a succession of States (whether

---

[71] See Arts. 19 to 23 VCLT: *supra* n. 1.   [72] Arts. 36 and 37 VCLT: *ibid.*

[73] On the assumption that their own rights and obligations are not impaired as a consequence: Art. 41 VCLT: *ibid.*

[74] See Art. 73 VCLT ('The provisions of the present Convention shall not prejudge any question that may arise in relation to a treaty from a succession of States'): *ibid.*

[75] *Supra* n. 1.

[76] See G. G. Fitzmaurice, Fourth Report on the Law of Treaties, Doc. A/CN4/120 (17 March 1959), p. 43.

through separation or unification) would not affect the binding character of treaty obligations insofar as the 'successor' could simply be treated as inheriting the obligations of the predecessor, much like a new government would inherit the obligations of the old. No additional act of consent would be needed, and all treaties would continue, so far as possible, in the adjusted social environment.[77] In this account, the analytic by which succession is to be conceptualised is one that pays attention to the question of identity: the successor State *is* the predecessor State for purposes of performing its international obligations.

The second, and contrasting, idea is that succession denotes the acceptance or imposition of treaty obligations assumed by one party, upon what is, to all intents and purposes, a third party to the original agreement. The term 'succession' being indicative merely of the historic social and political connections that bind the predecessor and successor States together (the fact, for example, that both exercised jurisdiction over the same space at different moments in time) and to the fact that, in some instances at least, the treaty obligations in question might already have been applied or executed on the territory of the successor. In this form, the regulatory architecture of succession would seek to operationalize the transfer or assignment of obligations from one party to another but in which case consent of both the successor State and other States parties would presumably be necessary.[78]

As if attempting to respond to the problem of identity (sameness/difference) that segments these two conceptions of succession, the VCSSRT cuts through the divergence in two different ways. In the first place, it posits a typology of social and political organization that differentiates between different kinds of political change along two lines: between, on the one hand, aggregative processes of unification or federation and dis-aggregative processes of dissolution and secession (with 'cession' as a hybrid) and, on the other, between processes that result in the formation of 'newly independent States' and those that do not. Here, a spatial analytics of expansion and contraction is overlaid by a more fundamental differentiation that conditions the effects of any change upon the identification of States as 'new' or 'old'. A presumption in favour of treaty continuity operates in case of 'old' but not 'new' States. In the second place, this organizational frame is then qualified by

---

[77] See, e.g., D. P. O'Connell, *State Succession in Municipal and International Law* (Vol. II) (Cambridge: Cambridge University Press, 1967), pp. 88–89.

[78] See McNair, *supra* n. 51, at p. 601, and G. G. Fitzmaurice, Fifth Report on the Law of Treaties, Doc. A/CN.4/130 (21 March 1960), p. 94.

a further functional typology by which different kinds of treaty are regarded as having different effects: bilateral treaties do not always survive; territorial and boundary treaties (or their 'regimes') generally do.[79] Succession to constituent instruments depends upon the 'rules of the organization' concerned (Article 4) and hence subject to the political and diplomatic processes governing admission.

The complex analytics put in play here has much to tell us about the imputed character of consent in case of treaties. In the first place, it forefronts one of the most self-evidential, but also most elusive, aspects of the question of consent: who is it that might be said to be consenting, and on whose behalf? In normal circumstances, the answer to both elements is usually a simple one: the 'State'. But it is equally clear, as has already been pointed out, that the State itself never consents in and of its own right but only through the medium of its representatives or agents. And it is here that the problem of succession arises: how, if that is the basis for consent, does it survive the reconfiguration of that relationship of authority? What conditions of political legitimacy are necessary for consent to have the effects prescribed? The general intuition, as Paul Reuter observed, was that:

> when the personality of the new State expresses a genuine and autonomous social reality, commitments are not transmitted, but when it has in fact had a part in the formation of its predecessor's commitments there is a substantial continuity and commitments are transmitted to the successor State.[80]

Yet, as the International Law Commission (ILC) ultimately appreciated, the kind of judgment required for sustaining this distinction could never satisfactorily be elaborated without drifting into arbitrariness (What level of participation is required? What indices determine genuine, as opposed to fictional, autonomy?). The final formula adopted for the Convention – that 'new States' were effectively those that enjoyed a right to self-determination – really just deferred the question.

In the second place, if the questions of political legitimacy and participation were to haunt the evaluation of whether treaties, in general, should continue, the Vienna Convention was to soften its implications in two different ways. On the one hand, new States were not entirely cast adrift but enjoyed, according to the ILC's controversial formula, a 'right

---

[79] Arts. 11 and 12 VCLT: *supra* n. 1. See, further, *Case Concerning Gabčikovo-Nagymaros Project (Hungary/Slovakia)* (1997) ICJ Rep. 7, at pp. 71–72.

[80] Reuter, *supra* n. 69, at p. 113.

of option' – a right to notify, by unilateral act, their succession to multi-lateral agreements under conditions not entirely dissimilar to that of accession (in the sense that new reservations might be made and its effect is to constitute the State a party from the date of notification)[81] but yet outside the process for accession that may otherwise be laid down in the agreement itself. 'New States', in that sense, were never entirely 'new'.[82] On the other hand, 'territorial' and 'boundary' regimes automatically continued irrespective of the political conditions underpinning the original expression of consent. The rationale for such regimes continuing to subsist despite the (potential) defects in consent was, at once, performative and constitutive. In the first instance, they were understood to be regimes whose validity was seen to stem from the fact of their materialisation. They were no longer simply 'agreements' contingent for their validity upon consent but were the products of their execution: regimes that had imprinted themselves on the territory creating rights and obligations *erga omnes*.[83] In the second place, their indelible character, furthermore, stemmed not merely from the fact that they gave permanence and security to the 'new' State – placing its borders beyond the field of political contestation – but from the fact that they also supplied its essential preconditions. The border, as Étienne Balibar succinctly put it, constituted one of the 'nondemocratic conditions of democracy'.[84]

In case of succession, thus, two implicit conditions of consent are laid bare, whose appearance in case of 'crisis' is only to highlight their absence otherwise. On one side, it would seem to demand a level of authenticity – demand that consent itself be rooted in a genuine, popular, social consciousness; that it be neither repressive nor authoritarian. On the other side, and in order for it to bear this democratic overtone, consent is dependent upon the spatial pre-configuration of the 'demos' in relation to which there is no possibility of collective agency: no consent could be given to that which made consent possible. If revolution has the habit of exposing the unspoken preconditions of political rule, the problem of succession does the same for treaties – they rely upon the idea of

[81] Arts. 17 to 23 VCRSST: *supra* n. 1.

[82] On the 'legal nexus', see M. Craven, *The Decolonisation of International Law: State Succession and the Law of Treaties* (Oxford: Oxford University Press, 2007), pp. 141–147.

[83] See *Case Concerning Gabčikovo-Nagymaros Project*, *supra* n. 79, at pp. 71–72 (paragraph 123) (the treaty 'inescapably created a situation in which the interests of other users of the Danube were affected'). See, also, the contribution to this volume of Waibel at pp. 201–236 (Chapter 8).

[84] É. Balibar, *We the People of Europe? Reflections on Transnational Citizenship* (Princeton, NJ: Princeton University Press, 2004), p. 109.

a positive, affirmative, social consensus underpinning the acts of governmental agencies (and by reference to which it may be measured) but yet
are conditioned upon the impossibility of any such social consensus
grounding itself (in the sense that some prior determination of its parameters is required).[85]

4.2   Freedom of Consent

Whilst succession poses the problem as to who may, or may not, have
consented, the problem of coercion goes more directly to the question of
its content. The legal regulation of the use of force in the twentieth
century, as Lauterpacht was to suggest, was central to 'the restoration
of the missing link of analogy of contracts and treaties, i.e. of the freedom
of will as a requirement for the validity of treaties'.[86] The earlier position,
as he was to explain, rendered any such equation problematic:

> [Since] war was permitted as an institution, it followed that the law was
> bound to recognize the results of successful use of force thus used. To this
> explanation, unimpeachable in logic, of the legal position there was added
> the cogent consideration that the adoption of a different rule would have
> removed the legal basis of all treaties imposed by the victor upon the
> defeated state and thus perpetuated indefinitely a state of war. While the
> persuasive power of these considerations could not be denied, it was clear
> that the disregard of the vitiating force of duress in the conclusion of
> treaties tended to constitute, in a real sense, a denial of the legal nature of
> treaties conceived as agreements based on the free will of the contracting
> parties.[87]

It was thus only by removing the possibility that war could be resorted to as
a legal remedy that it could be established that 'a treaty imposed by or as
a result of force or threats of force resorted to in violation of the principles of
these instruments of a fundamental character is invalid by virtue of the
operation of the general principle of law which postulates freedom of
consent as an essential condition of the validly of consensual
undertakings'.[88] Whilst jurists had been clearly reluctant to perfect this
move in the inter-war years (particularly insofar as the terms of the 1919

---

[85] E. Laclau, *Emancipation(s)* (London: Verso, 1996), pp. 1–19.
[86] H. Lauterpacht, *Private Law Sources and Analogies of International Law (with Special
Reference to International Arbitration)* (London: Longmans, Green & Co., 1927), p. 166.
[87] H. Lauterpacht, First Report on the Law of Treaties, Doc. A/CN.4/63 (24 March 1953),
p. 147.
[88] *Ibid.*, p. 148 (paragraph 3).

Treaty of Versailles itself would have been called into question),[89] Lauterpacht's intuitions were subsequently endorsed in the form of Article 52 VCLT, which renders void any treaty procured by the threat or use of force in violation of the principles of the United Nations Charter.[90]

In his discussion of the question at the ILC, however, Lauterpacht was to draw attention to the significance of the final phraseology of what was to become Article 52 VCLT. Inclusion of the phrase 'in violation of the principles of the Charter of the United Nations' was to draw attention to the fact that the problem of duress was to be situated within the framework of Charter principles governing coercion. As the Charter only prohibited the 'unlawful threat and use of force'[91] – and, hence, left open the possibility of defensive violence, force authorised by the

---

[89] 225 CTS 188. See, e.g., J. L. Kunz, 'The Meaning and Scope of the Norm *Pacta Sunt Servanda*', *AJIL*, 39 (1945), 180–197, at 185, and McNair, *supra* n. 51, at pp. 139–140. Such a position was also apparently upheld by Fitzmaurice in his reports to the ILC concerning the effect of duress: Third Report on the Law of Treaties, *supra* n. 2, at p. 26. But see Art. 4(3) of the Harvard Draft Convention on Rights and Duties of States in Case of Aggression, *AJIL Supp.*, 33 (1939), 819–909, at 895 ('A treaty brought about by an aggressor's use of armed force is voidable'). Concern over the Munich Agreement was clearly a considerable spur in this regards: see, e.g., Q. Wright, 'The Munich Settlement and International Law', *AJIL*, 33 (1939), 12–32, at 22–23 (arguing that the authors of the Munich Settlement had erred in the same way as had those of the Versailles agreement in placing substance before procedure).

[90] Cf. *Fisheries Jurisdiction Case*: United Kingdom v. Iceland (Jurisdiction) (1973) ICJ Rep. 3, at p. 14 (paragraph 24) ('There can be little doubt, as is implied in the Charter of the United Nations and recognized in Article 52 of the Vienna Convention on the Law of Treaties, that under contemporary international law an agreement concluded under the threat or use of force is void').

[91] Schmitt remarks that 'to demand of a politically united people that it wage war for a just cause only is either something self-evident, if it means that war can be risked only against a real enemy, or it is a hidden political aspiration of some other party to wrest from the state its *jus belli* and to find norms of justice whose content and application in the concrete case is not decided upon by the State but by another party, and thereby it determines who the enemy is'. See C. Schmitt, *The Concept of the Political* (Cambridge, MA: MIT Press, 1996), p. 49. He continues (at pp. 50–51) by remarking that the Kellogg-Briand Pact 'neither repudiated war as an instrument of international politics ... nor condemned nor outlawed war altogether'. This, he reasoned, followed from the fact that the declaration was subject to the specific exception of self-defence which, far from being a mere exception, gave the norm its concrete content – it was for each State to determine for itself the justification in question. He concluded, in that respect, that 'the solemn declaration of outlawing war does not abolish the friend-enemy distinction, but, on the contrary, opens new possibilities by giving an international *hostis* declaration new content and new vigour'. Thus (on p. 56) he concludes: 'the Geneva League of Nations does not eliminate the possibility of wars, just as it does not abolish states. It introduces new possibilities for wars to take place, sanctions coalition wars, and by legitimizing and sanctioning certain wars it sweeps away many obstacles to war'.

Council itself,[92] as well as the use of coercion falling short of 'armed force' itself[93] – the problem of duress, or palpable lack of consent, was obviously to re-appear. For Lauterpacht, the response was to be found in a differentiation between forms of coercion:

> Force ceases to have the character of mere coercion if it is exercised in execution of the law – as a legal sanction – or in accordance with the law. Although in such cases the element of consent on the part of the State concerned is lacking, the impersonal authority of the law on behalf of which – and in accordance with which – force is employed is properly deemed to supply, or to remedy, the absent element of consent.[94]

Lauterpacht's intention here seems to be to try to do two things. In the first place, and most obviously, he seems to want to distinguish the existence of coercion preliminary to the conclusion of an agreement from the identification of 'duress' as a feature that nullifies the effect of such an agreement. Only if the former is treated as 'unlawful' ('mere coercion') would the issue of duress come to be entertained.[95] And that would be the case even if there were no doubt as to the significance of the coercion in procuring the consent of the subordinate party. In the second place, he also wants to assign to the 'impersonal character of the law' a remedial capacity – a capacity to affirm the validity of consent 'as if' it had been freely given. 'Freedom of consent', in other words, is to be re-shaped: gone is any sense that it corresponds to a free exercise of will. Rather it assumes the character of a mere formal 'absence of constraint exercised otherwise than by law'.[96]

---

[92] Cf. Commentary to Arts. 49 and 70 VCLT, *YbILC* (1966–II), 246–247 and 268.

[93] On economic coercion, see, the Declaration on the Prohibition of Military, Political or Economic Coercion in the Conclusion of Treaties, annexed to the Final Act of the Vienna Conference on the Law of Treaties: Doc. A/CONF.39/26. An account of proceedings leading to the declaration may be found in C. Murphy, 'Economic Duress and Unequal Treaties', *Virginia JIL*, 11 (1970), 51–69.

[94] Lauterpacht, First Report on the Law of Treaties, *supra* n. 87, at p. 150 (paragraph 9). Brierly makes a similar point (*supra* n. 9, at p. 319): 'The true anomaly in the present law is not that it should be legal to coerce a state into accepting obligations which it does not like, but that it should be legal for a state which has been victorious in a war to do the coercing; and the change to which we ought to look forward is not the elimination of the use of coercion from the transaction, but the establishment of international machinery to ensure that when coercion is used it shall be in a proper case and by due process of law, and not, as present it may be, arbitrarily'.

[95] It is interesting to note the contrast between Art. 52 VCLT, which qualifies coercion of the 'State' in this way, to the unqualified terms of Art. 51 so far as concerns the coercion of a 'representative of the State': *supra* n. 1.

[96] Lauterpacht, First Report on the Law of Treaties, *supra* n. 87, at p. 149 (paragraph 6).

There are three particular consequences that seem to flow from this. The first is that the requirement that consent be 'free' is thereby largely conditioned by the extent to which the actions of the party exercising coercion are regarded as lawful or unlawful.[97] The focus is therefore shifted entirely away from the quality of consent exercised by the party experiencing duress: coerced consent may still be consent. In the second place, it offers an analytic in which coercion and consent are entirely separable – in which the presence or absence of unlawful coercion becomes, in a sense, an *ex post facto* qualification on the *effect* of consent. Unlawful coercion is something that has to be established as a way of impugning an agreement whose initial validity is the starting point. As the ICJ was to insist in the *Fisheries Jurisdiction Case*, any 'accusation' of coercion for purposes of disputing the validity of an agreement had to be accompanied by 'clear evidence' that went above and beyond, in that case, the mere presence of naval forces off the coast of the State concerned.[98] In the third place, and fairly obviously, in conflating 'duress' with the more general conditions that delimit unlawful threats and use of force, a whole host of other forms of economic and political pressure are immediate put beyond its reach.

If coercion and duress are separated in this way, however, the original argument that the prohibition of duress was essential for purposes of perfecting the analogy between the treaty and the contract by ensuring autonomous consent as a constitutive feature of treaty obligations was to become that much harder to maintain.[99] To the extent that coercion is rendered largely compatible with consent, the problem would no longer seem to be a problem of treaty law, but rather, as James L. Brierly suggests, 'a particular aspect of that much wider problem which pervades the whole system, that of subordinating the use of force to law'.[100] This idea is taken up by Sir Ian Sinclair, who, in his analysis of the Vienna Convention, suggests that:

---

[97] Under Art. 75 VCLT, provisions of the Vienna Convention 'are without prejudice to any obligation in relation to a treaty which may arise for an aggressor State in consequence of measures taken in conformity with the Charter of the United Nations with reference to that State's aggression': *supra* n. 1.

[98] *Fisheries Jurisdiction Case, supra* n. 90, at p. 14 (paragraph 24).

[99] Caflisch remarks that '[a]n imbalance of treaty obligations might carry a conclusive presumption or at least the suggestion that a party, on account of its political or economic dependence from its partner(s), did not enter into the treaty out of its own free will, for no 'reasonable State' can be assumed to have concluded an agreement disadvantageous to it'. See L. Caflisch, 'Unequal Treaties', *German YbIL*, 35 (1992), 52–80, at 53. This supposition is later rejected by the author as unfounded.

[100] Brierly, *supra* n. 9, at p. 319.

coercion of a State by the threat or use of force does not, strictly speaking, vitiate consent; it rather involves the commission of an international delict with all the sanctions attached thereto.[101]

In a positive sense, Sinclair seems to draw upon the point made by Lauterpacht to the effect that the nullification of an agreement following an unlawful act could, in some senses, be regarded as analogous to an obligation not to recognise an unlawful situation.[102] Whilst for Lauterpacht this was a crucial move in his articulation of the emergent prohibition on duress, for Sinclair it clearly works in a different direction. Having discussed the perils of giving heed to the idea of economic duress,[103] he goes on to suggest that 'consent' needed to be stripped of its associations with a factual 'absence of coercion' as Lauterpacht had suggested. Consent, rather, should be associated merely with the formal mode of acceptance of an instrument – signified by signature, ratification or accession – in which any investigation of the content of the 'agreement' was beyond the domain of law and the presence or absence of duress largely irrelevant.[104] Duress, for Sinclair, thus operates as an independent variable that may (or may not) render an agreement invalid 'by operation of law' rather than something that goes to an evaluation as to whether or not there has been an agreement in the first place.[105] He shares, in that sense, the view of Fitzmaurice, who, when proposing the distinction between formal and essential validity, was to

---

[101] Sinclair, *supra* n. 13, at p. 180. See, also, Reuter, *supra* n. 69, at pp. 180–181 ('Invalidity can . . . hardly be regarded as a result of vitiated consent; it is rather a sanction of an international offence').

[102] See, also, I. Brownlie, *International Law and the Use of Force by States* (Oxford: Clarendon Press, 1963), pp. 404–405 ('State practice in regard to the effect of duress is in part connected with the development of the principle of non-recognition of territorial acquisitions obtained by the threat or use of force').

[103] Sinclair, *supra* n. 13, at p. 178.

[104] See, e.g., Memorandum of the Solicitor for the Department of State, 30 June 1921, in which it was noted, in reference to German signature of the Treaty of Versailles, *supra* n. 89, that 'even though a vanquished nation is in effect *compelled* to sign a treaty, I think that in contemplation of law its signature is regarded as voluntary'. Cited in G. H. Hackworth, *Digest of International Law* (Vol. V) (Washington, DC: U.S. Govt. Printing Office, 1940), p. 158.

[105] This point is taken up by Nahlik, who notes that Sir Humphrey Waldock, Fourth Special Rapporteur of the International Law Commission for the Law of Treaties, 'chose to speak about *invalidity* only, with hardly anything stated about *validity* of treaties'. This 'negative' approach to the issue necessarily placed 'a presumption in favour of the validity and binding force of treaties. A treaty, *any* treaty, is presumed to be valid and in force *unless* one of the grounds listed in the convention has occurred'. See S. E. Nahlik, 'The Grounds of Invalidity and Termination of Treaties', *AJIL*, 65 (1971), 736–756, at 738 and 739–740.

suggest that the determination as to what is an agreement under international law is ultimately separable from (and, in some ways, prior to) the question as to whether or not it is a nullity.[106]

What seems to be revealed here is an array of at least three different ways of thinking about consent and its place in the law of treaties. The first formulation is that of an exercise of free will whose essential conditions are to be determined by the presence or absence of coercion (and perhaps including also the absence of mistake, error or fraud) but whose field of operation, it is reasoned, must necessarily be limited in view of the social desirability of certain forms of coerced agreements (peace treaties). The second is a formalised version of the first in which consent is conceptualised as contingent upon a distinction being made between lawful and unlawful coercion. 'Free will' here is not the free will of a radically autonomous agent but a legally regulated freedom the parameters of which are dependent upon the general constraints imposed by international law upon the use of force or other forms of coercion and in which consent is 'presumed' or its absence 'remedied' in cases in which coercion is lawful. The third is entirely procedural and in which consent is conceived, as Fitzmaurice puts it, as merely 'a method ... by which obligations arise or come into force' but which is yet independent of the binding force of the obligations once in place. Duress, so far as it attends to the problem of substantive validity, is entirely separable from the process of offering consent (through signature, ratification accession etc.).

For all their differences, all three of these accounts seek to do the same thing: to provide different ways of keeping the ideas of consent and coercion apart. Only by insulating the idea of consent in some way from the possibility of an entirely routine form of coercion can it survive as a means of providing the grounds for obligation. And this, in a sense, is encapsulated in Sinclair's fear that '[a]cceptance of the concept that economic pressure could operate to render a treaty null and void would ... put at risk any treaty concluded between a developing and a developed country'.[107] As a consequence, thus, one finds coercion itself being re-configured along a dynamic that excludes from view a range of forms of economic and non-armed coercion (as well, of course, as legitimate armed coercion) and consent being re-configured into an entirely formal or procedural idea separated from the social conditions that may impinge upon its substantive content.

---

[106] Fitzmaurice, First Report on the Law of Treaties, *supra* n. 13, at p. 109.
[107] Sinclair, *supra* n. 13, at p. 178.

5   The Limits of Consent

If, thus far, I have been dealing with the problem of the affirmation of free will through its denial, there is also the related issue of its limitation – of the circumstances in which consent is not denied or rendered dispensable but when consent is understood to encounter certain limits upon its effect. There are two possible categories here, both of which are essentially 'contextual' or 'environmental': on the one hand there are normative limits which putatively restrict the capacity of States to enter into agreements that violate some other, more fundamental, principle of international law (*jus cogens*);[108] on the other hand there are factual limits which circumscribe the effect of obligations by reference to some evaluation of the social conditions under which the obligations are to be put into operation. To the extent that the former is concerned with relationship between formal acts of consent and the extant legal environment that might putatively govern their effect, I have already covered much of the ground earlier in dealing with the question of coercion.[109] What I have not addressed is the putative relationship that might exist between the act of consent and its social, political or economic environment.

Within the Vienna Convention, two principles are given prominence here – one being the principle of supervening impossibility of performance;[110] the other, the principle of fundamental change of circumstances.[111] Both share an analytic[112] which seeks to relate the act

---

[108]   Arts. 53 and 64 VCLT: *supra* n. 1.

[109]   Reference, here, may also be made to Art. 32(2) VCLT, which specifies the relevant legal 'context' for purposes of interpretation: *ibid.*

[110]   Art. 61 VCLT: *ibid.* See, further, *Case Concerning Gabčikovo-Nagymaros Project, supra* n. 79, at pp. 56–64.

[111]   Art. 62 VCLT ('A fundamental change of circumstances which has occurred with regard to those existing at the time of the conclusion of a treaty, and which was not foreseen by the parties, may not be invoked as a ground for terminating or withdrawing from the treaty unless: (a) the existence of those circumstances constituted an essential basis of the consent of the parties to be bound by the treaty; and (b) the effect of the change is radically to transform the extent of obligations still to be performed under the treaty'): *ibid.* For an early appraisal, see, generally, C. Hill, *The Doctrine of* Rebus Sic Stantibus (Columbia, MO: University of Missouri, 1934). See, also, *Free Zones of Upper Savoy and District of Gex Case*: France v. Switzerland, 1932 PCIJ, Series A/B, No. 46, 97, at pp. 156–158; *Nationality Decrees in Tunis and Morocco*, 1923 PCIJ, Series B, No. 4, 29, and *Fisheries Jurisdiction Case, supra* n. 90, at p. 18.

[112]   As Fitzmaurice describes it: 'where a supervening impossibility does arise, a change of circumstances, and an essential one, must have occurred. But although the case of impossibility might therefore be represented as being one of *rebus sic stantibus*, it is clear that the latter principle is not limited to cases of actual impossibility'. See

of 'consenting' or 'promising' to a particular social and political (and perhaps even legal)[113] context and then offer the possibility of excusing one party from an obligation of performance by reason of some extraneous change in that external environment. It is only here that the act of consenting to obligation appears to be understood as a social experience as opposed to a highly formalised act. Consent not being the abstract formal decision of a legal actor in hypothetical space but that of a concrete, socially situated actor seeking to secure certain material objectives in a given political and social environment.

On the face of it, there is a significant contrast to be drawn here between the socially aware form of consent which is recognised in these principles and the more abstract or formal conception employed in case of duress, or indeed the more 'authentic' or 'consensual' idea that operates in case of succession. In case of duress, for example, a world is constructed in which power becomes visible only in case of unlawful violence. Other forms of economic and political pressure that might in practice be influential lack legibility. In case of succession, relations of domination and subordination might form the intelligible backdrop to the distinction between 'new' and 'old' States, but these are once again reduced to formal categories determined by whether the territory in question was formerly describable as 'dependent' prior to the moment of independence. It is not surprising, therefore, that in the drafting of the Vienna Convention, some States saw in the doctrine *rebus sic stantibus* a vital response to the problem of unequal or imposed treaties.[114]

But even then, appearances are somewhat deceptive – in case of fundamental change, what is in question is less the experience or intentions of the subject (which only remain relevant so far as determining whether the change was 'foreseen by the parties'),[115] still less with

Fitzmaurice, Second Report on the Law of Treaties, *supra* n. 5, at p. 60. See, also, Commentary to Art. 58, *YbILC* (1966–II), 255–256.

[113] See *Fisheries Jurisdiction Case, supra* n. 90, at p. 17.

[114] See, also, *Denunciation of the Sino-Belgian Treaty of 2 Nov. 1865*, 1929 PCIJ, Series A, No. 18, I, 52.

[115] Earlier authors had preferred to treat the 'clausula' as an implied term. See, e.g., Brierly, *supra* n. 9, at p. 336 ('the treaty is ended because we can infer from its terms that the parties, though they have not said expressly what was to happen in the event which has occurred, would, if they had forseen it, have said that the treaty ought to lapse'). Waldock and Fitzmaurice, amongst others, sought to provide it with an 'objective' basis. See Fitzmaurice, Second Report on the Law of Treaties, *supra* n. 5, at pp. 58–60. As Fitzmaurice describes it, the *rebus* may be considered 'as a rule which, irrespective of anything expressed or implied in the treaty, may give the parties a faculty to take steps directed to the revision or termination of the treaty, operates independently of the will of

a straightforward evaluation as to whether the transformation of the external environment made it implausible to insist upon continued performance.[116] Rather, it involves identifying the 'essential basis' for consent (quite independently of the question of motive) and then determining whether the change was such as to 'radically' transform the extent of obligations to be performed. The impugned treaty, in other words, has to be both obsolete *and* oppressive, not just one in isolation from the other.

This analytic appears to tell us two things about consent. First, it is to be recognised as having a social context from which the meaning of an act of consent partially draws sustenance. Consent has a time and place and certain material conditions to which it is invisibly tied. That context, however, does not condition consent in the sense of determining its formal validity or effect *ab initio* but emerges as a ground for termination only in circumstances in which it is deemed to have changed. Secondly, the central intuition would appear to be that the social/political context in which the expression of consent is embedded must be conceptualised as expressive of some kind of 'natural condition', such that any change in that *status quo* must be resisted, and resisted in the name of 'law'.[117] Whilst this may leave us with the impression that international law simply operates to conserve an existing order of power – visibly opposing attempts to question the authority of 'agreements' underpinned by 'legitimate' threats – the more important point, as I have been trying to suggest, is that it asks us to take seriously the world that 'consent to obligation' evokes into being.

---

the parties except at the point where a party invokes it'. See, also, H. Waldock, Second Report on the Law of Treaties, Doc. A/CN.4/156 and Add.1–3 (20 March, 10 Apr., 30 Apr. and 5 June 1963), pp. 79–85. See, generally, Commentary to draft Art. 59, *YbILC* (1966–II), 256–260 (esp. paragraph 7: 'In most cases the parties gave no thought to the possibility of a change of circumstances and, if they had done so, would probably have provided for it in a different manner . . . the theory of an implied term must be rejected').

[116] See, e.g., Brierly, *supra* n. 9, at p. 332 ('It may be, therefore, that if international law insists too rigidly on the binding force of treaties, it will merely defeat its own purpose by encouraging their violation').

[117] It is in this sense that the doctrine was closely related to the 'problem of peaceful change'. See, e.g., Q. Wright, 'Article 19 of the League Covenant and the Doctrine of "Rebus sic Stantibus"', *Proceedings ASIL*, 30 (1936), 55–73, at 59 ('Every legal system in a progressive society needs procedures for changing the law in order to keep it abreast of the sociological facts of the community, and procedures by which the members of the community can acquire and transfer rights within the law . . . But such extraordinary procedures must be resorted to with restraint and under the authority of the community as a whole, or the society will cease to be one of law').

6   Conclusion

If the regime of the law of treaties as articulated in the Vienna Convention(s) might be thought to organise itself around the legitimating idea of 'consent to obligation', consent is only nominally the starting point. Its principal function, one may imagine, is to immunise international legal obligation from a critique of power politics: instantiating in the form of the contract, the principle of sovereign equality and the idea of self-rule. Its pedagogy thus is one of virtue and restraint. It is clear, however, that even this idea of self-rule can never be just 'rule of the self'. It must always be conditioned, regularized, encased in rules and their exceptions and organised as a social category. And the Vienna Convention, one may think, does precisely that job. From this vantage point, one may simply ask how coherently it does that. How 'free' does it leave consent? What constraints may impinge upon it?

But there is another account of the Convention that I have been trying to sketch out here, which starts in a different place. Rather than suppose the pre-existence of a phenomenological category of State consent and then look at how it is organised and controlled, I have been trying to think of it as an idea (or set of ideas) produced or generated, in part at least, through the terms of the Vienna Convention. The hypothesis here is that State consent acquires meaning only at the point at which it is controlled or regularized – that it appears only through the act of its apparent limitation. From this standpoint, the Convention assumes a very different guise: operating as a way of enjoining us to believe in the reality of 'consent', inciting us to organise our conceptions of coercion in a way that does not displace the (apparent) reality of sovereign free will, encouraging the acting out of a set of ceremonial formalities the overall purpose of which being to generate the idea of faith, obligation and belief in law. To pursue this line of thought is to think of consent not as the beginning of our enquiry but as the end: as the ideational output of a machinery of consent-formation with its own forms of capital, labour and exchange.

6

Treaties as 'Living Instruments'

DANIEL MOECKLI AND NIGEL D. WHITE[*]

1 Use of the 'Living Instrument' Metaphor

To describe a legal instrument as a living organism is to employ a metaphor that is common in many national legal systems, especially in constitutional law.[1] In a case concerning the question of whether women were 'qualified persons' who could serve as members of the Canadian Senate, the Privy Council remarked that the constitution of Canada should be viewed as 'a living tree capable of growth and expansion within its natural limits'.[2] While recognising that women's exclusion from public office had a long history, the Privy Council asserted that this could not justify the practice as it did 'not think it right to apply rigidly to Canada of to-day the decisions and the reasonings therefor which commended themselves, probably rightly, to those who had to apply the law in different circumstances, in different centuries to countries in different stages of development'.[3] In the United States, the perhaps most important battle in constitutional scholarship pitches the 'living constitution', which can evolve and adapt to changes in social conditions through interpretation,[4] against the 'originalist constitution', whose meaning was fixed by its drafters and is immune to changes through judicial

---

[*] The authors are grateful to Raffael Fasel, Raphael Keller and Lea Raible for their research assistance.

[1] V. C. Jackson, 'Constitutions as "Living Trees"? Comparative Constitutional Law and Interpretive Metaphors', *Fordham L. Rev.*, 75 (2006), 921–960.

[2] *Edwards v. Attorney-General of Canada* [1930] AC 124, at p. 136.

[3] *Ibid.*, at pp. 134–135.

[4] See, e.g., D. A. Strauss, *The Living Constitution* (New York, NY: Oxford University Press, 2010); A. Winkler, 'A Revolution Too Soon: Woman Suffragists and the "Living Constitution"', *N.Y. Univ. L. Rev.*, 76 (2001), 1456–1526, and H. L. McBain, *The Living Constitution: A Consideration of the Realities and Legends of Our Fundamental Law* (New York, NY: Workers Bureau Education Press, 1927).

interpretation.[5] Similarly, it has been argued that the German *Grundgesetz* should be understood as a *'lebende Verfassung'*.[6]

Given the origin of the 'living instrument' metaphor in constitutional law, it is not surprising that, in international law, it has been used with regard to, first of all, those treaties that A. D. McNair characterised as 'treaties creating constitutional international law', particularly constituent treaties of international organizations.[7] The prime example of a constitutional treaty commonly described as a 'living instrument' is the 1945 Charter of the United Nations,[8] dealt with in Section 2 of this chapter; another one is the Marrakesh Agreement Establishing the World Trade Organization (WTO).[9]

However, the 'living instrument' metaphor is not confined to treaties constitutive of international organizations but has been used with regard to a range of further 'law-making treaties'[10] in many areas of international law, such as international environmental law and international humanitarian law. Treaties as diverse as the Treaty of Waitangi of 1840,[11] the Treaty on the Construction and Operation of the Gabčíkovo-Nagymaros Barrage System of 1977[12] and the Agreement on Trade-Related Aspects of Intellectual Property Rights (TRIPS) of 1994[13] have been explicitly described as 'living instruments'. The most important category of 'law-making treaties' that are

---

[5] See, e.g., A. Scalia, 'Originalism: The Lesser Evil', *Univ. Cincinnati L. Rev.*, 57 (1989), 849–865.

[6] W. Heun, *Die Verfassungsordnung der Bundesrepublik Deutschland* (Tübingen: Mohr Siebeck, 2012), p. 26.

[7] A. D. McNair, 'The Functions and Differing Legal Character of Treaties', *BYbIL*, 11 (1930), 100–118, at 112.

[8] 1 UNTS 16.

[9] 1867 UNTS 154. See the contribution to this volume of Pauwelyn and Van Damme at pp. 809–847 (Chapter 25). See, also, M. E. Footer, 'The WTO as a "Living Instrument": The Contribution of Consensus Decision-Making and Informality to Institutional Norms and Practices' in T. Cottier and M. Elsig (eds.), *Governing the World Trade Organization: Past, Present and Beyond Doha* (Cambridge: Cambridge University Press, 2011), pp. 217–240.

[10] On the different categories of treaties, see the contribution to this volume of Brölmann at pp. 79–102 (Chapter 4).

[11] *New Zealand Maori Council and Latimer v. Attorney-General and Others* [1987] 1 NZLR 641, at p. 663.

[12] Reproduced in ILM, 32 (1993), 1247–1258. See *Case Concerning Gabčíkovo-Nagymaros Project (Hungary/Slovakia)* (1997) ICJ Rep. 7, at pp. 114–115 (Separate Opinion of Vice-President Weeramantry).

[13] 1869 UNTS 299. See 'Commission Report Is Food for Thought on Intellectual Property – Supachai', WTO News, 17 Sept. 2002.

frequently characterised as 'living instruments' is, however, human rights treaties.[14] They are considered in detail in Section 3. It will be seen in the course of this analysis that the term 'living instrument' is no longer simply a straightforward metaphor deployed to show that treaties might grow but has become, itself, an evolving concept in the law of treaties. While the metaphor could be developed to the extent of identifying the 'signs of life' that make a treaty a 'living instrument', the concept of 'living instrument' is of greater significance because it embodies a legal understanding of a treaty in terms of its characterisation, interpretation and evolution.

Aside from constitutional and law-making treaties, the remaining bulk of treaties, including all 'contractual treaties', have not typically been described as 'living instruments'. The chapter aims to explore whether the 'living instrument' concept could usefully be applied to some of these treaties as well, making it of broad appeal. Section 4 therefore considers arms control law, an area of treaty provision that, at first sight, might appear to be the very antithesis of the 'living instrument' notion. While human rights treaties can be depicted as 'living instruments' in a conceptual sense, in arms control law the metaphor is not even deployed. However, the chapter will show that it may be appropriate to also think of arms control treaties in terms of the 'living instrument' metaphor.

While it is tempting to draw together all practice across treaties where the 'living instrument' characterisation has been used, this chapter focuses on treaties within the two areas of human rights law and arms control law in order to explore the understandings of 'living instrument' in greater depth. However, the chapter starts with a brief excursion into what is often viewed as the paradigmatic 'living instrument' – the 1945 Charter of the United Nations.

2   United Nations Charter

Constituent treaties of international organizations, which establish an organization and lay down rules, are the paradigmatic example of 'living instruments'. They adapt to changing social conditions, not automatically but through the ciphers of purposive interpretation by the organs of the organization. In the case of the United Nations, these consist mainly of States (in the Security Council, the General Assembly and the

---

[14] See the contribution to this volume of Chinkin at pp. 509–537 (Chapter 16).

Economic and Social Council) but also of individuals (the Secretariat headed by the Secretary-General), including judges (in the International Court of Justice).

Thus the United Nations Charter,[15] already as originally agreed in 1945 and before it was developed further, was a move away from the formalist position of the nineteenth century of the text being the sole source of information about the rights and duties of States. The Charter does contain statements on rights and duties of member States, for example in Article 2, but it also contains statements about the powers and responsibilities of the organs of the United Nations (for example in Chapters VI and VII in relation to the Security Council). Indeed, it was clear in 1945 that the political organs could add to the rights and duties of States by means of resolutions, interpreting wide phrases such as 'threat to the peace' (in Article 39) and 'measures not involving the use of armed force' (in Article 41). Thus, the Security Council can impose binding obligations on States in relation to matters of peace and security (Article 25) and the General Assembly in relation to matters of financing (Article 17).

It is clear that the development of the Charter as a 'living instrument' has pushed to the limit the rules on interpretation of treaties in Articles 31–33 of the 1969 Vienna Convention on the Law of Treaties (VCLT).[16] Those provisions supplement the textual approach with context (including subsequent agreement and practice) and purposes. In reality what this means is that while the text is the starting point, the changing understanding of that text is primarily driven by the practice not of all the member States but of majorities in political organs or by individuals working for the Secretariat (for instance, in interpreting the Charter's provisions on privileges and immunities)[17] or by the International Court of Justice (for instance, in interpreting the Charter to include the capacity to bring claims against States or the power of both the General Assembly and the Security Council to create peacekeeping forces).[18]

Edvard Hambro (writing as Pollux) recognised this as early as in 1946:

---

[15] 1 UNTS 16.   [16] 1155 UNTS 331.

[17] For instance, when negotiating a Status of Force Agreement (SOFA) with a host State. The model SOFA contains a number of clauses on privileges and immunities, though these may be modified for a particular operation: see U.N. Doc. A/45/594 (1990).

[18] *Reparation for Injuries Suffered in the Service of the United Nations* (Advisory Opinion) (1949) ICJ Rep. 174 and *Certain Expenses of the United Nations (Article 17, Paragraph 2 of the Charter)* (Advisory Opinion) (1962) ICJ Rep. 151.

> The Charter, like every written Constitution, will be a living instrument. It will be applied daily; and every application of the Charter, every use of an Article, implies an interpretation; on each occasion a decision is involved which may change the existing law and start a new constitutional development. A constitutional customary law will grow up and the Charter itself will merely form the framework of the Organization which will be filled in by the practice of the different organs.[19]

Christian Tomuschat supports this depiction by describing the United Nations as an 'entire system which is in constant movement, not unlike a national constitution whose original texture will be unavoidably modified by thick layers of political practice and jurisprudence'.[20] Rosalyn Higgins states further that 'the Charter is an extraordinary instrument, and a huge variety of possibilities are possible under it'.[21]

Subsequent practice is therefore a significant means of interpreting and developing the Charter. Nevertheless, sole reliance on practice as the test for legality is not acceptable,[22] since practice must be accompanied by normative intent and must be constrained by the purposes and principles of the Charter, which are broad but not unlimited. As stated by the International Court of Justice in the *Certain Expenses* advisory opinion in 1962, the purposes of the United Nations 'are broad indeed, but neither they nor the powers conferred to effectuate them are unlimited'.[23] It further held that 'when the Organization takes action which warrants the assertion that it was appropriate for the fulfilment of one of the stated purposes of the United Nations, the presumption is that such action is not *ultra vires* the Organization'.[24]

As well as the purposes, the text of the Charter will also provide limitations on its evolution. Perhaps the most important explicit limitation derives from Article 2(7) regarding intervention in the domestic affairs of States, but even the effect of this limitation has been restricted by a dynamic interpretation of what is domestic.[25] The amount of practice required to give a text a radically different meaning would

---

[19] Pollux, 'The Interpretation of the Charter', *BYbIL*, 23 (1946), 54–82.
[20] C. Tomuschat, 'Obligations Arising for States without or against Their Will', *Hague Recueil*, 241 (1993–IV), 195–374, at 251–252.
[21] R. Higgins, *Problems and Process: International Law and How We Use It* (Oxford: Clarendon Press, 1994), p. 184.
[22] S. Rosenne, *Developments in the Law of Treaties 1945–1986* (Cambridge: Cambridge University Press, 1989), p. 244.
[23] *Certain Expenses of the United Nations, supra* n. 18, at p. 168.   [24] *Ibid.*
[25] N. D. White, *Law of International Organisations* (Manchester: Manchester University Press, 2nd ed., 2005), pp. 89–98.

have to be significant in terms of volume and support, amounting to virtual agreement amongst the whole membership.[26] Nevertheless, any number of examples could be given for this, from the principles contained in Article 2, to the understanding of the General Assembly's powers under Chapter IV (to mandate peacekeeping forces, for instance), to those of the Security Council under Chapter VII (to massively expand the concept of threat to the peace in Article 39, to create *ad hoc* criminal tribunals, post-conflict administrations and legislation on terrorism and weapons of mass destruction under Article 41, to develop a military option that is not based on special agreement under Article 43 or a Military Staff Committee under Article 47), and to those of the Secretary General under Articles 97–99 (where he has long ceased to be simply the Chief Administrative Officer of the organization but has become the embodiment of diplomacy and initiative within the UN system).[27]

A simple example can be given where an interpretation by practice within the Security Council has been accepted by the wider membership and the International Court of Justice, and this relates to the understanding of the veto and when it operates under Article 27(3) of the Charter. In its *Namibia* advisory opinion of 1971, the International Court of Justice considered South African objections to the validity of the Security Council resolution which requested the opinion of the Court on the legality of the continued presence of South Africa in Namibia. Two permanent members had abstained on the resolution which, according to South Africa, therefore did not comply with the stipulations of Article 27(3) of the Charter that such decisions 'shall be made by an affirmative vote of nine members including the concurring votes of the permanent members'. After the Court had examined the proceedings of the Security Council, extending over a long period of time, it concluded that the 'practice of voluntary abstention by a permanent member' did not prevent the adoption of a valid resolution, so that only a negative vote by a permanent member constituted a veto preventing the adoption of a resolution. Although primarily relying on the practice of the Security Council, the Court also noted that there was support for this interpretation among the wider

---

[26] C. F. Amerasinghe, *Principles of the Institutional Law of International Organizations* (Cambridge: Cambridge University Press, 2nd ed., 2005), pp. 49–61.

[27] B. E. Urquhart, 'The Evolution of the Secretary-General' in S. Chesterman (ed.), *Secretary or General?: The UN Secretary-General in World Politics* (Cambridge: Cambridge University Press, 2007), pp. 15–32.

membership of the United Nations.[28] Although the practice did not produce an understanding that was contrary to the textual meaning (in particular the power of veto was not diminished by this practice), it did move the text a considerable way from its (admittedly rather ambiguous) literal meaning, and it also served the purposes of the United Nations by allowing its executive organ to take action in a greater number of situations than would have been possible had abstentions been treated as vetoes.[29]

Furthermore, despite some equivocation by the International Court in the *Namibia* opinion, within the UN system it is not the practice of member States that breathes life into the Charter but rather it is the practice of *the organs*.[30] This was recognised in an earlier opinion of the International Court of Justice on the practice of dealing with applications for membership in the political organs of the United Nations, when it stated that '*[t]he organs* to which Article 4 entrusts the judgment of the Organization in matters of admission have consistently interpreted the text . . .'.[31] However, in an earlier opinion of 1948 on membership, the Court had made it absolutely clear that such decisions still had to be exercised within the confines of the Charter:

> The political character of an organ cannot release it from the observance of the treaty provisions established by the Charter when they constitute limitations on its powers or criteria for its judgment.[32]

Thus, from an early stage, it was recognised that the Charter was a 'living' constitution that both allowed for freedom to develop its open-ended provisions but still provided limitations to prevent unrestricted growth. The growth has been provided primarily by the political organs of the United Nations in developing the broad purposes and powers given to them by the Charter, although the International Court of Justice has also made some significant contributions. In contrast, in the case of human

---

[28] *Legal Consequences for States of the Continued Presence of South Africa in Namibia (South West Africa) Notwithstanding Security Council Resolution 276 (1970)* (Advisory Opinion) (1971) ICJ Rep. 16, at p. 22.

[29] See, further, A. Zimmermann, 'Article 27' in B. Simma, D.-E. Khan, G. Nolte and A. Paulus (eds.), *The Charter of the United Nations: A Commentary* (Vol. I) (Oxford: Oxford University Press, 3rd ed., 2012), pp. 871–938, at pp. 912–916.

[30] B. Fassbender, 'The United Nations Charter as Constitution of the International Community', *Columbia JTL*, 36 (1998), 529–619.

[31] *Competence of the General Assembly for the Admission of a State to the United Nations* (Advisory Opinion) (1950) ICJ Rep. 4, at p. 9 (emphasis added).

[32] *Conditions of Admission of a State to Membership in the United Nations (Article 4 of the Charter)* (Advisory Opinion) (1948) ICJ Rep. 57, at p. 64.

rights treaties, it has been (quasi-)judicial organs created by these treaties that have breathed life into their provisions by interpreting them by reference to changing social mores and changing norms of international law.

3   Human Rights Treaties

A category of 'law-making treaties' that have been characterised as 'living instruments' from early on is human rights treaties. Judge Álvarez of the International Court of Justice thought already in 1951 that the 1948 United Nations Convention on the Prevention and Punishment of the Crime of Genocide[33] belonged to a category of 'multilateral conventions of a special character',[34] which 'must be interpreted without regard to the past, and only with regard to the future'.[35] According to him, such conventions are distinct from the preparatory work which preceded them: they 'have acquired a life of their own; they can be compared to ships which leave the yards in which they have been built, and sail away independently, no longer attached to the dockyard'.[36]

However, it was the European Court of Human Rights that gave real substance to the notion of an evolutive interpretation of human rights treaties and developed the idea that such treaties should be understood as 'living instruments'. The Court characterised the 1950 European Convention on Human Rights (ECHR)[37] as a 'living instrument' for the first time in 1978, and this notion has now become one of the central features of its approach to the interpretation of the Convention.[38] Although it took two more decades until the bodies supervising implementation of other human rights treaties started to take up the 'living instrument' idea, by today the 'living instrument' label tends to be attached to the category of human rights treaties as a whole.

---

[33] 78 UNTS 277.

[34] *Reservations to the Convention on the Prevention and Punishment of the Crime of Genocide* (Advisory Opinion) (1951) ICJ Rep. 15, at p. 51 (Dissenting Opinion of Judge Álvarez).

[35] *Ibid.*, at p. 53.   [36] *Ibid.*   [37] 213 UNTS 222.

[38] See, further, G. Letsas, 'The ECHR as a Living Instrument: Its Meaning and Legitimacy' in A. Føllesdal, B. Peters and G. Ulfstein (eds.), *Constituting Europe: The European Court of Human Rights in a National, European and Global Context* (Cambridge: Cambridge University Press, 2013), pp. 106–141.

3.1 ECHR

The first mention of 'living instrument' in Strasbourg's case law can be found in the judgment of *Tyrer v. United Kingdom*, handed down in 1978.[39] Anthony Tyrer was fifteen years old when a juvenile court sentenced him to three strokes of the birch in accordance with the legislation then in force on the Isle of Man. He was taken to a police station where he had to take down his trousers and underpants and bend over a table. He was held by two police officers whilst a third executed the punishment.[40] The European Court had to decide whether such judicially imposed corporal punishment amounted to 'degrading punishment' in breach of Article 3 ECHR. The Attorney-General for the Isle of Man argued that it did not, 'since it did not outrage public opinion in the Island'.[41] The Court rejected this argument, pointing out that the reason why the inhabitants of the island support corporal punishment may be precisely that they believe it to be degrading and thus an effective deterrent. In a passage that has since become one of the Court's standard formulations (at least its first part), it then went on to state:

> The Court must also recall that the Convention is a living instrument which, as the Commission rightly stressed, must be interpreted in the light of present-day conditions. In the case now before it the Court cannot but be influenced by the developments and commonly accepted standards in the penal policy of the member States of the Council of Europe in this field.[42]

The background and meaning of this passage are rather mysterious. In its decision in *Tyrer*, the European Commission of Human Rights had, in fact, neither described the Convention as a 'living instrument' nor referred to 'present-day conditions'. In addition, despite its insistence on this point, the Court did not explain what 'the developments and commonly accepted standards in the penal policy' of European States were. While it remarked rather incidentally – in a passage not relating to Article 3 ECHR – that corporal punishment was not used 'in the great majority of the member States of the Council of Europe',[43] there is no review of the legislation or legal developments in these States. Even more problematically, the Court did not give any reasons for its characterisation of the ECHR as a 'living instrument', which has now become one of its most important interpretive approaches: it did not explain why and

---

[39] *Tyrer v. United Kingdom*, No. 5856/72, Judgment of 25 Apr. 1978, Series A, No. 26.
[40] *Ibid.* (paragraphs 9–10).   [41] *Ibid.* (paragraph 31).   [42] *Ibid.*
[43] *Ibid.* (paragraph 38).

how much it matters that there are 'commonly accepted standards' and why the ECHR should be interpreted in the light of them.[44] In fact, it is clear from the Court's reasoning that the decisive factor for reaching its decision that Article 3 had been violated was not the development of common European standards at all. Instead, it was '[t]he very nature of judicial corporal punishment' that made it degrading, since 'it involves one human being inflicting physical violence on another human being'.[45]

A year later, in *Marckx v. Belgium*, the Court, although not explicitly describing the ECHR as a 'living instrument', referred to its judgment in *Tyrer* and repeated that the Convention 'must be interpreted in the light of present-day conditions'.[46] Accordingly, the Court attached no weight to the fact that 'at the time when the Convention of 4 November 1950 was drafted, it was regarded as permissible and normal in many European countries to draw a distinction in this area between the "illegitimate" and the "legitimate" family'.[47] In the meantime, the Court pointed out, the domestic law of the great majority of the Council of Europe member States had evolved and continued to evolve towards full recognition of maternal affiliation by birth alone with respect to 'illegitimate children'. While the Court admitted that two conventions aiming at establishing equality between 'legitimate' and 'illegitimate' children had only been ratified by a small number of members States, it thought it sufficient that there were signs of an 'evolution of rules and attitudes' 'amongst modern societies'.[48]

One of the Court's most famous invocations of the 'living instrument' notion was that in *Selmouni v. France* where it made it clear that what qualifies as 'torture' within the meaning of Article 3 ECHR may well change over the years:

> [H]aving regard to the fact that the Convention is a 'living instrument which must be interpreted in the light of present-day conditions' ... the Court considers that certain acts which were classified in the past as 'inhuman and degrading treatment' as opposed to 'torture' could be classified differently in future. It takes the view that the increasingly high standard being required in the area of the protection of human rights and fundamental liberties correspondingly and inevitably requires greater

---

[44] See, also, A. Mowbray, 'The Creativity of the European Court of Human Rights', *HRLR*, 5 (2005), 57–79, at 61.

[45] *Tyrer v. United Kingdom, supra* n. 39 (paragraph 33).

[46] *Marckx v. Belgium*, No. 6833/74, Judgment of 13 June 1979, Series A, No. 31 (paragraph 41).

[47] *Ibid.*   [48] *Ibid.*

firmness in assessing breaches of the fundamental values of democratic societies.[49]

Accordingly, the Court found the kind of ill-treatment that had occurred in this case to amount to torture, even though on application of the standards established in its previous case law it probably would have had to be classified as inhuman treatment.[50] This finding is a good illustration of the Court's use of the 'living instrument' notion insofar as it is typically invoked to support an extension of the Convention's protective scope.

By the time of writing, the ECHR has been described as a 'living instrument' in ninety-one judgments and decisions (fifty-five times the term appears in the majority's judgment/decision, twenty-six times in a separate opinion, ten times in both). The equivalent French term 'instrument vivant' was used in a further twenty-three judgements and decisions (twelve times in the majority's judgment/decision, eleven times in a separate opinion). In addition, not counting the judgments and decisions containing an explicit reference to 'living instrument' just referred to, the Court (or one of its members) has stated that the Convention must be interpreted in the light of 'present-day conditions' an additional thirty-six times (twenty-four judgments/decisions, twelve separate opinions), while the equivalent reference to 'conditions de vie actuelles' appears in two separate opinions. In total, therefore, the 'living instrument' idea has been invoked in 152 judgments and decisions.

The Court has used the 'living instrument' notion, for example, to characterise the death penalty as inhuman and degrading treatment in the sense of Article 3,[51] to qualify human trafficking as falling within the prohibition of slavery and forced labour of Article 4,[52] to limit the role of the executive branch in deciding on the release of prisoners under Article 5,[53] to read a right not to be compelled to join an association into Article 11[54] and to qualify the rejection of a lesbian woman's application to adopt a child as discriminatory and thus in violation of Article 14.[55]

---

[49] *Selmouni v. France*, No. 25803/94, Judgment of 28 July 1999, Reports 1999-V (paragraph 101).

[50] See *Ireland v. United Kingdom*, No. 5310/71, Judgment of 18 Jan. 1978, Series A, No. 25 (paragraph 167).

[51] *Al-Saadoon and Mufdhi v. United Kingdom*, No. 61498/08, Judgment of 2 March 2010, Reports 2010 (paragraphs 119–120).

[52] *Rantsev v. Cyprus and Russia*, No. 25965/04, Judgment of 7 Jan. 2010, Reports 2010.

[53] *Stafford v. United Kingdom*, No. 46295/99, Judgment of 28 May 2002, Reports 2002-IV.

[54] *Sigurdur A. Sigurjónsson v. Iceland*, No. 16130/90, Judgment of 30 June 1993, Series A, No. 264.

[55] *E.B. v. France* [GC], No. 43546/02, Judgment of 22 Jan. 2008.

The Court has relied on the 'living instrument' approach to interpret not only the substantive but also the procedural guarantees of the ECHR, such as those concerning interim measures[56] and the territorial jurisdiction of the Court.[57] In *Loizidou v. Turkey (Preliminary Objections)*, it explained that, just as the substantive guarantees, the procedural provisions 'cannot be interpreted solely in accordance with the intentions of their authors as expressed more than forty years ago'.[58]

The 'present-day conditions' that may influence the Court's interpretation of the Convention may consist of legal developments within the respondent State such as legislative reforms or changes in the case law of the domestic courts.[59] More often, however, the Court refers, as in *Tyrer* and *Marckx*, to the situation in other member States or sometimes, as in *Christine Goodwin v. United Kingdom*,[60] even to that in non-member States. In the latter case, the Court explicitly recognised that there was no 'common European approach' regarding the legal recognition of the new sexual identity of post-operative transsexuals but, based on a review of the legal situation in a number of non-European States, attached more importance to 'the clear and uncontested evidence of a continuing international trend' than to the lack of a common European standard.[61]

In recent years, the Court has also given increased weight to developments in international law.[62] In *Demir and Baykara v. Turkey* it expanded the 'living instrument' formula accordingly:

> [T]he Convention is a living instrument which must be interpreted in the light of present-day conditions, *and in accordance with developments in international law,* so as to reflect the increasingly high standard being required in the area of the protection of human rights, thus necessitating greater firmness in assessing breaches of the fundamental values of democratic societies.[63]

---

[56] *Mamatkulov and Askarov v. Turkey*, Nos. 46827/99 and 46951/99, Judgment of 4 Feb. 2005, Reports 2005-I.

[57] *Loizidou v. Turkey* (Preliminary Objections), No. 15318/89, Judgment of 23 March 1995, Series A, No. 310.

[58] *Ibid*. (paragraph 71).   [59] *Stafford v. United Kingdom, supra* n. 53 (paragraphs 69–80).

[60] *Christine Goodwin v. United Kingdom*, No. 28957/95, Judgment of 11 July 2002, Reports 2002-VI.

[61] *Ibid*. (paragraphs 56 and 84–85).

[62] See, already, *Golder v. United Kingdom*, No. 4451/70, Judgment of 21 Feb. 1975, Series A, No. 18 (paragraph 29) and *Loizidou v. Turkey* (Merits), No. 15318/89, Judgment of 18 Dec. 1996, Reports 1996-VI (paragraph 43).

[63] *Demir and Baykara v. Turkey* [GC], No. 34503/97, Judgment of 12 Nov. 2008, Reports 2008 (paragraph 146) (emphasis added).

In this case, concerning the right of civil servants to form trade unions, the Court referred very extensively to various international instruments, including ILO Conventions and the European Social Charter, to interpret Article 11 ECHR. The Turkish government objected that it had not ratified the respective provisions of the European Social Charter and that the Court was not entitled to create, by way of interpretation, new obligations not provided for in the ECHR. The Court stated that it had 'never considered the provisions of the Convention as the sole framework of reference for the interpretation of the rights and freedoms enshrined therein' but had also 'taken account of evolving norms of national and international law',[64] which 'show, in a precise area, that there is common ground in modern societies'.[65] Thus, it was 'not necessary for the respondent State to have ratified the entire collection of instruments that are applicable in respect of the precise subject matter of the case concerned'.[66] Similarly, in *Rantsev v. Cyprus and Russia* the Court drew upon the Protocol to Prevent, Suppress and Punish Trafficking in Persons, especially Women and Children and the Council of Europe Convention on Action against Trafficking in Human Beings to support its conclusion that trafficking in human beings falls within the scope of Article 4 ECHR, even though these instruments had not yet been in force at the relevant time.[67]

However, the Court has also made it clear that there are limits as to what the 'living instrument' method can achieve. In *Johnston v. Ireland*, it had to decide whether a right to divorce could be derived from Article 12 ECHR, guaranteeing the right to marry.[68] The Court recognised 'that the Convention and its Protocols must be interpreted in the light of present-day conditions' but held that it 'cannot, by means of an evolutive interpretation, derive from these instruments a right that was not included therein at the outset', particularly where the omission was deliberate.[69]

The 'living instrument' approach may also reach its limits where it conflicts with a systematic interpretation of the ECHR. In *Pretty v. United Kingdom*, the applicant, who suffered from a terrible, irreversible disease in its final stages, argued that Article 3 ECHR imposed a positive obligation on the State to sanction the assisted suicide of a terminally ill person.[70] The Court held otherwise, stating that while it 'must take

---

[64] *Ibid.* (paragraphs 67–68).   [65] *Ibid.* (paragraph 86).   [66] *Ibid.*
[67] *Rantsev v. Cyprus and Russia, supra* n. 52 (paragraph 282).
[68] *Johnston v. Ireland*, No. 9697/82, Judgment of 18 Dec. 1986, Series A, No. 112.
[69] *Ibid.* (paragraph 53).
[70] *Pretty v. United Kingdom*, No. 2346/02, Judgment of 29 Apr. 2002, Reports 2002-III.

a dynamic and flexible approach to the interpretation of the Convention, which is a living instrument, any interpretation must also accord with the fundamental objectives of the Convention and its coherence as a system of human rights protection'. Therefore, Article 3 ECHR had to be construed in harmony with Article 2 ECHR, the right to life.[71]

Finally, the Court will be reluctant to rely on the 'living instrument' method where the member States have taken it upon themselves to further develop and define the ECHR standards. *Soering v. United Kingdom* raised the question of whether imposition of the death penalty would amount to a violation of Article 3 ECHR.[72] While reaffirming that the Convention is a 'living instrument', the Court pointed out that Protocol No. 6 to the ECHR concerning the Abolition of the Death Penalty of 1983 showed that the intention of the State parties was to adopt the normal method of amendment of the text through a subsequent written and, in addition, optional instrument. Therefore, notwithstanding the special character of the Convention, Article 3 could not be interpreted as generally prohibiting the death penalty.[73]

As the Court has recently summarised its case law, the 'living instrument' approach 'does not ... mean that to respond to present-day needs, conditions, views or standards the Court can create a new right apart from those recognised by the Convention ... or that it can whittle down an existing right or create a new "exception" or "justification" which is not expressly recognised in the Convention'.[74] What qualifies as a 'new' right or exception is, however, a question of interpretation. Thus, some authors[75] have argued that the Court has, in fact, engaged in the creation of a new right that had been deliberately omitted from the Convention, when it held that the guarantee of freedom of association of Article 11 includes a 'negative right' not to be compelled to join an association.[76]

---

[71] *Ibid.* (paragraph 54).

[72] *Soering v. United Kingdom*, No. 14038/88, Judgment of 7 July 1989, Series A, No. 161.

[73] *Ibid.* (paragraph 103).

[74] *Austin and Others v. United Kingdom*, Nos. 39692/09, 40713/09 and 41008/09, Judgment of 15 March 2012, Reports 2012 (paragraph 53).

[75] G. Letsas, *A Theory of Interpretation of the European Convention on Human Rights* (Oxford: Oxford University Press, 2007), p. 65, and Baroness Hale of Richmond, 'Beanstalk or Living Instrument? How Tall Can the ECHR Grow?', Barnard's Inn Reading 2011 (www.supremecourt.gov.uk/docs/speech_110616.pdf).

[76] *Young, James and Webster v. United Kingdom*, Nos. 7601/76 and 7806/77, Judgment of 13 Aug. 1981, Series A, No. 44 (paragraph 53) and *Sigurdur A. Sigurjónsson v. Iceland*, *supra* n. 54.

3.2   Inter-American Instruments

The 'living instrument' method developed by the European Court of Human Rights has clearly influenced the interpretive approach of the Inter-American human rights bodies. Nevertheless, when the Inter-American Court of Human Rights, in 1989, for the first time emphasised the need for an evolutive interpretation of human rights instruments, this was backed up by a reference not to the European Court's case law but to the *Namibia* opinion of the International Court of Justice, according to which 'an international instrument must be interpreted and applied within the overall framework of the juridical system in force at the time of the interpretation'.[77] Therefore, the Inter-American Court thought that, to determine the legal status of the American Declaration of Human Rights,[78] it had to 'look to the inter-American system of today in the light of the evolution it has undergone since the adoption of the Declaration, rather than to examine the normative value and significance which that instrument was believed to have had in 1948'.[79]

In 1999, however, the Court did cite the European Court's judgments in *Tyrer, Marckx* and *Loizidou* to support its observation that 'human rights treaties are living instruments whose interpretation must consider the changes over time and present-day conditions'.[80] The Court held that such an evolutive interpretation is consistent with the general rules of treaty interpretation established in the VCLT and that international human rights law 'has made great headway thanks to an evolutive interpretation of international instruments of protection'.[81] Since then, the Inter-American Court has repeatedly made the following – or some similar – observation, mainly having in mind the 1969 American Convention on Human Rights (ACHR)[82]

---

[77] *Legal Consequences for States of the Continued Presence of South Africa in Namibia (South West Africa), supra* n. 28, at p. 31.

[78] Adopted by the Ninth International Conference of American States (1948), reprinted in *Basic Documents Pertaining to Human Rights in the Inter-American System*, OEA/Ser.L. V/II.82 Doc.6 Rev.1 at 17 (1992).

[79] OC-10/89, *Interpretation of the American Declaration of the Rights and Duties of Man within the Framework of Article 64 of the American Convention on Human Rights*, IACtHR Advisory Opinion of 14 July 1989, Series A, No. 10 (paragraph 37).

[80] OC-16/99, *The Right to Information on Consular Assistance in the Framework of Guarantees for Due Legal Process*, IACtHR Advisory Opinion of 1 Oct. 1999, Series A, No. 16 (paragraph 114). See, also, *ibid.* (paragraphs 7 and 10–11) (Concurring Opinion of Judge Cançado Trindade).

[81] *Ibid.* (paragraph 114).   [82] 1144 UNTS 123.

but also, in one case,[83] the 1989 Convention on the Rights of the Child (CRC):[84] 'The Court has pointed out, as the European Court of Human Rights has too, that human rights treaties are live instruments, whose interpretation must go hand in hand with evolving times and current living conditions'.[85]

The Inter-American Commission on Human Rights, for its part, referred to the 'living instrument' concept for the first time in 2000. In a case concerning the mandatory imposition of the death penalty for certain offences, the petitioners had argued that, just as the ECHR, 'the American Convention is a living, breathing and developing instrument reflecting contemporary standards of morality, justice and decency'.[86] The Commission, referring in a footnote to the European Court's 'living instrument' approach and citing *Tyrer*, held that 'a principle of law has developed common to those democratic jurisdictions that have retained the death penalty, according to which the death penalty should only be implemented through "individualized" sentencing'.[87] Exactly the same formulation and footnote can be found in a number of similar cases decided on the same day[88] and in 2001.[89] In 2002, the Commission, asserting that it was 'well-accepted' that 'human rights treaties are living instruments whose interpretation must consider changes over time and present-day conditions', held that the prohibition of executing persons below the age of eighteen had evolved into a norm of *jus cogens*.[90] As the

---

[83] *'Street Children' (Villagrán Morales et al.) v. Guatemala*, IACtHR Judgment of 19 Nov. 1999, Series C, No. 63 (paragraph 193).

[84] 1577 UNTS 3.

[85] *Mapiripan Massacre v. Colombia*, IACtHR Judgment of 15 Sept. 2005, Series C, No. 35 (paragraph 106). See, also, *Yakye Axa Indigenous Community v. Paraguay*, IACtHR Judgment of 17 June 2005, Series C, No. 125 (paragraph 125); *Mayagna (Sumo) Awas Tingni Community v. Nicaragua*, IACtHR Judgment of 31 Aug. 2001, Series C, No. 66 (paragraph 146) and *'Street Children' (Villagrán Morales et al.) v. Guatemala*, supra n. 83 (paragraph 193).

[86] Case 11.743, *Baptiste v. Grenada*, IACoHR Report 38/00 of 13 Apr. 2000, Annual Report 2000 (paragraph 31).

[87] *Ibid.* (paragraph 95 and fn. 59).

[88] Cases 12.023 and Others, *McKenzie et al. v. Jamaica*, IACoHR Report 41/00 of 13 Apr. 2000, Annual Report 2000 (paragraph 209 and fn. 87).

[89] Cases 11.826 and Others, *Lamey et al. v. Jamaica*, IACoHR Report 49/01 of 4 Apr. 2001, Annual Report 2001 (paragraphs 140–141 and fn. 52); Case 12.028, *Knights v. Grenada*, IACoHR Report 47/01 of 4 Apr. 2001, Annual Report 2001 (paragraph 87 and fn. 58) and Cases 12.067 and Others, *Edwards et al. v. Bahamas*, IACoHR Report 48/01 of 4 Apr. 2001, Annual Report 2000 (paragraph 152 and fn. 80).

[90] Case 12.285, *Domingues v. United States*, IACoHR Report 62/02 of 22 Oct. 2002, Annual Report 2002 (paragraph 103 and fn. 104). See, also, *ibid.* (paragraph 44 and fn. 30)

European Court has done for the ECHR, the Inter-American
Commission has suggested that the 'living instrument' concept is applicable with regard not only to substantive guarantees of human rights but
also to the procedural provisions of the ACHR.[91]

3.3   UN Instruments

Among the bodies supervising implementation of the *universal* human
rights treaties, the UN Human Rights Committee was the first, in 2002, to
apply the 'living instrument' method. In the landmark case of *Judge
v. Canada*, it had to decide whether Canada violated the author's right
to life under Article 6 of the International Covenant on Civil and Political
Rights (ICCPR)[92] by deporting him to the United States, where he had
been sentenced to the death penalty.[93] Nine years earlier the Committee
had held that the deportation of a person from a country which has
abolished the death penalty to a country where he or she faces capital
punishment does not *per se* amount to a violation of Article 6.[94] In *Judge*,
the Committee recognised that it 'should ensure both consistency and
coherence of its jurisprudence' but noted that in exceptional situations it
may be necessary to review the scope of application of the rights protected in the ICCPR, 'in particular if there have been notable factual and
legal developments and changes in international opinion in respect of the
issue raised'.[95] The Committee observed that, since its earlier decision,
there had been 'a broadening international consensus in favour of abolition of the death penalty, and in States which have retained the death
penalty, a broadening consensus not to carry it out'. The Committee
thought it significant that Canada's own practice reflected this consensus:
the Supreme Court of Canada had held that in such cases of removal the
government must, as a general rule, seek assurances that the death
penalty will not be applied. Considering 'that the Covenant should be
interpreted as a living instrument and the rights protected under it

(referring to the need to interpret the American Declaration in the light of present-day
conditions and citing *Tyrer, Marckx* and *Loizidou*).
[91] Interstate Case 01/06, *Nicaragua v. Costa Rica*, IACoHR Report 11/07 of 8 March 2007,
Annual Report 2007 (paragraph 205).
[92] 999 UNTS 171.
[93] *Judge v. Canada*, Communication No. 829/1998 of 5 Aug. 2002, U.N. Doc. CCPR/C/78/
D/829/1998.
[94] *Kindler v. Canada*, Communication No. 470/1991 of 30 July 1993, U.N. Doc. CCPR/C/48/
D/470/1991.
[95] *Judge v. Canada*, *supra* n. 93 (paragraph 10.3).

should be applied in context and in the light of present-day conditions',[96] the Committee departed from its previous findings and found a violation of Article 6.[97]

The Human Rights Committee has addressed similar interpretive issues in a series of cases concerning conscientious objection to compulsory military service. In *Yoon and Choi v. Republic of Korea*,[98] it deviated from its previous jurisprudence[99] and recognised that Article 18 ICCPR (guaranteeing freedom of conscience) implies a right to conscientious objection. To support this change in interpretation it argued that the understanding of Article 18, as that of any right guaranteed by the Covenant, evolved over time[100] and observed that 'an increasing number' of those States parties which had retained compulsory military service had introduced alternatives to that service.[101] In *Atasoy and Sarkut v. Turkey*, the State party argued that there were limits to evolutive interpretation: 'interpretation cannot go beyond the letter and spirit of the treaty or what the States parties initially and explicitly so intended'.[102] Nevertheless, the Committee reaffirmed its view that a right of conscientious objection, even though not explicitly referred to in Article 18, derives from this provision,[103] with one Committee member stressing in his individual opinion that the Committee 'must apply and interpret the Covenant as a living instrument'.[104]

The Committee on the Elimination of Racial Discrimination invoked the 'living instrument' concept in 2003 to support its conclusion that use of a term that was not considered offensive some time ago may be considered offensive today and thus violate the 1965 International Convention on the Elimination of All Forms of Racial Discrimination (ICERD).[105] In *Hagan v. Australia*, the petitioner had taken offence at the sign 'E.S. "Nigger" Brown Stand', which had been displayed since 1960 on

---

[96] *Ibid.*   [97] *Ibid.* (paragraph 10.6).
[98] *Yoon and Choi v. Republic of Korea*, Communications Nos. 1321/2004 and 1322/2004 of 3 Nov. 2006, U.N. Doc. CCPR/C/88/D/1321–1322/2004.
[99] See, e.g., *L.T.K. v. Finland*, Communication No. 185/1984 of 9 July 1985, U.N. Doc. CCPR/C/OP/2, (paragraph 5.2.) ('The Covenant does not provide for the right to conscientious objection; neither article 18 nor article 19 of the Covenant, especially taking into account paragraph 3(c)(ii) of [Art.] 8, can be construed as implying that right').
[100] *Yoon and Choi v. Republic of Korea, supra* n. 98 (paragraph 8.2).
[101] *Ibid.* (paragraph 8.4).
[102] *Atasoy and Sarkut v. Turkey*, Communications Nos. 1853/2008 and 1854/2008 of 29 March 2012, U.N. Doc. CCPR/C/104/D/1853–1854/2008 (paragraph 7.13).
[103] *Ibid.* (paragraph 10.4).   [104] *Ibid.* (paragraph 4) (Individual Opinion Salvioli).
[105] 660 UNTS 195.

a stand of a sporting ground in honour of a sporting personality who was neither black nor of aboriginal descent.[106] The Committee held

> that use and maintenance of the offending term can at the present time be considered offensive and insulting, even if for an extended period it may not have necessarily been so regarded. The Committee considers, in fact, that the Convention, as a living instrument, must be interpreted and applied taking into [sic!] the circumstances of contemporary society. In this context, the Committee considers it to be its duty to recall the increased sensitivities in respect of words such as the offending term appertaining today.[107]

The Committee has since reaffirmed in its General Recommendation 32 that '[t]he Convention, as the Committee has observed on many occasions, is a living instrument that must be interpreted and applied taking into account the circumstances of contemporary society', which made it imperative to read its text in a context-sensitive manner.[108]

The Committee on the Rights of the Child has equally invoked the 'living instrument' concept in a general comment. In its General Comment 8 concerning the right of the child to protection from corporal punishment, it has explained that, while the *travaux préparatoires* for the CRC did not record any discussion of corporal punishment during the drafting sessions, 'the Convention, like all human rights instruments, must be regarded as a living instrument, whose interpretation develops over time' and that in the seventeen years since the CRC was adopted, the prevalence of corporal punishment had become more visible.[109]

3.4   Assessment

As the preceding review demonstrates, in international human rights law, the 'living instrument' notion is used in a similar way as with regard to the UN Charter, namely primarily as a metaphor to justify a dynamic or evolutive interpretation.[110] Often it is invoked, as in *Marckx*, to support

---

[106] *Hagan v. Australia*, Communication No. 26/2002 of 20 March 2003, U.N. Doc. CERD/C/62/D/26/2002.

[107] *Ibid.* (paragraph 7.3).

[108] Committee on the Elimination of Racial Discrimination, General Recommendation No. 32 of 24 Sept. 2009, U.N. Doc. CERD/C/GC/32 (paragraph 5).

[109] Committee on the Rights of the Child, General Comment No. 8 of 2 March 2007, U.N. Doc. CRC/C/GC/8 (paragraph 20).

[110] On dynamic or evolutive interpretation, see M. Fitzmaurice, 'Dynamic (Evolutive) Interpretation of Treaties: Part I', *Hague YbIL*, 21 (2008), 101–153; M. Fitzmaurice, 'Dynamic (Evolutive) Interpretation of Treaties: Part II', *Hague YbIL*, 22 (2009), 3–31,

an interpretation that arguably deviates from the understanding that the drafters of the treaty had or, as in *Selmouni* and *Judge*, to explain a change in the case law.

One may question whether the 'living instrument' metaphor is a completely accurate description of this method of interpretation. The metaphor suggests that, similar to living organisms, legal instruments change their shape by themselves, when it is in fact the external social conditions that change, and the legal instruments are adapted to them.

Be that as it may, what is more important is the question as to the legality and legitimacy of this method of interpretation. When it comes to human rights treaties, international and regional courts or quasi-judicial bodies assume to a large extent the interpretive role that is played by States (or organs composed of States) with regard to other treaties. Where member States entrust a (quasi-)judicial body with supervising implementation of the treaty, they thereby also cede to it the interpretive authority over the treaty. The European Court of Human Rights,[111] the Inter-American Court of Human Rights[112] and the international human rights bodies[113] have all accepted that they are bound, to the same extent as States, to apply the rules of treaty interpretation codified in Articles 31 and 32 VCLT when interpreting the human rights conventions they are charged with supervising. In principle, it seems clear that the 'living instrument' method may be covered, and indeed required, by these rules. Article 31(1) VCLT requires a treaty to be interpreted 'in accordance with the ordinary meaning to be given to the terms of the treaty *in their context* and *in the light of its object and purpose*'. According to Article 31(3)(b) VCLT, 'any *subsequent practice* in the application of the treaty which establishes the agreement of the parties regarding its

---

and R. Bernhardt, 'Evolutive Treaty Interpretation, Especially of the European Convention on Human Rights', *German YbIL*, 42 (1999), 11–25.

[111] *Golder v. United Kingdom, supra* n. 62 (paragraph 29). For an overview, see M. E. Villiger, 'Articles 31 and 32 of the Vienna Convention on the Law of Treaties in the Case-Law of the European Court of Human Rights' in J. Bröhmer, R. Bieber, C. Calliess, S. Langenfeld, C. Weber and J. Wolf (eds.), *Internationale Gemeinschaft und Menschenrechte: Festschrift für Georg Ress* (Köln: Carl Heymanns Verlag, 2005), pp. 317–330.

[112] E.g. OC-16/99, *The Right to Information on Consular Assistance in the Framework of Guarantees for Due Legal Process*, IACtHR Advisory Opinion of 1 Oct. 1999, Series A, No. 16 (paragraph 58).

[113] See K. Mechlem, 'Treaty Bodies and the Interpretation of Human Rights', *Vanderbilt JTL*, 42 (2009), 905–947, at 919.

interpretation' must be taken into account. That subsequent practice may include State practice as well as the practice of supervisory bodies and may be used to establish original or changing intent.[114] Finally, Article 31(3)(c) VCLT provides that 'any relevant *rules of international law applicable* in the relations between the parties' are relevant for clarification of the meaning of that treaty.[115]

Application of the 'living instrument' method is rather unproblematic in cases where there have been obvious changes in State practice or relevant rules of international law and it is inevitable to interpret a given treaty in light of these changes. A good illustration of this is *Matthews v. United Kingdom,* which raised the question of whether elections to the European Parliament fall within the right to vote guaranteed by Article 3 of Protocol No. 1 to the ECHR. The European Court of Human Rights held that they did. Invoking the 'living instrument' metaphor, it stated that '[t]he mere fact that a body was not envisaged by the drafters of the Convention cannot prevent that body from falling within the scope of the Convention' and that it had to take into account structural changes mutually agreed by the contracting States.[116]

At the same time, the relevant human rights bodies have accepted that the requirements of State consensus and legal certainty impose limits on the use of the 'living instrument' method. As explained previously, the European Court has explicitly recognised that it may not engage in law-making by, for example, creating rights not intended by the original drafters of the ECHR[117] or engaging in creative interpretation in areas that have been singled out by the contracting States for reform by way of treaty amendment.[118] The Human Rights Committee has asserted that evolutive interpretation needs to be balanced against the need to 'ensure both consistency and coherence of . . . jurisprudence'.[119] In a similar vein, the European Court has acknowledged that, despite its 'living instrument' approach, 'in the interests of legal certainty and foreseeability it should not depart, without good reason, from its own precedents'.[120]

---

[114] See the contribution to this volume of Buga at pp. 363–391 (Chapter 12).

[115] Emphases added.

[116] *Matthews v. United Kingdom,* No. 24833/94, Judgment of 18 Feb. 1999, Reports 1999-I (paragraph 39).

[117] *Johnston v. Ireland, supra* n. 68 (paragraph 53) and *Austin and Others v. United Kingdom, supra* n. 74 (paragraph 53).

[118] *Soering v. United Kingdom, supra* n. 72 (paragraph 103).

[119] *Judge v. Canada, supra* n. 93 (paragraph 10.3).

[120] *Mamatkulov and Askarov v. Turkey, supra* n. 56 (paragraph 121).

Despite these assertions, the previous review of case law of relevant supervisory bodies reveals that it is, at the very least, questionable whether they can be said to have always complied with these restrictions. First, although there are frequent references to the alleged practice of States (be it the respondent State, other States parties or even non-States parties), only very rarely is evidence for that practice or its uniformity adduced. As explained previously, this already held true for *Tyrer*, where the 'living instrument' concept was established, and it equally applies to many of the subsequent cases. Second, in some of the cases the respective human rights body did, in fact, not even *claim* that the State practice concerned was uniform, despite the fact that Article 31(3)(b) VCLT requires the State practice to reflect *agreement* regarding a particular interpretation. The practice must be actively shared by at least some States parties and acquiesced in by the others.[121] Nevertheless, in *Christine Goodwin*, for example, the European Court explicitly recognised that there was *no* common European approach supporting its interpretation; it thought that it was sufficient that there was evidence of a 'continuing international trend' in non-European States. In *Marckx*, it satisfied itself with signs of an 'evolution of rules and attitudes' 'amongst modern societies'. The Human Rights Committee, in *Judge*, referred to a 'broadening international consensus' to justify a deviation from its previous jurisprudence and, in *Yoon and Choi*, to an 'increasing number' of States parties to read a right to conscientious objection into Article 18 ICCPR. Third, with regard to interpretation in the light of 'relevant rules of international law', the International Court of Justice allows, in certain cases, the consideration of rules that came into force after the conclusion of the treaty at issue.[122] However, Article 31(3)(c) VCLT states that the rules must be 'applicable in the relations between the parties', which also suggests that non-binding rules cannot be relied upon.[123] Nevertheless, the European Court has taken into account not only, as in *Demir and Baykara*, treaties that had not been ratified by the respondent State and, as in *Marckx*, treaties that had only been ratified by a very small number of States parties to the ECHR but also, as in *Rantsev*,

---

[121] M. E. Villiger, *Commentary on the 1969 Vienna Convention on the Law of Treaties* (Leiden: Martinus Nijhoff, 2009), p. 431.

[122] *Legal Consequences for States of the Continued Presence of South Africa in Namibia (South West Africa)*, *supra* n. 28, at p. 31, and *Case Concerning Gabčíkovo-Nagymaros Project*, *supra* n. 12, at pp. 67–68.

[123] Villiger, *supra* n. 121, at p. 433, and R. K. Gardiner, *Treaty Interpretation* (Oxford: Oxford University Press, 2nd ed., 2015), pp. 299–302.

even treaties that were not in force at the time the relevant facts occurred. Moreover, the Court regularly takes into consideration international materials that are not legally binding.[124]

This is not to argue that non-uniform State practice or non-binding rules may not be taken into consideration (they may still serve as supplementary means of interpretation according to Article 32 VCLT) but merely to point out that the weight given to these means of interpretation is rather extraordinary when it comes to human rights treaties. Such a special interpretive approach may be justified on the basis that human rights treaties have a special nature, calling for specialised rules of treaty interpretation, perhaps even 'interpretive rules that are beyond the VCLT paradigm'.[125] That human rights treaties fundamentally differ from other treaties, in that they create obligations of States towards individuals rather than between States, is beyond dispute today.[126] The Inter-American Court, for example, has explained:

> Since its first cases, the Court has based its jurisprudence on the special nature of the American Convention in the framework of International Human Rights Law. Said Convention, like other human rights treaties, is inspired by higher shared values (focusing on protection of the human being), they have specific oversight mechanisms, they are applied according to the concept of collective guarantees, they embody obligations that are essentially objective, and their nature is special vis-à-vis other treaties that regulate reciprocal interests among the States Parties.[127]

It may be added to the preceding list that, unlike most other types of treaties, human rights treaties are typically formulated in very general wording,[128] that they give effect to important moral principles[129] and that they, especially regional instruments, are in many respects similar to constitutions.[130]

---

[124] E.g. *Russian Conservative Party of Entrepreneurs and Others v. Russia*, Nos. 55066/00 and 55638/00, Judgment of 11 Jan. 2007 (referring to a resolution of the Parliamentary Assembly and a code of good practice adopted by the Venice Commission) and *Bekos and Koutropoulos v. Greece*, No. 15250/02, Judgment of 13 Dec. 2005 (referring to a report of the European Commission Against Racism).

[125] B. Çali, 'Specialized Rules of Treaty Interpretation: Human Rights' in D. B. Hollis (ed.), *The Oxford Guide to Treaties* (Oxford: Oxford University Press, 2012), pp. 525–548.

[126] See e.g. M. Craven, 'Legal Differentiation and the Concept of the Human Rights Treaty in International Law', *EJIL*, 11 (2000), 489–519.

[127] '*Mapiripán Massacre*' v. Colombia, supra n. 85 (paragraph 104).

[128] See Çali, *supra* n. 125, at p. 530.   [129] See Letsas, *supra* n. 75, at p. 79.

[130] See *Loizidou v. Turkey* (Preliminary Objections), supra n. 57 (paragraph 75) (describing the ECHR as 'a constitutional instrument of European public order').

Given the special object and purpose – and, as a consequence, character – of human rights treaties, it is indeed inevitable that their interpretation differs from that of other treaties, especially in that State consent can only play a limited role. Most importantly, whether the respondent State agrees with a given interpretation of a human rights treaty cannot be a decisive factor. Therefore, it is correct to conclude that it does not matter whether an evolutive interpretation is supported by the subsequent practice of the respondent State or its ratification of other treaties. The more difficult question is to what extent the 'present-day conditions' or standards that give rise to a particular interpretation must be shared among the States parties. The supervisory bodies have been very lenient in this regard, sometimes explicitly rejecting the notion that there must be a common approach supporting a change in interpretation. A good illustration – and at the same time justification – of this interpretive approach may be found in a separate opinion of Judge Garlicki of the European Court of Human Rights. Pointing out that the ECHR 'represents a very distinct form of international instrument' whose 'substance and process of application are more akin to those of national constitutions than to those of "typical" international treaties', he invoked the Court's 'living instrument' approach and observed that '[t]his may result (and, in fact, has on numerous occasions resulted) in judicial modifications of the original meaning of the Convention'. He went on to state:

> From this perspective, the role of our Court is not very different from the role of national Constitutional Courts, whose mandate is not only to defend constitutional provisions on human rights, but also to develop them . . . Thus, it is legitimate to assume that, as long as the member States have not clearly rejected a particular judicial interpretation of the Convention . . . the Court has the power to determine the actual meaning of words and phrases which were inserted into the text of the Convention more than fifty years ago.[131]

However, what Judge Garlicki failed to mention is that there are also important differences between constitutions and the ECHR, not the least of which concerns the legitimacy of an evolutive or dynamic approach to interpretation. In the case of a constitution, an evolutive interpretation by the constitutional court can be limited or corrected through the democratic process of amending the constitution. In the case of the ECHR as

---

[131] *Öcalan v. Turkey* [GC], No. 46221/99, Judgment of 12 May 2005, ECHR 2005-IV, partly concurring, partly dissenting opinion of Judge Garlicki (paragraph 4).

a multilateral treaty, in contrast, a State that objects to a particular interpretation may only withdraw from the Convention, which is normally a politically unrealistic option. An evolutive interpretation of a human rights treaty may thus not draw its legitimacy from the availability of a democratic corrective; it can only draw it from the consent of as many States parties as possible.

The supervisory bodies must be – and clearly are – aware that they must balance dynamic interpretation against the need for State support and expectations regarding legal certainty. Seen from this perspective, it becomes clear that invocations of the 'living instrument' notion are frequently intended precisely to garner State support for a particular interpretation. In *Tyrer*, for instance, there was no other reason for the Court to characterise the ECHR as a 'living instrument': its finding clearly suggests that all corporal punishment is inherently degrading, regardless of how many States have abolished it or what the public opinion on the matter is. The only reason for the Court to highlight developments in the member States, which, after all, needed to be taken into account when interpreting the Convention as a 'living instrument', was to generate support for its interpretation of Article 3. The same can be observed with regard to many of the other cases discussed previously: the 'living instrument' notion is not instrumental to the respective supervisory body's holding, but added as a kind of side-note to show that a particular understanding of the treaty is, in any event, reflected in State practice or international legal instruments or that there are, at least, signs of a trend towards such an understanding.

While such use of the 'living instrument' method is understandable, it often confuses things more than contribute to anything. Where, as in *Tyrer*, there are compelling reasons for a given interpretation, there is no need to invoke the 'living instrument' character of a treaty: if it is true that human rights give effect to 'higher shared values', it cannot matter whether States think a given treatment is degrading or not. When it *is* invoked, the respective supervisory bodies should, at the very least, take care to explain why and in how far exactly subsequent State practice or developments in international law matter and, of course, back up the alleged practice with evidence. It is not sufficient for them to merely cite the European Court's judgment in *Tyrer*: as explained previously, that judgment lacks any explanation of the 'living instrument' method of interpretation.

4   Arms Control Treaties

In the case of human rights treaties, the concept of 'living instrument' is used to explain (quasi-)judicial development of the relevant treaty, development which may well be ahead of State consensus. In the case of the UN Charter, interpretive development is in the hands of political organs and therefore puts the State back at centre stage, except that organs operate by way of majorities. The understandings of those majorities, for example as to what are the current threats to international peace, give the UN Charter life. The question remains as to whether treaties that do not have institutions (either judicial or political) at their heart can still be viewed as 'living instruments'. With regard to these treaties, the metaphor might not be invoked, but if they exhibit signs of life that allow them to develop to reflect wider changes then they are, to all intents and purposes, also 'living instruments'.

The argument in this section is that the concept of 'living instrument' is a metaphor that can be applied to a range of different types of treaties, so that it is untrue to say that this form of interpretive technique and understanding is confined to, say, human rights treaties or the UN Charter. Variation in interpretive techniques, and hence the amount of vitality within a treaty, is explicable on the basis of the different nature of the treaty being considered, whether they are contractual, law-making or constitutional. In general terms, this section illustrates the contention that, although the language of 'living instruments' is not used in relation to arms control treaties, the ideas and interpretive techniques involved are present in some of these treaties, although not in others.

In the modern era, treaty law purports to cover a range of different types of conventions. At the one end of the spectrum, there is the bilateral, contractual treaty. In the area of arms control, this is embodied by the now defunct Anti-Ballistic Missile (ABM) Treaty[132] and the Strategic Arms Reduction Treaties (START)[133] between the USA and the USSR/Russia.[134] In these treaties, there is greater certainty in the text as the terms were hammered out on a take-it-or-leave-it basis by the two parties. The rights and duties are relatively clear, and therefore, the text dominates the life of the treaty unless both parties agree on changes or, as

---

[132] 944 UNTS 13.   [133] 2264 UNTS 63.

[134] The analysis in this section draws on N. D. White, 'Interpretation of Non-Proliferation Treaties' in D. H. Joyner and M. Roscini (eds.), *Non-Proliferation Law as a Special Regime: A Contribution to Fragmentation Theory in International Law* (Cambridge: Cambridge University Press, 2012), pp. 87–118.

with the 1972 ABM Treaty between the USA and USSR/Russia, one party withdraws. This is not to state that the ABM Treaty was not an important treaty – it was the 'cornerstone of strategic stability' during the Cold War[135] – but it reflected the bilateral and bipolar nature of the Cold War. At the other end of the spectrum, there is a multiparty constitutional treaty that is both conventional and institutional,[136] laying down rules but also creating institutions and organs, paradigmatically the UN Charter discussed previously. However, as has been established when looking at human rights treaties, the metaphor of a 'living instrument' is not confined to those constitutional-type treaties but is also used with regard to certain law-making treaties that have an inbuilt dynamic, such as an expert committee or court, which can interpret the treaty in the light of changes in social conditions.

The question is whether there is any room for the idea of 'living instrument' in an area of law that is heavily State-dominated where clarity and certainty are important for the States parties. In these conditions, we might expect to find the opposite of 'living instruments' – lifeless, more accurately timeless, treaties under which States can operate in confidence, knowing that the obligations within them are not subject to change. However, as shall be seen, even arms control treaties can be – indeed, have to be – 'living instruments'; otherwise technological change would outstrip their normative reach. For instance, a prohibition on chemical weapons only works if we constantly re-evaluate our understanding of what chemical weapons are.

Unfortunately, arms control law is not populated with courts sitting in judgment, and thereby simultaneously applying and developing the rules contained in the three non-proliferation treaties to be considered in this section – the 1968 Nuclear Non-Proliferation Treaty (NPT),[137] the 1972 Biological Weapons Convention (BWC)[138] and the 1993 Chemical Weapons Convention (CWC).[139] They are all multilateral treaties, though the CWC is institutional as well as conventional, establishing the Organization for the Prohibition of Chemical Weapons (OPCW).

---

[135] J. B. Rhinelander, 'The ABM Treaty – Past, Present and Future (Part I)', *J. Conflict & Sec. L.*, 6 (2001), 91–114, at 92.

[136] The International Court of Justice has stated that the 'constituent instruments of international organizations are also treaties of a particular type ... Such treaties can raise specific problems of interpretation owing, *inter alia*, to their character which is conventional and at the same time institutional': *Legality of the Use by a State of Nuclear Weapons in Armed Conflict* (Advisory Opinion) (1996) ICJ Rep. 66, at p. 75.

[137] 729 UNTS 161.   [138] 1015 UNTS 163.   [139] 1974 UNTS 45.

This does not necessarily mean that only the CWC is a 'living instrument'; we have to go deeper to try to understand the nature of these treaties. In general terms, the overall purpose of these treaties is to address the 'horizontal proliferation of WMD' (weapons of mass destruction) with provisions 'proscribing possession, development, and transfer of both single-use WMD-related materials (i.e. those items and technologies primarily suited for use in WMD development programs) as well as dual-use WMD-related materials (i.e. items and technologies which have both civilian and military applications)'.[140] As well as aiming to prevent the proliferation of WMDs among a wider group of States, the treaties also aim to prevent the proliferation of weapons within States already possessing them ('vertical proliferation').[141]

In the seminal article written at the time of the NPT, Mason Willrich is clear about the significance of the treaty for achieving the 'goal of overriding importance in the nuclear era . . . the avoidance of nuclear war'.[142] The NPT was agreed in the Cold War period, when both superpowers desired to draw back from mutually assured destruction, and not only constituted a bargain between the superpowers on the possession and development of both nuclear weapons and nuclear power but was also law-making for the rest of the international community.

It is common to describe the NPT of 1968 as a 'grand bargain' between nuclear weapon States (NWS) and non-nuclear weapon States (NNWS). This suggests some sort of exchange between these two different groupings of States, thereby creating a static set of obligations and rights. Essentially, NWS were obliged not to provide WMD to NNWS and not to proliferate their own; indeed the obligation is to 'eventually disarm themselves of nuclear weapons'.[143] NNWS, on their side, agreed not to acquire nuclear weapons or to develop them themselves. 'In exchange for their commitment to forgo what would otherwise be their right, equal to that' of NWS, NNWS insisted not only on the recognition of their right to acquire 'nuclear technologies for the purpose of civilian power generation' but also on an obligation of NWS to help in the development of their civilian nuclear programmes.[144] In crude terms, the deal was for NWS to retain their right to nuclear weapons while NNWS gave up any right to

---

[140] D. H. Joyner, *International Law and the Proliferation of Weapons of Mass Destruction* (Oxford: Oxford University Press, 2009), p. xv.

[141] *Ibid.*

[142] M. Willrich, 'The Treaty on Non-Proliferation of Nuclear Weapons: Nuclear Technology Confronts World Politics', *Yale Law J.*, 77 (1968), 1447–1519, at 1449.

[143] Joyner, *supra* n. 140, at p. 8.   [144] *Ibid.*, at p. 9.

have them. In exchange for this deviation from sovereign equality, NWS promised to gradually disarm and to help develop peaceful uses of nuclear technology in NNWS. This bargain, according to Daniel Joyner, distinguishes the NPT as a contractual treaty from 'most other large multilateral treaties', for example, the Genocide Convention[145] and the 1982 United Nations Convention on the Law of the Sea,[146] which are law-making treaties where 'there is no consideration given between the States in exchange for the undertaking of obligations'.[147]

This suggests that the NPT is paradigmatically contractual, creating a certain (and static) set of rights and duties for both NWS and NNWS, a conception which does not seem to leave much room for the notion of 'living instrument'. While making an understandable argument, Joyner may be failing to distinguish between different forms of contract, in particular 'social contracts', which are much more profound than a contractual transaction whereby one party agrees to give up weapons if the other party does (as in the START). A social contract at the international level is found in the UN Charter, whereby the five Great Powers agreed to act as the world's police force in exchange for voting rights that no other member would possess. It is no coincidence that those five permanent members are the NWS at the heart of the NPT 'grand bargain', thus suggesting that the NPT is something more profound than an ordinary *traité-contrat*; indeed, it may be more constitutional than a *traité-loi* since it develops the 'grand bargain' found in the UN Charter by extending the inequality between the P5 and other members of the UN to the possession of nuclear weapons.[148] This suggests that although the NPT may be less dynamic than treaties that include within them modes for change (political, judicial or quasi-judicial organs), such foundational treaties will be adaptable to changing conditions if they are to keep their relevance; the question is how.

Of the five nuclear weapons States at the time of the NPT, three were original parties in 1968 (USA, USSR, UK), while two only became parties in 1992 (China and France). Further, though the treaty was originally adopted for twenty-five years, it was renewed indefinitely by consensus at the Review Conference in New York in 1995. This indicates that, despite the presence of a right of withdrawal (in Article X), in one sense the 'grand bargain' has become even stronger over the decades, though the

---

[145] *Supra* n. 33.   [146] 1833 UNTS 3.   [147] *Ibid.*
[148] See, further, T. M. Franck, *The Power of Legitimacy Among Nations* (Oxford: Oxford University Press, 1990), pp. 176–177.

spread of nuclear weapons to States outside the five indicates the strain it is under.[149] The essence of the NPT is that a handful of States have the right to nuclear weapons while others do not; but despite that inequality, the 'grand bargain', taken as a whole, is a constitutional treaty, and not only in an 'originalist' sense but in a 'living' sense. The NPT, like the CWC, has an institutional element (in the form of the IAEA) which assists in the development of the treaty by interpreting and applying it (especially Article III). As Richard Williamson states, the potential 'dual-use' capability of both nuclear materials and chemicals requires a 'high degree of intrusiveness' by the OPCW and the IAEA.[150] This dynamic interpretive element keeps the treaty alive, but this is perhaps not as important as the fluctuations in the 'grand bargain' underlying the NPT.

Thus, it is contended that the NPT forms part of the 'grand bargain' or social contract at the heart of the international legal and political order, alongside the UN Charter, and should be interpreted as a constitutional text, not a contractual one;[151] thereby placing equal emphasis on the purposes of the treaty, the practice of parties and the words of the provisions themselves. This is not the orthodox position, which portrays the 'grand bargain' in the NPT being a relatively straightforward exchange between two groups of States, which has remained static since 1968.[152] Under an 'originalist' interpretation of the NPT, all the elements of the bargain remain in place and in full force – that is, the obligations on NWS not to proliferate to NNWS (in Article I) and to negotiate nuclear disarmament (in Article VI) and in return the obligations on NNWS not to acquire nuclear weapons (in Article II), to develop peaceful uses of nuclear energy in accordance with Articles I and II (in Article IV) and to submit to safeguards agreements negotiated with the IAEA to prevent peaceful uses of nuclear energy being diverted to nuclear weapons pro-grammes (in Article III).

Joyner argues that this balance cannot be disturbed by subsequent interpretation and development. In fact, he argues that subsequent state-ments (after 1998, more vociferously after 11 September 2001) by some

---

[149] E. Louka, *Nuclear Weapons, Justice and the Law* (Cheltenham: Edward Elgar, 2011), pp. 98–122.

[150] R. L. Williamson, Jr., 'Hard Law, Soft Law, and Non-Law in Multilateral Arms Control: Some Compliance Hypotheses', *Chicago JIL*, 4 (2003), 59–82, at 72.

[151] But see M. J. Glennon, *The Fog of Law: Pragmatism, Security and International Law* (Stanford, CA: Stanford University Press, 2010), pp. 136–139, which argues strongly against 'entrenchment' of the NPT and instead argues for a more coercive counter-proliferation regime.

[152] Joyner, *supra* n. 140, at pp. 10–11.

NWS (especially the USA) emphasising non-proliferation obligations, and downplaying or eroding their disarmament obligations,[153] are incompatible with the NPT.[154] However, while it may be argued that in 1968 all the elements of the 'grand bargain' carried equal weight, as that was what was necessary to achieve the bargain, it is much more difficult to sustain that original understanding if that bargain is part of the international constitutional order, which should be open to development by the subsequent agreement and practice of States parties in accordance with changes in international relations. The avoidance of nuclear war by limiting the spread of nuclear weapons can be seen as the bottom line for the NPT, and this in itself would permit the prioritisation of non-proliferation over disarmament. However, the interpretation of constitutional treaties is driven not simply by a pragmatic understanding of the changing nature of international relations but by the changing understanding of States parties. Subsequent practice as a means of interpretation means that changes in emphasis within a constitutional regime must be supported by States parties. There is little indication from the five-yearly NPT Review Conferences that NNWS agree with NWS interpretations;[155] hence overall practice does not point to a changed understanding of the NPT. In fact, as Joyner points out, a purposive analysis of the NPT supports the original 'grand bargain' under which equal weight was to be given to all the elements,[156] including non-proliferation and disarmament. Thus, a constitutional approach to interpretation, which has regard to subsequent practice of the parties as well as the purposes of the treaty rather than just the text, produces a stronger reaffirmation of the 'grand bargain' than a textual approach.

Indeed, under a textual approach it is possible to read the non-proliferation provisions of Articles I and II NPT as embodying much firmer obligations on States parties (each NWS and NNWS 'undertakes not to . . .') than the disarmament obligation in Article VI (in which States parties 'undertake to pursue negotiations in good faith on effective measures relating to the cessation of the nuclear arms race at an early date and to nuclear disarmament'). The latter provision has been interpreted very narrowly indeed by one US representative on nuclear non-proliferation to mean that it contains no legal requirement to conclude negotiations,[157]

---

[153] *Ibid.*, at pp. 37–45.   [154] *Ibid.*, at p. 108.   [155] *Ibid.*, at pp. 45–46.
[156] *Ibid.*, at pp. 31–32 and 34.
[157] C. A. Ford, 'Debating Disarmament: Interpreting Article VI of the Treaty on Non-Proliferation of Nuclear Weapons', *Nonproliferation Rev.*, 14 (2007), 401–428, at 408.

disagreeing with the International Court of Justice in its advisory opinion of July 1996, which stated that 'there exists an obligation to pursue in good faith and bring to a conclusion negotiations leading to nuclear disarmament in all its aspects under strict and effective international control'.[158]

Thus, applying a constitutional approach to interpretation opens the NPT up to subsequent (re)interpretation by the parties. In fact, the consistent statements by NNWS (which are the vast majority of States parties to the NPT) that the different elements of the 'grand bargain' have equal weight in the treaty[159] are the key element in maintaining that interpretation. Focus has been on the States parties coming together in review conferences, differentiating the NPT from other constitutional treaties, such as the UN Charter where subsequent interpretation is undertaken by the political organs of the United Nations: the General Assembly, where all members are present; and the Security Council, where only fifteen members are present, including the P5. A difficult question in relation to the NPT is whether a constitutional approach to interpretation opens up the NPT for (re)interpretation by institutions which have responsibilities towards it. The IAEA can undoubtedly have an influence on the development of peaceful uses of nuclear power by NNWS through the development of safeguards agreements with NNWS under Article III NPT.[160] But can the Security Council have an influence on the non-proliferation elements in the exercise of its security functions? To admit this could be seen as allowing the NWS under the NPT (via their position as the P5 in the Security Council) to have an undue influence on the understanding of the obligations under the NPT. Security Council Resolution 1887 on nuclear non-proliferation and nuclear disarmament, adopted unanimously in September 2009, shows, as the title suggests, an emphasis on both non-proliferation and disarmament. The only equivocation in this regard is that while the resolution potentially regards violation of the non-proliferation provisions as a threat to international peace and security (and subject to Security Council competence and presumably measures), the obligation to disarm on NWS is not such a matter, though the resolution does call upon States to negotiate in good faith under Article VI NPT. But this simply reflects

---

[158] *Legality of the Threat or Use of Nuclear Weapons* (Advisory Opinion) (1996) ICJ Rep. 226, at pp. 263–264 (paragraph 99).

[159] D. H. Joyner, *Interpreting the Nuclear Non-Proliferation Treaty* (Oxford: Oxford University Press, 2011), p. 73.

[160] *Ibid.*, at pp. 92–93 (on IAEA's role under Art. III NPT). See, further, L. Rockwood, 'The IAEA's Strengthened Safeguard System', *J. Conflict & Sec. L.*, 7 (2002), 123–136.

the very nature of the inequality at the heart of the post-1945 international legal order, whereby the Great Powers (as NWS and as P5 members) are not subject to Security Council censure or measures. The resolution calls upon 'all States Parties to the NPT to cooperate so that the 2010 NPT Review Conference can successfully strengthen the Treaty and set realistic and achievable goals in all the Treaty's three pillars: non-proliferation, the peaceful uses of nuclear energy, and disarmament'.[161] Thus, the three pillars remain intact even when interpreted by the Security Council.

Equal emphasis on the three pillars of the NPT is also found in the final document of the 2010 NPT Review Conference,[162] which witnessed a return to consensus under the influence of President Obama and in light of a new START agreement between the USA and Russia. Thus, in 2009–2010, there was strong subsequent practice to support the continuation of the 'grand bargain' of the NPT, understood in a constitutional sense.

While the NPT can thus be characterised as a constitutional treaty, the BWC and CWC are 'merely' law-making treaties – though we still have to consider whether the presence of the OPCW makes a difference to the latter. The NPT is 'elevated' above the other arms control treaties for two reasons: first, the presence of the 'grand bargain' and, second, the fact that nuclear weapons are the most destructive and, paradoxically, are seen as the most legitimate of the WMD. This legitimacy is enhanced by the NPT itself,[163] which, unlike the other treaties, does not prohibit the WMD in question but just limits their proliferation. Nuclear weapons are allowed but only in the hands of the Great Powers, thereby acknowledging their central role in the international legal order.[164]

The BWC is a law-making treaty establishing a universal prohibition on the possession of such weapons, but because of the absence of institutional machinery, its implementation and its development has stagnated – it is not a 'living instrument'.[165] This is not untypical of law-making treaties agreed during the Cold War-era and can be contrasted with the CWC agreed in 1993, which, as well as containing a clear ban on chemical weapons, constituted the OPCW. Undoubtedly, it is important to have a ban on biological weapons, but, in the absence of similar

---

[161] At paragraph 6.   [162] Joyner, *supra* n. 159, at pp. 121–122.
[163] Joyner, *supra* n. 140, at p. 69.
[164] See further G. Simpson, *Great Powers and Outlaw States* (Cambridge: Cambridge University Press, 2004).
[165] Joyner, *supra* n. 140, at p. 123.

machinery, there is the obvious problem that non-proliferation depends solely on each State party accepting and implementing its obligations. Even under the later CWC, where there *is* oversight machinery, the lack of usage of the system that allows one State to challenge another[166] suggests that States are not always willing to look behind the veil of *pacta sunt servanda*.[167] However, dynamics are built into the CWC in other ways, with regular reviews of the operation of the convention by the conference of the parties, empowered 'to take into account any relevant scientific and technological developments'.[168] An Executive Council of the OPCW ensures the effective implementation of the CWC by, *inter alia*, supervising the Technical Secretariat.[169] This arm of the OPCW carries out inspections in States parties' territories on the basis of agreement between the organization and the State party[170] and in so doing is constantly interpreting the treaty. In addition, the treaty is kept up-to-date with changes in technology and scientific developments by any State party being allowed to propose amendments,[171] including to the Annex on Chemicals (which lists toxic chemicals and precursors).[172] Amendments, if accepted by the Executive Council, shall be made to the Annex if no State party objects. If there are objections, the proposal shall be considered at the next session of the Conference of the Parties and a decision shall be taken as a matter of substance,[173] which means by consensus, if possible, and, if not, by two-thirds majority.[174] As can be seen, there is a dynamism built into the CWC, which is largely State-led but also driven by technical expertise on the ground.

5 Conclusion

The notion of 'living instrument' has an intuitive appeal – as William Rehnquist once observed, only a necrophile would disagree that a living constitution is better than what must be its counterpart, a dead constitution.[175] The 'living instrument' metaphor may not be a completely accurate description for a legal instrument such as a treaty: it suggests that the treaty is alive when it is in fact the external

---

[166] Art. IX(9) CWC: *supra* n. 139.   [167] Joyner, *supra* n. 140, at p. 115.
[168] Art. VIIIB(22) CWC: *supra* n. 139.   [169] Art. VIIIC(31) CWC: *ibid.*
[170] Art. VIIID(39) CWC: *ibid.*   [171] Art. XV(1) CWC: *ibid.*
[172] Art. II(2)-(3) CWC: *ibid.*   [173] Art. XV(5) CWC: *ibid.*
[174] Art. VIIIB(18) CWC: *ibid.*
[175] W. H. Rehnquist, 'The Notion of a Living Constitution', *Texas L. Rev.*, 54 (1976), 693–706.

social conditions that are changing. However, those changing conditions may act to breathe life into treaties through the understandings and interpretations of organs (political, (quasi-)judicial or technical) and States parties. Thus, it is true to say that a treaty may have a 'living' element: namely, some internal features that allow interpretive actors (be they States or organs created by the treaty) to legitimately contribute to a developing understanding of its provisions, often as a result of external stimuli. Social change triggers change in the treaty through the medium of interpretive agents.

Thus, a treaty may indeed change in relation to changing social conditions and therefore justifiably be described as a 'living instrument'. However, this is only possible if the following two elements are present: first, it is a predominantly constitutional or law-making, rather than contractual, treaty; second, it has an inbuilt dynamic for change in the form of a court, a quasi-judicial body, a political organ, a technical body (such as the OPCW or the IAEA) or a regular (and active) conference of the State parties. It is the understanding of this body as a collective in relation to changed social conditions (and not the social conditions *per se*) that is the determinative factor. Under classical international law, only a 'living instrument' that is driven by the collective understandings of all the States parties could be seen as fully respecting the principle of consent. However, it is reasonable to conclude that, by agreeing to the establishment of a political organ of limited membership or one that adopts decisions by majority vote, States have accepted an erosion of their consent. This holds all the more true for a treaty that establishes a judicial or quasi-judicial organ, since the States parties have thereby accepted that the treaty will be developed by (quasi-)judicial interpretation.

Treaties with courts or quasi-judicial bodies are likely to have more 'life' than treaties that rely on a review conference of the State parties. However, the latter will more accurately reflect the views of States as to changing social conditions, so that any slight change in understanding will not only be indicative of signs of 'life' within a treaty but will *reflect* a change in State behaviour, something that is not guaranteed by dynamic judicial interpretation. Dynamic judicial interpretation of a treaty is an attempt to *influence* State behaviour to conform to changing social conditions. Courts employ the 'living instrument' notion as a legal concept to lend support to an interpretation of the treaty that may deviate from the original understanding of the State parties. This explains why human rights treaties are frequently described as 'living instruments', while arms control treaties are not. However, the analysis in this chapter shows that, in fact, there are also signs of 'life' in, for example, the NPT. These signs of 'life' are indicative of profound understandings by States of the precarious bargain that prevents mutual nuclear destruction. Even the apparently infertile soil of arms control treaties allows for limited 'life'.

7

Treaties and Their Preambles

JAN KLABBERS[*]

1 Introduction

Despite comprising the words with which most treaties open, preambles were long considered the appendices of international treaties: redundant, superfluous and rather risky in the wrong circumstances. Typically, the preamble is regarded as legally non-binding or, more accurately perhaps, as not giving rise to enforceable rights and obligations.[1] The preamble may enumerate some of the motives behind the conclusion of a treaty but is not considered to give rise to any practical legal effects: its role is generally considered to be largely metaphysical.[2] And yet the preamble may come to influence the standard interpretation of a text and even come close to being enforceable and should thus be composed with some care. Those who apply treaties tend to give meaning to the words used regardless of their place in the grander scheme of the treaty, and a promise made in the preamble may be as good as one made in the main body of text.

Since States may wish to manage 'the risks of international agreement',[3] the wording of preambles is often subject to intense negotiations,[4] creating the curious spectacle of heated debate on a part of an instrument that few profess to be really interested in. Martti

---

[*] I am indebted to Michael Bowman and Dino Kritsiotis for their many helpful suggestions.
[1] Surely, to claim that the parties may ignore or even go against the terms of a preamble would be difficult to justify, so in that sense, they are often regarded as legally binding.
[2] A rare exception is the decision of the Supreme Court of the Reich of 2 Sept. 1936, *In Re Kampfe*, reported in 8 Ann. Digest 428, at pp. 428–429. Here, the Supreme Court of Hitler's Germany held that a recital to provide legal assistance gave rise to a binding obligation but that specific modalities for legal assistance were lacking.
[3] See R. B. Bilder, *Managing the Risks of International Agreement* (Madison, WI: University of Wisconsin Press, 1981).
[4] Richard Gardiner notes that some preambles are negotiated with great care, whereas others are cobbled together by way of afterthought. See R. K. Gardiner, *Treaty Interpretation* (Oxford: Oxford University Press, 2nd ed., 2015), p. 206.

Koskenniemi has perceptively likened the preamble to both a celebration and a refusal.[5] On the one hand, it celebrates a text that it is not considered a relevant part of: witness the lofty language common to preambles, highlighting the moral achievement of the text that follows, none more so perhaps than the 1945 United Nations Charter's ideal 'to save succeeding generations from the scourge of war'.[6] On the other hand, the preamble also signifies a refusal: in Koskenniemi's pithy formulation: 'whatever it contains was not accepted as part of the text itself'.[7]

Not all treaties carry a preamble. In some cases, no agreement can be reached on the text of the preamble: the four Geneva Conventions of August 1949 form a celebrated example, as will be further discussed later. On other occasions, it may happen that the preamble is given such low priority that the negotiating States never get round to discussing it. This is said to have occurred with respect to the 1956 Protocol of Sèvres involving France, the United Kingdom and Israel, about which one commentator observes drily that it has no preamble 'because there was no time to compose one'.[8]

The academic literature on preambles is rather scarce. Anthony Aust pays scant attention to preambles,[9] and much the same applies to Paul Reuter[10] and even to A. D. McNair's classic study – the latter, its considerable size notwithstanding, does not contain an index entry on preambles.[11] The topic is also absent from the recent *Oxford Guide to Treaties*.[12] Commentaries on the 1969 Vienna Convention on the Law of

---

[5] See M. Koskenniemi, 'The Preamble of the Universal Declaration of Human Rights' in G. S. Alfredsson and A. Eide (eds.), *The Universal Declaration of Human Rights: A Common Standard of Achievement* (The Hague: Kluwer Law International, 1999), pp. 27–39. Note that this is not entirely in conformity with the Vienna Convention on the Law of Treaties, as will be discussed later.

[6] 1 UNTS 16. For a balanced discussion, see R. Wolfrum, 'Preamble' in B. Simma, D.-E. Khan, G. Nolte and A. Paulus (eds.), *The Charter of the United Nations: A Commentary* (Vol. I) (Oxford: Oxford University Press, 3rd ed., 2012), pp. 101–106. For a somewhat pedantic discussion, see H. Kelsen, 'The Preamble of the Charter – A Critical Analysis', *J. Politics*, 8 (1946), 134–159.

[7] Koskenniemi, *supra* n. 5, at p. 27.

[8] See A. Shlaim, 'The Protocol of Sèvres, 1956: Anatomy of a War Plot', *Int'l Aff.*, 73 (1997), 509–530, at 524.

[9] See, e.g., A. Aust, *Modern Treaty Law and Practice* (Cambridge: Cambridge University Press, 3rd ed., 2013), pp. 13, 207 and 210.

[10] See, e.g., P. Reuter, *An Introduction to the Law of Treaties* (Abingdon: Routledge, 2nd ed., 1995), p. 24.

[11] See A. D. McNair, *The Law of Treaties* (Oxford: Clarendon Press, 1961).

[12] See D. B. Hollis (ed.), *The Oxford Guide to Treaties* (Oxford: Oxford University Press, 2012).

Treaties (VCLT),[13] moreover, tend to discuss the preamble to that Convention itself but hardly address preambles in general.[14]

The Vienna Convention is ambivalent when it comes to the precise status of the preamble. It does not say anything on the form preambles should take, on what should or should not be included, on what counts as preamble, let alone on the legal effects of preambles. The word 'preamble' is mentioned only once, in the context of treaty interpretation, thus immediately suggesting that this is the only context in which the preamble is relevant. At first sight, Article 31(2) VCLT confirms that preambles are best seen as part of the 'context' of a treaty, mentioning the preamble in the same breath as annexes.[15] Yet it also suggests that the preamble and annexes are best seen as 'included' in the text of a treaty: the treaty's text then, including preamble and annexes, magically forms part of its own context.[16] This ambivalence can only be resolved by distinguishing a treaty from its substantive terms: on such a reading, the preamble forms part of the treaty but not of its substantive terms.

Terminology, too, is unstable. The various clauses that can be found in preambles are typically not referred to as norms or rules but rather as paragraphs, recitals or considerations. The latter term suggests a functional role: these are the 'considerations' that inspired the drafters. 'Paragraphs' and 'recitals', by contrast, would seem to be less purpose-oriented terms, although the former runs the risk of being confused for the component parts of treaty provisions – as in 'Article x, paragraph y'. With this in mind, I will generally refer to 'recitals', this being the least loaded term.

---

[13] 1155 UNTS 331.

[14] See O. Corten and P. Klein (eds.), *Les Conventions de Vienne sur le droit des traités: Commentaire article par article* (Vols. I–III) (Brussels: Bruylant, 2006) and *The Vienna Conventions on the Law of Treaties: A Commentary* (Vols. I–II) (Oxford: Oxford University Press, 2011). See, also, O. Dörr and K. Schmalenbach (eds.), *Vienna Convention on the Law of Treaties: A Commentary* (Berlin: Springer, 2012) and M. E. Villiger, *Commentary on the 1969 Vienna Convention on the Law of Treaties* (Leiden: Martinus Nijhoff, 2009).

[15] This is the standard reading: see, e.g., Gardiner, *supra* n. 4, at pp. 205–206, or the dissenting opinion of Judge Weeramantry in *Case Concerning the Arbitral Award of 31 July 1989*: Guinea-Bissau v. Senegal (Merits) (1991) ICJ Rep. 53, at p. 118 (holding that under the Vienna Convention the context of a treaty 'shall comprise in addition to the text, the preamble and certain other materials').

[16] The chapeau of Art. 31(2) VCLT reads: 'The context for the purpose of the interpretation of a treaty shall comprise, in addition to the text, *including* its preamble and annexes . . .' (emphasis added).

The purpose of the present chapter is to have a closer look at preambles, inspired by the impression that in recent years, preambles have grown considerably in size and in importance. The preamble is still not considered to give rise to enforceable rights and obligations yet somehow plays an indispensable role in international law and politics. Indeed, it is testimony to their relevance that sometimes recitals too come to be amended. An example is how the 1948 Treaty establishing the Western European Union was amended in 1954 to reflect the reintegration of Germany in post-war Europe. The 1948 preamble referred to the risk of German aggression; this was replaced in 1954 by a reference to the unity and progressive integration of Europe – the rewriting of history in one fell swoop.[17] A more recent example is that of the Protocol 15 to the European Convention on Human Rights, adding a new recital to the Convention's preamble introducing subsidiarity and solidifying the margin of appreciation doctrine.[18]

I will first take up the empirical claim that somehow the relevance of the preamble has grown considerably. Thereafter I will discuss the various legal effects that preambles may engender, which will be followed by the claim that a pivotal role for the preamble only makes sense on a reconceptualisation of the treaty as embodying disagreement.

Two caveats are in order. First, I will only discuss the preambles to treaties. Other instruments too often come with preambles: this applies to domestic legislation and constitutions[19] and applies in international affairs also to resolutions adopted by organs of international organizations, such as the General Assembly or Security Council,[20] as well as legislative instruments adopted within the European Union (EU).[21] It may even apply to what are ostensibly non-legally binding instruments: the

---

[17] 19 UNTS 51. The texts of the 1948 Brussels Treaty and the 1954 Paris Agreement can be found at www.weu.int.

[18] Protocol 15 is not yet in force: CETS No. 213.

[19] Notice how the preamble has become the venue for political debate in the Australian constitution (under construction) with regard to the position of indigenous Australians. See A. Twomey, 'The Application of Constitutional Preambles and the Constitutional Recognition of Indigenous Australians', *ICLQ*, 62 (2013), 317–342.

[20] Eric Suy pays considerable attention to the preambles of Security Council resolutions: see E. Suy, 'Le préambule' in E. Yakpo and T. Boumedra (eds.), *Liber Amicorum Mohammed Bedjaoui* (The Hague: Kluwer Law International, 1999), pp. 253–269, at pp. 263–268. See, also, Koskenniemi, *supra* n. 5.

[21] See, e.g., U. Grusic, 'Jurisdiction in Employment Matters under Brussels I: A Reassessment', *ICLQ*, 61 (2012), 91–126 (repeatedly referring to the preamble of an EU Council Regulation). A glorious example from EU law is Council Directive 2004/83/EC (on refugee protection), which boasts no less than 40 recitals!

1975 Final Act of Helsinki, a textbook example of such an instrument,[22] also comes with a preamble, as do instruments such as the 1990 Paris Charter for a New Europe.[23]

Second, what follows does not claim to be exhaustive of the available material. There are many cases by many courts and tribunals which contain a few lines on the relevance (*vel non*) of a treaty's preamble, and the recent proliferation of international tribunals makes it unworkable to identify all relevant cases within the confines of a book chapter. It would be even more unworkable to go through all treaties ever concluded (or even only all treaties currently in force) in order to gather metadata. What follows then represents a somewhat idiosyncratic overview, focusing largely on the practice of the International Court of Justice (ICJ) and its predecessor, the Permanent Court of International Justice (PCIJ), with a sprinkling of decisions from other courts and some non-judicial examples, and even the discussion of the relevant decisions of the ICJ is not comprehensive. The interest resides in fleshing out the main contours of the law relating to preambles and the latter's functions while allowing for the possibility of individual judicial decisions providing nuances or even falsification.

2   Changing Form and Substance

Historians with a penchant for the *longue durée* will appreciate that over the past five centuries or so both the form and substance of the preamble have undergone marked change. In terms of substance, preambles used to be, several centuries ago, little more than informative enumerations concerning the identity of those concluding treaties. As far as their form goes, moreover, while such enumerations could be lengthy (the names and titles of some of the plenipotentiaries could easily fill half a page),[24] they nonetheless remained limited to a few paragraphs.

Hence, it cannot exactly be claimed that preambles have traditionally always been brief and to the point. The preamble to the 1648 Treaty of Westphalia, for example, runs on for a considerable number of sentences, listing the revered authorities in whose names the treaty was to be

---

[22] ILM, 14 (1975), 1292–1299. See, further, Aust, *supra* n. 9, at p. 32.

[23] ILM, 30 (1991), 190–228. The form of the latter's preamble is more assertive than the usual aspirational nature of preambles, though; it does not have words such as 'mindful', or 'desiring', or 'considering' or 'recognizing'.

[24] See, e.g., the 1494 Treaty of Tordesillas between Spain and Portugal (http://avalon.law .yale.edu/15th_century/mod001.asp).

concluded.[25] Yet this particular preamble largely has the character of a *testimonium* (nowadays usually to be found at the close of a treaty and therewith marking a second appendix): there are few references to the goal of the Treaty of Westphalia in its preamble, unless one counts the somewhat oblique mention of the discords and disruptions that had plagued the Roman Empire in its opening sentence or the references to the glory of God and the benefit of the Christian world in its closing sentence.

Over the years, however, it became customary to add some *desiderata* to the preamble, although often still in combination with a *testimonium*. Already some of the Treaties of Utrecht (1713–1714) displayed such a combination, as witnessed by, e.g., the treaty between the United Kingdom and France.[26] It starts by listing the persons in whose name the treaty was concluded (Queen Anne for Great Britain, Louis XIV for France) and then provides a few reasons as to why the treaty was being concluded, referring to 'an earnest desire to increase the advantages of their subjects'.

The 1794 Jay Treaty between the United States of America and the United Kingdom reversed the order,[27] thus casting a shadow of the future. The brief preamble makes a few points about the desires of the two treaty-making nations (essentially: amity, commerce and navigation on the basis of reciprocity) and refers to the identities of the plenipotentiaries appointed by the King of Britain and the President of the USA. By contrast to the earlier practice, by now the *desiderata* were mentioned first.

The 1815 General Treaty of the Final Act of the Congress of Vienna still largely took the form of a *testimonium*: it enumerated the dignitaries concluding it and approved of their full powers and then immediately moved on to matters of substance. Still, the various treaties making up the total package agreed on in Vienna[28] do contain some matters that are recognisable as preambular recitals to today's international lawyer. Thus, the treaty between Russia and Austria mentions that their States were 'equally desirous of coming to an amicable understanding upon the measures most proper to adopt for consolidating the welfare of the Polish people' and 'wishing at the same time to extend the effects of this benevolent disposition to the provinces and districts which

---

[25] 1 CTS 271.   [26] 27 CTS 475.   [27] 52 CTS 243.

[28] The multilateral treaty was still relatively unknown and often consisted of sets of related bilateral treaties, although sometimes accompanied by a multilateral Final Act: 64 CTS 453.

composed the ancient kingdom of Poland'. The treaty between Prussia and Saxony, part of the same package, provided in its preamble that the parties were 'animated with the desire of renewing the ties of friendship and good understanding which have so happily subsisted between their respective states' and were 'anxious to contribute towards the re-establishment of order and tranquility [sic] in Europe'. Yet these were the only *desiderata* mentioned.

It was only later during the nineteenth century, it seems, that the preamble took on today's shapes with greater finality. A curious example is the 1868 St. Petersburg Declaration which, its designation notwith-standing, is a treaty.[29] Its preamble is almost as large as its dispositive, but this is partly due to the brevity of the latter: five recitals followed by five operative paragraphs.[30] The first Hague Convention of 1899, on the Pacific Settlement of International Disputes, has a nice list of some eight recitals.[31] The second, famously, not only lists a number of *desiderata* but also records the absence of agreement and proposes what became later known as the Martens clause in order to fill the resulting gap.[32] The third, however, has only one recital.[33]

It would seem that, over the years, two trends became established. The first is that the preamble has evolved from being something along the lines of a *testimonium* into a set of considerations and desires. The second is that the enumeration of considerations and desires has tended to become longer. The first trend seems to be more settled than the second: it is rare these days to see a recently concluded preamble which merely lists the names and positions of the representatives of the contracting parties. Instead, well-nigh all preambles now record the wishes and hopes of the contracting parties.

The second trend may be the more interesting, though, with many recently concluded treaties comprising ten or twelve or even more recitals. Recent high-profile treaties that fit this description include the 1998 Rome Statute of the International Criminal Court (eleven recitals),[34] the 1999 International Convention for the Suppression of the Financing of Terrorism (twelve),[35] the 1998 International Convention for the Suppression of Terrorist Bombings (eleven),[36] the

---

[29] 138 CTS 297.

[30] Note that the preamble of the 1928 Briand-Kellogg Pact is actually longer than the text of the Pact itself, both in terms of number of words used and in terms of recitals (four) versus articles (three): 205 CTS 233.

[31] 187 CTS 410.   [32] 187 CTS 429.   [33] 187 CTS 443.   [34] 2187 UNTS 90.

[35] 2178 UNTS 197.   [36] 2149 UNTS 284.

1997 Convention on the Law of the Non-navigational Uses of International Watercourses (twelve),[37] the 1995 Straddling Fish Stocks Agreement (ten),[38] the 1989 Convention on the Rights of the Child[39] (thirteen) and the 1978 Vienna Convention on Succession of States in Respect of Treaties (eleven).[40] In particular, environmental treaties tend to include quite a few recitals in their preambles. Partly, this may be due to the highly technical nature of the enterprise: the preamble can inform non-experts (judges, administrators, diplomats) of the considerations that formed part of the background. Partly, it may also be due to the deep political cleavages on how best to protect the environment. Examples include the 2001 Stockholm Convention on Persistent Organic Pollutants[41] (twenty recitals) and the 1992 Convention on Biological Diversity (twenty-three recitals).[42]

There are also recent treaties concluded with, seemingly, a more modest number of recitals. One example is the 2004 United Nations Convention on Jurisdictional Immunities of States and their Property,[43] with a modest five recitals, and the same number of recitals makes up the preamble to the 1994 Agreement establishing the World Trade Organization.[44] Moreover, at first glance the 2000 United Nations Convention against Transnational Organized Crime (the Palermo Convention) has no preamble at all.[45]

Yet these examples of relative brevity may well be deceptive. The Palermo Convention, for example, is preceded by a General Assembly Resolution which itself has a lengthy preamble of ten recitals and a further twelve operative provisions.[46] Likewise, the Convention on Jurisdictional Immunities also comes with a General Assembly resolution, with nine recitals and four operative paragraphs.[47] And while the Agreement establishing the WTO may have a modest preamble of its own, it is embedded in the Final Act Embodying the Results of the Uruguay Round of Multilateral Trade Negotiations (a further six paragraphs),[48] which is preceded by an eight-paragraph Marrakesh Declaration which itself has a preamble of five recitals.[49] Hence, Article

---

[37] ILM, 36 (1997), 700–720.   [38] 2167 UNTS 88.   [39] 1577 UNTS 3.   [40] 1946 UNTS 3.
[41] 2256 UNTS 119.
[42] 170 UNTS 79. The 2000 Cartagena Protocol to the Biodiversity Convention has an additional eleven recitals: 226 UNTS 208.
[43] ILM, 44 (2005), 801–814.   [44] 1865 UNTS 154.   [45] ILM, 40 (2001), 335–394.
[46] General Assembly Resolution 55/25 (8 Jan. 2001).
[47] General Assembly Resolution 59/38 (2 Dec. 2004).   [48] 1867 UNTS 3.
[49] Available at: www.wto.org/English/docs_e/legal_e/marrakesh_decl_e.htm.

1 of the Agreement establishing the WTO is preceded by no fewer than twenty-two recitals. Curiously, the preamble to the 1961 European Social Charter is followed not, as one would expect, by an enumeration of rights as such but by an enumeration of nineteen policy goals.[50] This enumeration in itself functions much like a preamble, in addition to the 'real' preamble.

While the preceding list is, admittedly, a small sample, nonetheless it suggests two things. First, it suggests that, as a general rule, the size of the preamble is a function of the measure of agreement underlying the convention at issue. Put differently: the more controversial the topic or the more ambitious or technically complicated the regime envisaged in the treaty, the longer the preamble tends to be. It is probably no coincidence that the convention on jurisdictional immunities comes with a smaller preamble than the Palermo Convention, even taking into account how both are embedded in General Assembly resolutions. And likewise, it is probably no coincidence that treaties addressing difficult and politically sensitive topics such as terrorism, criminal law or environmental protection tend to have lengthy preambles.

Second, the precise context of a treaty may well influence matters. Thus, a treaty concluded under General Assembly auspices will feel the need to refer in its preamble to the Assembly's work, and much the same will apply to treaties concluded under the auspices of other international organizations, such as the Council of Europe. By the same token, treaties that are additional to existing treaties will need to refer to the already existing framework, and large-scale renewals such as the Lisbon Treaty re-modelling the European Union will need to refer to what happened previously.[51] Sometimes also circumstances in a State party, or in the general environment of a treaty, may have changed considerably, to the extent relevant for a new treaty commitment. If so, those changes must also find a place in the treaty's preamble. Thus, the preamble to the treaty revising Benelux, concluded in 2008, refers to the federalisation of Belgium as well as to the creation and impact of the EU, two developments that had not occurred when the original Benelux treaty was concluded in 1958.[52] In short: treaties embedded within existing

---

[50] 529 UNTS 89.   [51] [2007] OJ C306/1.

[52] This deserves a nuance, of course, in that the EU goes back to 1951. Still, the 1958 Benelux treaty was based on an agreement concluded in 1944 and could have hardly anticipated the success of the EU. Such changes must be distinguished from David Cameron's pre-Brexit suggestion to make what may amount to a reservation to the Treaty establishing the European Union in order to reflect British discomfort with the idea of the EU moving to

frameworks may have longer preambles than treaties concluded independently, as the existing framework needs to be acknowledged.

It would seem to follow that as a general rule, the preambles to multilateral treaties might be longer and more complicated than those accompanying bilateral treaties. Still, this need not necessarily be the case: a glance at recent bilateral treaties concluded by Finland reveals that, in bilateral relations too, preambles can occasionally be quite extensive. Examples include a 2011 agreement with Sweden on services relating to icy waters (seven paragraphs).[53]

On the other hand, a 2005 agreement with China on extradition from and to Hong Kong contains but a single preambular recital,[54] as does a 2010 taxation treaty with Belize.[55] An agreement concluded in 2011 with Luxembourg on exchange of classified information has two recitals,[56] while a 2011 agreement with the Republic of Kosovo on readmission of citizens is a borderline example: it has three recitals, but these are quite lengthy.[57]

The point to make then is not so much that size matters by itself but that the nature of any preamble may be influenced by a number of forces. One is whether the matter to be regulated is politically sensitive. Another is whether the treaty is embedded within a larger framework. A third is the complexity of the substance of the agreement. And a fourth factor is whether the treaty is to be regarded as contractual or, perhaps better, whether it is based on what political scientists have called 'specific reciprocity'.[58]

The hypothesis is that if based on specific reciprocity, a treaty has no need for elaborate and lengthy preambles, as there is fairly little discord

---

become an 'ever closer union'. See 'Never Closer Union', *The Economist* (London), 21 Oct. 2015.

[53] Incorporated in Finnish law by means of Decree 77/2013. On Finland's approach to incorporating treaties generally, see J. Klabbers, 'Coming In from the Cold? Treaties in Finland's Legal Order' in T. Koivurova (ed.), *Kansainvälistyvä Oikeus: Juhlakirja Professor Kari Hakapää* (Rovaniemi: Lapin Yliopiston Oikeustieteiden Tiedekunta, 2005), pp. 143–152.

[54] Incorporated by means of Decree 68/2013.

[55] Incorporated by means of Decree 70/2013.

[56] Incorporated by means of Decree 60/2013.

[57] Incorporated by means of Decree 54/2013. Note that Finland recognised Kosovo's statehood in March 2008.

[58] The seminal article, distinguishing between specific and diffuse reciprocity, is R. O. Keohane, 'Reciprocity in International Relations' as reproduced in R. O. Keohane, *International Institutions and State Power: Essays in International Relations Theory* (Boulder, CO: Westview Press, 1989), pp. 132–157.

to gloss over. Put differently, a treaty based on specific reciprocity ('do ut des', in classic jargon, or 'tit for tat', in more colloquial terms) will normally be of limited scope and will reflect the agreement of the parties: you hand over the suspects I want to prosecute or allow my products on your markets, and I will do likewise. If not so based, however, then the parties need to find a place for their discord: they cannot rely on the treaty itself to cover all bases. Hence, they will aim to utilise the preamble in order to tilt things in their favour by having it refer to ideas and ambitions or a normative framework or perhaps even something of a definition. The preamble therewith becomes an extension of the *negotiandum*, and while it may be the case, as Koskenniemi suggests, that the preamble contains the things that were left out of the treaty itself, nonetheless its relevance is keenly felt by the parties: it functions as the garbage can of disagreement or the dumpster of discord.

3   Legal Effects

Preambles are generally considered not to give rise to any particular rights or obligations under international law, and this circumstance immediately raises the functionalist question: if not binding or enforceable, then what good are they? Why even have a preamble, and what are its legal effects if not the creation of rights or obligations? It would seem that preambles can serve broadly five functions. First, preambles may help with the interpretation of the precise terms of treaties. Second, preambles can help to identify what the treaty concerned aims to accomplish: its object and purpose.[59] Third, preambles can be informative. Fourth, a preamble may claim to reflect a specific state of affairs and may do so in language that is quite unequivocal. In such a case, it would be difficult for the parties to the treaty concerned to later deny that the state of affairs was considered to exist at least at the moment the treaty was concluded; hence, it might be creative of something not unlike an estoppel. This is unlikely to apply to rules of behaviour but may have a bearing on factual or conceptual issues. Finally, preambles can come very close to being legislative in nature.

---

[59] See, also, the contribution to this volume of Kritsiotis at pp. 237–302 (Chapter 9).

3.1   Aid in Interpreting a Provision

Courts and tribunals, including the ICJ and its predecessor, have on various occasions relied on the terms of a treaty's preamble in order to gain an understanding of the terms of a treaty. An early occasion arose when the PCIJ was asked to address whether the International Labour Organization (ILO) had the competence to address whether an ILO Convention prohibiting women from working at night also covered women in supervisory positions. While the text at issue seemed to make no distinction whatsoever between women engaged in manual work and women engaged in supervision, the Court nonetheless wondered whether such a distinction should not be made. One of the sources it looked at was the Convention's preamble, which did not seem to distinguish between manual and other work.[60]

A few years later, in the *Pajzs, Csáky and Esterházy Case*, something similar came up. When the newly created state of Yugoslavia had instigated agricultural reforms during the 1920s, it expropriated land against compensation. Hungary was bound to pay reparations under the Treaty of Trianon, and this issue became entangled with the position of Hungarian landowners in Yugoslavia.[61] A series of four agreements (the Paris Agreements) was concluded in 1930,[62] also involving Rumania and Czechoslovakia, and preceded by a General Preamble. Hungary was a signatory of the General Preamble but not of Paris Agreement IV (setting up a special fund, as did Agreement III). The General Preamble specified that all four agreements were inseparable and interconnected, and the preamble of Agreement IV further specified that with respect to Hungary, 'the questions relating to the agrarian reforms have been settled'. The latter clause was relied upon by the PCIJ in finding that the Paris Agreements thus fully covered the situation of Hungarian landowners, precluding any fresh claims or new demands for compensation.[63]

It is perhaps useful to underline though that recourse to the preamble is by no means always necessary – or considered necessary – in order to

---

[60] See *Interpretation of the Convention of 1919 Concerning Employment of Women during the Night* (Advisory Opinion), 1932 PCIJ, Series A/B, No. 50, 365, esp. at p. 375.

[61] 6 LNTS 188.   [62] 121 LNTS 69.

[63] See *The Pajzs, Csáky, Esterházy Case*: Hungary v. Yugoslavia (Merits), 1936 PCIJ, Series A/B, No. 68, 4, at p. 60. If there is something incongruous in using the preamble of a treaty as an argument against a State not party to that same treaty, it could nonetheless be claimed that given the interrelated nature of the four agreements and the wording concerned, this situation stopped short of transgressing the *pacta tertiis* rule.

determine the meaning of a treaty provision. Thus, in its *Mazilu* opinion, the ICJ could confidently state that the purpose of section 22 of the 1946 General Convention on Privileges and Immunities of the United Nations was 'evident',[64] despite the brevity of the Convention's preamble and the absence of any *travaux préparatoires*: section 22 was only added at a late stage during the negotiations.[65]

3.2   Aid in Identifying a Treaty's Object and Purpose

In the *Case Concerning Rights of Nationals of the United States of America in Morocco*, the ICJ used the preamble of a Convention so as to shed light on what that Convention aimed to accomplish, or its 'purposes and objects', as the Court put it. The preamble at issue was clear on this and inspired the Court to reach the conclusion that it cannot construct the Convention in a way which would go beyond 'its declared purposes and objects'.[66] In the same case, the Court also referred to the preamble of the 1906 Act of Algeciras and again did so with a view to identifying the purposes of that Act.[67] Broadly speaking then, the Court twice referred to preambles to shed light not on individual treaty provisions but on the object and purpose of the treaty.

Such an approach is perhaps the most common whenever preambles are invoked: they are often relied on to further elucidate the object and purpose of a treaty as opposed to the object and purpose of discrete treaty provisions. Arbitrator Borel in the *Case of the Kronprins Gustaf Adolf and the Pacific*, in 1932, looked at the preamble in order to ascertain the 'chief object' of a treaty and did so following a prompt by one of the parties.[68]

---

[64] See *Applicability of Article VI, Section 22, of the Convention on the Privileges and Immunities of the United Nations* (Advisory Opinion) (1989) ICJ Rep. 177, at p. 194 (paragraph 47).

[65] *Ibid.*, at pp. 193–194 (paragraph 46), in which the Court notes that 'the contemporary official records do not make it possible to ascertain the reasons for the addition'. The Convention's preamble, incidentally, merely recalls Arts. 104 and 105 of the UN Charter.

[66] See *Case Concerning Rights of Nationals of the United States of America in Morocco*: France v. United States of America (1952) ICJ Rep. 176, at p. 196. Note that that French text of the judgment speaks of 'buts' (plural) but contrary to the English text allows only for a single object, consistently speaking of 'l'objet'.

[67] *Ibid.*, at p. 197.

[68] See *The Kronprins Gustaf Adolf; The Pacific*: United States/Sweden, Award of 18 July 1932, reported in 6 Ann. Digest 372, at pp. 374–375. The USA had argued that the preamble suggested that the chief object of the treaty concerned was 'to safeguard the sovereignty' of the contracting parties. This, Arbitrator Borel held, went too far.

Five years later, the PCIJ followed suit, referring to the preamble of a treaty concluded between Holland and Belgium in 1863 in order to identify the treaty's 'purpose'.[69] The European Court of Human Rights launched much the same idea in the classic *Golder* case, noting that 'the preamble is generally very useful for the determination of the "object" and "purpose" of the instrument to be construed'.[70] Likewise, the arbitrators in *Beagle Channel* felt that preambles 'may be relevant and important to the manner in which the Treaty should be interpreted, and in order, as it were, to "situate" it in respect of its object and purpose'.[71] In its advisory opinion on the removal of the WHO's regional office from Alexandria, Egypt, the ICJ identified the purpose of the host agreement between the WHO and Egypt by invoking its preamble.[72] In an interesting variation, the ICJ used the preamble of a later treaty to confirm the scope of an earlier agreement: it relied heavily on the preamble of the 1843 Boundary Convention between the Netherlands and Belgium to confirm the proposition that the 1839 Treaty of London marking the separation of the same two States intended to settle the contested territorial status of several communes.[73]

Domestic courts too have utilised the preamble as providing clues with regard to the object of a treaty. One example is the Swiss Federal Tribunal, which has held that the 'objective' of a treaty may 'sometimes' be ascertained with the help of the preamble, which 'indicates the principles contained' in the treaty.[74] Much the same, it seems, was in the minds of the Federal Constitutional Court of (then) West Germany when confronted with the claim that the 1972 Treaty between the Federal Republic and the German Democratic Republic was unconstitutional. The Court invoked the preamble of the treaty, which held that it was without prejudice to outstanding questions of principle (such as that of

---

[69] See *Diversion of Water from the Meuse*: Netherlands v. Belgium, 1937 PCIJ, Series A/B, No. 70, 4, at p. 9.

[70] See *Golder v. United Kingdom*, Judgment of 21 Feb. 1975, reported in ILR, 57 (1980), 200–261, at pp. 216–217 (paragraph 34).

[71] See *Beagle Channel Arbitration*: Argentina v. Chile, 18 Feb. 1977, reported in ILR, 52 (1979), 93–288, at p. 132 (paragraph 19).

[72] See *Interpretation of the Agreement of 25 March 1951 between the WHO and Egypt* (Advisory Opinion) (1980) ICJ Rep. 73, at p. 84.

[73] See *Case Concerning Sovereignty over Certain Frontier Lands*: Belgium v. Netherlands (1959) ICJ Rep. 209, esp. at pp. 221–222.

[74] See *Frigerio v. Federal Department of Transport*, Swiss Federal Tribunal, Decision of 22 Nov. 1968, reported in ILR, 72 (1987), 679–689, at p. 685.

national unification), and held that the preamble was 'essential to the interpretation of the whole Treaty'.[75]

It should be noted that the case law demonstrates to be perfectly able to identify a treaty's object and purpose also without the aid of the preamble. Sometimes, this can be explained by the extreme brevity or even absence of the preamble concerned, as in *Affo v. Commander IDF (West Bank)* concerning the preamble-less Fourth Geneva Convention.[76] In other cases it would seem that matters are less obviously dependent on the preamble, and perhaps a stark example is the advisory opinion of the ICJ in *Reservations to the Convention on the Prevention and Punishment of Genocide*.[77] This opinion contains a lengthy exposition of the principles underlying the Convention as well as the objects of the Convention but only refers to the Convention's preamble once, and then without providing it with an argumentative role.[78]

Possibly the most momentous invocation of a preamble by a tribunal is the celebrated *Van Gend en Loos* decision of what is now the Court of Justice of the European Union. *Van Gend en Loos* 'ushered forth' the constitutional order of the EU[79] and is hailed as 'arguably the most important decision ever' of the Court of Justice of the European Union (CJEU) and 'one of the most revolutionary ever given by a court'.[80] As is well known, the Court held the EU (European Economic Community (EEC) at the time) to constitute a 'new legal order', and one of the elements which drove the Court to this conclusion was the preamble of the EEC Treaty which, by referring to peoples as opposed to governments, 'confirmed' that the EEC Treaty 'is more than an agreement which merely

[75] See *Re Treaty on the Basis of Relations between the Federal Republic of Germany and the German Democratic Republic, 1972*, Germany's Federal Supreme Court, Decision of 31 July 1973, reported in ILR, 78 (1988), 149–178, at p. 167.

[76] See *Affo and Another v. Commander Israel Defence Force in the West Bank*, Israel Supreme Court sitting as High Court of Justice, Decision of 10 Apr. 1988, reported in ILR, 83 (1990), 121–197.

[77] See *Reservations to the Convention on the Prevention and Punishment of the Crime of Genocide* (Advisory Opinion) (1951) ICJ Rep. 15, at pp. 23–24.

[78] The Court refers to the universal ambition of the Convention 'in order to liberate mankind from such a scourge', with the quoted words referring to the preamble of the Convention: *ibid.*, at p. 23. Hence, the preamble serves not as elucidation or argumentation but is referred to for the poignancy of its formulation.

[79] The characterisation is Joseph Weiler's: see J. H. H. Weiler, 'The Least Dangerous Branch: A Retrospective and Prospective of the European Court of Justice in the Arena of Political Integration' reproduced in J. H. H. Weiler, *The Constitution of Europe* (Cambridge: Cambridge University Press, 1999), pp. 188–218, at p. 202.

[80] See D. Chalmers, G. Davies and G. Monti, *European Union Law* (Cambridge: Cambridge University Press, 2nd ed., 2010), p. 14.

creates mutual obligations between the contracting states'.[81] The use of the verb 'to confirm' might suggest that the Court reached that conclusion independently from the preamble, but this seems unlikely, as no independent grounds are mentioned: most elements of the Court's reasoning (the preamble, the creation of institutions and the preliminary reference procedure) are said to 'confirm' the nature of the treaty. The one exception is the reference to organs through which the citizenry can participate in decision-making, such as the European Parliament and the Economic and Social Committee – these 'must be noted'.[82]

The literature sometimes also has resort to the text of a preamble in order to figure out what an agreement hoped to accomplish. One example is how Yoram Dinstein interprets the 1953 armistice agreement between North and South Korea, the Panmunjom Agreement,[83] as having the objective not so much of achieving a peace settlement but of a complete cessation of hostilities pending a final settlement.[84]

Perhaps the most imaginative use of a preamble by the negotiating States resides in the preamble of the 1946 International Convention for the Regulation of Whaling,[85] as analysed by Michael Bowman. The 1946 Convention builds upon the 1937 International Agreement for the Regulation of Whaling, which, according to its preamble, was mainly set up in the interests of the whaling industry.[86] This now was deemed unacceptable by the drafters of the 1946 Convention, who thus felt the need both to build on the 1937 Agreement and simultaneously to distance themselves from that earlier agreement and did so by stating in the preamble to the 1946 Convention that it was 'based on the principles embodied in the provisions' of the 1937 Agreement rather than, as could have been expected, under reference to 'the terms' of the 1937 Agreement

---

[81] See Case 26/62 *Van Gend en Loos v. Netherlands Inland Revenue Administration* [1963] ECR 1.

[82] *Ibid.* The CJEU does not always refer to preambles when investigating the object and purpose of a treaty. Thus, it has presented strong statements regarding the object and purpose of free trade agreements with third States without illustrating whence it derived its conclusions in, for instance, Case 194/81 *Hauptzollamt Mainz v. Kupferberg* [1982] ECR 3641.

[83] 4 UST 234.

[84] See Y. Dinstein, *War, Aggression and Self-Defence* (Cambridge: Cambridge University Press, 6th ed., 2017), p. 46. Puzzlingly, though, he adds that the claim that the Korean War is technically still ongoing in the absence of a final settlement is 'untenable', without further argument.

[85] 161 UNTS 72.

[86] 190 LNTS 79. Even maintaining the stock of whales was aspired to in order to safeguard the whaling industry's interests.

or 'the 1937 Agreement as a whole'.[87] In the end, then, it is at least arguable that the preamble dictates not just how the text must be understood but also how it must not be understood.

Identifying the object and purpose of a treaty with the help of the preamble sometimes shades into more overtly normative argument, both in the literature and (arguably) in judicial practice. Among the better-known examples from the literature is Bardo Fassbender's reliance, in part, on the preamble of the UN Charter in order to bolster his thesis that the Charter is a constitutional document, unlike other treaties.[88] Much the same approach is adopted with respect to both the UN Charter and the ill-fated Draft Treaty establishing a Constitution for Europe by the late Ronald St. John MacDonald.[89]

Without explicitly referring to the preamble of the UN Charter, a similar argument was utilised by the ICJ when justifying the creation of what was, at the time, the United Nations Administrative Tribunal. Responding to the argument that the General Assembly – or indeed the UN at large – lacked the explicit power to set up such a tribunal, the Court observed that it would 'hardly be consistent with the expressed aim of the Charter to promote freedom and justice for individuals and with the constant preoccupation of the United Nations Organization to promote this aim that it should afford no judicial or arbitral remedy to its own staff for the settlement of any disputes which may arise between it and them'.[90]

3.3   Informative Purposes

It sometimes happens that the preamble is relied upon as a source of information as to how to understand a certain instrument or situation, not so much in terms of substance (this would be covered by the interpretative function of preambles) but rather in terms of status. Two examples may perhaps help to clarify the point.

---

[87] See M. Bowman, '"Normalizing" the International Convention for the Regulation of Whaling', *Michigan JIL*, 29 (2008), 293–500, at 386–390. See, also, the contribution to this volume of Moeckli and White at pp. 136–171 (Chapter 6).

[88] See B. Fassbender, *The United Nations Charter as the Constitution of the International Community* (Leiden: Martinus Nijhoff, 2009), esp. at pp. 90–92.

[89] See R. St. John MacDonald, 'The International Community as a Legal Community' in R. St. John MacDonald and D. M. Johnston (eds.), *Towards World Constitutionalism* (Leiden: Martinus Nijhoff, 2005), pp. 853–909.

[90] See *Effect of Awards of Compensation Made by the United Nations Administrative Tribunal* (Advisory Opinion) (1954) ICJ Rep. 47, at p. 57.

In one of the many stages of the Namibia saga before the ICJ, South Africa argued that the Mandate over what was then commonly referred to as South West Africa was not a treaty and therewith remained outside the ICJ's jurisdiction. The Court disagreed, holding that while the Mandate was confirmed by means of a League of Nations Council resolution, the Mandate itself was to be regarded as a treaty: 'The Preamble of the Mandate itself shows this character'.[91] Four years later, the Court would nonetheless decline jurisdiction, again invoking the Mandate's preamble in support: the preamble, holding in its third recital that the Mandate was to be exercised 'on behalf of the League of Nations', suggested that the legal ties created by means of the Mandate were ties between the Mandatory and the League of Nations, not between the Mandatory and individual member States of the League.[92]

In its judgment in *Case Concerning Gabčikovo-Nagymaros Project* in September 1997, the ICJ found on the basis of the preamble of the *compromis* by which Hungary and Slovakia had brought the case that Slovakia had to be regarded as the sole successor to Czechoslovakia. The preamble had been explicit, recording the parties' agreement to 'bear in mind' that the Slovak Republic was 'the sole successor State to the rights and obligations relating to the Gabčikovo-Nagymaros Project'.[93] The Court drew the following conclusion: 'According to the Preamble to the Special Agreement, the Parties agreed that Slovakia is the sole successor State of Czechoslovakia in respect of rights and obligations relating to the Gabčikovo-Nagymaros Project'.[94]

In other words, both cases are examples of the Court using the preamble as a reliable source of information regarding either the status of the instrument at issue or the legal status of one of the parties to the proceedings. The preamble is not used as a source of rights or obligations *per se* but is held to be probative with regard to legal status.

---

[91] See *South West Africa Cases*: Ethiopia v. South Africa; Liberia v. South Africa (Preliminary Objections) (1962) ICJ Rep. 319, at p. 330.

[92] See *South West Africa Cases*: Ethiopia v. South Africa; Liberia v. South Africa (Second Phase) (1966) ICJ Rep. 6, at p. 24.

[93] The text of the *compromis* is reproduced in *Case Concerning Gabčikovo-Nagymaros Project (Hungary/Slovakia)* (1997) ICJ Rep. 7, at pp. 10–13 (paragraph 2).

[94] *Ibid.*, at p. 81 (paragraph 151).

3.4 The Declarative Function

Sometimes – albeit on rare occasions, it seems – preambles may contain a declaration relating to a certain state of affairs. This is not the same as the more common idea of referring in the preamble to a generally accepted primary rule or principle,[95] in the way that the 2001 Stockholm Convention on Persistent Organic Pollutants refers in its preamble to the idea of precaution (this can be seen as a reference to the precautionary principle, albeit not a terribly explicit reference) and to the idea of permanent sovereignty over natural resources. In such a case, the reference does not seem to do much work beyond locating the intentions of the drafters: the drafters are telling the world that they worked with these considerations – and others – in mind. Arguably, if repeated, such references may emanate a normative force of their own, but in isolation it seems their effect is limited.[96] Much the same applies to the example of the 1906 Act of Algeciras incorporating a generally accepted norm – and therewith doing fairly little work.[97]

Instead, the more proper declarative effect of some recitals may well be illustrated with the help of the preamble to the 1986 Vienna Convention on the Law of Treaties concluded with or between International Organizations (VCLTIO).[98] For much of their lifetime, the treaty-making capacity of international organizations was disputed: while the ICJ had stipulated in its *Reparation for Injuries* advisory opinion that the UN was to be considered as an international legal person, its analysis seemed limited in scope to the UN[99] and seemed based, in part, on inductive reasoning: the personality of the UN was derived, in part, from the circumstance that it had concluded a number of treaties.[100]

---

[95] On the distinction between primary and secondary rules of law, see H. L. A. Hart, *The Concept of Law* (Oxford: Clarendon Press, 1961).

[96] The example is taken from M. M. Mbengue, 'Preamble' in R. Wolfrum (ed.), *Max Planck Encyclopedia of Public International Law* (Vol. VIII) (Oxford: Oxford University Press, 2012), pp. 397–400, at p. 400, who does not mention the reference to permanent sovereignty and seems a bit too sanguine in his representation of precaution as a reference to a legal principle (although this may be due to the strictures of an encyclopedia entry).

[97] Also mentioned in Mbengue, *ibid.*, at p. 399 (referring to *Case Concerning Rights of Nationals of the United States of America in Morocco: supra* n. 66).

[98] ILM, 25 (1986), 543–592.

[99] See *Reparation for Injuries Suffered in the Service of the United Nations* (Advisory Opinion) (1949) ICJ Rep. 174, at p. 185 (referring to the UN as having been created by the 'vast majority' of States and somehow linking this to the UN's objective legal personality). The VCLTIO has fifteen recitals: *ibid.*

[100] *Ibid.*, at p. 179. Note that the Court was rather liberal here, strongly suggesting that the UN was a party to the 1946 Convention on the Privileges and Immunities of the United

What was left unclear was whether the treaty-making capacity of international organizations flowed from their constituent instruments or whether it derived from general international law. Article 6 VCLTIO leans towards the former option, suggesting that the rules of the organization are decisive. The preamble however suggests the opposite: '*Noting* that international organizations possess the capacity to conclude treaties, which is necessary for the exercise of their functions and the fulfilment [sic] of their purposes'. This now has generally been accepted as the dominant interpretation: international organizations derive a general treaty-making capacity from international law, while their specific treaty-making powers depend on their constituent instruments.[101]

By the same token, some preambles declare rules or principles that seem to be generally recognised, and a prime example is found in the preamble to the Vienna Convention on the Law of Treaties itself. Its third recital, the result of some serious negotiations, 'notes' that 'the principles of free consent and of good faith and the *pacta sunt servanda* rule are universally recognized'. Interestingly, while the *pacta sunt servanda* rule has found specific elaboration in Article 26 VCLT, the notions of good faith and free consent have not found such specific elaboration, operating more by way of cross-cutting principles. As Shabtai Rosenne has noted, good faith is referred to in five of the Vienna Convention's provisions,[102] whereas the principle of free consent can be said to inform most provisions addressing the validity of

---

Nations: 1 UNTS 15. Alas, while the UN may well be considered the main beneficiary of said Convention, it is not and has never been a party. Perhaps intriguingly, moreover, while the Court paid quite a bit of attention to the ambitions of the UN, at no point did it feel the need to invoke the Charter's preamble in support: the analysis is based mostly on Arts. 1 and 2: see *ibid.*, at pp. 178–179.

[101] See, e.g., J. Klabbers, *An Introduction to International Institutional Law* (Cambridge: Cambridge University Press, 2nd ed., 2009), p. 252. But see E. David, 'Préambule– Convention de Vienne de 1986' in Corten and Klein (eds.), *Commentaire* (Vol. I), *supra* n. 14, pp. 17–25, at p. 23, suggesting that the international legal personality of international organizations implies a *jus tractati* which, in turn, derives from either express or implied powers and therefore owes nothing to international law as such unless powers are themselves conceptualised as deriving from international law – but this comes very close to a theory of inherent powers of international organizations.

[102] See S. Rosenne, 'Good Faith in the Codified Law of Treaties' reproduced in S. Rosenne, *Developments in the Law of Treaties 1945–1986* (Cambridge: Cambridge University Press, 1989), pp. 135–179; a brief discussion of the drafting history of the third recital can be found at pp. 138–139. See, further, the contribution to this volume of Ong at pp. 710–747 (Chapter 22).

treaties: the main common ground of invalidity, it seems, is a defect in the consent of States.[103]

The same does not apply to some of the other recitals of the Vienna Convention's preamble. It refers, for instance, to the peaceful settlement of disputes but does so in aspirational rather than declaratory terms, while the reference to the principles contained in the UN Charter may play a role in embedding the Convention but does not do much work otherwise. What is nonetheless still noteworthy is the eighth recital, which declares, after some discussion, that the rules of customary international law 'will continue to govern questions not regulated' by the Vienna Convention itself.[104]

The general point here is not so much that the preamble can be legislative or, somehow, binding. After all, if it qualifies as a rule to begin with, a conferment of treaty-making capacity is a secondary rule of the system rather than a primary rule of international law, and cross-cutting references likewise may not immediately be reducible to rules.[105] Instead, the general point would be that preambles may provide building bricks when it comes to the identification of secondary rules (or principles) of law and, perhaps even more importantly, the concepts of international law. The problem with these is, after all, that they often defy attempts at legislation: one cannot legislate such things as treaty-making capacity or free consent or good faith in quite the same way as one can legislate against torture. Indeed, it would be inappropriate – and sometimes philosophically impossible – to do so explicitly: a treaty clause providing that, from now on, international organizations derive their treaty-making capacity from international law is bound to be problematic, partly because the circle of parties to the treaty may remain small and partly because it presupposes that States have the power to make the law as it applies to international

---

[103] See J. Klabbers, 'The Validity and Invalidity of Treaties' in Hollis (ed.), *supra* n. 12, pp. 551–575. The one exception is Art. 53. Arts. 46 to 52 all address a problem with the consent of States. A slight nuance is in place: some of the relevant provisions deal with the formation of consent on the domestic level and thus do not directly address the *freedom* of consent. See, further, the contribution to this volume of Craven at pp. 103–135 (Chapter 5).

[104] See, generally, H. Pazarci, 'Préambule – Convention de Vienne de 1969' in Corten and Klein (eds.), *Commentaire* (Vol. I), *supra* n. 14, pp. 1–16.

[105] Note how the ICJ has observed that good faith in itself is not capable of generating a legal obligation where otherwise none would exist. See *Border and Transborder Armed Actions*: Nicaragua v. Honduras (Jurisdiction and Admissibility) (1988) ICJ Rep. 69, at pp. 105–106 (paragraph 94).

organizations.[106] By contrast, there is nothing inappropriate in making an observation in a preamble ('noting'), and the force of the observation can hardly be affected by the limited amount of ratifications.[107]

3.5 The Legislative Function

Sometimes preambles can be said to have – or aspire to – something akin to a legislative effect. The 1928 Briand-Kellogg Pact provides in its preamble that parties resorting to war 'should be denied the benefits furnished' by the Pact, and at least one international lawyer of repute has interpreted this as a 'positive proposition of international law': as a matter of law, a breach of the Pact 'involves the forfeiture of the benefits' of the Pact.[108] Perhaps not too much should be made of this, in the sense that contemporary opinion seemed to hold that this applied to treaties at any rate in the form of the *inadimplenti non est adimplendum* principle,[109] and several parties held that the Pact would not affect their right to use force in self-defense.[110]

Likewise, the preamble to the 1961 European Social Charter oozes a legislative ambition. The Charter does not contain an explicit provision on equal treatment or non-discrimination (with the exception of equal pay for equal work in Article 4), but its preamble includes a general provision in aspirational but not too freewheeling terms: 'the enjoyment of social rights should be secured without discrimination on grounds of race, colour, sex, religion, political opinion, national extraction or social origin'.[111]

---

[106] One of the curiosities with the VCLTIO is precisely this: it aims to regulate the behaviour of organizations, but their expressions of consent to be bound have no immediate legal value, in that only State ratifications can bring the convention into force: *supra* n. 98.

[107] After all, the VCLTIO has yet to enter into force: *ibid.*

[108] See J. F. Williams, 'Recent Interpretations of the Briand-Kellogg Pact', *Int'l Aff.*, 14 (1935), 346–368, at 347.

[109] See the dissenting opinion of Judge Anzilotti in *Diversion of Water from the Meuse, supra* n. 69, at p. 50: the *inadimplenti* principle 'is so just, so equitable, so universally recognized, that it must be applied in international relations also'.

[110] See R. Lesaffer, 'Kellogg-Briand Pact (1928)' in R. Wolfrum (ed.), *Max Planck Encyclopedia of Public International Law* (Vol. VI) (Oxford: Oxford University Press, 2012), pp. 579–584.

[111] Note that as revised in 1996, the Charter says a little more, in that Article E now holds that 'differential treatment based on an objective and reasonable justification shall not be deemed discriminatory', which would suggest differential treatment without proper justification is seen as prohibited. See, also, Council of Europe, *Digest of the Case Law of the European Committee on Social Rights* (Strasbourg: Council of Europe, 2008). I am

A more recent potentially legislative effect can be found in some bilateral investment treaties. The 2011 investment treaty between Japan and Colombia may be said to contain a stand-still provision in one of its recitals: recital 4 recognises that prosperity and development can be achieved 'without relaxing health, safety and environmental measures of general application'.[112] It would be difficult to construe this in any manner other than a mutual promise not to relax existing measures. Put differently, should one of the parties reduce health or safety requirements, it may well be held in violation of the treaty. Note that, curiously perhaps, Article 21 of the same treaty expressly discourages the relaxation of health, safety and environmental standards (as well as the lowering of labour standards, missing from the preamble) in order to attract foreign direct investment but does so in language which can almost be deemed softer than the language contained in the preamble: the parties recognise that it 'is inappropriate' to try to attract foreign investment by lowering standards, and thus the contracting parties 'should not waive or otherwise derogate' from current standards, at least not for purposes of attracting foreign investment.

The idea behind Protocol 15 to the European Convention on Human Rights, briefly mentioned earlier, is obviously legislative. It introduces the idea of subsidiarity and solidifies the margin of appreciation doctrine, a doctrine developed by the Court which holds, in a nutshell, that national authorities might be better placed to assess locally prevailing circumstances than the Strasbourg Court itself.[113]

Perhaps the judgment of the ICJ in *Case Concerning Military and Paramilitary Activities in and against Nicaragua* deserves separate mention here, as it is arguable that the Court came quite close to assigning legal force to the recitals or, more precisely, to the object and purpose of the 1956 Treaty of Friendship, Commerce and Navigation between Nicaragua and the United States.[114] Having first warned that acts cannot be seen as having been intended to deprive a treaty of its object and

---

indebted to my colleague Jarna Petman, a former member of the Committee, for helpful discussion on this point.

[112] The 2007 BIT between the Netherlands and Burundi, drafted in French, contains a similar recital but without corresponding provision in the treaty itself. The third recital holds that development and fair treatment of investments can be achieved 'sans porter préjudice aux mesures applicables sur le territoire de chacune des Parties Contractantes à la protection de la santé, de la sécurité et de l'environnement'.

[113] A useful discussion of the doctrine is contained in G. Letsas, *A Theory of Interpretation of the European Convention on Human Rights* (Oxford: Oxford University Press, 2007).

[114] 367 UNTS 3.

purpose if those acts are envisaged in the text of the treaty itself,[115] it continued by holding that 'there are certain activities of the United States which are such as to undermine the whole spirit of a bilateral agreement directed to sponsoring friendship between the two States parties to it', such as direct attacks on ports or oil installations or the mining of ports: 'Any action less calculated to serve the purpose of "strengthening the bonds of peace and friendship traditionally existing between" the Parties, stated in the Preamble of the Treaty, could hardly be imagined'.[116]

4 Treaties and Disagreement: The Role of the Preamble

Treaties have traditionally been conceptualised as 'meetings of the minds': State A and State B would meet, agree to do X, put their agreement on paper, et voilà: a treaty was born. On such an understanding of the notion of treaty, the role of the preamble would be limited but clear: preambles are, in the words of Makane Moïse Mbengue, best seen as 'indicia of the intention of the parties to a treaty'.[117] And on such a conceptualisation, it does indeed make sense to speak, as Mbengue does, of a singular 'intention' behind a treaty: the States have reached agreement, and this agreement now manifests their common intention.[118]

Obviously, this conceptualisation of the notion of treaty owes much to inspirations from the classical model of contract law,[119] and obviously, this conceptualisation functions best when the treaty concerned can be classified as contractual in nature or can be seen to be based on specific reciprocity. In such a setting, the preamble may serve to decorate and embellish the transaction (I use the word 'transaction' advisedly) but will not do a lot of work: if States agree to do X in exchange for Z – and this has to be the presumption behind each and every contractual agreement – they do not really need the preamble. Hence, it should come as no

---

[115] See *Case Concerning Military and Paramilitary Activities in and against Nicaragua*: Nicaragua v. United States of America (Merits) (1986) ICJ Rep. 14, at p. 136 (paragraph 272).

[116] *Ibid.*, at p. 138 (paragraph 275). For further discussion, see J. Klabbers, 'Some Problems Regarding the Object and Purpose of Treaties', *Finnish YbIL*, 8 (1997), 138–160, at 155–159.

[117] See Mbengue, *supra* n. 96, at p. 397 (italics in original).

[118] Note that elsewhere he speaks, again in the singular, of preambles as explaining the 'policy rationale' behind the conclusion of a treaty: *ibid.*, at p. 399.

[119] This is not to say that this classical model is itself beyond criticism. See, e.g., P. S. Atiyah, *Essays on Contract* (Oxford: Clarendon Press, 1986) and J. Wightman, *Contract: A Critical Commentary* (London: Pluto Press, 1996).

surprise that bilateral treaties, often being contractual in nature, typically do not boast lengthy preambles, as the reciprocal promise to engage in mutually beneficial behaviour is its own reward. At best, sometimes a recital may be inserted to help convince a domestic audience but, as Aust notes, with respect to bilateral treaties there 'is seldom need for more than a few preambular paragraphs, if any'.[120]

Still, not all bilateral treaties can easily be classified as 'contractual' in nature. Some of these do not have as their object an exchange of goods or services or even territory but instead aspire to create a relationship of longer duration, and the clearest example here is made up of the large category of treaties on Friendship, Commerce and Navigation (FCN). In the same way as a marriage involves two individuals but can hardly be categorised as purely contractual, so too can FCN treaties not be seen as simple contractual arrangements based on a clearly identifiable 'do ut des'. It has been noted that the conclusion of FCN treaties is no longer common practice, its functions having been taken over by and large by more specialised (and sometimes multilateral) trade agreements and investment treaties,[121] but nonetheless, it is precisely the general nature of the relationship established by FCN treaties which has ensured that they have relatively often become objects of litigation.[122]

While some multilateral treaties can be regarded as contractual or can be re-characterised as embodying bilateral contractual relationships,[123] quite a few multilateral treaties nonetheless resist conceptualisation as contracts. International lawyers have aimed to capture this in launching categories of 'law-making' and 'institutional' treaties[124] in addition to contractual treaties, or speaking of 'normative multilateral instruments' or variations thereon,[125] but without being very successful at making the distinction airtight. Still, there is widely shared intuition that some

---

[120] See Aust, *supra* n. 9, at p. 366.

[121] See A. Paulus, 'Treaties of Friendship, Commerce, and Navigation' in R. Wolfrum (ed.), *Max Planck Encyclopedia of Public International Law* (Vol. IX) (Oxford: Oxford University Press, 2012), pp. 1140–1144.

[122] Given the general paucity of bilateral agreements (other than boundary treaties) making an appearance before the ICJ, FCN treaties appear to be fought over relatively often.

[123] A multilateral extradition treaty, e.g., will typically create bilateral extradition relationships between the state asking for extradition and the delivering state.

[124] McNair classically distinguished between treaties as conveyances, as contracts, as law-making instruments, and as charters of incorporation. See A. D. McNair, 'The Functions and Differing Legal Character of Treaties', *BYbIL*, 11 (1930), 100–118.

[125] See B. Simma, 'From Bilateralism to Community Interest in International Law', *Hague Recueil*, 250 (1994–IV), 221–384.

categories of treaties (in particular perhaps human rights treaties)[126] are different in nature from contractual arrangements.

In this light, it is hardly a coincidence that law-making treaties tend to have larger and more elaborate preambles than contractual treaties: if contractual treaties can be said to embody a 'meeting of the minds', a merging of intentions, this is less obviously the case with law-making treaties. Instead, law-making treaties aim to forge a common text out of the widely disparate intentions of the various participating States[127] and can thus hardly be said to represent a meeting of the minds except perhaps on an unhelpfully high level of abstraction.

Small wonder then that in particular law-making treaties are often accompanied by many reservations:[128] States that have 'lost out' during negotiations need a way to accommodate the treaty with their own intentions or with their own legal systems and prevailing local moralities.[129] Likewise, it is hardly a coincidence that environmental agreements (also difficult to reduce to purely contractual relations) have pioneered the idea of 'common, but differentiated responsibilities': while the overarching intention may be the same for all parties, their capacities will differ, as will their local sensibilities and sensitivities.[130]

If reservations and similar instruments (interpretive declarations, non-self-executing declarations) and the institution of 'common but differentiated responsibilities' represent two different techniques of accommodating political, economic and ethical differences between States,[131] the preamble may serve a similar function. Sometimes it is used as the receptacle for propositions that do not manage to acquire majority support during negotiations or for propositions that while acceptable in

---

[126] See M. Craven, 'Legal Differentiation and the Concept of the Human Rights Treaty in International Law', *EJIL*, 11 (2000), 489–519.

[127] This presumes that states can be said to have psychological conditions, such as intentions, to begin with.

[128] Emblematic is L. Lijnzaad, *Reservations to UN-Human Rights Treaties: Ratify and Ruin?* (Dordrecht: Martinus Nijhoff, 1994).

[129] The point is well-made by S. Marks, 'Three Regional Human Rights Treaties and the Experience of Reservations' in J. P. Gardner (ed.), *Human Rights as General Norms and a State's Right to Opt Out: Reservations and Objections to Human Rights Treaties* (London: British Institute of International & Comparative Law, 1997), pp. 35–63.

[130] See, also, the contributions to this volume of Bowman and French and Scott at pp. 392–439 (Chapter 13) and 677–709 (Chapter 21) respectively.

[131] A third may be the option of concluding a soft law arrangement rather than a treaty, although this should be approached with skepticism on theoretical as well as rule of law grounds. For discussion, see J. Klabbers, *The Concept of Treaty in International Law* (The Hague: Kluwer Law International, 1996).

principle elude a commonly accepted formulation. Conversely, some-times disputed topics cannot be agreed on at all, not even in the form of a preambular recital. An example from the drafting of the Vienna Convention itself is that a proposed recital referring to the 'right' of every State to enter into treaty relations was defeated: it stumbled over widespread disagreement as to the position of non-recognised States, which at the time was a highly topical issue.[132]

It may also happen that a proposed recital is defeated but given a place in another of the myriad documents that may accompany multilateral agreements.[133] An example is the French suggestion to include in the preamble to the 1951 Convention Relating to the Status of Refugees a clause expressing hope that the Convention would serve as guidance to all nations beyond the scope of the Refugee Convention itself.[134] This did not make it into the preamble (the United Kingdom eventually resisted, and France by then had changed its position) but was finally incorporated, in modified form, in a recommendation of the Conference of Plenipotentiaries accompanying the 1951 Refugee Convention.[135]

A famous set of examples where the entire preamble was ultimately defeated relates to the four 1949 Geneva Conventions.[136] While the ICRC had drafted a joint preamble for all four conventions which initially met with little objection, at some point during the negotiations things heated up. One set of delegates urged that references in the ICRC draft to the dignity of human beings should be accompanied by 'an affirmation of the

---

[132] See the brief rendition in Villiger, *supra* n. 14, at p. 45. In particular the status of East Germany was highly contested, which did not prevent western states from having extensive treaty contacts with the GDR. For in-depth discussion, see B. R. Bot, *Non-Recognition and Treaty Relations* (Leiden: A.J. Sijthoff, 1968).

[133] These may also often contain the sort of thing that states have a hard time really agreeing on. A classic example is the Declaration on the Prohibition of Military, Political or Economic Coercion in the Conclusion of Treaties, annexed to the Final Act of the UN Conference on the Law of Treaties: Doc. A/CONF.39/26 (and reproduced in Aust, *supra* n. 9, at pp. 436–437). This had to console those parties who argued for a broad notion of coercion in Art. 52 VCLT but lost out.

[134] 189 UNTS 150.

[135] For discussion see R. Alleweldt, 'Preamble to the 1951 Convention' in A. Zimmermann (ed.), *The 1951 Convention Relating to the Status of Refugees and Its 1967 Protocol: A Commentary* (Oxford: Oxford University Press, 2011), pp. 225–240, at pp. 230–231.

[136] 1949 Geneva Convention (I) for the Amelioration of the Condition of the Wounded and Sick in Armed Forces in the Field, 75 UNTS 31; 1949 Geneva Convention (II) for the Amelioration of the Condition of Wounded, Sick and Shipwrecked Members of Armed Forces at Sea, 75 UNTS 85; 1949 Geneva Convention (III) Relative to the Treatment of Prisoners of War, 75 UNTS 135 and 1949 Geneva Convention (IV) Relative to the Protection of Civilian Persons in Time of War, 75 UNTS 287.

divine origin of man', whereas other delegations urged the inclusion of a recital relating to punishment and sanctions. When advocates of both propositions proved uncompromising, the very idea of having a preamble was eventually given up altogether, unless one counts wording to the effect that the undersigned have agreed as follows as a preamble.[137]

5   By Way of Conclusion

Preambles have come to play, in part, a decorative function, and as noted previously, this is most obviously the case with bilateral treaties. While early preambles were mainly informative with respect to the identities of those concluding the treaty, at least since the nineteenth century preambles have come to decorate and embellish, reminding the parties of the lofty considerations that went into the treaty and that can be said to form its background.

It is in the nature of decorations and similar phenomena to highlight some things and hide other things from sight.[138] This may well apply across the board: when the decorated soldier is rewarded for her bravery on the battlefield, such may mask the circumstance that the battle was ill-considered or the commander's strategy backfired or her colleagues were not up to the task, and the university lecturer receiving a teaching award may be so lucky simply because her colleagues may be poor teachers. This naturally raises the question of what it is then that the modern-day preamble wishes to hide, and the most obvious answer, it would seem, is that the preamble glosses over fundamental disagreement between States.

States are located on different continents, in different climatic conditions, with different political traditions and religious inspirations and are

---

[137] See J. Pictet, 'Preamble' in J. Pictet (ed.), *Commentary to I Geneva Convention for the Amelioration of the Condition of the Wounded and Sick in Armed Forces in the Field* (Geneva: ICRC, 1952), pp. 18–23, esp. at pp. 20–21. Note that Pictet argues that common Art. 3 of the four Geneva Conventions functions as the practical equivalent of a preamble containing the main guiding principles underlying the Conventions (*ibid.*, at p. 23). See, also, T. Meron, 'The Geneva Conventions and Public International Law', *Int'l Rev. Red Cross*, 91 (2009), 619–625, at 623–624, and V.V. Pustogarov, 'The Martens Clause in International Law', *J. History Int'l L.*, 1 (1999), 125–135.

[138] Note how the word 'personality' (as in legal personality) derives from *persona*, i.e. mask, and simultaneously makes some things visible while hiding others from sight. For further reflection, see J. Klabbers, 'The Concept of Legal Personality', *Ius Gentium*, 11 (2005), 35–66.

sometimes even grouped as belonging to different civilisations. They have different, often incommensurate, interests; the sizes of their territory and populations differ, as do the effectiveness and political orientation of their governments. Small wonder then that in such a world, agreement is hard to come by, and small wonder then that States need to build in some safeguards when concluding their treaties. With many multilateral treaties, as noted earlier, the fiction that the treaty constitutes a meeting of the minds is just that – a fiction – and while legal fictions can be very useful, this is one fiction that possibly warrants some re-thinking. The more realistic outlook is captured in Philip Allott's glorious phrase according to which treaties are 'disagreement[s] reduced to writing',[139] and in these circumstances, the preamble plays a pivotal role.

[139] See P. Allott, 'The Concept of International Law', *EJIL*, 10 (1999), 31–50, at 43.

8

The Principle of Privity

MICHAEL WAIBEL*

1 Introduction

In May 1926, in *Certain German Interests in Polish Upper Silesia*, the Permanent Court of International Justice (PCIJ) said: 'A treaty only creates law as between the States which are parties to it; in case of doubt, no rights can be deduced from it in favour of third States'.[1] This is the classic statement of the privity, *pacta tertiis* or parties-only principle in international law.[2] Accordingly, treaties create (enforceable) obligations and rights only for the States parties to them. The Vienna Convention on the Law of Treaties (VCLT) codified the privity principle in its Articles 34, 35, 36 and 37.[3]

As this chapter shows, the PCIJ's axiomatic statement in *Certain German Interests* almost eighty years ago no longer fully reflects the effect of treaties on third parties in contemporary international law. Since then, the principle of privity of treaty has lost some of its sharp edges. The rise of *erga omnes* obligations and objective, status-creating treaties, the conferral of rights on non-State actors and their ability to directly enforce such rights as well as the turn towards informal international law beyond the law of treaties have tempered the traditional privity rule.[4] However, it

* I thank Neil Andrews, Sir Franklin Berman, Eirik Bjorge, Michael Bowman, Richard Gardiner, Neil Jones, Dino Kritsiotis, Jonathan Morgan, Barbara Miltner, Jasmin Moussa, Daniel Peat, Anneliese Quast Mertsch and Kate Parlett as well as participants of a seminar at the Lauterpacht Centre for International Law, University of Cambridge, for discussions and comments on earlier drafts. Finally, thank you to Hannah Dixie, Christina Gort, Hui-Min Loh, Teresa Mayr and Ridhi Kabra for research and editorial assistance.
[1] *Case Concerning Certain German Interests in Upper Silesia*: Germany v. Poland, 1926 PCIJ, Series A, No. 7, at p. 29.
[2] As explained later, these terms are often used interchangeably, but they are not exact equivalents.
[3] 1155 UNTS 331.
[4] On the turn from formal governance on the basis of treaties to informal governance, see N. Krisch, 'The Decay of Consent: International Law in an Age of Global Public Goods',

would be premature to sound the death knell of privity of treaty.[5] Privity remains an important structural characteristic on the inter-State plane.

This chapter explores the role played by privity in the law of treaties. Despite the imperfect analogy between contracts and treaties,[6] Section 2 compares and contrasts the functions of privity in domestic contract law and international law. Section 3 outlines the VCLT's approach to *pacta tertiis*. Section 4 discusses exceptions to privity of treaty, including objective regimes, international investment law and individual rights. Section 5 concludes.

2   Privity of Contract and Privity of Treaty

Privity in domestic law is a 'mysterious and undefined' term.[7] It originates from the Latin word '*privus*' (one's own) and the French word '*privauté*' (privacy).[8] Privity limits the right to bring an action to the promisee, and thereby privity prevents strangers from enforcing a contract.[9] Due to privity, contracts do create rights or obligations for third parties. Privity reflects the contract's character as a bilateral *vinculum juris* for enforcement purposes.[10] It is a formal element necessary for the enforcement of contractual bargains.

AJIL, 108 (2014), 1–40; J. Pauwelyn, R. A. Wessel and J. Wouters (eds.), *Informal International Lawmaking* (Oxford: Oxford University Press, 2012) and C. Brummer, *Minilateralism: How Trade Alliances, Soft Law and Financial Engineering Are Redefining Economic Statecraft* (Cambridge: Cambridge University Press, 2014).

[5] K. Zweigert and H. Kötz, *Introduction to Comparative Law* (Oxford: Oxford University Press, 3rd ed., 1998), p. 468.

[6] I. Seidl-Hohenveldern, *International Economic Law* (Dordrecht: Martinus Nijhoff Publishers, 1989), p. 32; H. Lauterpacht, *Private Law Sources and Analogies of International Law (with Special Reference to International Arbitration)* (London: Longmans, 1927) and D. W. Bowett, Review of Evangelos Raftopoulos, *Inadequacy of the Contractual Analogy in the Law of Treaties* (1990), BYbIL, 64 (1993), 439.

[7] A. L. Corbin, *Corbin on Contracts* (Vol. IV) (St. Paul, MN: West Publishing, 1950), p. 778.

[8] S. Johnson, 'A Dictionary of the English Language (1755)' quoted from V. V. Palmer, *The Paths to Privity: The History of the Third Party Beneficiary Contracts at English Law* (San Francisco, CA: Austin & Winfield, 1992), p. 7.

[9] R. Flannigan, 'Privity – The End of an Era (Error)', LQR (1987), 564–593; *John Price v. Easton*, 110 ER 518 (1833); *Tweddle v. Atkinson*, 121 ER 762 (1861); *Dunlop Pneumatic Tyre Co. Ltd. v. Selfridge & Co.* [1915] AC 847, at p. 853 ('only a person who was a party to a contract can sue on it. Our law knows nothing of a *jus quaesitum tertio* arising by way of contract'); *Coulls v. Bagot's Executor & Trustee Co. Ltd.* (1967) 119 CLR 460, at p. 478 (Barwick CJ) and N. Andrews, *Contract Law* (Cambridge: Cambridge University Press, 2nd ed., 2015), pp. 172–207.

[10] Other types of privity include privity of estate and privity of tenure: Palmer, *supra* n. 8, at pp. 6–10; Zweigert and Kötz, *supra* n. 5, at p. 465; J. Baker, 'Privity of Contract in the Common Law before 1860' in E. J. H. Schrage (ed.), *Ius quaesitum tertio* (Berlin: Duncker &

Privity of contract is sometimes regarded as an aspect of consideration. As a rule, only the person who has given consideration for a promise can enforce it. Consideration is 'some right, interest, profit, or benefit accruing to the one party, or some forbearance, detriment, loss or responsibility, given, suffered, or undertaken by the other'.[11] This definition illustrates that one of consideration's functions is to evidence the parties' intention to be bound reciprocally by their promises, though such intention is not sufficient for a promise to be supported by consideration.[12] Consideration has to be of some economic value, and various kinds of moral obligations (even if they provide evidence of intention) are excluded. Privity is thus the corollary of consideration because a person who has not provided consideration cannot bring an action under contract except in the case of contracts under seal.[13]

In contrast to contract law in common law jurisdictions, the term 'privity' is rarely used in international law.[14] The International Court of Justice (ICJ) has referred to the term 'privity' parenthetically in only four cases, namely *Libya v. Chad*, the *Nicaragua Case*, the *South West Africa Cases* and the *Anglo-Iranian Oil Co. Case*.[15] Judge Dreyfus in *District of Gex* was sceptical about the treaty-contract analogy in respect of privity:

Humblot, 2008), pp. 135–174, at p. 135; C. J. Tams, *Enforcing Obligations* Erga Omnes *in International Law* (Cambridge: Cambridge University Press, 2005), pp. 5 and 106 (*erga omnes* norms traditionally focus on enforcement) and E. A. Posner, 'Erga Omnes Norms, Institutionalization, and Constitutionalism in International Law', *J. Inst. Theor. Econ.*, 165 (2009), 5–23, at 5 (the difference between ordinary or two-party norms and *erga omnes* norms concerns enforcement).

[11] *Currie v. Misa* (1875) LR 10 Ex 153, at p. 162.

[12] *Stilk v. Myrick*, 2 Camp. 317; *Williams v. Roffey Bros & Nicholls (Contractors) Ltd.* [1991] 1 QB 1 and *Vantage Navigation Corporation v. Suhail and Saud Bahwan Building Materials LLC (The 'Alev')* [1989] 1 Lloyd's Rep. 138.

[13] M. P. Furmston, *Cheshire and Fifoot's Law of Contract* (London: Butterworth and Co. Publishers, 11th ed., 1981), pp. 74–75; *Dunlop v. Selfridge* [1915] AC 847; *John Price v. Easton*, 110 ER 518 (1833) and *Tweddle v. Atkinson*, 121 ER 762 (1861) (a 'stranger to the consideration of a contract' is barred from bringing a claim).

[14] R. K. Gardiner, *Treaty Interpretation* (Oxford: Oxford University Press, 2nd ed., 2015); E. Cannizzaro (ed.), *The Law of Treaties beyond the Vienna Convention* (Oxford: Oxford University Press, 2011); A. Aust, *Modern Treaty Law and Practice* (Cambridge: Cambridge University Press, 3rd ed., 2013); Tams, *supra* n. 10, and O. Corten and P. Klein (eds.), *The Vienna Conventions on the Law of Treaties: A Commentary* (Vols. I–II) (Oxford: Oxford University Press, 2012) contain no reference to 'privity'. The second edition of R. Wolfrum (ed.), *Max Planck Encyclopaedia of Public International Law* (Oxford: Oxford University Press, 2008) mentions 'privity' only five times.

[15] *Case Concerning the Territorial Dispute*: Libyan Arab Jamahiriya v. Chad (1994) ICJ Rep. 6, at p. 78 (paragraph 98) (Separate Opinion of Judge Ajibola) (quoting A.D.

the stipulation 'in favorem tertii' ... is well known in private law; but its forms vary infinitely in different municipal legislations ... In view of this diversity in the nature and legal effects of the stipulations 'in favorem tertii' in municipal law, there can be no question of transferring it as such into international law.[16]

Kindred notions in international law include the parties-only principle, *res inter alios acta* and *pacta tertiis* – though they all have somewhat different meanings. In contrast to privity, the *pacta tertiis* principle – that agreements neither harm nor benefit third parties – centres on obligations.[17] Consequently, it implies that a State party to one treaty cannot alter its obligations by concluding a second treaty with a third State. *Res inter alios acta* guarantees that even if the second treaty purports to affect rights and obligations under the first treaty, that first treaty remains valid between the States party to it. The second treaty cannot affect the right of third States.[18]

Despite the varying terminology and the rarity of references to 'privity' in international law, the idea underlying privity has long been influential, particularly in the law of treaties. Mutuality and reciprocity of rights and obligations have traditionally defined treaties, just like contracts in domestic law. The bond between States parties to a treaty is part and

---

McNair); *Case Concerning Military and Paramilitary Activities in and against Nicaragua*: Nicaragua v. United States of America (Provisional Measures) (1984) ICJ Rep. 169, at p. 196 ('fundamental rights of a State to live in peace, free of the threat or use of force against its territorial integrity or political independence, are rights of every State, *erga omnes*. They do not depend upon narrow considerations of privity to a dispute before the Court. They depend upon the broad considerations of collective security'); *South West Africa Cases*: Ethiopia v. South Africa; Liberia v. South Africa (Preliminary Objections) (1962) ICJ Rep. 319, at pp. 410–411 (Separation Opinion of Judge Jessup, quoting Hersch Lauterpacht for the proposition that '[p]rivity of contract is not a general principle of law'. According to Jessup, '[i]nternational law, not being a formalistic system, holds States legally bound by their undertakings in a variety of circumstances and does not need either to insist or to deny that the beneficiaries are "parties" to the undertakings') and *Anglo-Iranian Oil Co. Case*: United Kingdom v. Iran (Preliminary Objections) (1952) ICJ Rep. 93, at p. 112 ('there is no privity of *contract* between the Government of Iran and the Government of the United Kingdom') (emphasis added).

[16] *Free Zones of Upper Savoy and the District of Gex* (Advisory Opinion), 1929 PCIJ, Series A, No. 22, at p. 43.

[17] C. L. Rozakis, 'Treaties and Third States: Study in the Reinforcement of the Consensual Standards in International Law', *ZaöRV*, 35 (1975), 1–40, at 4.

[18] A. D. McNair, *The Law of Treaties* (Oxford: Clarendon Press, 1961), p. 321, and *Island of Palmas Case*: Netherlands v. United States, RIAA, Vol. II, 829–871, at p. 842.

parcel of the very idea of treaties whereby two or more States voluntarily enter into a relationship of trust.[19]

In international law, sovereignty and independence of States are the primary reason for privity of treaty. The International Law Commission (ILC) characterised the *pacta tertiis* principle as 'one of the bulwarks of the independence and equality of States'.[20] Privity limits liability in contract under domestic law and State responsibility in international law.

Privity of contract reflects the idea that the class of those who can enforce contractual rights needs to be strictly limited. Given the restrictions imposed by privity and consideration in contract, the English law of responsibility developed mainly through tort law.[21] The idea underlying privity continues to be influential even after the entry force of the 1999 Contracts (Rights of Third Parties) Act.[22] In domestic law, several causes of action may be available, whereas in international law the only ready alternative is custom, which by definition does not require privity of treaty.

By contrast, in international law, causes of action are considerably more limited. First, a claimant can rely on custom – where privity does not apply – only in some cases. Second, absent a specific treaty or customary obligation, States are rarely liable for their negligent acts or omissions.[23] For example, a State that negligently fails to supervise its financial system is not internationally responsible for the resulting financial crisis that has significant spillover effects on other States and individuals, unless it has violated a treaty or customary obligation.[24]

Third, many international obligations outside the human rights and investment context are owed only to other States, and only to a single State in the case of bilateral treaty. The class of eligible claimants is typically small, and traditionally, only States enjoy standing to bring claims. Fourth, the absence of a forum with jurisdiction over the claim

---

[19] D. J. Ibbetson, *A Historical Introduction to the Law of Obligations* (Oxford: Oxford University Press, 1999), p. 77.

[20] International Law Commission, Draft Articles on the Law of Treaties: Report of the Commission to the General Assembly, *YbILC* (1966–II), 227.

[21] M. Immenhauser, *Das Dogma von Vertrag und Delikt: zur Entstehungs- und Wirkungsgeschichte der zweigeteilten Haftungsordnung* (Cologne: Böhlau, 2006), p. 21.

[22] 1999 c. 31.

[23] Exceptionally, States may be held liable for omissions, as in *Corfu Channel Case*: United Kingdom of Great Britain and Northern Ireland v. Albania (Merits) (1949) ICJ Rep. 4.

[24] A. Hertogen, 'The Legal Implications of the GFC for Financial Services Liberalization' in M. Waibel (ed.), *The Legal Implications of Global Financial Crises* (Leiden: Martinus Nijhoff, forthcoming).

is common in international law. By contrast, those who suffer injury or damage in domestic law generally have a domestic forum to which they can turn for relief, subject to specific immunities. Standing is a necessary but insufficient condition for a successful claim. Fifth, *erga omnes* obligations apart,[25] States only enjoy standing in relation to breaches of international law that specifically affect them.[26]

Treaties are the main fountain of primary rules whose breach, if attributable to a State, can trigger State responsibility. Given the centrality of treaties in modern international law, the privity of treaty may be more constraining than privity of contract domestically and difficult to circumvent. The next section considers the codification of privity in the VCLT and its application.

3   Privity in the Vienna Convention on the Law of Treaties

The VCLT codifies the PCIJ's jurisprudence on treaties and third States. Section 4 of the VCLT, titled 'Treaties and Third States', has five articles: (1) Article 33 – the general principle of privity of treaty, (2) Article 35 – obligations of third States, (3) Article 36 – rights of third States, (4) Article 37 – revocation or modification of rights or obligations of third States and (5) Article 38 – the relationship to international custom.[27] At first sight, these provisions suggest that the privity principle is firmly established in international law, but as this section shows, this statement requires some qualification.

The VCLT defines 'third State' as a State not a party to the treaty.[28] A party to a treaty, according to the VCLT, is 'a State which expressed its consent to be bound . . . and for which the treaty is in force';[29] in the text of the 1986 Vienna Convention on the Law of Treaties between States and

---

[25] Art. 48 of the ILC's Articles on State Responsibility gives standing in narrow circumstances to non-injured States; cf. *Questions Relating to the Obligation to Prosecute or Extradite*: Belgium v. Senegal (Judgment) (2012) I.C.J. Rep. 422.

[26] 2001 ILC Articles on State Responsibility, Art. 42: Official Records of the General Assembly, Fifty-Sixth Session, Supp. No. 10 (A/56/10).

[27] *Supra* n. 3.

[28] Art. 2(1)(h) VCLT: *supra* n. 3. See, also, Art. 2(1)(h) of the 1986 Vienna Convention on the Law of Treaties between States and International Organizations or between International Organizations (VCLTSIO), ILM, 25 (1986), 543–592 ('"third State" and "third organization" mean respectively: (i) a State, or (ii) an international organization not a party to the treaty').

[29] Art. 2(1)(g) VCLT: *supra* n. 3. The VCLTSIO has identical provisions on third parties. See Arts. 34–38 VCLTSIO: *ibid.*

International Organizations or between International Organizations, 'party' is similarly defined as 'a State or an international organization which has consented to be bound by a treaty and for which the treaty is in force'.[30]

Article 34 VCLT reflects the principle of privity of treaty. It provides: 'A treaty applies only between the parties to it. A treaty does not create either obligations or rights for a third state without its consent and cannot infringe the rights of third states without their consent'.[31] Accordingly, in the absence of consent of the third State concerned, a treaty creates neither rights nor obligations for such a third State. Articles 35 and 36 VCLT set out the conditions under which rights and obligations under treaties may extend to third parties.

The principle of privity in international law has two aspects. First, treaties do not impose obligations on third States or otherwise modify their obligations except with their consent (the negative side of privity). Second, treaties do not confer benefits on third States without their consent (the positive side of privity).

The negative side of privity – that no obligations could be created for third States without their consent – has been and continues to be a significant constraint. This negative side is crucial for safeguarding the sovereignty and independence of States to which the ILC refers in the passage quoted previously.[32]

For a treaty to create obligations for third States under Article 35, two conditions must be met: (i) States parties must intend to establish such obligation and (ii) the third State must expressly accept the obligation in writing. Mere conduct by the third State is insufficient. When both conditions are met, a collateral agreement is formed between the parties to the treaty and the third State.[33] However, the third State remains a non-party to the treaty itself.

The VCLT speaks of a third *State* only. Articles 34 to 37 are designed to protect the sovereignty and independence of third States. They are not *prima facie* concerned with the rights of non-State actors, such as those of

---

[30] Art. 2(1)(g) VCLTSIO: *ibid.*

[31] McNair, *supra* n. 18, at p. 309 ('[b]oth legal principle and common sense are in favour of the rule') and Aust, *supra* n. 14, at p. 227 (the rule is 'obvious').

[32] *Supra* n. 20.

[33] M. Fitzmaurice, 'Third Parties and the Law of Treaties', *Max Planck Yb. UN Law*, 6 (2002), 37–137. According to Chinkin, the collateral agreement while legally binding is not a treaty in its own right: C. Chinkin, *Third Parties in International Law* (Oxford: Oxford University Press, 1993), p. 41.

individuals and investors. The sovereignty rationale does not extend to them. At best, the VCLT could apply to non-State actors by analogy,[34] yet there is a major qualitative difference between rights and obligations imposed on third party States and those imposed on third party non-State actors.

States may freely bestow rights and impose obligations on individuals subject to their jurisdiction through international treaties without requiring their consent, while to do so in respect of third States requires express assent.[35] According to Anthea Roberts, this difference can be understood in two related ways. First, the relationship between a State and its nationals is inherently vertical. This means that States 'have the power to determine whether to bring a case on behalf of their nationals, how to prosecute the case, whether and on what terms to settle, and what to do with any resulting compensation'.[36] States take decisions for individuals at the international level because they 'have not been granted the power to enforce their own rights or benefits before independent tribunals'.[37] This public law relationship between a State and its nationals does not threaten the sovereignty of third states. As a result, no issue of privity arises.

Second, and relatedly, individuals are themselves unable to become parties to a treaty, unlike third States. Even though States are able to confer substantive and procedural rights on individuals, and routinely do so for example under human rights and investment treaties, individuals as a rule lack the capacity to enter into treaties themselves.[38] While individuals are thus dependent on their home States for international engagement, other States could have opted to become a treaty party, with its attendant right and obligations, should they have so wished. By definition, a third State has chosen not to do so. To assert that third States nevertheless intended to be bound by such rights and obligations is problematic. It is for these reasons that privity applies strictly *vis-à-vis* third States but not with regard to individuals. This may go some of the way to explaining why the exceptions to privity in international investment law and individual are less controversial than the concept of objective regimes. Objective regimes focus on third States rather than individuals.

---

[34] A. Roberts, 'Triangular Treaties: The Extent and Limits of Investment Treaty Rights', *Harvard ILJ*, 56 (2015), 353–417, at 369.

[35] *Ibid.*, at 375.   [36] *Ibid.*, at 363.   [37] *Ibid.*

[38] T. Grant, 'Who Can Make Treaties? Other Subjects of International Law' in D. B. Hollis (ed.), *The Oxford Guide to Treaties* (Oxford: Oxford University Press, 2012), pp. 125–149, at p. 142.

At the same time, privity in the law of treaties has never been as constraining with respect to rights as privity of contract in English contract law and its progeny. States parties to a treaty have always been able to vest rights in third parties. All that mattered was their intention to do so, express or implied. The VCLT codified this permissive model for third party beneficiaries in Article 36.

Third States derive rights under Article 36 subject to two conditions: (i) parties must intend to vest a right in one or several States, or to States generally and (ii) the beneficiary third State(s) must assent. We do not lightly assume that State parties intended to confer rights on third States but the ordinary meaning of the terms of the treaty, its *travaux préparatoires*, diplomatic correspondence and pertinent resolutions and proposals of the parties can reveal such intent.[39] The conditions for States to derive rights are more liberal than the conditions related to obligations of third States.

The threshold for condition (ii) of assent by the third State is low. Assent is presumed. The rights then vest in the third State under a collateral agreement to the treaty.[40] Silence also amounts to assent.[41] In exercising the right, the third State implicitly accepts the offer made by the States parties. For rights, this presumption of assent is unproblematic because the third State can simply choose not to take advantage of the right.

Article 38 VCLT clarifies that privity does not extend to customary international law. It clarifies that custom does not represent a departure from privity. Accordingly, nothing prevents a rule contained in a treaty from subsequently becoming binding on third States by virtue of its transformation into customary international law. The same principle applies to antecedent customary international law. For example, when the United States did not ratify the 1982 United Nations Convention on the Law of the Sea (UNCLOS),[42] the question arose whether the United States would continue to enjoy access to international straits or whether only States parties to UNCLOS could exercise rights of passage after the

---

[39] L. T. Lee, 'The Law of the Sea Convention and Third States', *AJIL*, 77 (1983), 541–568.

[40] See P. Reuter, *Introduction to the Law of Treaties* (London: Pinter Publishers, 1989) and the Separate Opinion of Judge Negulsco in the *Free Zones Case: supra* n. 16, at pp. 28–39. See, also, the contribution to this volume of Craven at pp. 103–135 (Chapter 5).

[41] E. J. de Aréchaga, 'Treaty Stipulations in Favor of Third States', *AJIL*, 50 (1956), 338–357, at 339.

[42] 1833 UNTS 3.

entry into force of UNCLOS.[43] The United States has continued to enjoy these rights as a matter of customary international law.

Articles 34–38 VCLT received broad approval during the VCLT negotiations.[44] Some States, such as the United States, insisted that the provisions be formulated with more precision. The Netherlands opposed a broadly worded *pacta tertiis rule* because treaties concerning territory routinely affect the rights of third States. The drafters did not attempt to establish a differentiated privity regime. For example, they could have limited the parties-only rule to contractual treaties and exempted treaties establishing international organizations and status-creating treaties from the ambit of the *pacta tertiis* rule.[45]

Even though five articles in the VCLT relate exclusively to privity of treaty, they provide only general guidance and grey areas remain. For example, one difficulty is that the strict dichotomy between rights and obligations contemplated in Articles 35 and 36 VCLT is not as clear-cut in practice. In some cases, it may only become clearer over time whether particular treaty provisions comport not only rights but also obligations (e.g. for investment treaties examined in Section 4.2 later in this chapter). Furthermore, the extent to which the law of treaties knows exceptions to the privity principle is unclear – the subject of the next section of this chapter. It examines how objective regimes, investor rights and individual rights fit into the privity paradigm.

4 Exceptions to Privity of Treaty

In *German Interests in Polish Upper Silesia*, the PCIJ paradigmatically stated the privity principle. Lord Findlay, dissenting, advocated a trust-like exception. In his view, Poland, a third State with respect to the 1918 Armistice of Compiègne between the Allies and Germany,[46] benefited from a '*jus quaesitum*, a right acquired for the new State as soon as it should come into existence'.[47] Just like in domestic contract law, the privity principle in international law admits exceptions. This section examines three: objective regimes, investment arbitration and individual rights.

---

[43] Lee, *supra* n. 39, at 541–568 and 553–566.

[44] ILC Commentary, *YbILC* (1966–II), Pt. II, 851–852 (noting almost 'universal agreement' on the principle).

[45] J. M. McNeill, 'Regional Enforcement under the United Nations Charter and Constraints Upon States Not Members', *Cornell ILJ*, 9 (1975), 1–23.

[46] 224 CTS 286.   [47] *German Interests in Polish Upper Silesia, supra* n. 1, at p. 84.

4.1   Objective Regimes

Objective regimes typically provide and protect global or regional public goods.[48] They affect the relationship not just between the treaty parties *inter se* but between a group of States or even all States. Objective (or *erga omnes*) regimes have been controversial due to the attenuated consent requirement.[49] Examples of objective regimes are treaties creating rights *in rem*, such as territorial settlements and cessions,[50] boundary treaties[51] and treaties on internationalised territories.[52]

A specific example of an objective regime is the 1959 Antarctic Treaty.[53] Even though originally only twelve States signed the Antarctic Treaty, the treaty aims to establish an objective regime for Antarctica as a whole binding also third States. This regime rules out individual claims of sovereignty over Antarctica (Article IV), prohibits military bases (Article I), nuclear explosions and disposal of nuclear waste on Antarctica (Article V). While the treaty still falls short of universality, the fifty-one State parties strengthen the treaty's claim to having established an objective regime.

The concept of objective regimes emerged in the nineteenth century, when Europe's Great Powers 'alleged a regulatory competence for matters of international peace and security'.[54] By the twentieth century, the use of multilateral treaties to regulate matters of common interest had

---

[48]   P. Cahier, 'Le Problème des effets des traités à l'égard des Etats tiers', *Hague Recueil*, 143 (1974–III), 660–670; M. Ragazzi, *The Concept of International Obligations* Erga Omnes (Oxford: Oxford University Press, 1997), pp. 24–27, and R. Jennings and A. Watts (eds.), *Oppenheim's International Law* (Vol. I) (London: Longmans, 9th ed., 1992), p. 1205.

[49]   Chinkin, *supra* n. 33, at p. 36 (the Antarctic Treaty was a major source of controversy when the ILC debated the law of treaties).

[50]   1713 Treaty of Utrecht, 28 CTS 295; 1815 Declaration of the States Participating in the Congress of Vienna, 64 CTS 6, and the 1919 Treaty of Versailles, 225 CTS 188.

[51]   1978 Vienna Convention on Succession of States in Respect of Treaties, 1946 UNTS 3, Arts. 11 and 12; *Case Concerning the Territorial Dispute, supra* n. 15, at p. 37, and *Case Concerning the Territorial and Maritime Dispute*: Nicaragua v. Colombia (Preliminary Objections) (2007) ICJ Rep. 832, at p. 861 (paragraph 89).

[52]   E.g. the Åland Islands. Though formally part of Finland, a number of treaties have established that the Islands are autonomous, neutral and demilitarised. See, e.g., 1856 Convention on the Demilitarisation of the Åland Islands: 114 CTS 406.

[53]   402 UNTS 71; Aust, *supra* n. 14, at p. 112; A. Watts, *International Law and the Antarctic Treaty System* (Cambridge: Grotius Publications, 1992), pp. 295–298; R. E. Guyer, 'The Antarctic System', *Hague Recueil*, 139 (1973–II), 149–226; B. Simma, 'The Antarctic Treaty as a Treaty Providing for an "Objective Regime"', *Cornell ILJ*, 19 (1986), 189–209, at 195, and D. R. Rothwell, *The Polar Regions and the Development of International Law* (Cambridge: Cambridge University Press, 1996).

[54]   Tams, *supra* n. 10, at p. 82.

become more widespread,[55] considered 'a surrogate for the lacking international legislature'.[56] This shift indicated 'a gradual turning away from the strict consent approach'[57] of positivism. With status-creating treaties, in contrast to traditional 'dispositive or conveyance-type treaties',[58] 'the third party effect is not incidental, but intentional: creating a generally binding (objective) regime is the very essence of the treaty'.[59] Objective regimes 'enjoyed much support'[60] in the ILC until the ICJ's decision in *Barcelona Traction*,[61] after which the term's popularity began to wane. Consequently, the question of the validity of objective regimes in international law 'remains disputed in international legal scholarship'.[62]

Uncertainty as to precisely what constitutes an objective regime may well account for some of this controversy over its place in international law. The ambiguity of this notion means that it may be both overbroad and under-inclusive. First, Alexander Proelss has addressed its broad reach:

> if the dispositive character of the treaty concerned is cumulatively made dependent on the fact that all or the large majority of States have become parties to it, or that existence of the competence of the contracting parties to settle the respect matter with *erga omnes* is presumed vis-à-vis all third States which have not objected to the assertion made by the contracting parties to act in the general interest, the question arises whether there is really anything special about objective regimes as opposed to the inter partes validity of ordinary treaties.[63]

The label of objective regimes may thus appear devoid of explanatory power if it is applied too widely, i.e. to any treaty where third States have not expressly objected to being bound by its obligations. Proelss pointed to boundary treaties as a category frequently misunderstood as having

---

[55] Tams has pointed to the *Åland, Case of the S.S. 'Wimbledon', South West Africa (Status)* and *Reparations for Injuries Cases* as each recognising certain third-party effects of treaties: *ibid.*

[56] J. Delbrück, 'The Impact of the Allocation of International Law Enforcement Authority on the International Legal Order' in J. Delbrück and U. E. Heinz (eds.), *Allocation of Law Enforcement Authority in the International System* (Berlin: Duncker & Humblot, 1994), pp. 135–158, at p. 143 (fn. 33).

[57] *Ibid.*, at p. 143.   [58] Tams, *supra* n. 10, at p. 81.   [59] *Ibid.*   [60] *Ibid.*, at p. 83.

[61] *Case Concerning the Barcelona Traction, Light and Power Company, Limited (New Application: 1962)*: Belgium v. Spain (Second Phase) (1970) ICJ Rep. 3.

[62] A. Proelss, 'The Personal Dimension: Challenges to the *pacta tertiis* rule' in C. J. Tams, A. Tzanakopoulos and A. Zimmermann (eds.), *Research Handbook on the Law of Treaties* (Cheltenham: Edward Elgar Publishing, 2014), pp. 222–254, at p. 245.

[63] *Ibid.*

their legal basis in objective regimes despite actually stemming from 'the fact that only the States concluding the agreement have the competence to regulate the subject matter'.[64] They thereby demonstrate the misleading nature of the term's definition: not all treaties which affect third States constitute objective regimes and represent an exception to the *pacta tertiis* rule.

Second, the concept can also be criticised for its under-inclusivity, excluding from the label of objective regimes other types of treaties, such as those in the realms of international investment law and individual and human rights, which also display an 'objective'[65] character. Without any clear reasoning as to why certain treaties fall under the objective umbrella while others do not, it is hard to fully embrace the concept.

Objective regimes straddle the boundary between treaty and custom. They go back to the idea that some treaties have a public law and quasi-legislative rather than contractual character. Originally, the only way in which treaties could acquire binding force with respect to third States was through the passage of time and the transformation of the treaty creating an objective regime into custom. Third States are bound *qua* custom, not *qua* treaty.[66]

The VCLT does not contain special provisions on objective regimes. Special Rapporteur Humphrey Waldock suggested that the VCLT include an article on objective regimes.[67] Despite the absence of the term 'privity',[68] the idea was that such objective regime would bind third States. According to the Commentary on its draft articles, the ILC did consider whether treaties creating objective regimes should be addressed 'separately as a special case'.[69] Some members agreed with Waldock, sharing his view that 'the concept of treaties creating objective regimes existed in international law and merited special treatment in the draft articles'.[70]

However, others rejected any notion of these regimes forming a unique category in the law of treaties despite acknowledging that 'in certain cases treaty rights and obligations may come to be valid *erga omnes*'.[71] In light of this difference in opinion, which the ILC felt unable to reconcile, the

---

[64] *Ibid.*, at p. 246.
[65] The idea first surfaced in *Pfunders Case*: Austria v. Italy (App 788/60) (1961) 4 Yearbook 116 (EComHR).
[66] Lee, *supra* n. 39, at 565 ('the source of such effect remains custom, not the treaty').
[67] Draft Art. 63.   [68] Tams, *supra* n. 10, at p. 84.
[69] Draft Articles on the Law of Treaties with Commentaries: *YbILC* (1966–II), 231.
[70] *Ibid.*   [71] *Ibid.*

ILC included no special provision on objective regimes and deleted draft Article 63. Ultimately, the ILC rejected objective regimes as contrary to international law to the extent that they involve the imposition of obligations on third States by treaties to which they are not parties. Despite the lack of reference in the VCLT, a common view is that objective regimes have their proper place in international law.[72]

Instead, the ILC considered Article 38 as a sufficient basis for objective regimes to take effect *vis-à-vis* third States. Citing the examples of the Hague Conventions regarding the rules of land warfare, the agreements for neutralising Switzerland and treaties regarding international rivers and maritime waterways, the ILC commented that the rules were binding under custom, not treaty:[73]

> In none of these cases, however, can it properly be said that the treaty itself has legal effects for third States. They are cases where, without establishing a treaty relation between themselves and the parties to the treaty, other states recognised rules formulated in a treaty as binding customary law. In short, for the states the source of the binding force of the rule is custom, not the treaty.[74]

That these regimes become binding on third States only once the requirements for custom are met safeguards the principle of consent, at least as a matter of principle.

Conceptually, we can think of objective regimes in three ways – though all are in tension with privity of treaty.[75] The first approach considers that treaties can be valid *erga omnes* under Articles 36 VCLT, even though the ILC rejected to expressly incorporate the concept of objective regimes in the VCLT.[76]

---

[72] R. Rayfuse, 'The United Nations Agreement on Straddling and Highly Migratory Fish Stocks as an Objective Regime: A Case of Wishful Thinking?', *Australian YbIL*, 20 (1999), 253–278; I. Sinclair, *The Vienna Convention on the Law of Treaties* (Manchester: Manchester University Press, 2nd ed., 1984), pp. 104–105 and 358–364; S. P. Subedi, 'The Doctrine of Objective Regimes in International Law and the Competence of the United Nations to Impose Territorial or Peace Settlements on States', *German YbIL*, 37 (1994), 162–205, at 174; Tams, *supra* n. 10, at p. 83, and F. Salerno, 'Treaties Establishing Objective Regimes' in Cannizzaro (ed.), *supra* n. 14, pp. 225–243.

[73] *YbILC* (1966–II), 231.   [74] *YbILC* (1966–II), 230; see, also, Tams, *supra* n. 10, at p. 83.

[75] Simma, *supra* n. 53, at 196.

[76] Subedi, *supra* n. 72, at 162 (referring to regimes concerning the finality of boundaries, maintenance of peace and security in troubled areas, preservation of independence and existence of strategically located States and the regulation of the objects of common use and exploration).

The second, 'public law' approach originates in Sir Arnold McNair's Separate Opinion in the advisory opinion in *International Status of South-West Africa*.[77] It considers objective regimes as an emanation of the quasi-legislative power of a group of States to make certain treaties binding on third parties.[78]

The third approach suggests that customary law, recognition, acquiescence and estoppel together can create objective regimes.[79] This approach regards objective regimes as a 'variant of the thesis that customary international law may evolve from a widely accepted treaty on the basis of its "public law character"'.[80]

Common to all three approaches is the importance of intent in the creation of objective regimes.[81] Other conditions for the emergence of objective regimes include the regime's territorial character, the territorial competence of the parties (or alternatively consent – express or implied by third States) and the furtherance of the general interest of the international community.[82] According to Waldock's ILC draft, such consent need not be express and can be presumed after a certain time has expired.[83]

As we saw in Section 2, two scenarios need to be distinguished: (a) treaties creating *obligations* for third States under Article 35 VCLT and (b) treaties creating *rights* for third States under Article 36 VCLT. This distinction between rights and obligations predates the VCLT and already appears in the PCIJ's case law.

The PCIJ in *Case of the S.S. 'Wimbledon'* recognised that an objective regime could create *rights* for third States.[84] The Court found that Germany was obliged to guarantee free access through the Kiel Canal under Article 380 of the 1919 Versailles Treaty.[85] This 'self-contained

---

[77] *International Status of South-West Africa* (Advisory Opinion) (1950) ICJ Rep. 128, at pp. 146–163 (Separate Opinion by Sir Arnold McNair).

[78] *Ibid.*, at p. 153 (Separate Opinion of Sir Arnold McNair). See, also, E. Klein, *Statusverträge im Völkerrecht, Rechtsfragen territorialer Sonderregime* (Berlin: Springer, 1980). For criticism of this approach, see M. Fitzmaurice, 'Modifications to the Principles of Consent in Relation to Certain Treaty Obligations', *Austrian Rev. Int'l & European L.*, 2 (1997), 275–317.

[79] Simma, *supra* n. 53, at 202.   [80] Lee, *supra* n. 39, at 541.

[81] H. Waldock, Third Report on the Law of Treaties, Doc. A/CN.4/167 and Add.1-3 (3 March, 9 June, 12 June and 7 July 1964), p. 26. Cf., also, Subedi, *supra* n. 72.

[82] R. A. Barnes, 'Objective Regimes Revisited', *Asian YbIL*, 9 (2000), 97–145. See, also, the contribution to this volume of Miltner at pp. 468–505 (Chapter 15).

[83] Waldock, *supra* n. 81, at p. 33.

[84] *Case of the S.S. 'Wimbledon'*: France, Italy, Japan and United Kingdom v. Germany (Judgment), 1923 PCIJ, Series A, No. 1, at p. 22.

[85] *Supra* n. 50.

regime' was to 'provide easier access to the Baltic for the benefit of all nations of the world'.[86] Free access to the Kiel Canal also extended to vessels flying the flag of third States.[87] Germany, as a party to the Versailles Treaty, had obligations *vis-à-vis* third States, and third States had rights under the Versailles Treaty.

In his Separate Opinion in *South West Africa*, Judge Jessup affirmed that Article 5 of the Mandate for South West Africa concerning missionaries was a unilateral declaration for the benefit of the other Members of the League.[88] The Mandate and trusteeship system were important precursors for a move away from a strict privity requirement and towards the notion of objective regimes. Judge Jessup also considered the compromissory clause in Article 7 of the Mandate as a *stipulatio pour autrui* with respect to all members of the League of Nations.

In the context of examining the character of unilateral declarations, the ICJ insisted in *South West Africa* that international law took a much more flexible approach to legal undertaking than the formalism often found in domestic law:

> Most of these explanations of unilateral engagements are based upon some municipal system of contract law and reveal an anxiety to fit international law into a national suit of legal clothes. For this purpose there is at times laboured insistence upon identifying the parties. [. . .] '*Privity of contract* is not a general principle of law'. International law, not being a formalistic system, holds States legally bound by their undertakings in a variety of circumstances and does not need either to insist or to deny that the beneficiaries are 'parties' to the undertakings.[89]

In the *Nicaragua Case*, the Court similarly rejected a narrow conception of privity as a ground to decline standing to the United States. The Court explained that the rights of the United States were the rights of *all States*:

> the rights of the United States which are central to this case are the rights of all States which are central to modern international law and life: those

---

[86] *Case of the S.S. 'Wimbledon', supra* n. 84, at p. 23.

[87] J. Harrison, *Making the Law of the Sea: A Study in the Development of International Law* (Cambridge: Cambridge University Press, 2011), p. 8, and Ragazzi, *supra* n. 47, at pp. 24–27.

[88] *South West Africa Cases, supra* n. 15, at p. 409 (Separate Opinion of Judge Jessup). Art. 5 of the Mandate provided as follows: 'Subject to the provisions of any local law for the maintenance of public order and public morals, the Mandatory shall ensure in the territory freedom of conscience and the free exercise of all forms of worship, and shall allow all missionaries, nationals of any State Member of the League of Nations, to enter into, travel and reside in the territory for the purpose of prosecuting their calling'.

[89] *Ibid.*, at pp. 410–411 (Separate Opinion of Judge Jessup) (emphasis added).

that spring from 'the most fundamental and universally accepted principles of international law' invoked by Nicaragua in its Application. These fundamental rights of a State to live in peace, free of the threat or use of force against its territorial integrity or political independence, are rights of every State, *erga omnes*. *They do not depend upon narrow considerations of privity to a dispute before the Court.* They depend upon the broad considerations of collective security.[90]

Conversely, the privity principle protects third States against a treaty imposing *obligations* on them.[91] In *Free Zones of Upper Savoy*, the question was whether Article 435 of the Versailles Treaty could abrogate the special customs regime created for the free zones of Upper Savoy and the Pays de Gex under the 1815 Protocol of the Conference of Paris. The PCIJ held that 'Article 435 of the Treaty of Versailles is not binding upon Switzerland, who is not a Party to that Treaty, except to the extent to which that country accepted it'.[92]

Likewise, in *Case Relating to the Territorial Jurisdiction of the International Commission of the River Oder*, the PCIJ refused to find that the 1921 Barcelona Statute on the Regime of Navigable Waterways of International Concern was binding on Poland.[93] The question before the PCIJ was whether the jurisdiction of the international commission extended over tributaries to the River Oder on Polish territory. The Barcelona Statute was the 'General Convention drawn up by the Allies and Associated Powers, and approved by the League of Nations' referred to in Article 338 of the Versailles Treaty, implementing a regime of free navigation. Poland, as a third State *vis-à-vis* the Barcelona Statute, argued that the convention was *res inter alios acta*. Referring to the 'ordinary rule of international law [that] conventions ... are binding only by virtue of their ratification',[94] the PCIJ found that the Barcelona Statute could not affect the rights and obligations of Poland.

In *Island of Palmas*, Arbitrator Huber held that treaties concluded by Spain with other States were *res inter alios acta* which could not bind the Netherlands: 'It appears further to be evident that Treaties concluded by Spain with third Powers recognizing her sovereignty over the

---

[90] *Case Concerning Military and Paramilitary Activities in and against Nicaragua, supra* n. 15; ICGJ 106 (ICJ 1984), 10 May 1984 (emphasis added).

[91] A. Proelss, 'Article 34' in O. Dörr and K. Schmalenbach (eds.), *Vienna Convention on the Law of Treaties: A Commentary* (Heidelberg: Springer, 2011), pp. 605–644, at p. 607 (calling this case as the 'the litmus test' for Art. 34 VCLT).

[92] *Free Zones of Upper Savoy and the District of Gex: France v. Switzerland*, 1932 PCIJ, Series A/B, No. 46, at p. 141.

[93] 7 LNTS 35. [94] 1929 PCIJ, Series A, No. 23, at p. 20.

"Philippines" could not be binding upon the Netherlands'[95] and that '. . . whatever may be the right construction of a treaty, it cannot be interpreted as disposing of the rights of independent third Powers'.[96]

In *Brita GmbH v. Hauptzollamt Hamburg-Hafen*, the Court of Justice of the European Union (CJEU) found that products originating in the West Bank did not fall within the territorial scope of the EC-Israel Association Agreement.[97] The customs authorities of an importing EC Member State could refuse to grant preferential treatment to such products under the EC-Israel Agreement.[98] The CJEU explained that to construe the EC-Israel Agreement as implying that the Israeli customs authorities had competence in relation to products originating in the West Bank would impose on Palestinian customs authorities an obligation to refrain from exercising the competence conferred upon them by virtue of the similar EC-Palestine Liberation Organization (PLO) Protocol.[99] This would go against Article 34 VCLT and create an obligation for a third party – the PLO – without its consent.

The ILC in fact 'eschews [the term *erga omnes*] on the grounds that it has sometimes been confused with obligations to all parties to a treaty'.[100] The logical deduction from this is that the Commission considers *erga omnes* obligations to apply not simply to non-injured third States who are party to a treaty but additionally to non-injured *non-parties*. Christian Tams has considered this question further, noting that given 'the allegedly objective character of status treaties, the more interesting question is whether third States *not party* to the regime-creating treaty should have the same rights'.[101] Should this question be answered in the affirmative, as Tams notes, 'this would mean the recognition of a general interest of non-parties in seeing a treaty regime observed'.[102] Examples from international practice – such as the formal protest against violations of the

---

[95] *Islands of Palmas, supra* n. 18, at p. 850.   [96] *Ibid.*, at p. 842.

[97] Euro-Mediterranean Agreement establishing an association between the European Communities and their Member States, of the one part, and the State of Israel, of the other part: Official Journal, 21 June 2000, L/147/3.

[98] Case C-386/08 *Brita GmbH v. Hauptzollamt Hamburg-Hafen* (C-386/08), Judgment of 25 Feb. 2010.

[99] Euro-Mediterranean Interim Association Agreement on trade and cooperation between the European Community, of the one part, and the Palestine Liberation Organization for the benefit of the Palestinian Authority of the West Bank and the Gaza Strip, of the other part, signed in Brussels on 24 February 1997 (OJ 1997 L 187, p. 3).

[100] E. Brown Weiss, 'Invoking State Responsibility in the Twenty-First Century', *AJIL*, 96 (2002), 798–816.

[101] Tams, *supra* n. 10, at pp. 84–85 (emphasis added).   [102] *Ibid.*

Congo River regime by the United States despite having not itself acceded to said regime, and Waldock's broad draft Article 63 which outlined the 'right of *non-State parties* to respond against breaches',[103] essentially advocating a 'general right of response'[104] – suggest this is indeed the case. Furthermore, the *Åland Islands Case*,[105] in which the Committee of Jurists asserted every State interested has the right to insist upon compliance, further supports this contention. Tams explains:

> Although controversies about the concept as such have obscured the analysis of its enforcement regime, it has been shown that authorities supporting it were prepared to recognise a right of all States, *including non-parties*, to respond to breaches of the treaty-defined status ... Although the concept of status treaties remained controversial, the limited amount of evidence available *suggests that all States should be entitled to respond against breaches.*[106]

Admittedly, Tams stops one step short of asserting that his suggestion finds *conclusive* support in the case-law, though he has maintained that 'it was hard to ignore the trend towards the recognition of general legal interest in the observance of specific categories of obligations'.[107]

Objective regimes, though established in international law, remain difficult to reconcile with the fundamental requirement of consent and are in tension with privity of treaty. Courts have tried to safeguard the requirement of third States to consent by being more demanding in cases dealing with the negative side of privity (i.e. obligations) while often finding a way around a strict adherence to the privity rule in relation to the positive side of privity (i.e. rights). In sum, it seems that objective regimes are their own species of treaties with an attenuated privity principle. Just as objective regimes therefore do not fit neatly into the privity paradigm, neither does international investment law nor individual rights, examined in the next two subsections.

4.2 Investment Arbitration

Jan Paulsson has famously described modern investment arbitration as 'arbitration without privity'.[108] Privity (of treaty) has indeed disappeared from modern international investment law insofar as the treaty relationship between the investor and the host State is concerned. Investors are

---

[103] *Ibid.*   [104] *Ibid.*   [105] *Åland Islands Case* (1920) LNOJ Spec. Supp. No. 3.
[106] Tams, *supra* n. 10, at p. 87.   [107] *Ibid.*, at p. 96.
[108] J. Paulsson, 'Arbitration without Privity', *ICSID Rev.*, 10 (1995), 232–257.

not parties to the investment treaty – they are third party beneficiaries just like individuals under human rights treaties. Yet this subsection shows that investment tribunals can neither bypass privity of contract as it may apply to the investment contract, nor privity of treaty at the inter-State level.[109]

In *Anglo-Iranian Oil Company*, one of the few investment disputes to come before the ICJ, the Court stated categorically that the UK was not in privity of contract with Iran under a concession agreement. The UK had invoked the Court's jurisdiction based on Iran's acceptance of the UK's 1932 optional clause. In addition, the UK sought to rely on the 1933 concession contract between the Government of Iran and the Anglo-Persian Oil Company, contending that this agreement had '. . . a double character, the character of being at once a concessionary contract between the Iranian Government and the Company and a treaty between the two Governments'.[110]

The Court appeared to reject in principle the idea that a concession contract could simultaneously have a State party and a non-State party. As the UK was not privy to the concession contract, it had no standing to enforce the contract:

> The Court cannot accept the view that the contract signed between the Iranian Government and the Anglo-Persian Oil Company has a double character. It is nothing more than a concessionary contract between a government and a foreign corporation. The United Kingdom Government is not a party to the contract; there is *no privity of contract* between the Government of Iran and the Government of the United Kingdom. Under the contract the Iranian Government cannot claim from the United Kingdom Government any rights which it may claim from the Company, nor can it be called upon to perform towards the United Kingdom Government any obligations which it is bound to perform towards the Company. The document bearing the signatures of the representatives of the Iranian Government and the Company has a single purpose: the purpose of regulating the relations between that Government and the Company in regard to the concession. It does not regulate in any way the relations between the two Governments.[111]

---

[109] *Impregilo SpA v. Islamic Republic of Pakistan*, ICSID Case No. ARB/03/3, Decision on Jurisdiction, 22 Apr. 2005 (paragraph 216) and *Salini Costruttori S.p.A. and Italstrade S.p.A. v. Kingdom of Morocco*, ICSID Case No. ARB/00/4, Decision on Jurisdiction, 16 July 2001 (paragraph 61). See, further, J. Ho, 'State Responsibility for Breaches of Investment Contracts' (Unpublished Ph.D. Thesis, University of Cambridge, 2014), Chapter 3.

[110] *Anglo-Iranian Oil Co. Case*: United Kingdom v. Iran (Jurisdiction) (1952) ICJ Rep. 93, at p. 112 (emphasis added).

[111] *Ibid.* (emphasis added).

International investment law has been at the forefront of relaxing the privity of treaty principle in the investor-host State relationship. Conversely, at the level of investment contracts, privity of contract continues to play an important role. Investors are not in privity of treaty with the host State, given that their State of nationality and the host State conclude the investment treaty. Notwithstanding, investors have powerful procedural and/or substantive rights as beneficiaries under investment treaties. Under one theory, obligations under investment treaties are owed to investors; under another theory they are owed jointly to the home State and their investors.[112]

According to Melvin Eisenberg, the precise character of rights and obligations is irrelevant. Instead, he has suggested, the 'law of third-party beneficiaries is largely conceived as *remedial*, rather than substantive'.[113] It matters not, therefore, whether an investment contract imposed a right or obligation upon a third party but rather 'whether empowering the third party to enforce the contract is a necessary or important means to effectuating the contracting parties' performance objectives'.[114] On his view, privity is thus sidestepped by providing third parties with rights of action to enforce contracts to which they were not parties *only* when this accords with the intentions of the contracting parties.

Privity of treaty at the inter-State level remains an important ordering principle in international law. As the *Mihaly v. Sri Lanka* tribunal concluded, a Canadian investor could not invoke the ICSID Convention against Sri Lanka in breach of privity of treaty,[115] given that Canada was not a party to the ICSID Convention:

> It follows that as neither Canada nor Mihaly (Canada) could bring any claim under the ICSID Convention, whatever rights Mihaly (Canada) had or did not have against Sri Lanka could not have been improved by the process of assignment with or without, and especially without, the express consent of Sri Lanka, on the ground that *nemo dat quod non habet* or *nemo potiorem potest transfere quam ipse habet*. That is, no one could

---

[112] A. Roberts, 'State-to-State Investment Treaty Arbitration: A Hybrid Theory of Independent Rights and Shared Interpretive Authority', *Harvard ILJ*, 55 (2014), 1–70. See, also, W. M. Reisman, Expert Opinion in *Chevron v. Ecuador*, pp. 14–15 ('investment treaties, like human rights treaties, create rights for third party beneficiaries. The BIT is part of a species of treaties for the benefit of third parties').

[113] M. A. Eisenberg, 'Third-Party Beneficiaries', *Columbia L. Rev.*, 92 (1992), 1358–1430, at 1386 (quoted in Roberts, *supra* n. 34, at 373).

[114] *Ibid.*

[115] The International Centre for the Settlement of Investment Disputes (ICSID) is an organization established by the so-called ICSID Convention: 575 UNTS 159.

transfer a better title than what he really has. Thus, if Mihaly (Canada) had a claim which was procedurally defective against Sri Lanka before ICSID because of Mihaly (Canada)'s inability to invoke the ICSID Convention, Canada not being a Party thereto, this defect could not be perfected vis-à-vis ICSID by its assignment to Mihaly (USA). To allow such an assignment to operate in favour of Mihaly (Canada) would defeat the object and purpose of the ICSID Convention and the *sanctity of the privity of international agreements not intended to create rights and obligations for non-Parties*. Accordingly, a Canadian claim which was not recoverable, nor compensable or indeed capable of being invoked before ICSID could not have been admissible or able to be entertained under the guise of its assignment to the US Claimant. A claim under the ICSID Convention with its carefully structured system is not a readily assignable chose in action as shares in the stock-exchange market or other types of negotiable instruments, such as promissory notes or letters of credit. The rights of shareholders or entitlements negotiable instruments holders are given different types of protection which are not an issue in this case before the Tribunal. This finding is without prejudice to the right of Mihaly (Canada) to pursue its claims, if any, before another otherwise competent forum.[116]

A second illustration of the continued relevance of privity (of contract) is the *Bayindir* case. The investor brought a contract claim against the host State regarding the conduct of a State agency. Bayindir's alleged investment consisted of a contract with the National Highway Authority (NHA) to build the 'Pakistan Islamabad–Peshawar Motorway'. There was no privity of contract between Bayindir and Pakistan. The NHA was a separate legal entity in Pakistan with the capacity to sue and be sued in its own name. Bayindir invoked the rules of attribution in State responsibility, even though those rules do not apply to contract claims.

Pakistan objected to the tribunal's jurisdiction on the basis that the legal foundation of Bayindir's claims was the contract with the NHA, which provided for domestic arbitration for claims arising out of the contract. The tribunal remarked that 'Bayindir has abandoned the Contract Claims and pursues exclusively Treaty Claims. When an investor invokes a breach of a BIT by the host State (not itself party to the investment contract), the alleged treaty violation is by definition an act of "puissance publique"'.[117] The tribunal then concluded that the facts

---

[116] *Mihaly International Corporation v. Democratic Socialist Republic of Sri Lanka*, Award of 15 March 2002, ICSID Case No. ARB/00/2 (paragraph 24) (emphasis added).

[117] *Bayindir Insaat Turizm Ticaret Ve Sanayi AS v. Islamic Republic of Pakistan*, Decision on Jurisdiction, 14 Nov. 2005, ICSID Case No. ARB/03/29 (paragraph 187).

alleged by the investor were capable of amounting to a violation of the BIT.

According to Zachary Douglas, 'the tribunal stumbled before adopting the correct approach'.[118] The tribunal was silent on whether it needed to objectively analyse the foundation of Bayindir's claim (i.e. whether it sounded in contract or in the treaty). Without such an objective analysis and by simply adopting the investor's characterisation of the claim's foundation, 'tribunals have allowed claimants to bypass the principle of privity of contract by . . . invoking the rules of attribution in the law of State responsibility'.[119] The result is that the investor can sue the host State, even though only the State agency is the proper defendant for a contract claim.

As we have seen, privity has not been squeezed out of investment law entirely.[120] Investment treaty arbitration is thus only 'without privity' in the sense that there is no need for the investor to have concluded an agreement to arbitrate *ex ante* with the host State in an investment contract that provides a bilateral contractual between. Investors benefit from this offer to arbitrate and the treaty's substantive guarantees without being a party to the treaty. The investor simply accepts the host's State offer to arbitrate if and when needed.

4.3 Individual Rights

International human rights law is frequently considered a 'distinct jurisprudential phenomenon',[121] which stands at some distance from international law as a whole. As Christine Chinkin explains, human rights advocates have criticised the 'narrow perspective of the VCLT',[122] which they believe rejects 'human rights as the basis of an embryonic global or regional constitutional order'[123] in favour of 'accepted principles of general international law such as State consent and State responsibility'.[124] This subsection shows that human rights, and more generally individual rights, represent a third, limited exception to privity of treaty.

---

[118] Z. Douglas, *The International Law of Investment Claims* (Cambridge: Cambridge University Press, 2009), p. 271.

[119] *Ibid.* [120] Ho, *supra* n. 109, Chapter 3.

[121] L. Brilmayer, 'From "Contract" to "Pledge": The Structure of International Human Rights Agreements', *BYbIL*, 77 (2006), 163–202, at 164.

[122] See the contribution to this volume of Chinkin at pp. 509–537 (Chapter 16).

[123] *Ibid.* [124] *Ibid.*

The relationship between individual rights and privity is linked to the position of the individual in international law more generally. International legal personality has long been controversial. The decision of the PCIJ in *Jurisdiction of the Courts of Danzig*,[125] though a frequent reference point, left the extent, if any, of individual rights in international law open. The Court adopted a conservative posture, arguably to disguise the considerable ramifications of its decision. It held:

> It may be readily admitted that, according to a well established principle of international law, the [treaty], being an international agreement, cannot, as such, create direct rights and obligations for private individuals. But it cannot be disputed that *the very object of an international agreement, according to the intention of the contracting Parties, may be the adoption by the Parties of some definite rules creating individual rights and obligations and enforceable by the national courts.*[126]

Kate Parlett has suggested this passage represents a 'significant departure from the established view of international law which saw States as the exclusive beneficiaries of international rights and obligations',[127] thereby challenging the 'state-centric view of the international legal system'.[128] At one end of the spectrum of debate sits Hersch Lauterpacht, who argued that the consequence of the Court's statement in *Danzig* was the direct applicability of international law to individuals, thereby considerably broadening international legal personality.[129] At the other end is Dionisio Anzilotti, former President of the PCIJ, who believed the opinion merely reinforced the traditional States-only conception of international legal personality, where individuals exist only by virtue of their being nationals of a State and not as independent entities capable of possessing rights and obligations.[130]

Hans Kelsen summarised the two differing sides of this debate as follows. The traditional, State-centric view is that:

---

[125] *Jurisdiction of the Courts of Danzig (Pecuniary Claims of Danzig Railway Officials Who Have Passed into the Polish Service, against the Polish Railways Administration)* (Advisory Opinion), 1928 PCIJ, Series B, No. 15, at p. 17.

[126] *Ibid.*, at pp. 17–18 (emphases added).

[127] K. Parlett, 'The PCIJ's Opinion in *Jurisdiction of the Courts of Danzig*: Individual Rights under Treaties', *J. History Int'l. L.*, 10 (2008), 119–145, at 120.

[128] *Ibid.*

[129] R. Portmann, *Legal Personality in International Law* (Cambridge: Cambridge University Press, 2010), p. 68.

[130] *Ibid.*, at p. 72.

[without] any obligation on the part of the contracting parties to recognise the jurisdiction of a tribunal to which individuals have access in a case of a violation of their 'rights' by a state, it is misleading to speak of rights being conferred upon individuals by treaty. On this view, the rights thereby conferred by the treaty are solely the rights of the contracting parties, that is, the rights of states. *Nor is this conclusion altered by the fact that the purpose of the treaty is to protect certain interests of individuals.*[131]

In contrast, the view that favours international legal personality for individuals is thus:

individuals may be considered the subjects of international rights though they are without the 'faculty of independent action to enforce these rights'. 'The fact that the beneficiary of rights is not authorized to take independent steps in his own name to enforce them does not signify that he is not a subject of the law or that the rights in question are vested exclusively in the agency which possesses the capacity to enforce them'.[132]

Kelsen himself leaned towards the second view. However, he recognised that 'a distinction must be drawn between the procedural capacity of individuals and their status as the subjects of international rights'.[133] This distinction remains important in contemporary international law. We do not have to resolve the long-standing debate about the international legal personality of individuals and companies here.[134] Yet it is hard to deny that 'individuals themselves were increasingly given procedural capacity to vindicate their rights'.[135] This procedural entitlement to claims is particularly prominent in investment arbitration (as we saw in the previous subsection), but it also exists in the sphere of individual and human rights.

In 2001, in the *LaGrand Case*, the ICJ embraced the PCIJ's tentative recognition of individual rights in *Danzig* full force in respect of Article 36 of the 1963 Vienna Convention on Consular Relations:[136]

Article 36, paragraph 1, creates individual rights for the detained person in addition to the rights accorded the sending State, and . . . consequently the reference to 'rights' in paragraph 2 must be read as applying not only

---

[131] H. Kelsen, *Principles of International Law* (New York, NY: Holt, Reinhart and Winston Inc., 2nd ed., 1966) (R. W. Tucker ed.), pp. 231–232 (quoting H. Lauterpacht) (emphasis added).

[132] *Ibid.*, at p. 232.   [133] *Ibid.*

[134] J. E. Alvarez, 'Are Corporations "Subjects" of International Law?', *Santa Clara J. Int'l L.*, 9 (2011), 1–35, at 6–9.

[135] Tams, *supra* n. 10, at p. 51.   [136] 500 UNTS 95.

to the rights of the sending State *but also* to the rights of the detained individual.[137]

Since *LaGrand*, it has been widely recognised that individuals may acquire rights directly by virtue of treaties, provided States so intended. Yet State consent remains pivotal.[138] Parlett has explained the ramifications of this decision concisely:

> Such explicit recognition that individuals can be the beneficiaries of rights under treaties represents an exception to the notion of privity of treaty in international law: individuals are able to acquire rights from a process in which they play no participatory role, and as beneficiaries to rights emanating from treaties to which they are not parties. Individual rights do however remain dependent upon State consent, such that although individuals derive rights, obligations and capacities from international law, they 'remain subordinated in the international system, suspended between object and independent or autonomous subject.[139]

Having established that individuals can benefit from rights under international law provided the treaty drafters to intended, we now turn to consider human rights treaties in particular and their implications for privity of treaty.

Human rights treaties differ from more traditional treaties. While there is no accepted universal definition, they generally create (or recognise) objective obligations, not based on reciprocity.[140] Their intended beneficiaries are individuals rather than the States parties to human rights treaties. In short, they differ in object and in nature: aiming to supply individuals with effective protection and comprising 'a network of mutual, bilateral undertakings, objective obligations ... which benefit from a "collective enforcement"'[141] rather than 'mere reciprocal

---

[137] *LaGrand*: Germany v. United States of America (2001) ICJ Rep. 466, at p. 497 (paragraph 89) (emphasis added).

[138] Parlett, *supra* n. 127, at 145 (emphasis added). Cf., also, E. Katselli, 'Countermeasures by Non-Injured States in the Law on State Responsibility', Publication of the European Society of International Law (2005), p. 3 (www.esil-sedi.eu/sites/default/files/Katselli_0 .PDF).

[139] K. Parlett, *The Individual in the International Legal System: Continuity and Change in International Law* (Cambridge: Cambridge University Press, 2011), pp. 359–360.

[140] B. Simmons, *Mobilizing for Human Rights* (Cambridge: Cambridge University Press, 2009); W. Riphapen, Fourth Report on State Responsibility, YbILC (1983–II), Part One, 18 (paragraph 89), and B. Simma and D. Pulkowski, 'Of Planets and the Universe: Self-Contained Regimes in International Law', EJIL, 17 (2006), at pp. 483–529, at 511 and 526.

[141] Portmann, *supra* n. 129, at p. 169 (quoting *Ireland v. United Kingdom* (1978) ECHR 1 (paragraph 169)).

engagements between Contracting States',[142] human rights treaties are designed to ensure that third party individuals can invoke human rights obligations directly. In this respect, they go beyond the contract-based model of most other treaties.[143]

Notwithstanding, third States have no obligations under human rights treaties. The privity principle continues to operate with respect to human rights treaties – just as it does for investment treaties.

Individuals can not only possess rights in contemporary international law but also be subject to obligations. As the ICJ recognised in *Case Concerning Application of the Convention on the Prevention and Punishment of the Crime of Genocide*, 'genocide is an international crime entailing national and international responsibility on the part of *individuals and States*'.[144] The Court reasoned that the idea that 'international law imposes duties and liabilities upon individuals *as well as upon* States has long been recognised'.[145] The Court then underlined that this 'duality of responsibility continues to be a constant feature of international law',[146] drawing parallels with the Statute of the International Criminal Court, under which provisions imposing individual criminal responsibility have no bearing on State responsibility.[147] As pointed out by Judge Christopher Weeramantry in his Separate Opinion in the preliminary objections phase of that case, the beneficiaries of the Genocide Convention are not third parties:

> [t]he beneficiaries of the Genocide Convention, as indeed of all human rights treaties, are not strangers to the State which recognizes the rights referred to in the Convention. The principle that *res inter alios acta* are not binding, an important basis of the clean slate rule, does not therefore apply to such conventions. There is no vesting of rights in extraneous third parties or in other States, and no obligation on the part of the State to recognize any rights of an external nature. Far from being a transaction *inter alios*, such treaties promote the highest internal interests which any State can aspire to protect.[148]

---

[142] *Ibid.*   [143] Brilmayer, *supra* n. 121, at 163.

[144] *Case Concerning Application of the Convention on the Prevention and Punishment of the Crime of Genocide*: Bosnia and Herzegovina v. Serbia and Montenegro (2007) ICJ Rep. 43, at p. 111 (paragraph 163) (citing General Assembly Resolution A/RES/180 (II)) (emphasis added).

[145] *Ibid.*, at p. 116 (paragraph 172) (emphasis added).

[146] *Ibid.*, at p. 116 (paragraph 173) (emphasis added).   [147] *Ibid.*

[148] *Case Concerning Application of the Convention on the Prevention and Punishment of the Crime of Genocide*: Bosnia and Herzegovina v. Yugoslavia (Preliminary Objections) (1996) ICJ Rep. 595, at p. 651 (Separate Opinion of Judge Weeramantry).

This finding that individuals have standing to enforce rights to a convention to which they are not a party suggests that the concept of privity does not apply to the Genocide Convention (and perhaps human rights treaties more broadly), particularly as the judgment makes explicit that 'in a convention of this type, one cannot speak of individual advantages and disadvantages to States, *or of the maintenance of a perfect contractual balance between rights and duties*'.[149] The contractual concept of privity is one mechanism through which this 'perfect contractual balance' is traditionally ensured in synallagmatic treaties. In the same way that third States – those to whom Articles 34–37 VCLT is addressed – are not parties to that treaty, by definition the individual beneficiary/ obligor is not a party. Thus by bestowing individuals with rights, who are neither third parties to a treaty nor in a similarly contractual relationship of any kind, human rights treaties represent an exception to the concept of privity of treaty in international law.

Such a move away from the traditional contractual model in treaty law in the human rights context is particularly visible in European Court of Human Rights case-law. Roy Portmann, in evaluating the case-law and with particular attention to *Ireland v. The United Kingdom*[150] and *Bankovic v. Belgium*,[151] has noted the extent to which the Court emphasised the unique character of the European Convention of Human Rights (ECHR),[152] favouring the notion of an objective legal order, albeit one which remains 'firmly situated ... in the overall international legal system'.[153] The Court in *Bankovic* was aware that it must remain 'mindful of the Convention's special character as a human rights treaty',[154] yet still interpret the Convention 'as far as possible in harmony with other principles of international law of which it forms part', including the VCLT and the principle of privity of treaty.[155] It claimed to be 'conscious of the need to avoid "a regrettable vacuum in the system of human-rights protection"',[156] and outlined its obligation thus:

---

[149] Tams, *supra* n. 10, at p. 50.   [150] *Supra* n. 141.

[151] *Bankovic v. Belgium* (2001) ECHR 890.   [152] 213 UNTS 221.

[153] Portmann, *supra* n. 129, at pp. 171–172; cf. also B. Conforti, 'The Specificity of Human Rights and International Law' in U. Fastenrath, R. Geiger, D.-E. Khan, A. Paulus, S. von Schorlemer and C. Vedder (eds.), *From Bilateralism to Community Interest: Essays in Honour of Judge Bruno Simma* (Oxford: Oxford University Press, 2011), pp. 433–442, at p. 434.

[154] *Bankovic v. Belgium, supra* n. 151 (paragraph 57).   [155] *Ibid.*

[156] *Ibid.* (paragraph 80).

to have regard to the special character of the Convention as a constitutional instrument of *European* public order for the protection of individual human beings.[157]

However, the 'objective character' first surfaced in the Commission's argument in *Pfunders Case*,[158] in which Austria had lodged a complaint against Italy for violating the ECHR despite Austria not being a party to the ECHR at the time of the alleged breach. Austria could invoke the ECHR before the Commission, even though it was not in privity of treaty with Italy. The Court reasoned:

> the obligations undertaken by the High Contracting Parties in the Convention are essentially of an objective character, being designed rather *to protect the fundamental rights of individual human beings* from infringement by any of the High Contracting Parties than to create subjective and reciprocal rights for High Contracting Parties themselves.[159]

The Court further held that such rights and obligations established 'the system of collective guarantee', which on the facts of the case meant that although 'Italy had no obligations towards Austria under the Convention [this did] not debar Austria from now alleging a breach of the Convention'.[160] Most saliently for our purposes is the Court's statement that a State:

> undertakes to secure these rights and freedoms not only to its own nationals and those of other High Contracting Parties *but also to nationals of States not parties to the Convention and to stateless persons.*[161]

This objective character of the ECHR regime is strong evidence for human rights treaties representing an exception to privity of treaty: first, the explicit acknowledgement that individuals have enforceable rights, regardless of whether the State in which they reside – or whose nationality they hold – is a party to the relevant treaty; and, second, non-State parties have the ability to commence inter-State proceedings against other State parties to a treaty. However, as Eckart Klein has underscored, 'it is not convincing to argue that the "objective order" established by a human rights treaty gets *entirely absolved from its contractual basis*'.[162] Privity could indeed still play a role in the human rights sphere, albeit a lesser one than traditionally at play in treaty law.

---

[157] *Ibid.*   [158] *Pfunders Case, supra* n. 65.   [159] *Ibid.*, at p. 140 (emphasis added).
[160] *Ibid.*, at p. 142.   [161] *Ibid.*
[162] E. Klein, 'Denunciation of Human Rights Treaties and the Principle of Reciprocity' in Fastenrath, Geiger, Khan, Paulus, von Schorlemer and C. Vedder (eds.), *supra* n. 153, pp. 477–487, at pp. 483–484 (emphasis added).

If it is indeed the case that human rights treaties form absolute obligations in the form of an objective legal order distinct from any multilateral contractual basis, albeit under the umbrella of international law as a whole, arguably States should lack the option of unilateral denunciation of such treaties. As Chinkin has recognised elsewhere in this volume, 'there has been a bias in favour of continuity in determining that States are not free to withdraw from, or to terminate, their human rights treaty obligations in the absence of a termination or denunciation clause'.[163] The International Covenant on Civil and Political Rights (ICCPR),[164] for example, is a typical human rights treaty. Its very nature seems to prohibit denunciation. The Human Rights Committee issued General Comments on this very point, reasoning that the rights protected by the ICCPR 'belong to the people living in the territory of the State party'[165] and 'concern the endowment of individuals with rights'[166] and, therefore, should not be affected by any change in the make-up of a government or a State. Individuals could thus invoke ICCPR rights even after a State attempted to denounce the Covenant.[167] No issue of privity arises in this scenario because the State could not successfully denounce the treaty.

The special character of human rights treaties, and the conclusion that individuals can be beneficiaries of rights which they also have standing to enforce when violated, suggests a move towards the notion of community interest, away from any kind of analogy with the traditional contractual approach to treaty-making, premised upon bilateralism. Lea Brilmayer advocates such an intellectual shift. This area of the law has shifted from 'contract' to 'pledge' in her view. She defines the latter as 'parallel and independent commitments to respect pre-existing moral norms'[168] and explains the reason for according traditional treaties different treatment from human rights treaties as follows:

---

[163] Chinkin, *supra* n. 122.   [164] 999 UNTS 171.

[165] UNHRC, General Comment No. 24 (11 Nov. 1994) U.N. Doc. CCPR/C/21/Rev.1/Add.6. (paragraph 17).

[166] UNHRC, General Comment 26 (8 Dec. 1997), U.N. Doc. CCPR/C/21/Rev.1/Add.8/ Rev.1. (paragraph 4).

[167] North Korea attempted to denounce the Covenant in 1997. See UNHRC, 'Concluding Observations of the Second Periodic Report of the Democratic People's Republic of Korea' (26 July 2011), U.N. Doc. CCPR/CO/72/PRK, in which North Korea admitted defeat in the face of arguments from the Human Rights Committee.

[168] Brilmayer, *supra* n. 121, at 165.

> Reciprocity is not the glue that holds a rights regime together; the glue that holds a rights regime together is shared commitment to moral principle.[169]

Indeed, both the ICCPR's Human Rights Committee and the Inter-American Court of Human Rights have conceded 'how little human rights instruments resemble traditional-type treaties'.[170] The community interest view which prevails throughout her article is premised not upon the traditional contractual notion of standing but upon the doctrine of obligations *erga omnes*, which Brilmayer defined as:

> a corollary of the abandonment of the contractual reciprocity model of treaties, which sees reciprocal advantage to other state parties as the core rationale underlying international agreements. For rights agreements (in contrast to traditional contractual treaties) there is likely to be no state with a direct interest ... *The entire international community* is therefore equally responsible for ensuring compliance, *regardless of injury or benefit*.[171]

The treatment of obligations *erga omnes* confirms that human rights treaties operate beyond the traditional concept of privity. According to Article 48 of the Articles on State Responsibility for Internationally Wrongful Acts (ASR) of the ILC,[172] States can invoke responsibility for breaches of such obligations, those owed to the international community as a whole, despite having suffered no 'injury', which has been tradition-ally required. Brown Weiss claimed that this article 'is significant for what it does not say',[173] namely that 'Article 48 refers to the "international community as a whole", not to the international community of states as a whole',[174] which she argues 'conforms with the view that the interna-tional community now comprises important actors other than states'.[175] For example, individuals, thereby supporting our earlier argument that individuals are capable of possessing rights stemming directly from international law.

Two counter-arguments warrant consideration. First, the principles of Article 48 ASR are not restricted to human rights treaties but are of much wider application. This prompts criticism of Brilmayer's thesis that human rights treaties represent a *unique* category of pledges. Arguably, her thesis applies equally to other categories of treaty. Indeed, she

---

[169] *Ibid.*, at 170.　[170] *Ibid.*, at 173.　[171] *Ibid.*, at 180 (emphases added).

[172] Official Records of the General Assembly, Fifty-Sixth Session, Supp. No. 10 (A/56/10), Ch. V.

[173] Brown Weiss, *supra* n. 100, at 804.　[174] *Ibid.*　[175] *Ibid.*

expressly refers to international humanitarian law treaties throughout her article[176] as operating similarly, if not identically, to those in the realm of international human rights. In addition, she concedes that pledging 'now extends beyond its initial area of application'[177] to 'every subject matter where activists seek to use international law to further normative objectives'.[178]

This conclusion contradicts her thesis of a confined group of special human rights treaties which pose an exception to privity rules. Rather, as the concept of objective regimes, this definition seems overbroad and carries a risk of removing privity as an ordering principle altogether in countless areas of treaty law, as third parties may seek to claim rights whenever a treaty appears to vaguely further an undefined moral norm or promote an important public interest. Second, whether or not human rights treaties can be considered to operate beyond the traditional concept of privity will depend entirely upon how that concept is defined. Traditional privity rules have readily allowed for the conferral of rights upon non-parties in some circumstances; thus perhaps the reconceptualisation of human rights agreements as pledges rather than treaties so as to circumvent privity rules, led by Brilmayer, is ultimately unnecessary.

Unsurprisingly, the increased role of the individual in the international human rights sphere has evolved in parallel with a growing emphasis upon individual responsibility in international criminal law. It is now widely understood that individuals may acquire obligations directly under international law,[179] without incorporation into domestic law before these obligations can take effect. Elizabeth Wilmshurst has recognised that this 'presents a challenge for the application of treaty law',[180] posing difficulties in particular for privity. While, as previously discussed, the privity of treaty concerns third party States which have not been involved in the negotiation of the treaty, 'the individuals addressed by international criminal law are not parties to the treaties and have no capacity to become parties'.[181] The similarities with developments of international human rights law are evident. However, the individual's place in international criminal law is far from settled, as Wilmshurst acknowledges when she asks 'whether a connection with a State party is necessary in order for a treaty to be applicable in proceedings against an individual'.[182] It is to

---

[176] Brilmayer, *supra* n. 121, at 178 ('the reference, here, is to human rights and international humanitarian law treaties').
[177] *Ibid.*, at 165.   [178] *Ibid.*
[179] See the contribution to this volume by Wilmshurst at pp. 621–652 (Chapter 19).
[180] *Ibid.*   [181] *Ibid.*   [182] *Ibid.*

THE PRINCIPLE OF PRIVITY

this important question, yet to be conclusively addressed, or even consistently approached by the international courts, that we now turn.

The Statute of the International Criminal Court (ICC)[183] illustrates the controversy that arises over the role of individuals in international criminal law. Wilmshurst summarises the crux of the problem as follows:

> Immediately following the adoption of the ICC Statute, objections were made that the Statute was in conflict with treaty law on *pacta tertiis* in that the ICC was given jurisdiction over nationals of a State not a party to the Statute, without that State's consent, where a crime was committed on the territory of a State party.[184]

The essence of the objections from States was that their nationals could be internationally prosecuted despite the State itself not being a party to the Statute. There are three occasions when the Statute permits the ICC to exercise jurisdiction over matters occurring in the territory of a nonparty: when the territorial State or the accused's State of nationality consents or when the Security Council refers the case to the ICC. The latter is relevant for our purposes, as the language of Article 13(b) ICC Statute is ambiguous as to whether the referral powers of the Security Council extend to compelling non-parties to comply with provisions of the Statute.[185]

This raises two distinct questions regarding privity of treaty. The first is whether the ICC can exercise jurisdiction over nationals from a nonparty, who are present in the territory of a State party. The second is whether it can ever exercise jurisdiction with respect to the territory of a non-party.

There appears to be little doubt over the answer to the first. Dapo Akande has explained the *status quo*:

> It is clear that parties to the ICC possess a territorial criminal jurisdiction over nationals of non-parties where those non-party nationals commit a crime within the territory of the ICC party.[186]

The United States (a non-party to the Statute) contended that 'an assertion over [non-party] nationals would be a violation of the well-established principle that a treaty may not impose obligations on non-parties without

---

[183] 2187 UNTS 90.   [184] Wilmshurst, *supra* n. 179.

[185] Art. 13(b) of the ICC Statute provides that '[a] situation in which one or more of such crimes appears to have been committed is referred to the Prosecutor by the Security Council acting under Chapter VII of the Charter of the United Nations': *supra* n. 183.

[186] D. Akande, 'The Jurisdiction of the International Criminal Court over Nationals of Non-Parties: Legal Basis and Limits', *J. Int'l. Crim. Just.*, 1 (2003), 618–650, at 621.

the consent of those parties'.[187] Yet Akande correctly notes that 'there is no provision in the ICC Statute that requires non-party states (as distinct from their nationals) to perform or to refrain from performing any actions. The Statute does not impose any obligations or create any duties for non-party states'.[188] Rather than a departure from privity of treaty, therefore, this view indicates a shift away from nationality being the key determinant of jurisdiction, emphasising instead the importance of the territory in which events took place.

The second question is more controversial. The exercise of the ICC's jurisdiction over events that have occurred in the territory of a non-party does seem to interfere with the rights of that State. Ruth Wedgwood has argued that the exercise of such jurisdiction is objectionable:

> The lynchpin of the Rome treaty is supposed to be its foundation in consent. The proffered reason for creating a permanent criminal court by treaty, rather than through the exercise of the Security Council's Chapter VII powers, was that an institution of fundamental importance should have the solid grounding of direct statement agreement. To be sure, states have consented to the United Nations Charter which empowers the Council, but it was felt (philosophically and politically) that a framework institution like the ICC should ground its legitimacy on the immediate consent of the participating states. The exercise of third-party jurisdiction is in tension with that claim.[189]

Other commentators have argued that the ICC Statute violates the *pacta tertiis* principle[190] by exercising jurisdiction over, and thus imposing obligations upon, non-parties without their express consent. While on its face this may seem to conflict with traditional notions of privity, the counter-argument is that the third State in fact consented, albeit to the 1945 Charter of the United Nations,[191] which authorises interference with treaty-based rights and obligations of United Nations Member States rather than the ICC Statute. Concerns of non-parties thus seem largely unfounded: individual rights and obligations for non-parties in this context seem are dependent upon prior consent of the State.

Questions of privity in international criminal law have similarly arisen in the context of international immunities, particularly those of agents of States who are not parties to the ICC Statute. Wilmshurst has explained the dilemma:

---

[187] *Ibid.*, at 620.   [188] *Ibid.*
[189] R. Wedgwood, 'The International Criminal Court: An American View', *EJIL*, 10 (1999), 93–107, at 105.
[190] See Arts. 34 and 35 VCLT: *supra* n. 3.   [191] 1 UNTS 16.

Article 27 of the [ICC] Statute gives the Court jurisdiction in spite of any immunities otherwise attaching to the prospective defendant and thus, where the defendant is a representative or agent of a State, it can be seen to be in tension with the *pacta tertiis* principle.[192]

However, the overall impact on privity is limited by Article 98 of the Statute, which seeks to temper the impact of this provision by requiring State consent whenever a person benefitting from with international law immunities is required before the Court. As we witnessed in the international human rights sphere, State consent controls the extent of third party involvement in cases where privity of treaty ceased to operate.

Some notable comparisons between individual rights and each of the other exceptions to privity of treaty, namely objective regimes and investment arbitration, emerge.

The three preceding analyses of objective regimes are equally applicable to the individual rights exception to privity of treaty. The first approach to objective regimes considered that treaties could be valid *erga omnes* under Article 36 VCLT, despite the ILC rejecting calls to expressly incorporate any such provision. Obligations *erga omnes* have gained traction in international human rights law, with commentators rejecting the contractual, reciprocity-based model of traditional treaties in favour of entrusting the entire international community with obligations regardless of injury and which can be invoked even by States that are not themselves parties to the treaty. The second approach considered objective regimes as having a public rather than contractual character, therefore making certain treaties binding on third parties in departure from traditional requirements for privity. A similar notion of human rights treaties as objective in character has emerged. The third approach suggested that customary law is responsible for the creation of objective regimes, which is equally said of much of international human rights law. Once again, as we have seen in relation to individual rights, intent and State consent – express or implied – remains decisive. Even with international community interest in objective regimes and individual rights, privity gives way only to the extent that States so intend, or at the very least acquiesce to.

The investment law exception to privity of treaty also shares similarities with the individual rights exception. Investors are not parties to investment treaties; they are third party beneficiaries who are procedurally entitled to initiate arbitrations. This is analogous to those enforcement rights and standing enjoyed by individuals under human rights treaties. Both of these

---

[192] Wilmshurst, *supra* n. 179.

are examples of remedial rights of action, conceptually distinct from sub-stantive rights which investors and individuals may also be granted despite lacking any participatory role in the creation of these rights. The latter may provide the basis for an action, but the former are the rights which, crucially, empower parties to bring such action where a substantive right has been breached, despite the treaties not explicitly providing for a legal remedy. The imposition of substantive rights, without more, poses no threat to privity. Rather, it is in the remedial context that traditional rules on privity are challenged, as third parties acquire rights of action from treaties to which they were not party.

However, notably, privity remains an important ordering principle at the inter-State level in investment law. To a lesser degree, this is equally true in the context of individuals' rights in human rights law and, especially, of obligations in international criminal law.

5   Conclusion

Under the privity principle, now codified in Articles 34–37 VCLT, States parties to treaties do not have the power to bind third States, nor do third States have any rights under such treaties or standing to enforce such rights. Treaty obligations are owed not to the world at large but only to the States parties and, in some cases, to the nationals of treaty parties. Privity of treaty ensures that the burdens and benefits of treaties are confined to insiders and that outsiders are excluded.

Despite the rules on *pacta tertiis* in the VCLT, there is no principle in modern international law, if there ever was, according to which treaties would be restricted to reciprocal relationships and categorically bar third States or non-State actors from enforcing their rights. In English contract law, privity has long been an important bar to actions in contract by third parties. Yet the strictures of privity of contract were tempered by alternative avenues for relief such as tort and equity. Conversely, in international law a treaty claim is the primary, and often the only, cause of action available, and as a result, privity of treaty has rarely been applied in formalistic fashion.

Despite the growing role of *erga omnes* norms and the rise of invest-ment treaty arbitration and individual rights, all of which, set against the larger shift from bilateralism to multilateralism, have relaxed the doctrine of privity of treaty, the doctrine itself remains an important feature of the law of treaties. As this chapter has shown, it would be premature to proclaim the death of privity. Privity is here to stay.

9

The Object and Purpose of a Treaty's Object and Purpose

DINO KRITSIOTIS

1 Introduction

On seven occasions, the 1969 Vienna Convention on the Law of Treaties (VCLT) invokes the concept of a treaty's object and purpose: in perhaps its most celebrated iteration, Article 18 provides that '[a] State is obliged to refrain from acts which would defeat the object and purpose of a treaty when: (a) it has signed the treaty or has exchanged instruments constituting the treaty subject to ratification, acceptance or approval, until it shall have made its intention clear not to become a party to the treaty; or (b) it has expressed its consent to be bound by the treaty, pending the entry into force of the treaty and provided that such entry into force is not unduly delayed'.[1] The concept also arises twice in the context of reservations to treaties;[2] twice, too, with regard to the interpretation of treaties;[3] and, then, once apiece for the modification[4] and suspension of multilateral treaties.[5] On an altogether separate occasion, reference is made to 'the object *or* purpose' of a treaty: this is done for the purpose of defining the concept of 'material breach' in Article 60 as '(a) [a] repudiation of the treaty not sanctioned by the present Convention; or (b) the violation of a provision essential to the accomplishment of the object *or* purpose of a treaty'.[6]

---

[1] 1155 UNTS 331.

[2] Specifically, with regard to their permissibility/opposability: Arts. 19(c) and 20(2) VCLT: *ibid.*

[3] As part of its general rule on interpretation (Art. 31(1) VCLT) as well as its rule on interpretation of treaties that have been authenticated in two or more languages (Art. 33(4) VCLT): *ibid.*

[4] Art. 41(1) VCLT: *ibid.*   [5] Art. 58(1) VCLT: *ibid.*

[6] Art. 60(3) VCLT (emphasis added): *ibid.* Some appear, though, to gloss over this formulation, writing for example of the 'eight times' that the Vienna Convention puts the concept to use: D. S. Jonas and T. N. Saunders, 'The Object and Purpose of a Treaty: Three Interpretative Methods', *Vanderbilt JTL*, 43 (2010), 565–609, at 569 and 576. See, also, T. Giegerich, 'Article 60' in O. Dörr and K. Schmalenbach (eds.), *Vienna Convention on the Law of Treaties:*

The repeated references to a treaty's object and purpose – or to a treaty's object or purpose – are significant, for they either recast or confirm our understanding of the structure or, more appropriately, the anatomy of any given treaty by averting our gaze away from the four corners of its text – from our perennial obsessions with *lex scripta* – to something that is altogether more mercurial but which is also, if the Vienna Convention is to be believed, no less real than the written word. Indeed, the Vienna Convention is prone to suggest that the concept of a treaty's object and purpose is inherent in every treaty: in view of the span of provisions just mentioned, it matters not whether a treaty is bilateral or multilateral in terms of its design or reach,[7] and nor do its *materiae* alter the prospect of each treaty giving rise to an object and purpose. Almost by definition, a treaty possesses a 'spirit'[8] or 'ethos'[9] existing independent from its source text,[10] and with a certain lightness of touch, the Vienna Convention proceeds to sketch in the faintest of

---

A Commentary (Berlin: Springer, 2012), pp. 1021–1049, at p. 1031 ('[t]he object and purpose standard laid down in [Art. 60(3) VCLT]') and M. M. Gomaa, *Suspension or Termination of Treaties on Grounds of Material Breach* (The Hague: Kluwer Law International, 1996), p. 29 ('[t]he object and/or purpose of a treaty'). See, further, Report of the Study Group of the International Law Commission, Fragmentation of International Law: Difficulties Arising from the Divergence and Expansion of International Law (Finalized by M. Koskenniemi), A/CN/4/L/682 (13 Apr. 2006), p. 159 (paragraph 309); M. E. Villiger, *Commentary on the 1969 Vienna Convention on the Law of Treaties* (Leiden: Martinus Nijhoff, 2009), pp. 730–751; M. Fitzmaurice, 'Material Breach of Treaty: Some Legal Issues', *Austrian Rev. Int'l & European L.*, 3 (2001), 3–44, at 5; J. Klabbers, 'Some Problems Regarding the Object and Purpose of Treaties', *Finnish YbIL*, 8 (1997), 138–160, at 142; D. Azaria, *Treaties on Transit of Energy Via Pipelines and Countermeasures* (Oxford: Oxford University Press, 2015), p. 140, and V. Crnic-Grotic, 'Object and Purpose of Treaties in the Vienna Convention on the Law of Treaties', *Asian YbIL*, 7 (1997), 141–174, at 173.

[7] I.e. had it been confined to marking out the standard for permissible reservations: cf. Arts. 18 and 60 with 19(c) and 20(2) VCLT: *supra* n. 1.

[8] M. A. Rogoff, 'The International Legal Obligations of Signatories to an Unratified Treaty', *Maine L. Rev.*, 32 (1980), 263–299, at 269 and 299 – though consider R. K. Gardiner, *Treaty Interpretation* (Oxford: Oxford University Press, 2nd ed., 2015), p. 214 that '[c]aution, however, is advisable on this as the "spirit" may suggest a nebulous formulation of what animates the treaty. "Object and purpose" is a more specific point of reference'.

[9] See, further, A. Pronto and M. Wood, *The International Law Commission 1999–2009* (Vol. IV: Treaties, Final Draft Articles, and Other Materials) (Oxford: Oxford University Press, 2010), p. 742 (on the 'ethos' of a treaty) and Fragmentation Report, *supra* n. 6, at p. 141 (paragraph 277) (regarding treaties that 'share a similar object and purpose or carry a parallel "ethos"').

[10] Even though it has been said that it is 'intrinsic' to that text: Case A 28 *Federal Reserve Bank of New York v. Bank Markazi* (2000) 36 Iran-US Claims Tribunals Reports 5 (paragraph 58). Of course, it is always possible that the object and purpose of the treaty may be specified within its operative provisions, as is done with the 'objectives' of the 1992 Convention on Biological Diversity: 1760 UNTS 79 (Art. 1).

outlines the elements of this anatomy – of a treaty's preamble, its provisions, its schedules and annexes but also its 'object and purpose'.[11]

It cannot be said, however, that the *concept* of a treaty's 'object and purpose' is an invention of the Vienna Convention, for we find that the concept had already been addressed through a range of formulations including 'l'objet et la portée' ('the aim and the scope') of a treaty,[12] 'le but et l'objet' ('the aim and the object') of a treaty,[13] 'l'objet et le but' ('the aim and the object') of a treaty[14] and 'le sens et l'espirit des traités' ('meaning and spirit of the treaties'),[15] while the Harvard Research in International Law concluded in its 1935 Draft Convention on the Law of Treaties that '[t]wo or more of the States parties to a treaty to which other States are parties may make a later treaty which will supersede the earlier treaty in their relations *inter se*, only if . . . the latter treaty is not so inconsistent with the general purpose of the earlier treaty as to be likely to frustrate that purpose'.[16] Additionally, the Draft Convention referred to 'the general purpose which [a treaty] is intended to serve' for the exercise of its interpretation,[17] and it provided that '[a] treaty which expressly provides that the obligations stipulated are to be performed in time of war between two or more of the parties, or which by reason of its nature and purpose was manifestly intended by the parties to be operative in time of war between two or more of then, is not terminated or suspended by the beginning of a war between two or more of the parties'.[18]

Part of the commitment of this chapter will be to trace the concretisation of the concept in the specific terms of a treaty's *object and purpose* in

---

[11] Along similar lines, it is worth recalling at this point Ian Sinclair's observation that '[a] reservation is a declaration which is external to the text of a treaty': see I. Sinclair, *The Vienna Convention on the Law of Treaties* (Manchester: Manchester University Press, 2nd ed., 1984), p. 51. See, also, p. 23 of that work.

[12] *Competence of the ILO to Regulate, Incidentally, the Personal Work of the Employer*, 1926 PCIJ, Series B, No. 13, p. 18.

[13] *Interpretation of the Convention Between Greece and Bulgaria Respecting Reciprocal Emigration, Signed at Neuilly-sur-Seine on November 27th, 1919 (Question of the 'Communities')*, 1930 PCIJ, Series B, No. 17, p. 21.

[14] *Interpretation of the Convention of 1919 Concerning Employment of Women During the Night*, 1932 PCIJ, Series A/B, No. 50.

[15] *Minority Schools on Albania*, 1935 PCIJ, Series A/B, No. 64, p. 15. All of these examples, *supra* n. 12, n. 13 and n. 14, are helpfully recounted by I. Buffard and K. Zemanek, 'The "Object and Purpose" of a Treaty: An Enigma?', *Austrian Rev. Int'l & European L.*, 3 (1998), 311–343, at 315.

[16] *AJIL Supp.*, 29 (1935), 653–1226, at 661 (Art. 22(b)). See, further, M. Sørenson, 'The Modification of Collective Treaties without the Consent of All the Contracting Parties', *Nordisk Tidsskrift for International Ret*, 9 (1938), 150–173.

[17] Art. 19(a): *ibid.*, at 661. Also Art. 19(b): *ibid.*

[18] Art. 35(a): *ibid.*, at 664. Also Art. 35(b): *ibid.*, at 664–665.

the decades preceding the Vienna Convention on the Law of Treaties so that, by the time of the Vienna Convention itself, there was a much more concerted effort to roll out the significance of this concept for the law of treaties more generally – making it work, as the opening inventory to this chapter indicates, across a wide range of different contexts.[19] Still, with all of these stars now appearing in the constellation, the concept does remain 'a surprisingly elusive one',[20] quite possibly because in some quarters it is still unclear whether 'object' and 'purpose' are to be treated as separate and distinct propositions.[21] Others have maintained, however, that what is at stake is a term of art that frames a singular proposition denoting a sure set of pathologies or phenomena within treaty action.[22]

---

[19] For example, as against Art. 18 VCLT (*supra* n. 1), Art. 9 of the 1935 Draft Convention provided that '[u]nless otherwise provided in the treaty itself, a State on behalf of which a treaty has been signed is under no duty to perform the obligations stipulated, prior to the coming into force of the treaty with respect to that State; under some circumstances, however, good faith may require that pending the coming into force of the treaty the State shall, for a reasonable time after signature, refrain from taking action which would render performance by any party of the obligations stipulated impossible or more difficult': *supra* n. 16, at 658. Additionally, although the 1928 Havana Convention on Treaties contained provisions on interpretation (Art. 3), reservations (Arts. 6 and 7) and relations 'governed by rules other than those established in general conventions' (Art. 18), the concept of a treaty's object is nowhere to be found: *AJIL Supp.*, 29 (1935), 1205–1207.

[20] M. Bowman, '"Normalizing" the International Convention for the Regulation of Whaling', *Michigan JIL*, 29 (2008), 293–500, at 300. See, also, A. Aust, *Modern Treaty Law and Practice* (Cambridge: Cambridge University Press, 3rd ed., 2013), p. 209 ('as we have seen in relation to reservations to treaties, [the concept] can be elusive').

[21] As indicated most recently by the International Court of Justice when it made reference to a 'solution' that 'would be contrary to both the object and the purpose of the [1948] Pact [of Bogotá]': *Case Concerning Border and Transborder Armed Actions*: Nicaragua v. Honduras (Jurisdiction and Admissibility) (1988) ICJ Rep. 69, at p. 89 (paragraph 46). This formulation was picked up and used by Judge Oda in his separate opinion: *ibid.*, pp. 109–125, at pp. 112 and 124. See, also, the formulation contained in Art. 60(3) VCLT: *supra* n. 1. Indeed, Alain Pellet has been briefly tempted 'to decompose the concept of "the object and purpose of the treaty" by examining its object on the one hand, and its purpose, on the other hand': A. Pellet, 'Article 19 (1969)' in O. Corten and P. Klein (eds.), *The Vienna Conventions on the Law of Treaties: A Commentary* (Vol. I) (Oxford: Oxford University Press, 2011), pp. 405–488, at p. 449.

[22] The conclusion of Klabbers, *supra* n. 6, at 147–148 (that the *travaux préparatoires* 'clearly indicate that "object and purpose" is to be regarded as a single notion'). See, further, Buffard and Zemanek, *supra* n. 15, at 318–319 (noting 'a strong indication that [these] are separate and distinct elements which jointly designate a point of reference for interpretation' while observing, at 325, the German, Austrian and English tradition of treating 'object and purpose' as a 'joint notion' versus 'a stream of French doctrine which gives special attention to the distinction between object and purpose [l'objet et le but] of a treaty').

To make some headway with these issues, it is proposed that we examine the operating logic of the concept of a treaty's object and purpose at least in terms of its appeal in introducing an 'eminently objective standard' into the law of treaties where '[c]onformity or non-conformity with the object and purpose [of a treaty] seem to be independent of any State's opinions on the matter'.[23] We shall want to consider how this standard might have developed or deepened over time within the specific contexts brought to the fore by the Vienna Convention, and this approach informs the essential structure of the present chapter. It is hoped not only that each of these contexts spells out the particular implications that a treaty's object and purpose will have from circumstance to circumstance[24] but that, taken together, they will provide greater illumination on what this 'unique and versatile criterion' entails,[25] fundamentally enriching our understanding of the anatomy of treaties and the dynamics of treaty relations as they do so.

2 Reservations and *Reservations to the Genocide Convention* (1951)

Although the concept of a treaty's 'object and purpose' had long been known prior to the adoption of the Vienna Convention on the Law of Treaties of May 1969,[26] it was catapulted to prominence when the International Court of

---

[23] M. Koskenniemi, *From Apology to Utopia: The Structure of International Legal Argument* (Cambridge University Press, rev. ed., 2005), p. 369. Koskenniemi is keen to emphasize that this standard 'is not *wholly* objective' (*ibid.* (emphasis in original)) and that 'the [International] Court [of Justice] never outlined how such test could be undertaken, nor what criteria were relevant in it' (*ibid.*). See, also, J. K. Gamble Jr. and M. Frankowska, 'The Significance of Signature to the 1982 Montego Bay Convention on the Law of the Sea', *Ocean Dev. & Int'l L.*, 14 (1984–1985), 121–160, at 125. Note, too, H. Waldock, First Report on the Law of Treaties, Doc. A/CN.4/144 (20 March 1962), pp. 65–66 ('the principle [of object and purpose] is essentially subjective and unsuitable for use as a general test for determining whether a reserving State is or is not entitled to be considered to a multilateral treaty' while admitting that this does 'express a valuable concept to be taken into account both by States formulating a reservation and by States deciding whether or not to consent to a reservation that has been formulated by another State').

[24] C. A. Bradley, 'Treaty Signature' in D. B. Hollis (ed.), *The Oxford Guide to Treaties* (Oxford: Oxford University Press, 2012), pp. 208–219, at p. 213.

[25] Report of the International Law Commission, Fifty-Ninth Session (May-Aug. 2007), U.N. Doc. Supp. No. 10 (A/62/10), p. 68.

[26] See, further, H. W. Malkin, 'Reservations to Multilateral Conventions', *BYbIL*, 7 (1926), 141–162, at 142.

Justice delivered its advisory opinion in *Reservations to the Convention on the Prevention and Punishment of the Crime of Genocide* in May 1951.[27] The advisory opinion involved the Court responding to three 'abstract'[28] questions on the matter of reservations to treaties put to it by the General Assembly in November 1950 in the wake of some eighteen reservations that had been made by eight States to the 1948 United Nations Convention on the Prevention and Punishment of the Crime of Genocide.[29] The challenge facing Trygve Lie, the first Secretary-General of the United Nations, who served as the depositary to the Convention,[30] was whether States coming to the Convention with reservations could be counted among the number of States deemed necessary to bring the Convention into force.[31]

The Court commenced its analysis by recalling and emphasising the significance that consent has historically had in treaty relations: consent,

[27] *Reservations to the Convention on the Prevention and Punishment of the Crime of Genocide* (Advisory Opinion) (1951) ICJ Rep. 15. Note, though, that in his dissenting opinion, Judge Alejandro Alvarez wrote, *ibid.*, at p. 54, of 'the aims and objects of the Convention' ('les buts et objectifs de la Convention'). See, further, Klabbers, *supra* n. 6, at 140 (on the 'modern notion').

[28] *Ibid.*, at p. 21 – or, as it was put at another point, 'purely abstract' questions (*ibid.*, at p. 21). This was because '[t]hey refer neither to the reservations which have, in fact, been made to the Convention by certain States, nor to the objections which have been made to such reservations by other States' (p. 21). To refresh our memories, the three questions posited by the General Assembly were as follows:

 I. Can the reserving State be regarded as being a party to the Convention while still maintaining its reservation if the reservation is objected to by one or more of the parties to the Convention but not by others?

 II. If the answer to Question I is in the affirmative, what is the effect of the reservation between the reserving State and:
 (a) the parties which object to the reservation?
 (b) those which accept it?

 III. What would be the legal effect as regards the answer to Question I if an objection to a reservation is made:
 (a) by a signatory which has not yet ratified?
 (b) by a State entitled to sign or accede but which has not yet done so?

[29] 78 UNTS 277.

[30] Under Art. 11(2) of the Convention: *ibid.* Parry writes of how the Genocide Convention is 'remarkable for the cumbersome quality of its formal clauses', where notification of reservations is one of 'nine distinct duties': C. Parry, 'Some Recent Developments in the Making of Multi-Partite Treaties', *Transactions G. Soc.*, 36 (1950), 149–189, at 180.

[31] In accordance with Art. 13(2) of the Convention, it would come into force on the nineteenth day following the date of deposit of the twentieth instrument of ratification or accession: *ibid.* The Convention's entry into force – on 12 Jan. 1951 – was therefore imminent when the General Assembly referred its three questions to the Court on 16 Nov. 1950 (*supra* n. 28); the Convention contained no provision on reservations.

the Court said, not only was essential to realising a State's ambition to become part of a particular treaty but also was the mechanism for ensuring the 'integrity' of a treaty. The Court spoke of 'a generally recognised principle that a multilateral convention is the result of an agreement freely concluded upon its clauses'[32] and that, consequently,

> none of the contracting parties is entitled to frustrate or impair, by means of unilateral decisions or particular agreements, the purpose and *raison d'être* of the convention. To this principle was linked the notion of the integrity of the convention as adopted, a notion which in its traditional concept involved the proposition that no reservation was valid unless it was accepted by all the contracting parties without exception, as would have been the case if it has been stated during negotiations.[33]

Against this imperative of treaty integrity, the Court then considered what it called 'a variety of circumstances' that 'would lead to a more flexible application of this principle' in the specific context of the Genocide Convention,[34] emphasising 'a new need for flexibility in the operation of multilateral conventions' that would facilitate greater participation therein.[35] Indeed, the Court inferred from the first of the questions put to it by the General Assembly the existence of a 'faculty' to posit reservations to the Genocide Convention,[36] which was in fact, the Court said, 'contemplated at successive stages of the drafting of the Convention'.[37] The Court then turned its attention to the consequences of exercising this faculty, especially 'what kind of

---

[32] *Supra* note 27, at p. 21. See, also, the contribution to this volume of Craven at pp. 103–135 (Chapter 5).

[33] *Ibid.* (which, the Court said, 'is directly inspired by the notion of contract').

[34] *Ibid.* For further assessment of this theme of integrity, consider C. Redgwell, 'Universality or Integrity? Some Reflections on Reservations to General Multilateral Treaties', *BYbIL*, 64 (1993), 245–282, at 251. Though see, also, R. Goodman, 'Human Rights Treaties, Invalid Reservations, and State Consent', *AJIL*, 96 (2002), 531–560, at 535 ('the modern approach should be viewed as harmonizing – rather than choosing between – universality and integrity').

[35] *Supra* n. 27, at p. 22 (as manifested by '[m]ore general resort to reservations, very great allowance made for tacit assent to reservations, the existence of practices which go so far as to admit that the author of reservations which have been rejected by certain contracting parties is nevertheless to be regarded as a party to the convention in relation to those contracting parties that have accepted the reservations': *ibid.*, at pp. 21–22). See, further, D. R. Anderson, 'Reservations to Multilateral Conventions: A Re-examination', *ICLQ*, 13 (1964), 450–481.

[36] *Supra* n. 27, at p. 22.

[37] *Ibid.* (where 'the absence of an article providing for reservations' should not be taken to mean 'that the contracting States are prohibited from making certain reservations' as this can be explained 'by the desire not to invite a multiplicity of reservations').

reservations may be made and what kind of objections may be taken to them'.[38] For the Court, '[t]he solution of these problems must be found in the special characteristics' of the Convention itself – an approach that brought the Court into closer touch with 'the will of the General Assembly and the parties' to the Convention.[39] And, in the same breath, the Court maintained that the 'objects' – note the plural here[40] – of such a convention also had to enter the reckoning:

> The Convention was manifestly adopted for a purely humanitarian and civilizing purpose. It is indeed difficult to imagine a convention that might have this dual character to a greater degree, since its object on the one hand is to safeguard the very existence of certain human groups and on the other to confirm and endorse the most elementary principles of humanity. In such a convention the contracting States do not have any interests of their own; they merely have, one and all, a common interest, namely, the accomplishment of those high purposes which are the *raison d'être* of the convention. Consequently, in a convention of this type one cannot speak of individual advantages or disadvantages of States, or of the maintenance of a perfect contractual balance between rights and duties. The high ideals which inspired the Convention provide, by virtue of the common will of the parties, the foundation and measure of all its provisions.[41]

We can observe the equation the Court appears to draw in this passage between 'object' and 'purpose',[42] before it moved to articulate the mechanism for regulating 'the effects of objections to reservations',[43]

---

[38] *Ibid.*, at p. 23.

[39] *Ibid.* (as interpreted from: the origins and character of the Convention; the objects pursued by the General Assembly and the contracting parties; the relations which exist between the provisions of the Convention, *inter se*, and between those provisions and these objects). Note McNair's observation – in 1961 – that 'the practice of making reservations to multipartite treaties is now so common that some development in mechanism is required': A. D. McNair, *The Law of Treaties* (Oxford: Clarendon Press, 1961), p. 162. See, also, p. 168.

[40] Again, note the Court's reference to 'high purposes': *supra* n. 27, at p. 24.

[41] *Ibid.*, at p. 23. At a later point in its opinion (at p. 24), the Court made reference to 'the authority of the moral and humanitarian principles which are [the] basis [of the Convention]'.

[42] Indeed, also in the plural ('high purposes'): *ibid.* Similarly, at p. 24 (re: 'the acceptance of reservations which frustrate the purposes which the General Assembly and the contracting parties had in mind' and 'which may be quite compatible with those purposes').

[43] *Ibid.*, at p. 23. As against 'the conception of the absolute integrity of a convention' – which, the Court maintained (at p. 24), had not been 'transformed into a rule of international law'.

and it is in this context that it made its first reference to the concept of that treaty's 'object and purpose':

> The object and purpose of the Genocide Convention imply that it was the intention of the General Assembly and of the States which adopted it that as many States as possible should participate. The complete exclusion from the Convention of one or more States would not only restrict the scope of its application, but would detract from the authority of the moral and humanitarian principles which are its basis. It is inconceivable that the contracting parties readily contemplated that an objection to a minor reservation should produce such a result. But even less could the contracting parties have intended to sacrifice the very object of the Convention in favour of a vain desire to secure as many participants as possible. The object and purpose of the Convention thus limit both freedom of making reservations and that of objecting to them. It follows that it is the compatibility of a reservation with the object and purpose of the Convention that must furnish the criterion for the attitude of a State in making the reservation on accession as well as for the appraisal by a State in objecting to the reservation. Such is the rule of conduct which must guide every State in the appraisal which it must take, individually and from its own standpoint, of the admissibility of any reservation.[44]

What is especially interesting from these passages is how the Court develops an assured intimacy between the *intentions* of the General Assembly and States adopting the Convention and the *object and purpose* of the treaty: the Contracting States are there not just *qua* Contracting States to the Convention but also, and perhaps foremost, as designers or authors of the treaty. The Genocide Convention did not, of course, emerge from thin air: 'The high ideals which inspired the Convention provide', the Court reasoned, 'by virtue of the common will of the parties, the foundation and measure of all of its provisions'.[45] Yet, even with 'the foundation and measure of all of its provisions' in place, the Convention was still not able to yield an answer to the question of whether the aforementioned reservations were valid: for this, the Court had to read into the intention of the authors of the Convention as

---

[44] *Ibid.*, at p. 24. Indeed, in this formulation, the Court would appear to treat 'object' and 'purpose' as distinct propositions and *not* as interchangeable with one another or integrated into one generic concept or term of art: 'The object and purpose of the Genocide Convention imply' – not *implies*. Also, further in the same passage, '[t]he object and purpose of the Convention thus limit' – not *limits*. One is led to wonder whether these nuances somehow became lost once the Court *named* 'the object and purpose' of the Genocide Convention in this way: see, for instance, the remarks of Paul Reuter, *YbILC* (1964–I), 26 (paragraph 77).

[45] *Supra* n. 41.

refracted through the object and purpose of the Convention ('that as many States as possible should participate', or so deduced the Court).[46] It had to peer beyond the text – that is, beyond the provisions of the Convention – to its very object and purpose to see what this would 'imply': 'It is inconceivable', concluded the Court, 'that the contracting parties readily contemplated that an objection to a minor reservation should produce [the] result' of the 'complete exclusion from the Convention of one or more States'.[47]

We can appreciate that it is at this juncture that serious disagreement occurred *within* the Court, for Judges José Gustavo Guerrero, John Erksine Read, Hsu Mo and Sir Arnold McNair entered a joint dissenting opinion claiming that the approach before them would force 'a corresponding classification of the provisions of the Convention into two categories – of minor and major importance' in terms of their relation to the treaty's object and purpose.[48] Concerned, too, that 'no legal basis' existed for the scheme articulated by the Court,[49] these dissenting judges interrogated the operationalisation of a rule that 'hinges' on the identification of a treaty's object and purpose: 'What is the "object and purpose" of the Genocide Convention?', they asked pointedly. 'To repress genocide? Of course; but is it more than that? Does it comprise any or all of the enforcement articles of the Convention? That is the heart of the matter'.[50]

---

[46] *Supra* n. 44.

[47] *Ibid.* And, elsewhere, *supra* n. 27, at p. 24: 'Any other view would lead either to the acceptance of reservations which frustrate the purposes which the General Assembly and the contracting parties had in mind, or to recognition that the parties to the Convention have the power of excluding from it the author of a reservation, even a minor one, which may be quite compatible with those purposes'. Also: 'having regard to the character of the convention, its purpose and mode of adoption, it can be established that the parties intended to derogate from that rule by admitting the faculty to make reservations thereto': *ibid.*

[48] *Supra* n. 27, at p. 42.   [49] *Ibid.*

[50] *Ibid.*, at p. 44. For these dissenting judges, '[w]hen a new rule is proposed for the solution of disputes, it should be easy to apply and calculated to produce final and consistent results'. For its part, the International Law Commission was not far behind in its criticism of this mechanism: in its report on reservations to multilateral conventions to the General Assembly in 1951, the ILC concluded:

> 24. The Commission believes that the criterion of the compatibility of a reservation with the object and purposes of a multilateral convention, applied by the International Court of Justice to the Convention on Genocide, is not suitable for application to multilateral conventions in general. It involves a classification of the provisions of a convention into two categories, those which do and those which do not form part of its

Several observations now appear to be in order. First, there can be no doubting the centrality that the Court awarded to the concept of a treaty's object and purpose in its analysis: as A. D. McNair has observed, 'the [C]ourt, in effect, substituted for the requirement of the unanimous consent to a reservation the requirement that it must be "compatible with the object and purpose of the [Genocide] Convention"'.[51] A treaty's 'object and purpose' thus became the Court's 'uniform piece of machinery' for the task before it,[52] at the heart of which existed the treaty's integrity – or, we might say, its 'essence'.[53] That much remains clear; it is not disturbed by any incidental details that we might have teased from the advisory opinion of the Court.

Second, in setting down the object and purpose of a treaty as the 'criterion' for distinguishing valid from invalid reservations, it appears that we are none the wiser as to what the object and purpose of the Genocide Convention might in fact be – at least as it stood (or stood to be deciphered) at that point in time. To be sure, this determination might well have been regarded as surplus to requirements given the nature of the questions put to the Court by the General Assembly,[54] and, in any event, the Court did make mention of the 'object' of the Convention (which 'on the one hand is to safeguard the very existence of certain human groups and on the other to confirm and endorse the most elementary principles of humanity').[55] However, is this to be taken as the *totality* of the Genocide Convention's object and purpose? What if that totality is simply that which is stated in the preamble to the

> object and purpose. It seems reasonable to assume that, ordinarily at least, the parties regard the provisions of a convention as an integral whole, and that a reservation to any of them may be deemed to impair its object and purpose. Even if the distinction between provisions which do and those which do not form part of the object and purpose of a convention be regarded as one that it is intrinsically possible to draw, the Commission does not see how the distinction can be made otherwise than subjectively.

YbILC (1951–II), 128. The Commission was of the view, *ibid.*, at 129, that where a convention places 'no limit on the admissibility of reservations', the preferred approach would be for the text to 'establish a procedure in respect of the tendering of reservations and their effect'.

[51] McNair, *supra* n. 39, at p. 166. McNair is of course referring here to p. 27 of the advisory opinion: *supra* n. 27.

[52] As formulated by McNair: *supra* n. 39, at p. 170.

[53] E. T. Swaine, 'Treaty Reservations' in Hollis (ed.), *supra* n. 24, pp. 277–301, at p. 285.

[54] *Supra* n. 28.

[55] *Supra* n. 41 (in a context in which it also adverted to 'those high purposes which are the *raison d'être* of the convention').

Convention – that the Contracting Parties are convinced that 'international co-operation is required' for dealing with the crime of genocide?[56] What, then, is to be made of the 'prevention' and 'punishment' of this crime as per the Convention's title? And what if, hypothetically, part of the object and purpose of the Convention was the codification of international custom?[57] Was the Court itself even fully conscious of what it understood the 'special characteristics' of the Genocide Convention to be? For the Court does seem to hint at the potential complexity – the multidimensionality, if you will – of a treaty's object and purpose even in one as short as the Genocide Convention, comprising as it does a mere nineteen articles. '[E]ven less', chides the Court in one moment, 'could the contracting parties have intended to sacrifice the very object of the Convention in favour of a vain desire to secure as many participants as possible',[58] and yet it is that very 'vain desire' that the Court had earlier derived from '[t]he object and purpose of the Genocide Convention'.[59] From what the Court says, there is some sense that a treaty's 'object and purpose' awaits to be determined at different levels of engagement, taking on matters of *substance* ('to safeguard the very existence of certain human groups'),[60] the intended *structure* of legal relations (absent 'the maintenance of a perfect contractual balance between rights and duties')[61] and its projected *sphere of operation* ('as many States as possible should participate').[62]

Third, and perhaps most importantly of all, is the envisaged operationalisation of the Court's scheme: in short, just how was it meant to work in practice? Admittedly, once the object and purpose of the Genocide Convention is known, it does seem to follow – as was anticipated by the four dissenting judges – that different provisions of the Convention will relate to it in different ways or, rather, with differing strengths of connection. The Court said as much later in its advisory

---

[56] *Supra* n. 29. The preamble actually notes that genocide is a crime under international law – one that is 'contrary to the spirit and aims of the United Nations': *ibid.*

[57] See, further, P. Gaeta, 'On What Conditions Can a State Be Held Responsible for Genocide?', *EJIL*, 18 (2007), 631–648, at 642.

[58] *Supra* n. 44.   [59] *Ibid.* (i.e. 'that as many States as possible should participate').

[60] *Supra* n. 41.

[61] *Ibid.* This is brought on by the Court's emphasis of the 'character' of the Convention (*supra* n. 27, at p. 22), including the 'universal character both of the condemnation of genocide and of the co-operation required "in order to liberate mankind from such an odious scourge"': *ibid.*, at p. 23 (drawing on the formulation from the preamble of the Genocide Convention). See, further, McNair, *supra* n. 39, at p. 167.

[62] *Supra* n. 44.

opinion with its claim that '[i]t must clearly be assumed that the contracting States are desirous of preserving intact at least what is essential to the object of the Convention',[63] and when it spoke of 'the power of excluding from [the Convention] the author of a reservation, even a minor one, which may be quite compatible with those purposes'.[64] So, at least as far as (proposed) reservations are concerned, an apparent principle of *essentiality* is in operation,[65] with the Court having in mind that it is the *reserving* State that must activate the principle in the first instance: 'it is the compatibility of a reservation with the object and purpose of the Convention that must furnish the criterion for the attitude of a State in making the reservation on accession'. In the second instance, however, it is also the criterion which should inform 'the appraisal by a State in objecting to the reservation':[66] '[s]uch is the rule of conduct which must guide every State in the appraisal which it must make, individually and from its own standpoint, of the admissibility of any reservation'.[67]

Under this scheme, one can appreciate that 'whether a reservation is contrary to [a] treaty's object and purpose becomes a question lexically prior to whether States can object' thereto,[68] and this interpretation is very much supported by the Court's conclusion that '[a] State which has made and maintained a reservation which has been objected to by one or more of the parties to the Convention but not by others, can be regarded as being a party to the Convention *if the reservation is compatible with the object and purpose of the Convention*'.[69] However, the Court's scheme does seem to make some accommodation for any uncertainties that might result from the identification of the 'very'[70] object and purpose of a treaty, especially given the intricacies associated with that task. This is to say nothing of the essentiality of a proposed reservation to a treaty's object and purpose once that has been identified, since the Court seemed minded to involve States *other than the reserving State* in an exercise of

---

[63] *Supra* n. 27, at p. 27 (emphasis added).

[64] *Ibid.*, at p. 24. Again, plural: *supra* n. 40 (and accompanying text) and n. 42.

[65] One that 'implies a distinction between all obligations in the treaty and the core obligations that are the treaty's *raison d'être*': L. Lijnzaad, *Reservations to UN Human Rights Treaties: Ratify and Ruin?* (Dordrecht: Martinus Nijhoff, 1994), p. 83.

[66] *Supra* n. 27, at p. 24. [67] *Ibid.*

[68] B. Çalı, 'Specialized Rules of Treaty Interpretation: Human Rights' in Hollis (ed.), *supra* n. 24, pp. 525–548, at p. 535.

[69] *Supra* n. 27, at p. 29 (emphasis added). The Court's answer to Question I of the General Assembly: *supra* n. 28 (by seven votes to five).

[70] The Court's word: *supra* n. 44.

interaction and deliberation: in the Court's words, the 'criterion' of 'the compatibility of a reservation with the object and purpose of [a] Convention' must *also* ('as well as') inform 'the appraisal by a State in objecting to the reservation' if that should come to pass.[71]

***

And so the foundations were set for the rules on reservations that arrived with the Vienna Convention in May 1969 – which preserved the 'presumptive right for States to forge reservations',[72] and embraced the concept of a treaty's object and purpose for regulating the making of reservations more generally[73] (i.e. beyond the 'special characteristics' of the Genocide Convention that had so defined the Court's reasoning in the *Reservations* advisory opinion).[74] According to Article 19 VCLT, this faculty of States to formulate a reservation exists unless:

(a) the reservation is prohibited by the treaty;
(b) the treaty provides that only specified reservations, which do not include the reservation in question, may be made; or
(c) in cases not falling under sub-paragraphs (a) and (b), the reservation is incompatible with the object and purpose of the treaty.[75]

The inclusion of the concept or 'notion'[76] of a treaty's 'object and purpose' in this manner surely confirms its status as 'the equilibrium point between the necessity of preserving the essential core of the treaty and the willingness to facilitate membership of an as large as possible

---

[71] *Supra* n. 44. Also in the dispositif to Question II (by seven votes to five): 'if a party to the Convention objects to a reservation which it considers incompatible with the object and purpose of the Convention, it can in fact consider that the reserving State is not a party to the Convention'. *Supra* n. 27, at p. 29.

[72] Swaine, *supra* n. 53, at p. 285.

[73] Art. 19(c) VCLT: *supra* n. 1. Zemanek considers this an instance of the Court having 'initiated new custom': see K. Zemanek, 'Re-examining the Genocide Opinion: Are the Object and Purpose of a Convention Suitable Criteria for Determining the Admissibility of Reservations?' in N. Ando, E. McWhinney and R. Wolfrum (eds.), *Liber Amicorum Judge Shigeru Oda* (Vol. I) (The Hague: Kluwer Law International, 2002), pp. 335–348, at p. 335. See, also, McNair, *supra* n. 39, at p. 166 (a 'new test of the admissibility of reservations') and p. 167 ('this new criterion').

[74] *Supra* n. 27, at p. 23. Note Swaine's observation that the Court had not 'directly confront[ed] the question of whether an object-and-purpose test was hard-wired in all treaties (or, at least, in those that permitted reservations with less than unanimous consent)' where 'the Court's analysis seemed sufficiently context-sensitive to resist easy generalization, and it felt little cause to clarify anything beyond the result for the Genocide Convention itself – or, perhaps, for the greater class of human rights conventions to which it belonged': *supra* n. 53, at p. 283.

[75] Art. 19 VCLT: *supra* n. 1.   [76] Pellet, *supra* n. 21, at p. 445.

number of States to multilateral conventions',[77] as well as, ultimately, its significance for the law of treaties more generally,[78] notwithstanding the ritual uncertainties that continue to surround its actual 'content' and meaning.[79] Still, the strong and possibly symbolic message coming forward from the Vienna Convention is that States (and, in turn, international organizations)[80] do not have free reign to formulate any reservation of their choosing. In particular, when a treaty falls silent on prohibiting or authorising specific reservations to it,[81] that is not to be treated as an invitation for devising imaginative flights of fancy by a prospective treaty partner since the integrity – the normative integrity – of a treaty arrangement is there to be upheld as a matter of the law of treaties.[82] Of course, ironically or not, this is the position the Vienna Convention finds itself in since it contains no provision on reservations made against its own terms,[83] and the unadulterated technical nature of the Convention must give some pause for thought as to whether it might be 'virtually impossible' to determine its object and purpose.[84]

---

[77] *Ibid.*, at p. 445 (though, at pp. 419–420, noting that there is in fact a 'double equilibrium' for rules relating to reservations: 'between the prerequisites of universality and the integrity of the treaty' and 'between the liberty of the consent of the reserving State and that of the other States parties').

[78] Against, it must be said, some strong initial opposition within the International Law Commission 'as a *criterion* of a reserving State's status as a party to a treaty in combination with the objective criterion of the acceptance or rejection of the reservation by other States': Waldock, First Report on the Law of Treaties, *supra* n. 23, at p. 66 (original emphasis).

[79] Pellet, *supra* n. 21, at p. 445 (conceding, though, at p. 415, that '[t]his ambiguity, which has never been entirely removed . . . has undoubtedly allowed for the adoption of the system and is perhaps even the explanation of its relative success').

[80] See Art. 19 of the 1986 Vienna Convention on the Law of Treaties between States and International Organizations or between International Organizations: ILM, 25 (1986), 543–592.

[81] Authorised reservations are to be read as implicit prohibitions: Pellet, *supra* n. 21, at pp. 414 and 443–444.

[82] As Pellet remarks: Art. 19(c) VCLT 'guarantees, if not the *integral* application of its provisions, at least the *integrity* of its essential content': *supra* n. 21, at p. 420. See, also, *ibid.*, at pp. 409 and 427. One thinks of Lijnzaad's vivid image in this respect – that '[a] large number of reservations made by a great many States will turn a human rights instrument into a moth-eaten guarantee': *supra* n. 65, at p. 3.

[83] Sinclair, *supra* n. 11, at pp. 63–68. See, also, Aust, *supra* n. 20, at p. 124.

[84] Aust, *supra* n. 20, at p. 124. See *infra* n. 193 (and accompanying text). Not all is lost, however: Sinclair, *supra* n. 11, at pp. 67–68 ('[a] reservation to Article 66 [VCLT] or to the Annex [to the VCLT] might or might not eventually be determined to be incompatible with the object and purpose of the Convention; certainly, any such reservation, to use the words of the International Law Commission, "undermined the basis of the treaty or of a compromise made in the negotiations"'). Note, too, the Syrian Arab Republic's 'political statement' – Sinclair does not regard it as 'a reservation in the strict sense' – to Art. 81 VCLT ('[t]he present

Quite possibly, the Vienna Convention is making clear to authors of future treaties that a potential safeguard against untoward reservations will exist even if disagreement precludes a provision on reservations in their respective texts (Article 19(a) and (b) VCLT).[85] This will occur through the convenient vector of the treaty's 'object and purpose' (Article 19(c) VCLT). That said, it is not apparent from the Vienna Convention what consequences follow if a reserving State does not correctly 'intuit for itself'[86] that the reservation it has up its sleeve is *not* compatible with the aforementioned object and purpose.[87] If that State runs the risk of positing that reservation, will the reservation be void *ab initio* (as is proclaimed by the 'permissibility' school), or does it become subject to the Vienna Convention rules on objections (as *per* the 'opposability' school)?[88] Importantly, treaty practice either side of the Vienna Convention has explicitly embraced the concept of 'object and purpose' as a means of determining the permissibility of reservations, as in Article 20(2) of the 1965 United Nations Convention on the Elimination of All Forms of Racial Discrimination[89] and Article 28(2)

Convention shall be open for signature by all States Members of the United Nations or of any of the specialized agencies or of the International Atomic Energy Agency or parties to the Statute of the International Court of Justice, and by any other State invited by the General Assembly of the United Nations to become a party to the Convention, as follows: until 30 November 1969, at the Federal Ministry for Foreign Affairs of the Republic of Austria, and subsequently, until 30 April 1970, at United Nations Headquarters, New York') – that the provision 'is not in conformity with the aims and purposes of the Convention in that it does not allow all States, without distinction or discrimination, to become parties to it'. Sinclair, *supra* n. 11, at p. 65. This is significant because of its pluralisation of the 'aims and purposes' of the VCLT, but also because of its indication that 'the sovereign equality and independence of all States' as announced in the sixth preambular recital of the VCLT, forms part of that treaty's object and purpose.

[85] As occurred with Spain's proposal to prohibit reservations to Part V of the Vienna Convention ('Invalidity, Termination and Suspension of the Operation of Treaties') – which was rejected by sixty-two votes to nine, with thirty-three abstentions after 'strong objections' had been voiced by Brazil, Israel, the Soviet Union, India, the United Kingdom and Nigeria: Sinclair, *supra* n. 11, at p. 79. See, also, Aust, *supra* n. 20, at p. 122.

[86] As is wonderfully put by Swaine: *supra* n. 53, at p. 285.

[87] One of the contenders, we can presume, of the 'conceal[ed]' difficulties of the Vienna Convention régime: Sinclair, *supra* n. 11, at p. 62.

[88] See Arts. 20 and 21 VCLT: *supra* n. 1.

[89] 660 UNTS 195 ('[a] reservation incompatible with the object and purpose of this Convention shall not be permitted, nor shall a reservation the effect of which would inhibit the operation of any of the bodies established by this Convention be allowed'). Though the object and purpose of the Convention is not specified in the Convention, the formulation presented is instructive because it gives the impression that any inhibition of 'the operation of any of the bodies established by this Convention' does not pertain to the Convention's object and purpose.

of the 1979 United Nations Convention on the Elimination of All Forms of Discrimination Against Women.[90] This is interesting because these provisions could be viewed either as instances of what has emerged as Article 19(c) VCLT or, conceivably, as serving to define prohibited reservations in accordance with Article 19(a) VCLT (in which case, as with all prohibited reservations, there would be no 'need' for other States and international organizations to react 'for they have already expressed their objection to it in the treaty itself').[91]

The Vienna Convention invokes the concept of a treaty's 'object and purpose' on one other occasion in articulating its system on reservations, and this is to restrict the application of Article 19 VCLT in circumstances where 'it appears from the limited number of the negotiating States *and the object and purpose of a treaty* that the application of the treaty in its entirety between all the parties is an essential condition of the consent of each one to be bound by the treaty'; here, 'a reservation requires acceptance by all the parties'.[92] This reference to so-called 'plurilateral treaties'[93] or 'restricted multilateral treaties'[94] is further evidence of the

---

[90] 1249 UNTS 13 ('[a] reservation incompatible with the object and purpose of the present Convention shall not be permitted'). Additionally, Art. 29(2) provides that each State Party may 'declare that it does not consider itself bound' by Art. 29(1) of the Convention – relating to the dispute settlement mechanisms of negotiation, arbitration or judicial settlement. It is encouraging to note that, in terms of more recent practice, objections to reservations assume more of an explanatory character regarding compatibility with the Convention's 'object and purpose': J. Connors, 'Article 28' in M. A. Freeman, C. Chinkin and B. Rudolf (eds.), *The UN Convention on the Elimination of All Forms of Discrimination against Women* (Oxford: Oxford University Press, 2012), pp. 565–595, at pp. 576–577.

[91] Waldock, First Report on the Law of Treaties, *supra* n. 23, at p. 65.

[92] Art. 20(2) VCLT: *supra* n. 1 (emphasis added). This is why Pellet argues that Art. 19(c) VCLT 'displays a subsidiary character', i.e. 'only because it intervenes outside the hypotheses envisaged by paragraphs 2 and 3 of Article 20 of the Convention': *supra* n. 21, at p. 443. For Müller, Arts. 20(2) and 20(3) VCLT 'are nothing more than "savings clauses"', which 'exclude the applicability of the "flexible" regime to certain categories of treaties without specifying the applicable rules': D. Müller, 'Article 20 (1969)' in Corten and Klein (eds.), *supra* n. 21, pp. 489–537, at p. 519.

[93] See Aust, *supra* n. 20, at p. 125 (treaties 'negotiated between a limited number of States with a particular interest in the subject matter') and C. Walter, 'Article 20' in Dörr and Schmalenbach (eds.), *supra* n. 6, pp. 287–306, at p. 296.

[94] Sinclair, *supra* n. 11, at p. 33. Sinclair gives as 'obvious examples' the Treaty establishing the European Economic Community and the other basic European Community treaties: *ibid.*, at p. 34. Aust's example is that of the 1959 Antarctica Treaty, 402 UNTS 71: *supra* n. 20, at p. 125. Consider, too, the example of the North American Free Trade Agreement, 1867 UNTS 14: J. Brunnée, 'Treaty Amendments' in Hollis (ed.), *supra* n. 24, pp. 347–366, at p. 350. See, further, Walter, *supra* n. 93, at p. 298 ('treaties between riparian States relating to the development of a river basin or treaties relating to the building of a hydroelectric dam, scientific installations, etc') and, also, Azaria, *supra* n. 6, at pp. 103–104.

typologisation of treaties that occurs at various points within the Vienna Convention.[95] Plurilateral or restricted multilateral treaties as framed in Article 20(2) VCLT transcend the *materiae* of a given treaty by concentrating on its 'limited' circle of 'negotiating States';[96] it was only in order to bring greater definition to this principle – which, one hastens to contend, is more likely to rest on the intention of the parties than on the conjuring of an abstract numeric[97] – that reference was made to 'the object and purpose of a treaty' as well as to 'the application of the treaty in its entirety between all the parties [as] an essential condition of the consent of each one to be bound by the treaty'.[98] In this instance, the reservation will not be governed by the 'incongruent' model of 'bilateral treaty relations' that depends upon State objections to or acceptances of a reservation:[99] instead, that reservation will require 'acceptance by all the parties',[100] since '[t]he central purpose of [Article 20(2) VCLT] must be seen in the desire to maintain the unanimity rule for treaties where such a patchwork of different bilateral relations is unacceptable in view of their object and purpose'.[101]

***

Over time, however, this general regime came to be viewed as operating 'unsatisfactorily' for human rights treaties, which, Rosalyn Higgins wrote at the end of the Cold War, 'are not just an exchange of obligations between [S]tates where they can agree at will, in a web of bilateral obligations within a multilateral treaty, what bargains they find acceptable. Human rights treaties . . . reflect rights inherent in human beings, not dependent upon grant by the [S]tate'.[102] Of course, we are on familiar

---

[95] On this issue, see the contribution to this volume of Brölmann at pp. 79–102 (Chapter 4), and, further, A. V. Lowe, 'The Law of Treaties; Or, Should This Book Exist?' in C. J. Tams, A. Tzanakopoulos and A. Zimmermann (eds.), *Research Handbook on the Law of Treaties* (Cheltenham: Edward Elgar, 2014), pp. 3–15, at p. 12 (on 'categories of treaty for special treatment').

[96] Assuming these are separate considerations: see, further, B. H. Hoekman and P. C. Mavroidis, 'WTO "à la carte" or "menu du jour"? Assessing the Case for More Plurilateral Agreements', *EJIL*, 26 (2015), 319–343.

[97] See H. Waldock, Fourth Report on the Law of Treaties, Doc. A/CN.4/177 and Add.1 and 2 (19 March, 25 March and 17 June 1965), p. 51. Indeed, the International Law Commission discussed this in terms of 'treaties drawn up between very few States': *YbILC* (1965-II), 25. This, Walter maintains, 'can hardly be turned into a concrete figure': *supra* n. 93, at p. 296.

[98] Walter, *supra* n. 93, at p. 296.   [99] *Ibid.*, at p. 297.

[100] As per Art. 20(2) VCLT: *supra* n. 1.   [101] Walter, *supra* n. 93, at p. 297.

[102] R. Higgins, 'Human Rights: Some Questions of Integrity', *Modern L. Rev.*, 52 (1989), 1–21, at 11 (claiming that the 'principles' formulated for reservations 'did not of course

ground with this rhetoric of exceptionalism given the lauding of the 'special characteristics' of the Genocide Convention in *Reservations to the Convention on the Prevention and Punishment of the Crime of Genocide*,[103] and, in November 1994, the Human Rights Committee of the 1966 International Covenant on Civil and Political Rights (ICCPR)[104] issued General Comment No. 24(52), in which it actually sought to embellish the meaning of 'the object and purpose test' (as it called it)[105] of the Vienna Convention as applied to the ICCPR:[106]

> In an instrument which articulates very many civil and political rights, each of the many articles, and indeed their interplay, secures the objectives of the Covenant. The object and purpose of the Covenant is to create legally binding standards for human rights by defining certain civil and political rights and placing them in a framework of obligations which are legally binding for those States which ratify; and to provide an efficacious supervisory machinery for the obligations undertaken.[107]

have in mind at all treaties with their own built-in substantial limitations to the obligations undertaken' (*ibid.*, at 14) and remaining unconvinced that the Covenant's object and purpose 'can be the exclusive touchstone – for while I am ready to concede that purported reservations to non-derogable articles are contrary to the object and purpose of the treaty, it seems to me that so also can be certain reservations to articles [of the Covenant] that are in principle derogable' (*ibid.*, at 15)).

103 And of the 'special character of a human rights' treaty in Human Rights Committee, General Comment No. 24(52): General Comment on Issues Relating to Reservations Made upon Ratification or Accession to the Covenant or the Optional Protocol Thereto, or in Relation to Declarations under Art. 41 of the Covenant, U.N. Doc. CCPR/C/21/Rev.1/Add.6 (1994) (paragraph 18); '[a]lthough treaties that are mere exchanges of obligations between States allow them to reserve *inter se* application of rules of general international law, it is otherwise in human rights treaties, which are for the benefit of persons within their jurisdiction' (paragraph 8). See, also, Swaine's emphasis of 'the original human rights context in which [these] principles were forged': *supra* n. 53, at p. 278 (and at pp. 282-283 ('the characteristics of fundamental human rights conventions' like the Genocide Convention)). And Pellet: *supra* n. 21, at pp. 418 and 421. A. W. B. Simpson is of another view: 'Britain and the Genocide Convention', *BYbIL*, 73 (2002), 5-64, at 5 ('[t]he [Genocide] Convention belongs to international penal law, not to the international law of human rights').

104 999 UNTS 171.

105 General Comment No. 24(52), *supra* n. 103 (paragraphs 6, 9, 10 and 17).

106 And its First Optional Protocol, 999 UNTS 302 (*ibid.* (paragraphs 5, 13 and 14)); Second Optional Protocol, 1642 UNTS 414 (*ibid.* (paragraphs 5 and 15)) and declarations under Art. 41 ICCPR (*ibid.* (paragraph 17)). See, further, E. A. Baylis, 'General Comment 24: Confronting the Problem of Reservations to Human Rights Treaties', *Berkeley JIL*, 17 (1999), 277-329.

107 *Ibid.* (paragraph 7). They may not alone in this regard: see T. Meron, 'The Humanization of Humanitarian Law', *AJIL*, 94 (2000), 239-278, at 247-253, and, also, L. Brilmayer, 'From "Contract" to "Pledge": The Structure of International Human Rights Agreements', *BYbIL*, 77 (2006), 163-202.

As will be appreciated from this *motif*, and as is apparent from the tenor of General Comment No. 24(52) as a whole, this is an expansive and firmly articulated rendering of the ICCPR's 'object and purpose' so as to encompass (or so the Committee reasoned) reservations:

- 'that offend peremptory norms [of general international law]';[108]
- to 'provisions in the Covenant that represent customary international law';[109]
- to Article 1 ICCPR ('denying peoples the right to determine their own political status and to pursue their economic, social and cultural development');[110]
- to Article 2(1) ICCPR ('the obligation to respect and ensure rights, and to do so on a non-discriminatory basis')[111] and
- to Article 2(2) ICCPR ('[n]or may a State reserve an entitlement not to take necessary steps at the domestic level to give effect to the rights of the Covenant').[112]

---

[108] General Comment No. 24(52), *supra* n. 103 (paragraph 8).

[109] *Ibid.* It is in this context that the Committee mentioned that a State may not reserve the right to engage in slavery (Art. 8 ICCPR); to torture, to subject persons to cruel, inhuman or degrading treatment or punishment (Art. 7 ICCPR); to arbitrarily deprive persons of their lives (Art. 6(1) ICCPR); to arbitrarily arrest and detain persons (Art. 9 ICCPR); to deny freedom of thought, conscience and religion (Art. 18 ICCPR); to presume a person guilty unless he proves his innocence (Art. 15 ICCPR); to execute pregnant women or children (Art. 6(5) ICCPR); to permit the advocacy of national, racial or religious hatred (Art. 20(2) ICCPR); to deny persons of marriageable age the right to marry (Art. 23 ICCPR) or to deny to minorities the right to enjoy their own culture, profess their own religion, or use their own language (Art. 27 ICCPR): *ibid.*

[110] *Ibid.* (paragraph 9).   [111] *Ibid.*

[112] *Ibid.* This should not be taken to suggest, however, that the ICCPR's object and purpose precludes reservations to all protections: the Committee was of the view that 'while reservations to particular clauses of Article 14 [ICCPR] may be acceptable, a general reservation to the right to a fair trial would not be': *ibid.* Why this should be so is not immediately clear since all seven subparagraphs of Art. 14 ICCPR – '[a]ll persons shall be equal' (Art. 14(1)); '[e]veryone charged' (Art. 14(2)); 'everyone shall be entitled' (Art. 14(3)); '[i]n the case of juvenile persons' (Art. 14(4)); '[e]veryone convicted of a crime' (Art. 14(5)); 'the person who has suffered punishment' (Art. 14(6)) and '[n]o one shall be liable' (Art. 14(7)) – fit the Committee's mould of 'benefit[s] of persons within their jurisdiction' (paragraph 8). See, also, the Committee's statement that '[w]hile there is no automatic correlation between reservations to non-derogable provisions, and reservations which offend against the object and purpose of the Covenant, a State has a heavy onus to justify such a reservation' (paragraph 10).

Furthermore, the Committee concluded that '[t]he Covenant consists not just of specified rights, but of important supportive guarantees':

> These guarantees provide the necessary framework for securing the rights in the Covenant and are thus essential to its object and purpose. Some operate at the national level and some at the international level. Reservations designed to remove these guarantees are thus not acceptable. Thus, a State could not make a reservation to [Article 2(3)] of the Covenant, indicating that it intends to provide no remedies for human rights violations. Guarantees such as these are an integral part of the structure of the Covenant and underpin its efficacy. The Covenant also envisages, for the better attainment of its stated objectives, a monitoring role for the Committee. Reservations that purport to evade that essential element in the design of the Covenant, which is also directed to securing the enjoyment of the rights, are also incompatible with its object and purpose. A State may not reserve the right not to present a report and have it considered by the Committee. The Committee's role under the Covenant, whether under [A]rticle 40 or under the Optional Protocols, necessarily entails interpreting the provisions of the Covenant and the development of a jurisprudence. Accordingly, a reservation that rejects the Committee's competence to interpret the requirements of any provisions of the Covenant would also be contrary to the object and purpose of that treaty.[113]

The Committee thus did not hold back on the 'attendant requirements' for rights under the ICCPR to be 'ensured to all those under a State's jurisdiction',[114] and, following on from this, it stridently concluded that '[i]t necessarily falls to the Committee to determine whether a specific reservation is compatible with the object and purpose of the [ICCPR]':[115] 'necessarily' because, the Committee thought in part, 'it is an inappropriate task for States parties in relation to human rights treaties' to undertake.[116] This, then, in the Committee's view, had become a struggle for the soul – that is, a struggle for *realising* the object and purpose – of the ICCPR, jeopardised not so much by the vagaries of the concept but by the somewhat erratic practices of States in response to reservations to the ICCPR. Objections to these reservations have been 'occasional', the Committee said, brought on by the fact that States 'have not seen any legal interest in or need to object to reservations'.[117] For the

---

[113] *Ibid.* (paragraph 11). [114] *Ibid.* (paragraph 12). [115] *Ibid.* (paragraph 18).

[116] *Ibid.* (and 'in part because it is a task that the Committee cannot avoid in the performance of its functions'). At paragraph 17: the VCLT provisions 'on the role of State objections in relation to reservations are inappropriate to address the problem of reservations to human rights treaties'.

[117] *Ibid.* (paragraph 17). Said the Committee:

Committee, this struggle could not be resolved without engaging the question of 'the legal authority to make determinations as to whether specific reservations are compatible with the object and purpose of the [ICCPR]'.[118] The Committee boldly judged itself to be indispensable to that task, an approach that at its heart sought to recapture some of the initial promise of the concept's objectivity by injecting a measure of institutional coherence and discipline into the process while, at the same time, retaining the system of 'reservatory dialogue' encountered as far back as the *Reservations* advisory opinion.[119] To a greater or lesser degree, and in the view of the Committee, this dialogue must commence with – and within – the reserving State itself,[120] but it must also have an endpoint, and the Committee left us in no doubt as to where (or upon whose say-so) it thought that should be.

***

We have now almost come full cycle because, in the recent jurisprudence of the International Court of Justice, reservations to the Genocide Convention – specifically to the compromissory clause of Article IX of that Convention,[121] the focal point of many of the reservations that had

> The absence of protest by States cannot imply that a reservation is either compatible or incompatible with the object and purpose of the Covenant. Objections have been occasional, made by some States but not others, and on grounds not always specified; when an objection is made, it often does not specify a legal consequence, or sometimes even indicates that the objecting party nonetheless does not regard the Covenant as not in effect as between the parties concerned. In short, the pattern is so unclear that it is not safe to assume that a non-objecting State thinks that a particular reservation is acceptable. In the view of the Committee, because of the special characteristics of the Covenant as a human rights treaty, it is open to question what effect objections have between States *inter se.*

See, further, C. J. Redgwell, 'Reservations to Treaties and Human Rights: Committee General Comment No. 24(52)', *ICLQ,* 46 (1997), 390–412, at 394–399, 404 and 406.

[118] *Ibid.* (paragraph 16).   [119] Pellet, *supra* n. 21, at p. 479.

[120] Or so thought the Committee: 'States should institute procedures to ensure that each and every proposed reservation is compatible with the object and purpose of the Covenant'. General Comment No. 24(52), *supra* n. 103 (paragraph 20). For an appreciation of the broader significance of this General Comment, see M. Nowak, *U.N. Covenant on Civil and Political Rights: CCPR Commentary* (Kehl: N.P. Engel, 2nd rev. ed., 2005), pp. xxx–xxxvi.

[121] Art. IX provides that '[d]isputes between the Contracting Parties relating to the interpretation, application or fulfilment of the present Convention, including those relating to the responsibility of a State for genocide or for any of the other acts enumerated in [A]rticle III, shall be submitted to the International Court of Justice

inspired the request for the *Reservations* advisory opinion all those decades ago – have once again come to occupy the attention of the Court. By way of illustration, let us select the order of interim measures from July 2002 in *Case Concerning Armed Activities on the Territory of the Congo* (New Application: 2002) as well the (related) judgment on jurisdiction and admissibility given in the same case in February 2006.[122]

Upon initiating proceedings against Rwanda in May 2002, the Democratic Republic of the Congo (DRC) sought to challenge Rwanda's reservation to Article IX of the Genocide Convention[123] (which was one of several treaties invoked to found the jurisdiction of the Court).[124] Even though it had not objected to this reservation when Rwanda acceded to the Genocide Convention in April 1975,[125] the DRC's challenge was based on the ground (*inter alia*) that the reservation is incompatible with the object and purpose of the Convention in that 'its effect is to exclude Rwanda from any mechanism for the monitoring and prosecution of genocide, whereas the object and purpose of the Convention are precisely the elimination of impunity for this serious violation of international law'.[126] Rwanda, for its part, contended that there was no such incompatibility as its reservation related not to 'the substantive obligations of the parties to the Convention but to a procedural provision', and it cited the statistic that fourteen other States had maintained similar reservations to the Convention (with the majority of the 133 States parties to the Convention raising no objection in this regard).[127] It is therefore apparent that States may choose, for

---

at the request of any of the parties to the dispute': *supra* n. 29. See, further, W. A. Schabas, *Genocide in International Law: The Crime of Crimes* (Cambridge: Cambridge University Press, 2nd ed., 2009), p. 570.

[122] *Case Concerning Armed Activities on the Territory of the Congo* (New Application: 2002): Democratic Republic of the Congo v. Rwanda (Jurisdiction and Admissibility) (2006) ICJ Rep. 6.

[123] The reservation read simply: 'The Rwandese Republic does not consider itself bound by [A]rticle IX of the Convention'. In a communication received on 15 Dec. 2008, Rwanda informed the Secretary-General that it had decided to withdraw this reservation: https://treaties.un.org/Pages/ViewDetails.aspx?src=IND&mtdsg_no=IV-1&chapter=4&lang=en#27.

[124] *Case Concerning Armed Activities on the Territory of the Congo, supra* n. 122, at p. 220 (paragraph 2).

[125] As noted by the Court 'as a matter of the law of treaties': *ibid.*, at pp. 32–33 (paragraph 68).

[126] *Ibid.*, at p. 30 (paragraph 57).

[127] *Ibid.*, at p. 30 (paragraph 61). See, however, the discussion of A. Orakhelashvili, 'Case Concerning Armed Activities on the Territory of the Congo (Democratic Republic of the Congo v. Rwanda), Jurisdiction and Admissibility, Judgment of 3 February 2006', *ICLQ*, 55 (2006), 753–763, at 759–760.

essentially strategic reasons, to adopt entirely different formulations of the object and purpose of a treaty, given that concept's role as a crucial determinant of the validity of reservations to its provisions.

For the Court:

> Rwanda's reservation to Article IX of the Genocide Convention bears on the jurisdiction of the Court, and does not affect substantive obligations relating to acts of genocide themselves under that Convention. In the circumstances of the present case, the Court cannot conclude that the reservation of Rwanda in question, which is meant to exclude a particular method of settling a dispute relating to the interpretation, application or fulfilment of the Convention, is to be regarded as being incompatible with the object and purpose of the Convention.[128]

By fifteen votes to two, the Court went on to find it had no jurisdiction to entertain the application of the DRC,[129] but it is the position of five members of this majority – Judges Rosalyn Higgins, Peter Kooijmans, Nabil Elaraby, Hisashi Owada and Bruno Simma – as expressed in a joint separate opinion that is of particular interest to us here. These judges wanted to offer 'a proper reading'[130] of the Court's advisory opinion of May 1951 in order to counter the impression that has formed in recent years of the Court 'stipulating a régime of inter-State *laissez-faire* in the matter of reservations' – in which 'the object and purpose of a convention should be borne in mind both by those making reservations and those objecting to them, everything in the final analysis is left to the States

---

[128] *Ibid.*, at p. 32 (paragraph 67). In the order of July 2002, the Court had much more tentatively observed that the 'reservation does not bear on the substance of the law, but only on the Court's jurisdiction' – and, importantly, that 'it therefore does not appear contrary to the object and purpose of the Convention': *ibid.*, at p. 246 (paragraph 72); the Court had also indicated that Rwanda's reservation to the 1965 International Convention on the Elimination of All Forms of Racial Discrimination, *supra* n. 89, 'does not appear incompatible with the object and purpose of that Convention': *ibid.*, at p. 244 (paragraph 67).

[129] *Ibid.*, at p. 53 (paragraph 128). Seizing on the terms of Art. I of the Genocide Convention – that '[t]he Contracting Parties confirm that genocide, whether committed in time of peace or in time of war, is a crime under international law which they undertake to prevent and to punish' – Judge Abdul Koroma was of the view in his dissenting opinion that '[t]he object and purpose of the Genocide Convention is the prevention and punishment of the crime of genocide, and this encompasses holding a State responsible whenever it is found to be in breach of its obligations under the Convention': *ibid.*, at p. 57 (paragraph 12).

[130] Joint Separate Opinion of Judges Higgins, Kooijmans, Elaraby, Owada and Simma, *ibid.*, at p. 65 (paragraph 5).

themselves'.[131] In an opinion that bears considerable resemblance to General Comment No. 24(52) of the Human Rights Committee,[132] the judges suggested that, in May 1951, the Court was 'clearly not unaware of the hazards inherent in its answers, in the sense that they would entail a veritable web of diverse reciprocal commitments within the framework of a multilateral convention.'[133] They recalled the 'assumption' underpinning the advisory opinion 'of balancing the freedom to make reservations [with] the scrutiny and objections of other States' and went on to report that this has 'turned out to be unrealized: a mere handful of States do this'.[134]

In reflecting back on the advisory opinion in this way, these five judges demarcated precisely what was said and left unsaid by the Court on that occasion ('[t]o observe this reality is not to attempt to fragment a mythical overreaching law on all questions of reservations'),[135] but their ambition was to work through the intentions behind the 'assumption' of their predecessors.[136] Their finding suggests that the framework for making valid reservations as posited in May 1951 had not, in the end, optimised conditions for interactional *results* between States,[137] with only the faintest

---

[131]   *Ibid.* (paragraph 4). See, also, p. 69 (paragraph 15).

[132]   Not surprising given the common denominator of Rosalyn Higgins: see Nowak, *supra* n. 120, at p. xxx. See, also, Joint Separate Opinion of Judges Higgins, Kooijmans, Elaraby, Owada and Simma, *ibid.*, at p. 69 (paragraph 16).

[133]   *Ibid.*, at p. 66 (paragraph 9).

[134]   *Ibid.*, at p. 66 (paragraph 11). See, further, the data provided at *ibid.* (paragraph 10) (recording that twenty-eight reservations to the Genocide Convention have elicited objections from some eighteen States).

[135]   *Ibid.*, p. 68 (paragraph 13).

[136]   *Supra* n. 134. For consideration of reservations made in the absence of objections, see *Legality of Use of Force*: Yugoslavia v. Spain (Provisional Measures) (1999) ICJ. Rep. 761, at p. 772 (paragraphs 32–33) and *Legality of Use of Force*: Yugoslavia v. United States of America (Provisional Measures) (1999) ICJ Rep. 916, at p. 924 (paragraphs 24–25), where the 'said reservation' – i.e. by Spain and the United States to Art. IX of the Genocide Convention – 'had the effect of excluding that Article from the provisions of the Convention in force between the Parties'.

[137]   Though one may of course deduce this from evidence arising from litigation involving reservations – as the United States had done before the Court in *Legality of Use of Force* when, as the *reserving* State, it had 'contended that its reservation to Article IX [of the Genocide Convention] is not contrary to the Convention's object and purpose': *supra* n. 136, at p. 924 (paragraph 22). The United States was here making explicit what was presumably already implicit – otherwise, why would it have made the reservation if it had believed it was contrary to the object and purpose of the Genocide Convention? See Joint Separate Opinion of Judges Higgins, Kooijmans, Elaraby, Owada and Simma, *supra* n. 130, at pp. 69–70 (paragraph 18).

glimpses of a treaty's 'object and purpose' emerging from that process. This consideration weighed a great deal with these judges, as did the fact that it was the Genocide Convention – of all treaties – that was back in the crosshairs of the Court. 'It must be regarded as a very grave matter', the judges exhorted, 'that a State should be in a position to shield from international judicial scrutiny any claim that might be made against it concerning genocide'.[138] And this fed through to the final paragraphs of the joint separate opinion which kept the door open a chink on how the Genocide Convention may be interpreted in the future, as it is 'not self-evident that a reservation to Article IX [of the Convention] could not be regarded as incompatible with the object and purpose of the Convention and we believe that this is a matter that the Court should revisit for further consideration'.[139]

3   The Interim Obligation of Article 18 VCLT

Towards the end of its *Reservations* advisory opinion in May 1951, the International Court of Justice distinguished between those States entitled to sign or accede to the Genocide Convention (i.e. those that 'have a right to become parties' to the Convention) and those that had signed the Convention but had not yet ratified it.[140] It did so in order to deal with the final question put to it by the General Assembly,[141] finding that the latter position was 'different' because '[t]he case of the signatory State' triggered 'the question of the legal effect of signing an international convention'.[142] The Court shared its thoughts as follows:

> It is evident that without ratification, signature does not make the signa-
> tory State a party to the Convention; nevertheless, it establishes
> a provisional status in favour of that State. This status may decrease in
> value and importance after the Convention enters into force. But, both
> before and after the entry into force, this status would justify more

---

[138] Joint Separate Opinion of Judges Higgins, Kooijmans, Elaraby, Owada and Simma, *supra* n. 130, at p. 71 (paragraph 25) (where genocide was described as 'one of the gravest crimes ever known').

[139] *Ibid.*, at p. 72 (paragraph 29).

[140] *Supra* n. 27, at pp. 27–28 (where signature 'constitutes a first step to participation in the Convention': *ibid.*, at p. 28).

[141] See *supra* n. 28.   [142] *Supra* n. 27, at p. 28.

favourable treatment being meted out to signatory States in respect of objections than to States which have neither signed nor acceded. As distinct from the latter States, signatory States have taken certain of the steps necessary for the exercise of the right of being a party. Pending ratification, the provisional status created by signature confers upon the signatory a right to formulate as a precautionary measure objections which have themselves a provisional character. These would disappear if the signature were not followed by ratification, or they would become effective on ratification.[143]

This theme of the provisional status of the signatory State resonates with the rules subsequently incorporated within the Vienna Convention because it provides that a State that has signed a treaty or exchanged instruments constituting the treaty subject to ratification, acceptance or approval 'is obliged to refrain from acts which would defeat the object and purpose' until that point in time that it has 'made its intention clear not to become a party to the treaty'.[144] The same obligation obtains for a State that has expressed its consent to be bound by the treaty 'pending the entry into force of [that] treaty'.[145] In Article 18 VCLT, the provenance of the interim obligation is thus defined by two alternative sets of circumstance,[146] and, much like the Court had done before it, the Convention centres on this idea and develops a keen sense of how the relationship between a State and a treaty evolves at various points along

---

[143] *Ibid.*

[144] Art. 18(a) VCLT: *supra* n. 1. As *per* Art. 11 VCLT. Though the obligation is in fact stapled to acts of 'simple' as opposed to 'definitive' signature: Bradley, *supra* n. 24, at p. 212. *See*, further, Aust, *supra* n. 20, at p. 89 (who observes that '[i]f there is no indication, express or implied, of the need for ratification the treaty will be presumed to enter into force on signature').

[145] Art. 18(b) VCLT: *ibid.*

[146] A third circumstance featured at an earlier point in the history of the Vienna Convention, for the International Law Commission put its weight behind the obligation when a State 'has agreed to enter into negotiations for the conclusion of the treaty' – and 'while these negotiations are in progress'; this did not make it through to the Vienna Convention, however: *YbILC* (1966–II), 202. See, further, J. S. Charme, 'The Interim Obligation of Article 18 of the Vienna Convention on the Law of Treaties: Making Sense of an Enigma', *Geo. Wash. JIL & Econ.*, 25 (1992), 71–114; P. V. McDade, 'The Interim Obligation between Signature and Ratification of a Treaty: Issues Raised by the Recent Actions of Signatories to the Law of the Sea Convention with Respect to the Mining of the Deep Seabed', *Netherlands ILR*, 32 (1985), 5–47, and J. Klabbers, 'Strange Bedfellows: The "Interim Obligation" and the 1991 Chemical Weapons Convention' in E. P. J. Myjer (ed.), *Issues of Armed Control Law and the Chemical Weapons Convention* (The Hague: Kluwer Law International, 2001), pp. 11–29. See, however, Bradley, *supra* n. 24, at p. 213 ('signing obligation' and 'interim signing obligation'); p. 214 ('interim signing obligation') and pp. 214–215 ('signing obligation').

that treaty's chronological arc – from the moment of signature or exchange of instruments to the signaling of any changed intention toward a treaty and, in the event of expression of consent to be bound, the entry into force of a treaty 'provided that such entry into force is not unduly delayed'.[147]

It may seem curious that the Vienna Convention conceives of such an obligation in the first place, but evidence – indeed, 'a good deal of material' – was on hand well before the Convention came to pass showing that 'States which have signed a treaty requiring ratification have thereby placed certain limitations upon their freedom of action during the period which precedes its entry into force'.[148] And part of this evidence can be traced back to at least the nineteenth century when, in discussing the matter of treaties of peace, Arbitrator Lieber reasoned with considerable confidence in *Ignacio Torres v. the United States* that 'it is well understood that a peace is not a complete peace until ratified; that, as a matter of course, the ratifying authority has the power of refusing unless, for that time, it has given up this power beforehand, but there can be no doubt that so soon as peace has been preliminarily signed active hostilities ought to cease, according to the spirit of civilization and consistent with the very idea and object of the whole transaction, which is to stop the war and establish the peace'.[149] For its part, in commenting on the draft articles for the Vienna Convention, the International Law Commission mentioned that, in *Certain German Interests in Polish Upper Silesia*,[150] the Permanent Court of International Justice had accepted that 'a signatory State's misuse of its rights in the interval preceding ratification may amount to a violation of its obligations in respect of the treaty'.[151]

---

[147] *Supra* n. 145. Note that the Vienna Convention makes a distinction between the 'contracting State' ('a State which has consented to be bound by the treaty, whether or not the treaty has entered into force') under Art. 2(1)(f) and a 'party' ('a State which has consented to be bound by the treaty and for which the treaty is in force') under Art. 2(1)(g): *supra* n. 1.

[148] McNair, *supra* n. 39, at p. 199 (hence, *ibid.*, 'it must not be assumed that the signature pending the completion of ratification is devoid of all legal effect'). See, also, O. Dörr, 'Article 18' in Dörr and Schmalenbach (eds.), *supra* n. 6, pp. 219–235, at pp. 222–224.

[149] *See* J. B. Moore, *History and Digest of the International Arbitrations to Which the United States Has Been a Party* (Vol. IV) (Washington, DC: Govt. Printing Office, 1898), pp. 3798–3801. Importantly, all of the material collated by McNair, *supra* n. 39, at pp. 199–203, relates to situations 'pending ratification' (*ibid.*, at p. 200) or in the 'interval' between signature and ratification (*ibid.*, at p. 201).

[150] 1926 PCIJ, Series A, No. 7, p. 30.   [151] *YbILC* (1966–II), 202.

To be clear, then, the intention behind this provision of the Vienna Convention is not to bring forward the formal application of the terms of the treaty before the due date of that treaty's entry into force and still less is it to argue for the provisional or 'interim' application of those terms.[152] Rather, the organising impetus appears to be the optimisation of the conditions for the entry into force of the treaty: that is, to give it more than a good chance of the life intended for it.[153] In some measure, too, it does appear as though the principle of good faith is being actualised for the signatory State (as well as the State that has ratified prior to the treaty's entry into force),[154] which, alongside the principles of free consent and *pacta sunt servanda*, is 'universally recognized' according to the preamble of the Vienna Convention.[155] And, for D. P. O'Connell, 'good faith' must mean something more than just 'good form': '[i]t has equitable implications that the law cannot ignore [a]nd clearly [the] signature of a treaty is an act of good faith and not an empty gesture'.[156] The act of signature is thus responsible for 'bringing into play what may be called certain of the mechanics of treaty-making',[157] but within the broader scheme of the

---

[152] As is provided for in Art. 25 VCLT: *supra* n. 1. See, further, the chapter by Quast Mertsch in this volume at pp. 303–334 (Chapter 10).

[153] Its focus is on the 'commitment to the entire regime': Bowman, *supra* n. 20, at 353. For Bradley, the obligation is 'designed to ensure that one of the signatory parties . . . does not change the *status quo* in a way that substantially reduces either its ability to comply with its treaty obligation after ratification or the ability of the other treaty parties to obtain the benefit of the treaty': *supra* n. 24, at p. 215. See, also, Dörr, *supra* n. 148, at pp. 219–220 ('protects the negotiated instrument', but also, 'protects the legitimate expectation of the other participants').

[154] See the discussion of D. P. O'Connell, *International Law* (Vol. I) (London: Stevens & Sons, 1970), p. 222, and S. Rosenne, *Developments in the Law of Treaties 1945–1986* (Cambridge: Cambridge University Press, 1989), p. 149. The thinking, too, of Judge Fleischhauer in his assessment of Art. 18 VCLT in his dissenting opinion in *Gabčíkovo-Nagymaros Project (Hungary/Slovakia)* (1997) ICJ Rep. 7, at p. 206.

[155] In addition to this stipulation in the third preambular recital, the Vienna Convention makes several explicit references to good faith – in Art. 26 (*pacta sunt servanda*), Art. 31 (general rule of interpretation), Art. 46 (provisions of internal law regarding competence to conclude treaties) and Art. 69 (consequences of the invalidity of a treaty): *supra* n. 1.

[156] O'Connell, *supra* n. 154, at p. 222 (in a section in one of his two chapters on treaties entitled 'the legal nature of an unratified treaty'). For its 'moral' worth: H. Kelsen, *Principles of International Law* (New York, NY: Holt, Rinehart and Winston, 2nd rev. ed., 1962) (with R. W. Tucker), pp. 466–468. See, also, F. Dopagne, 'Article 28 (1969)' in Corten and Klein (eds.), (Vol. I), *supra* note 21, pp. 718–728, at p. 723.

[157] McNair, *supra* n. 39, at p. 203 (i.e. 'provisions indicating which States have a right to sign the treaty or to become a party to it by accession, or naming a headquarters Government charged with the receipt of instruments of ratification or accession, or permitting a special method of notifying the completion of an instrument of ratification'). It is in

Vienna Convention, this obligation does not emerge as an unusual occurrence. Rather, the Convention anticipates, as one supposes it must, 'matters arising necessarily before the entry into force of the treaty' such as the authentication of the text, the establishment of the consent of States to be bound by the treaty, the manner or date of the treaty's entry into force, as well as the specific functions of the depositary – which, the Convention states, 'apply from the time of the adoption of its text'.[158] Indeed, it could be said that, both apart from but also as a result of its interim obligation, Article 18 VCLT contains an auxiliary obligation which is the subject of infrequent comment, and that is that the signatory State must make its intention 'clear' that it will 'not become a party to the treaty' if that is the course of its choosing.[159]

***

As for the obligation at hand – 'to refrain from acts which would defeat the object and purpose of a treaty'[160] – this is evidently cast in negative terms and emphatically so: it is for the relevant State not to act in such a manner that would *defeat* the object and purpose of a treaty with which it is concerned. The language of 'defeat' in this context is strong to be sure,[161] especially when compared with alternative possibilities for framing this obligation (*viz.*, '[a] State is obliged to refrain from acts tending to frustrate

---

this context that McNair understands the Court's position on the final question put to it by the General Assembly: *supra* n. 28.

[158] Art. 24(4) VCLT: *supra* n. 1. See Rogoff, *supra* n. 8, at 268 ('with the possible exception of obligations arising from its procedural provisions, a treaty has no obligatory force prior to its entry into force'). On the adoption of the text of a treaty, see Art. 9 VCLT: *ibid.* See, further, A. Pellet, 'Entry into Force and Amendment of the Statute' in A. Cassese, P. Gaeta and J. R. W. D. Jones (eds.), *The Rome Statute of the International Criminal Court: A Commentary* (Vol. I) (Oxford: Oxford University Press, 2002), pp. 145–184, at p. 152, where it is suggested that, apart from the obligation in Art. 18 VCLT, signatory States are under 'the duty to examine [the] text [of the Statute] in good faith with an eye to determining their definitive position towards it (without their having the formal obligation to become parties). And if they decide to ratify, they must take the necessary steps to be able to meet their obligations on the date the Statute comes into force in relation to them'.

[159] See *supra* n. 147. And, presumably, constitutes an example of 'other matters arising necessarily before the entry into force of the treaty', on which Art. 24(4) VCLT does not purport to be exhaustive: *supra* note 1. See, further, Dörr, *supra* n. 148, at pp. 227–228.

[160] Art. 18 VCLT – and generic to both circumstances (a) and (b) mentioned in this provision. A comparator provision might be Art. 72(2) VCLT on the consequences of the suspension of the operation of a treaty: '[d]uring the period of the suspension the parties shall refrain from acts tending to obstruct the resumption of the operation of the treaty': *supra* n. 1.

[161] Bowman, *supra* n. 20, at 352–353. See, also, Aust, *infra* n. 165.

the object of a proposed treaty')[162] or set against other formulations appearing elsewhere in the Vienna Convention itself (such as the notion of in/compatibility with a treaty's object and purpose[163] or with the 'effective execution' of that object and purpose).[164] That said, the obligation is to some extent tempered by the notion of refraining from acts 'which *would* defeat the object and purpose of a treaty',[165] suggesting that it is not the position of the Vienna Convention that a treaty's object and purpose must be defeated as a matter of fact: it is sufficient that an act or course of action would, in the fullness of time, come to have the said effect.[166] The obligation, therefore, is not restricted to those acts which *do* defeat the object and purpose of a treaty. This nuance of Article 18 VCLT has perhaps got lost along the way,[167] but it is one that is echoed to a certain extent in the judgment of the International Court of Justice in *Case Concerning Military and Paramilitary Activities in and against Nicaragua* in June 1986: at one point in its ruling, the Court spoke of acts 'depriving' the treaty of its object and purpose,[168] and at another, it spoke of 'the obligation not to defeat the object and purpose of the treaty'.[169] However, the Court also

[162] General Assembly, Official Records, Twenty-First Session, Supp. No. 9, A/6309/Rev.1. See, further, W. Morvay, 'The Obligation of a State Not to Frustrate the Object of a Treaty Prior to Its Entry into Force: Comments on Art. 15 of the ILC's 1966 Draft Articles on the Law of Treaties', *ZaöRV*, 27 (1967), 451–462, at 453, 456 and 458. Another formulation in circulation at that time: 'one party to a treaty must not, pending ratification, do anything which will hamper any action that may be taken by the other party if and when the treaty enters into force'. See McNair, *supra* n. 39, at p. 200.

[163] Art. 19(c) VCLT (reservations) and Art. 58(1)(b)(ii) VCLT (suspension): *supra* n. 1.

[164] Art. 41(1)(b)(ii) VCLT (modification): *supra* n. 1. On this 'grammatical comparison', consider Dörr, *supra* n. 148, at p. 233.

[165] On this point, see Aust, *supra* n. 20, at p. 108 ('[t]he obligation is only to "refrain" (a weak term) from acts that would "defeat" (a strong term) the object and purpose of the treaty').

[166] See, in particular, Morvay, *supra* n. 162, at p. 458 ('the obligation is violated only by acts which are intended to frustrate the object of a treaty and not also by acts which frustrate it unintentionally'). Consider, too, the emphasis of J. Klabbers, 'How to Defeat a Treaty's Object and Purpose Pending Entry into Force: Toward Manifest Intent', *Vanderbilt JTL*, 34 (2001), 283–331.

[167] As *per* Dörr, *supra* n. 148, at p. 233 ('"defeating" the object and purpose'; cf. '[t]he obligation to refrain from acts that might affect a treaty that has been signed but not yet ratified': *ibid.*, at p. 222). A nuance not necessarily captured in the title given to Art. 18 VCLT ('[o]bligation not to defeat the object and purpose of a treaty prior to its entry into force').

[168] *Case Concerning Military and Paramilitary Activities in and against Nicaragua*: Nicaragua v. United States of America (Merits) (1986) ICJ Rep. 14, at p. 136 (paragraph 271) (the Court speaking of being able 'to entertain a claim alleging conduct depriving the treaty of its object and purpose'). See, also, p. 136 (paragraph 272). Also in this vein, acts 'tending to defeat' the object and purpose of a treaty: *ibid.*, at p. 137 (paragraph 273).

[169] *Ibid.*, at p. 138 (paragraph 276).

made reference to acts that are 'calculated to deprive'[170] or 'calculated to defeat'[171] or 'directed to defeating'[172] a treaty's object and
purpose,[173] and these are variations of a theme that seem to reflect
more closely the actual terms contained in Article 18 VCLT. They
hint, too, at the very real differences that exist in harnessing the
proper scope of obligation therein contained, but taken together, they
provide increasing indication that the concern might in fact be more
than the issue of *defeat* itself,[174] embracing, too, the *intention* (or
intentions) behind the relevant acts.[175]

Perhaps the most potent of recent examples to shed some light on this
interim obligation has come with the United States and its signature of
the 1998 Rome Statute of the International Criminal Court (ICC) on 31
December 2000.[176] On 6 May 2002, under the Administration of
President George W. Bush, the United States announced that it did 'not

---

[170] *Ibid.*, at p. 136 (paragraph 272) ('or to impede [the treaty's] due performance').

[171] *Ibid.*, at p. 138 (paragraph 276).   [172] *Ibid.*

[173] We must bear in mind, however, that, whatever echoes there may be of the Art. 18 VCLT
obligation, this discussion in the *Nicaragua Case* occurred in the context of customary
international law – and in respect of a bilateral treaty already in force between the
litigating States: see *infra* n. 194 and n. 196 (and accompanying text) – but the Court's
discussion does sharpen the focus on the way this provision of the Vienna Convention is
actually worded.

[174] Where the principle of good faith must loom large: *supra* n. 154. For Dörr, '[t]he interim
obligation . . . is basically an obligation of good faith': *supra* n. 148, at p. 220. Consider,
too, Art. 9 of the 1935 Draft Convention on the Law of Treaties ('under certain
circumstances . . . good faith may require that pending the coming into force of the
treaty the States shall, for reasonable time after signature, refrain from taking action
which would render performance by any party of the obligations stipulated impossible or
more difficult'): *supra* n. 16, at 778.

[175] Hence the references in the jurisprudence to 'calculation' (or derivatives thereof) and on
the formulation of Art. 18 VCLT itself: *supra* n. 144 ('would defeat'). See, further, *supra*
n. 166 (and accompanying text).

[176] 2817 UNTS 90. Note that Norway proposed Draft Art. 113 to the Statute – titled 'Early
Activation of Principles and Rules of the Statute' – which provided that '[p]ending the
entry into force of the Statute, States that have signed the Statute shall, in accordance
with applicable principles of international law, refrain from acts that would defeat the
object and purpose of the Statute. To this end, in ensuring the international prosecution
and suppression of crimes of international concern, States should pay due regard to the
relevant principles and provisions contained in the Statute including the performance of
their responsibilities in competent organs of the United Nations, with a view to accelerating the achievement of the shared goal of establishing the Court': Draft Statute for the
International Criminal Court, Arts. 108 to 116 – Report of the Preparatory Committee
on the Establishment of An International Criminal Court, Part 1, A/CONF.183/2/Add.1
(14 Apr. 1998), p. 166. While this proposal seemed to be of 'very broad scope' when
compared with Art. 18 VCLT, it was 'attenuated, to be sure, by the use of the conditional
(should), always disputable in a treaty text': Pellet, *supra* n. 158, at p. 152.

intend to become a party to the treaty' of the Statute[177] and that, '[a]ccordingly, the United States has no legal obligations arising from its signature' in December 2000.[178] This latter statement is quite revealing: the United States had come to the conclusion that an act of 'unsigning' was necessary in order to release it not from any 'obligations' under the Rome Statute as such but, rather, under the general law of treaties given its (ongoing) status as a signatory State (although this technical appreciation is not made explicit in these pronouncements).[179] And one can certainly understand the concerns of the United States: in the interval between signature and 'unsigning' the Rome Statute,[180] it had concluded a series of controversial 'bilateral non-surrender agreements' with numerous States who were either mere signatories to the Statute (and, thus, in the same legal position as the United States) or who had gone on to become parties to the Statute (which entered into force on 1 July 2002).[181] Typically, these agreements provided that '[p]ersons of one Party present in the territory of

---

[177] Subject to ratification under Art. 125(2) of the Statute: 'This Statute is subject to ratification, acceptance or approval by signatory States. Instruments of ratification, acceptance or approval shall be deposited with the Secretary-General of the United Nations'. The intention was announced by way of a letter from John R. Bolton, Under Secretary of State for Arms Control and International Security, to U.N. Secretary-General Kofi Annan: http://2001-2009.state.gov/r/pa/prs/ps/2002/9968.htm.

[178] *Ibid.*   [179] *Ibid.*

[180] See E. T. Swaine, 'Unsigning', *Stanford L. Rev.*, 55 (2003), 2061–2089, and, further, N. A. Lewis, 'U.S. Rejects Global Pact on War-Crimes Tribunal: Bush to "Unsign" Clinton-Era Agreement', *Int'l H. Trib.*, 7 May 2002, 1. Some have contested this language: M. Benzing, 'U.S. Bilateral Non-Surrender Agreements and Article 98 of the Statute of the International Criminal Court: An Exercise in the Law of Treaties', *Max Planck Yb. UN Law*, 8 (2004), 181–236, at 181. The term of 'unsigning' is not free from difficulty, for once signed, the signature of a treaty remains – and is still there, plain for all to see. What the Vienna Convention actually calls for is for the signatory State 'to ma[k]e its intention clear not to become a party to the treaty', and the effect of this expressed intention would be to neutralise the interim obligation contained in Art. 18: I owe this point to Michael Bowman who has sharpened my thinking on it. Note that the French delegate at the Vienna Conference suggested that 'the most obvious way for a State to make clear its intention not to become a party to the treaty was for it to frustrate the object of the treaty'. See United Nations Conference on the Law of Treaties, First Session, U.N. Doc. A/CONF. 39/11/Add.2 (26 March–24 May 1968), p. 100.

[181] The first of which was concluded between the United States and Romania – a party to the Statute – on 1 Aug. 2002. See www.amicc.org/docs/US-Romania.pdf. A helpful tabulation of these agreements is provided by J. Kelley, 'Who Keeps International Commitments and Why? The International Criminal Court and Bilateral Nonsurrender Agreements', *Am. Pol. Sci. Rev.*, 101 (2007), 573–589, at 574. See, also, Coalition for the International Criminal Court, 'Status of U.S. Bilateral Immunity Agreements (BIAs)' as of 11 Dec. 2006 (www.iccnow.org/documents/CICCFS_BIAstatus_current.pdf).

the other shall not, absent the expressed consent of the first Party, (a) be surrendered or transferred by any means to the International Criminal Court for any purpose, or (b) be surrendered or transferred by any means to any other entity or third country, for the purpose of surrender to or transfer to the International Criminal Court'.[182]

The lawfulness of this practice was taken up by James Crawford, Philippe Sands and Ralph Wilde in a joint legal opinion they prepared for the Lawyers' Committee for Human Rights and the Medical Foundation for the Care of Victims of Torture.[183] In their view, the object and purpose of the Statute 'is to put in place effective arrangements to prevent impunity for the crimes over which the ICC will have jurisdiction',[184] but they reasoned that this 'general' object and purpose is qualified by the Statute's reference to State and diplomatic immunity (under Article 98(1) of the Statute) and a certain class of agreements (under Article 98(2) of the Statute).[185] And, with respect to the behaviour of the United States:

> The question which arises is this: would the conclusion of a bilateral non-surrender agreement by a signatory to the ICC Statute prevent that State from performing its obligation to the Court and to other State parties to the ICC Statute? The answer would appear to be yes, both in relation to the category of persons addressed by a bilateral non-surrender agreement and the object and purpose of avoiding impunity. The better view, therefore, is that a signatory should avoid entering into a bilateral non-surrender agreement which may not be compatible with the ICC Statute and its Article 98.[186]

---

[182] See S. D. Murphy, 'Contemporary Practice of the United States Relating to International Law: International Criminal Law', *AJIL*, 97 (2003), 200 (where 'persons' are defined as 'current or former Government officials, employees (including contractors), or military personnel or other nationals of one Party').

[183] Their Joint Opinion in the Matter of the Statute of the International Criminal Court and in the Matter of Bilateral Agreements Sought by the United States under Article 98 (2) of the Statute is available at www.amicc.org/docs/Art98-14une03FINAL.pdf (where they conclude, at p. 21 (paragraph 45), that 'the limitation imposed by Article 98(2) concerns the relationship between the relevant person and the "sending State": the person who is present on the territory of the requested State Party must have a nexus with the 'sending State' which goes beyond mere nationality, and his or her presence must have been occasioned by some positive act of the sending State').

[184] *Ibid.*, at p. 12 (paragraph 26). And, at p. 13, 'avoiding impunity' (paragraph 28); at p. 14, '[t]he avoidance of impunity' (paragraph 32); at p. 16, 'guaranteeing subjection to a criminal justice process' (paragraph 34) and, also at 16, 'to remove impunity' (paragraph 33). For further discussion of the object and purpose of the Rome Statute, consider the contribution to this volume of Wilmshurst at pp. 621–652 (Chapter 19).

[185] *Ibid.*, at p. 16 (paragraph 33).

[186] *Ibid.*, at p. 24 (paragraph 55). Though the authors do admit the 'uncertainty' that surrounds whether this provision of the Vienna Convention 'reflects a rule of customary law and the extent of the obligation': *ibid.*, at pp. 23–24 (paragraph 54).

This approach bases its analysis upon an admixture of the object and purpose of the Rome Statute together with one of the provisions of the Statute; it contrasts with the position of the Parliamentary Assembly of the Council of Europe who, in September 2002, expressed great concern 'by the efforts of some [S]tates to undermine the integrity of the ICC treaty'[187] and considered that the exemption agreements in question 'are not admissible under the international law governing treaties ... according to which [S]tates must refrain from any action which would not be consistent with the object and the purpose of a treaty'.[188]

In a strange but satisfying sense, the interim obligation contained in Article 18 VCLT may have accelerated the act of 'unsigning' by the Bush Administration: it suggests that, in the view of the Administration, as long as the signature from December 2000 remained effective – or remained unaffected by an expressed contrary intention or action[189] – the United States would be bound by certain obligations as a matter of the general law of treaties (as opposed to the contents of the Rome Statute), and most importantly the interim obligation discussed in this section. However, if there is any truth to this claim,[190] it would have to be on the basis that the obligation expressed in the Vienna Convention – specifically Article 18(a) VCLT[191] – is reflective of customary international law, because the United States is only a signatory to the Vienna Convention on the Law of Treaties and has been so since 24 April 1970.[192] That signatory status is also

---

[187] Resolution 1300, Risks for the Integrity of the Statute of the International Criminal Court (25 Sept. 2002) (https://assembly.coe.int/nw/xml/XRef/Xref-XML2HTML-en.asp?fileid=17045&lang=en) (paragraph 9).

[188] *Ibid.* (paragraph 10) (which differs from the obligation as stated in Art. 18 VCLT: *supra* n. 1).

[189] *Supra* n. 177.

[190] A possibility that is presented by L. Boisson de Chazournes, A.-M. La Rosa and M. M. Mbengue, 'Article 18 (1969)' in Corten and Klein (eds.), (Vol. I), *supra* n. 21, pp. 369–403, at p. 396. See, also, C. A. Bradley, 'U.S. Announces Intent Not to Ratify International Criminal Court Treaty', *ASIL Insights* (May 2002) (regarding Under Secretary Bolton's 'implicit reference to the object and purpose requirement in Article 18 of the Vienna Convention').

[191] The Rome Statute had yet to enter into force; it did so on 1 July 2002.

[192] On Art. 18 VCLT as an exercise in codification, see Rogoff, *supra* note 8, at 284 and 287–288. See, further, Boisson de Chazournes, La Rosa and Mbengue, *supra* n. 190, at pp. 372–383; Gamble and Frankowska, *supra* n. 23, at 127–128; Dörr, *supra* n. 148, at pp. 220–221, and O'Connell, *supra* n. 154, at p. 205. An instance of the application of Art. 18 VCLT *qua* treaty obligation arose in *Öcalan* v. *Turkey* where the European Court of Human Rights observed, in the context of Turkey's signature of Protocol No. 6 to the European Convention on Human Rights, that its 'non-implementation of the capital sentence is in keeping with Turkey's obligations as a signatory State to this Protocol, in

significant here, because it raises in turn the unedifying prospect of deciphering what the interim obligation entails in respect of the Vienna Convention on the Law of Treaties itself,[193] which would necessitate some appreciation of what constitutes the object and purpose of the Vienna Convention!

***

It needs to be restated that Article 18 VCLT confines its obligation to the timepoints identified earlier in this chapter – of either the interval between signature and ratification or the period preceding the entry into force of a treaty. What, however, is to become of the object and purpose of a treaty once it enters into force?[194] In *Case Concerning Military and Paramilitary Activities in and against Nicaragua*, the International Court of Justice concluded as part of its *dispositif* that by committing certain attacks on Nicaraguan territory in 1983 and 1984 and by declaring a general trade embargo on Nicaragua in May 1985, the United States had 'committed acts calculated to deprive of its object and purpose' the 1956 Treaty of Friendship, Commerce and Navigation that it had reached with Nicaragua.[195] In so doing, the Court was responding to Nicaragua's claim that, amongst constituting violations of other provisions of international law, the actions of the United States

---

accordance with Article 18 of the Vienna Convention': App. No. 46211/99, 12 March 2003 (paragraph 185).

[193] For fourteen other States apart from the United States: Afghanistan, Bolivia, Cambodia, Côte d'Ivoire, El Salvador, Ethiopia, Ghana, Iran, Kenya, Madagascar, Nepal, Pakistan, Trinidad and Tobago and Zambia. Assuming, of course, the customary status of the obligation given the provision that the Vienna Convention makes on its own non-retroactivity. See Art. 4 VCLT: *supra* n. 1.

[194] A matter that carried some currency with Judge Fleischhauer in *Gabčíkovo-Nagymaros Project*: 'It follows from there that a State party to a treaty in force is not free to engage in – even on its own territory as Czechoslovakia did as from November 1991 – construction works which are designed to frustrate the treaty's very object, i.e., in the present case the creation and the operation of the Joint Project'. *Supra* n. 154, at p. 206. An important recent addendum from practice is also worth recounting here: the eighth preambular recitation of the Joint Comprehensive Plan of Action (JCPOA) – agreed between Iran, the five permanent members of the Security Council and Germany as well as the European Union in July 2015 and adopted in Oct. 2015 – provides that '[t]he E3/EU+3 and Iran commit to implement this JCPOA in good faith and in a constructive atmosphere, based on mutual respect, and to refrain from any action inconsistent with the letter, spirit and intent of the JCPOA that would undermine its successful implementation'. This passage is reproduced verbatim in the 28th operative paragraph of the JCPOA: www.state.gov/documents/organization/245317.pdf.

[195] *Nicaragua Case, supra* n. 168, at p. 148 (paragraph 292(10)) (by twelve votes to three). See, further, 367 UNTS 3.

were 'such as to defeat the object and purpose' of this bilateral agreement.[196]

The Court made clear that this claim was 'one not based directly on a specific provision' of the Treaty of Friendship, Commerce and Navigation but one that was related to 'a legal obligation of States to refrain from acts which would impede the due performance of any treaties entered into by them'.[197] In the words of the Court:

> if there is a duty of a State not to impede the due performance of a treaty to which it is a party, that is not a duty imposed by the treaty itself. Nicaragua itself apparently contends that this is a duty arising under customary international law independently of the treaty, that it is implicit in the rule *pacta sunt servanda*. This claim therefore does not fall under the heading of possible breach by the United States of the provisions of the 1956 Treaty, though it may involve the interpretation or application thereof.[198]

The fact that the Court found that this 'claim' does not 'fall under the heading of a possible breach' of the provisions of a treaty takes us back to the anatomy of a treaty mentioned above and edges us beyond its constituent provisions: it instructs us that a treaty mentioned might well comprise more than the sum of its constituent parts – including something other than its formal stipulations, something more than is visible to the naked eye. Seen in this light, the notion of a treaty's object and purpose acquires renewed vigour for, much like the 'duty' of a State 'not to impede the due performance of a treaty to which it is a party', it is there to sustain the conditions for the viability of the treaty *once it has entered into force*.[199] In proceeding down this path, the Court did sound an initial note of scepticism about what this claim would entail:

> The argument that the United States has deprived the Treaty of its object and purpose has a scope which is not very clearly defined, but it appears that in Nicaragua's contention the Court could on this ground make a blanket condemnation of the United States for all the activities of which Nicaragua complains on more specific grounds. For Nicaragua, the Treaty is 'without doubt a treaty of friendship which imposes on the Parties the obligation to conduct amicable relations with each other', and '[w]hatever the exact dimensions of the legal norm of "friendship" there can be no doubt of a United States violation in this case'. In other words, the Court is asked to rule that a State which enters into a treaty of friendship binds itself, for so long as the Treaty is in force, to abstain from any act toward the other party

---

[196] *Ibid.*, at p. 22 (paragraph 23). Cf. pp. 18–19 (paragraph 15). [197] *Ibid.* [198] *Ibid.*
[199] *Supra* n. 198. See, further, Bowman, *supra* n. 20, at 353.

which could be classified as an unfriendly act, even if such act is not in itself the breach of an international obligation.[200]

The Court was not disposed however to make any 'blanket condemnation' of the acts of the United States and, instead, in two very important paragraphs of the *Nicaragua* judgment, it moved to specify those activities that did in its view 'deprive' the Treaty of Friendship, Commerce and Navigation of its object and purpose.[201] As the Court explained in paragraph 275:

> it does consider that there are certain activities of the United States which are such as to undermine the whole spirit of a bilateral agreement directed to sponsoring friendship between the two States parties to it. These are: the direct attacks on ports, oil installations, etc. ... and the mining of Nicaraguan ports ... Any action less calculated to serve the purpose of 'strengthening the bonds of peace and friendship traditionally existing between' the Parties, stated in the Preamble of the Treaty, could hardly be imagined.[202]

And in paragraph 276:

> While [certain] acts of economic pressure are less flagrantly in contradiction with the purpose of the Treaty, the Court reaches a similar conclusion in respect of some of them. A State is not bound to continue particular trade relations longer than it sees fit to do so, in the absence of a treaty commitment or other specific legal obligation; but where there exists such a commitment, of the kind implied in a treaty of friendship and commerce, such an abrupt act of termination of commercial intercourse as the general trade embargo ... will normally constitute a violation of the obligation not to defeat the object and purpose of the treaty. The 90 per cent cut in the sugar import quota of 23 September 1983 does not on the other hand seem to the Court to go so far as constitute an act calculated to defeat the object and purpose of the Treaty. The cessation of economic aid, the giving of which is more of a unilateral and voluntary nature, could be regarded as such a violation only in exceptional circumstances. ... As to the opposition to the grant of loans from international institutions, the Court cannot regard this as sufficiently linked with the 1956 ... Treaty to constitute an act directed to defeating its object and purpose.[203]

---

[200] *Nicaragua Case, supra* n. 168, at pp. 136–137 (paragraph 273).

[201] *Ibid.*, at p. 138 (paragraph 275).   [202] *Ibid.*

[203] *Ibid.* (paragraph 276). As for the acts of economic pressure discussed at the start of this passage, the Court had itemised these at an earlier point in its judgment: cessation of economic aid (Apr. 1981); action to oppose or block loans to Nicaragua in the Bank for International Reconstruction and Development and the Inter-American Development Bank; modification of the system of quota for United States imports of sugar (Sept. 1983) and the total trade embargo (May 1985), i.e. prohibition of all imports from and exports to Nicaragua, the barring of Nicaraguan vessels from the United States ports and the

In its judgment, the Court therefore assesses, measure for measure, each of the actions of the United States as against the object and purpose of the Treaty of Friendship, Commerce and Navigation – and, through its reasoning, the Court came to confer a certain tangibility upon the concept of the Treaty's object and purpose as a juridical force over and above those of its twenty-five individual provisions. What is worth remarking, too, is *how* the Court chose to characterize the ongoing legal significance of a treaty's object and purpose after its entry into force: there is evident in its judgment an unmistakeable mirroring of the contents of Article 18 VCLT for the Court spoke of 'a violation of the obligation not to defeat the object and purpose of the treaty',[204] 'an act calculated to defeat the object and purpose of the Treaty'[205] and 'an act directed to defeating its object and purpose'.[206] Again, 'defeat of a treaty's object and purpose' does not appear to be the ultimate or exclusive question: the Court also directed itself toward the consideration of the calculation – and, presumably, the intention – of the recalcitrant State. This element should not be lost amongst the Court's description of 'acts of economic pressure' that are 'less flagrantly in contradiction with the purpose of the Treaty'[207] or its finding 'that the United States is in breach of a duty not to deprive the [Treaty of Friendship, Commerce and Navigation] of its object and purpose',[208] for in the *dispositif* of the judgment, the Court held very clearly that the United States had indeed 'committed acts calculated to deprive of its object and purpose the Treaty of Friendship, Commerce and Navigation' of January 1956.[209] Such

---

exclusion of Nicaraguan aircraft from air transportation to and from the United States. See *ibid.*, at pp. 69–70 (paragraphs 123–125).

[204] *Ibid.*

[205] *Ibid.* (and 'action less calculated to serve the purpose': *supra* n. 202). Also, 'an act calculated to deprive [the treaty] of its object and purpose': *ibid.*, at p. 141 (paragraph 280).

[206] *Supra* n. 203.

[207] *Nicaragua Case, supra* n. 168, at p. 138 (paragraph 276); see, also, *supra* n. 203.

[208] *Ibid.*, at p. 140 (paragraph 280) (in addition to 'acts which are in contradiction with the terms of the Treaty'). Or, indeed, of its summation of the 'claim' of Nicaragua – that 'the United States activities have been such as to deprive the [Treaty of Friendship, Commerce and Navigation] of its object and purpose': *ibid.*, at p. 138 (paragraph 275); see, also, *ibid.*, at p. 135 (paragraph 270) as this does not comport fully with what Nicaragua had claimed.

[209] *Ibid.*, at p. 148 (paragraph 292(10)). And, in the same sentence as its reference to the flagrant contradiction with the 'purpose' of the Treaty of Friendship, Commerce and Navigation, the Court said that 'such an abrupt act of termination of commercial intercourse as the general trade embargo of ... May 1985 will normally constitute a violation of the obligation not to defeat the object and purpose of the treaty': *ibid.*, at p. 138 (paragraph 276).

was the commitment 'of the kind implied in a treaty of friendship and commerce' said the Court,[210] and it would be engaged irrespective of the actual defeat of the object and purpose of Treaty of Friendship, Commerce and Navigation.

The Court's approach did not command the unanimous support of all colleagues: for Judge Shigeru Oda, the weight attached by the Court to the object and purpose of the Treaty of Friendship, Commerce and Navigation meant that it had 'misinterpreted' the concept of a treaty's object and purpose as 'introduced' by the Vienna Convention – a 'principle', he maintained, that 'requires compliance with the letter of obligations subscribed to, and not necessarily the avoidance of conduct not expressly precluded by the terms of the given treaty'.[211] In his dissenting opinion, Judge Stephen M. Schwebel regarded the 'narrower creative category' concerning acts 'tending to defeat the object and purpose of [a] [t]treaty' as 'an injudicious extension by the Court of the jurisdiction afforded it under a treaty of this kind',[212] and, for Judge Robert Jennings, 'the substance of the Court's decision … causes … unease': 'Either those acts are breaches of some provision of the Treaty [of Friendship, Commerce and Navigation] or they have nothing to do with the Treaty. The "object and purpose" of a treaty cannot be a concept existing independently of any of its terms'.[213] These are strong misgivings, of course, but they were not sufficient in the end to stall the allocation of a role for a treaty's object and purpose by the Court beyond the explicit terms of the Vienna Convention.

4   Interpretations of a Treaty's Object and Purpose

The next appearance of a treaty's object and purpose in the Vienna Convention comes with its rules regarding the interpretation of treaties,

---

[210] *Ibid.*, at p. 138 (paragraph 276). Although, for Judge Oda, the Court attributed this position to Nicaragua – and 'the Judgment does not make it clear whether [the Court] is espousing this point of view'. *Ibid.*, at p. 250 (paragraph 81). See, further, T. D. Gill, *Litigation Strategy at the International Court: A Case Study of the Nicaragua v. United States Dispute* (Dordrecht: Martinus Nijhoff Publishers, 1989), p. 264.

[211] *Ibid.*, at p. 250 (paragraph 81). Cf. Art. 60(3)(a) VCLT: *supra* n. 1.

[212] *Ibid.*, at p. 387 (paragraph 253). Also raised by Judge Oda: *ibid.*, at p. 250 (paragraph 81) ('It may furthermore be asked where the jurisdiction granted by a treaty clause would ever end if it were held to entitle the Court to scrutinize any act remotely describable as inimical to the object and purpose of the treaty in question').

[213] *Ibid.*, at p. 542. Although he, too, raised the issue of jurisdiction from this perspective: *ibid.*, at p. 540.

where it is provided that '[a] treaty shall be interpreted in good faith in accordance with the ordinary meaning to be given to the terms of the treaty in their context and in light of its object and purpose'.[214] Through to this point of the Convention, it might have been assumed that the treaty's object and purpose would have made itself known in the course of that treaty's text. This is not so, however, and we are greeted instead with silence on the matter of what constitutes the Vienna Convention's own object and purpose. To take another example, the preambular reference in the 1978 Vienna Convention on Succession of States in Respect of Treaties – to 'general multilateral treaties which deal with the codification and progressive development of international law and those the object and purpose of which are of interest to the international community as a whole is of special importance for the strengthening of peace and international cooperation' – does very little to illuminate what the object and purpose of *that* Convention is, notwithstanding the extensive reliance on that concept.[215] Incontrovertibly, we are confronted with the very real enigma that 'the object and purpose of a treaty [is] to be determined in light of its object and purpose!'[216]

In embarking upon this task, it is probably advisable to recall Alain Pellet's observation – in debt to Blaise Pascal – that '[s]uch a process undoubtedly requires more "*esprit de finesse*" than "*esprit de géométrie*", like any act of interpretation, for that matter – and this process is certainly one of interpretation'.[217] Pellet, as Special Rapporteur on Reservations to Treaties within the International Law Commission, was responsible for producing the International Law Commission's 2011

---

[214] Art. 31(1) VCLT: *supra* n. 1. Also, on plurilingual treaties, '[e]xcept where a particular text prevails in accordance with [Art. 33(1)], when a comparison of the authentic texts discloses a difference of meaning which the application of articles 31 and 32 does not remove, the meaning which best reconciles the texts, *having regard to the object and purpose of the treaty*, shall be adopted': Art. 33(4) VCLT (emphasis added): *supra* n. 1.

[215] 1946 UNTS 3 (fifth preambular recital); the 1978 Vienna Convention is a research marvel for present purposes because it contains eighteen – eighteen! – other references to the concept of a treaty's object and purpose – Arts. 15(b), 17(2), 17(3), 18(3), 18(4), 19(3), 19(4), 20(2)(a), 20(3)(a), 31(1)(b), 31(3), 32(6), 33(2), 33(5), 34(2)(b), 35(c), 36(3) and 37(2) – but nowhere does it identify its own object and purpose!

[216] W. A. Schabas, 'Reservations to Human Rights Treaties: Time for Innovation and Reform', *Canadian YbIL*, 32 (1994), 39–81, at 48. Though it is also true that the challenge of interpretation afflicts reservations made elsewhere under Art. 19 VCLT: Pellet, *supra* n. 21, at pp. 437 and 451 ('[u]ltimately, this is a problem of interpretation: the "general rule of interpretation" expressed in [Art. 31 VCLT] is applicable *mutatis mutandis* to the examination of the object and purpose of the treaty').

[217] *See* Report of the International Law Commission, Sixty-third Session (26 Apr.–3 June and 4 July–12 Aug. 2011), U.N. Doc. A/66/10/Add.1, pp. 359–360.

Guide to Practice on Reservations to Treaties, in which it is stated that '[t]he object and purpose of the treaty is to be determined in good faith, taking account of the terms of the treaty in their context, in particular the title and the preamble of the treaty. Recourse may also be had to the preparatory work of the treaty and the circumstances of its conclusion and, where appropriate, the subsequent practice of the parties'.[218] This is good as far as it goes, seeking to unite various morsels of the treaty anatomy in order to form a coherent proposition that is workable at law, and it suggests that a certain degree of circularity – or, perhaps, symbiosis – is implicated: we are to interpret the terms of the treaty by reference to its object and purpose (Article 31(1) VCLT); we are to interpret the treaty's object and purpose by reference to its terms (*Guide to Practice on Reservations to Treaties*).[219]

Ian Sinclair, perhaps more helpfully, has sought to structure the act of interpretation so that 'the reference to the object and purpose of the treaty [in Article 31(1) VCLT] is, as it were, a secondary or ancillary process in the application of the general rule of interpretation'.[220] It becomes a form of delayed reassurance for answers that might emerge from the principal method of ascertaining an 'ordinary meaning' in view of its 'context', although

> [i]t may be of course that the intellectual process is so overwhelmingly apparent that it must necessarily and from the very outset exercise a determining influence upon the search for the contextual 'ordinary meaning'; but this is likely to be a rare case, given that most treaties have no single, undiluted object and purpose but a variety of differing and possibly conflicting objects and purposes.[221]

This does seem to reduce the pressure on the function of the concept of a treaty's object and purpose as an immediate tool for exercises of treaty

---

[218] Guideline 3.1.5.1: *ibid.*

[219] As Pellet has correctly identified in the Commentary to the Guidelines, 'the basic problem is one of interpretation' – and, hence, 'it would appear legitimate, *mutatis mutandis*, to transpose the principles in [Arts. 31 and 32] of the Vienna Convention . . . and to adapt them to the determination of the object and purpose of the treaty': *supra* n. 217, at p. 361. The Commentary to the Guidelines identifies 'a number of highly disparate elements, taken individually or in combination' from the jurisprudence of the International Court of Justice that have helped it deduce the object and purpose of a treaty: title, preamble, treaty provisions, preparatory work on the treaty and from overall tenor': *ibid.*, at pp. 360–361.

[220] Sinclair, *supra* n. 11, at p. 130.

[221] *Ibid.* See, also, T. D. Grant, *Admission to the United Nations Charter Article 4 and the Rise of Universal Organization* (Leiden: Martinus Nijhoff, 2009), p. 130.

interpretation, but at the same time, it alerts us to the discomforting possibility that the concept might flourish in certain contexts but not, alas, in others (i.e. where there is 'no single, undiluted object and purpose'). Whereas this concept might bring clarity and insight, it might equally generate only conflict and irresolution. For example, what exactly is – what are – the object/s and purpose/s of the 1945 Charter on the United Nations?[222] And, more specifically, how might these resolve the intractable question of whether the right of self-defence in Article 51 of the Charter is confined to situations where 'an armed attack occurs' or whether the right permits anticipatory self-defence in some shape or form? Is the Charter's object and purpose – at least, in part – not to 'save succeeding generations from the scourge of war' as *per* its preamble?[223] What of the fact, also by way of the Charter preamble, 'that armed force shall not be used, save in the common interest'? But why, then, admit *any* right of self-defence at all? What of the establishment of conditions according to the Charter preamble 'under which justice and respect for the obligations arising from treaties and other sources of international law can be maintained'? Is this to be taken as support for the long-standing customary underpinning for a right of anticipatory self-defence in international law?[224] And are the purposes of the *United Nations* – to maintain international peace and security; to develop friendly relations among nations based on respect for the principle of equal rights and self-determination of peoples; to achieve international co-operation in solving international problems of an economic, social, cultural, or humanitarian character; to be a centre for harmonising actions of nations – as enunciated in Article 1 of the Charter to be read as elements of the object and purpose of the *Charter*?[225]

According to Sinclair, we must guard against the 'certain dangers' of considering 'that the search for the object and purpose of a treaty is in reality a search for the common intentions of the parties who drew up the treaty' – one of the interpretations made, it will be recalled, in the *Reservations* advisory opinion.[226] Here, he sounds a vital note of caution:

---

[222] 1 UNTS 16.

[223] *Ibid.* (first preambular recital). See, further, the discussion of T. Ruys, '*Armed Attack' and Article 51 of the UN Charter: Evolutions in Customary Law and Practice* (Cambridge: Cambridge University Press, 2010), pp. 59–60.

[224] R. Y. Jennings, 'The *Caroline* and McLeod Cases', *AJIL*, 32 (1938), 82–99.

[225] As argued by O. Dörr, 'Article 31' in Dörr and K. Schmalenbach (eds.), *supra* n. 6, pp. 521–570, at p. 546.

[226] *Supra* n. 27.

In the case of general multilateral conventions, a search for the common intentions of the parties can be likened to a search for the pot of gold at the end of a rainbow. Many of the parties will have acceded to the treaty and for that reason alone (because they have not taken part in the original framing of the text) must be assumed to have joined not on the basis of what the original negotiators intended but rather on the basis of what the text actually says and means. In addition, a dispute as to treaty interpretation arises only when two or more parties place differing constructions upon the text; by doing so, they are in reality professing differing intentions in regard to that text and, of necessity, professing to have had differing intentions from the very start. If this is the case, there can be no common intentions of the parties aside or apart from the text they have agreed upon. The text is the *expression* of the intention of the parties; and it is to that expression of intent that one must first look.[227]

***

Let us now try to explore some of these ideas through the jurisprudence of the International Court of Justice on these matters. The first example is *Case Concerning Oil Platforms* when Iran instituted contentious proceedings against the United States in November 1992, claiming *inter alia* that 'in adopting a patently hostile and threatening attitude towards the Islamic Republic [of Iran] that culminated in the attack and destruction of the Iranian oil platforms [in October 1987 and April 1988], the United States [had] breached the object and purpose' of the 1955 Treaty of Amity, Economic Relations and Consular Rights that it had agreed with Iran.[228] However, at the oral hearings stage of this case, Iran stated very clearly that 'its claim is strictly based on three very specific provisions' of the 1955 Treaty of Amity, Economic Relations and Consular Rights – namely Articles I, IV(1) and X(1) – and 'not on the violation of the object and purpose of the Treaty as a whole'.[229] This would release the Court from the challenge that had befallen it in the *Nicaragua Case*,[230] although the contested significance of Article I of the Treaty – which provides that '[t]here shall be firm and enduring peace and sincere friendship' between Iran and

---

[227] Sinclair, *supra* n. 11, at pp. 130–131.

[228] 284 UNTS 3. See *Case Concerning Oil Platforms*: Islamic Republic of Iran v. United States of America (Preliminary Objection) (1996) ICJ Rep. 803, at pp. 806–807 (paragraph 9(c)) and 808 (paragraph 12), and *Case Concerning Oil Platforms*: Islamic Republic of Iran v. United States of America (Merits) (2003) ICJ Rep. 161, at p. 170 (paragraph 18(c)) – which included, Iran claimed, Arts. I and X(1) of the 1955 Treaty and international law.

[229] *Case Concerning Oil Platforms* (Preliminary Objection), *ibid.*, at p. 809 (paragraph 13). Hence, the Court did not address this aspect in its *dispositif*: *Case Concerning Oil Platforms* (Merits), *ibid.*, at p. 218 (paragraph 125(1)).

[230] *Supra* n. 168.

the United States – meant that the Court had no option but to consider the treaty's object and purpose in order to interpret the scope and meaning of this particular provision. For Iran, this provision 'does not merely formulate a recommendation or desire ... but imposes actual obligations on the Contracting Parties, obliging them to maintain long-lasting peaceful and friendly relations',[231] and this would impose upon the Parties 'the minimum requirement ... to conduct themselves with regard to the other in accordance with the principles and rules of general international law in the domain of peaceful and friendly relations'.[232] For the United States, Article I constituted a mere 'statement of aspiration'.[233]

With the change in the substantive formulation of Iran's claims, we can begin to appreciate that the concept of a treaty's 'object and purpose' might in fact affect the structure of the process of interpretation as advanced by Sinclair, for there are going to be situations – as in the *Nicaragua Case* and potentially in *Case Concerning Oil Platforms* – where a treaty's object and purpose is front and centre of the dispute: it is integral to the actual claims being presented to the Court for adjudication. In the event, however, Iran progressively invested its energies in the substantive provisions of the Treaty of Amity, Economic Relations and Consular Rights, and this involved the Court scrutinizing the 'general formulation' of Article I of that Treaty – a provision which, the Court said, 'cannot be interpreted in isolation from the object and purpose of the Treaty in which it is inserted'.[234] Reflecting on the 'object' of the Treaty as understood from its preamble,[235] the Court undertook a brief assessment of kindred bilateral arrangements such as the 1955 Treaty of Friendship and Good Neighbourliness between the French Republic and the United Kingdom of Libya[236] and found that

---

[231] *Case Concerning Oil Platforms* (Preliminary Objection), *supra* n. 228, at p. 812 (paragraph 25).

[232] *Ibid.*, at p. 812 (paragraph 25) (i.e. 'in relation to the rules of general international law thus "incorporated" into the Treaty': *ibid.*, at p. 813 (paragraph 25)).

[233] *Ibid.*, at p. 813 (paragraph 26).   [234] *Ibid.*, at p. 813 (paragraph 27).

[235] Namely the 'encouraging [of] mutually beneficial trade and investments and closer economic intercourse generally' as well as the regulation of consular relations between two States: *ibid.*, at p. 813 (paragraph 27). On the importance of preambles for the object and purpose of investment treaties, see R. Dolzer and C. Schreuer, *Principles of International Investment Law* (Oxford: Oxford University Press, 2nd ed., 2012), p. 29, and, also, C. H. Schreuer, L. Malintoppi, A. Reinisch and A. Sinclair, *The ICSID Convention: A Commentary* (Oxford: Oxford University Press, 2nd ed., 2009), p. 117.

[236] *Case Concerning Oil Platforms* (Preliminary Objection), *supra* n. 228, at p. 813 (paragraph 27). This agreement came up for consideration in *Case Concerning the Territorial Dispute (Libyan Arab Jamahiriya/Chad)* (1994) ICJ Rep. 6, at pp. 25–26 (paragraph 52).

'the object and purpose of the Treaty of 1955 was not to regulate peaceful and friendly relations between the two States in a general sense':

> Article I cannot be interpreted as incorporating into the Treaty all of the provisions of international law concerning such relations. Rather, by incorporating into the body of the Treaty the form of words used in Article I, the two States intended to stress that peace and friendship constituted the precondition for a harmonious development of their commercial, financial and consular relations and that such a development would in turn reinforce that peace and that friendship. It follows that Article I must be regarded as fixing an objective, in the light of which the other Treaty provisions are to be interpreted and applied.[237]

The Court was therefore seeking to interpret the scope and meaning of Article I of the Treaty by reference to the treaty's object and purpose; it felt it could not do so, or not do so accurately, in the absence of this consideration, so it understood its 'interpreter's task' as 'not so much to give effect to the treaty's object and purpose, but rather *to give effect to its terms in light of that [object] and purpose*'.[238]

We can carry this thought forward to our second example, which is set in the context of a multilateral treaty: in *Whaling in the Antarctic*, Australia called upon the Court to declare that the Japanese Whale Research Program under Special Permit in the Antarctic Phase II (JARPA II) did not come 'within the meaning of Article VIII' of the 1946 International Convention for the Regulation of Whaling (ICRW) (which provides, in part, that 'any Contracting Government may grant to any of its nationals a specific permit authorizing that national to kill, take and treat whales for purposes of scientific research subject to such restrictions as to number and subject to such other conditions as the Contracting Government thinks fit').[239] That provision accordingly became the effective fulcrum for and of the whole case: Japan had originally taken the position that special permit whaling of the order envisaged by JARPA fell 'entirely outside the scope' of the 1946 Convention; it was to be regarded as 'free-standing' and 'would have to be read in isolation from the other provisions of the Convention'.[240] It later acknowledged, however, that Article VIII(1)

---

[237] *Case Concerning Oil Platforms* (Preliminary Objection), *supra* n. 228, at p. 814 (paragraph 28). Also, the United States had emphasised that its interpretation 'is called for in the context and on account of the "purely commercial and consular" character of the Treaty': *ibid.*, at p. 813 (paragraph 26).

[238] Bowman, *supra* n. 20, at 318 (emphasis in original).

[239] 364 UNTS 1953, Art. VIII(1). See *Whaling in the Antarctic: Australia v. France; New Zealand intervening* (2014) ICJ Rep. 226, at pp. 238–239 (paragraph 24).

[240] As reported by the Court: *ibid.*, at p. 250 (paragraph 52).

must be interpreted and applied consistently with the other provisions of the Convention, which would result in its forming an exemption from the duties thereby imposed.[241] For its part, Australia emphasised reading Article VIII in the context of the Convention as a whole, so that the conservation measures undertaken to realise its objectives must remain relevant for whaling for scientific purposes, which 'cannot have the effect of undermining the effectiveness of the regulatory régime as a whole'.[242] New Zealand (intervening) claimed that Article VIII provided a 'limited discretion' for Contracting Governments to issue special permits for the purpose of scientific research: it does not, however, 'constitute a blanket exemption for special permit whaling from all aspects of the Convention'.[243]

In its judgment, the Court recognised the extent to which both Australia and Japan had sought to invoke the object and purpose of the ICRW to 'buttress' their respective argumentation: the object and purpose of conservation (for Australia); the object and purpose of sustainable exploitation (for Japan).[244] This was done with a view to engineering the correct – or preferred – interpretation of Article VIII(1) ICRW: as recounted by the Court, for Australia, a restrictive interpretation of the provision was called for 'because it allows the taking of whales, thus providing an exception to the general rules of the Convention which give effect to its object and purpose of conservation'; for Japan, the Convention's commitment to sustainable exploitation meant that this was not the case.[245]

The Court was of the view that Article VIII ICRW forms 'an integral part of the Convention' which has to be interpreted in light of the object and purpose of the Convention and taking into account other provisions of the Convention (including its Schedule).[246] However, '[t]aking into

---

[241] *Ibid.*   [242] Again, as reported by the Court: *ibid.* (paragraph 53).

[243] *Ibid.* (paragraph 54).   [244] *Ibid.*, at p. 251 (paragraph 57).

[245] *Ibid.*, at pp. 251–252 (paragraph 57). As for New Zealand, it, too, argued for 'a restrictive rather than an expansive interpretation of the conditions in which the Contracting Government may issue a Special Permit under Article VIII' in order not to undermine 'the system of collective regulation under the Convention': *ibid.*, at p. 252 (paragraph 57). In its submissions to the Court, New Zealand had claimed that '[t]he object and purpose of the Convention was, and is ... to replace unregulated, unilateral whaling by States with a system of collective regulation through which the interests of the parties in the proper conservation and management of whales can be achieved': Written Observations of New Zealand (4 Apr. 2013), p. 12 (paragraph 25) (www.icj-cij.org/docket/files/148/17386.pdf).

[246] *Ibid.*, at p. 251 (paragraph 55). By Art. I of the Convention, the Schedule attached to it 'forms an integral part thereof': *supra* n. 239.

account the Preamble and other relevant provisions of the Convention',
the Court came to the conclusion that 'neither a restrictive nor an
expansive interpretation of Article VIII is justified': 'programmes for
purposes of scientific research should foster scientific knowledge; they
may pursue an aim other other than either conservation or sustainable
exploitation of whale stocks'.[247] Notable in this is the fact that the Court
did not itself in this moment explicitly refer to the 'object and purpose' of
the Convention.[248] However, its use of the word 'aim' here does
suggest that the 'object and purpose' of the Convention was not
far from its mind, and it also connects with the Court's earlier
dissection of the Convention's preamble, which in its view indicates
that the Convention 'pursues the purposes' of ensuring the conservation of all species of which whales while allowing for their sustainable exploration. Amongst the 'objectives' of the Convention, the
Court also said, was the Contracting Parties' decision in the final
preambular recital 'to conclude a convention to provide for the
proper conservation of whale stocks and thus make possible the
orderly development of the whaling industry' with the consequence
that '[a]mendments to the Schedule and recommendations by the
[International Whaling Committee] may put emphasis on one or
other objective pursued by the Convention but cannot alter its object
and purpose'.[249]

The conclusion of the Court that Article VIII(1) ICRW did not
warrant the interpretation placed on it by either Australia or Japan is
indicative of the duality stemming from the object and purpose of the
Convention – although the Court did not say this in so many words. This
element of duality in the object and purpose of the Convention meant
that it could not in the end prove dispositive in the exercise of interpreting the Convention, but even so, there are two crucial points we should
not miss in this regard. The first is that the Court disciplined its approach
toward the object and purpose of the Convention in that nowhere did it
make reference to the 'intention' of the authors of the Convention; the
Court's method derived from the contents of the preamble of the
Convention; it is this ('object and purpose') read together with 'other

---

[247] *Ibid.*, at p. 252 (paragraph 58).

[248] The Court does do so towards the end of its judgment when speaking of '[a]ny such
interpretation [that] would leave certain undefined categories of whaling activity beyond
the scope of the Convention and thus would undermine its object and purpose': *ibid.*, at
p. 294 (paragraph 229).

[249] *Ibid.*, at p. 251 (paragraph 56).

relevant provisions of the Convention' ('context') that led the Court to conclude that the interpretations of Article VIII(1) ICRW posited before it could not be supported. We thus seem to have a departure, a shift of sorts, from the *Reservations* advisory opinion with regard to the considerations that are regarded as relevant for a treaty's object and purpose to be construed.

The second point is the premium attached to the Convention's object and purpose in the separate and dissenting opinions attached to the judgment of the Court. These are especially interesting for revealing how some judges perceived the question of the Convention's object and purpose from the perspective of its *substance*. In the opinion of Judge Hisashi Owada, 'the object and purpose of the Convention is to pursue the goal of achieving the twin purposes of the sustainability of the maximum yield ... of the stocks in question and the viability of the whaling industry. Nowhere in this Convention is to be found the idea of a total permanent ban on the catch of whales'.[250] Judge Hanqin Xue was of the view that 'in granting special permits for killing, taking and treating whales for scientific purposes, the Contracting Party must avoid any adverse effect on the stock with a view to maintaining sustainable utilization and conservation of the resources, otherwise the very object and purpose of the Convention would be undermined, a point on which the Parties hold no different views'.[251] For Judge Julia Sebutinde, '[a Contracting Government] must exercise that discretion [in determining catch limits] consistent with the object and purpose of the ICRW, in that whales may be killed only to the extent necessary for achieving the stated goals of the scientific research programme'),[252] while others – such as Judge Antônio Augusto Cançado Trindade – advised against any attempt 'to reduce the object and purpose of the ... Convention to the protection or development of the whaling industry' on the grounds that it would be 'at odds with the rationale and structure of the ... Convention as a whole'.[253] And this meant that

---

[250] *Ibid.*, at p. 303 (paragraph 9). Also, '[a]ccording to the structure of the Convention as interpreted in light of its object and purpose, the Contracting Parties expressly recognize the need and the importance of scientific research for the purpose of supporting the "system of international regulation for the whale fisheries to ensure proper and effective conservation and development of whale stocks" ... as established by the Convention': *ibid.*, at p. 311 (paragraph 26).

[251] *Ibid.*, at p. 422 (paragraph 7).   [252] *Ibid.*, at p. 434 (paragraph 12).

[253] *Ibid.*, at p. 349 (paragraph 3). See, however: '[t]he object and purpose of the Convention point to, as a guiding principle, the conservation and recovery of whale stocks; not to be seen on an equal footing with the sustainable development of the whaling industry or the protection of commercial whaling': *ibid.*, at p. 351 (paragraph 7). In consequence:

Convention's object and purpose took on *more* than its *materiae* or competing materiae to consider the structure of legal relations there intended: Judge Mohamed Bennouna concluded that '[i]n order to strengthen the object and purpose of the Convention, it is clearly desirable that States parties should act within the institutional framework established'.[254] For Judge Abdulqawi Ahmed Yusuf, 'the Court should have assessed whether the continued conduct of JARPA II ... constitutes an anomaly, which may frustrate the object and purpose of the Convention in light of the amendments introduced to it in recent years which have resulted in an evolution of the regulatory framework of the Convention',[255] while Judge *ad hoc* Hilary Charlesworth spoke of 'the overarching object and purpose of the Convention ... which is to create "a system of international regulation" for the conservation and management of whale stocks' [sixth preambular recital]).[256] A treaty's object and purpose can therefore be more than one thing at any given moment in time: as a thing to be interpreted, it exists first and foremost in the eye of the beholder, and *Whaling in the Antarctic* demonstrates – just as the *Reservations* advisory opinion had done before it – that this cannot be taken for granted for, like any proposition of law, it is there to be interpreted, argued, contested and adjudicated.

5   On the Possibilities of Modification and Suspension

During its lifespan, there may come a point when '[t]wo or more of the parties to a multilateral treaty' conclude an agreement for its *modification* 'as between themselves alone',[257] a possibility that is anticipated by the Vienna Convention, as is the question of the *suspension* of a treaty.[258]

'[a] State party – Japan or any other – cannot act unilaterally to decide whether its programme is fulfilling the object and purpose of the ICRW, or the objective of conservation': *ibid.*

[254] *Ibid.*, at p. 347.   [255] *Ibid.*, at pp. 390–391 (paragraph 26).

[256] *Ibid.*, at p. 457 (paragraph 13).

[257] Art. 41(1) VCLT: *supra* n. 1. As opposed to the *amendment* of a multilateral treaty, which is initiated by a proposal 'as between all the parties' that 'must be notified to all the contracting States', where 'each one of which shall have the right to take part in: (a) [t]he decision as to the action to be taken in regard to such proposal and (b) [t]he negotiation and conclusion of any agreement for the amendment of the treaty': Art. 40(2) VCLT: *supra* n. 1. See, further, Sinclair, *supra* n. 11, at pp. 106–107.

[258] Art. 42(2) VCLT: *supra* n. 1 ('[t]he termination of a treaty, its denunciation or the withdrawal of a party, may take place only as a result of the application of the provisions of the treaty or of the present Convention. The same rule applies to suspension of the operation of a treaty').

The suspension of the operation of a treaty can occur 'in regard to all the parties or to a particular party',[259] but the Vienna Convention also envisages the suspension 'by agreement [as] between certain parties only',[260] both of which should be distinguished from the *termination* of a treaty.[261] We shall now deal with each of these possibilities in turn, as they provide the next occasions on which the Vienna Convention invokes the concept of a treaty's object and purpose: critically, as a unifying factor for the present analysis, both possibilities examined here relate to treaty action not involving 'all the parties'[262] to a treaty but to only a select – or, rather, self-selecting – cohort of those parties.[263]

As far as the modification of treaties is concerned, we can appreciate that there are certain parallels to be made with the system for reservations – a reservation, after all, is defined by the Vienna Convention as a unilateral statement made by a State 'whereby it purports to exclude or to *modify* the legal effect of certain provisions or the treaty in their application to that State'[264] – in that the original treaty is presented with a variable geometry of legal relationships as between its parties.[265] An agreement *inter se* is reached for modification by limited parties 'to vary provisions of a multilateral treaty in their mutual relations'.[266]

---

[259] Art. 57 VCLT: *supra* n. 1. And this suspension can occur '(a) [i]n conformity with the provisions of the treaty; or (b) [a]t any time by consent of all the parties after consultation with the other contracting States': *ibid.*

[260] Art. 58 VCLT: *supra* n. 1.

[261] The termination of a treaty may take place '(a) [i]n conformity with the provisions of a treaty; or (b) [a]t any time by consent of all of the parties after consultation with the other contracting States'. See Art. 54 VCLT: *supra* n. 1. The termination of a treaty can be implied from the conclusion of a later treaty 'if all the parties to it' conclude that later treaty or its provisions 'are so far incompatible with those of the earlier [treaty] that the two treaties are not capable of being applied at the same time'. See Art. 59(1)(a) and (b) VCLT: *supra* n. 1.

[262] *Supra* n. 257 and n. 259.

[263] And, indeed, are brought together in Art. 311(3) of the 1982 United Nations Law of the Sea Convention, 1833 UNTS 3.

[264] Art. 2(1)(d) VCLT: *supra* n. 1 (emphasis added). See, also, Art. 2(1)(d) VCLTSIO: *supra* n. 80.

[265] Note, however, Jonas and Saunders, *supra* n. 6, at 575 ('a modification, which is concluded between only a fraction of [S]tates party, is presumably less disruptive than a reservation, which the reserving [S]tate makes vis-à-vis all other [S]tates party').

[266] K. Odendahl, 'Article 39' in Dörr and Schmalenbach (eds.), *supra* n. 6, pp. 699–707, at p. 699. See, also, Sinclair, *supra* n. 11, at p. 185, and H. Aufricht, 'Supersession of Treaties in International Law', *Cornell Law Q.*, 37 (1952), 655–700, at 671. Though Koskenniemi adroitly observes that '*[i]nter se* agreements give rise to two types of legal relations: the "general" relations that apply between all the parties to the original treaty and the

The same might also be said, however, for a successful proposal to amend a given treaty, since the Vienna Convention is clear that an amending agreement 'does not bind any State already party to the treaty which does not become a party to the amending agreement',[267] and Sinclair remarks that the 'parallel' of the amending treaty 'with the effects of the reservations system embodied in the [Vienna] Convention is striking'.[268] That is why the International Law Commission approached the prospect of modification with considerable care and caution, and the track record did not allow modification to be presented in the most flattering light:

> Clearly, a transaction in which two or a small group of parties set out to modify the treaty between themselves alone without giving the other parties the option of participating in it is on a different footing from an amending agreement drawn up between the parties generally, even if ultimately they do not all ratify it. For an *inter se* agreement is more likely to have an aim and effect incompatible with the object and purpose of the treaty. History furnishes a number of instances of *inter se* agreements which substantially changed the régime of the treaty and which overrode the objections of interested States. Nor can there be any doubt that the application, and even the conclusion, of an *inter se* agreement incompatible with the object and purpose of the treaty may raise a question of State responsibility. ... the main issue is the conditions under which *inter se* agreements may be regarded as possible.[269]

"special" relations that apply between the States parties to the *inter se* agreement': Fragmentation Report, *supra* n. 6, at p. 155 (paragraph 301).

[267] Art. 40(4) VCLT: *supra* n. 1. As it most assuredly could not under Art. 34 VCLT, and Art. 40(4) VCLT goes on to provide that Art. 30(4)(b) VCLT applies in relation to such State: *supra* n. 1. Hence, Art. 39 VCLT: *supra* n. 1 ('[a] treaty may be amended by agreement between the parties'). See, also, Odendahl, *supra* n. 266, at p. 706, and, further, M. E. Villiger, *supra* n. 6, at p. 533.

[268] Following Paul Reuter: Sinclair, *supra* n. 11, at p. 106. See, further, P. Reuter, *Introduction au droit des traités* (Paris: Éditions A. Colin, 1972), p. 132. However, at the Vienna Conference, Max Sorenson (Denmark) did question the analogy between *inter se* modifications and reservations: this was 'more apparent than real', he maintained, arguing that '[a]t the time of the conclusion of a multilateral treaty, it might be justifiable to exclude the reservations but, as time passed, the need for *inter se* modifications could well become apparent': United Nations Conference on the Law of Treaties, First Session, *supra* n. 180, p. 207. See, further, the discussion of late reservations by Swaine, *supra* n. 53, at p. 289.

[269] International Law Commission, Draft Articles on the Law of Treaties with Commentaries, *YbILC* (1966–II), 235. In terms of the 'provision' alluded to in the (eventual) Art. 41 VCLT (i.e. 'derogation from which is incompatible with the effective execution of the object and purpose of the treaty as a whole'), the International Law Commission gave as an example 'an *inter se* agreement modifying substantive provisions of a disarmament or neutralization treaty [that] would be incompatible with its

How and why, then, is a treaty's 'object and purpose' relevant in this context? According to Article 41(1) VCLT, '[t]wo or more parties to a multilateral treaty may conclude an agreement to modify the treaty as between themselves alone if':

   a. the possibility of such modification is provided for by the treaty; or
   b. the modification in question is not prohibited by the treaty and:
      i. does not affect the enjoyment by the other parties of their rights under the treaty or the performance of their obligations;
      ii. does not relate to a provision, derogation from which is incompatible with the effective execution of the object and purpose of the treaty as a whole.

Where 'the possibility of such modification is provided for by the treaty' itself, the concept of a treaty's 'object and purpose' goes unmentioned. It does not – at least, not officially – come into play, presumably because the treaty authors will have taken this factor into account in designing the possibilities and arrangements for modification;[270] in this, there is perhaps some equation to be made with the situation of authorised reservations under Article 19(b) VCLT.[271] However, it is where 'the modification in question' is not prohibited in the treaty – a silence that

---

object and purpose and not permissible under the present article': *ibid.* The International Law Commission would later observe that modification 'involves ... a degree of "derogation" and "setting aside"': Fragmentation Report, *supra* n. 6, at p. 51 (paragraph 91).

[270] By way of example, consider Art. 311(3) UNCLOS: *supra* n. 264. This provision *does* mention that treaty's 'object and purpose' for any modification, though it is better viewed as an instance of authorised modification under Art. 41(1)(a) VCLT rather than Art. 41(1)(b) VCLT (but it does place additional demands on those parties seeking modification ('provided further that such agreements shall not affect the application of the basic principles embodied herein and that the provisions of such agreements do not affect the enjoyment by other States Parties of their rights or the performance of their obligations under this Convention')). See, further, J. Harrison, *Making the Law of the Sea: A Study in the Development of International Law* (Cambridge: Cambridge University Press, 2011), pp. 78–83. As an example of modification, General Assembly Resolution 48/263 (28 July 1994) is especially interesting for present purposes because in adopting the Agreement Relating to the Implementation of Part XI of UNCLOS (third operative paragraph), the General Assembly recognised the need to provide for the provisional application of that Agreement (tenth preambular recital) – and in the sixth operative paragraph of the Resolution, it called upon States, 'which consent to the adoption of the Agreement to refrain from any act which would defeat its object and purpose' – an unmistakable nod to Art. 18 VCLT: D. Anderson, *Modern Law of the Sea: Selected Essays* (Leiden: Martinus Nijhoff, 2008), p. 353.

[271] *Supra* n. 75. This includes 'contracting out' arrangements: see K. Odendahl, 'Article 41' in Dörr and Schmalenbach (eds.), *supra* n. 6, pp. 719–730, at p. 719, and, further, Sinclair, *supra* n. 11, p. 108.

recalls the rule contained in Article 19(c) VCLT[272] – that the Vienna Convention permits modification on the condition that it 'does not affect the enjoyment by the other parties of their rights under the treaty or the performance of their obligations'[273] and that it 'does not relate to a provision, derogation from which is incompatible with the effective execution of the object and purpose of the treaty as a whole'.[274]

In permitting modification to occur under these tightly bound circumstances, it is clear that the Vienna Convention is attempting to recognise and protect at least three constituencies of interest. First, by committing the general law to the possibility of modification in principle, the Convention recognises that, for future reference, '[t]wo or more' – but not all – of the parties to a multilateral treaty may satisfy their desire to modify their treaty relations 'as between themselves', and, so, it is the interest of the modifying States that provides the impetus for this provision.[275] Second is the interest of those parties to the original treaty not so intent on or involved in modification: under the treaty, rights are there to be enjoyed and obligations are waiting to be performed – and these are the rights and obligations of these 'other parties'.[276] There is also a third factor to register in this synopsis, however, and that is the *interest* of the treaty itself – note how, in the concern it expressed on the possibilities of modification, the International Law Commission spoke of 'the régime of the treaty' – presumably, as reflected in or projected by its object and purpose. The treaty has, after all, come into its own existence over and above the interests of either modifying or non-modifying States, and its 'object and purpose' somehow seem well-placed to mediate between these interests,[277] especially if *inter se* agreements

---

[272] *Ibid.*   [273] Art. 41(1)(b)(i) VCLT: *supra* n. 1.

[274] Art. 41(1)(b)(ii) VCLT: *ibid.* See A. Watts, *The International Law Commission 1949–1998* (Vol. II: The Treaties, Part II) (Oxford: Oxford University Press, 1999), p. 716. In which case the procedural obligation of Art. 41(2) VCLT – that 'the parties in question shall notify the other parties of their intention to conclude the agreement and of the modification to the treaty for which it provides' – arises: *supra* n. 1. Elias regards this latter obligation as a form of 'protection' for these 'other parties' (i.e. those not involved in the modification) – and not unmoored from the principle of good faith: T. O. Elias, *The Modern Law of Treaties* (Dobbs Ferry, NY/Leiden: Oceana Publications/A.W. Sijthoff, 1974), p. 97. On this point, see, further, Fragmentation Report, *supra* n. 6, at p. 154 (paragraph 300).

[275] Art. 41(1) VCLT: *supra* n. 1.   [276] Art. 41(1)(b)(i) VCLT: *supra* n. 1.

[277] Compare the position of McNair that 'as a matter of principle, no State has a legal right to demand the revision of a treaty in the absence of some provision to that effect contained in that treaty or in some other treaty to which it is a party' and that 'treaty revision is a matter of politics and diplomacy and has little, if any, place in this book' (*supra* n. 39, at p. 534) with that of Koskenniemi that 'Article 41 seeks a compromise between two requirements, that of meeting the needs of a limited number of parties wishing to

can be responsible for the 'development of the treaty, fully in line with its ethos and its object and purpose'.[278] The Vienna Convention thereby stands to preserve the 'inherently integral character' of the treaty in question.[279]

Additionally, it might be said that the potential vagueness of – or inherent within – the concept of a treaty's 'object and purpose' becomes a sudden strength in the sense that, as a moderating device within the life of a treaty, it is permissive and accommodating of the enterprise of modification while not being too prescriptive of the platforms for future action. It therefore does not foreclose unduly and too far in advance the options of those States intent on pursuing this course. And, in a recurring theme of this chapter, it is noticeable how the Vienna Convention relates the 'object and purpose' of a treaty to particular provisions occurring therein (for it is the derogation from individual provisions that must be found to be 'incompatible with the effective execution of the object and purpose of the treaty as a whole').[280] The upshot seems to be that different provisions of the same treaty resonate in different ways – and to

regulate their relations by *inter se* rules and that of allowing the other parties to continue applying the treaty in its initial form' (*supra* n. 6, at p. 156 (paragraph 303)). See, also, P. Reuter, 'Solidarité et divisibilité des engagements conventionnels' in Y. Dinstein and M. Tabory (eds.), *International Law at a Time of Perplexity: Essays in Honour of Shabtai Rosenne* (Dordrecht: Martinus Nijhoff, 1989), pp. 623–634, at p. 628.

[278] Fragmentation Report, *supra* n. 6, at p. 160 (paragraph 310).

[279] An observation made by Alan Boyle in respect of consensus/package deal treaties: 'Reflections on the Treaty as Law-Making Instrument' in A. Orakhelashvili and S. Williams (eds.), *40 Years of the Vienna Convention on the Law of Treaties* (London: British Institute of International & Comparative Law, 2010), pp. 1–28, at p. 6.

[280] The qualification of the treaty's object and purpose 'as a whole' is in fact unique within the Vienna Convention and could be viewed as a rhetorical reinforcement of the *concept* of the treaty's object and purpose: see, further, Bowman, *supra* n. 153; alternatively/ additionally, the formulation 'leaves open the possibility for minor modifications, which would in a way have the character of a simple "adjustment of what exists", detachable from the treaty as a whole, the object and purpose of which would not be compromised by this aggiornamento': A. Rigaux and D. Simon, 'Article 41 (1969)' in Corten and Klein (eds.), (Vol. II), *supra* n. 21, pp. 986–1008, at p. 1002. See, also, the distinction between 'the overall aim and purpose of the treaty' and '[the] treaty as a whole': McNair, *supra* n. 39, at pp. 380–381. In contrast, consider Art. 22(b) of the 1935 Draft Convention on the Law of Treaties ('[t]wo or more of the States parties to a treaty to which other States are parties may make a later treaty which will supersede the earlier treaty in their relations *inter se*, only if this is not forbidden by the provisions of the earlier treaty *and if the later treaty is not so inconsistent with the general purpose of the earlier treaty as to be likely to frustrate that purpose*'): *supra* n. 16 (emphasis added).

varying extents – with a treaty's object and purpose, whatever that might be.[281]

And this concentration on particular provisions of a treaty must surely bring to mind the question of the character of *obligation* that had informed some of the other work of the International Law Commission on the law of treaties. For 'in the case of obligations that could not be broken down into bilateral relationships, an *inter se* agreement might more easily be understood to be object and purpose of the treaty'.[282] So, in his discussion of the 'fundamental breach' of a treaty opening up the possibilities of its termination or suspension, Special Rapporteur Gerald Fitzmaurice identified: (i) reciprocal obligations – those based 'on contractual reciprocity consisting of a reciprocal interchange between the parties, each giving certain treatment to, and receiving it from, each of the others';[283] (ii) absolute or objective obligations – those of 'an absolute rather than a reciprocal character [involving] obligation[s] towards all the world rather than towards particular parties'[284] producing so-called 'integral treaties'[285] and, finally, (iii) interdependent (or 'fully interdependent type') obligations – where 'the participation of all the parties is a condition of the obligatory force of the treaty'[286] and the obligations 'are of such a kind that, by reason of the character of the treaty, their performance by any party is necessarily dependent on an equal and

---

[281] And, in another point I owe to Michael Bowman, there is an interesting question of the application of Art. 41(1)(b)(ii) VCLT that arises where the purported modification relates to several different provisions of a treaty and it is the cumulative effect which threatens the object and purpose of the treaty.

[282] Pronto and Wood, *supra* n. 9.

[283] G. G. Fitzmaurice, Second Report on the Law of Treaties, Doc. A/CN.4/107 (15 March 1957), p. 53 (or, at p. 30, 'obligations of the treaty which consist of a mutual and reciprocal interchange of benefits or concessions as between the parties' and, at p. 31, 'any obligations of the treaty which consist in a reciprocal grant or interchange between the parties of rights, benefits, concessions or advantages').

[284] *Ibid.*, at p. 54 (and, at p. 31, obligations 'of a self-existent character, requiring an absolute and integral application and performance under all conditions').

[285] Fitzmaurice also labelled these obligations 'self-existent', and they include 'certain standards or working conditions to prohibit certain practices in consequence of the conventions of the International Labour Organization ... or under maritime conventions as regards standards of safety at sea [and] in the Geneva Conventions of 12 August 1949 on prisoners of war and other matters': *ibid.*, at p. 54.

[286] *Ibid.*, at p. 36. And it is in this class that Fitzmaurice positioned disarmament treaties: 'the obligation of each party to disarm, or not to exceed a certain level of armaments, or not to manufacture or possess certain types of weapons, is necessarily dependent on a corresponding performance of the same thing by all the other parties, *since it is of the essence of such a treaty that the undertaking of each party is given in return for similar undertaking by the others'*. See *ibid.*, at p. 54.

corresponding performance by other parties'.[287] That these characterisations did not find their way into Article 41 VCLT[288] is not to say that they do not remain an invisible hand in guiding the meaning and import of a treaty's object and purpose: indeed, they may well transport us back to some of the reasoning underpinning the *Reservations* advisory opinion.[289]

***

Article 58 of the Vienna Convention deals with the suspension of the operation of a multilateral treaty as between '[t]wo or more parties to a multilateral treaty'.[290] As such, it is a variation or an extension of the thinking behind the law for modification of treaties. The operation of provisions of a treaty can be suspended 'temporarily and as between themselves alone' if provision is made for this in the relevant treaty,[291] or if the suspension is not prohibited in the treaty *and* two conditions are met: the suspension must not affect the other parties' enjoyment of their rights or performance of their obligations[292] and it must not be 'incompatible with the object and purpose of the treaty'.[293] The coincidence with the provision on modification in the Vienna Convention – Article 41 – should be clear.[294] At the Vienna Conference on the Law of Treaties, Shabtai Rosenne (Israel) commented that '[i]t was essential to avoid *inter se* suspension and *inter se* modification developing into concealed reservations that would evade the provisions of the draft articles on reservations'.[295] However, he thought it was important not to take the 'analogy' too far, for '[w]hat might be permissible in the cases envisaged [for modification] was not necessarily and automatically permissible in the cases contemplated [for suspension]'.[296] Additionally, it ought to be emphasised that the Vienna Convention does not make provision for the termination of a treaty *inter se*, but there is no reason why this should not

---

[287] *Ibid.*, at p. 31.   [288] Pronto and Wood, *supra* n. 9.

[289] *Supra* n. 27. It has been said that the advisory opinion 'presents one of the first signs of the distinction between bilateral and collective obligations': J. Pauwelyn, 'A Typology of Multilateral Treaty Obligations: Are WTO Obligations Bilateral or Collective in Nature?', *EJIL*, 14 (2003), 907–951, at 909.

[290] Art. 58(1) VCLT: *supra* n. 1.   [291] Art. 58(1)(a) VCLT: *supra* n. 1.

[292] Art. 58(1)(b)(i) VCLT: *supra* n. 1.   [293] Art. 58(1)(b)(ii) VCLT: *supra* n. 1.

[294] M.-P. Lanfranchi, 'Article 58 (1969)' in Corten and Klein (eds.), (Vol. II), *supra* n. 21, pp. 1311–1324, at p. 1318. See, also, Pauwelyn, *supra* n. 289, at 914.

[295] United Nations Conference on the Law of Treaties, First Session, *supra* n. 180, p. 349 (paragraph 21).

[296] *Ibid.* (though it is difficult to be more forthcoming on this because of 'scanty' State practice on this matter).

be permissible in principle – as long as it satisfies those conditions set forth in Articles 41 and 58 VCLT.[297]

A final point does seem to be in order: in addition to their reference to a treaty's 'object and purpose', Articles 41 and 58 VCLT require that the modification or suspension '[d]oes not affect the enjoyment by the other parties of their rights under the treaty or the performance of their obligations'.[298] There is a difficulty, here, in that this consideration is presented by the Vienna Convention as separate from that concerning a treaty's 'object and purpose',[299] when we have observed that a treaty's object and purpose may well incorporate in its remit and reckoning the overall structure of legal relations of that same treaty. Be this as it may, it is telling that this factor has often been explained in the literature by recourse to examples – whether in the form of 'a technical convention in the field of international communications which is essentially of a regulatory character',[300] and which therefore comports with the model of absolute or objective obligations mentioned earlier, or 'treaties containing reciprocal obligations . . . which provide for a mutual exchange of services or the right to specific treatment between all parties',[301] such as the 1963 Vienna Convention on Consular Relations (VCCR).[302] This, of course, is a modern paean to the contributions of Special Rapporteur Fitzmaurice, but, rising above the fray of these technicalities, the question to be asked is whether it is appropriate to essentialise the entire contents of treaties in quite this way: plainly, the 1963 Vienna Convention contains 'reciprocal obligations' for those States who are its parties, but is it confined to those 'reciprocal obligations'?[303] What of the 'individual rights' pronounced in

---

[297] As argued by Sinclair, *supra* n. 11, at p. 185.

[298] Respectively for modification (Art. 41(1)(b)(i) VCLT) and suspension (Art. 58(1)(b)(1)): *supra* n. 1.

[299] Which may prove to be 'unduly onerous in practice' according to Sinclair (regarding modification): *supra* n. 11, at p. 109.

[300] *Ibid.*   [301] Lanfranchi, *supra* n. 294, at p. 1317.

[302] 500 UNTS 95 (which 'logically results in a limitation on the possibility of *inter se* suspension': Lanfranchi, *supra* n. 294, at p. 1317).

[303] Note, however, the subtle qualification of the International Law Commission in its Fragmentation Report:

> There is no doubt about the relevance of the distinction between the two groups [i.e. reciprocal and non-reciprocal] of treaties. The 196[9] Vienna Convention on the Law of Treaties and the 1963 Vienna Convention on Consular Relations are examples of treaties containing essentially reciprocal obligations. The parties may at will derogate from those obligations in their relations *inter se*. This is not so in regard to a disarmament treaty, for example, where the performance by one party of its obligations is

Article 36 VCCR?[304] Do these constitute 'human rights'?[305] And does this make the VCCR a human rights treaty?[306] Furthermore, how might these questions be answered if we factor into the equation the object and purpose – or the objects and purposes – of the VCCR?[307]

6 The Question of Material Breach

Finally, to the question of 'material breach' and to Article 60 VCLT which operationalises the principle of *inadimplenti non est adimplendum* ('a party cannot be held to respect its obligations under a treaty if the other party refuses to honour them, and if both obligations form a synallagma').[308] Article 60 VCLT defines the concept of material breach as consisting in 'a repudiation of the treaty not sanctioned by the present Convention'[309] or 'the violation of a provision essential to the accomplishment of the object or purpose of the treaty'.[310] It proceeds to allocate a series of entitlements and remedies for the event of material breach: *other parties* may suspend the operation of the treaty in whole or in part or terminate it between themselves and the defaulting State or as between all parties;[311] *a party specially affected by the material breach* may suspend the operation of the

> a prerequisite for the performance by the other parties of theirs. A breach by one party is in effect a breach vis-à-vis all the other parties. A human rights convention, for its part, is an absolute or 'integral' treaty. The obligations it imposes are independent of any expectation of reciprocity or performance on the part of other parties of their obligations.

Fragmentation Report, *supra* n. 6, at pp. 160–161 (paragraph 312).

[304] As framed by the International Court of Justice: *Case Concerning Avena and Other Mexican Nationals*: Mexico v. United States of America (2004) ICJ Rep. 12, at p. 35 (paragraph 40). See, further, the contribution to this volume of Hampson at pp. 538–577 (Chapter 17) (and her engagement with Lea Brilmayer, *supra* n. 107).

[305] A point on which the International Court of Justice did not want to commit: *ibid.*, at p. 61 (paragraph 124).

[306] According to Pellet, the 'religious war' – or debate – on permissible reservations is in fact 'focused on reservations to normative treaties to the exclusion of those which envisage synallagmatic rights and duties of the parties': Pellet, *supra* n. 21, at p. 418.

[307] As discussed by the Court: *supra* n. 304, at p. 48 (paragraph 85). The VCCR, notably in its preamble, realises 'that the purpose of such privileges and immunities is not to benefit individuals but to ensure the efficient performance of functions by consular posts on behalf of their respective States': *supra* n. 302 (fifth preambular recital).

[308] B. Simma and C. J. Tams, 'Article 60 (1969)' in Corten and Klein (eds.), (Vol. II), *supra* n. 21, pp. 1351–1381, at p. 1353 ('an idea of negative reciprocity'). See, also, the contribution to this volume of Tams at pp. 440–467 (Chapter 14).

[309] Art. 60(3)(a) VCLT: *supra* n. 1.   [310] Art. 60(3)(b) VCLT: *supra* n. 1.

[311] Art. 60(2)(a) VCLT: *supra* n. 1.

treaty in whole or in part in its relations with the defaulting State[312] and, finally, *any party other than the defaulting State* may suspend the treaty in whole or in part with that State 'if the treaty is of such a character that a material breach of its provisions by one party radically changes the position of every party with respect to the further performance of its obligations under the treaty'.[313]

There are two points calling out for immediate attention here. The first relates to the unique disjunction that occurs in Article 60(3) VCLT of a treaty's object 'or' purpose: this is the only time that the Vienna Convention seems to separate out, and present as distinct and alternative propositions, the 'object or purpose' of a treaty – which stands in contrast to all other iterations of the concept of a treaty's object *and* purpose in the Vienna Convention. Yet, quite remarkably, a good share of the literature tends to skate over or even obscure this fact,[314] representing Article 60(3) VCLT as if it continues in the same untroubled vein as Articles 18, 19(c), 20(2), 31(3), 33(4), 41(1)(b)(ii) and 58(1)(b)(ii) VCLT.[315] Given these other references in the Vienna Convention, it is tempting to think that the formulation of a treaty's 'object or purpose' 'appears to have slipped in inadvertently, or [gone] unnoticed'.[316] However, to the extent that this quirk *has* been noticed,[317] there has been no major claim advanced that, with this formulation, the Vienna Convention is somehow attempting to break from the pattern of a concept of a treaty's 'object and purpose' and introduce or posit a rival – and, indeed, lesser – notion of a treaty's 'object or purpose' for determining a 'material breach'. For that is the next step that is available to us.[318]

As one reflects back upon the labours of the Special Rapporteurs on the law of treaties on this question, one can trace the evolution that occurs

---

[312] Art. 60(2)(b) VCLT: *supra* n. 1.   [313] Art. 60(2)(c) VCLT: *supra* n. 1.

[314] As identified *supra* n. 6.

[315] Consider, too, the International Court of Justice: in *Legal Consequences for States of the Continued Presence of South Africa in Namibia (South West Africa) Notwithstanding Security Council Resolution 276 (1970)*, delivered in June 1971, it correctly reproduced Art. 60(3) VCLT in paragraph 94 of its advisory opinion ('object or purpose') but then went on to view General Assembly Resolution 2145 (XXI) 'as the exercise of the right to terminate a relationship in case of a deliberate and persistent violation of obligations which destroys the very object and purpose of that relationship': (1971) ICJ Rep. 16, at p. 47 (paragraph 95).

[316] Klabbers, *supra* n. 6, at 148.

[317] See Klabbers, *ibid.*, and, also, Reuter, *supra* n. 277, at p. 628, and Bowman, *supra* 20, at 321.

[318] See, for example, Reuter, *ibid.*

from 'the purposes of a treaty' (Special Rapporteur Fitzmaurice on 'fundamental breach')[319] to 'the object and purpose of the treaty' (Special Rapporteur Waldock on 'material breach')[320] as well as to 'the objects or purposes of the treaty' and 'the object or purpose of the treaty' (International Law Commission on 'material breach').[321] What evidence there is suggests that there was a conscious effort on behalf of Special Rapporteur Waldock to systemize the concept of a treaty's 'object and purpose' from the law on reservations to the law on 'material breach',[322]

[319] Fitzmaurice, Second Report on the Law of Treaties, *supra* n. 283, at p. 31. Very helpfully:

> The breach must be a fundamental breach of the treaty in an essential respect, going to the root or foundation of the treaty relationship between the parties, and calling in question the continued value or possibility of that relationship in the particular field covered by the treaty . . . It must therefore be tantamount to a denial of the treaty obligation, and such as to either (*a*) destroy the value of the treaty for the other party; (*b*) justify the conclusion that no further confidence can be placed in the due execution of the treaty by the party committing the breach; or (*c*) render abortive the purposes of the treaty.

[320] H. Waldock, Second Report on the Law of Treaties, Doc. A/CN.4/156 and Add.1–3 (20 March, 10 Apr., 30 Apr. and 5 June 1963), p. 73. Again, very helpfully: 'Provided that, if a material breach of a treaty by one or more parties is of such a kind as to frustrate the object and purpose of the treaty also in the relations between the other parties not involved in the breach, any such other party may, if it thinks fit, withdraw from the treaty'. Indeed, part of Waldock's definition of 'material breach' in this report involved 'the failure to perform which is not compatible with the effective fulfilment of the object *and* purpose of the treaty': *ibid.* (emphasis added).

[321] Report of the Work of the International Law Commission on the Work of Its Eighteenth Session, Doc. A/CN.4/189 and Add.1 and 2, *YbILC* (1966–II), pp. 121 and 253.

[322] Waldock, in fact, seemed to be quite specific on the point of a treaty's 'object and purpose' in reflecting on how Special Rapporteur Fitzmaurice 'had seemed perhaps to put the concept of a "fundamental" breach rather high':

> The present draft, though inspired by the same general considerations, seeks to define a 'material' breach of a treaty by reference to the attitude adopted by the parties with regard to reservations at the time when they concluded the treaty; and, if they said nothing about reservations at the time, then by reference to the 'object and purpose' of the treaty – the criterion used for determining the power to make reservations in such a case. The reason, of course, is that, although the two questions are not identical, there is a certain connexion between the views of the contracting States concerning the making of reservations and their views concerning what are to be regarded as material breaches of the treaty. It therefore seemed logical, in formulating the present article, to take into account the rules regarding the making of reservations provisionally adopted by the [International Law] Commission . . .

Ibid., at 76. All other references in this (i.e. second) report are to a treaty's 'object and purpose': *ibid.*, at 76 (reservations), 77 (material breach), 78 (dissolution of a treaty in

and the unannounced and unexplained change from 'object and purpose' to 'object or purpose' is best treated as an instance of historical anomaly or, quite possibly, a rare drafting error.[323]

Setting this point or problem aside, our second observation relates to the requirement of Article 60(3)(b) VCLT – that the material breach must relate to a provision of a treaty 'essential to the accomplishment of [its] object or [and] purpose'. In other words, the stipulation is not, 'as could have been expected', to 'the *intensity, or gravity, of the breach* in question, but requires that the *provision* breached must have been essential for the accomplishment of the treaty's object and purpose',[324] further evidence of how the 'object and purpose' is being used to fillet the treaty into its component parts and weight each of them accordingly.[325] It is worth bearing in mind, though, that, in switching from 'fundamental breach' to 'material breach', Special Rapporteur Waldock made a remark that ought to have an important bearing on how we come to view a treaty's 'object and purpose' when used in this context:

> The word 'fundamental' might be understood as meaning that only the violation of a provision directly touching the central purposes of the treaty can ever justify the other party in terminating the treaty. But other provisions considered by a party to be essential to the effective execution of the treaty may have been very material in inducing it to enter into the

consequence of a supervening impossibility or illegality of performance) and 79 (doctrine of *rebus sic stantibus*). There are no references to 'object or purpose' in this report. See, also, H. Waldock, Fifth Report on the Law of Treaties, Doc. A/CN.4/183 and Add. 1–4 (15 Nov. 1965, 4 Dec. 1965, 20 Dec. 1965, 3 Jan. 1966 and 18 Jan. 1966), p. 36 (where Waldock recalls his earlier invocation of a treaty's 'object and purpose'). See, also, *ibid.*, at pp. 36–37 (material breach).

[323] For this is what was recommended to the conference (in draft Art. 57): A/CONF.39/11 and A/CONF/39/1 I/Add.1, p. 177. In its Draft Articles on the Law of Treaties with Commentaries, the International Law Commission states simply: '[t]he other and more general form of material breach is that in sub-paragraph (*b*), and is there defined as a violation of a provision essential to the accomplishment of any object or purpose of the treaty': *YbILC* (1966–II), 255.

[324] Simma and Tams, *supra* n. 308, at p. 1359.

[325] Judge Oda reflected on Art. 60(3) VCLT as follows: '[T]here is a degree of such violation justifying termination or suspension, and … the touchstone of that degree is that the *provision* violated should be essential to the accomplishment of a treaty's object and purpose. There is no suggestion that the undermining of the object and/or purpose, *independently* of any breach of a provision, would be tantamount to the violation of the Treaty'. See *Nicaragua Case, supra* n. 168, at p. 250 (paragraph 80). We should note that Art. 60(3) VCLT sets down a generic definition of 'material breach' – i.e. one that obtains in *both* bilateral and multilateral treaties as *per* Arts. 60(1) and 60(2) VCLT: see, further, F. L. Kirgis, Jr., 'Some Lingering Questions about Article 60 of the Vienna Convention on the Law of Treaties', *Cornell ILJ*, 22 (1989), 549–573, at 553.

treaty at all, even though these provisions may be of an entirely ancillary character. For example, a clause providing for compulsory arbitration in the event of a dispute as to the interpretation or application of the treaty is purely ancillary to the main purposes of the treaty, but may well be regarded by some parties as an essential condition for agreeing to be bound by the treaty. In that case a refusal to arbitrate would go to the root of the other party's consent to be in treaty relations with the default-ing State.[326]

Let us close this discussion by recalling that Article 60(5) precludes the application of the VCLT rules on – and, thus, qualifies the entitlements and remedies it provides for – material breach to 'provisions relating to the protection of the human person contained in treaties of a humanitarian character, in particular to provisions prohibiting any form of reprisals against persons protected by such treaties'. Its effect, therefore, is to render certain treaty provisions 'sacrosanct'.[327] At the instigation of Switzerland, an oral proposal was made at the Vienna Conference on the Law of Treaties with the 1949 Geneva Conventions in mind, which 'prohibited reprisals against ... protected persons and were virtually universal, but they were still the subject of some doubts and reservations': 'Such agree-ments', it was maintained, 'should not be exposed to termination or suspension that would endanger human life'.[328] The resulting quali-fication does bring back into sharp relief the importance of the 'special characteristics' of a given convention,[329] as well as Special

---

[326] Waldock, Second Report on the Law of Treaties, *supra* n. 320, at p. 75. Cf. Jiménez de Arechaga (Uruguay) who thought at the Vienna Conference on the Law of Treaties that the rule in Art. 60(3) VCLT was 'unduly restrictive' because 'where a treaty contained an arbitration clause, if one party ceased to apply that clause, the other party would be unable to invoke the violation of "a provision essential to the accomplishment of the object and purpose of the treaty"; yet it was a grave breach which ought to come under the rule in [Art. 57]': United Nations Conference on the Law of Treaties, First Session, *supra* n. 180, at p. 390.

[327] Simma and Tams, *supra* n. 308, at p. 587 (noting, *ibid.*, that '[t]he drafting history suggests that despite the curious wording, this exclusion is intended to cover provisions of international humanitarian law and international human rights law'). See, also, Giegerich, *supra* n. 6, at p. 1046 (Art. 60(5) VCLT 'immunizes certain treaty provisions against collective or individual termination and suspension in reaction to material breach').

[328] United Nations Conference on the Law of Treaties, First Session, *supra* n. 180, at p. 354. These were not the only agreements in the sights of Switzerland: 'In addition, there were conventions concerning the status of refugees, the prevention of slavery, the prohibition of genocide and the protection of human rights in general; even a material breach of those conventions by a party should not be allowed to injure innocent people'. *Ibid.*

[329] *Supra* n. 39.

Rapporteur Fitzmaurice's explication of 'integral treaties' – or those containing absolute or objective obligations – as

> the type of treaty in respect of which a fundamental breach by one party, in addition to giving no right of termination to the other parties, would not even justify a refusal to apply the treaty vis-à-vis the offending party (and where it would perhaps not in any case be practicable to operate such a refusal). Thus, a fundamental breach by one party of a treaty of a treaty on human rights could neither justify termination of the treaty, nor corresponding breaches of the treaty *even in respect of nationals of the offending party*. The same would apply as regards the obligation of any country to maintain certain standards of working conditions or to prohibit certain practices in consequence of the conventions of the International Labour Organisation; or again under maritime conventions as regards standards of safety at sea. The same principle is now enshrined in express terms in the Geneva Conventions of 12 August 1949 on prisoners of war and other matters [see, in particular, article 2 and other opening articles of each of the four Conventions]. Another type of case is where there exists an international obligation to maintain a certain régime or system in a given area [for example, the régime of the sounds and belts at the entrance to the Baltic Sea. See the Treaty of Copenhagen of 14 March 1857, and the Convention of Washington of 11 April 1857].[330]

7   Conclusion

This chapter has attempted to piece together some of the history and organising logic that has come to inform the concept of a treaty's 'object and purpose', before the Vienna Convention on the Law of Treaties consolidated but also expanded its significance for the modern law of treaties. We have explored the seven – or eight – occasions on which the Vienna Convention has put the concept to work to greater or lesser effect, but it should be said that, on the face of the diplomatic record, the final text of the Vienna Convention might well have understated its appeal as it stood at that point in time. Notwithstanding repeated concerns levelled

---

[330] Fitzmaurice, Second Report on the Law of Treaties, *supra* n. 283, at p. 54 (emphasis added). In his appraisal, Fitzmaurice juxtaposed 'the character of the treaty' alongside 'the obligation of any party': *ibid.* See, also, Sinclair, *supra* n. 11, at p. 190. And we can see Fitzmaurice's idea of 'interdependent' obligations – *supra* n. 286 – informing Art. 60(2)(c) VCLT ('if the treaty is of such a character that a material breach of its provisions by one party radically changes the position of every party with respect to the further performance of its obligations under the treaty'): *supra* n. 1.

against its indecipherability,[331] at the conference leading up to the Vienna Convention, Congo-Brazzaville (the Republic of Congo) proposed the inclusion of a provision to the effect that '[a]n error is a ground of invalidity of a treaty if it relates to the object and purpose of the treaty'.[332] Similarly, on behalf of twenty-two sponsors representing all regions of the world, Ceylon (Sri Lanka) proposed that '[e]very State has a right to participate in a multilateral treaty which codifies or progressively develops norms of general international law or the object and purpose of which are of interest to the international community'.[333] States have thus tended to be beholden to the concept as developed by the International Court of Justice in its *Reservations* advisory opinion:[334] a proposed amendment at the same conference to replace the words 'object and purpose' with 'character or purpose' in the provision on reservations did not meet with success.[335] There is also the question of whether a treaty's object and purpose is implicated by the provision on denunciation or withdrawal in Article 56 VCLT where reference is made to 'the nature of the treaty'.[336]

That the Vienna Convention – whose signature theme is one of flexibility in the cause of the stable flow of international relations – should embrace a concept of such pliability should not come as too much of a surprise. It appears that a treaty's 'object and purpose' affords choice opportunities for the Vienna Convention to pursue and even to achieve this flexibility because the concept does seem to incorporate a deliberative dimension that helps deepen the consciousness of a treaty's integrity. Of course, the Vienna Convention does not engage this concept in an identical manner on each of the seven/eight occasions on which it is invoked: a reservation must not be 'incompatible with the object and

---

[331] Including at the Vienna Conference on the Law of Treaties: Peru, for instance, observed that 'such vague concepts as "the object and purpose of the treaty" [which] called for . . . safeguards for their application': *ibid.*, at p. 436.

[332] *Ibid.*, at p. 289.

[333] Apparently identical with a proposal forthcoming from Syria: United Nations Conference on the Law of Treaties, Second Session, Vienna, 9 Apr.–22 May 1969 (New York, NY: United Nations, 1970), p. 181.

[334] E.g. the United Kingdom: United Nations Conference on the Law of Treaties, Second Session, *ibid.*, at p. 34. See, also, Cameroon, *ibid.*, at p. 30, and Mexico, *ibid.*, at p. 31.

[335] Co-sponsored by the United States: United Nations Conference on the Law of Treaties, Second Session, *ibid.*, at p. 35 ('because it had been uncertain whether the traditional reference to the object and purpose of the treaty was intended to cover the concept of the nature and character of the treaty').

[336] Art. 56(1)(b) VCLT: *supra* n. 1 (though this does seem to be a concept with a broader sweep). See, further, *ibid.*

purpose of the treaty'; a 'violation' is required of 'a provision essential to the accomplishment of the object or purpose of the treaty' for 'material breach' and the 'interim obligation' requires States 'to refrain from acts which would defeat the object and purpose of a treaty' between signature and ratification or between the period of consent to be bound and entry into force.[337] And at the same time that the concept of a treaty's 'object and purpose' underscores the integrity of a given treaty, the Vienna Convention intimates that that treaty is divisible into its respective provisions – each of which may well have different relationships with that treaty's object and purpose.[338]

Numerous intricacies have attended our understanding of the concept of a treaty's object and purpose as we move forward from the Vienna Convention. There is a complex portrait that has emerged of the object and purpose – or, better, the objects and purposes – of a treaty's object and purpose as set out in the Vienna Convention. It is true, then, that 'we have a criterion, and a unique, polyvalent criterion; but not a definition of this criterion' in our midst,[339] and, as argued in this chapter, much stands to be gained from understanding the invocation and relevance of the concept in each of these contexts. In the *Nicaragua Case*, too, we have seen a life for the object and purpose of a treaty beyond its entry into force,[340] adding even further hue to that complexity.[341] Even so, it may be no bad thing that a treaty's object and purpose is there to be interpreted, contested and even, in the course of time, recast, for those possibilities speak not only to the integrity of a given treaty but, also, to the opportunities for its growth and flourishing.

---

[337] And it is not always clear what these differences might/should entail – e.g. between a provision 'derogation from which is incompatible with the effective execution of the object and purpose of the treaty as a whole' (Art. 41(1)(b)(ii) VCLT) and that which is 'essential to the accomplishment' of a treaty's object or purpose (Art. 60(3) VCLT).

[338] See, in particular, Arts. 41(1)(ii) and Art. 60(3)(b) VCLT: *supra* n. 1. See, however, General Comment No. 24(52), *supra* n. 103, and, also, the position of the International Law Commission: *supra* n. 50.

[339] Pellet, *supra* n. 21, at p. 447.

[340] *Supra* n. 168. Against the voices of the decriers: *supra* n. 211 (Judge Oda), n. 212 (Judge Schwebel) and n. 213 (Judge Jennings).

[341] Bowman, *supra* n. 20, at 353.

10

Provisional Application of Treaties and the Internal Logic of the 1969 Vienna Convention

ANNELIESE QUAST MERTSCH*

1 Introduction

The provisional application of treaties is stipulated in Article 25 of the 1969 Vienna Convention on the Law of Treaties (VCLT).[1] It refers to the application of certain treaty provisions to relevant acts, facts and situations on a temporary basis prior to the treaty's entry into force. Since this occurs pending the treaty's entry into force, the legal effect of provisionally applied treaties has been accompanied by some uncertainty,[2] although the majority view regards these treaties as legally binding.[3]

---

* The author would like to thank Andrew Michie as well as the editors of this volume for their helpful comments and Lorand Bartels for bringing a piece of practice to her attention which is discussed in this chapter (*infra* n. 47).

[1] 1155 UNTS 331.

[2] The *pacta sunt servanda* principle, according to which a treaty is binding upon the parties to it, only applies from the entry into force of a treaty. The following refer to the uncertainty surrounding the legally binding force of provisionally applied treaties: G. Gaja 'Provisional Application of Treaties' in Report of the International Law Commission on the Work of its Sixty-third Session (2011), U.N. Doc. A/66/10, Annex C, pp. 330 (paragraph 2) and 331 (paragraph 4); A. Michie, 'The Role of Provisionally Applied Treaties in International Organisations', *Comp. & Int'l L.J. of Southern Africa*, 39 (2006), 39–56, at 56, and M. A. Rogoff and B. E. Gauditz, 'The Provisional Application of International Agreements', *Maine L. Rev.*, 39 (1987), 29–81, at 49–51 and 80. Furthermore, the point has been made that recourse to two different terminologies ('provisional entry into force' and 'provisional application') has also led to uncertainty and confusion regarding the concept of provisional application: see J. M. Gómez-Robledo, First Report on the Provisional Application of Treaties, A/CN.4/664 (3 June 2013), p. 4 (paragraph 16).

[3] For an overview of the majority view in practice and academic writings, see A. Quast Mertsch, *Provisionally Applied Treaties: Their Binding Force and Legal Nature* (Leiden: Koninklijke Brill NV, 2012), pp. 119–142, 161–173 and 198–217. See, also, Report of the International Law Commission on the Work of its Sixty-fifth Session (2013), U.N. Doc. A/68/10, p. 102 (paragraph 114). For the first minority view, according to which these treaties are non-legally binding, see, e.g., A. Geslin,

When legally binding,[4] the question of the legal regime applicable to these treaties arises,[5] and this chapter will focus on the (potential) application of Articles 18, 24(4) and 46 VCLT in relation to provisionally applied treaties. The reason for this particular focus is that these are among the VCLT provisions most often mentioned in relation to provisional application (second only to the question of the potential breach of these treaties and the antecedent question of their legal force and binding nature), and this chapter will try to identify some of the issues to which this could gives rise. In this way, the chapter is intended to contribute to the conceptualisation both of Article 25 VCLT and the Vienna Convention itself, or some of its provisions, as applied to provisionally applied treaties.

2 Background to the Provisional Application of Treaties

Treaties are the primary source of modern international law.[6] Once negotiated, their ability to effectively govern international relations depends significantly upon their timely entry into force. Yet entry into force can be delayed for a variety of reasons, including lengthy internal treaty-making procedures, lack of political support in parliament etc.[7] Where entry into force has been delayed or could not be awaited due to a need for swift action, provisional application has prevented stagnation and instead allowed States to move forward with the treaty regime. Among the more famous examples is the provisional application of the 1947 General Agreement on Tariffs and Trade,[8] Part XI of the 1982

La mise en application provisoire des traités (Paris: Pedone, 2005), pp. 319–330; P. Picone, *L'applicazione in via provvisoria degli accordi internazionali* (Naples: Eugenio Jovene, 1973), p. 184, and United Nations, *Final Clauses of Multilateral Treaties – Handbook* (New York, NY: United Nations, 2003) (https://treaties.un.org/doc/source/publications/FC/English.pdf), p. 44. For the second minority view, according to which the binding force of these treaties may vary, i.e. these treaties can be legally binding or non-legally binding, depending on the intention of the States concerned, see Quast Mertsch, *ibid.*, at pp. 177–180 and 241 (fn. 24).

[4] See the previous footnote on 'second minority view': Quast Mertsch, *ibid.*

[5] When these treaties are not intended to be legally binding, the question of the regime applicable to them arises as well, but then it might not necessarily be a 'legal' regime. This refers back to the debate on the framework and provisions applicable to soft law agreements and will not be addressed in the present chapter.

[6] M. Fitzmaurice and O. Elias, *Contemporary Issues in the Law of Treaties* (Utrecht: Eleven International Publishing, 2005), p. xiii.

[7] Rogoff and Gauditz, *supra* n. 2, at 31–32.   [8] 55 UNTS 308.

United Nations Convention on the Law of the Sea,[9] and some of the reform measures provided in Protocol 14 to the 1950 European Convention on Human Rights and Fundamental Freedoms.[10] In a bilateral context, provisional application has, for instance, enabled the United States and Cuba for the past thirty years to have a maritime boundary agreement in place, where the formal conclusion of the treaty appears impeded by political issues.[11] As is apparent from these examples, provisional application is an immensely useful tool – yet not without uncertainties or even difficulties.

The remainder of this introduction will take a brief look at the VCLT provision devoted to provisional application (Article 25 VCLT), shed some further light on the kinds of situations in which provisional application has frequently been used and, then, explore how provisional application works in all those situations – attempting, as it does, to reconcile the need for swift treaty application on the international plane with the often lengthy requirements imposed by internal treaty-making procedures. This last step prepares the later analysis in that it begins to set provisional application apart from both Articles 24(4) and 18 VCLT and explains why the invocation of Article 46 VCLT may be relevant in relation to consent to provisional application.

Article 25 VCLT – specifically on provisional application – provides as follows:

> 1. A treaty or part of a treaty is applied provisionally pending its entry into force if:
>   (a) the treaty itself so provides; or
>   (b) the negotiating States have in some other manner so agreed.
>
> 2. Unless the treaty otherwise provides or the negotiating States have otherwise agreed, the provisional application of a treaty or a part of a treaty with respect to a State shall be terminated if that State notifies the other States between which the treaty is being applied provisionally of its intention not to become a party to the treaty.

Broadly speaking, Article 25 VCLT is divided in two subsections: subsection one is devoted to how provisional application comes into being; subsection two is concerned with its termination. Neither the provision

---

[9] 1836 UNTS 3, Art. 7(2).   [10] CETS No. 194.
[11] 1977 Maritime Boundary Agreement between the USA and the Republic of Cuba, ILM, 17 (1978), 110–112, Art. V; for a subsequent agreement extending the provisional application, see, e.g., 9732 TIAS 840.

nor the VCLT elsewhere defines provisional application and its legal effects or provides more information on the legal regime applicable to it.[12] This leaves wide discretion and flexibility to States when determining the parameters of a particular provisional application regime.

Usually, recourse is had to provisional application in situations having the following two characteristics: first, there is a gap between the conclusion of the treaty negotiations on the one hand and the entry into force of the treaty on the other. (This is the case when the treaty does not enter into force upon signature but is subject to ratification, acceptance or approval etc.). Second, States are unwilling, for one reason or another, to await the treaty's entry into force and seek to apply the treaty provisions at an earlier point in time. Reasons for the unwillingness to await the treaty's entry into force[13] include: the urgency of the matter at the hand when the treaty is in response to a current or anticipated crisis; the need to ensure legal continuity between an earlier and later treaty on the same subject matter, where the earlier treaty is about to expire and the new treaty has yet to enter into force and, for instance, when ratification of the treaty in question is expected with great certainty, or great uncertainty. In these situations, provisional application enables States to bridge the gap to the treaty's entry into force, by applying the specified treaty provisions to relevant acts, facts and situations in the meantime. According to the 'UN Statement of Treaties and International Agreements Registered or Filed and Recorded with the Secretariat', each year approximately 3 per cent of registered treaties are subject to provisional application.[14]

To further prepare the ground for the later analysis, it is useful to explain how provisional application works. As provisional application advances the application of specified treaty provisions, the question arises as to how this is technically done – and how time is saved[15] compared with the entry into force of a treaty. The starting point of this analysis is

---

[12] Gaja, *supra* n. 2, at p. 330 (paragraph 2), and R. E. Dalton, 'Provisional Application of Treaties' in D. B. Hollis (ed.), *The Oxford Guide to Treaties* (Oxford: Oxford University Press, 2012), pp. 220–247, at p. 230.

[13] Gómez-Robledo, *supra* n. 2, at pp. 6–9 (paragraphs 25–35), and H. Krieger, 'Article 25' in O. Dörr and K. Schmalenbach (eds.), *Vienna Convention on the Law of Treaties: A Commentary* (Berlin: Springer, 2012), pp. 407–421, at pp. 408–411.

[14] (Monthly) Statement of Treaties and International Agreements Registered or Filed and Recorded with the Secretariat. See, also, Geslin, *supra* n. 3, at p. 347.

[15] For an alternative way to speed-up the constitutional treaty-making procedure, see, e.g., H. H. Koh, 'The Fast Track and United States Trade Policy', *Brooklyn JIL*, 18 (1992), 143–172.

the fact that on the international plane, provisional application, as opposed to entry into force, does not require an expression of consent to be bound in terms of Article 11 VCLT.[16] Frequently, the expression of consent to be bound (in terms of Article 11) is under constitutional law conditioned upon the prior completion of an internal treaty-making procedure.[17] Thus, it is only upon the completion of this internal treaty-making procedure that consent to be bound can be expressed. Provisional application, however, is an invitation to detach treaty application from these constitutional procedures, i.e. an 'invitation' to apply the treaty prior to the completion of the usual constitutional procedures, given that this is on a provisional basis and consent to be bound in terms of Article 11 VCLT has not yet been expressed.

Whether a State accepts this 'invitation', i.e. whether it does (or does not) await the completion of the usual treaty-making procedure for provisional application, is a matter which each domestic legal system can decide. Accordingly, the extent to which the advantages of provisional application are used differs from one State to another.[18] In some constitutional systems, a treaty subject to provisional application has to undergo the same internal treaty-making procedure as it would for an expression of consent to be bound in terms of Article 11 VCLT.[19] In these cases, provisional application enables application of the treaty from the moment of the completion of the internal treaty-making procedure, for instance while awaiting the deposit of the requisite number of instruments of ratification by the other States.[20] By contrast, in other constitutional systems, a treaty may be

---

[16] For a more detailed analysis of the distinction between provisional application and an expression of consent to be bound in terms of Article 11 VCLT, see the first two sections under Section 5.2.

[17] J. M. Ruda, *The Final Acceptance of International Conventions* (Muscatine, IA: Stanley Foundation, 1976), p. 23, and R. Jennings and A. Watts, *Oppenheim's International Law: Law of Peace* (Vol. I) (Harlow: Longmans, 9th ed., 1992), p. 1226.

[18] Evidence of this diversity in accommodating provisional application in national treaty law and practice can be found in a question on provisional application (and the answers thereto) contained in a Council of Europe questionnaire: Council of Europe and British Institute of International and Comparative Law (eds.), *Treaty Making: Expression of Consent by States to be Bound by a Treaty* (London: Kluwer Law International, 2001), p. 316.

[19] *Ibid.*, at p. 163 (Finland) and, also, at p. 192 (Iceland). On Austrian practice, see F. Trauttmansdorff, 'Der Abschluß völkerrechtlicher Verträge: einige Streiflichter aus der Österreichischen Praxis' in W. Karl and U. Brandl (eds.), *Völker- und Europarecht, 24. Österreichischer Völkerrechtstag* (Wien: Verlag Österreich, 2000), pp. 127–145, at p. 144.

[20] Trauttmansdorff, *ibid.*, at p. 144.

provisionally applied prior to the completion of the internal treaty-making procedures,[21] enabling provisional application for example from the moment of its signature, adoption or any other agreed moment thereafter.

By way of summary, the institution of provisional application is an invitation to detach the treaty's application from lengthy constitutional treaty-making procedures, i.e. to apply the treaty provisionally without prior completion of normally necessary internal procedures (leaving their completion for the later expression of consent to be bound in terms of Article 11 VCLT). A matter arising from this 'detachment' is whether provisional application undermines parliamentary powers relating to treaties.[22] This has been said to be the case when provisional application concerns a treaty whose entry into force (or rather the preceding expression of consent in terms of Article 11 VCLT) is under constitutional law subject to parliamentary approval. In these cases, the (provisional) application of the treaty may precede the parliamentary approval procedure, whereas normally, i.e. in case of the treaty's entry into force, the treaty's application would follow such approval. The key question, which different systems answer in different ways, would appear to be whether parliamentary approval is seen to substantially relate to the treaty's application, including provisional application, or only to the final expression of consent to be bound in terms of Article 11 VCLT. Be this as it may, it is clear that provisional application in various legal systems has given rise to constitutional tensions concerning parliamentary treaty-making powers. This is one of the reasons why the applicability of Article 46 VCLT in relation to provisionally applied treaties is a matter of interest, given that Article 46 enables a State to rely on certain violations of internal law in order to invoke the invalidity of the consent expressed in relation to that treaty.

---

[21] Council of Europe and British Institute of International and Comparative Law (eds.), *supra* n. 18, at pp. 274 (Switzerland); 183 (Greece) and 215 (Luxembourg); see, also, p. 263 (Spain).

[22] On Italian practice, see *Italian YbIL*, VII (1986–1987), 329; see, also, the Colombian reservation to Art. 25 (available at http://treaties.un.org/Pages/ViewDetailsIII.aspx? &src=TREATY&mtdsg_no=XXIII~1&chapter=23&Temp=mtdsg3&lang=en), and, further, Council of Europe and British Institute of International and Comparative Law (eds.), *supra* n. 18, at pp. 167 (France) and 281 (Turkey). For academic views, see Geslin, *supra* n. 3, at pp. 235–237, and D. Mathy, 'Article 25 (1969)' in O. Corten and P. Klein (eds.), *The Vienna Conventions on the Law of Treaties: A Commentary* (Vol. I) (Oxford: Oxford University Press, 2011), pp. 639–654, at pp. 643–646.

Yet, prior to looking at the possible invocation of Article 46 VCLT in relation to provisional application, the interplay of Article 25 with Articles 24(4) and 18 VCLT will be discussed.

3   Article 24(4) VCLT and the Scope of Provisional Application

Article 24(4) VCLT can be used to clarify the scope of provisional application. Article 24(4) governs the entry into force of treaties; it concerns the applicability of certain final clauses of a treaty from the adoption of the text of the treaty:

> The provisions of a treaty regulating the authentication of its text, the establishment of the consent of the States to be bound by the treaty, the manner or date of its entry into force, reservations, the functions of a depositary and other matters arising necessarily before the entry into force of the treaty apply from the time of the adoption of the text.

Article 24(4) VCLT and provisional application have in common that they provide for the application of certain treaty provisions prior to the treaty's entry into force. The difference between the two lies in the type of provision they affect. It has been said that Article 24(4) VCLT concerns certain of a treaty's final clauses whereas it is the treaty's substantive provisions that can potentially be the subject of provisional application.[23] This approach to the potential scope of provisional application will now be analysed, starting with a closer look at the type of provisions involved.

The substantive treaty provisions are those which regulate the treaty's subject matter and establish the legal regime negotiated by the parties (e.g. on trade, environment etc.); a treaty's final clauses are those which determine the parameters of the legal regime (when does it begin? when does it end? how can parties withdraw from it? can the rights and obligations be suspended? can the parties make reservations? what are the treaty's authentic languages and how will disputes be settled? etc.)[24] More accurately, there are five groups of final clauses, according to the United Nations' *Handbook on Final Clauses of Multilateral Treaties* (2003): Group I on the conclusion of treaties; Group II on the application of treaties; Group III on the amendment, revision and modification of

---

[23] J. Salmon, 'Les accords non formalisés ou "solo consensu"', *AFDI*, 45 (1999), 1–28, at 6. See, also, Quast Mertsch, *supra* n. 3, at p. 12. Some describe provisional application as being limited to a treaty's substantive provisions: see, e.g., Mathy, *supra* n. 22, at p. 640.

[24] On this distinction, see, e.g., S. Rosenne, *Breach of Treaty* (Cambridge: Grotius Publications, 1985), p. 3, and Mathy, *supra* n. 22, at pp. 649–650.

treaties; Group IV on the treaty's duration and Group V on the termination of treaties.[25]

Article 24(4) VCLT specifies that it concerns 'those matters arising necessarily prior to the treaty's entry into force'. This corresponds to those final clauses falling under Group I, including any clause on provisional application itself.[26] By contrast, the other final clauses, Groups II–V, are not covered by Article 24(4). They, like the treaty's substantive provisions, gain legal effect upon the treaty's entry into force.[27] Accordingly, again as with a treaty's substantive provisions, there may be a need to apply them prior to the treaty's entry into force – thus, to apply them provisionally. This, indeed, has been done with final clauses falling into Group II, namely dispute settlement clauses,[28] and is conceivable in relation to several other final clauses, including the ones on authentic languages, treaty suspension or possibly even modification and amendment. This shows that not only a treaty's substantive provisions but also some of its final clauses may be the subject of provisional application. Admittedly, to use the first-mentioned potential scope of provisional application (i.e. saying that Article 24(4) VCLT concerns final clauses and considering Article 25 VCLT solely in relation to a treaty's substantive provisions) is to rely on a familiar and easily accessible distinction, which might serve to establish an *initial* clear demarcation line between Articles 24(4) and 25 VCLT. However, this should not lead to the misconception that Article 25 VCLT is *limited* to a treaty's substantive provisions. As has been shown previously, provisional application would appear to be able to cover both a treaty's substantive provisions as well as, potentially, those final clauses falling into Groups II–V.

Furthermore, Article 24(4) VCLT can be seen to clarify another matter concerning the scope of provisional application. It is generally agreed that the final clauses covered by Article 24(4) VCLT are 'binding' and have full legal effect from the moment of the adoption of the treaty text.[29]

---

[25] For the UN *Handbook*, see *supra* n. 3.

[26] S. Rosenne, 'Final Clauses' in R. Wolfrum (ed.), *Max Planck Encyclopaedia of Public International Law* (Oxford: Oxford University Press, 2008) and I. Sinclair, *The Vienna Convention on the Law of Treaties* (Manchester: Manchester University Press, 2nd ed., 1984), p. 46.

[27] Rosenne, *supra* n. 26.

[28] 1991 Energy Charter Treaty, 2080 UNTS 95, Arts. 26 and 45, and 1946 Protocol of Provisional Application of the Fisheries Convention of 9 March 1964, 581 UNTS 76, and Art. 13 of said Convention.

[29] Rosenne: '[Art. 24(4)] clarified the question of the binding force of clauses relating to bringing the treaty into force. That binding force commences with the adoption of the

To the extent that one wishes Article 24(4) VCLT to retain its usual effect and significance also during provisional application, it follows that it carves out from the potential realm of provisional application those final clauses which apply from the moment of the adoption of the treaty. If so, provisional application can potentially cover all of a treaty's provisions, except those falling under Article 24(4) VCLT. This can be borne in mind when reading the opening phrase of Article 25 VCLT, that '[a] treaty or part of a treaty is applied provisionally . . .' (emphasis added). Strictly speaking, on this approach, it is not the 'entire'[30] treaty that is provisionally applied but only a part thereof. Nevertheless, it is common practice to refer to the provisional application of a 'treaty', and this technicality should in no way affect that; yet it might be borne in mind as an argument against a literal meaning of the opening phrase of Article 25 VCLT.

In conclusion, the interplay of Articles 24(4) and 25 VCLT helps to clarify the potential scope of provisional application. As has been shown, to say that an *entire* treaty can be subject to provisional application can be seen to be technically over-inclusive, whereas saying that only a treaty's *substantive* provisions can be subject to provisional application is technically under-inclusive.[31] A more precise and clearly less convenient description of the scope of provisional application is that it can cover all of a treaty's provisions *except* for those covered by Article 24(4) VCLT, i.e. substantive provisions *and* those final clauses belonging to Groups II–V.

After clarifying the scope of provisional application as derived from the interplay of Articles 24(4) and 25 VCLT, the analysis now turns to the interaction of Articles 18 and 25 VCLT and to the different views that have been expressed in this regard.

---

treaty text, regardless of whether or not or when the treaty as a whole comes into force'. See *supra* n. 26, at p. 1, and, also, p. 4; B. Cheng, *General Principles of Law as Applied by International Courts and Tribunals* (London: Stevens & Sons, 1953), p. 109; P. V. McDade, 'The Interim Obligation between Signature and Ratification of a Treaty', *Netherlands ILR*, 32 (1985), 5–47; T. O. Elias, *The Modern Law of Treaties* (Leiden: A.W. Sijthoff, 1974), p. 37, and Sinclair, *supra* n. 26, at p. 45.

[30] The wording of Art. 25 does not expressly refer to the 'entire' treaty or to the treaty 'as a whole': *supra* n. 1. However, it is submitted that mention of the alternative '[a] treaty *or* a part of a treaty is provisionally applied . . .' implies that the counterpart to 'part of a treaty' is the treaty as a whole.

[31] 'Over-inclusive' and 'under-inclusive' are terms borrowed from American constitutional law, meaning 'including more than is necessary or advisable' or 'including less than is necessary or advisable' respectively: E. Chemerinsky, *Constitutional Law: Principles and Policies* (New York, NY: Wolters and Kluwers, 5th ed., 2015), pp. 701–702.

4   Article 18 VCLT: Its Applicability and Role in Relation to Provisional Application

Often, either Article 18 VCLT or Article 25 VCLT is said to apply to a certain treaty. Yet the proposition has been made that both might apply to the same treaty at the same time. In response to this proposition, the following section analyses questions in relation to the interaction of these two provisions from the Vienna Convention, especially the applicability of Article 18 during the provisional application of a treaty as well as the role Article 18 can play in establishing or interpreting the provisional application regime.

It should be noted that in this chapter, Article 18 VCLT is viewed as customary international law,[32] and the expression 'Article 18 obligation' is shorthand for that obligation, irrespective of whether in a relevant case it would apply on the basis of the VCLT or as customary international law.

4.1   Delimitation of Articles 18 and 25 VCLT

Before looking at the different views expressed on the interaction of Articles 18 and 25 VCLT, the two provisions will briefly be delimited and compared in order to clarify their respective functions.

Article 18 stipulates the '[o]bligation not to defeat the object and purpose of a treaty prior to its entry into force' and reads as follows:

> A State is obliged to refrain from acts which would defeat the object and purpose of a treaty when:
>
> (a) it has signed the treaty or has exchanged instruments constituting the treaty subject to ratification, acceptance or approval until it shall have made its intention clear not to become a party to the treaty.

---

[32] M. L. Nash, 'Contemporary Practice of the United States Relating to International Law', *AJIL*, 74 (1980), 917–934, at 932; J. S. Charme, 'The Interim Obligation of Article 18 of the Vienna Convention of the Law of Treaties: Making Sense of an Enigma', *George Wash. JIL & Econ.*, 25 (1992), 71–114, at 76–85; McDade, *supra* n. 29, at pp. 13 and 25; M. A. Rogoff, 'The International Legal Obligations of Signatories to an Unratified Treaty', *Maine L. Rev.*, 32 (1980), 263–299, at 284; L. Boisson de Chazournes, A.-M. La Rosa and M. M. Mbengue, 'Article 18 (1969)' in Corten and Klein (eds.), *supra* n. 22, pp. 369–403, at pp. 382–383; O. Dörr, 'Article 18' in Dörr and Schmalenbach (eds.), *supra* n. 13, pp. 219–235, at p. 221; M. E. Villiger, *Commentary on the 1969 Vienna Convention on the Law of Treaties* (Leiden: Koninklijke Brill NV, 2009), p. 252, and H. Thirlway, *The Law and Procedure of the International Court of Justice* (Vol. I) (Oxford: Oxford University Press, 2013), p. 365.

(b) It has expressed its consent to be bound by the treaty, pending the entry into force of the treaty and provided that such entry into force is not unduly delayed.

Thus, provisional application and the obligation not to defeat a treaty's object and purpose prior to its entry into force both concern the effect of a treaty prior to its entry into force.[33] They are also both limited to treaties which do not enter into force immediately upon completion of the negotiations but where there is a gap between the conclusion of the treaty and its entry into force. They can be distinguished by the different effects treaties have prior to their entry into force as a consequence of either the Article 18 obligation or of a provisional application. In case of the Article 18 obligation, certain States are placed under an obligation roughly not to render the treaty inoperable or 'meaningless'[34] prior to its coming into force.[35] Accordingly, the obligation will often be one of abstention rather than of positive action.[36] Any conduct below the threshold of defeating the treaty's object and purpose is not covered by the obligation.[37] Thus, the obligation does not necessarily require States to refrain from conduct which, if the treaty was in force, would amount to a breach.[38] Furthermore, to the extent that positive action should be required under that obligation, it would generally fall short of applying the treaty's provisions to relevant acts, facts and situations.[39] It follows that the effect the treaty provisions have under the obligation within Article 18 VCLT is rather limited and indirect: they serve to establish the treaty's object and purpose, by way of an interpretation of the treaty and its provisions; but, generally, treaty provisions will not be given full effect in form of their direct application to relevant acts, facts and situations.

---

[33] In the VCLT the provisions relate to the period 'pending the treaty's entry into force' and 'prior to the treaty's entry into force'. See Arts. 25(1) and 18 (title) VCLT respectively: *supra* n. 1.

[34] Villiger, *supra* n. 32, at p. 249.

[35] Such conduct would not yet amount to a breach of the treaty because the treaty is not yet in force and, thus, not binding on the parties to it. It is this gap which the obligation not to defeat a treaty's object and purpose prior to its entry into force closes. See, further, the contribution to this volume of Kritsiotis at pp. 237–302 (Chapter 9).

[36] Nash, *supra* n. 32, at 933, and Villiger, *supra* n. 32, at p. 249.

[37] A. Aust, *Modern Treaty Law and Practice* (Cambridge: Cambridge University Press, 3rd ed., 2013), p. 108; O. Dörr, 'Codifying and Developing Meta-Rules: The ILC and the Law of Treaties', *German YbIL*, 49 (2006), 129–164, at 135, and Rogoff, *supra* n. 32, at 297.

[38] Aust, *supra* n. 37, at p. 108, and Dörr, *supra* n. 37, at p. 135.

[39] Villiger, *supra* n. 32, at p. 249, and Aust, *supra* n. 37, at p. 107.

This can be illustrated by the following hypothetical instances.[40] Where a disarmament treaty obliges its parties to reduce their armies by one-third, a signatory would comply with its Article 18 VCLT obligation as long as it did not, for instance, significantly increase its army. Thus, if it did nothing in particular with regard to its army, Article 18 VCLT would be fulfilled; and Article 18 VCLT would generally not oblige it to start complying with the treaty terms and reduce its army. To provide another example, if a State promises another in a treaty to deliver forest goods, the State would comply with its Article 18 VCLT obligation as long as, for instance, it did not destroy the forest or deliver all the goods derived therefrom to a third State. Again, under Article 18 VCLT, the State would not be required to begin performance of the delivery obligation; at best, the State might be required to maintain the forest so as to enable delivery of the forest goods when due, e.g. to undertake pest control to the extent necessary.

By contrast, the purpose of provisional application is precisely to allow the treaty's application prior to its entry into force[41] in situations where some or all of the States in question feel a need to act swiftly and choose not to await entry into force. Thus, if in relation to the preceding treaties the particular obligations were to be provisionally applied – i.e. as if the treaty was in force – the State in question would be required to perform those obligations during provisional application and preceding the treaty's entry into force, i.e. to reduce its army or deliver the forest goods.

This is not to say that in practice the distinction between Articles 18 and 25 VCLT will always be clear-cut. Yet, at least in theory, there is a clear distinction to be noted between provisional application and the obligation not to defeat a treaty's object and purpose.[42] Under Article 18 VCLT, the effects of a treaty prior to its entry into force are limited to preserving the treaty's core by prohibiting acts which would defeat its object and purpose. Provisional application, however, involves giving effect to the treaty in a much broader way by actually applying some of its provisions to relevant acts, facts and situations prior to the treaty's

---

[40] The treaty obligations in these instances, as well as their violations, are based on Villiger, *supra* n. 32, at p. 249.

[41] State practice indicates that provisional application involves the 'fulfilment' or 'performance' of the 'obligations' or the 'application' of the treaty: see Council of Europe and British Institute of International and Comparative Law (eds.), *supra* n. 18, at pp. 153 (Denmark); 192 (Iceland); 196 (Ireland); 211 (Lithuania) and 241 (Romania).

[42] Report of the International Law Commission on the Work of its Sixty-fourth Session (2012), U.N. Doc A/67/10, p. 106 (paragraph 147) and Nash, *supra* n. 32, at 933.

entry into force. Accordingly, as far as delimitation is concerned, the majority opinion in academic writings often describes the relationship between the two provisions by stating that Article 18 goes less far than Article 25 in terms of giving effect to the treaty or some of its provisions.[43]

4.2   Interaction of Articles 18 and 25 VCLT

Following the delimitation of Article 18 and 25 VCLT, the analysis can now turn to the potential simultaneous application and interaction of the two provisions.

4.2.1   Interaction of Articles 18 and 25 VCLT in Practice and Academic Writings

There is some support in practice and academic writings for the proposition that Articles 18 and 25 VCLT can apply simultaneously (i.e. to the same treaty). In relation to the 1977 Reciprocal Fisheries Agreement concluded between Canada and the United States,[44] the Canadian Legal Bureau made an incidental statement to such an effect.[45] According to the relevant Canadian memorandum, the Agreement had not yet entered into force. While the Parties appeared to have acted as though the Agreement was being applied provisionally, there had been no formal action – such as an exchange of notes – confirming this and on which to base more firmly an alleged material breach of the agreement by the United States. Turning to Article 18 VCLT as another potential basis for addressing the alleged breach, the Canadian memorandum went on to say that '*in any case* a State which has signed a treaty is obliged to refrain from acts which would defeat the object and

---

[43] Report of the International Law Commission, *ibid.*, at p. 106 (paragraph 147); Geslin, *supra* n. 3, at p. 330; Villiger, *supra* n. 32, at p. 252; A. Michie, 'Provisional Application of Non-Proliferation Treaties' in D. H. Joyner and M. Roscini (eds.), *Non-proliferation Law as a Special Regime: A Contribution to Fragmentation Theory in International Law* (Cambridge: Cambridge University Press, 2012), pp. 55–86, at p. 65, and, also, Dörr, *supra* n. 32, at p. 231. Cf. Rogoff and Gauditz, *supra* n. 2, at 49–51; Vienna Conference on the Law of Treaties, OR 1969, Plen. 11: India (paragraph 70). Finally, this is correct for legally binding provisionally applied treaties; when States agree in a non-legally binding manner to provisionally apply a treaty (in the same manner), then Art. 18 VCLT will be a *legal* obligation whereas the agreement to provisionally apply the treaty will be non-legally binding; in that instance, the delimitation is one between a legal and non-legally binding obligation.

[44] 1077 UNTS 55.

[45] M. D. Copithorne, 'Canadian Practice in International Law', *Canadian YbIL*, 16 (1978), 359–377, at 366–367.

purpose of the treaty ...'[46] Thus, based on a literal interpretation, the wording of the memorandum suggests that the Article 18 VCLT obligation would apply whether or not there had been provisional application of the treaty – or, more to the point here, even if there had been provisional application ('in *any* case'). Therefore, if the memorandum's language is accurate in this regard, it can be seen to express the understanding that Articles 18 and 25 VCLT can apply simultaneously with regard to the same treaty.

More direct support for the simultaneous application of Articles 18 and 25 VCLT is expressed in a letter dated 26 January 2010 from the then President-in-Office of the EU Council to the then President of the European Parliament.[47] The letter concerned the Agreement on the Processing and Transfer of Financial Messaging Data (TFTP Interim Agreement)[48] to be concluded and provisionally applied by the EU and the United States. The EU Parliament opposed the agreement and its provisional application on substantive and procedural grounds[49] and formally requested a two-week suspension of the envisaged provisional application.[50] In response to this, the President of the Council made the point that, upon signature, the Parties are bound by the Article 18 VCLT obligation and that this obligation would make it legally impossible to suspend the provisional application of the Agreement:

---

[46] *Ibid.*, at 366.   [47] PE 438.722/CPG/REP.

[48] Agreement between the EU and the USA on the Processing and Transfer of Financial Messaging Data from the EU to the US for Purposes of the Terrorist Finance Tracking Program [2010] OJ L8/11.

[49] The substantive grounds related to the level of protection provided in the agreement for the privacy/right to data of EU citizens, in terms of transparency, rights of access, rectification and erasure of inaccurate data, see http://ec.europa.eu/dgs/home-affairs/what-we-do/policies/crisis-and-terrorism/tftp/index_en.htm. The procedural grounds related to an alleged undermining of parliamentary powers by the Council in relation to the Agreement. The Agreement had been signed on the last day prior to the entry into force of the Lisbon Treaty, and some MEPs felt that this had been done in order to avoid compliance with the new rules and parliamentary rights regarding the conclusion of treaties under the Lisbon Treaty (including a veto power for treaties of this kind): see Letter from the President of the EU Parliament to President-in-Office of the Council of the European Union (15 Jan. 2010).

[50] Letter from the President of the EU Parliament to the President-in-Office of the Council of the European Union (21 Jan. 2010). Since there had been considerable delays in the submission of the final text to the Parliament, the EU Parliament had not yet had an opportunity to vote on the text of the agreement, and the agreement was scheduled to be provisionally applied from 1 Feb. 2010 onwards. The purpose of the suspension was to enable a vote prior to the commencement of the agreement's provisional application.

As a result of the signature of the TFTP Interim Agreement the Contracting Parties are obliged to refrain from acts that would defeat the object and purpose of the Agreement. It is *therefore* impossible to suspend the provisional application . . . .[51]

Leaving for later the question whether Article 18 VCLT can or should have the stated effect on the provisional application regime,[52] this quote can be seen to suggest that the Article 18 VCLT obligation applies in relation to and likely during[53] the treaty's provisional application. In other words, the quote can be seen to support the view that Articles 18 and 25 VCLT can apply to the same treaty at the same time. Furthermore, because the TFTP Interim Agreement provides for a provisional application of the (entire) agreement,[54] the quote would then also imply that Articles 18 and 25 VCLT apply to the same treaty provisions – i.e. overlap in their spheres of application – rather than applying to different parts or provisions of the TFTP Interim Agreement.

Moving from practice to scholarship, most of the literature dealing with both Articles 18 and 25 VCLT delimit the two from one another. The few writings that also consider their interaction agree that the two provisions complement one another, and seemingly assume or expressly stipulate that the two can indeed apply simultaneously.[55] The most explicit support for this view has been voiced by Andrew Michie. In a chapter on the provisional application of non-proliferation treaties, he considers the possibility of conduct breaching both Articles 25 and 18 VCLT, thus assuming that both provisions apply simultaneously.[56] He refers to this as a 'potential dual nature of the breach' and submits that it demonstrates the 'nexus' between Articles 18 and 25 VCLT. He does not explicitly deal with the question of an overlap of spheres of application, i.e. whether Articles 18 and 25 VCLT would apply to the same or different treaty provisions. But he does go on to mention that most non-

---

[51] See *supra* n. 47 (emphasis added).   [52] See Section 4.2.2.2.

[53] While this statement was made in anticipation of the treaty's provisional application, it is thought that the legal position expounded therein would have been maintained also during the provisional application.

[54] Art. 15(2) of the Agreement reads as follows: '*This Agreement* shall apply provisionally from . . .' (emphasis added).

[55] Boisson de Chazournes, La Rosa and Mbengue, *supra* n. 32, at p. 399; Michie, *supra* n. 43, at p. 66; see, also, M. Polkinghorn and L. Gouiffès, 'Provisional Application of the Energy Charter Treaty: The Conundrum' in G. Coop (ed.), *Energy Dispute Resolution: Investment Protection, Transit and the Energy Charter Treaty* (New York, NY: Huntington, 2011), pp. 249–282, at pp. 269–271.

[56] Unless otherwise indicated, this entire paragraph discusses points raised by Michie, *supra* n. 43, at p. 66.

proliferation treaties are provisionally applied in limited part only and that the core provisions of these treaties are not subject to provisional application.[57] Accordingly, his 'dual nature of the breach' does not necessarily imply an overlap of Articles 18 and 25 VCLT, but could also mean that they do apply at the same time but to different treaty parts or provisions. To illustrate this latter approach, a treaty's core provisions, for instance on trade, would be subject only to Article 18 VCLT, whereas, for instance, subordinate institutional provisions establishing a trade commission could be subject to Article 25 VCLT.

Others have relied on Article 18 VCLT and its obligation of good faith for interpreting an agreement on provisional application.[58] They thereby possibly adopt the view that Articles 18 and 25 VCLT apply simultaneously to the same treaty or, at the very least, that Article 18 VCLT provides guidance in establishing and interpreting the provisional application regime.

From this overview, two points can be extrapolated that shape the understanding of the interaction of Articles 18 and 25 VCLT: one is the question of the role of Article 18 VCLT when interpreting Article 25 VCLT, or rather the legal regime of provisional application. The other is the question of their simultaneous application and whether, in this event, they apply to the same treaty provisions or whether they have separate spheres of application, i.e. apply to different treaty parts or provisions. These two aspects of the interaction of Articles 18 and 25 VCLT will now be analysed in closer detail.

4.2.2   The Role of Article 18 VCLT in Interpreting the Provisional Application Regime

The preceding overview contains two instances in which the legal regime of provisional application is interpreted in light of Article 18 VCLT. According to one approach, Article 18 VCLT *determines* the legal regime;[59] according to another, Article 18 VCLT merely *guides or assists in* determining the provisional application regime.[60] This raises the question of what role, if any, Article 18 VCLT should play when it comes to interpreting the legal regime of provisional application.

---

[57]   Michie, *supra* n. 43, at p. 84.
[58]   Polkinghorn and Gouiffès, *supra* n. 55, at pp. 269–271: at the outset, the principle of good faith is deduced both from Arts. 26 and 18 VCLT, but the remainder of the analysis focuses on Art. 18 VCLT.
[59]   See *supra* nn. 47–51, and the corresponding text.
[60]   Polkinghorn and Gouiffès, *supra* n. 55, at pp. 269–271.

In an attempt at answering this question, recourse will be had to the *lex specialis* maxim, not as a conflict norm but as a broader analytical tool that describes different ways in which two potentially applicable norms can relate to one another and influence each other's interpretation.[61]

4.2.2.1   Articles 18 and 25 VCLT as *lex generalis* and *lex specialis*?

As a first step in this analysis, it will be examined whether Articles 18 and 25 VCLT can be understood as *lex generalis* and *lex specialis* in relation to the same subject matter.[62] Admittedly, the two are not usually described in this manner. However, they are at times considered in relation to one another, through statements that Article 18 goes 'less far' than Article 25 VCLT in terms of giving effect to the treaty preceding its entry into force.[63] Along these lines, the point could be made that they do relate to the same subject matter, in that they both concern the effects of certain treaties prior to their actual entry into force.[64] Regarding these treaties, Article 18 VCLT affords the standard protection, preserving the treaty's core by prohibiting conduct that would render the treaty meaningless. Thus, if States do not provide anything in their treaty with regard to the period pending the treaty's entry into force, this is the protection the treaty will receive per default.[65] Yet, if this is not enough, if States wish to give the treaty a more direct effect,[66] then they need to make this clear by agreeing on its provisional application. Such an agreement will then enable a more stringent effect of the treaty, in that certain of its provisions will be applied to relevant acts, facts or situations. Accordingly, it could be said that Article 18 VCLT provides the general rule, the standard protection, whereas Article 25 VCLT is the special regime, only applicable if so agreed and then providing for a more direct or specific effect of the treaty prior to its entry into force.

---

[61] International Law Commission, Report of the Study Group on Fragmentation of International Law: Difficulties arising from the Diversification and Expansion of International Law, Finalized by Martti Koskenniemi, U.N. Doc. A/CN.4/L.682 (2006), pp. 49–53 (paragraphs 88–97).

[62] G. Fitzmaurice, *The Law and Procedure of the International Court of Justice* (Vol. I) (Cambridge: Grotius Publications, 1986), p. 371, and Fragmentation Report, *supra* n. 61, at pp. 62–63 (paragraph 116).

[63] See *supra* n. 43.

[64] Report of the International Law Commission, *supra* n. 42, at p. 106 (paragraph 147).

[65] See *supra* n. 32 and corresponding text.

[66] Cf J. Pauwelyn, *Conflict of Norms in Public International Law: How WTO Law Relates to Other Rules of International Law* (Cambridge: Cambridge University Press, 2003), pp. 390 and 387–388, and Fragmentation Report, *supra* n. 61, at pp. 36–37 (paragraph 60).

Thus, Articles 18 and 25 VCLT could be conceived as *lex generalis* and *lex specialis* in relation to the effects of certain treaties prior to their entry into force. Now the question can be addressed whether their relationship under the *lex specialis* maxim is such that Article 18 VCLT should *determine* the legal regime of Article 25 VCLT as put forward by the EU Council.

4.2.2.2   *Lex specialis* as an Application or Elaboration of the *lex generalis*   It is submitted that *lex specialis* as an elaboration of the *lex generalis* describes a norm relationship that would support the EU approach expressed in the previously mentioned letter, according to which Article 18 VCLT controls the provisional application regime. *Lex specialis* as an elaboration of the *lex generalis* describes the situation where a general and a more specific provision relate to the same subject matter, where the latter is an application, development or supplement thereto.[67] In these cases, both rules apply, so that the specific one supplements the more general one.[68] While the more specific rule is the starting point of the interpretation, it should always be read and understood within the confines or against the background of the general standard.[69] The examples given for this type of normative relationship are the interpretation of domestic administrative rules in light of the legislation upon which they are based as well as the interpretation of a specific treaty in light of its framework convention.[70] Certainly, with regard to these examples, there is no doubt that there is a close relationship between the general and more specific rule and that the latter should be read against the background and within the confines of the former.

However, it is doubtful whether Articles 18 and 25 VCLT share this kind of bond. They clearly have commonalities, as has been pointed out earlier. Yet, that notwithstanding, provisional application is not normally perceived as building on Article 18 VCLT, in the sense that it would always contain (some part of) Article 18 VCLT and then provide a more or less substantial addition on top of that. Furthermore, the relationship is not such that a regime of provisional application can only be

---

[67] Fragmentation Report, *supra* n. 61, at pp. 49 (paragraph 88) and 54 (paragraph 98).

[68] Pauwelyn, *supra* n. 66, at p. 410, and C.J. Borgen, 'Treaty Conflicts and Normative Fragmentation' in Hollis (ed.), *supra* n. 12, pp. 448–471, at p. 466.

[69] Fragmentation Report, *supra* n. 61, at pp. 34–35 (paragraph 56) and pp. 54–55 (paragraph 99), and Pauwelyn, *supra* n. 66, at p. 410. See, also, Borgen, *supra* n. 68, at p. 466.

[70] Fragmentation Report, *ibid.*, at pp. 49 (paragraph 88) and 54 (paragraph 98), and Pauwelyn, *supra* n. 66, at p. 410.

understood by reference to the more general Article 18 VCLT obligation, and that writers and practitioners commonly and constantly refer to Article 18 VCLT when interpreting a provisional application regime. Accordingly, the interpretation put forward by the EU Council, according to which the legal regime of Article 25 VCLT is controlled or determined by Article 18 VCLT, may be questioned, since the relationship of the two provisions would not appear to be sufficiently close and symbiotic as to enable such an outcome.

4.2.2.3   *Lex specialis* as Informal Hierarchy between Articles 18 and 25 VCLT

Alternatively, recourse can be had to another emanation of the *lex specialis* maxim in order to conceptualise the relationship between Article 18 and 25 VCLT. At times, *lex specialis* is used to establish an informal hierarchy between two (or more) potentially applicable provisions.[71] This is the concept used for describing the relationship between the different sources of international law and, to the extent that the agreement on provisional application is set in relation to the customary Article 18 VCLT obligation, its application might be appropriate. Furthermore, it is submitted that this provides a more apt description of the role of Article 18 VCLT in interpreting the provisional application regime.

According to this understanding, the more specific provision is the starting point of interpretation and its main focus. In 'easy' cases, it will not be necessary to have recourse to the more general provision.[72] Only in 'hard' cases, the need might arise to look behind the more special rule. Then, the general rule can come into play, for instance, to fill a gap or to interpret undefined terms etc. When applied to the question underlying the EU Council statement – namely, whether a provisional application of a treaty is amenable to a suspension – it is submitted that this should first and foremost be answered by reference to the provisional application regime in question.[73] Should this be inconclusive, then the regime should be interpreted against the background of general international law, including the VCLT. In this specific case, the TFTP Interim Agreement not only contained a suspension clause,[74] the suspension clause also fell

---

[71] Fragmentation Report, *ibid.*, at pp. 47–48 (paragraph 85).

[72] Fragmentation Report, *ibid.*, at p. 48 (paragraph 86).

[73] Gómez-Robledo, *supra* n. 2, at pp. 5 (paragraph 20) and 10 (paragraph 36).

[74] Art. 14(1): *supra* n. 48. This could be used as an argument as to why suspension of provisional application would not normally defeat the treaty's object and purpose: it is difficult to conceive that a treaty would sanction action that could defeat its object and

within the range of provisions that were subject to provisional application.[75] Thus, the treaty's provisional application regime on the face of it would seem to allow a suspension of the provisionally applied treaty. Therefore, there would appear to be no need to have recourse to Article 18 VCLT in order to determine the possibility of a suspension of the provisional application of the TFTP Interim Agreement.

As was mentioned previously, academic writings have relied on Article 18 VCLT in order to establish an obligation of good faith for the provisional application regime.[76] At first sight, this choice would appear to stand to reason: Article 18 VCLT is a manifestation of an obligation of good faith, and Articles 18 and 25 VCLT both relate to the effects of treaties prior to their entry into force, i.e. have a similar temporal sphere of application. However, in the debate surrounding the legal nature and binding force of provisionally applied treaties, the view that conceptualised provisional application by relying on Article 18 VCLT was rejected.[77] The great majority, both in State practice and academic writings, adopted the view that relied instead on the principle of *pacta sunt servanda*, by positing that provisionally applied treaties, as indeed treaties in force, fell within the ambit of this principle.[78] Since the principle of *pacta sunt servanda* includes its own obligation to act in good faith, it might be more in line with the majority view to deduce the obligation of good faith during provisional application from Article 26 VCLT rather than 18 VCLT.

What, then, is the role of Article 18 VCLT in interpreting the provisional application regime? Article 18 VCLT may, for instance, provide useful guidance when issues with regard to Article 25(2) VCLT arise, given that the Article 25(2) VCLT clause was modelled after Article 18 VCLT.[79] However, unless there is such a particular reason, the present

---

purpose. Therefore, the sanctioning of a certain conduct can be taken to mean that, in principle, it is in conformity with the treaty (if done in accordance with the treaty).

[75] Arts. 14(1) and 15(2): *ibid.*   [76] See *supra* n. 58.

[77] Quast Mertsch, *supra* n. 3, at p. 51.   [78] See *supra* n. 3.

[79] Compare Art. 25(2) VCLT with Art. 18(a) VCLT regarding the element 'intention not to become a party to the treaty': *supra* n. 1. According to the Chairman of the Drafting Committee at the First Session of the Vienna Conference of the Law of Treaties, the text of then Art. 22(2) (today Art. 25(2) VCLT) was *inter alia* based on an amendment by Belgium: see 1968 CoW 72nd Meeting, p. 427 (paragraph 27). The Belgian delegate, when explaining the wording used in that amendment, underlined the fact that it was based on the terms employed in Art. 15 (today Art. 18 VCLT): see Belgium, 1968 CoW 26th meeting, p. 142 (paragraph 42). This was advantageous because, at least with regard to Art. 15, this wording had already been approved by the Committee in principle.

author would advocate a limited role of Article 18 VCLT in interpreting the provisional application regime. First and foremost, the legal regime of provisional application should be determined by reference to the relevant agreement on provisional application, Article 25 VCLT and the treaty in question; then recourse to the VCLT and to general international law may follow to the extent necessary. Yet, if there is any VCLT provision that does play a key role in determining the legal regime of provisional application, according to the majority view in practice and academic writings, it is Article 26 VCLT and not Article 18 VCLT.

4.2.3   Simultaneous Application

The following section raises matters pertaining to the simultaneous application of Articles 18 and 25 VCLT. Can Articles 18 and 25 VCLT apply at the same time to the same treaty, and if so, how can this be conceptualised? Is there an overlap, in the sense that whenever there is provisional application, there is always Article 18 VCLT – or some part thereof – in the background?[80] Or does Article 25 VCLT as *lex specialis* take the matter outside the sphere of application of Article 18 VCLT, so that the two operate in separate spheres of application?[81] Also, does this matter?

While a full analysis of this question on the basis of the *lex specialis* regime might prove useful, at this point only two thoughts are briefly developed. The first concerns coherence with the prevalent concept of provisional application; the second is of a pragmatic nature and aims at satisfactorily protecting a treaty pending its entry into force.

As has previously been mentioned, according to the majority view in practice and academic writings, provisionally applied treaties are seen as legally binding and as falling within the ambit of the *pacta sunt servanda* principle. If, now, the overlap approach assumes that Articles 18 and 25 VCLT share at least to some extent their spheres of application, then this could mean that during provisional application, both Articles 18 and 26 VCLT could apply to these treaties or to some of their provisions. If so, this would amount to more protection than non-provisionally applied

---

[80] See the Canadian and EU Council approach described in Section 4.2.1. This could be taken to correspond to the preceding *lex specialis* as application or elaboration of the *lex generalis* approach and has been criticised for not aptly describing the role Art. 18 VCLT has in interpreting the provisional application regime, see Section 4.2.2.2.

[81] This could be taken to correspond to the emanation of *lex specialis* as a conflict norm: see, e.g., Pauwelyn, *supra* n. 66, at pp. 391–409; Fitzmaurice, *supra* n. 62, at pp. 370–372, and Fragmentation Report, *supra* n. 61, at pp. 56–59 (paragraphs 103–107).

('normal') treaties enjoy.[82] In relation to these situations, either Article 18 or Article 26 VCLT applies – but not both. To be more precise, if Article 18 VCLT applies to those, then it is until their entry into force; at that moment, the temporal sphere of application of Article 18 ends and that of Article 26 VCLT begins.[83] It is not clear why this should be different for provisional application and whether it would be necessary to deviate from this general framework as laid out by the VCLT. Therefore, the coherence of the concept of provisional application and its conformity with the framework of the VCLT might be seen as a theoretical argument against generally overlapping spheres of application of Articles 18 and 25 VCLT.

On the other hand, a pragmatic approach would aim at a high level of protection for the treaty prior to its entry into force. If States agree on provisional application, rather than relying on the default protection of Article 18 VCLT, this is because they desire a strong protection of the treaty regime and the application of certain treaty provisions to relevant acts, facts and situations prior to the treaty's entry into force. However, when including a limitation clause,[84] the effect of the clause can be to entirely exclude provisional application by individual States, if in their constitutional systems provisional application is prohibited.[85] Similarly, if due to the absence of matching legislation, the provisional application of the treaty is severely limited, then it might be useful to be able to fall back on the default protection of the treaty under Article 18 VCLT. If, however, Article 25 VCLT is viewed as a *lex specialis* blocking recourse to the more general provision,[86] then this would leave States in an absurd

[82] This is even more so if one adheres to the view according to which upon a treaty's entry into force, Art. 26 VCLT 'continues' the obligation not to defeat a treaty's object and purpose; for a discussion thereof, see, e.g., Thirlway, *supra* n. 32, at pp. 364–369.

[83] See the wording of Art. 26 VCLT and the title of Art. 18 VCLT: *supra* n. 1.

[84] A limitation clause is a stipulation that determines the extent to which provisional application is to take place. Frequently, this is done by reference to internal law, the result of which is that the so specified internal law determines the extent to which a treaty is provisionally applied on the international plane. In other instances, financial considerations can additionally delimit provisional application, for instance when the States agree that a treaty will be provisionally applied 'insofar as their constitutional and budgetary regulations permit': see Quast Mertsch, *supra* n. 3, at pp. 4 and 95–102.

[85] *Yukos Universal Ltd v. Russian Federation* (Interim Award on Jurisdiction and Admissibility), PCA Case No. AA 227 (30 Nov. 2009), at pp. 110–111 (paragraph 301) and 115 (paragraph 311).

[86] This would involve the understanding of *lex specialis* as a conflict norm, where the more specific provisions take the matter outside the realm of the more general one. As a consequence, recourse to the more general norm could be excluded, even when the specific norm eventually is not applied, for the reason that the matter as such falls

situation: originally wanting more than Article 18 VCLT but eventually facing a weak provisional application regime, not even benefitting from the standard protection of Article 18 VCLT. To avoid this situation, even if a general overlap of spheres of application can be criticised on the previously noted grounds, it might be of interest to the concerned States to rely on the Article 18 VCLT protection, if the effect of a limitation clause is to exclude or severely limit the treaty's provisional application by some States.[87]

Based on the preceding analysis, the following instances of simultaneous application of the two provisions can be envisaged: first, if provisional application is limited to just one or a handful of provisions or concerns secondary provisions but not the core obligations of a treaty.[88] Then these few provisions are covered by provisional application, whereas the remainder of the provisions fall under Article 18 VCLT. Second, when provisional application covers the entire treaty but is subject to a limitation clause and the effect of the limitation clause is to exclude provisional application entirely. Similarly, when the limitation clause does not exclude but severely limits provisional application. For such instances, it is submitted that it might be in the interest of the States concerned to rely on the Article 18 VCLT obligation, given that the provisional application regime is rather weak. On the other hand, when the 'entire' treaty is subject to provisional application and the parties did not include a limitation clause, then there would appear to be neither any room nor any need for an application of Article 18 VCLT.

4.3   Conclusion on Article 18 VCLT

As has been shown earlier, there is some support in academic writings and practice for the simultaneous application of Articles 18 and 25 VCLT, although the conceptual framework underlying such application is in its early stages. For its further development, two suggestions have been outlined: on the one hand, to achieve consistency with the prevalent concept of provisionally applied treaties as falling within the scope of the *pacta sunt servanda* principle; on the other hand, to achieve a satisfactory

---

within the sphere of application of the *lex specialis*, and thereby *outside* the general one: see, e.g., Fitzmaurice, *supra* n. 62, at p. 370. However, for this reading, one might need to show a conflict between the two rules first.

[87] Ultimately, the possibility of such a fallback would need to be decided on the basis of the respective agreement on provisional application.

[88] Michie, *supra* n. 43, at p. 84.

level of protection for such instances in which the provisional application regime emerges to be weaker than anticipated – if, for instance, a limitation clause either entirely prevents provisional application of a treaty by certain States or severely limits it.

Regarding the role of Article 18 VCLT in interpreting the legal regime of provisional application, the approach has been questioned that would allow Article 18 VCLT to *determine* the legal regime of provisional application; similarly, recourse to Article 18 VCLT is unnecessary for establishing an obligation of good faith during provisional application. The more appropriate view is that the agreement on provisional application, Article 25 VCLT and the treaty in question should be the starting point and main focus for any determination of the legal regime of provisional application, supported by the VCLT and by general international law. If, with regard to the VCLT, one provision does play a more prominent role than others, then this should be Article 26 VCLT and not Article 18 VCLT, based on the prevalent concept of provisionally applied treaties.

5   Article 46 VCLT and Its Applicability in Relation to Provisional Application

The following section examines the question of the applicability of Article 46 VCLT in relation to provisional application. If applicable, Article 46 VCLT could be used to invalidate an expression of 'consent to the provisional application of a treaty'.[89]

Article 46 VCLT has to be read in conjunction with Article 27 VCLT.[90] The latter expresses the principle that internal law cannot be invoked to justify the non-compliance with a treaty; Article 46 (concerning provisions of internal law regarding competence to conclude treaties) is a limited exception thereto and reads as follows:

> 1. A State may not invoke the fact that its consent to be bound by a treaty has been expressed in violation of a provision of its internal law regarding competence to conclude treaties as invalidating its consent unless that

---

[89] The notion of 'consent to the provisional application of a treaty' here is distinct from 'consent to be bound' in terms of Art. 11 VCLT and is intended to cover all methods by which provisional application can be agreed: *supra* n. 1.

[90] On internal law and observance of treaties, which provides that '[a] party may not invoke the provisions of its internal law as justification for its failure to perform a treaty' – a rule that is 'without prejudice' to Art. 46 VCLT: *ibid.*

violation was manifest and concerned a rule of its internal law of fundamental importance.
2. A violation is manifest if it would be objectively evident to any State
   conducting itself in the matter in accordance with normal practice and
   good faith.

To ensure the stability and validity of treaty relations, the exception is
narrowly and negatively worded and contains very high hurdles.[91]
As a result, Article 46 VCLT is very difficult to successfully invoke.[92]

5.1 Overview

The question has been raised as to whether Article 46 VCLT can be
invoked if a State has consented to provisional application without
following the proper domestic procedure.[93] This is particularly relevant as in some domestic legal systems, provisional application gives
rise to considerable constitutional tensions.[94] It has, for instance, been
said to undermine parliamentary treaty-making powers, by transforming an *ex ante* treaty-approval procedure into an *ex post*
confirmation.[95]

Some of the scholarship on this topic assumes that Article 46 VCLT
can be invoked in relation to consent to provisional application.[96]
Furthermore, there is one decision by a Dutch appellate court which
concurs with this opinion in the abstract: the Dutch court refers to this
hypothetical option to bolster its analysis but does not actually apply
Article 46 VCLT to the consent to provisional application.[97] Finally, in

---

[91] T. Rensmann, 'Article 46' in Dörr and Schmalenbach (eds.), *supra* n. 13, pp. 775–804, at
pp. 778–779.

[92] Aust, *supra* n. 37, at pp. 273–274, and M. Schröder, 'Treaties, Validity' in Wolfrum (ed.),
supra n. 26, at p. 2.

[93] Report of the International Law Commission, *supra* n. 42, at p. 106 (paragraph 151), and
Quast Mertsch, *supra* n. 3, at p. xix.

[94] See *supra* n. 22, and Quast Mertsch, *supra* n. 3, at pp. 64–72; cf. Dalton, *supra* n. 12, at
p. 241.

[95] See penultimate paragraph of Section 2. See, also, Italian Parliamentary Practice in *Italian
YbIL*, 1 (1975), 294, and Quast Mertsch, *supra* n. 3, at pp. 65–66.

[96] R. Lefeber 'Treaties, Provisional Application' in Wolfrum (ed.), *supra* n. 26, at pp. 4–5. Cf.
S. M. Pounjin, 'The New Federal Law on International Treaties of the Russian Federation'
in R. Müllerson, M. Fitzmaurice and M. Andenas (eds.), *Constitutional Reform and
International Law in Central and Eastern Europe* (The Hague: Kluwer Law
International, 1998), pp. 267–278, at p. 275.

[97] *Management Board of the Social Insurance Bank v. X*, Higher Appeal Judgment, Case
No. 03/2625 AOW, accessed through Oxford Reports on International Law, Reporter:
Brölmann, 4.15.

the *Yukos Case*,[98] two of the claimants' witnesses differed in their opinion as to whether Article 46 VCLT could be so invoked: Michael Reisman submitted that this was so in principle,[99] whereas James Crawford rejected this approach.[100]

5.2   A Broad Interpretation of Article 46 VCLT?

By its own terms, Article 46(1) VCLT requires that a State has expressed its consent to be bound by a treaty. While there are several means of expressing consent to be bound, and States are free to devise other ones,[101] provisional application is not one of them. It is a distinct mechanism, as indicated in the VCLT: first, provisional application is not covered in the list of 'means of expressing consent to be bound by a treaty' in Article 11 VCLT nor in the following four provisions – Articles 12 to 15 VCLT – devoted to the most common means of expressing consent. More precisely, provisional application is not mentioned at all in the entire VCLT section dealing with the conclusion of treaties (Part II, Section 1) and instead is placed in the section devoted to entry into force and provisional application (Part II, Section 3).

Furthermore, expression of consent to be bound is a means by which a State expresses its intention to be bound by a treaty. This is the *final* step in treaty-making on the international plane, after which a State is considered a 'contracting State' in relation to the treaty in question (Article 2(1)(f) VCLT). By contrast, consent to provisional application is an *intermediary* step by which a State expresses its intention to apply a treaty to relevant acts, facts and situations *pending* its entry into force.

---

[98] Case brought by three shareholders of the Yukos Oil Corporation against the Russian Federation for various measures taken by the Russian Federation against the corporation (culminating in its bankruptcy), thereby allegedly adversely affecting the claimants' investments in Yukos. In the 2009 decision, the Arbitral Tribunal *inter alia* had to decide whether it had jurisdiction over the merits of the case on the basis of the provisionally applied Energy Charter Treaty: *Yukos Universal Ltd v. Russian Federation, supra* n. 85.

[99] Reisman argued that the Russian Federation could not invoke Art. 46 VCLT in relation to the provisional application of the Energy Charter Treaty (in an attempt at invalidating its consent thereto) because any alleged violation would not have been 'manifest': *Yukos Universal Ltd v. Russian Federation, supra* n. 85, at p. 84 (paragraph 236).

[100] When looking at the interplay of international treaties and internal law, Crawford stated that international law traditionally had been reluctant to allow internal (law) limitations to affect treaty provisions. In this context, he put forward the position that the scope of Art. 46 VCLT did not cover provisional application but only 'definitive acceptance': *Yukos Universal Ltd v. Russian Federation, supra* n. 85, at p. 80 (paragraph 220).

[101] See Art. 11 VCLT ('or by any other means if so agreed'): *supra* n. 1.

Consent to provisional application often precedes but may also succeed a State's expression of consent in terms of Article 11 VCLT – and, in both situations, it is a distinct act from the State's expression of consent to be bound in terms of Article 11 VCLT. It follows that the ordinary meaning of the terms of Article 46 VCLT does not cover consent to provisional application.

Additionally, the issue arises that Article 46 VCLT, as many other provisions of the VCLT,[102] normally applies to treaties in force.[103] Therefore, strictly speaking, one requirement in relation to the temporal sphere of application of these VCLT provisions is usually not met when their applicability to provisionally applied treaties is discussed. This is a general issue pertaining to the legal regime of provisional application[104] and as such may need to be analysed in a comprehensive manner that goes beyond the scope of this chapter. For present purposes, it suffices to refer to the *Kardassopolous Case*, where this matter was addressed by interpreting relevant provisions in a sense equivalent or analogous to their strict and literal meaning, on a *mutatis mutandis* basis.[105] If so done with regard to Article 46 VCLT, i.e. if broadening Article 46 VCLT to cover 'provisionally applied treaties' and 'consent to provisional application', the next potential stumbling block is the provision's nature as an exception to Article 27 VCLT – since exceptions are to be interpreted narrowly.[106] On the other hand, a broad interpretation of Article 46 VCLT might be acceptable if this does not undermine the overall aim

---

[102] Exceptions would be those VCLT provisions regulating the conclusion and entry into force of treaties: *ibid.*

[103] According to this view, prior to entry into force, consent can be withdrawn, so that there is no need to invoke Art. 46 VCLT: see, e.g., Aust, *supra* n. 37, at p. 109. See, also, Summary of Practice of the Secretary-General as Depositary of Multilateral Treaties (1999) (ST/LEG/7/Rev.1), p. 46 (paragraph 157).

[104] See, e.g., the different positions on this matter as expressed at the Vienna Conference on the Law of Treaties: VCLT termination provisions could apply: Waldock, 1968 CoW 27th Meeting, p. 145 (paragraph 20); VCLT termination provisions would not apply since a State could not denounce a treaty to which it was not a party: Belgium, 1968 CoW 26th Meeting, p. 142 (paragraph 42); see, also, Poland, 1968 CoW 27th Meeting, p. 144 (paragraph 3). In general, see, also, Gaja, *supra* n. 2, at p. 333 (paragraphs 9–10).

[105] *Kardassopoulos v. Georgia*, ICSID Case No. ARB/05/18, 6 July 2007, pp. 58–59 (paragraphs 220–222). The difference is that, here, the interpretation of VCLT provisions is at issue, in order to determine the legal regime of provisional application, whereas in the *Kardassopolus Case*, it was the interpretation of substantive law, i.e. of provisions of the (Energy Charter) treaty, subject to provisional application.

[106] *Singularia non sunt extendenda.* Specifically applying this maxim with regard to Art. 46 VCLT: Villiger, *supra* n. 32, at p. 590; and, in the context of provisional application, see Crawford (claimants' witness): *Yukos Universal Ltd v. Russian Federation, supra* n. 85, at

of Article 46 VCLT: the protection of the stability and validity of treaty relations against the invocation of internal law provisions.

To clarify, the preceding is not to say that Article 46 VCLT should never be applied to provisionally applied treaties but rather to raise points worth considering when contemplating such an application. The discussion whether indeed Article 46 VCLT should be so broadened is saved for last, following an examination of the remaining requirements of Article 46 VCLT.

5.3   Fundamental Importance of the Breached Provision

The requirement of the 'fundamental importance' of the breached provision relates to the nature of the violated provision and its underlying purpose or function. According to academic writings, provisions that are of fundamental importance include those on the separation of powers in relation to treaty-making, such as parliamentary control of the executive.[107] Therefore, if the internal procedure for provisional application requires consultation or cooperation with a legislative body[108] and this is not followed, this might qualify as violation of a norm of fundamental importance.

If the relevant domestic law only contains a provision that certain treaties require parliamentary approval for an expression of consent to be bound in terms of Article 11 VCLT[109] – in other words, there is no provision specifically regulating provisional application – it is submitted that an assessment of the legality of provisional application without/prior to such approval depends on the practice of the particular State. If provisional application has never been done before, or only rarely, it might be regarded as a violation thereof.[110] If, however, a(n unwritten)

---

p. 80 (paragraph 220). Cf. *Whaling in the Antarctic*: Australia v. Japan; New Zealand intervening (2014) ICJ Rep. 226, at pp. 249–252 (paragraphs 51–58).

[107] M. Bothe, 'Article 46 (1969)' in Corten and Klein (eds.), Vol. II, *supra* n. 22, pp. 1090–1099, at pp. 1094–1095, and Rensmann, *supra* n. 91, at pp. 790 and 794.

[108] See, e.g., the Japanese reporting requirement to the Committee on Foreign Affairs in both Houses of the Diet: T. Kawakami, 'National Treaty Law and Practice: Japan', *Studies in Transnational Legal Policy*, 30 (1999), 107–132, at 114.

[109] A. Bolintineanu, 'Expression of Consent to Be Bound by a Treaty in the Light of the 1969 Vienna Convention', *AJIL*, 68 (1974), 672–686, at 679.

[110] This, however, is not a necessity, if the requirement is for approval preceding *consent to be bound*. Accordingly, it could be argued that provisional application is not covered by the provision and that a procedure should be developed specifically for provisional application in order to fill the gap: see Quast Mertsch, *supra* n. 3, at pp. 70–72.

provisional application practice has been established for certain types of treaties and situations, then the legality of a provisional application would need to be assessed in light of this practice.[111] Provisional application in general would then be regarded as being in conformity with the relevant domestic law,[112] as long as it is in conformity with that practice.

In those situations where there are allegations that provisional application undermines parliamentary powers but the executive disagrees, a violation is alleged but not established, until the matter is resolved either between the concerned organs or by a relevant tribunal. Even if occurring at a later point, the practice is seen to have violated relevant domestic law, at the relevant time the violation arguably was not manifest (as is further required by Article 46 VCLT, see later).

In conclusion, to the extent that provisional application touches upon the separation of powers in relation to treaty-making, it is conceivable that an internal provision of fundamental importance is violated in the process.

5.4   Manifest Violation

As previously noted, the violation of the provision would need to be manifest. According to Article 46(2) VCLT, a violation is manifest if it would be objectively evident to any State conducting itself in the matter in accordance with normal practice and in good faith. The standard is an objective one,[113] and refers to any third State that would find itself in the same circumstances.[114] Manifest means 'clear' or 'obvious', and from this it follows that the violation needs to be easily ascertainable.

Many constitutions submit all or certain kinds of treaties to parliamentary approval.[115] While certain commonalities might exist among these constitutions, such as the principle to require parliamentary consent for treaties ceding territory/changing frontiers, treaties providing for binding dispute settlement on the international plane, or loan agreements, the practice still varies among States. Therefore, although

---

[111] Rensmann, *supra* n. 91, at pp. 785–786; see, also, Villiger, *supra* n. 32, at p. 591.

[112] See, for instance, Crawford stating as claimants' witness that it cannot be assumed that the mere existence of a constitutional requirement of ratification is inconsistent with provisional application: *Yukos Universal Ltd v. Russian Federation, supra* n. 85, at p. 80 (paragraph 220).

[113] Elias, *supra* n. 29, at pp. 149–150, and Aust, *supra* n. 37, at p. 274.

[114] Rensmann, *supra* n. 91, at p. 791, and Villiger, *supra* n. 32, at p. 591.

[115] Bolintineanu, *supra* n. 109, at p. 679, and Bothe, *supra* n. 107, at p. 1095.

the subject matter of a treaty can indicate that a treaty could be subject to parliamentary approval, it might still not be easily ascertainable whether this is so with regard to a particular State.[116] Furthermore, the practice within a specific State can be in flux, the written constitution can be supplemented or superseded by unwritten practice,[117] and it is not uncommon for experts to disagree on certain points of constitutional law and practice. In this regard, the International Court of Justice has held that 'there is no general legal obligation for States to keep themselves informed of legislative and constitutional developments in other States which are or may become important for the international relations of these States'.[118] Finally, the more complex the constitutional rule and practice, the less likely it is that a violation of a norm will be manifest.[119] For provisional application practice, this means that a manifest violation of a relevant procedure is rather unlikely: more often than not provisional application practice is unwritten,[120] and depending on the frequency with which a State uses provisional application, it is possible that the practice might not entirely be settled.[121] In such instances, a violation would generally not be easily ascertainable.

Of course, in some States there are written rules governing provisional application,[122] and again in other States, there is a long tradition of

[116] Bothe, *supra* n. 107, at p. 1095. See, for instance, the discussion of whether treaties relating to territory, if concluded in simplified form, should raise the question of compliance with internal law provisions: O. Elias, 'The Bakassi Peninsula Case and Article 46 of the Vienna Convention on the Law of Treaties' in Fitzmaurice and Elias, *supra* n. 6, pp. 372–388, at pp. 382–385.

[117] Rensmann, *supra* n. 91, at pp. 792–3.

[118] *Case Concerning Land and Maritime Boundary between Cameroon and Nigeria*: Cameroon v. Nigeria; Equatorial Guinea intervening (2002) ICJ Rep. 303, at p. 430 (paragraph 266).

[119] Both with regard to EU internal rules on treaty-making: Aust, *supra* n. 37, at p. 274, and Schröder, *supra* n. 92, at p.2.

[120] Quast Mertsch, *supra* n. 3, at p. 63.

[121] There are a number of States which have recourse to provisional application only in exceptional circumstances: see Council of Europe and British Institute of International and Comparative Law (eds.), *supra* n. 18, at pp. 127 (Belgium); 167 (France); 183 (Greece) and 281 (Turkey). Here, the question arises whether those circumstances are entirely settled.

[122] Examples are Art. 15, State Law on Approval and Promulgation of Treaties (Rijkswet goedkeuring en bekendmaking verdragen), Staatsblad, 1994, No. 542, and Art. 23, Federal Law on International Treaties of the Russian Federation, 1995, as printed in W. E. Butler, *The Law of Treaties in Russia and the Commonwealth of Independent States: Text and Commentary* (Cambridge: Cambridge University Press, 2002), p. 125. See, also, Art. 14, Law on International Treaties of the Republic Belarus, 1991, as printed in Butler at p. 280.

frequent recourse to provisional application.[123] In those instances, a deviation from those rules might be more easily ascertainable and could possibly satisfy the high standard of a manifest violation. In conclusion, a manifest violation of the domestic procedure of provisional application might be rare but should not generally be excluded.

5.5   Evaluation and Conclusion on Article 46 VCLT

These are some of the issues that might arise if Article 46 VCLT was to be extended to provisional application. It is to be expected that, due to the high hurdles contained therein, it would be very difficult to invoke the provision successfully, as is already the case in relation to treaties in force and consent to be bound in terms of Article 11 VCLT. Yet the question remains whether a broad interpretation covering provisional application could be reconciled with the overall aim of Article 46 VCLT. At this early stage in the debate, there are two points that the current author would like to raise. First, provisional application could be said to be comparable to consent to be bound in terms of Article 11 VCLT, and thus requiring similar protection, in that it is also a *binding* undertaking in relation to the treaty (even if intended to be temporary). As it is binding, the need might arise to invalidate such consent if it came about as prescribed by the remainder of Article 46 VCLT. To decide otherwise would create a gap in the legal regime of provisional application, since then provisional application could only be terminated but not invalidated by reason of a violation of an internal provision.

As a practical consideration, the point should be made that States are more likely to terminate provisional application rather than invoke the invalidity of the consent given thereto – as long as termination is sufficient for their needs and easy to bring about, see Article 25(2) VCLT. Therefore, the question of the applicability of Article 46 VCLT will mostly arise if termination (*ex nunc* effect) is insufficient and invalidity (*ex tunc* effect) is required, or if a more complex termination provision has been agreed replacing Article 25(2) VCLT and that provision is similarly difficult to invoke as Article 46 VCLT. By contrast, the question of the applicability of Article 46 VCLT may not arise when the agreement on provisional application contains a limitation clause that limits provisional application to the extent that it is in conformity with internal

---

[123] For a long list of Spain's provisionally applied treaties, see the Annexes in E. O. Calatayud, *Los tratados internacionales y su aplicación en el tiempo* (Madrid: Librería-Editorial Dykinson, 2004).

law.[124] In such a situation, if the domestic provisional application procedure was violated, then provisional application by the relevant State could be excluded on the basis of the limitation clause. Thus, the matter of the applicability of Article 46 VCLT would not arise. (Also, in these situations, a violation of the domestic provisional application procedure would be significantly easier to invoke than on the basis of Article 46 VCLT due to the absence of its hurdles.)

In conclusion, one strong argument for a broad interpretation of Article 46 VCLT is that consent to provisional application, when binding, is comparable to consent to be bound in terms of Article 11 VCLT and thus entitled to similar protection. Furthermore, it would only be a limited broadening due the reasons just adduced, so that it is rather unlikely that this broader interpretation would undermine the stability and validity of treaty relations.

6   Summary and Outlook

This chapter has examined the interaction of Article 25 VCLT with Articles 24(4), 18 and 46 VCLT. The interplay with Article 24(4) VCLT was used to clarify the potential scope of provisional application, i.e. to show what treaty provisions can potentially be subjected to provisional application. The interaction with Article 18 VCLT focused on two questions: the first was which role, if any, Article 18 VCLT should have in interpreting the provisional application regime, and the second was how a simultaneous application of Articles 18 and 25 VCLT to the same treaty can be conceptually conceived. Finally, the chapter examined whether and how Article 46 VCLT could be invoked in relation to consent to provisional application. The contribution is meant only as an initial enquiry into an entire field of open questions regarding the legal regime of provisional application in light of the VCLT. Part of the nature of provisional application is that it can amount to a 'prequel' of the treaty prior to its entry into force. This means that questions concerning the applicability of many more VCLT provisions during provisional application can arise or already have arisen – concerning preconditions of provisional application, interpretation, breach and dispute settlement, suspension, amendment or modification, termination and invalidity – and are waiting to be addressed in practice as well as academic writings.

---

[124] To the extent that the limitation clause amounts to a mutually agreed suspension of Art. 27 VCLT, it could be argued that also Art. 46 VCLT, being its exception, is inapplicable.

11

Characteristics of the Vienna Convention Rules on Treaty Interpretation

RICHARD GARDINER

1 Introduction: The Nature and Objectives of Treaty Interpretation

The provisions of the 1969 Vienna Convention on the Law of Treaties (VCLT) on the interpretation of treaties are commonly described as 'rules' though the word 'rule' only appears in the title of the first of these articles ('General rule of interpretation') and in the third paragraph of that article ('relevant rules of international law').[1] Does this general characterisation of these provisions as 'rules' affect the way in which they are understood, applied and criticised? This is difficult to assess, but examination of the main features of the provisions and how they work suggests that even if it may be formally correct to describe the provisions as 'rules', that term must be understood in a very loose sense. It is nevertheless a useful label for the framework and guiding principles which the provisions supply for interpretative reasoning.

In one of the more substantial works on treaty interpretation published in the first half of the twentieth century, Tsune-Chi Yü emphasised the need for a 'scientific' approach to treaty interpretation.[2] Some forty years later, in their extensive study of interpretation of international agreements, Myres S. McDougal and his colleagues Harold D. Lasswell

---

[1] 1155 UNTS 331, Arts. 31–33.

[2] T.-C. Yü, *The Interpretation of Treaties* (New York, NY: Columbia University Press, 1927). Other major works of the same era were: L. Ehrlich, 'L'Interprétation des Traités', *Hague Recueil*, 24 (1928), 1–146, whose study was based in large measure on classic writings in international law; Y.-T. Chang, *The Interpretation of Treaties by Judicial Tribunals* (New York, NY: Columbia University Press, 1933), seeking, at p. 19, 'to treat the subject scientifically' on the basis of case law; and the Harvard Codification of International Law, Part III, Draft Convention on The Law of Treaties, with commentaries at *AJIL Supp.*, 29 (1935), 653–1228, at 937–977, which emphasized the role of the purpose of a treaty in its interpretation.

and James C. Miller propounded what may be viewed as an approach grounded in social and political science.[3] Their conception of an international agreement was one of 'a continuing process of communication and collaboration between the parties in the shaping and sharing of demanded values'.[4] Such agreements were to be interpreted according to elaborate principles of content and procedure which, put in very general terms, favoured admitting anything found helpful in identifying the shared expectations of the parties and analysed within a framework of world public order.

The central questions addressed here are whether Articles 31 to 33 VCLT on treaty interpretation offer a 'scientific' approach and are effective as 'rules' to that end, or are properly viewed more as a combination of general principles, a starting point and a framework.[5] The latter seems the sensible conclusion. For, as Isabelle Van Damme has written of the Vienna rules:

> They reflect a more comprehensive catalogue of principles without purporting to be exhaustive. The general understanding is that treaty interpretation is not simply about the application of Articles 31 to 33 VCLT.[6]

What Yü had simply envisaged was that *all* available evidence should be brought to bear in the task of treaty interpretation:

> There is rather a demand for systematic, uniform recognition of the true source of evidence – whatever may be its form – as the only reliable major premise from which the interpreter is to derive sound conclusions. The fundamental principles of scientific interpretation, therefore, are based on ascertaining the genuine standard through sundry sources of evidence. The skill of tackling the problem lies not in marshalling or

---

[3] M. S. McDougal, H. D. Lasswell and J. C. Miller, *The Interpretation of Agreements and World Public Order: Principles of Content and Procedure* (New Haven, CT: Yale University Press, 1967). This text was re-issued with a new introduction and appendices in 1994; all page references that follow are to this edition. Of the role which McDougal saw for 'community policies' and 'human dignity' in treaty interpretation, Fitzmaurice commented: 'This, of course, however excellent, is not law but sociology': G. G. Fitzmaurice, '*Vae Victis* or Woe to the Negotiators! Your Treaty or Our "Interpretation" of It?', *AJIL*, 65 (1971), 358–373, at 372.

[4] McDougal, Lasswell and Miller, *supra* n. 3, at p. xxiii.

[5] For an interpretation of 'rule' and 'rules' in the VCLT, including a contextual study of use in, or in relation to, the rules on treaty interpretation, see R. K. Gardiner, *Treaty Interpretation* (Oxford: Oxford University Press, 2nd ed., 2015), pp. 35–41.

[6] I. Van Damme, 'Treaty Interpretation by the Appellate Body', *EJIL*, 21 (2010), 605–648, at 619 (footnote omitted).

combining rules, but rather in a keen observation of all the relevant facts and circumstances.[7]

While it may look as if the VCLT provisions are very much about 'marshalling or combining rules', they are not formulaic but merely identify the elements (as they present themselves in any given case) to which interpreters must apply their judgmental skills. Conversely, 'keen observation of all the relevant facts and circumstances' rather glibly passes over what is the test of relevance. Thus Yü is less clear over how to select and use evidence and how to find the standard for scientific interpretation. Duncan French has investigated the circumstances in which a tribunal can look 'beyond the primary text to rules of customary international law, other treaties between the parties, general principles of law, even documents of a "soft law" nature' and has noted that the flexibility which has been developed by tribunals is 'a flexibility that is (i) virtually incapable of strict classification; (ii) seemingly impossible to institutionalize; (iii) occasionally not recognized as anything other than "ordinary" treaty interpretation; (iv) sometimes condemned'.[8]

The proper application of the general rule in the VCLT does not suggest a literal or limited approach. A dictionary definition of a term which is being interpreted is *not* offered as a solution. A definition may provide a starting point, but the very first element of the general rule requires that selection of the general meaning be informed by the context and by the object and purpose of the treaty. Even if it can be argued that this remains a literal approach, in the sense of factors coming from within the treaty itself, further elements of the general rule, such as subsequent agreement, subsequent practice, relevant rules of international law and the supplementary means of interpretation, stand against McDougal's assessment of the Vienna rules as highly restrictive, with an 'insistent emphasis upon an impossible, conformity-imposing textuality'.[9]

1.1 Interpretation, Construction and Application

The starting point for an investigation of the potential roles of rules in treaty interpretation is identifying the nature and objective of interpretation. Humphrey Waldock, as the Special Rapporteur of the International

---

[7] Yü, *supra* n. 2, at p. 202.

[8] D. French, 'Treaty Interpretation and the Incorporation of Extraneous Legal Rules', *ICLQ*, 55 (2006), 281–314, at 282 and 313–314.

[9] M. S. McDougal, 'The International Law Commission's Draft Articles upon Interpretation: Textuality *Redivivus*', *AJIL*, 61 (1967), 992–1000.

Law Commission (ILC) on the law of treaties, endorsed an earlier description of interpretation: 'The process of interpretation, rightly conceived, cannot be regarded as a mere mechanical one of drawing inevitable meanings from the words in a text, or of searching for and discovering some preexisting specific intention of the parties with respect to every situation arising under a treaty . . . In most instances, therefore, interpretation involves *giving* a meaning to a text'.[10]

This contrasts with definitions or descriptions of interpretation centring on 'finding' in the sense of discovering the meaning. The difference between the latter and Waldock's 'giving' meaning to a text is twofold. The notion of *finding* the meaning steers in the direction of scrutinising the text to discern a meaning within it. Secondly, it tends in the direction of looking for the 'original' meaning of that text. While both of these elements play a part in the process envisaged by the VCLT, the notion of *finding* the meaning embodies a much narrower approach than that of the Vienna rules whose aim is better described in Waldock's notion of *giving* a meaning to the text. This is, first, because the principles in the Vienna rules are *not* exclusively 'textual' in the sense of aimed at drawing meaning solely from the text, despite that epithet being critically applied to them. Second, giving meaning is more apposite than finding meaning because the skill of the interpreter lies in deriving from the treaty the appropriate interpretation which words alone may not yield up without further discernment.

Also to be considered in the context of identifying the nature of interpretation is how it differs from application. All that need be addressed here is whether if the meaning is clear there is, as is sometimes argued, no need for interpretation. The first general maxim of Emer de Vattel in his elaborate code on treaty interpretation was that 'it is not permissible to interpret what has no need of interpretation'.[11] In a similar vein, A. D. McNair wrote:

> Strictly speaking, when the meaning of the treaty is clear, it is 'applied', not 'interpreted'. Interpretation is a secondary process which only comes into play when it is impossible to make sense of the plain terms of the treaty, or when they are susceptible of different meanings.[12]

---

[10] *YbILC* (1964–II), 53 (paragraph 1) (words from Part III of the Harvard Codification of International Law, *supra* n. 2, at p. 946 (original emphasis)).

[11] E. de Vattel, *The Law of Nations: Or Principles of the Law of Nature, Applied to the Conduct and Affairs of Nations and Sovereigns* (1758) (C. G. Fenwick trans.) (Washington, DC: Carnegie Institution, 1916), Bk. II, Ch. XVII at §263.

[12] A. D. McNair, *The Law of Treaties* (Oxford: Clarendon Press, 1961), p. 365 (fn. 1).

If the same essential ideas that prompted the observations of Vattel and McNair also underlie the concept of *acte clair*, it should be noted that both in the French system and in the jurisprudence of the Court of Justice of the European Union (CJEU), a finding that the meaning is clear is not a decision that no interpretation is necessary but rather that interpretation *by some other body* is not necessary.[13] Thus the effect is essentially procedural, determining whether the matter is one of interpretation to be referred to another tribunal or simply one of application of an interpretation made by a body which has jurisdiction to make definitive interpretations.

It is difficult to agree with the assertions of Vattel and McNair when one has had the benefit of Waldock's explanation of interpretation as giving meaning to the treaty. Before there can be any application, meaning must necessarily have been given to the terms of the treaty, however clear that meaning may seem or however simple the task of interpretation. It may, nevertheless, be instructive to examine briefly the idea that 'interpretation' is essentially textual and is distinct from a process of 'construction' leading to 'application'. The usefulness of drawing a distinction between interpretation and construction has been much explored in the context of the constitution of the United States under labels such as 'originalist' and 'constructivist' approaches.[14] As well as pointing to possible distinctions between interpretation, construction and application in the context of treaties, this debate between originalist and constructivist approaches carries over into intertemporal issues and evolutionary interpretation in the context of treaties, all of which are considered further in what follows.

1.2   Constitutional Approaches Transposed to Treaty Interpretation

Application of the distinction between interpretation and construction in analysis of constitutional interpretation includes identification of different aspects of textual content. Thus, Lawrence Solum contrasts 'semantic content' and 'legal content': semantic content he takes as 'the linguistic meaning of the text' whereas the legal content is the effect or doctrines

---

[13] For an account of the approach to *acte clair* in France, see F. G. Jacobs and S. Roberts (eds.), *The Effect of Treaties in Domestic Law* (London: Sweet & Maxwell, 1987), pp. 51–54.

[14] For a very helpful explanation of this, and an account of the debate in the USA of this topic, see L. B. Solum, 'The Interpretation-Construction Distinction', *Const. Comment.*, 27 (2010–2011), 95–118.

which the words or provisions produce.[15] Solum's example is the
US constitutional provision that Congress shall make no law abridging
the freedom of speech. 'Freedom' has a readily identified semantic meaning, but its legal content is what has led to a number of doctrines such as
that relating to prior restraint. Prior restraint is not present in the words
of the text, but principles precluding prior restraint in most circumstances have been found to be legal content of the regime envisaged by
the constitutional provision.[16]

A similar approach to problems over the meaning of a treaty has been
explored by Marko Milanovic in the context of the judgment of the
International Court of Justice (ICJ) in *Dispute Regarding Navigational
and Related Rights*[17] that 'commerce' meant only trade in goods in 1858
but also embraced trade in services, such as transportation and tourism,
in 2009.[18] In other words, the term's coverage has become extended to an
activity which was not current at the time at which the treaty was
adopted. '[T]he peril with such reasoning', wrote Milanovic, 'is that in
2050 or 2100 or whenever the word "commerce" might lose any relation
to the meaning of the word today or in 1858'.[19]

Thus Milanovic questioned what we are to do if a word has wholly
changed its meaning and the parties to a treaty are taken as having
intended the current meaning to be applied. Milanovic suggested that:
'The answer to this question lies, again, in the interpretation/construc-
tion distinction, and in the fixation of some core semantic meaning of
a word to the meaning that it had when it was written or uttered'. He
considered that the VCLT does distinguish in some way between interpretation and application, 'but perhaps not strongly enough', while '[t]he
ICJ's ruling above, of course, elides the distinction completely'.[20] Using
the example of the term 'cruel' in human right treaties and constitutional
provisions, Milanovic suggested that the meaning or interpretation has
not changed in, for example, the case of hanging in public or subjecting
juveniles to the death penalty. Such practices may have been viewed as
acceptable in 1789 and 1945, respectively, but are now open to being
understood to be cruel: 'This is not because the meaning of the word

---

[15] *Ibid.*, at 98–99.   [16] *Ibid.*, at 99–100.

[17] *Dispute Regarding Navigational and Related Rights*: Costa Rica v. Nicaragua (2009) ICJ
Rep. 213.

[18] M. Milanovic, 'The ICJ and Evolutionary Treaty Interpretation' www.ejiltalk.org/the-icj-
and-evolutionary-treaty-interpretation/ (14 July 2009).

[19] *Ibid.*   [20] *Ibid.*

'cruel' is different, or because its *interpretation* has changed; it is because our *application* of that meaning has been altered'.[21]

Applying this approach to *Dispute Regarding Navigational and Related Rights*, Milanovic wrote:

> If, however, the term commerce in 1858, then as now, semantically denoted an activity for profit that involves an exchange for money, but the term as interpreted was only *applied* to situations involving trade in goods, as only such situations in fact occurred, then there is no obstacle in construing the term 'commerce' more expansively to take into account the changing circumstances. This, however, has nothing to do with the changing meaning of the word, but with a change in the application or construction of that meaning.[22]

Leaving for elsewhere more detailed consideration of the intertemporal question, does this analysis work in showing a parallel division between interpretation and application on the one hand and between semantic meaning and legal content on the other? It looks very attractive, but one difficulty lies in the idea that 'some core semantic meaning' can be identified and a second in how the beguiling term 'construing' differs from interpreting (though it seems probable from the context that construing is to be equated with the meaning attributed to 'application or construction').

Even where a single treaty term is in issue, it may well not have a single fixed meaning at the time of the treaty's conclusion and may have a considerable history preceding the treaty quite apart from any development, not necessarily unitary, after its conclusion. In the present context, taking the English term 'commerce' as proxy for the Spanish word in the authentic text, it had different senses in the first five of its principal meanings in the *Oxford English Dictionary* (OED), each with a history stretching back at least two centuries before the *Dispute Regarding Navigational and Related Rights* case. The changing uses over some five centuries make it difficult either to identify any core semantic meaning fixed for 1858 or to say that any meaning has been definitively supplanted or finally abandoned since then (although the OED does sometimes identify some uses of a word as obsolete).

The suggestion of a distinction between interpretation and construction is not new. Yü gave critical attention to a study of it dating from the first half of the nineteenth century but found it

---

[21] *Ibid.* (original emphases).   [22] *Ibid.* (original emphasis).

unhelpful.[23] That rules distinguishing semantic meaning and legal content cannot readily be drawn up is implicit in the first element of the general rule of interpretation in the VCLT. This shows a low expectation of finding a single dictionary meaning useful. As noted previously, the general rule in the VCLT provides immediate guidance for selection of the ordinary meaning by reference to the context and to the object and purpose of a treaty. Waldock made this plain at the Vienna conference:

> With regard to the expression 'ordinary meaning', nothing could have been further from the [ILC]'s intention than to suggest that words had a 'dictionary' or intrinsic meaning in themselves. The provisions of [A]rticle 27, paragraph 1 [i.e. Article 31(1) VCLT] clearly indicated that a treaty must be interpreted 'in good faith' in accordance with the ordinary meaning of the words 'in their context'. The [ILC] had been very insistent that the ordinary meaning of terms emerged in the context in which they were used, in the context of the treaty as a whole, and in the light of the object and purpose of the treaty. So much so that, quite late in the [ILC]'s deliberations, it had even been suggested that paragraph 4 of [A]rticle 27 [i.e. Article 31(4) VCLT] could safely be omitted. It was said with some justice during those discussions that the so-called 'special' meaning would be the natural meaning in the particular context.[24]

Where an analysis based on the distinctions between semantic meaning and legal content may be helpful is in drawing the interpreter's attention to the possibility that in the case of a treaty framed in very general terms, the treaty may include its own express or implicit mandate for tackling vagueness and taking account of developments, linguistic or legal. An aspect of this in recent times has been dubbed 'evolutionary' or 'evolutive' interpretation, which is closely related to the idea that in some senses a treaty may be viewed as a 'living instrument'.[25] However, the suggested distinction between interpretation and application or construction does not look as if it provides a simple solution. For this is a point at which the framework provided by the VCLT requires the application of the interpreter's skill and judgment which cannot readily be encapsulated in general rules or principles.

---

[23] Yü, *supra* n. 2, at pp. 40–42 (citing F. Lieber, *Legal and Political Hermeneutics, or Principles of Interpretation and Construction in Law and Politics, with Remarks on Precedents and Authorities* (Boston, MA: Charles C. Little & James Brown, 1839)).

[24] Waldock, United Nations Conference on the Law of Treaties, First Session (26 March–24 May 1968), Official Records: Summary Records, p. 184 (paragraph 70).

[25] See the contribution to this volume of Moeckli and White at pp. 136–171 (Chapter 6).

1.3 Other Attempts at a Distinction between Interpretation and Application

A further avenue for investigating a possible border between interpretation and application is provided by Article 177 of the 1957 Treaty of Rome[26] (now Article 267 of the 2007 Treaty of the Functioning of the European Union).[27] This scheme by which national courts obtain from the European Court of Justice (ECJ) – or, now, the CJEU – a preliminary ruling on an issue of interpretation of relevant treaties and European instruments has been taken as leaving to the national courts the task of application of the relevant provisions in the light of the ECJ ruling. In the early *Bosch* case, it was argued that a request made by the Dutch Court could not be the proper subject of a preliminary ruling because the request was not restricted to a mere question of interpretation but, on its wording, called on the court to decide how the treaty applied to an actual case. The ECJ took the view that even if a request was made in a form which appeared to invite a ruling on a particular case, the Court would have no difficulty in abstracting from the request any questions of interpretation which it contained, and would respond to the request within the limits of its jurisdiction, that is to say, by limiting its ruling to interpretation of the treaty.[28]

However, as the Advocate-General put it in the following year in another case from the Netherlands: 'The limits between interpretation and application are sometimes difficult to distinguish'.[29] One of the Netherlands' arguments in the later case was that whether the chemical in question had been subjected to a higher tariff as a result of reclassification was a matter for application of Dutch law. However, the Court found that the question of whether a provision of the Treaty of Rome had direct application in national law and the question of whether an increase in customs duties contravened a prohibition of tariff increases when charged on the chemical as a result not of an increase in the rate but of a new classification were both questions which clearly involved interpretation of the treaty.

Subsequent cases show that while the Court avoids wording its rulings in the form of application to the particular facts of a case because the question for interpretation is posed in the context of specified facts, the formulation of the interpretation may make the outcome of its

---

[26] 298 UNTS 3.   [27] 2008 OJ C 115/47.
[28] Case 13/61 *Bosch v. Van Rijn* [1961] ECR 45, at p. 50.
[29] Case 26/62 *Van Gend en Loos v. Nederlandse Tariefcommissie* [1963] CMLR 105, at p. 120.

application a foregone conclusion. The approach taken by the ECJ may seem more concerned with the relationship between its jurisdiction and that of national courts, but the idea that interpretation requires giving meaning to a treaty's terms such that they can be applied to a particular case or set of facts is a realistic and functional approach. There is another point of contact between the doctrines of the ECJ and treaty interpretation. The concept of *acte clair* has a superficial similarity to the view expressed by McNair (that when a provision is clear, it is not interpreted but simply applied). However, this seems a blind avenue. *Acte clair* in the European context simply suggests that a fresh interpretation by the ECJ/ CJEU is unnecessary, while McNair's observation seems unconvincing because even if the meaning is uncontroversial, that meaning and the finding of its clarity constitute an interpretation.

Finally, another point at which an attempt was made to distinguish between interpretation and application occurred in the first draft of the provision which became Article 31(3)(c) VCLT. The ILC was presented with a projected draft to be located in the section of the draft articles dealing with the application and effect of treaties rather than their interpretation

> (1) A treaty is to be interpreted in the light of the law in force at the time when the treaty was drawn up.
> (2) Subject to paragraph (1), the application of a treaty shall be governed by the rules of international law in force at the time when the treaty is applied.[30]

This proposal was derived from the intertemporal law principle, and the ILC was not, therefore, considering how a change in meaning of a word might affect the interpretation of a treaty. Opinions were divided in the ILC debate whether there was a useful line to be drawn between interpretation and application in this context and, if so (or in any event), whether the two paragraphs of the draft contradicted one another. There was, however, sufficient unease for the attempt to include something of the sort to be abandoned and the interpretative aspects of the matter to be left to ultimate inclusion in Article 31(3)(c) VCLT and the concept of good faith.[31]

Following on from this description of interpretation, and whether anything useful about interpretation is to be gained by distinguishing it

---

[30] *YbILC* (1964–II), 8–9 (draft Art. 56 – and see Waldock's commentary thereto).
[31] For a fuller account, see Gardiner, *supra* n. 5, at pp. 296–298, and, also, the contribution to this volume of Ong at pp. 710–747 (Chapter 22).

from application and construction, there are several questions to which the answers may provide some indication of the nature and characteristics of the Vienna rules.

2 Questions Concerning the Vienna Convention Rules

2.1 What Do the Vienna Rules Aim to Achieve?

If treaty interpretation is 'giving' meaning to a treaty, do the Vienna rules provide a 'scientific' way of doing this? To suggest that they do seems misleading. Even if they provide indications of *what* is to be taken into account and, to a lesser extent, *how* certain factors are to be taken into account, the rules do not purport to be formulae or algorithms. Once again Waldock's account best expresses the aim:

> The [ILC] was fully conscious . . . of the undesirability – if not impossibility – of confining the process of interpretation within rigid rules, and the provisions of [the draft Articles] . . . do not appear to constitute a code of rules incompatible with the required degree of flexibility . . . any 'principles' found by the [ILC] to be 'rules' should, so far as seems advisable, be formulated as such. In a sense all 'rules' of interpretation have the character of 'guidelines' since their application in a particular case depends so much on the appreciation of the context and the circumstances of the point to be interpreted.[32]

The ILC itself in its Commentary on the drafts which became the Vienna rules noted that the first two of its Special Rapporteurs on the law of treaties had in their private writings expressed doubts as to the existence in international law of any general rules for the interpretation of treaties, but observed:

> Other jurists, although they express reservations as to the obligatory character of certain of the so-called canons of interpretation, show less hesitation in recognizing the existence of some general rules for the interpretation of treaties.[33]

This suggests that caution may be needed to distinguish between 'canons' and 'rules', but the ILC's distinction is not closely followed in practice or in commentary; nor is a clear distinction drawn between principles and rules. 'Canons' is a term which, when applied to interpretation,

---

[32] H. Waldock, Sixth Report on the Law of Treaties, Doc. A/CN.4/186 and Add. 1–7 (11 March, 25 March, 12 Apr., 11 May, 17 May, 24 May, 1 June and 14 June 1965), p. 94.

[33] Commentary on Draft Articles, *YbILC* (1966–II), 218 (paragraph 1).

commonly refers to maxims, presumptions and principles established by the practice of interpreters. 'Rules', as seen earlier, absorb some of the idea of principles while also in practice tending towards guidelines. It is probably more useful to assess the practice than the terminology. Thus after a period of increasing use of the Vienna rules, a more contemporary assessment suggests:

> [T]he structure of Articles 31 to 33 of the Vienna Convention has become the virtually indispensable scaffolding for the reasoning on questions of treaty interpretation, and this despite the intention of the authors of the Convention that it should not establish anything like a hierarchy of rules.[34]

The attractive part of this assessment is its description of the Vienna rules as 'scaffolding for the reasoning'. This is because it conveys the idea of the rules as a structure in some way supporting or ancillary to the substantive reasoning. The rules need to be seen as a system rather than as separate units. The general rule is *not* a sequence of separate rules but was designed by the ILC as a single composite rule, nor is there any hierarchy beyond the very light differentiation between the general rule and supplementary means in the latter's role to 'confirm' a meaning and the more circumscribed use of such supplementary means 'to determine' the meaning.[35]

2.2 Should the Vienna Rules Be Viewed as a Complete Code, or Would a More Extensive Set of Rules Be Useful?

As noted previously, Waldock characterised the draft articles which became the Vienna rules as not constituting a code but as consisting of 'rules' as much in the sense of 'guidelines' as prescriptive precepts. This seems to have been more of a response to a disinclination to go into the topic of treaty interpretation in great detail (if at all) rather than a reaction to the extensive and detailed sets of rules on treaty interpretation propounded by Hugo Grotius and Vattel. In more recent work on the topic, Yü had not suggested anything of the kind. The Harvard draft had only one article on interpretation expressing an essentially purposive approach, while the Institut de Droit International in its 1956 resolution

---

[34] H. Thirlway, 'The Law and Procedure of the International Court of Justice 1960–1989, Supplement 2006: Part Three', *BYbIL*, 77 (2006), 1–82, at 19.

[35] This is the differentiation which the American delegation at the Vienna conference, at the instigation of McDougal, sought to eliminate: see Gardiner, *supra* n. 5, at pp. 349–352.

adopted an approach similar in extent, though not in detail, to that ultimately recommended by the ILC.[36]

Roughly concurrent with the development of the VCLT was the work of McDougal on treaty interpretation. It is impossible to do justice to McDougal, Lasswell and Miller's massive code of principles of treaty interpretation in a short compass.[37] This was recognised by G.G. Fitzmaurice, who described it as an 'arresting and original' book but a 'very difficult work to assimilate and, partly for that reason, to be fair to'.[38] As with the Vienna rules themselves, if one extracts a single element from those designed to work as a set, the result is a travesty of the complete work. To give an illustration of the language and flavour, one could take the section in that book concerning 'Principle of the Largest Shared Audience'. This section, one of many in the chapter on 'Principles of Content', is in fact an extensive treatment of the notion of an 'ordinary meaning' of terms in a treaty, mainly through a review of cases of the Permanent Court of International Justice (PCIJ).[39] Fitzmaurice spots the connection between this principle and its deployment in the chapter on 'Principles of Procedure' where the following observation was made:

> The most frequent application of the lexical operation has been in analyses of the cultural features of the largest shared audiences of particular communications made in the agreement process. In recent years a more general form of this concern has emerged in which the explicit specification of lexical operations in relation to the largest shared audiences has become paramount.[40]

In his generally critical analysis, Fitzmaurice concludes that 'in the ideas underlying this passage, the language of which we have been criticizing, there is much of quite acceptable substance'.[41] What McDougal, Lasswell and Miller appear to be addressing in the principle of the largest shared audience includes the difficulty of identifying an ordinary meaning, the question of whether an ordinary meaning of a term in a treaty means ordinary in general estimation or that of those familiar with or specialists in the topic, and whether one can discern in a conclusion that a provision is 'clear' the genuine ground for the decision. The section concludes:

> It would be pointless to deny that a general consensus can on occasion be achieved as to 'plain' meanings ... Yet there would appear to be

---

[36] Session de Grenade, 19 Apr. 1956 (Rapporteur: H. Lauterpacht).
[37] For a very brief account, see Gardiner, *supra* n. 5, at pp. 71–74.
[38] Fitzmaurice, *supra* n. 3.   [39] McDougal, Lasswell and Miller, *supra* n. 3, at p. 216.
[40] *Ibid.*, at p. 319.   [41] Fitzmaurice, *supra* n. 3, at 368.

a limit to the usefulness of speculative hunches in areas of disagreement as to the 'real' plain or ordinary meanings. A more constructive
alternative would be for decision-makers to adopt a more thorough,
systematic examination of all relevant indices of the parties' expectations and of the significant community policies at stake in a particular
application, and to weigh these factors explicitly in decision. Such
a practice might both block claims of obfuscation or 'cloaking' of the
actual grounds of decision and promote decisions more in accord with
the genuine shared expectations of the parties and basic community
policies.[42]

To some extent, the need for this caution about the role of the ordinary
meaning has been borne out in the era of the Vienna rules but only or
mainly because the reference to ordinary meaning has been extracted
from its context and the totality of the general rule has remained unap-
preciated. While there may be a risk that some interpreters do try to pick
from the Vienna rules elements which cloak conclusions reached by
other means, McDougal, Lasswell and Miller's complaint of the lack of
systematic examination of relevant indices of parties' expectations might
actually be met by greater understanding and application of the Vienna
rules since negotiators would have a better idea of what fate to expect for
their work and interpreters would at least share a framework likely to
direct them to the main 'indices' of expectations.

More recently, Ulf Linderfalk has drawn up a set of rules for treaty
interpretation.[43] This is a detailed study of treaty interpretation resulting in a code of some complexity. As with McDougal, Lasswell and
Miller's work, it would not possible to do justice to it in a brief account
here. It is to be noted, however, that of Linderfalk's code Waibel has
observed:

> It would also have been useful, for example, if Linderfalk had broken
> down the 44 rules into categories and grouped them systematically.
> Moreover, there are too many rules for them to constitute a useful prac-
> tical guide for treaty interpreters – contradicting the practitioner's
> demand for simplicity. When preparing the drafts that became the
> VCLT, the ILC attempted to limit the number of interpretive rules.
> Linderfalk adopts the opposite approach.[44]

---

[42] McDougal, Lasswell and Miller, *supra* n. 3, at p. 252.

[43] U. Linderfalk, *On the Interpretation of Treaties: The Modern International Law as Expressed in the 1969 Vienna Convention on the Law of Treaties* (Dordrecht: Springer, 2007); for an example of one of the rules in this work, see text to n. 66 *infra*.

[44] M. Waibel, 'Demystifying the Art of Interpretation', *EJIL*, 22 (2011), 571–588, at 579.

2.3 Are the Vienna Rules Just a Statement of What Is to Be Taken into Account When Interpreting a Treaty, or Do They Also Give Guidance on How Material Which Is So Identified Is to Be Used?

Much of the content of the Vienna rules appears as specifications of *what* is to be taken into account in treaty interpretation; relatively few pointers are given to *how* these elements are to be used. If the rules are laconic as to the former, they are largely opaque as to the latter. Much depends on how the rules themselves are interpreted. One of McDougal's stronger points at the Vienna conference was how much reliance had to be placed on the preparatory work, and particularly on Waldock's explanations of the product of the ILC's deliberations, in order to understand how the nascent Vienna Convention was to work. McDougal noted:

> In parenthesis, it could be added that the mere presence at this Conference of Sir Humphrey Waldock, in the rôle of former Special Rapporteur, is the best testimony, not always mute, of the impossibility in application of the textuality approach. Time after time during the course of our deliberations, even with the preparatory work of the [ILC] before us, we have found it necessary to appeal to Sir Humphrey for enlightenment about the 'ordinary' meanings of the simple Convention before us. The tremendous clarity he has brought to our deliberations and the enormous influence he has had with us have been due, I submit, not to his skill in flipping pages of a dictionary or as a logician, but rather his very special knowledge of all the circumstances attending the framing of our draft Convention.[45]

McDougal's remark was made at the opening of the discussion of the draft provisions on interpretation. Appeals to Sir Humphrey for enlightenment were not particularly a feature of those debates, though he was invited to respond to points made. However, this was all part of the negotiating process. While it can hardly be suggested that treaty interpretation can rely on the availability of *oral* evidence from those who were privy to the thinking and discussions that led to the treaty, in contrast to what is so often the case, the preparatory work of the VCLT on treaty interpretation is generally helpful. To that extent, McDougal was right. Once reduced to the written record, Waldock's explanations would form part of the preparatory work which, when combined with the

---

[45] Statement of Professor McDougal, US Delegation, to Committee of the Whole, Vienna Conference, 19 Apr. 1968, as reproduced in 'Vienna Convention on the Law of Treaties', *AJIL*, 62 (1968), 1021–1027, at 1025.

ILC's Commentary and the preceding studies and debates, would thus be potentially useful.

What McDougal feared was that the draft articles would relegate such preparatory work to a completely subordinate role.[46] Yet the text of Article 32 VCLT, subsequent practice in relation to it, and the preparatory work relating to it, make clear that McDougal's fears were based on a misapprehension. Interpreters have sometimes found preparatory work helpful in understanding the Vienna rules themselves, and courts and tribunals do not appear to have resisted such resort. However, the Vienna rules are elliptical in places or drawn up in a manner which needs interpretative effort. The misunderstood possibility of using preparatory work 'to confirm' a meaning without the requirement to find ambiguity, obscurity etc. is a prominent example.[47] The ILC also left several matters to be rounded up in the concept of 'good faith', alone or in conjunction with another element in the rules.[48] One example is the principle of 'effectiveness', while the difficulty of including a general rule on time factors in treaty interpretation led to the much truncated provision in Article 31(3)(c) VCLT, and other unresolved matters, being left to the good faith of the interpreter.

A further issue is whether the rules only show what is to be considered rather than how to go about interpretation. This prompts investigation of two matters. First, how are the elements of Article 31 VCLT to be used? Second, does the relationship between Articles 31 and 32 VCLT work? It is easy enough to spot those elements of Article 31 VCLT which refer to material to be used for interpretative purposes. It is more difficult

---

[46] See J. D. Mortenson, 'Is the Vienna Convention Hostile to Drafting History?', *AJIL*, 107 (2013), 780–822.

[47] The ILC may itself have given the misleading impression, in its continuing (and otherwise very useful) work on subsequent agreements and practice, that *any* recourse to preparatory work is limited by the preconditions of ambiguity etc.: ILC Report on the Work of its Sixty-fifth Session (2013), A/68/10, Commentary on Draft Conclusion 1, p. 14 (paragraph 3); but see later ILC Commentary making clear the distinction between use of preparatory work to 'confirm' and to 'determine': ILC Report on the Work of its Sixty-sixth Session (2014), A/69/10, Commentary on Draft Conclusion 7, pp. 184–185 (paragraph 15).

[48] The principle of good faith extends, of course, throughout the VCLT and its role in relation to interpretation of another provision of the Convention has been noted in S. Karagiannis, 'Article 29 (1969)' in O. Corten and P. Klein (eds.), *The Vienna Conventions on the Law of Treaties: A Commentary* (Vol. I) (Oxford: Oxford University Press, 2011), pp. 731–758, at p. 735 ('the *a priori* application of a treaty on the entire territory of a contracting State can be seen as yet another form of the principle of the interpretation of treaties *in good faith* by contracting States (Arts. 26 and 31 of the Vienna Convention)') (original emphasis, footnote omitted).

to detect how this is to be done. For example, is there a difference between the apparently mandatory requirement in paragraph (1) of the article and the statement in paragraph (3) of what is to 'be taken into account together with the context'? Second, can one go straight to the preparatory material where the meaning seems clear on first reading or should the interpreter start with the ordinary meaning of 'take into account', study the relevant practice and any other elements from the general rule and then, if appropriate, look at supplementary means of interpretation? Taking elements into account clearly imports a margin of discretion. Since the elements of Article 31(3) VCLT are to be taken into account 'together with' the context, are those elements on exactly the same footing as the context? A reader of these provisions would note that this paragraph comes under the heading 'general rule' in the singular and that good faith in paragraph (1) applies to the whole operation. Thus the reader would gain an approximate interpretation of the role envisaged for the elements of Article 31(3) VCLT. The assiduous interpreter looking, for example, at subsequent practice would also find within the judgments of the ICJ endorsement of the ILC's statement:

> The importance of such subsequent practice in the application of the treaty, as an element of interpretation, is obvious; for it constitutes objective evidence of the understanding of the parties as to the meaning of the treaty.[49]

However, even taking such considerations together, they leave open sufficient grounds to justify at least seeking to 'confirm' from supplementary means any meaning provisionally reached as to the role of Article 31(3) VCLT or, possibly, even to 'determine' the meaning if its terms are thought to give a sufficiently nebulous account of the role of subsequent practice to leave the position 'obscure'. How much clearer it all becomes when the interpreter finds an explanation in the Commentary which the ILC submitted to the Vienna Conference to accompany its draft articles:

---

[49] *Case Concerning Kasikili/Sedudu Island*: Botswana v. Namibia (1999) ICJ Rep. 1045, at p. 1076 (paragraph 49), quoting from *YbILC* (1966–II), 221 (paragraph 15). In that case, the Court also noted that it had itself frequently examined the subsequent practice of the parties in the application of that treaty, giving a long list of relevant previous cases. The ILC is reviewing subsequent agreements and subsequent practice in relation to the interpretation of treaties; see, also, G. Nolte (ed.), *Treaties and Subsequent Practice* (Oxford: Oxford University Press, 2013) and, further, the contribution to this volume of Buga at pp. 363–391 (Chapter 12).

> The [ILC], by heading the article 'General rule of interpretation' in the singular and by underlining the connexion between paragraphs 1 and 2 and again between paragraph 3 and the two previous paragraphs, intended to indicate that the application of the means of interpretation in the article would be a single combined operation. All the various elements, as they were present in any given case, would be thrown into the crucible, and their interaction would give the legally relevant interpretation. Thus, Article 27 is entitled 'General *rule* of interpretation' in the singular, not 'General *rules*' in the plural, because the [ILC] desired to emphasize that the process of interpretation is a unity and that the provisions of the article form a single, closely integrated rule.[50]

While it is axiomatic, as indicated in this comment, that only where relevant elements are present in any given instance can those ingredients be included in the interpretative equation, it is equally clear that entirely piecemeal use of the Vienna rules was not what was intended. Thus, the first formulation by the UK Supreme Court in *Assange v. The Swedish Prosecution Authority* is out of line with the rules in stating that Article 31(3)(b) VCLT 'permits recourse, as an aid to interpretation, to "any subsequent practice in the application of the treaty which establishes the agreement of the parties regarding its interpretation"'.[51] This very much suggests an *à la carte* approach. Such is quite contrary to the concept of the general rule which does not simply 'permit recourse' as an 'aid' to interpretation. Subsequent practice has a much stronger role than that, for it potentially equates to agreement of the parties as to meaning and thus is authentic evidence of interpretation. Fortunately, subsequent references in the *Assange* judgment to Article 31(3)(b) VCLT do give a more faithful account of the provision.[52]

In fairness, it is easy to see that the bare words introducing the elements of Article 31(3) VCLT do not give a very clear indication of how those provisions relate to the rest of the general rule. This contrasts with the much clearer picture given by the ILC's Commentary of how the rule was intended to work. Does this suggest that the economy of expression in the Vienna rules is misplaced? More probably, it suggests that the rules need to be interpreted in the fuller and more liberal way in which it was envisaged they would apply to other treaties. That, however,

---

[50] United Nations Conference on the Law of Treaties: Official Records: Documents of the Conference, A/CONF.39/11/Add.2, p. 39 (paragraph 8) and *YbILC* (1966–II), 219 (paragraph 8) (original emphasis).

[51] [2012] UKSC 22 (paragraph 67). But cf. *Ministry of Justice, Lithuania v. Bucnys* [2013] UKSC 71.

[52] *Ibid.* (paragraph 106); see similarly paragraph 130 where Art. 31(3) VCLT is quoted.

does not answer the question of how in any given case, having identified the various elements (in the words of the ILC noted previously), their 'interaction would give the legally relevant interpretation'. In the work of the ILC, there are indications that subsequent agreement of the parties, and subsequent practice sufficient to evidence agreement, are to be regarded as 'authentic' interpretation since the parties are the masters of their treaty. Such an agreement could therefore usually be expected to trump other elements in the general rule. In practice, the issue is unlikely to be so clear-cut. Does the general rule allow fairly weak evidence of interpretative agreement through practice to be weighed against ambivalent context for selecting from a number of ordinary meanings? The Vienna rules have left that to the judgement of the interpreter, as in the *Assange* case, but they do at least give a guide to what elements should be considered.

A similar, or even more acute, example of the misleading impression that can be the result of economy of expression or from an over literal reading of a provision is the relationship between Articles 31 and 32 VCLT, and especially the role of the latter. McDougal considered that what he saw as the rigour of the ILC's insistence upon the 'primacy of the text' authorised only 'a minimum recourse to preparatory work'.[53]

The ILC's Commentary on the draft article which became Article 32 VCLT did little more than paraphrase its terms and explain that the word 'supplementary' emphasized that Article 32 VCLT does not provide for 'alternative, autonomous, means of interpretation but only for means to aid an interpretation governed by the principles contained in [A]rticle 27 [now 31]'.[54] In his observations in response to the later debate at Vienna, Waldock was more expansive:

> ... if the door were opened too widely to the use of preparatory work, very real dangers would arise for the integrity of the meaning of the treaty. The [ILC] had therefore considered that those elements of interpretation which had an authentic and binding character in themselves must be set apart in [A]rticle 27 [now 31]; some distinction must be drawn between them and the other elements, although *there had been no intention to discard recourse to preparatory work.*
>
> It was important to bear in mind that, under [A]rticle 28 [32], such supplementary means as preparatory work could be used 'in order to

---

[53] McDougal, *supra* n. 9, at 995.
[54] United Nations Conference on the Law of Treaties: Official Records: Documents of the Conference, A/CONF.39/11/Add.2, p. 43 (paragraph 19), and *YbILC* (1966–II), 223 (paragraph 19). See, further, Mortenson, *supra* n. 46.

confirm the meaning resulting from the application of [A]rticle 27 [31]',
apart from serving to determine that meaning in the cases envisaged in
subparagraphs (a) and (b) of [A]rticle 28 [32]. . . . *There had certainly been
no intention of discouraging automatic recourse to preparatory work for the
general understanding of a treaty.*[55]

This was in line with his earlier report that:

[t]his formulation [the precursor to Article 32] seemed to the [ILC] about as
near as it is possible to get to reconciling the principle of the primacy of the
text . . . with frequent and quite normal recourse to *travaux préparatoires*
without any too nice regard for the question whether the text itself is clear.
Moreover, the rule . . . is inherently flexible, since the question whether the
text can be said to be 'clear' is in some degree subjective.[56]

These extracts from the preparatory work give a better indication of the
range of permitted uses of the preparatory work than the words of the
provision itself. It is perhaps paradoxical that, as with the general rule, the
full flavour of Article 32 VCLT can only be fully grasped with the aid of
the preparatory work. Only the most literal and narrow reading of the
article could justify McDougal's criticism of the then draft rules as
allowing only 'a minimum recourse to preparatory work' and having an
'insistent emphasis upon an impossible, conformity-imposing textuality'.
The words used in Article 32 VCLT – particularly 'confirm' – allow for
much wider reference to preparatory work, as is itself confirmed by the
Vienna Convention's preparatory work. It is not too common for preparatory work to be much help, but the work of the ILC in preparation of
texts for diplomatic conferences stands in a rather special position if the
ILC's drafts are endorsed on the basis of the its commentary and use of
the detailed work of its Special Rapporteurs.

2.4 Does the Idea of Rules Suggest That They Will Always Lead to a Single Correct Interpretation of a Treaty Provision? What Conclusions May Be Drawn as to the Nature and Effect of the Rules from Differing Interpretations Being Placed on the Same Words by Courts and Tribunals?

There are now some instances of different tribunals reaching different
conclusions on interpretation of the same treaty language. On closer

---

[55] United Nations Conference on the Law of Treaties: Official Records, First Session,
Vienna, 1968: Summary Records, p. 184 (paragraphs 68–69 (emphasis added)).
[56] Waldock, *supra* n. 32, at p. 99.

examination, many of these exhibit differences in treaty relations sufficient, at least formally, to distinguish them. One example of quite clearly different outcomes from interpretation of the same term concerns the meaning of 'investment' as a possible determinant of jurisdiction of an 'ICSID' tribunal under Article 25 of the 1965 Convention on the Settlement of Investment Disputes between States and Nationals of Other States.[57] Yet even here, some caution is needed over treaty relations as cases typically address the link between Article 25 and one of the great number of differing bilateral investment treaties (BIT). In very general terms, Article 25 provides for the jurisdiction of the ICSID to extend to 'any legal disputes arising directly out of an investment', while the BITs tend to define 'investment' in detail and contain other provisions relevant to jurisdiction, commonly including advance consent.

Broadly speaking, ICSID tribunals investigating the meaning of 'investment' have fallen into two camps – those which view Article 25 as leaving it to the parties to a BIT to define 'investment', and thus the extent of their acceptance of ICSID jurisdiction, and those which consider that Article 25 has its own autonomous meaning or at least provides some outer boundaries to what falls within the jurisdiction of ICSID. The latter group includes those who have developed expanding menus of criteria of what constitutes an investment, broadly reflecting a 'constructivist' approach. The difference has also been interestingly analysed in terms of textual and teleological approaches.[58] Much depends on what reliance is to be placed on the preparatory work and how it is to be interpreted. However, what is suggested here is that even though different conclusions may be reached on the meaning of 'investment' in Article 25, the reasoning for the differing views is given greater coherence if proper use is made of the Vienna rule. Put in other words provided by Mahnoush Arsanjani and Michael Reisman:

> However much care parties may take to express their commitments with precision and to anticipate the various factual scenarios to which those commitments will relate, the predictability of the application of those commitments depends upon two things: first, upon a commonly accepted canon of interpretation and, second, upon the faithful application of that

---

[57] 575 UNTS 160 (establishing the International Centre for Settlement of Investment Disputes (ICSID)).

[58] J. Fellenbaum, 'GEA v. Ukraine and the Battle of Treaty Interpretation Principles over the Salini Test', *Arbitration International*, 27 (2011), 249–266. See, also, J. D. Mortenson, 'The Meaning of "Investment": ICSID's Travaux and the Domain of International Investment Law', *Harvard ILJ*, 51 (2010), 257–318.

canon by those called upon to construe the commitments in question, whether they be the parties in the course of performance or decision makers resolving a dispute about that performance . . .

International law's canon for interpreting international agreements is codified in the Vienna Convention on the Law of Treaties. Its provisions have become something of a *clause de style* in international judgments and arbitral awards: whether routinely and briefly referred to or solemnly reproduced verbatim, they are not always systematically applied. But a failure to apply the rules of interpretation properly may distort the resulting elucidation of the agreement made by the parties and do them an injustice by retroactively changing the legal regime under which they had arranged and managed their affairs.[59]

Such failure of systematic application of the rules may in part be attributable to continued analysis in terms of very general approaches to interpretation, such as the 'teleological approach' or the 'principle of effectiveness':

Indisputably, the PCIJ, the ICJ, and in their wake, the ECtHR and the ECJ, played a role in the development of the teleological method and the notion of effectiveness. However, this case law was still not widely affirmed at the time when the debates took place in the ILC, and the other interpretative means were generally used cumulatively without any clear line of action standing out.[60]

General approaches and principles have not always worked in favour of reception of the Vienna rules if they have been applied in substitution for a full application of the rules rather than as a harmonious gloss to assist their understanding.[61] Thus heed should be paid to the well-founded critical warning by Arsanjani and Reisman.

2.5   Does the Division between the General Rule and Supplementary Means Constitute a Fault Line in the Vienna Rules?

McDougal, as a member of the American delegation at the Vienna conference, argued for an amendment to the draft articles which would have put the general rule and the provision on supplementary means all

---

[59] M. H. Arsanjani and W. M. Reisman, 'Interpreting Treaties for the Benefit of Third Parties: The "Salvors' Doctrine" and the Use of Legislative History in Investment Treaties', *AJIL*, 104 (2010), 597–604, at 598–599.

[60] J.-M. Sorel and V. Boré Eveno, 'Article 31 (1969)' in Corten and Klein (eds.), *supra* n. 48, pp. 804–837, at p. 812.

[61] On the attention paid to the VCLT by certain international organizations and their associated courts and tribunals, see the chapters in Part II of this volume.

on the same footing. The idea was to ensure that all relevant evidence could be taken into account in the same way. This proposal was rejected. Have the Vienna rules led to relevant evidence being excluded?

As has been noted previously, when Article 32 VCLT is properly interpreted, relevant evidence is not excluded but is treated in different ways according to its relationship to the elements in the general rule. Article 32 VCLT does not only envisage recourse to preparatory work but also to circumstances of the conclusion of the treaty and other supplementary means This is confirmed from the work of the ILC in its commentary, by Waldock's account recorded at the Vienna conference and in his contributions to the ILC's preparation of the draft articles. This included use of preparatory work to help in *understanding* a treaty.[62] It is clear, however, that in many cases, preparatory work is unhelpful and a potentially dangerous source of misinterpretation. It was this, rather than any inclination to restrict the use of preparatory work, which led the ILC to propose the scheme which encourages free use to confirm a meaning but tightly circumscribed use to determine the meaning.

Such a distinction cannot resolve by rule the difficulties which often arise when reading preparatory work. Thus, in *Case Concerning Maritime Delimitation and Territorial Questions between Qatar and Bahrain* before the ICJ, the controversy was in reality about how to interpret the preparatory work rather than over whether to look at it.[63] In the arbitration *HICEE v. Slovak Republic*, the difference of opinion did not stem so much from the Vienna rules as from how to evaluate the material under consideration.[64] In issue was the phrase 'invested either directly or through an investor of a third State' in a BIT between the Netherlands and Czechoslovakia. Did this mean that the treaty applied wherever a corporate investor was the ultimate owner of any affected corporation in the host State, or did 'directly' mean that an investment in a corporation was not protected if the affected corporation was only a subsidiary of a company which the investor owned in the host State?

For the majority, the general rule of interpretation did not establish the meaning of 'directly', but they found help in Dutch Explanatory Notes produced from the respondent's archive which stated:

---

[62] See text accompanying *supra* n. 54 and n. 55.
[63] *Case Concerning Maritime Delimitation and Territorial Questions between Qatar and Bahrain* (Jurisdiction and Admissibility) (1994) ICJ Rep. 112. And see Gardiner, *supra* n. 5, at pp. 366–372.
[64] Case No. 2009–11 *HICEE B.V. v. Slovak Republic*, Partial Award, Permanent Court of Arbitration, 23 May 2011.

Normally, investment protection agreements also cover investments in
the host country made by a Dutch company's subsidiary which is already
established in the host country ('subsidiary'–'sub-subsidiary' structure).
Czechoslovakia wishes to exclude the 'sub-subsidiary' from the scope of
this Agreement, because this is in fact a company created by
a Czechoslovakian legal entity, and Czechoslovakia does not want to
grant, in particular, transfer rights to such company. This restriction
can be dealt with by incorporating a new company directly from the
Netherlands.[65]

Oversimplifying all the rest of the material and arguments, the significant
point is that the majority found the Explanatory Note helpful as supplementary means of interpretation and (effectively) conclusive.
The dissenting arbitrator considered that the context made it so clear
that the contrast in the BIT was between investment via an entity in
a third State and an investment not made that way that supplementary
means of interpretation were not needed. Does the fact that the Vienna
rules were deployed in considerable detail to produce diametrically
opposite results suggest that the rules have little value or that they need
to be much more detailed?

Taking the latter issue first, Linderfalk shows how detailed rules could
be formulated, his rule no. 22 stating that:

> (1) If, by using any ratification work of the treaty, a concordance can be
> shown to exist, as between the parties to said treaty, and with regard to the
> norm content of an interpreted treaty provision, then the provision shall
> be understood in such a way that it logically agrees with the concordance.
> (2) For the purpose of this rule, RATIFICATION WORK means any
> representation unilaterally produced by a state in the process of deciding
> whether to ratify a treaty or not.
> (3) [Defines 'parties'].[66]

This would cover the matter if one uses the analysis of the majority, but
the dissenting arbitrator could still be expected to have included the same
reasoning as he did, to show that there was no 'concordance'. For he said:
'In the end, unlike the Award, I cannot find "a concordance of views
between the two Contracting Parties" that "cannot be denied" ....'.[67]
More detailed rules would only really be helpful if they could be such
as to ensure certainty of outcome. It is likely that any detailed rules would

---

[65] *Ibid.* (paragraph 126).
[66] Linderfalk, *supra* n. 43, at pp. 249–255 and 392 (capitals in original).
[67] See Dissenting Opinion of Judge Charles N. Brower: *supra* n. 64, at p. 41 (paragraphs
26–41).

soon acquire their own interpretation in practice, just as the Vienna rules are doing at present. What the Vienna rules do contribute is help in providing a focus and a scheme according to which an interpreter's reasoning and judgment can be applied.

In its work on the draft articles on the law of treaties, there were several instances where the ILC was offered more detailed rules which became reduced in the process of development of the provisions. For example, in the case of Article 33 VCLT (treaties authenticated in two or more languages), Waldock initially proposed two draft articles: one for identifying relevant languages, the other for reconciling differences of meaning in different languages. Reconciliation involved two principles: first, if a term was capable of being given more than one meaning compatible with the objects and purposes of the treaty, a meaning common to both or all the texts was to be adopted. Second, if the ordinary meaning in one authentic text was clear and compatible with the objects and purposes of the treaty, while in another it was uncertain owing to the obscurity of the term, the former was to be adopted.[68] The ILC's consolidated and reduced text, though amplified at the Vienna conference, did not indicate quite so precise a rule as the second proposed by Waldock. Would such precision have proved helpful?

Perhaps the wisdom of setting out only rather general principles is shown by the situation which arose in *Kiliç v. Turkmenistan*.[69] A core issue was whether proper translation involves interpretation. The authentic text in English was syntactically deficient. It provided that a dispute 'can be submitted, as the investor may choose' to one of three tribunals:

> provided that, if the investor concerned has brought the dispute before the courts of justice of the Party that is a party to the dispute and a final award has not been rendered within one year.[70]

The equally authentic text in Russian, as at first translated into English for the case, worded the proviso in a similar way leaving it unclear whether

---

[68] Draft Art. 75(2) and (3), *YbILC* (1964–II), 62. The issue of whether the term 'preparatory work' can be applied to ILC material which was not included in documents for the conference which adopted the 1969 VCLT is not addressed here: see, further, Gardiner, *supra* n. 5, at pp. 114–116.

[69] ICSID Case No. ARB/10/1, *Decision of 7 May 2012 on Art. VII.2 of the 1997 Turkey-Turkmenistan Bilateral Investment Treaty*; the account here follows Gardiner, *supra* n. 5, at pp. 438–439, but cf. contrary interpretation in *Muhammet Çap v. Turkmenistan*, ICSID Case No. ARB/12/6, 13 Feb. 2015.

[70] *Ibid.* (paragraph 2.10).

there was an obligation to submit the dispute to the domestic courts.[71]
A later translation from the Russian 'made sense' of the provision by
eliminating the word 'if', so that the proviso clearly contained
a requirement to submit the case to the domestic court first

> on the condition that the concerned investor submitted the conflict to the
> court of the Party, that is a Party to the conflict, and a final arbitral award
> on compensation of damages has not been rendered within one year.[72]

The explanation for this changed translation was that the first translation
was simply a literal word-by-word translation, whereas a correct translation would reflect the fact that 'the "if" in the Russian text is part of the
correct syntax needed in Russian to create the conditional, but it does not
create a second or separate conditional'.[73]

Thus the tribunal was faced with a difference of translations. There was
a further discrepancy in that, in Russian, there was a reference to the
Turkish, Turkmen, English and Russian languages being authentic, while
in English there were stated to be authentic copies in only English and
Russian. No texts in Turkish and Turkmen signed by the parties were
produced, though there was an 'official' Turkish language text which
(translated into English) essentially matched the second Russian translation (making reference to a domestic court a precondition). The evidence
at the hearing of the issues over the authentic text and the meaning and
effect of the jurisdiction provision can, at its most favourable, best be
described as unsatisfactory. Put simply, and not in terms used in the
award, it seems that the Russian text could be made clear by 'proper'
translation, while the English text was syntactically hopeless. The tribunal
stated that it considered 'it to be necessary and proper for a translation to
convey accurately the complete sense of the Russian text when it is
translated into English'.[74]

The tribunal followed the general line of Article 33 VCLT, using it as
closely as it could, but had to do so in the face of the difficulties in
identifying the authentic text in different languages and the correct
meaning of the Russian one and in assessing the evidential value to be
placed on the Turkish 'version'. Perhaps all that can be said for what
could be achieved by 'rules' is that Article 33 VCLT may have helped to
establish some distinctions between a text authenticated in two different
languages and what might have been regarded as a 'version' in a third

---

[71] *Ibid.* (paragraph 2.11).   [72] *Ibid.* (paragraph 4.19).   [73] *Ibid.* (paragraph 4.20).
[74] *Ibid.* (paragraph 8.8).

language. Further, the Vienna rules did not prove restrictive in as much as they envisage consideration of 'the circumstances of conclusion', but the very general pointer for reconciling differences between languages was not much help. The key decision of the tribunal seems to have been accepting which translation of the Russian text into English was correct.

3   Concluding Observations

The very first contentious case heard by the PCIJ, the *Case of the S.S. 'Wimbledon'*, showed divergent approaches to treaty interpretation.[75] This could be portrayed as a contrast between the majority's 'textual' approach and the principal dissenters' use of extraneous matter. Oversimplified, this would suggest that the majority found clear and conclusive the statement that '[t]he Kiel Canal and its approaches shall be maintained free and open to the vessels of commerce and of war of all nations at peace with Germany on terms of the entire equality', while the two principal dissenters allowed the rights and obligations of a neutral State in time of war to trump the treaty provision.[76] The majority chose what could be said to have been a literal approach, while the dissenters took a more open approach.

However, neither description is quite right. True, the majority placed the prime emphasis on the text; but the judges evidently thought it necessary, in what was a very short judgment by modern standards, to devote quite some space to consideration of loosely comparable treaty regimes for the Suez and Panama canals and to study the relationship of obligations under those treaties to the law of neutrality. Hence, 'literal' is not a correct characterisation of this approach. Conversely, Judges Anzilotti and Huber in their joint dissent took pains to explain at the outset that they were not investigating whether the international law of neutrality displaced treaty obligations but whether the treaty itself was to be understood as meaning that the particular commitments applied in time of peace only. True, this led to consideration of the law of neutrality, but this was in the context of interpretation of provisions in the text of the treaty.

Would things have been different had the Vienna rules been used? Quite possibly, or even probably, the conclusions of the respective judges

---

[75] *Case of the S.S. 'Wimbledon'*: France, Italy, Japan and United Kingdom v. Germany (Judgment), 1923 PCIJ, Series A, No. 1, 20.

[76] *Ibid.* at p. 21 (referring to Art. 380 of the 1919 Treaty of Versailles, 225 CTS 188).

would have been the same, but at least they would have disclosed arguments and reasoning set in the same framework. For the dissenters could actually have found justification in Article 31(3)(c) VCLT for taking into account the extent to which the parties were beholden to obligations of general international law applying in their relations, while the majority would have needed to explain how the Suez and Panama canal treaties could legitimately provide a supporting role in their reasoning.

The Vienna rules do not aim to provide a 'scientific' approach to treaty interpretation. Describing them as 'rules' may give rise to unhelpful expectations and to a restrictive approach to their use. Hugh Thirlway's description of them as the 'virtually indispensable scaffolding for the reasoning on questions of treaty interpretation' is probably the best analogy to indicate their role.[77] Too much should not be claimed for the rules. Waldock as their architect made no very great claims for them. But since they apply and are to be used, it is as well that they be understood and used properly. Some of the less extreme criticisms made by McDougal would have proved well founded were the rules to be applied in an excessively formulaic way. Practice has shown that the relegation of preparatory work to a supplementary means of interpretation has not greatly restricted reference to preparatory work, though that practice is uneven and Article 32 VCLT is too easily misread. Further, the rules provide some points of reference in evaluating treaty interpretations. As Van Damme observes:

> The value of codifying these principles lies primarily in the fact that they introduce an element of accountability. The (limited) constraints of Articles 31 to 33 [VCLT] on the interpretive flexibility of the adjudicator are justified because a certain level of abstract predictability in interpretation contributes to the resolution of disputes in and outside courts and tribunals, and can possibly improve the drafting of treaties.[78]

A tentative conclusion is that the Vienna rules are now a useful and compulsory starting point for any treaty interpretation, but the need for the exercise of judgement within the framework of the rules takes the task of treaty interpretation well beyond application of rules. The description 'rules' should not be allowed to raise undue expectations and needs to be understood with not only an awareness of the limitations of the rules but also an understanding of their correct interpretation.

---

[77] See Thirlway, *supra* n. 34.   [78] Van Damme, *supra* n. 6, at 620 (footnotes omitted).

12

Subsequent Practice and Treaty Modification*

IRINA BUGA

'[T]oday's rule reflects in part yesterday's deviance; ... the cloth of obligation is partly cut from the pattern of non-conformity.'

– Sir Elihu Lauterpacht**

1 Introduction: The Effects of Subsequent Practice

Subsequent practice is a well-established tool for treaty interpretation that can serve as a guide to understanding the will of the parties,[1] initially aimed at shedding light on their original intention.[2] However, subsequent practice sometimes diverges from the provisions of a treaty to such an extent that it can no longer be said to constitute an act of treaty interpretation but rather one of *modification*. Such divergent practice can potentially also give rise to a supervening rule of customary law. Determining the point when the 'switch' from interpretation to modification occurs is an act of interpretation in itself. It poses difficulty to legal scholars and dispute settlement bodies alike – especially in light of the silence of the Vienna Convention on the Law of Treaties (VCLT)[3] in this regard – and impacts States' expectations as to their treaty obligations.

Treaties, the principal tool for regulating inter-State relations, are more than just dry parchments[4] or codifications of normative relations fixed in

---

* Many of the ideas and themes presented in this chapter are expanded upon in I. Buga, *Modification of Treaties by Subsequent Practice* (Oxford: Oxford University Press, 2018).
** E. Lauterpacht, 'The Development of the Law of International Organization by the Decisions of International Tribunals', *Hague Recueil*, 152 (1976–IV), 377–478, at 389.
[1] J.-P. Cot, 'La conduite subséquente des parties à un traité', *RGDIP*, 70 (1966), 632–666, at 663.
[2] See A. D. McNair, *The Law of Treaties* (Oxford: Clarendon Press, 1961), p. 424 (referring to this phenomenon as 'practical construction').
[3] 1155 UNTS 331.
[4] International Law Commission, Report of the International Law Commission on the Work of its 60th Session, Doc. A/63/10 (5 May–6 June, 7 July–8 Aug. 2008), Annex A, p. 365 (paragraph 1).

time.[5] A treaty is a continuous process – 'at most ... an approximate replica of a living practice, like a picture of a living person'.[6] To stay relevant, treaties must undergo modernisation to reflect technological developments, changing economic and social interests, the proliferation of international institutions and actors and evolving moral conceptions. They must allow for the possibility to redress shortcomings and ineffective compromises by the drafters. At the same time, States often have (highly) divergent interests, making it challenging to reach agreement on specific rules and further politicising the amendment process.[7] This makes formal treaty amendment procedures, especially in the case of large multilateral regimes in fields such as the law of the sea or human rights, extremely cumbersome if not altogether unfeasible.[8] This, in turn, makes it difficult for treaties to be adapted and continue fulfilling their purpose over time.[9]

The informal character of subsequent practice[10] may facilitate such treaty adaptation.[11] Its treaty modifying potential must, however, be examined with

---

[5] R. R. Baxter, 'Multilateral Treaties as Evidence of Customary International Law', *BYbIL*, 41 (1965–66), 275–300, at 299.

[6] K. Wolfke, 'Treaties and Custom: Aspects of Interrelation' in J. Klabbers and R. Lefeber (eds.), *Essays on the Law of Treaties: A Collection of Essays in Honour of Bert Vierdag* (The Hague: Martinus Nijhoff, 1998), pp. 31–39, at p. 35.

[7] Cf. McNair, *supra* n. 2, at p. 534; J.-M. Sorel and V. Boré Eveno, 'Article 31 (1969)' in O. Corten and P. Klein (eds.), *The Vienna Conventions on the Law of Treaties: A Commentary* (Vol. I) (Oxford: Oxford University Press, 2011), pp. 804–837, at p. 807.

[8] See, e.g., M. J. Bowman, 'Towards a Unified Treaty Body for Monitoring Compliance with UN Human Rights Conventions? Legal Mechanisms for Treaty Reform', *HRLR*, 7 (2007), 225–249, at 230-237; J. Arato, 'Treaty Interpretation and Constitutional Transformation: Informal Change in International Organizations', *Yale JIL*, 38 (2013), 289–357, at 355, and C. McLachlan, 'The Evolution of Treaty Obligations in International Law' in G. Nolte (ed.), *Treaties and Subsequent Practice* (Oxford: Oxford University Press, 2013), pp. 69–81, at p. 71.

[9] Similar discussions sometimes apply at the national level. For instance, too rigid a constitution, much like a rigid treaty, can hamper future developments. Constitutional legislators consequently often leave such matters to the sphere of unwritten law and practice.

[10] The term is used here in contradistinction to more formally prescribed 'subsequent agreements' under Art. 31(3)(a) VCLT: *supra* n. 3 (despite the admitted difficulty of precisely distinguishing between the two). In this sense, subsequent practice is taken to refer to the establishment of a *tacit* subsequent agreement. For an example of modification by subsequent agreement, see the contribution to this volume of Ong at pp. 710–747 (Chapter 22) (on the 1994 Implementation Agreement).

[11] Treaties do not have to be amended by means of an instrument of equivalent form or level of formality (thus, the existence of formal amendment procedures in the treaty does not exclude the possibility of modification by subsequent practice): International Law Commission, Draft Articles on the Law of Treaties with Commentaries, *YbILC* (1966-II), 249; M. J. Bowman, '"Normalizing" the International Convention for the Regulation of Whaling', *Michigan JIL*, 29 (2008), 293–499, at 337. Cf. J. Kammerhofer, *Uncertainty in International Law: A Kelsenian Perspective* (Abingdon: Routledge, 2011), p. 134.

caution and never be presumed to ensure that it does not go beyond the actual intention of parties to the treaty,[12] especially in the context of international organizations.[13] There is significant debate as to what type and degree of practice, as well as whose practice, should be able to influence a treaty. In recognition of the need to understand this elusive issue, the International Law Commission (ILC) has taken up consideration of the effect of subsequent practice upon treaties.[14] It was noted that despite its crucial importance, subsequent practice remains insufficiently explored.[15] Clarifying the process of how modification by subsequent practice operates – in other words, clarifying (part of the process of formation of) international law and the means of identifying it – would help, *inter alia*, to more accurately define States' expectations in relation to their treaty obligations and grant courts and tribunals an additional means of assessing the scope of disputing parties' obligations. This is a difficult task in light of the fact that the informal nature of subsequent practice is both its greatest advantage and its most significant drawback. However, these 'difficulties, and the concomitant legal uncertainty, though considerable, are not prohibitive'[16] – on the contrary, they constitute even more of a reason to investigate the phenomenon.

The term 'modification' is taken here to refer to the variation of treaty provisions by means of the parties' *implied* or *informal consent*, as the counterpart to formal treaty amendment. This term was also preferred by the ILC during the drafting of the Vienna Convention, in relation to the (ultimately deleted) article on 'modification of treaties by subsequent practice', discussed extensively later.[17] Formal procedures for treaty adaptation as laid down in Articles 39, 40 and 41 VCLT will be referred

---

[12] See, e.g., A. M. Feldman, 'Evolving Treaty Obligations: A Proposal for Analyzing Subsequent Practice Derived from WTO Dispute Settlement', *N.Y.U. J. Int'l L. & Pol.*, 41 (2009), 655–706, at 699, and S. Kadelbach, 'Domestic Constitutional Concerns with Respect to the Use of Subsequent Agreements and Practice at the International Level' in Nolte (ed.), *supra* n. 8, pp. 145–153. Cf. A. Guzman, 'Against Consent', *Virginia JIL*, 52 (2012), 747–790, at 753.

[13] See, e.g., Arato, *supra* n. 8, at 353 and 355. See, further, Section 2.1.

[14] See most recently G. Nolte, Fourth Report on Subsequent Agreements and Subsequent Practice in relation to the Interpretation of Treaties, U.N. Doc. A/CN.4/694 (2016), and the draft conclusions provisionally adopted by the Commission in ILC, Report of the International Law Commission on the Work of its 68th Session, U.N. Doc. A/71/10 (2016), Ch. VI.

[15] International Law Commission, Report of the International Law Commission on the Work of its 60th Session, *supra* n. 4, at p. 370 (paragraph 13).

[16] M. E. Villiger, *Customary International Law and Treaties: A Manual on the Theory and Practice of the Interrelation of Sources* (The Hague: Kluwer Law International, 2nd ed., 1997), p. 220 (paragraph 349).

[17] See, e.g., Art. 68 in International Law Commission, Draft Articles on the Law of Treaties, *YbILC* (1964–II), 198, and Art. 38 in International Law Commission, Draft Articles on the Law of Treaties, *YbILC* (1966–II), 182.

to as 'amendments' – a possible alternative might be 'revision', but this is often taken to imply large-scale changes to the original text. The term '*desuetude*' will be used to denote a situation in which a treaty (or provision thereof) is terminated by means of the tacit consent of the parties rather than by means of the formal procedures set out in Article 65 VCLT.[18] Moreover, treaty modification by the tacit agreement of *all* of the parties is different from 'modification *inter se*', i.e. between a subset of the parties only (see the terminology in Articles 40 and 41 VCLT). 'Modification' here will be employed as an overarching concept covering treaty change by subsequent practice in general.

First, the meaning of 'subsequent practice' will briefly be explained in light of Article 31(3)(b) VCLT.[19] Second, the role of subsequent practice as a means of treaty modification and its parameters will be explored, supplemented by examples drawn from within and outside of the judicial context. One key aspect is the ILC provision on treaty modification by subsequent practice proposed during the drafting of the Vienna Convention. Lastly, the potential treaty modifying effect of subsequent practice will be compared to that of subsequent customary law to determine the extent of their overlap. The chapter aims to outline certain aspects of the process of subsequent practice to serve the 'minimal ambition of informing practice about itself'[20] and elucidate some of the potential consequences of treaty modification through interpretative practice.

2   Subsequent Practice as a Means of Treaty Interpretation

2.1   'Relevant' Subsequent Practice under Article 31(3)(b) VCLT

The 'general rule of interpretation' in Article 31(3)(b) VCLT prescribes that there 'shall be taken into account, together with the context . . . any subsequent practice in the application of the treaty which establishes the agreement of the parties regarding its interpretation'. Subsequent practice is an established means of treaty interpretation, although its role in the interpretative process varies according to the interpretative policy preferred by different judicial bodies.[21] It also serves as the initial

---

[18]   See Art. 54 VCLT, *supra* n. 3, on treaty termination and, further, Section 3.

[19]   See, further, the contribution to this volume of Gardiner at pp. 335–362 (Chapter 11).

[20]   I. Venzke, *How Interpretation Makes International Law: On Semantic Change and Normative Twists* (Oxford: Oxford University Press, 2012), p. 265.

[21]   For a range of reasons, interpretive policies vary markedly across judicial bodies. See, e.g., O. K. Fauchald, 'The Legal Reasoning of ICSID Tribunals – An Empirical Analysis', *EJIL*, 19 (2008), 301–364, at 322–323 and 348–349; G. Abi-Saab, 'The Appellate Body and

reference point from which to distinguish its application as a source of treaty modification.

'Practice' refers to more than just State conduct in the classical sense; it covers a wide spectrum of acts, statements or omissions, which, to fall under Article 31(3)(b) VCLT, must directly relate to the 'application of the treaty' and – crucially – establish the 'agreement of [all] the parties' to a certain interpretation.[22] This requires at least some of the parties to actively contribute to the practice, and acceptance on the part of the rest – 'qualified passive conduct'.[23] Notions such as 'acquiescence' and 'estoppel' can play a significant role.[24] Overall, the more 'concordant, common and consistent' the practice,[25] and the higher the relevance of the participating States,

---

Treaty Interpretation' in M. Fitzmaurice, O. Elias and P. Merkouris (eds.), *Treaty Interpretation and the Vienna Convention on the Law of Treaties: 30 Years On* (Leiden: Koninklijke Brill NV, 2010), pp. 99–110, at p. 105, and G. Nolte, 'Subsequent Practice as a Means of Interpretation in the Jurisprudence of the WTO Appellate Body' in E. Cannizzaro (ed.), *The Law of Treaties Beyond the Vienna Convention* (Oxford: Oxford University Press, 2011), pp. 138–144, at pp. 139–140.

[22] Practice that does not satisfy these requirements will presumably fall under Art. 32 VCLT (supplementary means of interpretation): *supra* n. 3. Judicial bodies have often applied subsequent practice in this broader sense, without demonstrating e.g. the existence of an agreement: see, e.g., *supra* n. 14, and L. Crema, 'Subsequent Agreements and Subsequent Practice Within and Outside the Vienna Convention' in Nolte (ed.), *supra* n. 8, pp. 13–28, at pp. 17–18 and 27.

[23] M. E. Villiger, *Commentary on the 1969 Vienna Convention on the Law of Treaties* (Leiden: Koninklijke Brill NV, 2009), p. 432 (fn. 69) (adding that 'qualified passive conduct approximates to customary law'). See, also, H. Waldock, Sixth Report on the Law of Treaties, Doc. A/CN.4/186 and Add.1–7 (11 March, 25 March, 12 Apr., 11 May, 17 May, 24 May, 1 June and 14 June 1965), pp. 99 (paragraph 18) and 222 (paragraph 15). It has been argued that subsequent practice can even consist of the practice of one party only: see, e.g., U. Linderfalk, *On the Interpretation of Treaties: The Modern International Law as Expressed in the 1969 Vienna Convention on the Law of Treaties* (Dordrecht: Springer, 2007), p. 166, and L. Boisson de Chazournes, 'Subsequent Practice, Practices, and "Family-Resemblance": Towards Embedding Subsequent Practice in its Operative Milieu' in Nolte (ed.), *supra* n. 8, pp. 53–68, at p. 56.

[24] See, e.g., International Law Commission, Report of the International Law Commission on the Work of its 60th Session, *supra* n. 4, at p. 376 (paragraph 25), and I. Sinclair, 'Estoppel and Acquiescence' in V. Lowe and M. Fitzmaurice (eds.), *Fifty Years of the International Court of Justice: Essays in Honour of Sir Robert Jennings* (Cambridge: Cambridge University Press, 1996), pp. 104–120, at pp. 108–112.

[25] I. Sinclair, *The Vienna Convention on the Law of Treaties* (Manchester: Manchester University Press, 2nd ed., 1984), p. 137 (citing M. K. Yasseen, 'L'interprétation des traités d'après la Convention de Vienne sur le droit des traités', *Hague Recueil*, 151 (1976-III), 1–114, at 48). See, also, WTO, *Japan-Alcoholic Beverages*, Report of the Appellate Body (4 Oct. 1996), WT/DS8/AB/R, WT/DS10/AB/R, WT/DS11/AB/R, 13.

the higher its probative value will be.[26] The International Court of Justice (ICJ) has also stated that time is not in itself a decisive factor.[27] What matters is that the duration of the practice is sufficient to allow the content of the new rule or modification to crystallise and for States to become aware and react, achieving a 'certain stability of practice upon which States may come to rely'.[28]

Although the evidentiary value of certain forms of practice can be controversial – for instance, abstract verbal statements[29] or argumentation in judicial proceedings[30] – a broader definition of practice is preferred, given that 'consent to an international obligation can display the most diverse features'.[31] Moreover, the range of sub-State and non-State actors whose practice comes into consideration appears to be on the rise (notably, Article 31(3)(b) VCLT does not specify whose practice is to be taken into account).[32] The practice of domestic State branches, including national courts – arguably even that of lower-ranking officials as long as it is attributable to the State – falls under this provision.[33] There is also support to include the practice of international

---

[26] *North Sea Continental Shelf Cases*: FRG/Denmark; FRG/Netherlands (Judgment) (1969) ICJ Rep. 3, at p. 42 (paragraph 73) ('states whose interests are specially affected'); see, also, R. R. Baxter, 'Treaties and Custom', *Hague Recueil*, 129 (1970–I), 25–106, at 66, and Feldman, *supra* n. 12, at pp. 697–699.

[27] *North Sea Continental Shelf Cases*, *supra* n. 26, at p. 43 (paragraph 74).

[28] Villiger, *supra* n. 23, at p. 9.

[29] See, e.g., Villiger, *supra* n. 23, at pp. 5–6 and H. W. A. Thirlway, *International Customary Law and Codification* (Leiden: A.W. Sijthoff, 1972), p. 57. Cf. A. Cassese and J. H. H. Weiler (eds.), *Change and Stability in International Law-Making* (Berlin: Walter de Gruyter & Co., 1988), p. 24.

[30] See, e.g., Fauchald, *supra* n. 21, at p. 344.

[31] C. Tomuschat, 'Obligations Arising for States Without or Against Their Will', *Hague Recueil*, 241 (1993–IV), 195–374, at 277. See, further, L. Boisson de Chazournes, 'Qu'est-ce que la pratique en droit international?' in SFDI, *La Pratique et le Droit International* (Paris: Pédone, 2004), pp. 13–24, at p. 14.

[32] Cf. International Law Commission, Report of the International Law Commission on the Work of its 65th Session, Doc. A/68/10 (6 May–7 June and 8 July–9 Aug. 2013), paragraph 38 ('Conclusion 5').

[33] See, e.g., *Rights of Nationals of the United States of America in Morocco*: France v. USA (1952) ICJ Rep. 176, at p. 211; *Case Concerning Kasikili/Sedudu Island*: Botswana v. Namibia (1999) ICJ Rep. 1045, at pp. 1094–1095 (paragraph 74); G. Nolte, 'Jurisprudence of the International Court of Justice and Arbitral Tribunals of Ad Hoc Jurisdiction Relating to Subsequent Agreements and Subsequent Practice: Introductory Report for the ILC Study Group on Treaties over Time' in Nolte (ed.), *supra* n. 8, pp. 169–209, at pp. 197–198, and Venzke, *supra* n. 20, at p. 238. Cf. *Case Concerning Temple of Preah Vihear*: Cambodia v. Thailand (Merits) (1962) ICJ Rep. 6, at p. 30, and G. Haraszti, *Some Fundamental Problems of the Law of Treaties* (Budapest: Akadémiai Kiadó, 1973).

organizations,[34] as separate from that of their constituent States, as 'subsequent practice'.[35] However, even if its basis falls outside the scope of Article 31(3)(b) VCLT, 'institutional' practice supplements 'classical' State practice. Moreover, it could still qualify as relevant practice under Article 32 VCLT as a supplementary means of interpretation. The exclusion of such forms of practice would pose a limitation on the ability to analyse the modifying effect of practice across different types of treaty regimes.

2.2 Subsequent Practice, Evolutive Interpretation and the Doctrine of Implied Powers

The 'evolutionary treaty' approach is of special relevance to the topic of subsequent practice. Rooted primarily in Article 31(1) ('object and purpose', as well as 'ordinary meaning') and Article 31(3)(c) VCLT (other 'relevant rules of international law'),[36] evolutive interpretation

---

[34] It has been argued that the practice of human rights treaty bodies and 'autonomous institutional arrangements' (e.g. conferences of the parties) could also count as subsequent practice: see R. R. Churchill and G. Ulfstein, 'Autonomous Institutional Arrangements in Multilateral Environmental Agreements: A Little-Noticed Phenomenon in International Law', *AJIL*, 94 (2000), 623–659; Bowman, *supra* n. 11, at 332; K. Mechlem, 'Treaty Bodies and the Interpretation of Human Rights', *Vanderbilt JTL*, 42 (2009), 905–947, at 920–921; G. Ulfstein, 'Treaty Bodies and Regimes' in D. B. Hollis (ed.), *The Oxford Guide to Treaties* (Oxford: Oxford University Press, 2012), pp. 428–447, and G. Nolte, 'Report 3 for the ILC Study Group on Treaties over Time: Subsequent Agreements and Subsequent Practice of States Outside of Judicial or Quasi-Judicial Proceedings' in Nolte (ed.), *supra* n. 8, pp. 307–386.

[35] See, e.g., *Legal Consequences for States of the Continuing Presence of South Africa in Namibia (South West Africa) Notwithstanding Security Council Resolution 276 (1970)* (Advisory Opinion) (1971) ICJ Rep. 16, at p. 22 (paragraph 22); *Legality of the Use by a State of Nuclear Weapons in Armed Conflict* (Advisory Opinion) (1996) ICJ Rep. 66, at pp. 74–75 (paragraph 19); *Legal Consequences of the Construction of a Wall in the Occupied Palestinian Territory* (Advisory Opinion) (2004) ICJ Rep. 136, pp. 149–150 (paragraphs 27–28); J. E. Alvarez, *International Organizations as Law-Makers* (Oxford: Oxford University Press, 2005), pp. 88–89; J. Klabbers, 'Checks and Balances in the Law of International Organizations', *Ius Gentium*, 1 (2008), 141–164, at 151–152; Sorel and Boré Eveno, *supra* n. 7, at p. 826 and Venzke, *supra* n. 20, at p. 238. Cf. Art. 2(1)(j) of the 1986 Vienna Convention on the Law of Treaties between States and International Organizations or between International Organizations, ILM, 25 (1986), 543–592, and C. F. Amerasinghe, *Principles of the Institutional Law of International Organizations* (Cambridge: Cambridge University Press, 2nd ed., 2005), p. 53 (on the independent basis of organizational practice). But see, also, *Certain Expenses of the United Nations (Article 17, Paragraph 2, of the Charter)* (Advisory Opinion) (1962) ICJ Rep. 151, at p. 196 (Separate Opinion of Judge Spender).

[36] It should be noted that one of the likely primary purposes of the latter provision was to use subsequent practice to shed light on the parties' original intention, even where the question of evolutionary meaning does not arise. See, also, *supra* n. 2.

can serve the same purpose as subsequent practice, allowing treaties to develop over time. It looks to the parties' original intention to determine whether they meant to allow for the interpretation of the treaty in accordance with new developments[37] – including subsequent practice.[38] Even if it significantly changes the meaning of a provision, evolutive interpretation, unlike subsequent practice, does not amount to modification; it remains bounded by the four corners of the text.[39] Subsequent practice, on the other hand, can elucidate both the original as well as the *contemporary* intentions of the parties and may evidence the parties' agreement to *remove* a textual limit on the evolutionary potential of a treaty.[40]

Evolutionary treaty provisions are less susceptible to modification by subsequent practice. They contain an inherent 'adaptation' mechanism from their inception – even seemingly divergent subsequent practice may be 'read into' the drafters' intention to allow the treaty to evolve and thus be regarded as an element in the interpretative process rather than as a reflection of a tacit modifying agreement. It could be said that the more room there is for evolutive interpretation, the less room there may be for tacit modification by subsequent practice (and, in any case, the more difficult it becomes to draw the line between interpretation and modification).[41] However, subsequent practice can still go further – and impact the treaty more drastically – than evolutive interpretation.[42]

The effects of evolutive interpretation versus subsequent practice were highlighted in the relatively recent decision of the ICJ in *Dispute Regarding Navigational and Related Rights* between Costa Rica and Nicaragua.[43] One of the points in dispute involved interpreting the term 'commercial purposes' to determine the scope of Costa Rica's navigational rights on the San Juan River pursuant to the boundary treaty

---

[37] J. Arato, 'Subsequent Practice and Evolutive Interpretation: Techniques of Treaty Interpretation over Time and Their Diverse Consequences', *Law & Practice Int'l Courts & Tribs.*, 9 (2010), 443–494, at 445 and 466.

[38] See, e.g., *Aegean Sea Continental Shelf*: Greece v. Turkey (1978) ICJ Rep. 3, at p. 31 (paragraphs 74–75); Nolte, *supra* n. 33, at pp. 178 and 188, and International Law Commission, Report of the International Law Commission on the Work of its 65th Session, *supra* n. 32 (paragraph 38) ('Conclusion 3').

[39] See, e.g., A. Orakhelashvili, *The Interpretation of Acts and Rules in Public International Law* (Oxford: Oxford University Press, 2008), p. 291.

[40] Arato, *supra* n. 37, at 482.   [41] Nolte, *supra* n. 33, at p. 207.

[42] R. K. Gardiner, *Treaty Interpretation* (Oxford: Oxford University Press, 2nd ed., 2015), pp. 274–275.

[43] *Dispute Regarding Navigational and Related Rights*: Costa Rica v. Nicaragua (2009) ICJ Rep. 213.

between the two States. The Court acknowledged the doctrines of modification by subsequent practice and evolutive interpretation[44] but chose to base its reasoning solely on the latter.[45] It arrived at the conclusion that Costa Rica's right to pursue navigation for commercial purposes on the river had evolved to include services such as the transport of tourists.[46] It also found that, in accordance with this right, Nicaragua could not require visas for tourists aboard Costa Rican vessels despite its consistent practice of doing so.[47] As Judge Skotnikov points out in his Separate Opinion in that case, Nicaragua's practice of allowing Costa Rica to use the river for tourist navigation would have sufficed to establish the parties' agreement to include services within the meaning of 'commercial purposes'.[48] This could be said to constitute tacit modification by subsequent practice. Moreover, applying the doctrine of subsequent practice, Nicaragua would not have relinquished its right to require visas from tourists on Costa Rican vessels. Thus, the Court's conclusion on the basis of evolutive interpretation led to a broader, more 'dramatic reinterpretation' of Costa Rica's navigational rights than that reached by Judge Skotnikov through subsequent practice.[49] Reliance on subsequent practice would have been 'less speculative than conjecturing about what the parties had to foretell at the time of a treaty's conclusion',[50] minimising recourse to presumptions[51] and providing higher legitimacy.[52]

The implied powers doctrine is also important in this discussion. Much like evolutive interpretation, it constitutes a form of 'dynamic' (teleological) interpretation. It has already been explained that treaties establishing international organizations represent a special case for subsequent practice.[53] Implied powers apply when 'a term is being read into the organization's statute not in order to modify it . . . but in order to give effect to what they agreed by becoming parties to the constitutional treaty'.[54] Thus, implied powers, like evolutive interpretation, provide adaptation mechanisms to ensure that a treaty remains effective without, in principle, modifying it.

---

[44] *Ibid.*, at p. 242 (paragraph 64).   [45] *Ibid.*, at p. 243 (paragraphs 66–67).

[46] *Ibid.*, at p. 244 (paragraph 71).   [47] *Ibid.*, at pp. 257–258 (paragraph 115).

[48] *Ibid.*, at pp. 284–285 (paragraphs 8–10 of Separate Opinion of Judge Skotnikov) and pp. 298–299 (paragraph 16 of Declaration of Judge *ad hoc* Guillaume).

[49] Arato, *supra* n. 37, at 450.   [50] Venzke, *supra* n. 20, at pp. 232–233.

[51] *Dispute Regarding Navigational and Related Rights*, *supra* n. 43, at pp. 297–298 (paragraph 15 of Declaration of Judge *ad hoc* Guillaume).

[52] Nolte, *supra* n. 21, at p. 143.   [53] See Section 2.1.

[54] K. Skubiszewski, 'Implied Powers of International Organizations' in Y. Dinstein and M. Tabory (eds.), *International Law at a Time of Perplexity: Essays in Honour of Shabtai Rosenne* (Dordrecht: Martinus Nijhoff, 1989), pp. 855–868, at pp. 856–857.

Both doctrines rely on powers or objectives established by the original drafters[55] and find their limit in the text of the treaty. Lastly, both evolutive interpretation and implied powers can have far-reaching effects, pushing the boundary between interpretation and modification. The more room there is for an 'implicit' conferral of powers and therefore for 'adaptation' of the constitutive treaty by means of teleological interpretation, the less need there may be for tacit modification by practice. On the other hand, the significant attention paid to the practice of international organizations in the case law and doctrine suggests that these treaties may be adapted by means not envisaged by their founders.[56] One popular example is the tacit modification of Article 27(3) of the 1945 United Nations Charter[57] by the Security Council.[58]

3   Subsequent Practice as a Means of Tacit Treaty Modification

Even treaty regimes with only a small number of parties, such as the North America Free Trade Agreement (NAFTA) with its three States parties,[59] may, as discussed, prove difficult if not impossible to amend by means of formal processes.[60] But as the ILC points out, 'no legal relationship can remain unaffected by time',[61] and it has elsewhere been observed that *pacta sunt servanda* cannot rule out change'.[62] A first, isolated instance that deviates from the text may initially amount to a treaty violation. However, once that first deviation becomes part of a *sequence* of acts, it creates legitimate expectations as States come to rely on the new meaning of the impacted provision. In accordance with the principle of

---

[55] Some scholars thus distinguish between 'implied powers', founded on powers attributed to the organization at its creation, and 'customary powers', attributed subsequently by the parties: see H. G. Schermers and N. M. Blokker, *International Institutional Law: Unity within Diversity* (Leiden: Koninklijke Brill NV, 5th ed., 2011), p. 181 (§235), and N. D. White, *The Law of International Organisations* (Manchester: Manchester University Press, 2nd ed., 2005), p. 71.

[56] See, e.g., C. Brölmann, 'Specialized Rules of Treaty Interpretation: International Organizations' in Hollis (ed.), *supra* n. 34, pp. 507–524, at p. 512.

[57] 1 UNTS 16.   [58] Discussed in Section 3.2.1.   [59] ILM, 32 (1993), 289–456.

[60] Feldman, *supra* n. 12, at p. 656.

[61] International Law Commission, Report of the Study Group on Fragmentation of International Law: Difficulties arising from the Diversification and Expansion of International Law, Finalized by Martti Koskenniemi, U.N. Doc. A/CN.4/L.682 (2006), p. 241 (paragraph 476).

[62] Villiger, *supra* n. 16, at pp. 211–212, (paragraph 332). See, also, D. B. Hollis, 'Introduction' in Hollis (ed.), *supra* n. 34, pp. 1–10, at p. 2, and M. Byers, *Custom, Power and the Power of Rules: International Relations and Customary International Law* (Cambridge: Cambridge University Press, 1999), pp. 176–177.

good faith, the legitimate expectations of other parties shall be honoured.[63]

The potential modifying effect of subsequent practice was already acknowledged by the ILC during the drafting of the Vienna Convention.[64] The process has also been taken note of in the context of the recent discussions on subsequent practice,[65] which, at the time of writing, were ongoing.[66] Tacit modification by subsequent practice has been recognised by various international dispute settlement bodies.[67] Even national courts have taken up the issue.[68] Moreover, the majority of international law scholars recognise the process of modification by subsequent practice,[69]

---

[63] Villiger, *supra* n. 23, at p. 426.   [64] See Section 3.2 for a detailed discussion.

[65] Fragmentation Report, *supra* n. 61, at p. 116 (fn. 288).

[66] See, in particular ILC, Report on the Work of its 68th Session, U.N. Doc. A/71/10 (2016), Ch. VI, pp. 121–122 ('Conclusion 7', paragraph 3).

[67] See, e.g., *Dispute Regarding Navigational and Related Rights*, *supra* n. 43, at p. 242 (paragraph 64); *Case Concerning the Land and Maritime Boundary between Cameroon and Nigeria*: Cameroon v. Nigeria (Equatorial Guinea intervening) (2002) ICJ Rep. 303, at pp. 353–354 (paragraph 68); *Case Concerning the Land, Island and Maritime Frontier Dispute (El Salvador/ Honduras; Nicaragua intervening)* (1992) ICJ. Rep. 350, at pp. 408–409 (paragraph 80); *Air Transport Services Agreement Arbitration*: USA v. France, ILR, 38 (1969), 182–260, at pp. 249, 253 and 259; *Interpretation of the Air Transport Services Agreement between the United States and Italy*, RIAA, Vol. XVI, 75–108, at p. 100; *Arbitral Award in the Dispute Concerning Certain Boundary Pillars between the Arab Republic of Egypt and the State of Israel (Taba Arbitration)*, ILM, 27 (1988), 1421–1538, at 1481–1482 and 1489–1490 (paragraphs 209–210 and 235); *Decision Regarding Delimitation of the Border between Eritrea and Ethiopia*, RIAA, Vol. XXV, 83–195, at pp. 110–111 (paragraphs 3.6–3.10); *Soering v. UK*, App. No. 14038/88, Judgment of 7 July 1989 (paragraphs 103–104); *Öcalan v. Turkey*, App. No. 46221/99, Judgment of 12 March 2003 (paragraphs 196 and 198); *Öcalan v. Turkey*, App. No. 46221/99, Judgment of the Grand Chamber of 12 May 2005 (paragraph 163); *Al-Saadoon and Mufdhi v. UK*, App. No. 61498/08, Judgment of 2 March 2010 (paragraph 119); *Hassan v. United Kingdom*, App. No. 29750/09, Judgment of the Grand Chamber of 16 Sept. 2014 (paragraph 101), and Iran-US Claims Tribunal, *Islamic Republic of Iran v. United States of America*, Interlocutory Award No. ITL 83-B1-FT, 9 Sept. 2004, 2004 WL 2210709 (paragraph 132).

[68] See, e.g., German Federal Constitutional Court, Case Nos. 2 BvE 3/92, 5/93, 7/93 and 8/93 *1994 International Military Operations Case*, ILR, 106 (1997), 319–352, at 338.

[69] See, e.g., G. Fitzmaurice, 'The Law and Procedure of the International Court of Justice 1951–4: Treaty Interpretation and Other Treaty Points', BYbIL, 33 (1957), 203–293, at 225; Haraszti, *supra* n. 33, at pp. 143–145; M. Akehurst, 'The Hierarchy of the Sources of International Law', BYbIL, 47 (1975), 273–285, at 277; Yasseen, *supra* n. 25, at 51; Sinclair, *supra* n. 25, at p. 138; G. Di Stefano, 'La Pratique subséquente des états parties à un traité', AFDI, 40 (1994), 41–71, at 54–67; Wolfke, *supra* n. 6, at pp. 34–35; A. Aust, *Modern Treaty Law and Practice* (Cambridge: Cambridge University Press, 3rd ed., 2013), p. 264; Linderfalk, *supra* n. 23, at p. 168; M. Shaw, 'Title, Control, and Closure? The Experience of the Eritrea-Ethiopia Boundary Commission', ICLQ, 56 (2007), 755–796, at 776–777; Gardiner, *supra* n. 42, at pp. 243–245; Villiger, *supra* n. 23, at p. 429; Arato, *supra* n. 37, at 464; J. Harrison, *Making the Law of the Sea: A Study in the Development of International*

some of whom have even pointed to its customary law status.[70]

There is, however, debate as to how far such modifications can extend – can they go so far as to affect a treaty's object and purpose? The answer to this latter question appears to be affirmative,[71] subject to the critical limitations discussed in Section 3.2.[72] States may, for example, want to retain an existing treaty framework and its accompanying infrastructure but pursue new objectives. For instance, the 'new strategic concept' of the North Atlantic Treaty Organization (NATO) appears to go beyond the original purpose of the 1949 North Atlantic Treaty[73] – collective defence and deterrence oriented towards the Soviet Union. NATO's adaptation to a broad range of global issues and security tasks in recent years may indicate a marked modification by subsequent practice of its original mandate[74] – a question that has also

Law (Cambridge: Cambridge University Press, 2011), p. 95, and P. Sands, 'Article 39 (1969)' in Corten and Klein (eds.), Vol. II, supra n. 7, pp. 963–976, at p. 972.

[70] See, e.g., F. G. Jacobs, 'Varieties of Approach to Treaty Interpretation: With Special Reference to the Draft Convention on the Law of Treaties before the Vienna Diplomatic Conference', ICLQ, 18 (1969), 318–346, at 332; W. Karl, Vertrag und Spätere Praxis im Völkerrecht (Berlin: Springer, 1983), pp. 292–293, and J. Pauwelyn, Conflict of Norms in Public International Law: How WTO Law Relates to Other Rules of International Law (Cambridge: Cambridge University Press, 2003), p. 50. See, also, Summary Records of the Plenary Meetings and of the Meetings of the Committee of the Whole, U.N. Conference on the Law of Treaties, 1st Session (1968), U.N. Doc. A/CONF.39/C.1/SR.38, 211, 214 [38th Meeting of the Committee of the Whole].

[71] G. Fitzmaurice, 'The Law and Procedure of the International Court of Justice: Treaty Interpretation and Certain Other Treaty Points', BYbIL, 28 (1951), 1–28, at 8 (fn. 2) ('emergent purpose'); Fitzmaurice, supra n. 69, at 208; S. Rosenne, Developments in the Law of Treaties 1945–1986 (Cambridge: Cambridge University Press, 1989), p. 240; T. Sato, Evolving Constitutions of International Organizations (The Hague: Kluwer Law International, 1996), p. 33 and Bowman, supra n. 11, at 340–342 (citing the Ramsar Convention and the mandate of the World Organization for Animal Health as examples).

[72] For instance, modification should not 'disrupt the balance established under the general treaty between the rights and obligations of States parties thereto': see S. A. Sadat-Akhavi, Methods of Resolving Conflicts between Treaties (Leiden: Koninklijke Brill NV, 2003), p. 131, cited in Fragmentation Report, supra n. 61, at pp. 59–60 (paragraph 109). As with situations where formal amendment procedures have been triggered, the object and purpose will, in any case, carry implications for the threshold necessary for practice to establish agreement of the parties to the modification.

[73] 34 UNTS 243.

[74] See, e.g., L. Condorelli, 'Conclusions générales' in SFDI, La pratique et le droit international, supra n. 31, pp. 285–306, at p. 304; R. D. Asmus and R. C. Holbrooke, Re-reinventing NATO (Riga Papers) (Washington, DC: German Marshall Fund of the United States, 2006); S. C. Hofmann, Debating Strategy in NATO: Obstacles to Defining a Meaningful New Strategic Concept (Paris: Institut Français des Relations Internationales, 2008), pp. 1–4 and 11. Cf. C. Brölmann, 'Specialized Rules of Treaty

surfaced in national proceedings.[75] Similarly, the original purpose of the 1946 International Convention for the Regulation of Whaling[76] may have changed over time from a focus on sustainable management of resources to conservation in a broader sense.[77]

If subsequent practice can modify treaty provisions by means of a tacit agreement, it is also capable of tacitly terminating them – after all, 'amendment merges into termination at one extreme and into interpretation at the other'.[78] One must distinguish modification, which 'necessarily implies desuetude of the original conventional rule', and 'desuetude of a conventional rule alone, without substitution'.[79] The ILC has defined desuetude as 'the consent of the parties to abandon the treaty, which is to be implied from their conduct in relation to the treaty'.[80] It is the underlying agreement of the parties to terminate the treaty (or certain of its provisions), not the age[81] or prolonged non-application[82] of the instrument (although these are relevant factors in assessing the parties' intentions), that constitutes the basis for termination.[83] The same applies when a treaty falls into desuetude as a result of new customary law: it is not the customary norm as such that terminates the treaty provisions but rather the underlying consent of the treaty parties. During the drafting of the Vienna Convention, the ILC made clear that desuetude is already covered by Article 54(b) VCLT, according to which tacit termination can take place 'at any time by consent of all the parties after consultation with the other

---

Interpretation: International Organizations' in Hollis (ed.), *supra* n. 34, pp. 507–524, at p. 523. However, see G. Nolte, 'Die "neuen Aufgaben" von NATO und WEU: Völker- und verfassungsrechtliche Fragen', *ZaöRV*, 54 (1994), 95–123.

[75] German Federal Constitutional Court, Case No. 2 BvE 6/99 *PDS v. Federal Government*, 22 Nov. 2001, 104 at 151.

[76] 161 UNTS 72.   [77] See, e.g., Bowman, *supra* n. 11.   [78] Akehurst, *supra* n. 69, at 277.

[79] Villiger, *supra* n. 16, at pp. 206–208 (paragraphs 324 and 326).

[80] *YbILC* (1966-II), 237. Cf. M. G. Kohen, 'Desuetude and Obsolescence of Treaties' in Cannizzaro (ed.), *supra* n. 21, pp. 350–359, at pp. 351–352.

[81] Kohen, *supra* n. 80, at p. 355.

[82] There may be other explanations for the lack of application of a treaty, e.g. special political considerations or inertia, or simply the lack of occasion to apply it: *ibid.*, at pp. 356–357. It could even be argued that the lack of new practice confirms the treaty's continued relevance: *Nuclear Tests*: Australia v. France (1974) ICJ Rep. 253, at p. 381 (fn. 1) (Dissenting Opinion of Judge de Castro).

[83] Even the mutual non-compliance of parties to a bilateral treaty may be insufficient to terminate it: T. Giegerich, 'Article 54' in O. Dörr and K. Schmalenbach (eds.), *Vienna Convention on the Law of Treaties: A Commentary* (Berlin: Springer, 2012), pp. 945–962, at pp. 958–959 (paragraph 40), referring to *Case Concerning Gabčikovo-Nagymaros Project (Hungary/Slovakia)* (1997) ICJ Rep. 7, at p. 68 (paragraph 114).

contracting States'.[84] The parties can choose to do so implicitly – the ILC substituted 'agreement' with 'consent' in Article 54(b) precisely to allow for this possibility[85] – as long as the other parties become informed in good time.[86]

3.1   The Deleted ILC Article on Modification by Subsequent Practice

The ILC's *travaux préparatoires* of the Vienna Convention reveal that the process of treaty modification through subsequent practice had originally been included in Article 68 of the 1964 ILC Draft and subsequently in Article 38 of the 1966 ILC Draft.[87] In its final version, the article read: 'A treaty may be modified by subsequent practice in the application of the treaty establishing the agreement of the parties to modify its provisions'. ILC members did not much question the substance of this provision; prior versions had been adopted with widespread support.[88] Most agreed that it reflected 'long-standing and widely accepted practice'.[89] Their focus was mainly on the accuracy of its formulation, which was 'couched in general terms',[90] and on figuring out a proper place for it in the draft articles, in light of overlap with provisions on interpretation through subsequent practice,[91] formal amendment[92] and subsequent customary law.[93] The debates did not bring into doubt the principle of modification.[94]

At the 1968 session of the UN Conference on the Law of Treaties, however, a majority of State representatives expressed opposition to the article. One recurring argument was that it was indistinguishable in effect from Article 27(3)(b) – now Article 31(3)(b) VCLT – on interpretation

---

[84] *Supra* n. 3.   [85] *YbILC* (1966–I) (paragraph 94).

[86] *YbILC* (1966–II), 236; Villiger, *supra* n. 16, at p. 199–200 (paragraph 312); V. Chapaux, 'Article 54 (1969)' in Corten and Klein (eds.), Vol. II, *supra* n. 7, pp. 1236–1245, at p. 1244, and Giegerich, *supra* n. 83, at pp. 958–960 (paragraphs 40–44).

[87] See *supra* n. 17.   [88] See, e.g., *YbILC* (1964–I), 318 (paragraphs 45 and 49).

[89] Waldock, Sixth Report on the Law of Treaties, *supra* n. 23, at p. 88 (United States).

[90] *YbILC* (1966–I), 112 (paragraph 3). See, also, H. Waldock, Third Report on the Law of Treaties, Doc. A/CN.4/167 and Add.1–3 (3 March, 9 June, 12 June and 7 July 1964), p. 61 (paragraph 32).

[91] See, e.g., Waldock, Sixth Report on the Law of Treaties, *supra* n. 23, at p. 87, and *YbILC* (1966–I), 165 (paragraphs 26–27).

[92] See, e.g., *YbILC* (1966–I), 113 (paragraphs 9, 12 and 16) and 165–168 (paragraphs 31, 37, 55 and 61).

[93] See, e.g., Waldock, Third Report on the Law of Treaties, *supra* n. 90, at p. 62 (paragraph 33).

[94] Villiger, *supra* n. 16, at pp. 196–197 (paragraphs 306–307 and 310).

by subsequent practice.[95] Some feared modification by subsequent practice would circumvent domestic treaty approval procedures.[96] Another issue that was raised concerned the provision's lack of specificity.[97] It was feared that, unlike formal procedures, this would lead to uncertainty.[98] Many delegates at the time may not have been able to fully appreciate the necessity of overcoming obstacles to formal amendments.[99] Article 38 did contain certain safeguards: *all* the parties had to have accepted the practice, and 'certain delegations were not taking account of the final words "establishing the agreement of the parties to modify its provisions"'.[100] Humphrey Waldock also remarked that if more time had been available, the Commission might have re-examined the topic and drafted a more specific provision.[101] His statement speaks to the underlying value of the provision and to the mainly practical rather than substantive reasons on account of which it was considered problematic and deleted from the Vienna Convention.[102]

The article was ultimately excluded from the Vienna Convention, mainly on account of its overlap with other articles[103] and because it triggered questions deemed too difficult or risky to tackle under the heavy time constraints faced at the time.[104] Its exclusion has not detracted from the importance of subsequent practice as a source of dynamic evolution of the law, lying just beyond the sphere of the Vienna Convention.

---

[95] *Supra* n. 3. See, e.g., Summary Records of the Plenary Meetings and of the Meetings of the Committee of the Whole, U.N. Conference on the Law of Treaties, 1st Session (1968), U.N. Doc. A/CONF.39/C.1/SR.37 [37th Meeting of the Committee of the Whole] (paragraphs 57, 59 and 66) and 38th Meeting of the Committee of the Whole, *supra* n. 70 (paragraphs 28 and 48).

[96] 37th Meeting of the Committee of the Whole, *supra* n. 95 (paragraphs 63 and 68) and 38th Meeting of the Committee of the Whole, *supra* n. 70 (paragraphs 1, 17, 21, 36, 41 and 43; cf. paragraph 57).

[97] *Ibid.* (paragraphs 60–62) and 38th Meeting of the Committee of the Whole, *supra* n. 70 (paragraph 15).

[98] 38th Meeting of the Committee of the Whole, *supra* n. 70 (paragraphs 31 and 40–42).

[99] *Ibid.* (paragraph 53).

[100] *Ibid.* (paragraph 55) (Waldock). See, also, *YbILC* (1966–I), 219 (paragraph 31) and Feldman, *supra* n. 12, at pp. 671–672.

[101] 38th Meeting of the Committee of the Whole, *supra* n. 70 (paragraph 55).

[102] International Law Commission, Report of the International Law Commission on the Work of its 62nd Session, Doc. A/65/10 (3 May–4 June and 5 July–6 Aug. 2010), paragraph 352.

[103] See *supra* n. 91, n. 92 and n. 93 and accompanying text.

[104] I. Voicu, *De l'interprétation authentique des traités internationaux* (Paris: Pédone, 1968), p. 94.

3.2   Distinguishing Modification from Interpretation

Subsequent practice is a complex, multi-faceted issue because it covers so many areas and underlying principles of law. Tacit modifications cannot be deduced by means of abstract criteria. There is an array of factors at play to be applied on a case-by-case basis. The greatest difficulty lies in the fact that the processes of interpretation and modification by subsequent practice may seem indistinguishable in practice, but have very different legal effects. For instance, it has been argued that modifications could be considered to constitute an integral part of the treaty, with automatic legal effect in all situations in which the treaty is applied, whereas the parties' agreement to a given interpretation '*may* have a legal effect ... limited to the particular case at hand'.[105] If, on the other hand, a modification by subsequent practice is regarded as an *independent* source of legal obligation, a treaty may no longer constitute the basis of a dispute invoked pursuant to that treaty's compromissory clause, which can impact the ability of designated judicial bodies to assert jurisdiction.[106] Moreover, pursuant to the principle of non-retroactivity, a modification, unlike an interpretation, may not apply in a dispute in which the provision at issue was modified subsequent to the initiation of the proceedings.

A further complication is that States usually prefer that their practice be regarded as interpretation, especially where an organization like the United Nations or the World Trade Organization is involved – thus, tacit modification is often likely to take place under the guise of interpretative practice.[107] Moreover, dispute settlement bodies seem disinclined to acknowledge tacit modification by subsequent practice (with notable exceptions),[108] most likely due to the perception that States are wary of judicial bodies using tacit modification as a way of changing the law.[109] Instead, they often prefer recourse to alternative adaptation mechanisms, such as evolutive interpretation,[110] and favour explicit treaty rules over the more contentious process of identifying new customary law or implied agreement by

---

[105] Linderfalk, *supra* n. 23, at p. 168.

[106] See, e.g., *Arbitration Concerning Heathrow Airport User Charges (US v. UK)*, RIAA, Vol. XXIV, 1–359, at p. 59 (paragraph 6.8); Nolte, *supra* n. 33, at pp. 207–208, and J. Crawford, 'A Consensualist Interpretation of Article 31(3) of the Vienna Convention on the Law of Treaties' in Nolte (ed.), *supra* n. 8, pp. 29–33, at p. 33.

[107] See, e.g., Voicu, *supra* n. 104, at p. 89; Akehurst, *supra* n. 66, at 204, and Orakhelashvili, *supra* n. 39, at p. 105.

[108] See *supra* n. 67.

[109] S. D. Murphy, 'The Relevance of Subsequent Agreement and Subsequent Practice for the Interpretation of Treaties' in Nolte (ed.), *supra* n. 8, pp. 82–94, at pp. 83 and 87.

[110] See, e.g., *Costa Rica v. Nicaragua*, *supra* n. 43, discussed in Section 2.2.

subsequent practice.[111] Even when dispute settlement bodies do explicitly recognise a tacit modification, they fail to provide generalisable criteria for identifying it.[112]

3.2.1   The 'Natural and Ordinary Meaning' as the Point of Departure

The fact that the boundary between interpretative and modifying practice is often blurred does not mean that it cannot be established. This applies by analogy to determining whether an interpretative declaration to a treaty (purporting mainly to 'specify and clarify')[113] is actually a reservation in disguise (with the effect to 'exclude or modify').[114] The interpreter must examine the statement's substance and context to make the distinction.

A first step according to the ILC is to determine whether practice diverges significantly from the 'natural and ordinary meaning' of the provisions.[115] But the line between interpretation and modification can be blurred even when dealing with seemingly clear terms or situations.[116] For instance, the ICJ's *Wall* advisory opinion involved the interpretation of Article 12(1) of the United Nations Charter. The Court considered the 'increasing tendency' of the General Assembly and Security Council to 'deal in parallel with the same matter concerning the maintenance of international peace and security',[117] in particular with regard to 'recommendations',[118] as consistent with Article 12(1) of the Charter[119] – despite the fact that this practice is contrary to the clear wording of the article, which specifically precludes the General Assembly from making recommendations with regard to any dispute or situation in respect of which the Security Council is exercising the functions assigned to it under the Charter. This may indicate a tacit modification of the

---

[111] Pauwelyn, *supra* n. 70, at p. 141.   [112] See cases mentioned at *supra* n. 67.

[113] International Law Commission, Report on the Work of its 59th Session, Doc. A/62/10 (7 May–5 June, 9 July–10 Aug. 2007), p. 48.

[114] Art. 2(1)(d) VCLT: *supra* n. 3.

[115] Waldock, Third Report on the Law of Treaties, *supra* n. 90, at p. 61 (paragraph 25). See, also, *YbILC* (1964–II), 75.

[116] See, e.g., *Legal Consequences for States of the Continuing Presence of South Africa in Namibia, supra* n. 35; *Temple of Preah Vihear: supra* n. 33; *Eritrea-Ethiopia Arbitration, supra* n. 67, and *Taba Arbitration, supra* n. 67, as discussed previously. See, further, Nolte, *supra* n. 33, at p. 202.

[117] *Legal Consequences of the Construction of a Wall, supra* n. 35, at pp. 149–150 (paragraph 27).

[118] *Ibid.*, at pp. 148–152 (paragraphs 25–33).   [119] *Ibid.*, at p. 150 (paragraph 28).

Charter,[120] although the Court avoided construing it as anything more than 'accepted practice' amounting to an exercise of interpretation. Likewise, in the *Temple of Preah Vihear Case*,[121] there was a manifest divergence between the boundary line accepted by the parties in their subsequent practice and the one laid down in the bilateral treaty. The ICJ held that the subsequent practice, which was clearly at variance with the ordinary meaning of the text, constituted an authentic interpretation that prevailed over the relevant treaty clause. It did not refer to an outright modification. However, authentic interpretations constitute new legal enactments rather than mere interpretations.[122] The *Temple* judgment was also used by the ILC in support of the draft article on treaty modification by subsequent practice discussed earlier.[123]

As an example unrelated to judicial proceedings, subsequent practice seems to have expanded the definition of 'migratory species' under Article I(1)(a) of the Convention on Migratory Species (CMS)[124] to include species that become non-migratory due to climate change and certain classical sedentary species subject to 'transboundary, climate-induced range shifts', which are, *stricto sensu*, not covered by the Convention.[125] This seems to imply a broadening of the scope of the CMS regime to such an extent that it could arguably even affect the treaty's object and purpose – namely, to conserve *migratory* species.[126] In any case, it provides strong indication of a modification of Article I(1)(a) CMS by means of subsequent practice.

The ILC's approach of taking the text as the main point of departure also fails to account for the issue of ambiguous provisions – the wider the range of interpretations available, the more difficult it will be to tell when

---

[120] See, e.g., J. Liang, 'Modifying the UN Charter through Subsequent Practice: Prospects for the Charter's Revitalisation', *Nordic JIL*, 81 (2012), 1–20, at 10; Nolte, *supra* n. 33, at p. 180 and 201–202, and Arato, *supra* n. 8, at 326–327.

[121] *Temple of Preah Vihear*, *supra* n. 33, at p. 33.

[122] See, e.g., Waldock, Sixth Report on the Law of Treaties, *supra* n. 23, at p. 89 (paragraph 8); Orakhelashvili, *supra* n. 39, at p. 515, and Karl, *supra* n. 70, at p. 46.

[123] Waldock, Sixth Report on the Law of Treaties, *supra* n. 23, at p. 90 (paragraph 8).

[124] 1651 UNTS 333.

[125] M. J. Bowman, P. G. G. Davies and C. J. Redgwell, *Lyster's International Wildlife Law* (Cambridge: Cambridge University Press, 2nd ed., 2010), pp. 540–541, and A. Trouwborst, 'Transboundary Wildlife Conservation in a Changing Climate: Adaptation of the Bonn Convention on Migratory Species and Its Daughter Instruments to Climate Change', *Diversity*, 4 (2012), 258–300, at 287–288.

[126] See, e.g., the Preamble and Art. 2 of the CMS: *supra* n. 124.

a modification has occurred.[127] The same can be said of terms that are inherently 'evolutive' or can be expanded by means of implied powers (as seen in relation to Costa Rica v. Nicaragua previously).[128] Furthermore, modification is not only a process of altering existing provisions; it can also supplement them with a novel element or direction.[129] Practice that gives rise to a new obligation – or even to new institutional arrangements[130] – cannot be viewed only through a 'textual' lens; it forces the interpreter to take into account the context of the entire treaty regime and its underlying purposes.

One could take the example of the voting practice of the Security Council in relation to Article 27(3) of the UN Charter.[131] Article 27(3) requires the 'concurring votes' of the permanent members of the Security Council for certain decisions. In practice, the Council has taken 'concurring' to mean 'non-objecting', contrary to what was originally intended by the drafters.[132] This enabled it to recommend intervention in the 1950 Korean War in the Soviet Union's absence. The practice could be said to conform to the principle of effectiveness – the reinterpreted voting procedure allows the Council to adopt decisions faster while preserving the permanent members' veto power and perhaps also granting permanent members the discretion to support a politically sensitive decision without expressly endorsing it. From this vantage point, the Council's practice may be seen as 'dynamic' interpretation.[133] Indeed, in its *Namibia* advisory opinion, the ICJ

---

[127] What diplomats may refer to as 'constructive ambiguity' gives parties more freedom to interpret provisions in a way that better suits their interests. See, further, F. Salerno, 'Treaties Establishing Objective Regimes' in Cannizzaro (ed.), *supra* n. 21, pp. 225–243.

[128] *Supra* n. 43.

[129] Venzke, *supra* n. 20, at p. 236 (G. E. do Nascimento e Silva, 'Le Facteur Temps et les Traités', *Hague Recueil*, 154 (1977), 215–298, at 269).

[130] See, e.g., *Effect of Awards of Compensation Made by the UN Administrative Tribunal* (Advisory Opinion) (1954) ICJ Rep. 47, at pp. 56–58.

[131] See, generally, C. Stavropoulos, 'The Practice of Voluntary Abstentions by Permanent Members of the Security Council under Art. 27, Paragraph 3 of the Charter of the United Nations', *AJIL*, 61 (1967), 737–752.

[132] See, e.g., *Legal Consequences for States of the Continuing Presence of South Africa in Namibia*, *supra* n. 35, at p. 186 (Separate Opinion of Judge de Castro); G. Fitzmaurice, 'The Law and Procedure of the International Court of Justice, 1951–54: General Principles and Sources of Law', *BYbIL*, 30 (1953), 1–70, at 50; J. Klabbers, *The Concept of Treaty in International Law* (The Hague: Kluwer Law International, 1996), p. 16; Wolfke, *supra* n. 6, at p. 34; Aust, *supra* n. 69, at p. 243; Gardiner, *supra* n. 42, at p. 254, and J. E. Alvarez, 'Limits of Change by Way of Subsequent Agreements and Practice' in Nolte (ed.), *supra* n. 8, pp. 123–132, at p. 127.

[133] See, e.g., Amerasinghe, *supra* n. 35, at p. 55, and A. Zimmermann, 'Article 27' in B. Simma, D.-E. Khan, G. Nolte and A. Paulus (eds.), *The Charter of the United*

held that this voting practice falls within the interpretative bounds of the Charter[134] despite the fact that the *travaux préparatoires* say otherwise.[135] This allowed the Court to avoid any 'slippery slopes of reasoning' or claims of treaty breach.[136] A majority of scholars, however, appear to believe that Article 27(3) of the Charter has been effectively modified.[137]

3.2.2   Nature of the Treaty, Special Mechanisms and Non-derogability

The nature of the treaty and provisions in question constitutes an essential element in assessing the limits of modification by subsequent practice.[138] The Vienna Convention does not offer much guidance here, since it fails to distinguish between various types of treaties and treaty provisions (one fundamental provision is Article 64, which prevents derogation from *jus cogens* norms). One relevant consideration is whether a treaty is bilateral or multilateral. The distinction between interpretation and modification by subsequent practice is less controversial and easier to discern in the former case.[139] Many of the key illustrations of modification by subsequent practice fall within this category.[140] Nonetheless, there is no shortage of instances where large multilateral treaties have been modified by subsequent practice.[141] The operation of subsequent practice in multilateral treaty regimes merits closer attention due to the fact that the more States parties there are, the higher the threshold for establishing a tacit modification.[142] Older treaty regimes may also be more prone to tacit modification, due to a higher need for adaptation to modern developments

---

Nations: A Commentary (Vol. I) (Oxford: Oxford University Press, 3rd ed., 2012), pp. 871–938, at pp. 913–917.

[134] *Legal Consequences for States of the Continuing Presence of South Africa in Namibia*, *supra* n. 35, at p. 22 (paragraph 22).

[135] See, e.g., L. M. Goodrich, E. Hambro and A. P. Simons (eds.), *Charter of the United Nations: Commentary and Documents* (New York, NY: Columbia University Press, 3rd ed., 1969), p. 229; Aust, *supra* n. 69, at p. 216, and Gardiner, *supra* n. 42, at p. 245.

[136] Venzke, *supra* n. 20, at p. 73.   [137] See *supra* n. 124.

[138] See, further, the contributions to this volume of Brölmann, Moeckli and White and Bowman at pp. 79–102 (Chapter 4), 136–171 (Chapter 6) and 392–439 (Chapter 13) respectively.

[139] See, e.g., Murphy, *supra* n. 109, at p. 92.

[140] See e.g. *Temple of Preah Vihear*, *supra* n. 33; *Air Transport Services Agreement between the United States of America and France*, *supra* n. 64, and *Taba Arbitration*, *supra* n. 67.

[141] See, e.g., *Legal Consequences of the Construction of a Wall*, *supra* n. 35, and *Legal Consequences for States of the Continuing Presence of South Africa in Namibia*, *supra* n. 35. See, also, Nolte, *supra* n. 33, at p. 206.

[142] Some authors maintain that a higher threshold for consent (a higher degree of practice) is required when subsequent practice is taken to amount to a modification: Venzke, *supra* n. 20, at p. 237.

over time.[143] Moreover, adjustments by means of tacit modification may be more prevalent in 'rigid' treaty regimes in which formal procedures and the injection of new issues is more problematic than, for example, in the context of the World Trade Organization (WTO), where States are constantly negotiating new areas of international trade.[144]

As a note of caution, a distinction can be made between treaties that do and do not contain their own dispute settlement mechanism. Where this is the case, such as with the Court of Justice of the European Union, there is an accompanying tendency to develop specialised rules of interpretation (and modification) not applicable outside the context of that specific treaty regime.[145] For instance, WTO Panel and Appellate Body reports concerning subsequent practice must be understood in the context of the WTO framework, which contains its own rules and systemic limitations.[146]

Some treaties contain inbuilt adaptation mechanisms. The doctrines of evolutive interpretation and implied powers can be counted among them.[147] This qualification could apply in the case of treaties that describe a boundary in 'abstract' terms, without establishing an actual line, leaving the delimitation to a boundary commission. This could be taken to exclude other forms of specifying the boundary, including subsequent practice – a presumption disregarded in the aforementioned *Temple Case*[148] and refuted in the *Beagle Channel* arbitration.[149] Treaties – particularly multilateral environmental agreements – are also informally adapted through the practice of so-called 'autonomous institutional arrangements' (AIAs), such as conferences or meetings of the State parties. Such quasi-autonomous arrangements can modify treaty provisions by means of, *inter alia*, protocols and amendments.[150] Similarly, various treaty bodies, especially in the field of human rights, arguably engage in law-making through interpretative

---

[143] See *supra* n. 3, at p. 366 and Murphy, *supra* n. 109, at p. 94.

[144] Feldman, *supra* n. 12, at p. 702.

[145] See, also, the contribution to this volume of Koutrakos at pp. 933–965 (Chapter 29).

[146] See *supra* n. 21. See, further, International Law Commission, Report of the International Law Commission on the Work of its 60th Session, *supra* n. 4, at p. 379 (paragraph 33). See, also, the contribution to this volume of Pauwelyn and Van Damme at pp. 809–847 (Chapter 25).

[147] See Section 2.2.

[148] The Court held that the use of a certain map coupled with acquiescence had determined the course of the boundary, although the Boundary Commission had not delimited it.

[149] *Dispute Between Argentina and Chile Concerning the Beagle Channel*, RIAA, Vol. XXI, 53–264, at p. 187 (paragraph 169).

[150] See, e.g., M. J. Bowman, 'The Multilateral Treaty Amendment Process – A Case Study', *ICLQ*, 44 (1995), 540–549, at 544; Churchill and Ulfstein, *supra* n. 34, at 623, and A. Wiersema, 'The New International Law-Makers? Conferences of the Parties to

recommendations and resolutions.[151] Leaving aside the question of whether
the activities of such bodies can constitute 'subsequent practice' under
Article 31(3)(b) VCLT,[152] their impact on the evolution of treaties reduces
(but does not necessarily exclude) the need for modification by subsequent
practice.

As an example, the Meeting of States Parties to the 1982 United
Nations Convention on the Law of the Sea[153] (SPLOS)[154] adopted
a decision to extend the time limit specified in Article 4 of Annex II of
the Convention for coastal States' submissions to the Commission on the
Limits of the Continental Shelf (CLCS).[155] Formal amendment with
regard to the time limit was not an option for various legal and political
reasons.[156] The decision was formulated in the shape of an interpretation,
most likely to avoid the impression of a modification.[157] In 2008, SPLOS
again altered the submission requirements to allow certain States to
submit only preliminary information to the CLCS[158] – a possibility
clearly not contained in the Convention. Since this decision is likely to

---

Multilateral Environmental Agreements', *Michigan JIL*, 31 (2009), 231–287. See, further,
the contribution to this volume of French and Scott at pp. 677–709 (Chapter 21).

[151] See, e.g., Mechlem, *supra* n. 34, at 920–921; H. Keller and G. Ulfstein (eds.), *UN Human
Rights Treaty Bodies: Law and Legitimacy* (Cambridge: Cambridge University Press,
2012) and Ulfstein, *supra* n. 34, at pp. 436–437. See, also, the contribution to this volume
of Chinkin at pp. 509–537 (Chapter 16).

[152] See G. Nolte, 'Third Report for the ILC Study Group on Treaties over Time: Subsequent
Agreements and Subsequent Practice of States Outside of Judicial or Quasi-judicial
Proceedings' reproduced in Nolte (ed.), *supra* n. 8, pp. 307–386, at pp. 378 and 384.

[153] 1833 UNTS 3.   [154] See, further, e.g., Harrison, *supra* n. 69, at pp. 75–84.

[155] SPLOS, *Decision Regarding the Date of Commencement of the Ten-Year Period for
Making Submissions to the Commission on the Limits of the Continental Shelf Set out in
Article 4 of Annex II to the United Nations Convention on the Law of the Sea*, Doc. SPLOS/
72 (29 May 2001).

[156] A. G. Oude Elferink, '"Openness" and Article 76 of the Law of the Sea Convention:
The Process Does Not Need to Be Adjusted', *Ocean Dev. & Int'l L.*, 40 (2009), 36–50,
at 45.

[157] See, e.g., D. Freestone and A. G. Oude Elferink, 'Flexibility and Innovation in the Law of
the Sea – Will the LOS Convention Amendment Procedures Ever Be Used?' in
A. G. Oude Elferink (ed.), *Stability and Change in the Law of the Sea: The Role of the
LOS Convention* (Leiden: Martinus Nijhoff, 2005), pp. 169–222, at pp. 208–209;
A. G. Oude Elferink, 'Current Legal Developments: Meeting of States Parties to the
UN Law of the Sea Convention', *Int'l J. of Marine & Coastal L.*, 23 (2008), 769–798, at 770
and 777, and B. Kunoy, 'The 10-Year Time Frame to Disputed Areas', *Ocean Dev. & Int'l
L.*, 40 (2009) 131–145, at 132.

[158] SPLOS, *Decision Regarding the Workload of the Commission on the Limits of the
Continental Shelf and the Ability of States, Particularly Developing States, to Fulfil the
Requirements of Article 4 of Annex II to the United Nations Convention on the Law of the
Sea*, Doc. SPLOS/183 (20 June 2008).

make the CLCS procedure more effective,[159] it could be regarded as a merely minor procedural modification aimed at facilitating the substantive objectives of the treaty, but they constitute modifications nonetheless.[160] Indeed, tacit modification by subsequent practice may be more controversial if it affects substantive rather than procedural provisions of the treaty.[161] The same applies to 'essential' provisions[162] to the extent that the latter can be clearly identified[163] (a notion often linked to 'object and purpose', another enigmatic term).[164]

Individual treaties – or even subsequent practice in relation to a treaty 'creating an expectation of non-derogation'[165] – may contain specifications regarding modification or non-amenable provisions. Moreover, certain categories of treaties may constitute special cases in terms of non-derogability by subsequent practice. For instance, the concept of 'non-regression' limits the extent to which human rights and, arguably, environmental treaties can be modified. It implies that beneficiaries upon whom such rights have been conferred can no longer be deprived of them (even in cases of State succession).[166] Thus, it prevents modification to the detriment of the rights-holders.[167] There is also a prohibition on derogation from treaties benefiting third parties (e.g. investor protection under bilateral investment treaties).[168] A presumption of non-derogability also

---

[159] Oude Elferink, *supra* n. 157, at 774.   [160] Harrison, *supra* n. 69, at p. 80.

[161] *YbILC* (1966–I), 165–168 (paragraphs 18 and 64), and 37th Meeting of the Committee of the Whole, *supra* n. 95 (paragraph 69).

[162] J. Brunnée, 'Treaty Amendments' in Hollis (ed.), *supra* n. 34, pp. 347–366, at p. 351 and Bowman, *supra* n. 11, at 333.

[163] On the meaning of 'essential provisions', see, e.g., H. Waldock, Second Report on the Law of Treaties, Doc. A/CN.4/156 and Add.1–3 (20 March, 10 Apr., 30 Apr. and 5 June 1963), p. 75 (paragraph 11); *YbILC* (1966–II), 255 (paragraph 9) and S. Rosenne, *Breach of Treaty* (Cambridge: Grotius Publications, 1985), p. 21. See, also, e.g. Arts. 41(1)(b)(ii), 44(3)(b), 60(3)(b) and 62(1)(a) VCLT: *supra* n. 3.

[164] I. Buffard and K. Zemanek, 'The "Object and Purpose" of a Treaty: An Enigma?', *Austrian Rev. Int'l & European L.*, 3 (1993), 311–343. See, further, the contribution to this volume of Kritsiotis at pp. 237–302 (Chapter 9).

[165] Fragmentation Report, *supra* n. 61, at pp. 59–60 (paragraph 109).

[166] F. Pocar, 'Some Remarks on the Continuity of Human Rights and International Humanitarian Law Treaties' in Cannizzaro (ed.), *supra* n. 21, pp. 278–293, at p. 279.

[167] See, e.g., Human Rights Committee, General Comment No. 26 (1997), U.N. Doc. CCPR/C/21/Rev.1/Add.8/Rev.1 (paragraph 4); Fragmentation Report, *supra* n. 61, at p. 59 (paragraph 108); I. Hachez, *Le principe de standstill dans le droit des droits fondamentaux: une irréversibilité relative* (Brussels: Bruylant, 2008) and M. Prieur and G. Sozzo, *La non régression en droit de l'environnement* (Brussels: Bruylant, 2012).

[168] See, also, Art. 37 VCLT (*supra* n. 3) and, further, the contribution to this volume of Waibel at pp. 201–236 (Chapter 8).

applies to boundary treaties in light of the principle of stability of boundaries,[169] which has not impeded arbitral tribunals from upholding boundary modifications on the basis of subsequent practice. In fact, the Tribunal in the *Taba* arbitration relied on the stability of boundaries principle to sustain a modification of the boundary pillar on the basis of 'long accepted' practice on which the parties had come to rely – despite the clear requirements of the '1906 Agreement'.[170] Similarly, according to the Boundary Commission tasked with settling the dispute in the 2002 *Eritrea-Ethiopia* arbitration, subsequent practice served to mark a modification in the treaty-based relations between the parties.[171] Lastly, a tacit modification of a boundary treaty was also central to the ICJ's *Temple* judgment.[172]

Certain types of treaties and multilateral obligations (namely, 'non-reciprocal' ones) pose further limitations on the modifying potential of subsequent practice.[173] The nature of such obligations can be inferred from a treaty's object and purpose. For instance, the nature of the treaty may be such that any divergence from its substantive provisions would affect the non-participating parties' rights and obligations (this is the case, for example, under the WTO tariff schedules due to the 'most favoured nation' principle). This represents a 'non-reciprocal' treaty containing 'integral' obligations (every breach undermines the position of all the other parties), a subset of obligations *erga omnes partes*.[174] This also applies to obligations *erga omnes* generally. Human rights treaties, for instance, contain 'integral' or 'absolute' obligations that are 'independent of any expectation of reciprocity' from the other States

---

[169] See Shaw, *supra* n. 69, at 777. Cf. *Case Concerning the Territorial Dispute*: Libyan Arab Jamahiriya v. Chad (1994) ICJ Rep. 6, at p. 37 (paragraph 72); M. G. Kohen, 'The Decision on the Delimitation of the Eritrea/Ethiopia Boundary of 13 April 2002: A Singular Approach to International Law Applicable to Territorial Disputes' in M.G. Kohen (ed.), *Promoting Justice, Human Rights and Conflict Resolution through International Law: Liber Amicorum Lucius Caflisch* (Leiden: Martinus Nijhoff, 2006), pp. 767–779, at pp. 772–773. See, also, the contribution to this volume of Miltner at pp. 468–505 (Chapter 15).

[170] *Taba Arbitration, supra* n. 67 (paragraphs 210 (citing *Temple of Preah Vihear*) and 235).

[171] *Eritrea-Ethiopia Arbitration, supra* n. 67 (paragraphs 3.8, 3.10 and 4.60). Cf. Kohen, *supra* n. 160, pp. 772–773.

[172] See Section 3.2.1. See, also, Nolte, *supra* n. 33, at pp. 204–206.

[173] See, e.g., G. G. Fitzmaurice, Third Report on the Law of Treaties, Doc. A/CN.4/115 and Corr.1 (18 March 1958), p. 40 (paragraph 76), and J. Crawford, Third Report on State Responsibility, Doc. A/CN.4/507 (15 March, 15 June, 10 and 18 July and 4 August 2000), pp. 44–48 (paragraphs 99–108) and Nolte, First Report on Subsequent Agreements and Subsequent Practice in Relation to Treaty Interpretation, *supra* n. 14 (paragraph 16).

[174] See Crawford, Third Report on State Responsibility, *supra* n. 173, at p. 47.

parties.[175] *Inter se* modifications of non-reciprocal obligations are not permitted (see, also, Article 41(1)(b)(ii) VCLT),[176] and, generally, the threshold for modification by subsequent practice is much more difficult to attain in relation to such obligations.[177]

4   Tacit Modification by Means of New Customary International Law Conflicting with A Pre-existing Treaty Rule

Subsequent customary law is capable of modifying treaty obligations or, in other words, leading to their *disapplication*.[178] The drafting history of the Vienna Convention reveals that the ILC excluded the provision dealing with modification by customary law from the Draft Articles for two reasons: first, due to the difficulty associated with attempts at codifying the complex interplay between treaty and customary law, which was dealt with in a 'perfunctory' manner in the provision (without any indication of scope or conditions) and which the Commission had long agreed to try and avoid;[179] and second, due to the fact that many members preferred to leave the provision aside, on the understanding that the issue would be discussed in relation to the article on interpretation instead.[180] The drafting history nevertheless confirms that the process exists even if it never made it into the Vienna Convention.[181]

Customary law and treaties are equal in status and share a complex, dynamic relationship: treaties can lead to the creation of new customary law, just as new custom can lead to the expansive interpretation, modification or even *desuetude* of treaty provisions.[182] Their equality is manifested in many different ways in practice – if a customary norm

---

[175] Fragmentation Report, *supra* n. 61, at pp. 160–161 (paragraph 312). See, further, L. Brilmayer, 'From "Contract" to "Pledge": The Structure of International Human Rights Agreements', *BYbIL*, 77 (2006), 163–202. See, also, the contribution to this volume of Chinkin at pp. 509–537 (Chapter 16).

[176] *Supra* n. 3.   [177] Fragmentation Report, *supra* n. 61, at p. 195 (paragraph 385).

[178] See, e.g., *Fisheries Jurisdiction Case*: United Kingdom v. Iceland (Merits) (1974) ICJ Rep. 3, at pp. 22–24 (paragraphs 50–53); *Delimitation of the Continental Shelf between the United Kingdom and the French Republic*, ILR, 54 (1977), 6–133, at 47 (paragraph 47); *YbILC* (1966-II), 88–91; Fitzmaurice, *supra* n. 69, at 225; Byers, *supra* n. 62, at pp. 174–175 and Villiger, *supra* n. 23, at p. 433. Cf. Sands, *supra* n. 69, at pp. 973–974.

[179] *YbILC* (1966-I), 165–166 (paragraphs 28–29, 31, 37 and 39).

[180] *YbILC* (1966-II), 177 (paragraph 34) and 236 (paragraph 3.)

[181] Villiger, *supra* n. 23, at p. 15.

[182] *North Sea Continental Shelf Cases*, *supra* n. 26, at p. 41 (paragraph 71); Fragmentation Report, *supra* n. 61, at pp. 115–116 (paragraph 224); Wolfke, *supra* n. 6, at p. 31; Bowman, *supra* n. 11, at 305, and Byers, *supra* n. 62, at pp. 172–180.

and a treaty norm conflict, it will depend on their normative content, context and the parties bound by them which norm will prevail in a given case. Any preliminary inconsistencies between treaty and customary law may be resolved through harmonious interpretation, whether by reference to 'collision-rules' such as *lex specialis* and *lex posterior*[183] or, notably, by means of the principle of 'systemic integration' in Article 31(3)(c) VCLT.[184] This principle provides a way of reading new norms into the treaty without having to modify it. Accordingly, treaty modification by customary law can be said to have occurred when a non-identical customary rule emerges in respect of the subject-matter covered by a treaty, and interpretation pursuant to Article 31(3)(c) VCLT is no longer sufficient to account for the observed practice[185] (i.e. when the respective customary norm can no longer be considered 'secondary' to the treaty provision in question).

Just as treaties do not usually make explicit any departures from existing customary law, so too are States reluctant to admit that their practice departs from the provisions of a treaty in favour of a new, divergent customary norm. The *pacta sunt servanda* principle may give rise to a presumption against modification by subsequent custom.[186] This could also be understood in the sense that one must first try to reconcile the conflicting norms through interpretation.[187] However, legitimate expectations stemming from subsequent customary law should be capable of rebutting this presumption against change.[188] Treaties may be nearly impossible to amend, or customary rules may become so well established that States do not consider it necessary to codify them or amend conflicting older treaties. What is more, denying the possibility of treaty modification through customary law 'would seem to ignore the role and purpose of those many treaties which codify customary international law'.[189] It can also be argued that a higher threshold for practice is required for modification by subsequent custom: the practice must

---

[183] C. J. Borgen, 'Treaty Conflicts and Normative Fragmentation' in Hollis (ed.), *supra* n. 34, pp. 448–470, at p. 454.

[184] See, e.g., C. A. McLachlan, 'The Principle of Systemic Integration and Article 31(3)(c) of the Vienna Convention', *ICLQ*, 54 (2005), 279–320.

[185] P. Sands, 'Treaty, Custom and the Cross-Fertilization of International Law', *Yale Hum. Rts. & Dev. Law J.*, 1 (1998), 85–105, at 86.

[186] Byers, *supra* n. 62, at p. 176, and Villiger, *supra* n. 16, at pp. 217–219 (paragraphs 343–346).

[187] See, e.g., Fragmentation Report, *supra* n. 61, at pp. 207–208 (paragraph 412).

[188] Byers, *supra* n. 62, at pp. 109 and 176, and Villiger, *supra* n. 16, at p. 218 (paragraph 345).

[189] Byers, *supra* n. 62, at pp. 176–177.

establish agreement as to the content of the new customary rule as well as to the parties' intention to override the treaty rule (a 'double consent' requirement).

The arguments in favour of tacit modification by customary law must be qualified by certain important considerations. As highlighted during the ILC discussions,[190] a basic distinction can be drawn between customary law derived from treaty-oriented practice (which generally overlaps with modification by subsequent practice) and new customary law extrinsic to the treaty that conflicts with the rules codified therein (custom *contra legem*).[191] Granted, this distinction may pose difficulties in the case of treaties of near-universality, in relation to which new customary law can rarely be conceived as extrinsic. Subsequent customary law, with the exception of *jus cogens* norms, does not automatically modify treaties.[192] It must first be established from the practice in question that the parties so intended.[193] It is the tacit consent, not the custom *per se*, that leads to the modification or termination of the treaty. Otherwise, the treaty will remain unaffected as *lex specialis*.[194]

This mirrors the discussion on modification by subsequent practice – practice must be sufficient to establish the parties' implied agreement to modify the treaty, a similarity also noted in the ILC.[195] In this sense, newly emerged customary law is one of the multiple possible outcomes of subsequent practice in the application of a treaty.[196] One key difference as to its legal effect is that even if a later customary norm displaces an earlier treaty and becomes the applicable law on the issue, it does not become 'part and parcel of the treaty', maintaining a separate existence.[197]

[190] *YbILC* (1966–I), 166 (paragraph 41).

[191] Thus, one could seek evidence of a general practice of that custom *outside* of the practice of the parties to the respective treaty: Waldock, Third Report on the Law of Treaties, *supra* n. 90, at p. 34 (paragraph 24); Villiger, *supra* n. 16, at pp. 183–184 (paragraph 284), and Y. Dinstein, 'The Interaction between Customary International Law and Treaties', *Hague Recueil*, 322 (2006), 243–428, at 273 (paragraph 217).

[192] Again, this would endorse a hierarchy between customary and treaty law.

[193] Akehurst, *supra* n. 69, at 275–276, and N. Kontou, *The Termination and Revision of Treaties in the Light of New Customary International Law* (Oxford: Clarendon Press, 1994), pp. 132–133 and 145–146.

[194] Kontou, *supra* n. 193, at p. 147.

[195] *YbILC* (1966–I), 221 (paragraph 44). See, also, e.g., R. Kolb, *Interprétation et Création du Droit International* (Brussels: Bruylant, 2006), p. 507; Sands, *supra* n. 69, at p. 973 (paragraph 38) and Boisson de Chazournes, *supra* n. 23, at pp. 53–54 and 58.

[196] See, e.g., International Law Commission, Report of the International Law Commission on the Work of its 60th Session, *supra* n. 4, at p. 365 (paragraph 4), and Nolte, *supra* n. 152, at pp. 350–351.

[197] See, e.g., Pauwelyn, *supra* n. 70, at p. 142. This effect would presumably be coupled with the parallel modification or desuetude of the provision in question.

International obligations are becoming more and more extensive, intricate and intertwined. This raises the likelihood of conflicts between treaties and customary norms and, with it, the need for harmonisation through interpretation and, increasingly, informal modification. The answer to normative conflicts between subsequent customary law and pre-existing treaty provisions should be determined on a case-by-case basis, with regard to the quality and quantity of the respective practice and the object and purpose of the treaty in question and 'with minimal disturbance to the operation of the legal system'.[198]

5 Conclusion

In view of the silence of the Vienna Convention, there is clearly a need to learn to identify and classify the effects of subsequent practice. On the one hand, States have diverging interests, which poses a challenge for the law, both customary and conventional, to evolve accordingly and at a fast enough pace. On the other hand, the international community has become increasingly interdependent, which means that the acts of some States influence others and gradually gather sufficient momentum to steer the development of international norms. The workings of such processes are complex and often operate tacitly, making subsequent practice politically sensitive and controversial. The nuanced discussions in the ILC during the drafting of the Vienna Convention reveal not only the political difficulties inherent in delineating the effects of practice but also the abstract legal notions underlying it. The existence of the possibility of tacit modification through practice is reflective of the fragmented nature of international law. But this innate lack of homogeneity and hierarchy has its advantages: it allows for flexibility and contextual sensitivity, facilitating the progressive development of the law.[199] Thus, subsequent practice – in both its interpretative and modifying capacities – is a source of uncertainty and, at the same time, if used cautiously, a tool for facilitating greater coherence through treaty adaptation to new developments and customary law.[200]

The line between interpretative practice and law-making through practice is thin and inherently context-dependent. The same could be said of the distinction between modification by subsequent practice and

---

[198] Fragmentation Report, *supra* n. 61, at pp. 206–207 (paragraph 410).
[199] See by analogy *ibid.*, at pp. 248–256 (paragraphs 492–493).
[200] See by analogy M. Bos, *A Methodology of International Law* (Amsterdam/New York, NY/ Oxford: North-Holland, 1984), p. 127.

that by subsequent customary law. A deeper awareness of the nuances involved could enhance stability and clarity in the interpretation of treaty obligations and make international actors increasingly mindful of the consequences of their actions or reactions to an emerging practice. The interpreter should look not only at the extent to which the practice diverges from the text and its object and purpose but also, crucially, at factors regarding the age and field of the treaty and nature of the obligations involved as well as the presence of any special mechanisms for adaptation. It is also necessary to assess the extent to which the treaty could be considered evolutive, or, in the case of a constitutional treaty, susceptible to expansion by way of implied powers.

Thus, much depends on the type and subject matter of the treaty, the nature of the impacted obligations, the existence of other adaptation mechanisms and, generally, the legitimate expectations generated by the instrument. The balance between stability and change falls differently per treaty category and type of provision – for instance, the success of environmental law or law of the sea instruments depends especially on their 'dynamism'.[201] The question of whether subsequent practice has led to a treaty modification must be approached with caution, in view of the considerations discussed above, the general presumption against modification, and in light of the individual circumstances of each case.

The creation of international obligations is a dynamic, fluid process. Treaties must undergo transformation and modernisation even when recourse to formal procedures is unavailable; to say otherwise would be to underestimate the dynamism of State interactions and the organic development of international law through normative collisions between treaty and customary law. Subsequent practice can only be understood by means of a systematic exploration of its nature, repercussions and legal underpinnings in relation to treaty law. This should be the subject of further research. The aim of the present chapter is to contribute toward a better understanding of the variables involved and the recognition that – no matter how difficult to grasp in absolute terms – the process of tacit modification by subsequent practice is valid, vital and very much alive.

---

[201] Brunnée, *supra* n. 162, at p. 351.

13

Treaty Obligations, Universalized Norms and Differentiated Responsibilities

MICHAEL BOWMAN

1 Introduction

Within the traditional typology of treaties,[1] the distinction between *contractual* and *law-making* treaties is one of the most long-established and familiar.[2] In the former class – exemplified by the situation where two States enter into a mutual defence pact, exchange cultural missions or transfer sovereignty over territory, or a consortium of States pool their financial and technological resources to design and build a new aircraft – the instrument in question is seen essentially as a form of commercial bargain or inter-personal settlement of the kind that might be made by purely private parties within the context of a domestic legal system. In the latter case, by contrast, typically involving a larger constituency of States, the treaty is employed more as a public-law standard-setting device through which the absence of universal legislative authority within the international legal order can effectively be overcome: specifically, this is accomplished by the creation of a written instrument embodying generalised rules of conduct of the kind traditionally developed on the international plane through the medium of custom. In the archetypal treaty-contract, accordingly, obligations are individually tailored around the benefits that each particular State is undertaking to contribute to the overall project, whereas in the law-making type, obligations are characteristically standardised around specified norms of behaviour that everyone is expected to follow. Thus, treaty-contract obligations might be

---

[1] As to which, see the contribution to this volume of Brölmann at pp. 79–102 (Chapter 4).
[2] M. Shaw, *International Law* (Cambridge: Cambridge University Press, 8th ed., 2017), pp. 69–72. Recognition of this distinction, which is no less familiar in French (i.e. *traité-contrat/traité-loi*) and German (*vertrage/vereinbarung*), has been traced at least as far back as H. Triepel, *Völkerrecht und Landesrecht* (Leipzig: C.L. Hirschfeld, 1899): see S. Rosenne, *Developments in the Law of Treaties 1945–1986* (Cambridge: Cambridge University Press, 1989), pp. 181–190. For further discussion, see Brölmann, *ibid.*

likened to the separate staves detailing the individual instrumental parts on a musical score, whereas those of the standard-setting variety more closely resemble a mass-produced hymn sheet from which the entire congregation is expected to sing in unison.

1.1   The Limitations of Categorisation

Although these respective types of instrument and obligation may at first sight seem radically different in terms of their essential character and objectives, it has been suggested that they are not in reality susceptible to unambiguous division into discrete categories since, on closer inspection, 'there are many grey areas of overlap and uncertainty' between them.[3] International agreements may, indeed, incorporate obligations of both the law-making and the purely contractual kind, along with some which defy straightforward categorisation altogether. In addition, all of these duties are, through want of any other available mechanism, created through essentially the same functional device, *the treaty*. Furthermore, the precursory process of negotiation of such instruments may not necessarily differ substantially as between the two categories since, even in the case of law-making treaties, States are commonly intent upon driving hard bargains based on acute sensitivity to individual national interest.[4] For these and other reasons, the International Law Commission (ILC), having been charged with the task of elaborating a set of international legal modalities to govern the creation, activation, application, interpretation and termination of treaty instruments, resolutely resisted all exhortations to create separate regimes for these (or, indeed, other) supposed categories.[5] Instead, every species of legally binding written agreement concluded between States exclusively was in principle to fall

---

[3] See Shaw, *ibid.*, at p. 70.

[4] Rosenne, *supra* n. 2, at pp. 183–184. Consider, for example, the 1982 United Nations Convention on the Law of the Sea (UNCLOS), 1833 UNTS 3, as well as the 1992 Convention on Biological Diversity, 1760 UNTS 79, and the 1992 United Nations Framework Convention on Climate Change, 1771 UNTS 107, together with their respective protocols.

[5] Thus McNair, for example, had famously proposed that '[i]nadequate attention has been given by students of International Law to the widely differing functions and legal character of the instruments which it is customary to comprise under the term "treaty". It is suggested that this branch of the law would be in a more advanced state if more writers on the subject would study these essential differences and endeavour to provide for them instead of attempting to lay down rules applicable to treaties in general': A. D. McNair, 'The Functions and Differing Legal Character of Treaties', *BYbIL*, 11 (1930), 100–118, at 100.

within the framework of the 1969 Vienna Convention on the Law of Treaties (VCLT),[6] the first major product of their work in this area.

Nevertheless, it was plainly always intended that the single, ostensibly uniform, system of norms which it established be applied with a degree of sensitivity to the precise nature of the instrument under consideration, and it was accordingly designed with sufficient flexibility to make that possible. Indeed, there are instances where the rules themselves make explicit allusion to such factors. Article 5, for example, stipulates that the VCLT regime

> applies to any treaty which is the constituent instrument of an international organization and to any treaty adopted within an international organization *without prejudice to any relevant rules of the organization.*[7]

In addition, numerous articles of the Convention distinguish for specified purposes between multilateral and bilateral treaties,[8] while (cutting across the apparent simplicity of this distinction) significance is also attributed for certain purposes to treaties that have a 'limited number of negotiating States'.[9] In some cases, moreover, particular principles established by the Convention are judged to be inherently inappropriate for application to particular categories of treaty.[10]

Provisions such as these confirm that the ILC's denial of general and definitive normative significance to the broad functional category into which any particular treaty might fall was certainly not intended to render such questions of classification entirely irrelevant for legal purposes. In any event, quite apart from these nuances of legal technicality, there will always be a powerful *practical* utility in keeping in mind the general distinction between contractual and law-making instruments in view of their inherently different functions in international relations and the rather disparate characters of the obligations they typically create.

1.2   The Essential Character of Customary-Style Norms

Since treaties of the law-making type can so readily be conceived as written codifications of customary (or customary-style) norms,[11] the

---

[6] 1155 UNTS 331. See, in particular, Arts. 1 and 2(1)(a) VCLT.   [7] Emphasis added.

[8] Such references are particularly abundant in Parts IV and V of the Convention: *supra* n. 6.

[9] Article 20(2) VCLT, concerning reservations: *ibid.*

[10] See, e.g., Art. 60(5) VCLT, concerning termination for breach and humanitarian treaties, and Art. 62(2)(a) VCLT, concerning boundary treaties and the principle of *rebus sic stantibus: ibid.*

[11] In the Vienna Convention itself, note especially (i) Art. 4, which, while denying retrospective effect to the Convention *per se*, explicitly allows for the possible applicability of some of the rules set forth 'under international law independently of the Convention';

deontological character of the obligations they generate might be expected to be essentially similar. The precise relationship between the two has been considered by the International Court of Justice (ICJ) on several occasions, and most notably in the *North Sea Continental Shelf Cases* of 1969.[12] In the course of reaching their conclusion that the 'equidistance-special circumstances principle', established in Article 6 of the 1958 Geneva Convention on the Continental Shelf to govern the delimitation of such areas between neighbouring States,[13] could not be regarded as having attained the status of a rule of customary international law, so as to be binding even upon States that were not parties to the treaty itself, the Court saw fit to express severe doubts as to whether the rule in question was even *capable* of acquiring customary status.[14]

The Court's diffidence on this point related essentially to certain key features of the equidistance/special circumstances rule itself, as expressed in the treaty provision in question. The aspects highlighted[15] were (i) that recourse to the delimitation principle established by the provision was secondary to an obligation upon the States concerned to reach agreement on the matter, (ii) that the precise scope and role to be played by the 'special circumstances' element of the rule was profoundly uncertain and (iii) that the provision in question was susceptible to exclusion by the formulation of a reservation on the part of individual State parties. These features were judged to detract from the 'fundamentally norm-creating character' to be expected of genuine principles of customary law, 'which by their very nature, must have equal force for all members of the international community, and cannot therefore be the subject of any right of unilateral exclusion exercisable at will by any one of them in its own favour'.[16] This strongly suggests

(ii) Art. 38, which points out that the *pacta tertiis* rule elaborated in Part III, Section 4 does not preclude the applicability of any particular treaty obligation 'as a customary rule of international law, recognised as such' and (iii) Art. 43, which provides that the invalidity, termination, suspension or denunciation of any treaty does 'not in any way impair the duty of any State to fulfil any obligation embodied in the treaty to which it would be subject under international law independently of the treaty': *supra* n. 6.

[12] *North Sea Continental Shelf Cases*: FRG/Denmark; FRG/Netherlands (1969) ICJ Rep 3. See, also, *Case Concerning Military and Paramilitary Activities in and against Nicaragua*: Nicaragua v. United States (Merits) (1986) ICJ Rep. 14.

[13] 499 UNTS 311.

[14] See *North Sea Continental Shelf Cases, supra* n. 12, especially at pp. 38–39 (paragraph 63) and pp. 41–42 (paragraph 72).

[15] *Ibid.*, at pp. 41–42 (paragraph 72).   [16] *Ibid.*, at pp. 38–39 (paragraph 63).

that a key feature of customary-style norms was seen to be their *uniformly universalised* character.[17]

It seems reasonable to suppose, however, that the significance to be attributed to the three factors emphasised was essentially cumulative and evidential rather than independently definitive, since it is arguably only the second that seems of itself truly to undermine the principle's potential for customary status, and even then only if critical thresholds are crossed with regard to the nature and extent of the uncertainty disclosed. After all, some degree of uncertainty is inevitable in the articulation of *any* generalised norm of conduct, since it will usually be impossible to stipulate all of its ramifications and implications in advance, and it is therefore surely only where vagueness or ambiguity reach levels that render it impossible to discern any meaningful obligation at all that the normative quality of the commitment in question will be negated.[18] The other factors mentioned seem to be of very limited weight in themselves: the permissibility of self-exclusion from the application of particular customary norms by a 'persistent objector', for example, would seem to be a well-recognised (albeit restrictively defined) feature of the legal order[19] and a close parallel to the formulation of a substantive reservation to a law-making treaty. Equally, it is difficult to see why a putative customary norm could not validly be applicable only in default of agreement: indeed, *jus cogens* aside, it is surely the case that *any* customary norm is in principle capable of modification or exclusion by agreement between particular States, if only as amongst themselves.

In any event, and whatever may be the position with regard to customary rules, it seems beyond all doubt – not least from the specific example in issue in the Continental Shelf Convention noted previously – that those general behavioural norms which *are* enshrined in treaty form may in principle be the subject of modification, restriction or exclusion in

---

[17] If, however (as seems to be the case), customs may operate on a purely regional or other restricted basis, then the obligations in question would presumably be 'universalised' only within the particular sub-set of the international community to which they were applicable.

[18] The issue has been extensively explored by the European Court of Human Rights, for example, in relation to the requirement stipulated in several provisions of the 1950 European Convention for the Protection of Human Rights and Fundamental Freedoms (ECHR), 213 UNTS 221, that permissible exceptions to human rights norms must be 'prescribed by law': see especially the *Sunday Times Case* (1979) 2 EHRR 245 (paragraphs 49–53).

[19] This principle appeared to be accepted by the Court itself in *Fisheries Case*: United Kingdom v. Norway (1951) ICJ Rep. 116, at p. 131.

their applicability to particular parties. The legal device that comes most readily to mind for the purpose of achieving such a result is probably that mentioned in the case itself, i.e. the formulation by a State of a reservation with regard to the specific duty in question. Yet, the use of this device has itself traditionally been fraught with uncertainty and controversy.

2   The Evolution of the Reservations Controversy in International Law

The protracted saga surrounding the legal regime governing reservations might be regarded as having unfolded through several broad historical phases.[20] As the process of legislative-style treaty-making began to gather pace during the latter half of the nineteenth century, it was inevitable that instances would arise where individual States, unwilling to commit to the full array of obligations generated by such instruments, might seek to exclude themselves from the effect of those they found unacceptable and that the permissibility and implications of such action would have to be considered by other States involved. It is often suggested that the established position in customary law during this early period was essentially rigid and formalistic: just as a purported 'reservation' to a proposed bilateral treaty amounted in effect to a counter-offer which the other State concerned was free to accept or reject, so too a reservation to a multilateral agreement required the unanimous acceptance of all the other parties before the proponent could be deemed to have assumed its place amongst their ranks.[21]

From World War I onwards, however, the enhanced role of intergovernmental organizations within the international community (which was itself both a consequence and a cause of this increase in legislative-style activity) offered the opportunity for more systematic consideration of the issue. During this (second) phase, the reservations problem was accordingly

---

[20] For a similar point, see E. T. Swaine, 'Treaty Reservations' in D. B. Hollis (ed.), *The Oxford Guide to Treaties* (Oxford: Oxford University Press, 2012), pp. 277–301, at p. 281.

[21] See, e.g., J. M. Ruda, 'Reservations to Treaties', *Hague Recueil*, 146 (1975–III), 95–218, at 112; J. K. Koh, 'Reservations to Multilateral Treaties: How International Legal Doctrine Reflects World Vision', *Harvard ILJ*, 23 (1982–1983), 71–116, at 77, and C. J. Redgwell, 'Universality or Integrity? Some Reflections on Reservations to General Multilateral Treaties', *BYbIL*, 64 (1993), 245–282, at 246. In *Reservations to the Convention on the Prevention and Punishment of the Crime of Genocide* (Advisory Opinion) (1951) ICJ Rep. 15, four judges endorsed this view of customary law in a joint dissenting opinion, but the majority of the International Court explicitly denied, at p. 24, that 'the conception of the absolute integrity of a convention has been transformed into a rule of international law.'

brought squarely into the limelight within several of the institutions that were active at the time, though without producing any universally agreed solution. A committee of experts constituted by the League of Nations, for example, held essentially to the supposedly traditional view, qualifying it only to the extent that the instrument in question explicitly permitted reservations of any particular kind (a largely hypothetical possibility at the time, it seems, since multilateral treaties so rarely made express provision for reservations at all). The Pan-American Union (PAU),[22] by contrast, which by that time had already acquired substantial experience of multilateral treaty-making,[23] had pioneered a more flexible approach, whereby States enjoyed an essentially unrestricted right to formulate reservations, which would have the effect of modifying the scope of their treaty relations with parties which accepted them but where an objection thereto would have the effect of precluding the entry into force of the treaty between the reserving and objecting States.[24] These sharply contrasting approaches had not even come close to harmonisation, however, by the outbreak of World War II, after which the even greater proliferation of novel institutions markedly increased the incidence of conclusion of law-making treaties, thereby threatening to exacerbate still further the impact of the unresolved uncertainties in the law regarding reservations. At the same time, however, the emergence as part of this process of bodies such as the International Law Commission

---

[22] Now, of course, the Organization of American States (OAS).

[23] Co-operation between the newly independent States of Latin-America was evident from an early stage, with a suite of multilateral treaties on intellectual property concluded in 1889, and a succession of others following, duly published in the Pan-American Union Treaty Series and Pan-American Union Law & Treaty Series. An inter-American convention concerning the law of treaties was adopted as early as 1928: see PAULTS 34 and M. O. Hudson, *International Legislation* (Vol. IV) (Washington, DC: Carnegie Endowment for International Peace, 1931), p. 2378.

[24] For a fuller account of the PAU approach, see M. M. Whiteman (ed.), *Digest of International Law* (Vol. 14) (Washington, DC: U.S. Government Printing Office, 1970), pp. 141–144, and, for contrasting views regarding its merits, see G. G. Fitzmaurice, 'Reservations to Multilateral Conventions', *ICLQ*, 2 (1953), 1–26, and P. W. Gormley, 'The Influence of the United States and the Organization of American States on the International Law of Reservations', *Inter-Am. L. Rev.*, 7 (1965), 127–184. Gormley was, however, subsequently to concede (see 'The Modification of Multilateral Conventions by Means of "Negotiated Reservations" and Other "Alternatives": A Comparative Study of the ILO and Council of Europe' (Parts I and II), *Fordham L. Rev.*, 39 (1970–71), 59–80, and 413–446, at 61 (fn. 12)) that the PAU system had not worked particularly well even in its own context, and would be even less likely to operate successfully on a global basis. Note that all cross-references to Gormley in later footnotes in this chapter are to his article in the *Fordham Law Review*.

(ILC) and the International Court of Justice offered renewed hope for their effective resolution.

As it turned out, the opportunity to clarify and develop the law arose almost immediately. The ILC decided to embrace the law of treaties in its entirety as a priority topic for codification as early as 1949, while the following year the General Assembly charged the Court with resolving the legal uncertainties caused by the reservations which had been formulated by various States in relation to the 1948 United Nations Convention on the Prevention and Punishment of the Crime of Genocide.[25] Given the respective scales of the tasks assumed, it was no surprise that it was the deliberations of the Court which were brought to the speedier conclusion, with their advisory opinion in *Reservations to the Convention on the Prevention and Punishment of the Crime of Genocide*[26] moving the global legal regime some considerable distance towards accommodation of the PAU approach and thereby heralding the commencement of the third historical phase. More specifically, it found that a State that had formulated a reservation which had attracted objections from one or more of the other parties to the convention could nevertheless in principle be regarded as a party, provided always that the reservation was compatible with the overall object and purpose of the instrument; with that in mind, it remained open to an objecting State that disputed such compatibility to consider the reserving State as not a party as far as their relations *inter se* were concerned. It is noteworthy that the advice formally tendered by the Court in response to the questions put to it did not specifically address the possibility of objections framed on other grounds;[27] indeed, it had appeared to treat it as axiomatic that 'the compatibility of a reservation with the object and purpose of a Convention must furnish the criterion for the attitude of a State in making the reservation ... as well as for the appraisal by a State in objecting to the reservation'.[28] It had, however, touched upon alternative scenarios in passing, expressly recognising the possibility that in such

---

[25] 78 UNTS 277.

[26] *Reservations to the Convention on the Prevention and Punishment of the Crime of Genocide, supra* n. 21.

[27] Its other explicit findings were that a party which considered the reservation to be compatible with the object and purpose was (unsurprisingly) free to regard the reserving State as a party and that objections to reservations which had been formulated upon signature were without formal legal effect until the reserving State subsequently ratified its signature.

[28] *Reservations to the Convention on the Prevention and Punishment of the Crime of Genocide, supra* n. 21, at p. 24.

circumstances 'an understanding' between the reserving and objecting States might 'have the effect that the Convention will enter into force between them, except for the clauses affected by the reservation'.[29]

It soon became apparent, however, that that decision had failed decisively to put an end to all controversy; apart from anything else, the advice had commanded only the narrowest of majorities and was expressly limited to the case of the Genocide Convention itself. The whole question was therefore ripe for reconsideration by the ILC and duly received explicit attention in the provisions of the VCLT itself,[30] the adoption of which marked the beginning of a fourth identifiable phase of normative development of the reservations regime. Unfortunately, the provisions adopted have themselves been shown to fall short of their desired objective of decisively clarifying the legal implications,[31] resulting in the need for yet further rumination by the ILC on these matters, reflected ultimately in the recently published *Guide to Practice on Reservations to Treaties*.[32] Accordingly, the international community now stands at the threshold of a new, fifth, epoch as far as the legal regime governing reservations is concerned. Happily, the ongoing controversies regarding the respective substantive implications of these successive reservations regimes do not require detailed discussion here as they have already been extensively explored in the legal literature.[33] Furthermore, although there are reasonable grounds for hope that the

---

[29] *Ibid.*, at p. 27.   [30] See specifically Arts. 19–23 VCLT: *supra* n. 6.

[31] Amongst the issues which have emerged as being especially problematic in this context are (i) the preliminary question of the definition of reservations, and in particular the means by which they are to be distinguished from mere 'interpretative declarations'; (ii) the precise nature of the relationship between the provisions regarding 'permissibility' in Art. 19 VCLT and 'opposability' under Art. 20 VCLT; (iii) the related issue of whether a State which has formulated an invalid or impermissible reservation may be held to the treaty in any event, without the benefit of that reservation and (iv) the precise legal consequences that respectively ensue from the acceptance or rejection of reservations by other States.

[32] Published by the ILC, with Commentary, in its Report for its 63rd Session (2011), U.N. Doc. A/66/10/Add.1; U.N. GAOR, 66th Session, Supplement No. 10, and endorsed by the General Assembly in its Resolution A/RES/68/111 (16 Dec. 2013).

[33] An extensive bibliography is appended to the ILC report, *ibid.*, at pp. 603–630. Useful recent overviews of the topic can be found in Swaine, *supra* n. 20, and A. Aust, *Modern Treaty Law and Practice* (Cambridge: Cambridge University Press, 3rd ed., 2013), pp. 114–144, while invaluable discussion of the relevant articles of the VCLT can be found in O. Corten and P. Klein (eds.), *The Vienna Conventions on the Law of Treaties: A Commentary* (Vol. I) (Oxford: Oxford University Press, 2011), pp. 405–627. See, also, E. Cannizzaro (ed.), *The Law of Treaties Beyond the Vienna Convention* (Oxford: Oxford University Press, 2011), pp. 37–85.

new guidance will permit significant progress in this area, it may as yet be premature to attempt a meaningful appraisal.

In any event, the principal purpose of this chapter is actually very different: to be specific, rather than conducting yet another analytical study of the rules governing reservations themselves, it seeks to consider the impact of the evolving regime upon the treaty-making practice of States, seen particularly in the light of the pervasive and persistent pressure for the individualised modification or restriction of obligations of a *prima facie* universalised character that are generated by law-making conventions. Thus, it seeks specifically to examine the use of reservations contextually, as merely one particular means by which the differentiation of treaty obligations may be achieved, and thereby to reconceptualise the phenomenon in those terms. A key aim, accordingly, is to extend the focus to cover the various *alternative* mechanisms that may be available for achieving that objective and thereby hopefully to elucidate the *concept* and *process* of differentiation itself. This seems to be an issue which has been much less extensively explored in the literature.[34] To summarise, to the extent that the legal regime governing reservations during these various historical phases might be seen as generating significant problems or uncertainties, it might have been expected that States negotiating new law-making treaties would (i) respond to that perception by seeking to regulate the question explicitly, and in much greater detail, or (ii) explore the possibilities of using alternative mechanisms through which obligations might less problematically be differentiated. The discussion which follows therefore represents a tentative overview of practice that bears upon such matters.

3   Practical Responses to the Evolving Reservations Regime

During the first historical phase, through to the 1914–18 war, there is little evidence that the question of reservations was at the forefront of States' attention. Certainly, a preliminary survey of the principal law-making treaties of the era suggests that it was very seldom the subject of express provision.[35] The composition of the international community at

---

[34] A useful overview may be found in the ILC *Guide* itself, especially, perhaps, in the Commentary to Guidelines 1.1, 1.1.6, 1.5, 1.5.3 and 1.7.1. See *supra* n. 32. It is interesting that one of the more imaginative studies cited – that of Gormley, *supra* n. 24 – does not seem to command the ILC's wholehearted approval!

[35] See for example the 'Reservations' entry for treaties of this period in M. J. Bowman and D. J. Harris, *Multilateral Treaties: Index and Current Status* (London: Butterworths, 1984).

the time was, of course, very different from today, and the smaller number of legal subjects and rather greater degree of homogeneity amongst them may have served to facilitate the uniform adoption of universalised norms to some extent. On the other hand, it would be unwise to set too much store by this point, since experience suggests that there are remarkably few issues over which even broadly like-minded States can be guaranteed to steer clear of all equivocation or disagreement.[36] It seems clear that the practice of formulating reservations had begun to gather pace during this period,[37] prompting questions as to why so little attempt was made to deal with it explicitly and in advance. One possible explanation, proffered by the ICJ in the *Reservations* advisory opinion itself, is that the absence of clauses specifically addressing the question of reservations could be attributed to a desire not to encourage their proliferation,[38] but this does not, with respect, seem entirely convincing: after all, the tenor of the clause in question could well have been sharply restrictive or even prohibitive. In this vein, indeed, one of the few attempts formally to confront the matter can be found in the 1890 Convention for the Publication of Customs Tariffs,[39] Article 14 of which stated that accession 'shall imply adhesion to all the clauses'.

Perhaps, then, the dearth of such provisions in treaty regimes of the day is rather to be explained on the basis either of a failure to appreciate the full complexities of the legal and practical problems that the formulation of reservations and responses thereto might pose or, by contrast, a conscious judgment that these were likely to be outweighed by

---

[36] It has been pointed out that pious expectations of quibble-free negotiation have tended to be dashed even in such homogeneous organizations as the early Council of Europe: Gormley, *supra* n. 24, at 63.

[37] A perusal of the information readily to hand suggests that reservations are hard to find with respect to the major law-making instruments of the nineteenth century. They are certainly encountered in relation to the various conventions of that era concerning intellectual property, though generally on the part of States that did not become party until many years later. From around the turn of the twentieth century, by contrast, they began to become more frequent, as evidenced by practice with regard to the pre-war anti-slavery conventions and the Hague Conventions of 1899 and (more particularly) 1907 concerning dispute settlement and the conduct of warfare: 187 CTS 410 and 187 CTS 429; 205 CTS 233 and 205 CTS 277. See generally on this point Bowman and Harris, *supra* n. 35, Treaties 1–53. It would be interesting to see the results of a comprehensive, scientifically structured survey of such instances.

[38] *Reservations to the Convention on the Prevention and Punishment of the Crime of Genocide, supra* n. 21, at p. 22.

[39] 173 CTS 329.

the difficulties associated with the negotiation and drafting of suitable clauses to address them in advance. After all, the latter process would plainly be capable of generating considerable controversy on its own account, as a closer inspection of the Customs Tariffs Convention itself may reveal. On the one hand, the reference to unqualified commitment in the passage cited previously might naturally be read to *preclude* the formulation of reservations altogether, though, on the other, it might perhaps with equal legitimacy be understood to *permit* them on the basis that any mere 'implication' of such an outcome could be excluded by the expression of a clear contrary intention, of which the formulation of a reservation represented the clearest possible indication![40]

By the beginning of the second historical phase, as noted earlier, the incidence of the formulation of reservations had clearly begun to increase, and yet the propensity to incorporate clauses governing the matter did not at first sight appear to intensify so as to match this growing challenge – rather, the vast majority of law-making treaties maintained the traditional tendency towards silence on the matter. Yet, the evidence here must be treated with a degree of caution if it is not to be misunderstood, since within one institution at least (which in fact represented the most fertile source of international 'legislation' during this period), the silence in question could be attributed to the fact that the problem had been addressed by other means. To be specific, the International Labour Organization (ILO)[41] had virtually from its inception embraced a general policy of prohibiting reservations to its treaties,[42] rendering it unnecessary to address the matter specifically in the text of individual instruments.

---

[40] In the event, no State appears to have formulated a reservation, which may suggest that this latter interpretation was not the one that prevailed. In this context, note the phenomenon of 'package deal treaties', the 'inherently integral character' of which has to be 'preserved from ad hoc modification': see A. E. Boyle, 'Reflections on the Treaty as a Law-Making Instrument' in A. Orakhelashvili and A. Williams (eds.), *40 Years of the Vienna Convention on the Law of Treaties* (London: British Institute of International & Comparative Law, 2010), pp. 1–28. Ideally, this aspect will be signalled explicitly, as in Art. 309 UNCLOS, *supra* n. 4; Art. XVI(5) of the 1994 Agreement establishing the World Trade Organization, 1867 UNTS 3, and Art. 120 of the 1998 Rome Statute of the International Criminal Court, 2187 UNTS 90.

[41] In all, well over sixty legally binding agreements were adopted by the ILO during the inter-war period.

[42] See on this point the documents (i) *Admissibility of Reservations to General Conventions*, Memorandum by the Director of the International Labour Office, 8 LNOJ 882 (1927) and (ii) *Reservations to the Convention on the Prevention and Punishment of the Crime of Genocide*, Written Statement of the ILO (1951) ICJ Pleadings, Oral Arguments and Documents, at 216. For fuller discussion, see Gormley, *supra* n. 24, at 65–80, and the contribution to this volume by Trebilcock at pp. 848–880 (Chapter 26).

The justifications offered in support of its policy of prohibition were (i) that the fundamental purpose of the organization was the establishment of minimum conditions of labour designed to counter the detrimental impact of international competition and (ii) that it sought to achieve that goal not merely through inter-governmental collaboration but through a tripartite structure involving employers and employees as well. These considerations mandated a uniform standard of protection from which individual governments should not be free to depart on a purely unilateral basis.[43] On a practical level, the ILO's tendency to focus its legislative endeavours upon topics of a fairly specific, narrowly defined scope must have reduced the perceived need to formulate reservations in any event, so much so that the effective choice in many cases was simply to ratify of the treaty in full or remain aloof entirely.[44]

Yet for all this apparent zeal for uniform standards, the ILO also recognised the practical need for a degree of flexibility, which it achieved through a variety of means broadly envisaged under the terms of Article 19 of its Constitution,[45] paragraph three of which provided that:

> In framing any Convention or Recommendation of general application the Conference shall have due regard to those countries in which climatic conditions, the imperfect development of industrial organisation, or other special circumstances make the industrial conditions substantially different and shall suggest the modifications, if any, which it considers may be required to meet the case of such countries.

The ILO in fact displayed considerable ingenuity in devising mechanisms to give effect to this need for flexibility, including (i) the stipulation of obligations of a generalised character to be specified more

---

[43] The word 'unilateral' may carry a dual sense here, connoting governmental decisions taken independently not only of other governments but also possibly (and more importantly, perhaps, in this context) of the two non-governmental elements of national ILO delegations as well.

[44] Indeed, it seems to have been presented expressly in those terms by the organization itself when rejecting the relatively few attempts by States to propose and justify reservations during this era: see the 1951 Written Statement, *supra* n. 42 (paragraphs 228–230) and Gormley, *supra* n. 24, at 67.

[45] In addition to the key provision to be discussed in the text, Art. 19(7) made specific allowance for the position of federal States, while the paragraph immediately following allowed for the adoption of stricter domestic measures. This latter provision is interesting, since it appears to value the willingness of certain States to adopt *stricter* standards of protection more highly than the ILO's own general objective of *uniformity* of standards referred to previously. Strictly speaking, however, it falls beyond the scope of the present inquiry, since it does not entail the differentiation of *obligations* as such, but only the differentiation of performance.

precisely through national legislation, (ii) the adoption of conventions containing discrete parts or sections capable of separate acceptance, or permitting other forms of selective commitment and (iii) the incorporation within treaties of permissible exceptions or reserved powers.[46]

It was not only within the forum of the ILO, moreover, that diverse mechanisms of differentiation were employed, as examples can equally be found in treaties adopted under the aegis of other institutions. A particularly notable example is provided by the 1928 General Act for the Pacific Settlement of International Disputes,[47] which employed several of these devices concurrently. Thus, alongside a provision permitting the formulation of specified categories of reservation,[48] allowance was also made for the selective acceptance of separate chapters of the instrument (which addressed different methods of dispute resolution),[49] as well as for its partial denunciation at specified junctures, meaning that States were periodically afforded the opportunity to curtail the scope of their original acceptance if they chose to do so.[50] This serves to confirm that, even from a relatively early stage, there was significant awareness of both the existence and the potential utility of an array of formal mechanisms for securing the individualisation of ostensibly universalised legal obligations.

By the time of the third historical phase, it is plain that the uncertainties attendant upon the use of reservations had at last begun to exert a significant impact upon practice in the field of multilateral treaty-making generally. Thus, during the 1950s and 1960s, although the predominant tendency even then was to omit any reference to the problem at all,[51] there was undoubtedly an increased propensity to address the matter explicitly, particularly within treaties concluded under the aegis of the United Nations or its specialised agencies. The solutions adopted were distributed (albeit rather unevenly) along a broad spectrum from the recognition of a general power to formulate reservations to the absolute

---

[46] See, further, Gormley, *supra* n. 24, at 68 ff, and Section 4.1.1 *infra*.

[47] 93 LNTS 343. Concluded in Geneva, and also sometimes known as the General Act of Arbitration, it is not to be confused with the Pact of Paris, or Treaty providing for the Renunciation of War as an Instrument of National Policy, 94 LNTS 57, which was adopted a month earlier.

[48] Art. 39: *ibid*. Permitted reservations were restricted to the exclusion of certain specified categories of dispute.

[49] Art. 38: *ibid*.   [50] Art. 45(4): *ibid*.

[51] Again, for a broad impression of practice, see Bowman and Harris, *supra* n. 35, 'Reservations' entry for Treaties 249–553.

preclusion of any such option.[52] Intermediate approaches included the identification of particular provisions that were excluded from the general rule adopted, whether permissive or prohibitive.[53] In some cases, other forms of substantive restriction were imposed – for example, that reservations were permitted only to the extent that existing national legislation was incompatible with the requirements of the convention in question,[54] coupled sometimes with a requirement that they be withdrawn as soon as circumstances allowed.[55] In a few cases, highly specific solutions were adopted, including the negotiation and approval of reservations in advance and in some cases their formal incorporation into the text of the agreement itself or of some related document.[56]

The 1965 International Convention on the Elimination of All Forms of Racial Discrimination,[57] by contrast, famously adopted a solution which, while impliedly allowing for the formulation of reservations, provided expressly for the possibility of their non-acceptance by other parties.

[52] As to the former, treaties concluded under UN aegis quite frequently adopted a liberal attitude towards reservations – the 1952 International Convention to Facilitate the Importation of Commercial Samples and Advertising Material, 221 UNTS 255, explicitly allowed for their formulation 'to any provision' (Art. 14). In some contexts, however, they were clearly judged inappropriate, and accordingly prohibited: see Art. 9 of the 1956 Supplementary Convention on the Abolition of Slavery etc., 266 UNTS 3. For other early cases of outright prohibition, see, e.g., Art. 20 of the 1952 Universal Copyright Convention (depositary UNESCO), 216 UNTS 133; Art. 39 of the 1952 Convention Relating to Damage caused by Foreign Aircraft to Third Parties on the Surface (ICAO), 310 UNTS 181; Art. 15 of the 1953 Constitution of the European Commission for the Control of Foot and Mouth Disease (FAO), 191 UNTS 285, and Art. 9 of the 1955 Articles of Agreement of the International Finance Corporation (IBRD), 264 UNTS 117.

[53] By way of example, the three UN customs conventions of 18 May 1956 – 338 UNTS 103, 327 UNTS 123 and 319 UNTS 21 – each permitted reservations with respect to one specified provision alone; the 1954 Hague Convention Relating to Civil Procedure, 286 UNTS 265, allowed reservations to its Art. 17, without explicitly stating that no others were permitted; the 1957 Convention on the Nationality of Married Women, 309 UNTS 65, allowed reservations to all but its first two articles, while the 1954 Convention relating to the Status of Stateless Persons, 360 UNTS 117, specified some fourteen articles with respect to which the general power of formulating reservations was excluded.

[54] This is, of course, probably the most likely reason why a State might ever choose to formulate a reservation, but in these cases it was spelled out as a specific requirement: see, e.g., Art. 57 ECHR, *supra* n. 18, and Art. 26 of the 1955 European Convention on Establishment, 529 UNTS 141.

[55] As in both the treaties referred to in the previous note. Sometimes, moreover, this requirement was specified despite the absence of any express reference to domestic legislation: see, e.g., Art. 26 of the 1957 European Convention on Extradition, 359 UNTS 276, and Art. 23 of the 1959 European Convention on Mutual Assistance in Criminal Matters, 472 UNTS 185.

[56] For examples, see Section 4.1.2.   [57] 660 UNTS 195; see in particular Art. 20.

Further, reservations incompatible with the instrument's object and purpose, or inhibitive of the operation of any of the bodies established by it, were not permitted, and objections by two-thirds of the contracting parties were treated as conclusive of such illegitimacy. This approach plainly picks up quite specifically on the issues addressed in the emerging reservations regime but still falls short of resolving all uncertainties – the text itself does not make clear, for example, what is the implication of objection on grounds other than those specified, nor whether the two-thirds threshold is *the exclusive* or merely *a sufficient* criterion of incompatibility.

During the fourth historical phase, the establishment of the Vienna Convention regime had the potential to impact upon drafting practice in ways that might be regarded as both complicated and complicating: in one sense, by creating a reservations regime that could be applied in default of an agreed alternative, it could be said to have reduced the need for explicit provision in the treaty itself. At the same time, there were various, potentially contrasting, reasons why negotiating States might still have preferred to address the matter explicitly – namely, on the one hand, that they wished to specify categories of permitted or precluded reservations, as the VCLT regime itself expressly envisaged; or, on the other, that they perceived difficulties with that regime, and wished to avert them by regulating the matter explicitly. Furthermore, the VCLT itself did not actually enter into force for over a decade,[58] and even then a substantial majority of States remained outside the circle of those formally bound by its provisions.[59] In the event, therefore, no dramatic change in practice was evident regarding reservations specifically, as treaty-makers continued to resort to a broadly similar array of stratagems as before.

Within some organizations – most notably, perhaps, the International Maritime Organization (IMO) – the opportunity was sometimes taken to reaffirm explicitly certain aspects of the Vienna Convention regime – for example, that reservations took effect subject to reciprocity, or compatibility with the treaty's overall object and purpose, or must be formulated in writing, or that those made upon signature must be confirmed upon ratification.[60]

---

[58] To be precise, this occurred on 27 Jan. 1980, in accordance with Art. 84 VCLT: *supra* n. 6.

[59] Acceptance by 35 States was required, which, although a fairly high threshold for the entry into force of a multilateral treaty, still represented only a relatively small proportion of the international community as a whole.

[60] See respectively Art. 34 of the 1970 Convention on the Taking of Evidence Abroad in Civil or Commercial Matters, 847 UNTS 231; Art. 28 of the 1979 Convention on the

This tendency seems not to have lasted for long,[61] however – one obvious difficulty with it is that it may cast doubt on the intended applicability of those VCLT requirements that are *not* explicitly so endorsed. With such considerations in mind, perhaps, the drafters of the OAS's American Convention on Human Rights (ACHR), concluded just six months after the VCLT, sought to forestall any such problems by embracing its approach to reservations *en bloc*, explicitly stipulating that such statements were permitted only in accordance with the regime it established.[62] Needless to say, even that solution is not entirely problem-free, since it leaves unresolved any difficulties or uncertainties which may be inherent in the VCLT regime itself. In addition, it may conceivably cast doubt on the interpretation of other treaties concluded within the same organization that omit any such provision.[63] For whatever reason, the ACHR approach was not one that appears to have been replicated subsequently, whether within the OAS or elsewhere.

Once again, occasional attempts were made to address the matter in a more intricate fashion. In broadly similar vein to the approach adopted in the Racial Discrimination Convention, the 1971 Convention on Psychotropic Substances[64] expressly allowed reservations to certain provisions,[65] while treating others as permissible provided they did not

Elimination of All Forms of Discrimination against Women, 1249 UNTS 13; Art. 14 of the 1972 International Convention for Safe Containers, 1064 UNTS 3, and Art. 18 of the 1976 Convention on Limitation of Liability for Maritime Claims, 1456 UNTS 221.

[61] The entry into force of the VCLT itself in Jan. 1980 was possibly the key factor here. Thus, a clutch of OAS conflict of laws treaties concluded in 1979 (PAUTS 49–55; see further Bowman and Harris, *supra* n. 35, Treaties 742–748) contained a standard clause permitting reservations provided that they related to one or more specific provisions of the treaty in question and were not incompatible with its object and purpose; this latter requirement was omitted, however, from a similar group concluded in 1984 (PAUTS 62–65; see, further, Bowman and Harris, *ibid.*, Treaties 841–844). This was perhaps because it was deemed to be no longer necessary to make this point explicit, though it might equally be noted that only about ten OAU member States were actually parties to the VCLT by 1984 (with a similar number having the status of signatories).

[62] 1144 UNTS 123, Art. 75.

[63] Within the OAS itself, the treaties adopted in the years immediately following tended to omit altogether any clause addressing the question of reservations: see Bowman and Harris, *supra* n. 35, Treaties 576, 656–661, 686 and 712.

[64] 1019 UNTS 175.

[65] The particular provisions to which reservations could be made were explicitly identified by Art. 32(2): *viz.*, Art. 19(1) and (2) (concerning the right of treaty organs to address conduct endangering the Convention's aims); Art. 27 (concerning the general application of the Convention to overseas territories) and Art. 31 (concerning the unilateral reference of disputes to the ICJ). In addition, Art. 32(4) allowed most of the regulatory commitments under Art. 7 to be excluded with respect to the use of plants growing wild within

attract objection within twelve months by one-third of the existing parties.[66] In the event, while the former, unqualified, power has been quite widely utilised, it seems that only four of the 183 parties (Canada, Germany, Myanmar and Papua New Guinea) have ever sought to take advantage of the additional latitude provided by the latter, and no State has in any instance objected to the particular exemptions sought.[67] The approach adopted by the drafters might therefore be regarded either as a highly successful means of addressing particular national needs or conversely (though perhaps less plausibly) as an unnecessary exercise in over-elaboration.

What does seem clear is that during the phases following the *Reservations* advisory opinion, resort to *alternative* modes of differentiation became progressively more common, and a wider range of devices began to be employed in order to provide the flexibility which was judged desirable with respect to the scope and intensity of legal commitment. Perhaps it was hoped that some of these other techniques of differentiation would ultimately entail fewer practical complexities and legal uncertainties than resort to reservations. Yet while such an expectation may well have been broadly justified, it would certainly have been unwise to assume that these alternative devices would prove entirely free of practical complication, particularly if (as in the case of the 1928 General Act noted earlier) they were to be employed in combination. One consideration common to all of them is, of course, that they will typically have to be worked into the fabric of the regime during the negotiating phase of the treaty in question, which will obviously require a considerable degree of foresight and attention to detail on the part of the negotiating States.[68] Experience suggests, moreover, that achieving a satisfactory structure will not necessarily prove an easy task. Accordingly, in order to explore the potential difficulties more meaningfully, it will be necessary to attempt to identify the mechanisms in question in a more systematic fashion.

---

    a party's territory by certain communities which employed them in magical or religious rites: *ibid.*

[66] Art. 32(3): *ibid.*

[67] See generally the UN publication *Multilateral Treaties Deposited with the Secretary-General of the United Nations* (https://treaties.un.org/pages/ParticipationStatus.aspx).

[68] Of course, it may fairly be pointed out here that this element of anticipatory judgment will equally be required wherever a particular treaty seeks to substitute detailed provisions of its own regarding reservations for the general default regime of the VCLT itself.

4   Identifying the Mechanisms of Differentiation

To recapitulate, reservations are far from being the only means by which the duties imposed by standard-setting treaties may be 'individualised' or 'personalised' – that is to say, tailored more precisely to the needs of particular parties.[69] It would doubtless be difficult to present an exhaustive list of such devices, but the major instances can be categorised in accordance with the broad schema that follows. It should not be supposed, however, that the processes identified necessarily represent sharply defined or wholly discrete categories, for they are likely to overlap substantially and may even in some instances represent essentially the same process viewed from different perspectives.

4.1   Selective Opt-Out

As indicated previously, the nature of international law, and in particular its traditional preoccupation with individual State sovereignty, means that generalised, uniform norms of conduct cannot easily be imposed upon States but must typically be the subject of formal, individual acceptance. In the interests of extending the applicability of codified norms as widely as possible, the instruments through which they are elaborated are not necessarily presented on an uncompromising 'take-it-or-leave-it' basis but instead commonly offer the opportunity for qualified acceptance, whereby the applicability of duties that are especially problematic for particular States can be effectively excluded.[70] The principal mechanisms for achieving this outcome appear to be as follows.

4.1.1   Reservations *stricto sensu*

Reservations themselves represent the time-honoured and most familiar device, a point already highlighted in the preceding discussion concerning the gradual evolution over time of the legal regime which governs their operation. A key point to reiterate, however, with regard to that regime is that its significance is purely residual, with the consequence that, should they feel so inclined, treaty negotiators are perfectly free to adopt a different solution. Thus, they may (for instance) even now opt to

---

[69] 'Customised' is in some respects the ideal word but risks confusion in this particular context by virtue of its coincidental redolence with 'custom' as a source of legal obligation.

[70] On the other hand, as noted *supra* n. 40, certain treaties are devised quite explicitly as a form of 'package deal', to which no qualification or exception is permitted.

'turn back time' for the purposes of a particular treaty and demand that a reservation proposed by any particular State secure the explicit acceptance of all the existing parties and that, failing such endorsement, the proponent State shall not be deemed a party at all. Indeed, the 1993 FAO Agreement to Promote Compliance with International Conservation and Management Measures by Fishing Vessels on the High Seas is a modern example of a treaty which embraced precisely such a strategy.[71] Alternatively, drafters may simply seek to exploit the considerable operational leeway inherent in the VCLT regime itself by adopting any one of the range of responses that it permits, from remaining completely silent about the question of reservations – and thereby leaving the parties potentially at risk to any of its surviving uncertainties – to seeking to regulate the matter in exhaustive detail within the treaty in question.

Although, as indicated from the outset of this chapter, it is no part of its intention to undertake any extensive review of the substantive legal problems associated with the use of this mechanism, it may be appropriate to advert here to one or two issues of a more procedural character which have arisen in that connection. In particular, since the power to formulate reservations is conceived as an aspect of treaty acceptance,[72] it would seem logical that it may only be exercised as part of that process, a point which seems to be amply confirmed both by the substantive provisions of Article 19 VCLT and by the very definition of reservations advanced in Article 2.[73] Accordingly, when in 1996 the government of Estonia informed the depositary (the Council of Europe) that it wished to formulate reservations concerning certain species listed in the 1979 Bern Convention on the Conservation of European Wildlife and Natural Habitats,[74] to which it had acceded four years earlier, it was informed that it was now too late to do so, and that the proper course of action would be denounce the Convention entirely and then tender a new instrument incorporating the reservations in question.[75]

---

[71] 221 UNTS 91, Art. 12 (which provides, however, that failure to object within three months of notification of the proposed reservation shall be deemed acceptance).

[72] This point is frequently emphasised in the ILC Commentary in the passages cited previously, *supra* n. 32, and especially in paragraphs 6–9 of the Commentary to Guideline 1.1., but see also the text accompanying *infra* n. 77 and n. 78.

[73] In each case the crucial words are '. . . when signing, ratifying, accepting, approving or acceding to a treaty . . .'

[74] 1284 UNTS 209.

[75] Report of the Meeting of the Bureau of the Bern Convention (20 May 1996), Council of Europe Doc. T-PVS (96), 32.

While this advice seems to be entirely correct as a matter of law, a couple of points might be noted in that connection. The first is that a less formalistic perspective might have prompted the depositary to consult the parties generally in order to determine whether any of them would have objected to the establishment of a reservation at this belated juncture and, if not, to have regarded it as effective, on the basis that general acquiescence constitutes a validation of almost every ill, and certainly those of a formal or procedural nature.[76] On the other hand, given the seriousness of the biodiversity crisis which we currently face, it may have been advantageous that the Council of Europe Secretariat reacted in such a way as to uphold the rigour of the convention as far as possible. As the ILC Guidelines explicitly confirm, however, there should certainly be no objection in principle to allowing the formulation of reservations by a State party subsequent to its acceptance of a treaty if the other parties have no objection[77] or, more obviously still, if the treaty in question has explicitly countenanced that possibility in its final clauses, as did the 1928 General Act,[78] for example.

With regard, however, to the more formalistic solution canvassed previously, it is interesting to note that some commentators have specifically called into question the propriety in principle of a State denouncing a convention in order to reaccept shortly afterwards with the benefit of a freshly conceived reservation, especially in circumstances where that State is firmly believed, or has formally been found, to have committed certain breaches of treaty during the original period of its participation, and the reservation is designed specifically to protect it from charges of a similar kind in the future. Citing a handful of prominent examples of such action,[79] one author regards them as clear infringements of the principle of good faith.[80]

---

[76] Such acquiescence might, of course, relate to the untimely presentation of reservations generally, or to the particular proposal only. For discussion of UN depositary practice in this regard, see Swaine, *supra* n. 20, at p. 289.

[77] See Guideline 2.3. ff: *supra* n. 32.

[78] For a further example, see Art. 13 of the 1959 European Convention on Compulsory Insurance against Civil Liability in Respect of Motor Vehicles, 720 UNTS 119.

[79] These relate specifically to the Swiss interpretative declaration to Art. 6(1) ECHR, *supra* n. 18; the actions by Guyana and by Trinidad and Tobago with regard to the Optional Protocol to the ICCPR, 999 UNTS 302; Bolivian re-accession to the 1961 Single Convention on Narcotic Drugs, 520 UNTS 204, and Swedish attempts to avoid the impact of Chapter 1 of the 1963 Council of Europe Convention on the Reduction of Multiple Nationality and on Military Obligations in Cases of Multiple Nationality, 634 UNTS 221 (as to which, see *infra* n. 119 and n. 120 as well as accompanying text).

[80] B. Arp, 'Denunciation Followed by Re-Accession with Reservations to a Treaty: A Critical Appraisal of Contemporary State Practice', *Netherlands ILR*, 61 (2014), 141–165.

It should surely be borne in mind here, however, that the State in question (i) will typically be fully entitled to denounce the convention altogether, without re-acceding at all; (ii) will only be proffering at this stage a reservation that it was perfectly within its rights to have formulated at the time of its original acceptance; and in any event (iii) certainly cannot by this manoeuvre retrospectively free itself from any liability which it had incurred during its original period of participation.[81] It is therefore by no means obvious that it has necessarily done anything to undermine the convention's object and purpose or abused its rights in any other sense. To the extent that the outcomes of such behaviour are regarded as problematic, the solution would seem to lie in drafting future conventions in such a way as to exclude the possibility of its occurrence altogether, for example by excluding or restricting the opportunity for denunciation, or by prohibiting reservations of any description. Yet the price of such restriction may, of course, be simply to discourage the participation of certain governments in the convention altogether, a risk which established perceptions of State sovereignty essentially render inescapable. More generally, such controversies merely serve to re-emphasise the problems inherent in the use of reservations as such and may on that account strongly underline the virtue in exploring alternative solutions.

4.1.2 Pre-negotiated Exceptions/Reservations for Identified States

Since one of the principal problems associated with the use of reservations is the uncertain effect of responses by other States, this can plainly be circumvented by agreeing the matter in advance and entrenching that agreement in the treaty itself. A notable example of this approach is the 1950 International Convention for the Protection of Birds,[82] in which several States were successful in negotiating the insertion into the text of explicit allowances for their particular needs. Article 7, for example, which allowed for exceptions to be created from the protective regime of the Convention in the interests of science, education, falconry and the breeding of game birds, added that the 'provisions concerning transport contained in [A]rticles 3 and 4 shall not apply to the United Kingdom'.

---

[81] See on this point Art. 70 VCLT: *supra* n. 6.

[82] 638 UNTS 186. For discussion, see M. J. Bowman, P. G. G. Davies and C. J. Redgwell, *Lyster's International Wildlife Law* (Cambridge: Cambridge University Press, 2nd ed., 2010), pp. 201–203, and M. J. Bowman, 'International Treaties and the Global Protection of Birds: Part I', *J. Env. L.*, 11 (1999), 87–120, at 91–94.

In similar vein, Article 4 itself, which regulated, *inter alia*, the taking or destruction of wild birds' eggs, established a specific exception regarding the collection of lapwing eggs in the Netherlands, justifying it on the basis of 'exceptional local conditions'.

At the time of the treaty's adoption,[83] of course, the employment of this technique of pre-negotiated special exemption[84] had much to commend it, since the validity of any reservation formulated purely unilaterally would probably have been understood (at least within European circles)[85] to require the unanimous assent of the other parties in order to become effective, and therefore any such protection might just as well, and with greater certainty, be agreed in advance: it was not until the following year that the ICJ's *Reservations* advisory opinion heralded the arrival of a new, more flexible approach, which was later refined and elaborated more fully in the VCLT itself.

Yet even after these developments in the general law of treaties had occurred, the phenomenon of negotiating particular reservations in advance, and even of incorporating in the treaty explicit arrangements to cater for it, did not disappear entirely as a feature of treaty-making practice. Although the need for it had by now undoubtedly diminished, the precaution of securing advance general approval of any limitations desired by particular States upon their acceptance of treaty commitments still offered the distinct advantage of eliminating altogether the possibility of subsequent objections, with all their diverse unpredictable impacts. It follows that it retains considerable practical attraction, at least in circumstances where it is unlikely to cause undue delay to the progress of negotiations: accordingly, pre-arranged, individualised dispensations of this kind have continued to be employed, albeit only occasionally and in particular categories of treaty.

---

[83] That is, at the very end of the second temporal period noted earlier: the Convention was concluded barely a month before the General Assembly formulated its request for an advisory opinion in the *Reservations* case, *supra* n. 21, which took around six months to deliver.

[84] It should be noted that this type of provision goes some way beyond the technique labelled by Gormley, *supra* n. 24, as 'negotiated reservation', and is more strongly deserving of that description, because it is the specific reservation by a named State which is agreed and inserted into the text beforehand, not merely a clause permitting reservations of the particular category into which it falls.

[85] Although there is nothing explicit in the text to indicate it, the 1950 Convention was essentially a regional instrument concluded amongst European powers: Art. 11 did permit 'any' non-signatory State to accede, but no non-European State ever did so. See *supra* n. 82.

Thus, the 1960 Paris Convention on Third Party Liability in the Field of Nuclear Energy[86] required that any proposed reservation be formulated in advance of ratification/accession by the State concerned and made its admissibility dependent upon express acceptance by all signatories.[87] Those which had passed this particular test by the time of signature of the Convention itself were incorporated in an Annex.[88] A Supplementary Convention of 31 January 1963[89] repeated the requirement for advance acceptance of proposed reservations by all signatories and acceding governments but contented itself with a procedure of notification by the depositary of any reservations so accepted.[90]

In a similar fashion, opt-outs to particular provisions or entire policy areas of the basic agreements of the European Union are agreed in advance and incorporated as protocols to the parent instrument.[91] In this case, a number of factors of an overtly political character no doubt combine to render this a particularly attractive solution to the problem of differentiated commitment – *viz.*, (i) the radically *integrative* agenda of the institution in question; (ii) the perception of that aspiration by certain domestic factions and constituencies as striking at the very heart of each member State's national sovereignty and (iii) the highly charged and intensely politicised nature of the debate which is therefore certain to be generated by any significant change in existing arrangements. The approach in question arguably preserves the general ethos of a unified treaty regime, as entrenched in a formal constitutional document, while according a similarly high political profile to the negotiating 'success' of those who governments that wish to exempt themselves from its full implications.

Although the instruments specifically mentioned in this section were all designed essentially for operation within the European region, where

---

[86] 956 UNTS 263.

[87] Art. 18 – though paragraph 2 thereof dispensed with the requirement of approval in the case of any signatory that had not itself ratified the Convention within a period of twelve months from being notified of the reservation in question by the depositary: *ibid.*

[88] It is not expressly stated whether either this or the second Annex is formally to be regarded as part of the Convention, though the depositary itself (unlike certain other, unofficial, textual sources) places it before the testimonium clause in the published text: see www.oecd-nea.org/law/nlparis_conv.html.

[89] 1041 UNTS 358. The aim of the instrument was to increase the amount of compensation payable under the liability regime of the parent convention.

[90] As in the case of the parent convention, the relevant provision here is also Art. 18.

[91] For details, see in particular Protocols 15–22, 30–32, 34–35 to the consolidated version of the Treaty on European Union and the Treaty on the Functioning of the European Union, OJEU 2012/C 326/01.

the legal perception of the reservations issue has sometimes been thought to be distinctive, it should be noted that arrangements of this kind have also been initiated in regimes of intended global applicability. Within the Universal Postal Union (UPU), for example, the long-established practice (enshrined in Article 22(6) of that organization's Constitution),[92] has been that any member State wishing to avail itself of a reservation to any of the UPU's periodically negotiated, substantive agreements regarding postal services[93] must submit a proposal to that effect to the UPU Congress or the Postal Operations Council in accordance with an agreed procedure; if confirmed by the relevant forum, the reservation will be included along with any others in a Final Protocol to the agreement in question.

4.1.3   Express Provision for Reserved Powers

Specific instances of this technique have already been encountered in the earlier discussion, as where the parties to the 1950 Birds Convention were, by virtue of Articles 6 and 7, authorised to restrict or set aside the Convention's protective regime in defence of certain specified interests.[94] This general technique is, of course, extremely widely utilised, right across the range of treaties in all subject areas. In human rights conventions, for example, it is standard practice for the guarantees established to be qualified by a succession of permissible grounds for restriction or limitation of the rights in question, to which selective resort is permitted at the instance of individual parties. Within some jurisprudential traditions, moreover, recognition of the doctrine of the 'margin of appreciation' provides an additional dimension of individualisation of the protective regime.[95]

---

[92] 611 UNTS 7. It may possibly be significant that the Constitution itself dates from the pre-VCLT period. The approach has also, however, been replicated in regional postal treaties of a later era: see, e.g., the successive versions of the Asian-Pacific Postal Convention, dating from 1981, texts published by the Asian-Pacific Postal Union.

[93] These agreements are typically renegotiated on a five-yearly cycle: for the (relatively large) cluster of instruments from 1979, for example, see Bowman and Harris, *supra* n. 35, Treaties 759–762 and notes, and for the (much more streamlined) current arrangements, together with the Constitution and General Regulations of the UPU, and appended historical notes, see the UPU website at www.upu.int/.

[94] *Supra* n. 82. Note further that under Art. 6 certain more generalised powers of derogation were reserved specifically for Sweden, Norway, Finland, Iceland and the Faroe Islands, on account of the special economic conditions that prevailed there.

[95] For example, under the ECHR, as to which see S. Greer, 'The Margin of Appreciation: Interpretation and Discretion under the European Convention on Human Rights', Human Rights Files No. 17 (Council of Europe, 2000) and E. Frantziou, 'The Margin of Appreciation Doctrine in European Human Rights Law', UCL Policy Briefing, Oct. 2014.

Provision is also sometimes made for the temporary suspension of rights in appropriate circumstances.[96]

As noted previously, the ILO had also explicitly sanctioned the incorporation of reserved powers in its conventions, insisting (notwithstanding its arguably equal potential for undermining the organization's two key objectives identified there) that this practice was quite distinct from the phenomenon of reservations.[97] On the face of it, this assertion appears to be correct as a matter of principle, since a reservation is a quintessentially *unilateral* act, effected through an independent instrument of purely national provenance, whereby particular treaty obligations are modified or excluded for the protection of certain interests deemed important by the State in question; the establishment of reserved powers, by contrast, represents a *collective* recognition by the negotiating States, expressed in an instrument of international authorship and authenticity, that certain interests may have to be allowed priority over some or all of the commitments that have been agreed therein. Accordingly, resort to a reserved power is not so much 'to exclude or modify the legal effect of certain provisions of the treaty' (as the VCLT definition of reservations stipulates) as to *invoke and give effect* to certain of its provisions (to be specific, those that create the reserved powers in question).

Yet, upon closer examination the cogency of this explanation seems questionable, since the inevitable effect of invoking the provisions by which the reserved powers are created is undoubtedly to modify, exclude or restrict the effect of *other* provisions of the treaty in question – that is, after all, their very intention. This suggests that the substantive ground which separates these two processes is not in truth that extensive, and it may, moreover, be reduced still further – perhaps almost to vanishing point – if certain additional factors are introduced into the equation. Most obviously, wherever the convention in question expressly authorises the making of certain categories of reservation, then each instance of resort to such authority represents the exercise of a particular power collectively recognised in the instrument itself,[98] rendering it arguably a mere example of the wider category embracing resort to reserved powers generally. It might still perhaps be argued here that, in the case of reservations, the extent of the obligations to which the

---

[96] See, e.g., Art. 15 ECHR: *supra* n. 18.   [97] See text accompanying *supra* n. 41 to n. 46.

[98] Under the Vienna Convention regime, it could of course be argued that this is *always* the case with regard to reservations, the power to formulate them being implied for all parties provided the object and purpose is not thereby undermined.

reserving State *is* willing to commit is known specifically from the moment of its acceptance,[99] whereas the impact of reserved powers will not become known until they are actually exercised. The flaws in this argument are, however, (i) that the possibility of reservations being formulated *subsequent to acceptance* has certainly never been definitively excluded in principle[100] and, (ii) in any event, that some reservations do not entail the automatic and immediate exclusion of particular commitments but the mere retention of a faculty for such exclusion at some indeterminate future moment or upon some vaguely described contingency:[101] in such cases, therefore, they operate in a fashion which becomes difficult to distinguish from that displayed by certain reserved powers. Equally, although reservations must characteristically be notified to the other parties (either directly or *via* the depositary) in order to enable them to formulate a response, there are certainly cases of reserved powers which have been made subject to similar conditions.[102] Finally, any assumption that reservations represent a form of accommodation of peculiarly individual national interests, while reserved powers reflect policy issues of general concern, may be undermined by the fact that, in purely numerical terms, there may be more States wishing to formulate reservations of a particular ilk (and hence arguing during negotiations for the treaty for the authority to do so to be explicitly incorporated within it) than there are States wishing to exercise reserved powers of any particular character (even where little opposition was evident during negotiations to inclusion of the latter within the treaty in question).[103]

---

[99] That is to say, all those that are not excluded by the reservation in question.

[100] Although the ILC, as noted earlier, specifically acknowledges this point, it does not seem effectively to explore all of its possible implications.

[101] Note, for example, the Belgian reservation to the 1997 International Convention for the Suppression of Terrorist Bombings, 2149 UNTS 256, whereby '[i]n exceptional circumstances, [it] reserves the right to refuse extradition or mutual legal assistance in respect of any offence set forth in [Art.] 2 which it considers to be a political offence . . .' This may be compared with the more typical style of reservations to the Convention, formulated in a number of instances, whereby a state declared that it 'does not consider itself bound by' a particular provision (commonly Art. 20(1)).

[102] See, e.g., Art. 9 of the 1979 Bern Convention, *supra* n. 74, and Art. 3(5) and Art. 3(7) of the 1979 Bonn Convention on the Conservation of Migratory Species of Wild Animals, 1651 UNTS 333, for further discussion of which see text accompanying *infra* n. 108.

[103] As a striking example of the latter situation, certain of the reserved powers and exceptions to particular conservation provisions in the Bonn Convention, *ibid.*, (e.g., accommodation for the needs of traditional subsistence users) appear to have been inserted essentially at the behest of the United States, which ultimately opted not to participate in the convention at all!

All of this suggests that the very considerable substantive gulf between reservations and reserved powers that was perceived to exist by the ILO a century ago has been progressively shrunk as a result of treaty-making practice in the meantime, and arguably to the point that it can no longer be regarded as a clear difference of substance at all but only one of form. Yet the distinction seemingly remains critical, since anything identified as a reservation will be subjected to the regime of Articles 19–23 VCLT, the application of which, as history has demonstrated, may result in a wide variety of controversies.[104] Even on the assumption that the recently promulgated ILC Guidelines may help to avert or defuse many of these problems in the future, it will be valuable for treaty-makers to bear in mind the risk of certain residual difficulties remaining and, pondering the merits, resort to some other, potentially less troublesome, method for the differentiation of treaty obligations.[105] Yet success in any such venture will surely depend in no small measure upon the ease with which these various techniques may be distinguished, and it is in this respect that the ILC Guidelines themselves seem less than pellucid.

On the one hand, it is explicitly recognised that there is indeed an array of '*alternative* procedures' designed 'to achieve results *comparable* to those effected by reservations', and that these include 'the insertion in the treaty of a clause purporting to limit its scope or application'.[106] The words emphasised earlier, together with the Commentary accompanying the Guideline in question, seem to make it clear that these mechanisms fall outside the scope of the reservations regime. On the other hand, it is established that *what exactly is* a reservation must be regarded a matter of substance rather than form and that, by virtue of the Guidelines, a statement made 'in accordance with a clause expressly authorising the parties ... to exclude or modify the legal effect of certain provisions of the treaty' for the party formulating it 'constitutes a reservation' (albeit, obviously, one that is authorised).[107] Yet, although the Commission appears confident that these two categories are readily distinguishable, there are features of their Commentary which may call this conviction into question. Doubts arise in particular from their use of the wording 'clause purporting to limit [the] scope or application' of the treaty to illustrate the techniques that fall outside the reservations

---

[104] On this point, see, e.g., S. Marks, 'Reservations Unhinged: The *Belilos* Case before the European Court of Human Rights', *ICLQ*, 39 (1990), 300–327.

[105] The ILC Commentary, indeed, specifically encourages such eclecticism.

[106] See Guideline 1.7.1: *supra* n. 32.

[107] Guideline 1.1.6: *supra* n. 32. See, also, Art. 2(1)(d) VCLT: *supra* n. 6.

category, for the kinds of provision that are genuinely problematic to distinguish in this context are certainly not those whereby limits are set to the general scope of the obligations imposed: this, after all, represents an inevitable feature of the definition of *every* treaty obligation, and suggests that the ILC's focus should rather have been (as the actual examples it gives tend to confirm) upon those clauses which specifically '*permit the parties* to limit the scope or application' of the treaty in question and thereby, in common with reservations, risk depriving it of plenary effect on uniform terms.

Accordingly, all that truly seems to distinguish the exercise of such powers from action taken in reliance upon a reservation is (i) that reservations themselves must typically have been formulated upon acceptance and (ii) that written notification of the exercise of reserved powers, or intention to do so, is not generally required. As seen previously, however, both distinctions may be extinguished by express provision or subsequent agreement, leaving one to ponder whether the two concepts might not effectively have merged into another. As regards the first distinction, it seems especially noteworthy in this context that ILC Guidelines 2.3, 2.3.1 and 2.3.2, as explained by the Commentary, quite deliberately avoid any implication either that a post-acceptance reservation is not a *true* reservation (even declining to treat it as a special sub-category thereof) or that it only achieves that status upon 'acceptance' by the other parties. This strongly encourages the inference that the time of formulation is ultimately *not* an essential feature of the reservations concept. As to the second, various modern treaties now require that attempts to utilise exceptions or reserved powers be reported to the depositary or treaty secretariat for potential scrutiny by the relevant treaty organs.[108] This latter possibility has, of course, only become feasible during the epoch when treaty regimes have become more heavily institutionalised, and thereby assumed a decidedly more 'organic' character. Its effect, however, in combination with the other considerations mentioned earlier, does suggest that the process whereby reservations are distinguished from reserved powers may ultimately be more impressionistic than rigorously analytical.

Accordingly, and bearing in mind that the legal consequences of the distinction would seem to be highly significant, treaty-makers would

---

[108] See, e.g., Art. 9 of the 1979 Bern Convention, *supra* n. 74, and Art. 3(5) and Art. 3(7) of the 1979 Bonn Convention, *supra* n. 102. Note that under the former, the Council of Europe serves as both depositary and secretariat.

doubtless be well advised to give careful consideration to the kind of impression they are trying to create. In particular, if the implementational leeway to be allowed to States under any given treaty is granted in the form of reserved powers or permissible exceptions to the duties established, and the formulation of reservations categorically prohibited – as is commonly the case with many modern conservation treaties, for example – a good deal of unwanted legal complication and uncertainty may possibly be avoided. In particular, doubts regarding the very validity of a State's participation in the treaty should not arise, since these are essentially an artefact of the reservations regime itself.[109] Instead, any controversy will be transported instantly into the conceptual realm of breach of treaty and the lawfulness of the conduct of the State in question considered under that rubric. It was indeed on precisely this basis that the government of Japan was recently held by the ICJ to have violated its obligations under the 1946 International Convention on the Regulation of Whaling,[110] since its undisputed power to issue whaling permits for the purposes of scientific research (by way of exception to the moratorium on commercial whaling) had not been exercised in good faith.[111] A further interesting feature of this case is that it was indeed one where a requirement was imposed that any exercise of the power in question be reported – in this instance to the International Whaling Commission itself – and, furthermore, that this be done in advance.[112] Although the Commission has no actual authority to forbid the granting of such permits, it is noteworthy that some States have on occasion been willing to accede to exhortations to reconsider: unfortunately, the atmosphere within the organization has in recent times become so polarised that such amenability is no longer likely to be forthcoming. In general, however, this mode of collective monitoring of reserved powers may well prove more coherent and effective in a substantive sense than the highly

---

[109] If, however, reservations are not explicitly excluded, the risk of controversy is greatly enhanced, as is evidenced by the Icelandic government's questionable attempt to formulate a reservation on its re-accession to the 1946 Whaling Convention, as to which see A. Gillespie, 'Iceland's Reservation at the International Whaling Commission', *EJIL*, 14 (2003), 977–998.

[110] 161 UNTS 72.

[111] *Whaling in the Antarctic*: Australia v. Japan; New Zealand intervening (2014) ICJ Rep. 226.

[112] The requirement is established by paragraph 30 of the Schedule to the Convention, the implications of which are considered by the ICJ in *Whaling in the Antarctic, ibid.*, at pp. 296–298 (paragraphs 234–243).

fragmented, individualised pattern of responses which is likely to ensue under the reservations regime.[113]

That is not to suggest, however, that a reserved powers approach is inherently preferable, since it may possibly encourage a greater degree of divergence from the basic norms established by the treaty in question than would the toleration of reservations. Accordingly, the choice as to which of the two mechanisms to adopt within a given treaty may be conditioned by the degree of freedom which it is deemed appropriate to accord to States with regard to the obligations thereby established. The more important point here, however, is that everything will ultimately depend upon precisely how the two putative sets of provisions are actually drafted, and it is not difficult to imagine a reserved powers regime that afforded States very little room for manoeuvre. There could clearly be no objection in legal principle, for example, to a system whereby any specific exercise of reserved powers had actually to be approved in advance by the treaty bodies in question: the obstacles to the adoption of such a schema would lie exclusively in the realm of politics.

4.2   Selective Opt-In

Although the various procedures referred to previously entail the differentiation of conventional commitments through a process whereby particular governments 'opt out' of specified norms, it is by no means the only mode of achieving such an outcome, which may in appropriate cases equally result from a process of positive acceptance, or 'opting in'. This approach to differentiation may well be worth exploring in order to determine whether it entails fewer ancillary complications than do reservations, or alternative techniques of opting out. In one sense, of course, the very possibility of being bound by treaty obligations at all is dependent upon positive acceptance by the individual government in question through its expression of consent to be bound, but even where such acceptance has indubitably been established at a general level, there are various ways in which its precise scope or scale may be affected by the exercise of affirmative choice.

---

[113] That said, it will almost always occur at a later temporal juncture (i.e. following the reporting to the treaty body of the exercise of the relevant powers by the State in question) than would be applicable in the case of reservations, where the response will typically become apparent shortly after the deposit of the instrument of acceptance of the reserving State.

4.2.1 Partial Acceptance and 'Modular' Treaties

Although never especially common, the practice of allowing the partial acceptance of treaties was evidently sufficiently well established by the 1960s to merit specific recognition by the Vienna Convention,[114] in Article 17, and remains a possibility today. The only conditions established by the VCLT to govern this process are (i) that it must be permitted by the treaty itself or otherwise agreed by the parties thereto and (ii) that the State which seeks to rely upon such latitude must make clear to which provisions its acceptance relates.[115] As regards the former requirement, possibly the most obvious method of allowing partial acceptance is through the structuring of the treaty into distinct sections or 'modules' capable of separate acceptance. Of course, numerous treaties, including the VCLT itself, are divided into sections or parts for ease of reference or other purely presentational reasons, but this has no relevance for present purposes since there will be no intention or implication that selective acceptance of these various parts is possible. Genuine instances of modular treaty-making in this latter sense are relatively few in number.

As noted previously, however, one early example can be found in the 1928 General Act for the Pacific Settlement of International Disputes,[116] which contained separate numbered chapters addressing conciliation (Chapter I), judicial settlement (Chapter II) and arbitration (Chapter III), while ancillary provisions, together with the final clauses, appeared in Chapter IV. Under the terms of Article 38, accessions[117] applied automatically to Chapters I and IV but could at the option of the State concerned be extended additionally to Chapter II or to Chapters II and III. It will be evident from this that the possibility of a State confining its acceptance to Chapters I, III and IV alone was by clear implication excluded, an outcome which may at first glance appear curious but which a closer inspection of the instrument's structure reveals to have been quite deliberate. To be specific, Chapter III served only to set out the procedural modalities of arbitration, while the option to accept it in the first place (as an alternative to judicial settlement)

---

[114] This technique seems to have been a particular feature of treaties concerning social security: see, e.g., the ILO's 1952 Social Security (Minimum Standards) Convention (No. 102), 210 UNTS 131, and the Council of Europe's 1964 Code on Social Security, 684 UNTS 235.

[115] Paragraphs 1 and 2 of Art. 17 VCLT respectively: *supra* n. 6. [116] 93 LNTS 343.

[117] Somewhat unusually, 'accession' was the only means stipulated for the expression of consent to be bound: see Arts. 38–40, 43 and 44: *ibid.*

actually derived from Chapter II, so acceptance of the former without the latter would simply have made no sense.[118]

Although there was therefore no structural anomaly in the drafting of the General Act, it is evident that mishaps or oversights of this kind do sometimes occur in the treaty-making process and that modular instruments have not remained immune. For example, a 1963 Council of Europe convention concerning the reduction of cases of multiple nationality[119] contained two substantive chapters, one concerning the general question and one addressing the implications for military service specifically.[120] It was provided that States might restrict their acceptance to the latter aspect (Chapter II) only.[121] The Convention was not widely ratified, and when some years later it was judged necessary to revise it through the adoption of an amending protocol,[122] it was conceded in the accompanying Explanatory Report that there had been no logical reason for the parent treaty to have excluded the possibility of accepting Chapter I alone;[123] the amendments accordingly introduced such an option.[124]

Despite this experience, there is, of course, no reason to suppose that the modular approach is in any way peculiarly susceptible to drafting mishap, and it has continued to be employed occasionally both within the organizations that pioneered it (i.e. the ILO and the Council of Europe)[125] and elsewhere.[126] A variant of it occurs where certain basic obligations are contained in the body of the treaty and more specialised applications of its normative regime are then addressed in

---

[118] Arts. 17 and 18, located at the beginning of Chapter II, are the key provisions here: *ibid.*

[119] *Supra* n. 79.

[120] The Convention contained four chapters in all, the last of which comprised the final clauses: *ibid.*

[121] The relevant provision was Art. 7, designated as Chapter III of the Convention: *ibid.*

[122] 1977 Amending Protocol, ETS No. 95. Note also the contemporaneous Additional Protocol, ETS No. 96, the 1993 Second Amending Protocol, CETS No. 149, and the 2007 Agreement on the Interpretation of Article 12, ETS No. 43 ('related texts') (which allowed selective denunciation of the substantive chapters). The texts of all these instruments, together with the accompanying explanatory reports and status information, are obtainable from the Council of Europe's treaty website (www.coe.int/en/web/conventions/full-list).

[123] See, in particular, Section 3 of the Report.

[124] See Art. 3 of the Amending Protocol: *supra* n. 122.

[125] See, e.g., the 1977 ILO Convention No. 148 Concerning the Protection of Workers Against Occupational Hazards in the Working Environment Due to Air Pollution, Noise and Vibration, 1141 UNTS 107, and 1978 Additional Protocol to the 1968 European Convention on Information on Foreign Law, ETS No. 97.

[126] For example, the Hague Conference on Private International Law, under whose aegis a variety of treaties has been adopted.

Annexes.[127] One particular issue that may merit attention from the drafters of modular treaties, however, is whether the faculty of choice is formally presented on an 'opt-in' or 'opt-out' basis, since it appears, perhaps surprisingly, that this might conceivably generate substantive legal implications of some significance. In particular, if the desired latitude is framed in terms of an 'opt-out', any exercise of the option in question will, according to the ILC,[128] be tantamount to the use of a reservation, so that the VCLT regime which addresses such matters will automatically be brought into play. As a matter of principle, this conclusion may at first sight seem questionable, since the default rule established by the Vienna Convention itself for cases where the treaty under consideration is silent on the matter is, in the case of reservations, that they are permitted but, in the case of partial acceptance (the precise means being left unspecified), that it is not.[129] Yet, as the ILC itself points out, any risk of incoherence is removed by the fact that the latter rule is explicitly stated to operate 'without prejudice' to the former,[130] thereby removing any inherent legal impediment to modular opt-out arrangements being considered as reservations.[131]

The Commission then goes on to express its confidence that this characterisation will prove entirely unproblematic in practice, though here the ultimate correctness of their view may require a little more by way of demonstration. It is certainly true, as they suggest, that, wherever a treaty explicitly establishes a modular opt-out arrangement, the propriety of partial acceptance will by definition have been agreed in advance and therefore that any exercise of the option in question will constitute a *permissible* reservation. Yet that will not, of course, dispense with the

---

[127] 1978 Protocol relating to the 1973 Convention for the Prevention of Pollution from Ships (MARPOL 73/78), 1340 UNTS 61, and 1991 Protocol on Environmental Protection to the Antarctic Treaty, ILM, 30 (1991), 1461–1486.

[128] The point is perhaps never made quite as unequivocally as one might have hoped, but see Guideline 1.1.6 and Commentary (paragraphs 1–14); also Commentary to Guideline 1.5.3 (paragraphs 2 and 3): *supra* n. 32.

[129] Cf. Arts. 19 and 17 VCLT respectively: *supra* n. 6.

[130] See Art. 17(1), opening phrase, to which attention is explicitly drawn in the Commentary to Guideline 1.1.6 (paragraph 14): *supra* n. 32.

[131] It may be noted that there are treaties which explicitly treat them as such: see, e.g., the 1970 Convention on the Taking of Evidence Abroad in Civil or Commercial Matters, 847 UNTS 231, which treated the option to exclude the entire effect of Chapter II (concerning the taking of evidence by diplomatic and consular personnel operating abroad, rather than by letters of request to foreign authorities) exactly on a par with the only other permitted reservation, to Art. 4(2) (concerning the languages to be treated as acceptable for the drafting of such letters).

need to consider the responses of other States, since such reservations are the very category for which the objections procedure established by the VCLT was principally designed;[132] furthermore, there may conceivably have been States that would greatly have preferred that the treaty's substantive regime be applied in its entirety[133] and may even after its adoption be seeking a means of securing that result. However, it does not seem that they can do so through a simple objection to any particular exercise of the option, since the only effect[134] will be that the provisions to which the opt-out/reservation relates (i.e. the treaty 'module' in question) will 'not apply as between the two States to the extent of the reservation' – the very opposite of what the objecting State is striving to achieve. Guideline 4.3.8 duly confirms that 'the author of a valid reservation is not required to comply with the provisions of the treaty without the benefit of its reservation'.

Yet, the question remains whether there might be other means by which a party might demand performance of a modular treaty in its entirety. For example, rather than objecting to particular opt-outs as and when they occur, it might instead object in advance to the possibility of such exclusions being made at all – that is, by formulating a reservation to the opt out/reservations clause itself.[135] Such a reservation might well be deemed 'permissible' because it seems unlikely that it would have occurred to the drafters explicitly to foreclose such an unusual contingency in the treaty itself;[136] nor could it easily be seen as contrary to the object and purpose of the treaty, since its intent is manifestly quite the reverse – namely, to ensure the instrument's more fulsome implementation![137] In such circumstances, the provisions that would, 'to the extent of the reservation', either be 'modified' (in the event of acceptance by other States, whether tacit or explicit)[138] or simply 'not

---

[132] This may be inferred from the relationship between Arts. 19 and 20 VCLT, *supra* n. 6, and between Guidelines 2.6.2 and 4.5.1–2: *supra* n. 32.

[133] This possibility is, moreover, by no means fanciful: at the diplomatic conference at which the 1946 Whaling Convention, *supra* n. 110, was adopted, for example, several States (including some who were later to rely upon it) argued against the incorporation of a power to opt out of catch quotas that were from time to time agreed.

[134] Art. 21(3) VCLT: *supra* n. 6.

[135] Obviously, the deployment of such a reservation could normally only be accomplished at the time the state in question expressed its consent to be bound.

[136] It might, of course, have been precluded incidentally by a generic prohibition on reservations other than those expressly allowed by the treaty.

[137] The conclusion might be otherwise, however, if the opportunity for differential acceptance was of itself seen to be part of that object and purpose.

[138] Art. 21(1)(a) VCLT: *supra* n. 6.

apply' (in the event of objection)[139] would surely be the opt-out powers themselves, with the apparent result that any attempt by another State to use them to limit the scope of its acceptance would effectively be nullified.[140] This seems a highly implausible outcome, however, and the least to be expected is therefore that some means of countering it would be available.

One obvious possibility would be for the State which has exercised the power of modular opt-out not merely to object to the reservation which seeks to neutralise its effect but rather to treat it as precluding the entry into force of the treaty between itself and the State in question – this at least will ensure that there will be no party which can claim to hold it to performance of the treaty in its entirety. The principal drawback involved[141] will be that constant vigilance will be required on its part with regard to developments under the treaty (and appreciation of their legal significance) in order to enable the necessary action to be taken in due time. Perhaps, then, it could be spared this burden by arguing that its own entitlement under Guideline 4.3.8, cited previously, must prevail in any event, since the true effect of that provision for the reserving State (i.e. the one opposing opt-outs) in these circumstances is only that it is not itself 'required to comply with the provisions of the treaty without the benefit of its reservation' and not that it can, by virtue of its reservation, insist on full compliance by everyone else.

Although the suspicion remains that there might be yet further legal wrinkles to be encountered in this context, it is probably the case that the scenarios involved are by this stage so unlikely to occur as to render further exploration unproductive, but the general impression remains that, wherever strategies for affording choice to States with regard to the precise extent of the treaty commitments they adopt arise for consideration, preference should probably be given to those that demonstrate the lowest risk of straying into the domain occupied by reservations, notwithstanding the worthy efforts of the ILC to guide treaty-makers through that particular minefield. More specifically, it may be preferable to employ wording which speaks in terms of 'extending' acceptance to optional modules rather than 'excluding' or 'restricting' their

---

[139] Art. 21(3) VCLT: *supra* n. 6.

[140] To express the point in the terms of Guideline 4.3.8. itself, *supra* n. 32, the State that advanced a reservation to the opt-out clause would be no less entitled to 'the benefit of *its* reservation' than the opter-out was to its own!

[141] In addition, the opter-out will itself inevitably forfeit any entitlement to demand performance of the treaty by the state that formulated the reservation.

applicability. This is because, while arrangements of the latter kind will, by virtue of the 'without prejudice' clause at the beginning of Article 17, be brought within the sway of the reservations regime, those of the former will escape it: were this not the case, Article 17 would seem to have no independent *raison d'être* at all and should therefore properly have been omitted altogether or at least relocated to the reservations section of the VCLT. Thus, the difference between the opt-in and opt-out modes of presentation seems critical, though it must be admitted that there will probably always be a linguistically grey area in the middle where the proper categorisation of the arrangement is open to debate.

4.2.2 'Framework' Treaties

The practice of concluding treaties which commit their parties to only a limited array of (usually vague and broadly stated) obligations, amplified and enhanced through more specific and demanding duties contained in optional annexes, protocols or other subsidiary instruments, has now become relatively common, initially in the environmental field but increasingly in other areas as well.[142] In the scenario postulated for the purposes of this sub-section specifically, the supplementary instruments are adopted contemporaneously with the parent convention, as in certain of the United Nations Environmental Programme's regional seas conventions.[143] Technical legal complication associated with the differentiation of obligations should not arise here, since it is accomplished through the acceptance of separate legal instruments, and accordingly no scope is available for the impact of objections.

Although the use of modular and framework treaties introduces a welcome element of flexibility into the treaty-making process, such techniques plainly do not permit the specificity with which commitment can be individualised through the medium of reservations. Effectively, they allow selection from amongst pre-fabricated blocks of obligations concerning particular sub-aspects of the treaty's broader concerns rather

---

[142] For discussion, see N. Matz-Lück, 'Framework Conventions as Regulatory Tools', *Goettingen JIL*, 1 (2009), 439–458, and D. Bodansky, *The Framework Convention/ Protocol Approach* (Framework Convention on Tobacco Control Technical Briefing Series, Paper 1 (1999) WHO/NCD/TFI/99.1). See, further, the contribution to this volume by French and Scott at pp. 677–709 (Chapter 21).

[143] See, for example, the 1985 Convention for the Protection, Management and Development of the Marine and Coastal Environment of the East African Region (1993) UNEP Register 228, which had two contemporaneously adopted Protocols, and the 1992 Convention on the Protection of the Black Sea against Pollution, ILM, 32 (1993), 1110–1121, which had three: www.unep.org/regionalseas/programmes/.

than the exclusion of specific individual duties that are seen as peculiarly troublesome by particular States. In some cases, however, opt-in arrangements have been devised which arguably do rival reservations in terms of their potential for fine-grained selectivity.

4.2.3 The 'Smorgasbord' Approach

Of particular note in this regard are a group of Council of Europe conventions, commonly labelled 'charters',[144] under which the parties are formally obliged to accept only a specified minimum sample of obligations from a broad menu of choices but may opt to accept as many as they choose, rendering the precise composition of their individual packages of commitments potentially extremely diverse. A variant of this approach, encountered in the economic and social rights context and also in the customs field,[145] occurs where the selectivity offered relates not to individual treaty provisions but rather to clusters – or 'mini-modules' – thereof, each concerned with some particular aspect or application of the overall normative regime. These techniques accordingly form part of an extensive continuum of treaty formats that before long merges into the broader brush modular instruments that were considered in Section 4.2.1 and ultimately, indeed, into the sets of separate but related instruments that fall into the framework category.

Needless to say, the various techniques that offer a menu-style approach are most likely to be considered viable in circumstances where the individual packages of commitments in respect of which choice is available essentially entail successive, independent applications of certain basic normative principles rather than representing an integrated network of inter-related commitments, where such selectivity could not easily be permitted without causing the entire system to collapse.

---

[144] See, e.g., the 1961 European Social Charter, ETS No. 35; 1985 European Charter of Local Self-Government, ETS No. 122, and 1992 European Charter for Regional or Minority Languages, CETS No. 148.

[145] For examples of the former, see the 1952 Social Security (Minimum Standards) Convention, *supra* n. 114, and the 1964 Code on Social Security, *supra* n. 114, and Protocol, ETS No. 048, each of which contains ten Parts open to optional acceptance, and of the latter, see the 1973 International Convention on the Simplification and Harmonization of Customs Procedures, 950 UNTS 269, and the 1977 International Convention on Mutual Administrative Assistance regarding Customs Offences, 1226 UNTS 143, each of which contains numerous optional Annexes.

4.3 Structural Differentiation of Commitments

In the cases discussed previously, differentiation comes about as an incidental concomitant of the exercise of powers conferred upon individual States by particular treaties or in accordance with international law generally. In other instances, however, this diversification of commitment seems to represent a more deep-seated and integral feature of the network of obligations created and may even be specifically embraced or stipulated as the very foundation of the regulatory scheme envisaged. This tendency may be expressed through a variety of different forms or formulations, including the following.

4.3.1 Participation as Member of a Specified Constituency

In some cases, even though the regime established may be intended to provide more or less comprehensive regulation of a particular area of activity, it is envisaged from the outset that States will participate essentially as representatives of distinct constituencies. This is the case, for example, with respect to certain United Nations Conference on Trade and Development (UNCTAD) treaties, where States participate in the capacity either of (net) importers or exporters of the commodity concerned.[146] Equally, under the 1975 Lomé Convention[147] and its various successor agreements,[148] participation by States has always been in the capacity either of EEC/EU Member or ACP State as appropriate. Finally, under the 1988 Joint Protocol to the 1960 (OECD) Paris and 1963 (IAEA) Vienna Conventions[149] on liability for nuclear incidents (participation in which does not overlap at all) each party to the protocol agrees, on a reciprocal basis, to extend the benefit of the treaty by which it is itself bound to those States that are party to the other. In this particular instance, the two sets of duties are broadly similar, but in other cases within this category, the primary rights and duties established may differ markedly as between the respective groups, and the arrangement as a whole may even on occasion seem to resemble a multipartite version of a bilateral treaty-contract.

---

[146] See, e.g., the 2010 International Cocoa Agreement, U.N. Doc. TD/COCOA.10/5, especially Arts. 2(9–12), 4(2) and 54(2), though perhaps the more important implications of this distinction concern entitlements rather than obligations (see, e.g., Arts. 10 and 48).

[147] OJEC 1976 L 25/1.

[148] See currently the 2000 Cotonou Agreement, as revised 25 June 2005, European Commission Doc. DE-232 (2006), ISBN 92-79-00567-7.

[149] (1988) 42 *Nuclear Law Bulletin* 56. For the parent conventions, see respectively 8 *EYB* 203 and 1963 *UNJYB* 148.

4.3.2   Common but Differentiated Obligations

In this case the basic duties undertaken by parties may be *prima facie* uniform, but what they are understood to demand substantively of States may differ, and perhaps markedly. This differentiation may be achieved by a variety of mechanisms, *viz.*

i. *in accordance with general formulae or criteria designed for individualised application*: thus, substantive duties may be qualified or conditioned by expressions such as 'as far as possible and as appropriate' or 'in accordance with its particular conditions and capabilities', to take examples from the 1992 Convention on Biological Diversity.[150] A striking example from the field of human rights is Article 2(1) of the 1966 International Covenant on Economic, Social and Cultural Rights,[151] which provides:

> Each State Party to the present Covenant undertakes to take steps, individually and through international assistance and co-operation, especially economic and technical, to the maximum of its available resources, with a view to achieving progressively the full realization of the rights recognised in the present Covenant by all appropriate means . . .

The principal drawback, perhaps, with provisions of this kind concerns the enhanced difficulty of determining compliance, which has on occasions prompted doubts as to their very justiciability; on the whole, however, the problems in this regard do not appear to be insuperable.[152]

ii. *by reference to the identification of specified constituencies*: in other cases, the criteria of differentiation may centre upon the identification of particular constituencies, as explained in Section 4.3.1. Thus, under

---

[150] See respectively Arts. 5, 7–11, 14, 19 and Arts. 6 and 20: *supra* n. 4.

[151] 993 UNTS 3. In the case of civil and political rights, by contrast, the necessary flexibility is more likely to be provided by recourse to exceptions/reserved powers, as described in Section 4.1.3.

[152] The debate has, of course, been particularly lively and protracted in the field of economic and social rights itself, as to which see, e.g., F. Coomans (ed.), *Justiciability of Economic and Social Rights: Experience from Domestic Systems* (Maastricht: Intersentia, 2006); M. Langford (ed.), *Social Rights Jurisprudence: Emerging Trends in International and Comparative Law* (Cambridge: Cambridge University Press, 2009) and S. A. Yeshanew, 'Approaches to the Justiciability of Economic, Social and Cultural Rights in the Jurisprudence of the African Commission on Human and People's Rights: Progress and Perspectives', *African HRLJ*, 11 (2011), 317–340. For interesting examples of case law from other fields, see *Commonwealth of Australia v. State of Tasmania* (1983) 46 ALR 625 (conservation of natural heritage) and Ethiopia-Eritrea Claims Commission, Eritrea's Claim No. 17, ILM, 42 (2003), 1083–1115 (protection of PoWs).

the 1979 Bonn Migratory Species Convention (CMS), only the most generalised of obligations are imposed upon the parties as a whole, whereas primary responsibility for the conservation of particular species is allocated specifically to those that are 'Range States' of the taxa in question.[153]

iii. *by reference to the identification of individual parties*: in some cases, the particularisation of commitments is expressly taken right down to the level of the individual contracting party. For example, under some of the 'daughter' instruments of the CMS – which the Range States for all Appendix II-listed species are encouraged to conclude – each party accepts an array of broadly stated conservation commitments in the body of the text, but these are then significantly elaborated in terms of their implications for individual States by means of an appended action plan. Thus, certain specified States might be expected in particular to protect specified breeding or resting sites, others to control hunting within their territory, to regulate trade in relevant specimens more effectively, or to offer technical expertise to the plotting of precise migration routes and yet others some combination of the preceding tasks. Thus far, such arrangements have occurred primarily in 'soft-law' instruments,[154] but they are in principle available for all forms of ancillary CMS instrument. In a sense, such arrangements represent an ultimate fusion of the treaty-law and treaty-contract models.

4.3.3   'Two-Speed' Parallel Instruments

In this situation (most likely to occur, perhaps, in situations where powerful States find themselves in a minority on a politically charged issue), a regulatory instrument may appear in two (or possibly more) versions, one diluted in terms either of its substantive content or its legal status. The phenomenon is doubtless most familiar from the EU context,[155] but the *sui generis* nature of this institution perhaps renders

---

[153] *Supra* n. 102. As to the former, see Arts. 2 and 4(4), and, for the latter, Arts. 3(4), 3(5), 4(3) and 6(3); for the link between the two sets of obligations, see Art. 6(2) and, for the definitions of 'Party' and 'Range State', see Art. 1(1)(f, h, k).

[154] See, e.g., the 1993 and 1994 Memoranda of Understanding concerning Conservation Measures for, respectively, the Siberian Crane and the Slender-Billed Curlew: www.cms .int/.

[155] See, e.g., J.-C. Piris, *The Future of Europe: Towards a Two-Speed EU?* (Cambridge: Cambridge University Press, 2011). Such an arrangement was amongst the options considered by EU Member States during 2011–12, when seeking to tackle the sovereign

it less than ideal as an exemplar of treaty practice generally. Such arrangements are not unknown elsewhere, however: one example is the Agreed Minute informally endorsed by the United States in relation to the 1997 Agreement on Humane Trapping Standards,[156] since its support in principle for the safeguards agreed did not (on account of the domestic constitutional allocation of competence for the substantive matters covered) extend to the adoption of a legally binding commitment.

4.4 Inter-temporal Differentiation

In one sense, many of the arrangements outlined previously represent instances of the differentiation of obligations over time, since the actual disparities in commitment will only become evident in due course, as States gradually and successively express their consent to be bound and specify the precise scope of their undertakings or make use of the latitude offered by the terms of the instrument to utilise exceptions or formulate derogations. Yet, the juridical authority for such personalisation of commitment is established at a single, given moment – i.e. with the formal adoption of the instrument in question – and it is only the details of its application that await subsequent revelation. In some cases, however, the actual creation of this differentiable dimension of the commitments entailed will itself only occur subsequently, as the original obligations are authoritatively modified or supplemented in some way.[157]

4.4.1 Inter se Modification

For example, in circumstances where some particular sub-set of the parties to an existing multilateral treaty decide that the obligations established for some reason do not adequately fulfil their current aspirations (whether through being excessively or, by contrast, insufficiently rigorous, or simply inappropriate in some other respect) Article 41 VCLT explicitly endorses the possibility of their entering into an agreement to modify the treaty amongst themselves.[158] It thereby sanctions the

---

debt crisis within the Eurozone: see, generally, V. Miller, *The Treaty on Stability, Coordination and Governance in the Economic and Monetary Union: Political Issues* (House of Commons Research Paper 12/14, 27 March 2012).

[156] OJEU 1998 L042, approved by Council Decision 98/142; OJEU 1998 L219, approved by Council Decision 98/487. For discussion, see S. R. Harrop, 'The Agreements on International Humane Trapping Standards', *JIWLP*, 1 (1998), 387–394.

[157] See generally J. Brunnée, 'Treaty Amendments' in Hollis (ed.), *supra* n. 20, pp. 347–366.

[158] It does not seem to be required that the later agreement itself must satisfy the VCLT definition of a treaty, and therefore it could, for example, be purely oral.

emergence of a form of deontological differentiation which may be regarded as inter-temporal in the sense referred to previously, since the immediate source of the modified version of the duties in question is the later agreement rather than the original treaty.[159] Needless to say, the modification will be effective only as amongst the consenting group themselves, and this option will be foreclosed altogether if actually prohibited by the treaty in question or, even where this is not the case, if the modification will affect the other parties' enjoyment of their rights or performance of their obligations or relates to a provision derogation from which is incompatible with the effective execution of the treaty's object and purpose. With those contingencies in mind, Article 41(2) VCLT requires the sub-set in question to notify the other parties of their intentions.

4.4.2   Adventitious Incremental Acceptance of Revising Measures

Whereas the differentiation of treaty obligations is the very purpose of *inter se* modification, such disparity may also come about as the incidental by-product of a process that is actually designed to achieve a modified manifestation of uniform commitment. The inherent power to amend treaties offers the opportunity for the parties collectively to revise any existing regime, through the subsequent intensification, attenuation or redirection of the undertakings originally established. Yet although this process is formally defined by its openness to every party alike,[160] there is obviously no guarantee that they will all view the proposed change with equal enthusiasm: to cater for this eventuality, each regime will have to determine whether unanimity is required as a condition of the adoption of amendments. Very often it is not, but in any event such changes will typically require specific, formal acceptance by States in order to become binding upon them individually. In the absence of such action, they will remain bound by the original, unamended version of the treaty in their relations with other parties.[161] As a result, a differentiation of commitment will inevitably emerge amongst the parties to amended instruments, contingent upon their formal response to the amendment in question. What is more, those that have accepted it will find themselves in the position of owing contrasting sets of obligations to the different

---

[159] Of course, it might be argued that the possibility in principle of such modification is actually latent in every treaty from the outset.

[160] Art. 40(2) and Art. 40(3) VCLT: *supra* n. 6.

[161] Arts. 39 and 40 (4) VCLT (cross-referencing Art. 30(4) VCLT): *supra* n. 6.

categories of other parties, as defined by such responses. These rules can plainly give rise to situations of considerable complexity, especially where treaties are amended on numerous occasions: certain treaties of the World Intellectual Property Organization on intellectual property, for example, have undergone several large-scale revisions since their original adoption (commencing in the late nineteenth century), and for a variety of reasons States have not always displayed great alacrity in accepting the most recent version.[162] The 1886 Berne Convention for the Protection of Literary and Artistic Works[163] is an example. The current version is the 1971 Paris revision as amended in 1979,[164] but a handful of members of the Union established are still bound only by the earlier acts adopted in Stockholm in 1967,[165] Brussels in 1948[166] or even Rome in 1928.[167] While there may well be agreements where such diversity of obligation is tolerable in practical terms, there are sure to be others where it is not, and in order to avoid the problems that would otherwise arise in the latter context, it will be necessary to ensure that amendments cannot enter into force without unanimous agreement.[168]

4.4.3   Adventitious Incremental Exclusion of Revising Measures

Less commonly, the agreed arrangement will be that duly adopted amendments become binding upon treaty parties *automatically*, though deference to sovereignty usually ensures that they at least be given the opportunity to opt out of the new measure. Despite the very wide interpretation given by the ILC, as noted earlier, to its substantive scope, the concept of reservations presumably cannot be sufficiently compendious to embrace the process under discussion here, since the effect of an opt-out of the present kind is to exclude the applicability of the revising measure in its entirety, rather than 'the legal effect of certain [of its] provisions', as required by the VCLT definition. Accordingly, there should be little occasion to have regard to the VCLT reservations

---

[162] For current information regarding these treaties, see www.wipo.int/treaties/en. For many of them, however, the position is seemingly much less chaotic than it was twenty years ago: for comparison, see Bowman and Harris, *supra* n. 35, Treaties 4, 6, 12, 13, 94 and 348.

[163] 168 CTS 185.   [164] 1990 UKTS 63.   [165] 828 UNTS 221.   [166] 331 UNTS 217.

[167] 123 LNTS 233.

[168] Consider, for example, the various protocols to the European Convention on Human Rights, some of which impose such a requirement while others do not.

regime in this connection,[169] suggesting that there will typically be rather little difference in terms purely of juridical effect between opt-out and opt-in arrangements where inter-temporal differentiation through response to amendments is concerned.

The distinction may nonetheless remain critical in a variety of practical and political respects. Thus, as the treaty-making practice of various international institutions makes clear, the strategy of catering for sovereign sensibilities specifically through an 'opt-out' approach to the activation and application of formal amendments offers enormous benefits to the ongoing vitality of treaty regimes, since it allows inertia – arguably the most potent force of all in international affairs – to operate in favour of reform rather than against it. In the case of IMO treaties, for example, securing the actual entry into force of amendments which had been agreed in principle proved a herculean task under the original, orthodox approach which required their positive formal acceptance by individual treaty parties.[170] By contrast, the inclusion in later conventions of a 'tacit' amendment procedure, whereby agreed revisions take effect automatically for all States that do not exclude them, has seen a host of technical modifications become operative with near universal effect and scarcely a murmur of discontent.[171] Admittedly, however, such a strategy is unlikely to prove viable wherever the competitive advantage of States is centrally at stake, and in such circumstances it may therefore be necessary at least to offer States parties the opportunity to reconsider their own positions in the event of any specific exercise by a fellow party of a power to opt out of revising measures. This was the case, for example, regarding periodic quota revisions under the 1946 Whaling Convention,[172] where vested national interest has all too commonly prevailed over global protective concern.

---

[169] Though its applicability probably cannot be excluded altogether, for example where a party seeks not to exclude the effect of the amendment entirely but rather to accept it subject to qualifications.

[170] For discussion, see A. O. Adede, 'Amendment Procedures for Conventions with Technical Annexes: The IMCO Experience', *Virginia JIL*, 17 (1977), 201–215, and the contribution to this volume by Lost-Sieminska at pp. 907–932 (Chapter 28).

[171] Most remarkably, the 1974 Convention for the Safety of Life at Sea, 1184 UNTS 2, and its Protocols of 1978, 1226 UNTS 237, and 1988, IMO Doc HSSC/CONF/11, have collectively been the subject of well over 150 amendments to date: see www.imo.org/en/About/Conventions/StatusOfConventions/Pages/Default.aspx.

[172] *Supra* n. 110; see especially Art. 5(3).

5 Concluding Observations

The preceding discussion provides clear confirmation that, notwithstanding the basic general perception of multilateral norm-creating conventions as a means of imposing uniform standards of conduct upon the States that elect to become party to them, there is in fact ample capacity within the toolkit of international law to permit, at least to some degree, the personalised tailoring of the obligations accepted to meet the needs of individual States. As regards the latter perspective, the recent emergence of treaty regimes which incorporate not only general undertakings to which all parties must commit in principle but also detailed action plans which spell out more precisely what such commitments specifically entail for individual States represents a significant development in treaty-making, and one which brings about a virtual fusion of the long-recognised 'contractual' and 'law-making' categories of international agreement. It seems entirely possible that in the future this particular model of agreement may well become commonplace or even standard in certain subject areas of international legislative activity, providing further confirmation of the wisdom of the ILC in resisting all blandishments to provide specialised modes of legal regulation for the various different categories of treaty-instrument.

At present, however, the selective personalisation of generally applicable substantive obligations more commonly serves the purpose of rendering the treaty regimes that create them more palatable to individual States, and hence more likely to attract participation and support. Undoubtedly, there is a price to be paid for this element of flexibility, which is manifest in terms both of the dilution of the overall substantive effectiveness of the treaty regime in question and also of the increased technical complexity of the juridical inter-relationships amongst the parties that may result from recourse to the various mechanisms through which this differentiation of obligations may be generated. There are, however, means available through which the severity of these problems can be minimised, above all through the initial selection by treaty drafters of the optimum method of generating the flexibility desired. In general, the deployment of 'opt-in' arrangements may generate fewer technical problems than devices which permit opting-out, but where the latter cannot realistically be avoided, the incorporation of balancing measures, such as processes through which reservations may be reviewed and, where appropriate, withdrawn by the States that formulated them, merit serious consideration. Be that as it may, the disadvantages generated by the differentiation of legal obligations have generally been considered a price worth paying if increased participation is the result.

In some cases, of course, no amount of structural flexibility may ultimately prove sufficient to secure the level of engagement desired. The 1950 International Convention for the Protection of Birds, for example, was, as explained earlier, noteworthy for the range and diversity of the mechanisms of this kind that it employed, but this did not produce any noticeable alacrity on the part of States to assume its obligations: it attracted a mere ten parties in total and did not even enter into force until 1963.[173] Of the (seven) specified States, moreover, that were explicitly granted a certain latitude with regard to its application, only the Netherlands, Sweden and Iceland chose ultimately to participate. Nevertheless, the undeniable limitations of the Convention's attractiveness to States are probably attributable more to the slowness of the governments of the day to grasp the practical importance of trans-national co-operation for avian conservation as such[174] than to deficiencies in the particular drafting techniques employed to address any concerns they might have entertained over the fine detail of the regime.

The General Act for the Pacific Settlement of International Disputes – another imaginative experiment in the differentiability of legal undertakings – was scarcely more successful. It is easy to see why maximum flexibility should have been thought desirable in this case, since there was some virtue in securing *any* level of commitment on the part of States to pacific modes of dispute settlement, however restricted, but in the event the strategy did not prove sufficient to overcome the innate wariness of States in this area; the Act attracted only twenty-two acceptances in total, only two of which opted to make use of the modular latitude offered.[175] Following the dissolution of the Permanent Court of International Justice

---

[173] *Supra* n. 82. The Convention is still technically in force, but has for all practical purposes been superseded by other instruments (as to which see Bowman, Davies and Redgwell, *supra* n. 82, pp. 199–238) and was declared at the 1992 Rio Earth Summit to be effectively 'moribund': see P. H. Sand (ed.), *The Effectiveness of International Environmental Agreements* (Cambridge: Grotius Publications, 1992), p. 63.

[174] Some countries which ultimately declined to participate, such as the UK, responded instead by adopting national legislation which was, on the face of it, reasonably well conceived and comprehensive, but purely unilateral measures are unlikely to be truly effective for the protection of migratory species: for discussion of the historical development of protection at the international level, see Bowman, Davies and Redgwell, *ibid.*, and R. Boardman, *International Organisation and the Conservation of Nature* (London & Basingstoke: Macmillan, 1981), pp. 159–172.

[175] See https://treaties.un.org/pages/LONViewDetails.aspx?src=LON&id=567&chapter=30&lang=en.

and the League of Nations, the recurrent references to such institutions in the text of the Act rendered it uncertain whether it remained in force, and a number of parties opted to denounce the instrument once it was brought to their attention that it might be.[176] An appropriately revised version of the Act, concluded in 1949, was even less successful, attracting fewer than ten acceptances, though by that time alternative mechanisms for commitment to peaceful processes of dispute settlement were at least becoming available.[177]

Yet, despite these failures, there have doubtless been a great many more instances where the extension of a degree of individualised normative flexibility has been important in securing the participation of States which would probably have remained aloof in its absence. In a world of sovereign States, where commitment to exclusively national interests (whether real or imagined) still appears to carry more weight than priorities of genuinely global concern, the attraction of differentiable obligations is likely to remain strong, and the need for perspicacity and ingenuity on the part of treaty negotiators correspondingly crucial.

---

[176] These occurred for the most part in the mid-1970s, prompted by attempts by various States to rely upon the Act as a means of founding jurisdiction on the part of the International Court over particular disputes. In each case, however, the Court ultimately declined to reach a definitive determination of this general question, identifying a more specific reason why the Act could not be relied upon in each of the cases that came before them: see Case Concerning the Aerial Incident of 10 August 1999: Pakistan v. India (Jurisdiction) (2000) ICJ Rep. 12, at pp. 23–25 (paragraphs 26–28).

[177] At the regional level, for example, as to which see the 1957 European Convention for the Peaceful Settlement of Disputes, 320 UNTS 241, which, interestingly, adopted a very similar modular structure.

14

Regulating Treaty Breaches

CHRISTIAN J. TAMS

1 Introduction

Since 1946, States have registered 51,664 treaties with the United Nations.[1] A further 4,834 had been registered with the League of Nations.[2] To get an accurate picture of the reality of international treaty commitments, one would need to add non-registered treaties (a considerable number, which Paul Reuter at some point put at 25 per cent of the overall figure)[3] as well as treaties predating 1919. But for present purposes, the aggregate figure of 56,498 treaties registered with world organisations since 1919 may suffice. As States are not perfect, and as many treaties impose far-reaching obligations, it is hardly conceivable that there should have been a moment of perfect global compliance with treaty commitments: instead, on pure probability, and reversing a famous statement, one might perhaps say that 'almost all nations violate some of their treaties at least some of the time'.[4] Some of these breaches are dramatic (say, acts of aggression committed in breach of Article 2(4) of the 1945 United Nations Charter),[5] others are negligible, and many may in fact go unnoticed. But conversely, if States do 'disagre[e] on

---

[1] This figure relies on registration numbers – 51,664 being the number of the most recently registered treaty as of Nov. 2014. It does not include treaties amending or terminating prior treaties, which – while formally separate treaties – are registered under the same number as the parent treaty. (My thanks to the UN Treaty Section, and notably its head, Dr. Santiago Villalpando, for clarification on this point.) Details about United Nations practice are provided at: https://treaties.un.org/Pages/DB.aspx?path=DB/UNTS/page1_CIintro_en.xml.

[2] See https://treaties.un.org/Pages/LONOnline.aspx.

[3] P. Reuter, *Introduction to the Law of Treaties* (Abingdon: Routledge, 2nd ed., 1995), p. 54 (note accompanying paragraph 86).

[4] Cf. L. Henkin, *How Nations Behave: Law and Foreign Policy* (New York, NY: Columbia University Press, 2nd ed., 1979), p. 47 ('almost all nations observe almost all principles of international law and almost all of their obligations almost all the time').

[5] 1 UNTS 16.

a point of law or fact', and find themselves in a 'conflict of legal views or of interests',[6] their disagreement typically, at some level, relates to the interpretation or application of a treaty.[7]

Treaty breaches are not only common; the more relevant among them also are a source of friction in international relations. Of course, other parties can simply choose to ignore the treaty breach. But if they do not, they have a range of options, including protests; negotiations; coercive measures to put pressure on the responsible State or the 'freezing' of cooperation with it; the institution of legal proceedings before competent courts; the suspension of the treaty allegedly breached; in some instances, resort to self-defence, etc.[8] What course is taken depends on the circumstances of the case, the history of relations between the States concerned and, not least, the character and importance of the treaty allegedly being breached. But from the mere listing of possible options, it is quite understandable that (as was observed almost fifty years ago) treaty breaches 'pla[y] an important rôle in both international law and foreign office practice'.[9] Treaty breaches matter, as do responses to treaty breaches; and international law as a legal system needs to regulate both.

Because breaches and responses can be so very different, general international law can hardly be expected to regulate matters comprehensively. Particular treaties – any of the 56,498 referred to previously – set out the precise obligations imposed upon States, and often, treaties will regulate what should happen if these obligations are not complied with. With a few exceptions – outer limits notably set by Articles 52, 53 and 64 of the 1969 Vienna Convention on the Law of Treaties (VCLT)[10] – general international law does not restrict the freedom of States to agree on particular treaty commitments, and indeed, the mass of international treaty law covers international relations in their proverbial

---

[6] See *Mavrommatis Palestine Concessions*: Greece v. Great Britain, 1924 PCIJ, Series A, No. 2, at p. 11 (defining the notion of a 'dispute').

[7] See A. Aust, *Modern Treaty Law and Practice* (Cambridge: Cambridge University Press, 2nd ed., 2007), p. 352 ('most disputes between states, and especially those which are referred to international adjudication, involve, mainly or partly, the interpretation or application of a treaty').

[8] A. D. McNair provides a helpful list of six 'remedies for breach accruing to other party', which comprises unilateral abrogation, retaliatory suspension, claims for reparation before arbitral/judicial institutions, non-forcible measures to secure reparation, invocation of sanctions provided for by treaty, and prosecution of individuals: A. D. McNair, *The Law of Treaties* (Oxford: Clarendon Press, 1961), p. 539.

[9] R. B. Bilder, 'Breach of Treaty and Response Thereto', *Proceedings ASIL*, 61 (1967), 193–204.

[10] 1155 UNTS 331.

'infinite variety'. As far as responses are concerned, States remain largely free to design particular treaty rules of their liking. Major multilateral regimes – some of them specifically addressed in detailed contributions to this project – are heavily institutionalised; some rely on courts as enforcement agents; others place a premium on decentralised, private responses; some allow for sanctions, which others exclude; still others transfer procedural rights on non-State actors, etc.

Faced with this diversity and variety, the impact of a general regime governing treaty breaches and responses must remain limited. Still, such a general regime – a framework within which breaches and responses are to be addressed – does exist. However, this general regime has the character of a patchwork. Not only is it residual in scope, it is also incomplete and relatively incoherent. The main aspects of the regime are to be found in the international community's two main sets of 'meta-rules', its texts on the law of treaties and the law of responsibility. The subsequent contribution surveys the main elements of this patchwork and highlights the respective contributions of the law of treaties and the law of international responsibility to the general regime governing treaty breaches. In so doing, it seeks to shed light, not only on the substance of the applicable legal rules, but also on the architecture of the international regulation of treaty breaches.

2   The General Law of Treaties: Limited Guidance

Given its status as the central text on treaty law, one might expect the VCLT to regulate questions of treaty breaches and responses. However, it does so only in passing: in the words of Shabtai Rosenne, 'the provisions of the Convention, taken in their entirety, only touch the fringe of the legal and political problems which breach of a treaty ... will create'.[11] In fact, the term 'breach' appears in merely three provisions (Articles 60, 61, 62 VCLT) and is only central to one of them (Article 60 VCLT). The Convention's contribution to the regime of treaty breaches remains highly limited. More specifically, two features of the Convention deserve to be addressed: its decision not to define the notion of a 'breach of treaty' as such and its attempt to regulate – in Article 60 VCLT – one particular response to qualified treaty breaches.

[11] S. Rosenne, *Breach of Treaty* (Cambridge: Grotius Publications, 1985), p. 44. For a similar observation, see B. Simma, 'Reflections on Article 60 of the Vienna Convention on the Law of Treaties and Its Background in General International Law', *ÖZöR*, 20 (1970), 5–83, at 83.

2.1   A Law of Treaties without Rules on Treaty Breaches

The Convention notably provides limited guidance on what amounts to a breach of treaty. It does not attempt to define the term in the abstract but contents itself with addressing (and defining) one instance of a qualified breach, namely the notion of a 'material breach' as a ground justifying the suspension or termination of treaties (Article 60 VCLT). Yet as will be shown later, that definition is not only controversial; the instance of its regulation is also relatively irrelevant in practice. All this bears out Rosenne's observation: the VCLT 'only touch[es] the fringe' of treaty breaches.[12]

There are different aspects to its non-regulation. First, and unsurprisingly, the Convention as a 'treaty on treaties' of general application does not attempt to spell out the substantive obligations imposed by particular treaty clauses; this is a matter for each of the 56,498 particular treaties: for the 'primary rules'. It is worth noting, however, how little the general law of treaties as set out in the VCLT engages with the primary rules, i.e. the substance of treaty obligations. Unlike other general texts, it does not attempt to spell out general rules on attribution, which would define whose conduct – violative of a treaty commitment – could implicate a State.[13] Nor does the Vienna Convention categorise common types of treaties (sale; loans; exchanges, donations, cession of territory, treatment of investors, etc.)[14] with a view to defining or describing core obligations imposed by them – a point worth stressing because it is hardly ever made and because many domestic statutes consider this to be a key aspect of their regulation of contract law.[15] In contrast to domestic contract laws, the VCLT drafters decided not to standardise international treaties in their infinite variety. What they did was to distil general rules on treaty interpretation that would help identify the true meaning of a treaty provision (probably best regarded as a toolkit allowing diverse results to be reached)[16] and a set of fragmentary provisions on the temporal, spatial and personal scope of application of treaties.[17] But these are fairly

---

[12] Rosenne, *supra* n. 11, at p. 44.

[13] Contrast Section 3 of this chapter for brief comment on the approach adopted in the general rules on responsibility.

[14] See, further, the contribution to this volume of Brölmann at pp. 79–102 (Chapter 4).

[15] See, e.g., Arts. 1582–2061 of the French Code Civil and ss. 433–811 of the German Civil Code (BGB).

[16] Arts. 31–33 VCLT: *supra* n. 10. See, also, the contribution to this volume of Gardiner at pp. 335–362 (Chapter 11).

[17] See Arts. 28, 29 and 34 VCLT: *supra* n. 10.

cautious inroads into the substance of treaty obligations. The overarching impression is that of a convention that consciously stays clear of the substance of treaty obligations. Leaving substantive questions to the primary rules, its regulation of the notion of treaty breach is bound to be thin.[18]

Second, and perhaps a bit more surprisingly, the Convention consciously leaves to a side one major question of treaty law, namely that of responsibility for treaty breaches. During its debate, the International Law Commission (ILC) was relatively firm that 'the general principles governing the reparation to be made for breach of a treaty' would be addressed not within the project on the law of treaties but as part of the Commission's broader framework of State responsibility.[19] As is well known, this decision was formalised through Article 73 VCLT, according to which '[t]he provisions of the present Convention shall not prejudge any question that may arise ... from the international responsibility of a State'. The point is typically taken for granted but deserves to be mentioned as it sets international law apart from many domestic legal systems that differentiate between contractual and non-contractual responsibility.[20] It was based on a broad notion of responsibility that would not distinguish between violations of contractual and non-contractual obligations but treat treaty breaches as a sub-category of international wrongful conduct. This approach of course facilitated agreement on the law of treaties as a particularly thorny set of issues that did not have be addressed. At the same time, it means that the topic of the present contribution would come to be characterised essentially as a problem of responsibility rather than of treaty law.

---

[18] According to Rosenne, the drafters chose to focus on 'the treaty as an instrument' as opposed to 'the treaty as a source of obligation': *supra* n. 11, at pp. 3–8.

[19] *YbILC* (1966–II), 177.

[20] For clear restatements of the principle, see *Case Concerning the Difference between New Zealand and France Concerning the Interpretation or Application of Two Agreements, Concluded on 9 July 1986 between the Two States and Which Related to the Problems Arising from the Rainbow Warrior Affair*, RIAA, Vol. XX, 215–284, at p. 251 (paragraph 75): 'in the field of international law there is no distinction between contractual and tortious responsibility'. In its Commentary to Art. 12 of the Articles on State Responsibility, Official Records of the General Assembly, Fifty-Sixth Session, Supp. No. 10 (A/56/10), the ILC seemed to overstate the point when noting that 'there is no room in international law for a distinction, such as is drawn by some legal systems, between the regime of responsibility for breach of a treaty and for breach of some other rule, i.e. for responsibility arising *ex contractu* or *ex delicto*': J. Crawford, *The International Law Commission's Articles on State Responsibility: Introduction, Text and Commentaries* (Cambridge: Cambridge University Press, 2002), p. 127.

2.2 Responding to Treaty Breaches: Article 60 VCLT

Given the decision to 'outsource' questions of responsibility for treaty breaches, the VCLT was unlikely to provide much guidance on questions of remedies and redress. In fact, only one aspect was to be regulated, *viz.* the impact of a breach on the continuance of treaty relations between the parties. This aspect is addressed in Article 60 VCLT, which recognises that, under certain conditions, a treaty breach by one party may permit another party to suspend or terminate the treaty in whole or in part.

2.2.1 General Considerations

Article 60 is one of the crucial provisions of the Convention.[21] While the provision has hardly ever been applied, debates leading to its adoption helped shape contemporary thinking on questions of legal injury and, more generally, on the legal interests involved in multilateral treaties. Before addressing these and other aspects in more detail, it is worth clarifying the rationale of the provision: Article 60 VCLT is concerned not with the enforcement of international law nor with obtaining reparation or compensation (these matters being left to the law of State responsibility). The provision is based on the idea of 'inverse' or 'negative reciprocity' (also referred to as the principle *inadimplenti non est adimplendum*), according to which a party cannot be expected to respect its obligations under a treaty if the other party refuses to honour them. This logic informs Article 60 VCLT, which recognises an exception to the duty to perform treaties but only permits responses affecting the same treaty that allegedly had been breached. More specifically, the provision envisages two forms of responses: first, the partial or complete suspension of obligations under the relevant treaty, which temporarily 'releases the parties between which the operation of the treaty is suspended from the

---

[21] For commentary, see, e.g., M. M. Gomaa, *Suspension or Termination of Treaties for Grounds of Breach* (The Hague: Kluwer Law International, 1996); R. Pizillo Mazzeschi, 'Termination and Suspension of Treaties for Grounds of Breach' in B. Simma and M. Spinedi (eds.), *United Nations Codification of State Responsibility* (New York, NY: Oceana Publications, 1983), pp. 57–94; F. L. Kirgis, 'Some Lingering Questions about Article 60 of the Vienna Convention on the Law of Treaties', *Cornell ILJ*, 22 (1989), 549–573; D. W. Greig, 'Reciprocity, Proportionality, and the Law of Treaties', *Virginia JIL*, 34 (1994), 295–403; F. Capotorti, 'L'extinction et la suspension des traités', *Hague Recueil*, 134 (1971-III), 417–587; E. Schwelb, 'Termination or Suspension of a Treaty as a Consequence of its Breach', *Indian JIL*, 7 (1967), 309–334; Simma, *supra* n. 11, and B. Simma and C. J. Tams, 'Article 60 (1969)' in O. Corten and P. Klein (eds.), *The Vienna Conventions on the Law of Treaties: A Commentary* (Vol. II) (Oxford: Oxford University Press, 2011), pp. 1351–1378.

obligation to perform the treaty in their mutual relations during the period of the suspension'.[22] Within bilateral treaties and, exceptionally, by mutual accord, within multilateral regimes, Article 60 VCLT also allows for the partial or complete termination of the treaty, that is the permanent 'releas[e] [of] the parties from any obligation further to perform the treaty'.[23] Both suspension and termination only take effect prospectively, but both – unlike responses based on the law of State responsibility – involve the temporary or permanent extinction of a norm and (at least temporarily) remove the underlying legal bond between the parties to the dispute.[24] This may explain the VCLT's rather cautious approach: seeking to ensure the continued application of treaties, Article 60 formulates a very narrow exception that does not allow States to exit their treaty commitments lightly. This cautious approach in turn is manifest in three decisions taken during the drafting of Article 60 VCLT – which the subsequent sections revisit in turn.

2.2.2   The Requirement of a Material Breach

The narrow scope of Article 60 is evident first and foremost from the restriction to material breaches. In order to suspend or terminate a treaty, States must be able to point to a material breach by another party; non-material breaches, by contrast, are not actionable under the Vienna Convention regime.[25] The concept of 'material breach' itself is defined in Article 60(3) VCLT, which is two-pronged: it covers '(a) a repudiation of the treaty not sanctioned by the present Convention; or (b) the violation of a provision essential to the accomplishment of the object or purpose of the treaty'.

The essence of Article 60's restriction to material breaches is clear; however, the precise meaning of the two prongs of paragraph 3 is less so.

---

[22] Art. 72 VCLT: *supra* n. 10.   [23] Art. 70 VCLT: *supra* n. 10.

[24] Cf. J. Crawford, Third Report on State Responsibility, Doc. A/CN.4/507 and Add. 1–4 (15 March, 15 June, 10 and 18 July and 4 Aug. 2000) (paragraphs 334–325), with reference to the decision of the International Court of Justice in *Case Concerning Gabčíkovo-Nagymaros Project (Hungary/Slovakia)* (1997) ICJ Rep. 7, at p. 39 (paragraph 48); see, also, R. Provost, 'Reciprocity in Human Rights and Humanitarian Law', *BYbIL*, 65 (1994), 383–454, at 398–399.

[25] This was generally agreed for termination. By contrast, in his work, Sir Gerald Fitzmaurice had proposed to distinguish between suspension and termination and permit at least the partial suspension in response to 'lesser' breaches: see G. G. Fitzmaurice, Second Report on the Law of Treaties, Doc. A/CN.4/107 (15 March 1957), p. 30 (draft Art. 18) and G. G. Fitzmaurice, Fourth Report on the Law of Treaties, Doc. A/CN.4/120 (17 March 1959), p. 50 (draft Art. 37).

The first prong – paragraph 3(a) on 'repudiation' – has not prompted much debate. The *travaux préparatoires* suggest that it was meant to cover not only formal acts such as the official denunciation of a treaty but 'all the means available to a State attempting to free itself of obligations under a treaty'.[26] As Thomas Giegerich notes, '[t]hat would include all instances of invoking the invalidity, termination or suspension of a treaty', including the instances in which a recognised title of invalidity etc. is invoked, but its requirements are not met.[27] By contrast, if the Convention's requirements for the suspension, termination or invalidity are met, then the treaty can (of course) be repudiated, as the terms 'not sanctioned by the present Convention' in paragraph 3(a) make clear. In its *Namibia* advisory opinion, the International Court of Justice (ICJ) took the view that by openly disregarding obligations deriving from the 1922 mandate agreement, South Africa in fact had 'disavowed' it,[28] which in view of the Court's majority could be viewed as a repudiation.[29] But other than that, practice has remained sparse. In essence, the provision on repudiation seeks to capture those treaty breaches that concern the force of the treaty as a whole.

The second prong of the definition, contained in Article 60(3)(b) VCLT, is of broader scope. Under the terms of that clause, a breach is 'material' if it affects 'a provision essential to the accomplishment of the object or purpose of the treaty'. As has been observed frequently, this is a rather curious way of defining the term: it is not the breach that is qualified (as 'grave', 'systematic', 'widespread', etc.) but the character of the obligation breached. As a consequence, grave breaches of non-essential provisions do not give rise to a right to seek the suspension or termination (which seems acceptable), while trivial breaches of essential provisions could (which may perhaps be counter-intuitive).[30]

---

[26] See the statement by Roberto Ago (President): UNCLOT II 115.

[27] T. Giegerich, 'Article 60' in O. Dörr and K. Schmalenbach (eds.), *Vienna Convention on the Law of Treaties: A Commentary* (Berlin: Springer, 2012), pp. 1021–1050, at p. 1030.

[28] *Legal Consequences for States of the Continuing Presence of South Africa in Namibia (South West Africa) Notwithstanding Security Council Resolution 276 (1970)* (Advisory Opinion) (1971) ICJ Rep. 16, at p. 47 (paragraph 95).

[29] *Ibid.* See, also, the Separate Opinion of Judge de Castro at p. 218. It must be noted however that the Court did not clearly distinguish between the cases of 'repudiation' (Art. 60(3)(a) VCLT) and 'violations of essential provisions' (Art. 60(3)(b) VCLT). In an Annex to his dissenting opinion, at pp. 299–317, Sir Gerald Fitzmaurice criticised the majority's approach: in his view, South Africa had denied the existence of the obligation, which he considered (contrary to the view advocated in the text) to be distinct from its repudiation: at pp. 300–301 (paragraph 6).

[30] See the remarks in Greig, *supra* n. 21, at 342–343, and P. Malanczuk, *Akehurst's Modern Introduction to International Law* (New York, NY: Routledge, 7th ed., 1997), p. 143.

In applying this provision, the key question is to identify which provisions of a treaty are 'essential to the accomplishment of [its] object or purpose'. Where treaties have a neat and clear focus, possibly one expressed in the title or preamble, this can be an easy task: of course, a duty to extradite is 'essential' to the object and purpose of an extradition treaty, just as boundary treaties in essence seek to demarcate claims to territory. But that common-sense approach fails where treaties comprehensively address broad areas of international relations. (Which of the hundreds of provisions of the 1982 United Nations Convention on the Law of the Sea are essential to the accomplishment of that treaty's object and purpose?)[31] In the absence of clear guidance in State practice, that question eschews a clear answer.[32] The *travaux préparatoires* however at least provide one useful guideline: they suggest that while only breaches of qualified provisions trigger the right to suspend or terminate a treaty, for a provision to be essential, it need not necessarily regulate the central purpose of the treaty. This seems implicit in the Commission's decision to drop the term 'fundamental breach' (which had appeared in Fitzmaurice's draft articles)[33] and to replace it with 'material breach'. As the ILC's Commentary indicates, the change was intended to permit responses against breaches of provisions that are ancillary, but important.[34] Dispute settlement clauses are the most prominent example;[35] but the drafters' conscious decision to avoid the notion of 'fundamental breach' is of more general relevance: it might lead to an understanding of Article 60(3)(b) VCLT that recognises the need for a qualified breach but accepts that, within comprehensive agreements, there is room for different essential provisions.

While that may justify some measure of flexibility, the fact remains that Article 60 VCLT deliberately requires breaches to be qualified. Perhaps surprisingly, the Commission 'was unanimous that the right to terminate or suspend must be limited to cases where the breach is of a serious character'.[36] As in other provisions of the Convention, the overarching concern seems to have been with the continuance and

---

[31] 1833 UNTS 3.

[32] *See*, further, the contribution to this volume of Kritsiotis at pp. 237–302 (Chapter 9).

[33] See draft Art. 19(2) of Fitzmaurice, Second Report on the Law of Treaties, *supra* n. 25, at p. 31.

[34] ILC Commentary, *YbILC* (1966–II), 255 (paragraph 9) and, further, H. Waldock, Second Report on the Law of Treaties, A/CN.4/156 and Add.1–3 (20 March, 10 Apr., 30 Apr. and 5 June 1963), p. 75 (paragraph 11).

[35] See Waldock, Second Report on the Law of Treaties, *ibid.*

[36] *YbILC* (1966–II), 255 (paragraph 9).

stability of treaty relations; hence, responses releasing the party or parties from their obligations (if only temporarily) are not facilitated.

2.2.3 Standing to Respond to Material Breaches

If Article 60 VCLT continues to prompt debate, then this is largely because of its ambitious attempt at regulating which parties to a treaty can react against a prior breach. Article 60(2) VCLT formulates a general rule of standing, which – while discussed in the particular context of treaty suspension or termination – is considered to be of wider relevance.

The question to be addressed on the face of it seems rather straightforward. If a treaty is repudiated, or else materially breached, who would be able to seek its suspension or termination? In the context of bilateral treaties, this hardly requires much discussion: of course, the other party could, as it is affected by the prior non-performance. Yet this common-sense solution does not work – or at least does not work automatically – within the context of multilateral treaties. Against that light, the ILC – having opted to draw up a treaty law regime that in principle was unitary, as if all treaties were the same – was forced to engage with the implications of multilateralism in addressing what, really, is a niche aspect of the Vienna law of treaties.

The ILC's approach, as reflected in Article 60(2) VCLT, is a mix of pragmatism and principled considerations. Pragmatism reigns insofar as Article 60(2)(a) VCLT recognises the forces of near-unanimity: where all State parties to a multilateral treaty, with the exception of the defaulting State, collectively agree to terminate or suspend the treaty, they can do so.[37] Yet, especially in widely ratified treaties and those that do not establish institutions for deliberations among treaty partners, this is bound to be a rule for exceptional circumstances.[38]

In devising a regime for individual responses, the Commission – in line with its general concern for treaty stability – was much more cautious. According to Article 60(2)(b) VCLT, individual States can only respond to material breaches of treaties if those breaches 'specially affect' them (and even then are restricted to suspension). In essence, this means that, where

---

[37] For details, see Simma and Tams, *supra* n. 21, at pp. 1361–1362.

[38] In its 1971 *Namibia* advisory opinion, the ICJ seemed to interpret the termination of the mandate for South West Africa as an exercise of the right arising under Art. 60(2)(a) VCLT: however, even this stretched the wording of the provision, as the relevant General Assembly resolution was not adopted unanimously: see *Legal Consequences for States of the Continuing Presence of South Africa in Namibia (South West Africa), supra* n. 28, at p. 47 (paragraph 94).

a multilateral treaty obligation is breached, the multilateral treaty remains in force between all parties, while only States that have sustained some form of individual injury can respond. The notions of 'special effects' or 'individual injury' are not defined. As is indicated by the *travaux préparatoires*, the ILC – drawing on the work of Sir Gerald Fitzmaurice – mainly thought of obligations that bound more than two States but were to be performed between pairs of States.[39] Obligations under consular and diplomatic conventions illustrate the point: they bind most of the States in the world, but breaches will typically only be of concern between pairs of sending and receiving States; hence responses would have to stay within this reciprocal, or 'quasi-bilateral', treaty relationship.

Beyond these obligations, the traditional criterion of damage might help in identifying which treaty parties are 'specially affected'.[40] For example, a breach of a multilateral human rights convention individually injures the State of nationality of the victim, just as the illegal dumping of toxic substances on the high seas (in violation of a maritime convention) could individually injure a nearby coastal State most affected by the conduct. Finally, even within multilateral settings, international law may of course recognise a particular State's special status, e.g. as a protective power under a treaty.[41] In all these settings, the breach of a multilateral treaty obligation would specially affect one treaty party, and this specially affected State would be entitled to respond in line with Article 60(2)(b) VCLT.

However, that provision is equally relevant for what it does not say: in requiring some form of individual injury, however defined, the drafters opted against creating a general right, of all treaty parties, to respond to breaches of a multilateral obligation. Such a general right of response, initially envisaged in the first reading draft,[42] was considered to pose a threat to the stability of treaty relations, and hence not endorsed. At Vienna, delegates added a further layer of protection by expressly excluding the suspension or termination of 'provisions relating to the

---

[39] See Simma and Tams, *supra* n. 21, at p. 1364 for details and references.

[40] The following draws on B. Simma and C. J. Tams, 'Responding to Treaty Breaches' in D. B. Hollis (ed.), *The Oxford Guide to Treaties* (Oxford: Oxford University Press, 2012), pp. 576–604, at pp. 589–590.

[41] Art. 10(2) to and Annex IV of the 1946 Peace Treaty with Italy, 49 UNTS 3, provide an example in point in that they recognise Austria's special right to protect the German-speaking inhabitants of South Tyrol.

[42] See draft Art. 42(2)(a), adopted in 1963, pursuant to 'any other party' could respond to breaches of multilateral treaties by way of suspension: *YbILC* (1963–II), 204.

protection of the human person contained in treaties of a humanitarian character, in particular to provisions prohibiting any form of reprisals against persons protected by such treaties'.[43]

Or rather, it was only endorsed in respect of one particular – and very curious – category of multilateral obligations: according to Article 60(2)(c) VCLT, each and every treaty party can respond to material breaches of so-called integral or interdependent obligations, where the material breach 'by one party radically changes the position of every party with respect to the further performance of its obligations under the treaty'.[44] Just as Article 60(2)(b) VCLT, so Article 60(2)(c) VCLT has its roots in Fitzmaurice's attempt to classify treaty obligations. In essence, for a narrow circle of integral obligations, Fitzmaurice and the ILC were willing to accept that one party's material breach would justify responses by all other treaty parties acting individually.[45] The key question is how that narrow circle of obligations can be identified. Since Fitzmaurice's reports, the same, very few, examples keep being referred to, notably obligations under disarmament treaties and obligations not to acquire sovereign rights in certain areas, etc.[46] Perhaps, indeed, any breach of such obligations would 'radically chang[e] the position of every party with respect to the further performance of its obligations under the treaty'. But did this justify a special category; could this not have been dealt with as part of the flexible notion of 'special effects'? The ILC in its work on treaties felt a special rule was needed and was prepared exceptionally to admit a general right of response. But so narrowly did it define the exception that it barely takes away from the general (and restrictive) rule.

---

[43] See Art. 60(5) VCLT: *supra* n. 10. See, further, Simma and Tams, *supra* n. 21, at pp. 1366–1368, for critical comment.

[44] On integral obligations, see, e.g., Fitzmaurice, Second Report on the Law of Treaties, *supra* note 25, at pp. 30–31 (draft Art. 18) and 53–54 (draft Art. 19). For an analysis of Fitzmaurice's 'structural approach', see B. Simma, *Das Reziprozitätselement im Zustandekommen völkerrechtlicher Verträge* (Berlin: Duncker & Humblot, 1972); E. Decaux, *La Réciprocité en droit international* (Paris: L.G.D.J., 1980) and C. J. Tams, *Enforcing Obligations Erga Omnes in International Law* (Cambridge: Cambridge University Press, 2005), pp. 48–63.

[45] Sicilianos speaks of 'global reciprocity': L.-A. Sicilianos, 'The Classification of Obligations and the Multilateral Dimension of the Relations of International Responsibility', *EJIL*, 13 (2002), 1127–1145, at 1135.

[46] Further details are in M. Fitzmaurice and O. Elias, *Contemporary Issues in the Law of Treaties* (Utrecht: Eleven International Publishing, 2005), pp. 158–164, and Simma and Tams, *supra* n. 21, at pp. 1365–1366.

Summarising the Convention's approach, one might perhaps say that the Commission went out of its way to formulate a differentiated regime that would not only reflect differences between bilateral and multilateral treaties but also do justice to the different structures underlying multi-lateral obligations. In the latter respect, Article 60 VCLT draws on Fitzmaurice's earlier (and insightful) work, which the Vienna Convention otherwise hardly takes up. Yet, behind the facade of differ-entiation and nuance, this provision's approach to standing fundamen-tally remains restrictive: individual treaty parties should only be entitled to invoke a prior (material) breach as a ground justifying treaty action if that prior breach had specially affected them. This was obvious in the bilateral setting but otherwise required some form of individual injury or an exceptionally narrow type of integral obligation. All in all, the crucial debates on standing resulted in a narrow approach that restricted room for individual responses to breaches and that protected the integrity of treaties notwithstanding prior (material) breaches. Within the context of Article 60 VCLT, this may have been understandable; but where other forms of responses, based on different rationales, are concerned, the restrictive rule would come under pressure.

2.2.4   Cumbersome Procedures

In addition to requiring a qualified (material) breach and to restricting the circle of States entitled to respond to breaches, the Vienna Convention subjects responses based on Article 60 VCLT to a rather cumbersome procedure. Individual treaty parties seeking to respond to a material breach are not at liberty simply to suspend a treaty but have to activate the complex procedure prescribed in Articles 65 *et seq.* VCLT.[47] As is made clear in those provisions (which were hotly debated at Vienna),[48] treaty parties seeking to invoke Article 60 VCLT would have to notify their claims, would have to await the end of a cooling-off period of three months and would then be required to agree with the defaulting State on an amicable mode of dispute resolution. To make matters worse, failing agreement, the dispute would be submitted to mandatory con-ciliation according to Annex I to the Vienna Convention. All this is much more than a formality. In fact, the VCLT's responses to (material) treaty

---

[47] For detailed assessments see the contributions by H. Krieger, 'Article 65', 'Article 66', 'Annex to Article 66', 'Article 67' and 'Article 68' in Dörr and Schmalenbach (eds.), *supra* n. 27, pp. 1131–1177.

[48] Sinclair provides a detailed account: I. Sinclair, *The Vienna Convention on the Law of Treaties* (Manchester: Manchester University Press, 2nd ed., 1984), pp. 226–233.

breaches are placed in a 'procedural straightjacket' – which makes effective responses highly unlikely and swift responses virtually impossible.[49] While States have come to terms with the substantive imitation to material breaches as defined in Article 60(3) VCLT and often endorsed the regime of standing set out in Article 60(2) VCLT, it is indicative that they have boycotted the cumbersome procedural regime of Articles 65–68 VCLT, which does not seem to have been applied at all.[50] In light of this (non-)practice, the statement of the ICJ in *Case Concerning Gabčikovo-Nagymaros Project* that 'Articles 65 to 67 of the Vienna Convention on the Law of Treaties, if not codifying customary law, at least generally reflect customary international law and contain certain procedural principles which are based on an obligation to act in good faith' may not have be fully convincing (and in fact was prefaced by '[b]oth Parties agree that').[51] A decade later, the Court seems to have clarified matters by noting, in *Case Concerning Armed Activities on the Territory of the Congo* (New Application: 2002), that Article 66 (providing for compulsory conciliation) was not 'declaratory of customary international law'.[52] And indeed, given the complete absence of practice, it seems difficult to argue that the procedural requirements set out in Articles 65–68 VCLT should have attained customary status.

2.3   Concluding Thoughts

As is clear from the foregoing, the Vienna Convention indeed only addresses marginal aspects of the legal regime governing treaty breaches. Having decided that the big question – responsibility for treaty breaches – would not be treated as part of the law of treaties, the drafters could only

---

[49] Krieger is more positive: according to her, '[b]y emphasizing the stability of treaty regimes, the procedural requirements also contribute to the efficiency of treaty law': *supra* n. 47, at p. 1132.

[50] See, also, Krieger, *supra* n. 47, at p. 1134, and M. E. Villiger, *Commentary on the 1969 Vienna Convention on the Law of Treaties* (Leiden: Koninklijke Brill NV, 2009), pp. 813–814 ('mixed signals').

[51] *Case Concerning Gabčikovo-Nagymaros Project*, *supra* n. 24, at pp. 66–67 (paragraph 109).

[52] *Case Concerning Armed Activities on the Territory of the Congo* (New Application: 2002): Democratic Republic of Congo v. Rwanda (Jurisdiction and Admissibility) (2006) ICJ Rep. 6, at pp. 51–52 (paragraph 125). In the *Racke* case, which concerned the parallel problem whether responses based on the *clausula rebus sic stantibus* would require prior attempts at dispute settlement, the European Court of Justice adopted the same line of reasoning, holding that 'the specific procedural requirements there [i.e. in Art. 65 VCLT] laid down do not form part of customary international law': Case C-162/96 *Racke GmbH and Co. v. Hauptzollamt Mainz* [1998] ECR I-3655, [52]–[59].

deal with marginal issues. The one issue they did take up, namely the impact of breaches on the treaty relations between parties, was no doubt complex, but arguably Article 60 VCLT made things more complex. There is general agreement today that a breach as such does not end, nor suspend, treaty relations. But beyond that, Article 60 VCLT may have gone too far in its concern for treaty stability: its triad of limitations – the need for a qualified (material) breach, a nuanced rule on standing to respond and, above all, the cumbersome procedures governing responses – have choked Article 60 VCLT. And so it is telling that almost five decades after its wording was agreed in broad terms, the provision has yet to be applied properly. This in turn corroborates the general assessment of the relevance of the Vienna Convention regime. Not only does the Vienna Convention remain focused on the fringes of treaty breaches; insofar as it regulates fringe aspects, it does not do so successfully. Its relevance for the regime governing treaty breaches and responses remains highly limited.

3   The General Law of State Responsibility: The Governing Framework

Given its limitations, the law of treaties leaves a regulatory gap. To a large extent, this gap is filled by the law of international responsibility. The regime of State responsibility, shaped by the ILC's work between 1963 and 2001, supplies the conceptual framework within which international law addresses the key questions raised by treaty breaches. This should not be viewed as a hostile takeover: as noted earlier, the Vienna Convention consciously left to a side 'question[s] that may arise ... from the international responsibility of a State'.[53] However, the decision to address treaty breaches within the framework of responsibility comes at a price: it means that treaty breaches are treated not as a category in their own right but as part of the broader notion of internationally wrongful acts. In line with that, the key text on responsibility, the ILC's 2001 Articles on State Responsibility (ASR),[54] does not mention the terms 'treaty' and 'treaty breach'. Still, it contributes to their regulation in three important ways, which the subsequent sections take up.

---

[53] Art. 73 VCLT: *supra* n. 10.
[54] The ILC's Articles on State Responsibility, *supra* n. 20, are reproduced in Crawford, *supra* n. 20, at pp. 61–73.

3.1 Breach of Treaty: An Ancillary Role for the General Law of Responsibility

Just as the general law of treaties set out in the Vienna Convention, so the general regime of responsibility does not expressly define the notion of 'treaty breach'. However, where the Vienna Convention 'only touches upon the fringes',[55] the law of responsibility provides framework rules on core aspects. Notably, it defines the fundamental notion of an internationally wrongful act, of which treaty breaches are a crucial sub-category. According to Article 2 ASR, '[t]here is an internationally wrongful act of a State when conduct consisting of an action or omission: (*a*) is attributable to the State under international law; and (*b*) constitutes a breach of an international obligation of the State'.

Of the two requirements mentioned in Article 2 ASR, the general law of responsibility regulates only one – attribution – in a meaningful way: pursuant to Articles 4–11 ASR, some form of public conduct is required, while private conduct does not engage a State's international responsibility. With respect to treaty breaches, the same result will often follow from the formulation of treaty obligations. More generally, one might wonder whether conduct not attributable could 'constitut[e] a breach of an international obligation of the State'. But these matters need not be pursued: pragmatically, most commentators consider Articles 4–11 ASR to be useful, and as general rules, they can always be displaced.

With respect to the second element of an internationally wrongful act (non-compliance with an international obligation), the general regime of responsibility provides much less guidance. To be sure, Article 12 ASR clarifies that non-compliant conduct amounts to an internationally wrongful act irrespective of the source of the obligation breached.[56] But beyond that, notwithstanding the rather grandiose heading of 'Breach of

---

[55] Rosenne, *supra* n. 11, at p. 44.

[56] This is read into Art. 12 ASR, which provides: 'There is a breach of an international obligation by a State when an act of that State is not in conformity with what is required of it by that obligation, *regardless of its origin* or character': *supra* n. 20. The ILC's Commentary clarifies that the reference to 'origin' is meant to cover the sources of international law, including international treaties: see Crawford, *supra* n. 20, at pp. 126–127. As in other respects, the ILC's first reading text had been more detailed: according to draft Art. 17, as agreed in 1976 (*YbILC* (1976–II), 79), 'an act of a State which constitutes a breach of an international obligation is an internationally wrongful act regardless of the origin, whether customary, conventional or other, of that obligation'. And further, to avoid misunderstandings: 'The origin of the international obligation breached by a State does not affect the international responsibility arising from the internationally wrongful act of that State'.

an International Obligation', Part One, Chapter III (Articles 12–15 ASR) offers fairly little by way of clarification. The reason for this is well-known: the ILC's exercise, from the 1960s onwards, to devise a general ('secondary') regime has largely purged questions of substantive obligations from the law of responsibility. In the ILC's terminology, this is a matter for the 'primary rules' – i.e. in the present case, for particular treaties imposing obligations upon States, as interpreted and applied in line with the general law of treaties. What the ILC's text, notwithstanding its fascination with the primary-secondary divide, undertakes is to formulate some general rules on temporal law,[57] to spell out defences/justifications ('circumstances excluding wrongfulness')[58] and proclaim a rather ambitious (but surprisingly well-received)[59] set of rules against complicity.[60] But in the broader scheme of things, these are probably side issues. As the ILC noted, when determining whether a treaty has been breached, 'the principal focus will be on the primary obligation concerned'.[61] And further: 'There is no such thing as a breach of an international obligation in the abstract, and chapter III [as well as the ILC's text more generally] can only play an ancillary role in determining whether there has been such a breach'.[62]

3.2 'Breach of Treaty' as a Factor Shaping the Content of Responsibility

When it comes to the consequences of breaches, the general regime of responsibility is of more than ancillary relevance. Few treaties specifically spell out remedies;[63] so there is much more room for general rules regulating the consequences of breaches in the field of responsibility,

---

[57] Arts. 13 and 14 ASR: *supra* n. 20. [58] Arts. 20–27 ASR: *supra* n. 20.

[59] See the ICJ's judgment in *Case Concerning Application of the Convention on the Prevention and Punishment of the Crime of Genocide*: Bosnia and Herzegovina v. Serbia and Montenegro (2007) ICJ Rep. 43, at p. 217 (paragraph 420) (where Art. 16 ASR is said to 'reflec[t] a customary rule').

[60] Arts. 16–18 ASR: *supra* n. 20.

[61] Introductory Commentary to Chapter III of Part One ('The Internationally Wrongful Act of State') ASR: Crawford, *supra* n. 20, at p. 124.

[62] *Ibid.*

[63] The remedies regime of the WTO Dispute Settlement Understanding is perhaps the most prominent exception: seeking to 'secure the withdrawal of the measures concerned if these are found to be inconsistent with the provisions of any covered agreements' (Art. 3.7 of the Dispute Settlement Understanding, 1869 UNTS 401), it markedly differs from the general regime summarised in the text. For comment and further references, see C. J. Tams, 'Unity and Diversity in the Law of State Responsibility' in A. Zimmermann

and these form the heart of the regime of responsibility. In its Part Two, the ILC's text lays down an influential code of remedies, understood to make up 'the new legal relationship which arises upon the commission by a State of an internationally wrongful act'.[64]

In line with the ILC's approach to responsibility, this new legal relationship arises from all forms of legal wrongful conduct irrespective of the source of the obligations breached, and it arises automatically, i.e. immediately upon the commission of a wrongful act. Perhaps as a result, the ILC's code of remedies set out in Part Two is of considerable generality, indeed vagueness. Its main features are well known and can be summarised in four propositions. *First,* the natural consequence of any breach is that the wrongdoing State must cease its wrongful conduct, if it is still ongoing.[65] In exceptional instances, international law goes beyond cessation and requires the responsible State to give guarantees and assurances that the breach would not be repeated.[66] *Second,* apart from cessation and exceptionally guarantees and assurances, consequences are essentially aimed at remedying past wrongs. The overarching principle is that of reparation,[67] which according to the well-known *Chorzów Factory* formula requires the responsible State to 'wipe out all the consequences' of its wrongful conduct.[68] *Third,* and more specifically, reparation is traditionally considered to take three forms, whose availability depends on the type of breach in question:[69] restitution (re-establishment of the status quo ante); compensation (payment of indemnities) or satisfaction (in the case of non-material or moral damage).[70] Of these, restitution is said to enjoy primacy as a legal concept, while compensation is the most relevant remedy in practice.[71] Finally, *fourth,* particular severe breaches – namely 'serious breach[es] of an obligation arising under a peremptory norm of general

and R. Hofmann (eds.), *Unity and Diversity in International Law* (Berlin: Duncker & Humblot, 2006), pp. 437–470, at pp. 447–449.

[64] Introductory Commentary to Part Two ('Content of the International Responsibility of a State') ASR: Crawford, *supra* n. 20, at p. 191.

[65] Art. 30(a) ASR: *supra* n. 20.

[66] Art. 30(b) ASR: *supra* n. 20. See, also, *LaGrand Case*: Germany v. United States of America (2001) ICJ Rep. 466, at pp. 512–514 (paragraphs 124 and 125).

[67] Art. 31 ASR: *supra* n. 20.

[68] *Case Concerning the Factory at Chorzów* (Merits), 1927 PCIJ, Series A, No. 10, at p. 47, and *Case Concerning the Factory at Chorzów* (Claim for Indemnity) (Jurisdiction), 1927 PCIJ, Series A, No. 9, at p. 21.

[69] Arts. 34–37 ASR: *supra* n. 20.

[70] *Case Concerning the Factory at Chorzów* (Merits), *supra* n. 68, at p. 47.

[71] See e.g. Commentary to Art. 36 ASR: Crawford, *supra* n. 20, at pp. 218–219.

international law' – trigger special consequences: in addition to the regular remedies, they require bystander States not to recognise consequences of such qualified breaches but to 'cooperate to bring [them] to an end through lawful means'.[72]

As is clear from this briefest of descriptions, the ILC's code of remedies is so general that it can only meaningfully be applied in relation to specific sets of breaches. The general law of responsibility clarifies what remedy is owed, but in order to identify the content of the 'new legal relationship',[73] it is necessary to look at the particular breach in question. In this respect, the treaty breach can be said to shape the content of responsibility. Very often, the remedy set out in Part Two in fact is but the flipside of the breach. By way of illustration, where a State violates its duty not to use force against another State in violation of Article 2(4) of the 1945 United Nations Charter, the duty of cessation requires it to stop that particular treaty breach; similarly, where a domestic statute extending a State's territorial sea to 100 nautical miles has been passed in contravention of the United Nations Convention on the Law of the Sea, juridical restitution may require the rescinding of that statute. In these and similar settings, the general law of remedies requires the 'unmaking' of the treaty breach. In this respect, the ILC was right to note that '[e]vidently, the gravity of the breach may also affect the scope of the obligations of cessation and reparation'.[74] But the ILC's code of remedies remains influential because it lays down a framework for claims about the 'unmaking' of breaches: a framework that is of sufficient generality to have stood the test of time but that at the same time has prescriptive force – in prioritising restitution over compensation, in establishing guidelines for the calculation of quantum and in excluding humiliating forms of satisfaction (to summarise but a few of the choices made). The 'new legal relationship which arises upon the commission by a State of an internationally wrongful act'[75] is shaped by the (treaty) breach but defined by the general law of responsibility.

---

[72] Arts. 40 and 41 ASR: *supra* n. 20. And associated commentaries: Crawford, *supra* n. 20, at pp. 245–253. For details, see C. J. Tams and A. Asteriti, '*Erga Omnes, Jus Cogens*, and Their Impact on the Law of Responsibility' in M. Evans and P. Koutrakos (eds.), *The International Responsibility of the European Union: European and International Perspectives* (Oxford: Hart Publishing, 2013), pp. 163–188.

[73] Introductory Commentary to Part Two ASR: Crawford, *supra* n. 20, at p. 191.

[74] Commentary to Art. 33 ASR: Crawford, *supra* n. 20, at p. 209.

[75] Introductory Commentary to Part Two ASR: Crawford, *supra* n. 20, at p. 191.

3.3 Invoking Responsibility for Treaty Breaches

Rules on the invocation of State responsibility – laid down in Part Three of the ILC's text – provide the third and final pillar of the general regime governing treaty breaches. This third pillar consists of a mix of enabling and restrictive rules, which very much seeks to strike a balance between the competing interests of permitting effective responses (so that treaty breaches do meet with some reaction) and curbing abuses.

As is clear from the introductory comments, States can respond to treaty breaches in a number of ways, from massive coercive pressure to looking the other way. In addressing responses, international law seeks to provide guidance on two questions in particular: who can respond? and by what means? In addressing these questions, international law of course takes account of the character of the response. As regards the level of regulation, many of the more sophisticated rules on responses are treaty-based or institutionalised and hence outside the scope of the general regime. Especially in areas of advanced international regulation – such as trade, investment, environmental protection and human rights – contemporary international law is as much about providing adequate means of redressing breaches as it is about formulating treaty-based primary rules.[76] Where this is the case, predictably, the general regime will lose relevance, if it is not in fact completely disapplied.[77]

The gradual move towards treaty-based rules on responses is one factor explaining the rather straightforward nature of the general regime to be addressed in the following. The other, perhaps more powerful, is the decision purposefully not to regulate the most common responses to treaty breaches. As long as reactions, including those that bite, do not violate international law, they do not require to be justified but remain intrinsically lawful. By way of illustration, in an era of progressively shrinking *domaines réservés*, States simply need not establish any legal entitlement if they draw attention to human rights violations within

---

[76] This is brought out clearly by the various chapters in this volume, addressing heavily regulated areas of international relations: see, for example, the contribution to this volume of Pauwelyn and van Damme at pp. 809–847 (Chapter 25), and, further, Tams, *supra* n. 63.

[77] In fact, of McNair's list of six 'remedies for breach accruing to other party' mentioned in Section 1 of this chapter (and cf. McNair, *supra* n. 8, at p. 539) – unilateral abrogation, retaliatory suspension, claims for reparation before arbitral/judicial institutions, non-forcible measures to secure reparation, invocation of sanctions provided for by treaty and prosecution of individuals – two are treaty-based (sanctions, arbitral/judicial proceedings), while one (prosecution of individuals) either is treaty-based or can be seen as a non-forcible way to secure reparation.

another State, if they formulate strongly worded diplomatic démarches, if they seek not to support another State's candidate for high-profile international office or if they decide not to ratify a lucrative trade treaty coveted by another State. All these options remain legally open to all States, in response to any treaty breach, whether grave or not and irrespective of whether the responding States can claim to have been injured or affected under any of the much-discussed rules on standing. The governing principle is one of purposeful non-regulation: international law permits intrinsically lawful responses.

Both factors – the gradual move towards treaty-based responses and the deliberate decision to permit intrinsically lawful responses by any State – complement, but also side-line, the general regime. And as this is so, rules on the invocation of responsibility laid down in Part Three of the ILC's text – while much discussed – are perhaps not quite as influential in guiding responses than the general code of remedies set out in the preceding section. In essence, the ILC's text provides guidance on two aspects: *first*, it formulates a general test governing which States have standing to invoke the responsibility of another State for treaty breaches (or indeed other forms of wrongful conduct) through – in the ILC's words – 'measures of a relatively formal character',[78] that is, those that are *not* intrinsically lawful. And *second*, the ILC's text focuses on one particular type of 'measure of a relatively formal character': one that requires regulation and that is recognised under general international law, namely countermeasures. The subsequent sections summarise the legal position on both aspects, with a particular view to identifying differences and commonalities between the general regimes of treaty law and State responsibility.

3.3.1   A Liberal Regime of Standing to Invoke Responsibility

Just as in the 1960s, when a prior generation of Commission members discussed what was to become Article 60(2) VCLT, the ILC's debates on standing to respond to treaty breaches exposed sharp divisions about the role of individual States as 'enforcement agents' of international law. Especially during the second reading of the text on State responsibility, the ILC was guided by Article 60 VCLT. However, in a crucial respect, it went beyond the *acquis* of Article 60 VCLT. It managed to do both – being guided by, and yet overcoming, Article 60 VCLT – by opting to formulate two tests of standing. The first of these, Article 42 ASR, draws

---

[78] Commentary to Art. 42 ASR: Crawford, *supra* n. 20, at p. 256.

on the notion of an 'injured State', which, having suffered injury, is entitled to invoke another State's responsibility. And notwithstanding the differences between the responses – formal invocation of responsibility on the one hand, treaty suspension/termination on the other – Article 42 ASR effectively mirrors Article 60 VCLT: it identifies categories of legal injury that are much the same as those of Article 60, that is individual injury in the bilateral and quasi-bilateral context or because of the special effects of a breach (e.g. under bilateral treaties or multilateral treaties requiring to be performed reciprocally or causing particular damage to one State)[79] and general injury in the case of integral obligations based on the logic of 'global reciprocity'.[80] All this follows the approach governing the suspension or termination treaties in response to material breaches, which Article 42 ASR extends to the field of responsibility.

Yet unlike in the 1960s, a restrictive provision such as Article 42 ASR was only acceptable in the 1990s and early 2000s because it was complemented by a much more liberal provision, namely Article 48 ASR. Unlike Article 42 ASR, Article 48 ASR refers to 'legally interested' States: like injured States, legally interested States can invoke another State's responsibility through 'measures of a relatively formal character';[81] but unlike injured States, the ILC (controversially) suggests that they may not be able to do so by means of countermeasures.[82] Fears of abusive 'third party countermeasures' thus having been allayed, the ILC was willing to endorse a very liberal test. Hence, Article 48 ASR accepts that all treaty parties can respond to breaches of obligations 'owed to a group of States' if these have been 'established for the protection of a collective interest'. As the ILC's Commentary makes clear, 'collective interest treaties' are intended 'to foster a common interest, over and above any interests of the States concerned individually',[83] including treaties protecting 'the environment or security of a region (e.g. a regional nuclear-free-zone treaty or a regional system for the protection of human rights)'.[84] With respect to all of these treaties, each and every treaty party is entitled to respond to a treaty breach and demand a cessation of ongoing treaty breaches and reparation in the interest of the main beneficiaries of the obligation.[85]

---

[79] Art. 42(a) and (b)(i) ASR: *supra* n. 20.   [80] Art. 42(b)(ii) ASR: *supra* n. 20.
[81] Commentary to Art. 42 ASR: Crawford, *supra* n. 20, at p. 256.
[82] For comment see Section 3.3.2.
[83] Commentary to Art. 48 ASR: Crawford, *supra* n. 20, at pp. 277–278.   [84] *Ibid.*
[85] Art. 48(2) ASR: *supra* n. 20.

While Article 42 ASR reflects the concern for treaty stability, which informs Article 60 VCLT, Article 48 ASR thus accepts the need for decentralised responses against breaches of multilateral obligations. It reflects developments in international law since 1969, and notably the emergence and gradual recognition of community obligations, whether in the form of obligations *erga omnes*[86] or in multilateral treaties safeguarding global public goods.[87] While sometimes viewed as an instance of progressive development,[88] Article 48 ASR is based on solid preparatory work and, in fact, would be endorsed (if not expressly) by the ICJ in the 2011 judgment in *Questions Relating to the Obligation to Prosecute or Extradite* between Belgium and Senegal, in which the applicant was held entitled to bring international proceedings – without a doubt a 'measur[e] of a relatively formal character'[89] – in defence of the 'common interest', shared by all treaty parties, 'in [ensuring] compliance with these [treaty] obligations'.[90] All this suggests that international law has, over the course of the past decades, recognised the right of individual treaty parties to act in defence of collective treaty interests. Article 48 ASR reflects that new openness and stands in marked contrast to Article 60 VCLT.

3.3.2   Countermeasures: Retaining Flexibility

Whether that new openness should also be reflected in the regime of countermeasures remained controversial right until the end of the

---

[86] In its 1970 judgment in the *Barcelona Traction Case*, the ICJ accepted that all States can be held to have a legal interest in seeing certain fundamental rules complied with (which it termed obligations *erga omnes*): *Case Concerning the Barcelona Traction, Light and Power Co. Ltd.*: Belgium v. Spain (Second Phase) (1970) ICJ Rep. 3, at p. 32 (paragraphs 33–34).

[87] Simma pointedly speaks of 'workhorses of community interest': 'From Bilateralism to Community Interest', *Hague Recueil*, 250 (1994–VI), 217–384, at 322. Concluding his detailed study of multilateral treaties, Voeffray remarks that today, the idea of a 'public interest action' in defence of collective interests protected by treaties 'ne revêt … plus un caractère exceptionnel': F. Voeffray, *L'actio popularis – ou la défense de l'intérêt collectif devant les juridictions internationales* (Paris: Presses Universitaires de France, 2004), p. 383.

[88] See Commentary to Art. 48 ASR: Crawford, *supra* n. 20, at p. 279 (with respect to Art. 48 (2)(b) ASR), and, further, J. Crawford, 'Responsibilities for Breaches of Communitarian Norms: An Appraisal of Article 48 of the ILC Articles on Responsibility of States for Wrongful Acts' in U. Fasternrath, R. Geiger, D.-E. Khan, A. Paulus, S. von Schorlemer and C. Vedder (eds.), *From Bilateralism to Community Interest: Essays in Honour of Judge Bruno Simma* (Oxford: Oxford University Press, 2011), pp. 224–240.

[89] Commentary to Art. 42 ASR: Crawford, *supra* n. 20, at p. 256.

[90] *Questions Relating to the Obligation to Prosecute or Extradite*: Belgium v. Senegal (2011) ICJ Rep. 422, at p. 449 (paragraph 68).

ILC's project on responsibility. The eventual text, as agreed in 2001, remains ambivalent. Article 54 ASR simply records the Commission's – and the international community's – uncertainty when noting that the 2001 Articles do not 'prejudice the right of any State, entitled under [A]rticle 48, paragraph 1, to invoke the responsibility of another State, to take lawful measures against that State to ensure cessation of the breach and reparation in the interest of the injured State or of the beneficiaries of the obligation breached'.[91] That provision may perhaps have been overly cautious; but as is well known, the ILC considered it prudent not to endanger the adoption of its text by opting for a bolder approach. Other bodies have been less concerned: to mention just one, the Institut de Droit International in 2005 correctly recognised that where a State is responsible for a 'widely acknowledged grave breach of' a treaty protecting obligations *erga omnes*, 'all the States to which the obligation is owed ... are entitled to take non-forcible counter-measures under conditions analogous to those applying to a State specially affected by the breach'.[92] As has been discussed in more depth elsewhere, this position indeed is in line with international practice.[93] Yet given the ILC's ambivalence, this matter is certainly not beyond doubt.

While Article 54 ASR is ambivalent, the ILC's text is otherwise seen as a successful exercise in shoring up the legal regime of countermeasures. Articles 49–54 ASR, which lay down the condition for countermeasures adopted by *injured States* in the sense of Article 42 ASR, have met with considerable agreement. In essence, they affirm the traditional understanding of countermeasures as a flexible concept permitting the decentralised use of proportionate coercion against wrongful conduct, including breaches of treaties.

As is well known, such proportionate coercion may well take the form of the suspension of treaty obligations, i.e. the type of conduct regulated in Article 60 VCLT. As was noted previously, this does not mean that the two types of responses were exactly the same: based on the logic of law enforcement, countermeasures must be taken to 'induce the wrongdoing

---

[91] For critical comment, see, e.g., Sicilianos, *supra* n. 45, at 1139–1144, and Tams, *supra* n. 44, at pp. 198–249.

[92] Institut de Droit International, 'Resolution on Obligations and Rights Erga Omnes in International Law', *Annuaire de l'Institut de droit international*, 71 (2006), 289.

[93] For details, see Tams, *supra* n. 44, at pp. 198–249, and the earlier practice recorded in M. Akehurst, 'Reprisals by Third States', *BYbIL*, 44 (1970), 1–18, and J. I. Charney, 'Third State Remedies in International Law', *Michigan JIL*, 10 (1989), 57–101.

State to comply with its obligations under international law'[94] – and not so to redress a contractual imbalance. But in practice, that may be a very fine line, and the least that can be said is that in terms of their effects, responses under the two concepts can overlap. Given their proximity, the differences between the two legal regimes – of Article 60 VCLT on the one hand and countermeasures on the other – are quite remarkable. Where Article 60 VCLT places a premium on treaty stability, counter-measures are regulated with a view not to overregulate, not to 'choke' the potential for effective responses. This is illustrated by three crucial fea-tures of their regime – which given the abundance of scholarship on countermeasures may simply be listed here:

- *First*, and crucially in practice, countermeasures are not subject to a cumbersome procedural regime comparable to that of Articles 65 *et seq.* VCLT. Procedural conditions for countermeasures were discussed; but in the end, the ILC text retains only minimum requirements.[95] Notably, under Article 52 ASR, responding States are required to give 'advance warning' to the targeted State and provide it with an opportu-nity to respond to the claims underlying the dispute.[96]

- *Second*, equally fundamentally, as regards their 'trigger', countermea-sures are available against *all* treaty breaches: they presuppose an actual breach (as is regularly affirmed[97] so as to avoid misunderstandings to which the language in the *Case Concerning the Air Services Agreement of*

---

[94] *Case Concerning Gabčikovo-Nagymaros Project, supra* n. 24, at p. 56 (paragraph 85) and Art. 49(1) ASR.

[95] By contrast, during the ILC's first reading, Special Rapporteur Arangio Ruiz had sub-mitted far-reaching proposals: according to his draft Art. 12 and dispute settlement annex protest in 1993, States seeking to resort to countermeasures would have been required to exhaust 'all the amicable settlement procedures available under general international law, the United Nations Charter or any other dispute settlement instrument to which [a State seeking redress] is a party'; in addition, there would have been a system for 'post-countermeasures' dispute settlement. For details, see G. Arangio-Ruiz, Fourth Report on State Responsibility, Doc. A/CN.4/444 and Add.1–3 (12 and 25 May and 1 and 17 June 1992), p. 1, and G. Arangio-Ruiz, Fifth Report on State Responsibility, Doc. A/CN.4/453 and Add.1–3 (12 and 28 May and 8 and 24 June 1993), p. 1. The eventual ILC text retains none of these features.

[96] Art. 52(1) ASR provides that '[b]efore taking countermeasures, an injured State shall: (a) call upon the responsible State, in accordance with [Art.] 43, to fulfil its obligations under Part Two; (b) notify the responsible State of any decision to take countermeasures and offer to negotiate with that State': *supra* n. 20.

[97] See, e.g., Commentary to Art. 49 ASR: 'A State which resorts to countermeasures based on its unilateral assessment of the situation does so at its own risk and may incur respon-sibility for its own wrongful conduct in the event of an incorrect assessment'. See Crawford, *supra* n. 20, at pp. 284–285.

27 March 1946[98] might have given rise); however, there is no threshold requirement akin to that of a material breach. Any breach suffices.

- *Third*, as regards their scope, countermeasures offer responding States a much wider discretion in tailoring responses. Unlike Article 60 VCLT, the law of countermeasures does not prescribe which obligations can be disregarded in order to induce the targeted State back into compliance. There is no need to restrict responses to the same treaty, i.e. the one allegedly violated by the other State; and in fact, there is no need to restrict responses to treaty breaches at all. The response can be in the nature of a tit-for-tat, but it need not be, and there is no special regime governing 'reciprocal countermeasures'.

These three features illustrate the relative flexibility of the general regime of countermeasures. Compared to Article 60 VCLT, the law of State responsibility permits a wider range of responses and under less stringent conditions. To some extent, this flexibility is offset by exclusionary clauses[99] and the general requirement that countermeasures be proportionate.[100] But it is hard to avoid the impression that, when discussing the general regime of responsibility, the international law-making community *also* sought to avoid the over-regulation that is characteristic of Article 60 VCLT.

3.4   Concluding Thoughts

The foregoing considerations clarify that of the two main sets of 'meta-rules' devised by the ILC – the law of treaties and the law of international responsibility – the latter is of much greater relevance to the regulation of treaty breaches. As international law does not distinguish between 'responsibility arising *ex contractu* or *ex delicto*',[101] treaty breaches are treated as a sub-category of internationally wrongful acts and regulated within that broader framework. As a result, the provisions

---

[98] Cf. *Case Concerning the Air Services Agreement of 27 March 1946*, ILR, 54 (1979), 304–349, at p. 337 (paragraph 81).

[99] Notably, as clarified in Art. 50 ASR, countermeasures do not justify the non-performance of obligations imposed by rules of *jus cogens*; furthermore, they must not undermine agreed dispute settlement proceedings or affect the inviolability of diplomatic or consular premises or personnel: *supra* n. 20.

[100] Art. 51 ASR (requiring that 'the effects of a countermeasure . . . be commensurate with the injury suffered': *supra* n. 20) and *Case Concerning Gabčikovo-Nagymaros Project*, *supra* n. 24, at pp. 56–57 (paragraphs 85–87).

[101] Commentary to Art. 12 ASR: Crawford, *supra* n. 20, at p. 127.

of the ILC's Articles on State Responsibility in principle apply to treaty breaches and responses. Notably, they provide important default rules for determining attribution of conduct and consequences of treaty breaches. By contrast, because of the conscious limitations of the ILC's work on responsibility, they hardly help in determining the content of obligations. As regards the means of obtaining redress, the ILC's text lays down general rules of standing applicable to formal measures of invocation and implicitly accepts that below that threshold, all States can respond to treaty breaches. Just as the Vienna Convention, the general law of responsibility addresses only one particular response – countermeasures – which Articles 49–54 ASR regulate in a much more flexible way than Article 60 VCLT does for treaty suspension and termination.

4   Final Reflections

In the concluding chapter of his book on the Vienna Convention on the Law of Treaties, Sir Ian Sinclair compared the international community's approach to treaty law to an 'unintended triptych' in which the 1969 Convention formed the central panel flanked by the Conventions of 1978 (Succession)[102] and 1986 (International Organizations)[103] – the latter still incomplete at the time of his writing.[104] While the panels are different, perhaps the metaphor can be applied as well to the topic of the present inquiry: if so, the 'unintended triptych' of treaty breaches would comprise the general law of responsibility as the central panel, flanked by side panels representing particular treaty regimes and the Vienna Convention. Observers regarding this second triptych would presumably admire the complexity of the composition and might perhaps be puzzled and confused by the delicacy and diversity of the right-hand panel representing particular treaty regimes. By contrast, the left-hand panel depicting the general law of treaties might be considered to be a bit small and unduly modest.

In fact, looked at from a distance, this may be the most peculiar feature of the triptych – and it is certainly the most striking feature of the preceding analysis: of the three sets of rules analysed, the general law of treaties is by far the least important. Given the absence of practice under Article 60 VCLT, treaty breaches and responses thereto are almost exclusively governed by the general law of responsibility as complemented (and at times replaced) by particular treaty regimes. The central

[102] 1946 UNTS 3.   [103] ILM, 25 (1986), 543–592.   [104] Sinclair, *supra* n. 48, at p. 245.

choices explaining this state of affairs may be briefly recalled towards the end of this contribution: (i) the drafters' decision to treat treaty breaches, their consequences and the modalities for redressing them within the framework of responsibility (rather than as part of a special regime of responsibility for treaty breaches) and (ii) their unwillingness to engage with the substance of treaty obligations, let alone formulate core obligations characteristic of common types of treaties. Both decisions were plausible at the time of drafting and remain plausible today. Yet, taken together, they mean that solutions to the challenges posed by treaty breaches – essential questions that 'pla[y] an important rôle in both international law and foreign office practice'[105] – largely have to be sought outside the Vienna Convention regime.

[105] Bilder, *supra* n. 9, at 193.

15

Territory and Its Relationship to Treaties

BARBARA MILTNER

1 Introduction

The relationship between territory and treaties is a complex one that has evolved considerably over time. Treaties have long been relied upon to establish and govern relationships between States and territory, a practice that continues today. Some of the most obvious examples include treaties in which territorial claims are established, whether through assertions of sovereignty,[1] agreements over a boundary, establishment of jurisdictional or territorial authority or the creation of territorial regimes.[2] Treaties establishing jurisdictional mandates include former practices such as capitulations, which authorised the presence of a foreign military base, court or foreign consular agents in another State's territory.[3] Indeed, at least one scholar has argued that such treaty-based jurisdictional arrangements in foreign territory even predate the modern system of territorial sovereignty.[4] The variety and range of relationships to territory that treaties may govern are nearly endless; their possible variations expand and contract as parties' relationships to territory evolve over time.

---

[1] By virtue of Art. LXXI of the 1648 Treaty of Osnabrück (Treaty of Peace between the Holy Roman Empire and Sweden), France was awarded dominion and sovereignty over several bishoprics, including Metz, Toul and Verdun: 1 CTS 198.

[2] Such as the 1959 Antarctic Treaty: 402 UNTS 72.

[3] For the interesting example of a U.S. federal court in Shanghai, China, see K. Raustiala, *Does the Constitution Follow the Flag? The Evolution of Territoriality in American Law* (Oxford: Oxford University Press, 2009). Territorial mandates include mandates and trusteeships as well as the modern practices of international territorial administration and certain conduct under the responsibility to protect doctrine. See, respectively, A. Orford, *International Authority and the Responsibility to Protect* (Cambridge: Cambridge University Press, 2011) and R. Wilde, *International Territorial Administration: How Trusteeship and the Civilizing Mission Never Went Away* (Oxford: Oxford University Press, 2008).

[4] S. S. Liu, *Extraterritoriality: Its Rise and Its Decline* (New York, NY: AMS Press, 1969) (arguing that capitulations represent vestigial examples of the personality of laws).

The nature of these relationships is obscured by the fact that changes in technology frequently contribute to shifts in the treaty-territory relationship. The advent of modern cartography, for example, has enabled greater precision in claims to territory and the articulation of its status, whether for expressions of sovereignty, claims over new territory by a distant power or land transfers.[5] Boundary treaties, for example, remain a particular expression of this relationship between territorial sovereignty and the technologies underpinning it.

In addition to the changing technology, the relationship between territory and treaties is also informed by shifts in the very concepts that underpin our international legal system. Terms such as dominion, jurisdiction and sovereignty characterise and suggest relationships to territory that have not remained static over time. Nuanced shifts in the meaning of jurisdiction and its relationship to territorial sovereignty have been observed in such disparate contexts as that of the Holy Roman Empire and the United Nations' growing use of international territorial administration.[6] These conceptual shifts in turn prompt changes reflected in treaties and treaty practice. One such example is the territorialised conception of sovereignty that emerged in the apogee of colonial expansion in the early nineteenth century and the challenges it posed to traditional treaty-making practices.[7] This chapter argues that the protean character of territorial relationships has made them particularly challenging topics for codification because of the pace at which they evolve.

A brief word is in order regarding the placement of this chapter in the present volume between its division of the *conceptual* and *contextual* perspectives of treaty relations. In the modern law of treaties, territoriality is notoriously difficult to shoehorn because it defies clear divisions between conceptual and contextual aspects of treaty law. In a fitting tribute to the volume's overall organization, this chapter sets out to examine both: a conceptual aspect in Section 2 and a contextual aspect in Section 3. In this way, the ambiguous nature of territoriality serves to bridge the volume's two-part structure.

---

[5] S. Dorsett, 'Mapping Territories' in S. McVeigh (ed.), *Jurisprudence of Jurisdiction* (Abingdon: Routledge-Cavendish, 2007), pp. 137–158, and R. T. Ford, 'Law's Territory (A History of Jurisdiction)', *Michigan L. Rev.*, 97 (1999), 842–930.

[6] A. Orford, 'Jurisdiction without Territory: From the Holy Roman Empire to the Responsibility to Protect', *Michigan JIL*, 30 (2009), 981–1015. See, also, Wilde, *supra* n. 3.

[7] A. Anghie, *Imperialism, Sovereignty, and the Making of International Law* (Cambridge: Cambridge University Press, 2005), p. 70.

The second section of this chapter will survey the concept of the territorial scope of treaties through an examination of Article 29 of the 1969 Vienna Convention on the Law of Treaties (VCLT).[8] The International Law Commission's (ILC) drafting of this provision is revealing for the light it sheds upon the ambiguities of a treaty's application to territory and the difficulties faced by the ILC in articulating a provision so closely bound to objectionable colonial practices.[9] A third section will proceed to examine the ILC's codification, in the context of the 1978 Vienna Convention on the Succession of States in Respect of Treaties (VCSST),[10] of provisions relating to the special capacity of boundary and territorial treaties (in Articles 11 and 12 respectively) to survive instances of State succession. In each instance, the provisions at issue identify specific aspects of the relationship between treaties and territory against a backdrop of shifting practices. In the VCLT context, Article 29 established a formalised rule premised on the disappearance of fading colonial practices while simultaneously safeguarding their functionality. In the VCSST context, the effort was marked by an altogether different challenge: that of distilling a coherent rule from inconsistent, controversial and poorly understood State practice.

Notwithstanding the distinct contexts of territorial application on the one hand and boundary and territorial regimes on the other, some common points can be discerned. The most prominent of these is the conceptual and operational ambiguity in the topics under consideration. For the ILC members involved in the drafting and negotiations of these provisions, clear articulations of the meaning and function of these territorial concepts proved both rare and rarely agreed upon. These conceptual and functional ambiguities would create stumbling blocks for the drafters that were ultimately preserved in the language of the provisions eventually adopted. In both cases, such ambiguities have been fruitfully exploited to advantage contracting States by allowing practical solutions to modern challenges. As a result, these ambiguous 'territorial' clauses constitute highly adaptable resources that promote dynamic treaty participation and flexibility in inter-State relations.

---

[8] 1155 UNTS 331.
[9] On the relevance of drafting history as a source of a treaty's meaning, see J. D. Mortenson, 'The *Travaux* of *Travaux*: Is the Vienna Convention Hostile to Drafting History?', *AJIL*, 107 (2013), 780–822.
[10] 1946 UNTS 3.

2   Article 29 of the Vienna Convention on the Law of Treaties

2.1   *Historical Context and Backdrop*

The territorial application of treaties was first codified in Article 29 of the 1969 Vienna Convention on the Law of Treaties, but the interest in codifying the matter is much older. The topic was first considered by the League of Nations during the interwar period, and in the context of the United Nations, the ILC considered the topic at its first session. In the bilateral treaty context, the practice of States negotiating the territorial application of treaties emerged centuries earlier.[11]

Article 29 VCLT provides: 'Unless a different intention appears from the treaty or is otherwise established, a treaty is binding upon each party in respect of its entire territory'. On its face, the content of the provision seems unsurprising, even self-evident.[12] And yet complex issues remain.[13] Chief among them is the precise meaning of a treaty's application to territory. One possibility is that it signifies the territory that comprises the subject matter of a treaty, as the 1959 Antarctic Treaty[14] or the 1920 Spitsbergen (Svalbard) Treaty[15] might apply to the Antarctic or Spitsbergen. (If so, a subsequent question is whether non-territorial subject matter such as the moon, outer space or the high seas precludes territorial application.) Another possibility is the territorial locale of performance of treaty obligations, such as might apply to treaties of navigation or those regulating activities such as fishing or civil aviation. Still another meaning might involve the place where treaty obligations inhere,[16] regardless of where such obligations are to be performed. Accordingly, a contracting party to a human rights treaty might find itself bound by the instrument's provisions even when acting on the high seas or beyond its own territorial boundaries. Adding to this conceptual complexity was the political backdrop of the era in which the provision was being negotiated.

2.1.1   The Influence of Colonialism on the Territorial Application of Treaties: Colonial Clauses

By the time the drafting of Article 29 was seriously under way in the 1960s, the predominant sentiment in the ILC and the United Nations

---

[11] See the contribution to this volume of Lesaffer at pp. 43–75 (Chapter 3).

[12] *YbILC* (1966–II), 356.

[13] S. Karagiannis, 'Article 29 (1969)' in O. Corten and P. Klein (eds.), *The Vienna Conventions on the Law of Treaties: A Commentary* (Vol. I) (Oxford: Oxford University Press, 2011), pp. 731–758.

[14] *Supra* n. 2.   [15] 2 LNTS 8.   [16] See discussion in Section 2.2.

more generally was one of strident anti-colonialism.[17] Of particular relevance was the fact that the ILC had identified a treaty's territorial application as inextricably bound up with colonial clauses, the most consistent type of territorial application clause to appear in treaties.[18]

Colonial clauses were standard treaty provisions enabling States to modulate a treaty's application to dependent territories. The clauses authorised contracting parties to issue a declaration specifying the territories to be either included or excluded within the treaty's scope, depending on the language of the clause.[19] Early on, their role was to *include* dependent territories within a treaty's scope of application.[20] Eventually the clauses evolved to *exclude* dependencies that sought greater leeway in the negotiation of commercial treaties.[21]

Such clauses took many forms. Clauses in early multilateral treaties were elaborately worded to include dependencies in all their forms. The 1883 Paris Convention for the Protection of Industrial Property offers one such example:

> The contracting countries have the right to adhere at any time to the present Convention for their colonies, possessions, dependencies and protectorates, or for certain ones of them . . .[22]

Following the creation of the United Nations, colonialism began to fall into disfavour, and the use of colonial clauses in multilateral treaties became highly controversial.[23] Thereafter, such clauses took on

---

[17] Between 1960 and 1963, thirty former colonial dependencies were recognised for UN membership: www.un.org/en/members/growth.shtml. See, further, comments by ILC members El-Erian and Waldock at YbILC (1964–I), 47–48. See, also, T. O. Elias, *The Modern Law of Treaties* (Leiden: A.W. Sijthoff, 1974), pp. 51–52.

[18] Another lesser influence was the federal clause, discussed in the following section.

[19] Y.-L. Liang, 'Colonial Clauses and Federal Clauses in United Nations Multilateral Instruments', *AJIL*, 45 (1951), 108–128.

[20] J. E. S. Fawcett, 'Treaty Relations of British Overseas Territories', *BYbIL*, 26 (1949), 86–107, at 94.

[21] This was seen as early as the 1820s in France: P. Lampué, 'L'Application des Traités dans les Territoires et Départements d'Outre-Mer', *AFDI*, 6 (1960), 907–924. In the British Commonwealth, Canada and other Dominions actively sought exclusions from commercial treaties: see Fawcett, *supra* n. 20, and R. B. Stewart, *Treaty Relations of the British Commonwealth of Nations* (New York, NY: Macmillan Co., 1939).

[22] 38 Stat. 1658. This clause first appeared as Art. 16½ in the Convention as revised at the Washington, DC Revision Conference on 2 June 1911. See, further, 828 UNTS 107 (as amended).

[23] See, further, *YbILC* (1964–II), 15; Elias, *supra* n. 17, at pp. 51–55; Fawcett, *supra* n. 20, at p. 106; Lampué, *supra* n. 21, at p. 911; Y.-L. Liang, 'Notes on Legal Questions Concerning the United Nations: The Third Session of the International Law Commission – Review of its Work by the General Assembly', *AJIL*, 46 (1952), 483–503, and I. Sinclair, *The Vienna*

a simplified form, dropping lengthy categorical references in favour of what would become a common euphemism: 'territories for whose international relations a party is responsible'. This phrase enjoyed the benefit of simplicity[24] and also downplayed the connection to colonialism. Eventually, however, even this benign formula came to be viewed with 'increasingly bad odour at the United Nations'.[25] It was ultimately condemned for its colonial connotations and for being contrary to the principle of self-determination in the 1945 Charter of the United Nations.[26] As a result of this opposition, the insertion of territorial application clauses into treaties declined, leaving many treaties largely silent on the issue. What drafters sought to achieve through Article 29 VCLT was the articulation of a generally accepted rule addressing 'the cases where the parties have not made any special provision, either expressly or impliedly, in regard to the territorial scope of the treaty'.[27]

2.1.2 Federal Clauses as Precursor to Article 29 VCLT?

During the drafting of Article 29 VCLT, the ILC members also looked to federal clauses,[28] which they recognised as a variant of territorial application clauses capable of informing the future provision. Surprisingly, a closer look at the specific type of federal clauses in existence at that time suggests that reliance upon them was misplaced. The following section surveys the evolving form of federal clauses from their emergence to the present day. In doing so, it concludes that the ILC's portrayal of federal clauses as a 'species' of territorial application clauses was inaccurate for its time, if ultimately prescient.

At the time of the ILC's work during the 1960s, federal clauses enjoyed consistent form and operative effect. Their role was to regulate 'the extent of the obligations of a contracting State having a federal form of government in respect of the application of a multilateral instrument to its component parts'.[29] Such clauses originated in the context of bilateral treaties pertaining to matters of private international law and later expanded to multilateral conventions following the First World War.[30]

Convention on the Law of Treaties (Manchester: Manchester University Press, 2nd ed., 1984), p. 88.

[24] Elias, *supra* n. 17, at p. 51.   [25] *Ibid.*

[26] 1 UNTS 16, Arts. 1(2) and 55. See, also, *YbILC* (1964–I), 49.   [27] *YbILC* (1964–II), 15.

[28] *YbILC* (1964–II), 13; see, also, *YbILC* (1966–II), 64–65 (Netherlands) and, further, 213 (paragraph 4).

[29] Liang, *supra* n. 23, at p. 121.

[30] See the contribution to this volume of Trebilcock at pp. 848–880 (Chapter 26). See, also, I. Bernier, *International Legal Aspects of Federalism* (London: Longman Group Ltd., 1973), p. 174.

Federal clauses arose to meet the particular constitutional challenges faced by federal States in treaty implementation. Due to the
distribution of powers between federal and constituent units, some
federal States with plenary treaty-making power lack the concomitant treaty-implementation power necessary to ensure a treaty's full
performance. A federal State so placed would remain internationally
responsible for any breach by its constituent units, notwithstanding
its constitutional *inability* to guarantee treaty compliance. Enter the
federal clause.

2.1.2.1 Jurisdictional Clauses The first federal clause to appear in a
multilateral instrument emerged in the Constitution of the
International Labour Organization (ILO),[31] albeit with inauspicious
beginnings. The clause was so controversial as to nearly cause the
collapse of the ILO negotiations[32] and was sufficiently poorly drafted
as to require amendment in later years.[33] Nonetheless, the popularity of
the clause among federal States endured. Its first appearance in
a multilateral instrument of the United Nations would be in the 1951
Convention Relating to the Status of Refugees (Refugee Convention),[34]
excerpted later. This language constitutes a classic example of a federal
jurisdiction clause,[35] so named because it limits a State's responsibility
under a given treaty to *only* that subject matter within its legislative
competence:

---

[31] Section 405, Chapter XIII of the 1919 Treaty of Versailles, 225 CTS 188. Alternatively
enumerated as Art. 19(9), International Labour Office, *Constitution and Standing Orders
of the International Labour Organisation* (Geneva: Imprimerie Centrale, 1934).

[32] E. J. Phelan, 'The Commission on International Labor Legislation' in J. D. Shotwell
(ed.), *The Origins of the International Labor Organization* (Vol. I) (New York, NY:
Columbia University Press, 1934), pp. 127–198, at pp. 146 and 154, and R. B. Looper,
'"Federal State" Clauses in Multilateral Instruments', *BYbIL*, 32 (1955–1956), 162–203,
at 164.

[33] Art. 19(7), International Labour Office, *Instrument of Amendment Adopted by the
International Labour Conference at its 29th Session*, Vol. XXIX, Issue No. 4, Official
Bulletin (1946). See, also, Looper, *supra* n. 32, at pp. 171 and 179–184.

[34] 189 UNTS 150.

[35] See Bernier, *supra* n. 30, at pp. 177–178; H. Burmester, 'Federal Clauses: An Australian
Perspective', *ICLQ*, 34 (1985), 522–537, at 523; E. T. Swaine, 'Does Federalism Constrain
the Treaty Power?' *Columbia L. Rev.*, 103 (2003), 403–533; J. Trone, *Federal Constitutions
and International Relations* (St. Lucia, Qld.: University of Queensland Press, 2001),
pp. 12–13, and Report of the United Nations Secretary-General, Draft International
Covenant on Human Rights and Measures of Implementation: The Federal Clause,
U.N. Doc. E/CN.4/651 (1952), p. 4 (paragraph 11).

In the case of a Federal or non-unitary State, the following provisions shall apply:

(a) With respect to those articles of this Convention that come within the legislative jurisdiction of the federal legislative authority, the obligations of the Federal Government shall to this extent be the same as those of Parties which are not Federal States;

(b) With respect to those articles of this Convention that come within the legislative jurisdiction of constituent States, provinces or cantons which are not, under the constitutional system of the federation, bound to take legislative action, the Federal Government shall bring such articles with a favourable recommendation to the notice of the appropriate authorities of States, provinces or cantons at the earliest possible moment.

(c) A Federal State Party to this Convention shall, at the request of any other Contracting State transmitted through the Secretary-General of the United Nations, supply a statement of the law and practice of the Federation and its constituent units in regard to any particular provision of the Convention showing the extent to which effect has been given to that provision by legislative or other action.[36]

Accordingly, only those provisions within a federal authority's competence remain binding obligations, and these apply throughout its territory. The net result is that any treaty obligations outside a federal State's legislative competence are exempted from the State party's international responsibility.

The adoption of the federal clause in the Refugee Convention set a sort of institutional precedent within the United Nations, and similar clauses began to proliferate.[37] The clause continued to appear throughout the 1960s and early 1970s,[38] before eventually giving way to alternative formulations, including one with a genuine territorial basis.

During its use, however, the federal jurisdiction clause did not function as a territorial application clause. This is because it did not alter the *territorial* scope of a treaty's application *ratione loci.*

---

[36] Art. 41 of Refugee Convention: *supra* n. 34.

[37] 1954 Convention Relating to the Status of Stateless Persons, 360 UNTS 117, Art. 37. See, also, 1956 Convention on the Recovery Abroad of Maintenance, 268 UNTS 3, Art. 11, and 1958 New York Convention on the Recognition and Enforcement of Foreign Arbitral Awards, 330 UNTS 3, Art. 11.

[38] 1967 Protocol Relating to the Status of Refugees, 606 UNTS 267, Art. 34; 1978 American Convention on Human Rights, 1144 UNTS 123, Art. 28, and 1972 UNESCO Convention Concerning the Protection of the World Cultural and Natural Heritage, 1037 UNTS 151, Art. 34.

Rather, such federal jurisdiction clauses altered the substantive content of a federal State's treaty obligations by reducing its scope *ratione materiae*.[39] Given that federal jurisdiction clauses were the only type of federal clause in operation during the ILC drafting period, their contemplation as a potential *territorial* model constituted a decidedly poor fit.

2.1.2.2 'Territorial Units' Clauses   A second-generation federal clause, 'territorial units' gained traction in the early 1970s.[40] Popularised by Canada, these clauses have appeared in numerous private international law instruments including those drafted by such private international law bodies as the Hague Conference,[41] the United Nations Commission on International Trade Law (UNCITRAL)[42] and the International Institute for the Unification of Private Law (UNIDROIT).[43] Their formulation marks a distinct shift away from the 'jurisdictional' federal clauses typical of the earlier instruments already surveyed. Instead, territorial units clauses rely on a modality of territorial application more consistent with that of colonial

---

[39] Bernier argues that only federal clauses altering territorial scope are territorial, while those altering subject matter scope are not: Bernier, *supra* n. 30, at p. 173.

[40] A. Aust, *Modern Treaty Law and Practice* (Cambridge: Cambridge University Press, 3rd ed., 2013), p. 188; Burmester, *supra* n. 35; H. A. Leal, 'Federal State Clauses and the Conventions of the Hague Conference on Private International Law', *Dalhousie Law J.*, 8 (1984), 257–283; B. R. Opeskin, 'Federal States in the International Legal Order', *Netherlands ILR*, 43 (1996), 353–386, at 367–370, and Trone, *supra* n. 35, at pp. 13–15.

[41] Territorial units clauses became standard in Hague instruments after 1973. See, e.g., 1973 Convention on the Law Applicable to Products Liability, 1056 UNTS 192, Art. 14. Thereafter, see, e.g., 1985 Convention on the Law Applicable to Trusts and on their Recognition, 1664 UNTS 311; 2009 Convention on the International Protection of Adults, Reg. No. I-46241; 1996 Convention on Jurisdiction, Applicable Law, Recognition, Enforcement and Co-operation in Respect of Parental Responsibility and Measures for the Protection of Children, 2204 UNTS 95.

[42] See, e.g., 1988 Convention on the Limitation Period in the International Sale of Goods, as amended by the Protocol of 11 April 1980, 1511 UNTS 99, Art. 31; 1980 United Nations Convention on Contracts for the International Sale of Goods (CISG), 1489 UNTS 3, Art. 93, and 1995 United Nations Convention on Independent Guarantees and Stand-by Letters of Credit, 2169 UNTS 163, Art. 25.

[43] The earliest UNIDROIT Conventions contained no federal clause provisions. See, e.g., 1974 Hague Convention Relating to a Uniform Law on the International Sale of Goods, 834 UNTS 109. From 1973 onwards, the newer 'territorial units' variant of federal clauses was used: see, e.g., 1973 Convention Providing a Uniform Law on the Form of an International Will, ILM, 12 (1973), 1298–1311, Art. XIV(1); 2001 Convention on International Interests in Mobile Equipment, 2307 UNTS 285, Art. 52, and 2001 Protocol to the Convention on International Interests in Mobile Equipment on Matters Specific to Aircraft Equipment, 2367 UNTS 1, Art. XXIX.

clauses.[44] More generic 'territorial units' clauses are often defined by reference to a distinct legal system, as in this provision from the 1973 Convention Providing a Uniform Law on the Form of an International Will:

> 1. If a State has two or more territorial units in which different systems of law apply in relation to matters respecting the form of wills, it may at the time of signature, ratification, or accession, declare that this Convention shall extend to all its territorial units or only to one or more of them, and may modify its declaration by submitting another declaration at any time.
> 2. These declarations shall be notified to the Depositary Government and shall state expressly the territorial units to which the Convention applies.[45]

This clause enabled Canada to accede on behalf of each of its provinces at different times.[46] Such 'territorial units' clauses govern situations where the power to implement a treaty is allocated between two or more territorially distinct systems of law and grant the State party a right of territorially selective application of the instrument across its geographic units.

The effect of the 'territorial units' clause is therefore distinct from that of its 'jurisdictional' counterpart, which modulates the subject matter of treaty obligations while preserving their territorial applicability throughout the entirety of the federal State. In contrast, 'territorial units' clauses preserve treaty obligations as a whole while permitting territorial divisibility where different systems of law are 'applicable in relation to matters dealt with' in the treaty.

Accordingly, while the earliest federal clauses remained distinct from territorial clauses, the newer 'territorial units' variant amply qualifies as a territorial application clause.[47] Interestingly, courts have found such clauses to be so broadly framed as to extend to former colonial territories

---

[44] Art. 14 of Convention on the Law Applicable to Products Liability: *supra* n. 41 (emphasis added).

[45] Art. IX of Convention Providing a Uniform Law on the Form of an International Will: *supra* n. 43.

[46] Canada acceded on behalf of Manitoba and Newfoundland on 9 Feb. 1978; Ontario on 15 Sept. 1978; Alberta on 1 Dec. 1978; Saskatchewan on 8 Oct. 1982; Prince Edward Island on 22 March 1995; New Brunswick on 5 Dec. 1997 and Nova Scotia 27 May 2001.

[47] Aust, *supra* n. 40, at p. 188; Burmester, *supra* n. 35, at p. 525; Leal, *supra* n. 40, at p. 271; Opeskin, *supra* n. 40, at pp. 367–370, and Trone, *supra* n. 35, at pp. 14–15.

as well.[48] Taking a broader view, this development suggests that the language of Article 29 VCLT was indeed framed in sufficiently broad terms to accommodate a range of territorial contexts.

2.1.3   Drafting History of Article 29 VCLT

The ILC took up its drafting on the territorial scope of treaties in earnest during the peak years of anti-colonialism in the 1960s. Its work was guided by two working premises. The first was that the territorial scope of treaties would be primarily determined by State parties' intentions.[49] The second was to provide a residual rule to govern the territorial application of any treaty otherwise silent as to its territorial scope.[50]

Although the ILC's work on the law of treaties had begun in 1949, the issue of territorial application received little treatment until its third Special Rapporteur, G. G. Fitzmaurice, comprehensively developed the subject in 1959, in the form of an expository code.[51] At that time, the subject comprised four ponderous provisions relating to general principles, application to metropolitan territory, application to dependent territories and the determination of the status of such territories.[52] Perhaps not surprisingly, the ILC eventually abandoned the expository format, and the fourth Special Rapporteur, Sir Humphrey Waldock, consolidated the four proposed draft articles into a single provision in 1964.[53]

Waldock's consolidated draft provision[54] avoided Fitzmaurice's antiquated reference to specific categories of colonial dependencies and

---

[48]   Pourvoi No. 04-17726 *Telecommunications Products Case*, Cour de Cassation (France), Première Chambre Civile, 2 Apr. 2008 (www.globalsaleslaw.org/content/api/cisg/urteile/1651.pdf); *Innotex Precision Limited v. Horei, Inc., et al.*, 2009 WL 5174736, U.S. Dist. Ct. for the N. Dist. of Georgia, 17 Dec. 2009. Both judgments excluded applicability to Hong Kong of the Convention on Contracts for the International Sale of Goods based on CISG's absence from a list of treaties extending to Hong Kong. See, *contra*, Art. 93(4) CISG: *supra* n. 42.

[49]   See G. G. Fitzmaurice, Fourth Report on the Law of Treaties, Doc. A/CN.4/120 (17 March 1959) and H. Waldock, Third Report on the Law of Treaties, Doc. A/CN.4/167 and Add.1–3 (13 March, 9 June, 12 June and 7 July 1964).

[50]   J. E. S. Fawcett, *The British Commonwealth in International Law* (London: Stevens & Sons, 1963); A. D. McNair, *The Law of Treaties* (Oxford: Clarendon Press, 1961), p. 117, and Sinclair, *supra* n. 23, at pp. 89–90.

[51]   Fitzmaurice, Fourth Report on the Law of Treaties, *supra* n. 49, at p. 47.

[52]   *Ibid.* (draft Arts. 25–28 respectively).

[53]   Waldock, Third Report on the Law of Treaties, *supra* n. 49.

[54]   '[Art.] 58: Application of a treaty to the territories of a contracting State. A treaty applies with respect to all the territory or territories for which the parties are internationally responsible unless a contrary intention a) is expressed in the treaty; b) appears from the

adopted instead the standard phrase 'territory or territories for which the parties are internationally responsible'. It proposed a general rule wherein a treaty would apply throughout a party's territory, *except* where an express contrary intention existed within the treaty itself, the circumstances of its conclusion, or in a reservation. Yet the drafters failed to address exactly *how* a treaty applied to territory. Between 1964 and 1966, the draft provision underwent a series of changes to its text and title. Several challenges to the provision emerged, including confusion as to the meaning of territorial application of treaties.

2.2   Meaning of Territorial Application

In his accompanying Commentary, Waldock explained that the concept of territorial application was not concerned with territorial subject matter nor with the place of the performance of obligations. In his view, 'the "territorial application" of a treaty signifies the territories which the parties have purported to be bound by the treaty and which, therefore, are the territories affected by the rights and obligations set up by the treaty'.[55] For Waldock, 'the real problem was that of the territory with regard to which the treaty was binding, rather than the territory in which it was to be performed'.[56] Accordingly, the territorial application of the Antarctic Treaty, for example, was not Antarctica itself but the territory of each State party to the treaty that undertook to be bound by the treaty's obligations.

Notwithstanding Waldock's clear vision of territorial application as concerning 'territories affected by the rights and obligations set up by the treaty', confusion persisted among ILC members as to alternative meanings of territorial application. Some Commission members felt that not all treaties were susceptible to territorial application: treaties relating to the high seas or outer space, for example, did not involve any direct connection to territory at all,[57] while a treaty relating to Antarctica or the moon similarly bore no relationship to the territory of State Parties.[58] For those treaties, surely territorial application was limited to the subject matter of the treaty? Or its place of performance? ILC members

---

circumstances of its conclusion or the statements of the parties; c) is contained in a reservation effective under the provisions of [Arts.] 18 to 20 of these articles.' See Waldock, Third Report on the Law of Treaties, *supra* n. 49, at p. 12.

[55] *Ibid.*   [56] *Ibid.*, at p. 46.

[57] See, e.g., Statements by Ago, Tunkin, Yasseen and de Luna: *YbILC* (1964–I), 167–168.

[58] See, e.g., Statement by Ago, *YbILC* (1964–I), 51.

repeatedly debated these issues without clear resolution. Nor was it clear whether territorial application was relevant to treaties of friendship, of extradition or involving bilateral investment. Some ILC members simply felt that not all treaties were capable of territorial application because the issue engaged the State as a legal rather than a territorial entity.

The entrenched debate eventually prompted some concessions by Waldock, resulting in his ambiguous observation that '[c]ertain types of treaty, by reason of their subject matter, are hardly susceptible of territorial application in the ordinary sense'.[59] This explanation contradicted his earlier position that all treaties, regardless of their subject matter, remained capable of territorial application. It also sidestepped the crucial issue of what the 'ordinary sense' of territorial application might be. Such confusion would persist throughout the drafting period.

One is left to wonder how such a fundamental issue could remain unresolved by the ILC in its final adoption of Article 29 VCLT. The ILC's more recent work on its Guidelines to Reservations, discussed later, suggests that Waldock's view – that a treaty applies throughout the territory of the State where the obligations and rights inhere – was the correct one. Less contentious and more swiftly dealt with was the peripheral issue of extraterritorial application, which the ILC declined to address altogether on the grounds that 'to attempt to deal with all the delicate problems of extra-territorial competence in the present article would be inappropriate and inadvisable'.[60] Certainly the concept of territorial application of treaties had not matured sufficiently in 1969 to empower the ILC to explicitly accommodate the issue of extraterritorial application in Article 29 VCLT. By the time of the Vienna Conference, little further discussion of the draft provision took place. It was eventually amended by a Ukrainian proposal,[61] and the final text was adopted at the second session of the Vienna Convention by ninety-seven votes to none.[62]

And yet the ILC's refusal to weigh in on extraterritoriality may not have been as absolute as the Commentary would suggest. To begin with, the need to avoid language suggestive of colonial clauses prompted the ILC to replace the standard language 'territory or territories for which parties are internationally responsible' with 'entire territory'. The suggested alternatives discussed by the ILC, though eventually

---

[59] *YbILC* (1966–II), 213.   [60] *YbILC* (1966–II), 214.
[61] A/CONF.39/C.1/L.164. See also A/CONF.39/C.1/SR.72, pp. 428–429.
[62] A/CONF.39/SR.13, p. 55.

discarded as equally suggestive of colonialism, shed considerable light on the meaning of the phrase 'entire territory'.[63] These alternative proposals strongly suggest that the ambit envisioned for Article 29 VCLT contemplated that at least *some* extraterritorial application in the modern sense. This is because colonial clauses regularly encompassed some territories that, while not under a State's sovereign control, remained nonetheless under its jurisdiction for international relations purposes. Such was the case for foreign leased territory, overseas military bases, trust and non-self governing territories, and *condominia*. Just as standard colonial clause phrasing[64] encompassed these categories, so too did the general rule of Article 29 VCLT. Accordingly, although the drafters rejected any extraterritorial scope for Article 29 VCLT, they nonetheless impliedly endorsed its scope to extend to jurisdictional zones beyond a State's sovereign jurisdiction. This understanding further endorses Waldock's reading of territorial application as the place where treaty obligations inhere. Only this construction would be consistent with extending a treaty's application to leased territory in a foreign land, for example. Today, however, the territorial application of treaties appears to be developing in a context-specific manner.

2.3   Contemporary Issues from a Contextual Perspective

The territorial application of treaties has evolved since the adoption of Article 29 VCLT. One obvious shift has been in the decline of colonial clauses, which have since fallen into desuetude.[65] Another recent issue relates to the treatment and interpretation of territorial declarations – namely, whether they qualify as reservations or instead qualify as 'a different intention' under Article 29 VCLT. While a complete examination of the territorial application of treaties on a contextual basis would exceed the scope of this chapter, this section briefly canvasses three distinct modes of a treaty's territorial application to illustrate the

---

[63] Alternative phrasing included: 'territories under the jurisdiction of parties'; 'applicable to the whole of the territory over which a party to the treaty effectively exercised its sovereignty'; 'while a territory is or remains within the jurisdiction of a State party to a treaty …' and 'the whole area subject to the jurisdiction of the State, including any territory that might be geographically separate'. See *YbILC* (1964–I), 48–52.

[64] M. B. Akehurst, 'Treaties, Territorial Application', *Encyclopedia PIL*, 4 (2000), 990–992; Aust, *supra* n. 40, at p. 181, and Elias, *supra* n. 17, at p. 51.

[65] The Council of Europe continues to use colonial clauses in its treaties.

complexity of emerging issues and the absence of uniformity across various treaty regimes.

2.3.1 The International Legal Status of Territorial Declarations

In recent years, the question of how to construe territorial declarations has emerged as a timely topic. Until 2011, two influential institutions favoured treating territorial declarations as akin to reservations: the UN Secretary-General Treaty Depositary and the ILC's Special Rapporteur on Reservations to Treaties. This section briefly traces the positions taken by each, highlighting in particular their difficulties in attempting to reconcile the legal status of such declarations with Article 29 VCLT.

The Secretary-General's depositary practice recognises that 'in principle', Article 29 VCLT obliges State parties to apply a treaty throughout its entire territory in the absence of a territorial clause.[66] This presumption of full territorial application can be sidestepped by the 'constant practice of certain States' issuing territorial declarations. For treaties containing explicit territorial application clauses, UN Secretary-General depositary practice generally treats territorial declarations in the same manner as reservations,[67] calling them to the attention of governments where a declaration may conflict with a treaty provision.[68] Its practice is equally consistent with regard to silent treaties,[69] subject to the twin caveats that declarations contravene neither the nature of the treaty nor other special circumstances.[70] For both types of declarations, the UN Secretary-General applies the same principles to territorial declarations as he does to reservations, 'leaving it to the other parties to draw the legal

---

[66] Treaty Section of the Office of Legal Affairs, *Summary of Practice of Secretary-General as Depositary of Multilateral Treaties* (New York, NY, 1994; rev. ed. 1999), p. 83 (paragraph 276); see, also, Art. 29 VCLT ('Unless a different intention appears from the treaty or is otherwise established, a treaty is binding upon each party in respect of its entire territory'): *supra* n. 8.

[67] The Secretary-General does not recognise territorial declarations as formal reservations but rather treats them analogously to reservations where circumstances permit: *ibid.*, at p. 84 (paragraph 277). It also recognises a distinction between territorial declarations and territorial reservations: *ibid.*, at p. 85 (paragraphs 284–285).

[68] *Ibid.*, at p. 81 (paragraph 269).   [69] *Ibid.*, at p. 84 (paragraph 277).

[70] *Ibid.*, at p. 83 (paragraphs 274–275) (citing non-acceptance of territorial declarations to the 1946 Convention on the Privileges and Immunities of the United Nations, 1 UNTS 15, and the 1947 Convention on the Privileges and Immunities of Specialized Agencies, 33 UNTS 261, due to their special character as constitutive acts of an international organization).

consequences of such declaration that they may see fit.'[71] In the absence of State party objections, the depositary construes such declarations as 'establish[ing] a different intention within the meaning of [Article] 29'.[72]

Somewhat contradicting this position, however, is the depositary's treatment of declarations made *subsequent* to deposit of an instrument. The depositary interprets such declarations as creating an inference that 'prior to such notification, the treaty was *not* applicable to the Territories concerned'.[73] This position directly contradicts not only the general presumption of Article 29 VCLT but also the depositary's own claim of adherence thereto.[74] Accordingly, although the depositary claims that, 'in principle', Article 29 VCLT operates to apply a silent treaty throughout a party's entire territory, it nonetheless construes post-deposit declarations as creating a retroactively contrary inference of territorial *limitation* to the pre-declaration period.

The depositary's inconsistent position on the matter discredits its claim that territorial declarations amount to a different intention otherwise established under Article 29 VCLT. Surely if the point of construing such declarations as constituting 'different intentions' for purposes of Article 29 VCLT, they should reflect the territorial presumptions it prescribes. Yet the present depositary practice with regard to post-deposit declarations indicates that it fails to construe such declarations in conformity with that provision.

Similar to the Secretary-General, the ILC's Special Rapporteur on Reservations to Treaties also tended to treat territorial declarations as akin to reservations from 1998–2011.[75] This preliminary position faced several conceptual hurdles. First, the ILC had to reconcile the reality of actual State practice – altering the scope of an *entire* instrument – with

---

[71] *Ibid.*, at p. 84 (paragraph 277). But, see, *contra* H. W. Malkin, 'Reservations to Multilateral Conventions', *BYbIL*, 7 (1926), 141–162, at 153 (characterising French and British reservations to the 1912 International Opium Convention, 215 CTS 297, as 'not reservations in the ordinary sense but ... rather excluding declarations as regards colonies. In ordinary cases no question of the consent of the other signatories arises as regards such declarations'). Given that the Convention obligations regarding enactment of legislative prohibitions on exports (Art. 13) – and more generally concerning treaty signing and ratification (Art. 23) – explicitly extended to contracting Powers' 'countries, possessions, colonies and leased territories', this interpretation seems flawed.

[72] *Summary of Depositary Practice, supra* n. 66, at p. 85 (paragraph 285).

[73] *Ibid.*, at pp. 84–85 (paragraph 282) (emphasis added).

[74] *Ibid.*, at p. 83 (paragraph 276).

[75] Draft Guideline 1.1.8, 'Reservations having Territorial Scope': ILC, Third Report on Reservations to Treaties, A/CN.4/491/Add.3 (19 June 1998), p. 254 (paragraph 186). See, further, *YbILC* (1998–II), 99.

the fact that such declarations did not strictly qualify as reservations under the Vienna Convention.[76] Second, it had to concede that the strict *temporal* requirements of a true reservation (to occur at the time of becoming a contracting party) ran counter to the practice of making territorial declarations anytime, often years after accession.[77] Finally, it had to determine whether 'colonial reservations' really amounted to reservations when they did not require consent of other parties and were *territorial*, rather than *material* in scope.[78] Notwithstanding these hurdles, the ILC tentatively concluded that although they were not reservations in the strict sense, they could be 'assimilated to a reservation' by virtue of their limitation on the treaty's application.[79] Accordingly, it adopted the view that territorial declarations constitute reservations where they '*purport to exclude the legal effect of the treaty or of certain of its provisions in their application to that State*'.[80]

In 2011, the ILC reversed its position after receiving comments from several governments on the issue, including France, New Zealand and the United Kingdom. Notably, New Zealand argued that treating territorial declarations as reservations would be 'at odds with policy objectives supported by the United Nations'.[81] Such an approach, it argued, would require an unsatisfactory all-or-nothing approach to treaty adoption. New Zealand would either have to violate its own constitutional mandate to consult by requiring a treaty's application throughout its dependencies or be forced to delay accession pending consent of all dependencies. Both New Zealand and the United Kingdom claimed that territorial declarations were *not* reservations; rather, they were merely statements establishing a 'different intention' under Article 29 VCLT.[82]

This feedback prompted the ILC to reverse its position and redraft the relevant guideline to *exclude* territorial declarations from the ambit of reservations. The reformulated guideline is decidedly obscure on the matter:

> A unilateral statement by which a State purports to exclude the applica-
> tion of some provisions of a treaty, or of the treaty as a whole with respect
> to certain specific aspects, to a territory to which they would be applicable
> in the absence of such a statement constitutes a reservation.[83]

---

[76] *Ibid.*, at p. 250 (paragraphs 155–156).

[77] *Ibid.*, at pp. 253 and 254–255 (paragraphs 179 and 189 respectively).

[78] On the distinction between the territorial scope of a treaty and the territorial subject matter, rejecting that the two coincide, see Karagiannis, *supra* n. 13, at pp. 733–734.

[79] *YbILC* (1998–II), 257. See, also, 183.   [80] *Ibid.* (emphasis added); see, also, 93.

[81] A/CN.4/639/Add.1, at p. 9 (paragraph 4).

[82] *Ibid.*, p. 9 (paragraph 3) and p. 10 (paragraph 2).

[83] A/66/10/Add.1, Guideline 1.1.3, at p. 48.

Accordingly, territorial declarations excluding application of *some provisions* continue to qualify as a reservation.[84] So, too, do declarations purporting to exclude application of the treaty as a whole *with respect to certain specific aspects*, though this phrase is not explained.[85]

Yet a declaration is *not* a reservation where it excludes the application of the *treaty as a whole* to all or part of a State's territory. The Commentary explains that 'such declarations are not necessarily reservations' but rather a 'different intention' in the sense of [A]rticle 29'.[86] Disowning its former position, the Commentary notes that 'it would hardly seem possible to consider such declarations purporting to exclude the application of a treaty as a whole to a particular territory as actual reservations'.[87] The Commentary also identifies the political consequences as the basis for its decision to exclude such declarations from the ambit of reservations.[88] In short, the ILC's approach to reservations reflects a flexibility and willingness to readily accommodate practical challenges to treaty participation in matters of territorial application yet fails to make any case for its new approach.

Ultimately, the UN depositary and the ILC both struggle to articulate a clear basis for the view that territorial declarations qualify as different intentions under Article 29 VCLT. The depositary analyses territorial declarations to reservations in order to conclude that the constant practice of certain States, combined with lack of parties' objections thereto, operates to 'establish[] a different intention' under with Article 29 VCLT. In contrast, the ILC explicitly rejects the idea of territorial declarations as reservations while still concluding that they qualify as 'a different intention'. Both accord weight to State parties' intentions. While the ILC sees States' unilateral declarations themselves as determinative of a 'different intention', UN depositary practice goes further to require that parties' intention be 'established' by the absence of State party objections to such declarations. Accordingly, the ILC appears to consider a territorial declaration as a 'different intention' at the time it is unilaterally made, while the Secretary-General may not recognize such intention as 'otherwise established' until parties have had an opportunity – and subsequently declined – to exercise any objection thereto.

Whether such declarations lawfully qualify as a 'different intention otherwise established' yields little more than ambiguity. Certainly the

---

[84] This position is consistent with the Secretary-General's depositary practice. See *Summary of Depositary Practice, supra* n. 66, at p. 85 (paragraph 284).

[85] *Supra* n. 83, Guideline 1.1.3, at pp. 49–50 (paragraph 4).

[86] *Ibid.*, at p. 50 (paragraph 5).   [87] *Ibid.*, at p. 51 (paragraph 9).

[88] *Ibid.*, at p. 51 (paragraph 10).

depositary practice suggests little beyond an internally inconsistent approach. And the ILC's approach looks more reactionary than clearly reasoned, while the conspicuously absent explanation for its change of position leaves observers without any articulated basis for its reasoning. Instead, the more suitable question may be whether States that rely on territorial declarations issue them in a manner that reflects compliance with Article 29 VCLT. Here, the answer is a surprisingly mixed one.

2.3.1.1 State Practice Regarding Territorial Declarations to Silent Treaties As noted previously, the use of territorial declarations has sometimes accompanied ratification or accession to *silent* treaties. Such declarations implicate Article 29 VCLT, which provides that '*[u]nless a different intention* appears from the treaty or *is otherwise established, a treaty is binding* upon each party *in respect of its entire territory*'.[89] Whether a territorial declaration might constitute precisely such a 'different intention', and how it might become 'otherwise established', is less than clear from the provision's drafting history. Given that Article 29 VCLT was predicated on the rapid demise of colonial clauses, the current practice of territorial declarations to silent treaties may well have been unintended.[90]

In fact, the provision's drafting history remains decidedly ambiguous as to how a different intention might be 'otherwise established', as seen from comments by drafters,[91] governments[92] and specialised agencies

---

[89] Art. 29 VCLT (emphases added): *supra* n. 8. See, also, United Nations, *Final Clauses of Multilateral Treaties Handbook* (New York, NY: United Nations, 2003), p. 81.

[90] P. T. B. Kohona, 'Some Notable Developments in the Practice of the UN Secretary-General as Depositary of Multilateral Treaties: Reservations & Declarations', *AJIL*, 99 (2005), 433–450, at 449 (citing the practice as one example of changes 'not specifically envisaged in the Vienna Convention').

[91] Although an early draft of Art. 29 allowed for a contrary intention to be expressed 'from the circumstances of its conclusion *or the statements of the parties*' (see *YbILC* (1962–II), 12), this exception was later condensed into 'circumstances of its conclusion': *YbILC* (1964–I), 167 (emphasis added). In that form, it met with significant resistance by ILC members who sought to delete it as ambiguous. See statements by Tabibi, Tunkin, DeLuna, Pal and Lachs, at 167–168. Waldock was 'somewhat perturbed' (at 168) at suggestions to delete the clause, noting it was intended to cover matters mentioned in the *travaux préparatoires* but not the treaty itself. He later repeated this claim and emphasised that the clause should be broadly construed to ascertain a party's intention (at 233).

[92] Governments' comments also reveal conflicting views as to what the clause could permit, even among nations with a history of reliance on colonial clauses and territorial declarations. The Netherlands sought to amend the clause so as to explicitly authorise territorial declarations. *YbILC* (1966–II), 51. So, too, did Finland. A/Conf.39/6 at 14 (4 March 1968).

discussing it.[93] Nor have scholars found much clarity in this clause.[94] Two matters are clear, however. First, the practice of declarations with regard to otherwise silent treaties is both circumscribed[95] and relatively recent,[96] essentially coinciding with the VCLT drafting period. Second, notwithstanding indications of emerging support for the view that territorial declarations comprise 'a different intention ... otherwise established' under Article 29 VCLT,[97] a clearly reasoned basis for this approach remains undeveloped and State practice inconsistent.

The 1998 Rome Statute establishing the International Criminal Court contains no provision specifying its territorial scope of application.[98]

At the Vienna Conference, Australia understood that territorial declarations were included within the ambit of the clause, while the Netherlands expressly conditioned its support on the understanding that it would continue to be able to make such declarations. UN Conference on the Law of Treaties, 1st Session 1968–69, pp. 162–163.

[93] The UN Food and Agriculture Organization understood the provision to allow for territorial declarations (though its observation that each instrument 'should contain a clause' regarding territorial application suggests an understanding that the legal basis for such declarations be anchored in the treaty itself). A/Conf.39/5 (4 March 1968), p. 194. The Council of Europe was unclear whether the clause ('unless a different intention ... is otherwise established') could accommodate 'unilateral declarations' by parties. A/Conf.39/7 (27 March 1968), p. 31 (paragraph 2).

[94] K. Doehring, 'The Scope of the Territorial Application of Treaties: Comments on Art. 25 of the ILC's 1966 Draft Articles on the Law of Treaties', *ZaöRV*, 27 (1967), 483–490, at 485–486; Karagiannis, *supra* n. 13, at pp. 735–740, and Kohona, *supra* n. 90, at p. 449.

[95] *Final Clauses of Multilateral Treaties Handbook, supra* n. 89, at pp. 81–82 (describing the practice as 'exceptional', applying only to 'certain states' in 'some limited circumstances'). See, also, *Summary of Depositary Practice, supra* n. 66, at p. 84 (paragraphs 277–278) (noting that territorial declarations in silent treaties require the *absence* of any special circumstances – such as a constitutive treaty for an international organization – and other parties' objections).

[96] The United Kingdom Government explained: 'It has been the long-standing practice of the United Kingdom (since at least 1967), in relation to multilateral treaties which are silent on territorial application, to specify in the instrument of ratification (or accession) the territories in respect of which the treaty is being ratified (or acceded to).' Sixth Committee, *Comments from Governments on Reservations to Treaties*, A/CN.4/639/ Add.1 p. 10 (paragraph 4). In 1980, Sinclair described territorial declarations as having 'long been known and accepted' in State practice, but distinguished their use in silent treaties – by the United Kingdom – as a 'recent practice'. See Sinclair, *supra* n. 23, at pp. 90–91, and, also, *Summary of Depositary Practice, supra* n. 66, at pp. 83–85 (paragraphs 273–285) and *Final Clauses of Multilateral Treaties Handbook, supra* n. 89, at pp. 81–83 (observing that 'a practice has been developed' regarding the United Kingdom, the Netherlands, New Zealand and Denmark, extending to China since 1997 and 1999 in relation to Hong Kong and Macau respectively).

[97] *Summary of Depositary Practice, supra* n. 66, at p.85 (paragraph 285) and Karagiannis, *supra* n. 13, at pp. 735–740.

[98] 2187 UNTS 90.

Accordingly, one may construe its territorial application under Article 29 VCLT in two possible ways. First, the Rome Statute might necessarily apply throughout the 'entire territory' of each State party, on the basis that no different intention 'appears from the treaty'.[99] Alternatively, piecemeal territorial application might be permitted if a different intention (regarding the instrument's territorial scope) were somehow 'otherwise established'. Current State practice suggests that the latter interpretation is prevailing.

Commentators[100] have called attention to the fact that the United Kingdom, which ratified the Rome Statute on 4 October 2001, nonetheless felt free to issue a territorial declaration extending the Rome Statute to several of its dependencies in 2010, nearly a decade after ratification.[101] It then made a further declaration of extension in 2012 to the Isle of Man.[102] Nor is the United Kingdom alone in its piecemeal territorial application of the Statute. Denmark initially excluded the Faroe Islands and Greenland in 2001, then included them – in 2004 and 2006 respectively.[103] In contrast, the Netherlands extended the Statute to its Kingdom in Europe, the Netherlands Antilles and Aruba at the time it became a party;[104] while New Zealand declined to extend the Statute to Tokelau 'unless and until' it lodged a declaration to such effect.[105]

---

[99] A silent multilateral treaty is, by default, construed to apply to a party's entire territory. *Summary of Depositary Practice, supra* n. 66, at p. 85 (paragraph 276) and *Final Clauses of Multilateral Treaties Handbook, supra* n. 89, at p. 81. Territorial declarations to a silent treaty may meet with opposition depending on the nature of the treaty, including where 'the treaty is the constitutive act of an international organization'. See *Summary of Depositary Practice, supra* n. 66, at pp. 83–84 (paragraphs 274–275 and 277).

[100] W. Schabas, 'Territorial Declarations and the Rome Statute', Ph.D. Studies in Human Rights Blog, 10 Aug. 2010 (http://humanrightsdoctorate.blogspot.com/search?q=rome±statute) and M. Milanovic, The Territorial Scope of the Rome Statute, EJILTalk!, 11 Aug. 2010 (www.ejiltalk.org/the-territorial-scope-of-the-rome-statute/).

[101] In a declaration dated 11 March 2010, the United Kingdom sought to extend its ratification (effective as of that date) to include Anguilla; Bermuda; British Virgin Islands; Cayman Islands; Falkland Islands; Montserrat; Pitcairn, Henderson, Ducie and Oeno Islands; St. Helena, Ascension and Tristan da Cunha; the Sovereign Base Areas of Akrotiri and Dhekelia and Turks and Caicos Islands. See UN Status of Treaties database at: http://treaties.un.org/pages/ViewDetails.aspx?src=TREATY&mtdsg_no=XVIII-10&chapter=18&lang=en#9.

[102] United Kingdom Declaration dated 28 Nov. 2012, see https://treaties.un.org/pages/ViewDetails.aspx?src=TREATY&mtdsg_no=XVIII-10&chapter=18&lang=en#10.

[103] See UN Status of Treaties database at: https://treaties.un.org/pages/ViewDetails.aspx?src=TREATY&mtdsg_no=XVIII-10&chapter=18&lang=en#2

[104] See UN Status of Treaties database at: https://treaties.un.org/pages/ViewDetails.aspx?src=TREATY&mtdsg_no=XVIII-10&chapter=18&lang=en#6.

[105] See UN Status of Treaties database at: https://treaties.un.org/pages/ViewDetails.aspx?src=TREATY&mtdsg_no=XVIII-10&chapter=18&lang=en#7.

What is to be made of such declarations? They seem unlikely to constitute reservations, given the Rome Statute's prohibition[106] thereof and the ILC's recent change of position on the matter.[107] Alternatively, the treaty's silence on territorial application opens the possibility of 'a different intention ... otherwise established'. But *should* such unilateral declarations qualify as such?

On the one hand, the State practice cited here faces some hurdles from the Secretary General's depositary approach regarding territorial declarations to silent treaties. Although the depositary broadly treats such declarations analogously to reservations, it does so subject to two important caveats. First, a territorial declaration will not be accepted by the depositary where piecemeal territorial application is deemed to be inconsistent with the *travaux préparatoires*, precedent or nature of a treaty. A second exception involves 'other special circumstances'. One such special circumstance recognised by the depositary involves situations in which a treaty constitutes 'the constitutive act of an international organization', a criteria clearly applicable to the Rome Statute.

The Secretary-General's decision not to oppose any of these declarations, however, suggests that it considered them contrary neither to the nature of the treaty nor to its special circumstances as a constitutive document. And this view was ostensibly ratified by the absence of State party objections to the declarations. Yet an anecdotal look at these declarations demonstrates that they are not always issued in a manner that reflects compliance with Article 29 VCLT.

Take the example of the United Kingdom's 2001 ratification of the Rome Statute without an accompanying territorial declaration. No different territorial intention appeared from the treaty, nor was one 'otherwise established' in 2001. In accordance with Article 29 VCLT, the Rome Statute was presumptively binding in respect of the United Kingdom's entire territory as of 2001. But in March 2010, when the United Kingdom did issue a declaration, it did not act to *exclude* certain dependencies construed as presumptively included in 2001, as one might expect under a reading of Article 29 VCLT. Instead, the United Kingdom 'extended' its ratification to the territories named,[108] suggesting an understanding of its treaty obligations as *restricted* to the metropolitan territory until the time of its declaration, a premise entirely contrary to what Article 29 VCLT requires. In other

---

[106] 1998 Rome Statute of the International Criminal Court, 2187 UNTS 90, Art. 120.

[107] *Supra* n. 83.

[108] See Declaration at: https://treaties.un.org/pages/ViewDetails.aspx?src=TREATY&mtdsg_no=XVIII-10&chapter=18&lang=en#9.

words, the United Kingdom understood its treaty obligations in 2001 as limited to its metropolitan territory, until explicitly *extended* to additional territories in 2010. Its declaration of an additional extension to Isle of Man in 2012 further supports this interpretation. Despite its claims before the ILC, then, the United Kingdom practice regarding its territorial declarations does not support a reading that they amount to a different intention under Article 29 VCLT because they are not premised on its presumption of otherwise full territorial application.

The Netherlands' declaration suggests a similar lack of compliance with Article 29 VCLT. Made at the time of deposit, its declaration – '[f]or the Kingdom in Europe, the Netherlands Antilles and Aruba' – was arguably unnecessary, rendered superfluous under the Article 29 VCLT presumption of full territorial application. If the Netherlands similarly sought to have its territorial declarations construed as a different intention under the provision, why did it not structure its declarations to comport with Article 29's full territorial premise?

In contrast, the declarations made by Denmark and New Zealand demonstrate clear compliance with Article 29 VCLT by explicitly *excluding* certain named territories prior to subsequent inclusion at some later date. This practice supports an understanding that absent the declaration, each State's treaty obligations would otherwise extend to such territories.

The foregoing sections offer an ambiguous picture of the legal status of territorial declarations under international law. Neither depositary practice nor the ILC supports a view that they strictly qualify as formal reservations, though the former concedes that an analogous approach is practicable at present. And while both institutions claim to construe territorial declarations as amounting to a different intention under Article 29 VCLT, the approach ultimately lacks consistency, clarity, and support from the text and *travaux préparatoires* of Article 29 VCLT. Rather, today's inconsistently framed territorial declarations often belie such an understanding and reflect at best an *emerging* practice so far tolerated, absent a crisis developing in a territory whose ambiguous status brings the issue to the fore.

2.3.2   Membership beyond States

One way to promote expansive territorial application is to allow entities other than States to become parties to a treaty.[109] This device is not new;

---

[109] Notwithstanding that Art. 1 VCLT limits treaties to agreements between States parties, membership beyond States continues to flourish in practice: *supra* n. 8.

it has historical precedent in certain treaty regimes.[110] One modern example is the World Trade Organization, which invites membership from States as well as separate customs territories.[111] As originally framed, contracting parties to the 1947 General Agreement on Tariffs and Trade (GATT) were not States but 'governments',[112] who were to abide by its provisions on behalf of a 'separate customs territory'[113] and where separate tariffs or commercial regulations were to be maintained for a substantial part of its trade.[114] These broad membership rules have enabled non-sovereign entities to accede to GATT,[115] sometimes side-stepping politically charged issues in the process.[116] Such rules enabled Taiwan to become a WTO member in 2002, notwithstanding China's one-State policy and Taiwan's *de jure* status as a non-State.[117]

Taiwan's WTO membership was made possible under a special GATT provision allowing accession for 'a government acting on behalf of a separate customs territory possessing full autonomy in the conduct of its external commercial relations . . .'[118] An alternative provision enabled former territorial dependencies sponsored by a metropolitan authority to succeed on terms previously accepted by that authority.[119] These broad membership rules afford the WTO greater flexibility in membership and participation than organizations whose membership is confined to States alone,[120] particularly where terms such as 'customs territory' remain ambiguous.

---

[110] Since 1946, for example, the ILO Constitution has provided for membership by territorial dependencies: ILO Constitution, 15 UNTS 40, Art. 35.

[111] 1994 Marrakesh Agreement Establishing the World Trade Organization, 1867 UNTS 154, Art. XII(1).

[112] 55 UNTS 187, Art. XXXII(1).

[113] 'The rights and obligations arising under this Agreement shall be deemed to be in force between each and every territory which is a separate customs territory and in respect of which this Agreement has been accepted under Article XXVI . . .' See Art. XXIV(1) GATT: *ibid.*

[114] Art. XXIV(4) GATT: *supra* n. 111.

[115] GATT Analytical Guide, 'Art. XXXIII: Accession' (www.wto.org/english/res_e/book sp_e/gatt_ai_e/art33_e.pdf), p. 1017.

[116] H.-W. Cho, *Taiwan's Application to GATT/WTO: Significance of Multilateralism for an Unrecognized State* (Westport: Praeger, 2002), pp. 194–195.

[117] Taiwan joined the WTO under the name 'Separate Customs Territory of Taiwan, Penghu, Kinmen and Matsu', informally known as 'Chinese Taipei'.

[118] Art. XXXIII GATT: *supra* n. 111.

[119] Art. XXVI(5) GATT: *supra* n. 111. See, further, GATT Analytical Guide, Part B of 'Art. XXXIII': *supra* n. 115, at pp. 1025–1027.

[120] S. Charnovitz, 'Taiwan's WTO Membership and Its International Implications', *Asian J. WTO & Int'l. Health L. & Pol'y*, 1 (2006), 401–432.

Taiwan's political difficulties in securing WTO membership[121] remain emblematic of its challenges – as neither State, nor dependency, nor international organization – to participation in international regimes generally.[122] In the context of fisheries regimes, Taiwan has sometimes managed to participate successfully as a 'fishing entity',[123] albeit with mixed success.[124]

As with GATT, the 1982 United Nations Law of the Sea Convention (UNCLOS)[125] also allows for signature by entities other than States, including international organizations.[126] This expanded party approach has since been adopted in certain fisheries contexts. The 1995 United Nations Fish Stocks Agreement incorporates by reference to UNCLOS certain categories of 'entity' eligible to become parties[127] and adds 'other fishing entities'.[128]

---

[121] For background on Taiwan's WTO accession, see, generally, Cho, *supra* n. 116; P. L. Hsieh, 'Facing China: Taiwan's Status as a Separate Customs Territory in the World Trade Organization', *JWT*, 39 (2005), 1195–1221; P. L. Hsieh, 'An Unrecognized State in Foreign and International Courts: The Case of the Republic of China on Taiwan', *Michigan JIL*, 28 (2007), 765–814, and J. S. Mo, 'Settlement of Trade Disputes between Mainland China and the Separate Customs Territory of Taiwan within the WTO', *Chinese JIL*, 2 (2003), 145–174.

[122] For other international organizations of which Taiwan is a member, see Charnovitz, *supra* n. 120, at 403, and, also, Cho, *supra* n. 116, at p. 195.

[123] A. Serdy, 'Bringing Taiwan into the International Fisheries Fold: The Legal Personality of a Fishing Entity', *BYbIL*, 75 (2004), 183–221.

[124] Established by the 1993 Convention for the Conservation of Southern Bluefin Tuna, 1819 UNTS 360, the Commission for the Conservation of Southern Bluefin Tuna (CCSBT) granted Taiwan observer status until April 2001. At that time, the Commission adopted a resolution establishing an Extended Commission and an Extended Scientific Committee enabling membership beyond State parties ('any entity or fishing entity'). These entities enjoy the same voting rights and are subject to the same tasks and largely similar obligations. See Serdy, *supra* n. 123, at 195–198. The International Commission for the Conservation of Atlantic Tunas has passed resolutions in 1994 and 2001 granting renewable observer status for Taiwan as a recognised 'cooperating fishing entity'. See Serdy, *supra* n. 123, at 200–207. However, the Indian Ocean Tuna Commission (IOTC) has no means of accommodating Taiwan other than through *ad hoc* representation. Its underlying treaty, the 1993 Agreement for the Establishment of the Indian Ocean Tuna Commission, 1927 UNTS 329, allows membership by States and 'regional economic integration organizations', and observer status for intergovernmental and non-governmental organizations only: see Serdy, *supra* n. 123, at 207–209.

[125] 1833 UNTS 3.   [126] Art. 305 UNCLOS: *ibid.*

[127] 1995 Agreement for the Implementation of the Provisions of the United Nations Convention on the Law of the Sea of 10 December 1982 Relating to the Conservation and Management of Straddling Fish Stocks and Highly Migratory Fish Stocks (Straddling Fish Stocks Agreement), 2167 UNTS 88, Art. 1(2)(b)(i).

[128] Art. 1(3) of Straddling Fish Stocks Agreement: *ibid.*

When the Convention for the Conservation of Southern Bluefin Tuna[129] failed to adopt this expanded definition, its Commission was unable to promote participation and compliance by non-State fishing entities such as Taiwan. To correct its narrow membership rules, the Commission adopted a 2001 Resolution[130] creating duplicate institutional machinery (an Extended Commission and an Extended Scientific Committee) granting membership beyond Convention Parties to any 'entity or fishing entity' as well as to any 'regional economic integration organisation'.[131] This expanded membership has enabled varying degrees of participation by entities such as Taiwan and the European Community (as a formal Co-operating Non-Member without voting rights), thereby enabling broader participation in and compliance with the fisheries regime.[132]

2.3.3   Extraterritorial Application

Finally, a third form of territorial application stems from legal interpretations of the geographic scope of treaties or certain provisions within a treaty. In a slight twist, this issue has come to dominate determinations of a treaty's *extra*territorial application in the context of international human rights treaty law.[133] Much has been written in recent years about the territorial application of international human rights treaties, particularly in terms of their ability to apply extraterritorially, beyond a party's territory.[134] In part, this is due to the frequent presence of 'jurisdiction' clauses requiring a contracting party to secure treaty rights to the persons or territory within a State party's jurisdiction. These clauses may appear

---

[129] *Supra* n. 124.   [130] See Serdy, *supra* n. 123.

[131] The 2001 Resolution was replaced and repealed by a 2013 Resolution that supplemented membership rules to include those of regional economic integration organizations: Resolution to Establish an Extended Commission and an Extended Scientific Committee (replaced at the Twentieth Annual Meeting, 14–17 Oct. 2013).

[132] More recently, Hong Kong was included among a list of States invited to become observers at the Eighth Compliance Committee Meeting, suggesting that participation by non-State entities other than Taiwan is encouraged: Report of the Twentieth Annual Meeting of the Commission, 14–17 Oct. 2013 (paragraph 98).

[133] On human rights treaties generally, see the contribution to this volume of Chinkin at pp. 509–537 (Chapter 16).

[134] See, e.g., F. Coomans and M. T. Kamminga, *Extraterritorial Application of Human Rights Treaties* (Antwerp: Intersentia, 2004); M. Milanovic, *Extraterritorial Application of Human Rights Treaties: Law, Principles and Policy* (Oxford: Oxford University Press, 2011); K. Da Costa, *The Extraterritorial Application of Selected Human Rights Treaties* (Leiden: Martinus Nijhoff, 2013) and M. Gondek, *The Reach of Human Rights in a Globalising World: Extraterritorial Application of Human Rights Treaties* (Antwerp: Intersentia, 2009).

in a general framework provision governing the treaty as a whole,[135] in individual provisions with specified scope[136] or both.[137] Notwithstanding the varied language, structure, object and purpose, and drafting history of the instruments involved, international treaty bodies and tribunals have interpreted these clauses to produce nearly uniform extraterritorial results.[138] Two such examples involve the 1966 United Nations Covenant on Civil and Political Rights (whose geographic scope is governed by a single provision) and the 1984 United Nations Convention against Torture and Other Cruel, Inhuman or Degrading Treatment or Punishment (some of whose provisions are silent as to scope, while others apply to 'any territory under the jurisdiction of' a State party). Recently released memos from the Obama administration recommend formal recognition of the extraterritorial aspects of these treaty provisions as both legally sound and supported by broad consensus.[139] Some human rights instruments lacking such a clause and

[135] 1989 Convention on the Rights of the Child (CRC), 1577 UNTS 3, Art. 2(1); 1966 United Nations International Covenant on Civil and Political Rights (ICCPR), 999 UNTS 171, Art. 2(1) and 1950 European Convention for the Protection of Human Rights and Fundamental Freedoms (ECHR), 213 UNTS 221, Art. 1.

[136] 1965 United Nations International Convention on the Elimination of All Forms of Racial Discrimination (CERD), 660 UNTS 195, Arts. 3 and 6.

[137] In addition to a global jurisdiction clause in Art. 2(1), the 1984 United Nations Convention Against Torture and Other Cruel, Inhuman or Degrading Treatment or Punishment (CAT), 1465 UNTS 85, contains an identical jurisdictional phrase in several other provisions: Arts. 5, 7, 11–13 and 16.

[138] For the ICCPR, see *Legal Consequences of the Construction of a Wall in the Occupied Palestinian Territory* (Advisory Opinion) (2004) ICJ Rep. 136, at p. 180 (paragraph 111) and *Case Concerning Armed Activities on the Territory of the Congo*: Democratic Republic of the Congo v. Uganda (2005) ICJ Rep. 116, at p. 244 (paragraph 219). No international tribunal has yet interpreted the scope of the CAT, but its Committee has construed Art. 2(1) as one of extraterritorial application. General Comment No 2: Implementation of Article 2 by States Parties. No. CAT/C/GC/2, pt. (2008) (paragraphs 7 and 16). For CRC, see *Legal Consequences of the Construction of a Wall in the Occupied Palestinian Territory*, at p. 181 (paragraph 113); *Case Concerning Armed Activities on the Territory of the Congo*, at pp. 241 and 243–244 (paragraphs 211, 217 and 219). For CERD, see *Case Concerning Application of the International Convention on the Elimination of All Forms of Racial Discrimination*: Georgia v. Russian Federation (Order for Provisional Measures) (2008) ICJ Rep. 353, at p. 386 (paragraph 109). The ECHR's extraterritorial scope is well established: see, e.g., *Loizidou v. Turkey*, 20 EHRR 99 (ECtHR) (Preliminary Objections), Appl. No. 15318/89, 23 March 1995; *Cyprus v. Turkey*, App. No. 25781/94 J & D 2001-IV 10 (ECtHR [GC]-Merits), 10 May 2001; *R. (on the application of Al-Jedda) (FC) (Appellant) v. Secretary of State for Defence* [2007] UKHL 58 and *Al-Skeini and Others v. Secretary of State for Defence* [2007] UKHL 26.

[139] For detailed analysis discussing the bases for a revised position of the United States on the extraterritorial scope of the ICCPR and the CAT, see U.S. Dept. of State Office of the

otherwise silent as to their territorial scope[140] have been equally construed to involve extraterritorial obligations.[141] To further complicate
matters, many human rights treaties also contain additional provisions,
such as federal or colonial clauses, whose scope may limit the effect of
a jurisdiction clause.[142]

This broadly extraterritorial construction is not altogether unique to
human rights treaty regimes. Some international environmental
treaties[143] have also been interpreted to impose obligations on State

Legal Advisor, *Memorandum Opinion on the Geographic Scope of the International
Covenant on Civil and Political Rights* (19 Oct. 2010) and U.S. Dept. of State Office of
the Legal Advisor, *Memorandum Opinion on the Geographic Scope of the Convention
against Torture and Its Application in Situations of Armed Conflict* (21 Oct. 2013). Both
can be found at http://justsecurity.org/7946/forum-extraterritorial-application-human-
rights-treaties-analyzing-state-department-memos/.

[140] 1948 United Nations Convention on the Prevention and Punishment of the Crime of
Genocide (Genocide Convention), 78 UNTS 277; Refugee Convention, *supra* n. 34; 1966
United Nations International Covenant on Economic, Social and Cultural Rights
(ICESCR), 993 UNTS 3, and 1979 United Nations Convention on the Elimination of
All Forms of Discrimination against Women (CEDAW), 1249 UNTS 13.

[141] For the Genocide Convention, see *Case Concerning Application of the Convention on the
Prevention and Punishment of the Crime of Genocide*: Bosnia and Herzegovina
v. Yugoslavia (Preliminary Objections) (1996) ICJ Rep. 595, at p. 616 (paragraph 31)
and *Case Concerning Application of the Convention on the Prevention and Punishment of
the Crime of Genocide*: Bosnia and Herzegovina v. Serbia and Montenegro (2007) ICJ
Rep. 43, at p. 107 (paragraph 154). For the Refugee Convention, *supra* n. 34, Art. 33 (*non-
refoulement*) has been construed as extraterritorial in scope and applicable on the high
seas: *Haitian Centre for Human Rights et al. v. United States* (Inter-Am.Comm.H.R.,
13 March 1997) (paragraphs 157–158). But, see, *contra*, *Sale v. Haitian Centers Council*,
509 US 155, at p. 183 (U.S. Supreme Court 1993). For the ICESCR, see *Legal
Consequences of the Construction of a Wall in the Occupied Palestinian Territory, supra*
n. 138, at pp. 180–181 (paragraph 112). So far, no tribunal has examined the extraterritorial scope of CEDAW, *supra* n. 140, but its Committee recently issued a General
Recommendation on its extraterritorial application, asserting that State parties remain
under its obligations to persons 'within their territory or effective control, even if not
situated within the territory': General Recommendation No. 28 on the Core Obligations
of States Parties under Art. 2 CEDAW, No. CEDAW/C/2010/47/GC.2, pt. (2010)
(paragraph 12).

[142] On the relationship between the colonial clause and the jurisdiction clause of the ECHR,
see, e.g., L. Moor and A. W. B. Simpson, 'Ghosts of Colonialism in the European
Convention on Human Rights', *BYbIL*, 76 (2005), 121–194.

[143] Discussion of the extraterritorial scope of the 1979 Bern Convention on the
Conservation of European Wildlife and Natural Habitats, ETS No. 104, the 1971
Ramsar Convention on Wetlands of International Importance, 996 UNTS 245, and the
1972 Convention Concerning the Protection of the World Cultural and Natural
Heritage, 1037 UNTS 151, can be found in M. J. Bowman, P. G. G. Davies and
C. J. Redgwell, *Lyster's International Wildlife Law* (Cambridge: Cambridge University
Press, 2nd ed., 2010), pp. 323–326, 424–426 and 454–456 respectively.

parties either to refrain from certain extraterritorial conduct or to comply with conservation policies when acting outside their territory. As in the human rights context, the extent to which such treaty provisions can feasibly impose extraterritorial obligations remains unclear.

This section serves to highlight the complexities of territorial application in specific legal contexts. While not exhaustive,[144] it emphasises the enduring relevance of territoriality in the treaty context, its variability between and within different legal regimes and, most significantly, its continuing evolution in the modern era.

2.4 Conclusions

We conclude this section of the chapter by discussing the relevance of colonial clauses to the modern practice of territorial declarations and their ambiguous relationship to Article 29 VCLT today. It demonstrates that piecemeal territorial application not only persists and endures today, it does so in a decidedly less transparent manner than that of colonial clauses of a bygone era.

It is perhaps inevitable that the irreconcilable objectives of preserving parties' intentions and discouraging an unpopular colonial practice would result in equivalent practice by another name. Today, territorial declarations – now uncoupled from any treaty-based authorising clause – appear to embody a different intention 'otherwise established'. The practical result is the looming functional obsolescence of Article 29 VCLT's general rule of full territorial application in favour of its now dominant exception.

As a result of these developments, the territorial application of treaties is now moving to the margins of treaty practice, where it is achieved through the extramural device of unilateral declarations rather than negotiated treaty provisions. This development arguably runs contrary to premise of ILC drafters and the spirit of treaties as consensually negotiated instruments. And although the practice remains limited, it is expanding. Since 1997, China has been added to the UN depositary's list of countries that regularly rely on territorial declarations for differentiating treaty application to Hong Kong and Macau. The possibilities for further expansion remain. Importantly, future State practice is likely to be constrained only

---

[144] Territorial application in the context of the European Union is particularly complex. Excellent coverage of this issue is provided in D. Kochenov (ed.), *EU Law of the Overseas: Outermost Regions, Associated Overseas Countries and Territories, Territories Sui Generis* (The Netherlands: Kluwer Law International, 2011).

by State parties' objections on a treaty-by-treaty basis. The lack of objections at present suggests that the practice of territorial declarations is likely to continue, if not slowly expand, for some time to come.

3   Territorial Issues in State Succession of Treaties

3.1   Introduction

The first section of this chapter has examined the codification of the territorial application of treaties in the VCLT to canvass its conceptual aspects. Notably, that process suffered from the irreconcilable objectives of permitting a longstanding past practice while endeavouring to implement a remedial rule designed to produce a contrary result. The resulting provision was not only ambiguous to ILC members, who failed to agree on the meaning of territorial application of treaties, but difficult to apply given the dominance of its exception and the relative frailty of its residual rule. The present section switches gears to survey a particular *context* of territorial application of treaties: State succession.

Admittedly, the 'territorial project' undertaken in Article 29 VCLT remained incomplete in 1969. A multitude of related issues had been proposed and debated in relation to territorial application of treaties, only to be recognised as unsuitable for inclusion in the VCLT context. These included extraterritorial application (rejected as raising more issues than it addressed) and State succession – to be reprised in the VCSST of August 1978.[145] In this last context, territoriality would resurface with particular relevance.

In its examination of State succession in respect of treaties, the ILC began with a survey of the twin concepts of boundary and territorial treaties for their particular ability to survive State succession. One reason for treating these two topics so early on in the process reflected Special Rapporteur Waldock's decision to anchor the draft articles in the framework of the law of treaties[146] and to treat it as 'a *sequel* to the draft articles on the law of treaties rather than as one section of a single comprehensive codification of the several branches of the law applicable to succession of States and Governments'.[147] As one commentator explained, '[t]hey were problems of the law of treaties which arose in a special context – a succession of States.'[148]

---

[145] *Supra* n. 10.   [146] *YbILC* (1968–II), 222 (paragraphs 87 and 89).
[147] *Ibid.* (emphasis added).
[148] I. Sinclair, *The International Law Commission* (Cambridge: Grotius Publications, 1987), p. 67.

This approach was adopted in part due to doubts about any distinct legal discipline regarding State succession,[149] but it resulted from the guidance provided by the law of treaties for succession of States *in respect of treaties*. In this respect, Article 62(2)(a) VCLT[150] was of particular relevance for singling out boundary treaties as an exception to the rule permitting termination in the event of a fundamental change of circumstances.[151] Waldock explained his reliance on Article 62 VCLT in the State succession context by noting 'the same general considerations appear to apply, *mutatis mutandis*, to cases of "succession" even although in these cases the question of the continuance or termination of the treaty may present itself somewhat differently'.[152] Further, he recalled ILC discussions relating to territorial treaties involving the related question of so-called 'objective régimes',[153] which create rights *erga omnes*.[154] Within the VCLT context, the topic of objective regimes was partially resolved under Article 36[155] (governing third party rights),[156] but Waldock strongly believed that such regimes warranted further examination in the State succession context. Accordingly, the twin provisions on boundary and territorial treaties under the Vienna Convention on State Succession came to be seen as a continuation of a theme earlier abandoned as unresolved in 1964.[157]

It was the anomalous status of boundary treaties first discerned in the VCLT context that prompted Waldock to grant them a place among his first four draft articles on State succession, where he proposed that boundary treaties should 'remain untouched by the mere fact of

---

[149] *YbILC* (1968–II), 222 (paragraph 86).

[150] 'A fundamental change of circumstances may not be invoked as a ground for terminating or withdrawing from a treaty: (a) if the treaty establishes a boundary . . .'

[151] *YbILC* (1966–II), 256–260. See, also, S. Rosenne, 'Automatic Treaty Succession' in J. Klabbers and R. Lefeber (eds.), *Essays on the Law of Treaties: A Collection of Essays in Honour of Bert Vierdag* (The Hague: Kluwer Law International, 1988), pp. 97–106, at pp. 99–100.

[152] *YbILC* (1968–II), 92.

[153] An objective regime occurs when a treaty establishes territorially-based rights and obligations which attach to third States. For a formal definition, see *YbILC* (1964–II), 26–34. Their existence remains disputed: J. Crawford, *Brownlie's Principles of Public International Law* (Oxford: Oxford University Press, 8th ed., 2012), pp. 439–440.

[154] *YbILC* (1972–II), 49. See, also, S. Rosenne, *Developments in the Law of Treaties 1945–1986* (Cambridge: Cambridge University Press, 1989), p. 74.

[155] Art. 36 VCLT: *supra* n. 8.

[156] See the contribution to this volume of Waibel at pp. 201–236 (Chapter 8).

[157] See Rosenne, *supra* n. 154, at p. 74.

a succession'[158] while retaining the possibility of expanding the category to include a broader group of territorial treaties.

From the earliest stages, then, boundary and other territorial treaties became a central concept around which draft articles of State succession were negotiated. Problematically, early agreement as to their special status failed to secure consensus on their operation. Because of their unclear operation, boundary and territorial treaties become a focal point for discussions in the law of State succession in respect of treaties.

3.2 Boundary and Territorial Regimes Explained

Today, the Vienna Convention on Succession of States in Respect of Treaties contains two provisions specifically dealing with how a State succeeds to boundary and territorial treaties. The first of these is on boundary treaties:

> Art. 11: Boundary regimes[159]
> A succession of States does not as such affect:
> (a) a boundary established by a treaty; or
> (b) obligations and rights established by a treaty and relating to the regime of a boundary.

The second of these concerns a more ambiguous category:

> Art. 12: Other territorial regimes[160]
> 1. A succession of States does not as such affect:
>   (a) obligations relating to the use of any territory, or to restrictions upon its use, established by a treaty for the benefit of any territory of a foreign State and considered as attaching to the territories in question;
>   (b) rights established by a treaty for the benefit of any territory and relating to the use, or to restrictions upon the use, of any territory of a foreign State and considered as attaching to the territories in question.
> 2. A succession of States does not as such affect:
>   (a) obligations relating to the use of any territory, or to restrictions upon its use, established by a treaty for the benefit of a group of States or of all States and considered as attaching to that territory;
>   (b) rights established by a treaty for the benefit of a group of States or of all States and relating to the use of any territory, or to restrictions upon its use, and considered as attaching to that territory.

---

[158] *YbILC* (1968–II), 93.   [159] Art. 11 VCSST: *supra* n. 10.
[160] Art. 12 VCSST: *supra* n. 10.

3. The provisions of the present article do not apply to treaty obligations of the predecessor State providing for the establishment of foreign military bases on the territory to which the succession of States relates.

The significance of each of these provisions relates to their overall effect on a State's succession to treaties, which is to create specifically recognised exceptions to the general rule embodied by the clean slate doctrine.[161] But their significance extends beyond this to the peculiar feature shared by these treaties in the context of State succession. What is it about boundary and territorial regimes that gives them such special operative effect? What peculiar territorial characteristics enable them to receive different treatment in instances of State succession? ILC members repeatedly raised these questions during the drafting process.

3.3   Confusion in Principle and Practice

Between the two categories, boundary treaties enjoyed greater consensus from the outset in terms of their natural tendency to survive instances of State succession,[162] even if the means by which they achieved such effect could not be agreed upon. One prominent source of authority for this position was the *Case Concerning the Temple of Preah Vihear*, in which Cambodia and Thailand agreed that their boundary dispute was governed by a 1904 treaty between Siam and France.[163] The case has thus been cited for the fact that neither party disputed Cambodia's status as successor to France under boundary treaty.[164] Yet, agreement on the status of boundary treaties left unresolved the greater ambiguity surrounding territorial treaties as a whole. Did they consist of something other than boundary treaties? If so, what were their crucial features, and

---

[161] Whether this reflects State practice has been challenged: see Crawford, *supra* n. 153, at p. 438, and, also, Y. Makonnen, 'State Succession in Africa: Selected Problems', *Hague Recueil*, 200 (1986–V), 93–234, at 107–108.

[162] Crawford, *supra* n. 151, at pp. 439–440. See, also, International Law Association, *The Effect of Independence on Treaties: A Handbook* (London: Stevens & Sons, 1965), p. 361.

[163] *Case Concerning the Temple of Preah Vihear*: Cambodia v. Thailand (1962) ICJ Rep. 6. See Counter-Memorial of the Royal Govt. of Thailand, 29 Sept. 1961, p. 169. See, also, Reply of the Government of the Kingdom of Cambodia, 29 Nov. 1961, at p. 439 (paragraph 5). Cambodia asserted that while boundary provisions survived succession, political provisions governing peripheral issues such as dispute settlement procedures do not survive State succession. Prel. Obj. of the Royal Govt. of Thailand, 23 May 1960, at p. 145 (paragraph 40).

[164] See International Law Association, *supra* n. 162, at p. 214.

how did they operate to survive succession? On this issue, commentators disagreed.

Disagreement surrounding territorial treaties was so pervasive it extended even to the terminology used to reference them. In addition to the generic rubric of 'territorial' treaties,[165] other terms included: 'dispositive',[166] 'constitutive',[167] 'localized',[168] and 'real' treaties[169] as well as treaties creating 'objective' regimes.[170] They have been analogised to servitudes[171] and to conveyances.[172] The crucial features, or even the operative mechanism by which territorial treaties achieve their permanence, have been the subject of debate and controversy for decades.

Two precedents at the core of these debates proved highly influential to the formulation of the final provisions. The first was the *Åland Islands* case, in which Sweden sought enforcement of an 1856 treaty between France and Great Britain on one side and Russia on the other to forbid the latter from constructing military fortifications on the island.[173] The Committee of Jurists rejected Sweden's claim that the demilitarisation provision constituted a real servitude.[174] It found instead that the 1856 instrument had been attached to a subsequent peace treaty in such a manner as to give the 1856 treaty 'the character of a settlement regulating European interests'.[175] For the Committee, it was this *character* of the settlement accruing to European interests that generated the broader benefit accruing to Sweden as a third State. The features of this case, in

---

[165] E. J. S. Castrén, 'Aspets Récents de la Succession d'Etats', *Hague Recueil*, 78 (1951–I), 379–506.

[166] See International Law Association, *supra* n. 162.   [167] McNair, *supra* n. 50, at p. 256.

[168] C. W. Jenks, 'State Succession in Respect of Law-Making Treaties', *BYbIL*, 29 (1952), 105–144; M. Udina, 'La succession des états quant aux obligations internationales autres que les dettes publiques', *Hague Recueil*, 44 (1933), 704–758, and R. W. G. De Muralt, *The Problem of State Succession with Regard to Treaties* (The Hague: W.P. van Stockum & Zoon, 1954).

[169] R. Y. Jennings, *The Acquisition of Territory in International Law* (Manchester: Manchester University Press, 1963); J. M. Jones, 'State Succession in the Matter of Treaties', *BYbIL*, 24 (1947), 360–375, and F. A. Váli, *Servitudes in International Law* (London: Stevens & Sons, 1958).

[170] See Reports of the International Law Commission generally, 1968–1974.

[171] D. P. O'Connell, *State Succession in Municipal and International Law* (Vol. II: International Relations) (Cambridge: Cambridge University Press, 1967), pp. 17–23 and 231, and G. G. Fitzmaurice, 'The Juridical Clauses of the Peace Treaties', *Hague Recueil*, 73 (1948), 259–367, at 293–295.

[172] McNair, *supra* n. 50, at p. 256.

[173] *Report of the International Committee of Jurists on the Aaland Islands Dispute*, O.J. Spec. Suppl. No. 3 (5 Sept. 1920), at p. 3.

[174] *Ibid.*, at p. 18.   [175] *Ibid.*

which a territorial *régime* resulted in the creation of rights and obligations to the benefit of a larger community, went on to form the basis of Article 12(2) VCSST relating to the rights or obligations 'established by a treaty for the benefit of a group of States or of all States'.

The other influential precedent on Article 12 VCSST recognised the ability of territorial treaties to generate *localised* rights benefiting a single State rather than a group of States. This category created rights and obligations *'for the benefit of any territory of a foreign State'*.[176] This type of territorial regime was confirmed in the *Case of the Free Zones of Upper Savoy and the District of Gex*,[177] which recognised the ability of a *localised* territorial zone to survive state succession, even where its benefits only accrued to a single State or a part thereof. Article 12(1) is premised on this rule.

3.4   Post-Conference Analysis

The 1978 VCSST would not enter into force until November 1996, long after many relevant instances of State succession had transpired. The Convention has been criticised on many grounds, not only for its poor timing but for the inadequate foundational bases upon which the two provisions were established.[178]

Notwithstanding its swift and unequivocal support, Article 11 VCSST has encountered little subsequent development since its adoption. It has been neither applied nor interpreted by the International Court of Justice (ICJ). Yet if the rule is indeed an accurate articulation of customary international law, its codification may have been a factor in solidifying the heritability of boundaries. Consequently, parties to a boundary dispute may be more likely to concede the issue of a boundary's heritability, even among more complex boundary disputes.[179] In this sense, the lack of development of this provision may itself be a testament to its success.

---

[176] Art. 12(1) VCSST: *supra* n. 10.

[177] *Free Zones of Upper Savoy and the District of Gex*: France v. Switzerland (Second Phase), 1930 PCIJ, Series A, No. 24.

[178] M. Koskenniemi, 'Introduction: Report of the Director of Studies of the English-Speaking Section of the Centre' in P. M. Eismann and M. Koskenniemi (eds.), *State Succession: Codification Tested against the Facts* (The Hague: Martinus Nijhoff, 2000), pp. 65–132.

[179] See, e.g., *Case Concerning Kasikili/Sedudu Island*: Botswana v. Namibia (1999) ICJ Rep. 1045. See, also, *Case Concerning the Territorial Dispute*: Libyan Arab Jamahiriya v. Chad (1994) ICJ Rep. 6.

The legacy of Article 12 VCSST with regard to territorial treaties is more difficult to characterise. To date, the ICJ's only recognition of a territorial regime in the State succession context has been based on an interpretation of the provision as an expression of customary international law.[180] Since that time, subsequent ICJ cases have recognised territorial regimes as broadly relevant to construing a treaty's effect beyond the context of State succession.

In 2007, for example, the ICJ determined that a dispute over the sovereignty of certain islands between Nicaragua and Colombia was governed by a 1928 treaty between these two original parties. In support of its finding, the court noted as *obiter dictum* that even if the 1928 treaty had been terminated, Colombia's sovereignty over the islands, as provided for in the treaty, would remain unaffected:

> The Court recalls that it is a principle of international law that a territorial regime established by treaty 'achieves a permanence which the treaty itself does not necessarily enjoy' and the continued existence of that regime is not dependent upon the continuing life of the treaty under which the regime is agreed.[181]

This comment is significant for elevating recognition of territorial regimes to that of a general principle of international law, thereby granting it a place of prominence in international law well beyond the narrow State succession context. It bears mention that the authority relied by the Court in support of its position does not reference territorial regimes. Rather, it concerned *boundary* regimes akin to those dealt with under Article 11 VCSST. Together, these features point to the Court's willingness to construe territorial regimes more expansively and flexibly than the narrow State succession context.

In 2009, the ICJ again relied on the concept of territorial regimes, this time as an interpretive device to aid in construing the meaning of a treaty's terms. In a dispute over navigational rights on the San Juan River between Nicaragua and Costa Rica, the ICJ determined that the issue of navigational rights was governed by an 1858 treaty establishing Nicaragua's sovereignty over a portion of the San Juan River comprising a boundary between the two States.[182] That same treaty also recognised

---

[180] *Case Concerning Gabčikovo-Nagymaros Project (Hungary/Slovakia)* (1997) ICJ Rep. 7.

[181] *Case Concerning the Territorial Dispute*: Nicaragua v. Colombia (Preliminary Objections) (2007) ICJ Rep. 832, at p. 861 (paragraph 89) (internal citation to *Case Concerning the Territorial Dispute*: Libyan Arab Jamahiriya v. Chad omitted).

[182] *Dispute Regarding Navigational and Related Rights*: Costa Rica v. Nicaragua (2009) ICJ Rep. 213.

Costa Rica's rights of perpetual free navigation 'con objetos de comercio' thereon.[183] At issue was whether such commercial navigational rights were strictly limited to transport of commercial goods or could be more broadly construed to include commercial services such as passenger transport. In support of its conclusion that the Spanish term 'comercio' should enjoy an evolving meaning over time, the Court cited, among other factors, the parties' intention to create a lasting, permanent arrangement.[184] It found that Costa Rica's right of navigation itself was 'so closely linked with the territorial settlement defined by the Treaty – to such an extent that it can be considered an integral part of it – that it is characterised by the same permanence as the territorial regime *stricto sensu* itself'.[185]

The critical feature for the Court was the fact that Costa Rica's navigational rights were established on equal footing with Nicaragua's sovereignty without 'any hierarchy as between Nicaragua's sovereignty over the river and Costa Rica's right of free navigation'.[186] In essence, Costa Rica's commercial navigational rights were construed as part of the territorial regime precisely because they were established on par with Nicaragua's sovereign rights over the river.

These cases illustrate not only the progressive evolution of territorial regimes beyond the State succession context but their growing relevance to the ICJ as an interpretive aide to construing a treaty's terms and effects.

4 Conclusion

This chapter's discussion of the relationship between treaties and territory has been confined to a close examination of two territorial projects undertaken in the Vienna Convention framework: the territorial application of treaties under Article 29 VCLT and the State succession of boundary and territorial treaties in Articles 11 and 12 VCSST. The treatment in each showcases the remarkable breadth of that relationship. It also underscores the inherent difficulty in establishing rules that are not only historically accurate and contemporaneously relevant but equally resonant for the foreseeable (and unforeseeable) future. This challenge is amplified when one considers the unusual relevance of

---

[183] For further discussion of the term 'comercio', see the contributions to this volume of Gardiner and Buga at pp. 335–362 (Chapter 11) and 363–391 (Chapter 12) respectively.
[184] *Dispute Regarding Navigational and Related Rights, supra* n. 182, at p. 243 (paragraph 68).
[185] *Ibid.*, at p. 244 (paragraph 69).   [186] *Ibid.*, at pp. 237–238 (paragraph 48).

territory to modern conceptions of international law and its contributions to such foundational precepts as territorial sovereignty to the modern State.

In each case, the governing rules embody binary features of a major and minor premise, a dominant rule and an exception. For Article 29 VCLT, the primary purpose was to establish territorial applicability throughout the 'entire' territory of a State party as a new general rule designed to supplant the piecemeal territorial application of colonial clauses. An abrupt departure from past practice, the rule represented a political imperative in light of the anticolonial sentiments of the era. And yet its crucial exception ('unless a different intention . . . is otherwise established') is today capable of supplanting the general rule of treaty application throughout a party's entire territory. Accordingly, the most significant aspect of the provision's evolution has not led to conceptual refinement of what it means for a treaty to apply to territory. That concept remains poorly developed. Rather, the most significant development of Article 29 VCLT has occurred in regard to the breadth of its exception. A 'different intention . . . otherwise established' now includes unilateral declarations unmoored from anchoring treaty provisions granting it legitimacy and containing substantive rules whose premises contradict Article 29 VCLT.

In the State succession context, the primary rule was the permanence of treaty-based boundary regimes in Article 11 VCSST. Boundary regimes in State succession operated predictably and supported the clear objective of stability in international relations. As such, there has been little room for its evolution. In contrast, treaty-based territorial regimes fraught with ambiguity have enjoyed comparatively greater evolution and development, particularly by the ICJ. In particular, territorial regimes have evolved as a concept in their own right beyond the State succession context, capable of shedding light on the terms and effect of a given treaty. Much remains to be seen in this area.

Territory, and its relationship to treaties, remains a fascinating and under-developed topic. Perhaps predictably so, the most ambiguous of the topics examined here continue to generate the greatest dynamism in their meaning and effect.

PART II

Contextual Perspectives

16

Human Rights

CHRISTINE M. CHINKIN

1 Introduction

In its 1951 advisory opinion on *Reservations to the Convention on the Prevention and Punishment of the Crime of Genocide*, the International Court of Justice (ICJ) referred to the 'special characteristics' of a Convention 'manifestly adopted for a purely humanitarian and civilizing purpose'.[1] Judge Alvarez, dissenting, specifically indicated the emergence of new categories of conventions, those 'seeking to regulate matters of a social or humanitarian interest with a view to improving the position of individuals'.[2] Despite Judge Alvarez's claim that this category of treaty was 'formerly unknown', the 1948 United Nations Convention on the Prevention and Punishment of Genocide[3] was by no means the first humanitarian convention.[4] It was however at the forefront of the post–World War II international legal order and, like its exact contemporary the Universal Declaration of Human Rights (UDHR),[5] has its basis in the 1945 Charter of the United

---

[1] *Reservations to the Convention on the Prevention and Punishment of the Crime of Genocide* (Advisory Opinion) (1951) ICJ Rep. 15, at p. 21.

[2] *Ibid.*, at p. 51. In a more modern explication, human rights treaties 'represent a contribution to human dignity and global stability – as distinguished, for example, from a commercial or trading treaty'. See *Application of the Convention on the Prevention and Punishment of the Crime of Genocide*: Bosnia and Herzegovina v. Serbia and Montenegro (Preliminary Objections) (1996) ICJ Rep. 595, at p. 649 (Separate Opinion of Judge Weeramantry).

[3] 78 UNTS 277.

[4] E.g., dissenting Judges Guerrero, Sir Arnold McNair, Read and Hsu Mo described the 1926 Slavery Convention, 60 LNTS 253, as 'an important humanitarian convention': *Reservations to the Convention on the Prevention and Punishment of the Crime of Genocide, supra* n. 1, at p. 33. Another humanitarian convention 'with much in common with the Genocide Convention in point of structure' was the 1925 International Opium Convention, 81 LNTS 317: *supra* n. 1, at p. 34.

[5] The Genocide Convention was adopted one day before the UDHR: General Assembly Resolution 217A (III), U.N. Doc A/810 at 71 (10 Dec. 1948).

Nations.[6] By the time of the adoption of the Vienna Convention on the Law of Treaties (VCLT) in May 1969,[7] there was a range of instruments that could be categorised as appertaining to human rights,[8] including those adopted by the International Labour Organization,[9] the 1965 International Convention on the Elimination of All Forms of Racial Discrimination (ICERD),[10] the 1966 International Covenants on Civil and Political Rights (ICCPR)[11] and Economic, Social and Cultural Rights (ICESCR)[12] and, at the regional level, the European[13] and Inter-American[14] human rights conventions. But the 'International Human Rights Movement'[15] was still in its infancy in 1969, and human rights was not yet the significant component of international law and relations that it was later to become.[16] It is therefore not surprising that there is no 'special place' in the VCLT for human rights treaties, which – like all treaties – are widely accepted as instruments of public international law and subject to its terms. But 'human rights' are mentioned directly in the

---

[6] 1 UNTS 16. Art. 1(3) of the UN Charter includes among the purposes of the Organization 'promoting and encouraging respect for human rights and for fundamental freedoms for all'; the preamble to the Genocide Convention affirms that genocide is 'contrary to the spirit and aims of the United Nations': *supra* n. 3.

[7] 1155 UNTS 331.

[8] E. Schwelb, 'International Conventions on Human Rights', *ICLQ*, 9 (1960), 654–675, describes the diversity of human rights treaties in 1960, including proposals for treaties that never materialised.

[9] The character of labour treaties as human rights treaties is disputed: e.g., Craven does not see ILO treaties as human rights treaties. See M. Craven, 'Legal Differentiation and the Concept of the Human Rights Treaty in International Law', *EJIL*, 11 (2000), 489–519, at 497–498. ILO conventions are however the model for some of the features of human rights treaties: V. A. Leary, 'Lessons from the Experience of the International Labour Organisation' in P. Alston (ed.) *The United Nations and Human Rights: A Critical Appraisal* (Oxford: Clarendon Press, 1992), pp. 580–619.

[10] 660 UNTS 195.   [11] 999 UNTS 171.   [12] 999 UNTS 3.

[13] 1950 European Convention for the Protection of Human Rights and Fundamental Freedoms (ECHR), 213 UNTS 221.

[14] The Inter-American Convention on Human Rights (IACHR), 114 UNTS 123, was signed on 22 Nov. 1969, almost exactly six months after the signing of the VCLT. It came into force on 18 July 1978, nearly eighteen months earlier.

[15] L. Henkin, 'Human Rights and State "Sovereignty"', *Ga. J. Int'l & Comp. L.*, 25 (1995–1996), 31–45.

[16] 'Even in 1968 . . . such rights remained peripheral as an organizing concept and almost non-existent as a movement'. See S. Moyn, *The Last Utopia: Human Rights in History* (Cambridge, MA: Harvard University Press, 2010), p. 2; cf. A. Aust, *Modern Treaty Law and Practice* (Cambridge: Cambridge University Press, 3rd ed., 2013), p. 134 ('the era of modern universal human rights treaties only really began in 1966 with the two international covenants').

preamble to the VCLT as one of 'the principles of international law embodied in the Charter of the United Nations'[17] and indirectly in Article 60(5) VCLT as a 'humanitarian' exception to the general rule on the consequences of material breach.[18] The emergence of human rights law in international relations accelerated after the late 1970s,[19] making it contemporaneous with the growing acceptance of the VCLT as the codification of treaty law.

The legalisation and judicialisation of international human rights have founded arguments that human rights constitutes a sub-discipline of international law, a 'distinct jurisprudential phenomenon',[20] indeed a 'special law',[21] central to the anxieties about the fragmentation of international law.[22] The human rights world is a very different one from that envisaged by the VCLT: the latter is an empty, amoral world where States have reciprocal dealings only with other States, where there are no people hurt by States' actions and demanding reparations, no international institutions creating special mechanisms peopled by experts for monitoring and reporting and no non-governmental organizations (NGOs) demanding accountability. It is not surprising that human rights advocates are uncomfortable with the narrow perspective

---

[17] Cf. preamble of 1986 Vienna Convention on the Law of Treaties between States and International Organizations or between International Organizations, ILM, 25 (1986), 543–592. Pazarci comments that '[i]n this regard the preamble is of great significance', given that human rights are included within Arts. 1(3), 55 and 56 of the UN Charter as a 'purpose' to be promoted, not a foundational principle: H. Pazarci, 'Preamble (1969)' in O. Corten and P. Klein (eds.), *The Vienna Conventions on the Law of Treaties: A Commentary* (Vol. I) (Oxford: Oxford University Press, 2011), pp. 1–11, at p. 8.

[18] *Legal Consequences for States of the Continued Presence of South Africa in Namibia (South West Africa) Notwithstanding Security Council Resolution 276 (1970)* (Advisory Opinion) (1971) ICJ Rep. 16, at p. 55 (paragraph 96). On the effect of Art. 60(5) VCLT, see B. Simma, 'Reflections on Article 60(5) of the Vienna Convention on the Law of Treaties and Its Background in General International Law', *ÖZöR*, 20 (1970), 5–83.

[19] Moyn's argument that human rights emerged in the 1970s 'seemingly from nowhere' seems overstated, for instance in light of the antecedents such as those cited *supra* n. 4: see Moyn, *supra* n. 16, at p. 3.

[20] L. Brilmayer, 'From "Contract" to "Pledge": The Structure of International Human Rights Agreements', *BYbIL*, 77 (2006), 163–202, at 164.

[21] International Law Commission, Report of the Study Group on Fragmentation of International Law: Difficulties arising from the Diversification and Expansion of International Law, Finalized by Martti Koskenniemi, U.N. Doc. A/CN.4/L.682 (2006), p. 12 (paragraph 9).

[22] M. Koskenniemi and P. Leino, 'Fragmentation of International Law? Postmodern Anxieties', *Leiden JIL*, 15 (2002), 553–579.

of the VCLT.[23] They make claims for the supremacy of the 'special law' of human rights as the basis of an embryonic global or regional[24] constitutional order[25] that challenges accepted principles of general international law such as State consent[26] and State responsibility.[27] Further, NGOs feel a sense of ownership towards a human rights treaty for which they have campaigned. Somewhat inconsistently, they may lobby for the hard legal form but seek to ignore (and persuade others to ignore) what they perceive as legal formalities once a treaty has come into force.

This chapter explores some of these claims[28] and the extent to which the 'special character of a human rights treaty'[29] impacts upon the applicability of the VCLT or has been influential in the evolution of the modern law of treaties. It examines the threshold question of what constitutes a human rights treaty and looks at a number of significant areas where the applicability of the VCLT has been explored or contested,

---

[23] M. Scheinin, 'The Status of International Treaties on Human Rights', European Commission for Democracy through Law (Venice Commission), CDL-UD(2005)014 (Strasbourg, 8 Sept. 2005), p. 5.

[24] See, e.g., the European Court of Human Rights (ECtHR) has repeatedly described the ECHR as the 'constitutional instrument of European public order': *Loizidou v. Turkey* (ECtHR) (Preliminary Objections), Appl. No. 15318/89, 23 March 1995 (paragraph 75) and *Al-Skeini v. UK* (ECtHR GC), Appl. No. 55721/07, 7 July 2011 (paragraph 141).

[25] 'The interpretation and application of human rights treaties have indeed been guided by considerations of a superior general interest or *ordre public* which transcend the individual interests of Contracting Parties'. *Case Concerning Ahmadou Sadio Diallo*: Republic of Guinea v. Democratic Republic of the Congo (2010) ICJ Rep. 639, at p. 756 (paragraph 84 of Separate Opinion of Judge Cançado Trindade).

[26] See, e.g., 'considerations of a superior order (international *ordre public*) have primacy over state voluntarism': *Case Concerning Application of the International Convention on the Elimination of All Forms of Racial Discrimination*: Georgia v. Russian Federation (Preliminary Objections) (2011) ICJ Rep. 70, at p. 281 (paragraph 87 of Dissenting Opinion of Judge Cançado Trindade); 'Consent by an individual state would no longer be an absolute limit to state obligations under human rights treaties but would be pushed aside by an objectively binding "constitution"': Scheinin, *supra* n. 23, at p. 6.

[27] E.g., 'the whole conceptual universe of the law of the international responsibility of the State has to be reassessed in the framework of the international protection of human rights, encompassing the origin as well as the implementation of State responsibility, with the consequent and indispensable duty of reparation': *Questions Relating to the Obligation to Prosecute or Extradite*: Belgium v. Senegal (2012) ICJ Rep. 422, at p. 508 (paragraph 49 of Separate Opinion of Judge Cançado Trindade).

[28] For a full treatment, see especially O. de Frouville, *L'Intangibilité des Droits de l'Homme en Droit International: Régime Conventionnel des Droits de l'Homme et Droit des Traités* (Paris: Pedonne, 2004).

[29] Human Rights Committee (HRC), General Comment No. 24: Issues Relating to Reservations made upon Ratification or Accession to the Covenant or the Optional Protocols thereto, or in Relation to Declarations under Article 41 of the Covenant, U.N. Doc. CCPR/C/21/Rev.1/Add.6, 11 Apr. 1994.

in particular with respect to its impact on State obligations. It concludes that apparent deviation from the VCLT often in fact falls within its residual scope and that this flexibility has allowed for an expansive application of human rights treaties in order to enhance their scope of protection. Differences in approach may depend upon the identity of the decision-maker, for example specialist human rights bodies may be less ready to accept the constraints of treaty law than government officials or 'mainstream' bodies of international law such as the International Law Commission (ILC) or ICJ.

2   The Nature of Human Rights Treaties

2.1   What Is a Human Rights Treaty?

Any acknowledgement of the 'special' character of human rights treaties requires identification of treaties within this rubric.[30] However, while there are dozens of treaties that may be so categorised in the contemporary international legal order, 'the category of "human rights treaties" is ... far from homogeneous',[31] and there is no accepted definition of what constitutes a 'human rights' treaty. Matthew Craven argues that the very term creates a semantic problem: are we talking at any given moment about treaties (with all the international law baggage the form entails) 'or the fact that they instantiate human rights' (that is 'that they are premised upon the idea that the rights pre-exist not only the treaties themselves, but also explain or justify the competence of governments in relation to them')?[32]

With respect to form, a number of human rights treaties have been negotiated following an earlier non-binding declaration, demonstrating the importance to their proponents of the hard legal form.[33] UN human rights treaties have been developed through non-legal bodies such as the Commission on Human Rights (now Human Rights Council) or the Commission on the Status of Women, with input from expert bodies and NGOs and adoption by the UN General Assembly (GA). Thus, while

---

[30] E. W. Vierdag, 'Some Remarks about Special Features of Human Rights Treaties', *Netherlands YbIL*, 25 (1994), 119–142.

[31] A. Pellet, Second Report on Reservations to Treaties, U.N. Doc. A/CN.4/477 & Corr.1 & 2 and Add.1 & Corr.1–4 (10 May and 13 June 1996) (paragraph 82).

[32] Craven, *supra* n. 9, at 493 (footnotes omitted).

[33] E.g., in adopting the non-binding UDHR, the UNGA requested ECOSOC to ask the Commission on Human Rights to give priority to drafting a Covenant: UNGA Resolution 217 (III), 10 Dec. 1948.

they may have been 'discussed [in the GA] at length by all States, who have the opportunity to comment upon them as they see fit',[34] they have not necessarily been subject to the legal scrutiny commensurate with the binding legal obligation incurred by treaty form. In accordance with Article 1 VCLT, human rights treaties are between States, although exceptionally the 2006 Convention on the Rights of Persons with Disabilities allows for confirmation by a 'regional integration organization'.[35] Additional protocols to human rights treaties have been negotiated that create either new rights[36] or new procedures.[37] Protocols are not provided for in the VCLT but as treaties are themselves subject to its terms.

Attempts have been made to identify some defining features beyond their form and focus on the rights of individuals.[38] Article 64 IACHR allows States parties to consult the Inter-American Court of Human Rights (IACtHR) regarding the 'interpretation of . . . treaties concerning the protection of human rights in the American states'. In determining that the 1963 Vienna Convention on Consular Relations (VCCR)[39] concerns human rights, the Court relied upon the VCLT definition of a treaty[40] and noted the former's dual purpose: it recognises both the right of the State to assist its nationals and that of the individual to contact the consular officer to obtain assistance.[41] The Court concluded

---

[34] *Reservations to the Convention on the Prevention and Punishment of the Crime of Genocide, supra* n. 1, at p. 51 (Dissenting Opinion of Judge Alvarez).

[35] 2006 Convention on the Rights of Persons with Disabilities (CPD), 2515 UNTS 3, Art. 44. Art. 59(2) ECHR (as amended by Protocol No. 14) provides that the EU may accede to the Convention: *supra* n. 13.

[36] E.g., 1989 Second Optional Protocol to the ICCPR, Aiming at the Abolition of the Death Penalty, 1642 UNTS 414; 1989 Convention on the Rights of the Child (CRC), 1577 UNTS 3; 2000 Optional Protocol to the CRC on the Involvement of Children in Armed Conflict, 2173 UNTS 222, and 2000 Optional Protocol to the CRC on the Sale of Children, Child Prostitution and Child Pornography, 2171 UNTS 227.

[37] E.g., 1979 Convention on the Elimination of All Forms of Discrimination against Women (CEDAW), 1249 UNTS 13; 1999 CEDAW Optional Protocol (CEDAW OP), 2131 UNTS 83; 1984 Convention against Torture and Other Cruel, Inhuman or Degrading Treatment or Punishment (CAT), 1465 UNTS 85, and 2002 Optional Protocol to the CAT, 2375 UNTS 237.

[38] Although simply, 'human rights treaties *stricto sensu*: basically they are all concerned with the rights of the human being': *Application of the Convention on the Prevention and Punishment of the Crime of Genocide, supra* n. 2, at p. 637 (Separate Opinion of Judge Shahabuddeen).

[39] 596 UNTS 261.

[40] *The Rights to Information on Consular Assistance in the Framework of the Guarantees of the Due Process of Law* (IACtHR) (Advisory Opinion) OC-16/99, 1 Oct. 1999 (paragraph 71).

[41] *Ibid.* (paragraph 80).

that Article 36 VCCR 'endow[ed] a detained foreign national with individual rights that are the counterpart to the host State's correlative duties'.[42]
In comparable cases, the ICJ accepted that Article 36 bestows individual
rights but declined to determine whether they constitute human rights.[43]

The IACtHR's analysis suggests that human rights treaties have two
essential elements. First, like all treaties, a human rights treaty has
horizontal effect, regulating inter-State behaviour.[44] This characteristic
is exemplified by provision for inter-State complaint and dispute
resolution.[45] Indeed, the centrality of human rights in contemporary
international relations has encouraged the (unsuccessful) use of dispute
resolution clauses in human rights treaties to establish ICJ jurisdiction
where human rights are not core to the dispute.[46] Second, as
a 'framework enabling States to make binding unilateral commitments
not to violate the human rights of individuals within their jurisdiction',[47]
a human rights treaty represents a vertical relationship, a governmental
pledge[48] and limit to governmental power.[49] This feature of human rights
treaties is concretised at the international level by an individual

---

[42] *Ibid.* (paragraph 84).

[43] *LaGrand Case*: Germany v. United States of America (2001) ICJ Rep. 466, at p. 494
(paragraph 78) and *Case Concerning Avena and Other Mexican Nationals*: Mexico
v. United States of America (2004) ICJ Rep. 12, at pp. 60–61 (paragraph 124). See,
however, paragraph 34 of Separate Opinion of Judge Cançado Trindade in *Ahmadou
Sadio Diallo, supra* n. 25, at p. 739 ('I shall address this question, characterizing the right
to information on consular assistance as an *individual right*, within the conceptual
universe of human rights').

[44] HRC, General Comment No. 31: The Nature of the General Legal Obligation Imposed on
States Parties to the Covenant, U.N. Doc. CCPR/C/21/Rev.1/Add.13, 29 March 2004
(paragraph 2).

[45] '[W]e can nowadays reckon that we have before us as essentially a human rights case,
a case pertaining to the international protection of human rights. It is lodged with this
Court within the confines of an inter-State mechanism': *Ahmadou Sadio Diallo, supra*
n. 25, at p. 735 (paragraph 20 of Separate Opinion of Judge Cançado Trindade).

[46] *Case Concerning Armed Activities on the Territory of the Congo* (New Application: 2002):
Democratic Republic of the Congo v. Rwanda (Jurisdiction and Admissibility) (2006) ICJ
Rep. 6, at pp. 16–17 (paragraph 15) and *Case Concerning Application of the International
Convention on the Elimination of All Forms of Racial Discrimination, supra* n. 26. This can
lead to a formalistic analysis of disputes and of compromissory clauses in human rights
treaties.

[47] *The Effect of Reservations on the Entry Into Force of the American Convention on Human
Rights (Arts. 74 and 75)* (IACtHR) (Advisory Opinion) OC-2/82, 24 Sept. 1982, Ser. A,
No. 2 (paragraph 33).

[48] Brilmayer, *supra* n. 20.

[49] Human rights treaties 'restrict the power of governments over their own citizens. That is
their function'. See A. W. B. Simpson, *Human Rights and the End of Empire: Britain and
the Genesis of the European Convention* (Oxford: Oxford University Press, 2001), p. 12.

complaints mechanism and at the national level by their adoption as bills of rights core to the State constitutional framework.[50]

Traditionally international law had no stake in the substance of treaties, but this is changing and human rights law is at the forefront of this.[51] Human rights treaties are 'inspired by higher shared values (focusing on the protection of the human being)'[52] and 'embody essentially objective obligations'.[53] This results in a correlation between moral values and principles of the international legal order because, while the object and purpose of a human rights norm is humanitarian, it is also the maintenance of international peace and security.[54] This intersection has seen human rights become a cornerstone of post-conflict constitutional reordering within States[55] and territories[56] as well as within the Security Council's mandate under Chapter VII of the UN Charter.[57]

The broader term 'humanitarian' highlights the hybrid character of some treaties. Despite the accepted characterisation of the Hague Regulations[58] and Geneva 'Red Cross' Conventions as international humanitarian law,[59] 'a tendency may be detected in the Geneva

---

[50] S. Gardbaum, 'Human Rights as International Constitutional Rights', *EJIL*, 9 (2008), 749–768.

[51] F. Mégret, 'Nature of Obligations' in D. Moeckli, S. Shah and S. Sivakumaran (eds.), *International Human Rights Law* (Oxford: Oxford University Press, 2nd ed., 2014), pp. 96–118, at p. 99.

[52] *Case of the 'Mapiripán Massacre' v. Colombia* (IACtHR) (Merits, Reparations and Costs), 15 Sept. 2005.

[53] *Hilaire v. Trinidad and Tobago* (IACtHR) (Preliminary Objections) Ser. C No. 80, 1 Sept. 2001 (paragraph 94); cf. *Austria v. Italy* (EComm.HR), Appl. No. 788/60, YbECHR, 4 (1961), 116.

[54] F. Hampson, Working Paper Submitted pursuant to Sub-Commission Decision 1998/113, U.N. Doc. E/CN.4/Sub.2/1999/28 (1999) (paragraph 13). See, further, the contribution to this volume of Kritsiotis at pp. 237–302 (Chapter 9).

[55] E.g., Annex 6 of the 2005 General Framework Agreement (the Dayton Peace Accords) lists the human rights treaties to be made applicable in Bosnia and Herzegovina: ILM, 35 (1996), 89–152, at 130–136.

[56] E.g., UNMIK Regulation No. 2006/12 of 23 March 2006 on the establishment of the Human Rights Advisory Panel in Kosovo allows individuals to make complaints against the United Nations Interim Mission in Kosovo for violation of the UDHR and six human rights treaties.

[57] D. P. Forsythe, 'The UN Security Council and Human Rights: State Sovereignty and Human Dignity', *Friedrich-Ebert-Stiftung*, May 2012.

[58] Annexed to the 1907 Hague Convention (IV) Respecting the Laws and Customs of War on Land and Annex: 18 CTS 227.

[59] 1949 Geneva Convention (I) for the Amelioration of the Condition of the Wounded and Sick in Armed Forces in the Field, 75 UNTS 31; 1949 Geneva Convention (II) for the Amelioration of the Condition of Wounded, Sick and Shipwrecked Members of Armed Forces at Sea, 75 UNTS 85; 1949 Geneva Convention (III) Relative to the Treatment of

Conventions ... for their provisions to be considered not only as obligations to be discharged by the High Contracting Parties but as individual rights of protected persons'.[60] Indeed, some articles in the 1977 Additional Protocols appear directly to cross the line to human rights.[61] Correspondingly some human rights treaties guarantee fundamental rights in time of conflict, the domain of international humanitarian law.[62] There is a further fusion between human rights and international criminal law treaties. Some such treaties may be perceived as primarily human rights (for example, the Torture Convention),[63] while others as primarily international criminal law (for example, the Genocide Convention).[64] The mix within a single treaty of criminalisation of human rights violations, human rights complaints mechanisms, the assertion of individual criminal and State responsibility for violation, the obligation to extradite or prosecute, punishment of perpetrators and reparations for victims makes problematic any single label.

Space does not allow for consideration of the many variables of form, substance and processes found in treaties that might be understood as 'human rights' treaties. Accordingly, the chapter will focus on a small group, the 'core' UN human rights treaties for which independent expert monitoring bodies with multiple functions have been created[65] and the major regional treaties – the 1950 European Convention on Human Rights (ECHR),[66] the 1969 Inter-American Convention on Human Rights (IACHR),[67] the 1981 African Charter on Human and Peoples' Rights[68]

Prisoners of War, 75 UNTS 135 and 1949 Geneva Convention (IV) Relative to the Protection of Civilian Persons in Time of War, 75 UNTS 287.

[60] D. Schindler, 'The International Committee of the Red Cross and Human Rights', *Int'l Rev. Red Cross*, 19 (1979), 3–15; cf. the contribution to this volume of Hampson at pp. 538–577 (Chapter 17).

[61] E.g. the 'fundamental guarantees' contained in Art. 75 of 1977 Protocol Additional to the Geneva Conventions of 12 August 1949, and Relating to the Protection of Victims of International Armed Conflicts (Protocol I), 1125 UNTS 3, and Art. 4 of 1977 Protocol Additional to the Geneva Conventions of 12 August 1949, and Relating to the Protection of Victims of Non-International Armed Conflicts (Protocol II), 1125 UNTS 609.

[62] E.g., Art. 38 CRC (*supra* n. 36) and Art. 11 CPD (*supra* n. 35).   [63] *Supra* n. 37.

[64] *Supra* n. 3. 'The origins of the Convention show that it was the intention of the United Nations to condemn and punish genocide as "a crime under international law"': *Reservations to the Convention on the Prevention and Punishment of the Crime of Genocide, supra* note 1, at p. 23. 'The Convention belongs to international penal law, not to the international law of human rights': see A. W. B. Simpson, 'Britain and the Genocide Convention', *BYbIL*, 73 (2003), 5–64, at 5.

[65] Functions include considering States' reports, deciding upon individual complaints, inquiry, visits and issuing general comments or recommendations.

[66] *Supra* n. 13.   [67] *Supra* n. 14.   [68] OAU Doc. CAB/LEG/67/3 rev. 5 (27 June 1981).

and their Protocols. Other regional treaties follow the UN human rights treaty bodies model by also establishing an expert monitoring body;[69] this is perhaps the defining feature of human rights treaties, and the absence of such a body explains why the Genocide Convention, for instance, is not always so regarded.[70] The jurisprudence developed by the expert committees and the regional human rights courts enables an evaluation of the extent to which the VCLT is applied, which can be compared with the approach taken by international mainstream bodies.

2.2   Human Rights Treaties as 'Living Instruments'

The interpretation and application of human rights treaties have generated a large literature, especially with respect to the regional human rights courts whose jurisdiction covers all matters 'concerning the interpretation and application' of the relevant convention.[71] Such treaties present particular challenges: they are worded at a high level of abstraction with imprecise and indeterminate language, they do not prescribe States' obligations in any consistent form but rather provide for differing levels of commitment depending upon the context,[72] and they are not comprehensive. There are gaps that must be fleshed out. The language allows States a considerable discretion or margin of appreciation. They must retain their relevance in changing political, social and economic circumstances, even as they become ever more dated. In sum, they must be 'living instruments whose interpretation must consider the changes over time and present-day conditions'.[73] Since renegotiation is not a political

---

[69] E.g., 1987 European Convention for the Prevention of Torture and Inhuman or Degrading Treatment or Punishment, ETS No. 126, as amended by Protocol I and II, Art. 1, and 2011 Council of Europe Convention on Preventing and Combating Violence against Women and Domestic Violence (Istanbul Convention), CETS No. 210, Art. 66.

[70] '[T]he 1948 Genocide Convention differs from the core human rights treaties, however, in that it is not monitored by a body of independent experts equipped to build a jurisprudence that gives meaning to its clauses, and thus to contribute to the general development of human rights'. See O. De Schutter, *International Human Rights Law: Cases, Materials, Commentary* (Cambridge: Cambridge University Press, 2nd ed., 2014), p. 21.

[71] Art. 32 ECHR (*supra* n. 13); Art. 62(2) IACHR (*supra* n. 14), and Art. 28 of the 2008 Protocol on the Statute of the African Court of Justice and Human Rights, ILM, 48 (2009), 334–353.

[72] M. Hakimi, 'State Bystander Responsibility', *EJIL*, 21 (2010), 341–385, at 350.

[73] *Gomez Paquiyauri Brothers v. Peru* (IACtHR), Series C, No. 110, 8 July 2004 (paragraph 165). Cf. *Loizidou v. Turkey, supra* n. 24 (paragraph 71): 'That the Convention is a living instrument which must be interpreted in the light of present-day conditions is firmly rooted in the Court's case-law'. See, further, the contribution to this volume of Moeckli and White at pp. 136–171 (Chapter 6).

option, 'evolutive' interpretation is engaged to ensure their continued dynamism[74] and a principle of effectiveness employed to make the treaties' safeguards practical and effective,[75] for example through the formulation of positive obligations and procedural requirements.

Despite the distinctiveness of the effectiveness approach to the interpretation of human rights treaties, decision-makers within the regional human rights courts[76] and the UN human rights committees upon occasion explicitly indicate their reliance upon the VCLT articles on interpretation,[77] for instance the statement by the IACtHR that:

> the interpretation of any norm is to be done in good faith in accordance with the ordinary meaning to be given to the terms used in the treaty in their context and in the light of its object and purpose (Article 31 of the Vienna Convention on the Law of Treaties) and that an interpretation may, if necessary, involve an examination of the treaty taken as a whole.[78]

In other instances, the VCLT language is reflected but without any direct reference. Evolutive interpretation accords greater significance to the object and purpose of human rights treaties than to the ordinary meaning of the text,[79] the *travaux préparatoires*,[80] the historical context or the intentions of

---

[74] *The Rights to Information on Consular Assistance*, supra n. 40 (paragraph 114). See, further, R. Bernhardt, 'Evolutive Treaty Interpretation, Especially of the European Court of Human Rights', *German YbIL*, 42 (2009), 11–25, and G. Letsas, 'Strasbourg's Interpretive Ethic: Lessons for the International Lawyer', *EJIL*, 21 (2010), 509–541.

[75] E.g., *Nada v. Switzerland* (ECtHR GC), Appl. No. 10593/08, 12 Sept. 2012 (paragraph 182).

[76] M. Killander, 'Interpreting Regional Human Rights Treaties', *SUR Int'l J. on Hum. Rts.*, 7 (2010), 145–169. Villiger notes that the ECtHR consistently employs all techniques in Arts. 31 and 32 VCLT, while the IACtHR focuses on Art. 31(1) VCLT: M. E. Villiger, 'The Rules on Interpretation: Misgivings, Misunderstandings, Miscarriage? The "Crucible" Intended by the International Law Commission' in E. Cannizzaro (ed.), *The Law of Treaties beyond the Vienna Convention* (Oxford: Oxford University Press, 2011), pp. 105–122, at p. 116.

[77] A number of human rights treaties predate the coming into force of the VCLT, but the ECtHR, for example, has accepted that 'its [Arts.] 31 to 33 enunciate in essence generally accepted principles of international law': *Golder v. UK* (ECtHR, Plenary), Appl. No. 4451/70, 21 Feb. 1975 (paragraph 29).

[78] *The Rights to Information on Consular Assistance*, supra n. 40 (paragraph 72); cf. *Rantsev v. Russia and Cyprus*, Appl. No. 25965/04, 7 Jan. 2010 (paragraphs 274–275).

[79] *Ahmadou Sadio Diallo*, supra n. 25, at pp. 755–756 (paragraph 83 of Separate Opinion of Judge Cançado Trindade).

[80] But see *Bankovic v. Belgium and Others* (ECtHR GC), Appl. No. 52207/99, 12 Dec. 2001 (paragraph 65) where the ECtHR took a restrictive approach supported by the *travaux préparatoires* to determine 'the scope and reach of the entire Convention system of human rights' protection'.

the authors,[81] whether made explicit or not.[82] Nevertheless, it is seen as 'consistent with the general rules of treaty interpretation established in the 1969 Vienna Convention'.[83] Closely linked is the concept of an 'autonomous' interpretation of treaty terms,[84] meaning that they are not simply equated to their domestic law equivalent.[85] The European Court of Human Rights (ECtHR) has explained that if this were not the case and States were, for instance, free to classify an offence as 'disciplinary' or 'criminal' at their will, fundamental human rights provisions 'would be subordinated to their sovereign will'.[86] A conscious human rights approach opens the way to innovative jurisprudence. For example, Judge Cançado Trindade (a former President of the IACtHR) has asserted that States' obligations under human rights treaties must be of result, not merely of conduct, as this is the only way to make individual rights effective. Otherwise a State could claim that its conduct was appropriate but that other (internal or external) factors had prevented it from achieving full compliance with its obligations. Further, the Court cannot consider a case terminated because of the 'allegedly "good conduct" of the State concerned'.[87]

A purposive or evolutive methodology contrasts with the traditional international law approach which favours pursuance of 'a rather restrictive interpretation which gives as much precision as possible to the obligations of States Parties'.[88] It has not surprisingly been contested by some States. For

---

[81] 'It follows that these provisions cannot be interpreted solely in accordance with the intentions of their authors as expressed more than forty years ago'. See *Loizidou v. Turkey, supra* n. 24 (paragraph 71).

[82] Not many decision-makers are as explicit as Judge Alvarez: 'These conventions must be interpreted without regard to the past, and only with regard to the future'. See *Reservations to the Convention on the Prevention and Punishment of the Crime of Genocide, supra* n. 1, at p. 53.

[83] E.g., *Gomez Paquiyauri Brothers v. Peru, supra* n. 73 (paragraph 165).

[84] '[H]uman rights treaties have a normative character and that their terms are to be autonomously interpreted': *Ahmadou Sadio Diallo, supra* n. 25, at pp. 756–757 (paragraph 85 of Separate Opinion of Judge Cançado Trindade).

[85] *Mayagna (Sumo) Awas Tingni Community v. Nicaragua* (IACtHR), Ser. C, No. 79, 31 Aug. 2001 (paragraph 146): 'The terms of an international human rights treaty have an autonomous meaning, for which reason they cannot be made equivalent to the meaning given to them in domestic law'.

[86] *Engel and Others v. The Netherlands* (ECtHR), Appl. No. 5100/71, 8 June 1976 (paragraph 81) (the Court was referring to the designation of criminal offences for the applicability of Arts. 6 and 7 ECHR).

[87] *Questions Relating to the Obligation to Prosecute or Extradite, supra* n. 27, at pp. 505–508 (paragraphs 44–51 of Separate Opinion of Judge Cançado Trindade).

[88] *Ahmadou Sadio Diallo, supra* n. 25, at pp. 755–756 (paragraph 83 of Separate Opinion of Judge Cançado Trindade).

example, citing Article 31(1) VCLT as 'the fundamental rule of interpretation', the United States has rejected the extra-territorial application of certain human rights treaties.[89] It has argued that Article 2(1) ICCPR unambiguously applies only with respect to individuals 'who are both within the territory of a State Party *and* subject to that State Party's sovereign authority'.[90] It bolstered its position (that 'and' is conjunctive and does not denote either/or) by reference to the *travaux préparatoires* of the ICCPR in accordance with Article 32 VCLT.[91] In response, the Human Rights Committee (HRC), presumably imbued by the principle of effectiveness, regretted that the USA deemed the Covenant inapplicable 'to individuals under its jurisdiction and outside its territory'.[92] The United States responded similarly to the Committee against Torture's General Comment No. 2, rejecting the latter's assertion that Articles 3 to 15 of the 1984 Convention Against Torture and Other Cruel, Inhuman or Degrading Treatment or Punishment (CAT) are 'obligatory as applied to both torture and ill-treatment'. The United States considered this to be 'directly inconsistent with the express language of the Convention' and that 'there is no basis in international treaty law for the Committee to rewrite, in effect, the clear provisions of the treaty under the guise of interpretation'.[93]

Unlike the United States, in this instance neither the HRC nor the CAT referred to the VCLT articles on interpretation. There is no consistency in this regard, and it seems that there is simultaneously both an inherent recognition of the importance of the VCLT articles on interpretation and a rejection of any need for consistent reference to them. It has been argued, however, that compliance with the VCLT is a matter of obligation and necessity for the UN treaty bodies.[94] First, since States have to interpret human rights treaties in accordance with the VCLT, bodies performing this function in lieu of States should also have to do so. Second, although the statements of the treaty bodies are not legally authoritative, their 'special experience of handling problems in the

---

[89] USA, Third Periodic Report, U.N. Doc. CCPR/C/USA/3, 28 Nov. 2005, Annex I. See, further, the contribution to this volume of Waibel at pp. 201–236 (Chapter 8).

[90] *Ibid.*   [91] *Ibid.*

[92] Concluding Observations of the HRC, USA, U.N. Doc. CCPR/C/USA/CO/3/Rev.1, 18 Dec. 2006 (paragraph 3) and U.N. Doc. CCPR/C/USA/CO/4, 2 Apr. 2014 (paragraph 4).

[93] Observations by the USA on Committee Against Torture, General Comment No. 2: Implementation of Article 2 by States Parties, 3 Nov. 2008. The US has since reviewed its position: see U.N. Doc. CAT/C/USA/CO/3–5, 19 Dec. 2014 (paragraph 10) (www.state .gov/documents/organization/138853.pdf).

[94] K. Mechlem, 'Treaty Bodies and the Interpretation of Human Rights', *Vanderbilt JTL*, 42 (2009), 905–947, at 909.

human rights area'[95] gives their interpretations of human rights treaties persuasiveness and legitimacy, as recognised by the ICJ.[96] This is enhanced when they act in apparent conformity with the VCLT but is undermined when they lack any rigorous or coherent interpretive methodology.[97]

Specialist human rights bodies or individual judges[98] do not always favour an extensive interpretation of a human rights treaty. As a creature of international law, a human rights treaty cannot operate in a vacuum but must be interpreted in light of relevant principles of international law.[99] This is in accordance with Article 31(3)(c) VCLT and applies 'in particular' to 'rules concerning the international protection of human rights'.[100] Accommodation of the development of international law may be compatible with a dynamic approach[101] but may also be more restrictive.[102] Indeed, Alexander Orakhelashvili argues that restrictive interpretive trends can be discerned in the ECtHR, which the Court justifies on the basis of their conformity with international law.[103]

Drawing any firm conclusions about the applicability of the VCLT in the interpretation of human rights treaties is not easy. Rather, who is interpreting the treaty, for what purpose and the context are likely to determine the chosen approach to interpretation. While States may be expected to favour a positivist or dogmatic view that gives priority to the ordinary meaning of the words, the specialist human rights bodies are

---

[95] *Application of the Convention on the Prevention and Punishment of the Crime of Genocide, supra* n. 2, at p. 654 (Separate Opinion of Judge Weeramantry).

[96] *Ahmadou Sadio Diallo, supra* n. 25, at pp. 663–664 (paragraph 66).

[97] Mechlem, *supra* n. 94, at 905.

[98] E.g., Judge Fitzmaurice at first adopted a restrictive, textual approach, refusing to imply into the Convention 'a right or freedom which the Convention does not trouble to name': *Golder v. UK, supra* n. 77 (paragraph 28).

[99] E.g., *Sabeh El Leil v. France* (ECtHR GC), Appl. No. 34869/05, 29 June 2011 (paragraph 48).

[100] *Nada v. Switzerland, supra* n. 75 (paragraph 169).

[101] E.g., '[t]he Convention [CEDAW] is a dynamic instrument that accommodates the development of international law'. CEDAW Committee, General Recommendation No. 28 on the Core Obligations of States Parties under Article 2 of the Convention on the Elimination of All Forms of Discrimination against Women, U.N. Doc. CEDAW/C/ GC/28, 16 Dec. 2010 (paragraph 1).

[102] E.g., *Bankovic v. Belgium, supra* n. 80 (paragraphs 56 and 57) (international law principles of territorial jurisdiction engaged to limit the territorial scope of the ECHR) and *Al-Adsani v. UK* (ECtHR GC), Appl. No. 35763/97, 21 Nov. 2011 (State immunity does not constitute a disproportionate restriction on the right of access to a court).

[103] A. Orakhelashvili, 'Restrictive Interpretation of Human Rights Treaties in the Recent Jurisprudence of the European Court of Human Rights', *EJIL*, 14 (2003), 529–568.

more likely to seek a progressive interpretation that gives effect to and moves beyond the treaty text. This can be justified on ethical grounds: 'If the purpose of international human rights law is to make States accountable for the violation of some fundamental moral rights which individuals have against their government, then the purpose of human rights courts is to develop, through interpretation, a moral conception of what these fundamental rights are'.[104] In order to achieve 'the necessary clarity and the essential consistency of international law, as well as legal security', the ICJ believes it should 'take due account' of the interpretation given to human rights treaties by the bodies 'specifically created . . . to monitor the sound application of the treaty in question'.[105] Proponents of either a progressive or a regressive, an expansive or formalistic approach may cite the VCLT to support and legitimate their conclusion; lip service may be given to the VCLT by different decision-makers but with no guarantee that their outcomes will coincide.

3   Human Rights Treaty Norms as *Jus cogens*

Claims of *jus cogens* status for at least some provisions of human rights treaties underline the tension between treaty form and objective values. Elucidation of the legal implications of a determination of *jus cogens* might therefore have been anticipated in the context of human rights treaties. But this has not been the case. Judicial analysis has been limited[106] beyond a slow acceptance that at least some provisions of human rights treaties constitute *jus cogens*, including the prohibition of genocide,[107] torture[108] and discrimination.[109] The HRC has suggested

---

[104] Letsas, *supra* n. 74, at p. 540.

[105] *Ahmadou Sadio Diallo, supra* n. 25, at pp. 663–664 (paragraph 66).

[106] This is especially true of the ICJ. 'In any case, up to now, the Court has not shown much familiarity with, nor strong disposition to, elaborate on *jus cogens*; it has taken more than six decades for it to acknowledge its existence *tout court*, in spite of its being one of the central features of contemporary international law'. See *Questions Relating to the Obligation to Prosecute or Extradite, supra* n. 27, at p. 550 (paragraph 159 of Separate Opinion of Judge Cançado Trindade).

[107] E.g., *Case Concerning Armed Activities on the Territory of the Congo* (New Application: 2002), *supra* n. 46, at pp. 31–32 (paragraph 64) and *Jorgić v. Germany* (ECtHR), Appl. No. 74613/01, 12 July 2007 (paragraph 68).

[108] E.g., *Prosecutor v. Furundzija* (ICTY) IT-95-17/1-T, 10 Dec. 1998 (paragraph 153).

[109] The ICJ deemed 'the principles and rules concerning the basic rights of the human person, including protection from slavery and racial discrimination' to constitute obligations owed *erga omnes*: *Case Concerning the Barcelona Traction, Light and Power Company Ltd.*: Belgium v. Spain (New Application: 1962) (1970) ICJ Rep. 3, at p. 32

a much longer list.[110] The significance of *jus cogens* remains largely symbolic and hortatory. Other rights are stipulated to be non-derogable, although there is no absolute correlation between peremptory norm status, *erga omnes* obligations and non-derogability.

The place of human rights treaties in contemporary governance also portends clashes between domestic, regional and international legal orders.[111] The VCLT offers little assistance in resolving the dilemmas presented by the potential conflict between human rights norms and other substantive norms or procedural requirements, and decision-makers have to make their own determinations. For instance, at the international level claims of violations of human rights treaties have not over-ridden procedural bars to jurisdiction such as immunity.[112] The ECtHR and European Court of Justice (ECJ) have both sought to avoid a conflict between States' obligations under human rights treaties and those under Security Council resolutions. In *Al Jedda v. UK*, the ECtHR noted that Article 30(1) VCLT on conflict between successive treaties[113] gives priority to obligations under Article 103 of the UN Charter but does not render the 'lower-ranking' treaty null and void. Accordingly, States continue to be bound by the ECHR and must seek to

(paragraph 34); with respect to equality and discrimination the IACtHR went further considering that 'the principle of equality before the law, equal protection before the law and non-discrimination belongs to *jus cogens*': *Juridical Condition and Rights of the Undocumented Migrants*, Advisory Opinion, OC-18/03, Ser. A, No. 18, 17 Sept. 2003 (paragraph 101). Judge Cançado Trindade has noted the greater readiness of the IACtHR and international criminal tribunals to recognise *jus cogens*: '*Jus Cogens*: the Determination and the Gradual Expansion of its Material Content in Contemporary International Case-law', available at www.oas.org/dil/esp/3%20-%20cancado.LR.CV.3–30.pdf.

[110] HRC, General Comment No. 24, *supra* n. 29 (paragraph 8), although it has also asserted that there is 'no hierarchy of importance of rights' (paragraph 10).

[111] G. de Búrca, 'The European Court of Justice and the International Legal Order after *Kadi*', *Harvard ILJ*, 51 (2010), 1–49.

[112] 'The rules of State immunity are procedural in character ... [t]hey do not bear upon the question whether or not the conduct in respect of which the proceedings are brought was lawful or unlawful'. See *Jurisdictional Immunities of the State*: Germany v. Italy (Greece intervening) (2012) ICJ Rep. 99, at p. 140 (paragraph 93); cf. *Al-Adsani v. UK, supra* n. 102. In *Stichting Mothers of Srebrenica and Others v. The Netherlands*, the ECtHR similarly determined that according immunity to the UN 'served a legitimate purpose and was not disproportionate' and thus did not constitute a violation of Art. 6 ECHR: Appl. No. 65542/12, 27 June 2013.

[113] The ECtHR has rejected the 'later in time' aspect of Art. 30(3) VCLT, affirming that member States 'retain Convention liability in respect of treaty commitments subsequent to the entry into force of the Convention'. See *Bosphorus Hava Yollari Turzim v. Ticaret Anonim Sirketi v. Ireland*, Appl. No. 45036/98, 30 June 2005 (paragraph 154).

give effect to Security Council resolutions in a way that complies with the Convention.[114] Indeed, since promotion of human rights is a purpose of the UN,[115] there is a presumption that the Security Council does not intend to impose an obligation on States to act in breach of human rights. UN member States have a 'free choice'[116] with respect to how they give effect to Security Council resolutions within their domestic legal orders. In a case concerning implementation of anti-terrorist sanctions, the ECtHR held Switzerland in violation of the ECHR since it had failed to demonstrate that it had attempted 'as far as possible, to harmonise the obligations that they regarded as divergent'.[117] Also in a case concerning sanctions, the First Instance Court of the ECJ cited Articles 53 and 64 VCLT and held that Article 103 of the UN Charter gives Security Council resolutions priority over other international obligations with the exception of *jus cogens* norms.[118] On appeal, the ECJ found that it had no need to consider issues relating to rules of international law falling within the ambit of *jus cogens*,[119] although it found the applicable EC Regulation to constitute an unwarranted interference with the fundamental rights of the accused. By casting the judgment in terms of the distinct legal orders of the UN and the European Communities and on its own competence to review an EC Regulation for its compatibility with fundamental rights, the ECJ bypassed the possibility of articulating a human rights legal order and did not engage with questions raised by claims of *jus cogens*. This pragmatic approach that avoids direct conflict between human rights treaties and other legal obligations eschews any special status for human rights treaties, as such, while leaving open the possibilities of a determination of *jus cogens*.

4   States' Obligations

Various VCLT articles are generally applied to human rights treaties, especially where they involve standard, technical questions of treaty law, such as 'the way treaties come into existence, the simple idea that states

---

[114] *Al-Jedda v. the UK* (ECtHR GC), Appl. No. 27021/08, 7 July 2011 (paragraph 105).

[115] Art. 1(3) of the UN Charter: *supra* n. 6.

[116] *Nada v. Switzerland, supra* n. 75 (paragraph 176).   [117] *Ibid.* (paragraph 197).

[118] Case T-306/01 *Ahmed Ali Yusuf and Al Barakaat International Foundation v. Council of the EU and Commission of the EC* and Case T-315/01 *Yassin Abdullah Kadi v. Council of the EU and the Commission of the EC* [2005] OJ C 281.

[119] Joined Cases C-402/05 & C-415/05P *Yassin Abdullah Kadi and Al Barakaat International Foundation v. Council of the European Union and Commission of the European Communities* (paragraph 329).

are bound by treaties they ratify ... and that states should discharge their obligations in good faith'.[120] There are numerous examples of references to the VCLT with little or no discussion. For instance, the ICJ has accepted that Articles 27 and 28 VCLT apply to the CAT,[121] the HRC that Article 26 VCLT requires States parties to cooperate with itself in good faith,[122] and the Committee on Economic, Social and Cultural Rights (CESCR) that a 'party may not invoke the provisions of its internal law as justification for its failure to perform a treaty'.[123] The ICJ has suggested that the purpose of Article 60(5) VCLT, the only provision directly signifying the special nature of 'humanitarian' treaties, should guide the continued applicability of such treaties for the benefit of an affected population, despite the imposition of some sanction.[124] However, this approach has not been consistently adopted, causing Judge Parra-Aranguren to query why it was not followed so as to ensure the continued applicability of the Genocide Convention for the protection of the people of Bosnia-Herzegovina.[125]

However, some articles of the VCLT have generated considerable debate about States' obligations under human rights treaties. This section discusses a number of contexts where this has arisen. First is whether States can modify or withdraw from certain obligations through the adoption of reservations and interpretive declarations.

4.1   Reservations

The principle of voluntarism allows States to limit their obligations under treaties through entering reservations, but limited by the terms of Article 19 VCLT. Provisions addressing reservations in human rights treaties[126]

---

[120] Mégret, *supra* n. 51, at pp. 124 and 127.

[121] *Questions Relating to the Obligation to Prosecute or Extradite, supra* n. 27, at p. 457 (paragraph 100) and p. 460 (paragraph 113).

[122] HRC, General Comment No. 31, *supra* n. 44 (paragraph 3).

[123] CESCR, General Comment No. 9: The Domestic Application of the Covenant, U.N. Doc. E/C.12/1998/24, 3 Dec. 1998.

[124] *Legal Consequences for States of the Continued Presence of South Africa in Namibia, supra* n. 18, at p. 55 (paragraph 122).

[125] *Application of the Convention on the Prevention and Punishment of the Crime of Genocide, supra* n. 2, at p. 657 (Separate Opinion of Judge Parra-Aranguren).

[126] There is general acceptance of the Art. 2(1)(d) VCLT definition of a reservation; e.g., *Case Concerning Temeltasch* (European Commission on Human Rights, Decisions and Reports), Apr. 1983 (paragraphs 69–82); *Belilos v. Switzerland* (ECtHR), Appl. No. 10328/83, 29 Apr. 1988 (paragraph 42) and *T.K. v. France* (HRC), Communication No. 220/1987, 8 Nov. 1989.

are drafted in various terms. Some expressly incorporate the VCLT,[127] others reflect its language with respect to compatibility with the object and purpose of the convention,[128] expressly prohibit any reservation,[129] spell out which articles may be reserved,[130] impose conditions for reservations[131] or remain silent.[132] As is well known, there has been a long and disputed history with respect to the applicability of the VCLT articles on reservations to human rights treaties,[133] of which there are many.[134] This is made more complex by the VCLT's lack of 'clear and specific rules' with respect to the legal effects of an impermissible reservation.[135]

The controversy is rooted in both the object of human rights treaties (the effective protection of individuals) and their nature (comprising 'more than mere reciprocal engagements between Contracting States').[136] In the oft-cited words of the ICJ:

[127] E.g., Art. 75 IACHR allows reservations 'only in conformity' with the VCLT: *supra* n. 14.

[128] E.g., Art. 20(2) ICERD (*supra* n. 10); Art. 28(2) CEDAW (*supra* n. 37); Art. 51(2) CRC (*supra* n. 36); Art. 91 of the 1990 International Convention on the Protection of the Rights of All Migrant Workers and Members of their Families (CMWF), 220 UNTS 3, and Art. 46(1) CPD (impermissibility of reservations 'incompatible with the object and purpose' of the Convention) (*supra* n. 35).

[129] E.g., Art. 17 CEDAW OP: *supra* n. 37.

[130] E.g., Art. 78 of the Istanbul Convention: *supra* n. 69.

[131] E.g., Art. 64 ECHR: *supra* n. 13. The International Law Commission noted that this regime, 'is unquestionably *lex specialis* with respect to general international law': *Guide to Practice on Reservations to Treaties*, UNGAOR Sixty-Sixth Session, Supp. No. 10 (2011) 1, at p. 138.

[132] E.g., 2006 International Convention for the Protection of All Persons from Enforced Disappearance: G.A. Res. 61/177, U.N. Doc. A/RES/61/177 (2006).

[133] E.g., L. Lijnzaad, *Reservations to UN Human Rights Treaties: Ratify and Ruin?* (Dordrecht: Martinus Nijhoff, 1995); J. P. Gardner (ed.), *Human Rights as General Norms and a State's Right to Opt Out: Reservations and Objections to Human Rights Conventions* (London: British Institute of International & Comparative Law, 1997); R. Goodman, 'Human Rights Treaties, Invalid Reservations and State Consent', *AJIL*, 96 (2002), 531–560, and I. Ziemele (ed.), *Reservations to Human Rights Treaties and the Vienna Convention Regime: Conflict, Harmony or Reconciliation* (Leiden: Martinus Nijhoff, 2004).

[134] *Case Concerning Armed Activities on the Territory of the Congo* (New Application: 2002), *supra* n. 46, at p. 67 (paragraph 10 of Joint Separate Opinion of Judges Higgins, Kooijmans, Elaraby, Owada and Simma).

[135] A. Pellet, Fifteenth Report on the Law of Treaties, U.N. Doc. A/CN.4/624/Add.1 (31 March 2010) (paragraphs 400 and 401).

[136] *Ireland v. UK*, ILR, 58 (1978), 118–338, at p. 369. The IACtHR considered that only Art. 20(1) and 20(4) VCLT were relevant when applying Art. 75 IACHR 'because the object and purpose of the Convention is not the exchange of reciprocal rights between a limited number of States, but the protection of the human rights of all individual human beings within the Americas': *The Effect of Reservations, supra* n. 47 (paragraph 27).

> In such a convention the contracting states do not have any interests of their own: they merely have, one and all, a common interest, namely the accomplishment of those high purposes which are the *raison d'être* of the Convention. Consequently in a convention of this type one cannot speak of individual advantages or disadvantages to States, or of the maintenance of a perfect contractual balance between rights and duties.[137]

The differentiation between reciprocal and integral[138] treaty obligations has fostered detailed analyses of different meanings attributed to reciprocity, the relationship between reciprocity and the functions accorded to the 'objects and purposes' of a treaty in its interpretation and application, as well as differing conceptions of international law.[139]

The HRC has made a controversial and confrontational assertion of the special character of human rights treaties and that the VCLT provisions on objections to reservations 'are inappropriate to address the problem of reservations to human rights treaties'.[140] The Committee asserted that since human rights treaties do not form 'a web of inter-State exchanges of mutual obligations' but rather confer individual rights, the principle of mutual reciprocity 'has no place' in the legal regime for reservations to such treaties. Indeed, the inadequacy of the Vienna regime makes States reluctant to enter objections to reservations. The inclusion of expert monitoring bodies in human rights treaties was decisive for the Committee in determining that as a necessary part of its functions it must be competent to assess the compatibility of reservations with the object and purpose of the Covenant, a State prerogative under the VCLT, and also to sever incompatible reservations.[141] In indicating that reservations should be specific and transparent, the Committee also

---

[137] *Reservations to the Convention on the Prevention and Punishment of the Crime of Genocide, supra* n. 1, at p. 23.

[138] Sir Gerald Fitzmaurice defined classes of multilateral treaties, creating 'social' categories that 'do not lend themselves to differential application, but must be applied integrally': G. G. Fitzmaurice, Second Report on the Law of Treaties, U.N. Doc. A/CN.4/107 (15 March 1967), pp. 53 and 55 (paragraphs 115 and 128).

[139] Craven, *supra* n. 9, especially at 513–517; B. Simma and G. Hernandez, 'Legal Consequences of an Impermissible Reservation to a Human Rights Treaty: Where Do We Stand?' in Cannizzaro (ed.), *supra* n. 76, pp. 60–85, especially at pp. 66–68, and A. Paulus, 'Reciprocity Revisited' in U. Fastenrath, R. Geiger, D.-E. Khan, A. Paulus, S. von Schorlemer and C. Vedder (eds.), *From Bilateralism to Community Interest: Essays in Honour of Judge Bruno Simma* (Oxford: Oxford University Press, 2011), pp. 113–137.

[140] HRC, General Comment No. 24, *supra* n. 29 (paragraph 17).

[141] *Ibid.* See, also, HRC, General Comment No. 31, *supra* n. 44 (paragraph 5); HRC, General Comment No. 32: Right to Equality before Courts and Tribunals and to a Fair Trial, U.N. Doc. CCPR/C/GC/32, 23 Aug. 2007 (paragraph 5).

appears to be imposing additional criteria for acceptable reservations to those laid down in the VCLT.

Severance of a reservation from a State's acceptance of the relevant treaty, as first adopted by the ECtHR and followed by the HRC in General Comment No. 24, is also disputed.[142] The HRC's approach has not been explicitly followed by other of the UN human rights treaty bodies. However, in light of the many and far-reaching reservations to the 1979 Convention on the Elimination of All Forms of Discrimination against Women (CEDAW), the Committee on the Elimination of Discrimination against Women has also made clear to States its disquiet about reservations.[143] It has concluded that certain reservations are impermissible as contrary to the object and purpose of the Convention[144] but without purporting to sever the offending reservation from the State's acceptance of the Convention.

It is unusual to have such an express rejection of the appropriateness of the VCLT provisions as that by the HRC.[145] Not surprisingly, it was rejected by some States and has been scrutinised by the ILC since 1993 throughout its reference on reservations.[146] In its 2011 *Guide to Practice on Reservations to Treaties*,[147] the ILC finally decided not to apply different rules on reservations to human rights treaties, categorising them – along with other treaties, such as peace and environmental treaties – as 'containing numerous interdependent rights and obligations'.[148] In assessing the compatibility of a reservation with the object and purpose of such a treaty, Guideline 3.1.5.6 attempts to strike a balance between the interdependence of the rights and obligations, the importance of the reserved provision, and the impact of the reservation

---

[142] *Belilos v. Switzerland, supra* n. 126 (paragraph 60); *Loizidou v. Turkey, supra* n. 24 (paragraph 97) where, citing Art. 44 VCLT, the dissenting judges found it 'inappropriate' to do so; *ibid.*, at 33 (Joint Dissenting Opinion of Judges Gőlcuklu and Pettiti); Alain Pellet considered that this displayed an 'offhand attitude' towards State sovereignty and the requirement of consent: Pellet, Second Report on Reservations to Treaties, *supra* n. 31 (paragraph 230, fn. 419). But see Simma and Hernandez, *supra* n. 139, at p. 60 (supporting severance).

[143] CEDAW, General Recommendation No. 4: Reservations (6th Session, 1987); CEDAW, General Recommendation No. 20: Reservations to the Convention (11th Session, 1992).

[144] E.g. CEDAW, Concluding Observations, Israel, U.N. Doc. CEDAW/C/ISR/CO/5, 5 Apr. 2011 (paragraphs 8 and 9).

[145] The IACtHR also asserted that it would be 'manifestly unreasonable' to apply the entire legal regime of Art. 20 VCLT to Art. 75 IACHR; *The Effect of Reservations, supra* n. 47 (paragraph 34).

[146] For a summary of the process see Simma and Hernandez, *supra* n. 139, at pp. 69–85.

[147] International Law Commission, *Guide to Practice on Reservations to Treaties*, Doc. A/66/10.

[148] *Ibid.*, at p. 385 (with reference to Guideline 3.1.5.6).

on the treaty. The Guidelines implicitly highlight that what distinguishes human rights treaties is the existence of expert monitoring bodies and accept that such bodies may need to assess the permissibility of reservations to be able to discharge their functions. However, any such determination by a treaty monitoring body shall have 'no greater legal effect than that of the act which contains it'. Recognising the competence of the treaty bodies is, of course, without prejudice to the competence of States parties to do likewise, although States 'that have formulated reservations to a treaty establishing a treaty monitoring body shall give consideration to that body's assessment of the permissibility of the reservations'. In addition, there is a presumption of severability of impermissible reservations, allowing the reserving State to be considered a party to the Convention without the benefit of the reservation.[149]

Thus, the ILC has moved somewhat in the direction of the HRC and towards removing human rights treaties 'from the grip of the bilateralist paradigm and plac[ing] them into an objective, but equally consensualist framework'.[150] Nevertheless, it remains the case that 'it would be wrong to see human rights treaties as a special case. The problem of the legal effect of objections to reservations is the same for all multilateral treaties; it is just that the problem occurs more often, and more acutely, with human rights treaties because they seek to reconcile not just different national policies, but different social and religious systems'.[151]

4.2   Treaties and Third Parties

Without reference to the VCLT, the ECtHR has accepted the principle in Article 34 VCLT that 'a treaty does not create either obligations or rights for a third State without its consent'.[152] However, another shift away from the bilateral and voluntarist understanding of international obligations between States that is embedded in the VCLT towards one of promoting community interests concerns assertions of the binding nature of human rights treaties regardless of State consent. As early as

---

[149] *Ibid.*, Guideline 4.5.3 (paragraph 2). Severability applies 'unless the author of the invalid reservation has expressed a contrary intention or such an intention is otherwise established'.

[150] Simma and Hernandez, *supra* n. 139, at p. 84.   [151] Aust, *supra* n. 16, at p. 134.

[152] '[The ECHR] does not govern the actions of States not Parties to it, nor does it purport to be a means of requiring the Contracting States to impose Convention standards on other States'; *Al Skeini v. UK, supra* n. 24 (paragraph 141). See, further, the contribution to this volume of Waibel at pp. 201–236 (Chapter 8).

1951, the majority judges in the *Reservations* advisory opinion asserted that 'the principles underlying the Convention are principles which are recognized by civilized nations as binding on States, even without any conventional obligation'.[153] Nearly fifty years later, Judge Weeramantry emphasised that '[t]he human rights and humanitarian principles contained in the Genocide Convention are principles of customary international law' and that their embodiment in a treaty is irrelevant when determining their effect.[154] In *Barcelona Traction*, the Court noted that some *erga omnes* obligations have entered into 'the body of general international law' while 'others are conferred by international instruments of a universal or quasi-universal character'.[155] Article 38 VCLT recognises as an exception to the strict third party rule the possibility of a treaty provision becoming (or already being) binding upon non-party States as a rule of customary international law, but the Court offered no such analysis. Various explanations have been offered. Judge Alvarez had found the basis for the binding nature of 'these conventions signed by a great majority of States [which] ought to be binding upon the others, even though they have not expressly accepted them' in the interdependence of States and 'the existence of an international organization'.[156] Jonathan Charney argued that the process of passing through multilateral fora by-passes traditional modes of customary international law-making;[157] Louis Henkin considered that this non-conventional law is made 'purposefully, knowingly, wilfully';[158] Oscar Schachter argued that where the conduct is 'violative of the basic concept of human dignity', statements of condemnation are sufficient evidence of its status under customary international law;[159] Christian Tomuschat surmises that what is necessary is not a stock-taking of actual State practice but rather deductive reasoning: 'if human life and physical integrity were not protected, the entire idea of a legal order

---

[153] *Reservations to the Convention on the Prevention and Punishment of the Crime of Genocide, supra* n. 1, at p. 23.

[154] *Application of the Convention on the Prevention and Punishment of the Crime of Genocide, supra* n. 2, at p. 648 (Separate Opinion of Judge Weeramantry).

[155] *Case Concerning the Barcelona Traction, Light and Power Company Ltd., supra* n. 109, at p. 32 (paragraph 34).

[156] *Reservations to the Convention on the Prevention and Punishment of the Crime of Genocide, supra* n. 1, at pp. 52–53 (Dissenting Opinion of Judge Alvarez).

[157] J. I. Charney, 'Universal International Law', *AJIL*, 87 (1993), 529–551, at 549.

[158] Henkin, *supra* n. 15, at 31 and 37.

[159] O. Schachter, 'International Law in Theory and Practice', *Hague Recueil*, 178 (1982-V), 1–395, at 334–338.

would collapse';[160] and Judge Cançado Trindade asserts that the international *ordre public* must prevail over State voluntarism.[161]

4.3 Temporal Scope

Article 28 VCLT on the non-retroactivity of treaties has been applied in the context of human rights treaties. The ECtHR, for example has referred to Article 28 VCLT in asserting that '[i]t is beyond dispute that ... the provisions of the Convention do not bind a Contracting Party in relation to any act or fact which took place or any situation which ceased to exist before the date of the entry into force of the Convention with respect to that Party'.[162] The ICJ has adopted a similar approach.[163] Article 28 VCLT allows for a particular treaty to depart from this rule, but in its interpretation and application of CAT, the ICJ found nothing to suggest that a State must criminalise acts of torture that took place prior to the Convention's entry into force, although equally nothing in the CAT prevented Senegal from prosecuting Hissène Habré, former President of Chad, for acts of torture committed prior to the Convention's coming into force for Senegal, if it so chose. Judge Cançado Trindade took exception to the majority's position, seeing it as an 'undue invocation of non-retroactivity in relation to *continuing* wrongful situations of obstruction of access to justice'.[164] He considered that non-retroactivity 'gives effect to voluntarist reasoning, focused on the will of States within the confines of the strict and static inter-State dimension', which is inappropriate with respect to human rights treaties that focus on 'victimized human beings, who stand in need of protection'.[165] Judge Cançado Trindade was especially concerned about the impact of a principle of non-retroactivity on claims relating to human

---

[160] C. Tomuschat, *Human Rights between Idealism and Realism* (Oxford: Oxford University Press, 2nd ed., 2008), p. 38.

[161] *Case Concerning Application of the International Convention on the Elimination of All Forms of Racial Discrimination, supra* n. 26 (paragraph 87 of Dissenting Opinion of Judge Cançado Trindade).

[162] *Varnava v. Turkey* (ECtHR GC), Appl. No. 16064/90, 18 Sept. 2009 (paragraph 130); *Sargsyan v. Azerbaijan* (ECtHR GC), Appl. No. 40167/06, 14 Dec. 2011, and *Janowiec and Others v. Russia* (ECtHR), Appl. No. 55508/07, Judgment of 16 Apr. 2012 (paragraph 129).

[163] *Questions Relating to the Obligation to Prosecute or Extradite, supra* n. 27, at pp. 457–458 (paragraphs 100–102).

[164] *Ibid.*, at pp. 545–546 (paragraph 146 of Separate Opinion of Judge Cançado Trindade).

[165] *Ibid.*, at p. 553 (paragraph 166 of Separate Opinion of Judge Cançado Trindade).

rights violations committed during a period of oppression or conflict, as it undermines accountability and furthers a climate of impunity. This is a situation that the ECtHR has also faced. It has reasoned that there is a continuing procedural obligation to investigate a disappearance that is independent from the substantive obligation to find a violation of the Convention with respect to disappearances that occurred before the State in question had accepted the Court's jurisdiction.[166]

4.4 Continuity of States' Obligations

The continuity, or otherwise, of States' human rights obligations has arisen in different contexts, including changes in the composition of the State and a State's wish to denounce such obligations. The VCLT does not address the former situation,[167] but the HRC in particular has developed consistent practice and articulated principles that encompass both circumstances.[168] In response to the break-up of the former Yugoslavia, in 1992 the Committee required three successor States – Bosnia-Herzegovina, Croatia and Serbia-Montenegro – to submit urgent reports prior to any explicit acceptance of the ICCPR.[169] It repeated this stance in 1993, affirming that successor States were bound by the Covenant from their date of independence,[170] regardless of whether they had formally accepted this to be the case. Also in 1993, the Commission on Human Rights[171] encouraged successor States to confirm that they continued to be bound by the human rights treaties of the predecessor State. There are a number of justifications for this stance: the special nature of human rights treaties, the concept of universality and, especially, the need to avoid 'operational gaps'[172] in the protection of

---

[166] *Varnava v. Turkey, supra* n. 162 (paragraphs 136–150).

[167] The issue of whether a State succeeds to the obligations of a predecessor State is subject to the 1978 Vienna Convention on Succession of States in Respect of Treaties, 1946 UNTS 3. Art. 56 VCLT addresses denunciation and withdrawal: *supra* n. 7.

[168] The practice of the HRC has influenced State practice and that of the other treaty bodies; F. Pocar, 'Some Remarks on the Continuity of Human Rights and International Humanitarian Law Treaties' in Cannizzaro (ed.), *supra* n. 76, pp. 279–293, at p. 282.

[169] For the discussion within the Committee, see *ibid.*, at pp. 282–284.

[170] Report of the Secretary-General, Succession of States in respect of International Human Rights Treaties, U.N. Doc. E/CN.4/1995/80, 28 Nov. 1994 (paragraph 5). The Report also describes the practice of the Committee on the Elimination of Racial Discrimination.

[171] CHR Res. 1993/23, 5 March 1993, Succession of States in Respect of International Human Rights Treaties.

[172] *Application of the Convention on the Prevention and Punishment of the Crime of Genocide, supra* n. 2, at p. 637 (Separate Opinion of Judge Shahabuddeen).

rights vested in individuals. Human rights treaties are said 'to devolve with territory', and, accordingly, 'States continue to be bound by the obligations under the Covenant entered into by the predecessor State'.[173] Judge Weeramantry explained that '[h]uman rights and humanitarian treaties involve no loss of sovereignty or autonomy of the new State, but are merely in line with general principles of protection that flow from the inherent dignity of every human being which is the very foundation of the United Nations Charter'.[174] Indeed, Judge Weeramantry concluded that there is a principle of contemporary international law of automatic State succession to 'so vital a human rights convention as the Genocide Convention'.[175] The principle that rights cannot be taken away regardless of changes in the administration of territory has not been applied exclusively to States. The HRC and CESCR both requested the UN Interim Mission in Kosovo, a non-State authority, to report to them following that body's assumption of legislative and executive power and mandate to protect and promote human rights in Kosovo.[176]

Similarly, there has been a bias in favour of continuity in determining that States are not free to withdraw from or to terminate their human rights treaty obligations in the absence of a termination or denunciation clause.[177] Responding to North Korea's purported withdrawal from the ICCPR, the HRC noted that any such possibility 'must be considered in the light of applicable rules of customary international law which are reflected in the Vienna Convention on the Law of Treaties'.[178] The UN Legal Counsel had concluded that North Korea could not withdraw,

---

[173] HRC, Concluding Observations, United Kingdom of Great Britain and Northern Ireland (Hong Kong), CCPR/C/79/Add.69, 8 November 1996 (paragraph 4). In the case of Hong Kong, the Committee did not have to rely solely on this jurisprudence as the parties to the Joint Declaration had agreed that the ICCPR would remain in force after transfer of sovereignty to the People's Republic of China.

[174] *Application of the Convention on the Prevention and Punishment of the Crime of Genocide, supra* n. 2, at p. 648 (Separate Opinion of Judge Weeramantry).

[175] *Ibid.*, at p. 649. Judge Shahabuddeen did not decide whether this principle applies to human rights treaties in general: *ibid.*, at p. 637.

[176] Security Council Resolution 1244, 10 June 1999; Concluding Observations of the HRC, Kosovo (Serbia), U.N. Doc. CCPR/C/UNK/CO/1, 14 Aug. 2006; Concluding Observations of the ESCR, on the Initial Report of Serbia and Montenegro, U.N. Doc. E/C.12/1/Add.108, May 2005 (paragraph 9).

[177] 'Only very few human rights treaties do not have a termination clause': E. Klein, 'Denunciation of Human Rights Treaties and the Principle of Reciprocity' in Fastenrath, Geiger, Khan, Paulus, von Schorlemer and Vedder (eds.), *supra* n. 139, pp. 477–487, at p. 480.

[178] HRC, General Comment No. 26: Continuity of Obligations, U.N. Doc. CCPR/C/21/Rev.1/Add.8/Rev.1, 12 Aug. 1997 (paragraph 1).

unless all other parties to the Covenant agreed.[179] In language reflecting Article 56(1)(b) VCLT, the Committee stated that the ICCPR is not 'by its nature' the type of treaty 'where a right of denunciation is deemed to be admitted'. First, the Covenant is not of a temporary nature, and second, once accorded, Covenant rights belong to the people of the territory and remain with them unless there is an explicit provision allowing for withdrawal.[180] The same concern that people who have enjoyed human rights guarantees should not be subsequently deprived of those protections has motivated the ECtHR's decision that an occupier State party to the ECHR continues to be bound by the Convention in occupied territory within the Convention's legal space.[181] Eckart Klein notes that if the objective order and absolute obligations framed by human rights treaties are separate from the multilateral contractual basis, States do not have the option of unilateral denunciation. Nevertheless, if all States parties agreed to terminate the treaty they could do so, with the exception of obligations that had become binding as rules of customary international law.[182]

The objective that human rights obligations should not be easily undermined means that procedures for treaty amendment or revision[183] generally impose conditions 'somewhat more onerous and specific than the general or default' amendment provisions in the VCLT.[184] The political risk of seeking amendment of human rights treaties is high and is rarely attempted. Where amendment has been sought, formal acceptance has been slow. For instance, the General Assembly accepted in 1996 a proposal to amend Article 20(1) CEDAW by extending the meeting time for the Committee on the Elimination of Discrimination against Women.[185] The Resolution requires acceptance of the amendment by a two-thirds majority of States parties, a condition not necessitated by Article 40 VCLT or Article 26 CEDAW. Some sixteen

---

[179] Klein, *supra* n. 177, at p. 478.

[180] E.g., Art. 12 of the 1966 First Additional Protocol to the ICCPR, 999 UNTS 302; Art. 31 CAT (*supra* n. 37); Art. 89 CMWF (*supra* n. 128) and Art. 48 CPD (*supra* n. 35); indeed, '[o]nly very few human rights treaties do not have a termination clause': Klein, *supra* n. 177, at pp. 477 and 480.

[181] *Al Skeini v. UK, supra* n. 24 (paragraph 142). However, this does not mean that jurisdiction under the ECHR can never exist outside the territory covered by the Council of Europe Member States: *ibid.*

[182] Klein, *supra* n. 177, at pp. 483–485.

[183] E.g., Art. 51 ICCPR (*supra* n. 11); Art. 29 ICESCR (*supra* n. 12); Art. 23 ICERD (*supra* n. 10); Art. 26 CEDAW (*supra* n. 37); Art. 29 CAT (*supra* n. 37); Art. 50 CRC (*supra* n. 36); Art. 90 CMWF (after a period of five years) (*supra* n. 128) and Art. 47 CPD (Art. 47(3) is new) (*supra* n. 35).

[184] Gardbaum, *supra* n. 50, at 749 and 758.   [185] UNGA Res. 50/202, 23 Feb. 1996.

years later the amendment has not been accepted.[186] In practice, amendment is through the adoption of optional protocols or evolutive interpretation.

5 Conclusion

Following the adoption of the VCLT, multilateral treaty regimes have flourished, mainstreaming 'collective and universal values' into the international legal order,[187] including those for human rights, environmental law and disarmament. What distinguishes the former is not so much their substance but the existence of expert judicial or quasi-judicial bodies.[188] This has entailed human rights treaties being subject to more interpretation and practical application by experts from within the human rights world than is perhaps the case with any other conventional special regime. Their function is notionally 'limited to direct supervisory functions in respect of [the relevant] law-making treaty'[189] but is in fact directed towards establishing and upholding a public – even constitutional – international or regional order. This objective has grounded an open-ended, 'evolutive' approach to treaty interpretation that goes beyond the text and in developing the law.[190] While opinions emanating from the human rights courts and bodies are often accorded considerable weight, there is also disagreement from other decision-makers who prefer a 'traditionalist', positivist approach that rejects any deviation in favour of human rights. The current position is one of unarticulated compromise. On the one hand, the proliferation of human rights bodies has not precipitated a damaging fragmentation of international law. Although human rights bodies are not necessarily versed in treaty law, there is a good deal of reliance on the VCLT; either explicitly or implicitly it pervades the language and basis of decision-making. This is facilitated by the flexibility within the VCLT for human rights exceptionalism (Article 60(5)), for opting out and for managing normative conflict.

---

[186] I. Boerefijn, 'Article 20' in M. A. Freeman, C. Chinkin and B. Rudolf (eds.), *The UN Convention on the Elimination of All Forms of Discrimination against Women: A Commentary* (Oxford: Oxford University Press, 2012), pp. 513–518, at p. 516.

[187] E. Cannizzaro, 'Preface' in Cannizzaro, *supra* n. 76, pp. v–vi, at p. vi.

[188] Another distinction is that one State can 'spoil' the effectiveness of an environmental regime, but this is not the case with human rights treaties.

[189] *Loizidou v. Turkey, supra* n. 24 (paragraph 84).

[190] *Case Concerning Armed Activities on the Territory of the Congo* (New Application: 2002), *supra* n. 46, at p. 71 (paragraphs 22–23 of Joint Separate Opinion of Judges Higgins, Kooijmans, Elaraby, Owada and Simma).

Human rights bodies have sought harmony rather than confrontation with other areas of international law. Acceptance or otherwise by States of such an expansive approach depends upon political context: the USA views differently the HRC's insistence on the continuity of ICCPR rights when applied to the people of North Korea from that of its extraterritorial application when applied to itself. Neither is directly provided for within the Covenant. On the other hand, the ILC has maintained the integrity of treaty law while recognising the competence of the treaty bodies[191] and a presumption of severability of an impermissible reservation. The ICJ's approach has been mixed. As far back as the advisory opinion on the Genocide Convention in 1951, it was instrumental in identifying the special characteristics of humanitarian treaties and has upheld their extra-territorial application.[192] It has also distinguished their substantive content from procedural requirements, to the dissatisfaction of some human rights grounded judges. But the ICJ has jurisdiction over disputes relating to any area of international law and an obligation to apply principles of international law in many contexts, not just that of human rights. The conclusion is that the human rights treaty regime has not shifted from a 'purely treaty based regime' to a 'constitutional one'[193] but is rather a more flexible and pragmatic one that seeks 'to achieve the necessary clarity and the essential consistency of international law, as well as legal security, to which both the individuals with guaranteed rights and the States obliged to comply with treaty obligations are entitled'.[194]

---

[191] The rapporteur Alain Pellet had earlier responded aggressively to this position but later softened his position: Pellet, *Second Report on Reservations to Treaties*, *supra* n. 31 (paragraph 252(d)).

[192] *Legal Consequences of the Construction of a Wall in the Occupied Palestinian Territory* (Advisory Opinion) (2004) ICJ Rep. 136, at pp. 178–181 (paragraphs 107–113) and *Case Concerning Armed Activities on the Territory of the Congo:* Democratic Republic of the Congo v. Uganda (2005) ICJ Rep. 168, at pp. 242–243 (paragraph 216).

[193] Gardbaum, *supra* n. 50, at 753.

[194] *Ahmadou Sadio Diallo*, *supra* n. 25, at pp. 663–664 (paragraph 66).

17

Law of War/Law of Armed Conflict/
International Humanitarian Law

FRANÇOISE J. HAMPSON

1   Identifying the 'Context': Why Nomenclature Matters

The very way in which this area of public international law is described is a matter of dispute. Since this is relevant to an examination of treaties in this field, it is worth explaining why it is controversial. Until 1949, this area of law, as a whole, was known as the law of war.[1] It consisted of two strands.[2] There were rules on the conduct of hostilities and rules on the treatment of 'victims of war'. In this context, 'victims of war' refers to people adversely affected by the conflict and in the power of the opposing belligerent.[3] The second set of rules was known as international humanitarian law (IHL), and their object was to protect. The four Geneva Conventions of August 1949 referred to 'armed conflict' – rather than to 'war'.[4] From that date, the law of war became synonymous with the law of armed conflict in public international law. At the domestic level, the term

[1] See, generally, G. Best, *Humanity in Warfare* (New York, NY: Columbia University Press, 1980) and G. Best, *War and Law since 1945* (Oxford: Clarendon Press, 1994).

[2] Some would also include the *ius ad bellum* rules in the concept of the laws of war. It is submitted that this is unhelpful and risks undermining the generally accepted split between the *ius ad bellum* and *ius in bello*. The rules on the conduct of hostilities apply equally to all belligerents in international armed conflicts, irrespective of the lawfulness of the resort to armed force (see further later). Furthermore, the operation of the *ius ad bellum* in practice is subject to more political and policy influences than the *ius in bello*. In other words, it operates very differently as law. For these reasons, no consideration will be given to the *ius ad bellum* in this chapter.

[3] For example, the wounded and sick, the shipwrecked, POWs and civilians in the power of an opposing belligerent (the four categories covered by the four Geneva Conventions of 1949): see *infra* n. 4. It should be noted that protecting civilians generally from the effects of hostilities requires restriction on the conduct of hostilities by both sides. In other words, it does not form part of the rules on the protection of victims of war.

[4] Common Art. 2 of 1949 Geneva Convention (I) for the Amelioration of the Condition of the Wounded and Sick in Armed Forces in the Field, 75 UNTS 31; Geneva Convention (II) for the Amelioration of the Condition of Wounded, Sick and Shipwrecked Members of Armed Forces at Sea, 75 UNTS 85; Geneva Convention (III) Relative to the Treatment of

'war' might carry specific consequences. International humanitarian law was still used to describe rules on the protection of victims. From 1974–1977, a diplomatic conference met annually to update rules across the whole field. The resulting documents did not take the form of free-standing treaties. They were described as Additional Protocols to the 1949 Geneva Conventions, even though they were not limited to rules on the protection of victims.[5] Just because a mackerel is put into a box labelled apples, along with some apples, does not make the mackerel itself an apple. Nevertheless, from 1977, two things happened. First, the term 'international humanitarian law' started to be used to describe the field of law as a whole. This was something of a misnomer. It seems counter-intuitive to describe as 'humanitarian' rules on how to kill people and destroy things. It gave a misleading impression as to the contents of the law and may create unrealistic expectations. The use of the term became more and more widespread, until now it is the term used by the United Nations Security Council and General Assembly, the International Court of Justice (ICJ), the International Committee of the Red Cross (ICRC) and the human rights machinery of the United Nations. It is not the term used by a significant number of armed forces.[6] They still prefer either the 'law of war' or the 'law of armed conflict'. Second, a large majority of stakeholders, including some who used the term 'law of war' or 'law of armed conflict', appeared to treat all the rules contained in the Additional Protocols in the same way. They treated the mackerel as though it were an apple. In other words, the treaty provisions were treated in the same way *qua* treaty provisions, even though they belonged to two significantly different sub-fields. It will be shown that this has contributed to much of the confusion and disagreement between different stakeholders. Military lawyers treat the two strands of law differently, possibly without being conscious of doing so. Some governments and much of the UN appear to treat them in the same

Prisoners of War, 75 UNTS 135, and Geneva Convention (IV) Relative to the Protection of Civilian Persons in Time of War, 75 UNTS 287.

[5] 1977 Protocol Additional to the Geneva Conventions of 12 August 1949, and Relating to the Protection of Victims of International Armed Conflicts (Protocol I), 1125 UNTS 3, and 1977 Protocol Additional to the Geneva Conventions of 12 August 1949, and Relating to the Protection of Victims of Non-International Armed Conflicts (Protocol II), 1125 UNTS 609.

[6] The British Military Manual is published as UK Ministry of Defence, *The Manual of the Law of Armed Conflict* (Oxford: Oxford University Press, 2004); in June 2015, the U.S. Department of Defense published its *Law of War Manual* (www.dod.mil/dodgc/images/law_war_manual15.pdf).

way. This chapter will inevitably reveal and explore that fault line whilst looking at certain distinctive features of the treaty regime in the field. In this chapter, the law of armed conflict (LOAC) will be used to describe the area as a whole. IHL will be used to describe treaty provisions on the protection of victims.

The evolution in nomenclature raises a distinct but related question. Certain terms may change their meaning or may acquire a technical meaning over time. This intertemporal issue may be exacerbated when the change in meaning is reflected in treaty provisions which are ratified by some but not all States. One example is the word used to describe members of armed forces who are entitled to take part in the hostilities and to prisoner of war (POW) status if detained. Additional Protocol I uses the word 'combatant' to describe a person with those entitlements.[7] It does not mean merely someone who fights but someone who is entitled to fight. The United States has not ratified Additional Protocol I. It tends to use the vocabulary associated with the 1907 Hague Convention (IV) Respecting the Laws and Customs of War on Land and the Regulations annexed thereto.[8] For the United States, 'combatant' has no technical meaning and the term used to describe such a person is 'privileged belligerent'. This can lead to unnecessary difficulties in multinational coalitions, particularly where the United States is partnered with States which take the letter of the law seriously.[9]

2 Delimitation of the Field

This chapter will examine both treaties on the conduct of hostilities and treaties on the protection of victims. It will not include what are usually called disarmament treaties.[10] They are negotiated in a different forum and usually concern weapons of mass destruction. The 1925 Geneva Protocol for the Prohibition of the Use of Asphyxiating, Poisonous or Other Gases, and of Bacteriological Methods of Warfare (Geneva Gas Protocol)[11] will be included because it was not treated as a disarmament

---

[7] See, in particular, Arts. 43 and 44 of Additional Protocol I: *supra* n. 5.   [8] 205 CTS 277.

[9] C. H. B. Garraway, 'Interoperability and the Atlantic Divide: A Bridge over Troubled Waters', *International Law Studies*, 80 (2006), 337–355. A different confusion arises in those languages which cannot easily distinguish between fighters (i.e. someone who takes part in the fighting, with no implications as to status) and combatants. The French for fighter is 'combatant'. It is somewhat cumbersome to have to say 'quelqu'un qui se bat'.

[10] See the contribution to this volume of Tabassi and Elias at pp. 578–620 (Chapter 18).

[11] 187 CTS 453.

treaty.[12] Similarly, treaties restricting or prohibiting the use of conventional weapons will be included, even though certain of them involve banning the use, manufacture or stockpiling of the weapon in question. The chapter will not address any of the legal issues involved in United Nations or regional peace support operations. In other words, the context in which the relevant treaty rules will be considered is that of international armed conflict (IAC) between two or more States and non-international armed conflict (NIAC) between one or more States and one or more organised armed groups or between such groups themselves. The chapter will not consider displacement or humanitarian assistance, except to the extent that they are addressed by LOAC.[13]

Even with that delimitation, it leaves too many treaties to be examined all in depth. The principal focus will therefore be on the 1907 Hague Convention (IV), the four Geneva Conventions of 1949, the two Additional Protocols of 1977 and the 1980 Convention on Prohibitions or Restrictions of Use of Certain Conventional Weapons which may be Deemed to be Excessively Injurious or to Have Indiscriminate Effects (Certain Conventional Weapons Convention (CCWC))[14] and its Protocols.[15] Reference will also be made to other treaties, too, such as the 1925 Geneva Gas Protocol.[16]

3   A Summary of the Historical Development of LOAC Treaty Law

During the formative period of public international law, States only needed rules in a limited number of fields, owing to the comparatively

---

[12] It was negotiated in Geneva, even though it concerned the conduct of hostilities. It was adopted by the International Conference on the Control of the International Trade in Arms, Munitions and Implements of War, which was convened by the Council of the League of Nations. See, generally, A. Roberts and R. Guelff (eds.), *Documents on the Laws of War* (Oxford: Oxford University Press, 3rd ed., 2000), pp. 155–158.

[13] These represent two of the fields where the use of the term 'international humanitarian law' gives rise to confusion. The practitioners in these areas regard their work as humanitarian and therefore assume that it is one of the principal objects of IHL.

[14] 1342 UNTS 137.

[15] Five such protocols exist: 1980 Protocol (I) on Non-Detectable Fragments, 1342 UNTS 168; 1980 Protocol (II) Prohibiting Mines, Booby-Traps and Other Devices, 1342 UNTS 168 (as amended in 1996: 2048 UNTS 93); 1980 Protocol (III) Prohibiting Incendiary Weapons, 1342 UNTS 171; 1995 Protocol (IV) on Blinding Laser Weapons, 2024 UNTS 163, and 2003 Protocol (V) on Explosive Remnants of War, U.N. Doc. CCW/MSP/2003/2 (27 Nov. 2003).

[16] *Supra* n. 11.

few areas in which States encountered one another. In addition to diplomatic law and the law of the sea, those areas included war. This meant, first, that there was a significant body of customary law at the time when treaties started to be concluded in this field and, second, that the area was subject to treaty regulation much earlier than many other areas.[17] The starting point is often regarded as being the 1868 Declaration of St. Petersburg.[18] Until 1907, texts on the law of war were sometimes called treaties and sometimes declarations. It is not always clear why different terminology was chosen. Declarations could be ratified. It was clear that, subject to ratification, they were intended to be legally binding. The 1874 Brussels Declaration Concerning the Laws and Customs of War did not enter into force, but that was because many of the States involved in its drafting did not ratify it rather than on account of its status as a declaration.[19] Where they were both intended to give rise to legal obligations and entered into force, such instruments will be treated as treaties in this chapter. At around the same time as the St. Petersburg Declaration, the first treaty was concluded dealing with the protection of one category of victims – the military wounded.[20] From then until 1899, most of the focus was on a process of the consolidation of

---

[17] Best, *Humanity in Warfare, supra* n. 1, at pp. 1–29. See, also, T. Meron, *Human Rights and Humanitarian Norms as Customary Law* (Oxford: Clarendon Press, 1989); T. Meron, *Henry's Wars and Shakespeare's Laws: Perspectives on the Law of War in the Later Middle Ages* (Oxford: Clarendon Press, 1994) and T. Meron, *Bloody Constraint: War and Chivalry in Shakespeare* (Oxford: Oxford University Press, 1998). The concept of chivalry, including the prohibition of perfidy, still finds reflection in the current treaty rules. One of the reasons for the prohibition of certain weapons is that *soldiers* think them unfair, e.g. poisoned weapons.

[18] 138 CTS 297. Eight instruments are listed on the ICRC website dating between 1856 and 1898: https://ihl-databases.icrc.org/applic/ihl/ihl.nsf/vwTreatiesHistoricalByDate .xsp. Not all of them are treaties, and not all of the draft treaty texts entered into force.

[19] The Declaration is reproduced in D. Schindler and J. Toman (eds.), *The Laws of Armed Conflicts: A Collection of Conventions, Resolutions and Other Documents* (Dordrecht: Martinus Nijhoff, 3rd ed., 1988), pp. 25–34. The UK *Manual of the Law of Armed Conflict* does not appear to distinguish between treaties and declarations: *supra* n. 6.

[20] The first Geneva Convention – the 1864 Geneva Convention for the Amelioration of the Condition of the Wounded and Sick in Armies in the Field – which in fact pre-dated the St. Petersburg Declaration by four years, addressed the provision of medical care to wounded members of armed forces: 202 CTS 144. This represented the first step in the development of the unique role of the ICRC. The impetus which resulted in the treaty came principally from one, well-connected, Swiss citizen. Henry Dunant had been much marked by what he saw, as a spectator, of the 1859 Battle of Solferino. See, generally, H. Dunant, *A Memory of Solferino* (1862) (reproduced by the ICRC: www.icrc.org/eng/ assets/files/publications/icrc-002-0361.pdf).

customary law.[21] That work formed the basis for a number of treaty commitments adopted in 1899: the first Hague Peace Conference of that year adopted three conventions and three declarations.[22] The treaties on the military wounded and sick, shipwrecked members of the armed forces and POWs tended to be negotiated in Geneva. The Hague was the place where many negotiations on the conduct of hostilities (including rules on weapon use) and belligerent occupation were conducted. This resulted in the two strands becoming known respectively as 'the law of The Hague' and 'the law of Geneva'.

In 1907, a large number of treaties were concluded in The Hague regulating separate issues in separate treaties.[23] Some of them were consolidations of earlier treaties and others were new. They included Hague Convention (IV), which was designed to regulate war on land.[24] That treaty included provisions on belligerent occupation – framed from the perspective of the occupying power rather than the people subjected to belligerent occupation – and on POWs. Another important treaty was Hague Convention (V) Respecting the Rights and Duties of Neutral Powers and Persons in Case of War on Land.[25]

One of the main impetuses for the creation of new treaties or the updating of old ones has been the (recent) experience of hostilities. Another has been technological developments. After the First World War, however, events took a different course. The 'war to end

---

[21] See, for example, the 1874 Brussels Declaration: *supra* n. 19. See, also, the 1880 Oxford Manual on the Laws of War on Land (the product of the Institute of International Law), reproduced in Schindler and Toman (eds.), *supra* n. 19, at pp. 36–48.

[22] 1899 Hague Convention (I) for the Pacific Settlement of International Disputes, 187 CTS 410; 1899 Hague Convention (II) with Respect to the Laws and Customs of War on Land, 187 CTS 429, and 1899 Hague Convention (III) for the Adaptation to Maritime Warfare of the Principles of the Geneva Convention of 22 August 1864, 187 CTS 443. And the declarations: Declaration Concerning the Prohibition, for the Term of Five Years, of the Launching of Projectiles and Explosives from Balloons or Other New Methods of A Similar Nature, 187 CTS 453; Declaration Concerning the Prohibition of the Use of Projectiles Diffusing Asphyxiating Gases, 187 CTS 429, and Declaration on the Use of Bullets which Expand Easily or Flatten Easily in the Human Body, 187 CTS 459. This last Declaration deals with 'dum-dum' bullets and is still the legal basis for their prohibition in international armed conflicts. See, generally, F. Kalshoven, 'Arms, Armaments and International Law', *Hague Recueil*, 191 (1985–II), 191–342.

[23] Thirteen Conventions were adopted alongside one Declaration. Three of the Conventions revised earlier Conventions of 1899. The Declaration renewed the 1899 Declaration Concerning the Prohibition, for the Term of Five Years, of the Launching of Projectiles and Explosives from Balloons or Other New Methods of a Similar Nature, *ibid.*, which had expired.

[24] *Supra* n. 8.   [25] 205 CTS 299.

war'[26] was followed by the creation of the League of Nations in January 1920[27] and, eventually, the 1928 Kellogg-Briand Pact, which sought to outlaw war.[28] In that environment, there was considerable reluctance to address the issue of the conduct of hostilities. Rules were drafted to address aerial warfare and the protection of merchant shipping from submarine warfare, but they did not attract the ratifications necessary to enter into force.[29] One exception was the 1925 Geneva Gas Protocol, which was the product of the experience of the use of gas in the trenches.[30] Whilst that instrument sought to ban the use of such weapons, a large number of the States which ratified it made reservations which resulted in it becoming, in effect, a no-first-use treaty.[31] States reserved the right to use the weapon if the other side had used it first. This meant that it was legitimate to manufacture and stockpile the weapon. The inhibition regarding treaties on the conduct of hostilities did not apply to anything like the same extent in the case of treaties on the protection of victims of war. In July 1929, there was an important updating of the rules on the treatment of the military wounded and sick as well as POWs in two separate Geneva Conventions.[32] The latter treaty was fairly widely ratified and was in force during the Second World War on the Western Front. So, at the time of the outbreak of the Second World War, land warfare was regulated by a 1907 treaty but rules on the protection of victims were of much more recent origin.

The same process was at work after 1945. Even though the 1945 United Nations Charter contemplated the use of force in self-defence or as authorised by the Security Council,[33] there was a marked inhibition regarding the conclusion of treaties on the conduct of hostilities. Once again, however, this was not the case with rules on the protection of victims. In August 1949, four Geneva Conventions were concluded.[34]

---

[26] After H. G. Wells, *The War That Will End War* (London: Frank & Cecil Palmer, 1914).
[27] 225 CTS 195.   [28] Also known as the Pact of Paris: 94 LNTS 57.
[29] 1923 Hague Draft Rules on Aerial Warfare: reproduced in Schindler and Toman (eds.), *supra* n. 19, at pp. 207–217. See, also, 1936 London Procès-Verbal Relating to the Rules of Submarine Warfare Set Forth in Part IV of the Treaty of London of 22 April 1930: reproduced in Schindler and Toman (eds.), *ibid.*, at pp. 883–884.
[30] *Supra* n. 11.   [31] Roberts and Guelff (eds.), *supra* n. 12, at p. 155.
[32] 1929 Geneva Convention for the Amelioration of the Condition of the Wounded and Sick in Armies in the Field, 118 LNTS 303, and 1929 Convention Relative to the Treatment of Prisoners of War, 118 LNTS 343.
[33] 1 UNTS 16. See, in particular, Arts. 42 and 51.
[34] *Supra* n. 4. As of July 2015, each Convention had been ratified by 196 States. At an earlier stage, there was a question as to how to identify customary international law, when a treaty has been widely but not universally ratified, and in particular to distinguish

The first three dealt with issues already regulated by treaty. They updated the previous provisions in the light of the experience of the Second World War, addressing the military wounded and sick, the shipwrecked and the treatment of POWs. The fourth Convention broke new ground and, again, was based on the experience in the Second World War.[35] It dealt with civilians who were 'victims of war'. In other words, it concerned civilians who found themselves in the power of an opposing belligerent. It did not seek to protect civilians from the effect of hostilities. It sought to protect them from abuse at the hands of the other side. Broadly speaking, the treaty dealt with two situations. First, there were civilians who, at the outbreak of hostilities, were in the territory of the opposing belligerent (i.e. enemy aliens). Second, there were civilians living in their own territory but where the territory had been subjected to belligerent occupation. It will be recalled that Hague Convention (IV) of 1907 contains provisions on belligerent occupation, but they concerned principally what the belligerent occupant could and could not do in relation to enemy property.[36] The fourth Geneva Convention of 1949 addressed the relationship between the occupying power and the civilian population under its control.

One striking feature of the 1949 Geneva Conventions is that they included, for the first time, a provision which addressed non-international conflicts.[37] It was extremely rudimentary and essentially

subsequent treaty practice and state practice for the purposes of establishing custom. Now the question raised is as to the possible role of custom in IACs. This was a challenge for the authors of the ICRC Study into customary international humanitarian law when dealing with IACs: J.-M. Henckaerts and L. Doswald-Beck, *Customary International Humanitarian Law* (Vols. I–II) (Cambridge: Cambridge University Press, 2005).

[35] *Supra* n. 4.   [36] *Supra* n. 8.

[37] Common Art. 3 of 1949 Geneva Conventions (I)–(IV): *supra* n. 4. The ICRC Commentary to the Conventions, reflecting the view of Jean Pictet, calls it a 'convention in miniature': see J. Pictet, *Commentary to Geneva Convention for the Amelioration of the Condition of the Wounded and Sick in Armed Forces in the Field* (Geneva: ICRC, 1952), p. 48. This is singularly unhelpful. It gives the impression that it can be put into a box on its own and that no other provisions of the Conventions are relevant in relation to common Article 3. Obviously, it is subject to the general rules on entry into force, ratification etc., that are found at the end of each Convention. There is nothing which precludes the applicability of the rules on dissemination, implementation and enforcement to non-international armed conflicts, unless the content of the rule itself precludes such applicability. So, for example, the 'grave breach' regime only applies in international armed conflicts as the breaches in question are defined by reference to protected persons, a concept that only exists in IACs. Nothing, however, prevents the obligation to suppress all other violations of the Convention from applying to common Article 3. It is striking that, in an article published in 1990 specifically on the question of

dealt with the protection of persons in the power of the other side. A second remarkable feature of the provision – common Article 3 found in each of the Conventions – is that it claims to bind the parties to the non-international armed conflict, even though, by definition, at least one of those parties is a non-State actor.[38] It should be remembered that in 1948, the Universal Declaration of Human Rights,[39] the Convention on the Prevention and Punishment of the Crime of Genocide[40] and the American Declaration of the Rights and Duties of Man[41] were adopted and that the European Convention on Human Rights followed two years later.[42]

With one exception, the reluctance to update the rules on the conduct of hostilities continued until 1977. The exception was the safe or relatively uncontroversial subject of the protection of cultural property, which was addressed in the 1954 Hague Convention for the Protection of Cultural Property in the Event of Armed Conflict.[43]

penal repression ('suppression' does not necessarily involve penal proceedings), a member of the ICRC at no point mentioned the obligation to suppress: D. Plattner, 'The Penal Repression of Violations of International Humanitarian Law Applicable in Non-International Armed Conflicts', *Int'l Rev. Red Cross*, 30 (1990), 409–420, at 419. Indeed, it asserted that '[t]he *only* obligation explicitly stipulated in IHL applicable in noninternational armed conflicts is that the law must be disseminated (Art. 19 of Protocol II)' (emphasis added). The complaint is not that the author did not anticipate the finding that violations of common Article 3 were criminal in nature, which occurred a mere five years later at the hands of the ICTY. It is probable that any author writing at that time would have reached the same conclusion with regard to penal accountability. The complaint is rather that there was no acknowledgement of an existing obligation to suppress such violations, which could but need not involve criminal proceedings. It may be that viewing common Article 3 as detached from the rest of the Geneva Conventions – a 'convention in miniature' – contributed to that omission. See, generally, Section 4.7 of this chapter.

[38] An international armed conflict is defined in common Article 2 of the Geneva Conventions as being 'all cases of declared war or of any other armed conflict which may arise between two or more of the High Contracting Parties, even if the state of war is not recognized by one of them'. An armed conflict not of an international character therefore has to be one which does not have States on opposing sides. Under common Article 3 of the Geneva Conventions, an additional requirement is that the conflict has to occur in the territory of a High Contracting Party, though it is not stipulated that the High Contracting Party in question need itself be a party to the conflict. There are additional significant requirements in the case of Additional Protocol II (*supra* n. 5) which result in it only being applicable to a limited category of common Article 3 NIACs (*supra* n. 4).

[39] General Assembly Resolution 217A (III), U.N. Doc A/810 at 71 (10 Dec. 1948).

[40] 78 UNTS 277.   [41] OEA/Ser.L.V/II.82 Doc.6 Rev.1 at 17 (1992).   [42] 213 UNTS 221.

[43] 249 UNTS 240. Art. 19 of the Convention makes it clear that it applies in both IACs and NIACs. The 1954 (first) Protocol to the Convention addresses the export of cultural property and restitution of illegally exported objects: 249 UNTS 358. A (second) Protocol

By the 1970s, it had become clear that, owing to the process of decolonisation, a majority of armed conflicts were non-international in character. Much more was needed than the rudimentary provision of common Article 3. Additionally, an ever increasing proportion of the casualties of armed conflicts were civilians. To address that problem, it was not possible simply to adopt a fifth Geneva Convention. They were not victims of war in the usual sense and were not (necessarily) in the power of the other side. The threat came from the conduct of hostilities, including from their own side. That was the province of rules on the conduct of hostilities. In order to protect civilians, it was necessary to update the rules on that issue. By then, the treaty rules on the conduct of land and sea warfare were nearly seventy years old, and there were no binding treaty rules on air warfare other than the use of balloons![44] It was decided that the regulation of conventional weapons would be dealt with separately. Over four years, two Additional Protocols to the Geneva Conventions were then negotiated. Additional Protocol I, which applies in international armed conflicts, contains provisions both on the conduct of hostilities and on the protection of victims.[45]

was concluded in March 1999 to take account of the impact of the approach adopted in the 1977 Additional Protocols, *supra* n. 5, to create a system of enhanced protection in the case of cultural property of importance to the whole of humanity and to improve enforcement: 2253 UNTS 212.

[44] 1907 Hague Declaration (XIV) Prohibiting the Discharge of Projectiles and Explosives from Balloons, 204 CTS 403, which replaced the 1899 Declaration: *supra* n. 22. The 1923 Hague Draft Rules on Aerial Warfare were adopted but never entered into force; they nevertheless played a significant role in the development of customary international law: *supra* n. 29.

[45] Parts II on the wounded, sick and shipwrecked and Part IV (Section 3) on treatment of persons in the power of a party to the conflict clearly relate to the protection of victims of war in the traditional sense. The provisions on the care of the wounded, sick and shipwrecked now extend to both military and civilians, as does the protection of medical personnel and infrastructure. Part III clearly applies to the conduct of hostilities, being entitled methods and means of warfare. It includes provisions on combatant and POW status. It is less clear how Section 1 of Part IV – on the civilian population – and titled 'General Protection Against the Effects of Hostilities' and Section 2 – on 'Relief in Favour of the Civilian Population' – should be regarded. This raises a question about the importance of the structure of a treaty to an understanding of its content. It is submitted that, since Section 1 of Part IV has a direct impact on the conduct of military operations, it is better viewed as part of the rules on the conduct of hostilities. Its provisions appear to be integrated with Part III in the training of military personnel on the conduct of military operations. In the case of Section 2, it would depend on the circumstances and, in particular, whether the delivery of relief would interfere with the conduct of lawful military operations. Richard Gardiner suggests that headings and *chapeaux* form part of the context in which a treaty has to be interpreted: R. K. Gardiner, *Treaty Interpretation*

The hopes for a detailed elaboration of rules applicable in non-international armed conflict were frustrated, however, in part as a result of the acceptance that conflicts in the name of self-determination were to be treated as international.[46] Most States were not willing to accept significant restrictions on their freedom of man-oeuvre in purely internal conflicts. Additional Protocol II for the most part expands and elaborates the provisions in common Article 3 of the Geneva Conventions.[47] There are also some provisions on the conduct of hostilities, mostly addressing what cannot be done rather than what can be. A significant feature of Additional Protocol II is that it has a different and higher threshold for its applicability than common Article 3 of the Geneva Conventions. The latter just requires an armed conflict not of an international character occurring in the territory of one of the High Contracting Parties. It can be between the State and a non-State party or between two non-State parties. Additional Protocol II requires that the fighting occur in the territory of the State involved, that it should be between the territorial State and one or more non-State groups and that the non-State party should be under responsible command and exercise such control over part of the State's territory as to enable it to carry out sustained and concerted military operations and to implement the Protocol. This means that common Article 3 is applicable to all non-international armed conflicts whereas Additional Protocol II is only applicable to some of them. Subsequently, negotiations were conducted which resulted in the adoption of the CCWC and its original three Protocols.[48] The first dealt with non-detectable fragments, the second mines and booby traps and the third with incendiary weapons. The Convention takes a somewhat unusual form. The Convention itself is remarkably short.[49] What matter are the Protocols.[50]

(Oxford: Oxford University Press, 2nd ed., 2015), pp. 200–202. This presumably also applies to the organization of the treaty contents into parts and sections.

[46] Until the adoption of what became Art. 1(4) of Additional Protocol I, many new States were in favour of a substantial protocol on NIACs to regulate the conduct of the remaining decolonisation conflicts. Once that had happened, those same States realised that any new NIAC rules would have an impact on how they could deal with conflicts within their own territories.

[47] *Supra* n. 4.

[48] *Supra* n. 15. In some quarters, it is referred to as the 1981 treaty. The Conference adopted the text in 1980, after which it was passed to the UN General Assembly. It was only open for signature and ratification in 1981.

[49] *Ibid*. It contains eleven articles.   [50] *Supra* n. 15.

By 1977, the following human rights treaties had been adopted: the 1965 International Convention on the Elimination of All Forms of Racial Discrimination,[51] the 1966 International Covenant on Civil and Political Rights[52] and the 1966 International Covenant on Economic, Social and Cultural Rights.[53] At the regional level, the American Convention on Human Rights (Pact of San José) was adopted in November 1969.[54] A brief word is therefore necessary about the relationship between the law of armed conflict and human rights law, although it must be made clear that this is still a work in progress. It is apparent from the derogation clauses in certain human rights treaties that that body of law remains applicable in some fashion even during armed conflict. What is less clear is whether a human rights body will only find a violation of human rights law where there is a violation of the law of armed conflict. That may be the position in international armed conflicts, where there is a detailed body of treaty rules which has been universally (the Geneva Conventions) or widely (Additional Protocol I) ratified. It is less clear what human rights bodies will do in non-international armed conflicts. In many cases, the territorial State denies the applicability of the law of armed conflict. The human rights body may take account of the *fact* of armed conflict without needing to take account of the *law* of armed conflict. What if the State itself invokes the law of armed conflict in its defence? In the case of prohibitions under both bodies of rules, there should not be too much difficulty. The problem arises with regard to permissive rules, in other words where the law of armed conflicts permits behaviour prohibited under human rights law. For example, armed conflict lawyers might argue that they can target people based on status (i.e. the group to which they belong), not behaviour, in non-international armed conflicts, just as they can in international armed conflicts. Again, they may argue that they can intern in non-international armed conflicts, just as they can in international armed conflicts. In the case of non-international armed conflicts, however, the State cannot point to treaty rules. They would be relying on alleged customary law. It is as yet unclear how human rights bodies will handle such questions, but there are cases pending at the national and international level which will shed some light on the question.

Following the adoption of the 1977 Protocols and the CCWC, there was a period in which there was little treaty-making. There was a gradual increase in the number of parties to the 1977 Protocols, but not much

---

[51] 660 UNTS 195.   [52] 999 UNTS 171.   [53] 999 UNTS 3.   [54] 114 UNTS 123.

attention was paid to the CCWC. It seemed that States had forgotten about it rather than that they were opposed to it. From the mid-1990s, that changed. What was remarkable was the *cause* of the change. It was not – or not principally – experience of recent conflicts. It was not pressure from States. It was pressure from civil society, in the form of an extraordinary coalition of different types of groups. They included those opposed to the arms trade, human rights groups and development non-governmental organizations, frustrated at the inability of populations to return home at the end of a conflict owing to the risk from anti-personnel mines. Armed forces appear to have been disconcerted by the idea that popular pressure could lead to changes in LOAC rules. This pressure led, first, to a renewal of interest in the CCWC, which acquired additional protocols.[55] It also led to the extension of the applicability, first, of the revised second protocol and, then, of the Convention as a whole, to NIACs.[56] Many non-governmental organizations and some States were still frustrated at the limited progress made through the CCWC process. In a forum of like-minded States, they negotiated the Ottawa Convention on the Prohibition of the Use, Stockpiling, Production and Transfer of Anti-Personnel Mines and on Their Destruction (the Ottawa Convention on Anti-Personnel Mines),[57] which was adopted in December 1997. That text was adopted after the conclusion of the amended second Protocol to the CCWC.[58] In the case of cluster munitions, like-minded States negotiated their own treaty before the CCWC successfully completed international negotiations. The Convention on Cluster Munitions was adopted in Dublin in May 1998 and opened for signature in Oslo in December of that year.[59]

The mid-1990s also saw the creation of two *ad hoc* international criminal tribunals, one for the former Yugoslavia (ICTY) and the other for Rwanda (ICTR).[60] Their mandates included war crimes, in other words serious violations of the laws and customs of war, as well as 'grave breaches' of the Geneva Conventions.[61] Then, in July 1998, the Statute of the International Criminal Court was adopted in Rome.[62]

---

[55] *Supra* n. 15.
[56] Art. 1(2) of 1980 Protocol (II) Prohibiting Mines, Booby-Traps and Other Devices (as amended in 1996): *supra* n. 15; see, also, amended Art. 1 CCWC (as amended in 2001).
[57] 2056 UNTS 211.   [58] *Supra* n. 15.   [59] ILM, 48 (2009), 354–369.
[60] ICTY: Security Council Resolution 808 (22 Feb. 2003) and Security Council Resolution 827 (25 May 1993); ICTR: Security Council Resolution 955 (8 Nov. 1994). See, further, the contribution to this volume of Wilmshurst at pp. 621–652 (Chapter 19).
[61] *Ibid.*   [62] 2187 UNTS 90.

The Rome Statute included in its list of war crimes not only offences based on treaty law but, in the case of NIACs, a number of offences based on customary law. Since 1995, largely as a result of the work of the ICTY, a large body of customary LOAC rules applicable in NIACs has emerged.[63] The Rome Statute used a different definition of non-international armed conflict in relation to offences other than violations of common Article 3 of the Geneva Conventions. This affects particularly customary rules on the conduct of hostilities. The ICC definition is based on the case-law of the ICTY in the *Tadić Case*.[64] According to Article 8(2)(f) of the Statute, it applies to protracted armed conflict between governmental authorities and organised armed groups or between such groups.[65] These instruments of international criminal law will not be further considered in this chapter, but it should be remembered that they provide a means for the enforcement of LOAC treaty rules. It should also be remembered that LOAC itself is civil in character. Breaches of LOAC will only give rise to individual criminal liability if the violation also constitutes a war crime. Any and every violation of LOAC, however, represents a violation of international law by the relevant party. If a State wishes to argue that another State has violated the law of armed conflict, it would refer the case to the International Court of Justice or a regional human rights tribunal and not to a criminal court.[66]

This summary does not pretend to address all the treaties that come within the scope of this chapter. The goal was rather to show, admittedly in a sweeping and generalised form, what happened when and why. It is also helpful, in the light of what follows, to be aware of what was

---

[63] See, in particular, Henckaerts and Doswald-Beck, *supra* n. 34.

[64] *Tadić*, IT-94-1, Decision on the Defence Motion for Interlocutory Appeal on Jurisdiction (ICTY), 2 Oct. 1995.

[65] *Supra* n. 62.

[66] For example, *Case Concerning Trial of Pakistani Prisoners of War* (Pakistan v. India) before the ICJ (11 May 1973): Application Instituting Proceedings. The case was by agreement removed from the Court's list. *Case Concerning the Military and Paramilitary Activities in and against Nicaragua*: Nicaragua v. United States of America (Merits) (1986) ICJ Rep. 14 addressed the mining of harbours and the violation of common Art. 3 of the Geneva Conventions. See, also, *Case Concerning Armed Activities in the Territory of the Congo*: DRC v. Uganda (2005) ICJ Rep. 168. Inter-State cases have been brought before the European Court of Human Rights arising out of the armed conflicts between Cyprus and Turkey, Georgia and Russia, and Ukraine and Russia. A case was brought by Ecuador against Colombia before the Inter-American Commission if Human Rights but was the subject off a friendly settlement. In addition, individuals have brought complaints, seeking to hold States responsible for what are, in effect, violations of both human rights law and the law of armed conflict.

happening in relation to the development of human rights law and, to a lesser extent, international criminal law.

4 Particular Features of LOAC Treaties

For reasons of space, this cannot be an examination of all the detailed aspects of LOAC treaties. The focus is rather on those issues which pertain to particular aspects of the law of treaties in order to see how LOAC treaties address them as well as on certain features that are particular to LOAC treaties.

4.1 The Nature of LOAC Treaties

Some commentators suggest that no useful purpose is served by characterising treaties.[67] It is striking, however, that the first case of severance of an invalid reservation by a court occurred in relation to a human rights treaty and that the 'living instrument' doctrine found in that field favours the application of a teleological approach to interpretation.[68] This might suggest that human rights treaties have characteristics which distinguish them from other treaties. There is a rich literature on human rights treaties *qua* treaties.[69] Very much less has been written about the distinctive characteristics of LOAC treaties.

It is, in fact, quite difficult to characterise at least some LOAC treaties. Duncan Hollis distinguishes between contractual treaties, interdependent treaties and, citing Sir Gerald Fitzmaurice, 'inherent' treaty obligations.[70]

---

[67] R. Y. Jennings and A. Watts, *Oppenheim's International Law* (Vol. I: Peace) (London: Longman, 9th ed., 1992), p. 1203. See, further, the contribution to this volume of Brölmann at pp. 79–102 (Chapter 4).

[68] *Belilos v. Switzerland* (ECtHR), Appl. No. 10328/83, 29 Apr. 1988 (severance) and *Loizidou v. Turkey* (Merits), No. 15318/89, Judgment of 18 Dec. 1996 ('living instrument'). See, further, B. Çali, 'Specialized Rules of Treaty Interpretation: Human Rights' in D. B. Hollis (ed.), *The Oxford Guide to Treaties* (Oxford: Oxford University Press, 2012), pp. 525–548, and the contribution to this volume of Moeckli and White at pp. 136–171 (Chapter 6).

[69] See, in particular, the contribution to this volume of Chinkin at pp. 509–537 (Chapter 16).

[70] D. Hollis, 'Defining Treaties' in Hollis (ed.), *supra* n. 68, pp. 11–45, at pp. 38–39. Lea Brilmayer has referred to the move from contract to pledge and argues that the pledge features of human rights law (i.e. legally binding State commitments to a set of values) reduces the significance of contract in international law: 'From "Contract" to "Pledge": The Structure of International Human Rights Agreements', *BYbIL*, 77 (2006), 163–202. This is to undervalue the contractual aspect of human rights treaties. States are only bound if they ratify such treaties, and one incentive is the fact that other States have ratified. It is not so much the making of pledges but the doing so collectively with others that seems to be

Contractual treaties involve the reciprocal pairing of rights and treaties. Multilateral treaty obligations can be contractual in this sense. Interdependent treaties are those where one party's duty to perform depends on performance by all other parties. 'Inherent' treaty obligations are those where one party's obligation to perform is not linked to the performance of other parties. An obvious example is the majority of human rights treaties. These distinctions matter on account of the consequences of classification. For example, one would not expect reciprocal reliance on reservations or suspension of the obligation in the event of material breach in the case of 'inherent' treaty obligations, sometimes also known as treaties of an 'objective character'.[71] With these distinctions in mind, an attempt will be made to characterise the 1907 Hague Convention (IV), the 1925 Geneva Gas Protocol and the four Geneva Conventions of 1949. All these treaties lay down rules which are capable of constituting an international standard. They are not articulated in terms of 'if you do X, we will do Y'. To that extent, they do not appear to be either contractual or interdependent. Hague Convention (IV), however, by virtue of its 'general participation clause' in Article 2,[72] is interdependent with regard to its

important. The enforcement arrangements reflect a sense of mutual commitment. This is perhaps best reflected in the possibility that a non-victim State and not representing individual victims may nevertheless bring proceedings against another State. This has happened twice at the European level: the *Greek Case* (Denmark, Sweden, Norway and the Netherlands v. Greece), 3321–23 and 3344/67, and the *Turkish Case* (France, Norway, Denmark, Sweden and the Netherlands v. Turkey), 9940–9944/82. The form in which the commitment to certain values is manifested is a contractual form. When acceptance of individual petition was optional, a State could manifest its commitment to the values of the European Convention of Human Rights by ratification, but no individual could bring a complaint based on that commitment. It required a specific contractual undertaking to make that possible. There is a question as to the parties to the contract. Are they merely other State parties, or is there a contractual relationship with any monitoring and enforcement mechanism created under the treaty? There is no doubt that human rights treaties consist of pledges, but they do not *just* consist of pledges.

[71] This term appears to be used in at least two ways in the literature. The first use is to describe a treaty which will determine the issue for all States, whether or not they are parties. The example given is of treaties allocating territory (objective regimes). The treaty has an impact on States not party to it. The other meaning is that used in the human rights context, where it appears to mean that the parties are not creating a regime based on reciprocity: e.g. *Austria v. Italy*, 788/60, European Commission of Human Rights, 11 Jan. 1961 (treaties or commitments of an objective character). It will be used with the latter meaning in this chapter. Whilst this overlaps with the notion of *erga omnes* obligations, it is not coterminous with it. To rely on the treaty commitments made by State A, State B will need to be a party to the same treaty. See, generally, the contribution to this volume of Waibel at pp. 201–236 (Chapter 8).

[72] Otherwise known as the *si omnes* clause: 'The provisions contained in the Regulations referred to in Art. 1, as well as in the present Convention, do not apply except between

actual *applicability* in any armed conflict. The 1925 Geneva Gas Protocol, on the face of it, represents an international standard. The majority of the High Contracting Parties, however, have reserved the right to use the prohibited weapon if the other side uses it first. Therefore, by reservation, they have made its *application* reciprocal.[73] The Geneva Conventions of 1949 only apply during an armed conflict between States which have ratified them.[74] That is not inconsistent with their having an objective character, in the sense in which it is being used in this chapter. First, common Article 1 of the Conventions has been interpreted as imposing an obligation on all States parties to 'ensure respect' by other contracting parties.[75] This might be seen as creating a qualified form of *erga omnes* obligation, which has become unqualified as a result of the universal ratification of the Conventions. Second, belligerent reprisals are expressly precluded against protected persons as defined in each Convention.[76] This precludes the use of one of the tools usually available in the event of a material breach of LOAC. Third, as we shall see, States reacted in an unusual way to reservations which they believed to be incompatible with

Contracting Powers, and then only if all the belligerents are parties to the Convention'. See *supra* n. 8.

[73] This raises the relationship between a no-first-use treaty and belligerent reprisals. Where a treaty is *designed* as a no-first-use treaty, there is no need to take a position on belligerent reprisals. The violation of the obligation has the effect of suspending or terminating the obligation. The 1925 Geneva Gas Protocol was not designed to be such a treaty. It only became a no-first-use treaty as a result of the reservations made by ratifying States: Roberts and Guelff (eds.), *supra* n. 12. Had those reservations not been made, it would have been possible to invoke belligerent reprisals in response to a violation, on condition that the Protocol was not seen as coming within Art. 60(5) of the Vienna Convention on the Law of Treaties: 1155 UNTS 331.

[74] Their applicability during NIACs will be considered in Section 4.2.

[75] L. Boisson de Chazournes and L. Condorelli, 'Common Article 1 of the Geneva Conventions Revisited: Protecting Collective Interests', *Int'l Rev. Red Cross*, 82 (2000), 67–86. Frits Kalshoven has demonstrated that that was not the intended interpretation at the time of the adoption of the Geneva Conventions: 'The Undertaking to Respect and to Ensure Respect in All Circumstances: From Tiny Seed to Ripening Fruit', *YbIHL*, 2 (1999), 3–61. See, also, C. Focarelli, 'Common Article 1 of the 1949 Geneva Conventions: A Soap Bubble?', *EJIL*, 21 (2010), 125–171, and J.-M. Henckaerts, 'Article 1: Respect for the Convention' in International Committee of the Red Cross (ed.), *Commentary on the First Geneva Convention: Convention (I) for the Amelioration of the Condition of the Wounded and Sick in the Field* (Cambridge: Cambridge University Press, 2016), pp. 35–67 (paragraphs 153–173). Some States claim that they have no such obligation. Others appear to accept the principle but deny that its contents require them to take effective action if necessary.

[76] Art. 46 of Geneva Convention (I); Art. 47 of Geneva Convention (II); Art. 13(3) of Geneva Convention (III) and Art. 33 of Geneva Convention (IV): *supra* n. 4.

the object and purpose of the Conventions.[77] It is far from clear that the negotiators of the Geneva Conventions thought in terms of 'inherent' treaty obligations or obligations of an 'objective character'. Nevertheless, they have included provisions which have made it possible to apply such a designation to the Conventions after the event. It should be recalled that the Geneva Conventions only deal with the protection of victims; they do not address the conduct of hostilities.

This suggests that rules on the conduct of hostilities may have a different character from those on the protection of the victims of war. This presents a difficulty when dealing with Additional Protocol I, which contains rules in both categories. The negotiators do not seem to have been aware of the possible confusion between two different types of rules. After much heated debate, prohibitions of belligerent reprisals were included in relation to attacks against civilians and the civilian population and attacks against specially protected objects.[78] The United Kingdom, at the time of ratification, submitted a very precisely drafted reservation to the prohibition of belligerent reprisals against civilians.[79] No State has objected to the reservation, perhaps because they wish to keep their options open to act in like manner at some future point in time. That was a principal reason why the ICRC Study on *Customary International Humanitarian Law* reached the conclusion that it was not yet possible to say that the prohibition of belligerent reprisals against civilians was customary law.[80]

It is submitted that rules on the protection of victims of war impose 'inherent' obligations or ones of 'an objective character', but that rules on the conduct of hostilities may not have that character.

4.2   Who Is Bound by LOAC Treaties?[81]

In relation to who is bound by these treaties, LOAC displays some quite singular features. It is not suggested that States not party to these treaties are bound by them but, rather, that non-State groups are bound. The best

---

[77] See Section 4.4.

[78] Arts. 51(6), 52(1), 53(c), 54(4), 55(2) and 56(4) of Additional Protocol I: *supra* n. 5.

[79] For text of the reservation of the United Kingdom, see Roberts and Guelff (eds.), *supra* n. 12, at pp. 510–511 (reservation (*m*)).

[80] Henckaerts and Doswald-Beck, Vol. I, *supra* n. 34, pp. 520–523.

[81] See, generally, D. Bederman, 'Third Party Rights and Obligations in Treaties' in Hollis (ed.), *supra* n. 68, pp. 328–346.

known example occurs in NIACs but it is also necessary to consider certain examples in IACs.

It is submitted that the case of individuals being prosecuted before foreign courts for the commission of war crimes outside the territory of that court raises a different question; one of international criminal law. Where, for example, a private individual in State A, who does not belong to any armed force, shoots down an enemy pilot, baling out of an aircraft in distress and offering no resistance, he commits a war crime.[82] It is not that the individual has violated LOAC because that is only addressed to groups. It is rather that he has violated international criminal law, albeit that the substance of the prohibition is also reflected in LOAC.[83] International crimes are subject to universal permissive jurisdiction.

However, the same obligation may be imposed on members of a group as a result of LOAC. In that case, the group itself is bound by LOAC and the individual member of the group is bound both by LOAC and also by international criminal law.

For the most part, LOAC treaties apply to States and, through them, to members of the armed forces who fight for the State. That includes members of militia and volunteer corps who form part of the armed forces in time of armed conflict.[84] It also includes members of militia or other volunteer corps who, whilst not forming part of the armed forces, 'belong' to a party to the conflict and satisfy four cumulative criteria.[85] It is being assumed that persons entitled to POW status are combatants and, by virtue of their link with a party to the conflict, are covered by the State's assumption of legal obligations. So far, there is nothing out of the ordinary.

There is, however, a category of fighter who, by definition, does not 'belong' to the State, other than probably having its nationality, but who nonetheless qualifies for POW status. A *levée en masse* has been defined as the 'inhabitants of a non-occupied territory, who on the approach of the enemy spontaneously take up arms to resist the invading forces, without having had time to form themselves into regular armed units,

---

[82] Art. 42 of Additional Protocol I: *supra* n. 5.

[83] This needs to be distinguished from the issue of attribution under the law of State responsibility. A State is only responsible for behaviour legally attributable to it, not including the behaviour of private citizens. The issue being addressed here is not unattributable behaviour – see, for example, Art. 41 of the 1907 Hague Regulations (*supra* n. 8) – but individuals who cannot violate LOAC because they are not bound by it, even if they are bound by international criminal law.

[84] They are entitled to POW status. See Art. 4(A)(1) of Geneva Convention (III): *supra* n. 5.

[85] Art. 4(A)(2) of Geneva Convention (III): *ibid.*

provided they carry arms openly and respect the laws and customs of war'.[86] They are required to respect LOAC but do not form part of the fighting forces of the State. It is not clear on what basis they are required to comply with the rules, unless it is simply seen as a *quid pro quo*: if they want POW war status, they must comply. They remain free to fight in a way inconsistent with the rules, but they will then be subject to prosecution, by any State with jurisdiction, for any killings they commit.

The situation of those involved in a *levée en masse* can be contrasted with that of mercenaries. The definition of mercenary in Article 47 of Additional Protocol I is so cumbersome, with its six cumulative elements, that any person ultimately found to be a mercenary should sue his lawyer. A person is not a mercenary if he fights for or on behalf of the armed forces of a State. This reflects the fact that, under international law, there is no nationality requirement for belonging to the armed forces of a State. The position under domestic law may be different. A State's domestic law may make it a domestic crime to fight for a State of which you are not a national or for any organised armed group. Article 47 does not preclude a mercenary from having combatant or POW status but just says that he does not have the right to such status.

The more important anomaly is found in common Article 3 of the Geneva Conventions, which applies to non-international armed conflicts. 'Each party to the conflict' is obliged to apply its provisions.[87] By definition, at least one of those parties is a non-State group.[88] How can a treaty create obligations for an entity which is not merely not a party to the treaty but not even a State? It should be remembered that the obligations in question concern rules on the protection of victims of war. They do not include rules on the conduct of hostilities. The provision applies automatically and not on the basis of reciprocity. The ICRC Commentary on this provision raises the question but does not answer it.[89] It must be emphasised that there is no disagreement as to the result. Both States and commentators accept that common Article 3 is

---

[86] Art. 2 of the Regulations annexed to 1907 Hague Convention (IV): *supra* n. 8. See, also, K. Del Mar, 'The Requirement of "Belonging" under International Humanitarian Law', *EJIL*, 21 (2010), 105–124.

[87] See, generally, L. Zegveld, *The Accountability of Armed Opposition Groups in International Law* (Cambridge: Cambridge University Press, 2002), pp. 9–18, and S. Sivakumaran, 'Binding Armed Opposition Groups', *ICLQ*, 55 (2006), 369–394.

[88] *Supra* n. 38.

[89] Pictet, *supra* n. 37, at p. 51. See, also, *Commentary on the First Geneva Convention*, *supra* n. 75 (paragraph 504) and, generally, S. Sivakumaran, *The Law of Non-International Armed Conflict* (Oxford: Oxford University Press, 2012).

binding on non-State parties to the conflict. The least unsatisfactory argument suggests that every State is required to ensure that effect is given to its international obligations. A ratifying State must therefore ensure that any potential non-State armed group would be bound by common Article 3. In the case of dualist States, this would require domestic legislation. In that case, the group would be bound by national, rather than international, law. The State might not introduce specific implementing legislation, on the grounds that the conduct in question was already unlawful under national law for unrelated reasons.[90] Again, that would mean that any organised armed group was bound by existing national law. It is submitted that there is no doubt that non-State parties to a NIAC are bound by common Article 3 but that it is wholly unclear how this outcome has been brought about.

Additional Protocol II manages to avoid referring to those bound by its provisions whilst setting out the rules applicable to the situation in which it applies.[91]

If non-State parties to armed conflicts are bound by common Article 3 of the Geneva Conventions, does this automatically mean that they have some measure of international legal personality?[92] One of the principal preoccupations of States in negotiating both common Article 3 and Additional Protocol II was that the imposition of obligations on non-State actors would affect their status and give them some form of legitimacy.[93] Common Article 3 states expressly that it does not affect the status of the parties to the conflict. It also encourages those parties to 'endeavour to bring into force, by means of special agreements, all or part

---

[90] J. E. Viñuales, 'The Sources of International Investment Law' in S. Besson and J. d'Aspremont (eds.), *The Oxford Handbook on the Sources of International Law* (Oxford: Oxford University Press, 2017), pp. 1069–1094 (esp. Section III.2–3).

[91] The only party to which reference is made is the High Contracting Party – i.e. a State.

[92] At customary law, there is a concept of recognition of belligerency. In a high intensity NIAC, there may come a point at which the territorial State and/or third States wish to define their position in relation to the non-State party. In the case of third parties, they may wish to be able to invoke rights as neutrals. The effect of such recognition is to internationalise the conflict as between the recognising party and the non-State party. That is not what is at issue in acknowledging that a non-State actor has obligations under common Art. 3 of the Geneva Conventions.

[93] See Pictet, *supra* n. 37, at pp. 60–61, and Y. Sandoz, C. Swinarski and B. Zimmermann (eds.), *Commentary on the Additional Protocols of 8 June 1977 to the Geneva Conventions of 12 August 1949* (Geneva: ICRC/Martinus Nijhoff, 1987), p. 1344. See, also, M. Bothe, K. J. Partsch and W. A. Solf, *New Rules for Victims of Armed Conflicts: Commentary on the Two 1977 Protocols Additional to the Geneva Conventions of 1949* (The Hague: Martinus Nijhoff, 1982), pp. 605–608 and 624–629.

of the other provisions of the present Convention'.[94] That implies some measure of recognised capacity as between the fighting parties but does not, or not necessarily, involve third States. It involves either the State which is party to the conflict or another, non-State, actor. If the agreement does no more than to make some or all of the provisions of the Convention applicable to the parties, each party will have the same obligation. Yet, this raises the possibility, however unlikely, that by agreement the parties might accept different obligations. It should be noted that two recent treaties in particular *affect* non-parties but do not attempt to *bind* them: the Ottawa Convention on Anti-Personnel Mines[95] and the 2008 Dublin/Oslo Convention on Cluster Munitions[96] are unusual amongst LOAC treaties in that they expressly address the obligations of parties working alongside non-parties. This presents challenges in multinational obligations.

4.3   Differentiated Obligations[97]

In some fields of international law, it is common to find different obligations or obligations of different scope ascribed to the parties, usually as a result of varying levels of development and/or resources.[98] At first sight,

---

[94] The armed conflicts in Bosnia-Herzegovina were marked by a plethora of such agreements. The ICTY treated such agreements as giving rise to legal obligations. Whether this will act as a disincentive for the conclusion of such agreements in future remains to be seen. For a more recent example, see C. Smith, 'Special Agreements to Apply the Geneva Conventions in Internal Armed Conflicts: the Lessons of Darfur', *Irish YbIL*, 2 (2007), 91–104. See, also, Art. 3 VCLT: *supra* n. 73, and, further, T. Grant, 'Who Can Make Treaties? Other Subjects of International Law' in Hollis (ed.), *supra* n. 68, pp. 125–149, at pp. 141–142, and O. Corten and P. Klein, 'Are Agreements between States and Non-State Entities Rooted in the International Legal Order?' in E. Cannizzaro (ed.), *The Law of Treaties beyond the Vienna Convention* (Oxford: Oxford University Press, 2011), pp. 3–24. In addition to agreements, organised armed groups may make unilateral commitments: S. Sivakumaran, 'Lessons for the Law of Armed Conflict from Commitments of Armed Groups: Identification of Legitimate Targets and Prisoners of War', *Int'l Rev. Red Cross*, 93 (2011), pp. 463–482. See, also, the website of Geneva Call, a non-governmental organization that works with such groups to deliver unilateral commitments: www .genevacall.org/.

[95] *Supra* n. 57.   [96] *Supra* n. 59.

[97] See, generally, the contribution to this volume of Bowman at pp. 392–439 (Chapter 13).

[98] Environmental law is the obvious example: see, for example, Principle 7 of the Rio Declaration on Environment and Development ('States shall cooperate in a spirit of global partnership to conserve, protect and restore the health and integrity of the Earth's ecosystem. In view of the different contributions to global environmental degradation, States have common but differentiated responsibilities. The developed countries acknowledge the responsibility that they bear in the international pursuit to sustainable

this is fundamentally inconsistent with a basic customary principle of LOAC: the equality of belligerents.[99] The rules of IAC apply in the same way to the parties, even where one party has acted in violation of the *ius ad bellum*. That just serves to establish the clear distinction between the *ius ad bellum* and the *ius in bello*. In addition, it has long been accepted that, legally speaking, the parties are equal, having the same rights and obligations. That remains the case even where one party is much better resourced and equipped than the other. It is a reflection of the sovereign equality of States.[100]

The principle of equality of belligerents gives rise to real problems in the case of NIACs. First, as a matter of *domestic* law, the parties are not equal. The organised armed group may not commit an *international* crime by targeting the armed forces of the State or of another organised armed group, but its members are likely to commit a domestic crime. It could be charged as murder or even as treason. Mere membership of the group may be unlawful. At the same time, States are unwilling to accept *international* obligations which are not similarly binding on the other side. Common Article 3 is so rudimentary that it does not raise a problem with differentiated obligations. Additional Protocol II, with one possible exception, gives rise to the same result. Article 6 provides for penal prosecution of offences related to the conflict. It requires that proceedings be conducted before a court. It does not require that the

development in view of the pressures their societies place on the global environment and of the technologies and financial resources they command'). See, further, D. French and L. Rajamani, 'Global Responsibility, Differentiation, and An Environmental Rule of Law?' OUPBlog (22 Apr. 2014) (http://blog.oup.com/2014/04/global-responsibility-differentiation-environmental-rule-of-law-pil/) as well as the contribution to this volume of French and Scott at pp. 677–709 (Chapter 21).

[99] A. Roberts, 'The Equal Application of the Laws of War: A Principle under Pressure', *Int'l Rev. Red Cross*, 90 (2008), 931–962.

[100] There is one provision in Additional Protocol I which suggests that the principle may need to be qualified: Art. 54(5) permits a State to take action – a 'scorched earth' policy – in national territory and only in defence against invasion which it cannot undertake anywhere else: *supra* n. 5. This was included at the insistence of one State (France) which had experience of invasion. It is submitted that this is merely one of those 'blips' that occurs during the process of negotiation and does not undermine the general principle. It should be noted that the inclusion of the exception is significant support for the claim that the provisions of Additional Protocol I generally apply both outside and within the State's own territory. Otherwise, there would have been no need for the scorched earth exception. This shows that the rules on the conduct of hostilities are not just designed to protect foreign persons and territory. This is not sufficient to make the Hague rules objective in character but does suggest that there may be objective elements within those rules.

court be lawfully constituted, which would be impossible for the organised armed group but does require that the court offer essential guarantees of independence and impartiality. This will be challenging but not impossible for many organised armed groups.

One particular treaty, from outside the field of LOAC, has created differentiated obligations within LOAC. The 2000 Optional Protocol to the Convention on the Rights of the Child on the Involvement of Children in Armed Conflict[101] imposes different obligations on States and non-State parties. Under Article 4 of the Optional Protocol, armed groups should neither recruit nor use persons under eighteen years of age. States, on the other hand, are merely required under Article 1 to take all feasible measures to ensure that members of their armed forces under eighteen years of age do not take part in hostilities. That makes voluntary recruitment acceptable, on condition that those recruited do not take part in hostilities until they reach the age of eighteen. This raises a broader question of treaty law. Who is responsible for addressing the fact that a treaty rule in one area of international law may have and be designed to have an impact in a different area? Is it just up to States to harmonise their obligations and to make sure that the relevant constituencies are consulted, or is there an international law requirement that such consultations be carried out? It is possible, if not probable, that in many countries Foreign Ministries do not consult the armed forces before negotiating treaties which do not appear to be in the area of the law of armed conflict.

The possibility of differentiated obligations may have arisen not as a result of LOAC itself but as a result of the combined impact of LOAC and human rights law. In a NIAC, the State will have human rights obligations, possibly modified by derogation, as well as LOAC obligations. The non-State actor will not have human rights obligations but is increasingly seen as required to respect human rights principles.[102]

There may also be an issue of differentiated obligations in the case of customary LOAC rules applicable in NIACs. The more specific the alleged rule and the more it depends on the existence of a State-like infrastructure, the harder it will be for a non-State actor to comply. If equality of belligerents is to be preserved in NIACs as a matter of

---

[101] 2173 UNTS 222.

[102] The more that a non-State actor controls territory and exercises governmental functions, the more likely it is that human rights bodies will act as though it has obligations. Even where that is not the case, it is expected to respect human rights principles, as opposed to being found in violation of human rights rules. See, generally, D. Murray, *Human Rights Obligations of Non-State Armed Groups* (Oxford: Hart Publishing, 2016).

international law, even though as shown earlier it does not exist at the domestic level, it will inhibit the development of rules which the State is capable of applying. If, on the other hand, the test is what rules a State can respect, it will result in the adoption of rules which the non-State actor is, in many cases, incapable of applying.[103]

One area where differentiated obligations are virtually inevitable is in the field of enforcement. This will be discussed further in Section 4.7.

4.4   Reservations[104]

Until the advisory opinion of the ICJ in *Reservations to the Convention on the Prevention and Punishment of the Crime of Genocide* in May 1951,[105] the rule on reservations was that, unless the treaty provided otherwise, all States Parties had to accept a reservation before the reserving State could be regarded as a party.[106] There was no need to justify the objection – for example, by claiming that the reservation was incompatible with the object and purpose of the treaty. There was also no need to determine the effect of a reservation as between the reserving and objecting State. If the reservation was not accepted, the former did not become a party to the treaty unless it withdrew the reservation. In the case, the Court put considerable emphasis on the nature of the treaty in question: the Genocide Convention had a universalist goal and purpose in the sense that as wide a participation as possible was necessary to secure universal condemnation and co-operation. The treaty had a 'purely humanitarian and civilizing purpose', in the words of the Court.[107]

---

[103] M. Sassòli and Y. Shany, 'Should the Obligations of States and Armed Groups under International Humanitarian Law Really be Equal?', *Int'l Rev. Red Cross*, 93 (2011), 425–436, and R. Provost, 'The Move to Substantive Equality in International Humanitarian Law: A Rejoinder to Marco Sassòli and Yuval Shany', *Int'l Rev. Red Cross*, 93 (2011), 437–442.

[104] International Law Commission, *Guide to Practice on Reservations to Treaties*, UNGAOR Sixty-Sixth Session, Supp. No. 10 (2011). See, further, A. Pellet, 'Article 19 (1969)' in O. Corten and P. Klein (eds.), *The Vienna Conventions on the Law of Treaties: A Commentary* (Vol. I) (Oxford: Oxford University Press, 2011), pp. 405–482; D. Müller, 'Article 20 (1969)' *ibid.*, pp. 489–534, and D. Müller, 'Article 21 (1969)' *ibid.*, pp. 538–564.

[105] *Reservations to the Convention on the Prevention and Punishment of the Crime of Genocide* (Advisory Opinion) (1951) ICJ Rep. 15.

[106] The majority of the Court pointed out that the old understanding was 'directly inspired by the notion of contract': *ibid.*, at p. 21.

[107] *Ibid.*, at p. 23.

The only restriction to the making of reservations proposed by the majority was that the reservation had to be compatible with the object and purpose of the treaty. It was left to the International Law Commission to work out the practical implications of the case. The result finds expression in Articles 19–21 of the Vienna Convention on the Law of Treaties (VCLT).[108] It appears to put all the cards into the hands of the reserving State. Articles 20 and 21 deal with the consequences of an objection to a reservation. The provisions do not address expressly the consequences where the basis for the objection is that the reservation is incompatible with the object and purpose of the treaty. The objecting State has to decide what effects will flow from the reservation; silence will be deemed to be assent. The objecting State can accept the entry into force of the treaty with the reserving State but exclude the provision to which the reservation relates or it can oppose the entry into force of the treaty between the two States. There is no explicit reference to the possibility of severance of the reservation, even if it is inconsistent with the object and purpose of the treaty and, as such, is not a valid reservation.

In the past twenty years, the issue of reservations has become more controversial.[109] The main problems appeared to arise in the field of human rights law for a range of reasons. First, certain States had made vague but sweeping reservations at the time of ratification.[110] Second, many of the treaties have independent monitoring mechanisms. These entities of uncertain status in public international law needed to know how to handle such reservations.[111] Of what significance for their own

---

[108] *Supra* n. 73.

[109] See the contribution to this volume of Chinkin at pp. 509–537 (Chapter 16) and, also, C. Redgwell, 'Universality or Integrity? Some Reflections on Reservations to General Multilateral Treaties', 64 (1993), *BYbIL*, 245–282, and Çali, *supra* n. 68, at pp. 533–537. See, further, Z. Elibol and B. Çali, 'The ILC's Clever Compromise on the Validity of Reservations to Treaties: A Rejoinder to Marko Milanovic and Linos-Alexandre Sicilianos', EJIL:Talk!, 11 Apr. 2014.

[110] For example, some States ratified the 1979 Convention on the Elimination of Discrimination against Women, 1249 UNTS 13, with a reservation along the lines of 'subject to compatibility with Sharia law': see F. Hampson, 'Expanded Working Paper on the Question of Reservations to Human Rights Treaties', prepared in accordance with UNHRC Sub-Commission Decision 2001/17 (8 Aug. 2003): U.N. Doc. E/CN.4/Sub.2/2003/WP.2.

[111] General international law has not kept pace with the development, particularly since 1945, of a wide range of judicial or quasi-judicial mechanisms or bodies which include judicial or quasi-judicial functions. They exist in many fields of international law, not just human rights law. Can they contribute to the identification or even the creation of

deliberations was the acceptance by States of the reservations in question? In the case of the Human Rights Committee, it had to address the issue in order to exercise its functions. In relation to individual petition, it has to determine whether it has jurisdiction. The validity or effectiveness of a reservation could determine the question.[112] Where a human rights body determines that a reservation is incompatible with the object and purpose of the treaty, and is therefore not a legitimate reservation under the VCLT, what is it able to do about it? Faced with that question, the European Court of Human Rights had severed the invalid reservation. Human rights law and human rights bodies were seen as posing a challenge to the VCLT regime,[113] which appeared to put all the cards into the hands of the reserving State.

What is remarkable is that precisely this question had already arisen between States in relation to LOAC, but this had not been commented upon. Albania, the Byelorussian Soviet Socialist Republic, the People's Republic of China, the Democratic People's Republic of Korea, the Ukrainian Soviet Socialist Republic and the Union of Soviet Socialist Republics (USSR) all made the same reservation to Article 85 of Geneva Convention (III): POWs convicted of war crimes or crimes against humanity were to be treated in the same way as persons convicted in the country in question.[114] In other words, upon conviction, they would lose their status as POWs. The United Kingdom, Australia and New Zealand stated that they were 'unable to accept' the reservation. Whilst they 'regard all the above-mentioned states as being parties to the above-mentioned Conventions, they do not regard the above-mentioned reservations thereto made by those states as valid, and will therefore regard any application of any of those reservations as constituting a breach of the Convention to which the reservation relates'.[115] The last phrase represents severance of the invalid reservation, since they proposed to apply the provision without regard to the reservation. It should be noted that all

---

customary law? How authoritative are their interpretations of the treaties from which they derive their mandates?

[112] *Rawle Kennedy v. Trinidad and Tobago*, 845/1999, Admissibility Decision of 2 Nov. 1999 (paragraphs 6.6–6.7); see, also, Human Rights Committee, General Comment No. 24: Issues Relating to Reservations made upon Ratification or Accession to the Covenant or the Optional Protocols thereto, or in Relation to Declarations under Article 41 of the Covenant, U.N. Doc. CCPR/C/21/Rev.1/Add.6, 11 Apr. 1994.

[113] See, further, *supra* n. 104.   [114] Roberts and Guelff (eds.), *supra* n. 12, at pp. 362–369.

[115] Roberts and Guelff (eds.), *supra* n. 12, at p. 363 (Albania and Australia); p. 364 (Byelorussian SSR etc.); p. 366 (New Zealand) and p. 367 (United Kingdom).

three responses were made prior to the adoption of the VCLT.[116] The USSR and the other States affected contested the validity of the statement.[117]

There are a range of other, less controversial, reservations to the Geneva Conventions. In other words, there is no objection in principle to such reservations. Additional Protocol I has also attracted reservations and, in this case, they were made after the adoption of the VCLT. As far as the author is aware, no State has objected to a reservation on the grounds of incompatibility with the object and purpose of the Protocol.[118] As was mentioned previously, the United Kingdom made a qualified and very precisely drafted reservation to the prohibition of belligerent reprisals against civilians and the civilian population. Italy and a range of other States made what was claimed to be a statement of interpretation of Delphic obscurity. It stated: 'Italy will react to serious and systematic violations by an enemy of the obligations imposed by Additional Protocol I and in particular its Articles 51 and 52 [protection of the civilian population and of civilian property] with all means admissible under international law in order to prevent any further violation'.[119] This looks as though it is intended to be a reservation to the prohibition of belligerent reprisals. No State has, to the knowledge of the author, reacted to the reservations/statements of interpretation in question.

It would appear that reservations pose a similar type of challenge in LOAC as in human rights law. It should be noted that the objection of the United Kingdom to the Soviet reservation concerned a provision relating to the protection of victims of war. The United Kingdom's own reservation concerned a provision dealing with the conduct of hostilities. Reciprocity, and therefore the possibility of belligerent reprisals, may play a different role in that area of LOAC.

A particular difficulty has arisen in human rights law in determining with what a reservation must not be incompatible. Article 19 VCLT speaks of object and purpose in the singular. Can a treaty

---

[116] Which, according to Art. 4 VCLT, shall not apply retroactively; see, also, Art. 28 VCLT: *supra* n. 73.

[117] C. Pilloud, 'Reservations to the Geneva Conventions of 1949', *Int'l Rev. Red Cross*, 16 (1976), 107–124, and 16 (1976), 163–187.

[118] J. Gaudreau, 'The Reservations to the Protocols Additional to the Geneva Conventions for the Protection of War Victims', *Int'l Rev. Red Cross*, 85 (2003), 143–184.

[119] Roberts and Guelff (eds.), *supra* n. 12, at p. 507 (Italy: Reservation (H)); for the reservation of the United Kingdom, see *ibid.*, at p. 511. See, also, Henckaerts and Doswald-Beck, *supra* n. 34.

have only one object or purpose?[120] If so, it risks being defined with such a degree of generality as to afford little guidance and to leave a wide discretion to a decision-maker. If the singular object of a human rights treaty were the protection of the human person, would that not suggest that no reservations should be acceptable? Is it not better to have a State as a party, even with some reservations? In part, this depends on whether a treaty can have only one object or purpose and how that is defined. For example, would a reservation permitting a State to criminalise homosexuality be incompatible with the singular object and purpose of the International Covenant on Civil and Political Rights as a whole or the objects and purposes of the treaty in the plural or the object and purpose of the protection of the home and family life? If there were several objects and purposes, it might be easier to determine whether a reservation was incompatible with one of them.

The same problem arises with the law of armed conflict but in a less acute fashion. It is submitted that there are specific provisions that are less central to the overall object than others. Nevertheless, it is necessary to determine the possibly controversial question of the object and purpose of LOAC treaties. The object of rules on the conduct of hostilities is to strike a balance between military necessity and humanitarian considerations, with a tilt in the direction of military necessity. The object of the rules on the protection of victims is arguably not the protection of victims *simpliciter* but the protection of victims, taking account of military necessity. In this field, there is a tilt towards humanitarian considerations. If it were necessary to merge these slightly different objects in order to form a single object or purpose, it would have to be something like 'to strike a balance between military necessity and humanitarian considerations'. It would be difficult to obtain guidance from such a broad and vague formulation. This is not the place to enter into a discussion of what the law ought to be. It is submitted that there is a need to take account of both the object and purpose of the article to which a reservation has been made, the object(s) and purposes(s) of the treaty as a whole and the relationship between the two.

---

[120] D. S. Jonas and T. N. Saunders, 'The Object and Purpose of a Treaty: Three Interpretive Methods', *Vanderbilt JTL*, 43 (2010), 565–609. See, also, the contribution to this volume of Kritsiotis at pp. 237–302 (Chapter 9).

4.5   Consequences of Material Breach[121]

The general rule is contained in Article 60(1) VCLT: 'A material breach of a bilateral treaty by one of the parties entitles the other to invoke the breach as a ground for terminating the treaty or suspending its operation in whole or in part'.[122] Article 60(5) VCLT, however, provides that the normal rule does 'not apply to provisions relating to the protection of the human person contained in treaties of a humanitarian character, in particular to provisions prohibiting any form of reprisals against persons protected by such treaties'.[123] It will be remembered that, at the time when the VCLT was adopted, the two strands of LOAC were contained in separate treaties. Paragraph 5 of Article 60 VCLT was clearly a reference to IHL treaties, that is to say those on the protection of victims of war. That is reinforced by the reference to belligerent reprisals in the 1949 Geneva Conventions, which are prohibited against each category of protected person in the four treaties. No State has objected to those prohibitions of belligerent reprisals.

Article 60(5) VCLT strengthens the argument that the Geneva Conventions contain 'inherent' obligations or 'obligations of an objective character'. It is not clear whether the same consequence flows as is said to flow from the similar character of human rights obligations. It is said that States cannot rely on the basis of reciprocity on the reservation of other States, as would normally be the case, where the treaty is of such a character.[124] It is submitted that these two consequences of a particular type of treaty are dramatic. That suggests that it is worth

---

[121] B. Simma and C. J. Tams, 'Reacting against Treaty Breaches' in Hollis (ed.), *supra* n. 68, pp. 576–604, especially at pp. 587–588.

[122] *Supra* n. 73.

[123] *Ibid.* Simma and Tams, *supra* n. 121, indicate that this was intended to cover both international humanitarian law and human rights treaties: at p. 587 (fn. 57).

[124] *France, Norway, Denmark, Sweden, the Netherlands v. Turkey*, 9940–9944/82 (joined), ECommHR, Admissibility Decision of 6 Dec. 1983 (paragraphs 35–43): 'The Commission finds that the general principle of reciprocity in international law and the rule, stated in Article 21, para. I of the Vienna Convention on the Law of Treaties, concerning bilateral relations under a multilateral treaty do not apply to the obligations under the European Convention on Human Rights' and '[t]he Commission further recalls that the enforcement machinery provided for in the Convention is founded upon the system of 'a collective guarantee by the High Contracting Parties of the rights and freedoms set forth in the Convention', and that a High Contracting Party, when referring an alleged breach of the Convention to the Commission under Art. 24, 'is not to be regarded as exercising a right of action for the purpose of enforcing its own rights, but rather as bringing before the Commission an alleged violation of the public order of Europe' [*Austria v. Italy, supra* n. 71].

distinguishing between different types of treaties, if only to know when these consequences apply. It is not clear whether the results apply to the treaties in question as a whole or whether they can be restricted to only certain provisions. It is not clear that rules on the conduct of hostilities have the same character. This will be important in relation to those provisions of Additional Protocols I and II which apply to the protection of victims of war.

4.6   Interpretation[125]

Certain features of LOAC apply to both strands of the rules and distinguish IHL from human rights law. Others apply differently to the two strands.

4.6.1   Common Features

LOAC rules give rise to rights and obligations of parties to conflicts, rather than individual rights and responsibilities. The obligations of the party in whose control you are depends on the group to which you belong: civilian, combatant, wounded and sick, shipwrecked, POW or civilian in the power of the opposing belligerent. They are based on a balance between military necessity and humanitarian considerations.[126] That balance is tilted towards military necessity in the case of rules on the conduct of hostilities. This is illustrated by the acceptance of a measure of 'collateral casualties'. The balance is tilted towards humanitarian considerations in the case of rules on the protection of victims. In both cases, however, the rules represent a balance.

4.6.2   Rules on the Protection of Victims

The rules either require certain conduct or prohibit certain behaviour. They are not quite obligations of result, but if the prohibited result happens, the detaining power will have a lot of explaining to do. For example, if a POW dies, the Detaining Power will have to carry out an investigation, so as to be able to reassure the State of nationality and the Protecting Power (if any) that the death occurred naturally and was not as a result of any failing on its part.[127] There are echoes here of the

---

[125] Gardiner, *supra* n. 45; R. Gardiner, 'The Vienna Convention Rules on Treaty Interpretation' in Hollis (ed.), *supra* n. 68, pp. 475–506, and Çali, *supra* n. 68.

[126] A. Rogers, *Law on the Battlefield* (Manchester: Manchester University Press, 3rd ed., 2012), p. 3. See, also, US Department of Defense, *Law of War Manual, supra* n. 6, at p. 51.

[127] Art. 121 of Geneva Convention (III): *supra* n. 4.

approach of human rights law. In effect, the Detaining Power has not only a negative obligation to respect but a positive obligation to protect, all the time taking account of the context in which the activities are occurring. It is not clear whether there is any presumption in favour of protection in the interpretation of the rules. It is submitted that that would be inappropriate. The rules as they stand represent the agreed balance. That balance already takes account of the need for protection in the case of IHL rules. It should be remembered that the rules on the protection of victims principally apply away from the active battlefield.[128] The obligations do not significantly obstruct the conduct of hostilities, beyond requiring the necessary resources and planning. For that reason, it is possible to give more emphasis to protection in the rules themselves.

4.6.3   Rules on the Conduct of Hostilities

These rules are drafted in a completely different way. They are addressed to the mind of the military planner and commander at the time of the operation, and they tell him of what he has to take account and how. For that reason, they do not prohibit certain outcomes, except in the baldest terms.[129] They are not designed to be applied after the event, in the light of the result. They are designed to be applied at the time the attack occurs, and this must be taken into account in any subsequent determination as to existence of a violation. This has huge implications for enforcement and the finding of violation. Where the result of an attack is twenty dead civilians and a ruined home, it is not possible to determine on that basis alone whether a violation of the rules has occurred. It is not even possible to say that 'there is a violation unless . . . '. In order to find a violation, it is necessary to know what was targeted, for what reason, on the basis of what intelligence and using what weapons. It could be that the basement of the house was used as a command and control centre. It could be that the attacking force had no knowledge and could not be expected to have knowledge of the presence of the civilians. It could be that the attack killed thirty members of the opposing armed forces and took out an important communications facility. In that case, even if the death of the twenty civilians was foreseen, it might not have been excessive in relation to the direct and concrete military advantage anticipated. Or the attack

---

[128] Except for some of the rules on the treatment of the wounded and sick in Geneva Convention (I) and those provisions of Geneva Convention (III) which apply at the point of capture of the POW: *supra* n. 4.

[129] For example, the prohibition of targeting (i.e. launching an attack against, rather than simply causing harm to) civilians.

might have been based on faulty intelligence, where the attacking force could not reasonably have known that the intelligence was flawed. Or, again, the weapon may have misfired. Mistakes and material mistakes of fact occur in war as in other areas of the law. The rules work not by prohibiting an outcome but by identifying what needs to be taken into account. There is no scope for interpreting the rules in a way that favours protection. The rules have to be interpreted as they stand because they already represent the agreed balance.[130]

This suggests that there is no room for a 'living instrument' approach to interpretation. There is more scope for an interpretation favouring the object and purpose of the treaty in the case of provisions on the protection of victims, but even that has to respect the balance found in the rules and not create what are, in effect, new obligations. This gives rise to challenges either where the rules create a general framework but without specific details or where the rules do not address an issue at all.[131]

In exceptional cases, it may be that a subsequent rule of customary law and/or subsequent practice under a treaty totally displaces the original rule.[132] This is not the LOAC equivalent of the 'living instrument' doctrine found in human rights law. States are probably the only entities which can generate State practice: it is not open to a judge or decision-maker to 'discover' it. The application of the 'living instrument' doctrine

---

[130] This has sometimes proved a challenge to bodies more used to a more teleological approach to interpretation. *The Report of the United Nations Fact-Finding Mission on the Gaza Conflict* (the Goldstone Report), for example, reached conclusions as to the commission of war crimes where it knew the result of an attack but cannot have known what it needed to know to reach such a conclusion: A/HRC/12/48 (25 Sept. 2009). The *Report of the Detailed Findings of the Independent Commission of Inquiry established pursuant to Human Rights Council Resolution S-21/1* was much more nuanced: A/HRC/29/CRP.4 (24 June 2015).

[131] For example, Art. 109 of Geneva Convention (III) provides that the Detaining Power has the obligation to repatriate seriously wounded and seriously sick POWs: *supra* n. 4. It is not a right of a POW. The POW only has the right to object to repatriation during the conflict, under Art. 109(3). Nevertheless, the Working Group on Arbitrary Detention, in its United Nations Basic Principles and Guidelines on Remedies and Procedures on the Right of Anyone Deprived of their Liberty to bring Proceedings before a Court requires States to Provide POWs with a Right of Access to a Court to Challenge their Non-repatriation: A/HRC/30 (June 2015).

[132] Art. 118 of Geneva Convention (III) provides that POWs shall be released and repatriated without delay after the cessation of active hostilities: *supra* n. 4. This appears to create an obligation on the Detaining Power to repatriate POWs even against their will. State practice has so modified the rule that it is now possible for POWs to refuse repatriation. See, generally, the contribution to this volume of Buga at pp. 363–391 (Chapter 12).

may fly in the face of State practice and may, over time, change that practice.

In the case of rules on the conduct of hostilities, the rules have to be interpreted in the light of their ordinary meaning. In some cases, this may require special meaning to be given to technical terms.[133] Subsequent practice may be an important source of clarification.

There are real challenges in attempting to determine how LOAC rules are interpreted. First, there is a lack of authoritative judicial pronouncements. The ICJ rarely deals with cases which depend on the interpretation of the rules.[134] International criminal tribunals may shed light on the content of a LOAC rule, but they are interpreting a rule of international criminal law, even if it is one derived from LOAC.[135] Most of the interpretation of LOAC happens outside a judicial context. It is done by States. Military manuals provide an indication of how the State understands its legal obligations, but they are also based on policy considerations.[136] When interpreting a LOAC rule in a specific situation, the State's interpretation is likely to be self-interested rather than authoritative.[137] The ICRC is well placed to be more authoritative than most in its interpretations, but that depends on whether a particular interpretation is accepted by States.[138] It is for these reasons that the approach adopted in this chapter has been to derive the balance between

---

[133] Many of the terms used in Additional Protocol I have special meanings. Generally, the Protocol defines such terms (e.g. perfidy, ruses of war, combatants), but some are left undefined (e.g. military advantage): *supra* n. 5.

[134] In *Case Concerning Armed Activities in the Territory of the Congo*, there were no difficulties of interpretation: *supra* n. 66. Once the facts had been found, they represented a very clear violation of Art. 51 of Protocol I.

[135] For example, the test for the war crime of carrying out an indiscriminate attack in an IAC under the Rome State is that the civilian casualties were *clearly* excessive in relation to the military advantage anticipated: see Art. 8(2)(b)(iv) (emphasis added): *supra* n. 62. The LOAC test is excessive: Arts. 51(5)(b) and 57(2)(a)(iii) and (b) of Additional Protocol I: *supra* n. 5. It is understandable that war crimes are defined more narrowly than violations of LOAC. There is a real danger of distorting LOAC if international criminal law interpretations replace the express words of LOAC treaties.

[136] *Supra* n. 6.

[137] *International Humanitarian Law and the Challenges of Contemporary Armed Conflicts*, Document prepared by the ICRC for the 30th International Conference of the Red Cross and Red Crescent, Geneva, Switzerland, 26–30 Nov. 2007. See, also, *Int'l Rev. Red Cross*, 89 (2007), 719–757, at 720.

[138] For example, N. Melzer, *Interpretive Guidance on the Notion of Direct Participation in Hostilities under International Humanitarian Law* (Geneva: ICRC, 2009) attracted a good deal of criticism from military legal advisers of States: see the special issue of the *N.Y.U. J. Int'l L. & Pol.*, 42 (2010), 637–916.

ordinary meaning and an object and purpose approach to interpretation from the actual content of the treaty provisions.

LOAC contains as many areas of dispute between authentic texts in different languages as any other area of law. The phrase that has now become accepted in English as 'superfluous injury or unnecessary suffering' is the result of early treaty language which sometimes translated the French 'maux superflus' as superfluous injury and sometimes as unnecessary suffering![139] The text of Additional Protocol I is equally authentic in Arabic, Chinese, English, French, Russian and Spanish.[140] In English and French, the definition of a military objective is 'objects which by their nature, location purpose or use make an effective contribution to military action *and* whose total or partial destruction, capture or neutralization, in the circumstances ruling at the time, offers a definite military advantage' (emphasis added).[141] In the Spanish authentic text, the author believes that 'and' is rendered as 'or'.[142] The English text of Article 86(2) of Additional Protocol I provides for the responsibility of commanders for the acts of subordinates if 'they knew, or had information which should have enabled them to conclude' that the subordinate was committing or was going to commit a breach of the Conventions or Protocol.[143] The French text provides for responsibility 's'ils savaient ou possédaient des informations leur permettant de conclure'. In English, that would be 'if they knew or had information permitting them to conclude'.

It is submitted that, as a result of the way in which the relevant provisions are drafted and of the internal coherence of the two sub-fields of LOAC, provisions on the conduct of hostilities need to be interpreted in a significantly different way from those on the protection of victims. In the case of the former, more emphasis needs to be given to the terms of the treaty. In the case of the latter, there is more – albeit

---

[139] See, generally, Roberts and Guelff (eds.), *supra* n. 12, at p. 77 (fn. 3).

[140] Roberts and Guelff (eds.), *supra* n. 12, at p. 422.

[141] Art. 52(2) of Additional Protocol I: *supra* n. 5.

[142] 'Los ataques se limitarán estrictamente a los objetivos militares. En lo que respecta a los bienes, los objetivos militares se limitan a aquellos objetos que por su naturaleza, ubicación, finalidad o utilización contribuyan eficazmente a la acción militar *o* cuya destrucción total o parcial, captura o neutralización ofrezca en las circunstancias del caso una ventaja militar definida' (emphasis added). The Spanish Military Manual refers to the cumulative test, but it is understood that certain Central and Latin American military manuals refer to the alternative test. See, further, A. Jachec-Neale, *The Concept of Military Objectives in International Law and Targeting Practice* (London: Routledge, 2014), pp. 112–115.

[143] *Supra* n. 5.

limited – scope to take account of the object and purpose of the treaty. The object and purpose of the two types of provisions are slightly different and require that a different balance be achieved in balancing the different elements in the interpretation of the rules. It is not clear that human rights bodies are aware of the distinction in this regard between the two strands of LOAC.

4.7 Enforcement

The implementation and enforcement regime of the principal LOAC treaties applicable in IACs is unusual, partly as a result of the nature of the acts which constitute violations of the treaties. In many, but not all, cases, they constitute international crimes. It should nevertheless be remembered that LOAC itself is civil in nature.

1907 Hague Convention (IV) provides for implementation rather than enforcement. It states that '[t]he Contracting Powers shall issue instructions to their armed land forces which shall be in conformity with the Regulations respecting the laws and customs of war on land, annexed to the present Convention'.[144] It recognises, too, that '[a] belligerent party which violates the provisions of the said Regulations shall, if the case demands, be liable to pay compensation. It shall be responsible for all acts committed by persons forming part of its armed forces'.[145] It does not, however, provide for enforcement by the State in relation to violations committed by members of its own armed forces.

The 1949 Geneva Conventions were much more ambitious. There are identical provisions, *mutatis mutandis*, in the four Conventions. With regard to dissemination, there is an obligation 'in time of peace as in time of war, to disseminate the text of the present Convention as widely as possible in their respective countries, and, in particular, to include the study thereof in their programmes of military and, if possible, civil instruction, so that the principles thereof may become known to the entire population, in particular to the armed fighting forces, the medical personnel and the chaplains'.[146] Provision is also made for the conduct of an enquiry where one party alleged a violation by another party.[147] The Conventions divide violations into 'grave breaches' and other violations of the Conventions. The grave breaches listed in the Geneva

---

[144] Art. 1 of 1907 Hague Convention (IV): *supra* n. 8.
[145] Art. 3 of 1907 Hague Convention (IV): *supra* n. 8.
[146] Art. 47 of Geneva Convention (I): *supra* n. 4.
[147] Art. 52 of Geneva Convention (I): *supra* n. 4.

Conventions are defined in each of the four treaties. In relation to grave breaches, States are required to enact legislation to enable the punishment of such violations. States are 'under the obligation to search for persons alleged to have committed or to have ordered to be committed, such grave breaches, and shall bring such persons, regardless of their nationality, before its own courts'.[148] This represents the only case known to the author of universal mandatory jurisdiction. It is qualified by the provision that the State could, if it preferred, 'hand such persons over for trial to another High Contracting Party concerned, provided such High Contracting Party has made out a *prima facie* case'.[149] It is submitted that 'You must unless . . .' is a more onerous obligation than *aut dedere aut punire*.

In the case of all other violations of the Conventions – including, therefore, presumably violations of common Article 3 – States 'shall take measures necessary for the suppression of all acts contrary to the provisions of the present Convention'.[150] Suppression does not necessarily involve criminal proceedings, but it does require an investigation to determine whether there is a violation which needs to be suppressed and measures to put an end to the violation.

Additional Protocol I combines features of the regime in Hague Convention (IV) and the Geneva Conventions. States 'shall give orders and instructions to ensure observance of the Conventions and this Protocol, and shall supervise their execution'.[151] As part of the regime for the implementation of the Protocol, legal advisers are to be made available at the appropriate level to advise military commanders.[152] Again, there is a provision on dissemination, not only to the armed forces but also to the civilian population.[153] There is also a provision on the payment of compensation for violations.[154] The Protocol also develops the rules on enforcement found in the Geneva Conventions. It adds to the list of grave breaches, including certain violations of the rules on the conduct of hostilities.[155] It maintains the distinction between 'grave breaches' and all other violations, which, the Protocol provides, have to

---

[148] Art. 49 of Geneva Convention (I): *supra* n. 4.   [149] *Ibid.*
[150] Common Art. 49(3)/50(3)/129(3)/146(3) of Geneva Conventions (I), (II), (III) and (IV) respectively: *supra* n. 4.
[151] Art. 80 of Additional Protocol I: *supra* n. 5.
[152] Art. 82 of Additional Protocol I: *supra* n. 5.
[153] Art. 83 of Additional Protocol I: *supra* n. 5.
[154] Art. 91 of Additional Protocol I: *supra* n. 5.
[155] Art. 85 of Additional Protocol I: *supra* n. 5.

be 'suppressed'.[156] A commander bears legal or disciplinary responsibility where he knows or ought to know that a violation is being committed or is about to be committed and does nothing to prevent it.[157] This represents a specific articulation of an obligation to prevent. Article 87 (headed 'Duty of Commanders') is the flip side of this obligation: the State must ensure that the commanders prevent or suppress violations.[158] There is also provision for mutual assistance in criminal matters.[159] Two issues are not reflected in Additional Protocol I but are to be found in the Rome Statute: the responsibility of a commander for the acts of his subordinates and the defence of superior orders.[160] The Protocol also introduces the possibility of independent fact-finding.[161] The jurisdiction of the International Humanitarian Fact-Finding Commission (IHFFC) has to be accepted separately. It can be invoked not only by an opposing belligerent but by any other State that has accepted the jurisdiction of the IHFFC. In that regard, it resembles the provision for inter-State complaints before human rights bodies, which are not confined to States which claim to be the victim of the alleged violation.[162] The IHFFC has never yet been called upon to exercise its *ex officio* functions.

The framework for implementation and enforcement is less developed in the case of NIACs. The provision on the suppression of all violations which are not 'grave breaches' presumably applies to common Article 3 of the Geneva Conventions.[163] Violations of that article cannot constitute 'grave breaches' as the latter are defined in terms of protected persons, a category which only exists in IACs. Protocol II does not even contain that much. The only provision on implementation and enforcement is one on dissemination which simply states that '[t]he Protocol shall be as widely disseminated as possible'.[164] Since then, the Rome Statute has criminalised violations of common Article 3 and identified a number of international crimes in NIACs, including ones relating to the conduct of hostilities.[165] The list is less long than in the case of IACs. The lack of alternative, LOAC-specific forms of redress for violations may explain why, in recent years, there has been a trend towards using human rights

---

[156] Art. 86(1) of Additional Protocol I: *supra* n. 5.
[157] Art. 86(2) of Additional Protocol I: *supra* n. 5.
[158] Art. 87(3) of Additional Protocol I: *supra* n. 5.
[159] Art. 88 of Additional Protocol I: *supra* n. 5.
[160] Arts. 28 and 33 of Rome Statute: *supra* n. 62.
[161] Art. 90 of Additional Protocol I: *supra* n. 5.
[162] For example, the case referred to *supra* n. 124.   [163] *Supra* n. 4.
[164] Art. 19 of Additional Protocol II: *supra* n. 5.
[165] Art. 8(2)(c) and (e) of Rome Statute: *supra* n. 62.

machinery to obtain redress for what are violations of both human rights law and LOAC, where that is a possibility. This can only be done where the alleged perpetrator belongs to the State and not to an organised armed group.

The regime for implementation and enforcement, at least in the case of IACs, is unusual as compared to many other areas of civil (i.e. non-criminal) international law. It more closely resembles that associated with international criminal law treaties, including ones dealing with specific crimes. The regime envisages implementation of the rules and prevention of violations. It also requires domestic criminal proceedings and other measures of suppression of violations without specifying what they should be. The criminal proceedings involve not only ones against the State's own nationals, including members of its armed forces, but also the possibility of proceedings against foreigners for acts committed abroad against foreigners. Brief reference is made of the possibility of inter-State compensation for violations, but there is no express reference to the possibility of civil claims brought by individual victims of violations of the rules. This has been the subject of controversy, particularly with regard to 'comfort women'.[166] There is also the possibility of independent fact-finding. It should be remembered that LOAC itself is civil in character.

Whilst the IAC regime looks good on paper, one may question to what extent it has been implemented in practice, although it is undoubtedly the case that more attention has been paid to training, at least by some States, in recent years. Where a State has ratified the Rome Statute, it may take enforcement more seriously, if only to keep its armed forces away from the International Criminal Court. In the case of NIACs, there is nothing in the LOAC treaties on the prevention and sanctioning of violations.

5   Conclusion

It is submitted that LOAC contains two different strands. This does not just reflect the different content of the rules but has implications for how the relevant rules are treated under treaty law. The rules on the conduct

---

[166] F. Kalshoven, 'State Responsibility for Warlike Acts of the Armed Forces: From Article 3 of Hague Convention IV of 1907 to Article 91 of Additional Protocol I of 1977 and Beyond', *ICLQ*, 40 (1991), 827–858. See, also, Expert Opinions by F. Kalshoven, E. David and C. Greenwood in H. Fujita, I. Suzuki and K. Nagano (eds.), *War and Rights of Individuals: Renaissance of Individual Compensation* (Tokyo: Nippon Hyoron-sha Co., 1999).

of hostilities are not 'inherent' obligations or 'obligations of an objective character', although that appears to be coming under some pressure, notably from human rights bodies. Reciprocity plays a significant role in that field. The distinction between the two strands also seems to make a difference as to how reservations are handled, the consequences of a material breach of the treaty by the other side and as to how the relevant treaty provisions are interpreted. In other words, there is only one body of rules regulating armed conflict, but it contains within it two separate and distinctive legal regimes.

18

Disarmament

LISA TABASSI AND OLUFEMI ELIAS[*]

1 Introduction

Thousands of pages of commentary are published each year on arms control and disarmament, directed mainly to a specialised, technical audience and not commonly discussed or well understood by the general public. In a discourse dominated by political scientists and game theory, it is important to recall the legal framework and the milestones achieved over the past century which represent the context underpinning the political discourse – since these are often overlooked, dismissed, undermined or labelled as obsolete due to political or military necessity.[1] This is the place to argue that '[w]ords must mean something',[2] especially when the words are codified in multilateral treaties broadly adhered to and regulating sovereign freedom of action related to national security and defence, the legal means and methods of warfare and, possibly, the sustained existence of human and other species. In the present decade, a disarmament treaty has had a role in preventing armed intervention between States,[3] and the international organization established by that treaty to ensure the implementation of its provisions has won the Nobel Peace Prize for 2013.[4] The notion that

---

[*] The views expressed herein are those of the authors and are in no way intended to reflect the views of the organizations with which they are affiliated.

[1] See, notably, O. Meier and C. Daase (eds.), *Arms Control in the 21st Century: Between Coercion and Cooperation* (Abingdon: Routledge, 2013).

[2] Office of the Press Secretary (White House), Remarks by President Barack Obama, Hradcany Square, Prague, Czech Republic: www.whitehouse.gov/the_press_office/ Remarks-By-President-Barack-Obama-In-Prague-As-Delivered (5 Apr. 2009).

[3] 'Global Cop, Like It or Not: The American Administration Sees No Alternative to an Attack on Syria', *The Economist* (31 Aug. 2013), pp. 15–16, and 'Framework for Elimination of Syrian Chemical Weapons', U.S. State Department Media Note: www.state.gov/r/pa/prs/ps/ 2013/09/214247.htm (14 Sept. 2013); see, further, Section 9 of this chapter.

[4] The 2013 Nobel Peace Prize was awarded to Organization for the Prohibition of Chemical Weapons (OPCW) 'for its extensive efforts to eliminate chemical weapons': www .nobelprize.org/nobel_prizes/peace/laureates/2013/press.html.

disarmament is an essential component for international peace and security could hardly be demonstrated in more visible terms.

'Disarmament' as referred to here will include its various permutations as 'arms control' and 'non-proliferation'.[5] As a branch of international law, disarmament constitutes fragmentation within fragmentation: 'disarmament law' includes the various instruments regulating specific types of weapons, and each instrument is intended to advance, in varying degrees, the legal progression towards 'general and complete disarmament' (GCD), the overall goal agreed by the international community over fifty years ago.

That goal has remained immanent in disarmament treaties. Although in 1945 the drafters of the Charter of the United Nations excluded 'disarmament' as one of the purposes and principles of the United Nations, following the failure of the Covenant of the League of Nations on that point to prevent the Second World War, the 'regulation of armaments' is a task explicitly assigned by the Charter to both the United Nations General Assembly and the Security Council, with 'possible disarmament' assigned to the Security Council as well.[6] However, reacting to the first use of nuclear weapons against Japan that same year at the end of the war, the General Assembly, at its first Session, in its first resolution, requested proposals on 'the elimination from national armaments of atomic weapons and of all other major weapons adaptable to mass destruction'.[7] By 1959, the General Assembly had recognised the need for 'general and complete disarmament' under effective

---

[5] In this chapter, 'disarmament' also includes measures to reduce the level of national military capabilities or to ban altogether certain categories of weapons already deployed. The disarmament approach to arms limitations is premised on the assumption that armaments in and of themselves are a main source of tension and hostilities. 'Arms control' means measures placing political or legal constraints on the deployment and/or disposition of national military means. Its aim is to reduce the risk of inadvertent war by improving the capacity of adversaries to formulate more accurate assessments of each other's intentions. See, further, S. Tulliu and T. Schmalberger, *Coming to Terms with Security: A Lexicon for Arms Control, Disarmament and Confidence-Building* (Geneva: United Nations Institute for Disarmament Research, 2003), pp. 7–8. 'Weapons of mass destruction' means 'atomic explosive weapons radioactive material weapons, lethal chemical and biological weapons, and any weapons developed in the future which have characteristics comparable in destructive effect to those of the atomic bomb or other weapons mentioned above'. U.N. Doc. RES/S/C.3/30 (13 Aug. 1948). 'Chemical weapons' is defined in the 1993 Convention on the Prohibition of the Development, Production, Stockpiling and Use of Chemical Weapons and on Their Destruction: 1974 UNTS 45.

[6] Arts. 11(1), 26 and 47(1) of the 1945 United Nations Charter: 1 UNTS 16.

[7] General Assembly Resolution 1(I) (24 Jan. 1946).

international control as the most important question facing the world at that time.[8] Weapons would be retained only for the purposes of self-defence, border patrol and maintenance of internal order and for contributing to international peacekeeping missions.

The goal of GCD was vigorously pursued in the Ten-Nation Disarmament Committee (the predecessor to today's Conference on Disarmament), in joint statements on universal disarmament by the Soviet Union and the United States to the General Assembly[9] and national programmes.[10] Although GCD eventually became a propaganda and political tool during the Cold War, the goal of GCD was established in a series of separate, mutually reinforcing multilateral disarmament treaties: the 1963 Treaty Banning Nuclear Weapons Tests in the Atmosphere, in Outer Space and Under Water;[11] the 1967 Treaty for the Prohibition of Nuclear Weapons in Latin America and the Caribbean (Treaty of Tlatelolco);[12] the 1968 Treaty on the Non-Proliferation of Nuclear Weapons (NPT);[13] the 1971 Treaty on the Prohibition of the Emplacement of Nuclear Weapons and Other Weapons of Mass Destruction on the Seabed and the Ocean Floor and in the Subsoil Thereof;[14] the 1972 Convention on the Prohibition of the Development, Production and Stockpiling of Bacteriological (Biological) and Toxin Weapons and on Their Destruction (BWC);[15] the 1993 Chemical Weapons Convention (CWC);[16] the 1995 Southeast Asia Nuclear-Weapon-Free Zone Treaty (Treaty of Bangkok);[17] the 1996 African Nuclear Weapons Free Zone Treaty (Treaty of Pelindaba);[18] the 1996 Comprehensive Nuclear-Test-Ban Treaty;[19] the 2006 Central Asian Nuclear-Weapon-Free Zone Treaty[20] and the 2010 and 2013 drafts

---

[8] General Assembly Resolution 1378 (XIV) (20 Nov. 1959).

[9] US-Soviet Joint Statement of Agreement Principles of 20 Sept. 1961 (McCloy-Zorin Agreement): reprinted in Dept. of State Bull., 45 (1961), 589–590. See, further, A. Blunt, Research Note 5 of 1997–98 on United Nations: General and Complete Disarmament, Parliamentary Library of Australia (www.aph.gov.au/library/pubs/rn/1997-98/98rn05.htm).

[10] Principally, 'Freedom from War: The United States Program for General and Complete Disarmament in a Peaceful World', US Dept. of State Publication 7277, Disarmament Series 5 (Sept. 1961) (http://dosfan.lib.uic.edu/ERC/arms/freedom_war.html).

[11] Also referred to as the 'Partial' (PTBT) or 'Limited Test Ban Treaty' (LTBT), 480 UNTS 43, Preamble.

[12] 634 UNTS 281, Preamble.   [13] 729 UNTS 161, Art. VI.

[14] 955 UNTS 115, Preamble.   [15] 1015 UNTS 163, Preamble.   [16] *Supra* n. 5, Preamble.

[17] 1981 UNTS 129, Preamble.   [18] ILM, 35 (1996), 698–723, Preamble.

[19] ILM, 35 (1996), 1439–1478, Preamble.

[20] Text available at: http://disarmament.un.org/treaties/t/canwfz/text, Preamble.

of the (proposed) Nuclear Weapons Convention,[21] as well as in one international humanitarian law treaty (the 1980 Convention on Prohibitions or Restrictions on the Use of Certain Conventional Weapons Which May be Deemed to be Excessively Injurious or to Have Indiscriminate Effects (also known as the Inhumane Weapons Convention))[22] and a regional security arrangement.[23] Although the proposal for GCD as an Action Plan[24] was not adopted in the third General Assembly Special Session on Disarmament in 1988, the goal has been recalled and reinforced thereafter in successive, annual General Assembly resolutions under the GCD agenda item. The 2000 NPT Review Conference reaffirmed that 'the ultimate objective of the efforts of States in the disarmament process is general and complete disarmament under effective international control'.[25] As recently as 2009, in a summit meeting devoted to disarmament chaired by the President of the United States, the Security Council called upon all States 'to pursue negotiations in good faith ... on a Treaty on general and complete disarmament under strict and effective international control'.[26]

Treaties are the main source of disarmament law. Negotiated as State-centric, disarmament treaties have nonetheless survived and adapted to the paradigm shift that occurred globally after the terrorist attacks of 11 September 2001.[27] While the purpose of those treaties is directed at State actors, they are now also being implemented with a special focus on preventing proliferation among non-State actors as well, demonstrating that disarmament treaties, particularly those of unlimited duration, are living instruments.[28] The current and protracted debacle over the Islamic

---

[21] Preparatory Committee for the 2010 Review Conference of the Parties to the NPT, *Model Nuclear Weapons Convention: Working Paper Submitted by Costa Rica*, NPT/CONF.2010/PC.I/WP.17 (1 May 2007), Preamble.

[22] 1342 UNTS 137, Preamble.

[23] Final Act of the 1975 Helsinki Accords, ILM, 14 (1975), 1293–1298, Section 1(b)(i).

[24] Indian Prime Minister Rajiv Gandhi, 'A World Free of Nuclear Weapons', Address to the United Nations General Assembly, 9 June 1988: reproduced in *India and Disarmament: An Anthology* (New Delhi: Ministry of External Affairs, Govt. of India, 1988), pp. 280–294. The failure of the General Assembly to adopt the proposal was soon followed by India's decision to acquire nuclear weapons.

[25] Final Document of the 2000 Review Conference of the Parties to the NPT (NPT/CONF.2000/28 (Part I)), p. 15.

[26] Security Council Resolution 1887 (24 Sept. 2009) (paragraph 5).

[27] See, e.g., Security Council Resolutions 1368 (12 Sept. 2001), 1373 (28 Sept. 2001), 1377 (12 Nov. 2001), 1456 (20 Jan. 2003) and 1540 (28 Apr. 2004).

[28] See the contribution to this volume of Moeckli and White at pp. 136–171 (Chapter 6).

Republic of Iran's right to the peaceful use of nuclear energy under Article VI NPT has drawn attention to the operation of disarmament treaties and has prompted a spate of important contributions to the discourse on disarmament.[29]

One recent work has concluded that non-proliferation law is a special regime, although not a completely self-contained one since in most aspects, general international law continues to be applicable to it,[30] including the general rules of interpretation as codified in Article 31 of the 1969 Vienna Convention of the Law of Treaties (VCLT).[31] There is no question that disarmament law has been developed by treaties and that those treaties form a *lex specialis* – successive, progressive and interlinked. Limitations upon State sovereignty in the realm of national security will necessarily be very strictly interpreted and very much guarded. Absent an explicit commitment by the State itself, a State's sovereign discretion in matters of national security might defy all form of legal constraint[32] and even logic, for it anticipates extreme circumstances involving the survival of the State.[33] Disarmament obligations require a degree of precision and absolute predictability as they touch upon the very core of State sovereignty.[34] For these reasons, in the post-

---

[29] See, for example, the series of nine essays published in the *Bulletin of Atomic Scientists*, 'Agree to Disagree: Roundtable on Iran and the Bomb: Legal Standards of the IAEA', by D. H. Joyner, C. Ford and A. Persbo (Oct. to Dec. 2012): http://thebulletin.org/iran-and-bomb-legal-standards-iaea-0. See, also, D. H. Joyner, *International Law and the Proliferation of Weapons of Mass Destruction* (Oxford: Oxford University Press, 2009); D. H. Joyner, *Interpreting the Nuclear Non-proliferation Treaty* (Oxford: Oxford University Press, 2011); D. H. Joyner and M. Roscini (eds.), *Non-proliferation Law as a Special Regime: A Contribution to Fragmentation Theory in International Law* (Cambridge: Cambridge University Press, 2012); O. Meier and C. Daase (eds.), *supra* n. 1, and M. Sossai, 'Disarmament and Non-proliferation' in N. D. White and C. Henderson (eds.), *Research Handbook on International Conflict and Security Law: Jus ad Bellum, Jus in Bello and Jus Post Bellum* (Cheltenham: Edward Elgar, 2013), pp. 41–66; on the OPCW's role in preventing the re-emergence of chemical weapons once chemical disarmament has been completed, see OPCW, *The OPCW in 2025: Ensuring a World Free of Chemical Weapons* (OPCW Doc. S/1252/2015).

[30] D. H. Joyner and M. Roscini, 'Conclusions' in Joyner and Roscini (eds.), *supra* n. 29, pp. 270–277.

[31] 1155 UNTS 331.

[32] *Legality of the Threat or Use of Nuclear Weapons* (Advisory Opinion) (1996) ICJ Rep. 226, at p. 266 (paragraph 105(E)).

[33] See, in particular, the Declaration of President Bedjaoui, *ibid.*, at pp. 268–274 (paragraphs 2–5 and 22); Dissenting Opinion of Judge Weeramantry, *ibid.*, at pp. 520–554, and Dissenting Opinion of Judge Koroma, *ibid.*, at pp. 556–582. Cf. Dissenting Opinion of Vice-President Schwebel, *ibid.*, at pp. 311–329.

[34] As articulated in *Case Concerning Military and Paramilitary Activities in and against Nicaragua: Nicaragua v. United States of America* (Merits) (1986) ICJ Rep. 14, at p. 135

Charter system, disarmament treaties have been comprehensively drafted in the form of self-contained regimes with the treaty itself establishing, in particular: the specific mechanism for monitoring and determining compliance; the specific means for dispute resolution; specific sanctions for noncompliance; required circumstances for withdrawal; procedures for amendment, including fast-track 'changes'; and other specific procedures which will apply to the exclusion of general international law. From that perspective, it may be contended that the VCLT system has little left to offer.[35]

In this chapter, we recall the role accorded by Article 31(1) VCLT to the terms of the treaty in their context and in the light of the object and purpose of the treaty. In our view, for all disarmament treaties, reference to their context as well as their object and purpose in the broadest sense encompasses the progressive steps towards the goal of GCD as conceptualised under the Charter of the United Nations as a basic rule.[36] The issue to which this chapter is intended to make a contribution is the extent to which it can be said that the goal of GCD can be said to influence the operation of treaties in practice.

Two preliminary comments are necessary. Although 'disarmament' encompasses a broad range of measures to regulate arms,[37] owing to space limitations the following discussion will focus on the universal

(paragraph 269) ('in international law there are no rules, other than such rules as may be accepted by the State concerned, by treaty or otherwise, whereby the level of armaments of a sovereign State can be limited').

[35] See, generally, G. Lysen, 'The Adequacy of the Law of Treaties to Arms Control Agreements' in J. Dahlitz (ed.), *Avoidance and Settlement of Arms Control Disputes* (Geneva: United Nations, 1994), pp. 123–147, and T. Marauhn, 'Dispute Resolution, Compliance Control and Enforcement of International Arms Control Law' in G. Ulfstein, T. Marahun and A. Zimmermann (eds.), *Making Treaties Work: Human Rights, Environment and Arms Control* (Cambridge: Cambridge University Press, 2007), pp. 243–272.

[36] See, further, the contribution to this volume of Kritsiotis at pp. 237–302 (Chapter 9).

[37] See, further, B. Tuzukhamedov, 'Disarmament' in R. Wolfrum (ed.), *Max Planck Encyclopaedia of Public International Law* (Vol. III) (Oxford: Oxford University Press, 2012), pp. 150–159. Bilateral and regional arms control agreements to stabilize strategic offensive weapons are more contractual in nature, while the DDR (disarmament, demobilization and reintegration) treaties fall more neatly into the category of peace treaties and should be studied separately through that lens. The most recent universal instrument concluded in the conventional weapons field, the 2013 Arms Trade Treaty, which entered into force on 24 Dec. 2014, is aimed at establishing common international standards for regulating international trade in conventional arms (from battle tanks to small arms) and preventing illicit trade and diversion. It makes no reference to disarmament, except for the right of a State to seek assistance with disarmament: see U.N. Doc. A/CONF.217/2013/L.3 (27 March 2013).

multilateral regimes. Secondly, it will present selected issues arising in the implementation of disarmament treaties and consider how they relate to the application of the VCLT. Some of the larger and more complex issues have been exhaustively considered and commented upon elsewhere and are not discussed in this chapter. These include compliance with Article VI NPT by the Nuclear Weapons States;[38] compliance by the Islamic Republic of Iran with the NPT as a Non-Nuclear-Weapon State, its Safeguards Agreement with the IAEA and Security Council resolutions decided under Chapter VII of the United Nations Charter;[39] withdrawal

---

[38] In particular, see *Legality of the Threat or Use of Nuclear Weapons, supra* n. 32, at pp. 263–264 (paragraphs 98–99); International Law Association Committee on Nuclear Weapons, Non-proliferation and Contemporary International Law, Second Report on Legal Aspects of Nuclear Disarmament: Washington Conference 2014 (Washington, DC: 2014), pp. 1–19; D. Rietiker, 'The Meaning of Article VI of the Treaty on the Non-proliferation of Nuclear Weapons: Analysis under the Rules of Treaty Interpretation' in J. L. Black-Branch and D. Fleck (eds.), *Nuclear Non-proliferation in International Law* (Vol. I) (The Hague: T.M.C. Asser Press, 2014), pp. 47–84; A. Kmentt, 'How Divergent Views on Nuclear Disarmament Threaten the NPT', *Arms Control Today*, 10 (2013), 8–13; K. Davenport and M. Taylor, *Assessing Progress on Nuclear Nonproliferation and Disarmament* (Washington, DC: Arms Control Association Report, 2013); P. Kiernan, 'Disarmament under the NPT: Article VI in the 21st Century', *Michigan State Int'l L. Rev.*, 20 (2012), 381–400; Joyner, *Interpreting the Nuclear Non-proliferation Treaty, supra* n. 29; C. A. Ford, 'Debating Disarmament: Interpreting Article VI of the Treaty on the Non-proliferation of Nuclear Weapons', *Nonproliferation Rev.*, 14 (2007), 401–428; Assistant Secretary of State S. Rademaker, 'US Compliance with Article VI of the NPT', Statement at the Arms Control Association Panel Discussion (3 Feb. 2005); R. Thakur and G. Evans, *Nuclear Weapons: The State of Play* (Canberra: Centre for Nuclear Non-proliferation and Disarmament, 2013); Reaching Critical Will, The NPT Action Plan Monitoring Report (Geneva: Reaching Critical Will, 2015), pp. 22–55; Federation of American Scientists, *Status of World Nuclear Forces* (http://fas.org/issues/nuclear-weapons/status-world-nuclear-forces/); Stockholm International Peace Research Institute (SIPRI), *SIPRI Yearbook 2014: Armaments, Disarmament and International Security – Summary* (Oxford: Oxford University Press, 2014), pp. 12–14, at pp. 12–13.

[39] See, in particular, R. Einhorn, *Debating the Iran Nuclear Deal* (Washington, DC: Brookings Institute Research Report, 2015) (on the Joint Comprehensive Plan of Action (JCPOA) arrangement between Iran and the P5+1 countries, endorsed by the Security Council in Resolution 2240 (9 Oct. 2015)); P.-E. Dupont, 'Compliance with Treaties in the Context of Nuclear Non-proliferation: Assessing Claims in the Case of Iran', *J. Conflict & Sec. L.*, 19 (2014), 161–210; Arms Control Association, *Briefing Book: Solving the Iranian Nuclear Puzzle* (Washington, DC: Arms Control Association, 2013); N. Gerami and P. Goldschmidt, *Case Study: The International Atomic Energy Agency's Decision to Find Iran in Non-Compliance 2002–2006* (Washington, DC: Center for the Study of Weapons of Mass Destruction, 2012); D. H. Joyner, 'New IAEA DG Report on Iran Still Incorrect on the Legal Mandate of the IAEA', *Arms Control Law* (11 March 2013); D. H. Joyner, 'What If Iran Withdraws from the Nuclear Nonproliferation Treaty? Can They Do That?' *ESIL Reflections* (13 Dec. 2012); D. Albright, O. Heinonen and O. Kittrie, 'Understanding the IAEA's Mandate in Iran: Avoiding Misinterpretations',

from the NPT by the Democratic People's Republic of Korea (DPRK);[40] the interpretation of the CWC provisions on riot control agents and the application of the CWC to 'non-lethal weapons';[41] and the role of the Security Council under the Charter in disarmament and non-proliferation, including in respect of Israel, Iraq, India and Pakistan, the DPRK and, most recently, Iran.[42]

2 Definition of a 'Treaty'

Article 2(1)(a) VCLT provides that 'treaty' means 'an international agreement concluded between States in written form and governed by

---

ISIS Report (27 Nov. 2012); D. H. Joyner, C. A. Ford and A. Persbo, 'Iran and the Bomb: The Legal Standards of the IAEA', *Bulletin of the Atomic Scientists* (2012); D. H. Joyner, 'The IAEA Applies Incorrect Standards, Exceeding its Legal Mandate and Acting Ultra Vires Regarding Iran', *Arms Control Law* (13 Sept. 2012); and M. Veiluva, *Burdens of Proof: Iran, the United States and Nuclear Weapons – A Global View* (Charleston, SC: Booksurge Publishing, 2009).

[40] See, in particular, D. H Joyner and M. Roscini, 'Withdrawal from Non-proliferation Treaties' in Joyner and Roscini (eds.), *supra* n. 29, pp. 151–172; M. Asada, 'Arms Control Law in Crisis? A Study of the North Korean Nuclear Issue', *J. Conflict & Sec. L.*, 9 (2004), 331–355; G. Bunn and J. Rhinelander, 'The Right to Withdraw from the NPT: Article X Is Not Unconditional', *Disarmament Diplomacy*, 79 (2005), 39–42, and D. H. Joyner, 'North Korean Links to Building of a Nuclear Reactor in Syria: Implications for International Law', *ASIL Insights*, 28 Apr. 2008.

[41] See, e.g., W. Krutzsch and R. Trapp, 'Article II: Definitions and Criteria' in W. Krutzsch, E. Myjer and R. Trapp (eds.), *The Chemical Weapons Convention: A Commentary* (Oxford: Oxford University Press, 2014), pp. 73–104, at pp. 94–102; International Committee of the Red Cross, *Incapacitating Chemical Agents: Law Enforcement, Human Rights Law and Policy Perspectives* (Geneva: ICRC, 2012); J. D. Fry, 'Gas Smells Awful: U.N. Forces, Riot Control Agents and the Chemical Weapons Convention', *Michigan JIL*, 31 (2010), 475–559, and M. Sossai, 'Transparency as a Cornerstone of Disarmament and Non-proliferation Regimes' in A. Bianchi and A. Peters (eds.), *Transparency in International Law* (Cambridge: Cambridge University Press, 2014), pp. 392–416, at pp. 403–404.

[42] See, in particular, M. Wood, 'The Law of Treaties and the UN Security Council: Some Reflections' in E. Cannizzaro (ed.), *The Law of Treaties: Beyond the Vienna Convention* (Oxford: Oxford University Press, 2011), pp. 244–254; J. D. Fry, *Legal Resolution of Nuclear Non-proliferation Disputes* (Cambridge: Cambridge University Press, 2013), pp. 107–178; C. Stoiber, 'The United Nations Security Council and Nuclear Law' in OECD Nuclear Energy Agency (ed.), *International Nuclear Law: History, Evolution and Outlook* (Paris: OECD Publishing, 2010), pp. 91–104; Security Council Report, *The Security Council's Role in Disarmament and Arms Control: Nuclear Weapons, Non-proliferation and Other Weapons of Mass Destruction* (1 Sept. 2009) (www.securitycouncilreport.org); J. D. Fry, 'Dionysian Disarmament: Security Council WMD Coercive Disarmament Measures and Their Legal Implications', *Michigan JIL*, 29 (2008), 197–291, and I. Johnstone, 'Legislation and Adjudication in the UN Security Council: Bringing Down the Deliberative Deficit', *AJIL*, 102 (2008), 275–308, at 283–294.

international law, whether embodied in a single instrument or in two or more related instruments and whatever its particular designation'. The wording of the definition suggests that the term may be construed quite widely.

The Annex to the 1996 Resolution Establishing the Preparatory Commission for the Comprehensive Nuclear-Test-Ban Treaty Organization (CTBTO) (1996 Resolution) provides:

> 7. The Commission *shall* have standing as an international organization, authority to negotiate and enter into agreements and such other legal capacity as necessary for the exercise of its functions and the fulfilment of its purposes (emphasis added).

It has become evident that some States treat the 1996 Resolution as a legally binding treaty while other States consider it to be only 'politically binding'. According to one account, during the drafting of the 1996 Resolution in the Conference on Disarmament, at least one State asserted that the word 'shall' was inappropriate since the Resolution was intended to be politically binding, while other States disagreed: 'shall' remained in the final text of the Resolution.[43] Another commentator considered that the Resolution constitutes a supplementary treaty to the 1996 Comprehensive Nuclear-Test-Ban Treaty (CTBT).[44] Subsequent practice over two decades continues to reflect these diverging views, with the United Kingdom publishing the Resolution in its Treaty Series[45] and some of the other Member States not fully meeting its terms[46] and denying its enforceability. Such denials have serious impact since the activities of the CTBTO Preparatory Commission are global. Its mandate is to prepare for entry into force of the CTBT by, *inter alia*, constructing or establishing and provisionally operating, in eighty-nine States, the 347 facilities comprising the CTBT International Monitoring System (which is designed to detect nuclear explosions above 1 kiloton occurring any-where on the planet). Funded by its 183 Member States, as of 2016, it had expended over US$1 billion and, where possible, it has concluded facility agreements or arrangements with the States hosting those facilities. Some of those Member States have enacted national legislation to give effect to

---

[43] M. Asada, 'CTBT: Legal Questions Arising from Its Non-Entry-into-Force', *J. Conflict & Sec. L.*, 7 (2002), 85-122, at 106 (fn. 73).

[44] A. Aust, *Modern Treaty Law and Practice* (Cambridge: Cambridge University Press, 3rd ed., 2013), p. 157. The CTBT is available at 480 UNTS 43.

[45] 46 UKTS 1999.

[46] See Status of Arrears at http://ctbto.org/member-states/member-states-payments.

the facility agreement, enabling the Commission to import necessary equipment tax- and duty-free and exempt from customs restrictions.[47] Most of the Member States have not adopted any such national measures, and in some of them the CTBTO Preparatory Commission is being required to pay significant sums in direct or indirect taxes and customs duties in the course of activities, and in some cases it faces obstacles regarding customs clearance. There are cases in which the equipment has been held in customs or storage for days, weeks and even years. It has also faced obstacles in the issuance of necessary licenses or land permits to establish the facilities. The legal problem is not resolved by reference to the terms of the VCLT as the ordinary meaning of the written words of the 1996 Resolution are clear, the *travaux préparatoires* of the CTBT are silent, and subsequent practice is not consistent. Nor has it been resolvable in the Preparatory Commission or among leading commentators and authorities.[48] Intertwined with the sharp division over the interpretation of the legal status of the Resolution is the assertion by some States signatory that, irrespective of the terms of the Resolution, they assume no obligations whatsoever until entry into force of the CTBT. No similar divergence of views arose under the 1993 Resolution Establishing the Preparatory Commission for the Organization for the Prohibition of Chemical Weapons (OPCW Preparatory Commission), presumably because almost all its activities over its four-year existence were carried out in the Netherlands where it enjoyed legal capacity and privileges and immunities under its headquarters agreement.[49]

Oddly enough, most of the States which have revealed that they only consider the Resolution to be politically binding have nevertheless accredited a Permanent Mission to the CTBTO Preparatory Commission and submitted formal credentials for their respective Representatives in accordance with the Commission's Rules of Procedure. Such would not

[47] Australia, Canada, Mongolia, New Zealand, the Russian Federation, the United Kingdom. See *CTBT Legislation Database*: www.ctbto.org/member-states/legal-resources/.

[48] H. G. Schermers and N. M. Blokker, *International Institutional Law: Unity within Diversity* (Leiden: Koninklijke Brill NV, 5th rev. ed., 2011), pp. 1040–1044 (§§1617–1619), and A. Aust, 'The CTBTO Preparatory Commission – Legal Status and Responsibilities', CTBTO Spectrum, July 2004, pp. 10–11; cf. Asada, *supra* n. 43, at 105–113.

[49] See, further, J. Rautenbach and L. Tabassi, 'Legal Aspects of the Preparatory Commission for the OPCW' in I. R. Kenyon and D. Feakes (eds.), *The Creation of the Organization for the Prohibition of Chemical Weapons: A Case Study in the Birth of an International Organization* (Cambridge: Cambridge University Press, 2007), pp. 69–82.

normally be the practice if the organization did not have the status of an international organization established by treaty. Despite the differing views, the Commission itself has clearly proceeded in practice as if it were validly established by treaty, even to the extent of exercising treaty-making capacity with States and international organizations. For example, it has concluded and registered with the United Nations Secretary-General under Article 102 of the United Nations Charter the Headquarters Agreement with Austria; agreements with several of the eighty-nine States which are hosting CTBT monitoring stations and laboratories; a Relationship Agreement with the United Nations and co-operation agreements with a number of other international organizations (such as the United Nations Education, Scientific and Cultural Organization, the World Meteorological Organization and the Association of Caribbean States).

The CTBTO Preparatory Commission meets the criteria used in all three streams of doctrinal debate concerning the legal basis for international legal personality of international organizations: (a) the traditional view that it must be explicitly attributed;[50] (b) the 'objective legal personality' school that organizations which have an organ with decision-making power distinct from the subjective will of its member states possess international legal personality *ipso facto*, bestowed by international law and not by the intention of the parties (i.e. 'original personality, as do states')[51] and (c) the 'implied powers' school which holds that organizations empowered, for example, to conclude treaties have a derived legal personality (not *ipso facto* original).[52] In the opinion of the International Court of Justice (ICJ) in respect of the United Nations, 'by entrusting certain functions to [the organization], with the attendant duties and responsibilities, [the Member States] have clothed it with the competence required to enable those functions to be effectively discharged'.[53] The case of the Preparatory Commission proves Ian Brownlie's observation that as there is no process at the international level comparable to that of incorporation in municipal law, the primary

---

[50] See the discussion in Schermers and Blokker, *supra* n. 48, at pp. 988–989 (§1565) (citing as an example G. I. Tunkin, 'The Legal Nature of the United Nations', *Hague Recueil*, 119 (1966-III), 1–68, at 20–25).

[51] Schermers and Blokker, *supra* n. 48 (citing as an example F. Seyersted, *Common Law of International Organizations* (Leiden: Koninklijke Brill NV, 2008), pp. 43–64).

[52] Schermers and Blokker, *supra* n. 48, at pp. 988–989 (§§1565–1566) (citing *Reparation for Injuries Suffered in the Service of the United Nations* (Advisory Opinion) (1949) ICJ Rep. 174, at pp. 178–179).

[53] *Ibid.*

test is functional.[54] In any event, in practical terms, none of that doctrinal debate is helpful in the present context. The enjoyment of 'such other legal capacity as necessary for the exercise of its functions and the fulfilment of its purposes' implies cooperation by the Member State concerned to: (a) grant access to the treaty-stipulated location of the site and permits for construction of the facility; (b) grant the Preparatory Commission exemption from (or facilitate) customs clearance of the equipment for installation in the facility and (c) grant the Preparatory Commission exemption from taxes and duties in order to avoid the funnelling of the Commission's financial resources, derived from the public funding of its Member States, into the host State's national treasury. The failure to cooperate in the latter aspect makes it possible for a few States, which have been assigned by the treaty to host stations at the organization's expense, to recoup some or all of their financial contributions to the Preparatory Commission or even to make a profit.

Logically, the express terms of the Resolution in their 'ordinary meaning' (referring back to the VCLT) should eventually prevail. As the CTBT International Monitoring System draws closer to its operational readiness and completion, the divergence of intentions on the nature of the Resolution and the obligations of signatories will become ever more visible if facility construction reaches a standstill with the last few unbuilt monitoring stations. The host States of the last few unbuilt stations will be the object of attention by the governing body. If the reason given is the host State's denial of any obligations arising from the Resolution, the issue of the (non-)binding character of the Resolution may finally be debated. If the CTBTO Preparatory Commission is to complete its mandate to ensure the operationalisation of the Treaty's verification regime at entry into force of the CTBT, it will likely find itself under pressure to take action to interpret and resolve this legal and political problem.

3   Article 18 VCLT and the Interim Obligation Not to Defeat the Object and Purpose of a Treaty

Article 18 VCLT provides that '[a] State is obliged to refrain from acts which would defeat the object and purpose of a treaty when: (a) it has signed the treaty or has exchanged instruments constituting the treaty

---

[54] J. Crawford, *Brownlie's Principles of Public International Law* (Oxford: Oxford University Press, 8th ed., 2012), p. 170.

subject to ratification, acceptance or approval, until it shall have made its intention clear not to become a party to the treaty; or (b) it has expressed its consent to be bound by the treaty, pending the entry into force of the treaty and provided that such entry into force is not unduly delayed'.

The CTBT was opened for signature in 1996, and as of 2015, it had not entered into force. Nor is that prospect close at hand. In terms of Article 18 VCLT, are its 183 States signatories under the interim obligation not to defeat the object and purpose of the CTBT pending its entry into force? Would a nuclear weapon test explosion by any of the signatory States *defeat* the object and purpose of the CTBT? It has been argued that in terms of Article 18 VCLT, a State must not 'do anything that would prevent it from being able to fully comply with the treaty once it has entered into force' and that this does not require a State to abstain from *all* acts which will be prohibited once the treaty enters into force.[55]

Article 1 CTBT provides that '[e]ach State Party undertakes not to carry out any nuclear weapon test explosion or any other nuclear explosion, and to prohibit and prevent any such nuclear explosion at any place under its jurisdiction or control'. However, if one looks further, beyond the basic ban on testing, one sees in the preamble of the CTBT that the object and purpose of the comprehensive test ban are also to: (a) constrain the development and qualitative improvement of nuclear weapons, ending the development of advanced new types of nuclear weapons; (b) contribute effectively to the prevention of the proliferation of nuclear weapons in all its aspects, the process of nuclear disarmament and therefore the enhancement of international peace and security and (c) possibly contribute to the protection of the environment.[56]

Arguably, once a State has conducted a nuclear weapon test explosion, the *status quo* at the time of signature would fundamentally have been altered. There can be no restitution of the three elements drawn from the preamble of the CTBT. By virtue of the test, the testing State would be acquiring the knowledge either to improve its existing nuclear weapons (if it were a nuclear-weapons State) or to acquire nuclear weapons (if formerly a 'non-nuclear-weapons State'). The cumulative effect resulting from the heat and radiation of the blast would have affected the environment nearly permanently, in human terms.[57] The consequences of

---

[55] Aust, *supra* n. 44, at p. 108.

[56] CTBT, preambular paragraphs 5, 6, 9 and 10. See, further, *supra* n. 36.

[57] See, further, R. Johnson and D. Kimball, 'Who Needs the Nuclear Test Ban?', *Disarmament Diplomacy*, 59 (2001).

testing could be even more severe if the test triggered a series of earthquakes, a spate of testing by other States or a renewed nuclear arms race.

It has been written that 'the underlying principle behind [A]rticle 18 is not that signed treaties are binding; it is instead that fundamental fairness requires a State to refrain from undermining an agreement on which another State is relying . . .'[58] Reliance in this case may be derived from the consensus reached at the 1995 and 2000 NPT Review Conferences that systematic progress towards nuclear disarmament would be achieved under Article VI NPT by concluding the negotiations of the CTBT[59] and by respecting the moratorium on nuclear-weapon-test explosions or any other nuclear explosion pending its entry into force.[60] The States concerned – almost all in the world – can in principle legitimately rely on the agreement reached by them in the NPT Review Conferences and on the act of signature by each State signatory to the CTBT in respect of the other signatories *inter se.*

The *opinio juris* in this respect of one nuclear-weapon State – the United States – is found in the action taken in 1999 by Secretary of State Madeleine Albright when the United States Senate did not give its advice and consent to ratification of the CTBT: reportedly, she addressed letters to several foreign ministers, including those of China and the Russian Federation, in which she stated: 'I want to assure you that the United States will continue to act in accordance with its obligations as a signatory under international law'.[61] Another example is found in the statement two years later by the Minister for Foreign Affairs of Malta in the general debate of the Second Conference on Facilitating the Entry-into-Force of the CTBT, in which he said that under Article 18 VCLT, signatory States are bound not to defeat the object and purpose of the CTBT, which 'means they cannot conduct a nuclear test explosion'. No one is on record to have disputed this.[62] Indicative of the academic

---

[58] R. F. Turner, 'Legal Implications of Deferring Ratification of SALT II', *Virginia JIL*, 21 (1981), 747–784, at 777.

[59] Decision 2 on Principles and Objectives for Nuclear Non-proliferation and Disarmament, NPT/CONF.1995/32/DEC.2: www.reachingcriticalwill.org/legal/npt/1995dec.html#2.

[60] Practical steps for the systematic and progressive efforts to implement Article VI NPT, paragraph 15 of the Final Document of the 2000 Review Conference of the Parties to the NPT, *supra* n. 25.

[61] Quoted in Asada, *supra* n. 43, at 96 (citing 'The Imperial Presidency', *Washington Times*, 5 Nov. 1999).

[62] Statement of the Honourable Dr. Joe Borg, Minister of Foreign Affairs of Malta, Conference on Facilitating the Entry into Force of the CTBT, 11 Nov. 2001, quoted in Asada, *supra* n. 43, at 100.

opinion on this point is the outcome of the International Law Association's 1998 session – that it was 'the uncontested view after lengthy discussion ... that the special requirements of arms control lead to the application of a general rule that a State signatory will observe treaty provisions pending ratification and entry into force, whether or not the rule applies to all branches of the law'.[63]

The inherent weakness in relying on the interim obligation of Article 18 VCLT is its reversibility. While withdrawal clauses in arms control treaties have now become commonplace, primarily to increase the prospects for universality of participation in the treaties,[64] they incorporate criteria which must be met in order to justify a withdrawal as well as a time lag following which the withdrawal will become effective. For the interim obligation as conceived in the VCLT, there are no such explicit conditions. The State may simply withdraw its signature and, presumably with immediate effect, achieve a complete reversal to its *status quo ante*[65] depending upon prevailing circumstances. The only State practice on that point is the much-discussed retraction by the United States of its signature of the 1998 Statute of the International Criminal Court in May 2002.[66]

Article 18 VCLT also provides that the interim obligation expires if entry into force is unduly delayed. Since the CTBT was opened for signature in 1996, has any undue delay occurred? Arguably not, as the treaty has a built-in mechanism in its Article XIV to address a delay in entry into force. It requires the United Nations Secretary-General, acting as depositary, to convene a Conference of the States that have deposited their instruments of ratification, if the majority so request. The purpose of the Conference is for those States to consider the situation and decide what measures consistent with international law may be undertaken to accelerate the ratification process. Such a Conference has been requested on a biennial basis since 1999. Furthermore, the General Assembly annually adopts a resolution promoting the entry into force of the

---

[63] International Law Association, *Report of the Sixty-Eighth Conference* (Taipei: International Law Association, 1998), p. 177 (cited in the *Report of the Committee on Arms Control and Disarmament Law to the International Law Association London Conference* (2000), p. 8).

[64] Weapons of Mass Destruction Commission, *Weapons of Terror: Freeing the World of Nuclear, Biological and Chemical Arms* (Stockholm: Weapons of Mass Destruction Commission, 2006), p. 51.

[65] K. Bailey and R. Barker, 'Why the United States Should Unsign the Comprehensive Test Ban Treaty and Resume Nuclear Testing', *Comparative Strategy*, 22 (2003), 131–138.

[66] http://2001-2009.state.gov/r/pa/prs/ps/2002/9968.htm.

CTBT which is supported by the positive votes of nearly the entire membership of the United Nations.[67] The resolution '[u]rges all States that have not yet signed the Treaty, in particular those whose ratification is needed for its entry into force, to sign and ratify it as soon as possible'. Consequently, the Treaty has not fallen into desuetude.

A strong case can therefore be made that a nuclear weapon test explosion by a signatory State to the CTBT is prohibited pursuant to Article 18 VCLT.[68]

4   Provisional Application

Article 25 VCLT provides that a treaty or a part of a treaty can be applied provisionally pending its entry into force if the treaty itself so provides or the negotiating States have in some other manner so agreed.[69] Three examples from disarmament treaty practice relevant to Article 25 VCLT will be mentioned briefly here:

(a) The 1967 Treaty of Tlatelolco expressly provides in Article 28(2) that all signatory States shall have the imprescriptible right to waive, wholly or in part, the requirements for entry into force of the Treaty. It further provides that such a waiver would be effected by means of a declaration annexed to their respective instruments of ratification and which may be formulated at the time of deposit of the instrument or subsequently. It prescribes that for those States which exercise this right, the Treaty shall enter into force upon deposit of the declaration or as soon as those requirements have been met which have not been

---

[67] The 2015 resolution was adopted 181 votes in favour, one against (the DPRK) and three abstentions (India, Mauritius, Syria): U.N. Doc. A/RES/70/73 (7 Dec. 2015).

[68] This is in addition to the consideration that the *de facto* moratorium on nuclear testing has been respected by all States signatories. The only three States to conduct nuclear explosions since 1996 have not signed the CTBT – the DPRK, India, and Pakistan – nor are they party to any other instrument which would constrain their freedom to conduct a nuclear weapon test explosion (if one accepts that the DPRK's withdrawal from the NPT was valid). Nevertheless, after each test the Security Council requested the testing State(s) to halt testing. For a more complete discussion of Art. 18 VCLT and the CTBT as well as other aspects, see, further, L. Tabassi, 'The Nuclear Test Ban: *Lex Lata* or *Lege Ferenda?*', *J. Conflict & Sec. L.*, 14 (2009), 309–352. Cf. Asada, *supra* n. 43, and D. Jonas, 'The Comprehensive Nuclear Test Ban Treaty: Current Legal Status in the United States and the Implications of a Nuclear Test Explosion', *N.Y. Univ. J. Int'l L. & Pol.*, 39 (2007), 1007–1046.

[69] See, generally, A. Quast Mertsch, *Provisionally Applied Treaties: Their Binding Force and Legal Nature* (Leiden: Koninklijke Brill NV, 2012) and, further, the contribution to this volume of Quast Mertsch at pp. 303–334 (Chapter 10).

expressly waived. In practice, most States in Latin America and the Caribbean exercised their right to the waiver, incrementally rendering the region a nuclear-weapon-free zone far earlier than it would otherwise have been, as it took nearly thirty years for all States in the region to become parties to the Treaty. It has been suggested that the waivers contributed to reaching that achievement.

(b) On 12 September 2013, on the eve of the issuance of the report by the United Nations Mission to Investigate Allegation of the Use of Chemical Weapons in Syria,[70] Syria communicated to the United Nations Secretary-General its intention to provisionally apply the CWC. On 14 September 2013, Syria deposited its instrument of accession to the CWC, declaring that it 'shall comply with the stipulations contained [in the Convention] and observe them faithfully and sincerely, applying the Convention provisionally pending its entry into force [for it]'.[71] Bearing in mind the text of Article 25 VCLT, it is to be noted that the CWC does not expressly provide for provisional application – and, additionally, that the CWC is already in force.[72] The possibility existed that one or more States Parties to the CWC could object to Syria's declaration regarding provisional application. However, the Executive Council of the Organization for the Prohibition of Chemical Weapons (OPCW) noted Syria's declaration on provisional application and emphasised that such application gave immediate effect to the CWC in respect of Syria. It adopted a Decision on the Destruction of Syrian Chemical Weapons,[73] which provided special procedures to expedite the elimination of the Syrian chemical weapons programme.[74] In turn, the same day, the Security Council adopted Resolution 2118[75] which endorsed the OPCW Executive Council's decision and expressed its determination to ensure the destruction of Syria's chemical weapons program according to the expedited timetable. The preamble to Resolution 2118 also underscored Article 25 of the United Nations Charter, which establishes the obligation of Member States of the organization to accept and carry out decisions of the Security Council. These arrangements ensured a coordinated solution to the crisis and the expedited entry into force of the CWC for Syria.

---

[70] U.N. Doc. A/67/997–S/2013/553 (16 Sept. 2013).
[71] SG/SM/15279-DC/3451 (14 Sept. 2013).
[72] As of 29 Apr. 1997 – and as *per* Art. XXI CWC: *supra* n. 5.
[73] OPCW Executive Council Decision (EC-M-33/DEC.1) (27 Sept. 2013).
[74] See, further, Section 9.   [75] Security Council Resolution 2118 (27 Sept. 2013).

(c) The third example relevant to Article 25 VCLT is the CTBTO Preparatory Commission's provisional operation of the CTBT International Monitoring System. The Preparatory Commission was mandated to establish and, pending their formal commissioning, to *operate provisionally* as necessary the International Data Centre (IDC) and the International Monitoring System (IMS) networks provided for in the CTBT.[76] During 2002, the Preparatory Commission approved guidelines for the technical testing and provisional operation and maintenance of certified IMS stations, the global communications system and the International Data Centre. It emphasised that the pre-entry into force activities do not provide for verification of compliance with the CTBT, including monitoring for verification purposes.[77] Consequently, 'provisional operation of the IDC and IMS' is not to be confused with provisional application of the CTBT. Furthermore, the Preparatory Commission and its membership are of finite duration and are legally distinct from the CTBTO and its membership, which will only be established when the CTBT enters into force.[78]

Although some commentators have suggested that the international community could benefit from the provisional application of the CTBT,[79] and others have proposed that the Security Council could decide under Chapter VII of the Charter that the CTBT is provisionally applicable for all States pending its entry into force,[80] it has also been suggested that the CTBT could be amended to render less onerous the requirements for its entry into force.[81] However, neither the Preparatory Commission

---

[76] Resolution Establishing the Preparatory Commission for the CTBTO, CTBT/MSS/RES/1 (17 Oct. 1996), Annex, subparagraph 5(c) (emphasis added).

[77] Reports of the Preparatory Commission at its Eighteenth and Nineteenth Sessions, CTBT/PC-18/1 (21 Aug. 2002), Annex II, paragraphs 12 and 13, and CTBT/PC-19/1 (19 Nov. 2002), paragraph 17 and Annex II, paragraph 13(a).

[78] Cf. A. Michie, 'Provisional Application of Non-proliferation Treaties' in Joyner and Roscini (eds.), *supra* n. 29, pp. 55–87.

[79] See R. Johnson, *Unfinished Business: Negotiations of the CTBT and the End of Nuclear Testing* (Geneva: United Nations Institute for Development Research, 2009); A. Aust, 'The Comprehensive Nuclear-Test-Ban Treaty – The Problem of Entry into Force', *Japanese YbIL*, 52 (2009), 1–34, and R. Johnson, 'Is it Time to Consider Provisional Application of the CTBT?', *Disarmament Forum* (2006), 29–37.

[80] P. C. Szasz, 'The Security Council Starts Legislating', *AJIL*, 96 (2002), 901–905.

[81] UN Secretary-General Ban Ki-Moon, Statement to the NPT Review Conference (4 May 2010) on the need for 'an alternative mechanism to bring the treaty into effect' and Aust, *supra* n. 79, at 23–28.

nor its subsidiary bodies have been seized with that question and it has consequently not been pursued.

5 National Implementation Measures

Articles 26 and 27 VCLT imply that States Parties shall take positive steps to ensure that their treaty obligations are observed and enforced:

> Article 26. *Pacta sunt servanda.* Every treaty in force is binding upon the parties to it and must be performed by them in good faith.
>
> Article 27. Internal law and observance of treaties. A party may not invoke the provisions of its internal law as justification for its failure to perform a treaty . . .

In respect of law-making treaties, a State will need to enact national legislation to bind persons within its jurisdiction. An act is only punishable if prohibited at the time of its commission and the penalty applicable to it is prescribed by a law in force when the act occurred. Even in monist legal systems in which treaties in force automatically form part of the national legal code, criminal sanctions cannot be applied against persons violating treaty norms unless the national law so provides. The fundamental universal criminal law principles of *nullum crimen sine lege* and *nulle poena sine lege* require that a crime must be defined and the penalties established for the prohibition to become enforceable as a crime. Furthermore, criminal laws may not be applied by analogy.[82] Due to divergences in legal systems and penal policies, definitions of crimes (other than those defined in the 1998 Rome Statute of the International Criminal Court)[83] and establishment of penalties have not been included in multilateral treaties. It has been left to States Parties to transpose them into their criminal codes. As the United Nations Secretary-General has stated:

> It is not enough for States simply to give their consent to be bound by treaties. If the peoples of all nations are to participate in the emerging global legal order and enjoy its benefits, States must also respect and implement the obligations that the treaties in question embody. Realizing the promise of the framework of global norms developed by the international community is of critical importance. Without such a commitment the rule of law in international affairs will remain little more than a remote abstraction.

[82] *Consistency of Certain Danzig Legislative Decrees with the Constitution of the Free City* (Advisory Opinion), 1935 PCIJ, Series A/B, No. 65, 1, at pp. 14 and 19–20.

[83] 2187 UNTS 90.

... [A]ll too often ... national authorities ... simply lack the necessary expertise or resources to ensure that their obligations are properly implemented and applied – to draft and adopt the needed legislation, to put in place the necessary procedure and administrative arrangements, to train those involved in the application of such legislation, procedure and arrangements and to familiarize them with the international rules they are designed to implement. To support efforts to implement international treaty commitments we already provide Governments, on request, with assistance in drafting national laws and running training programmes in particular aspects of international law for those involved in its application ...[84]

The criticality of the adoption of national implementing measures for disarmament treaties has been taken in hand by Member States.[85] The rudimentary legal technical assistance programmes created in the relevant organizations to meet requests for legislative assistance have been augmented by significant voluntary contributions and scrutinised by Member States. Significant among these was an Action Plan requested by the first Review Conference for the CWC in 2003,[86] which resulted in a cutting-edge programme with a deadline of November 2005 for States to institute national implementation measures.[87] At its conclusion, although comprehensive implementing legislation was achieved in only approximately half of the membership, the Action Plan was considered to be a success since it created an unprecedented momentum among States Parties to implement the Convention effectively. The process under the Action Plan led to greater dialogue, organizational change and more intensive reporting as well as other concrete outcomes. An extensive and effective methodology for legislative assistance (questionnaires, gap analysis, documentary tools, on-site drafting assistance upon request and institutional support during the interministerial review and parliamentary approval process) has been acknowledged and replicated elsewhere. Momentum was sustained in part due to constructive support by Member States: it was not an exercise of naming and shaming States which had not yet adopted national implementing legislation.

[84] Report of the Secretary-General on the Work of the Organization, Supp. No.1 (A/55/1), 30 Aug. 2000, p. 37 (paragraphs 277–278).

[85] IAEA, CTBTO, OPCW, UNODC, as well as through government support to one non-governmental organization, VERTIC (www.vertic.org/).

[86] Subparagraph 7.83(h) of the 'Report of the First Special Session of the Conference of the States Parties to Review the Operation of the Chemical Weapons Convention (First Review Conference) 28 April–9 May 2003', OPCW Doc. RC-1/5 (9 May 2003).

[87] OPCW Conference of the States Parties Decision C-8/DEC.16 (24 Oct. 2003).

The challenge facing OPCW Member States was, and continues to be, to attract the political willingness of their parliaments to give priority to adopting the necessary legislation once it has been drafted.[88]

Thus, it is clear that in terms of compliance with disarmament treaties, States have moved beyond Article 27 VCLT. The issue is not whether or not a State can be excused if a treaty norm is violated in its jurisdiction: the emphasis is on prevention of violations through criminal sanctions, vigilance and enforcement. The instances of German chemical industry involvement in enabling the Libyan chemical weapons program in the 1980s[89] and key transfers in the Pakistani A.Q. Khan network enabling nuclear weapons programmes in a number of places,[90] coupled with fears of terrorist access to weapons of mass destruction in the post–11 September 2001 era, have led the international community to take a much more proactive stance on implementation of disarmament norms.

Principal among such efforts is Security Council Resolution 1540, adopted in April 2004, which went further than all previous resolutions on counterterrorism.[91] It required a number of measures, many of which were required pursuant to treaty obligations elsewhere, including the adoption of penal legislation criminalising the proliferation of nuclear, chemical and biological weapons by non-State actors and the improvement of export controls and enforcement measures at the borders. It was adopted under Chapter VII of the Charter and thus is binding on all Member States of the United Nations, thereby extending the substance of these obligations to Member States regardless of their participation (or lack thereof) in particular disarmament or nonproliferation treaties.[92] Paragraph 5 of Resolution 1540 also provides that none of the obligations set forth in the resolution would be interpreted so as to conflict with or alter the rights and obligations of States Parties to the NPT, CWC or BWC or alter the responsibilities of the International Atomic Energy Agency (IAEA) or the OPCW.

---

[88] See, further, L. Tabassi and A. Dhavle, 'Article VII: National Implementation Measures' in Krutzsch, Myjer and Trapp (eds.), *supra* n. 41, pp. 195–234.

[89] P. Rubenstein, 'State Responsibility for Failure to Control the Export of Weapons of Mass Destruction', *California WILJ*, 23 (1993), 319–372, at 327.

[90] M. Fitzpatrick, *Nuclear Black Markets: Pakistan, A.Q. Khan and the Rise of Proliferation Networks* (London: International Institute for Strategic Studies, 2007).

[91] See S. D. Murphy, 'Security Council Resolution on Nonproliferation of WMD', *AJIL*, 98 (2004), 606–608.

[92] See L. Tabassi, 'Impact of the CWC: Progressive Development of Customary International Law and Evolution of the Customary Norm against Chemical Weapons', *The CBW Conventions Bulletin* (March 2004), 1–7.

In the discussions in the OPCW on the follow-up to the Action Plan, some States Parties viewed Resolution 1540 as further reinforcement of the Action Plan and wanted specific reference to it by the Conference of the States Parties. This proposal was rejected by other States Parties which resisted any attempt to explicitly link the actions taken by the two separate organizations.

That rejection alludes to the history that the adoption of Resolution 1540 was met with some amount of criticism. The concept was initially announced by President George W. Bush in a speech to the General Assembly in September 2003, and after seven months of negotiations, the resolution (co-sponsored by France, the Philippines, Romania, the Russian Federation, Spain, the United Kingdom and the United States) was adopted. One-fourth of the entire United Nations membership appeared before the Security Council to speak to the proposed resolution. A number of States expressed several concerns, questioning the right of the Security Council to assume the role of prescribing legislative action by Member States, especially when the CWC, BWC and NPT already pre-scribed those obligations.[93] The action was also debated by a number of commentators.[94] Despite the criticism, States are generally cooperating with the '1540 Committee', which was established to oversee and report on implementation of the resolution.[95] In 2011, the Security Council renewed the mandate of the 1540 Committee for a further ten years.[96]

These developments indicate that the content of Article 27 VCLT is not only underscored but, as far as disarmament treaties are concerned, could be re-drafted as a positive obligation to adopt implementing measures for treaties in a timely and effective manner.

6   Interpretation and Application of Successive Treaties Relating to the Same Subject Matter

The step-by-step treaty progression towards the goal of GCD has inevi-tably led to successive treaties relating to the same subject matter, two cases of which will be commented on here.

---

[93] Egypt, India, Indonesia, the Islamic Republic of Iran, Namibia, Nepal, Nigeria, Pakistan, Singapore, South Africa, Switzerland: U.N. Doc. S/PV. 4950 (22 Apr. 2004).

[94] See, for example, E. Rosand, 'The Security Council as "Global Legislator": *Ultra Vires* or Ultra Innovative?', *Fordham ILJ*, 28 (2004), 542–590. Cf. Szasz, *supra* n. 80.

[95] Security Council Resolutions 1673 (27 Apr. 2006), 1810 (25 Apr. 2008), 1977 (20 Apr. 2011) and 2055 (29 June 2012). For further information: www.un.org/en/sc/1540/.

[96] Security Council Resolution 1977 (20 Apr. 2011).

6.1   The 1925 Geneva Protocol and the 1993
Chemical Weapons Convention

The Geneva Protocol for the Prohibition of the Use in War of Asphyxiating, Poisonous or Other Gases, and of Bacteriological Methods of Warfare, signed at Geneva on 17 June 1925, has long been considered to form part of customary international law.[97] As a treaty obligation, it is limited: it only bans the *use* in *international* armed conflict between the Parties to the Protocol, and as most of the Parties reserved the right to retaliate in kind if attacked with poison gas, the Geneva Protocol became essentially only a ban on *first use*. The CWC remedied that by establishing a comprehensive prohibition applicable in any circumstances and by not permitting any reservations to the articles of the Treaty.

The preamble of the CWC states: 'Determined for the sake of all mankind, to exclude completely the possibility of the use of chemical weapons, through the implementation of the provisions of this Convention, thereby complementing the obligations assumed under the Geneva Protocol of 1925 . . .' Article XIII CWC, on 'Relation to Other International Agreements', provides that '[n]othing in this Convention shall be interpreted as in any way limiting or detracting from the obligations assumed by any State under the [Geneva Protocol] . . .' Article XVI(3) CWC goes on to provide that '[t]he withdrawal of a State Party from this Convention shall not in any way affect the duty of States to continue fulfilling the obligations assumed under any relevant rules of international law, particularly the Geneva Protocol of 1925'.

Consequently, and consistent with Article 30 VCLT on the application of successive treaties relating to the same subject matter, both treaties apply in parallel: the Geneva Protocol and the CWC, together with the prohibition in customary international law.[98] Withdrawal from the CWC materially would not affect the ban on the use of chemical weapons.

---

[97] 94 LNTS 65. See, further, Section A of General Assembly Resolution 2603 (XXIV) (16 Dec. 1969) and Rules 74–76 of J.-M. Henckaerts and L. Doswald-Beck, *Customary International Humanitarian Law* (Vol. I: Rules) (Cambridge: Cambridge University Press, 2005), pp. 259–267. The use of gas in international or non-international armed conflict has also become an international crime falling within the jurisdiction of the ICC: Art. 8 of the Statute of the International Criminal Court, *supra* n. 83, and its amendment, Assembly of States Parties to the Rome Statute of the International Criminal Court, *Review Conference of the Rome Statute of the International Criminal Court, Kampala*, Official Records, RC/11 (31 May–11 June 2010), Part II, RC/Resolution 5: Amendments to Art. 8 of the Rome Statute: 2868 UNTS 195.

[98] See Henckaerts and Doswald-Beck, *supra* n. 97.

However, upon withdrawal, a State could resume development, production, stockpiling and transfer of chemical weapons, presumably with the condemnation of the remainder of most of the international community. Bearing that in mind, the General Assembly annually adopts a resolution which expresses its determination to act with a view to achieving effective progress towards GCD under strict and effective international control and calls upon States that have not done so to withdraw their reservations to the Geneva Protocol.[99] Considering that the maintenance of reservations allowing retaliatory use under the Geneva Protocol is inconsistent with adherence to the CWC, CWC States Parties have also begun making a similar call to motivate States to withdraw such reservations and requesting regular reporting on the progress towards doing so.[100]

6.2   The 1963 Partial or Limited Test-Ban Treaty and the 1996 Comprehensive Nuclear-Test-Ban Treaty

Article 1 of the 1963 PTBT or LTBT provides in part:

> Each of the Parties to this Treaty undertakes to prohibit, to prevent, and not to carry out any nuclear weapon test explosion, or any other nuclear explosion, at any place under its jurisdiction or control:
>
> (a) in the atmosphere; beyond its limits, including outer space; or under water, including territorial waters or high seas; or
> (b) in any other environment if such explosion causes radioactive debris to be present outside the territorial limits of the State under whose jurisdiction or control such explosion is conducted. It is understood in this connection that the provisions of this subparagraph are without prejudice to the conclusion of a Treaty resulting in the permanent banning of all nuclear test explosions, including all such explosions underground, the conclusion of which, as the Parties have stated in the Preamble to this Treaty, they seek to achieve.[101]

The 1996 CTBT makes reference in its preamble to the aspirations of the Parties to the PTBT and in nearly identical, but comprehensive, terms, provides in its Article I(1):

---

[99] The latest resolution is U.N. Doc. A/RES/69/53 (11 Dec. 2014).
[100] *The Geneva Protocol of 1925* (OPCW Document RC-3/NAT.7 (3 Apr. 2013)) and paragraph 9.31 of the *Report of the Third Special Session of the Conference of the States Parties to Review the Operation of the Chemical Weapons Convention* (OPCW Doc. RC-3/3 (19 Apr. 2013)).
[101] *Supra* n. 11, Art. 1(1).

> Each State Party undertakes not to carry out any nuclear weapon test
> explosion or any other nuclear explosion, and to prohibit and prevent any
> such nuclear explosion at any place under its jurisdiction or control.

Neither treaty defines 'nuclear weapon test explosion or any other nuclear explosion'. In terms of Article 31 VCLT, the ordinary meaning of the prohibition might lead one to initially contemplate whether the CTBT bans not only testing but the use of nuclear weapons as well. However, the CTBT preambular paragraphs suggest that the object and purpose of the CTBT is to achieve an end to nuclear testing as one of the highest priority objectives of the international community, to contribute effectively to the prevention of the proliferation of nuclear weapons and the process of nuclear disarmament.

In terms of context, the 1995 NPT Review Conference adopted in its Decision 2 on the Principles and Objectives for Nuclear Nonproliferation and Disarmament a programme of action specifying a deadline of one year for the Conference on Disarmament to complete negotiations on the CTBT. In order to meet that very ambitious deadline, the treaty drafters considered that it would not be possible to achieve consensus on definitions, as the NPT negotiations had proven definitions to be problematic. Thus the CTBT contains none. The text left unstated the precise parameters of the ban and postponed until the first CTBT Review Conference consideration of the possibility of permitting the conduct of underground nuclear explosions for peaceful purposes. The treaty is silent in respect of zero yield, low-yield testing, subcritical, hydrodynamic and inertial confinement fusion experiments, etc., or any necessary procedures to ensure stockpile safety until such time as nuclear disarmament is achieved. Commentators on the CTBT negotiations have suggested that the drafters arrived at the compromise text of the treaty within the one-year deadline by proceeding at the outset on the basis of the successful PTBT implementation or unwritten understandings underlying it.[102] At the time of transmitting the

---

[102] See, further, R. Johnson, *Unfinished Business: The Negotiation of the CTBT and the End of Nuclear Testing* (Geneva: United Nations Institute for Department Research, 2009), pp. 57–89; J. Ramaker, P. D. Marshall, R. Geil and J. Mackby, *The Final Test: A History of the Comprehensive Nuclear-Test-Ban Treaty Negotiations* (Vienna: Provisional Technical Secretariat of the Preparatory Commission CTBTO, 2003), pp. 55–71, and A. Schaper, 'The Problem of Definition: Just What Is a Nuclear Weapon Test?' in E. Arnett (ed.), *Implementing the Comprehensive Test Ban: New Aspects of Definition, Organization and Verification* (SIPRI Research Report No. 8, 1994), pp. 26–47.

PTBT to the United States Senate for ratification, the Message of President John F. Kennedy stated:

> ... the treaty language relates 'any nuclear weapon test explosion' to 'any other nuclear explosion', thus preventing evasion based on the contention that a particular detonation was not a weapon test but the explosion of an already tested device. The phrase 'any other nuclear explosion' includes explosions for peaceful purposes. Such explosions are prohibited by the treaty because of the difficulty of differentiating between weapon test explosions and peaceful explosions without additional controls. The article does not prohibit the use of nuclear weapons in the event of war nor restrict the exercise of the right of self-defence recognized in Article 51 of the Charter of the United Nations.[103]

While that message is categorical on the part of the United States, the negotiating history is clear: the final CTBT draft in the Conference on Disarmament was reached on the basis of a text in which different views of States, possessors and non-possessors and regional groupings were accommodated to the extent possible. It is also noted at this point that consensus was ultimately not reached in the Conference on Disarmament and the final draft was transmitted to the General Assembly by a State, not by the Conference on Disarmament. The work of the Preparatory Commission for the CTBTO in the ensuing two decades has focused on verifiability of the Treaty, constructing and provisionally operating the International Monitoring System and developing on-site inspection procedures, not on definitional issues.

7 Management of Compliance with Treaty Obligations

Some of the substantively fundamental deadlines[104] established by the CWC proved complex to meet in practice, for reasons unanticipated by the negotiators of the treaty. The intermediate deadlines for destruction

---

[103] *Message from the President of the United States Transmitting the Treaty Banning Nuclear Weapon Tests in the Atmosphere, in Outer Space, and Underwater* (8 Aug. 1963), 88th Congress, Senate, Doc. 99–118, p. 5.

[104] For example, the deadlines for submission of initial declarations, especially those related to the chemical industry, and notifications of transfers of chemicals; issuance of two-year multiple entry visas to inspectors and inspection assistants; issuance of a standing diplomatic clearance number for unscheduled aircraft; declarations of assistance to be provided under Art. X. Other obligations for which no specific deadline was provided also became problematic, e.g. adoption of national implementation measures and adjustment of national regulations in the field of trade in chemicals. See, further, Section 5 of this chapter.

of chemical weapons were the first critical ones that were not met for various reasons by some of the possessor States.[105] The delays were recognised within and outside the OPCW as a matter of concern; in December 2004, the United Nations Secretary-General's High-level Panel on Threats, Challenges and Change named the delays in destruction of chemical weapons stockpiles by CWC States Parties as one of the current threats to international peace and security.[106]

The CWC established a deadline of 29 April 2007 – ten years after entry into force of the treaty[107] – to complete destruction of all declared chemical weapons (the core obligation under the CWC). The treaty provided that the deadline was extendable once, upon approval of the OPCW Executive Council, for five years, i.e. to 29 April 2012.[108] The primary reason for establishing an absolute deadline was to remove any possible incentive for joining the treaty late: for States adhering to the treaty in the first decade, there was no possibility of extending destruction activities beyond that date.[109] Nevertheless, it became clear during that first decade that at least two of the so-called 'possessor States' would not meet the final extended deadline. The report of the Government of the United States in 2004 revealed that based on the (then) current schedule, the United States would not meet that deadline and estimated that the Russian Federation would not complete destruction of its stockpile until 2027.[110] The inability of those States to meet the destruction

---

[105] In 2004, citing plant safety issues, environmental requirements and funding shortfalls, the United States General Accounting Office indicated that the U.S. would be unable to complete the destruction of its chemical weapons stockpile even by the final extended deadline of 2012. See United States General Accounting Office (GAO) Report to the Chairman, Committee on Armed Services, House of Representatives, 'Nonproliferation: Delays in Implementing the Chemical Weapons Convention Raise Concerns About Proliferation', Report No. GAO-04-361 (March 2004), p. 10–11. The extremely high costs of chemical weapons destruction continued to plague the Russian Federation's ability to destroy its stockpile on time, despite increasingly significant voluntary contributions from other States. See, for example, SIPRI, *SIPRI Yearbook 2004: Armaments, Disarmament and International Security* (Oxford: Oxford University Press, 2004), p. 673, and the US GAO Report, at pp. 3 and 7–10, and extensions approved by the OPCW Conference of the States Parties, C-8/DEC.13 (2003). Faced with the technical complexities of destroying chemical weapons, both Albania and the Libyan Arab Jamahiriya sought and received extensions on their intermediate deadlines for destruction, respectively decisions C-9/DEC.8 and 7 (2004).

[106] High-level Panel on Threats, Challenges and Change, *A More Secure World: Our Shared Responsibility*, U.N. Doc. A/59/565 (2004), p. 40 (paragraph 114).

[107] *Supra* n. 5.   [108] Part IV(A) of the Verification Annex to the CWC: *supra* n. 5.

[109] Art. IV(6) CWC and Part IV(A)(26) of the Verification Annex: *supra* n. 5.

[110] US GAO Report, *supra* n. 105.

deadlines was a fundamental one that related to the central obligation set out in Article 1 CWC to destroy all chemical weapons.

The question that arose was how the organs of the OPCW could address the situation without amending the treaty deadline through pursuing the elaborate amendment procedures under the CWC.[111] During the discussions among Member States in 2011, at least one delegation was reportedly adamant that any amendment would have to be a formal one that strictly followed the CWC process.[112] Following protracted negotiations in the OPCW, a mechanism was adopted by the OPCW Conference of States Parties in December 2011. In a rare occasion of voting, the Conference approved a decision regarding the anticipated inability by Libya, the Russian Federation and the United States to meet the final extended deadline ('the Decision').[113] The vote was 101–1, with Iran voting against.[114] By adopting the Decision in advance of the final

---

[111] Art. XV CWC provides:

    2. The text of a proposed amendment shall be submitted to the Director General for circulation to all States Parties and to the Depositary. The proposed amendment shall be considered only by an Amendment Conference. Such an Amendment Conference shall be convened if one third or more of the States Parties notify the Director General not later than 30 days after its circulation that they support further consideration of the proposal. The Amendment Conference shall be held immediately following a regular [annual] session of the Conference unless the requesting States Parties ask for an earlier meeting. In no case shall an Amendment Conference be held less than 60 days after the circulation of the proposed amendment.

    3. Amendments shall enter into force for all States Parties 30 days after deposit of the instruments of ratification or acceptance by all the States Parties referred to under subparagraph (b) below:

        (a) When adopted by the Amendment Conference by a positive vote of a majority of all States Parties with no State Party casting a negative vote; and

        (b) Ratified or accepted by all those States Parties casting a positive vote at the Amendment Conference . . .

    Paragraphs 4 and 5 of Art. XV provide for a simplified procedure pursuant to which 'changes' could be made to provisions of the Annexes to the CWC (including the Verification Annex) 'if proposed changes are related only to matters of an administrative or technical nature'. These provisions cannot be considered applicable because the provisions relating to destruction deadlines – even those contained in the Verification Annex rather than the CWC itself (see, e.g., paragraphs 17 and 24 of Part IV(A) of the Verification Annex) – cannot properly be considered as being technical or administrative in nature: *supra* n. 5.

[112] See, e.g., OPCW Doc. C-16/NAT.17 (28 Nov. 2011).

[113] Decision on the Final Extended Deadline of 29 Apr. 2012, OPCW Doc. C-16/DEC.11 (1 Dec. 2011).

[114] D. Horner, 'Accord Reached on CWC's 2012 Deadline', *Arms Control Today*, 42 (Jan.–Feb. 2012), 38–39.

extended deadline, the Conference was not yet facing an actual situation of noncompliance, which has several explicit means of redress under the CWC, including bringing the matter to the attention of the Security Council.[115] Rather, it was establishing in advance a mechanism to deal with any failure to meet the deadline.

In the preamble to the Decision, the Conference recalled that the Executive Council 'as reported in EC-64/5 dated 3 May 2011 has already been addressing the concern in accordance with Paragraph 36 of Article VIII of the Convention that the final extended deadline of 29 April 2012 may not be fully met and that the matter has also been brought to the attention of the Conference'.[116] The final preambular paragraph states that the Conference adopted the Decision:

> [o]n the basis of the powers and functions of the Conference to take specific actions to promote the object and purpose of the Convention, to oversee implementation, or to ensure compliance with the Convention's provisions, and underlining that, in the event that the final extended deadline is not fully met, the destruction of the remaining chemical weapons of the possessor States concerned shall continue in accordance with the provisions of the Convention and its Annex on Implementation and Verification ('Verification Annex'), and with the application of the measures contained in this decision . . .

The Decision sets out obligations for the possessor States and underlined their obligations to complete the destruction as soon as possible and in

---

[115] Article XII CWC ('Measures to Redress a Situation and to Ensure Compliance, Including Sanctions'): *supra* n. 5.

[116] Paragraph 36 provides as follows:

> In its consideration of doubts or concerns regarding compliance and cases of non compliance, including, inter alia, abuse of the rights provided for under this Convention, the Executive Council shall consult with the States Parties involved and, as appropriate, request the State Party to take measures to redress the situation within a specified time. To the extent that the Executive Council considers further action to be necessary, it shall take, inter alia, one or more of the following measures:
>
> (a) Inform all States Parties of the issue or matter;
> (b) Bring the issue or matter to the attention of the Conference;
> (c) Make recommendations to the Conference regarding measures to redress the situation and to ensure compliance.
>
> The Executive Council shall, in cases of particular gravity and urgency, bring the issue or matter, including relevant information and conclusions, directly to the attention of the United Nations General Assembly and the United Nations Security Council. It shall at the same time inform all States Parties of this step.

accordance with the provisions of the CWC – and to report on the progress made. They are also subjected to an enhanced verification regime. For example, the possessor States 'are to invite' (in addition to the Chairperson of the Executive Council and the Director-General of the OPCW) a delegation which may include representatives of the Council and other 'observer' States to undertake periodic visits 'to obtain an overview of the destruction programmes being undertaken', thus supplementing the ongoing continuous monitoring of destruction activities performed by the OPCW Inspectorate under the CWC.

The procedure falls short of a formal amendment or modification of the CWC pursuant to its Article XV (Amendments). Apart from strong rhetoric from some Member States, none of the procedures associated with the provisions in the VCLT for breach or non-compliance or for amendment or modification of the treaty were invoked.[117] The failure to comply with obligations going to the object and purpose of the treaty were resolved by reference to the CWC itself and the fashioning of a solution within that context by the Member States.[118]

---

[117] For a detailed analysis of the legal implications of the OPCW's handling of the inability of the possessor States to meet the destruction deadlines, see M. Asada, 'The OPCW's Arrangements for Missed Destruction Deadlines under the Chemical Weapons Convention: An Informal Noncompliance Procedure', *AJIL*, 108 (2014), 448–474. After examining other possibilities, Asada concludes, at 459–460, that the Decision of the Conference is best seen as having been based on Art. VII(36)(c) CWC: he argues that the Decision 'was based directly on the text of a draft decision recommended by the Executive Council, which is exactly what Article VIII, paragraph 36(c) provides. That paragraph can thus be seen as a general provision enabling the [Conference] to take any measures recommended by the Executive Council to redress the situation and to ensure compliance – measures that go beyond those specifically enumerated in [Art.] XII. In particular, whereas [Art.] XII, paragraph 1, can deal only with "a situation which contravenes the provisions of [the] Convention" – that is, an actual contravention case – it can also, by acting on an Executive Council recommendation under [Art.] VIII, paragraph 36(c), address a situation that is still at the stage of "doubts or concerns" . . . If so, it would follow that the [Conference] is capable of acting not only reactively but proactively, and that the Conference decision of December 2011 was not a de facto amendment of the CWC but an application of its provisions'.

[118] The suggestion has been made that, as the Decision of the Conference 'does not present itself as an effort to address a treaty violation or to impose sanctions', the approach of the OPCW may be likened in several important respects to noncompliance procedures of the kind typically found in some treaties dealing with environmental protection. See Asada, *supra* n. 117, esp. at 461–468. See, also, E. Myjer, 'Non-compliance Procedures and Their Function in International Law: The Case of the Chemical Weapons Convention' in W. P. Heere (ed.), *Contemporary International Law Issues: New Forms, New Applications* (The Hague: TMC Asser Institute, 1998), pp. 355–363, and A. Rosas, 'Reactions to Non-compliance with the Chemical Weapons Convention' in M. Bothe, N. Ronzitti and A. Rosas (eds.), *The New Chemical Weapons Convention:*

8   Correction of Errors in Texts or Certified Copies of a Treaty

Article 79 VCLT establishes a procedure whereby clerical errors in the certified copies of treaties can be corrected.

Shortly after the CWC opened for signature in January 1993, discrepancies in the certified copy were noticed. The errors had occurred when text prepared with the word processing software used in Geneva in the Conference on Disarmament during the negotiations was converted to the word processing software used at the United Nations headquarters in New York to produce the certified copies for publication. Subsequently, a number of translation discrepancies were also detected which had occurred in the short timeframe in which the treaty text, negotiated in English, was translated into the other five languages for transmission by the Conference on Disarmament in its Report to the General Assembly. The Preparatory Commission for the OPCW decided to pursue the procedure stipulated in Article 79 VCLT for correction of the errors which successfully resulted in the issuance of Depositary Notifications[119] without incident.

In the case of the CTBT, the CTBTO Preparatory Commission has found that certain geographical coordinates for station locations were not feasible. The Preparatory Commission has been compiling a consolidated list of the erroneous or unsuitable locations, as and when they are identified during establishment of the CTBT International Monitoring System, and approving alternate locations which are deemed to better suit the purpose. Upon entry into force of the CTBT, the list will be communicated to the Conference of the States Parties at its first session, with the recommendation that the procedure under Article 79 VCLT be pursued in order to substitute corrected coordinates for the stations in the treaty text to reflect the actual coordinates of the stations established during the preparatory phase.[120]

9   Enhancement of Treaty Provisions by Other Treaties

When serious concerns about the Syrian chemical weapons stockpile were raised in 2012,[121] Syria was not party to the CWC, although it was

---

Implementation and Prospects (The Hague: Kluwer Law International, 1998), pp. 415–461.

[119] OPCW Doc. C-II/DG.8 (11 Nov. 1997) and Depositary Notifications C.N.246.1994. TREATIES-5 (31 Aug. 1994), C.N.359.1994.TREATIES-8 (27 Jan. 1995) and C.N. 454.1995.TREATIES-12 (2 Feb. 1996).

[120] CTBTO Doc. CTBT/INF.211.Rev.14.

[121] For information on Syria and CWC, see the special section on the website of the OPCW at www.opcw.org/special-sections/syria/.

bound to the prohibition of chemical weapons use under the Geneva Protocol and under customary international law. Under the authority conferred upon him by the General Assembly in November 1987[122] and the Security Council in August 1988,[123] the United Nations Secretary-General sought the assistance of the OPCW for an inspection in Syria. Paragraph 27 of Part XI of the Verification Annex to the CWC provides that '[i]n the case of alleged use of chemical weapons involving a State not Party to this Convention or in territory not controlled by a State Party, the Organization shall closely cooperate with the Secretary-General of the United Nations. If so requested, the Organization shall put its resources at the disposal of the Secretary-General of the United Nations'. The initial objective of the investigation was to confirm possession – not use – which meant that the cooperation between the OPCW and the United Nations was based on the Relationship Agreement between the two Organizations.[124] An inspection team was dispatched to Cyprus where it waited while the sites to be inspected and access thereto were negotiated with the Syrian government. In the meantime, it was alleged that chemical weapons were used; consequently, the CWC could be used as the legal basis for the OPCW's cooperation with the United Nations in an investigation of this apparent use under CWC.

While the United States contemplated armed intervention in Syria,[125] the Russian Federation negotiated a solution with the United States which resulted in an Agreed Framework for Elimination of Syrian Chemical Weapons.[126] Syria acceded to the CWC and declared that it would apply the CWC provisionally until it entered into force, to which no State Party objected.[127] As the timelines and other obligations set out in the CWC would now apply to the activities in Syria and possibly affect the particular arrangements agreed upon and considered necessary in view of the circumstances (involving OPCW's verification and monitoring of the destruction of Syria's chemical weapons in the midst of hostilities), the OPCW Executive Council decision on the destruction of Syrian chemical weapons was timed and coordinated with Security

---

[122] General Assembly Resolution A/RES/42/37C (30 Nov. 1987).

[123] Security Council Resolution 620 (26 Aug. 1988).

[124] Annexed to OPCW Executive Council decision EC-MXI/DEC.1 (1 Sept. 2000); also annexed to General Assembly Resolution A/RES/55/283 (24 Sept. 2001).

[125] 'Global Cop, Like it or Not', *supra* n. 3.

[126] Joint National Paper by the Russian Federation and the United States of America on the Framework for Elimination of Syrian Chemical Weapons, OPCW Doc. EC-M-33/NAT.1 (17 Sept. 2013).

[127] See, further, Section 4(b).

Council Resolution 2118 (adopted on the same day),[128] which resulted in the OPCW-UN Joint Mission[129] for the Elimination of the Chemical Weapons Programme of the Syrian Arab Republic. The interplay between the Agreed Framework, Resolution 2118, the decisions of the OPCW Executive Council and the CWC is of interest.

The Agreed Framework states that the parties to it 'determined that the most effective control' of Syrian chemical weapons 'may be achieved by the removal of the largest amounts of weapons feasible, under OPCW supervision, and their destruction outside of Syria, if possible'. It will be recalled, however, that pursuant to Article I(1)(a) CWC, States undertake 'never under any circumstances' to 'develop, produce, otherwise acquire, stockpile or retain chemical weapons, or transfer, directly or indirectly, chemical weapons to anyone'. The permissibility of the transfer of Syrian weapons notwithstanding, Article I(1)(a) CWC was explicitly ensured by the decision of the Security Council in paragraph 10 of Resolution 2118 'to authorize Member States to acquire, control, transport, transfer and destroy chemical weapons identified by the Director-General of the OPCW, *consistent with the objective of the Chemical Weapons Convention*, to ensure the elimination of the Syrian Arab Republic's chemical weapons programme in the soonest and safest manner'.[130] In addition to the measures envisaged under the Agreed Framework between the United States and the Russian Federation, the general plan for destruction submitted by the Syria in its initial declaration pursuant to Article III CWC stated reasons why Syria considered that the destruction of its chemical weapons 'would need to take place at facilities outside its territory, under strict verification by the OPCW, in order to meet the requirements set out in OPCW Executive Council decision EC-M-33/DEC.1'.[131] The authorisation by the Security Council of the removal

---

[128] *Supra* n. 75.

[129] Supplementary Arrangement Concerning Cooperation Between the United Nations and the OPCW for the Implementation of the OPCW Executive Council Decision EC-M-33/DEC.1 and Security Council Resolution 2118: *ibid*.

[130] Emphasis added. Art. 103 of the United Nations Charter, it will be recalled, accords primacy to obligations under the United Nations Charter over obligations in other treaties: *supra* n. 6.

[131] See the preamble to OPCW Executive Council decision on 'Detailed Requirements for the Destruction of Syrian Chemical Weapons and Syrian Chemical Weapons Production Facilities', OPCW Doc. EC-M-34/DEC.1 (15 Nov. 2014). The Decision reiterated the call to all States for voluntary contributions and assistance to the elimination of the Syrian chemical weapons programme. The destruction of the weapons outside the territory of Syria also raised a number of challenges. Albania rejected a proposal to transport the weapons to its territory; see J. Haber, 'Albania Considers OPCW Plan to Destroy Syria's

of the chemical weapons from the Syrian territory for destruction elsewhere was therefore considered to be a pragmatic solution – notwithstanding the prohibition of transfers contained in Article I(1)(a) CWC – to ensure the ultimate objective of the Convention.

A number of other elements of the Agreed Framework appeared to go beyond the text of the Convention. According to Article IV(8) CWC, Syria, for whom the Convention entered into force on 14 October 2013, would be required to destroy its chemical weapons 'as soon as possible' (unlike the deadlines applicable to States joining the CWC before 29 April 2007 discussed in Section 7). In contrast, the Agreed Framework envisaged 'the complete elimination of all chemical weapons material and equipment in the first half of 2014'. It may be doubted whether the drafters of the Convention envisaged the possibility for a possessor State to destroy its entire stockpile within less than a year. The OPCW Executive Council is responsible under Article IV(8) CWC for setting the timeframe for the destruction of the weapons and thereby determine what is meant by the phrase 'as soon as possible', but it is clear that, in deciding in its decision of 27 September 2013 that Syria shall 'complete the elimination of all chemical weapons material and equipment in the first half of 2014', the OPCW Executive Council took account of the requirements set out in the Agreed Framework.[132] Similarly, the Agreed Framework, paragraph 7 of Resolution 2118 and the OPCW Executive Council decision of 27 September 2013 all require Syria to allow inspectors 'immediate and unfettered right to inspect any and all sites in Syria'.[133] This language is considerably broader than the language used in the CWC and its Annexes.[134]

The object and purpose of the CWC in the context of the Syrian chemical weapons programme was achieved by supplementing its provisions with decisions of the OPCW Executive Council and Security Council Resolution 2118, both of which were informed by the Agreed Framework. It is noteworthy that the OPCW Executive Council, in its decision of 27 September 2013, explicitly stated that 'this decision is made

Chemical Weapons', *Foreign Policy Mideast Daily* (15 Nov. 2013). See, also, Letter to the Pancretan Commission against the Destruction of Syrian Chemical Weapons in the Enclosed Sea of the Mediterranean Sea: www.opcw.org/index.php?eID=dam_frontend_push&docID=17539 (29 July 2014).

[132] See paragraph 1(c) of EC-M-33/DEC.1 (27 Sept. 2013). Indeed, the preamble to this decision provides that the Council 'welcomes' the Agreed Framework.

[133] *Ibid.*, paragraph 1(e).

[134] See, e.g., Part II of the Verification Annex to the CWC ('General Rules of Verification'): *supra* n. 5.

due to the extraordinary character of the situation posed by Syrian chemical weapons and does not create any precedent for the future'.[135]

10   Convergence of Disarmament Law and International Humanitarian Law

At the end of the nineteenth century, the roots of what came to be known as international humanitarian law developed with the Martens Clause,[136] recognising that the methods and means of warfare were not unlimited. Weapons that were indiscriminate and deemed to cause unnecessary suffering were prohibited. The International Committee of the Red Cross became the leader in this movement, and its engagement resulted in, *inter alia*, the 1925 Geneva Protocol,[137] the four Geneva Conventions of 1949[138] and the Protocols thereto,[139] as well as the 1980 Convention on

[135] OPCW Doc. EC-M-33/DEC.1 (27 Sept. 2013), operative paragraph 3(d). At the time of writing, Security Council Resolution 2209 (6 March 2015) had expressed concern that the OPCW Fact-Finding Mission had concluded with a high degree of confidence that chemical weapons had been used in Syria in 2014; see, also, OPCW Doc. EC-M-48/DEC.1 (4 Feb. 2015). The resolution decided that measures would be imposed under Chapter VII in the event of future non-compliance with Security Council Resolution 2118: *supra* n. 75. This was followed by Security Council Resolution 2235 (2015) which created a further interplay between the two treaties in the form of the UN/OPCW 'Joint Investigative Mechanism'. Recognizing that the OPCW Fact-Finding Mission in Syria was not mandated to reach conclusions about the attribution of responsibility for the use of chemical weapons, the Security Council established the Joint Investigative Mechanism for one year (extendable) with the aim of identifying the 'individuals, entities, groups, or governments' responsible for the use who 'must be held accountable'. Governments were called upon to provide any information they possess on the perpetrators, organizers, sponsors or those otherwise involved in the use. The Security Council reaffirmed its decision to impose measures under Chapter VII in response to violations of Security Council Resolution 2118: *supra* n. 75.

[136] Introduced by the Russian delegate, F. F. van Martens, into the preamble of the 1899 Hague Convention (II) on the Laws and Customs of War on Land: 'Until a more complete code of the laws of war is issued, the High Contracting Parties think it right to declare that in cases not included in the Regulations adopted by them, populations and belligerents remain under the protection and empire of the principles of international law, as they result from the usages established between civilized nations, from the laws of humanity and the requirements of the public conscience': 187 CTS 429.

[137] *Supra* n. 97.

[138] 1949 Geneva Convention (I) for the Amelioration of the Condition of the Wounded and Sick in Armed Forces in the Field, 75 UNTS 31; 1949 Geneva Convention (II) for the Amelioration of the Condition of Wounded, Sick and Shipwrecked Members of Armed Forces at Sea, 75 UNTS 85; 1949 Geneva Convention (III) Relative to the Treatment of Prisoners of War, 75 UNTS 135, and 1949 Geneva Convention (IV) Relative to the Protection of Civilian Persons in Time of War, 75 UNTS 287.

[139] Protocol Additional to the Geneva Conventions of 12 August 1949, and Relating to the Protection of Victims of International Armed Conflicts (Protocol I), 1125 UNTS 3, and

Prohibitions or Restrictions on the Use of Certain Conventional Weapons (CCW),[140] which was concluded to prohibit the use of particularly inhumane weapons.

However, the meetings of the parties to the CCW to expand its coverage achieved results too conservative for many States Parties on certain issues, and thus far, this has led to negotiations of two treaties outside the CCW which also comprise the two most recent disarmament treaties: the 1997 Convention on the Prohibition of the Use, Stockpiling, Production and Transfer of Anti-Personnel Mines and on Their Destruction[141] and the 2008 Convention on Cluster Munitions.[142] Aimed largely at the protection of civilians and prevention of suffering from the consequences of the use of those weapons, these two international humanitarian law treaties established comprehensive prohibitions of those two categories of conventional weapons, including the destruction of existing stockpiles. On that point, they borrowed heavily from the more recent disarmament law treaties and can thus be said to represent a convergence of these two branches of the law. Although operating in furtherance of GCD, the goal was unarticulated in these two latest treaty texts. Both were also negotiated and concluded outside the Conference on Disarmament and enjoy wide adherence by the majority of States, but not those most interested – i.e. the main producers of those weapons. The two treaties have nevertheless had an effect on those producers as tolerance by the majority of international community for the actual use of those weapons no longer exists and any future use is likely to be widely condemned.

This represents a turning point as, previously, international humanitarian and disarmament law were treated as two separate branches of the law. This approach is evident from the July 1996 advisory opinion in *Legality of the Threat or Use of Nuclear Weapons*, in which the International Court of Justice examined the legality of nuclear weapons in respect of each branch.[143] As a general matter, the Court found the

---

Protocol Additional to the Geneva Conventions of 12 August 1949, and Relating to the Protection of Victims of Non-International Armed Conflicts (Protocol II), 1125 UNTS 609.

[140] *Supra* n. 22.   [141] 2056 UNTS 241.   [142] ILM, 48 (2009), 354–369.

[143] See *Legality of the Threat or Use of Nuclear Weapons, supra* n. 32, at pp. 256 (paragraph 75), 257 (paragraphs 78–79), 258–260 (paragraphs 83–86), 262–263 (paragraphs 95–97) and 266 (paragraph 105(2)). See, also, pp. 272–273 (paragraphs 19–22 of Declaration of President Bedjaoui); pp. 280–281 (Declaration of Judge Vereshchetin); pp. 285–286 (Declaration of Judge Ferrari Bravo); pp. 301–303 (Separate Opinion of Judge Ranjeva); pp. 306–309 (paragraphs 2–5 of the Separate Opinion of Judge Fleischhauer); pp. 320–322 and 329 (Dissenting Opinion of Vice-President Schwebel); pp. 558–559

threat or use of nuclear weapons unlawful under international humanitarian law[144] but reached a *non liquet* on their lawfulness in an extreme case of self-defence where the very survival of the State is at stake.[145] The spontaneous convergence of these two branches in the two treaties, outside the established fora and without the main players who produce those weapons, coupled with the almost immediate entry into force and widespread adherence to those treaties, is now spilling over into the area of nuclear disarmament. As human rights and international humanitarian law have become the standards by which global governance is measured, human security is challenging the primacy of national security/ State sovereignty. 'Humanitarian action' has developed into a multi-track diplomatic strategy which may possibly be leading to a delegitimisation of the doctrine of nuclear deterrence,[146] potentially also affecting the advisory opinion on *the Legality of the Threat or Use of Nuclear Weapons* – if it were ever to be revisited.

The United Nations Secretary-General has warned the Conference on Disarmament that it is in danger of being replaced by States which are resorting to alternative arrangements outside it.[147] During the period 2010–2016, the following twelve events were significant in that regard:

(i) For the first time, the 2010 NPT Review Conference expressed its deep concern at the catastrophic humanitarian consequences of any use of nuclear weapons and reaffirmed the need for all States at all times to comply with applicable international law, including international humanitarian law.[148]

(ii) In November 2011, the International Red Cross and Red Crescent Movement called for treaty negotiations to prohibit and eliminate

---

(Dissenting Opinion of Judge Koroma); pp. 585–591 (paragraphs 11–33 of the Dissenting Opinion of Judge Higgins); pp. 397–413 (Part III of the Dissenting Opinion of Judge Shahabuddeen) and pp. 476–512 (Part III of the Dissenting Opinion of Judge Weeramantry).

[144] *Ibid.*   [145] *Ibid.*, at p. 266 (paragraph 105(E)).

[146] R. Johnson, 'Arms Control and Disarmament Diplomacy' in A. F. Cooper, J. Heine and R. Thakur (eds.), *The Oxford Handbook of Modern Diplomacy* (Oxford: Oxford University Press, 2013), pp. 593–609, at p. 597; see, also, B. Docherty, 'Ending Civilian Suffering: The Purpose, Provisions, and Promise of Humanitarian Disarmament Law', *Austrian Rev. Int'l & European L.*, 15 (2010), 7–44.

[147] United Nations Secretary-General Ban Ki-Moon, 'Closing Statement to the High-Level Meeting on Revitalizing the Work of the Conference on Disarmament and Taking Forward Multilateral Disarmament Negotiations' (24 Sept. 2010). See, also, R. Rydell, 'Disarmament without Agreements?', *Int'l Negotiation*, 10 (2005), 363–380.

[148] NPT Review Conference 2010, Final Report (NPT/CONF.2010/50), Vol. I, Conclusion I.A.v.

nuclear weapons,[149] followed by adoption of a four-year action plan.[150]

(iii) Switzerland, with thirty-four other States, submitted a joint statement on the humanitarian dimension of nuclear disarmament in the General Assembly First Committee in October 2012.

(iv) The General Assembly established an Open-Ended Working Group on nuclear disarmament which met in Geneva during 2013 and produced a report.[151]

(v) Norway hosted the first Conference on the Humanitarian Impact of Nuclear Weapons in Oslo in March 2013, attended by 128 States (the P5/5 NPT Nuclear-Weapon States absent), international organizations and civil society.

(vi) The General Assembly convened a High-Level Meeting on Nuclear Disarmament in September 2013 at which the humanitarian initiative was discussed.[152]

(vii) New Zealand and 125 other States submitted a further Joint Statement on the humanitarian dimension of nuclear weapons in the General Assembly First Committee in October 2013.

(viii) Mexico hosted the second Conference on the Humanitarian Impact of Nuclear Weapons in Nayarit in February 2014, attended by 146 States (P5 again absent), international organizations and civil society.

(ix) New Zealand and 155 other States submitted a Joint Statement on the humanitarian consequences of nuclear weapons.

(x) Austria hosted the third Conference on the Humanitarian Impact of Nuclear Weapons in Vienna in December 2014, attended by 158 States, including India, Pakistan, the United Kingdom and the United States, international organizations and civil society, and subsequently launched a 'Humanitarian Pledge' which 127 States endorsed[153] and which the General Assembly welcomed.[154]

---

[149] International Red Cross and Red Crescent Movement, Council of Delegates Resolution CD/11/R1 (26 Nov. 2011).

[150] Council of Delegates Resolution CD/13/R1.

[151] U.N. Doc. A/68/514 (9 Oct. 2013), welcomed by the General Assembly in A/RES/68/46 and transmitted to the Conference on Disarmament and the Disarmament Commission for consideration.

[152] General Assembly Resolution A/RES/67/39 (4 Jan. 2013).

[153] www.bmeia.gv.at/en/european-foreign-policy/disarmament/weapons-of-mass-destruction/nuclear-weapons-and-nuclear-terrorism/vienna-conference-on-the-humanitarian-impact-of-nuclear-weapons/.

[154] General Assembly Resolution 70/48 (11 Dec. 2015).

(xi) On 7 December 2015, the General Assembly adopted Resolution 70/33 which convened an open-ended working group as a subsidiary body to address (*inter alia*) recommendations on other measures that could contribute to taking forward multilateral nuclear disarmament negotiations and to increase awareness and understanding of the complexity of and interrelationship between the wide range of humanitarian consequences that would result from any nuclear detonation.

(xii) On 14 October 2016, fifty-seven States co-sponsored a draft resolution in the General Assembly,[155] which expresses deep concern about the catastrophic humanitarian consequences of any use of nuclear weapons. If the resolution is adopted, the General Assembly will follow the recommendation of the open-ended working group and convene a United Nations conference in New York in 2017 to negotiate a legally binding instrument to prohibit nuclear weapons – leading towards their total elimination.

These milestones are encouraging and may foretell a treaty as the outcome of: (a) frustration with the impasse in the Conference on Disarmament and its failure to achieve any result since 1996 or even adopt its agenda since 2009; (b) fear that the continued stockpiling and possible renewal of the nuclear arms race could result in a nuclear accident or inadvertent, miscalculated or deliberate use and (c) *opinio juris* that the use of nuclear weapons under any circumstances will represent a violation of international humanitarian law and thus must be prohibited and eliminated.

The humanitarian initiative has been labelled as naïve, idealistic and futile, and it has been formally rejected by the P5/NPT Nuclear-Weapon States in the Conference on Disarmament. Among other points it was said that the initiative is not related to NPT goals and undermines the step-by-step process under way in the NPT Review Conference forum.[156] Consequently, similarly to the landmines and cluster munitions conventions mentioned earlier, the debatable possibility remains that a nuclear weapons convention could be concluded without the adherence of the producers and possessors of nuclear weapons as well as the States enjoying protection of the nuclear umbrella.

---

[155] U.N. Doc. A/C.1/71/L.41 (14 Oct. 2016).

[156] J. Borrie and T. Caughley, 'After Oslo: Humanitarian Perspectives and the Changing Nuclear Weapons Discourse' in J. Borrie and T. Caughey (eds.), *Viewing Nuclear Weapons through a Humanitarian Lens* (Geneva: United Nations Institute for Disarmament Research, 2014), pp. 95–115.

The tension between the majority's rejection of nuclear weapons and the minority which possesses or desires them continues unabated and is even augmented by the continued reliance of the possessors on the deterrent effect of nuclear weapons and the underscoring of their utility. While the DPRK holds its stockpile undisturbed, Iraq and Libya experienced coercive disarmament of their nascent nuclear weapons programmes and the Islamic Republic of Iran is under pressure to abandon the development of its technological capability. Under the 1994 Budapest Memorandum on Security Assurances,[157] Ukraine transferred to the Russian Federation the stockpile it inherited when the Soviet Union dissolved, in return for formal security assurances and guarantees of its territorial integrity and political independence. Twenty years later, it became the most recent example that there are no rewards for relinquishing the nuclear connection.

One study has hypothesised that four elements are necessary to increase the likelihood for the commencement and conclusion of negotiations of a convention on nuclear weapons and its entry into force: (i) scaled-up public consciousness (outcry) and industry support (for verification), (ii) intentional or accidental nuclear weapons use, (iii) political settlement (peace in the Middle East) and (iv) technological obsolescence (completion of the development of laser weaponry that can 'slice through cities and vaporise targets').[158] With the humanitarian initiative and the latest improvements in weapon technologies (autonomous lethal systems, hypersonic vehicles, cyberweapons, 'prompt global strike' (massive conventional strategic capabilities))[159] and the operational use of outer space, two of those conditions may be imminent.

11   Concluding Remarks

The issues discussed in this chapter show that, given the context in which they operate and the national interests involved, disarmament treaties raise several interesting issues for the law of treaties. The examples considered here demonstrate some of pragmatic solutions and arrangements that have been put in place to address problems

---

[157] Annexed to U.N. Doc. A/49/765 (19 Dec. 1994).

[158] C. Vestergaard, 'The Disarmament Factor: Toward a Typological Theory of WMD Disarmament', Doctoral Dissertation defended before the University of Copenhagen (Dec. 2010), pp. 200–242.

[159] Heinrich-Böll-Stiftung/Institute for Peace Research and Security Policy, *The Future of Arms Control* (Berlin: Heinrich-Böll-Stiftung, 2014).

that have arisen in order to ensure that the object and purpose of the treaty in question is achieved. It has been seen that, given the importance of disarmament in the work of the United Nations,[160] the Security Council in particular has played an important role, with its resolutions serving to enhance and supplement the provisions of treaties:[161] in one case, the prescriptions in a bilateral agreement informed the Security Council resolution which itself informed decisions of the policy-making organ of the relevant disarmament organization in supplementing the provisions of the relevant multilateral treaty regarding the obligations of a member State not party to the aforementioned bilateral agreement.[162] A major treaty of uncertain status is followed for several purposes as if there were agreement as to its status.[163] Pragmatic solutions have been adopted to manage (potential) issues of compliance with treaty obligations by invoking provisions of the treaty relating to the powers of the principal organs to achieve the objectives of the treaty rather than the provisions relating to treaty violations or imposition of sanctions.[164]

With regard to the challenge posed by nuclear weapons in particular, there was one significant development regarding the NPT. It will be recalled that, as part of the strategic bargain, Article VI NPT provides that each State Party 'undertakes to pursue negotiations in good faith on effective measures relating to cessation of the nuclear arms race at an early date and to nuclear disarmament, and on a treaty on general and complete disarmament under strict and effective international control'. Three decades later, in its advisory opinion in *Legality of the Threat or Use of Nuclear Weapons*, the ICJ made reference to Article 26 VCLT and declared that '[t]he legal import of [the Article VI NPT] obligation goes beyond that of a mere obligation of conduct; the obligation involved here is an obligation to achieve a precise result – nuclear disarmament in all its aspects – by adopting a particular course of conduct, namely, the pursuit

---

[160] See Section 1.   [161] See Sections 4(b), 5 and 9.

[162] Regarding the role of the Security Council in the operation of treaties in this field, D. H. Joyner and M. Roscini state that 'not only are there are special rules regarding treaty withdrawal present in non-proliferation treaties and in the legal practice of the UN Security Council but that there are also specialized interstitial norms present in the issue area of WMD proliferation that explain these rules, which differ from the general rules of international law and from specialized rules in other substantive areas of international law': see Joyner and Roscini, *supra* n. 29, at p. 168. While non-proliferation is not one of the issues considered in this chapter, it is clear that decisions of the Security Council play an important role in the operation and application of treaties in this field.

[163] See Section 2.   [164] See Section 7.

of negotiations on the matter in good faith'.[165] In the *dispositif* to the advisory opinion, the ICJ unanimously concluded that '[t]here exists an obligation to pursue in good faith and bring to a conclusion negotiations leading to nuclear disarmament in all its aspects under strict and effective international control'.[166] In April 2014, more than forty years after conclusion of the NPT, the Republic of the Marshall Islands instituted proceedings before the ICJ against the nine States that possess nuclear weapons.[167] The Marshall Islands filed applications against the five NPT nuclear States (China, France, Russia, United Kingdom and United States) for material breach of Article VI NPT and against four NPT non-parties (the DPRK, India, Israel, Pakistan), arguing that that provision now forms part of customary international law. In respect of the NPT nuclear States, the Marshall Islands argued that 'by not actively pursuing negotiations in good faith on effective measures relating to cessation of the nuclear arms race at an early date and to nuclear disarmament, [each Respondent] has breached and continues to breach its legal duty to perform its obligations under [NPT] and customary international law in good faith'. In respect of the NPT non-parties, the Marshall Islands argued that the obligations established in Article VI NPT are not merely treaty obligations; they also exist separately and apply to all States as a matter of customary international law. The Marshall Islands further argued that reliance upon their nuclear arsenals constitutes negative and obstructive conduct and that the quantitative build-up and qualitative improvements of arsenals constitutes all-out arms racing. The Marshall Islands requested the Court to order the Respondents to take all steps necessary to comply with their respective obligations under the NPT and customary international law within one year of its judgment, including the pursuit, by initiation if necessary, of negotiations in good faith aimed at the conclusion of a convention on nuclear disarmament in all its aspects under strict and effective international control. Three of the cases were heard by the Court: those against India, Pakistan and the United Kingdom.[168] All three Respondents replied by submitting

---

[165] *Legality of the Threat or Use of Nuclear Weapons, supra* n. 32, at pp. 263–265 (paragraphs 99–102).

[166] *Ibid.*, at p. 267 (paragraph 105(F)).

[167] See Press Release of the International Court of Justice, No. 2014/18: www.icj-cij.org /presscom/files/0/18300.pdf (25 Apr. 2014).

[168] In accordance with the Statute of the Court, only the Applications against India, Pakistan and the United Kingdom were entered in the Court's General List as those countries had accepted the compulsory jurisdiction of the Court. The Applications of the Republic of

objections to jurisdiction and admissibility. On 5 October 2016, the Court issued its verdict on the preliminary objections in all three cases, upholding the Respondents' objections to jurisdiction, finding, in each case, the absence of a dispute between the Parties and that it could not therefore proceed to the merits.[169] Each of the three decisions attracted fourteen declarations, separate or dissenting opinions from the judges. In upholding the objection of the United Kingdom to jurisdiction, the conclusion of the Court was only reached by the President's casting vote. Consequently, it is apparent that the Court remains deeply divided on the topic of nuclear weapons – reminiscent of the split in its advisory opinion in July 1996.[170]

The Marshall Islands cases represent an effort to determine the nature and extent of commitments undertaken by parties to a major treaty. The cases could have been significant if any of them had proceeded to the merits stage because this would have entailed a rare opportunity for *judicial* scrutiny of compliance with obligations under a disarmament treaty.

the Marshall Islands were transmitted to the governments of the other six, but as none consented to the Court's jurisdiction, none of those cases were entered on the General List. The Marshall Islands also filed a complaint in United States federal court for the continuing breach of Art. VI NPT as well as for depriving the Marshall Islands of the benefit of its bargain under the NPT, but the case was dismissed (and appealed) in 2015: *Republic of the Marshall Islands*, 79 F. Supp. 3d 1068 (N.D. Cal. 2015, 2 Apr. 2015); No. 4:14-CV-01885-JSW. For further discussion, see J. Maddox Davis, 'Promise Despite Overreach in Marshall Islands v. United States', *Emory ILR*, 30 (2016), 2063–2091.

[169] *Obligations Concerning Negotiations Relating to Cessation of the Nuclear Arms Race and to Nuclear Disarmament* (Marshall Islands v. India; Marshall Islands v. Pakistan; Marshall Islands v. United Kingdom) (Jurisdiction and Admissibility) (5 Oct. 2016).

[170] *Supra* n. 32.

19

International Criminal Law

ELIZABETH WILMSHURST

1 Introduction

Treaties are a major source of the law relating to genocide, crimes against humanity, and war crimes[1] and of the international courts and tribunals[2] which try those crimes. Treaty-based sources of international criminal law include the 1907 Hague Regulations,[3] the 1949 Geneva Conventions[4] (and their Additional Protocols)[5] and the 1948 United Nations Convention on the Prevention and Punishment of the Crime of Genocide,[6] all of which form, directly or indirectly, the basis for many

---

[1] This chapter adopts a definition of international criminal law restricted to the core crimes of genocide, crimes against humanity and war crimes and the international courts and tribunals which try these crimes. (See the similar approach adopted in R. Cryer, H. Friman, D. Robinson and E. Wilmshurst, *Introduction to International Criminal Law and Procedure* (Cambridge: Cambridge University Press, 3rd ed., 2014), pp. 3–27). The crime of aggression will be added to the list of crimes once the amendments to the International Criminal Court Statute adopted in 2010 at Kampala have entered into force.

[2] The chapter concerns primarily the International Criminal Tribunal for the Former Yugoslavia, the International Criminal Tribunal for Rwanda and the International Criminal Court. Occasional reference will also be made to the Special Court for Sierra Leone and the Special Tribunal for Lebanon. It includes developments through to March 2015.

[3] Annexed to the 1907 Hague Convention (IV) Respecting the Laws and Customs of War on Land, 118 LNTS 343.

[4] 1949 Geneva Convention (I) for the Amelioration of the Condition of the Wounded and Sick in Armed Forces in the Field, 75 UNTS 31; 1949 Geneva Convention (II) for the Amelioration of the Condition of Wounded, Sick and Shipwrecked Members of Armed Forces at Sea, 75 UNTS 85; 1949 Geneva Convention (III) Relative to the Treatment of Prisoners of War, 75 UNTS 135, and 1949 Geneva Convention (IV) Relative to the Protection of Civilian Persons in Time of War, 75 UNTS 287.

[5] Protocol Additional to the Geneva Conventions of 12 August 1949, and Relating to the Protection of Victims of International Armed Conflicts (Protocol I), 1125 UNTS 3, and Protocol Additional to the Geneva Conventions of 12 August 1949, and Relating to the Protection of Victims of Non-International Armed Conflicts (Protocol II), 1125 UNTS 609.

[6] 78 UNTS 277.

of the crimes within the jurisdiction of the international courts and tribunals. The Statutes of these courts and tribunals either are themselves treaties or are given binding effect by the 1945 United Nations Charter.

In establishing a system of international criminal justice, the Statutes of the international courts and tribunals include constitutive provisions establishing the court or tribunal, provisions regarding rights and obligations of States, and provisions which set out the jurisdiction of the court or tribunal and form or refer to a body of substantive law applicable to individuals rather than States. This chapter discusses the application of treaty law to the Statutes and to the treaties incorporated or applied by them by reference first to questions of individual criminal liability and second to inter-State relations. We leave to elsewhere in this volume questions regarding the constitutional provisions of international criminal law instruments.[7]

2 Individual Criminal Responsibility

2.1 The Application of Treaty Law

The international courts and tribunals apply a body of law which concerns individual criminal responsibility. The treaties contributing to this body of law do not simply direct States to incorporate in their domestic law offences applicable to individuals;[8] they address individuals directly by setting out a body of criminal law to be used by the international tribunals in relation to individual defendants. It is this feature of international criminal law that presents a challenge for the application of treaty law. Treaty law traditionally concerns instruments dealing with the rights and obligations of States; States (and international organizations) are the parties to treaties; treaty law has recourse to the intention of the treaty parties in interpreting the relevant instruments; the rules of privity concern third party *States* which have not been involved in the negotiation of the treaty.[9] But the individuals addressed by international criminal law are not parties to the treaties and have no capacity to become parties.

A preliminary issue is whether the treaties concerned are directly binding on individuals. It is well established that relevant parts of

---

[7] See the contribution to this volume of Moeckli and White at pp. 136–171 (Chapter 6).

[8] Some other treaties do just that: e.g. the 1971 Convention for the Suppression of Unlawful Acts against the Safety of Civil Aviation, 974 UNTS 178, and other so-called terrorism treaties.

[9] See the contribution to this volume of Waibel at pp. 201–236 (Chapter 8).

international humanitarian law can bind individuals, but the arguments as to why this is so sometimes rely on customary law as much as treaty law.[10] It has been suggested on the one hand that treaties *cannot* be a direct source of international criminal law[11] and, on the other, that 'there has been increasing willingness to interpret treaties as creating not only State responsibility but individual criminal liability as well'.[12] This is perhaps an area where the practice has outstripped the theory: the 'laws and customs of war' as found in treaty (and customary) law have long been applied by States directly to individuals,[13] and some of the practice of the international courts and tribunals supports the directly binding effect of treaty law on individuals. It has been argued that in this context the provisions of the Statutes of the *ad hoc* tribunals have to be distinguished from those of the Statute of the International Criminal Court (ICC),[14] the former being merely jurisdictional, the latter substantive: the

---

[10] See, e.g., T. Meron, *The Humanization of International Law* (Leiden: Brill 2006); the fact that the Nuremberg Tribunal considered as binding on individual defendants provisions of the 1929 Geneva Convention Relative to the Treatment of Prisoners of War, 118 LNTS 343, and 1907 Hague Convention (IV) Respecting the Laws and Customs of War on Land, *supra* n. 3, is used to support the argument that common Art. 3 of the 1949 Geneva Conventions creates individual criminal responsibility (at p. 114); but as later pointed out (at p. 116), it was only those provisions of the 1907 and 1929 Conventions that were declaratory of customary law that were considered as creating the basis for individual criminal responsibility.

[11] See, e.g., G. Mettraux, *International Crimes and the Ad Hoc Tribunals* (Oxford: Oxford University Press, 2005), pp. 7–9.

[12] Meron, *supra* n. 10, at p. 115.

[13] The International Committee for the Red Cross and Red Crescent (ICRC) Study on customary international humanitarian law states: 'Almost all military manuals and criminal codes refer to violations of both customary law and applicable treaty law'. See J.-M. Henckaerts and L. Doswald-Beck, *Customary International Humanitarian Law* (Vol. I: Rules) (Cambridge: Cambridge University Press, 2005), p. 572. On the applicability of treaties directly to individuals where that is the drafters' intent, see *Jurisdiction of the Courts of Danzing (Pecuniary Claims of Danzig Railway Officials Who Have Passed into the Polish Service, against the Polish Railways Administration)* (Advisory Opinion), 1928 PCIJ, Series B, No. 15, at p. 17. See, also, K. Partlett, *The Individual in the International Legal System: Continuity and Change in International Law* (Cambridge: Cambridge University Press, 2011), pp. 17–26. Cassese however argues that the privity rules in the Vienna Convention preclude non-State actors from becoming bound by treaties unless they accept to be bound: A. Cassese, 'The Status of Rebels under the 1977 Geneva Protocol on Non-International Armed Conflicts', *ICLQ*, 30 (1981), 416–439, at 428 ff. See, also, S. Sivakumaran, 'Binding Opposition Groups', *ICLQ*, 55 (2006), 369–394, arguing that it is the principle of legislative jurisdiction that allows rules to be binding on non-State armed groups. This is taken up further in J. Kleffner, 'The Applicability of International Humanitarian Law to Organised Armed Groups', *Int'l Rev. Red Cross*, 93 (2011), 443–461, casting doubt on some of the reasons given for asserting the binding nature of the law on armed groups.

[14] 2187 UNTS 90.

former are stated by their drafters to reflect customary international law
and thus merely to refer to pre-existing substantive law,[15] while the ICC
Statute departs from customary law in a few respects and to that extent
must create new obligations for individuals.[16] It may indeed be that in the
mind of the drafters, the Statutes of the *ad hoc* Tribunals only described
the jurisdiction of the courts and did not create substantive obligations
for individuals, the obligations being imposed by customary international law.[17] But the International Criminal Tribunal for Yugoslavia
(ICTY) itself has accepted that treaties can found criminal liability;[18]
even if the crimes provisions of its Statute are merely jurisdictional in
nature, the Tribunal's applicable law includes previous treaties, not
simply customary law. The Statute of the International Criminal
Tribunal for Rwanda (ICTR) criminalises violations of Additional
Protocol II although not all of it was at the time regarded as customary.[19]

---

[15] See, for example, the Secretary-General's Report which contains the Statute of ICTY (later
adopted by Security Council Resolution): Report of the Secretary-General Pursuant to
Paragraph 2 of Security Council Resolution 808 (1993), U.N. Doc. S/25704 (3 May 1993),
sections 5 and 6.

[16] Negotiators of the ICC Statute indicated that customary international law was regarded as
the basis for the definitions of crimes, but that that was not always the result is apparent:
see, for example, Cryer, Friman, Robinson and Wilmshurst, *supra* n. 1, at pp. 151–153.

[17] Report of the Secretary-General Pursuant to Paragraph 2 of Security Council Resolution
808 (1993), *supra* n. 15, at p. 9 (paragraph 34): 'In the view of the Secretary-General, the
application of the principle *nullum crimen sine lege* requires that the international
tribunal should apply rules of international humanitarian law which are beyond any
doubt part of customary law so that the problem of adherence of some but not all States to
specific conventions does not arise.'

[18] See Cryer, Friman, Robinson and Wilmshurst, *supra* n. 1, pp. 3–27, at pp. 9–10, referring
to *Kordić and Čerkez* (ICTY), IT-95-14/2-A (paragraphs 41–46) (which clarified *Tadić*
Decision on the Defence Motion for Interlocutory Appeal on Jurisdiction (ICTY), 2 Oct.
1995 (paragraph 143)) and noting that the ICTY Appeals Chamber has stated that the
position of the Tribunal is that treaties suffice for criminal responsibility, although 'in
practice the International Tribunal always ascertains that the relevant provision is also
declaratory of custom': *Galić* (ICTY Appeals Chamber), 30 Jan. 2006 (paragraph 85). As
pointed out in Cryer, Friman, Robinson and Wilmshurst, *supra* n. 1, statements in the
ICTY have not always been consistent: at least two ICTY Appeals Chamber judges have
taken the view that the ICTY only has jurisdiction over customary law offences: M.
Shahabuddeen, *International Criminal Justice at the Yugoslav Tribunal: A Judge's
Recollection* (Oxford: Oxford University Press, 2012), pp. 61–70, and *Galić* (ICTY
Appeals Chamber), 30 Jan. 2006, Partially Dissenting Opinion of Judge Schomburg
(paragraph 21).

[19] Art. 4 of the ICTR Statute: Report of the Secretary-General Pursuant to Paragraph 5 of
Security Council Resolution 955 (1994), U.N. Doc. S/1995/134 (13 Feb. 1995) (paragraph 12).

Further, the application of general principles of law by the tribunals has gone beyond customary international law.[20]

It would appear that international criminal law instruments, including those treaties that are incorporated in the relevant Statutes, can indeed be, under certain conditions, the basis for individual liability under international criminal law. This conclusion may present problems for the principle of *nullum crimen sine lege* (see Section 2.2.2.1 of the present chapter). It is of course only those treaties and those provisions which are *intended* to give rise to criminal responsibility which can do so.[21]

2.2 Interpretation

It is in relation to rules of interpretation in particular that this chapter considers the relevance of treaty law. The case law of the international courts and tribunals on the interpretation of the Statutes and other international instruments has been significant for the development of international criminal law – as well as providing a rich resource for a growing literature among international criminal lawyers.[22] The

---

[20] See, for example, cases cited in K. J. Heller, 'Two Thoughts on Manuel Ventura's Critique of Specific Direction', www.opiniojuris.org (http://opiniojuris.org/2014/01/10/two-thoughts-manuel-venturas-critique-specific-direction/) (10 Jan. 2014).

[21] See discussion in M. Milanovic, 'Is the Rome Statute Binding on Individuals? (and Why We Should Care)', *J. Int'l Crim. Just.*, 9 (2011), 25–52, at 47–51.

[22] See, for example, W. A. Schabas, 'Interpreting the Statutes of the Ad Hoc Tribunals' in L. C. Vohrah, F. Pocar, Y. Featherstone, O. Fourmy, C. Graham, J. Hocking and N. Robson (eds.), *Man's Inhumanity to Man: Essays on International Law in Honour of Antonio Cassese* (The Hague: Kluwer Law International, 2003), pp. 847–888; L. Grover, 'A Call to Arms: Fundamental Dilemmas Confronting the Interpretation of Crimes in the Rome Statute of the International Criminal Court', *EJIL*, 21 (2010), 543–583; D. Robinson, 'The Identity Crisis of International Criminal Law', *Leiden JIL*, 21 (2008), 925–963; M. Swart, 'Is There a Text in This Court? The Purposive Method of Interpretation and the ad hoc Tribunals', *ZaöRV*, 70 (2010), 767–789; K. Anderson, 'The Rise of International Criminal Law: Intended and Unintended Consequences', *EJIL*, 20 (2009), 331–358; D. Akande, 'Sources of International Criminal Law' in A. Cassese (ed.), *The Oxford Companion to International Criminal Justice* (Oxford: Oxford University Press, 2009), pp. 41–53, at pp. 44–49; P. Okowa, 'Interpreting Constitutive Instruments of International Criminal Tribunals: Reflections on the Special Court for Sierra Leone' in M. Fitzmaurice, O. Elias and P. Merkouris (eds.), *Treaty Interpretation and the Vienna Convention on the Law of Treaties: 30 Years On* (Leiden: Brill, 2010), pp. 333–356; D. Jacobs, 'International Criminal Law' in J. Kammerhofer and J. d'Aspremont (eds.), *International Legal Positivism in a Post-Modern World* (Cambridge: Cambridge University Press, 2014), pp. 451–474, and L. N. Sadat and J. M. Jolley, 'Seven Canons of ICC Treaty Interpretation: Making Sense of Article 25's Rorschach Blot', *Leiden JIL*, 27 (2014), 755–788.

approaches to interpretation found in this jurisprudence are drawn from the Vienna rules of treaty law[23] and from special rules appropriate to criminal trials. Antonio Cassese's judicial interpretations, including in the two *Tadić* decisions referred to later, led one commentator to observe that he transformed 'the ICTY Statute from an incomplete shopping list of ancient treaties, into a coherent progressive codification. Rules of interpretation provided him with many of the tools and the authoritative arguments necessary to carry out this task'.[24] His expansive interpretations were both praised and criticised[25] but have been particularly important to the development of international humanitarian law applicable in non-international armed conflict.

2.2.1   The Vienna Rules

The *ad hoc* Tribunals and the ICC have paid at least lip service to the application of the Vienna rules in the interpretative process. The ICTY early decided that its own Statute – contained in a report of the Secretary-General and adopted by Security Council Resolution 827 (1993)[26] – should be subject to the 'customary rules of interpretation codified in the Vienna Convention' on the Law of Treaties (VCLT);[27] the ICTR followed the same course with regard to its own Statute, contained in a Security Council resolution.[28] The Vienna rules were used, or at least

---

[23] Rules of interpretation as found in Arts. 31 to 33 VCLT: *infra* n. 27. See, further, the contribution to this volume by Gardiner at pp. 335–362 (Chapter 11).

[24] See Schabas, *supra* n. 22, at p. 848. See, also, R. Cryer, 'International Criminal Tribunals and the Sources of International Law: Antonio Cassese's Contribution to the Canon', *J. Int'l Crim. Just.*, 10 (2012), 1045–1061.

[25] For criticism, see, for example, Judge Li's separate opinion in *Tadić Jurisdiction*, where he maintained that the Court's decision regarding the wide scope of Art. 3 was 'in fact an unwarranted assumption of legislative power which has never been given to this Tribunal by any authority'.

[26] Security Council Resolution 827 (25 May 1993).   [27] 1155 UNTS 331.

[28] Security Council Resolution 955 (8 Nov. 1994). Early rulings by the ICTY can be found in: *Erdemovic*, Judgment, Separate Opinion of Judge McDonald and Judge Vohrah, IT-96-22-A, 7 Oct. 1997 (paragraphs 3–5) and *Tadić*, Decision on the Prosecutor's Motion Requesting Protective Measures for Victims and Witnesses, IT-94-1-T, 10 Aug. 1995, where the Trial Chamber stated: 'Although the Statute of the International Tribunal is a *sui generis* legal instrument and not a treaty, in interpreting its provisions and the drafters' conception of the applicability of the jurisprudence of other courts, the rules of treaty interpretation contained in the Vienna Convention on the Law of Treaties appear relevant' (paragraph 18). For the ICTR, see Decision on the Admissibility of the Prosecutor's Appeal from the Decision of a Confirming Judge Dismissing an Indictment against Theoneste Bagasora and 28 others, ICTR-98-37-A, 8 June 1998 (paragraphs 28–29).

referred to, in the interpretation not only of the Statute and treaties, but also the ICTY and ICTR Rules of Procedure and Evidence,[29] which are not agreements between States, nor agreements between States and international organizations, nor treaties within an international organization, but provisions adopted by the judges. The Vienna rules have even been applied to the ICTY Code of Professional Conduct for Counsel, apparently because it was made 'under' the Statute.[30]

Like the *ad hoc* Tribunals, the ICC has decided that the Vienna rules are applicable to the interpretation of its Statute[31] and to the ICC Rules of Procedure and Evidence[32] which, unlike those of the *ad hoc* Tribunals, were negotiated and agreed by governments. The Vienna rules have been referred to even though the ICC Statute has its own rules of interpretation for at least some of its provisions.[33]

Another example of reception of the Vienna rules is to be found in the case law of the Special Tribunal for Lebanon (STL). The Tribunal's Statute is attached to an agreement between Lebanon and the United Nations which never came into force as such, due to the political impasse in the country at the time; its provisions were brought into force by the Security

---

[29] *Erdemovic*, Judgment, Separate Opinion of Judge McDonald and Judge Vohrah, IT-96–22-A, 7 Oct. 1997; *Ramush Haradinaj et. al.* Decision on Prosecutor's Motion for Reconsideration of Relief Ordered Pursuant To Rule 68*bis*, ICTY IT-04-84bis-T, 27 March 2012 (paragraph 36) and ICTR-96–15-A, *Kanyabashi*, Joint Separate and Concurring Opinion of Judge Wang Tieya and Judge Rafael Nieto-Navia, 3 June 1999 (paragraph 11).

[30] 'The practice of interpreting the Statute and the Rules as a treaty should be equally applicable to the ICTY Code and Directive as instruments made under the Statute': *Slobodan Milosevic*, Decision on Assigned Counsel's Motion for Withdrawal, IT-02–54-T, 7 Dec. 2004.

[31] In *The Situation in the DRC*, the Prosecutor was claiming leave to appeal a decision for which no possibility of appeal was provided in the Statute. The Appeals Chamber held the Vienna Convention applicable, expressly referred to the Vienna rules and found that the interpretation of the Statute in accordance with the 'sense and spirit' led to the decision that a new right of appeal could not be created, and this view was confirmed by the *travaux préparatoires*: Judgment on Prosecutor's Application for Extraordinary Review of Pre-Trial Chamber's 31 March 2006 Decision Denying Leave to Appeal, ICC-01/04–168, 13 July 2006 (paragraph 33).

[32] Judgment on the Appeals of The Prosecutor and The Defence against Trial Chamber I's Decision on Victims' Participation of 18 Jan. 2008, ICC-01/04–01/06 OA 9 OA 10, 11 July 2008 (paragraph 55).

[33] Arts. 22 and 23 of the ICC Statute: *supra* n. 14; see, also, Section 2.2.2. It was not until the *Katanga* judgment that the ICC decided to address directly the tension between the Vienna rules and the Statute rules, concluding that there are limits set by the Statute to recourse to the Vienna rules: *Germain Katanga* (ICC-01/04–01/07–3436), 7 March 2014 (paragraph 50).

Council.[34] The Vienna rules were applied by the Tribunal to the interpretation of its Statute, 'whether the Statute is held to be part of an international agreement between Lebanon and the United Nations or is regarded instead as part of a binding resolution adopted by the Security Council under Chapter VII of the UN Charter'.[35] Its Rules provide expressly that they are subject to interpretation by the Vienna rules.[36]

The courts and tribunals have accepted the Vienna rules without much concern about their legal basis. The rules are not applicable *as treaty law* to the Statutes of the *ad hoc* Tribunals or to the STL Statute, all of which rely on Security Council resolutions.[37] The customary law status of the rules has on occasion been referred to in the Tribunals' case law,[38] as has the fact that they are drawn from or consistent with general principles found in domestic systems.[39] The application of the Vienna rules to the ICC Statute is said to be as treaty law,[40] though without a recognition that

[34] Security Council Resolution 1757 (30 May 2007).

[35] Interlocutory Decision on the Applicable Law: Terrorism, Conspiracy, Homicide, Perpetration, Cumulative Charging, AC STL-II-0l/1,16 Feb. 2011 (paragraph 28).

[36] The Rules (drafted by the judges) contain much more detailed principles of interpretation than the Statute itself (drafted by the UN Secretariat in consultation with the Security Council and the Lebanese government); the interpretation provision no doubt draws on the experience of the then President of the Tribunal, former ICTY President Cassese: '(A) The Rules shall be interpreted in a manner consonant with the spirit of the Statute and, in order of precedence, (i) the principles of interpretation laid down in customary international law as codified in Articles 31, 32 and 33 of the Vienna Convention on the Law of Treaties (1969), (ii) international standards on human rights (iii) the general principles of international criminal law and procedure, and, as appropriate, (iv) the Lebanese Code of Criminal Procedure. (B) Any ambiguity that has not been resolved in the manner provided for in paragraph (A) shall be resolved by the adoption of such interpretation as is considered to be the most favourable to any relevant suspect or accused in the circumstance then under consideration'.

[37] In the *Kosovo* advisory opinion, the ICJ clarified that the Vienna rules provide at least 'guidance' in the interpretation of Security Council resolutions. *Accordance with International Law of the Unilateral Declaration of Independence in Respect of Kosovo* (Advisory Opinion) (2010) ICJ Rep. 403, at p. 442 (paragraph 94). See, also, the contribution to this volume of Wood at pp. 790–808 (Chapter 24).

[38] For example, *Čelebići (Zejnil Delalic, Zdravko Mucic (a.k.a. 'Pavo'), Hazim Delic and Esad Landžo (a.k.a. 'Zenga'))*, IT-96–21-A, 20 Feb. 2011 (paragraph 67).

[39] *Nsengiyumva*, Joint and Separate Opinion of Judge McDonald and Judge Vohrah, 3 June 1999 (paragraph 14); and see, further, *Kanyabashi* Joint Separate and Concurring Opinion of Judge Wang Tieya and Judge Rafael Nieto-Navia, ICTR-96–15-A, 3 June 1999 (paragraph 11).

[40] 'The interpretation of treaties, and the Rome Statute is no exception, is governed by the Vienna Convention on the Law of Treaties'. *Judgment on Prosecutor's Application for Extraordinary Review of Pre-Trial Chamber I's 31 March 2006 Decision Denying Leave to Appeal*, ICC-01/04–168, 13 July 2006 (paragraph 33). See, also, Judge Kaul's dissent in *Situation in Kenya*, where he refers to the Convention as an 'applicable treaty' under Art.

as treaty law the Convention can apply only in the relations between the 'parties' to it; indeed in the context of individual criminal responsibility there is a question as to who the relevant 'parties' can be.

Another approach was taken in the STL by President Cassese, no doubt relying on his experience as one-time President of ICTY:

> It is true that the rules of interpretation that evolved in international custom and were codified or developed in the 1969 Vienna Convention on the Law of Treaties referred only to treaties between States, because at that stage the development of new forms of binding international instruments (such as agreements between States and rebels, or binding resolutions of the UN Security Council regulating matters normatively) had not yet taken a solid foothold in the world community. Those rules of interpretation must, however, be held to be applicable to any internationally binding instrument, whatever its normative source. This is because such rules translate into the international realm general principles of judicial interpretation that are at the basis of any serious attempt to interpret and apply legal norms consistently.[41]

As well as interpreting the international instruments which provide their Statutes, the courts and tribunals have used the Vienna rules to interpret the treaties which form the basis of their subject matter jurisdiction. An obvious question is whether a connection with a State party is necessary in order for a treaty to be applicable in proceedings against an individual. For example, is it appropriate for the ICC, in a prosecution for a war crime based on 1977 Additional Protocol I to the 1949 Geneva Conventions (I)–(IV),[42] to consider whether a State with jurisdiction over an individual is a State party to that treaty? Or is it relevant to consider the question only with regard to the State of nationality of the accused or on the territory of which the crime was committed – the two States of relevance for the purpose of the ICC's own jurisdiction under Article 12 of the Statute? Indeed, is the identity of States parties relevant at all? The issue has not been satisfactorily resolved by the courts.[43] On occasion, the ICTY has made reference to the relevance of States parties in the context of the *nullum crimen* principle but without explanation. Thus, in *Kordić and Čerkez*, the ICTY Appeals Chamber approved the

---

21 of the Statute, *supra* n. 14, which sets out the law applicable by the Court, and as customary international law: Decision Pursuant to Article 15 of the Rome Statute on the Authorization of an Investigation into the Situation in the Republic of Kenya, ICC-01/09–19-Corr, 31 March 2010 (paragraph 34).

[41] Interlocutory Decision on the Applicable Law: Terrorism, Conspiracy, Homicide, Perpetration, Cumulative Charging STL, AC STL-II-0l/1, 16 Feb. 2011.

[42] *Supra* n. 4.   [43] Milanovic, *supra* n. 21, at 47–52.

conviction of unlawful attack – a violation of Additional Protocol I – on the basis that '[t]he maxim of *nullum crimen sine lege* is also satisfied where a State is already treaty-bound by a specific convention, and the International Tribunal applies a provision of that convention irrespective of whether it is part of customary international law'.[44]

It would be fruitless to look for a consistent approach to interpretation, whether on the basis of the Vienna rules or otherwise. While there are frequent references to the Vienna rules in the case law of the *ad hoc* Tribunals, many other principles of interpretation have also been applied or at least referred to.[45] In two of the most important rulings of the ICTY in its early days, both from the *Tadić* case, the ICTY Appeals Chamber, differently constituted in the *Jurisdiction* decision[46] and the *Judgment*,[47] used diverse principles in reaching its decisions. In *Jurisdiction*, in determining that 'the laws or customs of war' (in Article 3) included crimes committed in internal as well as international armed conflict while the grave breaches provision (in Article 2) was applicable only to international armed conflict, the Court did not make express reference to the Vienna rules, but variously stated that it was using as interpretative tools the literal meaning of the text, statements made by government representatives in the Security Council, the 'general perspective' and historical context,[48] the object and purpose of the Statute,[49] customary international law,[50] 'logical and systematic construction',[51] and the intention of the drafters (the Security Council).[52] In his separate opinion, Judge Abi-Saab, while characterising the approach of the majority as following the principle of *effet utile*, reached a different view on the interpretation of

---

[44] *Kordić and Čerkez* (ICTY), 17 Dec. 2004 (paragraph 44). And see Milanovic, *supra* n. 21, at 38–47.

[45] For a short list of some interpretative principles used in the case law of the *ad hoc* Tribunals, see Grover, *supra* n. 22, and Schabas, *supra* n. 22.

[46] *Tadić* Decision On The Defence Motion For Interlocutory Appeal On Jurisdiction, ICTY, 2 Oct. 1995 ('*Tadić Jurisdiction*').

[47] *Tadić Judgment*, 15 July 1999 ('*Tadić Judgment*').

[48] *Tadić Jurisdiction, supra* n. 46 (paragraph 93).

[49] *Ibid.* (paragraphs 71–78); the Tribunal stated that the 'primary purpose' of the establishment of the Tribunal was 'not to leave unpunished any person guilty of a serious violation of international humanitarian law in the former Yugoslavia, whatever the context within which it may have been committed, and thus decided that crimes in internal armed conflict were included (paragraph 92).

[50] *Ibid.* (paragraphs 96–127 and 137); see, also, *Tadić Judgment, supra* n. 47 (paragraph 287).

[51] *Tadić Jurisdiction, supra* n. 46 (paragraph 137); see, also, *Tadić Judgment, supra* n. 47 (paragraph 284).

[52] *Tadić Jurisdiction, supra* n. 46 (paragraphs 74–77 and 137).

Article 2 by using what he regarded as subsequent practice and *opinio juris*. In *Tadić Judgment*, in determining whether the definition of crimes against humanity required a discriminatory intent, the Appeals Chamber, differently constituted but still with Judge Cassese on its bench, purportedly used some of the same tools,[53] but rejected the use of statements made in the Security Council as a legitimate means of interpretation in this instance. Making express reference this time to the Vienna rules, the Chamber found that the Council statements were not part of the 'context' and since, in the Chamber's view, the meaning was not ambiguous or obscure, they could not be resorted to as *travaux préparatoires*.[54] The approaches taken towards interpretation were crucial not only for the convictions in *Tadić* but also in establishing the jurisdiction of the Tribunal and in laying the way for future prosecutions of war crimes. The *Tadić* decisions were perhaps at the highwater mark of judicial creativity.

2.2.1.1 Article 31 VCLT

All the courts and tribunals have made reference to the components of the Vienna rules, while for the most part providing no analysis or system for their application. A few examples are given here from both old and more recent case law. As regards Article 31(1) VCLT, the *ad hoc* Tribunals have referred to ordinary meaning sometimes with surprising results;[55] the ICC has done the same.[56] 'Object

---

[53] *Tadić Judgment, supra* n. 47: ordinary meaning (paragraph 283); logical construction (paragraph 284); *effet utile* (paragraph 284); customary international law ('the principle whereby, in case of doubt and whenever the contrary is not apparent from the text of a statutory or treaty provision, such a provision must be interpreted in light of, and in conformity with, customary international law') (paragraph 284); object and purpose and aim of drafters (paragraph 285).

[54] *Ibid.* (paragraphs 298–304).

[55] See Appeals Chamber in *Tadić Jurisdiction* which extended the law of war crimes from international to non-international armed conflict, observing that a 'literal reading' of the laws or customs of war 'standing alone may lead one to believe that it applies to both kinds of conflict': *supra* n. 46 (paragraph 71). In *Blagojević et. al., Judgment*, ICTY-02-60-A, 9 May 2007, the Appeals Chamber gave a wide meaning to a provision of Additional Protocol I on the basis of the stated object and purpose of the Protocol and the 'ordinary and broad sense' (paragraphs 281–282).

[56] The 'plain' meaning of the Statute was referred to by Judge Fulford in his separate opinion in *Lubanga* (ICC-01/04–01/06, 14 March 2012 (paragraph 13)) in his rejection of the control of the crime theory adopted by the majority, which required him in his view to read in additional terms to the Statute. See, also, the concurring opinion of Judge Christine Van den Wyngaert in *Mathieu Ngudjolo Chui* (ICC-01/04–02/12–4, 18 Dec. 2012); her agreement with Fulford that the control of the crime theory should not be accepted was based on the 'ordinary meaning' of the Statute (paragraph 11).

and purpose' is referred to from time to time by the courts and tribunals, and the object and purpose of the Statutes have been variously described. The all-encompassing – 'to do justice, to deter further crimes and to contribute to the restoration and maintenance of peace'[57] – does not give much assistance to the interpreter. A reference to object and purpose has sometimes been used with circular effect. 'The aim of those drafting the Statute was to make all crimes against humanity punishable' said the Appeals Chamber in *Tadić Judgment*, purportedly relying on this to interpret the meaning of crimes against humanity, but thus begging the question at issue, the meaning of the crime.[58] And an early case before the ICTR resulted in a misconception: the Tribunal adopted a wide interpretation of the protected groups in *Akayesu*, drawing on what it inferred (wrongly) to be the aim of the drafters.[59]

A difficulty arises where the object and purpose of the treaties which provide the substantive jurisdiction of the court or tribunal differs from that of the relevant Statute. In *Tadić Judgment*, Geneva Convention (IV) Relative to the Protection of Civilian Persons in Time of War[60] was interpreted in accordance with an object and purpose which was stated to be 'the protection of civilians to the maximum extent possible'; the Chamber preferred the purposive approach over the fairly clear literal meaning.[61] But the *purpose* of the Tribunals' Statutes includes the

---

[57] *Tadić* Decision on The Prosecutor's Motion Requesting Protective Measures for Victims and Witnesses, 10 Aug. 1995 (paragraph 18), quoting the First Annual Report of the International Tribunal for the Prosecution of Persons Responsible for Serious Violations of International Humanitarian Law Committed in the Territory of the Former Yugoslavia since 1991, U.N. Doc. A/49/150 (1994) at paragraph 11. And see *Anto Furundžija Judgment*: the 'fundamental purpose of the Statute,' was described as 'to ensure fair and expeditious trials of persons charged with violations of international humanitarian law so as to contribute to the restoration and maintenance of peace in the former Yugoslavia', referring to paragraph 26 of Report of the Secretary-General Pursuant to Paragraph 2 of Security Council Resolution 808 (1993), *supra* n. 15, at p. 8: IT-95–17/1-A, 21 July 2000 (paragraph 280).

[58] *Tadić Judgment, supra* n. 47 (paragraph 285).

[59] The Trial Chamber decided that the intention was to 'ensure the protection of any stable and permanent group': ICTR-96–4-T, 2 Sept. 1998 (paragraph 516). For further assessment, see the contribution to this volume of Kritsiotis at pp. 237–302 (Chapter 9).

[60] *Supra* n. 4.

[61] *Tadić Judgment, supra* n. 47 (paragraphs 163–169). The definition of protected persons in Art. 4(1) of Geneva Convention (IV) Relative to the Protection of Civilian Persons in Time of War, *supra* n. 4, is those 'in the hands of a Party to the conflict or Occupying Power of which they are not nationals'. The Appeals Chamber expanded the definition by abandoning the plain meaning with its reference to nationality. The finding was followed in *Čelebići*, IT-96–21-A, *supra* n. 38 (paragraphs 71–73).

holding of fair trials,[62] which should include a requirement of strict construction.

The use of the purposive approach in criminal proceedings has come in for criticism. On the one hand it has been welcomed 'as promoting a certain humanitarian philosophy';[63] what is good for human rights interpretation is said to be good for the international tribunals, and the gap between human rights law and international humanitarian law is shrinking.[64] Others have pointed to the dangers for international criminal law of adopting a human rights approach to interpretation or one using a teleological victim-based interpretative reasoning:

> ... examination reveals that a technique commonly used in [international criminal law (ICL)] is (i) to adopt a purposive interpretive approach; (ii) to assume that the exclusive object and purpose of an ICL enactment is to maximize victim protection; and (iii) to allow this presumed object and purpose to dominate over other considerations, including if necessary the text itself.[65]

Darryl Robinson regards this is an illustration of the 'crisis of identity' for international criminal law; its subject-matter jurisdiction is largely drawn from international human rights law and international humanitarian law, for both of which practitioners readily use the interpretative approaches of protection for the victim or rights holder, while the system as a whole requires an interpretative approach which leads to a fair trial:

> The identity crisis theory helps to explain why an overwhelmingly liberal-minded profession endorses startlingly illiberal doctrines and developments. In a typical criminal law context, liberal sensitivities focus on constraining the use of the state's coercive power against individuals. In ICL, however, prosecution and conviction are often conceptualized as the fulfilment of the victims' human right to a remedy. Such a conceptualization encourages reliance on human rights methodology and norms.[66]

---

[62] See Arts. 20 and 21 of the ICTY Statute (*supra* n. 15) and Arts. 19 and 20 of the Rwanda Statute (*supra* n. 19).

[63] Swart, *supra* n. 22, at 775.

[64] *Ibid.* at 784. Swart, at 780, justifies wide teleological interpretations on the basis of a large community of international criminal lawyers, practitioners and law-makers and law-deciders: 'It can be argued that it is the implied consent of the international interpretive community that lends legitimacy to the Tribunals' use of the purposive approach and therefore to the lawmaking that takes place by employing the purposive approach'. For questions regarding the interpretation of human rights treaties, see the contribution to this volume of Chinkin at pp. 509–537 (Chapter 16).

[65] Robinson, *supra* n. 22, at 934.   [66] *Ibid.*, at 930.

Broad, victim-focused, dynamic interpretations lead to conflicts with the criminal law principles of interpretation which are discussed later.

To return to the Vienna rules, customary international law and international human rights law have frequently been called upon by the courts for interpretative purposes, whether or not by reference to the requirement in Article 31(3)(c) VCLT, that 'any relevant rules of international law applicable in the relations between the parties' are to be taken into account together with the context.[67] The *ad hoc* Tribunals have used the jurisprudence of the European Court of Human Rights to determine, for example, the content of torture and inhuman and degrading treatment.[68] Recourse to customary international law has amounted almost to a presumption in its favour,[69] sometimes as an assessment of whether the *nullum crimen* principle is being complied with (which shall be explored further later). The Tribunals have not always distinguished clearly between the application of human rights law or customary international law as source of law or as interpretative tool. These bodies of law can either be seen as filling gaps in the Statutes or as interpreting general terms; the two are sometimes employed interchangeably.[70] The ICC's special rules of interpretation include a requirement that 'the application and interpretation of law ... must be consistent with internationally recognised human rights',[71] although, unlike the reference in the

---

[67] It should be noted that the reference to 'parties' sits oddly in this context and exemplifies the uneasy match between the Vienna rules and the determination of criminal responsibility.

[68] See, for example, *Furundžija* (ICTY Trial Chamber II), 10 Dec. 1998 (paragraph 160), regarding the definition of torture.

[69] See Schabas, *supra* n. 22, at pp. 872–877 for discussion of the sometimes inconsistent approach of the ICTY on the issue.

[70] In *Kupreškić et al.*, the ICTY Trial Chamber declared, in interpreting the term 'persecution':

> any time the Statute does not regulate a specific matter, and the Report of the Secretary-General does not prove to be of any assistance in the interpretation of the Statute, it falls to the International Tribunal to draw upon (i) rules of customary international law or (ii) general principles of international criminal law; or, lacking such principles, (iii) general principles of criminal law common to the major legal systems of the world; or, lacking such principles, (iv) general principles of law consonant with the basic requirements of international justice. It must be assumed that the draftspersons intended the Statute to be based on international law, with the consequence that any possible lacunae must be filled by having recourse to that body of law.

Kupreškić et al., Judgment, 14 Jan. 2000, IT-95-16-T (paragraph 591) (Cassese again).

[71] Art. 21 (3) of the Statute: *supra* n. 10. See, further, R. Young, 'Internationally Recognised Human Rights before the ICC', *ICLQ*, 60 (2011), 189–208.

Vienna rules to take these materials into account, the ICC Statute imposes a *requirement* of consistency with human rights.[72]

2.2.1.2 Article 32 VCLT

As regards the use of *travaux préparatoires*, the international courts and tribunals have the same difficulties as many other interpreters in deciding what 'supplementary means' to call upon. In *Tadić Jurisdiction*, as we have seen, the Appeals Chamber used the statements made in the Security Council on adoption of the ICTY Statute as aids to the interpretation of provisions regarding war crimes, but in *Tadić Judgment*, the Chamber rejected the relevance of such statements for the interpretation of Article 5 on crimes against humanity, recognising that the interpretation followed by the Chamber was directly contrary to statements made in the Security Council.[73] The result in both instances was to give a wider scope to the provision in question. The STL, on the other hand, has taken into account statements made by members of the Security Council in relation to the adoption of the relevant resolutions, the Report of the United Nations Secretary-General on the Establishment of the Tribunal as well as the practice of the Security Council.[74]

Like many other courts, the international criminal courts and tribunals have not been consistent in deciding *when* resort may be had to the *travaux préparatoires*. While the norm may be that the separation of Articles 31 and 32 into general rule and supplementary means 'has not proved a bar to reference to preparatory work, circumstances of

---

[72] In *Lubanga*, the Trial Chamber had to consider the ambit of the war crime of recruiting or enlisting children or using them to 'participate actively in hostilities'. After referring to Art. 21(3) of the Statute, the Court interpreted the scope of the crime by reference to the jurisprudence of the SCSL, and to the 1989 United Nations Convention on the Rights of the Child, 1577 UNTS 3 (paragraphs 602–608). See, also, Judgment on Prosecutor's Application for Extraordinary Review of Pre-Trial Chamber I's 31 March 2006 Decision Denying Leave to Appeal, ICC-01/04–168, 13 July 2006, where the Court referred to Art. 14(5) of the International Covenant on Civil and Political Rights, 999 UNTS 171, and, in a footnote, to the American Convention on Human Rights, 1144 UNTS 123, as well as Protocol No. 7 to the European Convention on Human Rights, ETS 117, and decided that only final decisions of a criminal court on verdict or sentencing required an appeal under human rights law (paragraph 38).

[73] This was on the basis that 'although the statements may be interpreted as *travaux préparatoires* under customary law as codified in Art. 32 of the Vienna Convention, the *travaux préparatoires* may be resorted to only in cases of ambiguity or obscurity of the principal normative instrument'.

[74] Interlocutory Decision on the Applicable Law: Terrorism, Conspiracy, Homicide, Perpetration, Cumulative Charging STL AC STL-II-0l/1, 16 Feb. 2011 (paragraph 27).

conclusion or other supplementary means',[75] there has been some reticence by the international courts in using the *travaux préparatoires* except in cases of doubt or to confirm a meaning.[76]

One problem for the ICC is that there is a scarcity of *travaux préparatoires* for its Statute and it has suffered from – or enjoyed – a surfeit of interpretations of the Statute in the academic literature, drawing on the alleged intentions of negotiators. As one commentator has said, on occasion 'a reconstructed history appears to have eclipsed the actual drafting history'.[77]

2.2.2 Special Rules

While the courts and tribunals purport to use the Vienna rules (or not) in the same way as other courts, they also use special rules of interpretation which are appropriate to a body of criminal law.[78] The three main principles – *nullum crimen* (and *nulla poena*) *sine lege*, strict construction and *in dubio pro reo* (or interpretation in favour of the accused) – may be termed collectively the principle of legality. All three are expressly included in the ICC Statute,[79] along with the requirement, as we have seen, that the interpretation of the law must be consistent with internationally recognised human rights.[80] The special rules for the ICC allow

---

[75] R. K. Gardiner, *Treaty Interpretation* (Oxford: Oxford University Press, 2nd ed., 2015), p. 350.

[76] *Tadić Judgment, supra* n. 47 (paragraph 303); see, too, the ICC decision in *Situation in the DRC*, where the Court looked at the *travaux préparatoires* only to confirm a meaning reached by other means: Judgment on Prosecutor's Application for Extraordinary Review of Pre-Trial Chamber I's 31 March 2006 Decision Denying Leave to Appeal, ICC-01/04–168, 13 July 2006 (paragraph 40).

[77] D. Robinson, 'The Controversy over Territorial State Referrals and Reflections on ICL Discourse', *J. Int'l Crim. Just.*, 9 (2011), 355–384.

[78] *Pace* Gardiner, *supra* n. 23, this section does not distinguish between 'rules' and 'principles'.

[79] Arts. 22 and 23: *supra* n. 14. It can be said that there is a fourth rule of interpretation for the ICC – the use of its Elements of Crimes. The ICC Statute refers to the Elements variously as an additional aid to interpretation (in Art. 9) and as an additional body of law to be applied by the Court (in Art. 21(1)). The confusion between application and interpretation is for the time being resolved by the majority view in *Al Bashir*, which held that the Elements are applicable law and not merely an interpretative aid: ICC-02/05–01/09, 4 March 2009 (paragraphs 125–128). See Grover for the view that the Chamber did not acknowledge the effect of Art. 31(3) VCLT, which would require as interpretative aids both the use of the Elements of Crimes, which is a 'subsequent agreement between the parties', and custom, which contains relevant and applicable rules of international law: *supra* n. 22, at 577. That view supposes that Art. 31(3) VCLT overrides special rules laid down in the governing instrument, a view that is not widely shared.

[80] Art. 21(3): *supra* n. 14; the Article also provides that the interpretation and application of the law must be 'without any adverse distinction founded on grounds such as gender as

for a differentiation of interpretative techniques within the one legal instrument: the presumptions of criminal law expressly apply only to the definitions of crimes, but the rule regarding the use of international human rights applies to all of the provisions of the Statute.

Although not required by their Statutes, the *ad hoc* tribunals have referred to these principles on various occasions. The inclusion in the ICC Statute of the principles of strict construction and *pro reo* was undoubtedly motivated in part to avoid the judicial creativity exhibited in the first judgments of the ICTY.

2.2.2.1 *Nullum Crimen Sine Lege* The jurisdiction of some of the international courts and tribunals includes crimes committed before their Statutes came into force, notably the *ad hoc* Tribunals, the Special Court for Sierra Leone (SCSL) and the STL. For Security Council referrals, and where there is an *ad hoc* acceptance of jurisdiction by a non-party State, this is also the case for the ICC. The principle of *nullum crimen* is therefore an important one, both in assessing whether the relevant Statutes themselves refrain from creating or applying retroactive law and as a constraint on future law-making by the judges. In the *ad hoc* Tribunals, the principle has often supported an assumption that its subject-matter jurisdiction must be interpreted in conformity with customary international law,[81] flowing in part from the United Nations Secretary-General's report on the establishment of the ICTY which stated that 'the application of the principle *nullum crimen sine lege* requires that the international tribunal should apply rules of international humanitarian law which are beyond any doubt part of customary law'.[82]

---

defined in Article 7, paragraph 3, age, race, colour, language, religion or belief, political or other opinion, national, ethnic or social origin, wealth, birth or other status'.

[81] Thus in *Krštić*, in limiting the definition of genocide to acts seeking the physical or biological destruction of the group, the ICTY Trial Chamber reached its interpretation 'taking into account the state of customary international law at the time the events in Srebrenica took place,' referring to the principle of *nullum crimen* (paragraphs 541 and 580). In *Tadić Judgment*, the Appeal Chamber referred to '[t]he principle whereby, in case of doubt and whenever the contrary is not apparent from the text of a statutory or treaty provision, such a provision must be interpreted in light of, and in conformity with, customary international law. In the case of the Statute, it must be presumed that the Security Council, where it did not explicitly or implicitly depart from general rules of international law, intended to remain within the confines of such rules': *supra* n. 47 (paragraph 287; see, also, paragraph 296).

[82] Report of the Secretary-General Pursuant to Paragraph 2 of Security Council Resolution 808 (1993), *supra* n. 15, at p. 9 (paragraph 34).

Is *nullum crimen* a principle of interpretation or a substantive principle? While in *Vasiljević*, for example, the ICTY Trial Chamber used it as a principle of interpretation,[83] the SCSL in *Norman* would have been prepared to exclude the operation of a provision of the Statute itself on the basis of the principle.[84] It acted there as a jurisdictional limit.

In the ICC Statute, *nullum crimen* is a separate principle and is not described as merely interpretative (Article 22(1)).

2.2.2.2   Strict Construction

While the principle of strict construction was discussed in *Čelebići*,[85] its use by the Tribunals is scanty. It has been noted that 'the formulation and status of the rule ... in common law jurisdictions is not free from uncertainty, and it has been irregularly applied'.[86] The ICC, however, is required by its Statute to construe crimes within its jurisdiction strictly and not to extend them by analogy.[87] The Court applies the requirement of strict construction to the general principles of law, not merely to the definitions of crimes.[88]

2.2.2.3   *In Dubio Pro Reo*

The principle was explained in the STL Appeals Chamber as 'a corollary of the overarching principle of fair trial and in particular of the presumption of innocence' and applicable 'as a standard of construction when the Statute or the Lebanese Criminal

---

[83] *Vasiljević* (ICTY Trial Chamber), IT-98-32, 29 Nov. 2002 (paragraph 193).

[84] *Prosecutor v. Sam Hinga Norman*, Decision on Preliminary Motion based on Lack of Jurisdiction, SCSL-04-14-AR72(E), 31 May 2004. The crime of (conscripting and) enlisting soldiers under the age of fifteen was expressly within the Court's jurisdiction but the Court reviewed treaty law, customary law and the case law of other international tribunals to assess whether the principle of *nullum crimen* was breached by indicting the accused with the crime. 'It is the duty of this Chamber to ensure that the principle of non-retroactivity is not breached. As essential elements of all legal systems, the fundamental principle *nullum crimen* and the ancient principle *nulla poena crimes sine lege* need to be considered' (paragraph 25). In his dissenting judgment, Judge Robertson gave the view that the criminalisation of enlistment of child soldiers had not crystallised in customary international law until the adoption of the ICC Statute, and that he would therefore strike out the charge of enlistment in spite of the clear words of the SCSL Statute.

[85] *Čelebići*, IT-96-21-A, *supra* n. 38 (paragraphs 408 ff.).

[86] B. Broomhall, 'Article 22' in O. Triffterer (ed.), *Commentary on the Rome Statute of the International Criminal Court: Observer's Notes, Article by Article* (Munich/Oxford: C.H. Beck/Hart Publishing/Nomos, 2nd ed., 2008), pp. 713–729, at p. 724.

[87] Art. 22(2): *supra* n. 14. The principle was discussed in *Germain Katanga*, Judgment, ICC 01/04–01/07, 7 March 2014 (paragraph 52).

[88] For example, *Jean-Pierre Bemba Gombo*, Decision Pursuant to Article 61(7)(a) and (b) of the Rome Statute on the Charges of the Prosecutor Against Jean-Pierre Bemba Gombo, ICC-01/05–01/08, 15 June 2009 (paragraphs 369 (meaning of intent and knowledge) and 423 (meaning of superior responsibility)).

Code is unclear and when other rules of interpretation have not yielded satisfactory results'.[89] The Tribunal went on to reach a controversial decision which was markedly not in favour of the accused (and arguably did not conform with the principle of *nullum crimen*).[90] In the *ad hoc* Tribunals, the principle has been referred to in a few cases,[91] but in others it had no effect. Thus, in *Tadić Jurisdiction*, the approach used was clearly contrary to both a strict construction of Article 3 of the ICTY Statute – which would have confined the provision to international armed conflict – and to the principle of *pro reo*. Judge Robertson's dissenting opinion in *Norman* in the SCSL used this principle, as well as *nullum crimen*, to support his view that enlisting child soldiers should not be prosecuted.[92]

This principle is now mandatory for the ICC (Article 22(2) of its Statute) though explicitly only in relation to the definitions of the crimes, and only 'in case of ambiguity'. In logic, it should be applied to all provisions of the Statute relevant to the offence in question; the principle was referred to in *Mathieu Ngudjolo Chu* by Judge Van den Wyngaert in discussing the modes of liability as an 'essential safeguard to ensure both the necessary predictability and legal certainty that are essential for a system that is based on the rule of law'.[93] In *Katanga*, however, it was emphasised that the provision only benefited the accused if the meaning

---

[89] *Ibid.* (paragraphs 49–51). It is referred to expressly in the Rules of Evidence and Procedure; see *supra* n. 36.

[90] The Tribunal, in interpreting Art. 2 (terrorism) of its Statute, found contrary to the submissions of prosecution and defence, that although Art. 2 referred only to terrorism under national law, international law could 'assist in interpreting and applying Lebanese law'. It then imported into Lebanese law a wider offence of terrorism, having decided (against the preponderance of international criminal law commentary) that terrorism was a crime under customary international law. The ruling in effect created a new offence.

[91] For example, ICTY: *Tadić* Extension of Time Limit, 15 Oct. 1998 (paragraph 73): '. . . any doubt should be resolved in favour of the defence in accordance with the principle *in dubio pro reo*'; ICTR: *Akayesu*, ICTR-96-4-T, 2 Sept. 1998 (paragraphs 500–501): in a choice between the French and English versions of the Genocide Convention 'killing' or 'meurtre', the Chamber said that '[g]iven the presumption of innocence of the accused, and pursuant to the general principles of criminal law, the Chamber holds that the version more favourable to the accused should be upheld', choosing the French. And see cases cited at Schabas, *supra* n. 22, at p. 81; Schabas describes the cases he has identified as 'rare and essentially perfunctory references' to the principle, but that assessment can be doubted.

[92] See *supra* n. 84. 'If international criminal law adopts the common law principle that in cases of real doubt as to the existence or definition of a criminal offence, the benefit of that doubt must be given to the defendant, then this would appear to be such a case' (paragraph 6).

[93] *Mathieu Ngudjolo Chui*, Concurring Opinion (paragraph 19).

of an ambiguous term or provision cannot be resolved by reference to the Vienna rules or the complementary means of interpretation.[94]

2.2.3 Relationship between the Special Rules and the Vienna Rules

In spite of the widespread acceptance, whether expressly or impliedly, of the Vienna rules by the courts and tribunals, it has been argued that 'conceptually, the Vienna Convention should in fact be excluded as an interpretative tool for Statutes of international criminal tribunals'.[95] Identifying the differences between the Vienna rules and the principles applicable in criminal trials has become common in the literature.[96]

As we have seen, it is purposive interpretation under the Vienna rules which comes in for particular criticism. Designating the object and purpose of the Statutes as being the protection of victims can lead to a wide reading of the relevant crimes, thus conflicting with criminal law principles designed to protect the rights of the accused.

But the alleged faults of purposive interpretations are not necessarily to be laid at the door of the Vienna rules. An interpretation which looks over-expansive in the criminal law context may be due not to the use of the Vienna rules but to their abuse: a purely 'purposive' approach to interpretation extracts only one of the factors from Article 31 and ignores the others.[97] As an interpretative guide, the combination of the factors of ordinary meaning of a text, its context and its object and purpose is indicated by general principles of law – and common sense. Furthermore, some of the extreme examples of judicial creativity shown by the Tribunals, mentioned previously, are now in the past and will be avoided by the ICC for many of its cases as a result of the inclusion of Article 22(2) in the Statute.

It is not only purposive approaches to interpretation which are argued to get in the way of the criminal law principles. For example, the Vienna rules allow reference to the *travaux préparatoires* to resolve an ambiguity; but if there is ambiguity, Article 22(2) of the ICC Statute (and the same

---

[94] *Germain Katanga*, Judgment, ICC-01/04–01/07, 7 March 2014 (paragraph 53).
[95] Jacobs, *supra* n. 22, at p. 472.
[96] See for example, Sadat and Jolley, who counterpose the 'traditional methods of interpretation with the unique characteristics of the Rome Statute': *supra* n. 22, at 84.
[97] See for example the ILC Commentary, which makes it clear that object and purpose has to be closely related to identifying the ordinary meaning of a term: 'the ordinary meaning of a term is not to be determined in the abstract but in the context of the treaty and in the light of its object and purpose'. See *YbILC* (1966–II), 221 (paragraph 12).

principle as enunciated by other tribunals) requires that the meaning most favourable to the accused should be chosen, and this may conflict with travaux which point in a contrary direction.[98] None of the approaches to interpretation given in the Vienna rules recognises the criminal law principles, and any of the rules may be used to defeat the principles.

It may be argued that the Vienna rules are adequate if all the special principles necessary for a proper interpretative approach to criminal law are squeezed into the 'object and purpose' criterion in Article 31(1) VCLT; but, if so, the Vienna rules are of little use as universal guidance and risk losing their purpose as a unifying tool for the interpretation of treaties. Nor does a solution which proposes that criminal law interpretative principles be applied along with or as a subset of the Vienna rules resolve all difficulties. For example, *in dubio re* is applied in international criminal law only if other interpretative methods fail to solve the question, but applying, at a prior stage, a purposive approach which maximises victim protection may mean that there will not be an ambiguity left for this principle to resolve because all ambiguities have already been resolved against the accused.[99]

What is the relevance then of the Vienna rules to determinations of criminal responsibility? The problem of applying the rules to criminal trials has been addressed by many academics in the field of international criminal law.[100] There have been demands for the ICC to adopt clear methodologies of interpretation.[101] Instead of starting with the Vienna rules and trying to squeeze in the principles of criminal law, it may be thought to be more in conformity with the nature of this body of law to begin with the principles of international criminal law – bound up together as the principle of legality – and to adopt rules of interpretation in conformity with them.

Dov Jacobs, having first addressed the idea that a *lex specialis* approach would allow the principle of legality to be applied in preference to the Vienna rules at least so far as the ICC is concerned, also proposes an

---

[98] Akande, *supra* n. 22, at p. 45.   [99] Robinson, *supra* n. 22, at 934.

[100] For example, Schabas, *supra* n. 22, at p. 847, and Akande, *supra* n. 22. See, also, B. Van Schaak, '*Crimen Sine Lege*: Judicial Lawmaking at the Intersection of Law and Morals', *Georgetown Law J.*, 97 (2008), 119–192, at 135, and Grover, *supra* n. 22.

[101] Sadat and Jolley, *supra* n. 22, at 58 (it is 'vital that the Court develop a consistent methodology of interpretation, particularly as regards the "criminal code" embedded in the treaty' as a 'basic framework that balances traditional methods of interpretation with the unique characteristics of the Rome Statute'). And see Grover, *supra* n. 22, at 583.

approach which draws on the 'functional duality' of the Statutes and the fact that 'the nature of an instrument is not solely dependent on its mode of creation, but also on the institutional context in which it is applied'.[102] He goes on to say:

> Applied to the Statutes under consideration, this means that their mode of creation is in fact secondary. The fact that they are the legislative outcome of a treaty or a UN Security Council Resolution does not mean that they are international instruments in the specific context of the criminal proceedings that they allow. On the contrary, it is argued here that when a Judge applies the ICC Statute in criminal proceedings, for example, he is not applying it *qua* treaty, but applying it as the internal instrument for the functioning of the Court, which therefore does not automatically warrant, as usually claimed, the reference to the Vienna Convention as providing the rules of interpretation. If, on the other hand, two states were to disagree on the interpretation of a particular provision of the Statute, relating to head of state immunities for example, this would justify the application of the Vienna Convention because the ICC Statute would be considered as a treaty as between the two states.[103]

This echoes what has already been said in a separate opinion by one judge in the ICC. Judge Van den Wyngaert, in referring to Article 22(2) of the Statute (strict construction and *in dubio pro reo*), stated:

> [T]his article overrides the conventional methods of treaty interpretation, as defined in the Vienna Convention on the Law of Treaties, particularly the teleological method. Whereas these methods of interpretation may be entirely adequate for interpreting other parts of the Statute, I consider that for interpreting articles dealing with the criminal responsibility of individuals, the principles of strict construction and *in dubio pro reo* are paramount.[104]

This chimes with claims that in other bodies of law, the particular functions of treaties and of the different provisions within treaties should have an impact on the applicability of the Vienna rules.[105]

An attempt to marry the Vienna rules with the special rules of interpretation has been made by one Chamber of the ICC, which has addressed the challenge of applying the Vienna rules while respecting the principles of strict construction, the prohibition of arguing by

---

[102] Jones, *supra* n. 22, at p. 469.   [103] *Ibid.*, at p. 470.

[104] *Mathieu Ngudjolo Chui*, Concurring Opinion (paragraph 18). And see Grover, *supra* n. 22, at 543, calling for a differentiation of techniques depending on the different provisions within a single treaty.

[105] For analogies with human rights treaties on this point, see Chinkin, *supra* n. 64.

analogy, and *in dubio pro reo*, as required by Article 22 of the ICC Statute, as well as ensuring compatibility with international human rights law, as required by Article 21.[106] In its judgment in *Katanga*, the Chamber reaffirmed that the Vienna rules are indeed to be applied by the ICC. Making reference to many of the authors cited previously, the Chamber declared that a purposive approach to interpretation which took into consideration the requirement to end impunity could be contrary to the requirement of strict construction and *in dubio pro reo*. The Vienna rules identify or confirm one of the ordinary meanings of the text and do not give it an extraneous meaning.[107]

The resolution of the difficulty as to interpretative methods matters, of course. For international criminal courts and tribunals, the choice between one particular interpretative method and another may mean the difference between the imprisonment or freeing of an individual.

3 Intergovernmental Relations in International Criminal Law

The principal challenge for treaty law, as we have seen, is in that area of international criminal law which relates to questions of individual criminal accountability. The inter-State provisions of the Statutes, on the other hand, do not give rise to issues unfamiliar to other fields of international law, and for these provisions there is no reason to claim that international criminal law is a special body of law whose treaties should be subject to different treatment from others. The inter-State provisions and those governing the relations of States with the ICC give some interesting illustrations of the application of treaty law.

In disagreements about the interpretation of the inter-State provisions of the ICC Statute, the proponents of different views turn as a matter of course to the Vienna Convention to support their arguments. The term 'State' itself in the ICC Statute has given rise to argument. The debate arose first in connection with the attempted submission to jurisdiction by the Palestine Authority, and the arguments were littered with references to the Vienna Convention.[108] Article 12(3) of the Statute allows only

---

[106] *Germain Katanga*, Judgment, ICC-01/04–01/07, 7 March 2014 (paragraphs 43–57). Whether or not the interpretative approach discussed at the beginning of the judgment was followed in the judgment will no doubt be discussed in academic commentary.

[107] *Ibid.* (paragraphs 54–56).

[108] See, for example, 'Al-Haq Position Paper on Issues Arising from the Palestinian Authority's Submission of a Declaration to the Prosecutor of the International Criminal Court under Article 12(3) of the Rome Statute', and in response, 'Legal

'States' to make such a submission; the declaration lodged by the Palestinian National Authority on 22 January 2009[109] therefore required the Prosecutor to take a decision on whether Palestine was a State for this purpose. The Prosecutor decided that the declaration was not acceptable since the United Nations General Assembly had not accepted Palestine as being 'a State'. History has now moved on following General Assembly Resolution 67/19 of 29 November 2012, which accorded Palestine the status of an observer State in the UN, and the accession by Palestine to the Statute.

Immediately following the adoption of the ICC Statute, objections were made that the Statute was in conflict with treaty law on *pacta tertiis* in that the ICC was given jurisdiction over nationals of a State not a party to the Statute, without that State's consent, where a crime was committed on the territory of a State party. The underlying political objections were voiced by representatives of those States which opposed the Statute, principally the United States, while the relevance of Article 34 VCLT was debated in the literature.[110] The objection was legally without merit, since the Statute does not create obligations for States not parties to it. Although it is true that where ICC prosecutions concern the agents of a State not party to the Statute, the *interests* of the State may be very much affected, the fact that nationals of a non-party State can be prosecuted in an international court does not bind the State, and the State can in any event choose to bring a national prosecution itself and thereby prevent

Memorandum In Response to the Al-Haq Brief and opposing the Palestinian Authority's Attempt to Accede to ICC Jurisdiction', the first giving the purpose of the ICC Statute for the purpose of Art. 31 of the Vienna Convention as being to punish those who commit international crimes and to prevent impunity, thus justifying an expansive interpretation, and the second stating the purpose to be intentionally constrained, consistent with the notion of a court complementary to national legal systems, thus justifying a narrow interpretation. Both memoranda are available at www.icc-cpi.int/en_menus/icc/struc ture%20of%20the%20court/office%20of%20the%20prosecutor/comm%20and%20ref/ pecdnp/palestine/Pages/summary%20of%20submissions%20on%20whether%20the% 20declaration%20lodged%20by%20the%20palestinian%20nati.aspx.

[109] Available at www.icc-cpi.int/iccdocs/PIDS/press/Palestine_A_12-3.pdf.

[110] For a small selection from the large literature, see D. Akande, 'The Jurisdiction of the International Criminal Court over Nationals of Non-parties: Legal Basis and Limits', *J. Int'l Crim. Just.*, 1 (2003), 618–650; M. Morris, 'High Crimes and Misconceptions: The ICC and Non Party States', *Law & Contemp. Prob.*, 64 (2001), 13–66; F. Mégret, 'Epilogue to an Endless Debate: The International Criminal Court's Third Party Jurisdiction and the Looming Revolution of International Law', *EJIL*, 12 (2001), 247–268, and M. Scharf, 'The ICC's Jurisdiction over the Nationals of Non-party States: A Critique of the US Position', *Law & Contemp. Prob.*, 64 (2001), 67–117. See, further, the contribution to this volume of Waibel at pp. 201–236 (Chapter 8).

ICC proceedings. The jurisdiction given to the ICC by States parties is no more than they could themselves exercise; indeed, based as it is on nationality and on the *lex loci* it is more restricted than the universal jurisdiction generally admitted for international crimes. There is no conflict here with Article 34 VCLT.

An analogous objection has been raised in respect of the disregard by the ICC Statute of international law immunities enjoyed by agents of States not parties to the Statute. Article 27 of the Statute gives the Court jurisdiction in spite of any immunities otherwise attaching to the prospective defendant and thus, where the defendant is a representative or agent of a State, it can be seen to be in tension with the *pacta tertiis* principle. Another provision of the Statute – Article 98 – seeks to address this possible conflict by requiring the Court to seek consent from a relevant State when requiring the surrender of a person enjoying international law immunities. The matter came to a head in relation to the arrest warrant issued by the ICC against the President of Sudan.[111] The African Union resolved that its member States should not comply with the warrant, and a number of African States refused to effect an arrest when Al Bashir visited their countries. In proceedings before the ICC, Malawi argued that Sudan was not a party to the ICC Statute, and hence the provision of the Statute removing immunity (Article 27) was not applicable to Sudan; it noted also that it aligned itself with the position of the African Union.[112] The Pre-Trial Chamber rejected the argument. It noted the cases in which international courts had prosecuted heads of State as well as the findings of the Special Court for Sierra Leone in relation to former President Charles Taylor of Liberia.[113] It also noted the

---

[111] The arrest warrant was issued on 4 March 2009; a second arrest warrant was issued on 12 July 2010: ICC-02/05–01/09 *The Prosecutor v. Omar Hassan Ahmad Al Bashir* (www.icc-cpi.int/darfur/albashir).

[112] *Prosecutor v. Omar Hassan Ahmad Al Bashir*, Decision Pursuant to Article 87(7) of the Rome Statute on the Failure by the Republic of Malawi to Comply with the Cooperation Requests Issued by the Court with Respect to the Arrest and Surrender of Omar Hassan Ahmad Al Bashir ('Malawi Decision'), ICC-02/05–01/09–139, 12 Dec. 2011 (paragraph 8). This followed a decision of the Chamber authorising the arrest warrant where it addressed (briefly and unsatisfactorily) the position of Omar Al Bashir as Head of State: Decision on the Prosecution's Application for a Warrant of Arrest against Omar Hassan Ahmad Al Bashir, ICC-02/05-0l/09-3, 4 March 2009 (*supra* n. 73).

[113] The SCSL issued a warrant for the arrest of Charles Taylor, at the time the President of Liberia, in June 2003. He claimed that he was immune as a Head of State. The Appeals Chamber held that the SCSL was an 'international court' and, as such, was not barred from prosecuting serving Heads of State; this decision was reached although the Court was created by an agreement between the UN and Sierra Leone. The decision (at

large number of States Parties to the ICC, and held that a 'critical mass' had been reached, so that customary international law immunities were no longer applicable in this context.[114] The Chamber went on to hold that 'when cooperating with this Court and therefore acting on its behalf, States Parties are instruments for the enforcement of the *jus puniendi* of the international community'.[115] In this respect, the Malawi decision and the similar case concerning Chad[116] are interesting in that they purport to accord to the intergovernmental treaty which is the ICC Statute an almost constitutional status in the international community.[117] The Malawi decision mentioned the non-party State problem (which the Statute deals with in Article 98) but dismissed it – in an extraordinary illustration of misused purposive interpretation: 'To interpret Article 98(1) in such a way so as to justify not surrendering Omar Al Bashir on immunity grounds would disable the Court and international criminal justice in ways completely contrary to the purpose of the Statute Malawi has ratified'.[118]

Another question of treaty law arose from the opposition of the United States to the ICC in the early years of the Court. The then US administration secured from a number of States bilateral agreements which provided that no nationals, current or former officials, or military personnel of either party could be surrendered or transferred by the other State to the ICC.[119] Some of the States concerned were also parties to the ICC Statute. The bilateral agreements made reference to Article 98(2) of

---

paragraph 38) found that the agreement was one 'between *all* members of the United Nations and Sierra Leone. This fact makes the Agreement an expression of the will of the international community'. The Court thus found that it was an international court and that that entailed an absence of immunity for defendants: *Charles Ghankay Taylor*, SCSL-2993-01-I, A. Ch. 31 May 2004. The decision is criticised in Z. Deen-Racsmány, 'Prosecutor v. Taylor: The Status of the Special Court for Sierra Leone and Its Implications for Immunity', *Leiden JIL*, 18 (2005), 299–322; M. Frulli, 'The Question of Charles Taylor's Immunity', *J. Int'l Crim. Just.*, 2 (2004), 1118–1129; D. S. Koller, 'Immunities of Foreign Ministers: Paragraph 61 of the Yerodia Judgment as It Pertains to the UN Security Council and the International Criminal Court', *Am. Univ. Int'l L. Rev.*, 7 (2004), 30–41, and H. King, 'Immunities and Bilateral Agreements: Issues Arising from Articles 27 and 98 of the Rome Statute', *N.Z. J. Public & Int'l L.*, 4 (2006), 269–310.

[114] *Charles Ghankay Taylor, supra* n. 113 (paragraph 42).

[115] Malawi Decision, *supra* n. 112 (paragraph 46).   [116] *Ibid.*

[117] See the contribution to this volume of Moeckli and White at pp. 136–171 (Chapter 6).

[118] Malawi Decision, *supra* n. 112 (paragraph 41). The Malawi and Chad Decisions have been criticised for their treatment of Art. 98 of the Statute: D. Tladi, 'The ICC Decisions on Chad and Malawi: On Cooperation, Immunities, and Article 98', *J. Int'l Crim. Just.*, 11 (2013), 199–221.

[119] For the text of one example – that with East Timor – see *AJIL*, 97 (2003), 201–202.

the Statute,[120] and the United States maintained that, in accordance with that provision, the ICC would not be able to request a State to surrender a national of the United States to the Court once that State had entered into such an agreement with the United States. The agreements were concluded on a false premise, since Article 98(2) applies only to persons who are 'sent' by one State to another State,[121] so the agreements will not be effective to prevent the Court requesting the surrender of an individual covered by the agreement.[122] The requested State party will continue to be obliged to cooperate with the ICC by surrendering a person if asked to do so. Considered as a problem of treaty law, there is clearly a conflict of treaties here. A State party requested by the ICC to surrender a person covered by a bilateral agreement would face irreconcilable obligations.

A further example of tension between treaty obligations comes from Africa. Over 60 per cent of the membership of the African Union (AU) are parties to the ICC Statute, but there has long been some hostility within the AU to the Court. AU Assembly resolutions have been critical of the Court and in one respect at least have demanded action by its members which is inconsistent with the treaty obligations many of them have under the Statute: as we have seen, AU members are required not to cooperate in the arrest and surrender of President al

---

[120] Art. 98(2) precludes the Court from asking for the surrender of a suspect if that would require the requested State 'to act inconsistently with its obligations under international agreements pursuant to which the consent of a sending State is required to surrender a person of the State to the Court': *supra* n. 14.

[121] The provision was inserted in the Statute to address the problem of conflicting obligations where, for example, a State in which foreign military personnel are stationed has agreed under a status of forces agreement (SOFA) to accord the right to the sending State to exercise criminal jurisdiction over its troops for certain kinds of offences. Without Art. 98(2), such an agreement would conflict with the obligation in the ICC Statute to surrender suspects to the Court when so requested. The US attempt to interpret the reference in Art. 98(2) to a 'sending State' so as to refer to all nationals of that State relies erroneously on the use of that term in the 1963 Vienna Convention on Consular Relations, 21 UNTS 77: see D. Scheffer, 'Article 98 (2) of the Rome Statute: America's Original Intent', *J. Int'l Crim. Just.*, 3 (2005), 333–353, at 347–350.

[122] This view is reflected in the guidelines agreed upon by the EU Council: EU Council of Ministers 2459th Session, GAER Doc 12134/02 (30 Sept. 2002); reprinted in D. McGoldrick, P. Rowe and E. Donnelly (eds.), *The Permanent International Criminal Court: Legal and Policy Issues* (Oxford: Hart Publishing, 2004), pp. 430–431. On the subject generally, see M. Benzing, 'U.S. Bilateral Non-surrender Agreements and Article 98 of the Statute of the International Criminal Court: An Exercise in the Law of Treaties', *Max Planck Yb. UN Law*, 8 (2004), 181–236, and H. van der Wilt, 'Bilateral Agreements between the US and States Parties to the Rome Statute: Are They Compatible with the Object and Purpose of the Statute?', *Leiden JIL*, 18 (2005), 93–111.

Bashir.[123] Although the position is not entirely clear from the Constitutive Act of the African Union,[124] it appears that Assembly decisions are binding on AU members, and thus there is a conflict between the legal requirements to cooperate with the ICC and the obligations imposed by the Decisions of the African Union. While the 2010 AU decision would seem to allow a balancing of the AU resolution with the ICC obligations, that is not the case for the 2009 and later decisions.

It was again the opposition of the United States to the ICC that gave us a rare example of a State 'unsigning'[125] a treaty in order to indicate that it was no longer bound by the obligation that signatories to a treaty should 'refrain from acts which would defeat the object and purpose of a treaty'. While the announcement by the United States of its intention not to become a party to the Statute following its signature was greeted with dismay, the United States was being faithful to Article 18 VCLT in so doing – and Israel and, later, Sudan followed its lead.[126]

***

The procedures used at the 2010 Kampala Review Conference to amend the ICC Statute to allow prosecution of the crime of aggression have come under scrutiny for their compatibility with the Vienna Convention on the Law of Treaties. The procedures required by the Statute – the unamended Statute – differ according to the kind of amendment concerned. Amendments to the crimes provisions enter into force only for the States Parties which have accepted them (Article

---

[123] African Union, Assembly/AU/Dec/3(XIII), 3 July 2009 (paragraph 10), and Decision Assembly/AU/Dec.296 (XV) (2010); the latter decision however also required Member States to 'balance, where applicable, their obligations to the AU with their obligations to the ICC', which might be interpreted as allowing some latitude in complying with the earlier decision. Later Assembly decisions have reaffirmed the non-cooperation obligation (and have also required action by the ICC and the UN Security Council regarding the trial of the Kenyan President and Deputy President). See, also, Assembly/AU/Dec.334(XVI), 30–31 Jan. 2011 (paragraph 5) and Assembly/AU/Dec.547(XXIV) (paragraphs 18 and 19).

[124] OAU Doc. CAB/LEG/23.15 (11 July 2000).

[125] International law generally, and the Vienna Convention in particular, does not make any provision for 'unsigning' a treaty, and we put it therefore in quotation marks, although it is a useful term. For further discussion, see E. T. Swaine, 'Unsigning', Stanford L. Rev., 55 (2003), 2061–2089.

[126] The United States made its announcement during the first term of President George W. Bush's administration; Israel followed suit. Sudan was clearly influenced by the referral of the Darfur situation to the Court in doing the same.

121(5));[127] other amendments enter into force for all States Parties after seven-eighths of them have accepted them (Article 121(4)). The core of the amendments adopted at the Kampala Conference concerned the crimes provisions (allowing the Court jurisdiction over aggression), but additional provisions had to be included which could arguably be seen as coming within Article 121(4). The negotiators at the Conference had to choose between the two different entry into force provisions; they chose to adopt all the amendments by means of Article 121(5) – that is, the provision under which amendments bind only States Parties which accept them.[128] That was a perfectly acceptable procedure, justifiable on the basis that all the amendments were closely tied to the crimes provisions of the Statute.

The negotiators went further, however, and included in the amendments themselves a provision stating that the Court may not exercise jurisdiction over aggression by a State Party if the latter has previously declared that it does not accept such jurisdiction.[129] This conflicts with Article 121(5) of the Statute. It appears to be based on an assumption that the Court will have jurisdiction, once the amendments have entered into force, unless a State Party accepts the amendments and then opts out, with the further oddity that the opt-out seems to extend only to acts of aggression committed by the opting-out State. But the natural interpretation of Article 121(5) of the existing Statute leaves the nationals and territory of a State Party which does not accept the Kampala amendments in the first place unaffected by the Court's jurisdiction. The result of this rather extraordinary example of treaty (or amendment) drafting is that it is uncertain whether the nationals or territory of a State Party which does not accept the amendments are subject to the Court's jurisdiction.

Commentators have written varied accounts of the conflicting provisions and their interpretation.[130] The relatively clear wording of Article

---

[127] Which provides that '[a]ny amendment to article 5 of this Statute shall enter into force for those States Parties which have accepted the amendment one year after the deposit of their instruments of ratification or acceptance. In respect of a State Party which has not accepted the amendment, the Court shall not exercise its jurisdiction regarding a crime covered by the amendment when committed by that State Party's nationals or on its territory': *supra* n. 14.

[128] Resolution RC/Res. 6 (paragraph 1).   [129] Art. 15 *bis* (paragraph 4): *supra* n. 14.

[130] For a useful and critical analysis, see A. Zimmerman, 'Amending the Amendment Provisions of the Rome Statute', *J. Int'l Crim. Just.*, 10 (2012), 209–227. For a differing account, see C. Kreß and L. von Holtzendorff, 'The Kampala Compromise on the Crime of Aggression', *J. Int'l Crim. Just.*, 8 (2010), 1179–1217; among other points, the authors describe an interpretative approach by which Art. 121(5) does not preclude ICC

121(5) and its history lead to the conclusion that the nationals and territory of a State Party are *not* exposed to the Court's jurisdiction in respect of the crime of aggression until the State concerned accepts the Kampala amendments; if a State Party accepts the amendments it then has the choice of opting out, under Article 15 *bis*, but only in relation to acts of aggression it commits itself. A contrary view which has been expressed – and which was no doubt the view of many of the negotiators – is that States Parties which do not want their nationals to be tried for aggression will have to adopt the strange procedure of first accepting the amendments and then opting out. But this interpretation requires the effective amendment of Article 121 itself, and that is not possible except through the amendment procedure set out in Article 121(4).

The delegate from Japan at the Conference is reported as saying that Japan had serious doubts regarding the legality of the amendment procedures.[131] Indeed, the Vienna Convention's rules on amendments and its provisions protecting parties to a treaty from being bound by amendments to it except in accordance with the treaty's own provisions (Articles 40 and 41) were, arguably, ignored at Kampala. One commentator has criticised the procedure used on the basis that it raises 'fundamental issues of the law of treaties ... and could, in the long term undermine the legality and the effectiveness of the solution reached'.[132]

Another issue of contention concerns States which are not parties to the Statute. The Kampala amendments provide that the Court has no jurisdiction over the crime of aggression with respect to a State that is not a Party to the Statute 'when committed by that State's nationals or on its territory'.[133] The result is that the Court cannot try

---

jurisdiction over a national of a non-ratifying State Party when the alleged aggression was committed within the territory of a State Party that *has* ratified or accepted the amendment. This approach relies on Art. 12(2) of the Statute (which allows the Court to exercise its jurisdiction over the nationals of States that are not parties to the Statute whenever their acts are committed on the territory of a State Party) and conflicts with the history of the Rome Statute; see, e.g., M. Politi, 'The ICC and the Crime of Aggression: A Dream That Came Through and the Reality Ahead', *J. Int'l Crim. Just.*, 10 (2012), 267–288, at 280. See, also, S. D. Murphy, 'The Crime of Aggression at the International Criminal Court' in M. Weller (ed.), *The Oxford Handbook on the Use of Force in International Law* (Oxford: Oxford University Press, 2015), pp. 533–560.

[131] For reference to statements by Japan at the Review Conference and France at the subsequent ASP, expressing disagreement with the procedures used, see Politi, *supra* n. 130, at pp. 281–282.

[132] See Zimmermann, *supra* n. 130, at 210.

[133] RC/Res. 6, Annex I, Art. 15 *bis* (paragraph 5).

any of the nationals of such a State for the crime of aggression nor any aggression committed on their territory by others – unless the Security Council refers the situation to the Court. The removal of States not parties to the Statute from the ambit of the Court's aggression jurisdiction, while politically desirable, involves an amendment to the Statute which should have been effected by the slower procedure of Article 121(4). The Court itself may have to determine whether this attempt to amend the Statute has been successful, like the other defective amendments.

Together with the amendments to the Statute, the Conference adopted 'understandings regarding the interpretation' of those amendments.[134] These were intended to address concerns of particular governments regarding aspects of the definition and prosecution of aggression. These, too, have been the subject of controversy; their status has been analysed under the provisions of the Vienna Convention by reference to Articles 31, 32 and 41.[135] One conclusion is that 'the Understandings are nothing more than supplementary means of interpretation that the Court would have the right to ignore once the aggression amendments entered into force'.[136] This seems a little dismissive: the understandings reached are part of the context of the amendments and are likely to be used by the Court in determining the meaning of the amendments. Whether or not they will be useful in that regard is a separate question.

4   Conclusions

While the law of treaties is applied as a matter of course to inter-State treaty relations in the field of international criminal law and to the relations of States with the international courts and tribunals, its application to that autonomous body of law which concerns individual criminal responsibility presents challenges, particularly with regard to the interpretation of the relevant international instruments. One likely result of the developing differentiation in approaches to interpretation used on the one hand for the relations of States and, on the other, for individual criminal proceedings is a fragmentation of international law, particularly

---

[134] Annex III to Resolution RC/res.6.

[135] K. J. Heller, 'The Uncertain Legal Status of the Aggression Understandings', *J. Int'l Crim. Just.*, 10 (2012), 229–248.

[136] *Ibid.*, at 231.

with regard to the treaties providing the basis for the subject matter jurisdiction of the international courts and tribunals. The difference in outcome before the different courts in the *Tadić Case* (ICTY) and the *Nicaragua Case* (International Court of Justice) is notorious.[137] Such fragmentation is likely to increase but is inevitable due to the particular character of international criminal law.

---

[137] But the well-known difference of interpretation does not appear to have resulted from conscious use of different interpretative techniques by the ICTY and the ICJ: *Tadić Jurisdiction, supra* n. 46, and *Case Concerning Military and Paramilitary Activities in and against Nicaragua*: Nicaragua v. United States of America (Merits) (1986) ICJ Rep. 14, at pp. 62–65 (paragraphs 109–115).

20

International Investment Law

JULIAN DAVIS MORTENSON

1 Introduction

Since the middle of the twentieth century, the field of international investment protection has gone through a period of more or less continuous expansion. From a single bilateral investment treaty ('BIT') signed between Germany and Pakistan in November 1959,[1] international investment law has seen the proliferation of some 3,200 investment treaties governing the treatment of foreign investors by the host States where they do business.

As a historical matter, the substantive elements of modern investment law emerged from a loose network of customary international law protections that pre-existed the treaties now dominating the regime. Customary international law had long required host States to extend certain guarantees of decent treatment to foreign citizens within their jurisdiction. The systematic codification of these customary norms into a far-flung network of treaties began in earnest with the late nineteenth century emergence of so-called 'friendship, commerce, and navigation' treaties, which incorporated existing customary rules and adopted various new substantive requirements. The treaty network took its next step when BITs proper emerged in the mid-twentieth century, characterised principally by the extension of dispute resolution options to individual investors.[2]

As customary investment law was gradually codified at the retail level, the law of treaties began to loom much larger in meta-regulation of the

---

[1] 457 UNTS 24.

[2] K. Miles, *The Origins of International Investment Law: Empire, Environment and the Safeguarding of Capital* (Cambridge: Cambridge University Press, 2013), pp. 1–119; T. Weiler, *The Interpretation of International Investment Law: Equality, Discrimination and Minimum Standards of Treatment in Historical Context* (Leiden: Martinus Nijhoff, 2013) and K. J. Vandevelde, 'A Brief History of International Investment Agreements', *UC Davis JILP*, 12 (2005), 157–194.

regime. This chapter will explore some of the ways that the modern law of treaties interacts with the modern law of international investment protection. It will focus in particular on a handful of areas where the formal categories of treaty law map awkwardly onto the reality of modern investment law and adjudication.

Before turning to the law of treaties, it is necessary to begin with a further word on the basic unit to which that law is applied here: the individual bilateral investment treaty.[3] The basic structure of the modern BIT is well established. BITs generally create a set of substantive legal protections similar to the broad guarantees of fairness and due process found in many States' domestic constitutions. They typically prohibit expropriation without just compensation, while also promising 'fair and equitable treatment' – a sort of covenant of good faith and fair dealing. Many BITs include clauses guaranteeing both national treatment and most favoured nation treatment, which function in much the same way as their trade law cousins. And BITs often include a guarantee of 'full protection and security', which requires the host State, at a minimum, to provide adequate physical protection from violence and crime.[4]

While central to the modern investment regime, the substance of these protections is not actually the regime's more notable element in historical context. As noted previously, both treaties and customary law had long incorporated substantive protections for foreign investors. These protections were traditionally undercut, however, by a variety of restrictive doctrines and jurisdictional rules.[5] The signal innovation of the modern BIT – indeed, its defining feature as a category of agreement – removed many of these barriers by providing a direct remedy for the individual investor: mandatory dispute resolution through investor-State

---

[3] While investment guarantees are also included in a handful of important multilateral treaties, this chapter will for convenience simply use 'BITs' as shorthand for all investment treaties. The last two decades have seen particularly explosive growth in the number of BITs, with the total number rising from fewer than 500 in the late 1980s: United Nations Conference on Trade and Development, *World Investment Report 1996* (New York, NY/Geneva: United Nations, 1996), p. 147, to more than 3,200 by the end of 2013. See United Nations Conference on Trade and Development, *World Investment Report 2014* (New York, NY/Geneva: United Nations, 2014), p. 12.

[4] For a more in-depth survey of typical BIT protections, see R. Dolzer and C. Schreuer, *Principles of International Investment Law* (Oxford: Oxford University Press, 2008), pp. 79–194.

[5] In particular, investors' only recourse was typically to petition their home government for assistance; unless the host State agreed to arbitrate treaty disputes, investors could not bring direct claims themselves under international law: Vandevelde, *supra* n. 2, at 159–161.

arbitration, in which the individual investor and the host State faced off directly, without the intermediation of the investor's home State or any other international body.

As with all arbitration, no investment tribunal may be seised of a dispute until both parties – the aggrieved investor and the State defendant – have agreed to arbitrate. Typically, however, modern investment treaties contemplate neither an *ex post compromis* of existing disputes nor an *ex ante* dispute settlement contract. Rather, a typical BIT dispute resolution clause constitutes an open unilateral offer by each contracting State to arbitrate any future disputes that might arise with any qualifying foreign investor. This means that an aggrieved foreign investor can trigger binding BIT arbitration at her sole discretion, simply by filing a request for arbitration – even if she otherwise has no formalised legal relationship with the State. The open-endedness of these clauses is not unusual as such; any number of treaties contain *ex ante* dispute settlement clauses. But most unusual are these BIT clauses' one-sided nature, their contemplation of a private entity as the arbitral counterparty and their failure to require a formalised *ex ante* relationship between the defendant State and the aggrieved claimant.[6]

Taken as a body of treaty law, the signal characteristic of the investment law regime is its peculiar combination of pervasive similarity amidst relentless variation: the phenomenon that this chapter will describe as 'snowflakes in a blizzard'. These thousands of bilateral treaties are characterised by similar concerns, similar substance, similar enforcement structure and similar terms. And yet, the widely varying permutations of substantive guarantees, dispute resolution mechanics and covered activities mean that very few are *exactly* alike. The resulting structural tension between the requirements of contextually sensitive treatment and the demands of a systemically sensible administrative apparatus presents the defining challenge of applying the law of treaties to the investment context.

This chapter suggests that some of the most significant recurring treaty issues in international investment law emerge from this structural tension. To be sure, investment treaty disputes prompt all the usual

---

[6] For good discussion of the unusual mechanics of the BIT open consent mechanism, see *Churchill Mining Plc v. Republic of Indonesia*, ICSID Case No. ARB/12/14, Decision on Jurisdiction (24 Feb. 2014), paragraphs 155–231, and *Wintershall Aktiengesellschaft v. Argentine Republic*, ICSID Case No. ARB/04/14, Award (8 Dec. 2008), paragraphs 160(1)–160(3). See, also, generally J. Paulsson, 'Arbitration without Privity', *ICSID Rev.*, 10 (1995), 232–257.

disagreements about core substantive terms that characterize the adjudication of any substantive regime. But this chapter puts to one side the definitions of 'fair and equitable treatment', 'expropriation' or 'full protection and security' and emphasises instead the unique *structural* demands of applying, interpreting, and adjudicating treaty law in the international investment context.

On this background, the signal characteristic of the international investment law regime is multiplicity: a multiplicity of treaties, a multiplicity of claimants – and a multiplicity of tribunals. It is a measure of the sometimes awkward fit between the modern law of treaties and the modern law of investment protections that these various multiplicities seriously complicate at least three important aspects of treaty law: (1) the rules governing third-party beneficiaries, (2) the project of consistent interpretation in a decentralised system and (3) the distinction between multilateral and bilateral regimes. The remainder of this chapter will explore how the BIT ecosystem's peculiar combination of pervasive similarity and relentless variation plays out in each of these three areas. It will explore, in short, what the law of treaties can do when applied – over and over again, in predictably similar settings – to these snowflakes in a blizzard.

2 Third-Party Beneficiaries: Articles 34–38 of the Vienna Convention on the Law of Treaties

It is a fundamental presumption of modern treaty law that treaties do not create rights or obligations for 'third States' – i.e. States not party to the treaty in question.[7] Fully five articles of the Vienna Convention on the Law of Treaties (VCLT)[8] are devoted to this proposition and its implications.[9] Of particular relevance in the investment law context, Article 36 VCLT provides that 'a right arises for a third State' only if 'the parties to the treaty intend the provision to accord that right either to the third States, or to a group of States to which it belongs, or to all States, and the third State assents thereto'.

This focus on third *State* beneficiaries is, from the outset, an awkward fit for the realities of investment law. It has of course long been the conceit of many international law regimes that harm to individual persons is cognisable only as attributed to the injured person's home State.

---

[7] See, further, the contribution to this volume of Waibel at pp. 201–236 (Chapter 8).
[8] 1155 UNTS 331. [9] I.e. Arts. 34–38 VCLT: *ibid.*

And it is certainly true that investment law treaties do provide a concrete benefit for capital exporting States by providing additional protections for domestic capital when it is sent overseas. Yet, in the day-to-day reality of the regime, it is the individual investors who are the immediate beneficiaries of BIT protections, both in principle and (especially) when it comes to adjudicating alleged violations through mandatory investor-State arbitration procedures. Indeed, tribunals sometimes find a violation of the individual's substantive rights even when both State signatories agree that a given act does not violate the relevant BIT.[10]

That said, the third party considerations motivating Articles 34–38 VCLT are quite salient in modern investment law, with one key difference: it is *individuals* from third party States who are looking for the free ride. In this respect, the investment regime's core structural tension – of persistent differences among fundamentally similar agreements that all serve the same basic function – manifests in the form of aggressive efforts by investors to secure BIT protections negotiated by some other State than their own. These efforts respond to the facts that virtually all industrial countries have arranged BIT protections for their investors, that not all BITs are created equal and that not all investors' home States have a BIT with the State where those investors want to do business.

This section will focus on two ways that this pressure plays out doctrinally. First, it will discuss claimants' efforts to use most favoured nation clauses to pick and choose from a menu of treaty protections – not just those in the treaty that formally applies to their investment but those in all other treaties to which the host State is also party. Second, this section will discuss how tribunals deal with investors' use of strategic incorporation to invoke an attractive BIT which would not otherwise apply to the real party in interest.

In both cases, the background is set by the VCLT presumption that treaties do not create rights for third parties. And, yet, in both cases, tribunals regularly approve the application of provisions contained in a treaty that is 'third party' with respect to the home State (or at least what might seem to be the true home State) of the claiming investor. The practical consequence is that many investors are not limited to the unique permutations of the specific BIT that appears to apply to the economic substance of their activities. Instead, they can often pull in different BITs from elsewhere in the blizzard that offer more suitable

[10] See, e.g., *Pope & Talbot Inc. v. Canada*, Award on the Merits of Phase 2 (10 Apr. 2001), paragraph 116.

protections for their particular situation. This leads to a predictable levelling up of protections in practice, even if not fully in theory. And it systematically and pervasively upends the VCLT presumption that the effect of a treaty generally extends only to signatory States.

2.1   Most Favoured Nation (MFN) Clauses

Most favoured nation clauses are well known throughout international law,[11] perhaps especially in the trade context. A typical clause might guarantee that 'investments made by investors of one contracting party in the territory of the other contracting party ... shall be accorded treatment no less favourable than that accorded to investments made by investors of any third State',[12] or – with more specificity – that 'each Party shall accord to an investor of the other Party treatment no less favourable than that it accords, in like circumstances, to investors of a non-Party with respect to the establishment, acquisition, expansion, management, conduct, operation and sale or other disposition of an investment in its territory'.[13]

Essentially, MFN clauses allow foreign investors to claim any higher standard of protection that is granted by the host State to nationals of a third State. An example may help explain the stakes of such clauses in the context of the BIT blizzard. Imagine that an investor wishes to challenge a State's failure to follow through on its contractual obligations to the investor. As a matter of substantive investment law, this sort of challenge is often brought under what is known as an 'umbrella clause'.[14] But imagine that Treaty A – a BIT between the investor's home State and the host State where the investor is doing business – does *not* include an

---

[11]   *Anglo-Iranian Oil Co. Case*: United Kingdom v. Iran (Preliminary Objection) (1952) ICJ Rep. 93; *The Ambatielos Claim* (Greece, United Kingdom of Great Britain and Northern Ireland), RIAA, Vol. XII, 83–153, and *Case Concerning Rights of Nationals of the United States of American in Morocco*: France v. United States of America (1952) ICJ Rep. 176.

[12]   Agreement between the Government of the Kingdom of Norway and the Government of the Republic of Poland on the Promotion and Reciprocal Protection of Investments (5 June 1990), Art. IV(1) (http://investmentpolicyhub.unctad.org/IIA/mappedContent/treaty/2694).

[13]   Agreement between Canada and the Republic of Serbia for the Promotion and Protection of Investments (9 Jan. 2014), Art. 5(1) (http://investmentpolicyhub.unctad.org/IIA/country/35/treaty/3502).

[14]   Such clauses typically provide something like: 'either party shall observe any other obligation it may have entered into with regard to investments by nationals or companies of the other Party'. Agreement between the Federal Republic of Germany and the Islamic Republic of Pakistan for the Promotion and Protection of Investments: *supra* n. 1.

umbrella clause. Is the investor out of luck? Not if Treaty A includes an MFN clause. Because if the investor can identify some Treaty B – between the host State and a third State – that *does* include an umbrella clause, then the investor can claim the substantive protection of that umbrella clause.

Unless the MFN clause is structured so as to exclude certain types of protections,[15] an investor covered only by Treaty A can thus use an MFN to claim the benefit of Treaty B's fair and equitable treatment guarantee, its expropriation prohibition or any other substantive guarantee of protection.[16] What's more, even though we might think that the 'favourableness' of treatment should logically be assessed *en bloc*[17] – i.e. requiring investors to choose either the full package of protections under Treaty A or the full package of protections under Treaty B – in practice, tribunals regularly allow a mix-and-match approach.[18] This allows investors essentially to cook up their own made-to-order BITs, in which they can invoke both Treaty A's full protection and security clause and Treaty B's umbrella clause – even if the latter was added to Treaty B precisely so as to counterbalance its lack of the former.

While the consequences of the choice between mix-and-match and package deal interpretations of the MFN clause are significant, the noisiest debate about MFN clauses in the BIT context focuses on the procedural mechanics of dispute resolution.[19] Imagine, for example, that

---

[15] For an example, see *Sergei Paushok et al. v. Mongolia*, Award on Jurisdiction and Liability (28 Apr. 2011), paragraphs 562–573 (noting that the MFN text applied only to the treaty's 'fair and equitable treatment' guarantee and not to its umbrella clause).

[16] *Franck Charles Arif v. Moldova*, ICSID Case No. ARB/11/23, Award (8 Apr. 2013), paragraphs 393–396 (applying MFN clause to incorporate substantive protections from another treaty) and *Asian Agricultural Products Ltd. (AAPL) v. Republic of Sri Lanka*, ICSID Case No. ARB/87/3 (27 June 1990), paragraph 54 (similar).

[17] For an argument along these lines, see T. Cole, *The Structure of Investment Arbitration* (London: Routledge, 2012), pp. 104–107. For decisions that do adopt a 'package deal' view of MFN clauses, see *Hochtief AG v. Argentine Republic*, ICSID Case No. ARB/07/31 (24 Oct. 2011), paragraphs 59–72 and 98–99 (holding that MFN clause imports dispute settlement provisions as part of 'the whole scheme' of protections created by a different BIT) and *ICS Inspection and Control Services Limited v. Argentine Republic*, PCA Case No. 2010-9, Award on Jurisdiction (10 Feb. 2012), paragraphs 269 (n. 297) and 318–325 (similar).

[18] *Siemens AG v. Argentine Republic*, ICSID Case No. ARB/02/8, Decision on Jurisdiction (2 Aug. 2004), paragraphs 102 and 119–120 (rejecting 'the proposition that, since a treaty has been negotiated as a package, for other parties to benefit from it, they also should be subject to its disadvantages').

[19] For good overviews of this debate, see *Bilateral Investment Treaties 1995–2006, Trends in Investment Rulemaking* (2007), UNCTAD/IET/IIT/2006/5, pp. 39–42; *Garanti Koza LLP v. Turkmenistan*, ICSID Case No. ARB/11/20, Decision on the Objection to Jurisdiction

Treaty A contains an open offer to arbitrate investment disputes under the United Nations Commission on International Trade Law (UNCITRAL) rules, while Treaty B contains a consent to arbitration within the International Centre for Settlement of Investment Disputes (ICSID) along with its more iron-clad guarantee that States parties must 'enforce the pecuniary obligations imposed by [an] award . . . as if it were a final judgment of a court in that State'.[20] Or imagine that Treaty A includes an eighteen-month waiting period or an administrative exhaustion requirement and Treaty B does not. In both instances, the investor protected by Treaty A might prefer the 'better' remedial provisions under Treaty B – whether because the forum seems substantively more attractive or because it avoids additional delay. And on the logic of the MFN clause, the investor in this second example might well invoke Treaty B's consent to ICSID arbitration as a way to get around Treaty A's limitation to the UNCITRAL rules.

The case law on the application of MFN clauses to procedural provisions is divided. Tribunals often work hard to extract textual clues about whether any *particular* MFN should apply to procedural protections – whether concluding that it does[21] or that it does not.[22] But the real debate is about

---

for Lack of Consent (3 July 2013), paragraphs 40–42 and fn. 53–54; *ST-AD GmbH v. Bulgaria*, Award on Jurisdiction (18 July 2013), paragraphs 386–392, and *Wintershall Aktiengesellschaft v. Argentine Republic*, ICSID Case No. ARB/04/14, Award (8 Dec. 2008), paragraphs 179–184.

[20] 1965 Convention on the Settlement of Investment Disputes Between States and Nationals of Other States, 575 UNTS 159, Art. 51(1). For more on the unusual strength of this enforcement obligation, see R. P. Alford, 'Federal Courts, International Tribunals, and the Continuum of Deference', *Virginia JIL*, 43 (2005), 675–796, at 692.

[21] *RosInvestCo v. Russian Federation*, Award on Jurisdiction (1 Oct. 2007), paragraphs 126–139 (relying on MFN clause's application to protections relating to the 'use and management' of investments); *Garanti Koza LLP v. Turkmenistan*, ICSID Case No. ARB/11/20, Decision on the Objection to Jurisdiction for Lack of Consent (3 July 2013), paragraphs 39–46, 65–67 and 93–96 (close analysis of specific BIT text) and *National Grid v. Argentine Republic*, Decision on Jurisdiction (20 June 2006), paragraphs 81–83 (applying *expression unius* where dispute resolution was not included among exceptions to MFN obligation).

[22] *Renta 4 SVSA v. Russian Federation*, Award on Preliminary Objections (20 March 2008), paragraphs 69 and 119–120 (noting that MFN clauses can import procedural protections, but concluding that the particular clause at issue did not do so); *Sanum Investments Ltd. v. Lao People's Democratic Republic*, PCA Case No. 2013-13 (13 Dec. 2003), paragraphs 343–345 and 357–358 (concluding that MFN clause's specific reference to fair and equitable treatment means that it does not import procedural protections) and *Kilic v. Turkmenistan*, ICSID Case No. ARB/10/1, Award (2 July 2013), paragraphs 7.3.1–7.3.9 (noting that close reading of treaty structure shows that MFN clause applies only to substantive provisions listed above it and not to the dispute resolution provision listed below it).

whether MFN clauses should *generally* be presumed to apply to procedural rights. Some tribunals suggest that the treatment of an investment turns on its business experience in the regulated market: can the enterprise buy raw materials and sell goods; can it extract minerals; can it research and develop; can it acquire real estate and so on. Those adopting this perspective suggest that the 'treatment' of an investor and an investment presumptively begins and ends with the primary rules by which that investor and investments' behaviour is directly facilitated or constrained.[23] Many other cases take the opposite perspective, however, concluding that – particularly if domestic judiciaries are themselves capable of 'treating' an investor illegally under a BIT – there is no reason to exclude dispute resolution policy from the definition of 'treatment' or 'protection'.[24] Certainly, the investor who is permitted to go straight to dispute resolution receives superior protection of her interests, at least in that regard, than the investor who must twiddle her thumbs for eighteen months. Whatever the best answer, this struggle to apply VCLT third-party beneficiary concepts is a striking example of the systemic stresses imposed by so many claimants seeking the best package of protection from so many BITs.

[23] *ICS Inspection and Control Services Limited v. Argentine Republic*, PCA Case No. 2010-9, Award on Jurisdiction (10 Feb. 2012), paragraphs 297–304 (holding that MFN clause does not apply to procedure in absence of express provision to that effect); *Tecnicas Medioambientales Tecmed SA v. United Mexican States*, ICSID Case No. ARB(AF)/00/2 (29 May 2003), paragraph 69 (rejecting applicability of MFN clauses to procedure); *Wintershall Aktiengesellschaft v. Argentine Republic*, ICSID Case No. ARB/04/14, Award (8 Dec. 2008), paragraphs 190–197 (rejecting application of MFN clause to procedural provisions); *Salini Costruttori SPA v. Hashemite Kingdom of Jordan*, ICSID Case No. ARB/02/13 (15 Nov. 2004), paragraph 113–119 (MFN clause does not import procedure absent specific reference); *Plama Consortium Ltd. v. Republic of Bulgaria*, ICSID Case No. ARB/03/24, Decision on Jurisdiction (8 Feb. 2005), paragraphs 183–184 and 203–204; *Telenor v. Hungary*, ICSID Case No. ARB/04/15, Award (13 Sept. 2006), paragraphs 83 and 90–91, and *Austrian Airlines v. Slovak Republic*, Final Award (9 Oct. 2009), paragraphs 123–140 (refusing to expand scope of dispute resolution absent specific reference in MFN to procedure).

[24] *Emilio Maffezini v. Kingdom of Spain*, ICSID Case No. ARB/97/7 (25 Jan. 2000), paragraphs 44–64; *Gas Natural SDG v. Argentine Republic*, ICSID Case No. ARB/03/10 (17 June 2005), paragraph 49; *Siemens AG v. Argentine Republic*, ICSID Case No. ARB/02/8, Decision on Jurisdiction (2 Aug. 2004), paragraph 102 (elimination of eighteen-month waiting period *via* MFN clause); *Telefonica SA v. Argentine Republic*, ICSID Case No. ARB/03/20 (25 May 2006), paragraphs 102–103 (elimination of eighteen-month waiting period); *Suez et al. v. Argentina*, ICSID Case No. ARB/03/17, Decision on Jurisdiction (16 May 2006), paragraphs 63–66 (importing dispute resolution mechanism from a third party BIT) and *Hochtief AG v. Argentine Republic*, ICSID Case No. ARB/07/31 (24 Oct. 2011), paragraphs 59–72 (importing dispute resolution mechanism from a third party BIT).

2.2   Strategic Incorporation Decisions

Given how regularly sophisticated economic actors adjust their corporate structures with a view to regulatory or tax arbitrage, it is not surprising that they might sometimes do so with a view to favourable BIT coverage as well. Very few BITs speak directly to this question, for instance by specifying that the nationality of a corporate investor turns on whether it has a real presence in the place of incorporation.[25] Yet strategic incorporation pushes hard enough on the boundaries of privity-oriented third-party beneficiary norms to cause real discomfort. As Prosper Weil put it in a well-known dissent, logic might seem to dictate that 'economic and political reality [should] prevail over legal structure'.[26]

And yet it is close to black letter law that – at least as a default – substantive economic reality is irrelevant so long as a claimant satisfies the legal requirements for the requisite nationality, whether because of personal citizenship[27] or because of place of

---

[25] Treaty between the United States of America and Ukraine Concerning the Encouragement and Reciprocal Protection of Investment, with Annex and Exchange of Letters, Art. 1(2) (4 March 1994) (http://investmentpolicyhub.unctad.org/IIA/country/223/treaty/3054) (requiring real connection to signatory State); 1994 Final Act of the European Energy Charter Conference (Energy Charter Treaty), 2080 UNTS 95, Annex 1, Art. 17(1) (similar) and Treaty between the United States of America and the Argentine Republic Concerning the Reciprocal Encouragement and Protection of Investment, with Protocol, Art. 1(2) (similar) (14 Nov. 1991) (http://investmentpolicyhub.unctad.org/IIA/country/223/treaty/162); see, further, Amendment to the Protocol effected by Exchange of Notes at Buenos Aires on 24 Aug. 1992 and 6 Nov. 1992.

[26] *Tokios Tokeles v. Ukraine*, ICSID Case No. ARB/02/18 (29 Apr. 2004), paragraph 24 (Dissenting Opinion of Prosper Weil). See, also, e.g., I. Brownlie, *Principles of Public International Law* (Oxford: Oxford University Press, 6th ed., 2003), p. 465 ('As a whole the legal experience suggests that a doctrine of real or genuine link has been adopted, and, as a matter of principle, the considerations advanced in connection with the *Nottebohm* case apply to corporations') and R. Y. Jennings and A. Watts, *Oppenheim's International Law* (Vol. I: Law of Peace) (Harlow: Longmans, 9th ed., 1992), p. 861 ('In many situations, however, it is permissible to look behind the formal nationality of the company, as evidenced primarily by its place of incorporation and registered office, so as to determine the reality of its relationship to a State, as demonstrated by the national location of the control and ownership of the company').

[27] *Feldman v. Mexico*, ICSID Case No. ARB(AF)/99/1, Interim Decision on Preliminary Jurisdictional Issues (16 Dec. 2002), paragraph 36 (admitting NAFTA claims against Mexico by US resident who had permanent immigration status in Mexico); *Franck Charles Arif v. Moldova*, ICSID Case No. ARB/11/23, Award (8 Apr. 2013), paragraphs 355–360 (admitting BIT claims against Moldova by nationalised French citizen) and *Serafín Garcia Armas v. Republic of Venezuela*, PCA Case No. 2013-3, Decision on Jurisdiction (15 Dec. 2014), paragraphs 197–206 (admitting BIT claims against Venezuela by Venezuelan citizen with dual Spanish citizenship).

incorporation.[28] In fact, tribunals typically approve even incorporation strategies designed specifically to secure the protection of a favourable BIT. Such tribunals deny that it is a 'misuse of the privileges of legal personality'[29] to locate an investment vehicle partly on the basis of the BIT protections that are available. As one tribunal observed, 'it is not uncommon in practice, and – absent a particular limitation – not illegal to locate one's operations in a jurisdiction perceived to provide a beneficial regulatory and legal environment in terms, for examples, of taxation or the substantive law of the jurisdiction, *including the availability of a BIT*'.[30]

This is certainly true when investors incorporate their enterprise so as to secure BIT protections to which they would not otherwise be entitled.[31] Perhaps more surprisingly, it is true even with respect to

[28] *Tokios Tokeles v. Ukraine*, ICSID Case No. ARB/02/18 (29 Apr. 2004), paragraphs 29 and 56 (holding that since the foreign corporation was formed by citizens of the host State long before the BIT entered into force and without any effort to hide the investors' 'the only relevant consideration' is whether the corporate investor was properly established under the laws of its formal home State); *Saluka Investments BV v. Czech Republic*, Partial Award (17 March 2006), paragraphs 226–230 (not questioning real economic interest under Netherlands-Czech BIT where it was the Japanese corporation's ordinary business practice to operate through Dutch corporation for all European operations) and *ADC Affiliate Ltd v. Republic of Hungary*, ICSID Case No. ARB/03/16, Award (2 Oct. 2006), paragraphs 81 and 355–362 (accepting jurisdiction over corporation established by Canadian citizens in Cyprus for sole purpose of pursuing airport construction contract in Hungary).

[29] *Case Concerning the Barcelona Traction, Light and Power Company Ltd.*: Belgium v. Spain (Second Phase) (1970) ICJ Rep. 3, at p. 39 (paragraph 58) ('[T]he process of lifting the veil, being an exceptional one admitted by municipal law indicates that the veil is lifted, for instance, to prevent misuse of the privileges of legal personality').

[30] *Aguas del Tunari, SA v. Republic of Bolivia*, ICSID Case No. ARB/02/3, Decision on Jurisdiction (21 Oct. 2005), paragraph 330(d) (emphasis added) (accepting jurisdiction where US corporation had transferred its shares to Dutch holding company prior to filing an ICSID claim).

[31] *Mobil Corp. v. Venezuela*, ICSID Case No. ARB/07/27, Decision on Jurisdiction (10 June 2010), paragraphs 186–192 and 203–206 (holding that insertion of Dutch entity into corporate chain for the purpose of securing BIT protections would permit jurisdiction over new disputes, but not over existing ones); *Lao Holdings NV v. Lao People's Democratic Republic*, ICSID Case No. ARB(AF)/12/6, Decision on Jurisdiction (21 Feb. 2014), paragraphs 2, 49, 56, 68–70, 76, 79–83, 146 and 156–158 (accepting jurisdiction where investment was re-incorporated from Macao to the Dutch Antilles before the actual dispute arose); *Pac Rim Cayman LLC v. Republic of El Salvador*, ICSID Case No. ARB/09/12, Decision on Jurisdiction (1 June 2012), paragraphs 2.41 and 2.99–2.109 (accepting jurisdiction despite the fact that a 'principal purpose' of reincorporation was to secure BIT protection) and *Tidewater Inc. v. Republic of Venezuela*, ICSID Case No. ARB/10/5, Decision on Jurisdiction (8 Feb. 2013), paragraph 197 (accepting jurisdiction where corporate restructuring predated the reasonable foreseeability of BIT dispute).

citizens of the host State who incorporated a foreign investment vehicle so as to restructure their *home State* activity under a shell that enjoys the protections of international investment law.[32] Tribunals facing this latter fact pattern sometimes find ways to exclude the investment from BIT protection, such as by finding that the shell incorporation did not constitute a jurisdictional 'investment' because it did not involve a sufficient financial commitment in the place of incorporation. But even those tribunals have not challenged the proposition that host State citizens can trigger BIT protection for fundamentally local activity by incorporating outside the country.[33]

That said, such regulatory restructuring is not without its limits. As a fairly straightforward application of the presumption against retro-activity (Article 28 VCLT),[34] such re-incorporations cannot transform an existing municipal dispute into a new international dispute for the purpose of a BIT. So tribunals in such circumstances do examine whether a particular reincorporation or share transfer took place before the facts

---

[32] *Rompetrol Group NV v. Romania*, ICSID Case No. ARB/06/3, Decision on Jurisdiction and Admissibility (18 Apr. 2008), paragraphs 71 and 110 (accepting jurisdiction over Dutch vehicle used by Romanian citizens to pursue economic activities in Romania, on the ground that 'neither corporate control, effective seat, nor origin of capital has any part to play in the ascertainment of nationality under the Netherlands-Romania BIT'); *Libananco Holdings v. Republic of Turkey*, ICSID Case No. ARB/06/8, Award (2 Sept. 2011), paragraphs 98–101, 105 and 536 (conceding that Turkish investors managing their economic activity in Turkey through a holding company in Cyprus might be entitled to BIT protections, but denying jurisdiction since the relevant corporate restructuring took place after the investment dispute had already begun) and *Alpha Projektholding Gmbh v. Ukraine*, ICSID Case No. ARB/07/16, Award (8 Nov. 2010), paragraphs 335–339 and 343–345 (accepting jurisdiction over a BIT claim against Ukraine, where 50% of the shares in the complaining Austrian corporation were held by a Ukrainian investor).

[33] *KT Asia Investment Group BV v. Kazakhstan*, ICSID Case No. ARB/09/8, Award (17 Oct. 2013), paragraphs 7, 21, 90 and 120–124 (denying jurisdiction, not because the Dutch corporation was owned by a Kazakh citizen, but because the Dutch corporation's interest in the local investment vehicle was a gratis transfer rather than a genuine for-value exchange) and *Caratube International Oil Co. v. Kazakhstan*, ICSID Case No. ARB/08/12, Award (5 June 2012), paragraphs 455–456 (similar).

[34] Which provides that '[u]nless a different intention appears from the treaty or is otherwise established, its provisions do not bind a party in relation to any act or fact which took place or any situation which ceased to exist before the date or entry into force of the treaty with respect to that party'. For cases applying this in other circumstances, see, e.g., *Chevron Corp. v. Republic of Ecuador*, Interim Award (1 Dec. 2008), paragraphs 173–189 and 263–270; *Jan de Nul NV and Dredging International NV v. Arab Republic of Egypt*, ICSID Case No ARB/04/13, Award (6 Nov. 2008), paragraphs 132–133; *Nordzucker AG v. Poland*, Partial Award (10 Dec. 2008), paragraphs 107–110 and *Société Générale v. Dominican Republic*, LCIA Case No. UN 7927, Award on Jurisdiction (19 Sept. 2008), paragraphs 81–94.

giving rise to the BIT dispute arose.[35] In at least some cases, strategic reincorporation can also be precluded by the abuse of process doctrine. Tribunals taking this latter approach refuse to extend BIT jurisdiction if the claimant restructured its assets after a regulatory dispute had become reasonably foreseeable, even if the dispute had not yet formally materialised at the time of the restructuring.[36] This abuse of process doctrine is as close as the regime comes to expressing unease about strategic reincorporation in a world of many BITs.

3 Interpretation and the Evolution of Precedent: Article 32 of the Vienna Convention on the Law of Treaties

The investment law regime's signal characteristic of diversity amidst sameness is only compounded by its radical multiplicity of fully independent tribunals. This phenomenon is distinct from the multiplicity of *cases*. Domestic judiciaries adjudicate exponentially more cases than the investment system, and yet they are typically disciplined by the existence of a single court that has final say on the relevant law. By contrast, the investment law system is radically decentralised. Efforts to create an appellate body for investment law have so far come to naught,[37] notwithstanding the inconsistent awards that inevitably emerge from such decentralisation.[38]

---

[35] *Libananco Holdings v. Republic of Turkey*, ICSID Case No. ARB/06/8, Award (2 Sept. 2011), paragraphs 98–101, 105 and 536; *Mobil Corp. v. Venezuela*, ICSID Case No. ARB/07/27, Decision on Jurisdiction (10 June 2010), paragraphs 186–192 and 203–206; *Phoenix Action Ltd. v. Czech Republic*, ICSID Case No. ARB/06/5, Award (15 Apr. 2009), paragraphs 136–138 and 141–144 (denying jurisdiction where reincorporation was for the sole purpose of repackaging an existing dispute as a BIT claim) and *ST-AD GmbH v. Bulgaria*, Award on Jurisdiction (18 July 2013), paragraphs 307–312, 404–406 and 423 (denying jurisdiction where claimant had purchased an already-expropriated asset with a view to pursuing a BIT claim on the basis of that expropriation).

[36] *Renee Rose Levy v. Republic of Peru*, ICSID Case No. ARB/11/17, Award (9 Jan. 2015), paragraphs 180–195 (denying jurisdiction where corporate restructuring took place after dispute was already foreseeable); *Mobil Corp. v. Venezuela*, ICSID Case No. ARB/07/27, Decision on Jurisdiction (10 June 2010), paragraph 186–192 and 204–206 and *Banro American Resources v. Democratic Republic of Congo*, ICSID Case No. ARB/98/7, Award (1 Sept. 2000). *Cf. Lao Holdings NV v. Lao People's Democratic Republic*, ICSID Case No. ARB(AF)/12/6, Decision on Jurisdiction (21 Feb. 2014), paragraphs 76, 83, 116–119 and 146 (dictum) and *Pac Rim Cayman LLC v. Republic of El Salvador*, ICSID Case No. ARB/09/12, Decision on Jurisdiction (1 June 2012), paragraphs 2.41 and 2.99–2.109 (dictum).

[37] ICSID Secretariat, *Possible Improvements of the Framework for ICSID Arbitration* (22 Oct. 2004), paragraphs 20–23 and Annex (discussing appeal of establishing an appellate body).

[38] See, e.g., S. D. Franck, 'The Legitimacy Crisis in Investment Treaty Arbitration: Privatizing Public International Law through Inconsistent Decisions', *Fordham L. Rev.*, 73 (2005), 1521–1625. The problem is presumably mitigated to some degree by the repeat

A species of the fragmentation anxiety about international law more generally, this concern has particular bite in the investment regime, where extremely similar legal sources are continually interpreted by entirely independent tribunals.

The impact of this kind of decentralisation is sometimes felt when the same underlying dispute is litigated in parallel across multiple tribunals.[39] It also can happen, as with Argentina's turn-of-the-century economic crisis, that what amounts to a single event can injure a wide array of claimants, each of whom winds up with substantially similar legal claims. This can produce the occasional flash of what can only be taken as self-aware humour. In the words of the *Sempra v. Argentina* tribunal:

> A number of awards issued by ICSID tribunals have dealt with many issues concerning the measures adopted by the Respondent which have also been brought before this Tribunal. In some instances, counsel for each side has been the same as in previous cases and memorials have been written in similar or identical language. Members of this Tribunal have also sat in other such cases. On occasion, the wording used in the paragraphs that follow resembles that of prior awards. . . . The tribunal, however, has examined every single argument and petition on the basis of their merits in this proceeding.[40]

The more significant phenomenon from a systemic perspective, however, is the interpretation by many tribunals of similar or even identical language that appears in thousands of different BITs. Indeed, tribunals' standard disclaimer that they are 'not bound' by prior precedent is

player service of arbitrators on multiple cases. See, e.g., W. M. C. Weidemaier, 'Toward a Theory of Precedent in Arbitration', *Wm. & Mary L. Rev.*, 51 (2010), 1895–1958, at 1921.

[39] *Canfor v. United States*, Decision on Preliminary Question (6 June 2006), paragraph 3 (describing how softwood lumber dispute between USA and Canada had produced 'innumerable proceedings before NAFTA Article 1904 binational panels, WTO panels and the WTO Appellate Body, and the US Court of International Trade, which all involve highly complex issues of trade law', and noting that 'the present case was the result of a consolidation of three cases with numerous filings and a myriad of contentions'); *Cargill v. Mexico*, ICSID Case No. ARB(AF)/05/2, Award (18 Sept. 2009), paragraphs 102–103, 113 and 109 (noting parallel proceedings in multiple different fora); *Corn Products International v. United Mexican States*, ICSID Case No. ARB(AF)/04/01 (15 Jan. 2008), paragraph 47 (similar); *CME v. Czech Republic*, Partial Award (13 Sept. 2001), paragraphs 140–144, 298 and 302 (similar) and *Amto LLC v. Ukraine*, SCC Arb. No. 080/2005 (26 March 2008), Final Award, paragraph 71 (discussing related proceedings before the ECtHR).

[40] *Sempra v. Argentina*, ICSID Case No. ARB/02/16, Award (28 Sept. 2007), paragraph 76.

virtually always followed by the stipulation that such precedent does deserve 'serious consideration' – even if it emerges from the interpretation of a completely different BIT.[41] As a matter of international law, this claim is grounded either in the notion of judicial decisions as a subsidiary source of international law under Article 38 of the 1945 Statute of the International Court of Justice[42] or as a supplementary source of interpretive authority under Article 32 VCLT.[43] However you slice it, in the words of one arbitrator, 'there may not be a formal "stare decisis" rule as in common law countries, but precedent plays an important role. Tribunals and courts may disagree and are at full liberty to deviate from specific awards, but it is hard to maintain that they can and should not respect well-established jurisprudence'.[44]

The upshot of this is the gradual knotting together of precedent – or at least quasi-predictable majority and minority positions on any particular question – in a single system. And over time, that system thus clusters around more focused understandings of any particular BIT provision, notwithstanding that each individual treaty is just one iteration of a move that is repeated thousands of times across the system: an effort to protect investors by adopting similar, but not identical, textual provisions aimed at similar, but not identical, ends.

This mode of inter-treaty precedent extends even to the awkwardly reciprocal relationship between treaty jurisdiction under a BIT and adjudicatory jurisdiction under the selected forum. Especially when a claimant pursues ICSID arbitration, the adjudication of BIT claims often requires claimants to satisfy what is called a pair of 'double-barreled' requirements: the substantive requirements of the BIT and the access requirements of the arbitral forum. Both criteria must be satisfied in

---

[41] See, e.g., *Austrian Airlines v. Slovak Republic*, Final Award (9 Oct. 2009), paragraph 84; *Burlington Resources v. Republic of Ecuador*, Decision on Jurisdiction (2 June 2010), paragraphs 99–100; *Chevron Corp. v. Republic of Ecuador*, Interim Award (1 Dec. 2008), paragraphs 119–123; *Churchill Mining Plc v. Republic of Indonesia*, ICSID Case No. ARB/12/14, Decision on Jurisdiction (24 Feb. 2014), paragraph 85 and *Renta 4 SVSA v. Russian Federation*, Award on Preliminary Objections (20 March 2009), paragraphs 15–16.

[42] Attached to the 1945 Charter of the United Nations: 1 UNTS 16.

[43] *Canadian Cattlemen for Fair Trade v. United States*, Award on Jurisdiction (28 Jan. 2008), paragraphs 49–51; *Chevron Corp. v. Republic of Ecuador*, Interim Award (1 Dec. 2008), paragraphs 119–123, and *Enron Corporation Ponderosa Assets v. Argentine Republic*, ICSID Case No. ARB/01/3 (Annulment), Decision on Request for Stay (7 Oct. 2008), paragraphs 32–33.

[44] *International Thunderbird Gaming Corp. v. United Mexican States*, Award (26 Jan. 2006), paragraph 129 (Separate Opinion of Thomas Waelde).

order for the arbitral tribunal to have jurisdiction over the substantive claims.[45]

The most frequent disputes about 'double-barreled' jurisdiction involve one of two questions: whether an aggrieved claimant possesses the legally requisite *nationality* to bring a claim, and whether the claimant has made a jurisdictionally sufficient *investment* to qualify for international protection. In both cases, the two treaty instruments contain requirements that are conceptually distinct. Formally speaking, an asset might well qualify as an 'investment' under the 'any asset' formulation of the U.K.-Kazakhstan BIT,[46] and yet still fail to qualify as an 'investment' under Article 25 of the ICSID Convention.[47]

And yet, this formal instinct does not always play out in practice. It is not unusual for tribunals to suggest that interpretation of one treaty is directly affected by the content of the other; suggesting (for example) that since 'Article 25(1) [of the ICSID Convention] does not touch upon the definition of "investment"', it therefore 'does not operate to define the particular investment. That is a matter to be determined by the terms of the [BIT] the document relied upon as constituting the consent'.[48]

---

[45] For examples involving the 'investment' requirement of BITs and the ICSID Convention, see, e.g., *Franck Charles Arif v. Moldova*, ICSID Case No. ARB/11/23, Award (8 Apr. 2013), paragraphs 362–384; *Ambiente Ufficio v. Argentina*, ICSID Case No. ARB/08/9, Award (8 Feb. 2013), paragraphs 415–520; *El Paso Energy v. Argentine Republic*, ICSID Case No. ARB/03/15 (31 Oct. 2011), paragraphs 142–143; *Global Trading v. Ukraine*, ICSID Case No. ARB/09/11, Award (1 Dec. 2010), paragraphs 43–57; *KT Asia Investment Group BV v. Kazakhstan*, ICSID Case No. ARB/09/8, Award (17 Oct. 2013), paragraphs 160–173; *MCI Power Group v. Ecuador*, ICSID Case No. ARB/03/6, Award (31 July 2007), paragraphs 157–170; *Phoenix Action Ltd v. Czech Republic*, ICSID Case No. ARB/06/5, Award (15 Apr. 2009), paragraphs 74–75 and 81–99, and *Salini Costruttori SpA. v. Kingdom of Morocco*, ICSID Case No. ARB/00/4, Decision on Jurisdiction (23 July 2001), paragraphs 52–57 (23 July 2001). For examples involving the foreign control requirement under both BITs and the ICSID Convention, see, e.g., *Caratube International Oil Co. v. Kazakhstan*, ICSID Case No. ARB/08/12, Award (5 June 2012), paragraphs 326–343, and *KT Asia Investment Group BV v. Kazakhstan*, ICSID Case No. ARB/09/8, Award (17 Oct. 2013), paragraphs 95–96.

[46] Treaty between United States of America and Republic of Kazakhstan Concerning the Encouragement and Reciprocal Protection of Investment (12 Jan. 1994) (http://invest mentpolicyhub.unctad.org/IIA/country/223/treaty/2218).

[47] *Supra* n. 20. This gets more complicated when a particular BIT's only mandatory dispute resolution option is ICSID: the *effect utile* principle suggests that at least the BIT signatories believed that ICSID jurisdiction would extend to all assets covered by the BIT.

[48] See, e.g., *Gruslin v. Malaysia*, ICSID Case No. ARB/99/3, Award (27 Nov. 2000), para-graphs 13.5–13.6 ('Article 25(1) does not touch upon the definition of "investment" for the purposes of either the Convention or the IGA') and *Lanco International Inc. v. Argentine Republic*, ICSID Case No. ARB/97/6, Preliminary Decision on Jurisdiction (8 Dec. 1998), paragraph 48 (Since 'the term "investment" is not defined in the ICSID

Strictly speaking, this is a *non sequitur* – the best formulation of the expansive jurisdictional claim would begin with the proposition that the ICSID requirement is exceedingly loose and that the BIT therefore imposes the only serious limit regarding either 'nationality' or 'investment'. And yet the suggestion sometimes persists that the content of the ICSID 'investment' (or nationality) requirement might actually vary with the scope of 'investment' (or nationality) contemplated by any given BIT.

4 Multilateralising a Network of Successive Bilateral Treaties: Articles 30, 31 and 32 of the Vienna Convention on the Law of Treaties

The Vienna Convention drafters considered the possibility of adopting entirely separate rules for multilateral and bilateral treaties as a general matter, since it was understood that the two categories of agreement presented different challenges.[49] In the end, the drafters did not adopt a systematic distinction between the two types of treaty as a structuring principle of the VCLT itself. But they did make special provision for multilateral treaties in their treatment of several specific questions of treaty law.[50]

The distinction between bilateral and multilateral relations is straightforward: the former involves agreements between two parties, and the latter involves agreements among more than two parties. And yet, the investment law regime presses hard on this distinction, particularly for the purposes of interpretation.[51] The result has been something akin to an effectively *multilateral* regime that has emerged from a vast array of formally *bilateral* legal relations. The resulting quasi-hybrid has many features of a multilateral regime while maintaining a number of features that are profoundly at odds with genuinely multilateral coherence.

Convention', 'the bounds within which we operate in this case' are 'defined in the [relevant BIT]').

[49] For two examples, see, e.g., United Nations Conference on the Law of the Treaties, 2nd Sess., Vienna, 9 April–22 May 1969, Summary Record at pp. 213–220 (general discussion of whether to treat multilateral treaties separately) (10 Apr. 1969), U.N. Doc. A/ CONF.39/11/Add. 1 (1970) and H. Waldock, First Report on the Law of Treaties, U.N. Doc. A/CN.4/144, pp. 33–34 ('Distinctions of other kinds do exist, for example, between bilateral, plurilateral and multilateral treaties, and, where appropriate, these distinctions find a place in the draft articles').

[50] See, e.g., Arts. 40, 41, 55, 58, 60, 69 and 70 VCLT: *supra* n. 8.

[51] There is a framing issue lurking here. This could be viewed as a question of interpretation under Arts. 31 and 32 VCLT: *supra* n. 8. Alternately, it could be viewed as a question of treaty formation, or indeed of how to identify the substantive contents and boundaries of a treaty *qua* single agreement.

The strangeness of this hybrid is compounded by its regular application of sequentially successive treaties in a way that meshes awkwardly at best with the formal structure of Article 30 VCLT.

As a starting point, it is the rare international agreement that can avoid interaction with other sources of international law. In this sense, some problems of treaty interaction in investment law are not much different from similar questions in other areas. It is not strange for the WTO Appellate Body to review environmental treaties when interpreting WTO obligations,[52] or for the European Court of Human Rights to examine international humanitarian law when applying European human rights law.[53] So it comes as no surprise that the interpretation of investment treaty terms often involves attention to other sources of international law, whether the WTO/GATT agreements,[54] human rights law[55] or the European Union agreements.[56] To cite other sources is of course not to give them decisive influence; to the contrary, investment treaty tribunals sometimes discuss decisions from other regimes merely to distinguish

[52] See, e.g., *United States-Import Prohibition of Certain Shrimp and Shrimp Products*, AB-199-4, WT/DS58/AB/R (12 Oct. 1998), paragraphs 124–126 and 155–156.

[53] See, e.g., *Al-Jedda v. United Kingdom*, Application No. 27021/08, Judgment (7 July 2011), paragraphs 42–46 and 107.

[54] *Continental Casualty Co. v. Argentine Republic*, ICSID Case No. ARB/03/9, Award (5 Sept. 2008), paragraphs 192–199 (citing GATT and WTO precedent regarding meaning of 'necessity'); *Methanex Corp. v. United States*, Final Award, Part II-B (7 Aug. 2002), paragraph 6 (citing GATT precedent in the interpretation of NAFTA Chapter 11); *Corn Products International v. United Mexican States*, ICSID Case No. ARB(AF)/04/01 (15 Jan. 2008), paragraphs 121–125 (finding WTO 'like circumstances' doctrine relevant to 'national treatment' requirement of NAFTA Chapter 11) and *SD Myers v. Canada*, Partial Award (13 Nov. 2000), paragraphs 243–251 (adopting WTO approach to 'like circumstances' in applying 'national treatment' requirement of NAFTA Chapter 11).

[55] See, e.g., *Tecnicas Medioambientales Tecmed SA v. United Mexican States*, ICSID Case No. ARB(AF)/00/2 (29 May 2003), paragraphs 116 (note 134) and 122 (note 140) (employing ECHR to interpret NAFTA prohibition on 'expropriation, including with reference to the proportionality and public interest requirements').

[56] See, e.g., *Electrabel SA v. Republic of Hungary*, ICSID Case No. ARB/07/19, Decision on Jurisdiction and Liability (30 Nov. 2012), paragraphs 4.129–4.4.134 and 4.173–4.191 (seeking to interpret Energy Charter Treaty consistent with European Union agreements); *Oostergetel v. Slovak Republic*, Decision on Jurisdiction (30 Apr. 2010), paragraphs 72–88 (holding that the EC Treaty did not terminate existing Netherlands-Slovakia BIT as a later incompatible treaty under Art. 59 VCLT); *Ioan Micula v. Romania*, ICSID Case No. ARB/05/20, Award (11 Dec. 2013), paragraphs 178–186 and 813–827 (holding that Romania's obligation to comply with EU law constituted reasonable cause to change subsidies that were otherwise protected by the Romania-Sweden BIT); *Eureko BV v. Republic of Poland*, Partial Award (19 Aug. 2005), paragraphs 57–142, and *AES Summit Generation Ltd v. Republic of Hungary*, ICSID Case No. ARB/07/22 (23 Sept. 2010), paragraphs 7.2.1–7.6.12.

them. But this is typically because of particularised reasons to think the referenced treaty is genuinely different rather than because of any rigid determination to keep investment law in a silo.[57]

Of greater interest for present purposes are those instances where the terms of one BIT influence the interpretation of another BIT between two *different* parties. When interpreting the Germany-Argentina BIT, in other words, tribunals might sometimes ask about the wording of the Germany-Congo BIT – in fact, they might sometimes even investigate the structure of the France-Colombia BIT despite the fact that *neither* France *nor* Columbia had anything to do with the BIT actually at issue.

To understand better how this works, think about statutory interpretation in the domestic context. Imagine that in 1990, a domestic legislature enacted the Racial Equality Act, which protects the civil rights of racial minorities. The Racial Equality Act includes a judicial cause of action and stipulates that plaintiffs must exhaust administrative remedies before filing suit in court. Now imagine that five years later, the legislature enacts the Religious Freedom Act, which protects the civil rights of religious minorities. The Religious Freedom Act also includes a judicial cause of action but makes no reference to the exhaustion of administrative remedies – neither requiring them nor excusing their absence. What happens when a citizen files suit under the Religious Freedom Act, claiming violation of her religious rights? Does she have to exhaust administrative remedies before going to court? There would of course be complicated questions about the jurisdiction's baseline expectations of administrative law. But a thorough job of interpretation would require at least some reference to the differences in remedial structure between the Racial Equality Act and the Religious Freedom Act. The statutes deal with very similar topics, they include otherwise comparable judicial provisions, and they demonstrate two different ways of dealing with the same problem.[58]

---

[57] See, e.g., *Corn Products International v. United Mexican States*, ICSID Case No. ARB(AF)/04/01 (15 Jan. 2008), paragraphs 154–160 (distinguishing GATT Article XX precedent on countermeasures from customary international law precedent regarding countermeasures more generally) and *Cargill v. Mexico*, ICSID Case No. ARB(AF)/05/2, Award (18 Sept. 2009), paragraphs 193–194 and 203–210 (distinguishing NAFTA's reference to 'like circumstances' from GATT's reference to 'like products' on the grounds that characteristics unrelated to the product itself might be relevant to the NAFTA determination).

[58] For a real life example, see *West Virginia University Hospitals v. Casey*, 499 U.S. 83, 88–92 (1991) (comparing various fee shifting statutes to conclude that the legally relevant provision's failure to reference expert fees was significant).

One reason we do this in the domestic context – especially, but not only, when interpreting the second-in-time statute – is that we (heroically) infer something like a consistent legislative will, such that both variations and similarities among legislative mechanisms should be given effect. Whether described as the 'whole code canon' or simply representing a good sense effort to look at the same jurisdiction's law on similar subjects, this move is standard practice at the domestic level.

It is less clear that the move is sensible as a matter of modern treaty theory. The touchstone of VCLT treaty interpretation is the arrangement worked out by *these* parties to *this* treaty. A highly formalistic approach might thus fence out anything not demonstrably connected to the negotiated result between particular parties to a particular treaty – which constitutes not a link in a conceptually seamless web of municipal legislation but an international contract between sovereign States at a specific point in time. And, indeed, the strictest approach categorically refuses to offer *any* interpretive weight to other BITs. One NAFTA tribunal, disavowing interest in the litigants' reference to 'other BITs, the draft [Multilateral Treaty on Investment], [and] the Uruguay round', noted that '[t]hese agreements and sources are not the NAFTA, they did not involve entirely the same parties to the negotiation, at times raise inter-temporal discontinuities, and the extent to which they did not did not influence the NAFTA parties in the preparation of the NAFTA text is not well-established'.[59]

And yet, that view is the exception rather than the rule. Because in fact tribunals adjudicating BIT claims regularly reference provisions of BITs that are plainly inapplicable to the dispute being adjudicated. Indeed, it has become close to black letter law that 'it is proper to consider stipulations of earlier or later treaties in relation to subjects similar to those

---

[59] *Mobil Investments Canada Inc. v. Canada*, ICSID Case No. ARB(AF)/07/4, Decision on Liability and Principles of Quantum (22 May 2012), paragraphs 228 and 230. See, also, e.g., *Aguas del Tunari, SA v. Bolivia*, ICSID Case No. ARB/02/3, Decision on Respondent's Objections to Jurisdiction (21 Oct. 2005), paragraph 291 ('[t]he fact that a pattern might exist in the content of the BITs entered into by a particular State does not mean that a specific BIT by that State should be understood as necessarily conforming to that pattern rather than constituting an exception to that pattern') and *Rompetrol Group NV v. Romania*, ICSID Case No. ARB/06/3, Decision on Jurisdiction and Admissibility (18 Apr. 2008), paragraph 108 (rejecting relevance of 'impressive list of more-or-less contemporaneous Romanian BITs containing in express language restrictive definitions of the nationality of corporate investors', on the ground that it was merely 'positive confirmatory evidence of an intention to equip the present BIT with an unrestricted definition'). Cf. *Siemens AG v. Argentine Republic*, ICSID Case No. ARB/02/8, Decision on Jurisdiction (2 Aug. 2004), paragraph 106 (holding that comparative deviation from Germany's model BIT is irrelevant).

treated in the treaty under consideration' and that 'establishing the practice followed through [a] comparative law survey' is 'an extremely useful tool'.[60]

The simplest case involves instances where one party to the BIT at issue (call it Treaty A) has also adopted another BIT (call it Treaty B) that contains different terms or structure.[61] Under circumstances like these, the cross-treaty application of the *expressio unius* principle has been applied to infer significance from, for example, the omission of a reference to the customary international law standard,[62] the omission of an emergency exception,[63] the lack of an express reference to self-judging emergency provisions[64] or the applicability of a most favoured nation clause to dispute resolution procedures.[65] In each of these instances, the outcome turned at least in part on the fact that Treaty B specified the existence of the feature whose absence from Treaty A was deemed significant.

There are, naturally, many variations on this theme. The same move is sometimes deployed to emphasise the breadth, rather than the narrowness, of Treaty A.[66] Sometimes it matters that Treaty B existed before

---

[60] *Asian Agricultural Products Ltd. (AAPL) v. Republic of Sri Lanka*, ICSID Case No. ARB/87/3 (27 June 1990), paragraph 40.

[61] For a precursor in general international law, see *Case Concerning Oil Platforms*: Iran v. United States of America (Preliminary Objections) (1996) ICJ Rep. 803, at pp. 812–814 (paragraphs 24–28).

[62] *Azurix Corp. v. Argentine Republic*, ICSID Case No. ARB/01/12 (14 July 2006), paragraphs 358, 363 and 372 (citing other US FTAs that specify customary international law minimum standard).

[63] *BG Group v. Argentine Republic*, Final Award (24 Dec. 2007), paragraphs 385–387 (finding that the existence of an emergency provision in US-Argentina BIT suggests that the lack of a similar provision in the UK-Argentina BIT is significant).

[64] *El Paso Energy v. Argentine Republic*, ICSID Case No. ARB/03/15 (31 Oct. 2011), paragraphs 591–603 (reviewing other US treaty practice regarding self judging emergency clauses).

[65] *ICS Inspection and Control Services Limited v. Argentine Republic*, PCA Case No. 2010-9, Award on Jurisdiction (10 Feb. 2012), paragraphs 297–304 and 314–317 (surveying contemporary BIT practice regarding the application of MFN clauses to procedural questions).

[66] *Emilio Maffezini v. Kingdom of Spain*, ICSID Case No. ARB/97/7 (25 Jan. 2000), paragraphs 60–61 (comparing applicable MFN clause to the narrower MFN clauses contained in some other Spanish BITs); *KT Asia Investment Group BV v. Kazakhstan*, ICSID Case No. ARB/09/8, Award (17 Oct. 2013), paragraph 123 (noting that, in contrast to many Kazakhstan BITs, the applicable treaty does not specify a siege sociale rule for nationality) and *Philip Morris Brands SARL v. Republic of Uruguay*, ICSID Case No. ARB/10/7, Decision on Jurisdiction (2 July 2013), paragraphs 108 (n. 53) and 109 (discussing different BITs' wording of provisions requiring domestic litigation).

Treaty A; sometimes it does not.[67] Sometimes it matters that the comparator treaties were explicit on the point in debate; sometimes it does not.[68] But in each case, the interpreter acts as though there is at least a presumption that a party's drafting choices in Treaty B might affect the interpretation of that party's agreement in Treaty A with a completely different State.

Perhaps even more striking, tribunals regularly go further still, affording significance to BIT practice *generally* – even where that means reviewing a series of BITs that were concluded between States that had nothing to do with the BIT that actually applies. Here too, tribunals regularly look to the inclusion or exclusion of various restrictions and options as evidence in interpreting the BIT actually at issue.[69] It is not that every such excursion into third party practice bears interpretive fruit. But even when tribunals are unpersuaded by the actual evidence of the specific third party practice surveyed, its conceptual relevance is typically taken for granted. Some such tribunals focus on the temporal irrelevance of a Treaty B that was concluded after Treaty A.[70] Others find that no

---

[67] *El Paso Energy v. Argentine Republic*, ICSID Case No. ARB/03/15 (31 Oct. 2011), paragraphs 591–603.

[68] *Mondev International v. United States*, ICSID Case No. ARB(AF)/99/2, Award (11 Oct. 2002), paragraphs 110–112 (reviewing US transmittal statements regarding other BITs using similar 'fair and equitable treatment' language) and *SGS v. Philippines*, ICSID Case No. ARB/02/6, Decision on Jurisdiction (29 Jan. 2004), paragraphs 124–127 (doubting that the location of umbrella clause is significant, since an identically phrased clause appears in different places in other Philippine BITs).

[69] *Salini Costruttori SPA v. Hashemite Kingdom of Jordan*, ICSID Case No. ARB/02/13 (15 Nov. 2004), paragraph 117 (noting that United Kingdom BIT practice specifically includes procedural issues in the scope of its MFN provisions, and concluding that the lack of similar specificity in the applicable BIT should be given effect); *Wintershall Aktiengesellschaft v. Argentine Republic*, ICSID Case No. ARB/04/14, Award (8 Dec. 2008), paragraphs 166–167 (similar); *Saluka Investments BV v. Czech Republic*, Partial Award (17 March 2006), paragraph 204 (contrasting the relevant BIT's lack of any reference to customary international law to NAFTA's reference to customary international law in its 'fair and equitable treatment' provision); *Tokios Tokeles v. Ukraine*, ICSID Case No. ARB/02/18 (29 Apr. 2004), paragraphs 33–36 (noting that, in contrast to many other BITs, the relevant treaty does not expressly exclude investments controlled by an entity that does not have a substantial economic presence in its place of incorporation); *El Paso Energy v. Argentine Republic*, ICSID Case No. ARB/03/15 (31 Oct. 2001), paragraphs 591–592 and 602–603 (noting that BITs enacted after the ICJ's *Nicaragua* judgment often mention their self-judging character explicitly) and *Kilic v. Turkmenistan*, ICSID Case No. ARB/10/1, Award (2 July 2013), paragraphs 7.6.8–7.6.17 (emphasising the different wording of other BITs whose MFN provisions had been deemed to apply to dispute resolution).

[70] *El Paso Energy v. Argentine Republic*, ICSID Case No. ARB/03/15 (31 Oct. 2011), paragraph 591 (dismissing as irrelevant evidence of treaty practice that emerged after the

consistent pattern actually emerges from other BIT practice that could give rise to any reliable implications about Treaty A.[71] Still others find the precedents invoked too far afield to be of use for the interpretive question at issue.[72] Taken as a whole, however, the tribunals that give serious consideration to other BITs – even those to which *neither* signatory of the applicable BIT is a party – easily outnumber the tribunals that categorically refuse to consider such evidence.

The consequences are significant. Rather than taking each BIT as a thing unto itself, this approach situates each as an integral part of an overall ecosystem in which meaning is developed organically over time, with interpretive practices that resemble a domestic court's review of the 'whole code' promulgated by one legislature. To be clear, this is not necessarily inappropriate. At minimum, this kind of evidence seems obviously eligible for consideration as 'supplementary evidence' of meaning under Article 32 VCLT – which includes but is not limited to drafting history. But it comes far closer to Myres McDougal's vision of adjudication as the administration of a complex multifaceted system than to the purist's belief that arbitrators take cases one at a time, interpreting isolated text within hermetically sealed treaties.[73]

---

applicable BIT) and *Enron Corporation Ponderosa Assets v. Argentine Republic*, ICSID Case No. ARB/01/3, Award (22 May 2007), paragraphs 335–337 (similar).

[71] *Churchill Mining Plc v. Republic of Indonesia*, ICSID Case No. ARB/12/14, Decision on Jurisdiction (24 Feb. 2014), paragraphs 195–207 (finding that the signatories' other BIT practice was too varied to permit any conclusions about their baseline expectations) and *Plama Consortium Ltd. v. Republic of Bulgaria*, ICSID Case No. ARB/03/24, Decision on Jurisdiction (8 Feb. 2005), paragraph 195 (similar).

[72] *HICEE BV v. Slovak Republic*, Partial Award (23 May 2011), paragraphs 141–144 (dismissing similar treaty practice and statements regarding other treaties as insufficiently relevant to the point in dispute) and *National Grid Plc v. Argentine Republic*, Decision on Jurisdiction (20 June 2006), paragraphs 84–85 and 93 (describing the other treaty practice of the two signatories to the relevant BIT as conflicting and therefore inconclusive).

[73] Compare M. S. McDougal, H. D. Lasswell and J. C. Miller, *The Interpretation of Agreements and World Public Order: Principles of Content and Procedure* (New Haven, CT: Yale University Press, 1967), p. 41 (advocating an interpreter's 'obligation [to] examine the significance of every specific controversy for the entire range of policy purposes sought by the total system to which he is responsible') with, e.g., *Burlington Resources v. Republic of Ecuador*, ICSID Case No. ARB/08/5, Decision on Jurisdiction (2 June 2010), paragraph 100 ('Arbitrator Stern does not analyze the arbitrator's role in the same manner, as she considers it her duty to decide each case on its own merits, independently of any apparent jurisprudential trend'). For an excellent investigation of how this quasi-multilateralisation affects the operation of investment law as a control regime, see S. Schill, *The Multilateralization of International Investment Law* (Cambridge: Cambridge University Press, 2009).

5 Conclusion

In each of these respects, the sheer scale of the international investment regime – its massively multiple treaties, claimants and tribunals – seriously complicates the application of modern treaty law to modern investment law. The relentless similarity of BITs only highlights their persistent variations in both small details and large structure. In a system with many tribunals, many claimants and many sources of law – all brought to bear on an essentially similar problem of limiting the regulatory authority of domestic governments *vis-à-vis* foreign investors – the result is something like shadow multilateralism, with a persistent instinct for coherence and manageability even where that requires some inattention to black letter treaty law and formalistic VCLT categories.

The treaty problems canvassed here each emerge from efforts to tame and restrain the diversity of the BIT ecosystem in perhaps-unconscious service of something like the Benedict Kingsbury view of international administrative law – or, more controversially, the Myres McDougal understanding of judges as international administrators.[74] There is no getting around the fact that these efforts sometimes press hard on the black letter norms of modern treaty law. If we take seriously the challenges of sorting snowflakes in a blizzard, the system may have no other choice.

---

[74] Compare, e.g., B. Kingsbury, N. Krisch and R. B. Stewart, 'The Emergence of Global Administrative Law', *Law & Contemp. Prob.*, 68 (2005), 15–61, with McDougal, Lasswell and Miller, *supra* n. 73.

21

International Environmental Law*

DUNCAN FRENCH AND KAREN N. SCOTT

1 Introduction

An assumption is often made that treaty-making in the sphere of international environmental law is at the vanguard of more general developments in treaty law. Patricia Birnie, Alan Boyle and Catherine Redgwell, for example, describe the development of international environmental law as 'one of the most remarkable exercises in international law making, comparable only to the law of human rights and international trade in the scale and *form* it has taken'.[1] However, this assumption – though not without notable elements of accuracy, especially as regards progress by and within multilateral environmental agreements (MEAs) – risks caricaturing the supposed innovation and progression in the use of treaties to resolve many of the world's environmental problems. In particular, whereas key developments in matters such as amendment, breach, the relationship between treaty rules and institutional law have indeed been novel, much of what has been achieved so far either is merely a logical extension of developments in other fields of law or is much less innovative when considered alongside the challenges that remain. Moreover, the developments that have taken place – and by no means in all environmental treaties or in all subject matters of environmental law – invariably occur within the conceptual boundaries of *pacta sunt servanda* and the underlying principles of the 1969 Vienna Convention on the Law of Treaties (VCLT).[2] Thus innovations which have undoubtedly occurred do not challenge the underlying features of treaties in general international law.[3] Nevertheless, there

---

* This chapter was written prior to the conclusion of the 2015 Paris Agreement.
[1] See P. Birnie, A. Boyle and C. Redgwell, *International Law and the Environment* (Oxford: Oxford University Press, 3rd ed., 2009), p. 1 (emphasis added).
[2] 1155 UNTS 331.
[3] This is unsurprising when compared to other areas of law, such as human rights law, where there is an equal moral imperative towards global progress, if not convergence, but which would seem to be equally restricted by the established 'rules of the game'.

remains a growing body of opinion which seeks to argue that the nature and extent of the environmental problems facing the international community demands a much more radical response, including moving towards a form of international legislation, namely binding rules which have not otherwise been expressly consented to *ex ante*.[4] The issues of consent and treaty-making thus provide much of the central narrative of this chapter.

This chapter is divided into four sections. In the first section, we consider the extent to which such agreements can be characterised as law-making, or even constitutional, as opposed to being contractual, and the implications of this characterisation,[5] including the extent to which a limited focus on reciprocity affects both the underpinnings and operation of the treaties. We develop this theme in Section 2 of the chapter, in which we explore the notion of the 'treaty regime' with a particular focus on the operation and decision-making powers of the Conference of Parties (COP) and the consequent interaction between treaty law and international institutional law. In this section, we examine selected aspects of treaty-making including the nature of consensus, reservations and differentiated obligations. The third section of the chapter focuses on treaty change, with particular reference to innovations in amendment practices as a mode of development by some – but by no means all – MEAs. In the final section, we consider the role of the VCLT on the termination of MEAs, with particular reference to fundamental change of circumstances and material breach, before focussing on 'in-treaty' non-compliance procedures and other mechanisms. The chapter concludes with a return to the relationship between international environmental treaty law and the Vienna Convention and addresses the extent to which the latter's underlying rationale and operative provisions have an enduring relevance to MEAs as they traverse the divide between constitutional developments and traditional reciprocity.

2   (Non)-Reciprocity in International Environmental Law and the Creation of Obligations *Erga Omnes*

Multilateral environmental agreements are typically characterised as law-making or standard setting as opposed to contractual or synallagmatic. Treaty obligations are not generally reciprocal in the sense of being owed

---

[4] D. Bodansky, 'The Legitimacy of International Governance: A Coming Challenge for International Environmental Law', *AJIL*, 93 (1999), 596–624.
[5] See the contributions to this volume of Brölmann as well as Moeckli and White at pp. 79–102 (Chapter 4) and 136–171 (Chapter 6) respectively.

to an individual or even a group of parties but rather are owed to *all* parties or even to the international community as a collective. The term 'erga omnes' was famously adopted by the International Court of Justice (ICJ) in 1970,[6] and although environmental obligations were not highlighted by the ICJ in the *Barcelona Traction Case* as examples of *erga omnes* obligations[7] – hardly surprising given that 1970 marked the very beginning of the environmental movement – international environmental law provides perhaps the best illustration of the so-called move 'from bilateralism to community interest in international law'.[8] It is the notion of community interest, 'over and above any interests of the contracting parties individually'[9] that lies at the core of *erga omnes* obligations and that community or collective interest is explicitly acknowledged in a number of MEAs. The preambles to the 1992 United Nations Framework Convention on Climate Change (UNFCCC)[10] and the 1992 Convention on Biological Diversity (CBD),[11] for example, respectively describe climate change and the conservation of biodiversity as common concerns of humankind.[12] Implicitly, most if not all MEAs seek to serve the interests of the international community through their aim to protect the global environment.

The VCLT, however, provides little if any recognition of this very special category of multilateral agreement. The Convention adopts a primarily contractual approach to the creation, implementation and termination of treaties and where it does specifically address multilateral treaties, in respect of reservations or material breach for example, it effectively approaches such treaties as bundles 'of bilateral relations'.[13] Its recognition of a community or collective interest in a treaty is largely confined to developing principles to preserve that treaty – whether from

---

[6] *Case Concerning the Barcelona Traction, Light and Power Company Ltd.*: Belgium v. Spain (Second Phase) (1970) ICJ Rep. 3, at p. 32 (paragraphs 33 and 34).

[7] For a discussion of the examples of *erga omnes* obligations given in the *Case Concerning the Barcelona Traction, Light and Power Company Ltd.* (prohibition of aggression, genocide and protection from slavery and racial discrimination), see M. Ragazzi, *The Concept of International Obligations* Erga Omnes (Oxford: Clarendon Press, 1997), pp. 74–131.

[8] B. Simma, 'From Bilateralism to Community Interest in International Law', *Hague Recueil*, 250 (1994), 221–384, at 238.

[9] J. Pauwelyn, 'A Typology of Multilateral Treaty Obligations: Are WTO Obligations Bilateral or Collective in Nature?', *EJIL*, 14 (2003), 907–951, at 908. See, also, Simma, *supra* n. 8, at 298–299.

[10] 1771 UNTS 107.   [11] 1760 UNTS 79.

[12] See the contribution to this volume of Klabbers at pp. 172–200 (Chapter 7).

[13] Pauwelyn, *supra* n. 9, at 908.

the impacts of unduly wide reservations[14] or permitting too readily termination of, or withdrawal from, a treaty in response to breach[15] – rather than acknowledging its potential to impact on the rights and obligations of non-party States or the international community more generally. The VCLT largely dismisses the possibility that treaties may have legal consequences for non-party States without their express or implied consent,[16] and Sir Humphrey Waldock's proposal in 1964 that the Convention recognise so-called 'objective regimes' was explicitly rejected by the International Law Commission.[17]

Whilst the majority of MEAs confine their obligations to States parties, a significant minority nevertheless appear to provide for the application of treaty rules to non-party States. One of the oldest examples is the 1959 Antarctic Treaty,[18] which, in Article X, requires each of its Parties to 'exert appropriate efforts, consistent with the Charter of the United Nations, to the end that no one engages in any activity in Antarctica contrary to the principles' of the Treaty. The 1973 Convention on International Trade in Endangered Species (CITES)[19] permits Parties to trade with non-parties only where the non-party provides comparable documentation to that required by the Convention[20] and establishes a precedent for a similar condition under the 2000 Cartagena Protocol on Biosafety to the 1992 CBD,[21] the 2001 Stockholm Convention on Persistent Organic Pollutants (the POPs Convention)[22] and, most recently, the 2013 Minamata Convention on Mercury.[23] The 1987 Montreal Protocol on Substances that Deplete the Ozone Layer to the 1985 Convention for

---

[14] Art. 19(3) VCLT: *supra* n. 2.   [15] Art. 60 VCLT: *supra* n. 2.

[16] Arts. 34–36 VCLT: *supra* n. 2.

[17] F. Salerno, 'Treaties Establishing Objective Regimes' in E. Cannizzaro (ed.), *The Law of Treaties beyond the Vienna Convention* (Oxford: Oxford University Press, 2011), pp. 225–243, at pp. 226–227. See, further, E. David, 'Article 34 (1969)' in O. Corten and P. Klein (eds.), *The Vienna Conventions on the Law of Treaties: A Commentary* (Vol. I) (Oxford: Oxford University Press, 2011), pp. 887–896, at pp. 891 and 895, and, also, D. J. Bederman, 'Third Party Rights and Obligations in Treaties' in D. B. Hollis (ed.), *The Oxford Guide to Treaties* (Oxford: Oxford University Press, 2012), pp. 328–346, at pp. 341–345; G. M. Danilenko, *Law-Making in the International Community* (Dordrecht: Martinus Nijhoff Publishers, 1993), p. 63, and A. Proelss, 'Article 34' in O. Dörr and K. Schmalenbach (eds.), *Vienna Convention on the Law of Treaties: A Commentary* (Berlin: Springer, 2012), pp. 605–643, at pp. 622–628.

[18] 402 UNTS 71.   [19] 993 UNTS 243.

[20] Arts. II(4), III(1), IV(1), V(1) and X CITES: *supra* n. 19.   [21] 2226 UNTS 208, Art. 24.

[22] 2256 UNTS 119, Art. 3(2)(b)(iii).

[23] Not yet in force; Art. 3(6)(b). Text available at: www.mercuryconvention.org/Portals/11/ documents/conventionText/Minamata%20Convention%20on%20Mercury_e.pdf.

the Protection of the Ozone Layer[24] and the 1989 Basel Convention on the Control of Transboundary Movements of Hazardous Wastes and Their Disposal[25] go further and ban imports of controlled ozone-related substances from[26] and exports of waste to non-parties.[27] However, it is not clear that these provisions represent *in practice* genuine exceptions to the *pacta tertiis* rule as embodied in the VCLT.[28] Where a State not party to, for example, CITES or the POPs Convention agrees to transfer wildlife or persistent organic pollutants in accordance with the respective rules of those conventions, it has effectively accepted and agreed to be bound by that obligation as envisaged in Article 35 VCLT, provided that its acceptance is effected in writing. To the extent that acceptance pursuant to Article 35 VCLT has not taken place, or where a State party has imported pollutants or exported waste to a non-party in clear violation of the relevant convention, only the State party to that convention will incur responsibility for breach of that convention, unless it can be established that a separate obligation under customary international law exists and is applicable to the (non-Party) State in question.[29] Nevertheless, treaty provisions which restrict the rights of parties to trade or otherwise engage with third-party States provide an important incentive for third parties to ratify and thus obtain full rights under the convention in question, and to participate in its development and management.

The notion that all States and the international community as a whole have an interest in the protection of obligations *erga omnes* is as controversial as the assertion that such obligations are universally binding.[30] Notwithstanding the manifest interest individual States and indeed the international community as a collective have in holding parties to their obligations to protect the global environment, the VCLT makes no provision for such third-party intervention outside of the recognised 'exceptions' provided for in Articles 35 to 38 VCLT.[31] The ICJ in the

---

[24] 1522 UNTS 3.   [25] 1673 UNTS 126.   [26] Art. 4 of Montreal Protocol: *supra* n. 24.

[27] Art. 4(5) of Basel Convention: *supra* n. 25.

[28] Art. 34 VCLT: *supra* n. 2. See, generally, M. Fitzmaurice, 'Third Parties and the Law of Treaties', *Max Planck Yb. UN Law*, 6 (2002), 37–137.

[29] Art. 38 VCLT: *supra* n. 2.   [30] Ragazzi, *supra* n. 7, at p. 17.

[31] In contrast, Art. 48 of the 2001 International Law Commission Draft Articles on Responsibility of States for Internationally Wrongful Acts permits the invocation of responsibility by a State where the obligation is owed to the international community as a whole and allows that State to demand that the State in breach cease the wrongful conduct and provide appropriate reparation to injured States: Official Records of the General Assembly, Fifty-Sixth Session, Supp. No. 10 (A/56/10).

Barcelona Traction Case did not find it necessary to create a means of enforcing *erga omnes* obligations outside of the traditional principles of international law[32] and, twenty-five years later, confirmed its view that recognition of a right *erga omnes* does not automatically permit any State standing to vindicate that right.[33] In fact, there is little if any evidence to support the concept of an *actio popularis* with respect to *erga omnes* obligations.[34] By contrast however, the issue of standing appears to be unproblematic as between the parties to a MEA in respect of obligations *erga omnes partes*.[35] Although Article 60 VCLT requires parties to be especially affected in order to suspend a treaty in respect of a material breach, the Convention is silent on whether a party needs to be injured or otherwise affected in order to initiate dispute resolution proceedings in respect of a breach or interpretation of treaty obligations. Almost all MEAs provide for the peaceful resolution of disputes using existing fora such as the ICJ or Permanent Court of Arbitration or new institutions such as an arbitral tribunal established for the purpose, but none restrict such action to parties that have been injured or otherwise especially affected. This flexible approach to standing reflects and supports the community interest in achieving the objectives under environmental treaties and the challenges associated with ensuring compliance with the treaty if standing is restricted to those directly affected by the breach. This approach has received recent support from the ICJ in a different but analogous context, where the Court decided that Belgium did not need to prove a special interest in Senegal's alleged breach of the 1984 United Nations Convention against Torture and Other Cruel, Inhuman and

---

[32] *Case Concerning the Barcelona Traction, Light and Power Company Ltd., supra* n. 6, at p. 47 (paragraph 91).

[33] *Case Concerning East Timor: Portugal v. Australia* (1995) ICJ Rep. 90, at p. 102 (paragraph 29). Similarly, whilst the 2001 Draft Articles provide for the invocation of responsibility by a non-injured state in respect of *erga omnes* obligations under Art. 48, *supra* n. 31, the rights of non-injured States to intervene are limited to their ability to claim that the wrongful conduct cease and a demand for reparation on behalf of the injured state or 'of the beneficiaries of the obligation breached'.

[34] T. Stephens, *International Courts and Environmental Protection* (Cambridge: Cambridge University Press, 2009), p. 67. See, also, C. J. Tams, *Enforcing Obligations* Erga Omnes *in International Law* (Cambridge: Cambridge University Press, 2005), pp. 48–96.

[35] It is notable that in Advisory Opinion No. 17, the Seabed Disputes Chamber of the International Tribunal for the Law of the Sea stated that: 'Each State Party may also be entitled to claim compensation in light of the *erga omnes* character of the obligations relating to preservation of the environment of the high seas and in the Area'. See *Responsibility and Obligations of States Sponsoring Persons and Entities with Respect to Activities in the Area* (Advisory Opinion), at p. 54 (paragraph 180).

Degrading Treatment or Punishment[36] in order to initiate dispute resolution proceedings against Senegal in the ICJ in respect of those alleged breaches.[37] Further support for the notion of the *erga omnes partes* obligation can be found in Australia's decision to deliberately refrain from asserting any special interest in Japan's alleged breach of Article VIII of the 1946 International Convention on the Regulation of Whaling,[38] when initiating proceedings before the ICJ in 2010.[39] Moreover, in the absence of detailed rules relating to the consequences of a breach of treaty under the VCLT, and in light of the collective and community interest in the promotion of compliance with global environmental obligations, MEAs are developing increasingly innovative and sophisticated mechanisms for responding to issues of breach or, as they are more commonly referred to, non-compliance.

It is, however, worth noting that obligations under MEAs are not exclusively standard setting or legislative in character. Increasingly, obligations are differential in nature, and their application depends on issues of capacity or historic responsibility. For example, the 1997 Kyoto Protocol to the Framework Convention on Climate Change[40] imposes obligations to reduce emissions of greenhouse gases on States listed in Annex I to the Protocol, and the emissions reductions targets are specific to individual States. The 1987 Montreal Ozone Protocol, 1992 CBD, 2001 POPs Convention, 2000 Biosafety Protocol and 2010 Nagoya Protocol on Access to Genetic Resources and the Fair and Equitable Sharing of Benefits Arising from their Utilization to the Convention on Biological Diversity[41] all permit the capacity of States to be considered when assessing compliance and impose particular obligations on developed States in respect of technology and knowledge transfer. Two of the Agreements concluded under the auspices of the 1979 Bonn Convention on the

---

[36] 1465 UNTS 85.

[37] *Questions Relating to the Obligation to Prosecute or Extradite*: Belgium v. Senegal (2012) ICJ Rep. 422, at pp. 449–450 (paragraphs 68–69).

[38] 161 UNTS 72.

[39] *Whaling in the Antarctic*: Australia v. Japan: New Zealand Intervening (2014) ICJ Rep. 226. The Australian written proceedings are available at: www.icj-cij.org/docket/index .php?p1=3&p2=3&k=64&case=148&code=aj&p3=1. Australia's approach also pragmatically side-steps the dispute between Australia and Japan over the status of the waters off the coast of the area of Antarctica claimed by Australia as the Australian and Antarctic Territory.

[40] 2303 UNTS 148.

[41] Not yet in force. Text available at: www.cbd.int/abs/text/default.shtml.

Conservation of Migratory Species of Wild Animals (CMS)[42] – in respect of gorillas[43] and African-Eurasian waterbirds[44] – provide for action plans which specify the extent of each participating State's obligations in respect of habitat protection and hunting controls. Both agreements constitute essentially contractual undertakings by the relevant range States rather than setting out overall standards. In rare cases, MEA obligations are genuinely reciprocal or synallagmatic. For example, the extent to which developing countries are required to comply with their obligations under the 1992 UNFCCC is explicitly dependent upon the effective implementation of developed countries' obligations under the Convention in respect of financial resources and technology transfer.[45] This commitment is reiterated in Article 11 of the 1997 Kyoto Protocol and provides a precedent for a similar provision in the 2001 Stockholm Convention on POPs.[46] The extent to which these commitments constitute legally enforceable obligations rather than political aspirations is nevertheless debatable.[47] Finally, it is worth noting that all MEAs preserve the ultimate contractual right within the law of treaties: the right to withdraw from that treaty.

In conclusion, the paucity (though not complete absence) of reciprocal commitments within MEAs and the characterisation of environmental obligations as *erga omnes partes*, if not more generally *erga omnes*, have undoubtedly led to developments beyond those originally envisaged in the VCLT. As will be demonstrated later, MEAs have responded to the collective, community and arguably *erga omnes* interest in environmental obligations in a number of ways. First, techniques have been adopted to improve and speed up the development of treaties allowing States parties to more rapidly respond to changes in knowledge, environmental circumstances and ethical concerns. Examples of such techniques canvassed later in the chapter include the adoption of the framework convention/protocol model, the use of tacit and analogous consent procedures when adopting amendments, and the adoption of decisions and resolutions and other soft law instruments to develop or even amend

---

[42] 1651 UNTS 355.

[43] 2007 CMS Agreement on the Conservation of Gorillas and their Habitat. Text available at: www.cms.int/species/gorillas/agreement_text.html.

[44] 1995 CMS African-Eurasian Waterbird Agreement. Text available at: www.cms.int/species/aewa/aew_text.htm.

[45] Art. 4(7) UNFCCC: *supra* n. 10.

[46] Art. 13(4) of the Stockholm Convention: *supra* n. 22.

[47] M. Drumbl, 'Poverty, Wealth, and Obligation in International Environmental Law', *Tulane L. Rev.*, 76 (2002), 843–960, at 940.

the treaty. Second, States have adopted principles and concepts designed to preserve the integrity of treaties and the coherence of the environmental obligations they establish through, for example, restrictions on the use of reservations, tools of interpretation and a conservative approach to concepts such as fundamental change in circumstances. Third, issues of compliance and breach are increasingly addressed through a multilateral rather than bilateral process using designated internal institutions that emphasise a facilitative rather than coercive approach to compliance.

3 Aspects of Law-Making and the Creation of Environmental Regimes

3.1 The Creation of Environmental 'Regimes'

The term 'regime' has recently been liberated from its confinement to international relations scholarship by international lawyers seeking to describe the dynamic and innovative approach to law-making within the context of MEAs. Modern – and not so modern – MEAs typically adopt the following schema: a framework or overarching convention setting out guiding principles, general obligations and establishing institutions, developed by detailed protocols or annexes within which the substance of the instrument is often located and supplemented by formal decisions and resolutions adopted by the conference or meeting of the parties designed to guide or inform its implementation.[48] Such regimes have been developed to address climate change, ozone depletion, wildlife conservation, pollution prevention and ocean management among other environmental concerns and aim to protect the *erga omnes* nature of the treaty through developing efficient means to adopt, amend and develop its environmental obligations whilst simultaneously safeguarding the principles of sovereignty and State consent.[49]

[48] See, generally, T. Gehring, 'Treaty-Making and Treaty Evolution' in D. Bodansky, J. Brunée and E. Hey (eds.), *The Oxford Handbook of International Environmental Law* (Oxford: Oxford University Press, 2007), pp. 467–497, and P. C. Szasz, 'International Norm-making' in E. Brown-Weiss (ed.), *Environmental Change and International Law* (Tokyo: United Nations University Press, 1992), pp. 41–72.

[49] J. Brunnée, 'Reweaving the Fabric of International Law? Patterns of Consent in Environmental Framework Agreements' in R. Wolfrum and V. Röben (eds.), *Developments of International Law in Treaty Making* (Berlin: Springer, 2005), pp. 101–126, at p. 105. The framework convention/protocol approach has also been adopted in other sectors, notably health: see, in particular, D. Bodansky, *The Framework Convention/Protocol Approach* (Framework Convention on Tobacco Control Technical

The framework convention/protocol model is particularly well suited to complex or wide-ranging environmental problems where initial agreement on principles, concepts and basic obligations can provide an effective foundation for the development of more specific and concrete measures. The 1985 Vienna Convention on the Ozone Layer/1987 Montreal Protocol and 1992 UNFCCC/1997 Kyoto Protocol provide good examples of this incremental approach to regime creation. This model is also sufficiently flexible to permit specific environmental issues to be addressed by sub-groups of States where appropriate. For example, the 1979 Migratory Species Convention, which was one of the earliest framework MEAs, now provides the overarching framework for seven formal agreements between individual range States in respect of particular species such as cetaceans or gorillas and a further nineteen more informal memoranda of understanding. Highly technical agreements such as CITES, the 1998 Rotterdam Convention on Prior Informed Consent for Certain Hazardous Chemicals and Pesticides in International Trade[50] and the 2001 Stockholm Convention on Persistent Organic Pollutants make extensive use of annexes or appendices. As will be discussed later, most MEAs that follow such a model provide for a simplified amendment procedure in respect of technical annexes and appendices, which allows the instrument to be regularly updated in light of new information and changing attitudes. Both models embody a degree of novelty from the perspective of traditional treaty law, but neither can be characterised as a wholesale departure from it. Rather, they provide vigorous illustrations of the so-called 'living treaty'.[51]

By contrast, the third feature of MEAs – regime development through treaty institutions – does represent a more significant challenge to the traditional rules of treaty-making embodied in the VCLT. MEAs 'create their own institutional apparatuses',[52] often described as autonomous institutional arrangements[53] and in doing so 'become themselves machineries for the making and development of international environmental law'.[54] In this sense, they might be described as 'quasi-constitutional'

Briefing Series, Paper 1 (1999) WHO/NCD/TFI/99.1) and, further, the contribution to this volume of Granziera and Solomon at pp. 881–906 (Chapter 27).

[50] 2244 UNTS 337.   [51] Brunnée, *supra* n. 49, at p. 102.

[52] Gehring, *supra* n. 48 at p. 473.

[53] R. R. Churchill and G. Ulfstein, 'Autonomous Institutional Arrangements in Multilateral Environmental Agreements: A Little-Noticed Phenomenon in International Law', *AJIL*, 94 (2000), 623–659.

[54] Gehring, *supra* n. 48 at p. 474.

treaties.[55] Institutions typically established by MEAs include the conference or meeting of parties (COP/MOP), a secretariat, scientific bodies
and, in some cases, a financial mechanism and compliance body.[56] These
institutions, in particular, the COP/MOP, play a vital role in developing
the normative content of the regime.[57] For example, the COP established
by the 1992 UNFCCC is specifically mandated to adopt protocols[58] under
the Convention. A similar mandate is afforded to the COPs established
under the 1989 Basel Convention[59] and the 1992 Biodiversity
Convention.[60] However, whilst the locus of decision-making in respect
of the adoption of protocols in these cases has formally shifted from
individual States to an institution – the COP – no State party will
ultimately be bound by any protocol in the absence of its consent and
in accordance with its normal constitutional procedures.[61] Similarly,
treaty amendments adopted by the COP also have to be approved by
individual State parties in order for them to enter into force and become
binding. Even simplified or expedited treaty amendment procedures,
which are discussed further later, are originally consented to by States.
In practice, the COP/MOP provides a forum for decision-making and
does not normally act as an independent institutional decision-maker in
respect of the adoption of amendments and protocols.[62]

However, increasingly, treaty institutions are adopting binding or
non-binding decisions, often on a majority basis, which significantly
affect the scope and implementation of obligations undertaken by
State parties but which do not constitute formal amendment of that

[55] C. Brölmann, 'Specialised Rules of Treaty Interpretation: International Organisations' in
Hollis (ed.), *supra* n. 17, pp. 507–524, at p. 509.

[56] See, generally, G. Ulfstein, 'Treaty Bodies' in Bodansky, Brunée and Hey (eds.), *supra*
n. 48, pp. 877–889, and G. Ulfstein, 'International Framework for Environmental
Decision-making' in M. Fitzmaurice, D. M. Ong and P. Merkouris (eds.), *Research
Handbook on International Environmental Law* (Cheltenham: Edward Elgar, 2010), pp.
26–47.

[57] Churchill and Ulfstein, *supra* n. 53, at 623.   [58] Art. 17(1) UNFCCC: *supra* n. 10.

[59] Art. 15 of the Basel Convention: *supra* n. 25.   [60] Art. 23 CBD: *supra* n. 11.

[61] Nevertheless, it is worth noting that the shift towards institutional decision-making
effectively broadens the range of actors directly and indirectly involved in the process.
For example, at the fifteenth UNFCCC conference of the parties in Copenhagen in 2009,
over 20,000 individuals and 1,000 private organizations joined the 192 State delegations in
their efforts to negotiate a post-Kyoto instrument. See K. Raustiala, 'NGOs in
International Treaty Making' in Hollis (ed.), *supra* n. 17, pp. 150–174, at p. 150.

[62] See G. Handl, 'International "Lawmaking" by Conferences of the parties and other
Politically Mandated Bodies' in Wolfrum and Röben (eds.), *supra* n. 49, pp. 127–143.
A limited exception to this can be found under the 1987 Montreal Protocol, *supra* n. 24,
and this is discussed further later.

treaty. For example, in 1986, the CITES COP adopted a resolution creating a quota system permitting limited trade in Appendix I species, such as the leopard, subject to specified conditions.[63] The practical effect of this resolution was an informal amendment of CITES or, at a minimum, the adoption of a very particular interpretation of the obligation laid down in Article III of the Convention. Under the 1997 Kyoto Protocol the COP adopted, in 2001, the Marrakesh Accords, which established detailed rules relating to its implementation and undoubtedly shaped the interpretation and implementation of those provisions under the Protocol.[64] More significantly, the UNFCCC COP adopted the Copenhagen Accord in December 2009,[65] which, whilst soft in character, has been described as 'the most influential document that has emerged from the climate negotiations in the recent past'.[66] All non-compliance procedures adopted under MEAs to date have been established by means of a COP/MOP decision although in all but one case the original mandate for such a procedure can be found within the relevant treaty text.[67] Nevertheless, the procedures developed to address compliance under these regimes create, in many cases, significant new rights under international law for non-State actors to initiate proceedings and complex requirements on potentially *all* parties to support those States unable to comply. Perhaps the most audacious COP decision affecting the rights of treaty parties was the attempt, in 1994, to ban the transboundary movement of waste from OECD to non-OECD countries under the Basel Convention by means of

[63] M. Fitzmaurice, 'Expression of Consent to be Bound by a Treaty as Developed in Certain Environmental Treaties' in J. Klabbers and R. Lefeber (eds.), *Essays on the Law of Treaties: A Collection of Essays in Honour of Bert Verdiag* (The Hague: Martinus Nijhoff, 1998), pp. 59–80, at p. 75. See, now, Resolution Conf. 14.7 (Rev. CoP 15) *Management of Nationally Established Quotas.*

[64] Decisions 2-14/CP.7 (FCCC/CP/2001/13/Add.1 (21 Jan. 2002))

[65] Decision 2/CP.15 (FCCC/CP/2009/11/Add.1 (30 March 2010)).

[66] D. French and L. Rajamani, 'Climate Change and International Environmental Law: Musings on a Journey to Somewhere', *J. Env. L.*, 25 (2013), 437–461, at 446.

[67] The exception is the 1991 Espoo Convention on Environmental Impact Assessment in A Transboundary Context: 1989 UNTS 309. Although an NCP was established under the Convention in 2004 (see Decision III/2 *Review of Compliance* (2004); Decision IV/2 *Operating Rules of the Implementation Committee* (as amended by Decision V/4 *Review of Compliance* (2011)), there is currently no operative provision in the Convention which provides a specific mandate for the creation of an NCP. An amendment to the Convention was adopted in 2004 to remedy this omission and insert a new article into the Convention (Art. 14*bis*), but this amendment has yet to enter into force. See Decision III/7 *Second Amendment to the Espoo Convention* (2004) (not yet in force).

a decision only.[68] Concerns expressed by the parties over whether the COP could unilaterally alter parties' obligations under the Treaty[69] led the COP one year later to adopt the ban as an amendment to the Treaty.[70] Notably, that amendment has yet to enter into force. The extent to which MEA treaty bodies have the capacity to adopt decisions which impact on the treaty obligations of States is principally a matter for international institutional law rather than treaty law *per se*.[71] Indeed, their role within MEAs has been deliberately developed by the parties in order to 'overcome the cumbersome treaty-making process'.[72]

Moreover, soft law instruments and agreements intended to be non-binding are a growing feature of the typical environmental treaty regime. For example, particular sub-sets of parties to the 1979 Migratory Species Convention have adopted nineteen memoranda of understanding in respect of species such as sharks, elephants and flamingos,[73] as well as eleven action plans and seven co-called initiatives. Whilst formally non-binding,[74] these arrangements nevertheless have normative effect and, in the case of the memoranda of understanding, are clearly designed to reflect, and operate in the manner of, a typical treaty. More generally, MEA institutions are increasingly entering into formal cooperative agreements with one-another in order to share information and develop joint initiatives such as action plans.[75] The most active MEA in this respect is the 1992 CBD, which has formal relationships with eighteen other MEAs,[76] as well as over 140 memoranda of understanding with other bodies including scientific institutions, universities and botanical gardens.[77] This form of cooperation is by no means confined to biodiversity-focused MEAs, and similar agreements have been entered into by MEA institutions within the areas of pollution, environmental impact

---

[68] Decision II/12 (1994) available at: www.basel.int/TheConvention/ConferenceofthePart ies/ReportsandDecisions/tabid/3303/Default.aspx.

[69] Churchill and Ulfstein, *supra* n. 53, at 639.

[70] Decision III/1 (1995) *Amendment to the Basel Convention* available at: www.basel.int /implementation/legalmatters/banamendment/tabid/1484/default.aspx.

[71] G. Ulfstein, 'Treaty Bodies and Regimes' in Hollis (ed.), *supra* n. 17, pp. 428–447, at p. 428.

[72] *Ibid.*, at p. 435.   [73] See www.cms.int/species/index.htm.

[74] On the binding (or otherwise) nature of memoranda of understanding, see A. Aust, 'Alternatives to Treaty-Making: MOUs as Political Commitments' in Hollis (ed.), *supra* n. 17, pp. 46–72, and J. Klabbers, *The Concept of Treaty in International Law* (The Hague: Kluwer Law International, 1996).

[75] K. N. Scott, 'International Environmental Governance: Managing Fragmentation through Institutional Connection', *Melbourne JIL*, 12 (2011), 177–216, at 192–200.

[76] *Ibid.*, at 192.   [77] *Ibid.*

assessment and fisheries management.[78] The most extensive example of formal institutional cooperation has been developed by the Basel, Stockholm and Rotterdam Conventions – the so-called chemicals cluster – which have so far held two extraordinary joint meetings, in 2010 and 2013, at which joint decisions have been adopted designed to enhance joint work programmes and administrative synergies between the three conventions.[79] This quite remarkable set of initiatives raises important questions relating to the capacity of the treaty institutions to enter into such agreements, given that they are not generally considered to be international organizations as such,[80] the status of those agreements[81] and the impact of those agreements on the obligations of States, particularly where membership of the agreements cooperating is not coincidental. However, whilst these questions go beyond the parameters of this chapter,[82] there is little doubt that the legal landscape of the typical environmental regime today is increasingly complex, and the VCLT, whilst still preeminent in providing the overall framework for the management of these regimes, by no means constitutes the entirety of the background law.

3.2   The Meaning of 'Consensus' in International Environmental Law

Consent remains the bedrock on which all environmental regimes are built. However, within MEAs, the notion of consent has significantly diversified in order to respond to the need for rapid and more effective law-making.[83] This is nowhere more apparent than in the context of treaty amendment, which is discussed later in the chapter. In general, the preferred mode of decision-making within MEAs is consensus, followed by a majority vote where consensus cannot be achieved. This approach is adopted, for example, by Article 15 of the 1992 UNFCCC and replicated in the UNFCCC COP Rules of Procedure.[84] This model of decision-

---

[78] *Ibid.*, at 192–207.

[79] *Ibid.*, at 205–207. Reports of the 2013 Meeting and associated decisions can be found at: http://synergies.pops.int/2013COPsExCOPs/Overview/tabid/2914/mctl/ViewDetails/EventModID/9163/EventID/297/xmid/9411/language/en-US/Default.aspx.

[80] Churchill and Ulfstein, *supra* n. 53, at 623 and 632–634.

[81] Most MOUs are either silent on their status or explicitly state that they are non-binding. However, many contain clauses relating to termination, liability and the division of responsibilities suggesting that they are designed to have some legal effect as between the institutions if not States parties more generally.

[82] But see Scott, *supra* n. 75.   [83] Danilenko, *supra* n. 17, at p. 54.

[84] *Adoption of the Rules of Procedure*, FCCC/1996/CP/2 (22 May 1996).

making by consensus/majority vote is broadly followed by all MEAs although the rules relating to majority vote, in terms of whether three-quarters or other majority is required or where a majority must be achieved within particular State groupings, vary. No MEA provides a definition of consensus, although most confine the notion – and indeed the concept of the majority – to States physically present at the meeting in question. It is generally accepted that consensus occupies middle ground between unanimity and majority voting[85] and is a political rather than a formal legal concept.[86] As described by Thomas Gehring, consensus 'preserves the right of all parties to reject an undesired decision . . . but it does not require a positive vote by all parties'.[87] This understanding was, however, directly and controversially challenged in December 2010 when, at the Sixteenth UNFCCC COP, the Cancun Agreements[88] were adopted by consensus over the express opposition of Bolivia.[89] Two years later, at the Eighteenth COP in 2012, the Doha Amendments to the 1997 Kyoto Protocol were similarly adopted by consensus over the explicit opposition of Russia.[90] Thus far, apparently isolated to the particularly pressurised context of the climate change regime, this unusual approach to the concept of consensus has understandably created unease among certain UNFCCC parties.[91] Ultimately, neither Bolivia nor Russia is bound by these COP decisions, and both States can choose not to implement the Cancun Decisions or ratify the Kyoto amendments

---

[85] Gehring, *supra* n. 48, at p. 470.

[86] L. Rajamani, 'The Cancun Climate Agreements: Reading the Text, Subtext and Tea Leaves', *ICLQ*, 60 (2011), 499–519, at 516.

[87] Gehring, *supra* n. 48, at p. 470.

[88] 1/CP.16 (2010) *The Cancun Agreements: Outcome of the Work of the Ad Hoc Working Group on Long-Term Cooperative Action under the Convention.*

[89] See the *Report of the Conference of the Parties on its Sixteenth Session, Held in Cancun from 29 November to 10 December 2010*, FCCC/CP/2010/7 (paragraphs 47 and 48). Bolivia's position on the adoption of the Agreements was formally recorded in the Report.

[90] On Demand Webcast, Joint meeting of the Conference of the Parties (COP), 10th Meeting and the Conference of the Parties serving as the meeting of the Parties to the Kyoto Protocol (CMP), 10th Meeting (8 Dec. 2012): http://unfccc4.meta-fusion.com/kongresse/cop18/templ/play.php?id_kongresssession=5833&theme=unfccc. See, further, French and Rajamani, *supra* n. 66, at 449.

[91] In 2013, Russia, Belarus and the Ukraine attempted to raise the question of procedural decision-making in the Subsidiary Body for Implementation (SBI). Ironically, consensus on the issue was not achieved, and the question was not included on the SBI's agenda. See UNFCCC, Provisional Agenda and Annotations: Note by the Executive Secretary, Addendum, Supplementary Provisional Agenda (29 May 2013): U.N. Doc. FCCC/SBI/2013/1/Add.1 and (2013) 12 (580) Earth Negotiations Bulletin 17 (17 June 2013). See, also, French and Rajamani, *supra* n. 66, at 450.

respectively. Nevertheless, the 'consensus minus one' approach provides perhaps the clearest example to date of an *erga omnes* regime within which the international community as a collective has an interest over and above those of individual States.

3.3   Reservations to Multilateral Environmental Agreements

One of the most noticeable trends in many multilateral environmental agreements has been the move towards a general prohibition of unilateral reservations to the treaty's principal provisions.[92] Undoubtedly following the precedent of the 'package deal' approach of the 1982 United Nations Convention on the Law of the Sea (UNCLOS),[93] many – though not all – environmental treaties prohibit general reservations. The absence of reservations to the main text of a treaty was intended – and has clearly done much – to ensure the integrity of the treaty as well as arguably subsequently assisting the establishment of coherent legal regimes thereunder. As was recognised during the UNCLOS III negotiations, reservations seek to encourage universality of membership, though not without some risk to the nature and content of the commitments within a treaty. And although universality can be encouraged by other means – well-tested in the environmental field, including differentiation in commitments, and the provision of financial, technological and technical assistance – the existence of a general prohibition continues to be viewed as an important legal technique.[94]

However, the inclusion of such a general prohibition does not exist across all treaties and can certainly be contrasted with a number of the earlier environmental treaties such as the 1973 CITES and 1979 CMS, which prohibit general reservations but permit specific reservations

---

[92] On Art. 19 VCLT and the subject of reservations more generally, see A. Pellet, 'Article 19 (1969)' in Corten and Klein (eds.), Vol. I, *supra* n. 17, pp. 405–482; C. Walter, 'Article 19' in Dörr and Schmalenbach (eds.), *supra* n. 17, pp. 239–286; E. T. Swaine, 'Treaty Reservations' in Hollis (ed.), *supra* n. 17, pp. 277–301, and International Law Commission, 'Text of the Draft Guidelines constituting the Guide to Practice on Reservations to Treaties, as provisionally adopted by the International Law Commission' (2011) (available at: http://legal.un.org/ilc/guide/1_8.htm).

[93] 1833 UNTS 3, Art. 309. See, further, H. Caminos and M. Molitor, 'Progressive Development of International Law and the Package Deal', *AJIL*, 79 (1985), 871–890.

[94] This, of course, does not prevent States Parties issuing interpretative declarations, or such, at the time of signature or ratification, though their legal value is clearly less demonstrable than a reservation despite it often being difficult to distinguish between them notwithstanding formal attempts to demarcate their purposes.

limiting the application or scope of obligations in respect of individual species listed in appendices.[95] Though now viewed, especially by non-governmental organizations and indeed some international organizations, with some regret, such provisions remain fundamental to many States' strategic participation in such treaties. Moreover, such strategic considerations may play an increasingly important role in the current negotiations towards a new 2015 climate change agreement, where many of the previous assumptions in earlier MEAs would seem to be increasingly questioned. It would thus not be unexpected that a greater 'pick-and-mix approach' – which may include permitting reservations despite previous precedents – be part of the final compromise reached on that agreement.

Moreover, it must also be recalled that although there has been a trend towards general prohibitions on reservations in respect of the principal articles, this can be contrasted in a number of instances with other provisions within the same agreement, which permit States to vary – for want of a better word – their commitments in some way,[96] give States discretion on the means (but importantly not the principle) of dispute settlement[97] or, arguably most significantly, permit States parties to 'object' to future changes in technical annexes and appendices. The third issue is discussed later in this chapter when considering amendment, and all instances should be distinguished from reservations *per se* as understood by the VCLT. Nevertheless, it is worth noting that they serve a similar function, namely, permitting a State to remain party to the treaty without being bound in every detail, thus preserving sovereign autonomy. To this extent, the necessity for such an objection, 'opt out' or even, in some instances 'opt in' procedure – even in limited

---

[95] See, for instance, Art. XXIII CITES (*supra* n. 19) and Art. XIV CMS (*supra* n. 42). Both operate in largely the same fashion, whilst prohibiting so-called 'general reservations', permits '[a]ny State or regional economic integration organization may, on depositing its instrument of ratification, acceptance, approval or accession, enter a specific reservation with regard to the presence on either Appendix I or Appendix II or both, of any migratory species': e.g. Art. XIV(2) CMS (*supra* n. 42).

[96] Perhaps the best example of such a provision not termed a reservation, but having somewhat a similar role is Art. VIII ICRW, which allows States Parties to permit 'scientific whaling' which 'shall be exempt from the operation of this Convention'. See *Whaling in the Antarctic, supra* n. 39.

[97] See, for instance, Art. 14(2) UNFCCC: *supra* n. 10. Perhaps the best example is the complex structure created under Part XV of UNCLOS, both in terms of choice of procedure (Art. 287 UNCLOS (*supra* n. 93)) and optional exceptions to the scope of jurisdiction (Art. 298 UNCLOS (*supra* n. 93)).

circumstances – is considered legally and politically valuable for States in the face of future uncertainty and is not invariably viewed as undermining the integrity of the treaty. However, being able to object to changes and make reservations to technical annexes does – in principle and in substance – affect the primary commitments that States parties are obliged to respect under these agreements. Nevertheless, it would seem reasonable to conclude that *at present* there is a general consensus on the inclusion of a prohibition of reservations as against the main text of most multilateral environmental agreements.

3.4   Differentiation and International Environmental Obligations[98]

One of the most pronounced and noticeable aspects of treaty-making in the environmental field – again neither universally seen nor consistently applied – is the existence of differentiation between States parties in terms of the scope, nature and timing of the obligations contained within a treaty.[99] Discussion on this matter usually – if erroneously[100] – begins with the development of the principle of common but differentiated responsibilities (CBDR) during preparations for the 1992 United Nations 'Rio' Conference on Environment and Development and the parallel negotiations on a climate change convention to be opened for signature thereat. The principle – more commonly referred to now, certainly within the climate change context, as common but differentiated responsibilities and respective capabilities (CBDRRC) – has been a significant if not unique trait of many MEAs. Nevertheless, one must be careful not to generalise too readily.

First, though there is a reasonable time-line distinction between early environmental treaties, which paid scant regard to differentiation, and later agreements, especially those of the late 1980s/early 1990s, which utilised differentiation to a much greater extent, this pattern is not without exceptions and contradictions. For instance, whilst the 1987 Montreal Ozone Protocol, which was arguably the first international environmental agreement to permit differentiation between developed

---

[98] See more generally the contribution to the volume of Bowman at pp. 392–439 (Chapter 13).

[99] See P. Cullet, *Differential Treatment in International Environmental Law* (Burlington: Ashgate, 2003).

[100] D. French, 'Developing States and International Environmental Law: The Importance of Differentiated Responsibilities', *ICLQ*, 49 (2000), 35–60.

and developing countries in a structured manner (especially after the 1990 London Amendments),[101] other global treaties adopted around this time, such as the Basel Convention and other treaties dealing with hazardous materials and pollution control, have been much more restrained in the express differentiation that they permitted. The Basel Convention, for example, contains a number of provisions that can be characterised as cooperative rather than overtly differential[102] despite recognising, in its preamble, the great difficulties faced by developing countries when addressing the issue. The level, nature and extent of differentiation have thus varied in terms of environmental media and environmental harm, with global conventions on climate change and desertification[103] being an extreme rather than exemplars across environmental treaties as a whole. Indeed, the Seabed Disputes Chamber in Advisory Opinion Number 17, when asked whether developing country States Parties in the Area had less demanding environmental commitments placed upon them, drew an analogy with 'flags of convenience' to caution against such an approach:

> Equality of treatment between developing and developed sponsoring States is consistent with the need to prevent commercial enterprises based in developed States from setting up companies in developing States, acquiring their nationality and obtaining their sponsorship in the hope of being subjected to less burdensome regulations and controls.[104]

Second, there is a genuine question over what counts as differentiation. Though any provision which allows for variation in treatment between the parties might reasonably be considered as differentiation, a number of discrete forms have developed. These include differences in the substantive commitments (or whether such commitments exist for certain States parties),[105] permission for delayed compliance[106] or a legal

---

[101] The text of the London Amendments is available at: http://ozone.unep.org/new_site/en/ Treaties/treaties_decisions-hb.php?dec_id_anx_auto=780.

[102] See, for instance, Art. 4(13) of the Basel Convention, *supra* n. 25: 'Parties shall undertake to review periodically the possibilities for the reduction of the amount and/or the pollution potential of hazardous wastes and other wastes which are exported to other States, in particular to developing countries'.

[103] The 1994 Desertification Convention was, for instance, noticeable in incorporating annexes specific to separable geographic regions, with Regional Implementation Annex I on Africa being particularly significant – and substantive – in this regard: 1954 UNTS 3.

[104] Advisory Opinion Number 17, *supra* n. 35, at p. 54 (paragraph 159).

[105] See Art. 10 of the Kyoto Protocol: *supra* n. 40.

[106] See Art. 5 of the Montreal Protocol: *supra* n. 24.

requirement to act as a financial or technological 'donor' (in contrast to being a recipient of financial, technical and technological assistance).[107] Much of the controversy, certainly in the climate change regime, has centred almost exclusively on the first category, namely the extent and nature of commitments agreed.[108] Moreover, describing modalities of differentiation does not *per se* capture the crux of the debate in international environmental law over the past three decades. In particular, and perhaps most controversially, differentiation has largely been related synonymously with a division – however broadly defined – between developed and developing States and sometimes within sub-categories thereof.[109] Thus, while some treaties have permitted differentiation without explicit reference to developmental-status or permitted differentiation from any State Party,[110] the most contentious debates have been when this differentiation has been divided along developmental lines, however artificial these have become in some instances.[111]

Third, in addition to types and categories of differentiation, there is what might be referred to as different 'forms' of differentiation. Already mentioned has been structured differentiation, where the treaty itself sets out which obligations are differentiated and usually which States parties are to benefit. There is also so-called contextual differentiation,[112] best demonstrated by the 1992 CBD where some of its obligations are to be achieved 'as far as possible and as appropriate'.[113] This broadly worded differentiation gives discretion not just to defined groups of States but also within individual, national circumstances, with the 'as far as possible' supposedly providing a limitation to the 'as appropriate'. It also highlights that differentiation contributes to the perceived soft-ness in some international environmental law, namely the existence of normative

---

[107] The UNFCCC makes a distinction between Annex I parties (developed country parties and parties with economies in transition), which have further substantive commitments than developing country parties, and Annex II parties (which comprises only the developed country parties), which have additional financial obligations under the Convention, and subsequently under the Kyoto Protocol.

[108] Nevertheless, it would be wrong to marginalise the other forms of differentiation, as highlighted by Art. 4(7) UNFCCC: *supra* n. 10.

[109] See, for instance, Art. 4(8) UNFCCC: *supra* n. 10.

[110] The recently adopted 2013 Minamata Convention on Mercury, for instance, permits limited differentiation, but it is clearly available for all State parties to take advantage: *supra* n. 23.

[111] French and Rajamani, *supra* n. 66, at 440–441.

[112] D. Magraw, 'Legal Treatment of Developing Countries: Differential, Contextual and Absolute Norms', *Colorado J. Int'l Env. Law & Policy*, 1 (1990), 69–99.

[113] *Supra* n. 11.

obligations that lack the usual prescriptiveness that one would expect to find within a legally-binding treaty.[114]

A chapter such as this on treaty-making, however, is less concerned with the substance of the primary norms of differentiation – as the Vienna Convention itself is rarely concerned with any of the primary rules within a treaty – than with the role differentiation plays in influencing the secondary functions of treaty negotiation, interpretation, validity and termination as well as State responsibility.[115] It is at this point that the legal status of CBDR as a principle of international law becomes of interest.[116] Much is made of the political import of differentiation to achieve universal membership, especially encouraging developing country buy-in. What is less certain is how far differentiation is anything other than an operational precept rather than a legally binding principle. Certainly, a treaty such as the UNFCCC includes differentiation as a principle – in Article 3(1)[117] – which is to guide action,[118] but in terms of substance and normative impact, its influence remains disputed. Moreover, as the 'post-Kyoto' negotiations within the climate change regime have made clear, traditional divisions along developed/developing country lines have eroded in international environmental law, and as a working model, CBDRRC is no longer what it once was. Moreover, broadening out differentiation to range beyond purely legal obligation to include broader forms of assistance and support, including funding, differentiation in some form is arguably ingrained within both the ethos and the workings of international environmental law.

4 Treaty Amendment and Revision within International Environmental Law

The ability to amend a treaty in order to maintain its relevancy and ability to adapt to changing environmental and social conditions is as important as the ability to negotiate a treaty in the first place. Traditionally,

---

[114] See A. Boyle, 'Soft Law in International Law-Making' in M. Evans (ed.), *International Law* (Oxford: Oxford University Press, 4th ed., 2014), pp. 118–136, at pp. 126–128.

[115] In a very separate area, it is interesting to read the judgment of the Court in *Questions Relating to the Obligation to Prosecute or Extradite*, *supra* n. 37, at p. 460 (paragraphs 112–115) where Senegal's apparent lesser financial capacity to undertake an international criminal trial was not considered a relevant factor in mitigating its responsibility in that instance.

[116] See D. Shelton, 'Equity' in Bodansky, Brunnée and Hey (eds.), *supra* n. 48, pp. 639–662, at pp. 656–658.

[117] Art. 3(1) UNFCCC: *supra* n. 10.   [118] Art. 3 UNFCCC: *supra* n. 10.

amendment or modification[119] of treaties was deemed a matter of politics and diplomacy rather than law,[120] and there were few if any common rules on amendment in existence prior to the adoption of the VCLT.[121] The primary rule, as set out in the Vienna Convention, is that '[a] treaty may be amended by agreement between the parties'.[122] The importance of consent is reaffirmed in the case of multilateral treaties, where again the residual rule, unless the treaty expresses otherwise, is that '[t]he amending agreement does not bind any State already a party to the treaty which does not become a party to the amending agreement'.[123] Sovereign autonomy thus remains fundamental to treaty amendment, just as it is in the initial creation of the treaty.

As with other matters of treaty law within MEAs, on one level there is no radical departure from the traditional rules on treaty amendment within most environmental agreements. For example, although Article 29 of the 1992 CBD, which sets out the procedure for amendment of the convention, develops the rules contained in the Vienna Convention, particularly around the role of the COP and the balance between consensus and majority voting, ultimately consent is preserved as no amendment takes effect for that party without its 'ratification, acceptance or approval'.

This provision, which is fairly typical among MEAs, raises few problems from the perspective of the VCLT, which in any case sets out the default rules relating to amendment and modification.[124] Of greater significance is the practice within MEAs relating to the amendment, modification and adjustment of annexes and appendices associated with the treaty. MEAs dealing with nature conservation, transboundary pollution, marine pollution and hazardous materials commonly provide for technical annexes and appendices, which are generally integral to the treaty. The procedures relating to amendment of annexes and appendices

---

[119] The VCLT distinguishes between amendment of treaties, where the amendment is intended to apply to all parties (Art. 40) and modification, where the amendment operates as between a subgroup of parties (Art. 41): *supra* n. 2.

[120] A. D. McNair, *The Law of Treaties* (Oxford: Clarendon Press, 1961), p. 534.

[121] Odendahl, 'Article 40' in Dörr and Schmalenbach (eds.), *supra* n. 17, pp. 709–717, at p. 711. See, also, R. D. Kearney and R. E. Dalton, 'The Treaty on Treaties', *AJIL*, 64 (1970), 495–561, at 523.

[122] Art. 39 VCLT: *supra* n. 2.   [123] Art. 40(4) VCLT: *supra* n. 2.

[124] Arts. 39–41 VCLT: *supra* n. 2. For a history and recent assessment of these provisions, see Corten and Klein (eds.), Vol. II, *supra* n. 17, pp. 963–976, 978–984 and 986–1008, and Dörr and Schmalenbach (eds.), *supra* n. 17, pp. 699–707, at pp. 709–717 and 719–727.

vary significantly, and it is beyond the scope of this chapter to summarise them here.[125] Rather, a few general points will be made.

First, as noted previously, very often amendment procedures are intrinsically related to the secondary decision-making power of the relevant conference or meeting of the parties. While few, if any, treaties have so far gone down the route of endowing such institutional bodies with autonomous power, akin to legislative competence – at least, not beyond a narrow remit related to budgetary matters and, in some instances, non-compliance – many MEAs do give COPs a central role in considering and adopting amendments to technical annexes. There are however, clear limits to the role of the COP as 'law-maker' as illustrated by the objection of States to the 1994 decision of the COP to the Basel Convention, which sought to prohibit the movement of hazardous waste from OECD to non-OECD countries by means of a decision.[126]

Second, MEAs commonly use opt-out or tacit amendment procedures with respect to annexes and appendices. For example, amendments to the annexes of the 1985 Vienna Convention for the Protection of the Ozone Layer will automatically enter into force six months after their adoption for all those States which have not notified the depositary that they are unable to accept the amendment.[127] Similar provision is made for the amendment of annexes or appendices under the 1992 UNFCCC, 1973 CITES, 1989 Basel Convention, 1998 Rotterdam Convention, 2001 Stockholm POPs Convention, 1992 CBD and protocols, 1979 Bern Convention and 1979 Migratory Species Convention. This model has also been adopted by the 2013 Minamata Convention on Mercury, which goes so far as to provide that the adoption of a *new* annex will automatically enter into force for all those parties which have not objected to it one year after adoption.[128] Tacit and analogous amendment procedures serve a valuable function in facilitating the rapid updating of MEAs and maximising the likely acceptance of those amendments as States are forced to opt out rather than to opt in. However, in almost all MEAs, State consent and the principle of sovereignty is preserved as States may

---

[125] See M. Bowman, 'The Multilateral Treaty Amendment Process – A Case Study', *ICLQ*, 44 (1995), 540–559, and J. Brunnée, 'Treaty Amendments' in Hollis (ed.), *supra* n. 17, pp. 347–366.

[126] Discussed in Section 3.1 of this chapter.

[127] 1985 Vienna Convention for the Protection of the Ozone Layer, 1513 UNTS 323, Art. 10(2)(c).

[128] Art. 27(3) of the Minamata Convention: *supra* n. 23.

ultimately opt out and refuse to be bound by an amendment if they so choose. This procedure therefore simply provides an example of the 'any other means if so agreed' as envisaged in Article 11 VCLT. Nevertheless, one innovative example of a process of amendment that departs from the principle of State consent can be found in the Montreal Protocol on the Ozone Layer which, as revised in 1990, ensures that adjustments to the technical annexes which have been agreed, in the absence of consensus, by at least a two-thirds majority (including 'double' majorities of developed and developing countries) take effect for all States Parties with no further ability to opt-out.[129] This adjustment process has been used five times since 1990[130] but is thus far unique in international environmental law.

From a perspective of environmental effectiveness, it would seem that foreclosing – or limiting – the ability of States Parties to refuse to be bound by amendments, admittedly within the confines of the general parameters of *pacta sunt servanda*, is a positive trend. Indeed, certain fisheries conventions now require, even within their opt out system, for States parties to provide justification and cause for their decision, which holds States to account in a more meaningful way.[131] Nevertheless, States parties cherish their autonomy, and balancing this individual discretion with achieving global outcomes is resulting in a broad array of complex procedural rules around the issue of amendment to annexes. In matters, particularly, of the regulation of economic sensitivity, such rules reflect this careful balance between environmental protection and not losing competitive advantage.

Are these innovative approaches to treaty amendment exclusive or particular to environmental treaties?[132] Certainly, there are other examples of innovative amendment processes, including the 2005 International Health Regulations[133] and the 1993 Convention on the Prohibition of the Development, Production, Stockpiling and Use of

---

[129] Art. 4(9) of the Montreal Protocol: *supra* n. 24.

[130] Adjustments were made in 1990, 1992, 1995, 1997, 1999 and 2007. See http://ozone.unep .org/new_site/en/Treaties/treaties_decisions-hb.php?sec_id=343.

[131] See Art. 17(2) of the 2009 Convention on Conservation and Management of High Seas Fishery Resources in the South Pacific Ocean and the use of the objection procedure by the Russian Federation in 2013 (www.southpacificrfmo.org/objections/).

[132] See A. Aust, *Modern Treaty Law and Practice* (Cambridge: Cambridge University Press, 3rd ed., 2013), pp. 232–244, and Brunnée, *supra* n. 125.

[133] See Arts. 21(a) and 22 of the Constitution of the World Health Organization (WHO), under which the IHRs are adopted, and which provides for binding rules unless WHO member States opt out within a specified period: 14 UNTS 185.

Chemical Weapons and on their Destruction,[134] to name but two. Nevertheless, as a matter of course, it would seem that MEAs are more likely to provide for flexible amendment procedures, reflecting the need for greater adaptability to changing environmental circumstances. What remains uncertain is how far States parties are willing to develop these rules any further. The innovations in some fisheries treaties requiring States to justify their actions might be one area for further investigation, as might greater use of the processes employed within the International Maritime Organization.[135] However, there is a very clear prohibiting factor: States parties need to agree these procedures at the outset – consent is consequently preserved, and ultimately, States are inclined to restrict the occasions when it is displaced.

5   Termination of Multilateral Environmental Agreements

The ability to terminate or suspend a treaty, for whatever reason, is one of the most substantial powers given to a State party by the VCLT. The provisions on termination are thus some of the most normatively constrained provisions – together with those on validity – within the Vienna Convention. As with many other areas of law, matters of termination have arisen rarely within the broad context of the number of environmental treaties that exist. Nevertheless, on the issues of both fundamental change of circumstances and material breach, on which this part focuses,[136] the secondary rules are both influenced by and influencing the subject matter of the treaties. This is particularly apparent when considering the development of non-compliance procedures.

5.1   Fundamental Change of Circumstances

One of the most contested provisions in the Vienna Convention, certainly as regards termination, is *rebus sic stantibus*, which permits termination (and suspension) of a treaty on the grounds of a fundamental change of circumstances not foreseen by the parties at the time of

---

[134] Art. XV(4) and (5) establish an the expedited procedure for amendments to Annexes 'if proposed changes are related only to matters of an administrative or technical nature': 1974 UNTS 317.

[135] See, further, the contribution to this volume of Lost-Sieminska at pp. 907–932 (Chapter 28).

[136] This chapter will not address less controversial but doubtless more common mechanisms for the termination of treaties such as consent or the termination of a treaty implied by the conclusion of a later treaty (Arts. 54–59 VCLT: *supra* n. 2).

negotiation.[137] As is widely agreed, though this is a rule with significant historical pedigree and general doctrinal support,[138] the contours of the customary rule as reflected in the VCLT remain disputed. General judicial authority on the issue – notably by the International Court in the *Fisheries Jurisdiction Case*[139] – points to a restrictive reading of the rule. Nevertheless, as an accepted justification of termination, its potential relevance in the area of international environmental law is significant.

From an environmental perspective, several questions arise in respect of the potential application of Article 62 VCLT. Might a change to the environment such as an increase in sea levels and global temperatures caused by human-induced climate change be considered an unforeseen fundamental change in circumstances and justify the termination of a treaty? How scientifically certain must an environmental event be before a States party can claim fundamental change of circumstances? Must a States party wait for an event to have occurred – contrary to environmental ideas of prevention and precaution – before being able to rely on the principle of fundamental change of circumstances? The latter two questions raise the issue of foreseeability and, in an environmental context, the relevance of the precautionary principle. And, finally, what of contribution? In the case of climate change, would one State party's role in generating greenhouse gas emissions be sufficiently remote to avoid the application of Article 62(3) VCLT, which prohibits the invocation of the doctrine where there has been a breach of 'an obligation under the treaty or of any other international obligation'?

Though questions such as these are context-dependent upon the individual terms of the treaty, as well as the nature of the 'change' not foreseen, the ICJ has previously had the opportunity to consider some of the issues relating to environmental change and treaty law. In its 1997 judgment in *Case Concerning Gabčikovo-Nagymaros Project*, the ICJ was called upon to assess the Hungarian argument, *inter alia*, that the treaty in question – a 1977 bilateral treaty between Hungary and Czechoslovakia governing aspects of non-navigational uses of a section

---

[137] See, generally, M. Shaw and C. Fournet, 'Article 62' in Corten and Klein (eds.), Vol. I, *supra* n. 17, pp. 1411–1436; T. Giegerich, 'Article 62' in Dörr and Schmalenbach (eds.), *supra* n. 17, pp. 1067–1104, and M. Fitzmaurice, 'Exceptional Circumstances and Treaty Commitments' in Hollis (ed.), *supra* n. 17, pp. 605–633.

[138] See the literature cited *ibid*.

[139] *Fisheries Jurisdiction Case*: United Kingdom v. Iceland (Jurisdiction) (1973) ICJ Rep. 3, at p. 21 (paragraph 43): 'The change must have increased the burden of the obligation to be executed to the extent of rendering the performance something essentially different from that originally undertaken'.

of the River Danube – had been terminated owing to a fundamental change of circumstances.[140] Hungary argued that much had changed since the treaty's negotiation, including, significantly, 'progress of environmental knowledge and the development of new norms and prescriptions of international environmental law'.[141] The Court was not persuaded by this argument, noting in particular the treaty's own internal normative flexibility to respond to change, making 'it possible for the parties to take account of such developments and to apply them'.[142] This ability to reflect more recent developments in environmental knowledge was also a feature of the later decision in *Case Concerning Pulp Mills on the River Uruguay*.[143] Significantly, the Court went on to note in its 1997 judgment that '[t]he negative and conditional wording of Article 62 . . . is a clear indication moreover that the stability of treaty relations requires that the plea of fundamental change of circumstances be applied only in exceptional cases'.[144]

Beyond MEAs, there is a range of interesting questions as to how far environmental issues may come to be used by States parties to challenge their obligations undertaken in other areas of international law. Returning, for instance, to the preceding hypothetical example, might sea-level rise, or for that matter sea-temperature rise, be a sufficiently fundamental change in circumstances to disrupt a range of obligations under the Law of the Sea Convention?[145] Much would, of course, depend upon the severity of the impact. Similarly, might climate change influence to a sufficient degree, and without reasonable foreseeability, other treaties ranging from those that regulate navigational and non-navigational rights in international rivers to those that provide for free trade? At present, it is speculative whether the legal argument of fundamental change of circumstances could be made out. Nevertheless, as extreme environmental patterns emerge, settled legal obligations may be increasingly questioned.

The Court, in the *Gabčikovo-Nagymaros Case*, also had the opportunity to consider the issue of foreseeability, though under the separate

---

[140] *Case Concerning Gabčikovo-Nagymaros Project (Hungary/Slovakia)* (1997) ICJ Rep. 7.
[141] *Ibid.*, at pp. 64–65 (paragraph 104). [142] *Ibid.*, at pp. 65–66 (paragraph 107).
[143] *Case Concerning Pulp Mills on the River Uruguay*: Argentina v. Uruguay (2010) ICJ Rep. 14, at pp. 82–83 (paragraph 204).
[144] *Case Concerning Gabčikovo-Nagymaros Project*, *supra* n. 140, at p. 66 (paragraph 108).
[145] R. Rayfuse, 'Climate Change and the Law of the Sea' in R. Rayfuse and S. V. Scott (eds.), *International Law in the Era of Climate Change* (Cheltenham: Edward Elgar, 2012), pp. 147–174.

doctrine of necessity as a circumstance precluding wrongfulness. Hungary had argued 'ecological necessity' as a justification for breach.[146] Again, the Court – while not dismissing the possibility of such an argument – found it not proven in this particular case. And although its comments on foreseeability must be considered as primarily related to necessity as understood within State responsibility – at that time prior to the 2001 adoption of the ILC Draft Articles on State responsibility – what the Court says on the issue of foreseeability, and, in particular, the relationship between peril, risk and material damage,[147] seems of relevance to a broader range of issues, including termination and responsibility.[148]

Of course, the rules on necessity and fundamental change of circumstances are distinct, and each has its own purpose, limitation and threshold. But equally, both are based on the quality of the evidence presented and, within that, issues of risk and foreseeability. The ICJ has thus left open the possibility for States to argue the doctrine of fundamental change of circumstance – and, indeed, other rules of termination and State responsibility – in future cases, but the evidential and legal threshold for its application is clearly narrowed by the exceptional nature placed upon the rule by the International Court. As the Court noted, 'mere apprehension' is not enough.[149] Indeed, the overriding theme of the judgments in both the *Gabčikovo-Nagymaros Case* and *Pulp Mills on the River Uruguay Case* was that preserving the extant legal framework was invariably viewed as a preferable option.

5.2   Material Breach and Non-compliance

The rules relating to material breach as set out in Article 60 VCLT[150] constitute a complex regime and provide a rare example of where the Convention makes a limited distinction between law-making and

---

[146] *Case Concerning Gabčikovo-Nagymaros Project, supra* n. 140, at pp. 35–36 (paragraph 40).

[147] *Ibid.*, at pp. 41–42 (paragraph 54).

[148] See, further, the contribution to this volume of Fitzmaurice at pp. 748–789 (Chapter 23).

[149] *Ibid.*

[150] See, generally, T. Giegerich, 'Article 60' in Dörr and Schmalenbach (eds.), *supra* n. 17, pp. 1021–1049; M. M. Gomaa, *Suspension or Termination of Treaties on Grounds of Breach* (The Hague: Kluwer Law International, 1996); B. Simma and C. J. Tams, 'Article 60 (1969)' in Corten and Klein (eds.), Vol. II, *supra* n. 17, pp. 1351–1378, and B. Simma and C. J. Tams, 'Reacting against Treaty Breaches' in Hollis (ed.), *supra* n. 17, pp. 576–604. See, also, the contribution to this volume of Tams at pp. 440–467 (Chapter 14).

contractual treaties.[151] Taken as a whole, the provision seeks to balance the rights of the collective in supporting the stability of the agreement with the right of an injured party to obtain appropriate remedy and redress in the event of breach. The principle of *inadimplenti non est adimplendum*, or negative reciprocity, which underpins Article 60 VCLT,[152] is most clearly demonstrated in its requirement that a party can only unilaterally suspend a multilateral treaty as against the party in breach[153] where they have been especially affected by the breach[154] or where the breach radically changes the position of every party with respect to the further performance of their obligations under the treaty.[155] In short, the party wishing to suspend an agreement against a party in breach must have a 'particular interest' in the performance of the obligation in question 'which goes beyond that of the other parties to the treaty'.[156] This requirement, combined with the high-threshold definition of material breach,[157] would seem to render the application of Article 60 VCLT largely irrelevant to the typical MEA where obligations are generally *erga omnes partes* rather than clearly reciprocal in nature.[158] The question of whether the rules relating to material breach should, in principle, apply to standard setting or law-making treaties was vigorously debated during the negotiations of the Vienna Convention,[159] with Sir Gerald Fitzmaurice, in particular, advocating that a unilateral right either to suspend or to terminate a treaty as against a party in breach should not be available in respect of multilateral law-making treaties.[160] Whilst the

---

[151] Simma and Tams, in Corten and Klein (eds.), *supra* n. 150, at p. 1353.

[152] Giegerich, *supra* n. 150, at p. 1022.

[153] States parties to an agreement may choose to suspend or terminate a treaty against a party in breach or in its entirety by unanimous agreement (Art. 60(2)(a) VCLT: *supra* n. 2), but the possibility of unilateral termination of a multilateral treaty was specifically excluded.

[154] Art. 60(2)(b) VCLT: *supra* n. 2. [155] Art. 60(2)(c) VCLT: *supra* n. 2.

[156] Simma and Tams, in Corten and Klein (eds.), *supra* n. 150, at p. 1365.

[157] Art. 60(3) VCLT defines a material breach as a repudiation of the treaty not sanctioned by that treaty or a violation of a provision essential to the accomplishment to the object or purpose of that treaty: *supra* n. 2.

[158] The VCLT is silent on the consequences of a non-material breach and the extent to which an uninjured party may challenge a party in breach. As discussed previously, recent practice appears to support the right of any party to take action where the obligation can be categorised as *erga omnes partes*.

[159] Simma and Tams, in Corten and Klein (eds.), *supra* n. 150, at p. 1364, and E. Schwelb, 'Termination or Suspension of the Operation of a Treaty as a Consequence of Its Breach', *Indian JIL*, 7 (1967), 309–334, at 320–322.

[160] Giegerich, *supra* n. 150, at p. 1036. For a discussion of the pre-Vienna position on the right to respond to a breach of a treaty see S. Rosenne, *Breach of Treaty* (Cambridge: Grotius Publications, 1985), pp. 3–44, and Schwelb, *supra* n. 159.

overall principle advocated by Fitzmaurice was rejected on the basis that the distinction between contractual and law-making treaties is very difficult to draw in practice,[161] its spirit can nevertheless be found in Article 60(5) VCLT, which denies the right to suspend or terminate humanitarian treaties in the event of breach.[162] However, the very inclusion of Article 60(5) in the Convention supports the more general application of Article 60 VCLT to non-humanitarian multilateral law-making treaties, including MEAs, and this interpretation has received support from the ICJ.[163]

Responding, in part, to the relative lack of guidance provided by the VCLT in respect of breach, material or otherwise, more than twenty MEAs have developed or are in the process of developing internal procedures to deal with parties in breach or, as it is now commonly termed, in non-compliance with the treaty.[164] Typically, an MEA non-compliance procedure (NCP) is managed by a designated institution established by the treaty, and any party in non-compliance may be referred to that institution by other parties, by itself[165] or, increasingly, by a treaty institution such as the secretariat or meeting of the parties.[166]

---

[161] *Ibid.* It was also noted that law-making treaties permit States to withdraw at will notwithstanding their special characteristics and to prevent States from effectively withdrawing *vis-à-vis* an individual State in the event of a breach would be illogical.

[162] I. Sinclair, *The Vienna Convention on the Law of Treaties* (Manchester: Manchester University Press, 2nd ed., 1984), p. 190.

[163] In *Legal Consequences for States of the Continued Presence of South Africa in Namibia (South West Africa) Notwithstanding Security Council Resolution 276 (1970)* (Advisory Opinion) (1971) ICJ Rep. 16, at p. 47, the ICJ endorsed 'the general principle of law that a right of termination on account of breach must be presumed to exist in respect of all treaties except for those of a humanitarian character' (paragraph 96). See also p. 48 (paragraph 98).

[164] See, generally, J. Klabbers, 'Compliance Procedures' in Bodansky, Brunée and Hey (eds.), *supra* n. 48, pp. 995–1009; K. N. Scott, 'Non-compliance Procedures and Dispute Resolution Mechanisms under international environmental Agreements' in D. French, M. Saul and N. D. White (eds.), *International Law and Dispute Settlement: New Problems and Techniques* (Oxford: Hart Publishing, 2010), pp. 225–270, and T. Treves, L. Pineschi, A. Tanzi, C. Pitea, C. Ragni and F. Romanin Jacur (eds.), *Non-compliance Procedures and Mechanisms and the Effectiveness of International Environmental Agreements* (The Hague: TMC Asser Press, 2009).

[165] The first MEA to permit self-referral in non-compliance proceedings was the 1987 Montreal Ozone Protocol and this mode of initiating proceedings was used relatively extensively in the 1990s. See D. G. Victor, 'The Operation and Effectiveness of the Montreal Protocol's Non Compliance Procedure' in D. G. Victor, K. Raustiala and E. B. Skolnkioff (eds.), *The Implementation and Effectiveness of International Environmental Commitments: Theory and Practice* (Cambridge, MA: MIT Press, 1998), pp. 137–176.

[166] Almost 20 MEAs provide for the institutional initiation of NCPs and in practice, the overwhelming majority of proceedings have been initiated by institutions to date. See Scott, *supra* n. 164, at Appendix II.

In a minority of cases proceedings can even be initiated by an appropriately qualified NGO or an individual.[167] This multilateral as opposed to reciprocal response to breach, which is further enhanced by the increasing levels of public participation within non-compliance proceedings,[168] has been developed by MEAs operating in the areas of climate change, ozone depletion, wildlife protection, biodiversity conservation, pollution prevention and control and fisheries management among others.[169] Moreover, in contrast to the coercive approach which characterises the traditional response to a breach of treaty as developed by the law of treaties and the rules relating to countermeasures, non-compliance proceedings generally adopt a more facilitative approach, and measures adopted by compliance bodies are often designed to assist rather than to punish a State in non-compliance with its obligations.[170]

The relationship between NCPs and the more traditional rules relating to breach of treaty, dispute resolution and countermeasures is currently unclear.[171] Relying on Article 60(4) VCLT, it might be argued that the specialised rules developed by MEAs to deal with breach have priority over the default rules established by the law of treaties and countermeasures.[172] Such an interpretation would potentially preclude a party to an MEA responding to a party in breach of that MEA outside of the parameters of the NCP. However, most NCPs do not specify whether compliance

---

[167] For example, non-compliance proceedings can be initiated by individuals or appropriately qualified NGOs under the 1998 Aarhus Convention on Access to Information, Public Participation in Decision-Making and Access to Justice in Environmental Matters, 2161 UNTS 447, and the 1979 Bern Convention on the Conservation of European Wildlife and Natural Habitats, 1284 UNTS 209.

[168] Scott, *supra* n. 164, at pp. 249–251.

[169] For a comprehensive list of the MEAs that have developed or are in the process of developing non-compliance procedures, see Scott, *supra* n. 164, at Appendix I.

[170] Scott, *supra* n. 164, at pp. 244–247. The emphasis on facilitating compliance as opposed to penalising non-compliance supports a more general managerial approach to addressing implementation of and compliance with MEAs. See, further, A. Chayes and A. Handler Chayes, *The New Sovereignty: Compliance with Regulatory Agreements* (Cambridge, MA: Harvard University Press, 1995). It should be noted penal measures are by no means irrelevant and that a number of non-compliance procedures adopt a combined facilitative and coercive approach towards compliance. The NCP established under the 1997 Kyoto Protocol for example comprises both a Facilitative and an Enforcement Branch.

[171] See M. Fitzmaurice, 'Non-Compliance Procedures and the Law of Treaties' in Treves, Pineschi, Tanzi, Pitea, Ragni and Romanin Jacur (eds.), *supra* n. 164, pp. 453–481.

[172] Art. 55 of the 2001 Draft Articles similarly gives priority to specialised rules relating to countermeasures developed within individual regimes.

measures issued against a State in breach are formally binding,[173] and as noted earlier, most NCPs are established by decisions that are themselves non-binding. In at least one instance, a dispute between two parties over compliance with an MEA obligation was submitted to arbitration rather than being dealt with by the NCP.[174] Moreover, NCPs are regularly not intended to be comprehensive, and their scope may be limited to dealing with the consequences of designated treaty provisions. Commonly, treaty obligations to provide technical and financial assistance are excluded from the NCP mandate.[175] Non-compliance procedures therefore probably supplement rather than replace the traditional rules relating to treaties, countermeasures and dispute resolution and, consequently, run in tandem to these rules. This notwithstanding, NCPs established by MEAs appear in practice to increasingly provide the principal mechanism for addressing issues of breach[176] and in so doing are able to much more effectively respond to the non-reciprocal *erga omnes* nature of MEA obligations than the default rules relating to breach of treaties. As with the International Court's comments on the VCLT's provisions on fundamental change of circumstances, it is not the existence, but the residual nature, of the provisions on material breach that has allowed States Parties to find their own ways to preserve the integrity of the treaty rather than rely on the formal rules on treaty termination.

5   Conclusion

Having considered a broad spectrum of developments in international environmental treaty law, it is worth questioning where the Vienna

---

[173] Scott, *supra* n. 164, at p. 248.

[174] The dispute concerned the United Kingdom and Ireland over the opening of the MOX reprocessing plant at Sellafield and in particular, Ireland's allegation that the United Kingdom failed to comply with its obligation to provide appropriate information under Art. 9 of the 1992 Convention for the Protection of the Marine Environment of the North-East Atlantic ('OSPAR Convention'), 2354 UNTS 67. The dispute was submitted to arbitration and not to the NCP as provided for under Art. 23 of OSPAR: see *Dispute Concerning Access to Information under Article 9 of the OSPAR Convention*: Ireland v. United Kingdom (Final Award), ILM, 42 (2003), 1118–1186.

[175] Scott, *supra* n. 164, at pp. 239–241.

[176] It is notable that the most high-profile recent environmental dispute, between Australia and Japan over the interpretation and implementation of Art. VIII of the 1946 International Convention on the Regulation of Whaling, *supra* n. 38, concerns a regime that lacks a non-compliance mechanism. Negotiations within the ICRW for an NCP have been stalled since 2006. See the 2006 Report of the International Whaling Commission, Annex F, Appendix 5.

Convention on the Law of Treaties fits within this broader debate. Within the contention that international environmental treaty-making is progressing beyond general treaty law, there is a further – secondary and implicit – assumption that most multilateral environmental agreements extend beyond, deviate from or surpass the constitutional features of the Vienna Convention. As discussed earlier, there is a general view that the Vienna Convention does not embrace the more modern phenomena of 'law-making' treaties and related characteristics of objective standards and obligations *erga omnes* (or at least obligations *erga omnes partes*). But, as has been suggested, this view of the Convention is only partially accurate and is, for us, based somewhat on a misreading of the Convention. In particular, such a view marginalises the reality that the Vienna Convention provides on most matters minimum – or more accurately residual – secondary rules rather than fundamental, even non-derogable, principles. Thus, rather than being perceived in some form of conflict with the Vienna Convention, innovations within MEAs are consistent with the ethos and philosophy of the Convention, which does not intend to set out a set of universal rules applicable for all treaties but rather seeks to provide for default rules applicable where no other rules apply. The emerging framework of secondary, as well as primary, rules in MEAs is therefore particularly to be noted. The inevitable conclusion is that comparing MEAs with a supposed 'paradigm' as established by the Vienna Convention must be treated with caution. To that extent, international environmental law is a model of how States can adapt to changing, and challenging, circumstances within the parameters of the traditional normative framework.

22

International Law of the Sea

DAVID M. ONG

1 Introduction

The United Nations Convention on the Law of the Sea (UNCLOS) has recently celebrated the twentieth anniversary of its entry into force on 16 November 1994,[1] following on from the thirtieth anniversary of its adoption for signature and ratification on 10 December 1982.[2] The passing of these two historical milestones represents an appropriate time period to reflect upon and assess this significant treaty. UNCLOS has been variously described as a 'Constitution for the Oceans',[3] a 'world order treaty'[4] and a 'primary pillar of international law'.[5] Yet whether UNCLOS is in fact, and in law, living up to these billings remains to be seen. As Peter Prows notes, 'UNCLOS is more than just the treaty itself and requires more than just the formal validity of its law for normative force'.[6] Indeed, an extended consideration of UNCLOS shows that it exhibits features of a constitutional, framework-type treaty, a law-making

---

[1] 1833 UNTS 3.

[2] Adopted at the conclusion of the Third United Nations Conference on the Law of the Sea (UNCLOS III) in Kingston, Jamaica, having been negotiated between 1973 and 1982.

[3] See Remarks by Tommy T. B. Koh of Singapore, President of the Third United Nations Conference on the Law of the Sea at the Final Session of the Conference at Montego Bay, Jamaica, 'A Constitution for the Oceans' (www.un.org/Depts/los/convention_agree ments/texts/koh_english.pdf). Reproduced in M. H. Nordquist (ed.), *United Nations Convention on the Law of the Sea 1982: A Commentary* (Vol. I) (Dordrecht: Martinus Nijhoff, 1985), pp. 11–16.

[4] C. Tomuschat, 'Obligations Arising for States without or against Their Will', *Hague Recueil*, 241 (1993), 195–374, at 268–271.

[5] As one of 'seven pillars' of international law enumerated by Bederman: State responsibility, the Rome Statute of the International Criminal Court, diplomatic immunities, the law of the sea, the law of treaties, the Nuremberg Principles, and jurisdictional immunities of States: D. J. Bederman, 'Counterintuiting Countermeasures', *AJIL*, 96 (2002), 817–832, at 817.

[6] P. Prows, 'Tough Love: The Dramatic Birth and Looming Demise of UNCLOS Property Law (and What Is to Be Done about It)', *Texas ILJ*, 42 (2007), 241–309, at 243.

treaty and a codification treaty. As Hugo Caminos has observed, the preamble to the Convention itself denotes that it serves both the codification and progressive development of law in this field.[7] This chapter undertakes an assessment of this Convention through the lens of the law of treaties by considering a selection of the main themes, issues and challenges to treaty law and practice from the law of the sea. The topics covered are not intended to be comprehensive but instead chosen because they relate to issues of continuing importance for treaty law and general international law.

This analysis begins with a brief consideration of the place that UNCLOS holds in the relationship between treaty law and customary international law.[8] This relationship must first take on board the fact that the 1982 Convention was preceded by four related treaties, namely, the 1958 Geneva Conventions on the Law of the Sea,[9] as well as a further, abortive codification attempt in 1960, all of which was preceded by yet another unsuccessful codification exercise in the form of the 1930 Hague Codification Conference.[10] Moreover, the 1982 UNCLOS has itself arguably been subject to an amending instrument, namely, the 1994 Agreement Relating to the Implementation of Part XI of the United Nations Convention on the Law of the Sea (1994 Implementation Agreement).[11] A further, associated implementing treaty in this context is the 1995 Agreement for the Implementation of the Provisions of the United Nations Convention on the Law of the Sea of 10 December 1982 Relating to the Conservation and Managements of Straddling Fish Stocks and High Migratory Fish Stocks (Fish Stocks Agreement).[12]

The relationship between the Geneva Conventions and UNCLOS will be examined, first, by way of consideration specifically of the criteria for establishing the final limits of the continental shelf and, second, with

---

[7] H. Caminos, 'The Legal Régime of Straits in the 1982 United Nations Convention on the Law of the Sea', *Hague Recueil*, 205 (1987–IV), 9–246, at 184, referring to the seventh recital of the Preamble to UNCLOS. See, further, the contribution to this volume of Klabbers at pp. 172–200 (Chapter 7).

[8] R. Bernhardt, 'Custom and Treaty in the Law of the Sea', *Hague Recueil*, 205 (1987–V), 247–330.

[9] I.e. 1958 Geneva Convention on the Territorial Sea and the Contiguous Zone, 516 UNTS 205; 1958 Geneva Convention on the High Seas, 450 UNTS 11; 1958 Geneva Convention on Fishing and Conserving of the Living Resources of the High Seas, 559 UNTS 285, and 1958 Geneva Convention on the Continental Shelf, 499 UNTS 311.

[10] S. Rosenne, *League of Nations Conference for the Codification of International Law* (1930) (Dobbs Ferry, NY: Oceana Publications, 1975), p. 1414.

[11] 1836 UNTS 42.   [12] 2167 UNTS 3.

reference to the requirements for the removal of de-commissioned offshore installations from the continental shelf. Following the initial discussion over treaty relationships on law of the sea issues, the focus shifts
to the relationship between the 1982 UNCLOS and other treaties on
related subjects, specifically with regard to the choice between alternative
dispute settlement procedures. This issue arose between the 1982
Convention and the 1993 Convention for the Conservation of Southern
Bluefin Tuna,[13] which was the subject of the *Southern Bluefin Tuna
Case(s)* before the International Tribunal on the Law of the Sea
(ITLOS)[14] and an UNCLOS Annex VII arbitral tribunal.[15] A further
type of treaty relationship that will be examined here is the set of
UNCLOS provisions that make explicit reference to the term 'generally
accepted international rules and standards' but without actually identifying the relevant international agreements in which these 'international
rules and standards' are incorporated.[16] This relationship between
UNCLOS and other treaties on the same subject matter that provide
for the relevant 'international rules and standards' – or derivations
thereof – will initially be undertaken in the context of the removal of de-
commissioned offshore installations (as noted previously) but will also be
referred to in relation to the 1973/78 MARPOL International Convention
for the Prevention of Pollution from Ships for vessel operational discharge standards.[17]

Moving away from inter-treaty relationships *per se*, this chapter will
then examine the relationship between UNCLOS and the general principles of good faith and non-abuse of rights, from the perspective of the
underlying obligations of UNCLOS treaty performance as well as the
relevant treaty rules for interpreting relevant UNCLOS provisions.
The case study utilized to illustrate these relationships is the interaction
between Article 76 UNCLOS (on the criteria for continental shelf limits
beyond 200 nautical miles) and Article 82 UNCLOS (on revenue-sharing

[13] 1819 UNTS 360.
[14] Established under Annex VI of UNCLOS: *Southern Bluefin Tuna Cases*: New Zealand
v. Japan; Australia v. Japan (Provisional Measures) (1999) ITLOS Rep. 280.
[15] Established under Annex VII of UNCLOS: *Southern Bluefin Tuna Case*: Australia and
New Zealand v. Japan (Award on Jurisdiction and Admissibility), ILM, 39 (2000),
1359–1401.
[16] See Arts. 211(2), 211(5), 211(6)(c) and 226(1)(a) UNCLOS: *supra* n. 1. See, also, Art. 21(2)
UNCLOS ('generally accepted international rules or standards'); Arts. 60(3), 60(5) and
60(6) ('generally accepted international standards') as well as Arts. 21(4), 39(2)(a), 39(2)(b),
41(3), 53(8), 94(2)(a) and 94(5) ('generally accepted international regulations'): *ibid.*
[17] 1340 UNTS 184.

of proceeds from mineral resource exploitation beyond 200 nautical miles). Further examples of treaty interpretation issues arising from UNCLOS provisions, chosen here because they resonate with general international law debates on the interpretation and application of these phrases,[18] relate to, first, the 'nationality of ships' under Article 91 UNCLOS, as elaborated by the ITLOS in the *M/V 'Saiga' (No. 2)*[19] and related cases; and, second, the 'threat or use of force' under Article 301 UNCLOS, as addressed in the *Guyana/Suriname* arbitration award.[20] Finally, this contribution will summarize the relationship these two international law fields – the law of the sea and treaty law – with an eye to possible future developments.

2 Relationship between the 1958 Geneva Conventions, the 1982 UNCLOS and the 1994 Implementation Agreement

That the law of the sea has successfully undergone two major codification exercises since the end of World War II in itself testifies to the significance of this field of international law to the general conduct of international relations around world.[21] These two successful codification exercises yielded, respectively, the four 1958 Geneva Conventions[22] and the 1982 UNCLOS.[23] Since then, two further international agreements, namely, the 1994 Implementation Agreement[24] and the 1995 Fish Stocks Agreement,[25] have both modified the 1982 Convention as well as extended its coverage to include more detailed regulation of straddling and migratory fish stocks across and beyond

---

[18] See, further, the contribution to this volume of Gardiner at pp. 335–362 (Chapter 11).

[19] *M/V 'Saiga' (No. 2)*: Saint Vincent and the Grenadines v. Guinea (Merits) (1999) ITLOS Rep.

[20] *Arbitration between Guyana and Suriname*, Award of 17 Sept. 2007, RIAA, Vol. XXX, 1–144.

[21] A further (i.e. second) Law of the Sea negotiating conference was convened in 1960, ostensibly to address the following substantive topic: 'Consideration of the questions of the breadth of the territorial sea and fishery limits in accordance with resolution 1307 (XIII) adopted by the General Assembly on 10 December 1958' but, due to deep disagreements between coastal States eager to expand their limits of their territorial sea and fishery waters limits and distant-water fishing nations opposed to such extensions of maritime jurisdiction, this conference ended in stalemate. See: Second United Nations Conference on the Law of the Sea Geneva, Switzerland, 17 March–26 April 1960, Final Act of the Second United Nations Conference on the Law of the Sea, U.N. Doc. A/CONF.19/L.15. Extract from: Official Records of the Second United Nations Conference on the Law of the Sea (Summary Records of Plenary Meetings and of Meetings of the Committee of the Whole Annexes and Final Act).

[22] *Supra* n. 9.   [23] *Supra* n. 1.   [24] *Supra* n. 11.   [25] *Supra* n. 12.

the 200 nautical mile (nm)[26] limits of the Exclusive Economic Zone (EEZ). The 1958 and 1982 treaty regimes also represent two quite different examples of codification. The texts of the four Geneva Conventions were initially drafted by the International Law Commission (ILC) and then adopted with modifications by a Conference of Parties specifically convened for this purpose in 1958. The 1982 Convention, by contrast, is the product of an arguably ground-breaking treaty-making process,[27] having been negotiated almost from scratch through a series of biannual multilateral negotiation rounds beginning in 1973 and stretching over a period of nearly a decade, culminating in the adoption of the Convention text on 10 December 1982.

The 1982 UNCLOS entered into force on 16 November 1994, exactly one year following Guyana's ratification as the sixtieth contracting State to this Convention.[28] However, it is at least arguable that UNCLOS may never have entered into force (at all) were it not for the adoption by the United Nations General Assembly of the Implementation Agreement on 28 July 1994.[29] Writing soon after the Convention entered into force, Bernard H. Oxman noted that the fear that few, if any, industrial States would participate in the Convention was eliminated with the conclusion of this Agreement and its endorsement by the General Assembly.[30] Presently, the United States, Turkey, Venezuela and Iran are among the few prominent States that are still not parties to the Convention, although Iran was an initial signatory State in December 1982.[31] Presciently, Oxman also cautioned about the distinction between *substantial* ratification and *global* ratification of UNCLOS, observing that '[t]he position

---

[26] According to the 'Guidelines for the Presentation of Navigation-related Symbols, Terms and Abbreviations' (T2-OSS/2.7.1) of International Maritime Organization (IMO), the abbreviation for the 'Nautical Mile' is 'NM'.

[27] The innovative elements of the negotiation by consensus and package-deal approach to multilateral treaty-making at UNCLOS III have been highlighted by B. Buzan, 'Negotiating by Consensus: Developments in Technique at the United Nations Conference on the Law of the Sea', *AJIL*, 75 (1981), 324–348; H. Caminos and M. R. Molitor, 'Progressive Development of International Law and the Package Deal', *AJIL*, 79 (1985), 871–890, and G. Plant, 'The Third United Nations Conference on the Law of the Sea and the Preparatory Commission: Models for United Nations Law-Making?', *ICLQ*, 36 (1987), 525–558.

[28] As stipulated by Art. 308(1) UNCLOS: *supra* n. 1.

[29] *Supra* n. 11. This Agreement currently has 145 parties.

[30] B. H. Oxman, 'The Rule of Law and the United Nations Convention on the Law of the Sea', *EJIL*, 7 (1996), 353–371, at 355.

[31] See www.un.org/depts/los/reference_files/status2010.pdf.

that the Convention is the best evidence of the customary international law of the sea is a useful one for filling the gap pending global ratification, and may even be useful thereafter for dealing with such non-parties as remain. But, from the perspective of strengthening the rule of law, the customary law position is no substitute for the goal of global ratification. If the past is any guide at all, customary law is unlikely to provide a regime for the sea that entails the stability and restraint we associate with the rule of law. Moreover, customary law may well omit important technical details and almost certainly omits key structural elements of the Convention'.[32] This argument against over-reliance on customary international law as a substitute for the lack of universal adherence to a multilateral treaty is well-founded[33] and will be revisited when we compare the provisions of UNCLOS on the continental shelf limits beyond 200 nautical miles with the provisions for continental shelf limits previously established by the 1958 Continental Shelf Convention.

An additional controversy which has arisen concerns the extent to which the text of the 1982 Convention affords opportunities for States parties to push forward with legislative initiatives that arguably represent a further evolution of the law of the sea. Examining Australian practice for example, Warwick Gullett has recently postulated two reasons why Australia's domestic laws do not implement UNCLOS provisions precisely on certain issues: first, the inherently varying forms of domestic law implementation processes operative within individual States parties and, second, and more significantly, the 'desire by the Australian government to contribute to the development of the international law of the sea in areas where [UNCLOS] provisions are open to a range of interpretations'.[34] According to Gullett, this latter phenomenon is manifest in Australian efforts to enhance its enforcement jurisdiction over illegal fishing by foreign-flagged vessels within its 200 nautical mile EEZ.[35] In this regard, Australia has entered into a bilateral agreement

---

[32] Oxman, *supra* n. 30, at 355.

[33] The seventh recital of the Preamble to UNCLOS provides as follows: 'Believing that *the codification and progressive development of the law of the sea achieved in this Convention* will contribute to the strengthening of peace, security, cooperation and friendly relations among all nations in conformity with the principles of justice and equal rights and will promote the economic and social advancement of all peoples of the world, in accordance with the Purposes and Principles of the United Nations as set forth in the Charter' (emphasis added): *supra* n. 1.

[34] W. Gullett, 'Legislative Implementation of the Law of the Sea Convention in Australia', *Univ. Tasmania L. Rev.*, 32 (2013), 184–207, at 184.

[35] *Ibid.*, at 199–203.

with France to allow the right of hot pursuit against the flagships of third States to continue into the territorial seas of Australia and France.[36] This agreement arguably modifies the right of hot pursuit under Article 111(3) UNCLOS which expressly states that '[t]he right of hot pursuit ceases as soon as the ship pursued enters the territorial sea of its own State or of a third State'.

While UNCLOS does allow for inter-party modification of its provisions under Article 311(3), this is subject to the provision that such modifying agreements, *inter alia*, are compatible with the effective execution of UNCLOS itself, do not affect the application of the basic principles embodied therein and, finally, *do not affect the enjoyment by other States Parties of their rights* or the performance of their obligations under this Convention.[37] These restrictions on the modification of rights and/or obligations for third parties within UNCLOS are in line with Article 41 of the 1969 Vienna Convention on the Law of Treaties (VCLT)[38] as well as the law regarding treaties and third States contained in Articles 34–38 VCLT.[39] On this basis, the present Australia-France bilateral agreement raises concerns about the extension of coastal State enforcement jurisdiction over the flagships of third States (which are not parties to this bilateral agreement) within the territorial sea of another State.[40] The Government of Australia claims that this agreement represents 'a 21st century definition of hot pursuit' and, moreover, that furthering such legal concepts through the conclusion of bilateral (and other) agreements might eventually lead to the inclusion of such concepts within the Convention itself.[41]

---

[36] Art. 4 of the Treaty between the Government of Australia and the Government of the French Republic on Co-operation in the Maritime Areas adjacent to the French Southern and Australian Territories (TAAF), Heard Island and the McDonald Islands, Canberra, 24 Nov. 2003. Text available at *Int'l J. of Marine & Coastal L.*, 19 (2004), 545–553.

[37] Art. 311(3) UNCLOS: *supra* n. 1. See, further, I. Buga, 'Between Stability and Change in the Law of the Sea Convention: Subsequent Practice, Treaty Modification, and Regime Interaction' in D. R. Rothwell, A. G. Oude Elferink, K. N. Scott and T. Stephens (eds.), *The Oxford Handbook of the Law of the Sea* (Oxford: Oxford University Press, 2015), pp. 46–68.

[38] 1155 UNTS 331.

[39] See, further, the contribution to this volume of Waibel at pp. 201–236 (Chapter 8).

[40] For a detailed discussion of the issues raised by these concerns, see W. Gullett and C. Schofield, 'Pushing the Limits of the Law of the Sea Convention: Australian and French Co-operative Surveillance and Enforcement in the Southern Ocean', *Int'l J. of Marine & Coastal L.*, 22 (2007), 545–583, at 565–567.

[41] Gullett, *supra* n. 34, at 205, citing Alexander Downer, (then) Australian Minister for Foreign Affairs, 'The UNCLOS: Ten Years of Benefits for Australia', in a speech delivered at a Symposium on 'Strategic Directions for Australia and the Law of the Sea', Canberra, 16 Nov. 2004.

Moving on from the implications of the passage of UNCLOS for the relationship between treaty and custom of the law of the sea, a further treaty law issue that should be touched upon, if only in passing, is the legal status of the 1994 Implementation Agreement in relation to the 1982 Convention itself. According to E. D. Brown, this Agreement, being the outcome of informal consultations sponsored by the United Nations Secretary-General, in effect substantially amends the seabed mining regime laid down in Part XI of UNCLOS.[42] Commenting on the legal implications of both the 1994 Implementation Agreement and the 1995 Fish Stocks Agreement, Alan Boyle notes that 'these agreements interpret, amplify, and develop the existing provisions of UNCLOS. They also provide examples of what is in effect, though not in form, *inter se* amendment of the Convention'.[43] However, describing the 1994 Agreement as an amendment of UNCLOS has been criticized by others. For example, Ambassador Henrique Valle, (then) Deputy Permanent Representative of Brazil to the United Nations, sees this 'as loose language that might suit certain purposes, but the fact remains: the Convention has not been amended'.[44] Rather, he stresses the fact that the 1994 Agreement relates to the implementation of Part XI of UNCLOS, with Part XI applying not as envisaged in the Convention but as provided for in this Agreement. In this context, he refers to Article 2 of the Agreement which states that 'the provisions of this Agreement and Part XI shall be interpreted and applied together as a single instrument'.[45] This more cautious appraisal of the relationship between the 1982 UNCLOS and the 1994 Agreement is echoed in David Anderson's assessment that 'the Agreement modifies in effect the terms of Part XI'.[46] Anderson clarifies this observation by restating the legal status of the 1994 Agreement and its relationship with the 1982 UNCLOS, especially Part XI as follows: 'The agreement is clearly a treaty, governed by the Vienna Convention of the Law of Treaties. Although it does not expressly amend any provisions of Part XI, there is

---

[42] E. D. Brown, 'The 1994 Agreement on the Implementation of Part XI of the UN Convention on the Law of the Sea: Breakthrough to Universality?', *Marine Policy*, 19 (1995), 5–20.

[43] A. Boyle, 'Further Development of the Law of the Sea Convention: Mechanisms for Change', *ICLQ*, 54 (2005), 563–584, at 565.

[44] H. R. Valle, 'The Negotiation Process' in M. H. Nordquist and J. N. Moore (eds.), *Entry into Force of the Law of the Sea Convention* (The Hague: Martinus Nijhoff, 1995), pp. 47–53, at p. 52.

[45] *Ibid.*

[46] D. Anderson, *Law of the Sea: Selected Essays* (Leiden: Martinus Nijhoff, 2008), p. 53.

no doubt that the agreement will result in the terms of Part XI being implemented, interpreted and applied in a new way, as described in the annex. International courts and tribunals, as well as international organisations, called upon in the future to interpret or apply the terms of the Convention will be legally obliged to have regard also to the terms of the agreement'.[47]

On reflection, it is possible to suggest that the reluctance of commentators to pronounce definitively upon both the legal status of the 1994 Agreement and its relationship with the 1982 Convention is at least in part due to the logistical difficulties of re-convening the States parties as required for the formal treaty amendment procedure under Articles 312 and 313 UNCLOS. As Andrew Serdy notes, '[w]hile UNCLOS can be amended by procedures set out in Articles 312 and 313, no risk-averse government wants to be the first to reopen the delicate compromise text for the sake of one desired improvement, given that it would prompt many others to follow suit, risking the unravelling of much of the painstaking work on other provisions and leaving the world worse off overall'.[48]

A further agreement in the same vein is the Fish Stocks Agreement, which was adopted in August 1995 by the United Nations Conference on Straddling Fish Stocks and Highly Migratory Fish Stocks.[49] However, unlike the 1994 Implementation Agreement, there is no direct link between the Fish Stocks Agreement and the 1982 Convention itself with respect to establishing consent to be bound. In other words, parties to the Fish Stocks Agreement do not necessarily have to be parties to the 1982 Convention (or the 1994 Implementation Agreement, for that matter). Indeed, the Fish Stocks Agreement arguably allows entities that might not be able to join the 1982 Convention itself nevertheless to become party to this Agreement: its Article 1(3) explicitly provides that, in addition to the States, international organizations and other entities that can become parties to the 1982 Convention, '[t]his Agreement applies *mutatis mutandis* to other fishing entities whose vessels fish on the high seas'.[50]

---

[47] *Ibid.*, at p. 322.

[48] A. Serdy, Review of James Harrison, *Making the Law of the Sea: A Study in the Development of International Law* (Cambridge: Cambridge University Press, 2011), *Mod. L. Rev.*, 75 (2012), 469–474, at 469.

[49] Entered into force 11 Dec. 2001, i.e. thirty days after the date of deposit of the thirtieth instrument of ratification or accession (in this case, the accession of Malta) in accordance with Art. 40(1) of the Agreement. As of 10 Oct. 2014, there are eighty-two parties to the Fish Stocks Agreement: www.un.org/Depts/los/reference_files/status2010.pdf.

[50] *Supra* n. 12.

This provision was undoubtedly directed at Taiwan/Chinese Taipei, which has one of the world's largest long line fishing fleets and is thus a significant harvester of tuna and other highly migratory species. Indeed, the Letter of Transmittal of the Straddling Stocks Agreement from Secretary of State Warren Christopher to President Bill Clinton dated 24 January 1996 notes that Article 1(3) of the Agreement (which refers to 'other fishing entities'), together with Article 17(3) (which refers to 'the fishing entities' mentioned in Article 1(3)), provides a mechanism through which Taiwan and its fishing vessels could be brought 'within the ambit of' regional fisheries organizations.[51] However, as the European Parliament has noted, although Taiwan supports the Fish Stocks Agreement, it is unable to become party to this Agreement because 'all but 25 or so States recognise the authorities in Beijing, not Taipei, as speaking for Taiwan, and most of such treaties require their parties to be States or meet other qualifying criteria, such as being a member of the United Nations or one of its specialised agencies, which again Taiwan cannot satisfy'.[52] Thus, Taiwan is unable to join the Fish Stocks Agreement – and, indeed, most treaties to which the People's Republic of China is already a party – due to wider political difficulties raised by the general non-recognition of Taiwan as a State under international law rather than any lack of specific treaty provision for its participation within the Fish Stocks Agreement.

Nevertheless, regional fisheries management organizations such as the Inter-American Tropical Tuna Commission (IATTC) have attempted to accommodate Taiwan within their decision-making organs for their conservation efforts through the use of different legal designations, such as 'fishing entity' or 'separate customs territory'. Building on its designation as a 'separate customs territory' for membership of the World Trade Organization (WTO), Taiwan was of the view that the WTO model would be the best solution for Taiwan's participation in the IATTC, according to Dustin Wang.[53] Ultimately, though, a compromise wrought between China and Taiwan resulted in the nomenclature of 'Chinese

---

[51] United States Senate, *Agreement for the Implementation of the United Nations Convention on the Law of the Sea of 10 December 1982 Relating to Fish Stocks*, Treaty Doc. 104–24, 104th Congress, 2nd Session, pp. v–xvi, at p. x.

[52] See *Perspectives for the United Nations Fish Stocks Agreement*, Study Requested by the European Parliament's Committee on Fisheries, IP/B/PECH/IC/2006_159 (Brussels: European Parliament, 2007), p. 71.

[53] D. Kuan-Hsiung Wang, 'Taiwan's Participation in Regional Fisheries Management Organizations and the Conceptual Revolution on Fishing Entity: The Case of the IATTC', *Ocean Dev. & Int'l L.*, 37 (2006), 209–219, at 211.

Taipei' to describe Taiwan, and this was used alongside the term 'fishing
entity' under Article XXXVIII of the 2003 Antigua Convention for the
Strengthening of the Inter-American Tropical Tuna Commission established by the 1949 Convention between the United States and the Republic
of Costa Rica for the purpose of enabling membership of the IATTC,[54] but
not for becoming a party to the Convention itself.[55]

Let us now examine two case studies that afford greater detail and
understanding on the relationship between the 1982 UNCLOS and 1958
Continental Shelf Convention; these concern, first, the final limits of the
continental shelf and, second, the removal of de-commissioned offshore
installations.

2.1   Final Limits of the Continental Shelf

Returning to the legal relationship between the 1982 UNCLOS and 1958
Geneva Conventions, Article 311(1) UNCLOS makes it clear that '[t]his
Convention shall prevail, as between States Parties, over the Geneva
Conventions on the Law of the Sea of 29 April 1958'. This is in keeping
with the *lex posterior* rule on successive treaties dealing with the same
subject matter, as codified by Article 30 VCLT.[56] In particular, Article
30(3) VCLT provides that '[w]hen all the parties to the earlier treaty are
parties also to the later treaty but the earlier treaty is not terminated or
suspended in operation under [A]rticle 59 [VCLT], the earlier treaty
applies only to the extent that its provisions are compatible with those
of the later treaty'. While this provision clearly establishes that the 1982
Convention supersedes the 1958 Conventions for parties to both of these
treaties, it is equally clear from this formulation of the rule that non-
parties to the 1982 Convention – such as Colombia, Turkey and the
United States – are not bound by this treaty, whether or not the 1982
Convention significantly changes the previous position on a particular
legal issue under the relevant 1958 Convention. As Article 30(4) VCLT
goes on to provide: 'When the parties to the later treaty do not include all
the parties to the earlier one … (b) as between a State party to both
treaties and a State party to only one of the treaties, the treaty to which
both States are parties governs their mutual rights and obligations'.[57]

---

[54] (2006) OJ EU 224/22 (under Art. I(7) of the Antigua Convention).
[55] Under Art. I(6) of the Antigua Convention: *ibid.*   [56] *Supra* n. 38.
[57] For an extended discussion, see A. Orakhelashvili, 'Article 30 (1969)' in O. Corten and
     P. Klein (eds.), *The Vienna Conventions on the Law of Treaties: A Commentary* (Vol. I)
     (Oxford: Oxford University Press, 2011), pp. 764–800, at pp. 791–798.

A good example of the continuing significance for non-parties to the 1982 UNCLOS of the 1958 Geneva Conventions, and especially that on the continental shelf,[58] relates to the relevant provisions of the latter for the final, outermost limits of the continental shelf. Article 1(a) states in part that, for the purpose of the Convention, the term 'continental shelf' refers 'to the seabed and subsoil of the submarine areas adjacent to the coast but outside the area of the territorial sea, to a depth of 200 metres or, beyond that limit, to where the depth of the superjacent waters admits of the exploitation of the natural resources of the said area' – an arguably open-ended criterion, subject only to the practical limits of marine technology. However, for parties to *both* 1958 Continental Shelf Convention and the 1982 UNCLOS, the continental shelf limits beyond 200 nautical miles are now governed by Article 76 of the latter convention. This not only provides the criteria for delineation but also establishes alternative means for fixing the outermost limits of the continental shelf beyond 200 nautical miles, which 'either shall not exceed 350 nautical miles from the baselines from which the breadth of the territorial sea is measured or shall not exceed 100 nautical miles from the 2,500 metre isobath, which is a line connecting the depth of 2,500 metres'.[59]

According to the *lex posterior* rule, non-parties to UNCLOS that are nevertheless still parties to the 1958 Continental Shelf Convention are bound only by the relevant provisions of that – i.e. the 1958 – Convention. The simple and open-ended nature of the final limits of the continental shelf in the preceding provision under the 1958 Convention contrasts vividly with the technically specified final limits of continental shelf jurisdiction under the 1982 Convention. Article 311(6) UNCLOS, which states that 'there shall be no amendments to the basic principle relating to the common heritage of mankind set forth in Article 136 and that States parties to this Convention shall not be party to any agreement in derogation thereof', is also limited in application to States parties to UNCLOS itself. Even the explicit recognition by these non-parties to UNCLOS of the deep sea-bed 'Area' as being subject to the principle of the common heritage of mankind under General Assembly Resolution 2749 (XXV) only provides for the application of this principle 'beyond the limits of national jurisdiction'.[60] This arguably affords these non-parties to UNCLOS the continuing discretion to establish their own

---

[58] *Supra* n. 9.   [59] As provided in Article 76(5) UNCLOS: *supra* n. 1.
[60] General Assembly Resolution 2749 (XXV) (12 Dec. 1970): Declaration of Principles Governing the Sea-Bed and the Ocean Floor, and the Subsoil Thereof, beyond the Limits of National Jurisdiction.

limits of national jurisdiction for their respective continental shelves under the 1958 Continental Shelf Convention, to which they are still party, and which is still in force.

The legal position of non-State parties to UNCLOS in relation to their continental shelf limits beyond 200 nautical miles is arguably buttressed by the carefully worded pronouncements of the International Court of Justice (ICJ), which clearly seek to confine the application of the criteria and requirements of Article 76 UNCLOS to State parties of that convention. Adjudicating on Nicaragua's claim for continental shelf entitlement beyond 200 nautical miles in the *Territorial and Maritime Dispute Case*,[61] the Court observed that, in a previous case concerning the *Territorial and Maritime Dispute between Nicaragua and Honduras in the Caribbean Sea*, it had stated that 'any claim of continental shelf rights beyond 200 miles [by a State party to the 1982 UNCLOS] must be in accordance with Article 76 UNCLOS and reviewed by the Commission on the Limits of the Continental Shelf'.[62] However, it is possible to discern an attempt at disambiguation by the ICJ here, as the passage quoted from the earlier, *Nicaragua v. Honduras* judgment did not, in its original form, actually include the words contained in square brackets as reproduced previously: these were only inserted in the later *Nicaragua v. Colombia* decision. The qualification they contain was made explicit there presumably because one of the litigants (Colombia) was not a party to UNCLOS.

Thus, despite the burgeoning number of State parties to UNCLOS,[63] the legal position of a non-party State *vis-à-vis* the 1982 Convention continues to raise interesting issues, especially in this aspect of the law of the sea, due to the inherent nature of the sovereign rights and jurisdiction over the continental shelf under international law, as codified by Article 77 UNCLOS. With regard to the *St. Pierre and Miquelon* award,[64] for example, Malcolm Evans has observed that it is interesting that the Court of Arbitration seems to have accepted that both Article 76 UNCLOS and Article 136 UNCLOS (common heritage of mankind)

---

[61] *Territorial and Maritime Dispute*: Nicaragua v. Colombia (2012) ICJ Rep. 624.

[62] *Ibid.*, at pp. 668–669 (paragraph 126) (citing (2007) ICJ Rep. (II), p. 759 (paragraph 319)).

[63] UNCLOS has 166 Parties as of 10 Oct. 2014: www.un.org/Depts/los/reference_files/status2010.pdf.

[64] *Canada/France (Saint Pierre and Miquelon) Delimitation of Maritime Areas Arbitration*, Decision of 10 June 1992, by a Court of Arbitration Established by Agreement on 30 March 1989, ILM, 31 (1992), 1145–1219.

represented customary international law, even though neither France nor Canada had ratified the Convention at that point in time.[65] Ted McDorman concurs with this, while holding the view that non-parties to UNCLOS must nevertheless fulfil the criteria of Article 76 UNCLOS to effectuate a continental shelf claim beyond 200 nautical miles.[66] He notes that there is no UNCLOS provision that prohibits non-parties from submitting their claims for consideration by the Commission on the Limits on the Continental Shelf (CLCS) – an institutional innovation anticipated by Article 76(8) UNCLOS. This is notwithstanding Tommy Koh's authoritative view as President of the UNCLOS III negotiation process that non-party States could not utilise these conventional criteria as customary international law to justify their extended claims to an outer continental shelf beyond 200 nautical miles because 'the article contains new law in that it has expanded the concept of the continental shelf to include the continental slope and the continental rise'.[67] The authoritative report of the International Law Association (ILA) Committee on the Limits of the Outer Continental Shelf (CLIOCS) has also determined that non-parties to UNCLOS do not have a right to make Article 76 submissions to the CLCS.[68] In any case, McDorman suggests that it is more difficult to assign customary status to the institutional role of the Commission in confirming adherence to Article 76 requirements by a non-party coastal state.[69] Equally important for the present discussion is the relationship between coastal State submissions relying on the Article 76 criteria for claiming a continental shelf area beyond 200 nautical miles and the Article 82 revenue-sharing obligation of UNCLOS on proceeds from mineral exploitation in this area. This relationship will be considered in further detail in Section 4 in relation to the pre-eminent non-party State to the 1982 UNCLOS – namely, the United States.

---

[65] Which, in any event, was not in force at the time of the decision: M. D. Evans, 'Less Than an Ocean Apart: The St Pierre and Miquelon and Jan Mayen Islands and the Delimitation of Maritime Zones', *ICLQ*, 43 (1994), 678–696 (noting Prosper Weil at paragraph 42 of his Dissenting Opinion in this case, where he doubted the customary law status of Art. 76(4)–(9) UNCLOS).

[66] T. L. McDorman, 'The Role of the Commission on the Limits of the Continental Shelf: A Technical Body in a Political World', *Int'l J. of Marine & Coastal L.*, 17 (2002), 301–324, at 303–304.

[67] See Koh, *supra* n. 3. See, further, the contribution to this volume of Lost-Sieminska at pp. 907–932 (Chapter 28).

[68] Conclusion 16 of ILA Committee on the Legal Issues of the Outer Continental Shelf (CLIOCS), Toronto Conference Report (2006).

[69] McDorman, *supra* n. 66.

2.2   Removal of De-commissioned Offshore Installations

Apart from the major difference highlighted previously in the provisions for the outermost limits of the continental shelf jurisdiction accruing to coastal and island States, there are other significant differences in the provisions of the 1958 and 1982 Conventions. For example, in relation to the disposal of offshore installations at the end of their production life, Article 5(5) under the 1958 Continental Shelf Convention provides that '[d]ue notice must be given of the construction of any such installations, and permanent means for giving warning of their presence must be maintained. Any installations which are abandoned or disused must be entirely removed'. By contrast, Article 60(3) UNCLOS provides as follows:

> Due notice must be given of the construction of such artificial islands, installations or structures, and permanent means for giving warning of their presence must be maintained. Any installations or structures which are abandoned or disused shall be removed to ensure safety of navigation, taking into account any generally accepted international standards established in this regard by the competent international organization. Such removal shall also have due regard to fishing, the protection of the marine environment and the rights and duties of other States. *Appropriate publicity shall be given to the depth, position and dimensions of any installations or structures not entirely removed.*[70]

The implication of the last sentence of this provision is that such offshore installations/structures are not required to be completely removed from the seabed, whereas the 1958 Convention does require the entire removal of abandoned or disused structures.

The different removal requirements in these regimes are arguably mitigated by the fact that the International Maritime Organization (IMO) has produced guidelines and standards for the removal of such installations/structures.[71] As Youna Lyons points out, however, the 1989 IMO Guidelines for the Removal of Offshore Installation and Structures on the Continental Shelf and in the Exclusive Economic Zone are not designed to be mandatory except if considered within the scope of Article 208 UNCLOS, which addresses 'pollution from seabed activities subject to national jurisdiction'.[72] Article 208, in summary, requires that coastal

---

[70] Emphasis added.   [71] IMO Resolution A.672(16) (19 Oct. 1989).

[72] Y. Lyons, 'Abandoned Offshore Installations in Southeast Asia and the Opportunity for Rigs-to-Reefs', Centre for International Law Working Paper, National University of Singapore, presented at a Conference on The Regulation of Continental Shelf Developments: Rethinking International Standards, Halifax, 21–22 June 2012

States shall adopt laws and regulations to prevent, reduce and control pollution of the marine environment from artificial islands, installations and structures under their jurisdiction, pursuant to Articles 60 and 80 UNCLOS.[73] Such laws, regulations and measures shall be no less effective than international rules, standards and recommended practices and procedures[74] to prevent, reduce and control pollution of the marine environment, for which States, acting especially through competent international organizations or diplomatic conference, shall establish global and regional rules, standards and recommended practices and procedures.[75] In this regard, it should be noted that, within its Resolution adopting these Guidelines, the IMO Assembly held that they represent the 'generally accepted international standards' referred to in Article 60 UNCLOS, as well as establishing the IMO as 'the competent organization to deal with this subject'.[76] Again, it should be noted that non-parties to the 1982 Convention that are still parties to the 1958 Continental Shelf Convention are bound by the terms of the earlier – i.e. 1958 – Convention, even though they exert a stricter requirement than the 1982 Convention. Moreover, pursuant to Article 30(4)(b) VCLT, States parties to UNCLOS will, unless they have denounced the 1958 Convention, remain bound by its stricter provisions *vis-à-vis* States that are only parties to the 1958 Convention.

The relationships between UNCLOS and related agreements in the maritime sphere, including those that provide for relevant international standards such as the 1989 IMO Guidelines, are delved into more deeply in the next section of this chapter. In this respect, Article 208 and several other similarly-worded provisions of the 1982 Convention perform significant roles in establishing and maintaining the relation between the framework or umbrella aspects of UNCLOS and various other, regional and/or subject-specific treaties and international instruments that actually establish the particular international standards concerned, in ways that have implications for the law of treaties as well. Anderson is clear about both the legal significance of this treaty relationship structure as well as its future implications, stating that UNCLOS 'represents a framework which links together the fundamental rules of law of the sea (notably those on the scope and limits of national jurisdiction) with other conventions (notably the IMO Conventions on the technical

---

(http://cil.nus.edu.sg/wp/wp-content/uploads/2013/03/Youna-Lyons-Abandoned-Offshore-Installations.pdf).

[73] Art. 208(1) UNCLOS: *supra* n. 1.   [74] Art. 208(3) UNCLOS: *supra* n. 1.
[75] Art. 208(5) of UNCLOS: *supra* n. 1.   [76] *Ibid.* See, also, *supra* n. 16.

aspects of safety and environmental protection). This inter-linkage holds good whether the other conventions were adopted before or after 1982'.[77] These treaty relationships will be examined in more detail later, especially in terms of whether the operation of Article 211 UNCLOS has resulted in the 'incorporation by reference', within the 1982 Convention, of the vessel-source discharge standards provided in the relevant annexes to the 1973/78 MARPOL treaty on the Prevention of Pollution at Sea from Ships.

3   Relationship between the 1982 UNCLOS and Other Treaties

3.1   General Provisions in the 1982 UNCLOS and the 1969 VCLT

As alluded to previously, Article 311(1) UNCLOS governs the prevailing relationship between the 1982 Convention and over the 1958 Geneva Conventions on the Law of the Sea. However, in 'relation to other conventions and international agreements', Article 311(2) provides that '[t]his Convention shall not alter the rights and obligations of States Parties which arise from other agreements compatible with this Convention and which do not affect the enjoyment by other States Parties of their rights or the performance of their obligations under this Convention'. Article 311(5) further provides that '[t]his article does not affect international agreements expressly permitted or preserved by other articles of this Convention'. More specifically, in relation to obligations for dispute settlement under related general, regional or bilateral agree-ments, Article 282 UNCLOS stipulates that '[i]f the States Parties which are parties to a dispute concerning the interpretation or application of this Convention have agreed, through a general, regional or bilateral agreement or otherwise, that such dispute shall, at the request of any party to the dispute, be submitted to a procedure that entails a binding decision, that procedure shall apply in lieu of the procedures provided for in this Part, unless the parties to the dispute otherwise agree'.

These provisions do not detract from the generally accepted legal relationship between successive treaties on the same subject matter, as codified in Article 30 VCLT,[78] but neither do they provide specific guidance for resolving the issues that can arise between States on the relationships between treaties on similar subjects. In particular, a definitive account of the legal relationship between *lex generalis* and

---

[77] Anderson, *supra* n. 46, at p. 252.   [78] See *supra* n. 54 and n. 55.

lex specialis is not provided, either generally for the law of treaties within the VCLT or specifically for the law of the sea, in the 1982 UNCLOS. The legal issues arising from this relationship were included by the ILC within the mandate of its Study Group on Fragmentation of International Law, chaired by Martti Koskenniemi, which reported to the ILC in April 2006.[79] According to Koskenniemi, '[t]here are two ways in which law may take account of the relationship of a particular rule to general one. A particular rule may be considered an *application* of a general standard in a given circumstance. ... Or it may be considered as a *modification, overruling* or a *setting aside* of the latter. The first case is sometimes seen as not a situation of normative conflict at all but is taken to involve the *simultaneous* application of the special and the general standard. Thus, only the latter is thought to involve the application of a genuine *lex specialis*'.[80] However, following a (re-) consideration of various authorities, including the ILC Commentary on the Draft Articles on State Responsibility, relevant jurisprudence of the European Court of Human Rights and the ICJ decision in the *Case Concerning the Gabčikovo-Nagymaros Project*,[81] Koskenniemi concludes that the proper approach to the *lex specialis/lex generalis* relationship is that 'the *lex specialis* [is] applicable even in the absence of direct conflict between two provisions and where it might be said that both apply concurrently'.[82] Moreover, '[i]t follows that whether a rule is seen as an "application", "modification" or "exception" to another rule, depends on how we view those rules in the environment in which they are applied, including what we see as their object and purpose. Because separating "application" from "setting aside" would be artificial and distort the context in which the question of *lex specialis* emerges'.[83]

3.2 Case Studies: The Relationship between lex generalis *and* lex specialis

The *lex generalis/lex specialis* relationship within the law of the sea is examined in the following case studies concerning, first, the *Southern*

---

[79] International Law Commission, Report of the Study Group on Fragmentation of International Law: Difficulties arising from the Diversification and Expansion of International Law, Finalized by Martti Koskenniemi, U.N. Doc. A/CN.4/L.682 (2006).

[80] *Ibid.*, at p. 49 (paragraph 88) (footnotes omitted).

[81] *Case Concerning the Gabčikovo-Nagymaros Project (Hungary/Slovakia)* (1997) ICJ Rep. 7.

[82] *Ibid.*, at pp. 50–51 (paragraph 91).   [83] *Ibid.*, at p. 53 (paragraph 97).

Bluefin Tuna (SBT) case(s) and, secondly, the relationship between Article 211 UNCLOS and the 1973/78 MARPOL Treaty, Annex 1 of which provides for the generally accepted rules and standards for vessel-source oil pollution.

3.2.1   The Southern Bluefin Tuna Cases

This case study will focus on the implications of the *SBT* case on jurisdiction and admissibility issues before different judicial bodies on the law of the sea. Specifically, the *SBT* case raised the issue of whether the dispute settlement provision in a regional fisheries conservation agreement – namely, the 1993 Convention for the Conservation of Southern Bluefin Tuna (CCSBT)[84] – should be allowed to prevail over the corresponding dispute settlement provisions in Part XV of UNCLOS, as between State parties to both these treaties. On 15 July 1999, Australia and New Zealand initiated arbitration proceedings against Japan under Annex VII of UNCLOS regarding the conservation and management of the Southern Bluefin Tuna (SBT) stock. Japan objected to the jurisdiction of the arbitral tribunal constituted at the request of both Australia and New Zealand; it argued instead that the dispute settlement provisions of the 1993 CCSBT, to which all three States were parties, should apply instead, unless and until all three parties to the dispute agreed to be subject to the dispute settlement provisions under the 1982 Convention, to which they were all also parties. On the other hand, Australia and New Zealand asserted that they were within their rights to bring Japan to the dispute settlement mechanisms of UNCLOS rather than that of the 1993 CCSBT.

Prior to these jurisdiction and admissibility issues being adjudicated and pending the constitution of this UNCLOS Annex VII arbitral tribunal, the applicant parties also requested ITLOS to prescribe provisional measures, as allowed by Article 290(5) UNCLOS. In its provisional measures decision,[85] the ITLOS ordered the parties to refrain from experimental SBT fishing[86] and also found that the arbitral tribunal would have *prima facie* jurisdiction to decide the dispute.[87] However, the arbitral tribunal that was later constituted to hear the case noted the parties' agreement that the dispute fell under the CCSBT concluded

---

[84] 1819 UNTS 360.
[85] *Southern Bluefin Tuna Cases* (New Zealand v. Japan; Australia v. Japan), Cases No. 3 & 4. ITLOS, Provisional Measures, Order, 27 Aug. 1999.
[86] *Ibid.* (paragraphs 2–5 and 35).   [87] *Ibid.* (paragraph 5).

between the parties in 1993.[88] The tribunal rejected Japan's assertion that the CCSBT as a *lex specialis* 'subsumed, discharged and eclipsed' any UNCLOS provisions generally relevant to the dispute.[89] It recognised that support exists in both international law and domestic legal systems for the application of *lex specialis* to prevail over general provisions of an antecedent treaty or statute but found that: (1) it is 'a commonplace of international law and State practice' that several treaties can bear upon a particular dispute and (2) an act may violate obligations under more than one treaty.[90] On this basis, it held that both the CCSBT and UNCLOS were applicable to the dispute.[91] The arbitral tribunal then noted that the parties agreed in Article 16 CCSBT to seek a settlement by peaceful means of their choice and concluded that this provision did not preclude UNCLOS procedures.[92] It went on to find, however, that Article 16 CCBST required the consent of all parties for adjudication or arbitration under UNCLOS procedures and that the present arbitral tribunal therefore lacked compulsory jurisdiction to reach the merits of the dispute.[93] Furthermore, it revoked the provisional measures issued by the ITLOS.[94] Justice Keith dissented from the majority decision of the arbitral tribunal, asserting that Article 16 CCBST did not preclude UNCLOS compulsory binding procedures on the ground that it would otherwise have to be capable of dealing with all SBT disputes between the parties, including the interpretation and application of UNCLOS.[95]

3.2.2 Part XII of UNCLOS and References to 'Generally Accepted International Rules and Standards'

Shabtai Rosenne has written about the IMO 'interface' with the 1982 UNCLOS, defining this word in the present context as how 'independent and often incompatible systems interact or communicate with each other'.[96] According to Liu Nengye, the many references to, *inter alia*,

---

[88] *Southern Bluefin Tuna Case* (New Zealand v. Japan; Australia v. Japan), Arbitral Tribunal Award, 4 Aug. 2000, RIAA, Vol. XXIII, 1–57, at pp. 9–12 (paragraph 23) and 40 (paragraph 50).

[89] *Ibid.*, at pp. 22–23 (paragraphs 38(a–c)) and 40–41 (paragraphs 51–52).

[90] *Ibid.*, at pp. 40–41 (paragraph 52).   [91] *Ibid.*

[92] *Ibid.*, at pp. 42–43 (paragraphs 54–56).

[93] *Ibid.*, at pp. 43–44 (paragraphs 57–59), 46 (paragraph 65) and 48–49 (paragraph 72).

[94] *Ibid.*, at pp. 46–47 (paragraph 66) and 48–49 (paragraph 72).

[95] Separate Opinion of Mr. Justice Keith: *ibid.*, at pp. 51 (paragraph 10), 52 (paragraphs 13–15) and 57 (paragraph 30).

[96] S. Rosenne, 'The International Maritime Organization Interface with the Law of the Sea Convention' in M. H. Nordquist and J. N. Moore (eds.), *Current Maritime Issues and the International Maritime Organization* (The Hague: Martinus Nijhoff, 1999), pp. 251–268, at p. 251.

'international rules and standards' clearly establish 'an obligation for the [UNCLOS] States parties to apply the IMO rules and standards'.[97] This UNCLOS-IMO interface will now be examined in terms of the inter-treaty relationship between UNCLOS and the 1973/78 MARPOL Convention.[98] The 1973 International Convention on the Prevention of Marine Pollution from Ships, as modified by the 1978 Protocol relating to it, is the most comprehensive and important of all the IMO conventions in this area and the first one to provide comprehensive and exhaustive guidelines for ship builders and ship owners to follow in order to actively prevent vessel-source oil pollution. Annex I of MARPOL is concerned with vessel-source oil pollution and came into force at the same time as the main body of the 1973/78 MARPOL. This inter-treaty relationship is especially pertinent within the 200 nautical mile EEZ, where, as Yoshifumi Tanaka observes, the spatial scope of coastal State jurisdiction has been significantly expanded,[99] both in a prescriptive and an enforcement sense. Thus, in the 200 nautical mile EEZ, coastal States can legislate to give effect to 'generally accepted international rules and standards' for ship-generated pollution established, *inter alia*, 'through the competent international organization'.[100] Tanaka confirms the general view that the competent international organization within this context is the IMO. Moreover, while there is no clear definition of 'generally accepted international rules and standards', he notes that 'it can reasonably be presumed that those rules include the first two annexes to MARPOL because these instruments are widely ratified'.[101] This legislative technique is called 'incorporation by reference' and forms a useful pathway for the continuing significance of UNCLOS in the future as it incorporates whatever 'generally accepted international rules and standards' are in place at any given point in time, i.e. as and when these are upgraded within their respective agreements, without any corresponding requirement to amend or modify the relevant UNCLOS provisions themselves.

---

[97] L. Nengye, 'International Legal Framework on the Prevention of Vessel-Sourced Pollution', *China Oceans L. Rev.*, 2 (2010), 238–263, at 247. See, further, *supra* n. 16, and, also, C. Redgwell, 'The Never Ending Story: The Role of GAIRS in UNCLOS Implementation in the Offshore Energy Sector' in J. Barrett and R. Barnes (eds.), *Law of the Sea: UNCLOS as a Living Treaty* (London: British Institute of International & Comparative Law, 2016), pp. 167–186.

[98] See *supra* n. 17.

[99] Y. Tanaka, *The International Law of the Sea* (Cambridge: Cambridge University Press, 2012), p. 281.

[100] Art. 211(5) UNCLOS: *supra* n. 1.   [101] Tanaka, *supra* n. 99, at p. 280.

The question remains as to whether the particular provisions that are 'incorporated by reference' are applicable and binding upon UNCLOS State parties that are not themselves parties to the specific international standard-setting instrument that these UNCLOS provisions are referring to. Ostensibly, the rules for third States encapsulated in Articles 34–38 VCLT apply in these situations to deny the application of these international standard-setting instruments to UNCLOS State parties that are not also parties to these instruments. These VCLT provisions obviate third States from having to comply with treaties that are not expressly (in the case of obligations) or impliedly (in the case of rights) accepted by these States. However, a rejoinder to this strict, doctrinal approach is to note that these 'incorporation by reference' provisions are not actually creating new obligations or rights for these UNCLOS State parties but instead merely *specifying* the appropriate standards of behaviour for these parties in the implementation of their UNCLOS obligations, both under Part XII and elsewhere in the Convention. Viewed in this way, this iteration of the *lex generalis/lex specialis* relationship is arguably not far removed from the 'framework treaty-protocol' approach that characterises many recent environmental treaties.[102]

4 Treaty Interpretation of UNCLOS Provisions and the Principle of Good Faith under International Law

Moving away from inter-treaty relationships, we now examine the application of treaty law rules of interpretation to selected provisions from UNCLOS.[103] The present discussion will focus on a specific aspect of the rule(s) of treaty interpretation applicable to UNCLOS as well as all other treaties. This concerns the requirement upon States both to interpret and to apply in good faith treaties that are binding upon them. This requirement is evident in the initial statement on the general rule of interpretation provided in Article 31(1) VCLT, namely, that '[a] treaty shall be interpreted in good faith in accordance with the ordinary meaning to be given to the terms of the treaty in their context and in the light of its object and purpose', and is buttressed by the articulation of the principle of *pacta sunt servanda* in Article 26 VCLT, that '[e]very treaty in force is binding upon the parties to it and must be performed by them in good faith'. Thus, in the VCLT, the good faith obligation relates to both the

---

[102] See the contribution to this volume of French and Scott at pp. 677–709 (Chapter 21).
[103] See the contribution to this volume of Gardiner at pp. 335–362 (Chapter 11).

performance of any treaty in force by a State party as well as the *inter-pretation* of any of the terms of that treaty.

Coming to UNCLOS, however, we find that the notion of good faith as an obligation of performance is supplemented by the additional require-ment that such performance cannot result in an abuse of rights. Article 300 UNCLOS, entitled 'Good Faith and Abuse of Rights', provides: 'States Parties shall fulfil in good faith the obligations assumed under this Convention and shall exercise the rights, jurisdiction and freedoms recognised in this Convention in a manner which would not constitute an abuse of right'. This relationship between good faith and non-abuse of rights will be examined in terms of the interaction between Article 76 UNCLOS (on the final limits of the continental shelf) and Article 82 UNCLOS (providing for revenue-sharing between coastal States and land-locked, less-economically developed States of the proceeds from mineral resource production in the continental shelf beyond 200 nautical miles). This link between the extension of sovereign rights and jurisdic-tion occasioned by a successful coastal State application to the CLCS under Article 76 UNCLOS and the revenue-sharing requirement under Article 82 UNCLOS is confirmed by authoritative accounts of the UNCLOS III negotiations process as well as several commentators since. To cite Koh once again, 'this concession (of the inclusion of the continental slope and rise within the legal definition of the continental shelf) to the broad margin states was in return for their agreement for revenue-sharing on the continental shelf beyond 200 miles'.[104] More recently, Atsuko Kanehara, too, has highlighted the connection between these two provisions in the negotiation process of UNCLOS, while lamenting the lack of clear language and practical guidance for effectuat-ing this link within the Convention itself.[105] In this regard, it should be pointed out that this link between Articles 76 and 82 UNCLOS is not explicitly articulated in the actual text of either of the provisions in question.

Of particular interest in this context is the practice of the United States as the most significant non-party State to UNCLOS. In addition, it is widely expected that the first successful exploitation of hydrocarbon

---

[104] Koh, *supra* n. 3.

[105] A. Kanehara, 'The Revenue-Sharing Scheme with respect to the Exploitation of the Outer Continental Shelf under Article 82 of the UNCLOS – A Plethora of Entangling Issues', Text of Presentation at Seminar on the Establishment of the Outer Limits of the Continental Shelf beyond 200nm under UNCLOS – Its Implications for International Law, Ocean Policy Research Foundation, on 27 Feb. 2008, at pp. 1–2.

resources occurring beyond the 200 nautical mile limit will take place in the continental shelf area of the United States located in the waters of the Gulf of Mexico. Furthermore, very little State practice, apart from the US federal law contractual provisions cited later, has explicitly linked these two aspects of the continental shelf regime beyond 200 nautical miles. Since scholars are divided as to whether the United States should consider itself bound by the criteria and procedure established by Article 76 UNCLOS, it is worthwhile examining US official practice in this regard. Following a US government inter-agency review of the UNCLOS III negotiations ordered by newly elected President Ronald Reagan, he announced, *inter alia*, that '[o]ur review has concluded that while most provisions of the draft [Law of the Sea] Convention are acceptable and consistent with United States interests, some major elements of the deep seabed mining regime are not acceptable'.[106] More specifically in relation to the continental shelf regime, J. Ashley Roach and Robert W. Smith have asserted that the United States 'has recognized [A]rticle 76 as reflecting customary international law'.[107] However, closer scrutiny of the published position of the United States on this issue arguably reveals a more nuanced engagement with *certain* aspects of Article 76 UNCLOS rather than with that provision in its entirety.[108] Specifically, the US Policy statement provides in part: 'The United States has exercised and shall continue to exercise jurisdiction over its continental shelf in accordance with and to the full extent permitted by international law as reflected in Article 76, paragraphs (1), (2), and (3). At such time in the future that it is determined desirable to delimit the outer limit of the continental shelf of the United States beyond two hundred nautical miles from the baseline from which the territorial sea is measured, such delimitation shall be carried out in accordance with paragraphs (4), (5), (6), and (7)'.[109] Thus, the US Policy statement eschews reference to the requirement for coastal State submission to

---

[106] Statement on United States Participation in the Third United Nations Conference on the Law of the Sea, 29 Jan. 1982, reproduced in G. Peters and J. T. Woolley, *The American Presidency Project* (www.presidency.ucsb.edu/ws/?pid=42853).

[107] J. A. Roach and R. W. Smith, *United States Responses to Excessive Maritime Claims* (The Hague: Martinus Nijhoff, 2nd ed., 1996), p. 201, referring to a Memorandum dated 17 Nov. 1987, of the US Federal Government Interagency Group on the Law of the Sea and Ocean Policy, sent from Assistant Secretary John D. Negroponte to Deputy Legal Adviser Elizabeth Verville, State Department File No. P89 0140-0428.

[108] See Policy Governing the Continental Shelf of the United States of America, attached to the preceding Memorandum, reproduced in Roach and Smith, *ibid.*, at pp. 201–202.

[109] *Ibid.*, at pp. 201–202.

the CLCS and the procedure for establishing the final outer limits of its continental shelf by reference to the Commission's recommendations under Article 76(8) UNCLOS. Despite the lack of putative US engagement with the CLCS, Roach and Smith nevertheless affirm the significant role played by the Commission in this procedure by going beyond the wording of Article 76(8) UNCLOS itself and unequivocally asserting that 'the limits of the continental shelf established by a coastal State on the basis of these (CLCS) recommendations are final and bind-ing *on all States Parties to the Convention and on the International Seabed Authority*'.[110] Neither is the Article 82 UNCLOS revenue-sharing obliga-tion specifically mentioned in this US Policy statement, although it may be possible to infer this duty as among those explicitly accepted by the USA when the statement confirms that '[t]he United States shall continue to exercise its rights and *duties* pertaining to its continental shelf in accordance with international law'.[111] In any case, the relationship between possible extension of US seabed jurisdiction beyond 200 nautical miles (in line with Article 76 UNCLOS criteria) and its Article 82 UNCLOS obligations is already reflected in US federal offshore oil and gas contractual terms.[112] Indeed, as the International Seabed Authority technical report notes, '[s]ince at least 2001, and most recently at the time of writing in 2008, the Minerals Management Service (MMS) of the Department of the Interior, US Federal Government, has advised lessees in successive rounds of leasing that contingent royalty payment provi-sions would apply if the United States becomes a party to [UNCLOS], prior to or during the life of a lease'.[113]

At this juncture, Article 300 UNCLOS on good faith and non-abuse of rights may be recalled to provide some guidance for an interpretation in favour of the conjunction of the extension of continental shelf jurisdiction beyond 200 nautical miles under Article 76 UNCLOS and the revenue-sharing duty under Article 82 UNCLOS. The analytical pathway is as follows: first, Article 26 VCLT requires that treaties must be performed in good faith while the general rule of treaty

---

[110] *Ibid.*, at p. 203 (emphasis added).   [111] *Ibid.*, at p. 202 (emphasis added).

[112] See Western Planning Area, Oil & Gas Lease Sale 207 (20 Aug. 2008): Final Notice of Sale Stipulation No. 4–Law of the Sea Convention Royalty Payment, Box 1, ISA Technical Study No. 4 (2009), pp. 7–8.

[113] *Ibid.*, at pp. 5–6. Following regulatory failures exposed by the 2010 Deepwater Horizon disaster, the MMS was divided into three new federal agencies: the Bureau of Ocean Energy Management, the Bureau of Safety and Environmental Enforcement and the Office of Natural Resources Revenue, by the United States Secretary of the Interior, Ken Salazar, through Secretarial Order No. 3299, on 19 May 2010.

interpretation provided in Article 31 VCLT also makes explicit reference to this principle. Next, Article 300 UNCLOS provides that its obligations be fulfilled in good faith and, also, that the rights, jurisdiction and freedoms recognised by UNCLOS shall be exercised in a manner that would not constitute an abuse of such rights. According to Richard McLaughlin, this provision has been interpreted so as to 'restrict both the unnecessary or arbitrary exercise of rights, jurisdiction and freedoms, as well as the misuse of powers by the contracting parties' to UNCLOS.[114] Thus, the provisions of this article as a whole require not only the application of this fundamental principle of international law, and indeed of law generally, but, also, the non-abuse of rights.[115] Applying the principle of good faith and its corresponding requirement of non-abuse of rights to the acknowledged legal relationship between Articles 76 and 82 UNCLOS, it is submitted here that where a coastal State – whether party or non-party to UNCLOS – chooses to formalise its continental shelf limits beyond 200 nautical miles, then the principle of good faith will guide these States towards both fulfilling the criteria laid down in Article 76 UNCLOS on this matter and complying with the revenue-sharing duty under Article 82 UNCLOS. Moreover, non-compliance of this revenue-sharing obligation under Article 82 UNCLOS would arguably constitute an abuse of the exercise by the coastal State of the sovereign rights and jurisdiction over natural resources in the continental shelf beyond 200 nautical miles through its reliance on Article 76 UNCLOS. In this way, it can possibly be seen why the non-abuse of rights was expressly linked to the principle of good faith under Article 300 UNCLOS, by contrast with its iteration in Article 31 VCLT. Doctrinal support for this line of argument can be drawn from Bin Cheng's

[114] R. J. McLaughlin, 'Maritime Boundary Delimitation and Co-operative Management of Transboundary Hydrocarbons in the Ultra-Deep Waters of the Gulf of Mexico' in S.-Y. Hong and J. M. Van Dyke (eds.), *Maritime Boundary Disputes, Settlement Processes and the Law of the Sea* (Leiden: Martinus Nijhoff, 2009), pp. 199–230, at p. 213 (fn. 76) (citing R. J. McLaughlin, 'UNCLOS and the Demise of the United States' Use of Trade Sanctions to Protect Dolphins, Sea Turtles, Whales and Other International Marine Living Resources', *Ecology L. Quarterly*, 21 (1994), 1–78, at 57).

[115] An example of a claim of the abuse of rights can be discerned from the *Barbados/Trinidad & Tobago* arbitral decision, where the tribunal considered whether recourse by Barbados to arbitration under Art. 287 UNCLOS and Art. 1 of Annex VII of UNCLOS constituted an abuse of right but ultimately concluded that this unilateral invocation of third-party dispute settlement procedures under UNCLOS did not amount to an abuse of this right. See *Barbados/Trinidad & Tobago*, Award of 11 Apr. 2006, RIAA, Vol. XXVII, 147–251, at p. 64 (paragraph 208).

exposition of the interdependence of rights and obligations,[116] as high-lighted in both the *North Atlantic Coast Fisheries Case* between Great Britain and the United States[117] and the *Certain German Interests in Polish Upper Silesia Case* between Germany and Poland.[118] In both these cases relating to the exercise of treaty rights that are circumscribed by certain restrictions, Cheng argues that the principle of good faith requires that such rights not be exercised in a manner that constitutes an abuse of any restrictions to these rights. The test for whether such abuse has occurred is the reasonableness of the exercise of these rights in the face of their respective restrictions.[119] Willem Riphagen has suggested that Cheng's reliance on the non-abuse of rights as part of the application of the good faith principle to the exercise of rights by a State resonates better as a counter-balancing argument in the era of complete or absolute sovereignty of States rather than the present era.[120] However, this does not negate its application as a conditional limitation on the exercise of sovereign rights in the continental shelf regime beyond 200 nautical miles, in the form of Article 82 UNCLOS.

The preceding discussion concerned the principle of good faith and non-abuse of rights as obligations both of interpretation and performance of relevant UNCLOS provisions. The next two examples of treaty interpretation will focus on the way in which specific phrases within UNCLOS have been interpreted and applied in maritime disputes between different States in order to compare the approach adopted by UNCLOS-based tribunals with that adopted under general international law and by the International Court of Justice.

4.1 Nationality of Ships: The M/V 'Saiga' (No. 2) Case

The pre-eminent judicial body established by the 1982 UNCLOS regime – namely, the International Tribunal on the Law of the Sea (ITLOS) – was presented with its first set of cases as a result of the capture by Guinea of a flagship of St. Vincent and the Grenadines, the *M/V Saiga*.[121] During

---

[116] B. Cheng, *General Principles of Law as Applied by International Courts and Tribunals* (Cambridge: Cambridge University Press, 1953; reprinted 2006), pp. 123–125.

[117] *The North Atlantic Coast Fisheries Case* (Great Britain, United States), RIAA, Vol. XI, 167–226.

[118] *Case Concerning Certain German Interests in Polish Upper Silesia*: Germany v. Poland (Merits), 1926 PCIJ, Series A, No. 7, 19.

[119] Cheng, *supra* n. 116, at p. 125.

[120] A. Cassese and J. H. H. Weiler (eds.), *Change and Stability in International Law-Making* (Berlin/New York: Walter de Fruyter, 1988), p. 36.

[121] *M/V 'Saiga' (No. 2): supra* n. 19.

the proceedings on the merits, ITLOS had to undertake a close examination of a significant issue arising from the nationality of ships, namely, the requirement of a 'genuine link' between the vessel and the State claiming it as a flagship of that State. Article 91(1) UNCLOS states, *inter alia*, that '[t]here must exist a genuine link between the [flag] State and the ship'.[122] In this case, Guinea argued that there was no such link between the *Saiga* and St. Vincent, as St. Vincent lacked the necessary prescriptive and enforcement standing to assert its flag State jurisdiction over the foreign owner and operator to fulfil its obligations as a flag State. Specifically, Guinea objected to the admissibility of the claim by St. Vincent, arguing, *inter alia*, that (a) the ship was not registered in St. Vincent at the time of the arrest in October 1997; (b) there was no genuine link between St. Vincent and the ship and, finally, (c) the injured individuals and companies were not nationals of St. Vincent. Guinea maintained that the *Saiga* was a ship without nationality at the time of the arrest since St. Vincent's provisional certificate of registration expired on 12 September 1997 and its permanent certificate of registration was not issued until 28 November 1997. Guinea concluded that, in the absence of a 'genuine link', it was not bound to recognise claims asserted by the applicant.

As Rachel Baird has noted, '[i]n essence, Guinea argued that the existence of a "genuine link" was a prerequisite for the recognition of nationality'.[123] However, as she then goes on to observe, neither the 1958 Geneva Convention on the High Seas nor the relevant provisions of UNCLOS explicitly support such a proposition. While Article 5 of the High Seas Convention, which was the predecessor to Articles 91 and 94 UNCLOS, does state that '[t]here must exist a genuine link between the State and the ship', it then goes on to provide that 'in particular, the State must effectively exercise its jurisdiction and control in administering technical and social matters over ships flying its flag'. The absence of this phrase in Article 91 UNCLOS arguably dilutes the 'genuine link' requirement between a ship and its flag State, as there is no longer any specific need for the flag State to show effective jurisdiction over these matters to prove the 'genuine link' between them. Moreover, as Baird observes, 'Article 5 of the Convention on the High Seas did not retain the

---

[122] This provision replicates most of the text of Art. 5 of the 1958 Geneva Convention on the High Seas: *supra* n. 9.

[123] R. Baird, 'Illegal, Unreported and Unreported Fishing: An Analysis of the Legal, Economic and Historical Factors Relevant to Its Development and Persistence', *Melbourne JIL*, 5 (2004), 299–334, at 316.

recommendation made by the International Law Commission when formulating the 1956 Draft Articles on the Law of the Sea'.[124] Article 29 of these Draft Articles provided that 'for the purposes of recognition of the national character of the ship by other States, there must exist a genuine link between the state and the ship'.[125] This emphasis on a 'genuine link' between a State and legal individual was first introduced in the *Nottebohm Case* before the International Court of Justice,[126] at around the time that the ILC Draft Articles were being formulated. The subsequent absence of any references to nationality in Article 5 of the 1958 High Seas Convention and in Articles 91 and 94 UNCLOS arguably mirrors the rapid movement in general international law away from the requirement of a 'genuine link' between a State and an individual for the purpose of asserting diplomatic protection over the individual by the State.[127]

In the *M/V 'Saiga' (No. 2) Case*, St. Vincent cited various facts providing evidence of a 'genuine link' between the vessel and itself, as the flag State asserting jurisdiction over the vessel. Among these facts were that: (a) the owner of the *Saiga* was represented in St. Vincent by a company formed and established there; (b) the ship was subject to the supervision of Vincentian authorities to secure compliance with IMO safety and pollution conventions and (c) the ship's seaworthiness was subject to regular surveys conducted at least annually by reputable classification societies authorised for that purpose by its flag and that St. Vincent made vigorous efforts to protect the *Saiga* before and throughout the present dispute.[128] On these bases, the Tribunal decided that St. Vincent had produced sufficient evidence to support its assertion that the *Saiga* was a ship entitled to fly its flag at the time of the incident that gave rise to the dispute. Moreover, the Tribunal noted that '[i]n addition to making references to the relevant provisions of the Merchant Shipping Act, [it] has drawn attention to several indications of Vincentian nationality on the ship or carried on board. These include the inscription of "Kingstown" as the port of registry on the stern of the vessel, the documents on board and the ship's seal which contained the words "SAIGA

---

[124] *Ibid.*, at 317.
[125] YbILC (1956–II), 278–279. Of course, an alternative interpretation of this omission might be that it simply removes a limitation on the relevance of the 'genuine link' principle.
[126] *Nottebohm Case*: Liechtenstein v. Guatemala (Second Phase) (1955) ICJ Rep. 4.
[127] *Flegenheimer Claim*, ILR, 25 (1958), 91–167.
[128] *M/V 'Saiga' (No. 2)*: *supra* n. 19 (paragraph 78).

Kingstown" and the then current charter-party which recorded the flag of the vessel as "Saint Vincent and the Grenadines".[129] Although the dissenting judges attached importance to the failure to produce documents that the ship had been removed from Maltese registration, the majority accepted as sufficient St. Vincent's statement that, as required by its laws, its authorities had received satisfactory evidence from the owner that the ship's registration in the country of last registration (Malta) had been closed.[130] Finally, the Tribunal also invoked policy considerations for its decision, concluding that '[i]n the particular circumstances of this case, it would not be consistent with justice if the Tribunal were to decline to deal with the merits of the dispute'.[131] The specific policy consideration here was the concern that too strict an application of the 'genuine link' requirement for finding flag State jurisdiction would deny many States the ability to secure the prompt release of vessels they regarded as subject to their jurisdiction and control as well as effectively render these vessels without nationality or stateless (also described as unregistered or flagless ships). As Allyson Bennett has noted, '[b]ecause stateless vessels do not have a flag state, no state can exercise control over them on the high seas or provide diplomatic protection on their behalf'.[132]

The difficulties faced by the Tribunal in the M/V 'Saiga' (No. 2) Case on the connected issues of nationality of ships, 'genuine link' and flag State jurisdiction, have resurfaced in several more so-called 'prompt release' cases under Article 292 UNCLOS. Most contentiously, in The 'Grand Prince' Case,[133] ITLOS, by a narrow majority decision of twelve to nine, declined jurisdiction to hear a prompt release application from Belize on the basis, inter alia, that '[t]he documents placed before it by the parties disclose on their face contradictions and inconsistencies in matters relating to expiration of the provisional patent of navigation, de-registration of the vessel and suspension of de-registration, all of which give rise to reasonable doubt as to the status of the vessel when the Application was made'.[134] This allowed it to conclude that '[t]he documentary evidence submitted by the applicant fails to establish that *Belize*

---

[129] *Ibid.* (paragraph 67). However, in their separate opinions, several judges in the majority, including Judges Mensah, Wolfrum, Nelson and Rao, expressed substantial disagreement with the analysis in this paragraph.

[130] *Ibid.* (paragraphs 60 and 70).   [131] *Ibid.* (paragraph 73(d)).

[132] A. Bennett, 'That Sinking Feeling: Stateless Ships, Universal Jurisdiction, and the Drug Trafficking Vessel Interdiction Act', *Yale JIL*, 37 (2012), 433–461, at 439.

[133] *The 'Grand Prince'* (Belize v. France), ITLOS Judgment, Case No. 8, 20 Apr. 2001.

[134] *Ibid.* (paragraph 76).

was the flag State of the vessel when the (prompt release) Application was made. Accordingly, the Tribunal finds that it has no jurisdiction to hear the Application'.[135] The apparent refusal on the part of the Tribunal to treat the discrepancies in the factual evidence produced by Belize in support of its flag State jurisdiction in the same way as it treated similar evidentiary discrepancies in relation to St. Vincent in the *M/V 'Saiga' (No. 2) Case* prompted a strongly worded dissenting opinion from nine ITLOS judges.[136] In this dissent, these judges first noted that the Tribunal had not indicated any intention to deviate from the reasoning in its earlier decisions relevant to the issue of the nationality of ships,[137] and, then, they reminded the majority judges of that reasoning as follows:

> In the *M/V 'Saiga' (No. 2) Case*, the Tribunal concluded, on the basis of the evidence before it, that Saint Vincent and the Grenadines had discharged the initial burden of establishing that the *Saiga* had Vincentian nationality at the time of its arrest, despite the fact that its Provisional Certificate of Registration had expired. . . . Dealing with the effect of the expiry of the patent of navigation, the Tribunal notes in passing the means by which the competent authorities could have extended the registration of the *Grand Prince* (paragraph 84 of majority Judgment). Following on the statements of the Belize authorities in the documents referred to above, this listing of possible means should have satisfied the Tribunal as to the registration of the *Grand Prince* on the basis of the Tribunal's reasoning in the *M/V 'SAIGA' (No. 2) Case.*[138]

The Joint Dissenting Opinion concludes as follows:

> In summary, we are of the view, firstly, that it cannot be concluded, on the basis of the documents before the Tribunal, that the registration of the *Grand Prince* had been revoked by the Belize authorities. Secondly, we are of the view that the statements of the competent Belize authorities that the *Grand Prince* was registered in Belize suffice to discharge the initial burden of establishing that it had Belize nationality, given that the Belize legislation provided for means by which the validity of provisional registration could be extended beyond the period of the provisional patent of navigation. Accordingly, we are of the view that the Tribunal has jurisdiction to entertain the Application.[139]

Of much more concern from a treaty interpretation perspective is the view expressed in the Joint Dissenting Opinion concerning the

---

[135] *Ibid.* (paragraph 93) (emphasis added).
[136] See Joint Dissenting Opinion of Judges Caminos, Marotta Rangel, Yankov, Yamamoto, Akl, Vukas, Marsit, Eiriksson and Jesus in *The 'Grand Prince': supra* n. 133.
[137] *Ibid.* (paragraph 6).   [138] *Ibid.* (paragraphs 9 and 11).   [139] *Ibid.* (paragraph 14).

Tribunal's interpretation of Article 292 UNCLOS. The point at issue was whether the flag State of the vessel at the time the prompt release application is made under the terms of this provision must be the same as the flag State at the time the vessel is detained. The Joint Dissenting Opinion stated as follows:

> A more general point of interpretation of the Convention, going beyond the scope of the present case, is raised by the fact that the decision of the Tribunal proceeded from the assumption that the applicant in a proceeding under [A]rticle 292 of the Convention must be the flag State at the time the application is submitted. In the circumstances of prompt release proceedings, the flag State at the time of detention, and at the time when an allegation is made of non-compliance with the provisions of the Convention on prompt release, would ordinarily still be the flag State at the time of making an application under article 292. The reasoning of the Tribunal to justify this as a legal requirement under article 292 is, however, not convincing. Regrettably, the deliberations in the present case have not allowed a full treatment of the consequences of this approach in various other circumstances which could be contemplated ... The decision of the Tribunal has the effect, perhaps unintended, when depriving Belize of its rights as a flag State, albeit for the limited purposes of actions under article 292 of the Convention, also of condoning a system under which a flag State can in certain circumstances absolve itself of its duties as a flag State, including those laid down in article 94 of the Convention. It will be recalled that, under article 94, paragraph 1, every State must effectively exercise its jurisdiction and control in administrative, technical and social matters over ships flying its flag. It certainly cannot suffice for a flag State to seek to comply with this obligation merely by revoking, without more, the registration of ships flying its flag. The Tribunal should not have dealt as it did with a matter with such important consequences without the benefit of full consideration of the legal questions involved.[140]

Again, however, it is possible to suggest that wider policy considerations may have played a part in the majority decision in this case, as Bernard H. Oxman and Vincent P. Bantz have observed, 'although the opinion does not address the matter, the instant case involved the reflagging of a fishing vessel, a problem that has attracted international concern'.[141] As the ITLOS judgment noted: 'According to the Applicant (*Belize*), at the time of its detention, the vessel was going to be reflagged and registered in Brazil where the vessel had been allocated a fishing

---

[140] *Ibid.* (paragraphs 15 and 16).
[141] B. H. Oxman and V. P. Bantz, 'The "Grand Prince" (Belize v. France), Judgment, ITLOS Case No. 8', *AJIL*, 96 (2002), 219–225, at 222.

licence'.[142] Given the often tenuous links between re-flagged fishing vessels in particular, and their *ersatz* flag States,[143] it is perhaps understandable that the majority of the Tribunal judges were reluctant to accept that there was a 'genuine link' between the *Grand Prince* and Belize as its flag State for the purposes of its prompt release application, especially as it was in the process of being reflagged to another flag State. Thus, the significance of the 'genuine link' requirement as initially stated by the ICJ in the *Nottebohm Case* returns to prominence in this context.

4.2   Threat or Use of Force: The Guyana/Suriname Arbitration

Article 301 UNCLOS, a provision that is entitled 'Peaceful Uses of the Seas', almost replicates Article 2(4) of the 1945 Charter of the United Nations in providing that when 'exercising their rights and performing their duties under this Convention, States Parties shall refrain from any threat or use of force against the territorial integrity or political independence of any State, or in any other manner inconsistent with the principles of international law embodied in the Charter of the United Nations'.[144] In the course of its maritime boundary dispute with neighbouring Suriname, Guyana claimed that Suriname had breached both this provision of UNCLOS as well as Article 2(4) of the Charter in using or threatening to use force in its international relations against the territorial integrity of Guyana, arguing that the Charter provision remains applicable in the context of territorial or maritime boundary disputes. The immediate background to the incidents leading up to Guyana's specific claims against Suriname on the threat or use of force were authoritatively summarized by the Arbitral Tribunal convened under Annex VII of UNCLOS,[145] as follows: Guyana claimed that Suriname had rejected Guyana's repeated offers of immediate high-level negotiations concerning offshore exploratory activities by Guyana's licensee CGX. Instead, it resorted to the use of force on

---

[142] The 'Grand Prince', supra n. 133 (paragraph 33).

[143] See M. Fitzmaurice, 'Natural Resources Management: Protecting Fisheries in the 21st Century' in E. Blanco and J. Razzaque (eds.), *Natural Resources and the Green Economy: Redefining the Challenges for People, States and Corporations* (Leiden: Martinus Nijhoff, 2012), pp. 191–244, at p. 219.

[144] Supra n. 1. Art. 2(4) of the United Nations Charter provides that '[a]ll Members shall refrain in their international relations from the threat or use of force against the territorial integrity or political independence of any state, or in any other manner inconsistent with the Purposes of the United Nations': 1 UNTS 16.

[145] Arbitration between Guyana and Suriname, supra n. 20.

3 June 2000 to expel Guyana's licensee – the CGX exploratory rig and drill ship *C.E. Thornton* – and threatened similar action against other licensees, namely Esso E. & P. Guyana and Maxus.[146] Guyana also made an interesting claim regarding the proportionality of the alleged threat or use of force by Suriname, suggesting that in the context of the small-scale military capabilities of Guyana and Suriname, Guyana viewed Suriname's threat or use of armed force as significant and amounting to an internationally wrongful act, engaging the international responsibility of Suriname.[147]

According to Guyana, Suriname's conduct had resulted in both material and non-material injury to Guyana. First, Guyana claimed to have suffered material injury in the form of loss of foreign investment in offshore exploration, licensing fees and other sources of income and foregone benefits in the development of Guyana's offshore resources. This blocked the development of Guyana's offshore hydrocarbon resources, for which injuries Guyana claimed full reparation in accordance with international law.[148] Second, Guyana claimed compensation for non-material losses occasioned by the adverse effect of Suriname's action on Guyana's standing as a nation.[149]

The Annex VII Arbitral Tribunal was therefore required to assess the factual events brought before it by the two parties and decide whether such a violation of the prohibition of the threat or use of force had actually occurred. In its award, the arbitral tribunal began by addressing the interpretation of the phrase 'threat or use of force' as follows: 'With respect to the question of whether the CGX incident constituted a threat of force, the Tribunal considered it helpful to examine the statements of some of the main participants in that incident'.[150] It is notable that, even at this initial stage of its deliberations on this issue, the Arbitral Tribunal had apparently already narrowed the scope of its legal enquiry to the issue of whether a 'threat of force' had occurred rather than an actual *use* of force as initially claimed by Guyana. The Tribunal then addressed the question as to whether this threat of force breached the terms of UNCLOS and the United Nations Charter as well as general international law. In this regard, it observed that the ICJ has thrown some light on the circumstances where a threat of force can be considered illegal, by declaring in its advisory opinion in *Legality of the Threat or Use of Nuclear Weapons* in July 1996 that:

---

[146] *Ibid.* (paragraph 426). [147] *Ibid.* (paragraph 266). [148] *Ibid.* (paragraph 426).
[149] *Ibid.* (paragraph 266). [150] *Ibid.* (paragraph 432).

Whether a signalled intention to use force if certain events occur is or is not a 'threat' within Article 2, paragraph 4, of the Charter depends upon various factors. If the envisaged use of force is itself unlawful, the stated readiness to use it would be a threat prohibited under Article 2, paragraph 4. Thus it would be illegal for a State to threaten force to secure territory from another State, or to cause it to follow or not follow certain political or economic paths. The notions of 'threat' and 'use' of force under Article 2, paragraph 4, of the Charter stand together in the sense that if the use of force itself in a given case is illegal – for whatever reason – the threat to use such force will likewise be illegal. In short, if it is to be lawful, the declared readiness of a State to use force must be a use of force that is in conformity with the Charter.[151]

The Arbitral Tribunal then proceeded to draw a distinction between legitimate law enforcement action on the part of a coastal State and the illegal use of force, when it affirmed that 'force may be used in law enforcement activities provided that such force is unavoidable, reasonable and necessary'.[152] However, as Patricia Jimenez Kwast notes, the difficulty involved in making this distinction when applied to action at sea is due to the fact that 'many states would consider the use of armed force against a ship flying its flag, in contrast to cases involving the forcible exercise of police powers, to be an attack upon the state'.[153] Kwast explores the issues raised by this distinction in the use of force on land as opposed to its use at sea by initially noting that in the *Nicaragua Case* before the ICJ, the Court considered it 'necessary to distinguish the most grave forms of the use of force (those constituting an armed attack) from other less grave forms'.[154] Although Kwast accepts, that in that case, the ICJ was solely concerned with different variations in the level of 'force', she observes that 'it is precisely the line between such 'less grave' use of force and the use of police force at sea that may at times be a particularly difficult one to draw'.[155] With regard to the

---

[151] *Ibid.* (paragraph 439) (citing *Legality of the Threat or Use of Nuclear Weapons* (Advisory Opinion) (1996) ICJ Rep. 226, at p. 246 (paragraph 47), and noting further that scholarly opinion is in line with this proposition: see I. Brownlie, *International Law and the Use of Force by States* (Oxford: Clarendon Press, 1963), p. 364).

[152] *Ibid.* (paragraph 445) (citing *S.S. 'I'm Alone' (Canada/United States)*, RIAA, Vol. III, 1609–1618, at p. 1615; *Red Crusader (Commission of Enquiry, Denmark–United Kingdom)*, XXIX RIAA 521–539, and *M/V 'Saiga' (No. 2): supra* n. 19).

[153] P. J. Kwast, 'Maritime Law Enforcement and the Use of Force: Reflections on the Categorisation of Forcible Action at Sea in the Light of the Guyana/Suriname Award', *J. Conflict & Sec. L.*, 13 (2008), 49–91, at 58.

[154] *Case Concerning Military and Paramilitary Activities in and against Nicaragua*: Nicaragua v. United States of America (Merits) (1986) ICJ Rep. 14, at p. 101 (paragraph 191).

[155] Kwast, *supra* n. 153, at 60.

Tribunal's finding that the warning by the Suriname Navy to leave the area or face the consequences was sufficient to constitute a *threat* of the use of force in contravention of international law, she suggests that, in this particular context, 'the nature of the threatened force is to be seen as a reference to the category of "less grave forms" of armed force that may occur in the context of border incidents'.[156] Also, in this context, Dino Kritsiotis has suggested that *threats* of force can also be calibrated according to their gravity within a spectrum ranging from less grave to grave threats as per the ICJ's schemata for uses of force.[157] However, the fact that this threat of force occurred in a disputed area of maritime jurisdiction does not seem to have been emphasized by the Arbitral Tribunal itself in this part of its award. Indeed, Kwast herself admits that this characterization of the *threat* of the use of force by Suriname as related to a 'border incident' is not discernible from the precise paragraph when the Tribunal holds that it is illegal,[158] but instead would seem to follow from an earlier paragraph of the award that refers to the alternatives of the operation of 3 June 2000 being either a 'border incident' or a case of 'law enforcement activity'.[159] Thus, it is difficult to accept that this relatively low threshold for a breach of the prohibition against the threat of force is necessarily to be applied only in situations of territorial or maritime boundary disputes. More significantly, the Tribunal implicitly acknowledged the difficulties involved in distinguishing between these two types of forcible action – border incidents and law enforcement activity – by its initial emphasis on the subjective perception of the participants involved. Having considered various statements from those involved in the actual incident, the Tribunal then held as follows: 'The testimony of those involved in the incident clearly reveals that the rig was ordered to leave the area and if this demand was not fulfilled, responsibility for unspecified consequences would be theirs. There was no unanimity as to what these "consequences" might have been. The Tribunal is of the view that the order given by Major Jones (Commander Staff Support of the Suriname Air Force and Navy), to the rig constituted an explicit threat that force might be used if the order was not complied with.'[160] Finally, the Tribunal also noted the Surinamese defences of its actions in the specific incident as follows: 'Suriname has maintained that the measures it undertook on 3 June 2000

---

[156] *Ibid.*, at 61.
[157] D. Kritsiotis, 'Close Encounters of A Sovereign Kind', *EJIL*, 20 (2009), 299–330.
[158] See *Arbitration between Guyana and Suriname, supra* n. 20 (paragraph 445).
[159] *Ibid.* (paragraph 410).   [160] *Ibid.* (paragraph 439).

were of the nature of reasonable and proportionate law enforcement measures to preclude unauthorized drilling in a disputed area of the continental shelf. It asserted that it was quite normal for coastal States to undertake law enforcement activities in disputed areas (usually in relation to fisheries) and also to do so against vessels under foreign flags including the flag of the other party to the dispute, unless specific arrangements exist.'[161] However, in the circumstances of the present case, the Tribunal was of the view that the action mounted by Suriname against the Guyanese-licensed ship seemed more akin to a threat of military action rather than a mere law enforcement activity.[162]

A number of implications of the Tribunal's decision on this aspect of the *Guyana v. Suriname* award can be noted: first, the distinction between the prohibition(s) against the 'threat' and the 'use of force' itself, which was confirmed by the ICJ in its *Legality of the Threat or Use of Nuclear Weapons* advisory opinion, has been clearly maintained and clearly applied for the purposes of establishing the culpability of Suriname in this case. A second point concerns the Tribunal's reliance, as a matter of evidence, on the testimony of the alleged victims of the threat of force as opposed to the reassurances of the Surinamese naval/coastguard officers that they were never going to use force against the Guyanese drill ship operators during the incident. The subjective approach of the Tribunal – emphasizing the viewpoints and perspectives of the potential victims of the alleged threat as well as their apprehensions concerning its violent nature – when placed alongside the de-coupling of the prohibition of the threat of the use of force from that concerning the actual use of force, arguably introduces an unduly low threshold for the finding of an international law violation for the former prohibition and, therefore, the international responsibility on the part of the threatening State. It remains to be seen whether this approach to the interpretation of the relevant phrase will find favour before other international tribunals if or when they are called upon to adjudicate on similar factual situations regarding threats of force.

5   Conclusions

Summing up, the 1982 Convention has over the years presented a number of challenges to the overarching discipline of the law of treaties. Chief among these, as highlighted in the preceding pages, has been:

---

[161] *Ibid.* (paragraph 411).   [162] *Ibid.* (paragraph 445).

1. the nature of the treaty relationship between the previous, 1958 Geneva Conventions, the 1982 UNCLOS, and subsequent 1994 Implementation Agreement;
2. the relationship between the 1982 Convention and other treaties on subject matters related to that covered in UNCLOS; and
3. the relationship between the 1982 UNCLOS and 1969 VCLT rules on the interpretation of UNCLOS provisions.

The last of these topics also takes on board the role of the principle of good faith, coupled with the obligation not to abuse rights, and the possible application of the 1982 Convention to non-parties, such as the United States. On each of these issues, the potential for fragmentation of the discipline has been glimpsed, but on the whole, these developments in the law of the sea would seem to have kept within the discretionary margins of what would be acceptable under the law of treaties. In particular, UNCLOS-related State practice and jurisprudence is evolving in ways that are apparently unobjectionable to most States around the world, whether they are parties to UNCLOS or not. On this note, it is as well to remind ourselves that the approach adopted in the negotiations to the 1982 Convention was that of a 'negative' consensus, in the sense that, where there was no strenuous objection to a proposed treaty text, then all the States represented were deemed to have acquiesced to that text. In this vein, it is possible to conclude that, barring future scientific and technological breakthroughs that revolutionize the outlook for the political economy of the sea, future developments in the law of the sea will continue along this implicitly consensus-driven evolutionary path that will not challenge the overriding precepts of the law of treaties.

23

The Law of Treaties, the Law of State Responsibility and the Non-performance of Treaty Obligations: A View from the Case Law

MALGOSIA FITZMAURICE

1 Introduction

The relationship between the law of treaties and the law of State responsibility, deliberately left open by Article 73 of the 1969 Vienna Convention on the Law of Treaties (VCLT),[1] has been one of the most widely discussed questions of international law. The general theoretical aspects of this relationship, insofar as they impact upon the process of responding to alleged breaches of treaty by another party, have already been revisited earlier in this edited collection,[2] so the aim of the present chapter is more specific: namely to examine the extent to which this issue has been illuminated through the medium of litigation practice, especially before the International Court of Justice (ICJ).

It is believed that the forensic setting of argument, counter-argument and judgment offers a particularly interesting context for the investigation of the relationship between these distinct frameworks of normative assessment. It does so for two, somewhat contrasting, reasons. On the one hand, the need to reach a decisive conclusion on a specific controversy offers the opportunity for the concrete and detailed application of the relevant principles in a way that abstract discussions may find difficult to match. On the other hand, however, the intensity of the perceived need to defend the national interests which are at stake in the litigation in question may not be conducive to the most objective and coherent framing and presentation of the legal issues by the parties themselves. These countervailing considerations render it difficult to predict how much genuine light litigation practice is

---

[1] 1155 UNTS 331.
[2] See the contribution to this volume by Tams at pp. 440–467 (Chapter 14).

likely to shine on the vexed relationship between the law of treaties and the law of State responsibility.

It should be made clear from the outset that this chapter will focus on the relevant case law relating to the relationship between the law of treaties and State responsibility only in so far as that relationship impacts upon the question of the non-performance of treaty obligations. It will not deal with breaches of other international obligations, such as those deriving from customary international law. The law of countermeasures and other justifications for non-performance, as codified in the 2001 Articles on Responsibility of States for Internationally Wrongful Acts (ASR) of the International Law Commission (ILC),[3] are of course applicable in the event of breaches of norms of customary international law; in this chapter, however, they will be dealt with only in so far as they have some bearing upon the consequences of breach of *treaty* obligations.

With these qualifications in mind, this chapter will deal with the case law relating to the law of treaties regarding non-performance of a treaty obligation, including impossibility of performance and fundamental change of circumstances, as well as the law of State responsibility regarding countermeasures and other justifications for non-performance such as *force majeure* and state of necessity. It will also address the so-called exception of non-performance, referred to here as the *exceptio* (or in full *exceptio non adimplenti contractus* or *exceptio inadimplenti non est adimplendum*) which remains difficult to locate squarely within either of these frameworks of legal response. On the basis of this case law, the attempt will be made to draw some general conclusions at a macro-level concerning the behaviour of States in their selection of particular defences in order to justify their non-performance of treaty obligations. Another distinction which may usefully be borne in mind at this stage is based on the intrinsic nature of the various measures open to States seeking to respond to breaches of treaty obligation. While all of these measures are essentially defensive in character, some involve a positive counter-initiative in the sense that they are designed to bring about the suspension or actual termination of a treaty under the Vienna Convention or, alternatively, to induce a State which breaches its treaty obligation back into compliance through applying a certain degree of coercion upon them (under the law of State responsibility). By contrast, purely passive defences include the invocation of a state of necessity or *force majeure*, which serve simply as justifications for non-performance.

---

[3] Official Records of the General Assembly, Fifty-Sixth Session, Supp. No. 10 (A/56/10), Ch. V.

The most complex and the least understood of these matters concerns the triangular relationship between the exception of non-performance, material breach and countermeasures. To help us undertake this analysis, a brief introductory explanation of each of these three institutions and their interrelationship will be presented, beginning with the exception of non-performance. The circumstances in which recourse to this principle is possible have never been clearly established. Despite its Latin formulation, the *exceptio* does not, according to James Crawford and Simon Olleson, seem actually to have been part of the Roman legal system in a general sense. Rather, it was reflected only in certain specific instances, in particular the *exceptio mercis non traditae*.[4] It was not until later, in the twelfth century, that a general rule was extrapolated from these particular instances by the glossators and their followers.

The lack of agreement – confusion, even – regarding the precise legal nature of this concept was clearly visible during the discussions within the ILC during the codification of the rules of State responsibility, where it was mooted that the *exceptio* be retained as Article 30*bis* of the Articles – a suggestion which ultimately failed.[5] As a general matter, it was suggested that this exception has a character similar to countermeasures and also to *force majeure* and that it typically appears as a feature of synallagmatic relations.[6] In the context of the law of treaties, the *exceptio*, according to the ILC, related to non-performance of a treaty and was applicable in cases where, without suspension or termination of the instrument in question, a State was nonetheless released from performance of certain obligations,[7] at least temporarily. The inclusion of a special provision relating to non-performance of treaty obligations in the VCLT was accepted, but this emerged as Article

---

[4] J. Crawford and S. Olleson, 'The Exception of Non Performance: Links between the Law of Treaties and the State Responsibility', Australian *YbIL*, 21 (2000), 55–74, at 66. Classical Roman law knows the '*exceptio mercis non traditae*' where the mechanism calls for the raising of the defence by the defendant. This principle, also known as the defence of non-performance, later found application in many legal systems and traditions, such as section 320 of the Bürgerliches Gesetzbuch (BGB); Art. 1426 of the Spanish Código Civil; Art. 82 of the Swiss Code des Obligations and Art. 1460 of Italy's Codice Civile. See, further, F. Parisi, M. Casini and B. Luppi, 'Enforcing Bilateral Promises: A Comparative Law and Economics Perspective', *European Rev. Private L.*, 2 (2013), 412–450, at 431.

[5] Part I of the Draft Articles was adopted in 1980: *YbILC* (1980–II), Part Two, 26–61. See, also, J. Crawford, 'Revising the Draft Articles on State Responsibility', *EJIL*, 10 (1999), 435–460, at 456–457.

[6] J. Crawford, Second Report on State Responsibility, U.N. Doc. A/CN.4/498/Add.2 (30 Apr. 1999), pp. 40–48 (paragraphs 314–329).

[7] *Ibid.*, at p. 46 (paragraph 324).

60 VCLT – a provision that is confined to cases of 'material breach'. The consequences of breach of obligation generally were left to be addressed in the Articles on State Responsibility.[8] Crawford and Olleson express the view that the *exceptio* – which might conceivably still be applicable in the case of non-material breaches of treaty – 'has fallen between the two instruments'.[9] If it is assumed that the *exceptio* belongs to the law of treaties, the further question may be posed as to 'whether it should be regarded as a rule of international law at all, or simply as a potential source of treaty interpretation'.[10]

As for the 'material breach' of a treaty, this is defined in Article 60(3) VCLT, which states that it 'consists in (a) a repudiation of the treaty not sanctioned by the [VCLT] or (b) the violation of a provision essential to the accomplishment of the object or purpose of the treaty'. In other words, separate possibilities are envisaged for the occurrence of a material breach; conditions (a) and (b) are not to be taken as cumulative.[11] Once a material breach has occurred in accordance with this definition, it entitles the other party in the case of a bilateral treaty 'to invoke the [material] breach as a ground for terminating the treaty or suspending its operation in whole or in part' (Article 60(1) VCLT). According to Article 60(2) VCLT, the material breach of a multilateral treaty entitles:

    a. the other parties by unanimous agreement to suspend the operation of the treaty in whole or in part or to terminate it either:
      i. in the relations between themselves and the defaulting State, or
      ii. as between all the parties;
    b. a party specially affected by the breach to invoke it as a ground for suspending the operation of the treaty in whole or in part in the relations between itself and the defaulting State;
    c. any party other than the defaulting State to invoke the breach as a ground for suspending the operation of the treaty in whole or in part with respect to itself if the treaty is of such a character that a material breach of its provisions by one party radically changes the position of every party with respect to the further performance of its obligations under the treaty.

---

[8] G. G. Fitzmaurice, Second Report on the Law of Treaties, *YbILC* (1957–II), 16–70.
[9] Crawford and Olleson, *supra* n. 4, at 66.   [10] *Ibid.*
[11] M. M. Gomaa, *Suspension or Termination of Treaties on Grounds of Breach* (Leiden/The Hague: Martinus Nijhoff, 1996), p. 25.

The difference between paragraphs (b) and (c) can be explained on the basis that the latter relates to treaties in which every party has an interest in ensuring performance (so-called 'integral treaties').[12]

Whereas material breach has its foundation in the law of treaties, countermeasures are responses of States to a breach of treaty which derive their authority from the law of State responsibility. Article 49 ASR defines the object of countermeasures as limited to the non-performance for the time being of international obligations of the State taking the measures towards the responsible State, which shall, as far as possible, be implemented in such a way as to permit the resumption of performance of the obligations in question.[13] The measures taken must be proportionate or commensurate to the injury suffered,[14] with other stringent conditions attached to their use.[15] In similar fashion to Article 60(2)(c) VCLT, Articles 42 and 48 ASR respectively concern the invocation of responsibility by the injured State or by another State. These provisions entitle such States to demand cessation of the breach and that reparation be made to the injured State itself or to the beneficiaries of the obligation breached.

Although proportionality is not one of the conditions specified in Article 60 VCLT for responding to material breach, the view has been expressed that it is built into that process implicitly by virtue of (i) the restrictive definition of material breach in Article 60(3) VCLT and (ii) the limitations that are imposed on recourse to suspension and termination, which are such as to render them 'not a disproportionate response'.[16]

---

[12] L.-A. Sicilianos, 'The Relationship between Reprisals and Denunciation or Suspension of a Treaty', *EJIL*, 4 (1993), 341–359, at 348.

[13] Art. 49(2) ASR: *supra* n. 3.   [14] Art. 51 ASR: *supra* n. 3.

[15] Art. 52 ASR: *supra* n. 3. This provision states:

1. Before taking countermeasures, an injured State shall:
   (a) call upon the responsible State ... to fulfil its obligations ...
   (b) notify the responsible State of any decision to take countermeasures and offer to negotiate with that State.
2. Notwithstanding paragraph 1(*b*), the injured State may take such urgent counter-measures as are necessary to preserve its rights.
3. Countermeasures may not be taken, and if already taken must be suspended without undue delay if:
   (a) the internationally wrongful act has ceased; and
   (b) the dispute is pending before a court or tribunal which has the authority to make decisions binding on the parties.
4. Paragraph 3 does not apply if the responsible State fails to implement the dispute settlement procedures in good faith.

[16] Gomaa, *supra* n. 11, at pp. 119 and 121. In his view, proportionality is automatically applied when the measures contained in this Article are activated. This is achieved by

This is not the only similarity between material breach and counter-measures: the threat of termination or suspension (or, indeed, actual suspension), where permitted under Article 60 VCLT, may be seen as coercive measures to the extent that they are aimed at influencing the defaulting State to reconsider its action(s) and to resume performance in good faith – not unlike the logic underpinning countermeasures. The existence of these similarities might help to explain the confusion that has been evident in arguments presented before international courts and tribunals by States attempting to justify their non-performance of treaty obligations by reference to alleged breaches by other parties.

2 'The Exception of Non-performance' in International Law

In-depth theoretical consideration of the concept of the *exceptio* can be found elsewhere.[17] As mentioned earlier, it is in essence a form of response by a State to another party's demand for performance of a treaty obligation that relies on a corresponding breach by that other State. Its legal character is, however, unspecified and not very well defined.[18] Additionally, the invocation of the *exceptio* does not involve the same procedural requirements as in case of the material breach.[19]

There are a number of cases before courts and tribunals in which the parties to the dispute have relied on the *exceptio*. Crawford and Olleson mention three in which it was discussed,[20] albeit inconclusively. Two of them are *Diversion of Water from the Meuse*[21] and *Appeal Relating to the Jurisdiction of the ICAO Council*.[22] The third is the *Case Concerning the Gabčikovo-Nagymaros Project*, where the principle of the exception of non-performance was expressly mentioned by judges in separate and

---

virtue of combined effect of the relationship between Art. 60(1), (2) and (3) VCLT: *supra* n. 1.

[17] See Crawford and Olleson, *supra* n. 4, and, further, D. W. Greig, 'Reciprocity, Proportionality and the Law of Treaties', *Virginia JIL*, 34 (1994), 295–403. See, also, the contribution to this volume by Tams at pp. 440–467 (Chapter 14).

[18] See, in particular, the Separate Opinion of Judge Simma in *Application of the Interim Accord of 13 September 1995*: the former Yugoslav Republic of Macedonia v. Greece (2011) ICJ Rep. 644, at pp. 695–708.

[19] As occurred in *Application of the Interim Accord of 13 September 1995: ibid.*; to be discussed later.

[20] Crawford and Olleson, *supra* n. 4, at 63.

[21] *Diversion of Water from the Meuse*: Netherlands v. Belgium, 1937 PCIJ, Series A/B, No. 70, 4.

[22] *Appeal Relating to the Jurisdiction of the ICAO Council*: India v. Pakistan (1972) ICJ Rep. 46.

dissenting opinions.[23] This latter case is an excellent illustration of the general confusion and misconceptions surrounding the fields of State responsibility and the law of treaties, and it will be discussed further on in this chapter.

In *Diversion of Water from the Meuse*, the issue related to the complaint by the Netherlands concerning the diversion of water by Belgium from a lock situated in Belgian territory for several purposes, including irrigation. The Netherlands alleged that Belgium was in breach of a bilateral treaty of May 1863;[24] Belgium responded that its use of water was not wrongful at all in light of similar actions that had been undertaken by the Netherlands on its side. Belgium additionally argued that the Netherlands, by erecting certain works contrary to the treaty provisions, had in any event forfeited its right to invoke the treaty against Belgium. By a substantial majority, the Permanent Court of International Justice (PCIJ) agreed that Belgium was not in breach of the treaty, rendering moot any particular justifications it had offered.[25] There was some discussion in the separate and dissenting opinions of Belgium's additional plea in this regard, but there was no uniformity of approach toward the *exceptio*: in his separate opinion, for example, Judge Altamira did not support the view that the obligations of the two parties were synallagmatic. According to him, it followed that Belgium could not rely on the conduct of the Netherlands as a circumstance precluding wrongfulness.[26] On the other hand, Judge Anzilotti expressed the view that the *exceptio* was so widely recognised in practice and equitable as a matter of principle that it 'must be applied in international relations also'.[27] He further noted that the principle was a general principle of law within the meaning of Article 38 of the Statute of the PCIJ.[28] For his part, Judge Hudson held the view that the principle of equity underlay the synallagmatic contractual relationship and that therefore it justified non-performance.[29] The principle *inadimplenti non est adimplendum* could be applied by an international court in certain very restricted circumstances with respect to an identical or reciprocal obligation.[30]

As for the *Appeal Relating to the Jurisdiction of the ICAO Council*, this concerned, in part, a discussion of the material breach of a treaty. The ICJ approached this principle with caution and maintained the view that the

---

[23] *Case Concerning the Gabčíkovo-Nagymaros Project (Hungary/Slovakia)* (1997) ICJ Rep. 7.
[24] 127 CTS 441.   [25] *Diversion of Water from the Meuse, supra* n. 21, at p. 32.
[26] *Ibid.*, at pp. 38–39 (Separate Opinion of Judge Altamira).
[27] *Ibid.*, at p. 50 (Dissenting Opinion of Judge Anzilotti).   [28] *Ibid.*
[29] *Ibid.*, at p. 76 (Individual Opinion of Judge Hudson).   [30] *Ibid.*, at p. 77.

mere allegation by one party that a material breach has been committed does not permit the automatic unilateral termination or suspension of a treaty under Article 60 VCLT – and certainly not so as to deprive a relevant treaty body of jurisdiction over a dispute regarding the application or interpretation of that treaty. As far as the principle of *inadimplenti non est adimplendum* was concerned, this was raised by Judge de Castro in his separate opinion. While discussing material breach of a treaty enshrined in Article 60 VCLT, he made the following observation in a footnote:

> It should not be overlooked that the rule [concerning an injured party's entitlement to invoke the breach as a ground for suspending or terminating a treaty in accordance with Article 60 VCLT] opens the possibility of raising the *exceptio inadimplenti non est adimplendum*. The breach of an obligation is not the cause of the invalidity or termination of the treaty. It is a source of responsibility and of new obligations or sanctions. Alongside this, it is the material breach of a treaty which entitles the injured party to invoke it in order to terminate or suspend the operation of the treaty.[31]

Judge de Castro further mentioned this principle in connection with the discussion of the legal character of Article 60 VCLT, which, in his view, was 'a principle which follows from the contractual nature of treaties ... The rules of international law are not outside treaties, they give legal force to treaty rules ... Article 60 is a complement and the sanction of the principle *pacta sunt servanda*. It is the breach of rights or obligations having their source in the agreement which lies at the root of the *exceptio non adimpleti*'.[32]

Subsequent to the publication of Crawford and Olleson's study, the principle of reciprocity in the case of non-performance – or, one can say, the *exceptio* – was implicitly invoked during the *Case Concerning Oil Platforms*, though only during the pleadings and not in the judgment of the ICJ.[33] This case was brought before the Court in November 1992 by the Islamic Republic of Iran against the United States. It concerned a dispute arising out of the destruction by US warships of three offshore oil production complexes, owned and operated for commercial purposes by the National Iranian Oil Company. In its Application to the Court,

---

[31] *Appeal Relating to the Jurisdiction of the ICAO Council, supra* n. 22, at p. 127 (Separate Opinion of Judge de Castro).

[32] *Ibid.*, at p. 129.

[33] *Case Concerning Oil Platforms*: Islamic Republic of Iran v. United States (Merits) (2003) ICJ Rep. 161.

Iran contended that these acts constituted a 'fundamental breach' of various provisions of the Treaty of Amity, Economic Relations and Consular Rights between the United States and Iran, which was signed in Tehran on 15 August 1955 and entered into force on 16 June 1957,[34] as well as of general international law.[35] The Application invoked, as a basis for the Court's jurisdiction, Article XXI(2) of the Treaty.

Counsel for the United States, Stephen Mathias, pleaded before the Court that the breach of a reciprocal obligation by Iran of this Treaty precluded the possibility for Iran of objecting to corresponding non-performance on the part of the United States. He argued that 'the consequence of Iran's own wrongful conduct is that Iran may not invoke the 1955 Treaty',[36] with reference made to *Diversion of Water from the Meuse*.[37] Yet, although it was submitted that the actions of the United States were adopted in response to unlawful action by Iran under the Treaty,[38] it was not suggested that they constituted either countermeasures or action taken in response to a material breach of the treaty.[39] Reliance was placed instead on the statement once made by Sir Gerald Fitzmaurice – that 'the failure of one State to perform its international obligations in a particular respect will ... *disentitle that State from objecting to ... corresponding non-performance*'[40] – suggesting that the argument was based on the *exceptio*. This apparent invocation of the *exceptio* was, however, only supplementary to the pleadings of the United States and was not in the end addressed in the judgment of the Court, which focused on other arguments.

More recently still, the *exceptio* was relied upon extensively before the ICJ in the dispute between the Former Yugoslav Republic of Macedonia (FYROM) and Greece.[41] On 17 November 2008, the FYROM initiated proceedings against Greece before the ICJ, after it had made an unsuccessful request to join NATO during the April 2008 NATO Summit in

---

[34] 284 UNTS 3.   [35] *Case Concerning Oil Platforms, supra* n. 33, at p. 166 (paragraph 1).

[36] CR 2003/18, Public Sitting in the *Case Concerning Oil Platforms* (Islamic Republic of Iran v. United States of America): www.icj-cij.org/docket/files/90/5181.pdf (5 March 2003), p. 11 (paragraph 26.4).

[37] *Ibid.* (specifically the Individual Opinion of Judge Hudson in that case: *supra* n. 21).

[38] *Ibid.*, at p. 11 (paragraph 26.4) and p. 12 (paragraph 26.7).

[39] *Ibid.*, at pp. 12–13 (paragraph 26.9).

[40] For his Fourth Report on the Law of Treaties: *YbILC* (1959–II), 70 (emphasis in original).

[41] *Application of the Interim Accord of 13 September 1995, supra* n. 18. See, further, A. Tzanakopoulos, 'Legality of Veto to NATO Accession: Comment on the ICJ's Decision in the Dispute between FYR Macedonia and Greece', www.ejiltalk.org/legality-of-veto-to-nato-accession/ (7 Dec. 2011).

Bucharest, Romania. The FYROM alleged that Greece had objected to its admission because of the unresolved dispute over the name 'Macedonia',[42] which, it claimed, was in direct violation of the Interim Accord of 13 September 1995 designed to facilitate the bilateral relationship between the two countries pending the conclusion of a permanent agreement.[43] The Accord provided in Article 11(1) that Greece would refrain from objecting to the FYROM's application for admission to any universal or regional organization to which Greece was a member; however, by the same provision, Greece reserved 'the right to object to any [such] membership ... if and to the extent [the FYROM] is to be referred to in such organization or institution differently than in paragraph 2 of United Nations Security Council resolution 817 (1993)'.[44]

Given the Court's findings that the behaviour of Greece could not be justified under the terms of Article 11(1), it became necessary to address the supplementary arguments that Greece had put forward to meet that contingency. In particular, it alleged that the FYROM had itself committed breaches of Articles 5, 6 and 7 of the Interim Accord that justified retaliatory action on Greece's part. In an attempt to anticipate these arguments, the FYROM had contended that (i) '[t]he Respondent's nonperformance cannot be explained on the basis of a suspension of Article 11(1) of the Interim Accord for material breach' – thus basing itself on Article 60 VCLT – and (ii) that '[t]he Respondent's violation of Article 11(1) cannot be excused as a lawful countermeasure to a precedent wrongful act by the Applicant'.[45] Greece, however, initially argued that it was not seeking to rely on either of these grounds.

With regard to Article 60 VCLT specifically, it noted that it had never claimed any intent to suspend or terminate the operation of the Interim Accord in whole or in part. Indeed, it had steadily and consistently

---

[42] 'Macedonia' is the name of a historical and geographical region that extends mainly between Greece, Bulgaria and FYR Macedonia. Greece objected to FYROM's use of the name of one of the administrative regions of Greece.

[43] 1891 UNTS I-32193 (with Related Letters and Translations of the Interim Accord in the Languages of the Contracting Parties).

[44] *Ibid.* In paragraph 2 of Security Council Resolution 817 (7 Apr. 1993), the Security Council recommended to the General Assembly 'that the State whose application is contained in document S/25147 be admitted to membership in the United Nations, this State being provisionally referred to for all purposes within the United Nations as "the former Yugoslav Republic of Macedonia" pending settlement of the difference that has arisen over the name of the State'.

[45] Memorial of the FYROM, Vol. I, Section III (www.icj-cij.org/docket/files/142/16354.pdf), 20 July 2009, pp. 94–100.

maintained that the Accord was in force and ought to be fully respected on the basis of the principle *pacta sunt servanda*.[46] Rather, Greece committed itself to the more general principle of reciprocity according to which *non adimplenti non est adimplendum*, 'which means that as long as the FYROM does not comply with its obligations under the 1995 Accord, Greece is entitled not to comply with its own obligations under the same instrument'.[47] Greece explained that '[t]he *exceptio inadimpleti contractus* must not be confused with the ground for suspension and termination of a treaty dealt with in Article 60 of the Vienna Convention or with countermeasures (even though the conditions for having recourse to countermeasures [were] also met). It is merely a defence against a claim of non-performance of a conventional obligation'.[48]

In contrast to the *exceptio*, which 'is a defence which can be invoked at any time in response to a claim by another State',[49] the purpose of countermeasures is to induce a State which is responsible for an internationally wrongful act to comply with its international obligations.[50] It is therefore understandable that Greece argued that these three international law institutions have a common purpose or ambition – namely, to address unlawful conduct by another State. However, and equally importantly, the conditions triggering the exception of non-performance are different from and less strict than the conditions for suspending a treaty or adopting countermeasures.[51] The *exceptio* is broader than Article 60 VCLT as it is not confined to material breaches and does not have any procedural requirements attached to it.[52] Furthermore, the *exceptio* suspends the execution by the injured party only of the obligation that is the counterpart or the reciprocal

---

[46] Counter-Memorial of Greece, Vol. I (http://www.icj-cij.org/docket/files/142/16356.pdf), 19 Jan. 2010, pp. 163–164 (paragraph 8.2).

[47] *Ibid.*, at pp. 163–164 (paragraphs 8.2 and 8.3).   [48] *Ibid.*, at p. 164 (paragraph 8.6).

[49] *Ibid.* See, also, F. Fontanelli, 'The Invocation of the Exception of Non-performance: A Case-Study on the Role and Application of General Principles of International Law of Contractual Origin', *Cambridge JICL*, 1 (2012), 119–136. This article offers an interesting analysis of this principle. First of all, it approaches the principle as *lex specialis*, to be invoked where there is a gap in the rules of international law applicable between the parties (*ibid.*, at 128). The author submits (*ibid.*, at 130) that the *exceptio* could fill gaps both in the law of treaties and, to a greater degree, in the law of State responsibility: it focuses more on the legality of a party's reaction to non-performance than upon the question of the continuance of the parties' contractual obligations.

[50] *Supra* n. 13.

[51] Counter-Memorial of Greece, Vol. I, *supra* n. 46, at pp. 164–165 (paragraph 8.7).

[52] *Ibid.*, at pp. 165–166 (paragraph 8.10) and at pp. 174–177 (paragraph 8.27).

engagement of the non-performed obligation in the context of this case.[53] Suspension under Article 60 VCLT, by contrast, suspends the execution of the obligations of the treaty for both parties, with termination putting an end to them definitively. This is why Greece went on to claim before the Court that '[i]t would be paradoxical that the victim of a treaty breach has no choice but to suspend or terminate it'.[54] The result of the application of the *exceptio* is different: the treaty will remain in force between the parties but the injured party will be able to withhold the execution of those of its own obligations which are synallagmatic to the ones not performed by the other party.

The *exceptio* is also different from countermeasures, as it is a specific feature of certain mutual or synallagmatic obligations and not a general circumstance precluding wrongfulness, as explained by Special Rapporteur on State Responsibility James Crawford.[55] Furthermore, in cases of the withholding of performance under the principle *inadimplenti non est adimplendum*, the requirement of proportionality is substituted by a more specific criterion, namely the typically synallagmatic principle of *quid pro quo* (*corrispettivo*).[56] The *exceptio* is based on the principle of reciprocity and may, moreover, be invoked at any time, even during judicial or arbitral proceedings, without giving prior notice of default to the non-performing party.[57] The *exceptio* is not a self-standing provision included in the Vienna Convention, nor does it form part of the provision on material breach in Article 60 VCLT. Ultimately, it is characterised by the flexibility inherent in reciprocal obligations: it affords an opportunity for the injured party to use the defence offered in case of the breach of a treaty obligation not only as an immediate response to the wrongdoing but also subsequently as a defence during proceedings initiated by the wrongdoer.[58]

---

[53] *Ibid.*, at pp. 167–168 (paragraph 8.13).   [54] *Ibid.*, at pp. 166–167 (paragraph 8.11).

[55] International Law Commission, Draft Articles on Responsibility of States for Internationally Wrongful Acts, with Commentaries: *YbILC* (2001–II), Part Two, 72; cited in Counter-Memorial of Greece, Vol. I, *supra* n. 46, at pp. 170–171 (paragraph 8.17). Fontanelli, however, is of the view that the strictly synallagmatic character of this principle narrows its legal structure. He explains that *exceptio* is seldom dependent on the link of synallagma – all contracts are reciprocal – and is more frequently reliant on a requirement of minimum gravity of the breach. In essence the *exceptio* relieves the aggravated non-performing party from his/hers contractual responsibility: *supra* n. 49, at 131.

[56] Counter-Memorial of Greece, Vol. I, *supra* n. 46, at p. 171 (paragraph 8.19).

[57] ICSID Tribunal, *Klöckner v. Cameroon*, Award of 21 Oct. 1983, 14 ILR 211 (as cited in Counter-Memorial of Greece, *ibid.*, at pp. 172–173 (paragraph 8.22)).

[58] Counter-Memorial of Greece, Vol. I, *supra* n. 46, at pp. 173–174 (paragraph 8.25).

For its part, the FYROM doubted whether the *exceptio* could be characterised as a general principle of international law. Furthermore, it rejected the argument that its own obligations under the Interim Accord were to be regarded as synallagmatic with Greece's obligation in Article 11(1) of the Accord. It also did not accept that the *exceptio* could justify non-performance under the law of State responsibility.[59] In short, Article 60 VCLT provides the set of rules relating to material breaches of treaties and the *exceptio* is not recognised under the law of State responsibility. In order to meet these points, Greece found it necessary to modify the argument that it had originally advanced involving reliance on the *exceptio* exclusively.

The Court observed that there had been an evolution of the argument of Greece. Its ultimate position before the Court – that any disregard of obligations under the Interim Accord could be justified as a response to a material breach of the Interim Accord – contrasted with its initial position 'that it was not seeking to suspend the Interim Accord in whole or in part pursuant to the 1969 Vienna Convention'.[60] Greece was now asserting that 'partial suspension' of the Accord was justified under Article 60 VCLT because of the materiality of the breaches of the FYROM.[61] It accepted that certain procedural requirements – from Article 65 VCLT – obtained in this event but argued that if a State is suspending part of a treaty 'in answer to another party … alleging its violation', *ex ante* notice is not required.[62]

Greece also made the argument that any disregard of obligations under the Interim Accord could be justified as a countermeasure.[63] On this front, too, the Court noted that Greece's position had 'evolved' during the proceedings: 'Initially', said the Court, Greece 'stated that it did not claim that any objection to the [FYROM's] admission to NATO was justified as a countermeasure', whereas it later adopted the position that its 'supposed objection would fulfil the requirements for countermeasures'.[64] Greece described its stance toward the defence of countermeasures as 'doubly subsidiary', which the Court understood to mean 'that it would play a role only if the Court found [Greece] to be in breach of the Interim Accord and if it concluded that the *exceptio* did not preclude the wrongfulness of [Greece's] conduct'.[65] On that basis, it

---

[59] *Application of the Interim Accord of 13 September 1995, supra* n. 18, at pp. 679–680 (paragraphs 115–117).
[60] *Ibid.*, at p. 681 (paragraph 118).   [61] *Ibid.*   [62] *Ibid.*
[63] *Ibid.*, at p. 682 (paragraph 120).   [64] *Ibid.*   [65] *Ibid.*

proceeded to argue the defence of countermeasures in terms of Article 49 ASR.[66]

The Court analysed Greece's allegations relating to breaches of various provisions of the Interim Accord by FYROM. It concluded that Greece had only established one such breach.[67] It then addressed Greece's contention that the *exceptio* principle precluded the Court from finding that Greece had breached its own obligations under Article 11(1) of the Interim Accord. According to the Court, since Greece had failed 'to establish that the conditions which it has itself asserted would be necessary for the application of the *exceptio* have been satisfied in this case' – namely, the prior breach of a synallagmatic obligation – it was unnecessary for the Court to determine whether that doctrine forms part of contemporary international law.[68] As for the breach by the FYROM that it had found earlier,[69] the Court was of the view that this 'incident' could not 'be regarded as a material breach within the meaning of Article 60 of the 1969 Vienna Convention'.[70] Additionally, 'the Court considers that [Greece] has failed to establish that the action it took in 2008 in connection with the [FYROM's] application to NATO was a response to the breach of Article 7, paragraph 2, approximately four years earlier. Accordingly, the Court does not accept that [Greece's] action was capable of falling within Article 60 of the 1969 Vienna Convention'.[71]

In relation to the claim of countermeasures, it will be recalled that Greece had ultimately argued that its objection to FYROM's admission to NATO could be justified as a proportionate countermeasure in response to breaches of the Interim Accord by the FYROM.[72] However, in the light of the breach of only one provision of the Interim Accord by FYROM, the Court rejected Greece's claim that its objection to FYROM's admission to NATO could be justified as a countermeasure: the Court was not persuaded that Greece's objection 'was taken for the purpose of achieving the cessation of the [FYROM's] use of the symbol' prohibited by the

---

[66] *Ibid.*, at p. 682 (paragraphs 121–122).

[67] *Ibid.*, at p. 690 (paragraph 161) (Greece 'has demonstrated that the Applicant used the symbol prohibited by Article 7, paragraph 2, of the Interim Accord in 2004'). Art. 7(2) of the Interim Accord provides: 'Upon entry into force of this Interim Accord, the Party of the Second Part shall cease to use in any way the symbol in all its forms displayed on its national flag prior to such entry into force': *supra* n. 43.

[68] *Application of the Interim Accord of 13 September 1995*, *supra* n. 18, at p. 690 (paragraphs 161).

[69] *Supra* n. 67.

[70] *Application of the Interim Accord of 13 September 1995*, *supra* n. 18, at p. 691 (paragraphs 163).

[71] *Ibid.* [72] *Supra* n. 66.

Interim Accord.[73] It therefore found that there was no reason for it to consider any of the arguments advanced by the parties with respect to the law governing countermeasures with the additional justifications submitted by Greece meeting with no success.[74]

***

As the preceding discussion and the relevant case law demonstrate, the legal character of the exception of non-performance in international – and, for that matter, in national – law remains very unclear. Notwithstanding scholarly attempts such as those of Crawford and Olleson to offer an explanation of its complex legal character, and notwithstanding the international case law brought forward for review in this chapter, the present author is of the view that the place of the *exceptio* in the modern law of treaties is not well defined or articulated. Even the elementary question as to whether the *exceptio* is an institution of the law of treaties or of the law of State responsibility appears to remain a point of controversy – as is intimated in Judge de Castro's definition of the *exceptio non adimplenti* as having its roots in the breach of rights and obligations deriving from an agreement.[75]

It is also apparent that, in *Application of the Interim Accord of 13 September 1995*, the argument based on the *exceptio* was quite extensive, as opposed to the *Case Concerning Oil Platforms* and *Diversion of Water from the Meuse*, where it assumed a much more subsidiary role. In all other cases that we have examined, it was only individual judges who, in their separate and dissenting opinions, analysed the meaning and operation of this principle. Among these was Judge Simma, who in his Separate Opinion in *Application of the Interim Accord of 13 September 1995*, declared the 'pre-Vienna Convention *exceptio*' dead in light of the emergence of the sophisticated and mature Article 60 VCLT.[76] This amounted to a departure from his earlier position that such an exception could fill the gap between material and non-material breaches.[77] On reflection, he regarded Article 60 VCLT as 'truly exhaustive, that is, totally eclipsing

---

[73] *Application of the Interim Accord of 13 September 1995, supra* n. 18, at p. 692 (paragraph 164) (i.e. Art. 7(2) thereof: *supra* n. 67).

[74] *Application of the Interim Accord of 13 September 1995, supra* n. 18, at p. 692 (paragraph 164).

[75] *Supra* n. 31 and n. 32.

[76] *Application of the Interim Accord of 13 September 1995, supra* n. 18, at p. 706 (paragraph 26) (Separate Opinion of Judge Simma).

[77] B. Simma, 'Reflections on Article 60 of the Vienna Convention on the Law of Treaties and Its Background in General International Law', *Österreichische Zeitschrift für öffentliches Recht*, 20 (1970), 5–83, at 59–60.

the earlier non-written law of the functional synallagma operating behind treaties'.[78] He favours the view that, at present, non-material breaches in the law of treaties are remedied by recourse to countermeasures.

The present author agrees that a plausible case can be made that the *exceptio* has been subsumed by Article 60 VCLT. Yet, even if the *exceptio* is indeed dead, it has died a heroic death, as it has left in place the heritage of reciprocal (*do ut des*) synallagmatic obligations,[79] which has informed the foundations for material breach in the modern law of treaties. At the same time, an argument may possibly be made to the effect that the *exceptio* is not entirely dead and that it may still perform a useful role in cases of breaches of treaty obligation which do not lend themselves to be remedied either by the law of treaties or by recourse to the measures available under the law of State responsibility. In particular, there may still be circumstances in which it is appropriate for one party to withhold performance of its own obligation in response to a failure by the other party to perform a reciprocal or interdependent obligation, even though recourse to the codified justifications may not be permissible. Effectively, the State in question would be arguing that the occasion for its own performance has not yet arisen. There seems no doubt that a treaty might expressly permit such a response,[80] so the key question is whether the *exceptio* might be relied upon to render it permissible by implication. Plainly, the answer will depend critically upon the interpretation of the treaty in question.

3   Justification of Non-performance under the Codified Law of Treaties and of State Responsibility

The thorny issue concerning the relationship between the law of treaties and the law of State responsibility arose during the codification of both

---

[78] *Application of the Interim Accord of 13 September 1995, supra* n. 18, at pp. 699–700 (paragraph 11) (Separate Opinion of Judge Simma).

[79] B. Simma and C. Tams, 'Article 60 (1969)' in O. Corten and P. Klein (eds.), *The Vienna Conventions on the Law of Treaties: A Commentary* (Vol. I) (Oxford: Oxford University Press, 2011), pp. 1351–1381, at p. 1354.

[80] A possible example – at least on one interpretation – is Art. 20(4) of the 1992 United Nations Convention on Biological Diversity, 1760 UNTS 79 ('[t]he extent to which developing country Parties will effectively implement their commitments under the Convention will depend on the effective implementation by developed country Parties of their commitments under the Convention related to financial resources and transfer of technology and will take fully into account the fact that economic and social development and eradication of poverty are the first and overriding priorities of the developing country Parties').

subjects, in connection with the provisions concerning the suspension and termination of treaties and the circumstances precluding wrongfulness. There are many cases, including the *Case Concerning the Air Service Agreement of 27 March 1946 between the United States of America and France*[81] and, most notably, *Case Concerning the Rainbow Warrior Affair*[82] and the *Gabčikovo-Nagymaros* case,[83] which are excellent illustrations of the continuing misconceptions regarding these two pillars of international law. To recapitulate, countermeasures and termination or suspension under Article 60 VCLT are both responses to breaches of a treaty and, in the latter case, perhaps a modern manifestation of the *exceptio*. By contrast, other justifications for non-performance, as codified in Articles 61 and 62 VCLT as well as in ASR on circumstances precluding wrongfulness, are not grounded exclusively in the internal dynamics of the duty-relationships existing between States. They depend rather upon invocations of some additional factor or contingency external to this relationship, such as a change of circumstances or collateral impact upon essential interests not explicitly envisaged by the particular duties in issue.

3.1 Breach of Obligations by Other Party

Far from clarifying the uncertainties here, the relevant case law seems if anything to have muddled the question further. The *Air Service Agreement Case* concerned a bilateral Air Service Agreement of 27 March 1946 between France and the United States providing for civil air flights between these two countries.[84] In April 1960, the parties then entered into an Exchange of Notes relating to this Agreement, authorising designated American carriers to fly to Paris from the West

---

[81] *Case Concerning the Air Service Agreement of 27 March 1946 between the United States of America and France*, XVIII RIAA 417–493. See, further, L. Fisler Damrosch, 'Retaliation or Arbitration – or Both? The 1978 U.S.-France Aviation Dispute', *AJIL*, 74 (1980), 785–807.

[82] *Case Concerning the Difference between New Zealand and France Concerning the Interpretation or Application of Two Agreements, Concluded on 9 July 1986 between the Two States and Which Related to the Problems Arising from the Rainbow Warrior Affair*, XX RIAA 215–284.

[83] *Case Concerning the Gabčíkovo-Nagymaros Project, supra* n. 23. See, further, R. Lefeber, 'The Gabčikovo-Nagymaros Project and the Law of State Responsibility', *Leiden JIL*, 11 (1998), 609–623, and M. Fitzmaurice, 'The *Gabčikovo-Nagymaros* Case: The Law of Treaties', *Leiden JIL*, 11 (1998), 321–344.

[84] 139 UNTS 114.

Coast of the United States *via* London. In 1978, Pan American World Airlines (PanAm), a designated carrier, announced its resumption of a West Coast-London-Paris service, but with a change of gauge in London, where passengers would transfer from a larger to a smaller plane. However, in March 1978, France objected to this arrangement on the basis that it constituted a breach of the 1946 Agreement (which permitted certain gauge changes within the territory of the two parties but contained no provision concerning such changes in the territory of a third State).[85]

A further French objection was issued in May 1978. PanAm continued to operate its service, but on 3 May 1978, one of its Boeing 727 aircraft was surrounded by French police after its arrival at Orly Airport in Paris, with passengers and freight not allowed to disembark. Thereafter, PanAm suspended its flights. The following day, the United States proposed that the dispute be referred to arbitration on the basis of a *compromis*.[86] In the meantime, the United States, in contravention of the 1946 Agreement, had triggered a procedure which led to the issuance of an Order under the Economic Regulations of the Civil Aeronautics Board prohibiting flights by French-designated carriers to the West Coast of the United States from Paris *via* Montreal so long as the French ban on PanAm flights continued. However, following the signing of the *compromis*, this prohibition was not actually implemented.

In its arbitral award, the Tribunal decided that carriers of the United States were indeed entitled under the 1946 Agreement to operate with a change of gauge in London. It is useful to reflect a little further on the argumentation put forward before the arbitral tribunal that led to this decision. In its pleadings, the United States indicated that it considered the termination or suspension of the bilateral treaty as the ultimate response to breach of a treaty:

> If a trivial or a nonmaterial breach gave the aggravated party an excuse to terminate all treaty obligations, the rule *pacta sunt servanda* would seriously be impaired. However, where the sanction to be invoked is a simple reciprocal withdrawal of rights, the rule of proportionality provides an adequate safeguard.[87]

---

[85] The relevant provision is section 6 of the Annex: *ibid.*

[86] As recounted by the Arbitral Tribunal in *Case Concerning the Air Service Agreement of 27 March 1946, supra* n. 81, at p. 420 (paragraph 4–5).

[87] US Memorial, 1978 Digest of U.S. Practice in International Law, Dept. of State Publication No. 9162 (1980), p. 772.

This is an oblique statement which can be interpreted in various ways. The reference to reciprocity might suggest an invocation of the *exceptio* of non-performance. On the other hand, the question of proportionality might indicate that the United States considered the use of counter-measures an appropriate response in the event of a non-material breach but did not exclude recourse to a possible suspension or termination of a treaty in the event of a material breach. While both France and the United States in their pleadings attempted to differentiate in principle between measures anchored in the law of treaties and those rooted in the law of State responsibility, there was some confusion as to the precise legal characterisation of the measures that were adopted.[88]

The arbitral tribunal's decision did not dwell on the legal differences between these two regimes. The tribunal focused on two points: first, the principle of the legality of countermeasures and, second, the limits of such measures in light of either the existence of machinery for negotiation or of a mechanism for judicial settlement. As to the first point, the tribunal confirmed the legality of countermeasures under international law:

> If a situation arises which, in one State's view, results in the violation of an international obligation by another State, the first State is entitled, within the limits set by the general rules of international law pertaining to the use of armed force, to affirm its rights through 'counter-measures'.[89]

The tribunal also stated that it was of no interest in this case to

> introduce various doctrinal distinctions and adopt diversified terminology dependent on various criteria, in particular whether it is the obligation allegedly breached which is the subject of the counter-measures or whether the latter involve another obligation, and whether or not all the obligations under consideration pertain to the same convention.[90]

What was of crucial importance, the tribunal confirmed, was the substantive requirement that countermeasures must be 'equivalent' and 'proportionate'.[91] Given the lack of evidence submitted by the parties, the most that it could say was that the US action did not seem to be clearly disproportionate. Furthermore, and this is with respect to the second

---

[88] For example, France appeared to argue that resort either to countermeasures or to suspension under the law of treaties was conditioned by a requirement of necessity: *Case Concerning the Air Service Agreement of 27 March 1946, supra* n. 81, at pp. 427–428 (paragraphs 17–18).

[89] *Ibid.*, at p. 443 (paragraph 81).　　[90] *Ibid.*, at p. 443 (paragraph 82).

[91] *Ibid.*, at pp. 443–444 (paragraph 83).

point adverted to earlier, the tribunal explained that contemporary international law does not endorse the view that when a party enters negotiations to resolve a(n) (ongoing) dispute, it is automatically prohibited from adopting countermeasures, especially when such countermeasures are accompanied by an offer for a procedure that promises the possibility of accelerating the solution of the dispute.[92] It is only the actual setting up of an arbitral tribunal or actual recourse to judicial proceedings that leads to disappearance of the possibility of countermeasures.

The arbitral award in the *Case Concerning the Rainbow Warrior Affair* is equally inconclusive with respect to solving the question concerning the relationship between the law of treaties and the law of State responsibility (i.e. countermeasures). The agreement in question concerned the detention of two officers of the French Secret Service on Hao, an island in the Pacific Ocean. They were detained there as part of a prison sentence that had been imposed by a criminal court in New Zealand for the bombing of a civilian vessel, the *Rainbow Warrior*, in Auckland harbour in July 1985. The position was taken by France that both officers had to be evacuated from the island before the expiry of the agreed term of three years, owing in one case to a medical emergency and in the other to personal matters (as well as to medical emergency). New Zealand argued that the evacuation of both officers and France's prevention of a consultation with a New Zealand medical doctor failed to follow the terms of the agreement.

The parties' arguments focused respectively on the law of treaties (New Zealand) and the law of State responsibility (France). New Zealand was of the view that the actions of France should be analysed in light of the provisions relating to the fundamental change of circumstances as enshrined in the VCLT.[93] In contrast, France's pleadings were based on circumstances precluding wrongfulness – that is, of *force majeure* and distress.[94] The arbitral tribunal took note of the provisions of Article 60 VCLT (material breach) as well as Article 26 VCLT (*pacta sunt servanda*).[95] It was primarily concerned with the question of whether there had been a breach of an international obligation – as well as with the extent of the breach. The tribunal explained that the alleged breach of the obligation, which had its roots in the law of treaties, did not in principle preclude the application of the law of State responsibility: after all, this set

---

[92] *Ibid.*, at p. 445 (paragraph 91).
[93] *Case Concerning the Rainbow Warrior Affair, supra* n. 82, at pp. 249–250 (paragraph 73).
[94] *Ibid.*, at pp. 250–251 (paragraph 74).   [95] *Ibid.*, at p. 251 (paragraph 75).

of rules relates to breaches of international obligation regardless of their source, 'since in the international law field there is no distinction between contractual and tortious responsibility, so that any violation by a State of any obligation, of whatever origin, gives rise to State responsibility and consequently, to the duty of reparation'.[96] Ultimately, however, the defences invoked by France were not, on the facts, sufficient to preclude the wrongfulness of its conduct.

The issue concerning the relationship between the material breach of a treaty and the responsibility of the wrongdoing State featured more extensively in the judgment of the International Court of Justice in the *Gabčikovo-Nagymaros* case in September 1997.[97] For that reason, the case deserves detailed analysis. The dispute concerned the construction of a system of dams and locks in the Bratislava-Budapest section of the Danube River, on the basis of the 1977 Treaty Concerning the Construction of and Operation of the Gabčikovo-Nagymaros System of Locks (which did not contain any clause on termination).[98] The portion of the river in question formed a natural frontier between Hungary and the Slovak Republic, with Cunovo and Gabčikovo located on Slovak territory and Nagymaros situated on Hungarian territory. The system's objective was to achieve the broad utilisation of natural resources of the Bratislava-Budapest section of the Danube for the development of water resources, energy, transport, agriculture and other sectors of the national economy of both parties. The parties were mindful of the protection of the environment and of the upholding of the Danube's water quality when erecting the system of locks.[99] The whole system was intended to constitute 'a single, operational system of works', with the work based on a principle of joint management and financing in which both parties participated in equal measure.[100]

The subsequent collapse of communism prompted negative attitudes towards the project, however. Above all, doubt was expressed about its economic viability as well as its effects on the environment. This resulted in the decision by Hungary to suspend the project in May, July and October 1989.[101] In view of these actions, Czechoslovakia adopted

[96] *Ibid.*   [97] *Case Concerning the Gabčíkovo-Nagymaros Project, supra* n. 23.
[98] Reproduced in ILM, 32 (1993), 1247–1258.
[99] In particular, Arts. 15, 19 and 20 of the 1977 Treaty relating to water quality, nature protection and fisheries respectively: *Case Concerning the Gabčíkovo-Nagymaros Project, supra* n. 23, at p. 36 (paragraph 41).
[100] *Ibid.*, at pp. 13–24 (paragraphs 10–20).
[101] For further details of these suspensions (and their respective durations), see *ibid.*, at p. 35 (paragraph 22).

a unilateral solution which became known as 'Variant C'. This solution included the construction at Cunovo of an overflow dam and of a levee connecting that dam to the south bank of the bypass canal. The provisional solution was followed by a decision by the Government of Czechoslovakia to continue the construction of the Gabčikovo Project. In November 1991, work began on Variant C, and in May 1992, the Government of Hungary transmitted a Note Verbale to the Government of Czechoslovakia terminating the 1977 Treaty.[102] Czechoslovakia proceeded to dam the River Danube in October 1992,[103] and after Slovakia became an independent State on 1 January 1993,[104] Hungary and the Slovak Republic agreed to submit the case to the Court in April 1993.[105]

In its written pleadings before the Court, Hungary contended *inter alia* that Czechoslovakia had violated several provisions of the 1977 Treaty by refusing to enter into negotiations with Hungary to adopt the Joint Contractual Plan so as to include new developments in environmental protection. However, these provisions were specifically designed to oblige the parties to take appropriate measures necessary for the protection of water quality, of nature and of fishing interests on a continuous basis. The view was expressed in the judgment that while both parties in principle indicated a willingness to undertake further research,[106] Czechoslovakia refused to interrupt the work on Variant C, which (according to Hungary) would prejudice the outcome of negotiations. Hungary relied on Variant C as a basis for invoking the material breach of the treaty by Czechoslovakia.

The facts of this case proved to be the most fertile ground for analysing the convoluted relationship between material breach of treaty, countermeasures and even, according to Crawford and Olleson, the exception of non-performance. As they argue, this question 'arose in a rather specific and unusual form'.[107] This exception can only be applied in the case of an interrelated treaty obligation, where its application, Crawford and

---

[102] With effect from 25 May 1992: *ibid.*, at pp. 25–27 (paragraph 23). See, further, Text of Hungarian Declaration Terminating Treaty, ILM, 32 (1993), 1259–1290.

[103] *Case Concerning the Gabčikovo-Nagymaros Project, supra* n. 23, at pp. 25–27 (paragraph 23).

[104] *Ibid.*, at p. 27 (paragraph 25).

[105] By virtue of the Special Agreement for Submission to the International Court of Justice of the Differences between the Republic of Hungary and the Slovak Republic concerning the Gabčikovo-Nagymaros Project: *ibid.*, at p. 27 (paragraph 25). The Special Agreement was jointly notified to the International Court of Justice in a letter of July 1993 by Hungary and the Slovak Republic: *ibid.*, at p. 10 (paragraph 1).

[106] *Ibid.*, at pp. 47–51 (paragraphs 61–67). [107] Crawford and Olleson, *supra* n. 4, at 64.

Olleson suggest, may possibly overlap with the law of countermeasures.[108] It was found by the Court that Czechoslovakia had only violated the Treaty when it diverted the waters of the Danube into the bypass canal in October 1992.[109] However, in merely constructing the works which led to the operation of Variant C, Czechoslovakia had not acted unlawfully.[110] It was held that the notification of termination of the 1977 Treaty in May 1992 by Hungary was therefore premature, since at that time Czechoslovakia had not yet breached the 1977 Treaty.[111] It was also concluded that Hungary was not entitled, at the time it did, to invoke any such a breach of this Treaty as a ground for terminating it.[112]

Moreover, Hungary's declaration purporting to terminate the 1977 Treaty was not, the Court found, undertaken in accordance with the principle of good faith.[113] In fact, both parties agreed that Articles 65 to 67 VCLT, if not specifically codifying customary international law, at least generally reflected it and contained certain procedural principles that were, all told, based on the principle of good faith.[114] By its own conduct, Hungary had prejudiced its right to terminate the 1977 Treaty. It was forcefully asserted in the judgment that 'this would still have been the case even if Czechoslovakia, by the time of the purported termination, had violated a provision essential to the accomplishment of the object and purpose of the Treaty'.[115] Thus, the Court applied the rules and procedures relating to material breach in a very rigorous manner, by insisting on the observance of procedural as well of substantive requirements. The judgment indicates that the Court strongly supported the principle of the stability of treaties and that it approached all rules concerning the possibility of a unilateral termination, including those relating to material breach, with great caution.

In addition to this aspect of the judgment, the Court made several remarks on the relationship between the law of treaties and the law of State responsibility. In particular, it stated, in line with the approach of the ILC, that:

> [a] determination of whether a convention is or is not in force, and whether it has or has not been properly suspended or denounced, is to be made pursuant to the law of treaties. On the other hand, an evaluation of the extent to which the suspension or denunciation of a convention,

---

[108] *Ibid.*

[109] *Case Concerning the Gabčíkovo-Nagymaros Project, supra* n. 23, at p. 66 (paragraph 108).

[110] *Ibid.*, at pp. 79–80 (paragraph 146).   [111] *Ibid.*, at p. 66 (paragraph 108).

[112] *Ibid.*, at p. 76 (paragraph 132).   [113] *Ibid.*, at pp. 78–79 (paragraph 142).

[114] *Ibid.*, at pp. 66–67 (paragraph 109).   [115] *Ibid.*, at p. 67 (paragraph 110).

seen as incompatible with the law of treaties, involves the responsibility of the State which proceeded to it, is to be made under the law of State responsibility. Thus the Vienna Convention ... on the Law of Treaties confines itself to defining – in a limitative manner – the conditions in which a treaty may lawfully be denounced or suspended; while the effects of a denunciation or suspension seen as not meeting those conditions are, on the contrary, expressly excluded from the scope of the Convention by operation of Article 73. It is moreover well established that, when a State has committed an internationally wrongful act, its international responsibility is to be involved whatever the nature of the obligation it has failed to respect.[116]

Hungary's pleadings appeared to assimilate the arguments based on the law of treaties with those based on State responsibility in certain respects. For example, necessity was advanced as a ground for terminating a treaty, whereas its proper place is in the law of State responsibility.[117] Hungary also argued in its written pleadings that the termination of the 1977 Treaty operated as a countermeasure in response to the unilateral modification of the Treaty by Czechoslovakia.[118] A further argument advanced by Hungary was to the effect that the termination of the 1977 Treaty was not only justified by the plea of material breach by Czechoslovakia but also permissible on the grounds of Czechoslovakia's violation of environmental obligations under general international law. The Court, however, held as follows:

> As to that part of Hungary's argument which was based on other treaties and general rules of international law, the Court is of the view that it is only a material breach of a treaty itself, by a State party to that treaty, which entitles the other party to rely on it as a ground for terminating the treaty. The violation of other treaty rules or rules of general international law may justify the taking of certain measures, including countermeasures, by an injured State, but it does not constitute a ground for termination under the law of treaties.[119]

It may be noted that Crawford and Olleson argue that the Court's reasoning was incorrect concerning the suspension of the 1977 Treaty by Hungary: they argue that, in fact, the Treaty was not suspended – in other words, that the requirements of Article 65 VCLT were not fulfilled – and that Hungary never purported to suspend it and was not entitled to do so under the law of treaties.[120] They introduce a distinction between the

---

[116] *Ibid.*, at p. 38 (paragraph 47).   [117] As to which see Section 3.3.
[118] See Text of Hungarian Declaration Terminating Treaty, *supra* n. 102, at 1285–1288.
[119] *Case Concerning the Gabčíkovo-Nagymaros Project, supra* n. 23, at p. 65 (paragraph 106).
[120] Crawford and Olleson, *supra* n. 4, at 65.

suspension of the 1977 Treaty and Hungary's 'unwillingness' to comply with some of its provisions through suspension of some of the works required by the Treaty,[121] arguing that there is a difference between suspension of a treaty and the refusal to comply with the terms of a treaty.[122] In their view, the legally justified suspension of a treaty places the treaty in a sort of limbo.[123] Conduct inconsistent with the terms of a treaty in force – even if justified as a countermeasure – does not have the effect of suspending the treaty: the treaty continues to apply and the party resorting to countermeasures must continue to justify its own non-performance by reference to the criteria governing countermeasures throughout the period of its non-compliance.[124]

***

It would appear from these cases that the International Court of Justice has missed several opportunities to explain the daunting and vexed relationship between the *exceptio non adimplenti contractus*, material breach and countermeasures.[125] The *Gabčikovo-Nagymaros Case* has prompted a comment lamenting 'the unwillingness of the Court to further examine a question so vital for the continuous and effective functioning of the international legal order',[126] an omission that this author also finds regrettable. It may be recalled once more that the case law examined here indicates that States are far from certain which legal arguments to rely upon in cases of a breach – those arising from Article 60 VCLT or countermeasures. The present author therefore suggests that the theoretical and neat classifications of the ILC and many scholars have not been faithfully reflected in the practice of States and still less in the relevant case law.

---

[121] *Ibid.*   [122] *Ibid.*   [123] *Ibid.*

[124] *Ibid.*, at 66. Where the treaty is suspended under Art. 60 VCLT, *supra* n. 1, then it may be said to come into a sort of abeyance, whereas under the *exceptio*, its status as a source of obligation is not really affected at all – it may simply be that one party is arguing that, on the proper interpretation of the instrument, its own performance has not yet fallen due on account of the other party's failure to perform its correspondent or interdependent obligation. Presumably, also, the party invoking the *exceptio* will remain bound to perform any of its own obligations that cannot be considered interdependent with the obligation breached by the other side (though, admittedly, this may be difficult to distinguish in practice from the situation where a treaty is suspended only in part on account of material breach, as envisaged by Art. 60 VCLT).

[125] *Supra* n. 18.

[126] K. Wellens, 'The Court's Judgment in the *Case Concerning Gabčikovo-Nagymaros Project (Hungary/Slovakia)*: Some Preliminary Reflections' in K. Wellens (ed.), *International Law: Theory and Practice: Essays in Honour of Eric Suy* (The Hague/Boston/London: Martinus Nijhoff Publishers, 1998), pp. 765–800, at p. 781.

3.2 Other Justifications of Non-performance

This part of the chapter deals with the existence of 'exceptional circumstances' that States can invoke to avoid, or extinguish, their treaty obligations, as drawn from the VCLT and the ASR. The following doctrines that may serve this purpose will be analysed: supervening impossibility of performance (Article 61 VCLT),[127] fundamental change of circumstances (Article 62 VCLT),[128] *force majeure* (Article 23 ASR)[129] and necessity (Article 25 ASR).[130]

---

[127] Art. 61 VCLT, *supra* n. 1, provides:

1. A party may invoke the impossibility of performing a treaty as a ground for terminating or withdrawing from it if the impossibility results from the permanent disappearance or destruction of an object indispensable for the execution of the treaty. If the impossibility is temporary, it may be invoked only as a ground for suspending the operation of the treaty.
2. Impossibility of performance may not be invoked by a party as a ground for terminating, withdrawing from or suspending the operation of a treaty if the impossibility is the result of a breach by that party either of an obligation under the treaty or of any other international obligation owed to any other party to the treaty.

[128] Art. 62 VCLT, *supra* n. 1, provides:

1. A fundamental change of circumstances which has occurred with regard to those existing at the time of the conclusion of a treaty, and which was not foreseen by the parties, may not be invoked as a ground for terminating or withdrawing from the treaty unless:
   a. the existence of those circumstances constituted an essential basis of the consent of the parties to be bound by the treaty; and
   b. the effect of the change is radically to transform the extent of obligations still to be performed under the treaty.
2. A fundamental change of circumstances may not be invoked as a ground for terminating or withdrawing from a treaty:
   a. if the treaty establishes a boundary; or
   b. if the fundamental change is the result of a breach by the party invoking it either of an obligation under the treaty or of any other international obligation owed to any other party to the treaty.
3. If, under the foregoing paragraphs, a party may invoke a fundamental change of circumstances as a ground for terminating or withdrawing from a treaty it may also invoke the change as a ground for suspending the operation of the treaty.

[129] Art. 23 ASR, *supra* n. 3, provides:

1. The wrongfulness of an act of a State not in conformity with an international obligation of that State is precluded if the act is due to *force majeure*, that is the occurrence of an irresistible force or of an unforeseen event, beyond the control of the State, making it materially impossible in the circumstances to perform the obligation.
2. Paragraph 1 does not apply if:
   (a) the situation of *force majeure* is due, either alone or in combination with other factors, to the conduct of the State invoking it; or
   (b) the State has assumed the risk of that situation occurring.

[130] Art. 25 ASR, *supra* n. 3, provides:

3.2.1   Supervening Impossibility of Performance

The doctrine of supervening impossibility of performance has generally received comparatively little attention when compared to fundamental change of circumstances.[131] Both Special Rapporteurs Gerald Fitzmaurice and Humphrey Waldock presented their views on this matter, and subsequent ILC discussion addressed the questions concerning how widely to define the notion of 'impossibility', how to distinguish it in turn from fundamental change of circumstances and how to differentiate it from the law of State responsibility.[132] Fitzmaurice's examples of this doctrine referred to the extinction of the physical object to which the treaty related, such as the disappearance of an island owing to the subsidence in the seabed; the permanent drying up of a river; the destruction of a railway by an earthquake; or the destruction of a plant, installation, canal, lighthouse, etc.[133] For Waldock, the doctrine of supervening impossibility of performance, like that concerning fundamental change of circumstances, belongs to the cohort of reasons available to States for terminating or suspending a treaty resulting from events unrelated to the conduct of the parties (in contrast to those which were the result of such conduct which produced a material breach of a treaty).[134]

The ILC's attempt to make a significant distinction between the law of treaties and the law of State responsibility on the question of supervening impossibility of performance ultimately proved inconclusive.[135]

1. Necessity may not be invoked by a State as a ground for precluding the wrongfulness of an act not in conformity with an international obligation of that State unless the act:
   (a) is the only way for the State to safeguard an essential interest against a grave and imminent peril; and
   (b) does not seriously impair an essential interest of the State or States towards which the obligation exists, or of the international community as a whole.
2. In any case, necessity may not be invoked by a State as a ground for precluding wrongfulness if:
   (a) the international obligation in question excludes the possibility of invoking necessity; or
   (b) the State has contributed to the situation of necessity.

[131] For an in-depth discussion, see M. Fitzmaurice, 'Exceptional Circumstances and Treaty Commitments' in D. Hollis (ed.), *The Oxford Guide to Treaties* (Oxford: Oxford University Press, 2012), pp. 605–633.

[132] See ILC Report, *YbILC* (1966–II), 254 (paragraph 5). See, also, ILC Report, *YbILC* (1963–II), 207 (paragraph 4).

[133] Fitzmaurice, Second Report on the Law of Treaties, *supra* n. 8, at 50.

[134] H. Waldock, Second Report on the Law of Treaties, *YbILC* (1963–II), 78 (paragraph 1).

[135] Official Records, 1st Session, 62nd Meeting, p. 361 (paragraphs 2–5).

The Commission generally viewed supervening impossibility of performance under the rubric of *force majeure* – in other words, belonging to the realm of State responsibility rather than to the law of treaties.[136] Pierre Bodeau-Livinec and Jason Morgan-Foster have tried more recently to draw very hard and fast lines distinguishing supervening impossibility of performance from *force majeure*.[137] They have explained that Article 61 VCLT – which requires 'the permanent disappearance or destruction of an object indispensable for the execution of the treaty'[138] – 'should give rise to easier and more objective determination than *force majeure*, which is brought about by any unforeseen event in the circumstances'.[139] Furthermore, they are of the view that supervening impossibility of performance stands at the confluence of the law of treaties and of State responsibility. If it is an event which materially prevents performance, it fits within the framework of Article 61 VCLT; however, as a legal doctrine, it has been placed by the International Law Commission among the circumstances precluding wrongfulness within the realm of State responsibility.[140] The authors admit that this differentiation could result in difficulties of application, but it seems necessary 'to maintain the theoretical distinction that preserves the restrictive meaning of impossibility of performance in Article 61 [VCLT], insofar as admission of *force majeure* in the context of the Vienna Convention would have weakened the stability of treaties'.[141]

Supervening impossibility of performance under the rubric of *force majeure* was in fact pleaded before the PCIJ in two cases decided on the same day – *Case Concerning the Payment in Gold of the Brazilian Federal Loans*[142] and *Case Concerning the Payment of Various Serbian Loans Issued in France*[143] – but the Court rejected the claims in both of these

---

[136] See *YbILC* (1980–I), 3 (paragraph 8).

[137] P. Bodeau-Livinec and J. Morgan-Foster, 'Article 61 (1969)' in Corten and Klein (eds.), Vol. II, *supra* n. 79, pp. 1382–1408.

[138] *Supra* n. 127.   [139] Bodeau-Livinec and Morgan-Foster, *supra* n. 137, at p. 1397.

[140] *Supra* n. 3.

[141] Bodeau-Livinec and Morgan-Foster, *supra* n. 137, at p. 1398. At *ibid.*, and by way of example:

> a State having contributed to the disappearance of an object indispensable to a treaty could possible invoke *force majeure* if the situation was due to its conduct but essentially result from other factors; the wrongfulness of the act of the State thus excluded, the restriction of [Art.] 61(2) [VCLT] would no longer apply to it and the grounds in [Art. 61(1) VCLT] could be invoked to terminate the treaty.

[142] *Case Concerning the Payment in Gold of the Brazilian Federal Loans*: France v. Brazil, 1929 PCIJ, Series A, No. 21.

[143] *Case Concerning the Payment of Various Serbian Loans Issued in France*: France v. Serb-Croat-Slovene State, 1929 PCIJ, Series A, No. 20.

cases. In the *Brazilian Federal Loans Case*, the Government of Brazil issued three loans between the years 1909 and 1911 in the form of bearer bonds. The bonds were mainly offered for subscription in France. Although there were some discrepancies in the wording of the relevant documents, the Court ultimately interpreted all three loans to require repayment in gold francs, which had ceased to be available as such in 1914. As the French franc depreciated in value, protests arose when the bonds continued to be paid in depreciating paper currency and not in valuable gold. In 1924, the French government intervened on behalf of the bond holders and asked the Brazilian government to repay the capital of the loans and the interest due thereon, on the basis of the value of the French franc in gold at the time the bonds were issued. The Brazilian Government refused, and the case was submitted to the Court by France. In the view of the Court, '[t]he economic dislocation caused by the Great War has not, in legal principle, released the Brazilian Government from its obligations. As for gold payments, there is no impossibility because of inability to obtain gold coins, if the promise be regarded as one for the payment of gold value. The equivalent in gold value is obtainable'.[144]

With a similar set of facts before it, the Court took the same view in the *Serbian Loans Case*:

> It cannot be maintained that the war itself, despite its grave economic consequences, affected the legal obligations of the contracts between the Serbian Government and the French bond holders. The economic dislocations caused by the war did not release the debtor State, although they may present equities which doubtless will receive appropriate consideration in the negotiations and – if resorted to – the arbitral determination for which Article II of the Special Agreement provides.[145]

Although gold francs as stipulated in the contract were no longer available as gold coins *in specie*, it could be hardly be said for this reason that the obligation of the Treaty was discharged on the ground of impossibility of performance. It is interesting to note that the Court named this paragraph of its analysis *force majeure*, but further in the same paragraph, the Court talks about 'impossibility of performance' as coterminous with *force majeure*,[146] which is one more example of synergy between the law of State responsibility and the law of treaties.

---

[144] *Case Concerning the Payment in Gold of the Brazilian Federal Loans, supra* n. 142, at p. 120.

[145] *Case Concerning the Payment of Various Serbian Loans Issued in France, supra* n. 143, at pp. 39–40.

[146] *Ibid.*

Undoubtedly, the most relevant modern case applying the doctrine of supervening impossibility of performance is the *Gabčikovo-Nagymaros Case*.[147] Here, Hungary specifically sought to rely on Article 61 VCLT, arguing that the essential object of the 1977 Treaty – namely, the joint economic investment undertaken by the two parties, which was to be compatible with environmental protection – had permanently disappeared and that 'the Treaty had thus become impossible to perform'.[148] The Court, however, decided that Hungary's interpretation of supervening impossibility of performance was in conformity neither with the terms of its formulation in Article 61 VCLT nor with the intentions of the diplomatic conference that adopted the Vienna Convention.[149] The Court decided not to engage in the discussion as to whether the term 'object' in Article 61 could encompass the disappearance of a legal regime: it found, instead, that 'even if that were the case, it would have to conclude that in this instance that régime had not definitively ceased to exist'.[150] The Court pointed out – as it did repeatedly throughout its judgment – that the 1977 Treaty included provisions enabling the parties to make necessary adjustments between economic and environmental issues.[151] Moreover, the Court observed that the impossibility of joint exploitation was in fact caused by Hungary's failure to carry out most of the work for which it was responsible under the treaty. The Court relied on Article 61(2) VCLT to prohibit Hungary from invoking impossibility of performance when it resulted from a party's own breach of an obligation under a treaty.[152]

3.2.2 Fundamental Change of Circumstances

The notion that a State may terminate or suspend its treaty obligations if circumstances have changed fundamentally since the treaty entered into force – the doctrine known in international law as *rebus sic stantibus* – has received extensive attention from States, courts and scholars;[153] it also constituted a substantial part of the work of Special Rapporteurs

---

[147] *Case Concerning the Gabčikovo-Nagymaros Project, supra* n. 23.

[148] *Ibid.*, at p. 59 (paragraph 94).   [149] *Ibid.*, at p. 63 (paragraph 102).

[150] *Ibid.*, at p. 64 (paragraph 103).

[151] *Ibid.* (citing, specifically, Arts. 15, 19 and 20 of the 1977 Treaty: *supra* n. 98).

[152] *Ibid.*

[153] See, in particular, O. J. Lissitzyn, 'Treaties and Changed Circumstances (*Rebus Sic Stantibus*)', *AJIL*, 61 (1967), 895–922; G. Haraszti, 'Treaties and the Fundamental Change of Circumstances', *Hague Recueil*, 146 (1975–III), 1–93, and R. Müllerson, 'The ABM Treaty: Changed Circumstances, Extraordinary Events, Supreme Interests and International Law', *ICLQ*, 59 (2005), 509–539.

Fitzmaurice and Waldock during the ILC's codification of the law of treaties.[154] Today, it is undoubtedly considered part of customary international law,[155] which has been codified in Article 62 VCLT.[156] Nevertheless, although recognising the doctrine's existence, international tribunals have rarely applied it, so it is from this angle that we shall approach examples from the case law.

In the *Gabčikovo-Nagymaros Case*, in addition to claiming supervening impossibility of performance as discussed earlier, Hungary also identified several substantive elements which it claimed had fundamentally changed by the time of its notification to the Government of Czechoslovakia of termination of the 1977 Treaty. These elements included: (i) the notion of 'socialist integration', for which the treaty had initially been a vehicle, had since ceased to exist; (ii) the 'single and indivisible operational system', which had been substituted by a unilateral scheme; (iii) the fact that the basis of the planned joint investment had been frustrated by the emergence of both States as market economies; (iv) the change in Czechoslovakia's attitude, which turned the framework treaty into an immutable form; and, finally, (v) the transformation of a treaty consistent with 'environmental protection' into 'a prescription for environmental disaster'.[157] Slovakia argued that the changes identified by Hungary had not altered the nature of the obligations under the treaty from those initially undertaken, so that Hungary had not been entitled to terminate the treaty in the way it had claimed.[158] The Court rejected Hungary's argument on the following basis:

> The changed circumstances advanced by Hungary are, in the Court's view, not of such a nature, either individually or collectively, that their effect would radically transform the extent of the obligations still to be performed in order to accomplish the Project. A fundamental change of

---

[154] See Fitzmaurice, Second Report on the Law of Treaties, *supra* n. 8, at 32, and Waldock, Second Report on the Law of Treaties, *supra* n. 134, at 80.

[155] *Case Concerning the Gabčikovo-Nagymaros Project, supra* n. 23, at p. 64 (paragraph 104). As opposed to the procedural requirements set down in Art. 65(1) to 65(3) VCLT for invoking the doctrine of fundamental change of circumstances (which also apply in the event of material breach): neither do these attract the force of custom nor do they present an indispensable element of the doctrine as formulated in Art. 62 VCLT: *supra* n. 1.

[156] Note, though, the observation of Malcolm Shaw and Caroline Fournet that, as formulated in Art. 62 VCLT, it is to be understood in a restrictive and rigorously limited manner: M. N. Shaw and C. Fournet, 'Article 62 (1969)' in Corten and Klein (eds.), Vol. II, *supra* n. 79, pp. 1411–1433, at p. 1419.

[157] *Case Concerning the Gabčikovo-Nagymaros Project, supra* n. 23, at pp. 59–60 (paragraph 95).

[158] *Ibid.*, at pp. 60–62 (paragraph 96).

circumstances must have been unforeseen; the existence of the circumstances at the time of the Treaty's conclusion must have constituted an essential basis of the consent of the parties to be bound by the Treaty. The negative and conditional wording of Article 62 of the Vienna Convention on the Law of Treaties is a clear indication moreover that the stability of treaty relations requires that the plea of fundamental change of circumstances be applied only in exceptional cases.[159]

One case before an international tribunal in which the plea of fundamental change of circumstances was upheld was *Racke v. Hauptzollamt Mainz* in the European Court of Justice (ECJ).[160] This case arose from the suspension by the Council of Ministers of the European Communities (EC) of a Cooperation Agreement between the EC and Yugoslavia in 1991, following the outbreak of hostilities in that region.[161] The ECJ gave a preliminary ruling on the validity of the suspension, in which it listed two conditions for successfully claiming fundamental change of circumstances. First, the Court identified the essential basis for the parties' consent, finding that 'the maintenance of a situation of peace in Yugoslavia, indispensable for neighbourly relations, and the existence of institutions capable of ensuring implementation of the cooperation envisaged by the Agreement throughout the territory of Yugoslavia constituted an essential condition for initiating and pursuing that cooperation'.[162] The ECJ found that these conditions no longer existed on the facts before it. Second, the ECJ emphasised that the fundamental change of circumstances must have radically transformed the extent of obligations undertaken by the parties. In this respect, the ECJ ruled that it was sufficient that no purpose was being served by continuing to grant preferences with a view to stimulating trade in circumstances where Yugoslavia was breaking up, since 'the customary international law rules in question [do] not require an impossibility to perform obligations'. Accordingly, the plea of fundamental change of circumstances was

---

[159] *Ibid.*   [160] Case C-162/96 *Racke v. Hauptzollamt Mainz* [1998] ECR I-3655.

[161] It should be recalled that Art. 73 VCLT provides, *inter alia*, 'that the provisions of the Convention do not prejudge any question that may arise in regard to a treaty from the outbreak of hostilities between States': *supra* n. 1. In 2011, the International Law Commission produced a set of Draft Articles on the Effects of Armed Conflicts on Treaties with Commentaries: U.N. Doc. A/66/10, GAOR, 66th Sess., Supp. No. 10 (2011). For background reading, consider R. Rank, 'Modern War and the Validity of Treaties: A Comparative Study', *Cornell Law. Q.*, 38 (1953), 321–355. See, further, A. N. Pronto, 'The Effect of War on Law – What Happens to Their Treaties When States Go to War?', *Cambridge JICL*, 2 (2013), 227–241.

[162] *Racke v. Hauptzollamt Mainz*, *supra* n. 160 (paragraph 53).

upheld, since no 'manifest error of assessment' existed in the Council's appreciation of the situation and its invocation of the plea.[163]

One may note that the ECJ was not as strict as the International Court of Justice in its application of the doctrine of fundamental change of circumstances.[164] As Arnold Pronto has explained, as a matter of law, the possibility that treaties may be terminated by armed conflict is implicitly retained in the Vienna Convention by virtue of the provision regarding the invocation of fundamental change of circumstances (Article 62).[165] He is of the view that war (or armed conflict)[166] may fall within this provision despite the fact that from the traditional point of view this eventuality was considered a distinct ground for termination or withdrawal.[167] However, according to the same author, there has been a shift in the law over the past century, so that it is no longer accepted that war (or armed conflict) automatically has such an effect on a treaty.[168]

3.2.3 Force Majeure

The plea of *force majeure* is defined in a restrictive manner in Article 23 ASR.[169] In its commentaries on the ASR, the International Law Commission mentions numerous examples of the application of *force majeure*, most of which concern the incidence of natural phenomena such as floods or loss of part of a State's territory. Other instances have arisen out of a combination of the two.[170] *Force majeure* requires more than just a burdensome situation, as the arbitral tribunal in *Case Concerning the Rainbow Warrior Affair* explained.[171] One must add that if the State invoking the doctrine itself brought about the situation

---

[163] *Ibid.* (paragraph 52).

[164] Even though Article 73 VCLT specifically excludes the outbreak of hostilities from its scope, *Racke* also illustrates how questions may still arise as to whether such a situation qualifies as a fundamental change of circumstances.

[165] Pronto, *supra* n. 161, at 234.

[166] Note the Vienna Convention formulation of 'the outbreak of hostilities between States': *supra* n. 161.

[167] See, in particular, A. D. McNair and A. D. Watts, *The Legal Effects of War* (Cambridge: Cambridge University Press, 4th ed., 1966).

[168] Pronto, *supra* n. 161, at 235. See, also, the general principle of Art. 3 of the 2011 ILC Draft Articles on the Effects of Armed Conflicts on Treaties: '[t]he existence of an armed conflict does not *ipso facto* terminate or suspend the operation of treaties: (a) as between States parties to the conflict; (b) as between a State party to the conflict and a State that is not'. See *supra* n. 161.

[169] *Supra* n. 129.   [170] *YbILC* (2001–II), Part Two, 76–78.

[171] *Case Concerning the Rainbow Warrior Affair, supra* n. 82.

in question, it cannot rely on the plea of *force majeure*. This causal link must be close, however, requiring more than just a mere contribution.[172]

In the *Rainbow Warrior Case*, France argued that even though its actions had not been in strict accordance with the letter of the relevant agreement, its international responsibility was not engaged because the law of State responsibility recognised the doctrines of *force majeure* and of distress.[173] These doctrines, France argued, exonerated it. The tribunal decided, however, that, within international law, *force majeure* was cast in absolute terms and that it applied only where circumstances rendered compliance by a State with an international obligation impossible. It did not apply where – as was the case before the tribunal – circumstances merely made compliance more difficult or burdensome.[174] The plea of distress was also relied upon by France in relation to the evacuation of Major Mafart and Captain Prieur from the island of Hao. The tribunal explained the requirements for the invoking of such a circumstance precluding wrongfulness. First of all, distress had to be distinguished from the more controversial plea of necessity, where departure from international obligations is justified on the ground of the vital interests of the State concerned. In its view, distress can be invoked in circumstances involving a choice between breach of international obligation and a serious threat to the life or physical integrity of a State organ or of persons entrusted to its care. For distress to be applicable, three conditions were required: (i) the existence of exceptional medical or other circumstances of an elementary nature of extreme urgency, provided that a prompt recognition of the existence of those circumstances was subsequently sought from, or demonstrated by, the other party; (ii) the re-establishment of the original situation of compliance in Hao as soon as the circumstances of emergency had disappeared and, finally, (iii) a good faith attempt to obtain the consent of New Zealand under the terms of the

---

[172] *Case Concerning the Gabčikovo-Nagymaros Project, supra* n. 23, at p. 39 (paragraph 48).

[173] Art. 24 ASR provides:

   1. The wrongfulness of an act of a State not in conformity with an international obligation of that State is precluded if the author of the act in question has no other reasonable way, in a situation of distress, of saving the author's life or the lives of other persons entrusted to the author's care.
   2. Paragraph 1 does not apply if:
      (a) the situation of distress is due, either alone or in combination with other factors, to the conduct of the State invoking it; or
      (b) the act in question is likely to create a comparable or greater peril.

   Supra n. 3.

[174] *Case Concerning the Rainbow Warrior Affair, supra* n. 82, at pp. 252–253 (paragraph 77).

relevant agreement.[175] On the facts before the tribunal, these conditions had not been met.

3.2.4 State of Necessity

Like fundamental change of circumstances, the doctrine of necessity is formulated negatively in Article 25 ASR.[176] The plea of necessity may not be invoked unless the act done out of necessity is the 'only way for the State to safeguard an essential interest against grave and imminent peril; and does not seriously impair an essential interest of the State or States towards which the obligation exists, or of the international community as a whole'.[177] Similarly, it cannot be invoked if the international obligation in question excludes the invocation of necessity or if the State in question contributed to the situation of necessity in some way. A state of necessity frequently constitutes a separate ground for a State to attempt to terminate or suspend treaty obligations, as in the *Gabčikovo-Nagymaros Case*. In this respect, the plea exemplifies the difficult relationship between the law of treaties and the law of State responsibility, as theoretical differences between these two areas of the law may in practice be very challenging for States to discern. In this case, Hungary justified its termination of the 1977 Treaty by suggesting that such action safeguarded its essential interests, specifically the health and vital interests of the population in the Szigetköz region of the country.[178] Hungary further argued that the ecological dangers posed by the 1977 Treaty were (i) of an 'exceptional' character and threatened a 'major interest' of the State; (ii) 'imminent' and (iii) impossible to avert by means other than termination.[179] The exceptional character of the interests involved severe pollution, a threat to the quality of drinking water, agriculture and the essential interest on the part of Hungary in maintaining its natural environment. Hungary also emphasised the imminent nature of the peril, particularly after Czechoslovakia put into operation Variant C. Finally, Hungary stressed the unavoidable character of its decision to terminate the project. In view of these considerations, Hungary argued that the termination of the 1977 Treaty was the last possible legal reaction to Czechoslovakia's unlawful and persistent refusal to engage in negotiations – a refusal that

---

[175] *Ibid.*, at p. 255 (paragraph 79).
[176] *Supra* n. 130. See, further, T. Yamada, 'State of Necessity in International Law: A Study of International Judicial Cases', *Kobe J. Law*, 34 (2005), 107–158.
[177] *Ibid.*
[178] *Case Concerning the Gabčikovo-Nagymaros Project, supra* n. 23, at p. 43 (paragraph 56).
[179] *Ibid.*, at p. 42 (paragraph 54).

was only underscored by Czechoslovakia's perseverance with Variant C despite Hungary's urgent invitations to discontinue the construction of Variant C as highly damaging and incompatible with the 1977 Treaty.[180] Furthermore, Hungary stressed that it had not contributed to the occurrence of this state of necessity.

The Slovak Republic offered a vigorous reply, arguing that an 'ecological state of necessity' did not exist – either at the time of the suspension of the works or at the time of Hungary's termination notice. It even expressed doubts as to whether there could be an 'ecological state of necessity', since such a plea would come to seriously undermine the stability of the law of treaties.[181] In any case, the Slovak Republic suggested that when the 1977 Treaty was concluded, the best possible evidence of the project's expected environmental impact was offered. It also claimed that Hungary did not believe that a state of necessity existed when it unlawfully suspended, abandoned and terminated its performance under the 1977 Treaty. According to its memorial, '[t]o invoke a State of ecological necessity, a State must believe it exists and it must have held that deep and genuine belief at the moment it decided to act contrary to its international obligations'.[182] The Slovak Republic asserted that Hungary's actions were in fact dictated by financial difficulties and its own perceptions of its energy needs rather than by a state of necessity.[183] Finally, it argued that by invoking the state of necessity, Hungary had ignored the provisions of the 1977 Treaty, which had its own dispute settlement procedure based on objective data and its own built-in mechanism for the constant monitoring of environmental conditions. The Slovak position was that '[f]ull use of such mechanisms therefore precluded the unobserved development of any situation which could be characterised as a state of necessity and any negative developments could be resolved within the 1977 Treaty framework'.[184]

The Slovak Republic therefore adopted 'a subjective approach' to necessity – that is, one requiring a true belief on the part of the State in

---

[180] J. Crawford, *The International Law Commission's Articles on State Responsibility: Introduction, Text and Commentaries* (Cambridge: Cambridge University Press, 2002), p. 184.

[181] Peter Tomka, Verbatim Record of Oral Arguments in *Case Concerning Gabčikovo-Nagymaros Project* (The Hague: 15 Apr. 1997), CR.97/15, p. 60.

[182] Memorial Submitted by the Slovak Republic to the ICJ for *Case Concerning Gabčikovo-Nagymaros Project* (2 May 1994), Vol. I, p. 324.

[183] *Ibid.*, at p. 325.

[184] Memorial Submitted by the Slovak Republic to the ICJ for *Case Concerning Gabčikovo-Nagymaros Project* (2 May 1994), Vol. I, p. 325.

question (here, Hungary) – that a state of necessity did in fact exist.[185] Its position suggested that the dispute settlement procedure contained in the Treaty could preclude the emergence of a situation of necessity.[186] In this respect, the Slovak Republic revealed the complexities of this doctrine and the lack of agreement on the part of States as to what can constitute a plea of necessity, as the two conditions pleaded are not a part of Article 25 ASR (previously Draft Article 33 ASR). The Court itself analysed the state of necessity against the background of Article 33 of the 1980 Draft Articles of the ILC,[187] ascertaining that necessity was recognised by customary international law as a circumstance precluding wrongfulness.[188] It was confirmed that the state of necessity was not limited to the traditional grounds for the purposes of its invocation, such as a grave danger to the existence of the State itself.[189] Following the ILC's findings, it was also acknowledged that safeguarding the ecological balance could be considered an 'essential interest' of all States. However, the judgment confirmed the exceptional character of necessity as a circumstance precluding wrongfulness and the stringent conditions attached to a State's invoking it.

The existence in 1989 of the threat of 'a grave and imminent peril' was, in this light, questioned, along with whether Hungary's suspension and termination of the treaty and the abandonment of the works constituted the only method of safeguarding its essential interest against this peril. Regarding the erection of the Gabčikovo-Nagymaros barrage system, it was stated by the Court that 'serious though these uncertainties might have been, they could not, alone, establish the objective existence of a "peril" in the sense of a component element of a state of necessity'.[190] The Court further explained that 'peril' in this context 'certainly evokes the idea of "risk"; that is precisely what distinguishes "peril" from material damage'.[191] A state of necessity can only exist with a 'peril', 'duly established' at 'the relevant point in time'.[192] For the Court, 'the mere apprehension of a possible "peril" could not suffice' to establish a state of necessity,[193] and this follows from the requirement that a 'peril' must at

---

[185] *Ibid.*   [186] *Ibid.*, at p. 322.
[187] Draft Articles on State Responsibility: Text of the Articles of Part 1 (Arts. 1–35) of the Drafts Adopted by the International Law Commission at its 25th to 32nd Sessions: *YbILC* (1980–II) (Part Two), 30.
[188] *Case Concerning the Gabčikovo-Nagymaros Project, supra* n. 23, at p. 65 (paragraph 105).
[189] *Ibid.*, at p. 41 (paragraph 53).   [190] *Ibid.*, at pp. 41–42 (paragraph 54).
[191] *Ibid.*, at pp. 42–43 (paragraph 55).   [192] *Ibid.*, at pp. 41–42 (paragraph 54).
[193] *Ibid.*

the same time be 'grave' and 'imminent' (where "'[i]mminence" is synonymous with "immediacy" or "proximity" and goes far beyond the concept
of "possibility"').[194]

According to the ILC, an 'extremely grave and imminent peril' must be
a threat to a State's interest at the actual time. In the view of the Court,
however, a 'peril' appearing over a long period of time might be considered 'imminent' 'as soon as it is established, at the relevant point in
time, that the realisation of that peril, however far off it might be, is not
thereby any less certain and inevitable'.[195] Against this background, the
Gabčikovo-Nagymaros system of locks and barrages was analysed. As far
as the Nagymaros portion of the project was concerned, the Court viewed
the dangers alleged by Hungary as being of an uncertain character and
therefore saw no 'grave and imminent' peril at the time of its suspension
and abandonment of the works.[196] It was observed, moreover, that the
peril invoked by Hungary had already been present before 1989 and
could not be ascribed entirely to the work on the Nagymaros dam; the
Court stressed that even if the system's erection had created serious risks,
Hungary had at its disposal other means besides the project's suspension
and abandonment.[197] The use of these more costly techniques was 'not
determinative of the state of necessity'.[198] The Court invoked similar
reasoning to deny Hungary's plea of necessity with respect to the quality
of certain ground and surface water and the effects on fauna and flora.[199]
Finally, it was stated that even if it had been established that there had
been a state of necessity in 1989 linked to the performance of the 1977
Treaty, Hungary would not have been permitted to rely upon it because it
had contributed, by act or omission, in bringing about that state of
necessity.[200]

3.3 Distinguishing Supervening Impossibility of Performance, Fundamental Change of Circumstances, Force Majeure and Necessity

In the view of the present author, the relationship between the law of
treaties (in particular, the doctrines of supervening impossibility of
performance and fundamental change of circumstances) and the law
of State responsibility (in particular, the doctrines of *force majeure*, state
of necessity and distress) remains unresolved. Certain commentators have

---

[194] *Ibid.* [195] *Ibid.* [196] *Ibid.*, at pp. 42–43 (paragraph 55). [197] *Ibid.* [198] *Ibid.*
[199] *Ibid.*, at pp. 43–44 (paragraph 56). [200] *Ibid.*, at pp. 45–46 (paragraph 57).

advanced the view that there is a clear distinction between the law of treaties and of State responsibility by relying on the different objectives of these two systems – that is, on their functional separation which guarantees their coherence.[201] Notwithstanding this functional separation, certain common points of contact remain regarding the provisions on the termination or suspension of a treaty under the VCLT and defences in the law of State responsibility.[202] Difficulties, however, remain with respect to a clear-cut determination as to which set of rules applies to these points of contact. Decisions such as *Case Concerning the Rainbow Warrior Affair* show that rigid divisions between these two regimes are frequently not observed in practice.

From the theoretical point of view, at least it is correct to say that the provisions of the VCLT concern the existence of a treaty as a whole and of treaty obligations, while the rules of State responsibility deal with consequences of non-fulfilment of a specific obligation, including those deriving from a treaty.[203] In the *Gabčikovo-Nagymaros Case*, the Court adopted such a rigid distinction between the law of treaties and the law of State responsibility. The Court said as follows:

> A determination of whether a convention is or is not in force, and whether it has or has not been properly suspended or denounced, is to be made pursuant to the law of treaties. On the other hand, an evaluation of the extent to which the suspension or denunciation of a convention, seen as incompatible with the law of treaties, involves the responsibility of the State which proceeded to it, is to be made under the law of State responsibility.[204]

The award in *Case Concerning the Rainbow Warrior Affair* offers a very useful illustration of a case in which the claims of circumstances precluding wrongfulness and provisions on treaty termination were blurred. The tribunal accepted the French position and reasoned that the breach of a treaty could be justified on the basis of the general law of State responsibility, even where there had existed no basis to terminate the treaty under the law of treaties. As Susan Marks has argued, this 'puts into question the continued operation of the provisions of the Vienna

---

[201] P.-M. Dupuy, 'Droit des traités, codification et responsabilité internationale', *AFDI*, 43 (1997), 7–30, at 29.

[202] F. I. Paddeu, 'A Genealogy of *Force Majeure* in International Law', *BYbIL*, 82 (2011), 381–494, at 467.

[203] *Ibid.*, at 467.

[204] *Case Concerning the Gabčikovo-Nagymaros Project, supra* n. 23, at pp. 38–39 (paragraph 47).

Convention relating to the termination, suspension and invalidity of treaties'.[205] She has explained further that:

> If a state wishing to avoid its obligations under a treaty can justify breaching the treaty by reference to the full range of excuses known to the law of state responsibility, why should it pay any heed to the stricter grounds and procedures applicable under the law of treaties?[206]

However, several scholars favour the approach adopted by the arbitral tribunal in *Case Concerning the Rainbow Warrior Affair*:

> The circumstances precluding wrongfulness cannot logically be precluded by the existence of provisions concerning termination, suspension or impossibility of performance, as circumstances precluding wrongfulness cancelled not the operation of the treaty, but only the liability for what was unquestionably illegal conduct. The regimes are to be considered as complements to one another: a state whose act of termination or suspension is incompatible with the law of treaties may still escape responsibility if it can rely on the general excuses under the law of state responsibility.[207]

Marks' position does not enjoy full support in theory, State practice or the relevant jurisprudence – especially the *Gabčikovo-Nagymaros Case*. The prevailing view supports a strict distinction between State responsibility and the law of treaties. A determination as to whether a convention is or is not in force, and whether it has or has not been properly suspended or denounced, is to be made pursuant to the law of treaties, whereas an evaluation of the extent to which the suspension or denunciation of a convention, seen as incompatible with the law of treaties, gives rise to liability is to be made under the law of State responsibility. Accordingly, as noted previously, a State whose act of termination or suspension is incompatible with the law of treaties may still escape responsibility if it can rely on the general excuses under the law of State responsibility.

The plea of fundamental change of circumstances gives rise to similar confusion and misconceptions in terms of its relationship with the state of necessity. The predominant view is that the invocation of a state of necessity does not terminate treaty relations but only serves as a justification for non-compliance. The rules of State responsibility

---

[205] S. Marks, 'Treaties, State Responsibility and Remedies', *Cambridge Law J.*, 49 (1990), 387–390, at 388.
[206] *Ibid.*
[207] M. Agius, 'The Invocation of Necessity in Intertnational Law', *Netherlands ILR*, 56 (2009), 95–135, at 113.

such as necessity could be treated as emergency rules that do not affect treaty relations between States and are temporary in character.[208] But this distinction does not reflect State practice or, indeed, the case law, including the *Gabčikovo-Nagymaros Case*. Necessity is often pleaded as a ground for the termination of a treaty, and the treaty itself (as we know) contains primary rules. Even if one adheres to the view that under the law of treaties the treaty remains in force, the rules of State responsibility – such as the rules on necessity – preclude the wrongfulness of a State's non-performance of its treaty commitments and prevent the responsibility of that State from arising. In doing so, they to a certain extent defeat the stability of treaties and the fundamental principle of *pacta sunt servanda*.[209]

The difficulties regarding the clear-cut distinction between these two regimes may be due to the fact that 'although each set of norms to some degree regulates the same fields and the same situations[,] the law of State responsibility is separate from the law of treaties'.[210] '[N]evertheless, international practice has confirmed that whenever State responsibility is incurred, the State has a right to invoke the circumstances precluding wrongfulness, as well as defences under the law of treaties'[211] and that 'it would seem correct to come to the conclusion that the law of treaties contains a gateway leading into the law on state responsibility, thus making the pleas of circumstances precluding wrongfulness available, independently of the determination made under the law of treaties'.[212] Furthermore, it has been said that:

> [e]vidently, there is a blurred distinction between these concepts. The conflation could stem from the overlap between the law of treaties and the law on state responsibility; the risk of confusing concepts that are linguistically close . . . or a desire to cover as many defences as possible in one integrated legal defence strategy.[213]

In light of the difficulties concerning the clear functional division between these two areas of international law, a correct conclusion seems to be that the choice of a mechanism will depend on the particular circumstances of a case and on the intentions of the parties. The incontrovertible conclusion is that the law of State responsibility,

---

[208] *Ibid.*, at 113–114.

[209] *Case Concerning the Gabčikovo-Nagymaros Project, supra* n. 23, at pp. 38–39 (paragraphs 46–47).

[210] M. Agius, 'The Invocation of Necessity in International Law', LL.M. Dissertation, University of Uppsala (2006), p. 43.

[211] *Ibid.*   [212] *Ibid.*, at p. 44.   [213] Agius, *supra* n. 207, at p. 112.

including a defence of non-performance, applies to an alleged breach of an obligation under international law, irrespective of the source of this obligation.[214]

4 Conclusion

In conclusion, it may be said that while the relationship between the various sets of rules is reasonably clear in principle, it may happen that their application in practice sometimes operates in such a way as to erode that clarity. In principle, the rules precluding wrongfulness do not normally affect the treaty's continuance in operation. However, if there is only one important obligation left to perform and the State in question will have a permanent justification (such as an ongoing state of necessity) not to perform it, then for most practical purposes the treaty is at an end. This may be particularly relevant where the treaty has a fixed time duration, as held – arguably wrongly – in *Case Concerning the Rainbow Warrior Affair*.[215] The case has also evidenced that the forensic context is seemingly such as to cause states to twist or confuse the rules in their determination to escape liability.

---

[214] Paddeu, *supra* n. 202, at 460.

[215] In that context, it is interesting to speculate whether New Zealand might have been better advised (i) to agree to the evacuation on condition that the individuals were returned to serve their full terms of imprisonment once the personal emergency was over or (ii) to suspend the treaty at the first sign of a breach by France – would that equally have had the effect of suspending the running of the three-year period?

24

Security Council Resolution 687 (1991)

MICHAEL WOOD*

1 Introduction

The aim of the present chapter is to look into the interconnections between the work of the United Nations Security Council and treaty law and practice: it is for this reason that it appears as one of the studies on the *contextual* dimension of the modern law of treaties in this volume. In order to achieve this purpose, it considers, among other things, the possible application of concepts drawn from the law of treaties in the specific context of Security Council Resolution 687 (1991) of 3 April 1991.[1] This was the 'ceasefire' resolution,[2] intended to bring the 1991 Gulf Conflict to an end. Like many a peace settlement, it imposed heavy obligations on the vanquished. Like many a peace settlement, it cast a long shadow and spawned endless disputes, eventually leading to further conflict. For almost twelve years, from its adoption on 3 April 1991 to the invasion of Iraq on 19 March 2003, Resolution 687 (1991) served as a framework for the myriad of efforts 'to restore international peace and security in the region',[3] efforts largely conducted by or with the assent of the Security Council – until, that is, the March 2003 invasion. Resolution 687 (1991) had a long and active life, a life to which it is not possible to do justice within the confines of this chapter.[4] It led to

---

* The author wishes to thank Matina Papadaki (Research Fellow, Max Planck Institute Luxembourg) for her valuable assistance in the preparation of this chapter.

[1] The Resolution was adopted by twelve votes to one (Cuba) with two abstentions (Ecuador and Yemen).

[2] On the meaning of the term 'ceasefire' in Security Council Resolution 687 (1991), see Section 4.

[3] Security Council Resolution 678 (1990) (29 Nov. 1990), operative paragraph 2.

[4] Among writings specifically on Resolution 687 (1991), see S. Sur, 'La résolution 687 (3 avril 1991) du Conseil de sécurité dans l'affaire du Golfe', *AFDI*, 37 (1991), 25–97; L. D. Roberts, 'United Nations Security Council Resolution 687 and Its Aftermath: The Implications for Domestic Authority and the Need for Legitimacy', *N.Y.U. J. Int'l L. & Pol.*, 45 (1993),

many legal arguments, some of which resembled or were at least inspired by arguments that arise in the life of a treaty.

These debates have been somewhat overshadowed by the controversy over the interpretation of a resolution adopted some eleven years later, Security Council Resolution 1441 (2002) of 8 November 2002,[5] which was central to the question of the legality of the March 2003 invasion of Iraq.[6] Yet that debate was not about Resolution 1441 (2002) in isolation but turned on the interpretation of a series of resolutions, including Resolution 678 (1990) of 29 November 1990[7] and Resolution 687 (1991) as well as Resolution 1441 (2002). A key factor in interpreting Resolution 1441 (2002) concerned who was to determine whether a breach of Resolution 687 (1991) was sufficiently grave as to authorise the resumption of hostilities that had terminated with the ceasefire imposed by Resolution 687 (1991) (a 'material breach').

There is already some writing on the role of the Security Council in relation to treaties.[8] The aim of the present chapter is to explore certain provisions of the 3 April 1991 resolution. It should be recalled that the resolution was adopted very early in the post–Cold War period, a period which saw a remarkable revival in the work of the Security Council.[9] Yet, while the 1991 resolution was in many respects innovative, it also reflected a degree of caution – caution that has since been thrown to the winds

---

593–626; R. Wedgwood, 'The Enforcement of Security Council Resolution 687: The Threat of Force against Iraq's Weapons of Mass Destruction', *AJIL*, 92 (1998), 724–728; N. Jalilossoltan, 'Désarmement de l'Irak en vertu de la résolution 687 (1991) du Conseil de sécurité de l'ONU', *AFDI*, 46 (2000), 719–740; C. Hindawi, 'D'une guerre à l'autre ou un retour sur les ambiguïtés de la résolution 687 (1991) du Conseil de sécurité', 37 *Études internationales*, 37 (2006), 357–382, and D. Battistella, '687 (1991): Iraq et Koweït' in M. Albaret, E. Decaux, N. Lemay-Hébert and D. Placidi-Frot (eds.), *Les grandes résolutions du Conseil de sécurité des Nations unies* (Paris: Dalloz, 2012), pp. 121–136.

[5] Adopted unanimously.

[6] Among the many writings on the question, see in particular S. D. Murphy, 'Assessing the Legality of Invading Iraq', *Georgetown Law J.*, 92 (2004), 173–258. For the present author's contemporaneous view, see various documents made public by the United Kingdom Iraq Inquiry ('Chilcot Inquiry'); see, also, his written and oral evidence to that Inquiry (www .iraqinquiry.org.uk/).

[7] The Resolution was adopted by twelve votes to two (Cuba and Yemen) with one abstention (China).

[8] S. Talmon, 'Security Council Treaty Action', *Revue hellénique de droit international*, 62 (2009), 65–116, and M. Wood, 'The Law of Treaties and the UN Security Council: Some Reflections' in E. Cannizzaro (ed.), *The Law of Treaties beyond the Vienna Convention* (Oxford: Oxford University Press, 2011), pp. 244–255.

[9] The thaw in the Security Council seems to parallel that in East-West relations, cooperation among the permanent members is often thought to have begun with the drafting of Security Council Resolution 598 (1987) (20 July 1987) (on the 1980–88 Iran-Iraq War).

(some would say). For example, while it imposed the international bound-ary agreed in the contested 1963 Agreed Minutes between the State of Kuwait and the Republic of Iraq Regarding the Restoration of Friendly Relations, Recognition and Related Matters,[10] it merely 'invited' Iraq to ratify certain other treaties. Later resolutions went further, imposing upon States obligations set forth in treaties to which they were not parties.[11]

Security Council resolutions, while not treaties, share some of their characteristics. In certain respects, of course, they have important advan-tages over treaties, not least in terms of timeliness: timeliness of adoption, application, interpretation and amendment, and termination.[12] But there are also disadvantages, including in terms of clarity and legitimacy.[13]

The chapter considers briefly (in Section 2) the background and content of Resolution 687 (1991). Section 3 then recalls the approach to the interpretation of Security Council resolutions adopted by the International Court of Justice. Section 4 addresses the Resolution's nature as a ceasefire – not a peace treaty – and goes on to review the circum-stances in which the use of force might be used to enforce Iraq's obliga-tions under the resolution. Section 5 offers some modest conclusions.[14]

---

[10] 1964 UNTS 326.

[11] See, e.g., Security Council Resolution 1624 (2005) (14 Sept. 2005) on terrorist financing and Security Council Resolution 1757 (2007) (30 May 2007) on the Special Tribunal for Lebanon.

[12] See the various contributions in V. Popovski and T. Fraser (eds.), *The Security Council as Global Legislator* (London: Routledge, 2014). Specifically on the termination of Security Council resolutions, see, also, J. Galbraith, 'Ending Security Council Resolution', *AJIL*, 109 (2015), 806–821.

[13] For a moderate approach (despite its title), see A. Tzanakopoulos, *Disobeying the Security Council* (Oxford: Oxford University Press, 2011). On the obscure notion of 'legitimacy', see A. E. Roberts, 'Legitimacy versus Legality: Can Uses of Force Be Illegal but Justified?' in P. Alston and E. MacDonald (eds.) *Human Rights, Intervention, and the Use of Force* (Oxford: Oxford University Press, 2008), pp. 179–213.

[14] The chapter does not cover all treaty issues arising in connection with the resolution, in particular the relationship of the resolution to certain treaties mentioned therein. Security Council Resolution 687 (1991) refers to various treaties and in various ways: the 1963 Agreed Minutes between the State of Kuwait and the Republic of Iraq Regarding the Restoration of Friendly Relations, Recognition and Related Matters, 1964 UNTS 326 (effectively confirming their validity); the 1925 Geneva Protocol for the Prohibition of the Use in War of Asphyxiating, Poisonous or Other Gases, or of Bacteriological Methods of Warfare, 94 LNTS 65 (which Iraq was politely 'invited' to ratify); the 1968 Treaty on the Non-Proliferation of Nuclear Weapons, 729 UNTS 161 (Iraq 'invited' to reaffirm uncon-ditionally its obligations thereunder); the 1972 Convention on the Prohibition of the Development, Production, and Stockpiling of Bacteriological (Biological) and Toxin Weapons and on Their Destruction, 1015 UNTS 163, and the 1979 International Convention Against the Taking of Hostages, 1316 UNTS 205.

2 Background and Content of Security Council Resolution 687 (1991)

The 1991 Gulf Conflict was precipitated by Saddam Hussein's unlawful invasion of Kuwait on 2 August 1990 and his unlawful occupation of Kuwait and purported incorporation of Kuwait into Iraq.[15] The Security Council immediately condemned Iraq's invasion of Kuwait and demanded the immediate and unconditional withdrawal of its forces.[16] A coalition prepared to eject Iraq from Kuwait in exercise of the right of collective self-defence of Kuwait, but the legal basis shifted when the Security Council authorised Member States cooperating with Kuwait to take all necessary means 'to uphold and implement resolution 660 (1990) and all subsequent relevant resolutions and to restore international peace and security in the area' ('Operation Desert Storm', to give it its American name).[17] Following the successful military action in January and February 1991, the Council on 2 March 1991 noted 'the suspension of offensive combat operations by the forces of Kuwait and the Member States cooperating with Kuwait pursuant to resolution 678 (1990)',[18] and, then, a month later, on 3 April 1991, imposed a formal ceasefire, which took effect on 11 April 1991.[19]

---

[15] The Security Council decided 'that annexation of Kuwait by Iraq under any form and whatever pretext has no legal validity, and is considered null and void': Resolution 662 (9 Aug. 1990), operative paragraph 1.

[16] Security Council Resolution 660 (1990) (2 Aug. 1990).

[17] Security Council Resolution 678 (1990) (29 Nov. 1990). On the debate concerning this resolution and the distinction between collective self-defence and Security Council authorisation, see D. Bowett, 'Collective Security and Collective Self-Defence: The Errors and Risks of Identification' in M. R. Montaldo (ed.), *El derecho internacional en un mundo en transformación: liber amicorum en homenaje al profesor Eduardo Jiménez de Aréchaga* (Vol. I) (Montevideo: Fundación de Cultura Universitaria, 1994), pp. 425–440; F. Berman, 'The Authorization Model: Resolution 678 and Its Effects' in D. M. Malone, (ed.) *The UN Security Council: From the Cold War to the 21st Century* (Boulder, CO: Lynne Reiner Publishers 2004), pp. 153–165, and M. Wood, 'Collective Security and Collective Self-Defence: Key Distinctions' in M. Weller (ed.), *The Oxford Handbook on the Use of Force* (Oxford: Oxford University Press, 2015), pp. 649–660. On the resolution more generally, see E. Rostow, 'Until What? Enforcement Action or Collective Self-Defense?', *AJIL*, 85 (1991), 506–516; C. Denis, 'La résolution 678 (1991) peut-elle légitimer les actions menées contre l'Irak postérieurement à l'adoption de la résolution 687 (1991)?', *RBDI*, 31 (1998), 485–537; E. Convergne, '678 (1991): Iraq et Koweït' in Albaret, Decaux, Lemay-Hébert and Placidi-Frot (eds.), *supra* n. 4, pp. 111–120, and O. Corten, *Le droit contre la guerre* (Paris: Pedone, 2nd ed., 2014), pp. 594–610.

[18] Security Council Resolution 686 (2 March 1991), fifth preambular paragraph.

[19] See Letter from the President of the Security Council to the Permanent Representative of Iraq to the United Nations: S/22485 (11 Apr. 1991) ('[t]he members of the Security

Resolution 687 (1991) lays down in some detail the terms for the ceasefire, which were to be accepted by Iraq before the ceasefire took effect (which it did on 11 April 1991).[20] It deals with a wide range of matters, and had some notoriety as the longest and most complex Security Council resolution yet adopted.[21] It has twenty-six preambular and thirty-four operative paragraphs. After operative paragraph 1, which reaffirms all previous resolutions, the operative part is divided into nine sections:

A. The inviolability of the international boundary and the allocation of islands between Iraq and Kuwait, as set out in the Agreed Minutes Between the State of Kuwait and the Republic of Iraq Regarding the Restoration of Friendly Relations, Recognition and Related Matters (the validity of which had been contested by Iraq).[22]
B. The deployment of a United Nations force in a demilitarised zone either side of the international boundary.
C. Disarmament obligations in the fields of chemical and biological weapons, ballistic missiles, and nuclear weapons, with intrusive inspection procedures (led by the International Atomic Energy Agency (IAEA) and a subsidiary organ of the Security Council, the United Nations Special Commission (UNSCOM) – later the United Nations Monitoring, Verification and Inspection Commission (UNMOVIC)).
D. Return of Kuwaiti property seized by Iraq.
E. Iraq's liability for direct loss, damage and the depletion of natural resources or injury to foreign Governments, nationals and corporations as a result of Iraq's unlawful invasion and occupation of Kuwait and the creation of a fund to pay compensation for resulting claims.

Council have ... asked me to note that the conditions established in paragraph 33 of resolution 687 (1991) have been met and that the formal cease-fire referred to in paragraph 33 of that resolution is therefore effective').

[20] *Ibid.* For Iraq's acceptance, see Letters dated 6 April 1991 from the Permanent Representative of Iraq to the Secretary-General (S/22456) and 10 April 1991 from the Permanent Representative of Iraq to the President of the Security Council, transmitting the decision of the National Assembly of Iraq adopted on 6 April 1991 accepting Resolution 687 (S/22480).

[21] The regrettable trend towards ever lengthier (and hence less intelligible and focused) Security Council resolutions seems unstoppable, though they have not yet reached the dimensions of some General Assembly resolutions: by way of example, see Resolution Adopted by the General Assembly on 29 Dec. 2014, A/RES/69/245 (which has forty-five preambular and 313 operative paragraphs).

[22] See, in particular, M. Mendelson and S. C. Hulton, 'The Iraq-Kuwait Boundary', *BYbIL*, 64 (1993), 135–195.

F. Modifications of the sanctions imposed on Iraq.

G. Repatriation of all Kuwaiti and third-country nationals.

H. International terrorism.

I. Ceasefire and decision 'to take such further steps as may be required for the implementation of the present resolution and to secure peace and security in the area'.

The key provisions of Resolution 687 (1991), for present purposes, are those contained in section I (paragraphs 33 and 34), in which the Security Council:

> 33. *Declares* that, upon official notification by Iraq to the Secretary-General and to the Security Council of its acceptance of the provisions above, a formal cease-fire is effective between Iraq and Kuwait and the Member States cooperating with Kuwait in accordance with resolution 678 (1990);
>
> 34. *Decides* to remain seized of the matter and to take such further steps as may be required for the implementation of the present resolution and to secure peace and security in the area.[23]

Resolution 687 (1991) has been summarised in the following terms:

> Resolution 687 set out the steps which the Council required Iraq to take in order to restore international peace and security in the area. Resolution 687 suspended, but did not terminate, the authority to use force in resolution 678. The United Kingdom's position was that a determination by the Security Council that Iraq was in material breach of its obligations under resolution 687 was capable of reviving the authorisation to use force in resolution 678.[24]

---

[23] Mention should also be made of Security Council Resolution 688 (1991) (5 Apr. 1991), adopted just two days after Security Council Resolution 687 (1991), in the face of the looming humanitarian catastrophe created by the flight from northern Iraq of large numbers of Kurds under attack by Saddam Hussain: see A. Pellet, '668 (1991): Iraq' in Albaret, Decaux, Lemay-Hébert and Placidi-Frot (eds.), *supra* n. 4, pp. 137–148. Resolution 688 (1991) was not expressed to be adopted under Chapter VII of the United Nations Charter, and did not authorise the use of force: it was part of the background to the United Kingdom's 'humanitarian intervention' argument for the safe havens and no-fly zones: see M. Wood, 'The International Law on the Use of Force: What Happens in Practice?', *Indian JIL*, 53 (2013), 345–367, at 360–365.

[24] *Legality of Military Action in Iraq: Disclosure Statement Made by the Cabinet Office and the Legal Secretariat to the Law Officers* (Annex 6 to the Information Commissioner's Enforcement Notice of 22 May 2006, addressed to the Legal Secretariat to the Law Officers): reproduced in *BYbIL*, 77 (2006), 831–837 (paragraph 6). This Disclosure Statement details the processes culminating in the Attorney General reaching 'the clear conclusion that the better view was that there was a lawful basis for the use of force without a second resolution' (Legal Secretary's record of 13 March 2003), and the Attorney General's written statement to Parliament of 19 March 2003.

3   The Interpretation of Security Council Resolutions

The extent to which the customary international law rules of treaty interpretation, reflected in Articles 31 and 32 of the 1969 Vienna Convention on the Law of Treaties (VCLT),[25] may be applied to the interpretation of Security Council resolutions was addressed by the International Court of Justice in its *Kosovo* advisory opinion of July 2010. The key passage reads:

> ... the Court must recall several factors relevant in the interpretation of resolutions of the Security Council. While the rules on treaty interpretation embodied in Articles 31 and 32 of the Vienna Convention on the Law of Treaties may provide guidance, differences between Security Council resolutions and treaties mean that the interpretation of Security Council resolutions also require[s] that other factors be taken into account. Security Council resolutions are issued by a single, collective body and are drafted through a very different process than that used for the conclusion of a treaty. Security Council resolutions are the product of a voting process as provided for in Article 27 of the Charter, and the final text of such resolutions represents the view of the Security Council as a body. Moreover, Security Council resolutions can be binding on all Member States (*Legal Consequences for States of the Continued Presence of South Africa in Namibia (South West Africa) notwithstanding Security Council Resolution 276 (1970), Advisory Opinion, I.C.J. Reports 1971*, p. 54, para. 116), irrespective of whether they played any part in their formulation. The interpretation of Security Council resolutions may require the Court to analyse statements by representatives of members of the Security Council made at the time of their adoption, other resolutions of the Security Council on the same issue, as well as the subsequent practice of relevant United Nations organs and of States affected by those given resolutions.[26]

In an article published in 1998, the present author referred to a number of differences between Security Council resolutions and treaties relevant in the context of interpretation.[27] These included the following:

---

[25]   1155 UNTS 331.

[26]   *Accordance with International Law of the Unilateral Declaration of Independence in Respect of Kosovo* (Advisory Opinion) (2010) ICJ Rep. 403, at p. 422 (paragraph 94). The Seabed Disputes Chamber of the International Tribunal for the Law of the Sea has also referred to the Vienna rules when interpreting binding 'instruments that are not treaties': *Responsibilities and Obligations of States with Respect to Activities in the Area* (Advisory Opinion) (2011) ITLOS Rep. 10, at p. 21 (paragraphs 59–60).

[27]   M. Wood, 'The Interpretation of Security Council Resolutions', *Max Planck Yb. UN Law*, 2 (1998), 73–95, and M. Wood, 'The Interpretation of Security Council Resolutions, Revisited', *Max Planck Yb. UN Law*, 20 (2016), 3–35.

- Given the way Security Council resolutions are drafted, less reliance can be placed upon preambular language as a tool for the interpretation of the operative part;[28]
- Security Council resolutions are often not self-contained but refer to and incorporate by reference other documents (reports of the United Nations Secretary-General, for example);
- Security Council resolutions are often part of a series and can only be understood as such. They look forward and back;
- There are no 'parties' to a resolution, only the Security Council, and the various references in the Vienna rules to the 'parties' to a treaty are not easy to apply in the context of an Security Council resolutions;
- Given the way they emerge and that for the most part Security Council resolutions are intended to be political documents, one should not expect them to be drafted with the same attention to legal detail and consistency as is normally the case with treaties;
- Under the rules of the VCLT, there shall be taken into account, together with the context, any relevant rules of international law applicable in the relations between the parties.[29] Quite apart from the fact that there are no parties to Security Council resolutions, the impact of other rules of international law may be subject to Article 103 of the 1945 Charter of the United Nations;[30]
- The VCLT's distinction between the general rule in Article 31 and supplementary means of interpretation in Article 32 is likely to be less significant in the case of Security Council resolutions than in the case of treaties, given the importance of the historical background for the interpretation of resolutions. Any serious effort at interpreting a resolution will need to have regard to all the available *travaux préparatoires* and to the circumstances of the resolution's adoption.[31]

Some of the preceding points are matters of degree. For example, treaties may also refer to other documents or be part of a series, but this happens much less frequently than with Security Council resolutions. Other

---

[28] On preambles, see E. Suy, 'Le préambule' in E. Yakpo and T. Boumedra (eds.), *Liber Amicorum Mohammed Bedjaoui* (The Hague: Kluwer Law International, 1999), pp. 253–269 (dealing with preambles to Security Council resolutions at pp. 263–268). See, also, the contribution to this volume of Klabbers at pp. 172–200 (Chapter 7).

[29] Art. 31(3)(c) VCLT: *supra* n. 25.   [30] 1 UNTS 16.

[31] See C. Greenwood, 'New World Order or Old? The Invasion of Iraq and the Rule of Law', *Modern L. Rev.*, 55 (1992), 153–178, at 166 ('it is impossible properly to understand the text of any Security Council resolution without reference to the debates which preceded it').

points noted previously, such as the non-existence of parties, clearly distinguish the interpretation of treaties from the interpretation of Security Council resolutions as well as preclude the direct transposition by analogy of many rules on of the law of treaties.

These differences also become apparent when considering subsequent agreements and subsequent practice.[32] In the case of treaty interpretation, particularly in the case of long-lived and active treaties, subsequent agreements and subsequent practice may play an important role. As far as Resolution 687 (1991) is concerned, it was certainly long-lived and had an active life. However, since subsequent agreements and subsequent practice as elements of treaty interpretation presuppose an agreement on interpretation among the parties to the treaty, they do not apply directly to resolutions of the Security Council. The equivalent in the case of Security Council resolutions would be subsequent decisions of the Council establishing the Council's understanding of the interpretation of the resolution or subsequent practice of the Council likewise establishing the Council's understanding. Subsequent decisions would principally be found in later resolutions, while subsequent practice of the Council takes a variety of forms, including Presidential statements and letters, as well as practice of subsidiary organs of the Council, such as sanctions committees or the Counter-Terrorism Committee. Given the nature of the Council's activities, it seems likely that subsequent decisions and subsequent practice play a greater role in the case of the interpretation of resolutions than do subsequent agreements and subsequent practice in the interpretation of treaties.

4   The Nature of Resolution 687 (1991) and the Use of Force to Remedy a Breach

This is not the occasion to discuss the nature of Security Council resolutions as compared with other sources of international legal obligation such as treaties or unilateral declarations of States. In any event, it may be difficult to generalise. Security Council resolutions include a great variety of provisions, from legally binding decisions (within the meaning of Article 25 of the Charter of the United Nations) to internal operational decisions (for example, establishing a subsidiary organ or

---

[32] Art. 31(3)(a) and (b) VCLT: *supra* n. 25. See, also, the International Law Commission's current work on '[s]ubsequent agreements and subsequent practice in relation to the interpretation of treaties' and, further, the contribution to this volume of Buga at pp. 363–391 (Chapter 12).

recommending candidates for United Nations Secretary-General). They may range from 'treaty-like' instruments, such as the Statutes of the International Criminal Tribunals for the Former Yugoslavia[33] and Rwanda,[34] to policy statements not unlike those to be found in General Assembly resolutions.

As far as Resolution 687 (1991) is concerned, it has occasionally been suggested by writers that it is a peace treaty.[35] That cannot be right. While some of its provisions cover issues that might be found in a peace treaty (boundary demarcation, a demilitarised zone, reparation, arms limitation and disarmament), it is neither a peace treaty between belligerents, as it was imposed by the Security Council,[36] nor even an equivalent or substitute for a peace treaty. The use of the term 'ceasefire' is significant.[37] Its key provision in this regard – paragraph 33 set out earlier – established

---

[33] Security Council Resolution 827 (25 May 1993).

[34] Security Council Resolution 955 (8 Nov. 1994).

[35] C. Gray, 'After the Ceasefire: Iraq, the Security Council and the Use of Force', *BYbIL*, 65 (1994), 135–174, at 144 ('despite the terminology used in Resolution 687, it is clearly more than a mere suspension of hostilities. The substance is that of a peace treaty') and O. Schachter, 'United Nations Law in the Gulf Conflict', *AJIL*, 85 (1991), 452–473, at 456 (arguing that it is similar to the Treaty of Versailles).

[36] See J. Yoo, 'International Law and the War in Iraq', *AJIL*, 97 (2003), 563–575, at 569.

[37] Terms such as 'ceasefire', 'cessation of hostilities', 'armistice' and '(peace) settlement' are not used consistently; the effect of any particular instrument depends upon its terms and context, not the name given to it – though its name can be an important pointer. See, generally, J. K. Kleffner, 'Peace Treaties' in R. Wolfrum (ed.), *Max Planck Encyclopedia of Public International Law* (Vol. VIII) (Oxford: Oxford University Press, 2012), pp. 104–105; C. Bell, 'Ceasefires' in R. Wolfrum (ed.), *Max Planck Encyclopedia of Public International Law* (Vol. II) (Oxford: Oxford University Press, 2012), p. 10–18, at p. 11, and Y. Dinstein, 'Armistice' in *Max Planck Encyclopedia of Public International Law* (Vol. I) (Oxford: Oxford University Press, 2012), pp. 642–643. The terms 'cease-fire', 'truce' and 'armistice' have not been used by the Security Council consistently or with specific technical meaning: see S. D. Bailey, 'Cease-Fires, Truces, and Armistices in the Practice of the UN Security Council', *AJIL*, 71 (1977), 461–473. The Security Council is not alone in not using terms with precision: C. Greenwood, 'Scope of Application of International Humanitarian Law' in D. Fleck (ed.), *The Handbook of International Humanitarian Law* (Oxford: Oxford University Press, 2nd ed., 2008), pp. 45–78, at p. 67 ('the dividing line between ceasefires, armistices and other forms of suspensions of hostilities has become increasingly blurred') and Bell, *ibid.* ('[t]he terms truce, armistice, ceasefire, and cessation of hostilities are often used colloquially as interchangeable. While historically each term captured similar but distinct situations on a continuum from war to peace, with both the start of war and the end of war characterized by formal declarations, their meaning has changed over time, erasing clarity as to the distinctions between each term and leading to some overlap between terms. A number of writers have noted the flexible use of the term ceasefire by the UN, and the tendency to collapse pre-Charter concepts of truce, armistice, and even *peace treaties* into the term "ceasefire" so that each of the concepts has now become virtually indistinguishable') (citations omitted).

(upon Iraq's acceptance of the terms) 'a formal cease-fire',[38] between Iraq and 'the Member States cooperating with Kuwait in accordance with resolution 678 (1990)'.

Even more crucial was the answer to the question: Who was authorised by the Council to determine that the ceasefire had broken down and that 'the Member States cooperating with Kuwait under resolution 678 (1990)' could resume hostilities against Iraq?

The main legal justification[39] of the invasion in March 2003 turned on Iraq's breach of its weapons of mass destruction obligations under Resolution 687 (1991) and subsequent resolutions, in particular its repeated failure to cooperate fully with the weapons inspectors.[40] It was never seriously suggested that as a general matter the breach of legal obligations deriving from binding Security Council resolutions, adopted under Chapter VII of the Charter of the United Nations, gives rise to a right to enforce such breach through the use of force. That is clearly not the law, any more than a breach of treaty obligations gives rise to a right to use force.[41] The legal consequences of an internationally wrongful act are not affected by the origin of the obligation breached, be it customary, treaty or other.[42]

---

[38] Operative paragraph 1 expressly states that the goals of the resolution include a formal ceasefire.

[39] There were also hints of a self-defence argument in certain US statements, including their March 2003 letter to the President of the Security Council (S/2003/351), but this does not seem to have been a serious argument on the facts, and was not relied upon by any other members of the alliance. See, further, D. Kritsiotis, 'Arguments of Mass Confusion', *EJIL*, 15 (2004), 233–278. References to 'regime change' or retaliation for Saddam Hussein's attempted assassination of former President George H. Bush in in Kuwait in April 1993 were largely political rhetoric.

[40] The fact that weapons of mass destruction and ballistic missiles were not found following the invasion does not affect the legal argument, which was based not on the possession of such weapons but on failure to cooperate with the inspectors.

[41] See, for example, *Case Concerning Military and Paramilitary Activities in and against Nicaragua*: Nicaragua v. United States of America (Merits) (1986) ICJ Rep. 14, at p. 134 (paragraph 267) ('where human rights are protected by international conventions, that protection takes the form of such arrangements for monitoring or ensuring respect for human rights *as are provided for in the conventions themselves*') and pp. 134–135 (paragraph 268) ('*the use of force could not be the appropriate method to monitor or ensure such respect*') (emphases added).

[42] See *YbILC* (2001–II), Part Two, 55 ('the origin or provenance of an obligation does not, as such, alter the conclusion that responsibility will be entailed if it is breached by a State, nor does it, as such, affect the regime of State responsibility thereby arising. Obligations may arise for a State by a treaty and by a rule of customary international law or by a treaty and a unilateral act': paragraph 4 of the Commentary to Art. 12 of the Articles on State Responsibility). See, further, the contribution to this volume of Tams at pp. 440–467 (Chapter 14).

The Security Council itself may authorise the use of force to enforce its resolutions, as it has frequently done, for example, in connection with sanctions resolutions.[43] The popular idea that breach of a binding Chapter VII resolution gives rise to a right to use force is one of a number of myths about Chapter VII of the Charter of the United Nations.[44]

In 2002/2003, the question turned on whether a breach of Resolution 687 (1991) – the ceasefire resolution – could revive the authorisation to use force given by the Security Council in Resolution 678 (1990) (the 'revival' argument). If it could, the next – and crucial – questions were what kind of breach could revive the authorisation to use force and who was to determine that the breach was of such a nature as to lead to such revival. The United States and the United Kingdom held opposing views on that last question: Who decides?[45]

As early as August 1992, the United Nations Legal Counsel, Dr Carl-August Fleischhauer, had given written advice on the interpretation of Resolution 687 (1991) as regards the use of force, in which he argued that its authorisation by Resolution 687 was of a continuing nature – that is, if the obligations included therein were violated, the ceasefire would come to an end and use of force would again be authorised. He gave a further opinion in January 1993.[46] Ralph Zacklin, United Nations Deputy Legal Counsel throughout the relevant period, has described the influence of the Fleischhauer opinions as follows:

---

[43] For one example among many, see Security Council Resolution 665 (1990) (25 Aug. 1990), calling on States 'to use such measures commensurate to the specific circumstances as may be necessary . . . to halt all inward and outward maritime shipping in order to inspect and verify their cargoes and destinations and to ensure strict implementation of the provisions related to such shipping laid down in resolution 661 (1990)'.

[44] M. Wood, *The UN Security Council and International Law* (Sir Hersch Lauterpacht Memorial Lectures, 7–9 Nov. 2006): paragraphs 31–33 of First Lecture (www.lcil.cam .ac.uk/sites/default/files/LCIL/documents/lectures/2006_hersch_lecture_1.pdf).

[45] Wedgwood, *supra* n. 4.

[46] The substance of Dr. Fleischhauer's advice was subsequently made public in Ralph Zacklin's Hersch Lauterpacht Memorial Lectures of Jan. 2008, and is now reproduced in the book based on those lectures: R. Zacklin, *The United Nations Secretariat and the Use of Force in a Unipolar World: Power v. Principle* (Cambridge: Cambridge University Press, 2010). The Fleischhauer advice is described at pp. 18–20 of that work, and its application discussed at pp. 20–22 and pp. 145–146. There was a further legal opinion of the United Nations Legal Counsel, in Jan. 1993, which concluded that the Presidential statements of 8 and 13 Jan. 1993 made it clear on balance that the serious consequences included all necessary means. As Zacklin goes on to note at pp. 20–22, the UN's semi-official 1996 'Blue Book' cited the Presidential statements as the basis for the 1993 airstrikes: *The United Nations and the Iraq-Kuwait Conflict 1990–1996* (Vol. IX) (New York, NY: United Nations Blue Books, 1996).

The legal opinions of August 1992 and January 1993 did not constitute authoritative interpretations of Security Council resolutions but they had considerable significance in terms of the Secretariat's interpretation of the inter-play of the decisions to authorize use of force and the establishment of the cease-fire. They came to be seen, even in 1993, as the basis for the argument that a resumption of the use of force could not be automatic. Not everyone agreed, and the United States in particular did not share the interpretation, but many Council members did.[47]

These matters were considered on many occasions following the adoption of Resolution 687 (1991), including in January 1993, December 1998 and 2002/2003. In each case, the breach was a failure to cooperate with the weapons inspectors.

On 7 January 1993, Iraq notified UNSCOM that it could no longer use the Habbaniyah airfield, thus preventing short-notice inspections. The President of the Security Council quickly denounced the action as an 'unacceptable and material breach of the relevant provisions of Resolution 687 (1991), which established the cease-fire and provided the conditions essential to the restoration of peace and security in the region'.[48] In a further Council statement on 11 January 1993, Iraq was warned that 'serious consequences' would flow from 'continued defiance'.[49] On 13 January 1993, the United States, United Kingdom and France conducted air raids on sites in southern Iraq.[50]

In 1997/1998, when Iraq was seriously obstructing the inspectors, the Security Council found Iraq to be in 'flagrant violation' of its obligations[51] and warned that 'serious consequences' would follow from Iraq's failure to allow inspections.[52] After United Nations Secretary-General Kofi A. Annan had secured a Memorandum of

---

[47] Zacklin, *supra* n. 46, at p. 22.   [48] S/25081 (8 Jan. 1993).   [49] S/25091 (11 Jan. 1993).

[50] R. W. Apple, Jr., 'U.S. and Allied Planes Hit Iraq, Bombing Missile Sites in South in Reply to Hussein's Defiance', *N.Y. Times*, 14 Jan. 1993, A1, and B. Gellman and A. Devroy, 'Military Action against Iraq Signaled by Administration', *Wash. Post*, 14 Jan. 1993, A1. This was followed by further strikes on 17 and 18 Jan. 1993. See Letter to Congressional Leaders Reporting on Iraq's Compliance with United Nations Security Council Resolutions (19 Jan. 1993): reproduced in *Public Papers of George Bush* (Vol. 2) (Washington, DC: Govt. Printing Office, 1993), pp. 2269–2270.

[51] Security Council Resolution 1134 (1997) (23 Oct. 1997); Security Council Resolution 1137 (1997) (12 Nov. 1997) and Security Council Resolution 1205 (1998) (5 Nov. 1998).

[52] S/PRST/1997/49 (29 Oct. 1997) ('The Security Council condemns the decision of the Government of Iraq to try to dictate the terms of its compliance with its obligation to cooperate with the Special Commission. The Security Council warns of the serious consequences of Iraq's failure to comply immediately and fully with its obligations under the relevant resolutions').

Understanding from Iraq,[53] the Council in Resolution 1154 (1998) of 2 March 1998 warned that any failure by Iraq to provide 'immediate, unconditional and unrestricted access' would 'have the severest consequences'. Again, on 31 October 1998, in Resolution 1205 (1998), the Council '[c]ondemn[ed] the decision by Iraq of to cease cooperation with the Special Commission as a flagrant violation of resolution 687 (1991) and other relevant resolutions'. These resolutions were followed, in December 1998, by intensive bombing in and around Baghdad (Operation Desert Fox), lasting just a few days.[54]

On the last occasion – in 2003 – the advice of the United Kingdom's Attorney General of 7 March 2003 (first leaked, then officially made public) went into the issues in some depth, and it is worth quoting some key passages:

> 9. Law Officers have advised in the past that, provided the conditions are made out, the revival argument does provide a sufficient justification in international law for the use of force against Iraq. That view is supported by an opinion given in August 1992 by the then UN Legal Counsel, Carl-August Fleischauer [sic]. However, *the UK has consistently taken the view (as did the Fleischauer [sic] opinion) that, as the cease-fire conditions were set by the Security Council in resolution 687, it is for the Council to assess whether any such breach of those obligations has occurred. The US have a rather different view: they maintain that the fact of whether Iraq is in breach is a matter of objective fact which may therefore be assessed by individual Member States.* I am not aware of any other state which supports this view. This is an issue of critical importance when considering the effect of resolution 1441.
>
> 10. The revival argument is controversial. It is not widely accepted among academic commentators. However, I agree with my predecessors' advice on this issue. Further, I believe that the arguments in support of the revival argument are stronger following adoption of resolution 1441. That is because of the terms of the resolution and the course of the negotiations which led to its adoption. Thus, preambular paragraphs 4, 5 and 10 recall the authorisation to use force in resolution 678 and that resolution 687 imposed obligations on Iraq as a necessary condition of the cease-fire. Operative paragraph (OP) 1 provides that Iraq has been and remains in material breach of its obligations under relevant resolutions, including the

---

[53] S/1998/166 (27 March 1998).

[54] F. X. Clines and S. L. Myers, 'Attack on Iraq: The Overview; Impeachment Vote in House Delayed as Clinton Launches Iraq Air Strike, Citing Military Need to Move Swiftly', *N.Y. Times*, 17 Dec. 1998, A1.

resolution 687. OP 13 recalls that Iraq has been warned repeatedly that 'serious consequences' will result from continued violations of its obligations. *The previous practice of the Council and statements made by Council members during the negotiation of resolution 1441 demonstrate that the phrase 'material breach' signifies a finding by the Council of a sufficiently serious breach of the cease-fire conditions to revive the authorisation in resolution 678 and that 'serious consequences' is accepted as indicating the use of force.*

11. I disagree, therefore, with those commentators and lawyers, who assert that nothing less than an *explicit* authorisation to use force in a Security Council resolution will be sufficient.[55]

The US position, admitting a unilateral decision, was set out by Ruth Wedgwood (writing of threats of force by the United States in 1997/98):

Was the United States entitled under international law to threaten the use of military force to gain Iraqi compliance with disarmament obligations? We need not enter into the continuing debate over the limits of individual and collective self-defense. Defenders of the United States position have available at least two powerful quasi-constitutional arguments in support of the legitimacy of the threat of force against Iraq to maintain the UN weapons inspection regime: these are the conditional nature of the 1991 cease-fire, and prior practice under the UNSCOM regime, in particular, the use of force in 1993 to deter Iraqi interference with inspections . . .

---

[55] Attorney General's Advice on the Iraq War – Iraq: Resolution 1441: reproduced in *ICLQ*, 54 (2005), 767–778, and *BYbIL*, 77 (2006), 819–829 (emphases added). For the legal justifications of the UK, USA and Australia, see their respective letters to the President of the Security Council: S/2003/350 (20 March 2003), S/2003/351 (20 March 2003) and S/2003/252 (20 March 2003). Furthermore, on the UK legal position: Attorney General's Written Answer to a Parliamentary Question, 17 March 2003, Hansard, 646 HL Debs., WA 2, and FCO Paper 'Iraq: Legal Basis for the Use of Force' reproduced in *BYbIL*, 73 (2003), 792–796, and *ICLQ*, 52 (2003), 811–814; 'Review of Intelligence on Weapons of Mass Destruction' (Butler Review, July 2004, HC 898), paragraphs 366–387; 'Legality of Military Action in Iraq: Disclosure Statement made by the Cabinet Office and the Legal Secretariat to the Law Officers', at Annex 6 to the Information Commissioner's Enforcement Notice of 22 May 2006, addressed to the Legal Secretariat to the Law Officers, reproduced in *BYbIL*, 77 (2006), 831–837. On the US legal position: W. H. Taft IV and T. F. Buchwald, 'Preemption, Iraq, and International Law', *AJIL*, 97 (2003), 557–563 (without the usual disclaimer); State Department Press Briefing on UN Security Council Resolution 1441 (www.staff.city.ac.uk/p.willetts/IRAQ/BRIEF.HTM) and *Digest of United States Practice in International Law 2002* (Washington, DC: Dept. of State, 2002), pp. 937–945. On the Australian legal position: 'Memorandum of Advice on the Use of Force against Iraq to the Commonwealth Government: 18 March 2003', *Melbourne JIL*, 4 (2003), 78–182.

Iraq's calculated defiance of these cease-fire terms in the 1997–1998 confrontation allowed the United States to deem the cease-fire in suspension and to resume military operations to enforce its conditions . . .[56]

Wedgwood relied on what she considered to be the 1993 precedent to support her view that there was no need for the Security Council to ascertain a material breach. However, on that occasion, it was the Council that had determined the breach.[57]

These various long-held legal positions underlie the structure and the wording of the key provisions of Resolution 1441 (2002) and the arguments about whether it revived the authorisation to use force without a subsequent decision of the Security Council. This is not the occasion to rehearse these arguments, which have been canvassed fully in the evidence to the Chilcot Inquiry and in the literature.[58]

As was the case on earlier occasions,[59] Resolution 1441 (2002) employs the term 'material breach', which echoes Article 60 VCLT.[60] Ireland, for example, made it abundantly clear that it conceived the term as stemming

---

[56] Wedgwood, *supra* n. 4, at 725–726.

[57] See, also, Yoo, *supra* n. 36, at 571 ('In sum, well-established principles of UN Security Council practice, treaty law, and armistice law allowed the United States to suspend the cease-fire in response to Iraq's material breaches of Resolution 687. The United States then could rely on Resolution 678 to use "all necessary means" to bring Iraq into compliance. Nothing in Resolution 1441 suggested that the Security Council needed to adopt any additional resolution to establish the existence of further material breaches to provide the basis for the use of force under Resolution 678. Indeed, Resolution 1441 left intact Resolution 678's reference to the use of force. Resolution 1441 neither revoked Resolution 678's language concerning the use of "all necessary means" against Iraq, nor terminated its effect in any way').

[58] For a detailed British analysis of the arguments surrounding Resolution 1441 (2002), see letter of 9 Dec. 2002 from the FCO Legal Adviser to the Legal Secretariat to the Law Officers (www.iraqinquiry.org.uk/media/43707/document2010-01-27-100553.pdf). For an extended analysis of many of the arguments surrounding the revival doctrine and Resolution 1441 (2002), see Murphy, *supra* n. 6. The Chilcot Inquiry published its twelve-volume report on 6 July 2016 (www.iraqinquiry.org.uk/the-report/).

[59] In Resolution 707 (1991) (15 Aug. 1991), the Security Council '*[c]ondemn[ed]* Iraq's serious violation of a number of its obligations under section C of resolution 687 (1991) and of its undertakings to cooperate with the Special Commission and the IAEA, which constitutes a material breach of the relevant provisions of resolution 687 which established a cease-fire and provided the conditions essential to the restoration of peace and security in the region' (operative paragraph 1).

[60] Though not in the French version, which characterises Iraq's conduct as being in '*violation patente*' of its obligations, while the French version of Art. 60 VCLT employs the term '*violation substantielle*'. In the Spanish as in the English text the language of Art. 60 VCLT is employed ('*violación grave*'): *supra* n. 25.

from Article 60 VCLT and that it was rightly used and should be resorted to again in case Iraq continues to defy its obligations deriving from Resolution 687.[61]

In relation to the use of force and the revival argument, statements before and after the vote on Resolution 1441 (2002) affirmed the rejection of 'any automaticity in the use of force'.[62] The United States and the United Kingdom equally rejected 'automaticity' and 'hidden triggers'. Bulgaria, Cameroon, China, Mexico and Syria also emphasised this point.[63]

The term 'material breach' was the clearest term to convey the underlying idea behind the revival argument, since it was the term of art used in Article 60 VCLT,[64] which is defined in Article 60(3) as consisting in '(a) a repudiation of the treaty not sanctioned by the present Convention; or (b) the violation of a provision essential to the accomplishment of the object or purpose of the treaty'.

Nevertheless, earlier practice (such as in 1993, 1994 and 1998) showed that it was the idea rather than the actual terminology that mattered. On those occasions, reference had been made to 'flagrant violation', 'serious consequences' and 'the severest consequences'. What mattered was that the Council had used language that all concerned understood to mean that the breach was sufficiently serious as to justify the use of force. It has to be noted again that Security Council resolutions are 'rarely self-contained'.[65] The references to previous resolutions and the parallels

---

[61] U.N. Doc. S/PV. 4644 (8 Nov. 2002) ('As the concept of material breach is a key element of this resolution, let me make it clear that Ireland's understanding of this concept is in accordance with the definition contained in the 1969 Vienna Convention on the Law of Treaties ... There is no doubt, on the basis of this definition, that Iraq has been in material breach of its obligations. We fully expect this same definition to be applied in determining whether any further material breach has occurred, should it become necessary to do so').

[62] Joint Statement by China, France and the Russian Federation issued as a Security Council document after the meeting at which Resolution 1441 (2002) was adopted: S/2002/1236 (8 Nov. 2002); see, also, United States statement at the Council meeting: U.N. Doc. S/PV. 4644 (8 Nov. 2002)

[63] U.N. Doc. S/PV. 4644 (8 Nov. 2002).

[64] See Memorandum by Professor Christopher Greenwood, CMG, QC, The Legality of Using Force Against Iraq, 24 Oct. 2002 (www.publications.parliament.uk/pa/cm200203/cmselect/cmfaff/196/2102406.htm) ('Accordingly, my conclusion is that military action against Iraq would be justified if: – ... (2) The Security Council indicated that Iraq was in material breach of Resolution 687 (1991) and that breach entailed a threat to international peace and security, in which case action would be justified within the framework of Resolution 678 (1990)') (three disjunctive conditions are provided).

[65] Wood (1998), *supra* n. 27, at 93.

drawn between similar situations are an invaluable interpretative tool. Thus, it is in this context that Resolution 1441 (2002) has to be seen.

Article 60 VCLT does not apply directly to breaches of mandatory Security Council resolutions. It is the basic idea behind Article 60 that applies – the idea that a material breach gives rise to a right to terminate the instrument or suspend its operation. But the detailed terms of Article 60 (which are in any event of a residual nature)[66] and the elaborate associated procedures in Articles 65 to 68 VCLT cannot apply, even by analogy, in the case of the material breach of a Security Council resolution.[67] The main reason for this is that a resolution has no parties, unless the Security Council and the States and others upon whom the resolution imposes obligations are viewed as such. In the case of Resolution 687 (1991), the Council and Iraq could indeed be seen as 'parties', which is consistent with the position that it was for the Council itself to determine whether there had been a material breach and to specify the consequences that flowed therefrom.

5 Conclusions

The critical question under Resolution 687 (1991) was who decides whether there has been a material breach such as to justify the use of force. The answer was connected with the nature of the resolution and the ceasefire that it established. We have seen the differing views of the United States and the United Kingdom, and the position taken by the United Nations Legal Counsel. A further clear indication is given in its last paragraph – operative paragraph 34 – under which the Security Council decided that it would 'take such further steps as may be required for the implementation of the present resolution and to secure peace and security in the area'. It was for the Security Council, not one or more members of the 'coalition of the willing', to determine whether there was a material breach, as had happened in 1993 and 1998. And it was for the Security Council to take any steps required for the implementation of Resolution 687 (1991).

We have tried to summarise in this chapter some of the differences between treaty interpretation and the interpretation of Security Council

[66] Art. 60(4) VCLT reads: 'The foregoing paragraphs are without prejudice to any provision in the treaty applicable in the event of a breach'.

[67] Efforts to explain matters by reference to the detailed provisions of Art. 60 VCLT are therefore beside the point. See, e.g., M. Weller, *Iraq and the Use of Force in International Law* (Oxford: Oxford University Press, 2010), pp. 106–119.

resolutions, which seem particularly relevant to the interpretation of Resolution 687 (1991). That resolution is a typical example of a resolution that has to be read as part of a series, stretching back to Resolution 660 (1990) and forward to Resolution 1441 (2002) and beyond. The interpretation of Resolution 687 (1991) was under constant scrutiny over this twelve-year period, which resulted in many subsequent decisions and much subsequent practice. And the fact that a resolution is an act of an organ of an international organization, not an agreement between two or more States, becomes even more significant when it is a resolution imposing a ceasefire.

The present chapter has touched on one aspect of Resolution 687 (1991). Its many interesting provisions would also benefit from further analysis, now that it is no longer at the centre of ongoing political controversy and the complete story of its life is known.

25

The World Trade Organization

JOOST PAUWELYN AND ISABELLE VAN DAMME

1 Introduction

The relation between the law of treaties and the law of the World Trade Organization (WTO)[1] is described usually in terms of their separateness. Indeed, the conventional view is that the 1969 Vienna Convention on the Law of Treaties (VCLT)[2] is mainly, if not exclusively, applied in the WTO for purposes of treaty interpretation. In this chapter, we propose to adopt a broader approach by focusing on the reception of the law of treaties, and not merely Articles 31 to 33 VCLT, in WTO law against the historical background of the 1947 General Agreement on Tariffs and Trade (GATT 1947).[3] We argue that the VCLT applies in the WTO for purposes other than treaty interpretation and that this was already the case at the time when the GATT 1947 was (provisionally) applied. We show that use and references to the VCLT are visible prior to the creation of the WTO and the application of Article 3.2 of the Understanding on Rules and Procedures Governing the Settlement of Disputes (DSU) according to which the WTO dispute settlement bodies are to clarify the WTO covered agreements 'in accordance with customary rules of interpretation of public international law'.[4]

International law governing trade consists primarily of treaties, whether multilateral, plurilateral, regional or bilateral. It is thus mostly treaty-based and therefore subject to the law of treaties. WTO panels and the Appellate Body have generally given the law of treaties a favourable reception and, unless the WTO covered agreements provide for a rule that departs from the VCLT, they

---

[1] WTO Agreement: Marrakesh Agreement Establishing the World Trade Organization, 1867 UNTS 154.
[2] 1155 UNTS 331.   [3] 55 UNTS 194.   [4] 1869 UNTS 401.

have applied the law of treaties as providing a necessary set of rules to complement the covered agreements and ensure their effectiveness. Despite the structural debate about the relation between the WTO covered agreements and other parts of international law, the law of treaties thus performs an essential function of setting forward the meta-rules governing treaty relations between WTO Members. That use of the law of treaties, as the analysis in this chapter demonstrates, is often 'conservative' in the sense that panels and the Appellate Body rely especially on parts of the law of treaties that are widely accepted and do not lead to controversies. Typically, no inquiry is made into the customary international law status of a provision of the VCLT.[5] Usually, the provisions of the VCLT used are those with respect to which another international court or tribunal (typically, though not exclusively, the International Court of Justice and/or its predecessor) has already established that status and given some explanation of their content. If there is uncertainty about a provision's customary international law status, the relevance of a provision is examined before any inquiry into its status as a source of international law.[6]

Yet the interaction is not a one-way street. As one of the more active branches of international law, the practice and jurisprudence of the WTO can contribute to the further development and refinement of the law of treaties. This chapter examines the extent to which that has already happened.

---

[5] A rare instance of a case where that was done is: Panel Report, *Korea – Measures Affecting Government Procurement* ('*Korea – Government Procurement*'), WT/DS163/R, adopted 19 June 2000, DSR 2000:VIII, 3541, paragraph 7.126 (fn. 769) (on the basis of a judgment of the European Court of Justice, the Panel found that Art. 65 VCLT does not constitute customary international law) and paragraph 7.123 (on Art. 48 VCLT).

[6] See, for example, Panel Report, *European Communities – Measures Affecting the Approval and Marketing of Biotech Products* ('*EC – Biotech Products*'), WT/DS291/R, WT/DS292/R, WT/DS293/R, Corr. 1 and Add.1, 2, 3, 4, 5, 6, 7, 8, 9, adopted on 21 Nov. 2006 (fn. 251). See also, by analogy, the Appellate Body's use of the International Law Commission's Articles on State Responsibility in Appellate Body Report, *United States – Definitive Anti-dumping and Countervailing Duties on Certain Products from China* ('*US – Anti-dumping and Countervailing Duties (China)*'), WT/DS379/AB/R, adopted 25 March 2011. See, further, I. Van Damme, 'The Appellate Body's Use of the Articles on State Responsibility in US – Anti-dumping and Countervailing Duties (China)' in C. Chinkin and F. Baetens (eds.), *Sovereignty, Statehood and State Responsibility: Essays in Honour of James Crawford* (Cambridge: Cambridge University Press, 2015), pp. 363–388.

The chapter develops these themes and arguments by testing the 'two-way street' hypothesis in respect of the character and design of WTO treaties; the conclusion, provisional application and amendment of GATT/WTO treaties; the interpretation of WTO treaties; the application of WTO treaties and, finally, the consequences resulting from the breach of WTO treaties.

Whilst the focus of this chapter is not solely on the use of the law of treaties in WTO dispute settlement, that is nonetheless a context that illustrates well the reception of the law of treaties in this area of international law. Therefore, we start with some statistics on references to the VCLT in GATT and WTO dispute settlement reports.

2 Some Numbers

In WTO jurisprudence to date (1996–2016) – counting a grand total of 329 reports on record (206 panel reports and 123 Appellate Body reports)[7] – explicit references to twenty-two of the eighty-five articles of the VCLT have been made in the legal findings of panel or Appellate Body reports.[8] The VCLT has been expressly mentioned no fewer than 401 times in the legal findings of those reports (and thus not counting party arguments). Whilst the most frequent reference is to the VCLT articles on treaty interpretation (Article 31 (general rule of interpretation): 162 times; Article 32 (supplementary means of interpretation): 139 times and Article 33 (interpretation of treaties authenticated in two or more languages): twenty-four times), other VCLT provisions have also had an impact (for example, Article 18 (obligation not to defeat the object and purpose of a treaty prior to its entry into force): six times; Article 26 (*pacta sunt servanda*): fifteen times; Article 27 (internal law and observance of treaties): ten times; Article 28 (non-retroactivity of treaties): twenty times; Article 30 (application of successive treaties relating to the same subject-matter), five times; Article 60 (material breach),

---

[7] See www.worldtradelaw.net (as of 20 Feb. 2016).

[8] More specifically, Arts. 2, 7, 15, 18, 25, 26, 27, 28, 29, 30, 31, 32, 33, 34, 41, 44, 48, 59, 60, 65, 66 and 70 VCLT (Article Citation Index, WTO reports referring to the VCLT by VCLT Article, www.TradeLawGuide.com, survey conducted on 20 Feb. 2016).

three times and Article 70 (consequences of the termination of a treaty), twice).[9]

Whilst only concluded in May 1969 and in force since January 1980, the VCLT was mentioned in no fewer than fifteen GATT panel reports[10] (out of a total of eighty-three GATT panel reports available in or after 1980 or 100 GATT panel reports issued in or after 1969).[11] The first such reference is in a US argument on 'subsequent practice' in the *DISC* case, circulated in 1976 but adopted only in 1981.[12] The first reference to the VCLT in a GATT panel's reasoning was in the 1985 *Canada – Gold Coins* dispute.[13] This was a reference not to Articles 31 to 33 VCLT (interpretation of treaties) but to Article 27 VCLT (internal law is not a justification for failure to perform a treaty). Out of the fifteen GATT panel reports referring to the VCLT, ten refer to VCLT provisions on treaty interpretation, and eight refer also or exclusively to other VCLT provisions (in particular, Articles 27, 28, 30, 45 and 58).

Other than the *DISC* case, all references to the VCLT in GATT panel reports were made in reports *post*-dating the entry into force of the VCLT. Out of the twenty-five GATT panel reports circulated between 1992 and 1995 (the final years of operation of the GATT 1947), thirteen explicitly mentioned the VCLT and, in many other reports, panels used or applied the VCLT without doing so in explicit terms. Indeed, the former Director of the Legal Affairs Division of the GATT, in charge of GATT dispute panels from 1989 to 1995, has stated that GATT panels were often hesitant to refer expressly to the VCLT for fear of upsetting certain GATT

---

[9] See Article Citation Index, WTO reports referring to the VCLT by VCLT Article, www .TradeLawGuide.com, survey conducted on 20 Feb. 2016, counting the total number of citations for each VCLT provision.

[10] Based on a search for 'Vienna Convention on the Law of Treaties' in the www .TradeLawGuide.com text search function limited to GATT 1947 & 1979 Codes, Jurisprudence. This includes any reference to the VCLT in parties' arguments and panels' reasoning.

[11] Numbers of GATT panel reports are drawn from www.worldtradelaw.net.

[12] Report of the Panel on *United States Tax Legislation (DISC)*, 2 Nov. 1976, paragraph 42, adopted on 7–8 Dec. 1981, BISD 23S/98 and 28S/114.

[13] Panel Report on *Canada – Measures Affecting the Sale of Gold Coins*, L/5863, 17 Sept. 1985, unadopted, paragraph 53.

Contracting Parties, especially those which had not (yet) ratified the VCLT (such as the United States).[14] Of course, at the time, a single GATT Contracting Party could block the adoption of a panel report. Against that background, panellists were writing their reports with an eye on making them 'politically acceptable' for the entire GATT membership (not, as WTO panels do today, with the objective of making their reports appeal proof before the WTO Appellate Body or legally sound in the eyes of the readers of those reports). In the 1989 GATT panel report on *US – Restrictions on Imports of Sugar*, for example, neither the parties nor the panel explicitly referred to the VCLT. Yet, when reading that panel's findings, it is clear that the panel interpreted Article II of the GATT 1947 in a manner that scrupulously weighed all the relevant elements mentioned in Articles 31 and 32 VCLT, referring first to text and 'ordinary meaning' before looking at the issue 'in the light of the purpose of the General Agreement', considering the issue in 'context' and then turning to 'the practice' of the GATT parties and, finally, to 'the drafting history'.[15]

Despite their relative character, these numbers show (i) that contrary to conventional wisdom, extensive references have been made not only to VCLT rules on treaty interpretation but also to a large number of other VCLT provisions and (ii) that GATT panels also used the VCLT, especially during the final years of the GATT 1947 (1992–1995), both explicitly and implicitly and in respect of both VCLT rules on treaty interpretation and other VCLT provisions. As a result, the conventional view according to which GATT panels did not apply the VCLT rules on treaty interpretation, prior to the inclusion of Article 3.2 of the DSU, might be mistaken.[16] If anything, it seems that Article 3.2 of the DSU confirmed GATT panel practice rather than overruled it.

---

[14] Presentation by F. Roessler at the Conference 'Legal Affairs Division at 30', WTO, Geneva, on 28 June 2012.

[15] GATT Panel Report on *United States – Restrictions on Imports of Sugar*, adopted 22 June 1989, BISD 36S/331, paragraphs 5.2–5.6.

[16] See, for example, GATT Panel Report, *United States – Restrictions on Imports of Tuna*, DS29/R, 16 June 1994, unadopted, paragraph 5.18. See, also, GATT Panel Report, *United States – Imposition of Countervailing Duties on Certain Hot-Rolled Lead and Bismuth Carbon Steel Products Originating in France, Germany and the United Kingdom*, 15 Nov. 1994, unadopted, SCM/185, paragraph 368.

3 Character and Design of WTO Treaties

The WTO 'treaties' consist of the Marrakesh Agreement Establishing the World Trade Organization (or 'WTO Agreement')[17] and 'agreements and associated legal instruments' attached in the form of four annexes to the WTO Agreement. All of these agreements and certain other legal instruments are considered to be an integral part of the WTO Agreement and binding on all WTO Members (with the exception of Annex 4, discussed later).[18] In principle, WTO membership is conditional upon acceptance to be bound by all of these treaties and other instruments. Annexes 2 and 3 contain, respectively, the DSU[19] and the Trade Policy Review Mechanism.[20] Annex 1, by contrast, is further divided into three parts dealing with trade in goods, trade in services and trade-related aspects of intellectual property rights. The first part of the first annex, containing multilateral agreements on trade in goods, further consists of a set of separate treaties. In addition, some of these agreements need to be read together with, for example, the schedules of concessions and commitments (for each WTO Member) attached to them, protocols and certifications relating to tariff concessions, annexes containing notes and supplementary provisions, decisions on waivers, GATT decisions forming part of the WTO agreements,[21] so-called 'Understandings', etc. For newly acceded Members, in particular, Accession Protocols and Working Party Reports set forth legally binding provisions that co-exist with the other treaties. A fourth annex contains agreements and associated legal instruments that are 'part' of the WTO Agreement but only for those WTO Members that have agreed to accept them (the so-called 'plurilateral agreements').[22]

The general structure of the WTO treaties looks like this:

---

[17] *Supra* n. 1.   [18] Art. II:2 of the WTO Agreement: *supra* n. 1.   [19] *Supra* n. 4.

[20] 1869 UNTS 480.

[21] For example, the Enabling Clause or Decision of 28 Nov. 1979 on Differential and More Favourable Treatment, Reciprocity and Fuller Participation of Developing Countries (L/4903). That GATT decision forms part of the GATT 1994 on the basis of paragraph 1(b)(iv) of Annex 1A of the WTO Agreement. See, also, Appellate Body Report, *European Communities – Conditions for the Granting of Tariff Preferences to Developing Countries*, WT/DS246/AB/R, adopted 20 April 2004, DSR 2004:III, 925, paragraph 90 (fn. 192).

[22] Art. II:3 of the WTO Agreement: *supra* n. 1. See, further, 1915 UNTS 103.

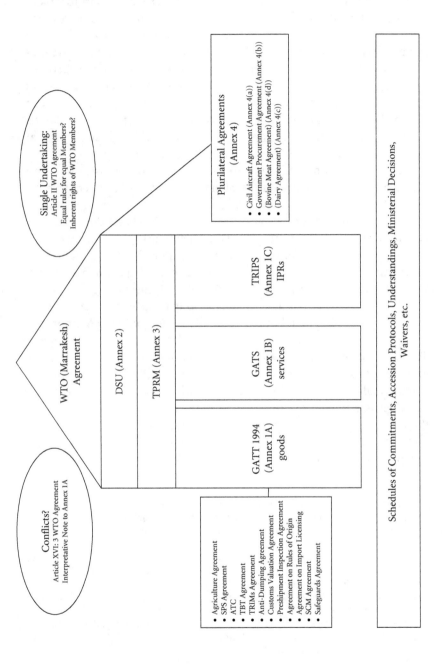

Single Undertaking:
Article II WTO Agreement
Equal rules for equal Members?
Inherent rights of WTO Members?

Conflicts?
Article XVI: 3 WTO Agreement
Interpretative Note to Annex 1A

WTO (Marrakesh)
Agreement

Plurilateral Agreements
(Annex 4)

- Civil Aircraft Agreement (Annex 4(a))
- Government Procurement Agreement (Annex 4(b))
- (Bovine Meat Agreement) (Annex 4(d))
- (Dairy Agreement) (Annex 4(c))

DSU (Annex 2)

TPRM (Annex 3)

GATT 1994
(Annex 1A)
goods

GATS
(Annex 1B)
services

TRIPS
(Annex 1C)
IPRs

- Agriculture Agreement
- SPS Agreement
- ATC
- TBT Agreement
- TRIMs Agreement
- Anti-Dumping Agreement
- Customs Valuation Agreement
- Preshipment Inspection Agreement
- Agreement on Rules of Origin
- Agreement on Import Licensing
- SCM Agreement
- Safeguards Agreement

Schedules of Commitments, Accession Protocols, Understandings, Ministerial Decisions,
Waivers, etc.

While the WTO covered agreements are heterogeneous in form and structure, they all satisfy the elements of the definition of a treaty in Article 2(1)(a) VCLT.[23] Leaving aside these elements, it is difficult, if not impossible, to characterise the WTO covered agreements as treaties that, depending on their content, are either law-making or contractual – assuming that that is a valid distinction to be made between types of treaty in public international law.[24] None of the treaties as a whole can be labelled as constitutional, administrative, contractual or legislative. Many provisions are prescriptive; others recognise existing rights of States in international law or, as a matter of WTO law, create new rights.[25] They can be addressed to Members or to the institution and concern the relation between Members and between Members and the institution.

Even if an obligation is owed to all other Members, the reciprocal character of such an obligation does not necessarily prevent that (with respect to certain types of provision) two or more Members may agree, for example, to waive a right that the WTO covered agreements protect. One example, taken from a procedural context, is the requirement under Article 17.10 of the DSU that Appellate Body proceedings shall be confidential and the implied, but corresponding, right of WTO Members to respect of the confidentiality of the proceedings in which they appear. The Appellate Body accepts that parties to a dispute may forego that right provided this does not affect the right of third participants to confidentiality.[26] This is thus a situation where two or more Members can agree to waive a right insofar as it applies between them and of which the covered agreements are constitutive while observing the obligation owed to other Members to respect their same right. While formally waiving an obligation owed to the entire WTO membership requires

---

[23] A 'treaty' for the purposes of the VCLT is 'an international agreement concluded between States in written form and governed by international law, whether embodied in a single instrument or in two or more related instruments and whatever its particular designation': *supra* n. 2.

[24] See, further, the contribution to this volume of Brölmann at pp. 79–102 (Chapter 4), and, also, J. Pauwelyn, 'A Typology of Multilateral Treaty Obligations: Are WTO Obligations Bilateral or Collective in Nature?', *EJIL*, 14 (2003), 907–952.

[25] See, generally, M. E. Footer, *An Institutional and Normative Analysis of the World Trade Organization* (Leiden: Martinus Nijhoff, 2005), pp. 271–326.

[26] Appellate Body, *Canada/United States – Continued Suspension of Obligations in the EC – Hormones Dispute* ('*Canada/US – Continued Suspension*'), WT/DS321/AB/R, WT/DS320/AB/R, adopted 14 Nov. 2008, Procedural Ruling of 10 July to Allow Public Observations of the Oral Hearing, paragraphs 6 and 7.

a decision by the Ministerial Conference in accordance with Article IX:3 and 4 of the WTO Agreement (by three-quarters of WTO Members; in practice, consensus is required), there may be circumstances where the content of the right permits two or more WTO Members to waive as between themselves the reciprocal obligation of mutual respect for that right. The extent to which that reasoning can be extended to other rights established under the WTO Agreement, other than such procedural rights, remains uncertain. Nor is it clear whether it matters whether such an agreement is reached outside or inside the context of the WTO. Thus, in *Peru – Agricultural Products*, the Appellate Body did 'not exclude the possibility of articulating the relinquishment of the right to initiate WTO dispute settlement proceedings in a form other than a waiver embodied in a mutually agreed solution'.[27] That case concerned whether such a relinquishment could have been reached in a free trade agreement between two WTO Members outside the WTO. However, the Appellate Body added that relinquishment of the DSU right to a panel (as regards the settlement of specific disputes) in such a form needed to be 'in relation to, or within the context of, the rules and procedures of the DSU'.[28]

It should be added, however, that, pursuant to Article XIII of the WTO Agreement, a WTO Member may also decide not to apply the WTO treaties in their entirety to one or more other WTO Members. Crucially, however, such non-application can only be invoked 'at the time either becomes a Member' and can be withdrawn subsequently by the Member invoking Article XIII. It is a type of flexibility that is not entirely unlike a reservation.[29]

The fact remains that, as a matter of the law of treaties, panels and the Appellate Body generally consider the WTO covered agreements to form a homogeneous set of treaties even though these treaties can diverge widely in terms of their content, structure, wording and the process through which they are concluded. So far, panels and the Appellate Body have neglected to call into question the proposition that the law

---

[27] Appellate Body, *Peru – Additional Duty on Imports of Certain Agricultural Products* ('*Peru – Agricultural Products*'), WT/DS457/AB/R, adopted on 31 July 2015, paragraph 5.25.

[28] *Ibid.* (paragraph 5.25 (fn. 106)).

[29] See further, for example, M. Footer, 'Article XXXV GATT' in R. Wolfrum, P.-T. Stoll and H. P. Hestermeyer (eds.), *WTO – Trade in Goods* (Leiden: Martinus Nijhoff, 2011), pp. 762–765 (and references included therein, in particular to reports of the ILC's Special Rapporteur on Reservations).

of treaties, as it is codified in the VCLT, applies to all forms of WTO law in the same manner. Consistent with that approach, the Appellate Body has attempted, for example, to interpret schedules of commitments according to the same methodology applied in interpreting, for example, the GATT 1994.[30] Schedules of commitments contain the specific concessions made by each individual WTO Member to its trading partners during multilateral trade rounds but also during bilateral or plurilateral negotiations outside a round or membership negotiations. They exist for goods, services, agriculture and government procurement and form integral parts of the WTO covered agreements. Article II of the GATT 1994 sets out the main disciplines governing goods schedules. Changes in tariff bindings need to be negotiated by each WTO Member with its trading partners, possibly in combination with an offer of compensation for trading partners' loss in trade as a result of the change (pursuant to Article XXVIII of the GATT 1994). Schedules negotiations need to be pursued on a reciprocal and mutually advantageous basis; concessions are to be bound and need to be applied on a most-favoured-nation (MFN) basis.[31] On the ground that they are an integral part of the WTO Agreement, the Appellate Body interprets schedules like any other WTO treaty language. It is evident that a text with treaty authority, even if it consists of lists of products in a schedule, be given meaning based on the words used in that text. While it might be true that, depending on the type of tariff negotiation involved, certain obligations in schedules are of a bilateral and contractual character, these obligations are then taken to the multilateral level ('multilateralised') on the basis of the WTO Agreement itself. The term 'integral part' used in the WTO Agreement – and repeatedly emphasised by the Appellate Body – then prevails over the general characterisation of the obligations concerned.[32] Whatever is the case with standard multilateral treaty texts (where the assumption of a common intention of all the parties may be a fiction anyway), the presumption that 'treaty language' (that is, authoritatively agreed treaty texts) reflects the common intentions of its drafters does

---

[30] 1867 UNTS 187.
[31] Art. II:7 of the GATT 1994, *supra* n. 30; Art. XX:3 of the General Agreement on Trade in Services (GATS), Annex 1B of the Marrakesh Agreement Establishing the World Trade Organization, 1869 UNTS 183, and Art. 3.1 of the Agreement on Agriculture, Annex 1A of the Marrakesh Agreement Establishing the World Trade Organization, 1867 UNTS 410. See, also, Art. XXIV:12 of the Agreement on Government Procurement, 1867 UNTS 194 (which is a plurilateral agreement).
[32] Pauwelyn, *supra* n. 24, at 926.

not readily apply to all 'treaty language', and schedules of commitments might prompt an alternative characterisation. Schedules are not unilateral declarations but are more like multilateral acts of a special character; similar to reservations, they are more unilateral than other treaty language.[33]

In the context of WTO dispute settlement, the paradigm of the unity of WTO law[34] nonetheless enables panels and the Appellate Body to interpret and apply the covered agreements as if they form a single treaty text, applicable to all WTO Members. It is this sole treaty text that (in principle) can be used as a basis for establishing jurisdiction and which has been in practice the applicable law to resolve disputes between WTO Members. The paradigm as such likely could not apply if the applicable law were to be defined more widely so as to include other norms of international law (which might bind only a sub-set of WTO Members) or WTO law were to be interpreted differently depending on the WTO Members in dispute (and the outside norms or conduct in which those disputing parties might have engaged) or in the case of disputes arising under plurilateral agreements. In those circumstances, techniques of interpretation based on the (aspired) internal coherence or intra-effectiveness of the agreements when read as a whole, even if not apparently supported by their wording, could no longer be sustained as being intended by all WTO Members in agreeing to be bound by those texts constituting WTO law. Given the diversity of commitments between and amongst WTO Members under existing WTO treaties, diverse application and interpretation or variable geometry, depending on the facts and the WTO Members involved, form a logical alternative.

Unlike the constitutive texts of some other powerful international or regional organizations (in particular the European Union),[35] the WTO Agreement does not provide a general basis for WTO bodies to adopt secondary norms of WTO law (other than decisions by WTO organs implementing or administering existing WTO treaties) and for judicial review of such decisions. Although the WTO is an organization consisting of a detailed institutional structure wherein competences are mostly substance-based and is tasked with facilitating, among others, the

---

[33] See, further, I. Van Damme, 'The Interpretation of Schedules of Commitments', *J. World Trade*, 41 (2007), 1–54.

[34] This paradigm is to be distinguished from that of the 'single package'. The latter reflects the principle applied during the Uruguay Round negotiations to the effect that nothing is agreed until everything is agreed.

[35] See the contribution to this volume of Koutrakos at pp. 933–965 (Chapter 29).

implementation and administration of the covered agreements, either those bodies have no generally defined legislative powers or, where decision-making powers are attributed to a WTO body,[36] there is uncertainty about the legislative status of such decisions and their use remains limited.[37] Despite those features, WTO treaties are increasingly read in the light of declarations, decisions, guidelines, and other products of the activities within those bodies. Through those instruments, WTO Members often agree on how to apply or interpret parts of the treaty text and thereby further develop existing rules. Increasingly, panels and the Appellate Body acknowledge the interpretive relevance of such instruments and seek a basis in the VCLT for that approach. In that context, the Appellate Body in *US - Tuna II (Mexico)* decided that a Technical Barriers to Trade Committee Decision on Principles for the Development of International Standards, Guides and Recommendations[38] was a subsequent agreement between the parties regarding the interpretation of the Agreement on Technical Barriers to Trade[39] and therefore could, based on Article 31(3)(a) VCLT, be used to interpret Article 2.4 of that agreement.[40] In another report, the Appellate

---

[36] For example, Art. 12.1 of the Agreement on the Application of Sanitary and Phytosanitary Measures (SPS), 1867 UNTS 493, states that the SPS Committee 'shall carry out the functions necessary to implement the provisions' of that agreement and Art. 12.4 attributes power to the same committee to 'develop a procedure to monitor the process of international harmonization and the use of international standards, guidelines or recommendations'.

[37] For an extensive study of those powers, see, for example, P. J. Kuijper, 'WTO Institutional Aspects' in D. Bethlehem, D. McRae, R. Neufeld and I. Van Damme (eds.), *The Oxford Handbook of International Trade Law* (Oxford: Oxford University Press, 2009), pp. 79–128.

[38] Decision of the Committee on Principles for the Development of International Standards, Guides and Recommendations with relation to Arts. 2, 5 and Annex 3 of the Agreement, in WTO document G/TBT/1/Rev.9, Decisions and Recommendations adopted by the WTO Committee on Technical Barriers to Trade since 1 Jan. 1995, 8 Sept. 2008, 37–39; and WTO document G/TBT/1/Rev.10, 9 June 2011, 46–48.

[39] 1868 UNTS 120.

[40] Appellate Body Report, *United States - Measures Concerning the Importation, Marketing and Sale of Tuna and Tuna Products* ('*US - Tuna II (Mexico)*'), WT/DS381/AB/R, adopted on 13 June 2012, paragraphs 371–378. Compare with an apparently more restrictive approach adopted in *EC - Bananas III (Article 21.5 - Ecuador II)/ EC - Bananas III (Article 21.5 - US)*, finding that multilateral authoritative interpretations adopted pursuant to Art. IX:2 of the WTO Agreement are most akin to subsequent agreements. Appellate Body Reports, *European Communities - Regime for the Importation, Sale and Distribution of Bananas - Second Recourse to Article 21.5 of the DSU by Ecuador*, WT/DS27/AB/RW2/ECU, adopted 11 Dec. 2008, and Corr.1/*European Communities - Regime for the Importation, Sale and Distribution of Bananas - Recourse to Article 21.5 of the DSU by the United States* ('*EC - Bananas III (Article 21.5 - Ecuador II)/*

Body construed the Doha Ministerial Declaration as a 'subsequent agreement' to guide its interpretation of a 'reasonable interval' in Article 2.12 of the Agreement on Technical Barriers to Trade (TBT Agreement).[41] Those decisions might signal that the Appellate Body is willing to endorse the position that the meaning of the complex treaty structure agreed upon in the Uruguay Round needs constant revision and 'updating' as a result of action of WTO Members in various committees and other bodies – even though the mechanism in question cannot be characterised as a formal waiver,[42] authoritative interpretation or amendment adopted pursuant to the procedures explicitly provided for in the WTO Agreement itself (outside the context of WTO treaty negotiations).

Despite the fact that the agreements themselves provide for conflict of norm rules defining how they apply together,[43] the legal fiction that these treaties form an integral part is increasingly tested, especially in the context of the relation between the GATT 1994 and the other agreements on trade in goods contained in Annex 1A to the WTO Agreement as well goods related disciplines in Accession Protocols.

The approaches taken by the Appellate Body in two recent cases illustrate this well. The first case is *China – Various Raw Materials*. The Appellate Body was asked to consider the application of the general exceptions clause in Article XX of the GATT 1994 as a legal basis to justify an export duty that is otherwise inconsistent with China's Accession Protocol. That Accession Protocol neither confirmed nor excluded the application of Article XX of the GATT 1994. The omission of a provision governing the availability of an exception

---

EC – Bananas III (Article 21.5 – US)'), WT/DS27/AB/RW/USA and Corr.1, adopted 22 Dec. 2008, paragraphs 390–391.

[41] Appellate Body Report, *United States – Measures Affecting the Production and Sale of Clove Cigarettes ('US – Clove Cigarettes')*, WT/DS406/AB/R, adopted 24 Apr. 2012, paragraph 268. For the TBT Agreement: 1868 UNTS 120.

[42] For example, in *EC – Bananas III (Article 21.5 – Ecuador II)/EC – Bananas III (Article 21.5 – US)*, the Appellate Body disagreed with the Panel that the Doha Art. I Waiver was a subsequent agreement seemingly because it was neither an agreement bearing specifically on the interpretation of a treaty nor an agreement specifying how existing rules or obligations need to be applied. Appellate Body Reports, *EC – Bananas III (Article 21.5 – Ecuador II)/EC – Bananas III (Article 21.5 – US)*, supra n. 40, paragraphs 390–391.

[43] For example, Art. XVI:3 of the WTO Agreement provides that '[i]n the event of a conflict between a provision of this Agreement and a provision of any of the Multilateral Trade Agreements, the provision of this Agreement shall prevail to the extent of the conflict': *supra* n. 1. The general interpretative note to Annex 1A states: 'In the event of conflict between a provision of the [GATT 1994] and a provision of another agreement in [Annex 1A], the provision of the other agreement shall prevail to the extent of the conflict'.

to justify the imposition of an export duty on grounds that such a measure protects interests defined in Article XX could arguably be read in different ways. The Appellate Body resolved the interpretive uncertainty by resorting to a strict, formalist approach to treaty interpretation. Ultimately, its reasoning was based on the consideration that, in the absence of an explicit confirmation of the application of Article XX of the GATT 1994 and where the Protocol itself provides for specific exceptions, China is precluded from justifying an otherwise WTO-inconsistent export duty with reference to Article XX. That reasoning illustrates the difficulty facing the Appellate Body – but, also, panels – to reconcile the treaty text with the function and characteristics of particular treaty obligations. An exception clause like that found in Article XX seeks to balance the interest of trade liberalisation against legitimate interests justifying certain trade restrictions. Neither Article XX nor any other part of the covered agreements is constitutive of those legitimate interests. Instead, by joining the WTO, a WTO Member accepts that those interests may be pursued only if in accordance with the obligations in the covered agreements, including the conditions that, for example, define the required connection between the measure and the stated objective.

The Appellate Body refused to endorse this approach despite its earlier confirmation in *China – Audiovisual Products* of the general principle that it is the sovereign right of States to regulate trade, which is restricted only to the extent that a State accepts limitations on that right by acceding to the WTO.[44] Through this prism, which reflects a foundational principle of international law, the Appellate Body in *China – Audiovisual Products* did not construe the meaning of the WTO agreements on the basis of some rigid structure of interpretive steps. It articulated views on the balance of powers between WTO members and the depth and scope of their regulatory freedom. By contrast, in *China – Various Raw Materials*, the Appellate Body essentially refused to read the disciplines on trade in goods in the Accession Protocol together with those set out in the GATT 1994 to which China has also acceded. The main reason therefore was that the former did not expressly confirm China's right to rely on Article XX of the GATT 1994, with respect to those export duties. In particular, 'there [was] no language in Paragraph 11.3 [at issue in *Various Raw Materials*] similar to that found in Paragraph 5.1 of China's

---

[44] Appellate Body Report, *China – Measures Affecting Trading Rights and Distribution Services for Certain Publications and Audiovisual Entertainment Products* ('*China – Audiovisual Products*'), WT/DS363/AB/R, adopted 19 Jan. 2010, esp. paragraph 222.

Accession Protocol [at issue in *China – Audiovisual Products*]' (namely '[w]ithout prejudice to China's right to regulate trade in a manner consistent with the WTO Agreement').[45] No explanation was given of why it was not relevant to consider instead whether the text of the Accession Protocol expressly excluded China's pre-accession right to use trade instruments for legitimate policy goals such as those enumerated in Article XX or its newly acquired obligation to do so only in a manner consistent with the disciplines assumed under the latter provision.

Shortly after *China – Various Raw Materials*, the Appellate Body in *US – Clove Cigarettes* used the preambular language in the TBT Agreement, in particular the phrase '[d]esiring to further the objectives of GATT 1994', to construe the general relationship between that agreement and the GATT 1994.[46] The Appellate Body read that phrase to mean that 'the two agreements overlap in scope and have similar objectives' and as indicating that 'the TBT Agreement expands on pre-existing GATT disciplines and emphasizes that the two agreements should be interpreted in a coherent and consistent manner'.[47] It followed also from the fifth and sixth recitals that the TBT Agreement explicitly recognised a WTO Member's right to regulate in order to pursue certain legitimate objectives provided that right was exercised in accordance with that agreement. The balance between that right and the desire to avoid creating unnecessary obstacles to international trade, the Appellate Body found, 'is not, in principle, different from the balance set out in the GATT 1994, where obligations such as national treatment in Article III are qualified by the general exceptions provision of Article XX'.[48] That balance, found between Article III:4 as qualified by the exceptions in Article XX of GATT 1994, is reflected in a single provision in the TBT Agreement.[49]

Ultimately, the different approaches and outcomes in *China – Various Raw Materials* and *US – Clove Cigarettes* can be reconciled only by accepting the distinction made between, on the one hand, a provision or agreement prescribing an obligation that is a development of an existing WTO obligation and, on the other hand, a provision or agreement that creates an obligation additional to those found in existing agreements (and without being based thereon).

---

[45] Appellate Body Report, *China – Measures Related to the Exportation of Various Raw Materials* ('*China – Various Raw Materials*'), WT/DS394/AB/R, WT/DS395/AB/R, WT/DS398/AB/R, adopted on 22 Feb. 2012, paragraph 291.

[46] Appellate Body Report, *US – Clove Cigarettes*, *supra* n. 41, paragraphs 90–91.

[47] *Ibid.* (paragraph 91).   [48] *Ibid.* (paragraph 96).   [49] *Ibid.* (paragraph 109).

The distinction is subtle and possibly difficult to justify. Had China's Accession Protocol included preambular language to the effect of confirming the objectives of the WTO, arguably there would be no basis for the distinction.[50] Indeed, it is difficult to argue that disciplines on export duties are *not* a further, more progressive development of the WTO's objectives as well as of existing disciplines governing trade instruments applied at the border.[51] The tension (and possibly contradiction) between the two cases shows that, when interpreting WTO rules that apply generally to all WTO Members (such as the GATT 1994 or the TBT Agreement), the Appellate Body progressively attempts to strengthen the unity of WTO law whereas, when interpreting WTO rules that apply only to some WTO Members (such as China's Accession Protocol), it conservatively enforces the separateness of those provisions or agreements. The Appellate Body has yet to explain how it separates additional obligations from those constituting a development of an existing commitment.

4   Conclusion, Provisional Application and Amendment of GATT/WTO Treaties

The WTO was established and the WTO covered agreements were concluded against the background of the longstanding but provisional application of the GATT 1947, its interpretation and amendment, as well as a series of treaties that were concluded by some GATT Contracting Parties and intended to co-exist with the GATT 1947. The provisional application of the GATT 1947[52] predates the drafting and entry into force of the VCLT, which expressly provides in Article 25 for the possibility of the provisional application of a treaty.[53]

---

[50] See, also, J. Qin, 'The Challenge of Interpreting "WTO-PLUS" Provisions', *J. World Trade*, 44 (2010), 127–172, at 139–140. On the importance of preambles more generally, consider the contribution to this volume of Klabbers at pp. 172–200 (Chapter 7).

[51] See, also, Qin, *ibid.*, at 157–158.

[52] For a brief history of the circumstances surrounding the provisional application of the GATT 1947, see J. H. Jackson, 'History of the General Agreement on Tariffs and Trade' in R. Wolfrum, P.-T. Stoll and H. P. Hestermeyer (eds.), *Max Planck Commentaries on World Trade* (Vol. 5: Trade in Goods) (Leiden: Martinus Nijhoff, 2011), pp. 1–24, esp. at pp. 5–16. For a more detailed history, see D. A. Irwin, P. C. Mavroidis and A. O. Sykes, *The Genesis of the GATT* (Cambridge: Cambridge University Press, 2008), and 'Provisional Application of the General Agreement' in the GATT Analytical Index, pp. 1071–1084.

[53] See the contribution to this volume of Quast Mertsch at pp. 303–334 (Chapter 10).

In accordance with that provision, '[a] treaty or part of a treaty is applied provisionally pending its entry into force if ... the treaty itself so provides; or ... the negotiating States have in some other manner so agreed'.[54] Article 25 was included as a recognition of the 'practice which occurs with some frequency [at the time of drafting the VCLT]' and was based on the consideration that '[c]learly, the "provisional" application of the treaty will terminate upon the treaty being duly ratified or approved in accordance with the terms of the treaty or upon it becoming clear that the treaty is not going to be ratified or approved by one of the parties'.[55] The documentation available does not show that the provisional application of the GATT 1947 formed part of the practice that was the basis of the International Law Commission's (ILC) codification of the law of treaties on provisional application.[56]

Consistent with the norm subsequently codified in Article 25(1) VCLT, consent to the provisional (partial) application of the GATT 1947 was expressed in a distinct agreement, namely the Protocol of Provisional Application of the General Agreement on Tariffs and Trade,[57] providing for the provisional application of Parts I and III of the GATT 1947 as well as of Part II of the GATT 1947 to the fullest extent not inconsistent with existing legislation.

Apart from its longstanding application, the particularity of the GATT 1947 is that its provisional application was a pragmatic response to the risk that some States would not, according to their internal laws, ratify another treaty, the Havana Charter for An International Trade Organization.[58] There was therefore a triangular link between the protocol on provisional application, the treaty being provisionally applied

---

[54] Art. 25(1) VCLT: *supra* n. 2.   [55] *YbILC* (1962–II), 182.

[56] More recent work of the ILC shows, by contrast, a deep interest in the (mostly interpretive) practices of the WTO. See, for example, the ongoing work of the ILC on 'treaties over time' and the 'provisional application of treaties'. For an overview of the work done so far, see Report of the International Law Commission, Sixty-fourth session (7 May–1 June and 2 July–3 Aug. 2012), A/67/10, Chapter VII (provisional application of treaties) and Chapter X (treaties over time) as well as the First Report by the Special Rapporteur, A/CN.4/660, and International Law Commission, 'Report of the Study Group on Fragmentation of International Law: Difficulties arising from the Diversification and Expansion of International Law', finalised by Martti Koskenniemi, U.N. Doc. A/CN.4/L.682 (2006) (and taken note of by the Sixth Committee of the General Assembly, Doc. A/61/454, paragraph III.4). See, also, the ILC's focus on the practice of international organizations and the value of decisions of international courts or tribunals in the context of its study on 'Formation and evidence of customary international law' (see, for example, A/CN.4/659 and A/67/10, Chapter VIII).

[57] 55 UNTS 308.   [58] U.N. Doc. E/Conf. 2/78.

and the treaty causing the provisional application. The obligation to respect the rule *pacta sunt servanda* in performing obligations owed under the protocol and indirectly under the GATT 1947 was found to co-exist with the obligation to refrain from undermining the object and purpose of the Havana Charter (that is, the treaty causing the GATT 1947 to be provisionally applied).[59]

The GATT 1947 thus provisionally applied pending its entry into force, which never in fact occurred.[60] Nor did any Contracting Party seek to terminate it, although withdrawals were made.[61] Pending its entry into force, the institutional architecture constructed around the GATT 1947 nonetheless produced a considerable body of practice under the agreement[62] and the GATT 1947 was complemented by other stand-alone treaties that did enter into force, such as the agreements resulting from the Tokyo Round (on, for example, technical standards, subsidies or anti-dumping).

The signature of the 'Final Act Embodying the Results of the Uruguay Round of Multilateral Trade Negotiations'[63] and the adoption of associated Ministerial Decisions initiated the transition from the GATT 1947

---

[59] In this chapter, we do not consider the reception of the GATT 1947 as a treaty being provisionally applied in the domestic legal orders of Contracting Parties to that agreement.

[60] During the provisional application of the GATT 1947, discussions about its definitive application continued. In 1966, the Director-General even noted that many Contracting Parties appeared prepared to accept the GATT 1947 under its Art. XXVI provided that they could confidently expect that a sufficient number of other Contracting Parties would do the same. See GATT Contracting Parties, *Definitive Application of the GATT – Note by the Director-General*, L/2611 (24 March 1966).

[61] See, e.g., Liberia's withdrawal from the GATT 1947 in accordance with Paragraph 7 of the Terms of Accession of the Annecy Protocol (G/45 (16 April 1954)); Portugal's withdrawal from the Customs Valuation Agreement (VAL/34 (5 Feb. 1988)); Syria's withdrawal from the GATT 1947 in accordance with Paragraph 5 of the Protocol of Provisional Application (GATT/CP/118 (6 Aug. 1951)); the United States' withdrawal from the Agreement on Import Licensing Proceedings pursuant to Art. 5(7) of that agreement (LIC/24 (26 Jan. 1995)).

[62] That is sometimes referred to as the 'GATT acquis'. In that regard, Art. XVI:1 of the WTO Agreement states: 'Except as otherwise provided ... the WTO shall be guided by the decisions, procedures and customary practices followed by the Contracting Parties to GATT 1947 and the bodies established in the framework of GATT 1947'. Paragraph 1(b)(iv) of the language of Annex 1A incorporating the GATT 1994 into the WTO Agreement, 1867 UNTS 190, provides that 'other decisions of the Contracting Parties to GATT 1947' which have entered into force under the GATT 1947 before the date of entry into force of the WTO Agreement are part of the GATT 1994 and thus treaty language (rather than serving as 'guidance').

[63] The WTO Agreement, the Ministerial Declarations and Decisions and the Understanding of Commitments in Financial Services form an integral part of the Final Act.

to the WTO.[64] By signing the Act, representatives agreed to submit the WTO Agreement to their internal ratification procedures and to adopt the Ministerial Declarations and Decisions.[65]

In preparing the transition from the GATT 1947 and additional treaties to the WTO Agreement, which incorporates the GATT 1994 as an annex,[66] the GATT Secretariat identified three solutions for determining the terms of a contracting party's commitments following the entry into force of the WTO Agreement. A Contracting Party may (i) withdraw from the GATT 1947 and become a WTO Member, (ii) remain a GATT 1947 Contracting Party and not become a WTO Member and (iii) remain a GATT 1947 Contracting Party and become a WTO Member. In each of these circumstances, issues would arise regarding the relationship between rights and obligations under the GATT 1947 and those under the WTO Agreement and, in particular, their coexistence and the replacement of the former by the latter.[67] The Secretariat's analysis demonstrated familiarity with the principles governing the withdrawal and denunciation of treaties but also showed that it considered the VCLT to offer an incomplete and unsatisfactory solution for the necessary transition. Apart from those two options, the Secretariat proposed that all Contracting Parties may withdraw from the GATT 1947 and associated treaties. That option was available, pursuant to Article 54 VCLT, 'even if, as is the case for the GATT 1947 and the Tokyo Round Agreements, the treaty does not explicitly provide for its termination'.[68] Relying also on Article 59 VCLT, the Secretariat considered that 'once all contracting parties to the GATT 1947 or all parties to a Tokyo Round Agreement for which there is a successor agreement annexed to the WTO Agreement have become Members of the WTO, the GATT 1947 or the respective Tokyo Round Agreement could be considered terminated'.[69] It also referred to Article 70 VCLT, which describes the consequences of treaty termination and denunciation or withdrawal 'unless the treaty

---

[64] Paragraph 6 of the Marrakesh Declaration of 15 Apr. 1994.

[65] Paragraph 2 of the Final Act. Acceptance of the WTO Agreement as a whole was open by signature or otherwise: paragraph 4 of the Final Act. See, also, Decision on the Acceptance of and Accession to the Agreement Establishing the World Trade Organization.

[66] *Supra* n. 62.

[67] Preparatory Committee for the World Trade Organization Sub-Committee on Institutional, Procedural and Legal Matters, *Transitional Arrangements – Note by the Secretariat* PC/IPL/W/5 (7 Sept. 1994), paragraph 3.

[68] *Ibid.* (paragraph 6).

[69] *Ibid.* (paragraph 7). Yet, technically it would be appear sufficient that only one party remains in order to conclude that a treaty is terminated.

otherwise provides or the parties otherwise agree'.[70] The Secretariat interpreted the VCLT so as to mean that 'it would appear that the principles of Article 70 apply also in the case foreseen in Article 59 [VCLT]' and added the difficulty that 'Article 70 gives little guidance on how to determine the exact scope of these unaffected rights and obligations'.[71]

In assessing how to respond to those transitional issues, the default position was thus the application of the VCLT, and the discussion focused on whether that set of generally applicable provisions was sufficient to organise the entry into force and compliance with the newly agreed upon WTO covered agreements. If that discussion appears to have been an afterthought of the Uruguay Round trade negotiations, it nonetheless was the subject of considerable debate and resulted in the adoption of a series of transitional decisions on the co-existence and withdrawal of treaty obligations.[72] These decisions and the debates surrounding them show that GATT Contracting Parties did not call into question the application of the VCLT to the possible succession of the GATT 1947 or withdrawal from it. In particular, Articles 30 and 70 VCLT formed the starting point for considering how to organise the transition from the GATT 1947 and the Tokyo Round Codes[73] to the WTO Agreement.[74] Uncertainty regarding the meaning of those provisions and the objective of ensuring continuity between obligations, despite the discontinuity of the formal sources in which they appeared, caused the Contracting Parties to adopt transitional decisions and thereby preempt possible undesirable outcomes if the VCLT were to be applied.[75] In doing so, the practice developing from this transition from the GATT

---

[70] *Ibid.* (paragraph 9).   [71] *Ibid.*

[72] See, for example, P. M. Moore, 'The Decisions Bridging the GATT 1947 and the WTO Agreement', *AJIL*, 90 (1996), 317–328, and G. Marceau, 'Transition from the GATT to WTO – A Most Pragmatic Operation', *J. World Trade*, 29 (1995), 147–163. See, in particular, GATT Contracting Parties, Transitional Co-existence of the GATT 1947 and the WTO Agreement – Decision of 8 Dec. 1994 adopted by the Preparatory Committee for the WTO and the Contracting Parties to GATT 1947, L/7583 (13 Dec. 1994).

[73] These codes were agreements concluded during the Tokyo Round negotiations (1973–1978) concerning subsidies and countervailing measures (interpreting Arts. 6, 16 and 23 of the GATT 1947), technical barriers to trade, import licensing procedures, government procurement, customs valuation (interpreting Art. 7 of the GATT 1947), anti-dumping (Art. 6 of the GATT 1947 and replacing the Kennedy Round codes (1964–1967)), bovine meat, international dairy and trade in civil aircraft. GATT 1947 Contracting Parties were not obliged to become also a party to these stand-alone agreements.

[74] *Supra* n. 1.   [75] See, Moore, *supra* n. 72, and Marceau, *supra* n. 72, at 152.

1947 to the WTO Agreement demonstrates the flexibility of the law of treaties and an alternative way of conceptualising such treaty relations.

The treaties resulting from the Uruguay Round are difficult to amend.[76] Article X of the WTO Agreement provides different types of voting rules and, depending on the agreement at issue and the type of the amendment (that is to say, whether the amendment would alter the rights and obligations of the Members), different rules determine how amendments take effect. In principle, an amendment only enters into force after two-thirds of the Member States have deposited formal instruments of acceptance with the Director General.[77] In certain circumstances, all Member States need to do so.[78] Separate rules apply also for the amendment of plurilateral agreements.[79] For some treaties concluded within the WTO framework, there are no rules concerning their amendment.[80] It is thus, as a matter of WTO law, not necessary that 'all agree on everything' before amendments can be made and take effect for (some) WTO Members.[81] In any event, some WTO Members might find it unnecessary to express their consent to an amendment because they may yield (some) benefits as a free-rider through the operation of the MFN principle.[82]

---

[76] Art. II:4 of the WTO Agreement expressly addresses the relation between the GATT 1947 and the GATT 1994: *supra* n. 1. The latter is considered to be legally distinct from the GATT 1947. Contracting parties to the GATT 1947 as of the date of entry into force of the WTO Agreement (as well as the European Communities, now the European Union) became original WTO Members if they accepted the WTO covered agreements and had schedules of concessions and commitments attached to the GATT 1994 and GATS. Other States and separate customs territories can become WTO Members through accession. See Arts. XI:1 and XII of the WTO Agreement: *supra* n. 1.

[77] Art. X:3 of the WTO Agreement: *supra* n. 1.

[78] See, e.g., Arts. X:2 and X:5 of the WTO Agreement: *supra* n. 1.

[79] Art. X:10 of the WTO Agreement provides that '[a]mendments to a Plurilateral Trade agreement shall be governed by the provisions to that Agreement'. With regard to the application of the 1994 Agreement and the amendments in the Protocol, the applicable rules set out in paragraph 3 of the Decision of 30 March 2012 echo those expressed in Art. 30(4) VCLT: *supra* n. 2. Members who are a party to the Information Technology Agreement are currently also negotiating an amendment of that agreement which would result in an extended product coverage.

[80] No such rules are found in China's Accession Protocol. For a discussion, see Qin, *supra* n. 50, at 133–135.

[81] In principle, amendments only take effect for those Members that have accepted them upon acceptance by two thirds of the Members (Art. X:3 of the WTO Agreement) but exceptions to that rule exist (see Arts. X:4 and X:5 of the WTO Agreement): *supra* n. 1.

[82] See, e.g., M. Kennedy, 'Legal Options for a Sustainable Energy Trade Agreement', International Centre for Trade and Sustainable Development (Geneva: Switzerland, 2012) (www.ictsd.org) and H. Nottage and T. Sebastian, 'Giving Legal Effect to the Results of WTO Trade Negotiations: An Analysis of the Methods of Changing WTO Law', *J. Int'l Econ. L.*, 9 (2006), 989–1016, at 993.

If the amendment confers additional benefits, non-parties to it may also claim those benefits with reference to MFN; if the amendment adds obligations, it cannot be opposed to non-parties.

Putting aside the struggling Doha Round negotiations (which, if successful, might result in a wide set of amendments), more than one example of formal amendment now exists.[83] Through the adoption in 2001 of the Doha Declaration on the Trade-Related Aspects of Intellectual Property Rights (TRIPS) Agreement and Public Health (and in particular its paragraph 6), WTO Members instructed the TRIPS Council to find a solution for WTO Members with insufficient or no manufacturing capacities in the pharmaceutical sector and which therefore face difficulties in using compulsory licensing under the TRIPS Agreement.[84] That solution was an amendment with the effect of waiving obligations of the exporting Member under Article 31(f) of the TRIPS Agreement[85] in certain circumstances. It was first implemented through a decision[86] but is intended to become permanent through a Protocol Amending the TRIPS Agreement dated 6 December 2005, subject to its acceptance by two-thirds of WTO Members. That majority has not yet been reached to date.[87]

The second example is more recent. In 2012, the parties to the Government Procurement Agreement completed their review of that agreement (as foreseen by it)[88] and agreed to a series of amendments (set out in the protocol) and a series of decisions.[89] With regard to the application of the 1994 agreement and the amendments in the Protocol,

---

[83] Outside the context of the WTO covered agreements, some WTO Members are also negotiating amendments of, for example, the product scope of the Information Technology Agreement. Whilst initially negotiated outside the WTO, this agreement (aimed at cutting tariffs in the information technology sector) was concluded by a group of WTO Members through the adoption of a Ministerial Declaration at the Singapore Ministerial Conference. Its membership is growing. However, unlike the Government Procurement Agreement, *supra* n. 31, and the Agreement on Trade in Civil Aircraft, 1869 UNTS 508, it is not a plurilateral agreement.

[84] WT/MIN(01)/DEC/2 (20 Nov. 2001). For the TRIPS Agreement: 1869 UNTS 299.

[85] *Ibid.*

[86] Decision on Implementation of Paragraph 6 of the Doha Declaration on the TRIPS Agreement and Public Health WT/L/540 (30 Aug. 2003).

[87] See, further, M. Kennedy, 'When Will the Protocol Amending the TRIPS Agreement Enter into Force?', *J. Int'l Econ. L.*, 13 (2010), 459–473.

[88] *Supra* n. 31.

[89] WTO Committee on Government Procurement, Adoption of the results of the negotiations under Art. XXIV:7 of the Agreement on Government Procurement, following their verification and review, as required by the Ministerial Decision of 15 Dec. 2011 (GPA/112), paragraph 5 (GPA/113, 2 Apr. 2012).

the applicable rules set out in paragraph 3 of the Decision of 30 March 2012 echo those expressed in Article 30(4) VCLT. It remains unclear when that protocol and those decisions will enter into effect. The experience in the WTO helps to illustrate that ratification can be as challenging and as protracted a process as negotiation.

A final example is amendment in the form of the inclusion of an entire new agreement in Annex 1A to the WTO Agreement. As a result of the decision of the Ministerial Conference of 27 November 2014, an Agreement on Trade Facilitation is to be added and will enter into force when the requirements under Article X:3 of the WTO Agreement are satisfied.[90]

Departing from the paradigm of a single package nonetheless remains politically difficult though practically unavoidable. Sustaining the model of the Uruguay Round negotiations seems no longer feasible in part because the agreements resulting from that round, while being characterised and used in dispute settlement as forming a single coherent set of treaty rules (although committing individual WTO members in different ways, depending on, for example their schedules, status as developing countries etc.), no longer correspond to a set of treaty rules on which all (now) WTO Members have agreed. Some (parts of the) agreements have been terminated, others have been amended[91] or have evolved through the rules provided for in Article X of the WTO Agreement or other means for changing their content (such as decisions of the Ministerial Conference or other WTO institutional bodies), and new treaty rules have been added.[92] Moreover, these treaty norms must be read against the background of an increasing production of instruments by either the WTO itself or its Members which, while not constituting treaty law or secondary legislation, nonetheless are in varying degrees of normative relevance – in terms of the day-to-day implementation and operation of WTO law as well as of WTO dispute settlement. The importance that was attached to a decision of the TBT Committee in *US – Tuna II (Mexico)*, which we discussed in setting out the character and design of the WTO treaties, illustrates this well.

---

[90] Protocol Amending the Marrakesh Agreement Establishing the World Trade Organization, WT/L/940 (28 Nov. 2014).

[91] The first treaty amendment agreed by WTO Members was the Protocol Amending the TRIPS Agreement: WT/L/641. The period during which instruments of acceptance can be deposited has been extended several times.

[92] See, for example, Kennedy, *supra* n. 82.

The instruments through which WTO membership is obtained also illustrate these developments. The terms of acceding to the WTO are set out primarily in a new Member's Accession Protocol and complemented by a Working Party Report. To take again an example related to China's accession, the former is a treaty concluded between the People's Republic of China and the WTO and is thus governed by the 1986 Vienna Convention on the Law of Treaties between States and International Organizations or between International Organizations.[93] The Working Party Report is neither a treaty nor a legislative instrument. Through a technique of incorporation into the Accession Protocol,[94] certain paragraphs of those reports may nonetheless become normative and enforceable before WTO panels and the Appellate Body, despite the fact that their wording is not always prescriptive in a manner that is comparable to how WTO treaty rules are drafted. The binding terms of those protocols and reports might confirm existing treaty disciplines or add new ones. A new Member thus can be presumed to have acceded to the WTO and to have become a party to the WTO covered agreements on those terms (some of which may not apply to other Members). Neither the processes through which this is done nor their rationale is the subject of this chapter. The result is however an explicit (political) choice for there to be variable terms of membership. That choice has been reinforced by the Appellate Body's decision to interpret those additional terms in a separate manner from how it usually reads the covered agreements. Indeed, as the discussion previously on *China – Various Raw Materials* has shown, the Appellate Body departed from its usual attempt to ensure that the agreements operate effectively together by deciding that China did not have the right to avail itself of Article XX of the GATT 1994 as a defence in relation to export duties found to be inconsistent with Paragraph 11.3 of its Accession Protocol.[95] Leaving aside the policy implications of that choice, the Appellate Body's reasoning arguably endorses the development of WTO law as evolving towards a set of sources that is neither exclusively treaty-based nor uniformly applicable to all WTO Members and therefore can no longer be interpreted and applied as if the subject of that exercise was a single treaty (in terms of formal source) or single and uniform set of rules (in terms of material source). Even if the status quo resulting from the Uruguay Round is clearly abandoned and an alternative model of (formal and

---

[93] ILM, 25 (1986), 543–592 (which has not yet entered in force).   [94] WT/L/432.
[95] *Ibid.*

material) sources of WTO law has not yet emerged, it has become evident that the form of WTO law is transforming.[96]

In this context, it is also relevant to consider treaty activity on trade matters, that is, the negotiation and conclusion of bilateral, regional and multilateral trade agreements, outside the context of the WTO. In *Peru – Agricultural Products*, the Appellate Body inquired into whether a free trade agreement between Peru and Guatemala (the disputants) could be relied on for interpretive purposes and/or as a valid basis for relinquishing the right to initiate WTO dispute settlement proceedings or changing the substantive content of the Agreement on Agriculture (and thus modifying the WTO covered agreements as between those parties). It was not convinced that such *inter se* modification would be subject to Article 41 VCLT (on '[a]greements to modify multilateral treaties between certain of the parties only').[97] That was so because 'the WTO agreements contain specific provisions addressing amendments, waivers, or exceptions for regional trade agreements, which prevail over the general provisions of the Vienna Convention, such as [A]rticle 41'.[98]

Against that background, it may be an anomaly that (many) WTO Members continue to insist on negotiating agreements based on the notion that all must agree on everything. Indeed, that negotiation technique seems idealistic compared with the realism reflected in the WTO Agreement as to the rules that apply to the amendment and other evolutions of the treaties agreed upon during the previous multilateral trade negotiations.

5 Interpretation of WTO Treaties

The WTO covered agreements offer guidance on how they should be interpreted.[99] Guidance is found in the DSU,[100] the Agreement on

---

[96] See, for example, Kennedy, *supra* n. 82, and Nottage and Sebastian, *supra* n. 82, at 1010–1012.

[97] Appellate Body, *Peru – Agricultural Products, supra* n. 27, paragraph 5.111.

[98] Appellate Body, *Peru – Agricultural Products, supra* n. 27, paragraph 5.112. For a detailed analysis and critique of this Appellate Body report, see J. Pauwelyn, 'Interplay between the WTO Treaty and Other International Legal Instruments and Tribunals: Evolution after 20 Years of WTO Jurisprudence' (https://papers.ssrn.com/sol3/papers.cfm?abstract_id=2731144).

[99] For a more detailed discussion of the interpretation of the WTO covered agreements, see I. Van Damme, *Treaty Interpretation by the WTO Appellate Body* (Oxford: Oxford University Press, 2009).

[100] *Supra* n. 4.

Implementation of Article VI of the General Agreement on Tariffs and Trade 1994 (the Anti-dumping Agreement)[101] and the WTO Agreement.[102] Article 3.2 of the DSU states that 'Members recognize that it serves to preserve the rights and obligations of Members under the covered agreements, and to clarify the existing provisions of those agreements in accordance with customary rules of interpretation of public international law'. Article 17.6(ii) of the Anti-dumping Agreement restates in its first sentence that language of the DSU. Its second sentence adds particular guidance on how to interpret the Anti-dumping Agreement: 'Where the panel finds that a relevant provision of the Agreement admits of more than one permissible interpretation, the panel shall find the authorities' measure to be in conformity with the Agreement if it rests upon one of those permissible interpretations'.[103] Finally, Article IX:2 of the WTO Agreement confirms that the general principle concerning the relationship between judicial interpretation and authoritative interpretation also applies to the WTO covered agreements: 'The Ministerial Conference and the General Council shall have the exclusive authority to adopt interpretations of this Agreement and of the Multilateral Trade Agreements'.[104]

Since not all WTO members signed and ratified the VCLT, the DSU negotiators decided to refer in Article 3.2 of the DSU to the customary rules on interpretation; the alternative being to mention Articles 31 to 33 VCLT.[105] The Appellate Body confirmed in its first reports that Articles 31 and 32 VCLT have attained the status of 'customary rules of interpretation of public international law'.[106] It later made the same point

---

[101] 1868 UNTS 201.   [102] *Supra* n. 1.   [103] *Supra* n. 101.   [104] *Supra* n. 1.

[105] Some WTO members cannot become parties to the VCLT because they are not States or are not recognised as States.

[106] Appellate Body Report, *United States – Standards for Reformulated and Conventional Gasoline* ('*US – Gasoline*'), WT/DS2/AB/R, adopted 20 May 1996, DSR 1996:I, 3, at 16–17; Appellate Body Report, *Japan – Taxes on Alcoholic Beverages* ('*Japan – Alcoholic Beverages II*'), WT/DS8/AB/R, WT/DS10/AB/R, WT/DS11/AB/R, adopted 1 Nov. 1996, DSR 1996:I, 97, at 104; see also, e.g., Appellate Body Report, *European Communities – Customs Classification of Certain Computer Equipment* ('*EC – Computer Equipment*'), WT/DS62/AB/R, WT/DS67/AB/R, WT/DS68/AB/R, adopted 22 June 1998, DSR 1998:V, 1851 R, at paragraph 84; Appellate Body Report, *United States – Import Prohibition of Certain Shrimp and Shrimp Products* ('*US – Shrimp Products*'), WT/DS58/AB/R, adopted 6 Nov. 1998, DSR 1998:VII, 2755, at paragraph 114, and Appellate Body Report, *Korea – Definitive Safeguard Measure on Imports of Certain Dairy Products* ('*Korea – Dairy Products*'), WT/DS98/AB/R, adopted 12 Jan. 2000, DSR 2000:I, 3, at paragraph 81.

about Article 33 VCLT.[107] Arguably, even absent the explicit reference to customary principles of interpretation, panels and the Appellate Body would apply the principles in Articles 31 to 33 VCLT, as well as those not codified in that convention but nonetheless widely accepted and applied as part of the law of treaty interpretation,[108] in interpreting the WTO treaty language.[109]

The need for the rule in Article 3.2 of the DSU is often explained as being based on the practice of GATT panels to ignore the interpretive principles set out in the VCLT and to make undue use of negotiating history.[110] The numbers and GATT panel quotes set out earlier belie the idea that somehow GATT panels consistently deviated from VCLT rules. Instead, and especially during the final years of the GATT 1947, the VCLT was commonly referred to and used. If anything, therefore, Article 3.2 confirmed rather than overruled GATT panel practice. Whether the provision was aimed at ensuring wider reception of the law of treaties (beyond treaty interpretation) in the WTO is doubtful, though such a legal basis might not be necessary for applying customary international law. Considered in context, Article 3.2 has also helped panels and the Appellate Body in asserting the judicial function in the

---

[107] Appellate Body Report, *United States – Final Countervailing Duty Determination with Respect to Certain Softwood Lumber from Canada* ('*US – Softwood Lumber IV*'), WT/DS257/AB/R, adopted 17 Feb. 2004, DSR 2004:II, 571, at paragraph 59; Appellate Body Report, *Chile – Price Band System and Safeguard Measures Relating to Certain Agricultural Products* ('*Chile – Price Band System*'), WT/DS207/AB/R, adopted 23 Oct. 2002, DSR 2002:VIII, 3045 (Corr.1, DSR 2006:XII, 5473), at paragraph 271, and Appellate Body Report, *European Communities – Anti-dumping Duties on Imports of Cotton-Type Bed Linen from India – Recourse to Article 21.5 of the DSU by India* ('*EC – Bed-Linen (Article 21.5 – India)*'), WT/DS141/AB/RW, adopted 24 Apr. 2003, DSR 2003: III, 965, at paragraph 123 (fn. 153).

[108] Such as the principle of effectiveness.

[109] In circumstances where there is no formal treaty basis for defining the applicable law so as to include customary international law on treaty interpretation, the application of such law can be explained by reference to the function of interpretation. States, which otherwise are bound – whether or not on a treaty basis or under customary international law – to interpret treaties in accordance with that law, ask a third party to interpret the treaty provisions that bind them. They delegate the interpretive exercise to a third party whose decision on that question of interpretation they accept as to be binding upon them. The function of the third party's interpretation is thus to replace separate findings of an individual State in that regard. It would be odd if international courts or tribunals would not apply the rules applicable to States if they had not deleted the interpretive authority to a third party.

[110] P. J. Kuijper, 'The Law of GATT as a Special Field of International Law: Ignorance, Further Refinement or Self-contained System of International Law?', *Netherlands YbIL*, 25 (1994), 227–257, at 229–232.

WTO and in enforcing the relationship between the covered agreements and other treaties and general international law.

Also, interpretations of Article 17.6(ii) of the Anti-dumping Agreement have shown that the Appellate Body has refused to apply the principle laid down therein apparently on the ground that it is irreconcilable with the task which a treaty interpreter, like a WTO panel or the Appellate Body, is asked to perform.[111] That is clear from the Appellate Body's description of the interpretive exercise in *US – Continued Zeroing*:

> A word or term may have more than one meaning or shade of meaning, but the identification of such meanings in isolation only commences the process of interpretation, it does not conclude it. Nor do multiple meanings of a word or term automatically constitute 'permissible' interpretations within the meaning of Article 17.6(ii). Instead, a treaty interpreter is required to have recourse to context and object and purpose to elucidate the relevant meaning of the word or term. This logical progression provides a framework for proper interpretative analysis. At the same time, it should be kept in mind that treaty interpretation is an integrated operation, where interpretative rules or principles must be understood and applied as connected and mutually reinforcing components of a holistic exercise.[112]

That holistic exercise also involves that a panel, before it can even consider the second sentence of Article 17(ii), must first apply customary rules of interpretation 'to see what is yielded by a conscientious application of such rules including those codified in the Vienna Convention'.[113] That exercise must be aimed at 'narrowing' the range instead of 'generating' competing interpretations.[114] The application of the second sentence of Article 17.6(ii) becomes relevant only after the completion of that exercise.[115] At the same time, the Appellate Body considers that 'the rules and principles of the Vienna Convention cannot contemplate interpretation with mutually contradictory results'.[116] What this suggests is that the application of Articles 31 to 33 VCLT by the WTO dispute settlement

---

[111] For a recent critique, see M. Cartland, G. Depayre and J. Woznowski, 'Is Something Going Wrong in the WTO Dispute Settlement?', *J. World Trade*, 46 (2012), 979–1016, at 988–989.

[112] Appellate Body Report, *United States – Continued Existence and Application of Zeroing Methodology* ('*US – Continued Zeroing*'), WT/DS350/AB/R, adopted 19 Feb. 2009, paragraph 268.

[113] *Ibid.* (paragraph 271) (original emphasis).

[114] *Ibid.* (paragraph 273) (original emphasis).   [115] *Ibid.* (paragraph 271).

[116] *Ibid.* (paragraph 273).

bodies cannot result in two opposing interpretations of a word or phrase, whilst each can be explained by reference to the principles articulated in those provisions and in that sense is 'permissible'.

The Appellate Body has struggled nonetheless with the functions of guidance and justification of principles of interpretation and there exists a concern about excessive formalism. Initially, the Appellate Body used Articles 31 to 33 VCLT to explain every step of its reasoning, though other principles of treaty interpretation were also used but less openly. By adopting this strategy, the Appellate Body succeeded in making its early decisions transparent and intelligible – even if sometimes at the cost of finding its own authoritative voice. As claims and arguments became more complex and were made under various agreements, it became increasingly difficult to maintain that strategy. At times, excessive formalism showed the limitations of the principles codified in Articles 31 to 33 VCLT, causing the Appellate Body to search for (not always successfully) a more balanced approach in explaining its conclusion about the meaning of the treaty. The expectation that the Appellate Body will explain and justify every step in its reasoning by reference to, preferably, Articles 31 to 33 VCLT has not entirely disappeared. It seems as if the conclusion that the meaning is evident, as it often is, became intolerable. Treaty interpretation by the WTO Appellate Body, and, in fact, by any court or tribunal, can never be reduced to a mere synthetic application of Articles 31 to 33 VCLT and the WTO practice of using this part of the law of treaties shows this well.

Compared to that of other courts and tribunals, the function of the Appellate Body was not neatly defined at its inception. The DSU created a dispute settlement system without making a conscious decision to refer third party resolution of disputes between WTO members to a judicial body. In many respects, establishing a body responsible for reviewing panels' decisions and reasoning on issues of law was an ambitious experiment, but no clear sense of purpose or direction was established for this new institution. The chorus of 'security and predictability' and 'not adding or diminishing the rights and obligations' in Article 3.2 of the DSU is often used to describe the unique mandate of panels and the Appellate Body. However, it is difficult to imagine that a judicial dispute settlement system would not be entrusted with the tasks of preserving the integrity and respecting the text of the treaty it is mandated to uphold and apply to the resolution of disputes. In other words, the uniqueness of Article 3.2 of the DSU should not be overestimated. The thrust of the provision is unquestioned – that is, that treaties should be interpreted in accordance with the law of treaty interpretation and without changing them, also in other contexts of international dispute settlement.

6   Application of WTO Treaties

The basic principles governing the observance and application of treaties set out in Articles 26 to 30 VCLT have been used in varying degrees in GATT and WTO dispute settlement. Where considered to be relevant, Articles 26 and 27 VCLT on the observance of treaties are used without further inquiry[117] – though in certain reports, Article 27 VCLT appears to have been used also as a basis for stating what is now Article 6 of the 2001 Articles on Responsibility of States for Internationally Wrongful Acts (ASR) on attribution.[118] For example, the GATT panel in *US – Malt Beverages* relied on, for the purposes of interpreting Article XXIV:12, 'the general principle of international treaty law that a party to a treaty may not invoke the provisions of its internal law as justification for its failure

---

[117]   On Art. 26 VCLT, see, for example, Appellate Body Report, *United States – Continued Dumping and Subsidy Offset Act of 2000* ('*US – Offset Act (Byrd Amendment)*'), WT/DS217/AB/R, WT/DS234/AB/R, adopted 27 Jan. 2003, DSR 2003:I, 375, paragraphs 296 to 298 (accepting, at paragraph 297, that 'there is a basis for a dispute settlement panel to determine, in an appropriate case, whether a Member has not acted in good faith'); Appellate Body Report, *European Communities – Trade Description of Sardines* ('*EC – Sardines*'), WT/DS231/AB/R, adopted 23 Oct. 2002, DSR 2002:VIII, 3359, paragraph 278; Panel Report, *United States – Import Prohibition on Certain Shrimp and Shrimp Products* ('*US – Shrimp*'),WT/DS58/R and Corr.1, adopted 6 Nov. 1998, as modified by Appellate Body Report WT/DS58/AB/R, DSR 1998:VII, 2821 (fn. 644), and Panel Report, *United States – Continued Suspension of Obligations in the EC – Hormones Dispute* ('*US – Continued Suspension*'), WT/DS320/R, adopted 14 Nov. 2008, as modified by Appellate Body Report WT/DS320/AB/R, DSR 2008:XI, 3891, paragraphs 7.316–7.317.

[118]   Appellate Body Report, *United States – Measures Relating to Zeroing and Sunset Reviews – Recourse to Article 21.5 of the DSU by Japan* ('*US – Zeroing (Japan) (Article 21.5 – Japan)*'), WT/DS322/AB/RW, adopted 31 Aug. 2009, paragraph 182; Panel Report, *Australia – Measures Affecting Importation of Salmon – Recourse to Article 21.5 of the DSU by Canada* ('*Australia – Salmon (Article 21.5 – Canada)*'), WT/DS18/RW, adopted 20 March 2000, DSR 2000:IV, 2031 (fn. 146); Panel Report, *Canada – Measures Affecting the Importation of Milk and the Exportation of Dairy Products* ('*Canada – Dairy*'), WT/DS103/R, WT/DS113/R, adopted 27 Oct. 1999, as modified by Appellate Body Report WT/DS103/AB/R, WT/DS113/AB/R, DSR 1999:VI, 2097 (fn 424); Panel Report, *Canada – Measures Affecting the Sale of Gold Coins (Canada – Gold Coins)*, L/5863 (not adopted), paragraph 53, and GATT Panel Report, *United States – Measures Affecting Alcoholic and Malt Beverages (US – Malt Beverages)*, DS23/R – 39S/206, adopted on 19 June 1992, paragraph 5.79. For the ASR: U.N. Doc. A/CN.4/SER.A/2001/Add.1 (Part Two).

to perform a treaty obligation'.[119] As support for the existence of this general principle, the GATT Panel referred to the 'example' of Article 27 VCLT. WTO panels and the Appellate Body have also endorsed the application of the principle.[120]

Unlike Articles 26 and 27 VCLT, the provisions governing non-retroactivity and the territorial scope of treaties state expressly that they apply only insofar as no different intention appears from the treaty or is otherwise established. While panels and the Appellate Body accept that those provisions apply as default rules, the focus of their inquiry is often on whether a contrary intention is reflected in the covered agreements.[121] If no such intention is found, Articles 28 and 29 VCLT are used conservatively.

In *US – Footwear from Brazil*, the Panel interpreted Article VI:6(a) of the GATT 1947 to mean that the obligation expressed in that provision applied also to pre-existing decisions to impose countervailing duties without injury determinations.[122] That interpretation was confirmed by reference to Article 28 VCLT, which, according to the Panel, provided that 'new treaty provisions did not bind parties in relation to any act or fact which had taken place before the date of entry into force of the treaty'. On the other hand, 'the treaty provisions did bind parties in relation to a situation which had arisen from a previous act ... which situation continued to exist'.[123] Similarly, the Appellate Body has interpreted Article 28 VCLT so as to mean that it 'necessarily implies that, absent a contrary intention, treaty obligations do apply to any "situation"

---

[119] GATT Panel Report, *US – Malt Beverages, supra* n. 112, paragraph 5.79; see also GATT Panel Report, *Canada – Gold Coins, supra* n. 112, paragraph 27.

[120] See, for example, Appellate Body Report, *US – Zeroing (Japan) (Article 21.5 of the DSU – Japan), supra* n. 112, paragraph 182 (fn. 463). The rule has also been misunderstood. In *US – Section 301 Trade Act*, the Panel found that Art. XVI:4 of the WTO Agreement 'goes a step further than Article 27 [VCLT]' because it 'not only precludes pleading conflicting internal law as a justification for WTO inconsistencies, but requires WTO Members actually to ensure the conformity of internal law with its WTO obligations'. Panel Report, *United States – Sections 301–310 of the Trade Act of 1974 ('US – Section 301 Trade Act')*, WT/DS152/R, adopted 27 Jan. 2000, DSR 2000:II, 815, paragraph 7.41 (fn. 652).

[121] See, as regards Art. 27 VCLT, for example: Decision by the Arbitrator, *Canada – Export Credits and Loan Guarantees for Regional Aircraft – Recourse to Arbitration by Canada under Article 22.6 of the DSU and Article 4.11 of the SCM Agreement ('Canada – Aircraft Credits and Guarantees (Article 22.6 – Canada)')*, WT/DS222/ARB, 17 Feb. 2003, DSR 2003:III, 1187, paragraph 3.104.

[122] GATT Panel Report, *US – Footwear from Brazil*, SCM/94, not adopted, paragraph 4.5.

[123] *Ibid.*

which has not ceased to exist – that is, to any situation that arose in the past, but continues to exist under the new treaty'.[124]

By contrast, Article 30 VCLT has been used in limited cases. With regard to that provision, the case law is underdeveloped. Unlike Articles 28 and 29 VCLT, it does not expressly provide for the possibility that parties might agree on a separate rule though the ILC commentary does not appear to preclude this – provided that that rule is not contrary to the principle according to which a treaty cannot bind a third party (or *pacta tertiis non nocent*).[125] The provision applies solely to successive treaties relating to the same subject-matter and which are in force. It thus does not apply to the relation between the GATT 1947 and the WTO covered agreements: the former no longer applies and therefore no conflict between them can emerge.[126] The WTO covered agreements, insofar as they can be considered to relate to the same subject matter, form part of a single treaty, were concluded at the same time and, if necessary, are governed by separate rules on how they co-exist.

The application of Article 30 VCLT is thus limited to circumstances where the WTO covered agreements form, using the date of adoption as a benchmark, either the earlier or the later treaty. As regards the first category, the later treaty may take various shapes. It may be a bilateral, regional or multilateral agreement concluded outside the WTO insofar as

---

[124] Appellate Body Report, *Canada – Term of Patent Protection* ('*Canada – Patent Term*'), WT/DS170/AB/R, adopted 12 Oct. 2000, DSR 2000:X, 5093, paragraphs 70 to 74. See also Appellate Body Report, *Brazil – Measures Affecting Desiccated Coconut* ('*Brazil – Desiccated Coconut*'), WT/DS22/AB/R, adopted 20 March 1997, DSR 1997:I, 167, paragraphs 44 and 45; Appellate Body Report, *EC Measures Concerning Meat and Meat Products (Hormones)* ('*EC – Hormones*'), WT/DS26/AB/R, WT/DS48/AB/R, adopted 13 Feb. 1998, DSR 1998:I, 135, paragraph 128, and Appellate Body Report, *EC – Sardines, supra* n. 111, paragraph 200.

[125] See paragraph 4 of the Commentary on (then) Art. 26 in ILC, 'Draft Articles on the Law of Treaties with Commentaries 1966', *YbILC* (1966–II), 214–215. See, further, the contribution to this volume of Waibel at pp. 201–236 (Chapter 8).

[126] Though Art. XVI:1 of the WTO Agreement states that '[e]xcept as otherwise provided under this agreement or the Multilateral Trade Agreements, the WTO shall be guided by the decisions, procedures and customary practices followed by the CONTRACTING PARTIES to GATT 1947 and the bodies established in the framework of GATT 1947': *supra* n. 1. That appears to have been the reason why the Appellate Body in *EC – Poultry* did not see any reason to have recourse to either Art. 59(1) or Art. 30(3) VCLT as regards the reason the relation between the Oilseeds Agreement – a bilateral agreement negotiated by the (then) European Communities and Brazil under Art. XXVIII of the GATT 1947 – as part of their resolution of the GATT dispute in *EEC – Oilseeds*. Appellate Body Report, *European Communities – Measures Affecting the Importation of Certain Poultry Products* ('*EC – Poultry*'), WT/DS69/AB/R, adopted 23 July 1998, DSR 1998:V, 2031, paragraphs 79–81.

its relation to the WTO covered agreements is not governed by those agreements themselves (such as Article XXIV of the GATT 1994) – this follows from *Peru – Agricultural Products* (though that case concerned Article 41 VCLT) – or it may be a plurilateral agreement. Leaving aside whether those treaties can be characterised as relating to the same subject-matter as one of the WTO covered agreements and whether that quality must be established solely based on the subject of the rights and obligations they set out,[127] the WTO covered agreements do not contain any clause to the effect that another (earlier or later) agreement shall prevail. Contrary to Article 30(2) VCLT, there may be scope to apply Article 30(3) VCLT. Assuming all WTO Members are party to a later treaty on, for example, export restrictions on foodstuffs, 'the earlier treaty applies only to the extent that its provisions are compatible with those of the later treaty'. If the later treaty contains more permissive or stricter rules on using such measures in that context, as a matter of the law of treaties, it will prevail over the relevant provisions in the GATT 1994. If only some WTO Members are party to a subsequent treaty modifying, for example, WTO disciplines on export restrictions by making them more detailed in relation to foodstuffs, Article 30(4) VCLT describes in relation to 'successive treaties' the consequences resulting from such an agreement for the treaty relations as between parties and between parties and non-parties. By contrast, if the later agreement can be characterised as 'modifying' the earlier treaty, the extent to which it is acceptable to conclude such a later treaty depends on the fulfilment of the conditions set forth in Article 41 VCLT.

But what is the position as a matter of WTO law? That will depend on the extent to which the WTO considers itself to be competent to consider matters concerning the later treaty. Insofar as the treaty was 'institutionalised' as a plurilateral agreement, panels and the Appellate Body can take jurisdiction in disputes over that agreement. If the treaty is concluded and enters into force outside the WTO institutional or treaty framework, disputes concerning that agreement fall outside the jurisdiction of panels and the Appellate Body. Nonetheless, such an outside WTO treaty might still have normative relevance, be it as part of the applicable law, as interpretative guidance or as a legal fact.[128] A WTO

---

[127] See, for example, J. Pauwelyn, *Conflict of Norms in Public International Law: How WTO Law Relates to Other Rules of International Law* (Cambridge: Cambridge University Press, 2003), pp. 364–367.

[128] See J. Pauwelyn, 'The Role of Public International Law in the WTO: How Far Can We Go?', *AJIL*, 95 (2001), 535–578.

Member whose imports have suffered from the measures imposed under the later (outside WTO) treaty might nonetheless seek to enforce, for example, Article XI:1 of the GATT 1994 against a Member that acted upon that later treaty. In that context, the use of Article 30 VCLT as well as that of the principle of *lex specialis* argue in favour of resolving the dispute by giving effect to the later treaty that prescribes in more specific terms the application of restrictions to exports of foodstuffs as between the disputing parties. Doing so would imply the recognition that the applicable law in WTO dispute settlement is not limited to the WTO covered agreements. So far, panels and the Appellate Body have not taken a clear position on this matter, which likely explains the underdeveloped state of the case law on Article 30 VCLT. The Appellate Body has nonetheless accepted in *Peru – Agricultural Products* that a later agreement outside the WTO clarifying *inter se* the WTO covered agreements may be interpretively relevant subject to the conditions that such an interpretation is not *contra legem*, serves to establish the common intentions of all WTO Members and 'bears specifically' on terms used in the WTO treaty.[129] Whether such an agreement may satisfy these conditions remains unsettled. What is clear, however, is that the permissibility of such an agreement (or provisions thereof) depends on the WTO covered agreements themselves (rather than Article 41 VCLT).[130]

By contrast, were another treaty to be added to Annex 1A of the WTO Agreement and were it to provide more flexible rules on using export restrictions on foodstuffs, the *lex posterior* principle reflected in Article 30 VCLT likely would apply (at least for that agreement's relation to earlier Annex 1A agreements for which no explicit conflict clauses are included).

As regards the second category, if a bilateral treaty precedes the adoption of the WTO covered agreements and concerns the same subject matter, Article 30(4)(a) VCLT provides that, as between the bilateral treaty partners, the earlier treaty applies only to the extent that its provisions are compatible with those of the later treaty. As between a bilateral treaty partner and another WTO Member who is not a party to that treaty, the WTO covered agreements apply because it governs the parties' mutual rights and obligations.[131] In *EC – Hormones (Article 22.6 – EC)*, the Arbitrators were asked to consider the status of a bilateral agreement (containing the results of

---

[129] Appellate Body, *Peru – Agricultural Products, supra* n. 27, paragraphs 5.94, 5.95 and 5.101.

[130] Appellate Body, *Peru – Agricultural Products, supra* n. 27, paragraph 5.113.

[131] Art. 30(4)(b) VCLT: *supra* n. 2.

bilateral negotiations on concessions) that was then multilateralised through a binding schedule. In those circumstances, the earlier treaty – that is, the bilateral agreement – was superseded by the multilateral schedule. The Arbitrators reasoned that '[c]onsidering the GATT/ WTO specific circumstances of their conclusion, the bilateral agreements [and in particular the quota allocation to one Member] would appear to be incompatible with the multilateral ... schedule [and in particular the quota allocation to two Members]'.[132] A different conclusion was reached by the Panel in *Japan – Film*, where the Panel considered Japan's argument that the Schedules annexed to the Marrakesh Protocol prevail over Schedules that entered into force under the GATT 1947 because the former were a later agreement.[133] The Panel found there was 'nothing inherently incompatible ... between the earlier and later agreed tariff concessions', adding that '[s]uch a conflict would only seem to exist if the subsequent concessions were less favourable than prior concessions'.[134] Hence, Article 30 VCLT did not apply.

7 Consequences Resulting from the Breach of WTO Treaties

WTO law does not use the notion of 'breach'.[135] Instead, it is the nullification or impairment of benefits accruing under the covered agreements that gives rise to remedies. Nullification or impairment of benefits can result in a complaint of either the violation or non-violation of the obligations assumed under those agreements. The first type of complaint, if successful, is considered *prima facie* to constitute a case of nullification or impairment.[136] It is the result of the failure of another Member to carry out its obligations under the covered agreements.[137] The second type of

---

[132] Decision by the Arbitrators, *European Communities – Measures Concerning Meat and Meat Products (Hormones), Original Complaint by the United States – Recourse to Arbitration by the European Communities under Article 22.6 of the DSU* ('EC – Hormones (US) (Article 22.6 – EC)'), WT/DS26/ARB, 12 July 1999, DSR 1999:III, 1105, paragraph 51.

[133] Panel Report, *Japan – Measures Affecting Consumer Photographic Film and Paper* ('*Japan – Film*'), WT/DS44/R, adopted 22 Apr. 1998, DSR 1998:IV, 1179, paragraph 10.65.

[134] Panel Report, *Japan – Film*, supra n. 125, paragraph 10.65.

[135] See, further, the contribution to this volume of Tams at pp. 440–467 (Chapter 14).

[136] Art. 3.8 of the DSU: *supra* n. 4.

[137] See Art. XXIII:1(a) of the GATT 1994: *supra* n. 30; Appellate Body Report, *European Communities – Measures Affecting Asbestos and Asbestos-Containing Products* ('*EC – Asbestos*'), WT/DS135/AB/R, adopted 5 Apr. 2001, paragraph 185.

complaint results from the application of any measure that does not conflict with those obligations.[138] It is available when '[t]he improved competitive opportunities that can legitimately be expected from a tariff concession [are] frustrated not only by measures proscribed by the [GATT] but also by measures consistent with that Agreement'.[139] Article 26.1 of the DSU sets out separate rules on the consequences resulting from such a finding. To date, no such complaint has been successful. Only in exceptional circumstances will Members be challenged for action not in contravention of the rules they negotiated and agreed to follow. Whether those circumstances must be understood as corresponding with or be closely related to the notion of a 'fundamental change in circumstances' described in Article 62 VCLT is doubtful.[140] The latter is, under limited conditions, a ground for terminating, withdrawing and possibly suspending the operation of the treaty.[141] Those remedies do not correspond with those set out in Article 26(1) of the DSU and the conditions for their application differ.

If a complainant bringing a violation complaint is successful, it may be authorised to suspend concessions where prompt compliance by the defendant is not practicable and the parties do not agree on compensation. A 'material' breach of the covered agreement is thus neither necessary nor sufficient to suspend the operation of part of those agreements. In that regard, the rules in the DSU differ from Article 60 VCLT, in particular its second paragraph.[142] Article 60(4) VCLT accommodates that possibility.

---

[138] A variation of this second type is the complaint resulting from the existence of any other situation other than the action or inaction resulting in a violation or non-violation complaint. See Art. XXIII:1(c) of the GATT 1994 (*supra* n. 30) and Art. 26.1 of the DSU (*supra* n. 4). Unlike the ILC Articles (which apply to wrongful acts), remedies under WTO law may thus be adopted in response to a measure that does not violate the covered agreements.

[139] Appellate Body Report, *EC – Asbestos, supra* n. 129, paragraph 185 (quoting the Panel Report in *EEC – Oilseeds*).

[140] An argument in favour of that position is made in F. Roessler, 'Should Principles of Competition Policy Be Incorporated into WTO Law through Non-violation Complaints?', *J. Int'l Econ. L.*, 2 (1999), 413–421, at 416–417, and A. von Bogdandy, 'The Non-Violation Procedure of Article XXIII:2 GATT – Its Operational Rationale', *J. World Trade*, 26 (1992), 95–111, at 110–111.

[141] Art. 62(1) and Art. 62(3) VCLT: *supra* n. 2.

[142] Unlike the DSU, Art. XXIII of the GATT 1994 – stating the original GATT 1947 conditions for finding nullification or impairment of benefits and the use of countermeasures – qualifies the circumstances in which countermeasures can be used: they must be serious enough to justify such action: *supra* n. 30.

Under WTO law, if disputants cannot agree on a mutually agreed solution that conforms with WTO law,[143] the general principle is that a third party (a panel and, possibly, the Appellate Body) must find a violation of the covered agreements and recommend the defendant Member to comply. Such a finding and recommendation create an obligation to immediately withdraw the measure (or at least the inconsistency on which the finding was based). That is the remedy of cessation.[144] If that is not practicable, compensation and suspension of concessions or other obligations are temporary measures that can be used to induce compliance.[145] Whilst the exact purpose of suspension of concessions was subject to debate,[146] the Appellate Body in *Canada/US – Continued Suspension* appears to have resolved it in favour of the position that they are to be used to induce compliance and not to rebalance concessions.

Neither action may be taken unilaterally: compensation must be agreed upon by the disputants whilst suspension of concessions or other obligations must be authorised by the DSB. Whether it is acceptable (and under what conditions) to take any other type of unilateral action for the same reasons that justify compensation or suspension remains uncertain.[147]

Both types of action are forms of countermeasures.[148] They do not affect the substantive (treaty) obligations that were the subject of the violation or non-violation and, in that respect, especially suspension of concessions differs from the legal consequences resulting from the breach

---

[143] See W. Alschner, 'Amicable Settlements of WTO Disputes: Bilateral Solutions in a Multilateral System', *W. Trade Rev.*, 13 (2014), 65–102.

[144] See also Art. 30 ASR: *supra* n. 112.

[145] See Art. 3.7 of the DSU and its interpretation by the Appellate Body in *Canada/US – Continued Suspension, supra* n. 26, paragraph 302. See, also, Art. 22.1 of the DSU: *supra* n. 4. Similarly, Art. 49(2) ASR provides that an injured State may take countermeasures that are defined as being 'limited to the non-performance for the time being of international obligations of the State taking the measures towards the responsible State': *supra* n. 112.

[146] See, for example, debate between J. H. Bello, 'The WTO Dispute Settlement Understanding: Less Is More', *AJIL*, 90 (1996), 416–418, and J. H. Jackson, 'The WTO Dispute Settlement Understanding – Misunderstandings on the Nature of Legal Obligation', *AJIL*, 91 (1997), 60–64; J. H. Jackson, 'International Law Status of WTO Dispute Settlement Reports: Obligation to Comply or Option to "Buy Out"?', *AJIL*, 98 (2004), 109–125.

[147] See Art. 23 of the DSU; Panel Report, *European Communities – Measures Affecting Trade in Commercial Vessels* ('*Korea – Commercial Vessels*'), WT/DS301/R, adopted 20 June 2005, paragraph 7.196.

[148] See Arts. 22.2 and 23.2 of the DSU: *supra* n. 4.

of a treaty that are described in the VCLT, notably in Article 60.[149] The DSU subjects the suspension of parts of the treaty to particular practical rules as regards to its authorisation, form, level and implementation.[150]

8 Conclusion

It is probably true that the contribution of the GATT and the WTO to the development of the law of treaties is yet to become visible. In codifying the law of treaties in the VCLT, the ILC was remarkably silent in commenting on the practice of GATT Contracting Parties in assuming and performing their treaty obligations under the GATT 1947 as well as other trade-related agreements during the long history of the provisional application of the GATT 1947. Few references were made to the treaty practices resulting from the GATT 1947 in the preparatory work of the ILC when codifying the law of treaties.[151] By contrast, in its recent work aimed at revisiting parts of those codified rules, it has become impossible for the ILC to ignore the WTO treaties and even the historical example of the GATT 1947.[152]

What has brought about that change? The WTO dispute settlement system, and especially the Appellate Body's use of the VCLT in its interpretive practices, has made WTO law more visible and accessible through its recurrent interpretation and application of the same set of treaties. However, the ILC is also studying in some detail the provisional application of the GATT 1947 whereas the latter was mostly ignored when Article 25 VCLT was drafted and, in its work on the topic of treaties

---

[149] See J. Crawford, *The International Law Commission's Articles on State Responsibility: Introduction, Text and Commentaries* (Cambridge: Cambridge University Press, 2002), p. 282.

[150] The DSU limits the form and level of permissible countermeasures that otherwise are available under the Articles of State Responsibility. Arbitrators have nonetheless interpreted the covered agreements against the background of the articles on state responsibility in a manner suggesting that the commonalities between the WTO covered agreements and that part of general international law might be as relevant as their separateness.

[151] See, for example, Practice of the United Nations Secretariat in relation to certain questions raised in connexion with the articles on the law of treaties: Note by the Secretariat, Doc. A/CN.4/121, *YbILC* (1959–II), 82 (on the practice of signing 'ad referendum'); Depository practice in relation to reservations: Report by the Secretary General submitted in accordance with General Assembly Resolution 1452 B (XIV), A/5687, *YbILC* (1965–II), 74, at 77, 86–87, 89 and 96 (on reservations).

[152] *Supra* n. 53.

over time, it will also be hard to neglect how the GATT 1947 evolved over time. This historical inquiry into the GATT 1947 is valuable to both public international law and WTO law. First, through this inclusive approach, it represents a departure from a long-standing conception that international trade law is not a classic topic of public international law. The practice of States in relation to treaties on trade is now perceived to be relevant to assessing the status quo regarding States' practice in applying the law of treaties. Revisiting the use of the law of treaties under the GATT 1947 might also help, as this chapter has shown, to test the flexibility of customary international law on treaties. Second, this type of historical enquiry shows that, despite common perceptions, the inclusion of the reference to customary international law on treaty interpretation in Article 3.2 of the DSU was not a turning point in how international trade law relates to the law of treaties. Undeniably, the particularities of the use of the VCLT in interpreting the WTO covered agreements represent a remarkable result of the instructions in Article 3.2 of the DSU directed at panels and the Appellate Body. The intensity of the use of the VCLT in this area stands in contrast with the underdeveloped practice in the WTO as regards other parts of the law of treaties, but even there, as this chapter has shown, GATT/WTO jurisprudence has built a clear bridge to the VCLT.

26

The International Labour Organization

ANNE TREBILCOCK*

1 Introduction and Background

The International Labour Organization's approach to the law of treaties has been coloured by both its structural features and its long history. Chapter XIII of the Treaty of Versailles created the International Labour Organization (ILO) in 1919,[1] fifty years before the adoption of the Vienna Convention on the Law of Treaties (VCLT)[2] and well before decolonization or the emergence of newer fields of public international law. While reviewing the most notable features of the ILO's extensive treaty-related practice (adoption, submission, ratification, revision, reservations, monitoring of implementation, interpretation), this chapter briefly explores a topical issue the Organization is now facing in relation to treaty interpretation. Finally, it offers some observations about the ILO and *lex specialis* in relation to the VCLT.

Since 1919, the International Labour Conference has established a large body of international labour standards, and the Organization has entered into multiple agreements with other institutions and with many of its member States.[3] The original idea of having the ILO act as a supranational organization adopting international labour legislation that would have been binding, subject only to an opting out clause,[4]

---

* The author gratefully acknowledges comments from participants at the Sept. 2012 workshop at the University of Nottingham organised by the editors of this volume as well as from Claire La Hovary and Guido Raimondi on an earlier draft. Appreciation is also expressed to the ILO Archives and the United Nations Law Library in Geneva. All views and any possible errors remain the author's alone.

[1] 225 CTS 188.   [2] 1155 UNTS 331.

[3] ILO Conventions and Recommendations are available at www.ilo.org under 'labour standards'; inter-organizational agreements are found under the Office of the Legal Adviser on the ILO website.

[4] This was put forward by the authors of the first British draft of the Constitution. Later, G. Scelle continued to refer to ILO Conventions as 'international legislation': see F. Maupain, 'The ILO's Standard-Setting Action: International Legislation or Treaty

gave way to agreement on a less ambitious constitutional construct built around ratification of Conventions by sovereign States. But with an important difference: the adoption of these treaties is not done by States alone, but with the voting participation of representatives of Employers and of Workers. This feature accounts for much of the ILO's particular 'take' on the law of treaties. It may also explain in part why the ILO was keen to be involved with both the VCLT and the 1986 Vienna Convention on the Law of Treaties between States and International Organizations and between International Organizations (VCLTSIO).[5] The ILO, of course subject to customary and general international law, has relied on its *lex specialis* as an organization to nuance its application of the 'Vienna rule(s)' in relation to several of the issues addressed by these treaties.

2   The ILO as a Generator of International Law

2.1   The ILO as a Treaty-Making Institution

By the end of 2015, the International Labour Conference had adopted 189 Conventions, six Protocols and 203 Recommendations.[6] However, as the result of official revisions of some Conventions and several 'pruning' exercises by the Conference and the ILO Governing Body, far lower numbers of these instruments are considered by the ILO as being 'up-to-date'. With the entry into force in August 2013 of the 2006 Maritime Labour Convention,[7] which revised a number of earlier instruments, the total of up-to-date Conventions fell to 68, with five of them supplemented by the same number of Protocols. (Some Recommendations stand on their own, while others complement Conventions; in neither case are Recommendations treaties). Moreover, the ILO Governing Body is setting into motion a new Standards Review Mechanism with a view to

---

Law' in V. Gowlland-Debbas, H. Hadj-Sahraoui and N. Hayashi (eds.), *Multilateral Treaty-making: The Current Status of Challenges to and Reforms Needed in the International Legislative Process* (Leiden: Martinus Nijhoff, 2000), pp. 129–135.

[5] ILM, 25 (1986), 543–592.

[6] The topics addressed range from fundamental labour standards (see later) to occupational safety and health, social security and labour market governance. While most instruments are of general application, some are aimed at specific categories, such as domestic workers, nurses, seafarers or indigenous peoples. See J.-M. Servais, *International Labour Law* (The Hague: Wolters Kluwer, 4th ed., 2014) and J.-M. Thouvenin and A. Trebilcock (eds.), *Droit international social: Droits économiques, sociaux et culturels* (Vol. II) (Brussels: Bruylant, 2013).

[7] ILM, 45 (2006), 792. See, also, ILM, 53 (2014), 933–1018.

arriving at a 'robust and effective' body of international labour standards.[8] This is partly in response to the concerns of some that the ILO may have too many instruments that are poorly ratified, thus blunting the impact of the system overall.[9] That view is open to debate,[10] and the topic remains sensitive, as workers' representatives fear an erosion of hard-won labour rights and a retreat from the ILO's purpose of improving labour conditions.[11] Thus, future streamlining of the body of ILO standards is to be undertaken in line with several guiding principles, including non-reduction of the protection afforded by relevant ratified Conventions and decision-taking by consensus.[12]

2.2   The ILO as a Generator of 'Soft Law'

Furthermore, the International Labour Conference has generated a huge body of 'soft law' in the form of Recommendations, resolutions and, on five occasions, declarations.[13] Most notable in terms of its

---

[8] GB. 312/LILS/5 (Nov. 2011), paragraph 1; see, also, GB.323/5, Record of Decision (March 2015), establishing a tripartite working group under the Standards Review Mechanism, GB.310/LILS/3/1 (rev.) (March 2012) and GB.313/LILS/5 (March 2012), as well as the conclusions of the 1995–2002 'pruning' exercise at www.ilo.org/wcmsp5/groups/public/-ed_norm/-normes/documents/genericdocument/wcms_125644.pdf.

[9] See, e.g., A. Wisskirchen, 'The Standard-Setting and Monitoring Activity of the ILO: Legal Questions and Practical Experience', *International Labour Rev.*, 144 (2005), 253–289, at 261–263.

[10] See, for instance, B. Langille, 'Imagining Post "Geneva Consensus" Labor Law for Post "Washington Consensus" Development', *Comp. Labor L. & Policy J.*, 31 (2010), 523–552, and A. Trebilcock, 'Setting the Record Straight About International Labor Standard Setting', *Comp. Labor L. & Policy J.*, 31 (2010), 553–570. For a recent diagnosis of the challenges facing the traditional tools used by the ILO in the context of globalisation, see F. Maupain, *The Future of the International Labour Organization in the Global Economy* (Oxford: Hart Publishing, 2013).

[11] This is one of three purposes set out in the preamble to the Constitution, the other two being establishment of universal and lasting peace based upon social justice and the avoidance of a 'race to the bottom' ('the failure of any nation to adopt humane conditions of labour is an obstacle in the way of other nations which desire to improve the conditions in their own countries'); see also Arts. 1(1) and 19(8) of the ILO Constitution and the 1944 Declaration Concerning the Aims and Purposes of the International Labour Organization (also known as the Declaration of Philadelphia).

[12] The entire list of the objectives, outcomes, guiding principles and framework for the exercise appears in GB.12/LILS/5 (Nov. 2011), paragraphs 8–11.

[13] The Conference adopted the Declaration of Philadelphia in May 1944, the Declaration on Apartheid in July 1964, the Declaration on Equality of Opportunity and Treatment for Women Workers in June 1975, the Declaration on Fundamental Principles and Rights at Work in June 1998 and the Declaration on Social Justice for a Fair Globalization in June 2008. In addition, the ILO Governing Body adopted the Declaration on Social

impact, the Declaration on Fundamental Principles and Rights at Work was adopted by the International Labour Conference on 18 June 1998. Based on the reporting obligation of Member States under Article 19(5)(e) of the ILO Constitution in relation to measures taken on Conventions they have not ratified,[14] the Declaration calls upon Member States to 'respect, promote and realize, in good faith and in accordance with the Constitution' four sets of principles.[15] These are freedom of association and the effective recognition of the right to collective bargaining, the elimination of all forms of forced or compulsory labour, the effective abolition of child labour and the elimination of discrimination in respect of employment and occupation. The Declaration has emerged as a key soft law instrument, with the principles also now widely embraced outside the ILO.[16] Within the ILO, the 1998 Declaration and the 2008 Declaration on Social Justice for a Fair Globalization have been used as platforms for expanded technical cooperation programmes in member States. This is the case as well for selected ILO Conventions and Recommendations.[17] The 1998 Declaration also spurred the now almost universal ratification of the eight core Conventions relating to the Declaration principles.[18]

Policy and Multinational Corporations in 1977 and has either adopted or taken note of many guidelines, manuals and codes of practice.

[14] See L. R. Helfer, 'Monitoring Compliance with Unratified Treaties', *Law & Contemp. Prob.*, 71 (2008), 193–218.

[15] ILO Declaration on Fundamental Principles and Rights at Work, adopted by the International Labour Conference on 18 June 1998, paragraph 2. For a detailed examination, see C. La Hovary, *Les droits fondamentaux au travail: Origines, statut et impact en droit international* (Paris: Presses Universitaires de France, 2009). A brief description appears in A. Trebilcock, 'The ILO Declaration on Fundamental Principles and Rights at Work: A New Tool' in R. Blanpain and C. Engels (eds.), *The ILO and the Social Challenges of the 21st Century* (Deventer: Kluwer Law International, 2001), pp. 105–116.

[16] See for example the Global Compact, www.unglobalcompact.org/AboutTheGC/TheTenPrinciples/index.html; the United Nations Guidelines on Principles on Business and Human Rights, U.N. Doc. A/HRC/17/31 (21 March 2011), endorsed by the Human Rights Council in Res. 17/4 of 16 June 2011, the updated OECD Guidelines on Multinational Enterprises (www.oecd.org/daf/inv/mne/48004323.pdf) and the International Finance Corporation's Performance Standard 2 (labour and social conditions) in its Policy on Environmental and Social Sustainability (www.ifc.org).

[17] For recent examples, see J. M. Diller, 'Pluralism and Privatization in Transnational Labour Regulation: Experience of the International Labour Organization' in A. Blackett and A. Trebilcock (eds.), *Research Handbook on Transnational Labour Law* (Cheltenham: Edward Elgar, 2015), pp. 329–342.

[18] These are the 1930 Convention Concerning Forced or Compulsory Labour Convention (No. 29), 39 UNTS 55; the 1948 Freedom of Association and Protection of the Right to Organize Convention (No. 87), 68 UNTS 17; the 1949 Right to Organize and Collective

In addition, a tracking system based on country annual reporting and baselines has kept attention focused on the issues in non-ratifying States. Thematic reports on the principles – originally known as Global Reports – have, since the adoption of the 2008 Declaration on Social Justice for a Fair Globalization, become part of a periodic recurrent discussion at the annual ILO Conference.

3 The ILO and the 1969 and 1986 Vienna Conventions

3.1 The ILO's Interest in the 1986 Vienna Convention

In addition to the ILO's own contribution to the creation of substantive international labour law and human rights, the Organization has concluded many agreements with other organisztions and its member States. Agreements with States generally address issues involving ILO operational activities and/or the financing or implementation of technical cooperation. Those concluded with international and regional inter-governmental organizations focus on various forms of collaboration in particular fields or practical arrangements relating to staff.[19]

In a document prepared for the Governing Body about the VCLTSIO, the ILO Secretariat indicated that, 'while the 1969 Convention applied, without prejudice to the relevant rules of the organization which constitute a *lex specialis*, to the Constitution of the ILO and to international labour Conventions which are treaties exclusively between States, the 1986 Convention applies where the ILO would be one of the parties to

---

Bargaining Convention (No. 98), 96 UNTS 257; the 1957 Abolition of Forced Labour Convention (No. 105), 320 UNTS 291; the 1958 Discrimination (Employment and Occupation) Convention (No. 111), 362 UNTS 31; the 1973 Convention Concerning Minimum Age for Admission to Employment (No. 138), 1015 UNTS 297, and the 1999 Convention Concerning the Prohibition and Immediate Action for the Elimination of the Worst Forms of Child Labour (No. 182), 2133 UNTS 161. All the same, the singling out of 'principles concerning the fundamental rights which are the subject of' those 'Conventions recognized as fundamental both inside and outside the Organization' sparked an academic storm around whether the focus on the selected Conventions was desirable or indeed legally justifiable: see P. Alston, '"Core Labour Standards" and the Transformation of the International Labour Rights Regime', *EJIL*, 15 (2004), 457–521; B. Langille, 'Core Labour Rights: The True Story (Reply to Alston)', *EJIL*, 16 (2005), 409–437; F. Maupain, 'Revitalization not Retreat: The Real Potential of the 1998 ILO Declaration for the Universal Protection of Workers' Rights', *EJIL*, 16 (2005), 439–465, and La Hovary, *supra* n. 15, at pp. 33–53.

[19] Many of these are available through the Office of the ILO Legal Adviser on the ILO website; see www.ilo.org/public/english/bureau/leg/rel_org.htm.

a treaty or agreement ...'[20] Although the ILO had not experienced difficulties in relation to such agreements, it welcomed the specific legal framework as a contribution to 'removing ambiguities and doubts which might adversely affect the legal security of its transactions'.[21] Following discussion of the matter, the Governing Body authorised the Director-General to sign the 1986 instrument. The International Labour Conference then authorised the deposit of an act of formal confirmation. The document submitted to the Conference as a basis for this decision recalled that the Convention, which rested on 'the broadest possible application of the general rules governing the law of treaties between States',[22] contained 'special clauses addressing the specific nature and requirements of international organizations such as the ILO. Most of these special provisions are designed to take into account the 'rules of the organization'.[23] The decision was thus built upon a position the ILO had advocated in relation to the 1969 Vienna Convention (see Section 3.2 in this chapter).

The document put before the Conference marshaled another argument for the ILO to deposit an act of formal ratification of the VCLTSIO. Noting that the Convention confirms the status of international organizations as subjects of law in the international legal order, the document added that 'this consideration is all the more significant in the case of an international organization like the ILO which is of a tripartite structure'.[24] The ILO was among the first of the United Nations Specialized Agencies to submit, on 21 July 2000, a formal act in relation to the Convention. However, the treaty has as yet received only thirty-one of the thirty-five State ratifications it needs to enter into force.

3.2 The ILO's Role in Shaping Article 5 VCLT and Preservation of lex specialis

The considerable and unique treaty experience accumulated by the ILO by the time preparations were underway for the VCLT led the Organization to advocate preservation of its *lex specialis* in the context of the 1969 instrument.[25] This occurred through adoption of Article 5 VCLT, which provides that:

---

[20] G.B.235/IO/2/4 (March 1987), cited in International Labour Conference, 88th Session, 2000, *Provisional Record*, No. 5, Appendix I, p. 5/5.

[21] *Ibid.*   [22] *Ibid.*, at p. 5/3 (paragraph 8).   [23] *Ibid.* (paragraph 9).

[24] *Ibid.*, at p. 5/4 (paragraph 15).

[25] See Statement of the ILO (Mr. Jenks), 1 Apr. 1968, in ILO Archives, File No. UN 1020–100; reproduced in United Nations Conference on the Law of Treaties, 1st

> [t]he present Convention applies to any treaty which is the constituent
> instrument of an international organization and to any treaty adopted
> within an international organization *without prejudice to any relevant*
> *rules of the organization* (emphasis added).

The preparatory works for the Convention noted the need for 'a reservation regarding the application of the rule in question in the case of
constituent instruments of international organizations and sometimes
also of treaties drawn up within an organization'.[26] The Commission's
commentary on the text of what later became Article 5[27] referred to it as
'a general reservation covering the draft articles as a whole'.[28] Originally
extending to the 'established rules of an organization', the reservation in
the end covered 'only constituent instruments and treaties actually drawn
up within an organization'.[29]

The text of Article 5 is attributed to Sir Humphrey Waldock,[30] who as
Expert Consultant did indeed propose it to the International Law
Commission.[31] However, its origin was apparently the ILO, which in
1967 submitted a written statement 'in its capacity as depositary of certain
treaties'.[32] Commenting on the draft final articles prepared by the
International Law Commission, the ILO statement pointed out these
areas of difference between its rules and those laid down in the draft:
authentication of Conventions, their revision, reservations and acceptance
of obligations. The ILO expressed its understanding that under the draft of
what would become Article 5, 'these various categories of rules will

---

Session, 1968, Official Records, pp. 36–37. He recalled the number of ILO Conventions
and ratifications, along with the network of obligations governed by the ILO Constitution
and by a 'well-established body of practice'.

[26] E. Yemin, 'International Treaties Adopted within International Organizations (with
Special Reference to the ILO)', unpublished paper prepared for the Hague Centre for
Studies and Research on International Law and International Relations (1970; rev. 1972)
(copy on file with the author). And see H. Waldock, Fourth Report on the Law of Treaties,
A/CN.4/177, reproduced in R. G. Wetzel and D. Rauschning, *The Vienna Convention on*
the Law of Treaties: Travaux Préparatoires (Frankfurt am Main: Alfred Metzner Verlag,
1978), pp. 90–91.

[27] The notion was first reflected in draft Art. 48, which was then moved to the introduction
as Art. 4. Art. 4 was in turn renumbered Art. 5 at the time of adoption of the Convention.

[28] International Law Commission, Eighteenth Session, Report of the Commission to the
General Assembly (UNGA 1966), p. 191.

[29] *Ibid.*   [30] *Ibid.*, at p. 90.

[31] H. Waldock, Fourth Report on the Law of Treaties, in Wetzel and Rauschning, *supra*
n. 26, at pp. 90–91.

[32] Letter from ILO Director-General David Morse to the Secretary-General of the United
Nations, dated 18 May 1967, in ILO Archives, UN File No. 1001, Jacket 1 (01/
1950–12/1973).

continue to apply to the Constitution of the Organization and the instruments adopted within the International Labour Organization, including international labour Conventions, even where they differ from the draft articles on the law of treaties'.[33] Even today, Article 5 is known informally within the institution as 'the ILO clause'. Kirsten Schmalenbach confirms its function as 'primarily that of a general reservation clause'.[34]

In advance of the first diplomatic Conference of the VCLT, C. Wilfred Jenks,[35] then Principal Deputy Director-General and former Legal Adviser of the ILO, corresponded with C. A. Stravropoulous, Under-Secretary and Legal Counsel of the United Nations, on the issue.[36] The ILO designated an official who could follow the entire proceedings; he kept Jenks updated on progress and even arranged for the time-slot in which Jenks could present the ILO statement to the Conference. The ILO Secretariat was pleased with the outcome of what eventually emerged as draft Article 5.[37] Jenks' oral statement elaborated on the divergences on the issues already mentioned and added the question of informal interpretations (see Section 4.6). Jenks spoke eloquently in favour of a provision that would both state the rule and the exception, thus 'ensuring that codification does not operate as a bar rather than a stimulus to the progressive development of international law'.[38] Since then, the Organization has continued to pursue its own approach to weighing the various elements of the VCLT in relation to its own practice.

4 Special Features of ILO Practice in Relation to Treaties

4.1 Structural Features Related to Adoption of Treaties and Authentication of Texts

The structural features of the ILO, notably its governing organs (International Labour Conference, ILO Governing Body) and its

---

[33] *Ibid.*

[34] K. Schmalenbach, 'Article 5' in O. Dörr and K. Schmalenbach (eds.), *Vienna Convention on the Law of Treaties: A Commentary* (Berlin: Springer, 2012), pp. 89–99, at p. 89.

[35] Jenks, a law graduate of the University of Cambridge, had joined the ILO Legal Division in 1931 and served as Legal Adviser as from 1940 to 1953, before being named Deputy Director-General. He was elected Director-General in 1970 and served until he died in office in 1973.

[36] Letters of 21, 27 and 28 Feb., 22 March and 22 Apr. 1968, in ILO Archives, Mr. Jenks, BIT XXVII, Comprehensive File 11 Oct. 1967–31 Dec. 1968.

[37] Exchange of correspondence between Mssrs. P. P. Fano, Director, ILO Rome Office, and Jenks, 10 and 22 Apr. 1968; Jenks' memo to the Director-General, both in ILO Archives, File No. UN 1020–100.

[38] Statement of ILO to VCLT Conference, 1 Apr. 1968, p. 6.

secretariat (International Labour Office), along with various treaty-related rules in the ILO Constitution, have marked its treaty practice. Both the Conference, which is the supreme organ, and the Governing Body are tripartite: representatives of employers' and of workers' organizations take decisions alongside those of governments. Each of the ILO's 185 Member States is invited to send a conference delegation consisting of two government delegates, one employer delegate and one worker delegate (the '2–1-1' formula) along with non-voting advisers. Conventions are adopted upon receiving a majority of two-thirds of the favourable votes cast in plenary by the delegates present at the International Labour Conference (Article 19(2) of the ILO Constitution). Thus, adoption of an instrument is possible only with the support of delegates from the employer and/or worker ranks, in addition to those from government. An adopted instrument is signed by both the President of the Conference[39] and the Director-General of the ILO. This feature deviates from the dominant model reflected in Articles 7 to 12 VCLT, which focuses on consent and signature by representatives of States. This distinction has certain consequences in relation to reservations (see Section 4.3).

Unlike open-ended treaty negotiations, the development of international labour standards follows a schedule set by the ILO Governing Body, taking into account the Standing Orders of the Conference. Without entering into detail, the Governing Body can place a standard-setting item on the agenda of the Conference for a single or a double discussion, i.e. for examination at either one or two sessions of the annual meeting.[40] In either case, the Conference committee charged with examining a proposed standard operates under extreme time pressure. Often, the Employer and Worker groups have worked out their main positions in advance; regional or other groupings of States may do the same. Sometimes the Secretariat organises informal briefing sessions or off-the-record consultations prior to the Conference.

The Conference committee normally works on the basis of a text proposed by the secretariat following its internal consultation on substantive and legal issues and then written consultation of ILO

---

[39] This has usually been a Government delegate, but on occasion an Employer or Worker delegate has been elected President.

[40] While the General Conference normally takes place once a year, special maritime sessions have traditionally been held in addition to address such issues. Proposals are under consideration by the ILO Governing Body that could lead to changes in the Standing Orders so as to provide additional means of standards preparation.

constituents.[41] Unlike in the plenary, this Committee takes decisions by simple majority, and the votes of governments, employers and workers are equally weighted. Its report contains in an annex a draft which has gone through its own drafting committee (convened by the Legal Adviser). The technical Committee's reporter submits the report to the plenary, and the chair and vice-chairs of the committee make statements, but there is no further discussion of the report. Following prior publication of a draft instrument, a record vote is taken to establish whether the required majority has been met.[42] A final review of the text of an adopted Convention is then rapidly done by the Conference Drafting Committee, primarily to spot printing errors or any remaining discordance between the French and English versions.[43] At this point, the Director-General begins to exercise the depositary functions for a Convention, as stipulated in standard final provisions that were approved in 1946.[44] These provisions cover future revision of a Convention, automatic denunciation of a revised instrument, depositary functions and notification to Members and the United Nations Secretary-General when ratifications occur. They also stipulate the default number of ratifications required for entry into force (two), but the Conference can increase this number.[45] In several cases, especially in the maritime field, the Conference has set a higher ratification level that also includes a ship tonnage threshold.

The preparatory works of a Convention will thus normally include the official documents prepared by the Office in advance of the discussion, the report of the Conference Committee set up to handle the agenda item

---

[41] The Office sends questionnaires and reports to Governments, which are requested to consult with national organizations representing Employers and Workers in preparing replies or comments (these organizations can also provide comments directly to the Office). The entire process is set out in the Standing Orders of the Conference, Section E (Arts. 34–40).

[42] Since for each member State the Governments have two votes to the one vote each of the Employer and Worker delegates, some Conventions have been adopted, particularly in the last twenty years, without the support of most of the Employer delegates (often through abstention rather than a 'no' vote, through which it is possible to prevent the necessary quorum from being attained for adoption).

[43] Spanish is the third official language of the Conference, but not of the Conventions.

[44] 1946 Final Articles Revision Convention (No. 80), 38 UNTS 3. See, also, International Labour Organization, *Manual for Drafting ILO Instruments* (Geneva: International Labour Organization, 2006; rev. on line 2011) and available through www.ilo.org/pub lic/english/bureau/leg/manual.htm, which presents a full examination of final clauses and provides the gender-neutral texts versions used since the mid-1990s: paragraphs 41–73.

[45] The ILO Governing Body reviewed practice in relation to the final provisions of Conventions when it took note of GB.313/LILS/2 (20 Feb. 2012) at its Session in March 2012 (see GB.313/LILS/PV, March 2012).

at each session, the record of the plenary, the recorded vote of each delegate present and, of course, the text as adopted in English and French. A standard clause in Conventions provides that the two languages are equally authoritative, as is the case for the ILO Constitution.[46]

4.2   Submission and Ratification

The ILO Constitution contains an unusual submission requirement: no later than eighteen months from adoption of a Convention, it must be brought 'before the authority or authorities within whose competence the matter lies, for the enactment of legislation or other action' (Article 19(5)(b)). In addition, under a 1946 amendment to the Constitution, even in the absence of ratification, a State may be asked to report on 'the position of its law and practice in regard to the matters dealt within the Convention' and to indicate difficulties which prevent or delay ratification (Article 19(5)(e) of the ILO Constitution). The Governing Body of the ILO identifies the instruments on which it will request such reports. The Committee of Experts on the Application of Conventions and Recommendations (CEACR) then prepares a 'general survey' of these reports which is discussed by the Committee on the Application of Standards (CAS) of the International Labour Conference. These two bodies also review whether submission requirements have been met.

As in other treaty regimes, the act of ratification is a voluntary one for which State consent is required. If the Member State 'obtains the consent of the authority ... it will communicate the formal ratification of the Convention to the Director-General ...' (Article 19(5)(d) of the ILO Constitution). A State that has ratified the 1976 Tripartite Consultation (International Labour Standards) Convention (No. 144)[47] must have procedures in place that will permit consultation of representatives of employers and workers on, *inter alia*, 're-examination at appropriate intervals of unratified Conventions ... to consider what measures might be taken to promote their implementation and ratification as appropriate' (Convention No. 144, Article 2 and Article 5(1)(c)).[48]

---

[46] See International Labour Organization, *Manual for Drafting ILO Instruments, supra* n. 44, at paragraphs 71–72. Compare Art. 33(3) VCLT ('The terms of the treaty are presumed to have the same meaning in each authentic text'): *supra* n. 2.

[47] ILM, 15 (1976), 1076–1080.

[48] Convention No. 144: *ibid.*, considered by the ILO to be a priority as a 'governance' Convention, has been ratified by 139 States (as of 11 June 2015).

The Director-General of the ILO examines the instrument submitted by the State before registering the ratification (cf. Article 77 VCLT). An instrument must clearly identify the Convention, include any required declarations, be signed in the original by a person with authority to engage the State and clearly convey the Government's intention that the State will be bound by the Convention and its undertaking to fulfil the relevant requirements of the Convention in light of Article 19(5)(d) of the ILO Constitution.[49] While ratification is open only to ILO Member States – thereby excluding multilateral organizations – withdrawal from the Organization does not terminate a State's obligations under a ratified Convention (Article 1(5) of the ILO Constitution). Denunciation of a Convention is possible under the conditions stipulated in it, most commonly in a one-year window opening at ten-year intervals following the date it first entered into force.

4.3   Reservations, Declarations and 'Flexibility Devices'

Before registration can occur, the Secretariat ascertains that the instrument of ratification is not accompanied by any reservations, since they are not permitted in ILO treaty practice. If a reservation is included, the Government will be quietly invited to submit a new instrument of ratification without it. The reasons, set as early as the 1920s,[50] relate to the purpose and structure of ILO standard-setting and have been confirmed on many occasions. The most notable post–World War II expressions of this appeared in the ILO's submission in relation to advisory proceedings before the International Court of Justice in *Reservations to the Convention on the Prevention and Punishment of the*

---

[49] International Labour Organization, *Handbook of Procedures Relating to International Labour Conventions and Recommendations (Rev. 2012)* (Geneva: International Labour Organization, 2012), p. 13.

[50] See materials cited in the Memorandum submitted by the International Labour Organization to the International Court of Justice in *Reservations to the Convention on the Prevention and Punishment of the Crime of Genocide* (Advisory Opinion) (1951) ICJ Rep. 15 (International Labour Organization, *Official Bulletin*, Vol. XXXIV (1951), pp. 274–312, and the written statement of the ILO submitted to the International Court of Justice also appears in ICJ Pleadings (1951), see esp. pp. 235–236). The ILO position and sources are reflected in Chapter VII of the Report of the 52nd Session of the International Law Commission (www.legal/un.org/ilc/reports/2000/English/chp7), pp. 109–111. See, also, J. Klabbers, 'On Human Rights Treaties, Contractual Conceptions and Reservations' in I. Ziemele (ed.), *Reservations to Human Rights Treaties and the Vienna Convention Regime: Conflict, Harmony or Reconciliation* (Leiden: Martinus Nijhoff, 2004), pp. 149–182, at pp. 179–180.

Crime of Genocide,[51] and the ILO Statement to the VCLT Conference described previously. Essentially, the option of making reservations has been excluded because (i) international labour Conventions are adopted by the delegates to a tripartite Conference, not by plenipotentiaries of States as signatories; (ii) there is therefore no mechanism in place for the objection to reservations entered by States, in light of the impossibility of consulting non-governmental delegates on such questions at a later stage and (iii) the ILO Constitution already contemplates that in framing Conventions – which are intended in part to avert unfair competition – the Conference shall have due regard 'to those countries in which climatic conditions, the imperfect development of industrial organization, or other special circumstances make the industrial conditions substantially different [so as] to suggest the modifications, if any, which it considers may be required' (Article 19(3) of the ILO Constitution). This latter provision, along with other 'flexibility devices' (see later), was thus used in lieu of possible reservations. The 1951 memorandum couched the special ILO rules in terms of recognised principles of international law and international practice in relation to treaties. It stressed the constitutional obligation of submission of Conventions as adopted by the Conference to the member States, i.e. without reservations. Jan Klabbers has pointed out that a reservation to a labour Convention might mean more relaxed domestic labour laws, thereby creating an arguable comparative advantage[52] (which would be contraindicated by the ILO Constitution).

In its examination of reservations, the International Law Commission found the ILO's reasoning for its 'respectable tradition' to be 'somewhat less than convincing',[53] and the characterisation of the ILO's position has been nuanced by Guido Raimondi.[54] In the ILO's view, some of the functions that reservations may serve are taken into account through various 'flexibility devices' in a number of ILO Conventions.[55] Indeed, many Conventions

---

[51] See Memorandum submitted by the International Labour Organization, ICJ Pleadings, *supra* n. 50, at pp. 228–231.

[52] Klabbers, *supra* n. 50, at p. 168.

[53] International Law Commission, Chapter VII (2000), p. 110.

[54] G. Raimondi, 'Réserves et conventions internationales du travail' in J.-C. Javillier, B. Gernigon and G. Politakis (eds.), *Les normes internationales du travail: un patrimoine pour l'avenir: Mélanges en l'honneur de Nicolas Valticos* (Geneva: International Labour Organizations, 2004), pp. 527–539.

[55] For an exploration of the topic, see G. Politakis, 'Deconstructing Flexibility in International Labour Conventions' in Javillier, Gernigon and Politakis (eds.), *supra* n. 54, pp. 463–496. The *Manual for Drafting ILO Instruments*, *supra* n. 44, examines flexibility measures in paragraphs 133–163.

provide latitude in the means of their application by a ratifying State (by legislation, court decision, arbitral awards, etc.). And for a few Conventions, it is possible to accept only parts of the instrument upon ratification (differentiated obligations),[56] such as the branches of social security protection to be covered under the 1952 Social Security (Minimum Standards) Convention (No. 102).[57] A number of Conventions permit declarations that specify categories of workers or of undertakings that may be excluded from the scope upon ratification by that country.[58] A few Conventions require a declaration, such as to specify the minimum age for employment or the required minimum number of days of annual leave, within boundaries set by the instrument.[59] Flexibility measures may thus concern the scope of the obligation undertaken or the means by which it will be applied. ILO practice appears internally consistent over time in relation to reservations, with apparently no change after the entry into force of the VCLT. Indeed, the VCLT Conference was well informed of this deviation from its Articles 19 to 23 provisions and can be seen as having at least tacitly accepted it.

4.4   Revision of Conventions; Abrogation

Today, ILO Conventions contain provisions which permit their revision and replacement by ratification of a subsequently adopted Convention; under the standard final provisions, the result is *ipso jure* denunciation of the earlier instrument unless otherwise provided. This was not the case for the first twenty-seven Conventions adopted by the ILO, however. In addition, since space on the Conference agenda is limited, it may take considerable time for an instrument to be revised in the manner foreseen by the Conference Standing Orders. These were two factors that led the Conference in 1997 to adopt an amendment to the ILO Constitution, under which the Conference is now able to abrogate *vis-à-vis* the ILO all legal effects of a Convention 'if it appears that the Convention has lost its purpose or that is no longer makes a useful contribution to attaining the objectives of the Organization'.[60] This basically non-controversial

---

[56] See, further, the contribution to this volume of Bowman at pp. 392–439 (Chapter 13).

[57] 210 UNTS 131.

[58] This may be subject to a requirement of consultation with national employers' and workers' organizations in relation to such an exclusion. A list of such Conventions appears in the *Handbook* of the International Labour Organization, *supra* n. 49, at pp. 15–17.

[59] The *Handbook* contains a list of such Conventions: *supra* 49, at pp. 13–14.

[60] International Labour Conference, 85th Session, 1997 (www.ilo.org/public/english/bureau/leg/manual.htm).

amendment finally won the two-thirds majority of Member States' ratifications required for its entry into force on 8 October 2015.[61]

In the meantime, the ILO took what Felice Morgenstern has termed 'practical measures'.[62] For instance, pending entry into force of the constitutional amendment, a procedure was later approved for the 'withdrawal' of obsolete Conventions which had not entered into force, and of selected Recommendations.[63] Before this, certain Conventions were 'shelved' in line with Governing Body decisions to declare them 'out-of-date'. Whether 'withdrawn' or 'out-of-date', these Conventions are no longer promoted for ratification, and reports on their application are no longer requested of governments.[64] All of these mechanisms have been accompanied by constitutional and consultation guarantees reflecting the ILO's tripartite structure. The 2006 Maritime Labour Convention incorporates its own novel mechanism for its revision, using an opting-out clause inspired by the practice of the International Maritime Organization.[65] This variety in ILO practice goes well beyond what the VCLT contemplated – in Article 40 – in its codification of customary international law on amendment of multilateral treaties.

4.5   Implementation and Monitoring

A State ratifying an ILO Convention undertakes to 'take such action as may be necessary to make effective the provisions of such Convention' (Article 19(5)(d) of the Constitution). In addition to the supervisory

---

[61] The ILO registered the 125th ratification on 3 Dec. 2015, and several instruments are being abrogated, making it only one ratification short of entry into force (assuming no change in the number of Member States). Note: the 1986 constitutional amendment, which has also not entered into force, would raise the ratification requirement for such amendments from two-thirds to three-fourths of member States. On the significance of the two amendments, see GB.323/LILS/2 (March 2015).

[62] F. Morgenstern, *The Legal Problems of International Organizations* (Geneva: International Labour Organization, 1982), p. 114. She reported that the impossibility of abrogation absent a constitutional amendment was confirmed during an in-depth review of international labour standards done between 1974 and 1977.

[63] International Labour Conference, 88th Session, 2000, *Provisional Record*, No. 6–2.

[64] However, when ratified, they may still be subject to representations and complaints regarding failure to give effect to their provisions, pursuant to Arts. 24 and 26 of the ILO Constitution. This will also be the case for Conventions that may be abrogated in line with the 1997 Constitutional amendment.

[65] *Supra* n. 7. See, further, M. L. McConnell, D. Devlin and C. Doumbia-Henry, *The Maritime Labour Convention, 2006: A Legal Primer to an Emerging International Regime* (Leiden: Martinus Nijhoff, 2011).

machinery in place to review regular reporting (the CEACR and the CAS), if a State party to a Convention 'has failed to secure in any respect the effective observance within its jurisdiction', a representation may be filed under Article 24 of the Constitution by an 'industrial association of employers or of workers'. Moreover, any State having also ratified the Convention, the Governing Body, or a delegate to the Conference has the right to file a complaint under Article 26 of the Constitution if a ratifying State is in its view not 'securing the effective observance' of the Convention in question. An Article 26 complaint may also be pursued by the ILO Governing Body on its own motion or upon receipt of a complaint from a delegate to the International Labour Conference (Article 26(4)).

To examine complaints, the Constitution foresees establishment of a Commission of Inquiry whose report should include 'findings and recommendations' on steps to be taken to meet the complaint within a specified time (Article 28).[66] Each government concerned by the complaint shall indicate within three months whether it accepts the recommendations and if not, whether it proposes to refer the complaint to the International Court of Justice (ICJ) (Article 29). The ICJ may affirm, vary or reverse any of the findings or recommendations of the Commission of Inquiry (Article 32). If the State involved does not seek ICJ review, the Commission of Inquiry's findings and recommendations are the last word. But if the State rejects the findings without going to the ICJ or does not implement the recommendations, there is risk of a stalemate that can have an ultimately delegitimising effect on the procedures. This situation has led the institution to consider various alternatives (e.g. establishing the tribunal foreseen by Article 37(2) of the Constitution, seeking an advisory opinion from the ICJ[67] or adopting a resolution encouraging member States to take other action).[68]

---

[66] B. Vukas, 'Some Remarks Concerning the Commissions of Inquiry Established under the ILO Constitution' in Javillier, Gernigon and Politakis (eds.), *supra* n. 54, pp. 75–82.

[67] Although the ILO depended upon the Council of the League of Nations to take this step before the founding of the United Nations, the Agreement between the UN and the ILO authorises the ILO to do so on its own 'on legal questions arising within the scope of its activities other than questions concerning the mutual relationships of the Organization and the United Nations or other specialised agencies' (see its Art. IX(2)).

[68] See, for instance, Resolution concerning the measures recommended by the Governing Body under Art. 33 of the ILO Constitution on the subject of Myanmar (International Labour Conference, 88th Session, 2000), partially lifted by a resolution adopted at the 101st Session in 2012.

In contrast to the plethora of expert committees or arbitration panels that have emerged for separate treaties in other areas of public international law, the ILO features a unitary system in relation to the review of the application of all ratified ILO Conventions, in addition to what is constitutionally foreseen in the case of an alleged breach. The Constitution calls for regular State reporting, supplemented by input from employer and worker organizations, and as noted permits representations and complaints (Articles 22 to 34). Over the years, these provisions have been augmented by procedures created by the International Labour Conference or the ILO Governing Body, in particular by establishing the Committee of Experts on the Application of Conventions and Recommendations (CEACR), the Conference Committee on the Application of Standards (CAS) and the Committee on Freedom of Association (CFA), each with its own special function.[69] The composition of the CAS and the CFA is tripartite, but the CFA has a neutral external chair. The Governing Body appoints members of the CEACR on the basis of their competence, impartiality and independence; many distinguished jurists and judges have served on it.

4.6   Interpretation

While Articles 31 and 32 VCLT largely represent customary international law, ILO practice in regard to the interpretation of treaties has a few nuances of its own. Under the ILO Constitution, only the International Court of Justice is competent to render an official 'interpretation' (Article 37). Yet, views on the meaning of provisions of ILO Conventions are also provided informally during the consideration of their adoption, prior to their ratification by an ILO member State and after a Convention has entered into force for a ratifying State. The function performed by these views thus differs, reflecting both the different stages at which they are given and the ILO entity involved.

Under Article 37(1) of the ILO Constitution, 'any question or dispute relating to the interpretation' of the Constitution or any Convention adopted in pursuance of its provisions 'shall be referred

---

[69] A short explanation of these 'regular' and 'special' procedures may be found in International Labour Organizations, *Rules of the Game: A Brief Introduction to International Labour Standards* (rev. ed., 2014) (www.ilo.org/wcmsp5/groups/public/-ed_norm/-normes/docu ments/publication/wcms_318141.pdf). The CEACR and CAS were established in 1926; the CFA in 1952.

for decision to the International Court of Justice'.[70] This article also provides for the possible establishment of 'a tribunal for the expeditious determination of any dispute or question relating to the interpretation of a Convention' (Article 37(2)). None has ever been set up, but the idea of doing so has enjoyed a revival in recent years.[71] Any applicable 'judgment or advisory opinion' of the ICJ is termed 'binding' on such a tribunal. And while no 'question or dispute' has been referred to the ICJ, its predecessor, the Permanent Court of International Justice, was called upon, pursuant to Article 423 of the Treaty of Versailles, to provide an interpretation of an ILO Convention in *Interpretation of the Convention of 1919 Concerning Employment of Women during the Night (No. 4)*[72] and, on several occasions, of its Constitution.[73]

In the face of reluctance to engage the ICJ, member States' need for interpretation has been filled through unofficial means: by the ILO Secretariat before and after adoption, by the ILO Committee of Experts on the Application of Conventions and Recommendations and by Commissions of Inquiry. As Francis Maupain has concluded, aside from what Article 37 of the ILO Constitution foresees, 'there is no mechanism that permits resolution of a problem of interpretation so as to create a binding obligation *erga omnes*: the opinions of the Office can give a universal interpretation – just as the Committee of Experts can – but these opinions are not binding. The conclusions of a Commission of Inquiry – including the interpretations it may be led to give – can become

---

[70] In the equally valid French version, it reads: 'toutes questions ou difficultés relatives à l'interprétation ... seront soumises à l'appréciation'.

[71] J. Fraterman, 'Article 37(2) of the ILO Constitution: Can an ILO Interpretive Tribunal end the Hegemony of International Trade Law?' *Georgetown JIL*, 42 (2011), 879–922. In 2014, the ILO Governing Body was informed in some depth about both options under Art. 37(1) and (2) of the Constitution: see GB.322/INS/5 (Oct. 2014).

[72] *Interpretation of the Convention of 1919 Concerning Employment of Women during the Night (No. 4)* (Advisory Opinion), 1932 PCIJ, Series A/B, No. 50, 365. The Permanent Court of International Justice found that women managerial employees were covered by the gender-based prohibition on night work established by the Convention.

[73] *Designation of the Workers' Delegate for the Netherlands at the Third Session of the International Labour Conference* (Advisory Opinion), 1922 PCIJ, Series B, No. 1; *Competence of the ILO in Regard to International Regulation of the Conditions of the Labour of Persons Employed in Agriculture* (Advisory Opinion), 1922 PCIJ, Series B, No. 2; *Competence of the ILO to Examine Proposals for the Organization and Development of the Methods of Agricultural Production* (Advisory Opinion), 1922 PCIJ, Series B, No. 3, and *Competence of the International Labour Organization to Regulate, Incidentally, the Personal Work of the Employer* (Advisory Opinion), 1926 PCIJ, Series B, No. 13.

binding, but their scope is limited to the case at hand'.[74] These ILO bodies are not courts and are thus not required to provide reasoned opinions, although sometimes their explanations are extensive. All the same, the CFA handles 'cases', the CEACR speaks of 'cases of progress', some authors refer to the 'jurisprudence' of the supervisory bodies,[75] and national courts have cited them.[76] The confusion inherent in this situation continues to dog the institution.[77]

One further aspect of the ILO Constitution is relevant in the context of interpretation. As Klabbers has noted, 'the *pacta sunt servanda* rule not merely stipulates that treaties are binding, but also that they shall be performed in good faith ... this is also why the notion of good faith is included in the general rule on interpretation as laid down in [A]rticle 31 [VCLT]'.[78] This is implicitly embraced by the ILO Constitution's reference to a State taking 'such action as may be necessary to make effective the provisions of' a ratified Convention (Article 19(5)(d)) and a Member State's acceptance of the obligations of the Constitution (Article 1(4)).

4.6.1   Interpretation Issues Arising during the Adoption Process

During the drafting phase of a Convention in Committee discussions, queries may arise in relation to the meaning of certain terms or phrases used in the proposed text as well as to procedural matters. The Standing Orders of the Conference permit a motion in committee to ask for the opinion of the Chairperson, the Secretariat or the Legal Adviser of the Conference (Article 63(2)(f)); this is also possible in the plenary (Article 15(2)(f)). Legal opinions provided on terminology are sometimes cited later when it comes to questions of interpretation. When called upon to give legal advice to Committees, the Legal Adviser may cite the elements

---

[74] F. Maupain, 'L'interprétation des conventions internationales du travail' in R. J. Dupuy (eds.), *Mélanges en l'honneur de Nicolas Valticos, Droit et justice* (Paris: Pedone, 1999), pp. 567–583, at p. 573 (author's translation).

[75] C. La Hovary, 'Showdown at the ILO? A Historical Perspective on the Employer Group's 2012 Challenge to the Right to Strike', *Industrial Law J.*, 42 (2013), 1–31.

[76] See, e.g., E. Gravel and Q. Delpech, 'International Labour Standards: Recent Developments in Complementarity between the International and National Supervisory Systems', *International Labour Rev.* 147 (2008), 403–415.

[77] See A. A. Dijkoff and F. J. L. Pennings, 'The Interpretation of International Labour Standards' in F. Pennings (ed.), *International Social Security Standards: Current Views and Interpretation Matters* (Antwerp: Intersentia, 2007), pp. 149–174, at pp. 164–166.

[78] J. Klabbers, 'Virtuous Interpretation' in M. Fitzmaurice, O. Elias and P. Merkouris (eds.), *Treaty Interpretation and the Vienna Convention on the Law of Treaties: 30 Years On* (Leiden: Koninklijke Brill NV, 2010), pp. 17–38, at p. 37.

of interpretation found in the VCLT. And in 1993, when the Office prepared a document on interpretation for the Governing Body, it set out the essence of the VCLT rule on the subject.[79] During informal consultations that took place on the basis of a 'non-paper' on interpretation of international Labour Conventions in 2009, the VCLT was again referred to, but in a way that reiterated the ILO's own approach to the interpretation of its Conventions, with its greater reliance on the preparatory works.

In addition, the Office of the Legal Adviser has compiled the *Manual for Drafting International Labour Instruments*; it provides an overview of actual and recommended practice in the elaboration of ILO Conventions and Recommendations. The *Manual* reviews the meaning of terms used recurrently in ILO instruments while promoting consistency in terminology and structure.[80] Originally prepared in 2006 by the Office of the Legal Adviser and examined by a tripartite group of experts, the nonbinding Manual was submitted to the Governing Body for information.[81] It contrasts ILO practice on preambles with the interpretative value of preambles as expressed in the VCLT on the other.[82] In the ILO, preambles have rarely been used to interpret the scope of a given provision of a Convention. For purposes of ILO instruments, 'the Legal Adviser has consistently recalled that the preamble is non-binding in nature and that its primary function is to set out the context of the instrument'.[83] It may also shed light on the object and purpose of a Convention or place ILO instruments in a wider framework.[84] Sometimes, Committees have spent considerable time on preambular language, while in other instances its content has been kept to a minimum.[85] One factor leading to longer preambles in the ILO is the larger body of already existing legal

---

[79] GB.256/SC/2/2 (1993).

[80] See International Labour Organization, *Manual for Drafting ILO Instruments, supra* n. 44: Part I (formal structure), Part II (substantive content) and Appendix 7 (on terms), pp. 112–124.

[81] GB.297/12(Rev.) (Nov. 2006), pp. 1–2.

[82] See International Labour Organization, *Manual for Drafting ILO Instruments, supra* n. 44: Part I, Section 1.2. (paragraphs 11–12).

[83] *Ibid.* (paragraph 11). See, e.g., Report of the Committee on Maternity Protection, International Labour Conference, 88th Session (2000), *Provisional Record*, No. 20 (paragraph 68).

[84] International Labour Organization, *Manual for Drafting ILO Instruments, supra* n. 44: Part I, Section 1.2. (paragraphs 23–24).

[85] On the phenomenon of preambles more generally, see the contribution to this volume of Klabbers at pp. 172–200 (Chapter 7).

instruments to which a new Convention will tend to refer.[86] This may help to clarify the interrelationship between treaties.[87]

4.6.2 Interpretation by the International Labour Conference

As a matter of general international law, the International Labour Conference – as the body having adopted a treaty – would theoretically have the implicit authority to interpret it,[88] subject of course to Article 37 of the ILO Constitution, which does not attribute this power to the Conference. It appears that the Conference has done so on only one occasion. In 2011, it adopted the Resolution concerning gender equality and the use of language of legal texts in the ILO. In it, the Conference resolved that:

1. ... gender equality should be reflected through the use of appropriate language in official legal texts of the Organization. This can be achieved among others through the use of the principle applied in paragraph 2.

2. ... in the ILO Constitution and other legal texts of the Organization, in accordance with applicable rules of interpretation, the use of one gender includes in its meaning a reference to the other gender unless the context otherwise requires.[89]

As guidance applying to all Conventions, however, this 'horizontal interpretation'[90] differs from others which are normally set in a particular factual situation involving a single instrument. The Conference may have the opportunity to answer the question in future in relation to the 1952 Social Security (Minimum Standards) Convention (No. 102),[91] which

---

[86] For example, contrast the preamble to the 2011 Convention Concerning Decent Work for Domestic Workers (No. 189), ILO PR No.15A, with the shorter one in the 1958 Discrimination (Employment and Occupation) Convention (No. 111), *supra* n. 18. Cross-references to existing instruments are a way of forestalling a possible erosion in the level of protection being afforded.

[87] See, further, Art. 30 VCLT: *supra* n. 2.

[88] O. Dörr, 'Article 31' in Dörr and Schmalenbach (eds.), *supra* n. 34, pp. 521–570, at pp. 530–532.

[89] International Labour Conference, 100th Session, 2011, Resolutions adopted by the Conference, also reproduced in International Labour Organization, *Manual for Drafting ILO Instruments*, *supra* n. 44, at p. 133 (Annex 10). The *Manual* provides guidance on gender-neutral drafting (paragraphs 254–266).

[90] Cf. J. Arato, 'Subsequent Practice and Evolutive Interpretation Techniques of Treaty Interpretation over Time and Their Diverse Consequences', *Law & Practice Int'l Courts & Tribs.*, 9 (2010), 443–494.

[91] *Supra* n. 57.

contains provisions that the Committee on the Application of Standards has termed 'gender biased' and reflecting 'an obsolete model of the male breadwinner'.[92] The Governing Body has been called on to determine the 'most appropriate means of interpreting gender-sensitive language' in the light of the 2011 Conference Resolution.[93] The ILO may also, depending on the outcome of the International Law Commission's work on treaties over time,[94] wish to take account of the Commission's conclusions as it looks for ways to resolve the issues arising under Convention No. 102.

4.6.3   'Informal Opinions' or 'Clarifications' Provided by the ILO Secretariat

Since the beginning of the ILO, insights into the meaning of provisions of various Conventions have been voiced through statements made by the Secretariat (the International Labour Office) in response to individual requests by member States considering ratification of an adopted instrument. Indeed, in the early years of the institution, the Governing Body noted that a Government's 'tacit acceptance of an interpretation acted on by a Member and communicated through the *Official Bulletin* constitutes important authority which can always be invoked for that interpretation'.[95]

Between 1921 and 2002, 147 informal opinions on the meaning of provisions of Conventions were published in the *Official Bulletin*, on a range of topics and instruments (space constraints prevent greater specificity). Memoranda of the International Labour Office containing 'informal opinions' or 'clarifications' were published under the rubric of 'Interpretations of Decisions of the International Labour Conference'. Somewhat curiously in an age of greater transparency, no response provided to a member State's request has appeared publicly since 2002.[96]

---

[92] International Labour Conference, Report of the Committee on the Application of Standards, Part I, International Labour Conference, 100th Session, 2011, *Provisional Record*, No. 18, p. I/35.

[93] *Ibid.*

[94] See the First Report on Subsequent Agreements and Subsequent Practice in Relation to Treaties (as the work on treaties over time has been renamed), in A/CN.4/660 (19 March 2013), and draft conclusions considered at the Commission's 65th Session, reported in U.N. Doc. A/68/10 (2013), pp. 9–48 (as well as later reports).

[95] Minutes of the 9th Session of the Governing Body of the ILO (1921), pp. 365–366 (cited by C. W. Jenks, 'The Interpretation of International Labour Conventions by the International Labour Office', *BYbIL*, 20 (1939), 132–141).

[96] Nonetheless, the *Handbook* still states that when a request is for a formal or official opinion and the issue raised is likely to be of general interest, a Memorandum by the Office will be published in the *Official Bulletin*. See International Labour Organization,

In contrast to the secondary reference to preparatory work under Article 32 VCLT, such material has been a primary means of 'interpretation' for the ILO Secretariat, along with the ordinary meaning of terms in their context and the object and purpose of the instrument (Article 31). An examination of internal documents available in the ILO Archives sheds some light on whether this practice was influenced by the VCLT. In 1952, the Director-General issued an Instruction (No. 45) on the procedure concerning requests for interpretations of Conventions and Recommendations, setting out the internal arrangements for preparation of a memorandum to be addressed to the State requesting an interpretation. ILO technical divisions were to prepare a detailed paper on the basis of the preparatory work of the instrument in question, information concerning measures taken with a view to putting it into effect, any observations of the CEACR and all available technical information. The paper was to include 'earlier interpretations on identical or similar points', with mention made of the International Labour Code, an ILO reference work covering the period up to 1951. 'When a request for an interpretation raises a question of terminology, the English and French terms of the instruments under discussion shall be studied and compared. [They] are of equal authority and must be read in conjunction in order to determine the meaning of the Convention' (paragraph 6). Later instructions included a similar provision.

The Office memorandum was to be drawn up, after citation of (a) the relevant provisions of the Convention and (b) the request received, along the following lines: '(c) In appropriate cases, a study of the terms involved, in accordance with [paragraph] 6 above, (d) An account of the preparatory work and the various technical data, (e) Conclusions' (paragraph 7). The reply was to contain 'the usual reservation that the Constitution of the International Labour Organization confers no special competence upon the International Labour Office to give an authentic interpretation of the provisions of Conventions adopted by the International Labour Conference'. If the requests raised 'questions of general interest' or were 'of some importance', the replies were to be brought to the attention of the Governing Body and later published in the *Official Bulletin*.

As in some later versions, this Instruction stated that the 'Office will not, for the time being, give any opinion on requests for the

---

Handbook, *supra* n. 48, at p. 42. (Each year, the *Official Bulletin* communicates selected information and documents of the Organization).

interpretation of the Freedom of Association and Protection of the Right to Organize Convention, 1948 (No. 87), and the Right to Organize and Collective Bargaining Convention, 1949 (No. 98), in view of the special procedure instituted by the Governing Body for dealing with complaints in the matter of freedom of association' (paragraph 12).[97]

These instructions were reformulated on 11 January 1968, when the Director-General issued the Procedure concerning requests for interpretation of Conventions and Recommendations (Director-General's Instruction No. 337). The Instruction referred to the following sources to be examined: 'any earlier interpretations relating to the problems raised, references to any relevant observations of the Committee of Experts on the Application of Conventions and Recommendations and other competent supervisory bodies' (paragraph 4) and 'a note on the technical aspects of the problems raised which lie within [the] competence [of the technical branch], taking into account 'the preparatory work which preceded the adoption', 'the extent to which law and practice in countries other than the one making the request may assist in clarifying the problems at issue', 'earlier interpretations and any observations of a supervisory body' 'and other relevant technical information and technical considerations' (paragraph 6). The introductory letter was to state 'the usual reservation' (paragraph 9). The prescribed format for the reply called for (i) citation of the provisions involved and (ii) the essence of the request for an interpretation, followed by '(iii) in appropriate cases, a study of the terms involved; (iv) an account of the preparatory work and the various technical data; (v) conclusions' (paragraph 9).

The 1952 and 1968 Instructions demonstrate the approach taken to (unofficial) interpretation prior to the adoption of the VCLT. They are clear expressions of the ILO's unique approach to some aspects of treaty law. In Jenks' oral statement to the VCLT Conference, he mentioned that ILO practice 'has somewhat freer and more generous recourse to the preparatory work than that of the Convention [VCLT]'.[98] While heavy reliance is placed on the meaning of the terms used in the particular context, the preparatory works are cited even when it is stated that the meaning is clear. This practice can be seen as a way to enhance 'ownership' by the ILO constituents of the views expressed by the Secretariat. Indeed, as Jenks had noted, the criterion of intent, to be deduced from the context in which the terms are used and the object and purpose of the

---

[97] References for both of these Conventions can be found at *supra* n. 18.
[98] Jenks' oral statement to the VCLT Conference, 1968, p. 4.

[ILO] Convention as it relates to the intent of the tripartite Conference, was key.[99]

The 1968 Instruction was replaced by a 1987 Circular,[100] prepared almost twenty years after adoption of the VCLT. It had dropped references to Conventions Nos. 87 and 98[101] but otherwise echoed the earlier Instructions. In preparing a draft reply to a request for interpretation of a Convention or Recommendation, the technical unit was instructed in 1987 to take account of: '(a) the preparatory work ... (b) the extent to which law and practice in countries other than the one making the request may assist in clarifying the problems at issue; (c) any earlier interpretations and any comments of a supervisory body; (d) any other relevant technical information and technical considerations'. The circular reproduced the same reservation clause and the identical prescribed format for the reply as the 1968 Instruction. It repeated that interpretations in the form of a memorandum were to be brought to the attention of the Governing Body and later published in the *Official Bulletin* (paragraph 13). Between 1968 and 1987, then, little or no impact of the VCLT can be seen in ILO policy on (unofficial) interpretations issued by the Secretariat.

This is hardly surprising when one looks at the ways in which ILO procedures diverge from the model of Article 31 VCLT. In his analysis, Edward Yemin pointed to these issues:

> (1) where Article 31 refers to the intention of the parties .... Office interpretation refers to the intention of the tripartite International Labour Conference; (2) the context of the treaty as defined in Article 31, paragraph 2 (a), of the Vienna Convention, in Office interpretations, includes agreements made by the Conference, not by the parties to the Convention; (3) instruments of the nature referred to as part of the context in Article 31, paragraph 2 (b) ... do not appear to be permissible in ILO treaty practice; (4) subsequent agreements between parties to a treaty (Article 31, paragraph 3) regarding its interpretation do not appear to be permissible in respect of international labour Conventions, unless the Convention concerned provides for such agreements; (5) the

---

[99] *Ibid.*

[100] Procedure concerning requests for interpretations of Conventions and Recommendations, International Labour Organization Circular, No. 40, Series 9, 15 Sept. 1987, p. 3.

[101] *Supra* n. 18. However, it remains the case that 'the Office has generally considered it inappropriate to express an opinion on the interpretation of standards' in the field of freedom of association. See International Labour Organization, *Handbook, supra* n. 49, at p. 43, citing *Minutes of the Governing Body*, 122nd Session (1953), p. 110.

preparatory work leading up the adoption of international labour Conventions and Recommendations is a primary means of interpretation in Office opinions, which are referred to often in the first instance to demonstrate the meaning of a provision.[102]

In addition, the reference to law and practice of other countries, as contemplated by the ILO Circulars, has no equivalent in the VCLT rule on interpretation. Furthermore, following the adoption of the VCLT, the ILO Legal Adviser Francis Wolf included the special ILO practice of unofficial interpretations in his list of what was shielded by Article 5.[103] This is of course supported by the International Law Commission's characterisation of it as a 'general reservation' applicable to the entire Convention. In practical terms, the main difference is the reliance on preparatory works in the first instance of an interpretation provided by the ILO secretariat.

4.6.4   'Interpretation' or 'Explanation' by the ILO Supervisory Bodies

As alluded to in the Office Instructions, the supervisory bodies established by the ILO in relation to the application of ratified Conventions also provide indications to member States as to how a particular provision is to be applied in their own circumstances. The line between monitoring application and interpretation is not always a bright one, however. In particular, the comments that the CEACR addresses to member States, as well as the findings of *ad hoc* Commissions of Inquiry in their examination of Article 26 complaints, usually involve some measure of appreciation about the meaning of provisions of Conventions in relation to particular situations. On occasion, the CEACR also makes a general observation in relation to the application of a Convention in its examination of Article 22 reports.[104] Like the Secretariat with its informal opinions, the independent CEACR also takes care in its reports to note that it is only the ICJ that can render an authoritative or definitive opinion interpreting an ILO Convention, and

---

[102] Yemin, *supra* n. 26, at pp. 45–46.

[103] Mission Report of F. Wolf, referring to Jenks' statement, in ILO Archives, File No. UN 1020–100, p. 4.

[104] See, for example, the CEACR general observation that sexual harassment falls under the prohibition of sex discrimination in the 1958 Discrimination (Employment and Occupation) Convention (No. 111): *supra* n. 18. See, further, *Report of the Committee of Experts on the Application of Conventions and Recommendations*, International Labour Conference, 91st Session, Report III (Part 1A) (Geneva: International Labour Organization, 2003), pp. 463–464.

that its views are non-binding.[105] Statements to this effect appear in the Committee's introduction to its observations on the application of Conventions in particular States and in its General Surveys on the law and practice in ratifying and non-ratifying countries. The ILO International Labour Standards Department currently refers to the comments of the CEACR that involve the meaning of provisions of Conventions as 'explanations'.[106]

In 2011, the CEACR itself explained that 'it has to consider and express its views on the legal scope and meaning of certain provisions' of Conventions 'in order to fulfil the mandate with which it has been entrusted of supervising the application of ratified Conventions. The examination of the meaning of the provisions of Conventions is necessarily an integral part of the functioning of evaluating and assessing the application and implementation of Conventions'.[107] In doing so, it 'constantly and consistently bears in mind all the different methods of interpreting treaties recognized under international public law and in particular' under the VCLT. Thus 'the Committee has always paid due regard to the textual meaning of the words in light of the Convention's purpose and object as provided for by Article 31 [VCLT], giving equal consideration to the two authoritative languages of ILO Conventions, namely the English and French versions (Article 33 [VCLT])'.[108] In addition, 'in accordance with Articles 5 and 32 VCLT, the Committee takes into account the Organization's practice of examining the preparatory work leading to the adoption of the Convention'.[109] The Committee added that this was especially important in view of the role that the tripartite constituents play in standard-setting.

Since 2013, the Committee has drawn attention to several principles, the first being that its mandate 'logically and inevitably requires an assessment, which in turn involves a degree of interpretation of both the national legislation and the text of the Convention'.[110] Another was

---

[105] See, for instance, *Report of the Committee of Experts on the Application of Conventions and Recommendations*, International Labour Conference, 102nd Session, Report III (Part 1A) (Geneva: International Labour Organization, 2013), p. 10 (paragraph 26) and p. 14 (paragraph 36).

[106] See International Labour Organization, *Handbook, supra* n. 49, at p. 42.

[107] *Report of the Committee of Experts on the Application of Conventions and Recommendations*, International Labour Conference, 100th Session, Report III (Part IA), (Geneva: International Labour Organization, 2011), p. 9 (paragraph 11).

[108] *Ibid.* (paragraph 12).   [109] *Ibid.*

[110] *Report of the Committee of Experts on the Application of Conventions and Recommendations*, International Labour Conference, 102nd Session, Report III

its concern for ensuring equal treatment for all States and for uniformity to maintain principles of legality and predictability in relation to application. It is clear from these statements that the CEACR's approach is inspired by elements of the VCLT interpretation rule, which it apparently sees as its lodestone. As an independent body, its distinct twist on the matter differs somewhat from the practice of the Secretariat in its informal 'clarifications'. In light of Articles 5, 31 and 32 VCLT, this is perfectly acceptable in the ILO context. Other human rights bodies have been criticised for acting inconsistently with the Vienna rule on interpretation,[111] so the CEACR is acting prudently by relying on it in relation to its own observations.

4.6.5   The Recent Controversy over Interpretation and the Right to Strike

However, the CEACR's disclaimers and explanations of its approach to 'interpretation' have not protected it from attack, as seen most evidently at the June 2012 International Labour Conference and its *sequelae*. At each of its regular sessions, the Conference sets up a Committee on the Application of Standards (CAS), which engages in a tripartite discussion of selected elements of the CEACR's reports. Under the time constraints, the CAS can discuss only a small fraction of the comments made by the CEACR in relation to the effect given to particular Conventions in selected countries. Thus a tentative choice is usually made shortly before the meeting (with a list agreed by the Employer and Worker Vice-Chairpersons and the Committee Chairperson) and put before the Committee for approval. In June 2012, however, the Employer delegates on the Committee refused to include any comments involving the right to strike under Convention No. 87,[112] since they objected to interpretations by the CEACR concerning freedom of association on this point.[113]

(Part 1A) (Geneva: International Labour Organization, 2013), p. 12 (paragraph 33). The principles were recalled in its 2014 and 2015 reports.

[111] See K. Mechlem, 'Treaty Bodies and the Interpretation of Human Rights', *Vanderbilt JTL*, 42 (2009), 905–947.

[112] *Supra* n. 18.

[113] The statements to which they objected appeared in another report of the CEACR, known as the 2012 General Survey. See *Report of the Committee of Experts on the Application of Conventions and Recommendations: Giving Globalization of a Human Face*, General Survey on the fundamental Conventions concerning rights at work in light of the ILO Declaration on Social Justice for a Fair Globalization, International Labour Conference, 101st Session, Report III (Part 1B) (Geneva: International Labour Organization, 2012), pp. 46–50.

This led to an unprecedented stalemate which resulted that year in no discussion of any individual country cases in relation to any Convention (aside from the special arrangement involving follow-up on forced labour in Myanmar).

Immediately following the Conference, the Governing Body was invited to 'take appropriate follow-up as a matter of urgency, including through informal tripartite consultations'.[114] Several such consultations have taken place, with some *ad hoc* accommodations reached, but the issues have not yet been fully resolved. At the October 2013 session of the Governing Body, the Director-General noted that the questions raised were of 'even existential importance for the ILO'.[115] The roots of the controversy go back to the end of the Cold War, in a story too long to be told here.[116] At this writing, it is unclear when the crisis will stop casting a pall over some aspects of the ILO standards supervisory system.

In the Conference Committee 2012 discussion, the Employer spokesperson had argued that '[t]he mandate of the Committee of Experts was to comment on the application of Convention No. 87 and not to interpret a right to strike into Convention No. 87. . . . If the Constitution were to be applied, given the absence of any reference to a right to strike in the actual text of Convention No. 87, then internationally accepted rules of interpretation required Convention No. 87 to be interpreted without a right to strike'.[117] The Employers saw the CEACR as making policy and reportedly feared its 'interpretation of the right to strike becoming an internationally accepted human right to strike'.[118] This strangely ignored its explicit mention in Article 8(1)(d) of the 1966 International Covenant on Economic, Social and Cultural Rights[119] and its relation to ILO Conventions.[120] The Employers also opposed referral of the question to

---

[114] GB.315/INS/4 (15 June 2012).

[115] Report of the Legal Issues and *International Labour Standards Section, 319/LILS/PV/ Draft* (Geneva: International Labour Organization Governing Body, Oct. 2013), paragraph 40.

[116] See La Hovary, *supra* n. 75.

[117] International Labour Conference, *Report of the Committee on the Application of Standards*, 101st Session (Geneva, May–June 2012), *Provisional Record*, No. 19, Part I, p. 34 (paragraph 146).

[118] *Ibid.*, at p. 35 (paragraph 148) and p. 37 (paragraph 153).   [119] 993 UNTS 3.

[120] In a document included in the *Official Bulletin* of the International Labour Organization, it was pointed out that although 'ILO instruments do not expressly guarantee the right to strike, a substantial body of established ILO principles on this question exists, some derived from the general provisions of Conventions dealing with freedom of association and industrial relations, others developed within the framework of special supervision procedures relating to trade union rights'. See 'Comparative Analysis of the International

the ICJ, since in their view the ILO tripartite constituents supervised labour standards, and the (tripartite Governing Body) Committee on Freedom of Association[121] provided a separate supervisory procedure.[122] These positions were essentially restated and elaborated upon at later meetings.

At the Employers' suggestion, the tripartite constituents set out their views on standards supervision-related issues, including on the application and interpretation of particular Conventions, at the December 2012 meeting of the CEACR,[123] which normally operates *in camera*. The CEACR then included the divergent views of the Employer and Worker Vice-Chairs of the Applications Committee in its report to the 2013 International Labour Conference. In that report, the CEACR also recalled its 2011 statement concerning interpretation, as well as its own independence, objectivity and impartiality.[124] During discussion of the CEACR report in the 2013 CAS, the Employers voiced their disappointment with the position taken by the Expert Committee.

At the 2012 Conference, the Workers and Governments had responded respectively with shock and regret over the deadlock.[125] Since then, formal and information consultations have explored a number of options. A tripartite meeting on the right to strike and Convention No. 87 took place in February 2015 and the Governing Body examined its final report a month later.[126] One idea that has been put on the back burner due to a lack of consensus is possible referral of a question to the ICJ for an advisory opinion.[127] Several related issues

---

Covenants on Human Rights and International Labour Conventions and Recommendations', *Official Bulletin*, LII (1969) 2, p. 214 (paragraph 152). The principles here included the CEACR's reading, in relation to strikes, of Arts. 3, 8 and 10 of ILO Convention No. 87: *supra* n. 117, at p. 193 (paragraph 57).

[121] The Committee on Freedom of Association (CFA), a tripartite body established by the ILO Governing Body, with a neutral chair, has acknowledged a right to strike, albeit it with some permissible limitations. The CFA's mandate is to examine complaints of violation of freedom of association under constitutional principles, thus involving any Member State, whether or not it has ratified relevant ILO Conventions. See B. Gernigon, A. Odero and H. Guido, *ILO Principles Concerning the Right to Strike* (Geneva: International Labour Organization, 2000), p. 62.

[122] *Supra* n. 117, at p. 35 (paragraph 147).

[123] *Supra* n. 117, at p. 37 (paragraph 152) (regarding the employers' suggestion).

[124] CEACR Report III (Part 1A), ILC, 2013, p. 13 (paragraph 33(a)).

[125] *Supra* n. 117, at pp. 37–44 (paragraphs 154–185).

[126] See GB. 323/INS/5/App. II (March 2015) and background documents referred to therein.

[127] See GB.322/INS/5 (Oct. 2014) for further details. The alternative of establishing a tribunal under Art. 37(2) of the ILO Constitution was considered at the same time.

are also now under scrutiny, such as clarifying the relationship between various ILO supervisory bodies.[128] In the meantime, some *ad hoc* solutions have been found prior to each International Labour Conference while consensus is sought on the larger questions.

In terms of the substantive issue, respected commentators have expressed their views that a right to strike clearly exists in international law, albeit with some permissible restrictions, and that this right is implicit and has long been recognised, including under Convention No. 87.[129] Even before this controversy arose at the Conference, Achim Seifert and Manfred Weiss had examined in detail the question of the right to strike under Convention No. 87 from the perspective of Article 31(3)(b) VCLT.[130] This provision envisages taking into account, together with the context, 'any subsequent practice in the application of the treaty which establishes the agreement of the parties regarding its interpretation'.[131] The authors explored the consistent practice and its duration of the ILO supervisory bodies on this issue and its acceptance by member States. They concluded that, overall, there was much to say in support of recognition of a right to strike under Article 3 of Convention No. 87.[132] This provision stipulates in its first paragraph that 'Workers' and employers' organizations shall have the right to ... organise their administration and activities and to formulate their programmes'. One of the activities of trade unions is obviously the calling of strike action as a means of pressure to achieve their aims through collective (associative) action. Article 10 of Convention No. 87 (it defines 'organization' under

---

[128] See GB.323/5 (March 2015), decision on the fifth item of the agenda (clause (h)).

[129] *Supra* n. 18. See, e.g., J. R. Bellace, 'The ILO and the Right to Strike', *Int'l Labour Rev.* 153 (2014), 29–70; K. Ewing, 'Myth and Reality of the Right to Strike as a "Fundamental Labour Right"', *Int'l J. Comp. Labour L. & Industrial Relations*, 29 (2013), 145–166; L. Swepston, 'Crisis in the ILO Supervisory System: Dispute over the Right to Strike', *Int'l J. Comp. Labour L. & Industrial Relations*, 29 (2013), 199–218, and La Hovary, *supra* n. 75. See, also, the background document prepared for the tripartite meeting on the right to strike: TMFAPROC/2015 (Geneva, 23–25 Feb. 2015).

[130] A. Seifert and M. Weiss, 'Der Streik im Recht der Internationalen Arbeitsorganisation' in T. Dieterich, M. Le Friant, L. Nogler, K. Kezuka and H. Pfarr (eds.), *Individuelle und kollektive Freiheit im Arbeitsrecht: Gedächtnisschrift für Ulrich Zachert* (Baden Baden: Nomos, 2010), pp. 130–146, esp. at pp. 137–140. (This was written in partial response to the German version of the article by Wisskirchen at *supra* n. 9.) More recently, Reingard Zimmer has taken a view similar to that of Seifert and Weiss in this context: see R. Zimmer, 'Wirkungsweise, Auslegung und Implementierung von ILO-Standards' in W. Däubler and R. Zimmer (eds.), *Arbeitsvölkerrecht: Festschrift für Klaus Lörcher* (Baden Baden: Nomos, 2013), pp. 29–41, at p. 38.

[131] *Supra* n. 2. See, further, the contribution to this volume of Buga at pp. 363–391 (Chapter 12).

[132] Seifert and Weiss, *supra* n. 130, at p. 141.

the Convention as meaning one 'for furthering or defending the interests of workers or employers') has also been invoked in support of the existence of the right to strike under this instrument.[133]

All in all, this protracted debate gives considerable food for thought for the Organization on the roles of different bodies[134] as well as on the relationship between fundamental principles and provisions of Conventions relating to them (as with freedom of association). It is also a source of some concern about how the VCLT has on occasion been invoked by the employers to support rather dubious inferences.[135] The questioning of the informal interpretation role of the supervisory bodies in the ILO reflects resistance by business to binding rather than voluntary application of human rights at work, with possible repercussions beyond the current controversy in this institution.[136]

5   Summing Up

While the ILO certainly faces its own set of challenges, 'thanks to an ingenious constitutional framework it also has the capacity to reinvent itself from the inside to meet the expectations of its founders and become a more effective social regulator of the global economy'.[137] In recent years, the ILO has taken important steps towards maintaining the relevance of its treaty-making action. From a legal perspective, the adoption of the 1997 Amendment to the ILO Constitution (on abrogation of obsolete Conventions) and of the 1998 Declaration on Fundamental Principles and Rights at Work, together with the revision of a number of older international labour standards, represent the most significant measures so far. The ILO's rejection of reservations to Conventions is unlikely to change, since the Organization will soon celebrate its 100th year of operation without them. Other innovations may however arise in the context of the soul-searching around the ILO standards system that is accompanying the right to strike controversy.

---

[133] See, for instance, the discussion of the right to strike in the CEACR's General Survey 2012, *supra* n. 113, at pp. 46–49.

[134] On this aspect, see especially J. Bellace, 'Hoisted on Their Own Petard? Business and Human Rights', *J. Industrial Rel.*, 56 (2014), 442–457, and Swepston, *supra* n. 129.

[135] For critiques, see, e.g., Ewing (*supra* n. 129), Seifert and Weiss (*supra* n. 130) and Zimmer (*supra* n. 130).

[136] Swepston points to the potential harm to supervision carried out by other bodies of the UN system: *supra* n. 129, at 218.

[137] Maupain, *supra* n. 10, at p. 243.

The ongoing debate over interpretation of ILO Conventions by its various entities poses issues of direct interest to application of the VCLT rule and the future of the ILO standards system. How the various parts of the ILO (the Conference, the Governing Body, the supervisory mechanisms and the Secretariat) resolve these issues will involve tacit or explicit choices that could lean towards either relying heavily on its *lex specialis* or employing more mainstream treaty interpretation rule(s). This is an enviable choice. The *lex specialis* defended by the ILO in the VCLT negotiations has clearly permitted the Organization to continue finding its own creative solutions for a variety of treaty law issues, in line with its Constitution and unique tripartite structure. This validates the intent of Article 5 VCLT, which is reflected as well in the 1986 instrument.[138] At the same time, there may be a risk of over-reliance on *lex specialis* in a way that turns the institution in on itself, possibly isolating it from the modern developments in international treaty law to which the independent CEACR may have a more open ear. The new developments include the International Law Commission's ongoing examination of subsequent practice and a dynamic or evolutive approach to interpretation which – while still debated – appears to be gaining ground, particularly when it comes to human rights treaties.[139] After all, application of the Vienna rule – itself flexible – involves an art, not a science.[140] Whatever decisions are taken, they should remain true to both the ILO's constitutional purpose of pursuing social justice and to general international law as applicable to it.

---

[138] *Supra* n. 5.

[139] See, e.g., M. Fitzmaurice, 'Dynamic (Evolutive) Interpretation of Treaties' in M. Kohen, R. Kolb and D. L. Tehindrazanarivelo (eds.), *Perspectives of International Law in the 21st Century: Liber Amicorum Professor Christian Dominicé in Honour of His 80th Birthday* (Leiden: Martinus Nijhoff, 2012), pp. 101–153. See, also, Arato, *supra* n. 89, who points out that such an approach can have consequences distinct from invoking subsequent practice in an interpretation.

[140] Dörr, *supra* n. 88, at p. 522.

27

The World Health Organization

EGLE GRANZIERA AND STEVEN A. SOLOMON

1 Introduction

Normative activities in public health law matters are wide-ranging, encompassing a number of ideological paradigms, international organizations and instruments which are mainly predicated upon one teleological end: creating and facilitating a climate in which all individuals may realise their health potential. Given this expansive landscape, norms and standards established by intergovernmental organizations and their interaction with international conventions, in particular, the 1969 Vienna Convention on Treaties (VCLT),[1] reflect diverse normative views.

The relationship between international public health organizations, such as the World Health Organization (WHO), and its Member States mirrors the Hobbesian tradition in so far as States seek to ensure the viability of their domestic health policies through collective action. The logic of this contracting mechanism is grounded by the notion that pathogens know no geographical boundaries. As globalisation continues to connect people and places, the geographical barriers that once provided a shield against infectious diseases no longer do so. Consequently, key methods for promoting a country's protection against communicable diseases and countering the negative externalities created by our globalised world include collective action, cooperation and international contracting mechanisms.[2]

Further strengthening these methods, the international community has embraced the view that health is fundamental to the attainment of

---

[1] 1155 UNTS 331.

[2] In Sept. 2016, global leaders met at the United Nations General Assembly in New York to commit to fighting antimicrobial resistance together; this was only the fourth time in the history of the organization that a health topic was to be discussed at the General Assembly (HIV, non-communicable diseases and Ebola were the others): www.who.int/antimicro bial-resistance/events/UNGA-meeting-amr-sept2016/en/.

peace and security. Such a view seeks to fill the gaps created by domestic and transnational economic disincentives that are in conflict with global health policies.

The developing canon of health-related norms aimed at governing and addressing global public health needs and issues does not operate in isolation. To this end, the importance of understanding the ideological frameworks as well as the accompanying dynamics between States helps to illuminate some of the problems associated with and the general aversion to the creation of internationally binding instruments among globally integrated health organizations and their respective Member States. A robust understanding of the international diplomatic state of affairs and its guiding principles can suggest an efficacious way forward when drafting and implementing new frameworks. Further, considering that in the international public health sector treaty law plays a limited role in establishing norms on health matters, understanding the under-lying character of the relationship between States and their incentives is of fundamental importance.

The operative framework for global health law and its interaction with public international law is thus coloured by three dominant landscapes: formal sources of international law; socio-economic factors and, finally, domestic political appetite. While the latter two factors are important, the focus of the chapter will be on the formal international legal processes that guide health law and its institutions.

International health law-making is similarly vulnerable to the well-known handicaps of public international law. As is the case in international law generally, health norms and standards and the related organizations fall prey to the voluntary nature associated with them, diluted treaty agreements which lack enforcement mechanism among sovereign States, as well as competing national health agendas and their correlative financing structure.

The World Health Organization, however, is in a unique position to serve as a platform for promoting and developing international law related to health. As the directing and coordinating authority on inter-national health work of the United Nations system,[3] the WHO takes the lead in global health matters with the aim of establishing a world where people everywhere and at every age enjoy the highest possible level of health. In this context, the WHO's actions are every bit as ambitious and innovative as the notion of health contained in the preamble of its

---

[3] Art. 2(a) of the Constitution of the World Health Organization, 14 UNTS 185.

Constitution, which defines health as a 'state of complete physical, mental and social wellbeing and not merely the absence of disease and infirmity'.[4]

The World Health Organization, however, is not the only multilateral organization dealing with health matters. A number of international institutions, within and outside the United Nations system, promote global public health in different ways and contribute either to establishment of legal frameworks for health or to their implementation.

2   International Legal Instruments

The normative framework of international public health takes a variety of forms: hard law sources (i.e. legally binding instruments such as treaties, conventions, agreements and regulations) which co-exist together with soft law ones (i.e. non-legally binding instruments) such as resolutions and other act of a recommendatory nature. A third category is constituted by acts of international organizations. The analysis in this section is limited to selected samples of hard law instruments which address health issues.

The development of 'health law' did not happen accidentally. It was a response to growing problems and worldwide concerns. Health law developed and develops as a reaction to the historic and continuing threat of diseases and other threats to public health. States started to more formally consider health problems as global problems at the end of the nineteenth century when the first regional health organizations were established to achieve common goals.[5]

The pressures to achieve common goals are even greater today as globalisation moves or enhances the mobility of people, products and pathogens ever further and faster. It is often said that disease knows no borders, and this is ever more the case. Freedom and ease of movement distinguishes our time, making the threat of communicable diseases increasingly significant. And, indeed, examples such as SARS, Avian Flu and H1N1 have shown how vulnerable the world can be. Coupled with the growing epidemic of non-communicable diseases, which constitutes an emerging worry for not only developed but also middle- and

---

[4] Preamble of the Constitution of the World Health Organization: *ibid.*

[5] It is worth mentioning the Pan Arab Regional Health Bureau and the Pan American Sanitary Organization (later renamed the Pan American Health Organization). The latter still exists today and also functions as the Regional Office for the Americas of the World Health Organization.

lower-income countries, the global aspects of disease and the necessity of a global response have never been greater. Tackling such health problems and reducing their burden can be achieved through different avenues. The conclusion of treaties has been one of them at both global and regional levels.

As noted previously, the WHO is not the only actor in the public health arena. A variety of other stakeholders, at global and regional level, contribute to the development of international health law. States remain the main subject of public international law and intergovernmental organizations have been the driving forces in that context without necessarily having a mandate exclusively focused on health matters. Without any intention to be exhaustive, we will cite some of them whose impact, in our view, has been significant for advancing the affirmation and implementation of the right to health.

In doing so, we will focus on human rights, environmental and trade instruments. We will start from international organizations having a mandate to protect human rights. The promotion and protection of health are also closely linked to the protection and fulfilment of human rights. A number of human rights instruments contain rules on the protection of public health. One of the major achievements in international public health is the treaty adopted by the Council of Europe on 8 December 2010 – namely, the Convention on the Counterfeiting of Medical Products and Similar Crimes involving Threats to Public Health ('Medicrime Convention').[6] This instrument, which aims at combating counterfeit of medical products and similar crimes involving threats to patients' health and medical products, is ultimately designed to protect patients' health, as well as medical products relevant thereto. The Medicrime Convention establishes as offences (provided appropriate elements of intent are present) the manufacturing of counterfeits (Article 5); the supplying, offering to supply, and trafficking in counterfeits (Article 6); the falsification of documents (Article 7); 'similar crimes' involving threats to public health (Article 8) and aiding or abetting and attempt (Article 9). Additionally, it requires the adoption of necessary legislative and other measures to facilitate the cooperation and exchange of information among different competent authorities (Article 17) and imposes a duty of international cooperation in criminal matters and on prevention (Articles 21 and 22).

---

[6] CETS No. 211.

Secondly, the close link between environmental and health issues has yielded important treaty developments in the public health arena. For example, the management of hazardous wastes, in order to avoid adverse effects which may derive from them, has been regulated by the 1989 Basel Convention on the Control of Transboundary Movements of Hazardous Wastes and their Disposal.[7] The Convention aims at reducing the generation of hazardous wastes and restricting their transboundary movements and it emphasises the promotion of environmentally sound management of hazardous wastes. The overarching principle governing the Convention is the protection of human health. In its preamble, the parties to the Convention recognise 'the growing threat to human health and the environment posed by the increased generation and complexity, and transboundary movement of hazardous wastes and other wastes' and 'that the most effective way of protecting human health and the environment from the dangers posed by such wastes is the reduction of their generation to a minimum in terms of quantity and/or hazard potential'. Hence, the health component plays a major role. Similarly, the 2001 Stockholm Convention on Persistent Organic Pollutants,[8] while prohibiting or requiring parties to take measures to reduce or eliminate releases from intentional production and use of chemicals, makes clear in its preamble the determination of the parties to the Convention 'to protect human health and the environment from the harmful impacts of persistent organic pollutants'. Also, the 1992 United Nations Framework Convention on Climate Change recognises that adverse effects of climate change may have an impact on health and that parties shall take climate change considerations into account and employ appropriate methods with a view to minimising adverse effects on public health.[9]

Finally, consideration is given to the interactions between the heath and trade law, with a particular attention to the legal instruments of the World Trade Organization, namely, the Agreements on Technical Barriers to Trade (TBT),[10] on the Application of Sanitary and Phytosanitary Measures (SPS),[11] on Trade-Related Intellectual Property Rights (TRIPS)[12] and on Trade in Services (GATS).[13] Article 2(2) of the TBT Agreement requires that 'Members shall ensure that technical regulations are not prepared, adopted or applied with a view to or with the effect of creating unnecessary obstacles to international trade. For this purpose, technical regulations shall not be more trade-restrictive than necessary to

---

[7] 1673 UNTS 126.   [8] 2256 UNTS 119.   [9] 1771 UNTS 107, Art. 4(1)(f).
[10] 1868 UNTS 120.   [11] 1867 UNTS 493.   [12] 1869 UNTS 299.   [13] 1869 UNTS 183.

fulfil a legitimate objective, taking account of the risks non-fulfilment would create'. Health is listed among the legislative objectives. Similarly, Article 2(1) of the SPS Agreement provides that 'Members have the right to take sanitary and phytosanitary measures necessary for the protection of human, animal or plant life or health, provided that such measures are not inconsistent with the provisions of this Agreement'. Additionally, the 2001 Doha Declaration on the TRIPS Agreement and Public Health, adopted by the WTO Ministerial Conference on 14 November 1991, states: 'We agree that the TRIPS Agreement does not and should not prevent Members from taking measures to protect public health. Accordingly, while reiterating our commitment to the TRIPS Agreement, we affirm that the Agreement can and should be interpreted and implemented in a manner supportive of WTO Members' right to protect public health and, in particular, to promote access to medicines for all'.[14] The principles of non-discrimination and of national treatment are relevant for health in the context of TRIPS and the GATS. As far as TRIPS are concerned, accessibility of medicines and vaccines and the protection of patent rights may have significant impact on public health considerations. Recent times have shown tension between the trade and health sector related to the need to balance between and among different interests and different actors.

3   The Fragmentation of International Health Law

The question of whether 'health' has or not a complete and satisfactory *corpus iuris* is difficult to answer. As described previously, and as is the case in other branches of public international law, health has experienced the phenomenon of 'fragmentation' according to which assorted aspects of health law can be found in different legal instruments existing in a variety of normative arenas. Since the Second World War, public international law, including international health law, has faced a significant expansion of its normative framework and acceleration in the production of norms.[15] Some authors have indicated that explosion of legal norms was due to the need of international law to prove its existence.[16]

---

[14] Document WT/MIN(01)/DEC/W/2 (14 Nov. 2001).
[15] E.-L. Comtois-Dinel, 'La fragmentation du droit international: vers un changement de paradigme?' *Lex Electronica*, 11 (2006), 1–22, at 2.
[16] M. Prost and P. Kingsley Clark, 'Unity, Diversity and the Fragmentation of International Law: How Much Does the Multiplication of International Organizations Really Matter?', *Chinese JIL*, 5 (2006), 341–370, at 342.

Nowadays this preoccupation seems to be overcome by events. International lawyers are perhaps now less concerned in justifying and proving the existence of this new legal system, and more concerned about finding solutions to matters of substance.[17] 'Fragmentation' of international health law may therefore be seen as simply a practical consequence of problem solving efforts in different arenas. At the same time, some authors see in the fragmentation a threat to the unity and coherence of public international law[18] and, as a consequence, an element of weakness within the international legal system when taken as a whole. Others, reflecting on the practical elements of international legislative efforts, consider it as reflecting the maturity of the system and, hence, as a natural consequence of the pluralism of norms.[19]

'Fragmentation', however, may be best understood as due to a number of factors – operating either independently or in combination. It is somehow inevitable as it reflects the dynamics of a newly established legal order whose peculiarity lies in the variety of law-making fora and the lack of a sole adjudicator. In that sense, the international legal system differs from domestic and national legal systems. As a consequence, coordination mechanisms, as well as remedies, operating within national boundaries, are not transposed to the international level.

Perhaps first among these factors is the proliferation of 'different centres of power' and, in particular, of international organizations, which, even marginally, deal with health matters. As described earlier, a number of entities have promoted the adoption of legal frameworks having a significant impact on health. It has already been stated that health is a complex issue and requires a coordinated response. International law, as a legal system, is somewhat artificially subdivided into different branches.[20] The establishment of field-specific or 'territorial' organizations should not hinder the achievement of common objectives and the coherence of the entire system. Even in cases where overlap among the mandates of different organizations are possible, it is not readily apparent that such overlapping produces negative consequences

---

[17] *Ibid.*, at 342 and 343.

[18] See, further, M. Koskenniemi and P. Leino, 'Fragmentation of International Law: Postmodern Anxieties?', *Leiden JIL*, 15 (2002), 553–579.

[19] See, further, International Law Commission, Report of the Study Group on Fragmentation of International Law: Difficulties arising from the Diversification and Expansion of International Law, Finalized by Martti Koskenniemi, U.N. Doc. A/CN.4/L.682 (2006), p. 11 (paragraph 8 (fn. 13)).

[20] *Ibid.*, at pp. 8–10 (paragraphs 1–4).

with respect to the attainment of the common outcome. In other words, the proliferation of international organizations, which create rules to be applied in self-contained systems, should not necessarily be negatively perceived. If overlaps and duplications may happen, they may well push those organizations to cooperate and strengthen their coordination.

Secondly, fragmentation is also closely linked to the globalisation of public health issues and needs. While the proliferation of organizations should be understood in terms of creation of legal rules, globalisation also concerns the implementation of those rules. It is evident that the action of States and/or organizations alone may not be adequate to comprehensively address such implementation. The globalisation of public health involves States, international organizations and non-State actors and underlines the importance of establishing coordinated frameworks to pursue common interests and values. An interaction among the different actors is, thus, unavoidable. Such an interaction may take different forms, including the establishment of legally binding rules governing their relations and functioning, and, with increasing frequency, it involves the concluding of soft law instruments. This is why international organizations often conclude instruments of both types among themselves in order to join forces for facing common problems. In the public health context, this is often the case not only in emergencies that require urgent deployment of financial and human resources but in the everyday fight for ensuring the enjoyment of the highest attainable standard of health is one of the fundamental rights of every human being.

Thirdly, the lack of a sole adjudicator at international and national level may contribute to the incoherence of the system. Some commentators have seen, in the multiplication of judicial and quasi-judicial mechanisms at international level, a growing risk. For example, successive presidents of the International Court of Justice have noted, while welcoming the creation of new tribunals, that conflicts may emerge among different instances and that forum-shopping opportunities may generate unwanted confusion whose effect may be to jeopardise the unity and integrity of public international law.[21]

As far as the health system is concerned, however, commentators have inclined towards a positive approach when it comes to the roles of tribunal and other dispute resolution mechanisms on tobacco-related

---

[21] Most famously in the statement of Judge Gilbert Guillaume, President of the International Court of Justice, to the United Nations General Assembly on 26 Oct. 2000 (www.icj-cij .org/court/index.php?pr=%2084&pt=3&p1=1&p2=3&p3=1).

matters. Part of the confidence of those commentators resides in the fact that the WHO Framework Convention on Tobacco Control[22] is a science- and evidence-based treaty which 'establishes scientific and medical determination that compensate for any judicial limitations in this regard'.[23]

4   The Constitutional Normative Function of the World Health Organization

The very first truly global legal instrument dealing with health matters is the Constitution of the World Health Organization.[24] Adopted by the International Health Conference on 22 July 1946 and entering into force on 7 April 1948 when the number of acceptance required by its Article 80 was reached, it is a treaty delineating a very innovative concept of health which is intended not only as the absence of infirmity but includes mental and social well-being.[25] A founding act of the Organization, the WHO

---

[22] 2302 UNTS 116.

[23] C. M. Flood and T. Lemmens, 'Global Health Challenges and the Role of Law', *J. Law, Medicine & Ethics*, 41 (2013), 9–15, at 11.

[24] *Supra* n. 3.

[25] The WHO Constitution describes health as 'a state of complete physical, mental and social well-being and not merely the absence of disease or infirmity' and 'the enjoyment of the highest attainable standard of health is one of the fundamental rights of every human being without distinction of race, religion, political belief, economic or social condition'. *Ibid.* Additionally, as emphasised in the General Comment No. 14 on the right to the highest attainable standard of health adopted in May 2000 by the Committee on Economic Social and Cultural Rights of the United Nations, the right to health is 'fundamental human right indispensable for the exercise of other human rights' which is 'health is closely related to and dependent upon the realization of other human rights . . . including the rights to food, housing, work, education, human dignity, life, non-discrimination, equality, the prohibition against torture, privacy, access to information, and the freedoms of association, assembly and movement' and 'embraces a wide range of socio-economic factors . . . and extends to the underlying determinants of health, such as food and nutrition, housing, access to safe and potable water and adequate sanitation, safe and healthy working conditions, and a healthy environment': U.N. Doc. HRI/GEN/1/Rev.6 at 85 (2003). Similar affirmations of the right to health are contained in variety of instruments adopted at the global level such as Art. 25 of the Universal Declaration of Human Rights, G.A. Res. 217A (III), U.N. Doc. A/810 at 71 (1948), and Art. 12(1) of the 1966 International Covenant on Economic, Social and Cultural, 999 UNTS 3. At the regional level, see Art. 16 of the 1981 Banjul Charter on Human and Peoples' Rights, OAU Doc. CAB/LEG/67/3 Rev.5; Art. 10 of the 1988 Additional Protocol to the American Convention on Human Rights in the area of Economic, Social and Cultural Rights Inter-American Commission on Human Rights (Protocol of San Salvador), OAS Treaty Series No. 69 (1988), and Art. 11 of the 1961 European Social Charter, 529 UNTS 89. On this matter, see A. Wilson and A. S. Daar, 'A Survey of International Legal Instruments to

Constitution sets out the objectives of the Organization and its subsequent institutional design, and it gives the organization the legal capacity and authority to provide a forum for developing and establishing international health norms and frameworks by providing a significant standard setting and regulatory power to its main governing body, the World Health Assembly (WHA). With that purpose in mind, three main categories of normative instruments have been recognised: conventions and agreements, regulations and recommendations.[26] We shall deal with each of these in turn.

4.1   Conventions and Agreements

Article 19 of the WHO Constitution provides the WHA with the authority to adopt, by two-thirds majority, conventions and agreements on any matter falling within the competence of the Organization. Such conventions and agreements create legally binding obligations on Member States of the Organization. Once adopted by the WHA, each Member State undertakes to take action in relation to the acceptance of the agreement or convention. Such action needs to be taken within eighteen months after the adoption by the WHA. Each Member shall notify the Director-General of the action taken, and if it does not accept such convention or agreement within the time limit, it will furnish a statement of the reasons for non-acceptance.[27]

The WHO Framework Convention on Tobacco Control represents the first and sole normative instrument adopted on the basis of Article 19 of the WHO Constitution. Put another way, in more than sixty years from the establishment of the WHO, its Members have only once selected an opt-in, legally binding treaty mechanism for the protection of public health. Interestingly, the States parties to this Convention (a different constituency than the WHO membership owing to the opt-in nature of the instrument) have acted rather more quickly to adopt analogous, legally binding treaty mechanisms. Under Article 33 of the WHO Framework Convention on Tobacco Control, authority is given to the

---

Examine Their Effectiveness in Improving Global Health and in Realizing Health Rights', *J. Law, Medicine & Ethics*, 41 (2013), 89-102.

[26] Art. 2(k) of the WHO Constitution lists among the functions of the Organization the authority 'to propose conventions, agreements and regulations and make recommendations with respect to international health matters and to perform such duties as may be assigned to the Organization and are consistent with its objectives': *supra* n. 3.

[27] Art. 20 of the WHO Constitution: *supra* n. 3.

Conference of the Parties, its main governing body, to adopt protocols and the first such document adopted has been the Protocol to Eliminate Illicit Trade in Tobacco Products of November 2012.[28]

4.2   The Regulations

In addition to the authority provided for under Article 19, Article 21 of the WHO Constitution grants to the WHA the authority to establish regulations in a limited number of areas, such as with regard to 'procedures designated to prevent the international spread of diseases' and standards with regard to pharmaceutical products. Such regulations are legally binding instruments under international law. They come into force at the same time for all WHO Member States, except for Members having notified rejections or reservations in a given time-frame – that is, they bind all Members except those that 'opt out'.[29] Examples of this kind of instrument are the so-called Nomenclature Regulations[30] and the International Health Regulations,[31] the latter having been recently revised in 2005.

4.3   Recommendations

Article 23 provides the WHA with the authority to adopt, by simple majority, recommendations on matters falling within the competence of the Organization. The resolutions, the most common instrument used by the WHA, are indeed recommendatory in both form and nature. Such instruments do not constitute legally binding decisions in a strict international legal sense. At the same time, the recommendatory nature of the WHA resolutions does not mean that they are devoid of any effect. They have considerable force as an international political matter and often include specific implementation requirements. Recommendations under Article 23 become effective immediately upon adoption by a simple majority of the Health Assembly. When the Health Assembly adopts a complex set of recommendations, it often refers to them in terms of 'strategy' or 'framework' or 'plan of action' or 'code'. As to their structure, usually, WHA resolutions are composed of a preamble setting general principles and recalling previous WHA resolutions or international instruments on the relevant subject matter as well as by operative

---

[28] ILM, 52 (2013), 365–396.   [29] Art. 22 of the WHO Constitution: *supra* n. 3.
[30] Resolution WHA20.18 (22 May 1967).   [31] Resolution WHA58.3 (23 May 2005).

paragraphs. The latter normally request or urge Member States to act or refrain from acting in the relevant and specific context and ask the WHO Director-General to take actions which are clearly defined in the text of the operative paragraph itself.

5 Legal Considerations on WHO Normative Action

Given the legally binding nature of regulations and conventions, it is often asked on what basis Member States choose the appropriate legal instrument. It should be considered that, while regulations are to be adopted in matters specifically listed in Article 21 of the WHO Constitution, conventions may concern a wider range of areas of work of the Organization. In addition, a critical consideration is political in nature and depends on the assessment and decision of the WHO membership.

Consequently, notwithstanding the language contained in the WHO General Programme of Work for 2006–2015,[32] which indicated that the WHO will 'continue to lead in facilitating the drafting and adaptation of international legal instruments'[33] and that considers that one of the WHO's core functions is setting norms and standards and promoting and monitoring their implementation, WHO Member States remain generally reluctant, at least as a collective, to negotiate and adopt legally binding instruments. However, and as mentioned previously, in 2005 the Health Assembly revised the 1969 International Health Regulations (IHR) which entered into force as a legally binding instrument across the globe on 15 June 2007.[34] 'The purpose and scope of these Regulations are to prevent, protect against, control and provide a public health response to the international spread of disease in ways that are commensurate with and restricted to public health risks, and which avoid unnecessary interference with international traffic and trade'.[35] Yet a relatively unexamined question regarding the 2005 IHR is whether they should be understood as an international agreement within the meaning of the Vienna Convention on

---

[32] World Health Assembly, Eleventh Programme of Work, 2006–2015, Doc. 59/25, Annex 2, adopted by Resolution WHA59.4 (27 May 2006). The General Programme of Work is a programmatic document which defines the broad direction for WHO's work and describe challenges and possible measures to face those challenges.

[33] *Ibid.*, at p. 25.   [34] *Supra* n. 31.   [35] Art. 2 of the IHR (2005): *ibid.*

the Law of Treaties or whether they should be taken as a 'legislative' act issued by the Health Assembly – thus falling outside the ambit of the Vienna Convention for purposes such as interpretation.

While views on this vary, it is clear that the Vienna Convention's definition of 'treaty'[36] is broad to the point that it could, in theory, encompass every text used by States and International Organizations to create legally binding obligations among themselves,[37] and the 2005 IHR are no exception. In fact, they are considered an agreement with an international character, expressed in a written form among the WHO and its Members States, concluded with the intention to create obligations that are binding under international law. The fact that they are called 'Regulations' should not alone affect its international character, as 'in itself[,] the name does *not* determine the status of the instrument; what is decisive is whether the negotiating [S]tates intended the instrument to be or not to be legally binding'.[38]

Defenders of the non-treaty nature of the IHR may argue, however, that treaties are contracts and that it is within the very nature of a contract to require an affirmative expression of the will of each of its parties to be bound by it. Consequently, the 2005 IHR would not be a treaty, but a legislative act issued by the Health Assembly on the basis of authority delegated to it by WHO Member States through their acceptance of the Constitution and their membership in the WHO. In other words, WHO Member States have accepted in advance to be bound, as a legislative matter, by decisions of the Health Assembly adopted under the terms of Articles 21 and 22 of the Constitution. This view is strengthened by the fact that regulations may be adopted by a simple majority vote of the Health Assembly. Even States that abstained from or voted against

---

[36] Art. 2(1)(a) VCLT: '"Treaty" means an international agreement concluded between States in written form and governed by international law, whether embodied in a single instrument or in two or more related instruments and whatever its particular designation': *supra* n. 1. Art. 2(1)(a) of the 1986 Vienna Convention on the Law of Treaties between States and International Organizations or between International Organizations defines a treaty as 'an international agreement governed by international law and concluded in written form: (i) between one or more States and one or more international organizations; or (ii) between international organizations, whether that agreement is embodied in a single instrument or in two or more related instruments and whatever its particular designation': ILM, 25 (1986), 543–592.

[37] J. Salmon, 'Les accords non formalisés ou "solo consensus"', *AFDI*, 45 (1999), 1–28, at 10.

[38] A. Aust, *Modern Treaty Law and Practice* (Cambridge: Cambridge University Press, 3rd ed., 2013), p. 20 (emphasis in original).

a particular regulation will be bound by it unless they positively 'opt out' as an active expression of consent to be bound is not required.[39]

However, the theory of contracts also shows that, regarding consent, what is important is the manifestation of the will to be bound, which in some cases could be evidenced by the silence or acquiescence of the parties. In other words, consent to be bound could also be given in an implied form. Indeed, acquiescence may be seen as a form of consent attributed to a State facing a given situation.[40]

In the case of the 2005 IHR, the WHO's Constitution introduces the 'opting out' mechanism, as explained earlier. Therefore, silence from Members States or the choice to not 'opt out' could be interpreted as an 'act' evidencing their will to be bound by the Regulations. Consent, therefore, might be understood as having been given by Member States' passive acquiescence. The International Court of Justice has, in different cases, recognised the legal effect of silence, i.e. in *Case Concerning Military and Paramilitary Activities in and against Nicaragua* of November 1984[41] and *Case Concerning the Temple of Preah Vihear* of June 1962.[42]

---

[39] However, it should be noted that Art. 64 of the 2005 IHR allows States that are not members of the WHO to become a party: *supra* n. 31. Therefore, for such States, there is no previous delegation of authority to the WHA. Thus, a positive action to 'opt in' is required for them to be a party.

[40] Salmon, *supra* n. 37, at 15.

[41] *Case Concerning and Paramilitary Activities in and against Nicaragua*: Nicaragua v. United States of America (Jurisdiction and Admissibility) (1984) ICJ Rep. 392, at p. 410 (paragraph 39). The Court noted that Nicaragua, even though it 'did not at any moment explicitly recognize that it was bound by its (1929) recognition of the (Permanent) Court's compulsory jurisdiction ... neither did it deny the existence of this undertaking ... Having regard to the public and unchanging nature of the official statements concerning Nicaragua's commitment under the Optional-Clause system, the silence of its Government can only be interpreted as an acceptance of the classification [of the State which has accepted the compulsory jurisdiction of the Court under Art. 36(5) of the Court's Statute] thus assigned to it. It cannot be supposed that that Government could have believed that its silence could be tantamount to anything other than acquiescence'.

[42] *Case Concerning the Temple of Preah Vihear*: Cambodia v. Thailand (Merits) (1962) ICJ Rep. 6, at p. 23 ('In fact, as will be seen presently, an acknowledgment by conduct was undoubtedly made in a very definite way; but even if it were otherwise, it is clear that the circumstances were such as called for some reaction, within a reasonable period, on the part of the Siamese authorities, if they wished to disagree with the map or had any serious question to raise in regard to it. They did not do so, either then or for many years, and thereby must be held to have acquiesced. *Qui tacet consentire videtur si loqui debuisset ac potuisset*').

In sum, on one hand it is arguable that the possibility offered to individual States by the WHO Constitution to choose not to be bound by regulations by 'opting out' cannot be equated to a positive expression of consent to be bound by a treaty. It would, rather, have a different function, namely, to safeguard the sovereignty of individual States which for a variety of reasons are not in a position to become bound by those instruments. But in any case, the concept of active 'consent' – a key element of 'treaty-ness'[43] – would be missing. And thus regulations adopted under Article 21 of the WHO Constitution might be better seen as 'legislative' in nature.[44]

[43] See, further, the contribution to this volume of Craven at pp. 103–135 (Chapter 5).

[44] There are other examples of the delegation of legislative authority to intergovernmental bodies by Member States of international organizations or by States Parties to certain treaties, including the authority to bind those States. Nevertheless, the WHO case differs in some aspects from those other examples. For instance, the enforcement resolutions adopted by the Security Council of the United Nations under Chapter VII of the Charter of the United Nations. Such resolutions are unconditionally binding for the States to which they are addressed by virtue of Articles 25 and 48 of the Charter: 1 UNTS 16. There is no 'opt out' mechanism unless otherwise decided by the Security Council on a case-by-case basis. Consequently, these examples should be considered as legislative acts and not international agreements. The same can be said regarding the Meeting of the Parties to the 1987 Montreal Protocol on Substances that Deplete the Ozone Layer which, under Art. 9 thereof, provides for the adoption by a qualified majority vote of adjustments and reductions to production and consumption levels of certain controlled substances: 1522 UNTS 3. Such decisions become binding after six months on all Parties without possibility of objections.

Further, the International Whaling Commission, established under the 1946 International Convention for the Regulation of Whaling, may under Art. V thereof, amend the schedule attached to the Convention, which forms an integral part of it and regulate important conservation issues such as hunting seasons, designation of sanctuary areas as well as size limits for hunted whales: 161 UNTS 72. Amendments enter into force after ninety days for all Parties but are subject to an objection procedure under which individual Parties may refuse to be bound by them. However, in this case the objections allowed are made on the amendments and not on the schedule attached to the Convention, nor on the Convention itself.

Finally, and one of the most similar cases to the WHO's, is the Council of the International Civil Aviation Organization, which may adopt by a two-thirds majority 'international standards' under Arts. 37 and 38 of the 1944 Chicago Convention on Civil Aviation: 15 UNTS 295. International standards become mandatory after three months unless a majority of contracting States register their disapproval by that deadline. Individual States, however, may also notify ICAO that they find it impracticable to comply with any such standard, in which case they will not be bound by them. The fact that a majority of contracting States which register their disapproval within the deadline period could render the 'international standards' not mandatory for all Members States, including the ones who had not manifested any position of disapproval, shows the legal nature of the 'international standards' adopted under Arts. 37 and 38 of the Chicago Convention. Whereas in the case of the 2005 IHR, once they were adopted by a simple

On the other hand, perhaps the act of not 'opting out' may be reasonably seen as a positive form of expressing consent that would bring such regulations under the Vienna Convention. Article 11 VCLT, which sets out a relatively exhaustive enumeration of the classic means to express consent to be bound in international law, also and importantly introduces the notion of indeterminate modalities through the expression 'any other means if so agreed'. Arguably, such 'other means' include the WHO Constitution's 'opting out' mechanism.

This position has, moreover, has been expressed as follows: '[T]he agreement does not have to be express: it is enough for it to be implicit in the text of the treaty or otherwise established, for example, by conduct. Thus it is possible for a treaty to be adopted, without signature or any other procedure, and enter into force *instantly* for all the adopting States'.[45]

As we have seen, the 2005 IHR, and an 'international agreement' within the meaning of the Vienna Convention of the Law of Treaties,[46] have both similarities and dissimilarities. The 2005 IHR may reasonably be regarded as a legislative act issued by the Health Assembly and not as a treaty. But unless and until the IHR are tested by formal questions of interpretation or breach, the issue regarding the 'opting out' mechanism and the concept of 'consent', and its status as a treaty, will likely remain an open one.

In other areas, the Health Assembly has been reluctant to establish new agreements under Article 19 of the WHO Constitution, which are very clearly treaties within the meaning of the Geneva Conventions. This occurred most recently at the 65th World Health Assembly held in Geneva in May 2012, when the WHO's membership could not find consensus on an initiative to enter into negotiations for developing a binding agreement based on Article 19 of the WHO Constitution to address issues on research and development for health needs of developing countries.[47] The proposal for a legally binding instrument was one of the recommendations formulated by the Consultative Expert Working Group on Research and Development: Financing and Coordination

---

majority, they entered into force and bound all WHO Members States (as no Member State 'opted out'). Furthermore, the fact is that even if a majority of States had rejected the 2005 IHR after its adoption by the Health Assembly, it would not have affected the Regulations itself. In any case, the IHR would have continued to remain in effect. This can be explained by their contractual nature as an international agreement.

[45] Aust, *supra* n. 38, at p. 104 (emphasis in original).   [46] *Supra* n. 36.
[47] World Health Assembly, Official Records, WHA65/2012/REC3.

(CEWG).[48] In its report presented to the Sixty-Fifth World Health Assembly in May 2012,[49] the CEWG expressed the view that recommendations were not 'sufficient due to the collective action problem of providing global public goods and since stringer commitments and monitoring and enforcement mechanism are needed'[50] and suggested the establishment of a convention providing effective financing and coordination mechanisms to promote research and development. Even though recognising that poor people continue to suffer from the lack of effective health technologies and market failure to address that need, the Health Assembly considered that times were not mature for such a negotiation and preferred facilitating and instead requested the Director-General of the Organization to hold an open-ended meeting of Member States and, where applicable, regional economic integration organizations to further assess the feasibility of the recommendations of the Consultative Expert Working Group on Research and Development: Financing and Coordination.[51] This process is intended to enable the WHO's membership to better understand whether a binding instrument is needed or whether other proposals may address pending needs in that area.

The same hesitation regarding hard law mechanisms has been seen in regard to WHA action on alcohol related matters. Notwithstanding calls for the development of a framework convention on alcohol control (and attendant arguments that other international conventions on different topics had been adopted and had proven to be successful in protecting public health),[52] the membership of the World Health Organization

---

[48] The CEWG was established by Resolution WHA63.28 (21 May 2010). Its work builds on the work done by another working group which was established by Resolution WHA61.21 (24 May 2008) in order to examine financing and coordination of research and development as well as proposals for new and innovative sources of funding to stimulate the research of certain types of diseases. The work carried out by this first working group was only partially welcomed by WHO Member States which underlined the divergence between their expectations and the outcome of the Group. For this reason, the WHO's membership decided to establish the CEWG whose mandate is clearly delineated in Resolution WHA63.28 and whose composition was approved by the members of the Executive Board of the World Health Organization at its session prior establishment of the group itself by the Director-General of the Organization.

[49] See the Report of the Consultative Expert Working Group on Research and Development: Financing and Coordination, contained in Doc. A65/24 (http://apps.who.int/gb/e/ e_wha65.html).

[50] Ibid., at p. 113.

[51] World Health Assembly, 'Follow Up of the Report of the Consultative Expert Working Group on Research and Development: Financing and Coordination', Resolution WHA65.22 (26 May 2012).

[52] 'A Framework Convention on Alcohol Control', The Lancet, 370 (2009), 1102.

again chose a soft law approach, adopting in May 2010 the Global Strategy to reduce the harmful use of alcohol which – legally speaking – represents a set of recommendations.[53] The majority of WHO Member States felt that a legally binding instrument was not needed to address the harm caused by the use of alcohol. Alcohol is different from tobacco: while a safe use of alcohol can be foreseen, use of tobacco is always harmful. Thus, a difference in the attitude to tackle these two issues was justified. At the same time, the weight and impact of a global strategy should not be underestimated: the new global strategy allows Member States to re-evaluate their control alcohol policies[54] so that effective actions can be shaped. That cannot be disregarded, nor can the coordinating and political force of the new global strategy.

Following the same trend, the World Health Assembly adopted in May 2011 a document of paramount importance in promoting global health security, the Pandemic Influenza Preparedness Framework (PIP Framework).[55] As recalled by the WHO Director-General Margaret Chan 'this has been a long journey to come to this agreement, but the end result is very significant victory for public health'.[56] And, as further described by the Assistant Director-General of Health Security and Environment of the WHO, 'the framework provides a much more coherent and unified global approach for ensuring that influenza viruses are available to the WHO system for monitoring and development of critical benefits such as vaccines, antiviral drugs and scientific information while, at the same time, ensuring more equitable access to these benefits by developing countries'.[57] The new system helps ensure more equitable access to affordable pandemic influenza and other related benefits in addition to ensuring the continued sharing of viruses. It reflects a willingness to create a bold response to the need for cooperation among different stakeholders, including those of the private sector. The PIP Framework applies to the sharing of H5N1 and other influenza viruses with human pandemic potential and the sharing of benefits. The scope seems to be limited, but in reality it responds to a very specific

---

[53] Resolution WHA63.13, Global Strategy to Reduce the Harmful Use of Alcohol (21 May 2010).

[54] T. F. Babor, 'Public Health Science and the Global Strategy on Alcohol', *WHO Bulletin*, 88 (2010), 643.

[55] Doc. A64/8 and Resolution WHA64.5 (24 May 2011).

[56] WHO Press, 'Landmark Agreement Improves Global Preparedness for Influenza Pandemics' (www.who.int/mediacentre/news/releases/2011/pandemic_influenza_prep_20110417/en/index.html).

[57] *Ibid.*

need of the worldwide public health community: to allow surveillance activities and effective responses to potential outbreaks of pandemic flu viruses which may cause very serious health and political consequences if not tackled in a coordinated way globally. It is worth noting that WHO Member States have – as already in past occasions – chosen to adopt the Framework under Article 23 of the WHO Constitution as clearly indicated in the resolution adopting the PIP Framework.[58] As a consequence, the PIP Framework does not alter the current legal status quo.[59] Consequently, the PIP Framework is not a legally binding instrument, but a set of recommendations which contain two standard model agreements – the standard Material Transfer Agreements (SMTAs) – aimed at, on the one hand, governing transfer of PIP biological materials among members of the WHO Global Influenza Surveillance and Responses System (GISRS)[60] and, on the other, establishing rights and obligations regarding the transfer of biological material from GISRS to parties outside GISRS.[61] Accordingly, the Framework presents a peculiarity being a document of a recommendatory nature which contains, with respect to the latter SMTA (known as SMTA2), a model agreement that creates legally binding obligations on the contracting parties – the WHO on the one side and the recipient of materials from the WHO network, be they private or public, on the other side.[62] It should further be considered that these agreements are 'standard' in the sense that certain of their terms are repeated in every case, but key elements, such as what a particular flu vaccine manufacturer will bring to the table, may differ based on a predetermined range of options.

Acts of a recommendatory nature can then eventually acquire another legal value in different legal system: this is the case of the Codex Alimentarius Food safety standards in the WTO content. The Joint FAO/WHO Programme on Food Standards, widely known as Codex Alimentarius, was established in 1963 by the WHO together with the Food and Agriculture Organization of the United Nations. The Programme has its own form of governance which differs from the governance of the two parent organizations. Its principal organ is the

---

[58] See Resolution WHA 64.5: *supra* n. 55.

[59] L. O. Gostin and D. P. Fidler, 'WHO's Pandemic Influenza Preparedness Framework: A Milestone in Global Governance for Health', *J. Am. Med. Assoc.*, 306 (2011), 200–201.

[60] SMTA 1.   [61] SMTA 2.

[62] B. Molenaar, 'Pandemic Influenza Preparedness Framework: Negotiations in the Open-Ended Working Group Slowly Moving Forward', *Health Diplomacy Monitor*, 2 (2011), 14–16, at 15.

Codex Alimentarius Commission, whose task is to administer the Programme. In its work, the said Commission is supported by the Executive Committee and by a number of Committees, in addition to a dedicated Secretariat housed in the FAO building in Rome.

One of the main tasks of the Programme is protecting the health of consumers and ensuring fair practices in the food trade. This aspect had already been duly highlighted by the United Nations General Assembly which, in its April 1985 guidelines on consumer protection, stated that '[w]hen formulating national policies and plans with regard to food, Governments should take into account the need of all consumers for food security and should support and, as far as possible, adopt standards from the Food and Agriculture Organization of the United Nations and the World Health Organization Codex Alimentarius' (Annex to General Assembly Resolution 39/248). In quite recent times, food standards developed by the Codex Alimentarius Commission have also acquired great significance in the trade area. Indeed, the Agreement on the Application of Sanitary and Phytosanitary Measures, adopted within the context of the World Trade Organization, explicitly mentions those standards as 'the preferred international measures for facilitating international trade in food'. This shows the capacity and credibility of the Programme in establishing science-based food safety standards and its interaction with other sectors and organizations.

6   The Modern Law of the Treaties and International Health: Key Issues

6.1   Preliminary Considerations

Notwithstanding the bold vision and capacity of the WHO Constitution, as shown by the long-standing practice of the Organization, WHO's Member States have traditionally been hesitant to adopt internationally binding legal instruments. This is, however, not surprising since international obligations are widely perceived among representatives of States as impinging, and to some necessary extent do impinge on, the sovereignty of Member States. It has also evident that the preference of States for non-legally binding international instruments often reflects a desire to maintain the *status quo*, often non-legal in nature, and the flexibility of political as opposed to legally binding commitments.[63] Difficulties encountered by States in formalising technical requirements in

---

[63] See, further, J.D. Sachs, 'From Millennium Development Goals to Sustainable Development Goals', *The Lancet*, 379 (2012), 2206–2211.

a rapidly evolving sector and in negotiating instruments and 'lack of normative tradition in WHO's governing bodies, which makes many delegations and ministries of health unfamiliar and uncomfortable with negotiating and debating international legal instruments',[64] together with the WHO's science-oriented culture[65] contribute to this skepticism towards hard law instruments.

Nevertheless, it is irrefutable that the law of the treaties plays an important role in addressing health issue. Notwithstanding the caution of the WHO in adopting legally binding instruments, other intergovernmental organization have shown how treaties can contribute, even indirectly, to achieve public health goals.

In order to assess the effectiveness of the law of the treaties in addressing the needs of the global public health community, it is necessary to understand what those needs are and what is the best instrument to be used to achieve a satisfactory outcome. The normative experience of the WHO seems to indicate that international agreements are not the preferential option to tackle public health issues. This does not mean that the law of treaties does not provide guidance in matters dealt with in the public health arena. It should be recognised that this body of law provides a certain degree of flexibility since many provisions allow States to depart from the rules of the law of the treaties itself.[66] Additionally, 'despite its limitations (hard) law serves multiple positive functions, from raising awareness and debate, to promoting commitments, to stimulating action, to articulating norms and standards, to constructing mechanisms for achieving identified end and erecting structure to promote/enforce action and compliance'.[67]

6.2 'Hard Law' versus 'Soft Law'

The concepts of 'hard law' and 'soft law' are by now well-known to all those exposed and/or familiar with public international law. Broadly

---

[64] G. L. Burci and C.-H. Vignes, *World Health Organization* (The Hague: Kluwer International Law, 2004), p. 155.

[65] D. Fidler, 'The Future of the World Health Organization: What Role for International Law?', *Vanderbilt JTL*, 31 (1998), 1079–1126.

[66] A. Aust, 'Vienna Convention on the Law of the Treaties (1969)' in R. Wolfrum (ed.), *Max Planck Encyclopedia of Public International Law* (Vol. X) (Oxford: Oxford University Press, 2012), pp. 712–713.

[67] S. H. E. Harmon, 'International Public Health Law: Not So Much WHO as Why, and Not Enough WHO and Why Not?', *Medicine, Health Care and Philosophy*, 12 (2009), 245–255.

speaking, these two terms are used to contrast legally binding instruments (such as treaties, conventions, international agreements and regulations) with non-legally binding instruments (such as resolutions and any other act of a recommendatory nature).[68] Although instruments within the two categories seem to be very different, and are so from a strict normative perspective, they have, nevertheless, a lot in common. First of all, they are the result of the will of States to reach a common goal. Secondly, they are negotiated in a contractual style, if not as actual contracts, then often with painstaking attention to detail and with lawyerly precision in the use of language. And, perhaps most importantly, they establish expectations between and among States regarding actions to be taken or refrained from, along with consequences, even if only within a political realm, for failures in meeting those expectations.

It would be naive to think that only legal considerations are guiding States' actions in the public health arena when choosing the most suitable tool to achieve results of common interest. As already indicated previously, practical rather than legal considerations drive the actions of States vis-à-vis the adoption of all instruments, both legally binding and not.

Yet the differentiation between hard law and soft law reveals an implicit negative judgement on the effectiveness of non-legally binding instruments. The preference for treaties and conventions is linked to the credibility of the process for developing those instruments at international level and the required internal procedures for ratification at national level. In addition, they are considered 'stronger' than recommendations contained in resolutions. These arguments seem, however, to have less force if consideration is given to contemporary dynamics of global diplomacy, particularly in the health arena. Indeed, even recommendations which go into effect immediately, i.e. without undergoing a ratification process, are marked by highly complex and detailed negotiation processes. By whatever name they are referred to, such complex recommendations are normatively influential, even if not technically binding under international law. They have political authority and standing as instruments of normative bodies, such as the World Health Assembly, and they establish commitments, sometimes of a general nature but more and more of a highly specific and measurable nature. They are, furthermore, closely linked to the credibility of the

[68] See, further, C. M. Chinkin, 'The Challenge of Soft Law: Development and Change in International Law', *ICLQ*, 38 (1989), 850-866.

Organization and to the confidence Member States have in the means the Organization uses for achieving its objectives.

One of the most recent examples of complex set of recommendations is the adoption of the already cited WHO Global Code of Practice on the International Recruitment of Health Personnel.[69] Protracted negotiations until the early morning of the date of its adoption demonstrate that States attach a great significance and weight to recommendations of the WHO's governing bodies. The principles and norms set by resolutions provide guidance to the members of an organization and – upon adoption – the expectation that those recommendations will be followed and duly implemented.

Another aspect, which relates to the 'power and weight' of international agreements versus resolutions, should also be considered further. In recent times, it has become evident that States are reticent to depart from the status quo even when they commit to enter into negotiations for developing new legally binding instruments. States often propose use of qualifiers and expressions aimed at diluting the obligations they are negotiating. The insertion of expressions such as 'as appropriate' and 'subject to national law'[70] if, on the one hand, contributing to quicker possible solutions, on the other hand, provide the State with a great flexibility as to the fulfilment of the obligations contained in the instrument. The 'hard law' instrument with such qualifiers becomes somewhat softer on close inspection. To this, it should be added that many internationally, legally binding instruments – in particular adopted under the auspices of the WHO – do not provide for enforcement mechanisms. The lack of those mechanisms affects to a certain extent their credibility and leaves the obligation to comply largely to the good will of States.

7   Conflicts of Treaties in International Health Law

In order to tackle the problem related to the conflict of treaties, there is a need to identify such conflict. The most common definition of conflict of norms is a conflict between two norms where a party to two

---

[69] Resolution WHA63.16 (21 May 2010). See, further, A. L. Taylor and I. S. Dhillon, 'The WHO Global Code of Practice on the International Recruitment of Health Personnel: The Evolution of Global Health Diplomacy', *Global Health Governance*, 5 (2011), 1–24.

[70] E. Bertorelli, S. A. Solomon and N. Drager, 'Instruments of Health Diplomacy' in T. E. Novotny, I. Kickbusch and M. Told (eds.), *21st Century Global Health Diplomacy* (Singapore: World Scientific Publishing, 2013), pp. 97–130.

international legal instruments 'cannot simultaneously comply with its obligations under both treaties'.[71] This narrow definition of conflict of norms has undergone some criticisms.[72] Some have objected that this definition does not take into consideration the fundamental functions of the norms. In particular, in looking at three major functions of norms – obligations, prohibitions and permissions – a critical question is whether a conflict of law only exists in case of incompatibilities between obligations and prohibitions or whether it also extends to permissions. It is, in fact, one of the main objections made against the narrow definition of conflicts discussed previously, since incompatibilities between permissions and obligations and permissions and prohibitions may lead, in practice, to the same consequence of a conflict between obligation and prohibitions which is the inapplicability of the norm. Therefore, 'it excludes incompatibilities that appear analogous to the mutual incompatibility between obligations and prohibitions'.[73]

Most of the doctrine makes reference to the conflict of norms without specifying whether the conflict operates within the same or different legal systems. Conversely, a part of the doctrine has made an interesting distinction between conflicts of norms – which operate within the same system – and conflicts of laws – which operate between different systems.

Conflicts of norms are traditionally present at domestic or national level. Prerequisites for qualifying a situation as a conflict of norms should be the existence of a sole legislator and a single overarching system. Conflict rules are based on the existence of the hierarchy of norms and on considerations *ratione materiae* and *ratione temporis*. As a consequence, while principles such as *lex superior derogate legi inferiori* operate where a hierarchical relation between norms exists, since it states that the superior rule trumps ordinary law, *lex posterior derogate lege anterior* and *lex speciali derogate lex generalis* may be applied exclusively within the same systems of law and values. Balancing different interests is thus only possible within the same legal system.

---

[71] W. C. Jenks, 'The Conflict of Law Making Treaties', *BYbIL*, 30 (1953), 401–453, at 425–426.

[72] See E. Vranes, 'The Definition of "Norm Conflict" in International Law and Legal Theory', *EJIL*, 17 (2006), 395–418, and, also, J. Pauwelyn, *Conflict of Norms in Public International Law: How WTO Law Relates to Other Rules of International Law* (Cambridge: Cambridge University Press, 2003), pp. 170–171.

[73] Vranes, *supra* n. 72, at p. 404.

At the same time, conflicts may also exist between and among different legal systems. A practical case of conflict of law is currently pending before the World Trade Organization. The WHO Framework Convention on Tobacco Control is currently undergoing its first test in front of an international instance. On 13 March 2012, Ukraine requested consultations with Australia through the World Trade Organization on the recently approved Australian legislation involving trademark restrictions and plain packaging requirements on tobacco products. Cuba, the Dominican Republic, Honduras and Indonesia have subsequently joined have challenged the Australian legislation by arguing that the measures appear to be inconsistent with Australia's obligations under the TBT Agreement, the TRIPS Agreement and GATT 1994.

In November 2011, Australia became the one of the most forward-leaning countries regarding the regulation of packaging of tobacco products in the interest of public health by providing that all promotional text be prohibited and establishing the colour and the printing of tobacco company logo and brand information. Justification for this new legislation lies, *inter alia*, on a number of provisions of the Convention, including Articles 5, 11 and 13. While Article 5 lists general obligations requiring Parties to the Convention to 'develop, implement, periodically update and review comprehensive multisectorial national tobacco control strategies, plans and programmes in accordance' with the Convention, Article 11 requires Parties to adopt and implement effective measures on packaging and labelling of tobacco products, including health warnings and other appropriate messages. Additionally, Article 13 of the WHO FCTC requires Parties to implement comprehensive bans on tobacco advertising, promotion and sponsorship to be intended as 'means of any form of commercial communication, recommendation or action with the aim, effect or likely effect of promoting a tobacco product or tobacco use either directly or indirectly'.

In the case at hand, there is a tension between the need to achieve a legitimate health objective and the restriction of international trade and intellectual property rights which reflects the tension among different legal instruments: the WHO FCTC, on one side, and the WTO legislation, on the other.

8   Conclusion

Public health is a complex topic which cannot be considered in isolation. The interplay between health and other sectors such as trade or environment – only to mention two of them – has become evident not only within the global health community but to national officials dealing with issues from trade and environment to development and security. For many centuries, States have sought to address national needs by protecting their own territories from spread of diseases. Now those efforts are no longer effective.[74] It is, rather, abundantly clear that globalisation to be understood as 'the process of increasing economic, political and social interdependence, and global integration that occurs as capital, traded goods, people, concepts, images, ideas and values diffuse across national boundaries'[75] produces consequences in the health context with implications across a wide array of governmental responsibility. The international cooperation in public health matters among and between States and other relevant stakeholders needs to be governed by normative and institutional mechanisms guided by the principle of universalism as well as practical and unavoidable political considerations.

Offering a universal mechanism to achieve such a significant objective, the WHO Constitution sets the overarching principles aimed at guiding the WHO's action to ensure the coherent and effective development of frameworks of cooperation, both binding and non-binding, both within and outside of the Vienna Convention on the Law of Treaties, among the different actors populating the health arena and across the spectrum of existing and emerging public health challenges.

---

[74] S. Chichevalieva, *Developing a Framework for Public Health Law in Europe* (Copenhagen: WHO Regional Office for Europe, 2011), p. 10.
[75] A. Taylor, 'Global Governance, International Health Law and WHO: Looking Towards the Future', *WHO Bulletin*, 80 (2002), 975–980.

28

The International Maritime Organization

DOROTA LOST-SIEMINSKA*

1 Introduction

Shipping is one of the oldest and most international trading industries in the world, while regulations applying to this mode of transport date back as far as the eighth century.[1] Ships are often owned by more than one person or entity and the daily operational management of vessels is contracted out to agents, managers and charterers who are likely to be spread across the globe, often operating from multiple jurisdictions. Seafarers manning today's global merchant fleet come from various countries, ship-owners can be insured anywhere in the world, and they have numerous other worldwide connections. The international dimension of shipping was the reason why the international community recognised the need for conformity and unity in standards from a very early stage in the industry.

The first maritime treaties governing this diverse and globally important industry date back to the nineteenth century and were developed during the Industrial Revolution. The rapid rise in international

* The author would like to thank Dr. Rosalie P. Balkin, Director of the Legal Affairs and External Relations Division of the International Maritime Organization (1998–2013), for her constant support and many discussions. The author would also like to thank Dino Kritsiotis and Michael Bowman for their valuable comments and suggestions. All views expressed in this chapter are of the author only and do not represent official position of IMO in any matter.

[1] The first known source of maritime law is the law of Rhodes. Roman maritime law was based on it, as well as the maritime code of the later Eastern Empire, dating from the seventh or eighth century. This code was called the 'Rhodian Sea Law'. Together with the 'Rolls of Oléron', dating from the twelfth century, these codes created the basis of *lex maritima*, which developed as part of the *lex mercatoria*. The commercial highway and the centre of the western world were in the Mediterranean and this is where European maritime law began to evolve as a comprehensive body of law: W. Tetley, 'The General Maritime Law – The Lex Maritima (with a Brief Reference to the Ius Commune in Arbitration Law and the Conflict of Laws)', *Syracuse J. Int'l L. & Comm.*, 20 (1994), 105–145.

commerce that followed the revolution resulted in the adoption of a number of conventions related to shipping, including safety, tonnage measurement, the prevention of collisions, signalling and other matters.[2] The sinking of the *Titanic* in April 1912 was a major impetus behind extensive safety regulations. The first International Convention for the Safety of Life at Sea (SOLAS) was adopted in January 1914;[3] however, it was not until 1948 that a conference was convened by the United Nations in Geneva, spurred on by the new spirit of global unity after the Second World War, which led to the adoption of the Convention on the Inter-Governmental Maritime Consultative Organization (IMCO).[4] This organization changed its name to the International Maritime Organization (IMO) in May 1982.[5] By the time it had come into existence in 1958,[6] several important international conventions had already been developed, including the International Convention for the Safety of Life at Sea in June 1948,[7] the International Convention for the Prevention of Pollution of the Sea by Oil in May 1954[8] and treaties dealing with load lines and the prevention of collisions at sea.[9]

The majority of conventions adopted under the auspices of the IMO fall into three main categories: maritime safety; the prevention of marine pollution; liability and compensation, particularly for damage caused by pollution. There are, moreover, a number of other conventions dealing with other matters relating to shipping including facilitation, tonnage measurement, unlawful acts against shipping and salvage. The IMO is

---

[2] On 28 July 1879, nineteen States adopted joint rules in London for an international signal code, and on 1 Sept. 1880, an international convention was devised to establish the first rules for preventing collisions. The first convention on health and safety for steam packet navigation was signed on 28 July 1881 and the first International Maritime Conference was held between 16 Oct. and 31 Dec. 1889. See, further, P. Boisson, *Safety at Sea: Policies, Regulations* (Paris: Bureau Veritas, 1999).

[3] 219 CTS 177. The full text of the Convention may be found at the website of the IMO Maritime Knowledge Centre (www.imo.org/KnowledgeCentre/Pages/Default.aspx).

[4] 289 UNTS 3.

[5] Amendments to the title and the substantive provisions of the Convention on the International Maritime Organization, adopted by the Assembly of the Organization by Resolution A.358 (IX) of 14 Nov. 1975 and A.371 (X) of 9 Nov. 1977 (rectification of Resolution A.358 (IX)).

[6] For more information on the history of the IMO, see A. Blanco-Bazan, 'IMO – Historical Highlights in the Life of a UN Agency', *J. Hist. Int'l L.*, 6 (2004), 151–176.

[7] 164 UNTS 113.   [8] 1327 UNTS 3.

[9] 1966 International Convention on Load Lines, 640 UNTS 133, and 1960 International Regulations for Preventing Collisions at Sea, TIAS 5813. Texts of treaties of historical importance as well as *travaux préparatoires* of IMO conferences may be found at the website of the IMO Maritime Knowledge Centre, *supra* n. 3.

responsible for keeping the majority of these conventions up to date. It is also tasked with developing new conventions as and when a compelling need is demonstrated. The creation of the IMO coincided with a period of tremendous change in world shipping and it has been extremely active from the start, developing new conventions and ensuring that existing ones keep pace with changes in commercial and operational practice as well as environmental and safety technology. The IMO is now responsible for almost fifty international conventions and agreements. Membership is open to all States, and the IMO currently has over 170 members.[10]

This chapter focuses on the peculiarities of the treaty-making process within an international organization – specifically the IMO – touching briefly on the adoption of treaties and the ratification process before turning to the amendment procedure as provided in the 1969 Vienna Convention on the Law of Treaties (VCLT)[11] and in the practice of States acting under the auspices of the IMO.

2   The Treaty-Making Process

The drafting of conventions, agreements and other suitable instruments is expressly recognised in Article 2 of the IMO Convention as one of the principal means by which the Organization may seek to achieve its purposes as set out in Article 1 of the Convention. These are:

(a) [t]o provide machinery for co-operation among Governments in the field of governmental regulation and practices relating to technical matters of all kinds affecting shipping engaged in international trade; to encourage and facilitate the general adoption of the highest practicable standards in matters concerning the maritime safety, efficiency of navigation and prevention and control of marine pollution from ships; and to deal with administrative and legal matters related to the purposes set out in this Article;

(b) [t]o encourage the removal of discriminatory action and unnecessary restrictions by Governments affecting shipping engaged in international trade so as to promote the availability of shipping services to the commerce of the world without discrimination; assistance and encouragement given by a Government for the development of its national shipping and for purposes of security does not in itself constitute discrimination, provided that such assistance and

---

[10] With three Associate Members (the Faroe Islands, Hong Kong and Macao): for up-to-date data, consult http://www.imo.org/en/About/Membership/Pages/Default.aspx.
[11] 1155 UNTS 331.

encouragement is not based on measures designed to restrict the freedom of shipping of all flags to take part in international trade;

(c) [t]o provide for the consideration by the Organization of matters concerning unfair restrictive practices by shipping concerns in accordance with Part II;

(d) [t]o provide for the consideration by the Organization of any matters concerning shipping and the effect of shipping on the marine environment that may be referred to it by any organ or specialized agency of the United Nations;

(e) [t]o provide for the exchange of information among Governments on matters under consideration by the Organization.[12]

2.1   Role of IMO Organs (in the Treaty-Making Process)

Treaty-making at the IMO takes place through its various organs: the Assembly, the Council, the Maritime Safety Committee (MSC), the Legal Committee (LEG), the Marine Environment Protection Committee (MEPC), the Technical Cooperation Committee (TCD) and the Facilitation Committee (FAL).[13] Developments in shipping and other related industries are discussed by Member States and observer delegations in committee sessions and the need for a new convention or amendments to existing conventions can be raised by any of them. The Secretariat of the IMO plays a supportive role for these statutory bodies.[14] The IMO operates on the basis of reaching consensus, which is often achieved by compromise. In the rare event that a vote is needed, each member of the IMO has one vote and decisions are taken by a majority of the members that are present and eligible to vote; for decisions where a two-thirds majority vote is required, a two-thirds majority of those present is required. Member States which fail to meet

---

[12] *Supra* n. 4.

[13] For more information about the rules of international organs, see H. G. Schermers and N. M. Blokker, *International Institutional Law: Unity with Diversity* (Leiden: Martinus Nijhoff, 5th rev. ed., 2011), pp. 121-235 (§§155–290). For specific information on the Maritime Safety Committee, see *ibid.*, at pp. 303–304 (§397).

[14] The role of the Secretariat is described *ibid.*, at §§434–545. Richard Gardiner, in *Treaty Interpretation* (Oxford: Oxford University Press, 2nd ed., 2015), pp. 125–129, expresses the opinion that international organizations have their own legal advisers as part of their respective Secretariats who can give advice on the interpretation of treaties. The Legal Office of the IMO Secretariat has, on several occasions, received requests to provide legal advice on the interpretation of a convention. However, these are not binding interpretations and States Parties are not obliged to take such interpretations into account. See Legal Advice on the Draft Assembly Resolution on the Application of the BWM Convention, Document MEPC 65/2/18, as well as Document 65/22 (paragraph 2.24).

their financial obligation to the IMO have no vote in the Assembly, the Council or the committees, unless the Assembly, at its discretion, decides otherwise.[15]

The Assembly is the highest governing body of the IMO and consists of all the members. It is the responsibility of the Assembly to recommend the adoption of regulations and any guidelines or amendments. The Assembly also decides whether to convene international conferences. It can also adopt international conventions or amendments to international conventions developed by the committees or other organs of the IMO, following the appropriate procedure.

The Council is the executive organ of the IMO and has forty members elected by the Assembly.[16] It usually meets twice a year to consider the draft work programme, which also includes plans for adopting new instruments or amending existing ones as well as proposals and recommendations from the committees. Drafts prepared by the committees are then submitted to the Council and, in turn, transmitted to the Assembly.[17]

The five committees contain all the members and meet at least once a year. The MSC is the oldest and principal technical body of the IMO. It drafts proposals for safety regulations and amendments to safety regulations.[18] Issues that relate to the prevention and control of marine pollution from ships are discussed at the MEPC which, like the MSC,

---

[15] Art. 61 of the IMO Convention: *supra* n. 4.

[16] Ten members of the Council are States that have the greatest interest in providing international shipping services; ten are other States with the greatest interest in international seaborne trade; the other twenty are States that are not elected under the previous criteria but have special interests in maritime transport or navigation and whose election to the Council will ensure the representation of all the major geographic areas of the world. Originally the Council was composed of sixteen Members. The current number of the Members of the Council was decided in 1993 by the Assembly Resolution A.735 (18).

[17] This role of the Council is envisaged in Arts. 29, 34 and 39 as well as Arts. 44 and 49 of the IMO Convention: *supra* n. 4. The Council then considers the decisions of the committees reflected in the reports and transmits the reports with any comments and recommendations to the Assembly. The Council also notes the adoption of the amendments to mandatory instruments. See, for example, Document C. 110/11 (13 June 2013), Consideration of the Report of the Marine Environment Protection Committee.

[18] It also develops recommendations and guidelines, and considers any matters relating to navigational aids, the construction and equipment of vessels, manning from a safety standpoint, rules for the prevention of collisions, handling dangerous cargo, maritime safety procedures and requirements, hydrographic information, log books and navigational records, marine casualty investigation, salvage and rescue, and any other matters directly affecting maritime safety. See Art. 28 of the IMO Convention: *supra* n. 4.

adopts and amends draft regulations, recommendations and guidelines.[19] The FAL deals with issues concerned with the facilitation of international maritime traffic.[20] Legal matters are considered by the LEG, which prepares and agrees drafts of international conventions.[21] All the drafts and proposals that are prepared by these committees are then submitted to the Council for approval. The TCD considers issues relating to the implementation of technical cooperation projects, and it is the only committee that does not submit any drafts of international regulations to the Council. However, it plays a vital role in the implementation of international instruments, particularly in developing countries, for whose benefit this technical cooperation is designed.[22]

2.2   Adoption of Treaties

Article 9 VCLT sets out rules for the adoption of a treaty and requires the consent of all the States participating in its drawing up or adoption by the vote of two-thirds majority of the States present and voting, if the process takes place at an international conference.[23] In IMO practice, the treaty-making process begins when a compelling need for a new treaty has been established and is initiated by a submission from a Member State during one of the committee meetings and thereafter reflected in the Strategic Plan of the IMO.[24] As already stated, after their development in the relevant committee, proposals for and amendments to treaties are then submitted to the Council for approval. In the case of new treaties, the Assembly decides whether to convene a diplomatic conference.[25] Treaties and protocols to them are in practice adopted at the diplomatic

---

[19]   Art. 38 of the IMO Convention: *supra* n. 4.

[20]   Art. 48 of the IMO Convention: *supra* n. 4.

[21]   Art. 33 of the IMO Convention: *supra* n. 4.

[22]   Art. 43 of the IMO Convention: *supra* n. 4.

[23]   For a detailed discussion of Art. 9 VCLT, see F. Hoffmeister, 'Article 9' in O. Dörr and K. Schmalenbach (eds.), *Vienna Convention on the Law of Treaties: A Commentary* (Berlin: Springer, 2012), pp. 137–148, at p. 139. Adoption of a treaty is also discussed by A. Aust, *Modern Treaty Law and Practice* (Cambridge: Cambridge University Press, 3rd ed., 2013), pp. 79–83.

[24]   The requirement to demonstrate a compelling need for a new treaty is contained in the guidelines on the organization and method of work which each IMO committee adopts. See, for example, Guidelines on the Organization and Method of Work of the Legal Committee: LEG.1/Circ.7 (11 May 2012).

[25]   More information on the adoption of treaties in the United Nations system may be found at: https://treaties.un.org/pages/Overview.aspx?path=overview/glossary/page1_en.xml.

conference by consensus, although rules of procedure of the conference would require a two-thirds majority.[26]

As for amendments, the majority of treaties adopted under the auspices of the IMO provide for the revision or amendment to be adopted by the convening of a conference without specifying any further requirements as to the amendment procedure or the organ responsible for it.[27] However, some treaties specify the amendment procedure in an extremely detailed way and prescribe the IMO organ responsible for adoption.[28] The nature of this amendment procedure will be discussed in greater depth later in this chapter.

2.3   Ratification and Entry into Force

The adoption of a treaty only marks the conclusion of the first stage of a long process. Before the treaty comes into force, individual governments must express their consent to be bound by it.[29] As provided in Article 11 VCLT, governments may express their consent in a variety of ways: signature, exchange of instruments constituting a treaty,

---

[26] In his commentary to Art. 9(2) VCLT, Sinclair notes the general agreement that the rule reflected in this article did not automatically apply to treaties adopted within an international organization, if the relevant rules of the organization provided otherwise: I. Sinclair, *The Vienna Convention on the Law of Treaties* (Manchester: Manchester University Press, 2nd ed., 1984), p. 36. The rules adopted at IMO conferences would usually provide for a two-thirds majority. See, for example, Provisional Rules of Procedure for the International Conference on the Revision of the HNS Convention, Document LEG-CONF.17/2 (5 Oct. 2009), but the final text was adopted by consensus: LEG-CONF.17/RD.2 (30 Apr. 2010), Records of Decisions of the Plenary and LEG-CONF.17/12 (1 June 2010), Final Act of the International Conference on the Revision of the HNS Convention.

[27] See, for example, Art. 22 of the 2002 Protocol to the 1974 Athens Convention relating to the Carriage of Passengers and Their Luggage by Sea (PAL PROT 2002), IMO Doc. LEG/CONF.13/20; Art. 20 of the 1976 Convention on Limitation of Liability for Maritime Claims (LLMC 1976), 1456 UNTS 221; Art. 23 of the 2003 Protocol to the International Convention on the Establishment of an International Fund for Compensation for Oil Pollution Damage (FUND PROT 2003), IMO Doc. LEG/CONF.14/20, and Art. 32 of the 1989 International Convention on Salvage, 1953 UNTS 165.

[28] A very detailed amendment procedure is provided for in Art. VIII of the 1974 International Convention for the Safety of Life at Sea (SOLAS), 1184 UNTS 278, and in Art. 16 of the 1973/1978 International Convention for the Prevention of Pollution from Ships (MARPOL), 1340 UNTS 62. On MARPOL, see, further, *infra* n. 51.

[29] For more information on the consent to be bound by a treaty, see Aust, *supra* n. 23, at pp. 87–113. See, also, M. Fitzmaurice, 'The Practical Working of the Law of Treaties' in M. D. Evans (ed.), *International Law* (Oxford: Oxford University Press, 4th ed., 2014), pp. 166–197.

ratification, acceptance, approval or accession – or 'by any means if so agreed'. The most common method in the IMO is by signature subject to ratification, followed by the ratification, or acceptance, approval and accession thereto.

A particularly interesting issue concerning consent to be bound can be found in the 2010 Protocol to the 1996 International Convention on Liability and Compensation for Damage in Connection with the Carriage of Hazardous and Noxious Substances by Sea (known as the 2010 HNS Convention).[30] Article 20(4) of this instrument provides that '[a]n expression of consent to be bound by this Protocol shall be accompanied by the submission to the Secretary-General [of the IMO] of data on the total quantities of contributing cargo liable for contributions received in that State during the preceding calendar year in respect of the general account and each separate account'.[31] Article 20(5) further provides that an expression of consent that is not accompanied by the data referred to in Article 20(4) will not be accepted by the Secretary-General of the IMO.

This presents somewhat of a novel situation in the practice of the IMO and for the depositary in particular, and the procedure for fulfilling the ratification requirements of this convention is likely to raise some interesting issues. The ratification process begins in the government administration of a State and normally makes its way through to the national parliament (or other appropriate organ). Once a given parliament consents to be bound by a treaty, and the treaty has been given effect under domestic implementing legislation where required, the government submits an instrument of ratification (or accession) to the depositary.

This potentially creates a challenge in some jurisdictions, since the procedure for reporting contributing cargo data – referred to in Article 20(4) and as mentioned earlier – requires a decision from the HNS Fund

---

[30] ILM, 35 (1996), 1415–1436. The original International Convention on Liability and Compensation for Damage in Connection with the Carriage of Hazardous and Noxious Substances was adopted in May 1996, but has never come into force. This is mainly due to the complicated provisions on the reporting requirement, which needs to be met prior to entry into force. The 2010 Protocol to the 1996 International Convention on Liability and Compensation for Damage in Connection with the Carriage of Hazardous and Noxious Substances is designed to resolve the practical problems that had prevented many States from ratifying the original Convention. The full consolidated text of the Convention, as amended by the 2010 Protocol (i.e. the 2010 HNS Convention), may be found at www.hnsconvention.org.

[31] An HNS workshop held at IMO Headquarters in 2012 adopted Guidelines on Reporting of HNS Contributing Cargo which were subsequently endorsed by the IMO Legal Committee at its 100th Session in Apr. 2013. The text of the Guidelines may be found at www.hnsconvention.org.

Assembly to ensure uniformity in annual cargo reporting. This Assembly cannot be convened until the treaty enters into force. This means that a ratifying State needs to adopt reporting regulations prior to ratification and therefore also prior to the entry into force of this Convention. The reason why such reports have to be submitted is that there are two requirements for the entry into force of the Convention. First, it has to be ratified by at least twelve States.[32] Second, these twelve States must have identified contributors that have received individually 20,000 tonnes or more contributing cargo in the preceding year and, collectively, there must be a total quantity of at least 40 million tonnes of cargo contributing to the general account.[33]

The question arises whether the depositary has any control or any right of verification of the data report. The 2010 HNS Convention is silent about the role of the depositary in this respect.[34] Does this mean that any report that accompanies the instrument of ratification submitted by a State must be accepted by the depositary, regardless of its format, quality or attestation by the State that the report is indeed accurate? Moreover, are there any powers conferred on the Secretary-General of the IMO to intervene where the report appears inaccurate? There is no doubt that the depositary can refuse to accept the instrument when the State has not submitted a report at all. An instrument of ratification that is not accompanied by the relevant data would not be counted as valid and therefore would not contribute to the total number of Contracting States for any relevant purpose, including bringing the Protocol into force.[35] Presumably, where the data report is obviously and comprehensively defective, the depositary could refuse to accept the instrument on the ground that the State has failed to implement in good faith its obligations under the Convention.

---

[32] Art. 21(1) of 2010 HNS Convention: *supra* n. 30.

[33] See, also, the contribution to this volume of Trebilcock at pp. 848–880 (Chapter 26).

[34] Art. 53 of 2010 HNS Convention: *supra* n. 30.

[35] Similar issues arise in other treaties: for instance, under Art. 2(4) of the 1971 Ramsar Convention on Wetlands of International Importance Especially As Waterfowl Habitat, 996 UNTS 245, each Contracting Party must designate at least one wetland to be included in the List when signing this Convention or when depositing its instrument of ratification or accession. An instrument which failed to do so would presumably be rejected. For further details, see M. J. Bowman, P. G. G. Davies and C. J. Redgwell, *Lyster's International Wildlife Law* (Cambridge: Cambridge University Press, 2nd ed., 2010), pp. 406–407.

3 Amendment of Treaties

In view of the rapid pace of change in the circumstances and demands of modern shipping activities, it is important that treaties are capable of being amended in expeditious fashion. However, while IMO treaties have very frequently been amended, a number of significant practical problems have been encountered in the application of amendment procedures.

3.1 Entry into Force of Amendments

In early IMO conventions, amendments only came into force after a certain proportion – usually two-thirds – of contracting States had accepted them.[36] This commonly meant that more acceptances were required to amend a convention than were originally required to bring it into force because the total number of States Parties to the convention might well have increased in the meantime. This classical amendment procedure has caused the IMO particular difficulties. For example, the amendments to the 1960 SOLAS Convention entered into force twelve months after the date on which the amendment was accepted by two-thirds of the contracting governments, including two-thirds of the governments represented on the MSC.[37] This did not appear to be a difficult target to reach when the Convention was adopted because it only required acceptance by fifty countries for its entry into force, seven of which had fleets consisting of at least 1 million gross tons of merchant shipping. But by the late 1960s, the number of parties to the SOLAS Convention had reached eighty and the tonnage was continuously rising as new countries emerged and began to develop their shipping activities. As the number of parties rose, so did the total number required to amend

---

[36] As T. O. Elias indicated in *The Modern Law of Treaties* (New York, NY/Leiden: Oceana Publications/A.W. Sijthoff, 1974), p. 93, treaties concluded within the framework of an international organization or under their auspices will almost invariably contain definitive provisions for amendment procedures. See, further, M. N. Shaw, *International Law* (Cambridge: Cambridge University Press, 8th ed., 2017), p. 706, and J. Crawford, *Brownlie's Principles of Public International Law* (Oxford: Oxford University Press, 8th ed., 2012), p. 386.

[37] I. A. Shearer, *Starke's International Law* (London: Butterworths, 11th ed., 1994), p. 426, noted that '[g]enerally, unanimity is required for the adoption of the amendments, but the trend since 1945 is towards allowing amendment of multilateral conventions by a majority, if this is the interest of the international community. The main difficulty has been in getting the parties to proceed promptly to ratification of the proposed modification'.

the Convention – and, as might have been expected, many governments took far longer to accept amendments than they did to ratify the parent convention. In addition, technology in the shipping industry was changing so rapidly that the 1960 Convention was amended six times after it entered into force in 1965 and, in 1974, a completely new convention was adopted to incorporate all these amendments (and other minor changes). It has subsequently been modified on numerous occasions.

In practice, this percentage requirement led to long delays in bringing amendments into force. To remedy the situation, a new amendment procedure called 'tacit acceptance' was introduced whereby an amendment enters into force at a specified date, unless objections to the amendment are received from a specific number of parties before that date.[38] Tacit acceptance was designed to amend provisions of a technical nature, usually contained in the annexes and appendices of treaties. The classical acceptance procedure therefore remained for non-technical articles.[39] As expected, the tacit acceptance procedure has greatly sped up the amendment process. Amendments generally enter into force within 18 to 24 months. In comparison, none of the amendments adopted for the 1960 SOLAS Convention between 1966 and 1973 received sufficient acceptances to satisfy the requirements for entry into force.

---

[38] Curtis A. Bradley refers to tacit amendments as 'unratified treaty amendments that are changes to treaties proposed by international bodies that become binding upon parties to the treaty without the expectation of a national act of ratification' in 'Unratified Treaty Amendments and Constitutional Process' (6 Feb. 2006), unpublished manuscript on file with the author, prepared for Duke Workshop on Delegating Sovereignty (https://law .duke.edu/publiclaw/pdf/workshop06sp/bradleyc.pdf). See, also, Aust, *supra* n. 23, at pp. 237–238.

[39] The history of tacit acceptance dates back to 1968 when the Council agreed to establish a working group to analyse the working methods of the IMO. The most important part of this analysis concerned the procedures for amending the various conventions. The study examined the procedures of four other United Nations agencies: the International Civil Aviation Organization (ICAO), the International Telecommunications Union (ITU), the World Meteorological Organization (WMO) and the World Health Organization (WHO). It showed that all of these organizations were able to amend technical and other regulations, which then became binding on Member States, without a further act of ratification or acceptance being required. The results of the working group's findings proved that the classical amendment system made it difficult to keep conventions up to date. There was general agreement that tacit acceptance offered the best way forward. There was some concern about what would happen if a large number of countries did reject an amendment, so committee members agreed that tacit acceptance should only apply to the technical content of conventions.

The tacit acceptance procedure has now been incorporated into the majority of the IMO's technical conventions and has been extended to other instruments, including those dealing with limits of liability for oil pollution damage as well as other maritime claims.[40] Its effectiveness is most noticeable in the case of the SOLAS and MARPOL Conventions, which have been amended on many occasions.[41] Tacit acceptance facilitates the quick and simple modification of conventions to keep pace with rapidly evolving technology in the shipping world. It also provides a welcome element of certainty as to the date upon which an amendment will become effective rather than leaving this to the vagaries of the timing of individual acceptances. In reality, the classical amendment procedure meant that many amendments would never have entered into force and, as a consequence, every State would have adopted its own national rules for shipping safety and environmental protection, inevitably leading to chaos.

Although the SOLAS Convention and Chapter I can only be amended using the classical amendment procedure, an amendment to most of the chapters (which constitute the technical parts and the core of the Convention) is 'deemed to have been accepted at the end of two years from the date on which it is communicated to Contracting Governments', unless the amendment is objected to by more than one-third of contracting governments or contracting governments owning not less than 50 per cent of the world's gross merchant tonnage.[42] The MSC may vary this period by up to one year. Similarly, the

---

[40] The Legal Committee used the tacit acceptance procedure for the first time at its 82nd Session (16–20 Oct. 2000) in order to increase the limitation amounts and compensation amounts in the 1992 Protocol to Amend the 1969 International Convention on Civil Liability for Oil Pollution Damage (CLC), 1956 UNTS 255, and the 1992 Protocol to Amend the International Convention on the Establishment of An International Fund For Compensation for Oil Pollution Damage, 1996 ATS 3, respectively. This procedure is laid down in Art. 15 of the Final Clauses of the 1992 Protocol to the CLC and in Art. 33 of the Final Clauses of the 1992 Protocol to the Fund Convention. On this occasion, the proposal to increase the limits was submitted by one quarter of the States Parties to both treaties and circulated six months before LEG 82. The committee considered and adopted the amendments on 18 Oct. 2000. No objection or comments of a procedural nature were raised by other States Parties after the circulation of the proposal and the amendments entered into force.

[41] MSC (the Committee responsible for the SOLAS Convention) and MEPC (the Committee responsible for the MARPOL Convention) meet usually twice a year. At each meeting new amendments to both treaties are adopted. So far, 147 resolutions were adopted to amend the SOLAS Convention and seventy-five resolutions to amend the MARPOL Convention.

[42] See Art. VIII of SOLAS: *supra* n. 28.

MARPOL provides for an amendment to be deemed to have been accepted at the end of a period determined by the appropriate body at the time of its adoption, which period shall not be less than ten months.[43] Again, to block the entry into force of such amendments, they must be objected by not less than one-third of the parties or by parties owning not less than 50 per cent of the world's gross merchant tonnage.

Both the SOLAS and MARPOL Conventions provide for two options: amendment after the consideration by the Organization and amendment by the Conference of Parties. In the first scenario, IMO committees are involved in the consideration of proposed amendments; in the second scenario, only the parties consider the amendments.[44]

3.2 Adoption of Amendments

3.2.1 The Respective Roles of IMO Organs and States Parties

The general rule governing amendments of multilateral treaties can be found in the Vienna Convention on the Law of Treaties.[45] In accordance with Article 40 VCLT, both the decision as to whether to take action on a proposal to amend a treaty and the negotiation and conclusion of any agreement for its amendment is, subject to the provisions of a particular treaty, left for the parties. The situation is different when a treaty assigns specific functions concerning the procedure for amendments to an international organization.

As already mentioned, the MARPOL and SOLAS Conventions contain provisions on the basis of which the respective committees consider proposals for amendments that are eventually adopted by a two-thirds majority of parties. This procedure creates more problems than may appear from the literature on this subject.[46] The rules of procedure of the committees provide for a simple majority of the Members present and voting to take decisions, but this is 'subject to the provisions of any

---

[43] See Art. 16 of MARPOL: *supra* n. 28.

[44] For discussion, see M. Fitzmaurice and P. Merkouris, 'Amendment and Modification of Non-proliferation Treaties' in D. H. Joyner and M. Roscini (eds.), *Non-proliferation Law as a Special Regime: A Contribution to Fragmentation Theory in International Law* (Cambridge: Cambridge University Press, 2012), pp. 17–54. See, also, Aust, *supra* n. 23, at p. 235.

[45] For a more detailed analysis, see K. Odendahl, 'Article 40' in Dörr and Schmalenbach (eds.), *supra* n. 23, pp. 709–718, at p. 714.

[46] See, for example, J. Harrison, *Making the Law of the Sea: A Study in the Development of International Law* (Cambridge: Cambridge University Press, 2011), p. 189.

treaty'.[47] The relevant provisions require a two-thirds majority of parties (in the case of the MARPOL Convention) or Contracting Governments (in the case of the SOLAS Convention) for the amendments to be adopted.[48]

The relationship between the States Parties to the MARPOL Convention and the MEPC as the body responsible for this Convention is a good example of the procedural difficulties that may arise when it comes to any decision on amendments. There are currently 171 States eligible for membership of the committee: 170 Members of the Organization and one State that is a non-Member of the Organization but is a Party to the MARPOL Convention. Of those States, only seventy-five are parties to the 1997 Protocol (MARPOL Annex VI). We may very well imagine the situation in which the majority of the committee will have different view than the two-thirds of the parties.

It is well-established IMO practice that all decisions, including the adoption of amendments, are taken by consensus. Oona Hathaway and her collaborators, while rightfully acknowledging this fact, are nevertheless mistaken in proclaiming that the treaties provide for the amendments to be adopted by a two-thirds majority of the appropriate body.[49] Both the SOLAS and MARPOL Conventions leave no doubt that a two-thirds majority of the parties adopts amendments. In two recent cases where the delegations were unable to reach consensus, a discussion arose about the role of the committee and the role of the parties. This discussion is presented later.

3.2.1.1 The Role of the MEPC and the Parties versus that of the Assembly

The question of the role played by the Assembly, the MEPC and the parties in the amendment procedure under the MARPOL Convention arose during the discussion on greenhouse gas

---

[47] See Rule 27 of the Rules of Procedure of the Marine Environment Protection Committee and Rule 26 of the Rules of Procedure of the Maritime Safety Committee.

[48] The role of the IMO committees has also been discussed by M. J. Kachel, 'Competencies of International Maritime Organizations to Establish Rules and Standards' in P. Ehlers and R. Lagoni (eds.), *International Maritime Organisations and Their Contribution Towards a Sustainable Marine Development* (Hamburg: Lit Verlag, 2006), pp. 21–52, at p. 34.

[49] O. Hathaway, H. Nix, S. S. Sanghvi and S. Solow, 'Tacit Amendments', White Paper for Yale Law School Centre for Global Legal Studies (Nov. 2011) (www.law.yale.edu/documents/pdf/cglc/TacitAmendments.pdf), p. 14.

emissions from shipping.[50] Article 16(2) stipulates that an amendment proposed by a party to the Convention shall be submitted to the Organization and circulated to all Members and all parties before being submitted to an appropriate body by the Organization for consideration, after which the amendments shall be adopted by a two-thirds majority of only the parties to the Convention which are present and voting. In this instance, all parties to the Convention, whether or not members of the IMO, are entitled to participate in the proceedings of the appropriate body – in this case, as mentioned, the MEPC. The MARPOL Convention is a very specific instrument that consists of protocols and six annexes that are optional and therefore require separate acceptance.[51]

It was agreed that MARPOL Annex VI was an appropriate vehicle for enacting mandatory energy efficiency measures to ensure that ships minimised their emissions. The Committee prepared the draft mandatory regulations at the request of a number of States Parties to MARPOL Annex VI, with a view to their adoption at an MEPC meeting. At the subsequent session, the Committee considered all issues relating to the proposed amendments. Fifty-nine of the then sixty-four parties to

---

[50] This discussion was caused by the controversy arising in connection with the adoption of the mandatory global greenhouse gas reduction regime, where two opposite opinions about common but differentiated responsibilities were expressed. Some delegations made statements supporting the principle of common but differentiated responsibilities recognized in the United Nations Framework Convention on Climate Change (UNFCC) and opposing non-differentiated application of energy efficiency measures by both developing and developed countries. However, many delegations thought that common but differentiated responsibilities that apply at the UNFCC cannot apply for shipping due to the fact that the vast majority of ships and shipping companies may have owners in developed countries but be registered in developing countries. This means that the application of common but differentiated responsibilities in the case of the reduction of greenhouse gas from ships would jeopardise the effect of this measure. As a result, it was decided that ships flying the flag of developing countries assume the same responsibilities in maritime emission reduction as developed countries in accordance with the principle of 'no more favourable treatment' (NMFT). See Document MEPC 62/5/10. This principle means that all ships, whether flying the flag of a State Party to a convention or not, shall comply with this convention whilst entering the port of a State Party. See, further, the contribution to this volume of Bowman at pp. 392–439 (Chapter 13).

[51] Originally, the International Convention for the Prevention of Pollution from Ships (MARPOL) was adopted in Nov. 1973, but this treaty has never entered into force. In 1978, a Protocol was adopted which is now treated as a parent convention: 1340 UNTS 61. It has six annexes that deal with different kinds of pollution from ships. Interestingly, some of these annexes are optional and, according to Art. 14(1) of the Convention, a State may at the time of signing, ratifying, accepting, approving or acceding to the Convention declare that it does not accept any or all of Annexes III, IV and V. Subject to this, the parties to the Convention are bound by any annex in its entirety. Annex VI was adopted in 1997 in the form of a Protocol, and therefore requires separate ratification/acceptance. More information is available at www.imo.org.

MARPOL Annex VI were present at the session of the Committee and eligible to vote. The Committee did not reach a consensus and the amendments were eventually adopted by a two-thirds majority of the parties.[52]

However, at the following Assembly meeting – comprising all 170 Member States – the view was expressed by several delegations that the adoption of these amendments was a departure from the established procedures and customs of the IMO; it was stated that consensus was required to adopt this amendment. One delegation stressed that consensus was important when voting eligibility was restricted to sixty-four Member States Parties to MARPOL Annex VI, therefore excluding more than 100 other Member States of the IMO from the decision-making process. Another delegation not only supported this view, but stated that the amendments were actually adopted by a minority. Several countries took the view that the Assembly, as the superior body of the IMO, was entitled to ask the Committee to review the matter in order to find a consensus solution that would reflect Member States' obligations in relation to the IMO and other international instruments and ensure the integrity of the climate change regime.

Nevertheless, the vast majority of delegations was convinced that all the rules of procedure had been duly followed and that the Assembly, although a superior IMO body, did not have the mandate to question a decision taken by the States Parties at the meeting of the Committee.[53] Those delegations insisted that in reaching its decision on energy efficiency requirements, the Committee had complied with its rules of procedure and the amendment procedure required by the MARPOL Convention.

This discussion obviously had a political slant, with the attempt made by several countries to use the Assembly as a forum to overrule the decision taken by States Parties (most of whom were developed countries). This is not an uncommon scenario in the life of an international organization. On this occasion, the interpretation of the provisions of the instrument in compliance with the law of treaties prevailed. But if the political will had been stronger, the treaty-making rules could have been jeopardised. Although the Assembly was fully entitled to express its

---

[52] See Document MEPC 62/24: Report of the Marine Environment Protection Committee on its Sixty-Second Session.

[53] The mandate for the Committee's work is set out in Assembly Resolution A.963 (23) on IMO Policies and Practices Related to the Reduction of Greenhouse Gas Emissions from Ships.

views, it could not overrule the parties to a treaty by modifying it or ordering it to be modified, even though the treaty had been negotiated within the framework of one of the Assembly's subsidiary bodies. It would have set an undesirable and dangerous precedent if the Assembly had condemned a decision made in full compliance with an international treaty by the parties to that treaty.[54]

3.2.1.2 The Role of the MEPC versus that of the Parties

As stated previously, decisions of the Committee are taken by a simple majority of the members of the Committee, but amendments to the MARPOL Convention are eventually adopted (where there is no consensus) by a two-thirds majority of only the parties. At its spring session in 2014, the MEPC debated a proposal to amend Regulation 13 of MARPOL Annex VI. There were three options on the table.[55] In preparation for the session, the need arose to clarify the voting procedure in case the Committee was unable to reach consensus.

Putting aside the question which proposal should be voted first,[56] the main problem was determining who would decide which option to send to the drafting group to be eventually adopted: the Committee or the parties? According to Article 16(2)(c) of the Convention, the Committee shall 'consider' the amendments. Does this 'consideration' also include voting on the options before the final adoption? In other words, is the Committee empowered to impose on the parties the amendment that they will eventually adopt? The Convention is silent on this point. The Rules of Procedure of the MEPC leave it for the Committee to decide on procedural matters, but this is 'subject to the provision of any treaty'.

Bearing in mind that it would be easy for the parties to reject the option preferred by the majority of the Committee if they wished so to do, it

---

[54] IMO Assembly Summary Record of the Seventh Plenary Meeting A27/SR7.

[55] Documents MEPC 66/6/3; MEPC 66/6/6 and MEPC 66/6/10.

[56] One proposal was originally submitted to the previous session of the Committee, already approved and circulated six months prior to the session for adoption, whilst two other proposals were submitted only to this session. The question which proposal should be voted first involved interpretation of Rules 40, 43 and 44 of the Rules of Procedure of MEPC. Rule 40 states that if two or more proposals relate to the same question, the Committee shall vote on the proposals in the order in which they have been submitted – whereas Rule 44 applies to situations when two or more amendments are moved to a proposal and resolves that in this situation the Committee shall first vote on the amendment furthest removed in substance from the original proposal and then on the amendments next furthest removed therefrom, until all amendments have been put to the vote.

seems right that, even at the pre-adoption stage, it is up to the parties to decide which proposal they wish to adopt. Otherwise, the prerogative of the parties would be illusory. If the intention of the parties to the Convention was to empower the Committee to amend treaty provisions, surely this would have been expressly provided. The intention, however, was to empower the Committee to only 'consider' but not to take any decision on the adoption.

In practice, the vast majority of delegations that took part in the considerations within the Committee were parties to MARPOL Annex VI. Eventually, a compromise was reached and the amendments were adopted by consensus.

4   Novel Challenges for the Law of Treaties

The controversies described earlier can at least be fitted reasonably comfortably within the traditional framework within which the law of treaties is traditionally analysed and discussed. In recent years, however, certain problems have arisen which appear to pose a more fundamental challenge to that familiar framework. They relate to provisional application and tacit acceptance as applied in certain recent instruments.

4.1   The Ballast Water and Sediments Convention and Provisional Application of the Tacit Acceptance Procedure

It took more than fourteen years of complex negotiations between IMO Member States to adopt the International Convention for the Control and Management of Ships' Ballast Water and Sediments (BWMC) by consensus in February 2004.[57]

---

[57] IMO Doc BWM/CONF/36, Annex. Since the introduction of steel hulled vessels around 120 years ago, water has been used as ballast to stabilise vessels at sea. Ballast water is pumped in to maintain safe operating conditions throughout a voyage. This practice reduces stress on the hull, provides transverse stability, improves propulsion and manoeuvrability and compensates for weight lost due to fuel and water consumption. While ballast water is essential for safe and efficient modern shipping operations, it may pose serious ecological, economic and health problems due to the multitude of marine species carried in ships' ballast water. These include bacteria, microbes, small invertebrates, eggs, cysts and larvae of various species. The transferred species may survive to establish a reproductive population in the host environment, becoming invasive, out-competing native species and multiplying into pest proportions. The problem of invasive species in ships' ballast water is largely due to the expanded trade and traffic volume over the past few decades and since the volumes of seaborne trade continue to increase, the problem may not yet have reached its peak. The spread of invasive species is now recognised as one

The Convention has not yet come into force, and some of the dates specified for the entry into force of the new standards are already approaching.[58] It will be impossible for ships to comply with the new standards unless the dates are somehow amended. On the basis of Article 25(1)(b) VCLT, which provides for the provisional application of a treaty, one delegation proposed the provisional application of Article 19 BWMC in order to change the dates of implementation of specific regulation of the Convention.[59]

Like Article VIII of the SOLAS Convention, Article 19 BWMC provides for the amendment procedure of the treaty, allowing both the classical amendment procedure and the tacit acceptance procedure outlined previously. The proposal suggests that the Convention could be amended by the provisional application of the tacit acceptance procedure. It states further that this would first require the negotiating States to the BWMC to agree on the provisional application through an Assembly resolution, thereby opening the way to initiating the amendment procedure. The amendment would then be agreed by the MEPC, and it would be binding for all contracting States.[60]

The question of the legality of this proposal was considered by the MEPC. The basic principles concerning provisional application are set out in Article 25 VCLT. The main purpose of provisional application is

---

of the greatest threats to the ecological and the economic well-being of the planet. The Convention aims to prevent the spread of harmful aquatic organisms from one region to another by establishing standards and procedures for the management and control of ships' ballast water and sediments. Under the Convention, all ships in international traffic are required to manage their ballast water and sediments to a certain standard, using a ship-specific ballast water management plan. All ships are also required to carry a ballast water record book and an international ballast water management certificate. The ballast water management standards will be phased in over a period of time. As an intermediate solution, ships need to exchange ballast water mid-ocean. However, most ships will eventually need to install an on-board ballast water treatment system. Source: www.imo.org.

[58] At the time of writing this chapter, there were forty-three contracting parties to the BWMC – meaning that the criterion of the number of States needed for entry into force had been met. However, the second requirement, namely 35 per cent of the world's tonnage, had not yet been met. The BWMC entered into force in Sept. 2017 in accordance with the terms of Art. 18 BWMC.

[59] Regulation B-3 sets a schedule for ships to implement specific requirements of ballast water management depending on the date of the ship's construction.

[60] In the practice of the IMO, recourse to provisional application was made during the privatisation process of INMARSAT in 1990s. At that time consultations with Member States over the issue disclosed that, while many accepted provisional application, others were prevented by their constitutions from doing so without special legislation.

the immediate entry into force of the whole treaty or of certain provisions of a treaty. This practice now appears to be well-established in international law.[61] There are two ways of securing provisional application. The treaty itself may provide for provisional application; the clause enabling this would normally be stipulated in the final provisions of the treaty. An alternative procedure that would have the same effect would be for the States concerned to enter into an agreement in a separate protocol or in some other manner to bring the treaty into force provisionally without having to insert such a clause into the treaty itself.[62]

Provisional application is utilised when there is some urgency to implement a treaty or some of its provisions before the treaty is ratified and definitively enters into force. It is also used where the negotiators are certain that the treaty will obtain the domestic approval required for ratification; to achieve continuity between successive treaty regimes; to attain consistency of obligations among the parties when amending or modifying the treaty; to circumvent political or other obstacles to the entry into force of a treaty or, in the context of preparatory institutional arrangements, for a new international organization.

Unfortunately, Article 25 VCLT lacks legal precision. Nothing in the Vienna Convention expressly defines 'provisional application' or indicates what it means for a treaty (or part thereof) to be 'applied provisionally'. There are also no rules on the point in time when the agreement on provisional application should be concluded.[63] The agreement to apply a treaty provisionally is either included in the treaty itself or its conclusion immediately follows the adoption of a treaty. In practice, provisional application means the immediate application of the substantive rules contained in the treaty. It has been a well-established rule in the history of provisional application that only the substantive provisions of a treaty may be provisionally applied. In relation to the provisional application of final clauses, G. G. Fitzmaurice stated that 'prior to its entry into force, a treaty has an operative effect ... so far as concerns those of its provisions that

---

[61] See, further, the contribution to this volume of Quast Mertsch at pp. 303–334 (Chapter 10).

[62] See Elias, *supra* n. 36, at p. 38.

[63] Report of the Correspondence Group on the Assembly resolution on the Application of the International Convention for the Control and Management of Ships' Ballast Water and Sediments: MEPC 65/2/11 (2004).

regulate the processes of ratification, acceptance and similar matters, and the date and manner of entry into force itself'.[64]

The BWMC does not provide for provisional application, as the negotiating States did not foresee the need for it. An additional agreement between negotiating States would therefore have to be concluded in order to provisionally apply the Convention in whole or in part. Assuming there is a will to apply Article 19 BWMC provisionally, questions about who would conclude the agreement on provisional application – as well as who would amend the Convention – would be raised. The Vienna Convention on the Law of Treaties provides that only negotiating States can agree on provisional application and defines the 'negotiating State' as a State which takes part in drawing up and adopting the text of a treaty.[65] Therefore, those States present at the diplomatic conference in 2004 would have to decide on provisional application. Some of these States would certainly not agree to it as their domestic law does not provide for such a possibility.[66] The proposal suggested that the negotiating States that agree on provisional application would subsequently be treated as 'States Parties' to the Convention. However, at the time that this proposal was considered, there were thirty-nine contracting States that have already expressed their consent to be bound by the BWMC. If some of those States did not agree on provisional application, this would mean that a (negotiating) State that was not bound by the

---

[64] G. G. Fitzmaurice, First Report on the Law of Treaties, Doc. A/CN.4/101 (14 March 1956), p. 116. He further stated that 'logically, a treaty which, *ex hypothesi*, is not yet in force cannot provide for its own entry into force – since, until that occurs, the clause so providing can itself have no force. . . . by tacit assumption invariably made, the clauses of a treaty providing for ratification, accession, entry into force, and certain other possible matters, are deemed to come into force separately and at once, on signature – or are treated as if they did – even though the substance of a treaty does not'. For more information on the considerations of the International Law Commission in that matter, see Sinclair, *supra* n. 26, at p. 45.

[65] The full provision – of Art. 25 VCLT – reads:

  1. A treaty or a part of a treaty is applied provisionally pending its entry into force if:
     a. The treaty itself so provides; or
     b. The negotiating States have in some other manner so agreed.
  2. Unless the treaty otherwise provides or the negotiating States have otherwise agreed, the provisional application of a treaty or a part of a treaty with respect to a State shall be terminated if that State notifies the other States between which the treaty is being applied provisionally of its intention not to become a party to the treaty.

  See *supra* n. 11.

[66] Provisional application clauses are not generally favoured, since many States still have to obtain parliamentary consent on provisional application: Aust, *supra* n. 23, at pp. 154–156.

whole treaty but only by one, provisionally applied, article (i.e. Article 19 BWMC) would have the right to amend the treaty, while a State that is a contracting State but has not agreed on the provisional application of Article 19 BWMC would have no right to amend the treaty. This would be a highly undesirable situation.

As stated previously, only the substantive provisions of a treaty may normally be applied provisionally. In this case, it was proposed that only the article that provides for the tacit acceptance procedure would be so applied. Although Article 25 VCLT does not limit provisional application to substantive articles only,[67] this experience has been unique since it involves the provisional application of a procedural provision.

It should be strongly emphasised that the amendment procedure cannot be applied while the Convention is not in force. Only States Parties to the Convention have the right to amend it. States that have agreed to provisionally apply only one article should not have the right to amend the whole treaty. A formal proposal to amend the Convention has to come from the parties after the entry into force of the Convention, so that the amendment procedure can be put into motion. The proposed interpretation of Article 25 VCLT jeopardises the general rule that only parties can amend a treaty (Article 39 VCLT), as there are no parties until the Convention is in force (Article 2(1)(g) VCLT defines a 'party' as 'a State which has consented to be bound by the treaty and for which the treaty is in force'). Therefore, the amendment procedure of Article 19 BWMC cannot be applied before the Convention enters into force.

The provisional application of multilateral treaties creates major uncertainties. The international rules on provisional application should certainly be interpreted to facilitate the entry into force of a treaty, but not at the price of confusion about the legal consequences concerning the rights and obligations of negotiating States, contracting States and States Parties. The option of provisional application should also not be used to jeopardise the amendment procedure of a treaty. The proposed selective provisional application – which only some States might accept – would also lead to inconsistency and uncertainty about the application of the whole treaty. The amendment procedure provided for in Article 19 BWMC makes immediate amendment impossible, since in order for the amendment to come into force a considerable amount of time is required, which makes the provisional application pointless in any event.

[67] *Supra* n. 65.

4.2 The New Regulation on Polar Shipping: Using Tacit Acceptance to Bring a 'New Treaty' into Force

The melting of the perennial sea ice cover has accelerated since the late 1990s and the loss of seasonal sea ice is opening new shipping routes.[68] The possibility of intense vessel traffic has raised concerns about the safety of navigation in polar areas as well as the protection of this very sensitive environment.[69] A Canadian proposal to develop a mandatory instrument regulating shipping in Arctic waters has been deliberated for more than twenty years.[70] Meanwhile, the Guidelines for Ships Operating in Arctic Ice-Covered Waters were adopted by the MSC and MEPC in December 2002.[71] This is known as the Polar Code.

The proposed Polar Code includes certain requirements that fall within the existing subject matter of the SOLAS Convention and some that fall within the MARPOL Convention (Annexes I to VI), the BWMC and the 2001 International Convention on the Control of Anti-Fouling Systems for Ships (AFS).[72] During the consideration of the Code, the question arose as to how it could be made mandatory.[73]

The first option to make this Code mandatory was to amend the SOLAS Convention by adding a new chapter on ships operating in polar waters, in which the entire Code – in the form of an Assembly resolution – would be incorporated by reference in the regulations and subject to the tacit acceptance procedures of the SOLAS Convention. The main advantage of this solution was that the Code could be brought into force and implemented as a stand-alone document under a single existing convention through the efficiency of the tacit acceptance procedures of Article VIII(b). However, this option also had several

---

[68] W. Maslowski, J. C. Kinney, M. Higgins and A. Roberts, 'The Future of the Arctic Sea Ice', *Annual Rev. Earth & Planetary Sci.*, 40 (2012), 625–654.

[69] A. Johnston, M. Johnston, J. Dawson and E. Stewart, 'Challenges of Arctic Cruise Tourism Development in Canada: Perspectives of Federal Government Stakeholders', *J. Maritime L. & Comm.*, 43 (2012), 335–347.

[70] P. Kikkert, 'Promoting National Interest and Fostering Cooperation: Canada and the Development of a Polar Code', *J. Maritime L. & Comm.*, 43 (2012), 319–334.

[71] IMO Maritime Safety Committee Circular 1056 and Marine Environment Protection Committee Circular 399.

[72] IMO Doc. AFS/CONF/26.

[73] The challenge of amending several treaties simultaneously in order to incorporate a single, uniform modification has been encountered in other contexts as well, e.g. the human rights context: see M.J. Bowman, 'Towards a Unified Treaty Body for Monitoring Compliance with UN Human Rights Conventions? Legal Mechanisms for Treaty Reform', *HRLR*, 7 (2007), 225–249.

disadvantages: the Code would be subject to the scope of application of the SOLAS Convention – that is, only to ships engaged on international voyages except where otherwise provided – and some States Parties to the SOLAS Convention might not be happy with including an issue that primarily relates to environmental protection within the framework of SOLAS. This material would not be germane to the overall object and purpose of SOLAS,[74] and the full range of new requirements might not fall neatly into the structure of their domestic legislation.

A second option was to expand the scope of the amendment process by (a) adding a new chapter to the SOLAS Convention on ships operating in polar waters to make parts of the Code relating to ship safety mandatory; (b) amending one or more annexes of the MARPOL Convention to address ships operating in polar waters, depending on the subject matter of the new requirements and subject to the germaneness requirement of Article 16(7) in order to address the environmental protection aspects of the Code; (c) amending the AFS Convention to address anti-fouling issues which are specific to polar waters under the Code and (d) developing amendments to the BWMC to be held for adoption once the Convention comes into force. This approach would address the key safety and environmental protection aspects of the Code. But the entry into force of the Code would be fragmented, with different sets of States Parties and different timelines and procedures for entry into force of any future revisions to the Code.

A third option was to develop a new convention altogether on ships operating in polar waters with the Code either (a) incorporated by reference and subject to the amendment requirements of the new convention or (b) attached as an annex to the new convention. This new convention could explicitly state that its requirements are in addition to those that might apply to a particular ship pursuant to the SOLAS, MARPOL, BWM(C) and AFS Conventions.[75]

The main advantage of this last option was that the full range of supplementary requirements for ships operating in polar waters, whether related to safety or environmental protection, would be covered by a single instrument. However, depending on the entry into force requirements, the date when the Code becomes mandatory would be uncertain. In addition, the Code would not apply to ships entitled to fly the flag of

---

[74] See, further, the contribution to this volume of Kritsiotis at pp. 237–302 (Chapter 9).
[75] These options were discussed at the MEPC meeting in May 2011. See Document: MEPC 62/11/4.Add.1.

States not party to the new convention (except to the extent the NMFT principle might apply under Port State Control provisions).[76]

Although there is a need for comprehensive regulation of polar shipping, the IMO Member States did not agree on the adoption of a new treaty. The trivial reason was that even if adopted, the new free-standing treaty would have very little chance of ever coming into force, as it would only directly serve the interest of a handful of States.[77] It was therefore decided that it would be much more practical to dissect the Code and adopt it in the form of annexes to the existing treaties using the tacit acceptance procedure.[78]

5   Conclusion

The broadly stated provisions of the VCLT do not answer all possible questions, or even give guidance for the solution of all of the practical treaty-related problems arising within the life of an international organization. This chapter has made this point evident with particular respect to the International Maritime Organization. The clear intention of States has been to embrace a very practical path in order to respond to the challenges of a complex and rapidly changing world. The practice of States Parties to the various IMO treaties with regard to the amendment process, for example, has created a new approach to the adoption of a treaty. The 'classical' procedures concerning treaty adoption and amendment no longer seem to be the practical way of reaching agreement in multilateral relationships. Instead, States have chosen to circumvent time-consuming methods by adopting innovative schemes and strategies involving tacit acceptance.

As already mentioned, tacit acceptance was originally designed for adopting new technical requirements resulting from rapidly changing technology. It is now also used to increase the limits of liability, to add

---

[76] On NMFT – no more favourable treatment – see *supra* n. 50.

[77] There are nine Member States of the IMO interested in regulating the shipping in polar areas: Argentina, Canada, Denmark/Greenland, Finland, Iceland, Norway, the Russian Federation, Sweden and the United States.

[78] In Nov. 2014, at its Ninety-Fourth Session, the Maritime Safety Committee adopted the safety part of the Polar Code. It also adopted an amendment to the SOLAS Convention, adding a new Chapter XIV through which the Code will be made mandatory: see Resolutions MSC.385(94) and MSC.386(94). At is Sixty-Eighth Session in May 2015, the Marine Environment Protection Committee adopted the environmental part of the Code and the associated MARPOL amendments: see Resolutions MEPC.264(68) and MEPC.265(68). The Polar Code entered into force in Jan. 2017 by virtue of the tacit acceptance procedure.

new chapters to treaties (in the form of annexes) and even, perhaps, to adopt a 'new treaty' (again in the form of annexes to an existing treaty). Tacit acceptance is now so appealing to States that it was even proposed to provisionally apply one article of a treaty providing for this simplified amendment procedure in order to amend the treaty before its entry into force.

The question arises as to whether use of the tacit acceptance procedure in all cases where there is a need to amend a treaty, or even adopt a new convention, fully complies with the law of treaties, as codified by the Vienna Convention on the Law of Treaties. It could be argued that tacit acceptance as a procedural rule has its roots in the standard concept of acquiescence in international law. Acquiescence takes the form of silence or the absence of protest in circumstances which generally call for a positive reaction signifying an objection. Tacit acceptance is a procedure written into the treaty through which the States Parties to that treaty *prima facie* agree on its application by expressing their consent to be bound. States that agreed to adopt a treaty providing for tacit acceptance of amendments have in effect already given their consent for this procedure to be applied in the future. These States may always object to amendments so adopted, thereby excluding themselves form their application and if a sufficient number of States do so object, the amendment will not enter into force at all. However, in the practice of an international organization, it may well be that States do not always object to the application of such a procedure even in circumstances where it goes beyond the original purpose for which that procedure was established and may therefore seem to jeopardise certain basic principles of the law of treaties.

29

The European Union

PANOS KOUTRAKOS

1 Introduction

The relationship between the law of treaties and the European Union (EU) may be approached in different ways. These may include the extent to which the European Court of Justice (ECJ) draws upon the 1969 Vienna Convention on the Law of Treaties (VCLT)[1] in its case law.[2] This chapter will adopt a broader approach and will examine the function of treaties within the Union's deeply idiosyncratic legal order. Its focus will be two-fold: it will examine the treaties which set out the primary rules governing the EU and their role as the foundation of the contested nature of the Union on the basis of the case law of the Court of Justice; it will also provide an overview of the treaty-making activity of the Union and will highlight the process of the negotiation, conclusion and application of treaties as a legal terrain in which EU institutions and the Member States compete for an increased international presence.

This chapter is structured in four main parts. First, it returns to the nature of the EU as a creature of international law and examines the elevated status that the Union's constitutive treaties have acquired over the years. Secondly, it outlines the range of treaties which the European Union concludes and identifies some threads in the Union's practice. Thirdly, it focuses on the internal challenges for the EU and its Member States that treaty-making raises. Fourthly, it examines the implications of treaty-making for the legal position of Member States as a matter of EU law and explores the different ways in which the Union's treaty-making activity imposes constraints on the international role of Member States.

---

[1] 1155 UNTS 331.

[2] See P. J. Kuijper, 'The European Courts and the Law of Treaties: The Continuing Story' in E. Cannizzaro (ed.), *The Law of Treaties beyond the Vienna Convention* (Oxford: Oxford University Press, 2011), pp. 256–278.

2   The Internal Function: Treaties as the Foundation
of the European Union

It is a fact sometimes forgotten by fervent federalists that the European
Union is based on a treaty. Signed on 25 March 1957, the Treaty of Rome
entered into force on 1 January 1958 and created the European Economic
Community, that is, what may have appeared to be yet another international organization.[3] And yet, it took the Court of Justice only five years
to make it clear that that treaty was fundamentally distinct from all other
treaties. In its first seminal judgment, in *Van Gend en Loos*
in February 1963, the Court of Justice stressed the centrality of the legal
position of individuals under the new legal rules and held that:

> the Community constitutes a new legal order of international law for the
> benefit of which the states have limited their sovereign rights, albeit within
> limited fields, and the subjects of which comprise not only Member States
> but also their nationals.[4]

Having pointed out both the international law foundation and the ambitious scope of the Community, the Court highlighted with stark clarity
the unique character of the Treaty of Rome in *Costa* the following year:

> By contrast with ordinary international treaties, the EEC Treaty has
> created its own legal system which, on the entry into force of the Treaty,
> became an integral part of the legal systems of the Member States and
> which their courts are bound to apply.[5]

Having underlined the extraordinary character of the Community's
constitutive document, the preceding extract suggests that the system
which the latter establishes is somewhat autonomous. This is partly based
on its specific legal features and their normative implications for the
Member States:

> By creating a Community of unlimited duration, having its own
> institutions, its own personality, its own legal capacity and capacity
> of representation on the international plane and, more particularly,
> real powers stemming from a limitation of sovereignty or a transfer
> of powers from the States to the Community, the Member States have
> limited their sovereign rights, albeit within limited fields, and have
> thus created a body of law which binds both their nationals and
> themselves.[6]

---

[3] 298 UNTS 3.
[4] Case 26/62 *Van Gend en Loos v. Nederlandse Tariefcommissie* [1963] ECR 1.
[5] Case C-6/64 *Costa v. ENEL* [1964] ECR 585, at p. 593.   [6] *Ibid.*

These specific legal characteristics of the Treaty, on the one hand, and the transfer of sovereignty which they entail, on the other, are viewed as the foundations of the autonomy of the Community, and later the Union, legal system:

> ... the law stemming from the Treaty, an independent source of law, could not, because of its special and original nature, be overridden by domestic legal provisions, however framed, without being deprived of its character as Community law and without the legal basis of the Community itself being called into question.[7]

The notion of the Union legal order as a distinct part of international law gave rise to a process of constitutionalisation which then led gradually and inexorably to the constitutional maturity and complexity of the current EU legal order.[8] It has enabled the Court of Justice to introduce the main principles which shape the relationship between the EU legal order and the Member States and which also determine the legal status of individuals. In addition to the principles of supremacy and direct effect, mentioned previously,[9] such principles include the liability of national authorities for a violation of EU law,[10] the gradual transformation of national courts into EU courts,[11] and the reliance upon general principles and fundamental human rights as a matter of EU law against both EU and national measures.[12]

This development of the internal characteristics of the EU[13] has been premised on the constitutional function which the Court of Justice attributes to the Treaty setting out the primary rules of the Union. First

---

[7] *Ibid.*

[8] On the notion of the treaty as a living instrument, see the contribution to this volume of Moeckli and White at pp. 136–171 (Chapter 6).

[9] See A. Dashwood, 'From *Van Duyn* to *Mangold* via *Marshall*: Reducing Direct Effect to Absurdity?', *CYbELS*, 9 (2006–2007), 81–109.

[10] See M. Dougan, 'The Vicissitudes of Life at the Coalface: Remedies and Procedures for Enforcing Union Law before the National Courts' in G. de Búrca and P. Craig (eds.), *The Evolution of EU Law* (Oxford: Oxford University Press, 2nd ed., 2011), pp. 407–438.

[11] See A. Arnull, 'Judicial Dialogue in the European Union' in J. Dickson and P. Eleftheriadis (eds.), *Philosophical Foundations of European Union Law* (Oxford: Oxford University Press, 2012), pp. 109–133.

[12] See G. de Búrca, 'The Evolution of EU Human Rights Law' in de Búrca and Craig (eds.), *supra* n. 10, pp. 465–498, and T. Tridimas, *The General Principles of EU Law* (Oxford: Oxford University Press, 2nd ed., 2006).

[13] For an analysis of this process, see K. Alter, *Establishing the Supremacy of European Law: The Making of an International Rule of Law in Europe* (Oxford: Oxford University Press, 2001) and B. de Witte, 'Direct Effect, Primacy, and the Nature of the Legal Order' in de Búrca and Craig (eds.), *supra* n. 10, pp. 323–362.

reflected by its interpretation and application over the years, this function was acknowledged expressly in the early 1990s. Addressing the question of whether the conclusion of the 1992 European Economic Area (EEA) Agreement[14] and the adjudication system which it provided were consistent with the Community's rules of that time, the Court referred to the Community's founding Treaty, as amended by the Single European Act in 1987, as 'the constitutional charter of the Community based on the rule of law'.[15]

This notion of autonomy attracted attention more recently when the Court of Justice relied upon it and, rather spectacularly, annulled EU measures implementing United Nations Security Council Resolutions requiring the freezing of assets of individuals and organizations suspected of financing international terrorism. The story of the case law of the Court and its aftermath has been told often and well.[16] For the purposes of this analysis, suffice it to focus on the main thread of the line of reasoning in *Kadi I*:

> an international agreement cannot affect the allocation of powers fixed by the Treaties or, consequently, the autonomy of the Community legal system, observance of which is ensured by the Court by virtue of the exclusive jurisdiction conferred on it by Article 220 EC [now Article 19 TEU], jurisdiction that the Court has, moreover, already held to form part of the very foundations of the Community (see, to that effect, *Opinion 1/91* [1991] ECR I-6079, paragraphs 35 and 71, and Case C-459/03 *Commission v Ireland* [2006] ECR I-4635, paragraph 123 and case law cited).[17]

The notion of autonomy set out in *Kadi* in the late 2000s may appear to serve a different function from that first referred to in *Costa* in the early 1960s. The latter was intended to bolster the normative features of the nascent legal order in order to enable it to withstand challenges from national law. The former was intended to protect one of the main policy characteristics of the mature legal order from interference originating beyond the Union. Whilst apparently distinct, these internal and external

---

[14] 1801 UNTS 3.

[15] *Opinion 1/91 (re: EEA Agreement)* [1991] ECR I-6079 (paragraph 21).

[16] See, for instance, G. de Búrca, 'The EU, the European Court of Justice and the International Legal Order after *Kadi*', *Harvard ILJ*, 51 (2010), 1–49; C. Eckes, *EU Counter-Terrorist Policies and Fundamental Rights: The Case of Individual Sanctions* (Oxford: Oxford University Press, 2009) and T. Tridimas, 'Terrorism and the ECJ: Empowerment and Democracy in the EC Legal Order', *European L. Rev.*, 34 (2009), 103–126.

[17] Joined Cases C-402/05 P and C-415/05 P *Kadi and Al Barakaat* [2008] ECR I-6351 (paragraph 280).

functions of autonomy[18] are not easy to distinguish. This is the case not only in conceptual but also in policy terms. After all, the EU's judges render their judgment with an eye to national courts and, in the *Kadi* cases,[19] in full awareness of the potential role that national judges might be called upon to assume if judicial review in Luxembourg was viewed as deficient. Be that as it may, the emphasis of the Court of Justice on the autonomy of the EU legal order has been criticised as being underpinned by a certain hostility to international law. In particular, it has been viewed as indicative of a long-standing approach which has enabled the EU's judiciary to be, at best, selective in its reliance upon and application of international law.[20]

It is noteworthy that, in its construction of autonomy, the Court of Justice is at pains to refrain from any hierarchy-based assessment of the Union legal order in its relationship with international law. In fact, both judgments in *Kadi I* and *II* stress that the constitutional foundations of the Union legal order as set out in its constitutive Treaties bestow upon the EU courts jurisdiction which is confined to ascertaining compliance of EU acts with fundamental human rights. According to the judgment in *Kadi I*:

> any judgment given by the Community judicature deciding that a Community measure intended to give effect to such a resolution [adopted by the United Nations Security Council] is contrary to a higher rule of law in the Community legal order would not entail any challenge to the primacy of that resolution in international law.[21]

This attempt to separate strictly judicial review of United Nations law from that of EU measures implementing United Nations law is a constant thread of the judgment:

---

[18] See J. W. van Rossem, 'The Autonomy of EU Law: More Is Less?' in R. A. Wessel and S. Blockmans (eds.), *Between Autonomy and Dependence: The EU Legal Order under the Influence of International Organisations* (Berlin: Springer, 2013), pp. 13–46, at p. 17. On the idea of an 'objective regime' in the law of treaties, see the contribution to this volume of Waibel at pp. 201–236 (Chapter 8).

[19] See, also, Joined Cases C-584/10 P, C-593/10 P and C-595/10 P *Kadi II*, ECLI:EU:C:2013:518 (where the Court annulled, on appeal, the delisting of Kadi on the grounds of violation of fundamental human rights by the EU institutions).

[20] See G. de Búrca, 'The ECJ and the International Legal Order: A Re-evaluation' in G. de Búrca and J. H. H. Weiler (eds.), *The Worlds of European Constitutionalism* (Cambridge: Cambridge University Press, 2012), pp. 105–149, and J. Klabbers, 'Völkerrechtsfreundlich? International Law and the Union Legal Order' in P. Koutrakos (ed.), *European Foreign Policy – Legal and Political Perspectives* (Cheltenham: Edward Elgar, 2011), pp. 95–114.

[21] Joined Cases C-402/05 P and C-415/05 P *Kadi, supra* n. 17 (paragraph 288).

It is not a consequence of the principles governing the international legal order under the United Nations that any judicial review of the internal lawfulness of the contested regulation in the light of fundamental freedoms is excluded by virtue of the fact that that measure is intended to give effect to a resolution of the Security Council adopted under Chapter VII of the Charter of the United Nations.[22]

The logic of this approach is based on the premise that the special status of the Treaties establishing the EU and the ensuing autonomy of EU law would not amount to a threat to the principle of international law and the hierarchies which this has introduced.[23] In fact, this underpins the entire body of the Court's case law on smart sanctions.[24] This approach reminds us that the EU's judiciary is not prepared to interpret the autonomy of the legal order as a normative construct which would remove EU law from international law. It also enables the Court to maintain its 'wisely agnostic attitude' on the nature of the Union's legal order.[25] This is supported by the rules on the revision of the Treaty of European Union (TEU)[26] and the Treaty on the Functioning of the European Union (TFEU) – last amended by the Treaty of Lisbon.[27] Set out in Article 48 TEU and providing for a complex set of procedures, these rules reflect the public international law character of the EU's constitutive Treaties and the central position of the Member States which must ratify any Treaty amendment subject to their individual constitutional requirements. The Lisbon Treaty introduces for the first time simplified revision procedures (Article 48(6)–(7) TFEU) which facilitate the amendments of parts of TEU and TFEU subject to a unanimous decision of the European Council. However, these may not be relied upon in order to transfer further competences from the Member States to the Union.[28]

---

[22] *Ibid.* (paragraph 299).

[23] See, also, the analysis in G. Pavlakos and J. Pauwelyn, 'Principled Monism and the Normative Conception of Coercion under International Law' in M. Evans and P. Koutrakos (eds.), *Beyond the Established Legal Orders: Policy Interconnections Between the EU and the Rest of the World* (Oxford: Hart Publishing, 2011), pp. 317–341.

[24] See Case C-548/09 P *Bank Melli Iran v. Council* [2011] ECR I–11381 (paragraph 105) and Joined Cases C-584/10 P, C-593/10 P and C-595/10 P *Kadi II, supra* n. 19 (paragraph 67).

[25] B. de Witte, 'The European Union as an International Legal Experiment' in de Búrca and Weiler (eds.), *supra* n. 20, pp. 19–56, at p. 41.

[26] 1747 UNTS 3.   [27] 2008 OJ C 115/47.

[28] One such amendment has been made by the European Council Decision 2011/199/EU ([2011] OJ L 91/1) adding a third paragraph to Art. 136 TFEU about the establishment of a stability mechanism by Member States whose currency is the euro. This amendment, and its basis on Art. 48(6) TFEU, were sanctioned by the Court in Case C-370/12 *Pringle* ECLI:EU:C:2012:756.

The interpretation of the principle of the autonomy of the EU legal order by the Court of Justice has a strong institutional, or rather self-referential, dimension.[29] Whilst it accepts, in principle, that a treaty setting up a judicial body with jurisdiction binding on the institutions of the parties, including the EU's judiciary, may be compatible with the EU's primary rules, the Court of Justice has been less than enthusiastic in its approach to such arrangements in practice. In *Opinion 1/91*, it rejected the draft agreement establishing the European Economic Area because it would set up a court which could end up ruling on the division of competence between the EU and the Member States.[30] In *Mox Plant*, the initiation of a dispute between two EU Member States before an arbitral tribunal set up under the 1982 United Nations Convention on the Law of Sea[31] was deemed to 'involve a manifest risk that the jurisdictional order laid down in the treaties and, consequently, the autonomy of the Community legal system may be adversely affected'.[32] In *Opinion 1/09*, it held that the establishment of a European and Community Patents Court would impinge on the right of national courts to refer questions about EU patent law to the Court of Justice.[33]

More recently, in December 2014, and most controversially, the Court held in *Opinion 2/13* that the draft agreement on the Union's accession to the European Convention of Human Rights (ECHR), negotiated between 2010 and 2013, was incompatible with the Union's primary law.[34] This Opinion provides one of the most comprehensive statements on the autonomy of EU law. In an analysis starting from the very beginning of European integration, with references to the *van Gend en Loos* and *Costa* judgments, the Court held that the essential characteristics of EU law 'have given rise to a structured network of principles, rules and mutually interdependent legal relations linking the EU and its Member States, and its Member States with each other'.[35] The powers of the Court are central to the functioning of this network and an international agreement may affect them 'only if the indispensable conditions for safeguarding the essential character of those powers are satisfied and, consequently, there

---

[29] De Witte refers to 'a subtext of selfishness': B. de Witte, 'A Selfish Court? The Court of Justice and the Design of International Dispute Settlement beyond the European Union' in M. Cremona and A. Thies (eds.), *The European Court of Justice and External Relations Law: Constitutional Challenges* (Oxford: Hart Publishing, 2014), pp. 33–46, at p. 39.

[30] *Opinion 1/91, supra* n. 15.   [31] 1833 UNTS 3.

[32] Case C-459/03 *Commission v. Ireland (re: Mox Plant)* [2006] ECR I–4635 (paragraph 154).

[33] *Opinion 1/09* [2011] ECR I–1137.   [34] *Opinion 2/13* ECLI:EU:C:2014:2454.

[35] *Ibid.* (paragraph 167).

is no adverse effect on the autonomy of the EU legal order'.[36] In practical terms, this meant that 'it should not be possible for the [European Court of Human Rights] to call into question the Court's findings in relation to the scope *ratione materiae* of EU law, for the purposes, in particular, of determining whether a Member State is bound by fundamental rights of the EU'.[37] The Court concluded that its jurisdiction would be undermined by the draft agreement: it would not be in a position to guarantee at all times that national standards of protection of fundamental rights would not compromise the level of protection provided for by the Union's Charter of Fundamental Rights[38] or the primacy, unity and effectiveness of EU law;[39] the application of the Convention would violate the principle of mutual trust as it would compromise the assumption that every EU Member State observes fundamental rights; a procedure in the draft agreement about the Court's prior involvement might risk circumventing the preliminary reference procedure laid down in Article 267 TFEU.[40]

Whilst ostensibly about the protection of human rights and the implementation of Article 6(2) TEU which requires that the Union should accede to ECHR, *Opinion 2/13* is not really about human rights. It is about the institutional and procedural arrangements negotiated carefully – and with input from the Court of Justice itself – in order to ensure that the interpretation of EU law would be a matter left for the Court of Justice. The concept of autonomy is, therefore, viewed through a narrow Court-centred lens, and the co-operation with the European Court of Human Rights is treated suspiciously, even though the relationship between the two courts has been deeply symbiotic.

---

[36] *Ibid.* (paragraph 183).   [37] *Ibid.* (paragraph 186).   [38] 2010 OJ C 83/02.

[39] The Court referred to Case C-399/11 *Melloni* EU:C:2013:107 (paragraph 60).

[40] The Court also held that that draft agreement compromised its exclusive jurisdiction under Art. 344 TFEU and found problematic other parts of the agreement setting out an elaborate co-respondent mechanism before the European Court of Human Rights and providing for the ECJ's prior involvement. For an analysis of the draft agreement, see J. Heliskoski, 'The Arrangement Governing the Relationship between the ECtHR and the CJEU in the Draft Treaty on the Accession of the EU to the ECHR' in Cremona and Thies (eds.), *supra* n. 29, pp. 223–248, and T. Lock, 'Walking on a Tightrope: The Draft ECHR Accession Agreement and the Autonomy of the EU Legal Order', *Common Market L. Rev.*, 48 (2011), 1025–1054. See, also, P. Gragl, *The Accession of the European Union to the European Convention on Human Rights* (Oxford: Hart Publishing, 2013).

3   The External Function: Treaties as an Instrument for Policy-Making

The analysis so far has focused on the internal function of the Treaty establishing the then European Economic Community and all the subsequent treaties amending and replacing it, up to and including the current Treaty on the European Union and the Treaty on the Functioning of the European Union. Setting out the primary rules which govern the EU, these Treaties have been viewed by the European courts as constitutional documents which establish the autonomy of the EU legal order, the latter being understood in terms of its relationship with both national and international law. This section broadens up its approach and focuses on treaties negotiated, concluded and applied by the European Union in its capacity as a subject of international law.

Over the years, the Union has been an active player on the international scene. Both the number and the range of treaties negotiated and concluded by the EU are impressive.[41] In the period between 1 January 2009 and 30 June 2012, it signed 118 treaties.[42] This is not surprising given the ambition which the Union exudes when it comes to its international role. For instance, the Laeken Declaration on the Future of the European Union, initiating the process of reform of the Union's Treaties in 2001 which led to the Treaty of Lisbon, referred prominently to 'Europe's new role in a globalised world' and raised the question: 'Does Europe not, now that is finally unified, have a leading role to play in a new world order, that of a power able both to play a stabilising role worldwide and to point the way ahead for many countries and peoples?'[43]

Its treaty-making record covers, amongst others: treaties which pursue integration in well-defined areas and whose normative characteristics follow closely the EU constitutional and policy framework;[44]

---

[41] See the treaties office database of the European External Action Service: http://ec.europa.eu/world/agreements/default.home.do. On the factors which may determine whether the EU would act by negotiating an international agreement or adopt unilateral legislation, see B. de Witte and A. Thies, 'Why Choose Europe? The Place of the European Union in the Architecture of International Legal Cooperation' in B. Van Vooren, S. Blockmans and J. Wouters (eds.), *The EU's Role in Global Governance: The Legal Dimension* (Oxford: Oxford University Press, 2013), pp. 23–38.

[42] These figures are based on the treaties office database on the website of the European External Action Service.

[43] European Council, 14–15 Dec. 2001, 2.

[44] See the European Economic Area Agreement: [1994] OJ L 1/3. See the analysis in T. Blanchet, R. Piipponen and M. Westman-Clément, *The Agreement on the European Economic Area (EEA)* (Oxford: Clarendon Press, 1994).

association agreements which were then transformed into instruments of eventual accession to the Union;[45] treaties establishing an association with groups of countries with which Member States have had historical links;[46] stabilisation and association treaties with the West Balkan countries which were negotiated following the end of the civil wars occurring there in the 1990s;[47] association treaties with the countries in the Mediterranean region (the Euro-Mediterranean Agreements);[48] treaties with countries from the former Soviet Union (the Partnership and Cooperation Agreements);[49] framework cooperation treaties providing for trade and economic cooperation[50] and cooperation treaties.[51]

An exhaustive analysis of the treaty-making activity of the Union is beyond the scope of this chapter.[52] Instead, this analysis will highlight certain threads which have emerged recently. The Union has shown over the years a preference for the development of increasingly structured frameworks of cooperation with groups of countries whose geography and political circumstances give rise to common policy interests. Examples of such structured cooperation include the Union for the Mediterranean, which covers the countries in North Africa and the Middle East,[53] and the Stabilisation and Association Process, which

---

[45] See, for instance, the association agreements with the Central and Eastern European countries which acceded in the 2000s (such as Hungary: [1993] OJ L 347/2). See, more generally, M. Cremona (ed.), *The Enlargement of the European Union* (Oxford: Oxford University Press, 2003) and C. Hillion (ed.), *EU Enlargement: A Legal Approach* (Oxford: Hart Publishing, 2004).

[46] See the Cotonou Agreement with the Caribbean, Pacific and African countries in [2000] OJ L 317/3.

[47] See, for instance, the treaty with the Former Yugoslav Republic of Macedonia in [2004] OJ L 84/13.

[48] See, for instance, the treaty with Jordan in [2002] OJ L 129/3.

[49] See, for instance, the treaty with Ukraine in [1998] OJ L 49/3.

[50] See, for instance, the treaty with Brazil in [1995] OJ L 262/54.

[51] See, for instance, the treaty with Cambodia in [1999] OJ L 269/18.

[52] For a typology of treaties concluded by the EU, see *Commentaire Megret* (Vol. 12: Relations extérieures) (Brussels: Editions de l'université de Bruxelles, 2005), pp. 293–324. For an analysis of bilateral treaties in particular, see M. Maresceau, 'Bilateral Agreements Concluded by the European Community', *Hague Recueil*, 309 (2004), 125–451. For an analysis of the links between the EU third countries, see P. Koutrakos, *EU International Relations* (Oxford: Hart Publishing, 2nd ed., 2015), pp. 379–407.

[53] See the principles for its establishment as set out in the Paris Summit for the Mediterranean (July 2008) (www.ue2008.fr/webdav/site/PFUE/shared/import/07/0713_declaration_de_paris/Joint_declaration_of_the_Paris_summit_for_the_Mediterranean-EN.pdf).

covers West Balkan countries.[54] These initiatives grew organically from the conclusion and application of agreements concluded between the EU and its Member States and the third countries concerned, namely the Euro-Mediterranean Agreements in the case of the Union for the Mediterranean, and the Stabilisation and Association Agreements in the case of the Stabilisation and Association Process. These agreements are still the nucleus of the structured forms of cooperation around which the contracting parties have established a dense institutional framework aiming to monitor cooperation between the parties.

The development of these forms of cooperation is not only based on the common policy objectives which the Union's bilateral relationships share in a given region. It also illustrates the ambition of the Union to undertake a greater role in its neighbourhood and to export its model of integration whilst taking into account the widely divergent policy contexts of each case. It is noteworthy, for instance, that a central aspect of these frameworks is regional cooperation and the development of closer economic and political links between the Union's interlocutors. Other recent forms of structured cooperation with groups of third countries include the Eastern Partnership[55] and the Northern Dimension.[56]

The most ambitious and interesting form of structured cooperation between the EU and third countries is the European Neighbourhood Policy (ENP).[57] Drawing upon, but developed beyond, existing treaties

---

[54] This involves the links between the EU and its Member States and the Western Balkan countries: see COM (1999) 235 final On the Stabilisation and Association Process for Countries of South-Eastern Europe (Brussels, 26 May 1999) and the Final Declaration of the Zagreb Summit in November 2000 (www.consilium.europa.eu/ueDocs/cms_Data/docs/pressdata/en/er/Declang4.doc.html).

[55] See COM (2008) 823 final Eastern Partnership (Brussels, 3 Dec. 2008) and the Prague Joint Declaration on the Eastern Partnership (7 May 2009) (www.rpo.gov.pl/pliki/12659747270.pdf), which defines the main goal of the Partnership as the creation of 'the necessary conditions to accelerate political association and further economic integration between the European Union and interested partner countries' (paragraph 2).

[56] See the Northern Dimension Policy Framework Document adopted at Helsinki in Nov. 2006 (http://eeas.europa.eu/north_dim/docs/nd_framework_document_2006_en.pdf), which defines the main aim of the initiative as 'providing a common framework for the promotion of dialogue and concrete cooperation, strengthening stability, well-being and intensified economic cooperation, promotion of economic integration and competitiveness and sustainable development in Northern Europe' (paragraph 10).

[57] See COM (2003) 104 fin. Wider Europe-Neighbourhood: A New Framework for Relations with Our Eastern and Southern Neighbours (Brussels, 11 March 2003). The ENP has been reviewed by COM (2006) 726 fin. On Strengthening the European Neighbourhood Policy (Brussels, 4 Dec. 2006), COM(2007) 774 fin A Strong European Neighbourhood Policy (Brussels, 5 Dec. 2007), COM(2010) 207 Taking Stock of the

between the EU and its eastern and southern neighbours (namely the Partnership and Cooperation Agreements in the case of the former and the Euro-Mediterranean Agreements in the case of the latter), it provides the overall framework within which the EU structures its relations with its immediate neighbours.[58] The scope of this arrangement is broad and covers economic, social, political, transport, energy and security objectives. Its function is based on regular agreements reached between the EU and each ENP partner on reform targets in any of these areas and for which the EU provides financial and technical assistance. The ENP is underpinned by two main principles: differentiation (that is, the definition of objectives on the basis of the specific needs of each ENP partner country) and joint ownership (that is, the definition of each set of objectives with the agreement of each ENP partner rather than the prescriptive imposition of reforms from the EU).[59]

The record of the ENP in policy terms has not escaped criticism. An editorial in the *Financial Times* in September 2007 pointed out that, 'not for the first time, the European Union created a muddle and called it a policy, the European Neighbourhood Policy ... which is a mix of jumble and evasion'.[60] Such criticism is by no means rare following the events which have been developing in northern Africa since late 2010.[61]

European Neighbourhood Policy (Brussels, 12 May 2010), COM(2011) 303 A New Response to a Changing Neighbourhood (Brussels, 25 May 2011), JOIN(2013) 4 final European Neighbourhood Policy: Working towards a Stronger Partnership (Brussels, 20 March 2013).

[58] These include Algeria, Egypt, Israel, Jordan, Lebanon, Libya, Morocco, the Palestinian Authority, Syria and Tunisia, and Armenia, Azerbaijan, Belarus, Georgia, Moldova and Ukraine.

[59] From the voluminous literature on ENP, see S. Blockmans, 'Friend or Foe? Reviewing EU Relations with Its Neighbours Post Lisbon' in P. Koutrakos, (ed.), *The European Union's External Relations a Year after Lisbon* (2011/3 CLEER Working Paper No. 3), pp. 113–124; M. Cremona and C. Hillion, 'L'Union fait la force? Potential and Limitations of the European Neighbourhood Policy as an Integrated EU Foreign and Security Policy', EUI Working Papers, Law No. 2006/39; M. Cremona and G. Meloni (eds.), *The European Neighbourhood Policy: A Framework for Modernisation?* (EUI Working Paper No. 21) and B. Van Vooren, *EU External Relations Law and the European Neighbourhood Policy: A Paradigm for Coherence* (Abingdon: Routledge, 2012).

[60] *Financial Times* (London), 5 Sept. 2007, p. 12.

[61] For the Union's response, see COM (2011) 303 fin *A New Response to a Changing Neighbourhood* (Brussels, 25 May 2011). See the analysis in J. Wouters and S. Duquet, 'The Arab Uprisings and the European Union: In Search of a Comprehensive Strategy', *YbEL*, 32 (2013), 1–36, and the criticism in S. Blockmans, 'The ENP and "More for More" Conditionality: Plus que ça change ...' in G. Fernández Arribas, K. Pieters and T. Takács (eds.), *The European Union's Relations with the Southern-Mediterranean in the Aftermath of the Arab Spring* (2013/3 CLEER Working Paper No. 113), pp. 53–59.

The policy is characterised by the intense proceduralisation which has become the hallmark of various strands of the Union's external action. In legal terms, however, the ENP is an interesting experiment. For instance, it makes extensive use of soft law which determines both the content and the pace of integration between the EU and its partner countries.[62] For the purposes of this chapter, the ENP provides an interesting example of a policy framework which develops from and draws upon a set of bilateral treaties concluded between the EU and its Member States and neighbouring countries and then combines them with a range of legally binding and soft law instruments in order to maximise its impact in its neighbourhood. Viewed from this angle, the conclusion of treaties enables the Union to experiment with the legal armoury which would enable it to meet its ambition on the international scene.

The analysis so far has focused on the Union's reliance upon bilateral treaties for the development of structured forms of cooperation with groups of countries. Another interesting function of the Union's treaty-making activity is its increasing alertness to the need to establish links between internal and external policy-making. In October 2006, the Commission adopted a document titled *Global Europe: Competing in the World*.[63] In policy terms, this seeks to refocus the Union's external economic relations in order to stimulate growth and create jobs in Europe. In practical terms, it prioritises the negotiation of Free Trade Agreements (FTAs) with countries such as South Korea, India and Russia and organizations such as the Association of Southeast Asian Nations, Mercosur and the Gulf Cooperation Council. This direction is justified on economic considerations – such as the market potential of these actors, their level of protection against EU export interests and the impact on EU markets and economies of their links with the EU's competitors.

The interesting feature of this initiative is its ambition. Such FTAs are wider in scope than traditional trade agreements because, rather than focusing on straightforward trade restrictions such as tariffs, they aim to reach the highest possible degree of liberalisation in areas such as services and investment, intellectual property rights and competition. They also aim to include provisions on regulatory convergence and cooperation, labour and environmental standards and good governance in financial,

---

[62] See B. Van Vooren, 'The European Union as an International Actor and Progressive Experimentation in its Neighbourhood' in Koutrakos (ed.), *supra* n. 20, pp. 147–171.

[63] COM (2006) 567 fin (Brussels, 4 Oct. 2006).

tax and judicial areas. It is in the light of the preceding information that
they are labelled Deep and Comprehensive FTAs (DCFTAs).

The EU has concluded such agreements with South Korea,[64]
Ukraine,[65] Moldova[66] and Georgia[67] (with the three latter countries,
the EU has concluded association agreements which include provisions establishing a Deep and Comprehensive Free Trade Area). The
conclusion and entry into force of the Agreement with Ukraine has
followed a somewhat truncated pattern. A couple of days prior to
the signing of the agreement with Ukraine, the Ukrainian
Government announced that it would not sign the Agreement after
all. Demonstrations erupted in Kiev in November 2013 which led to
the violent response by and the ensuing resignation of the government as well as the annexation of Crimea by Russia. The political
provisions of the Association Agreement were signed in March 2014
with the parties agreeing on the provisional application of some of
its rules,[68] whilst the trade provisions of the agreement (which were
about the establishment of the Deep and Comprehensive Free Trade
Area between the EU and Ukraine) were signed three months later.
Whilst the parties also agreed to the provisional application of the
previously noted parts of the Agreement,[69] the provisional application of the trade provisions in particular was delayed until 1
January 2016.[70] These episodes of the unusually eventful life of the
Agreement between the EU/Member States and Ukraine suggest that
the EU is sufficiently flexible to rely upon the mechanism of the
provisional application of treaties in order to respond to geopolitical
pressures that seek to limit the treaty-making power of the EU.[71]
It should be recalled, too, that Russia had been hostile to the
negotiation and conclusion of the Agreement, as it considered it

---

[64] [2011] OJ L 127/6.   [65] [2014] OJ L 161/3.

[66] [2014] OJ L 260/4. A considerable part of the Agreement has applied provisionally since 1
Sept. 2014 pursuant to Art. 3 of Council Dec. 2014/492/EU [2014] OJ L 260/1.

[67] [2014] OJ L 261/4. A considerable part of the Agreement has applied provisionally since 1
Sept. 2014 pursuant to Art. 3 of Council Dec. 2014/494/EU [2014] OJ L 261/1.

[68] Namely on fundamental human rights and the rule of law, political dialogue and its final
provisions on its implementation: Council Dec. 2014/295/EU [2014] OJ L 161/1, Art. 4.

[69] Along with justice and home affairs, economic and financial co-operation Council
Dec. 2014/668/EU [2014] OJ L 278/1, Art. 4.

[70] Council Dec. 2014/691/EU [2014] OJ L 289/1. Up until the date of entry of the provisional
application of the trade provisions, Ukrainian business had access to EU markets, but EU
products will not have not access to the Ukrainian market.

[71] On the provisional application of treaties, see the contribution to this volume of Quast
Mertsch at pp. 303–334 (Chapter 10).

a threat to its sphere of influence in the Caucasus. The various episodes of the life of the Agreement must also be understood in the light of the considerable tension between the West and Russia (the EU and the United States have imposed a wide range of sanctions on the latter), tensions in the Eastern part of Ukraine and the constant threat of further destabilisation in the area. The Union's response in relation to the application of its Agreement with Ukraine suggests realism in so far as the EU is keen to instrumentalise legal mechanisms in order to pursue specific policy objectives whilst avoiding long-term political challenges. It also suggests that the exercise of the Union's treaty-making power, whilst governed by principles of striking complexity, is also deeply political and, potentially, controversial.[72] This is borne out by the referendum in the Netherlands on the conclusion of the Agreement between the EU and its Member States and Ukraine. In April 2016, voters rejected the conclusion of the Agreement in a non-binding referendum which, nonetheless, the Netherlands Government stated that it would take into account.[73] In their effort to salvage the Agreement, the Member States agreed to address concerns about its impact (such as on movement of persons and the financial support to the Ukraine).[74] In political terms, the referendum also illustrates the increasing prominence of the Union's treaty-making activity in domestic political debates. This development is borne out by the controversy surrounding the negotiation of the Transatlantic Trade and Investment Partnership Agreement[75] and the spectacular manner in which the signature and provisional application of the EU-Canada Comprehensive Economic and Trade Agreement (CETA) were nearly prevented by the Walloon Parliament.[76]

---

[72] For instance, whilst an Association Agreement, including a Deep and Comprehensive Free Trade Area, had also been negotiated with Armenia, the latter decided not to complete the process and, instead, has joined the Customs Union with Russia, Belarus, Kazakhstan and Kyrgyzstan.

[73] S. Castle, 'Dutch Voters Reject Deal between E.U. and Ukraine', *N.Y. Times*, 7 Apr. 2016, A4.

[74] Decision of the Heads of State or Government of the 28 Member States of the European Union, meeting within the European Council, Annexed to the European Council Conclusions on Ukraine (15 Dec. 2016).

[75] See, for instance, by J.-F. Morin, T. Novotná and M. Telo (eds.), *The Politics of Transatlantic Trade Negotiations: TTIP in a Globalized World* (Farnham: Ashgate, 2015).

[76] For the text of CETA, see [2017] OJ L 11/23. See also the Joint Interpretative Instrument: [2017] OJ L/113.

The EU has also completed negotiations of a Comprehensive Economic and Trade Agreement with Canada[77] and Vietnam,[78] while further negotiations are under way with India, Malaysia, Thailand and Japan as well as ASEAN and Mercosur. Finally, a comprehensive free trade agreement with Singapore has been finalised but not yet signed, as the European Court of Justice has been asked to rule on whether the Agreement falls within the Union's exclusive competence.[79]

In relation to such agreements, two points are worth making. First, when the initiative for this new generation of treaties was articulated in 2006, the economic and political climate in the Union was profoundly different. The Treaty of Lisbon had been signed, and the EU was basking in the comfort which the establishment of the Eurozone had created and was preparing for another round of enlargement. Therefore, it was confident and exuded success and ambition. The intervening years have not been kind. The financial crisis has caused unprecedented problems, with the possibility of sovereign default for at least one Member State; extraordinary economic, legal and political efforts to safeguard the euro and the very existence of the Eurozone put in doubt. This crisis has been allowed to assume existential dimensions for the Union. In the new economic and political climate, the conclusion of comprehensive trade agreements has acquired new urgency for the EU. The implementation of this policy priority, however, has encountered considerable legal and political obstacles. Reference has already been made to the process of signature and ratification of the Agreements with Ukraine and Canada. The following section will set out the legal complexities that characterise the Union's treaty-making activity.

Secondly, there is a clear linkage between the realignment of its treaty-making ambition in the economic sphere and the achievement and consolidation of the Union's internal market objectives. Whilst internal policy-making and external activity have always been intrinsically linked

---

[77] The text of the Agreement is available here: http://trade.ec.europa.eu/doclib/docs/2016/february/tradoc_154329.pdf. It attracted considerable attention because, once its text had been agreed upon and sent for legal revision, it emerged with a considerable change in the area of investment dispute settlement: rather than providing for investment arbitration, it establishes a permanent tribunal for investment disputes. This policy choice reflects the EU's recent decision to advocate permanent investment tribunals instead of arbitral tribunals.

[78] The text of the Agreement is available here: http://trade.ec.europa.eu/doclib/cfm/doclib_section.cfm?sec=714.

[79] The text of the Agreement is available here: http://trade.ec.europa.eu/doclib/press/index.cfm?id=961.

both at a constitutional and substantive level,[80] this link has gradually become more apparent as one of the foundations of the EU's treaty-making activity.[81] This suggests another function of treaties in the EU's external relations: in addition to their role as the starting point for and the nucleus of increasingly structured forms of cooperation with groups of countries, they facilitate the consolidation and, most importantly, the export of its regulatory policies.

4 Treaty-Making as the Terrain for Legal Disputes

The EU is endowed with international personality under Article 47 TEU. However, the treaty-making capacity which this entails is governed by the principle of conferred competence. In accordance with Article 5(2) TEU:

> Under the principle of conferral, the Union shall act only within the limits of the competences conferred upon it by the Member States in the Treaties to attain the objectives set out therein. Competences not conferred upon the Union in the Treaties remain with the Member States.

In practical terms, the principle of conferred competence suggests that the negotiation and conclusion of a treaty by the EU must be based on a substantive legal basis set out in the Treaties – that is, either the TEU or the TFEU – which confers on the Union the competence to negotiate and conclude the treaty in question. The implications of the choice of the appropriate legal basis are considerable as the latter determines the procedures pursuant to which secondary measures are adopted and the input of the Union institutions in decision-making.[82] As the Court of Justice pointed out in *Opinion 2/00*, 'the choice of the appropriate legal basis has constitutional significance'.[83] It indicates compliance with the principle of conferred competence and determines the nature and extent of Union competence. In the words of the Court of Justice:

---

[80] See M. Cremona, 'The External Dimension of the Single Market: Building (on) the Foundation' in C. Barnard and J. Scott (eds.), *The Law of the Single European Market: Unpacking the Premises* (Oxford: Hart Publishing, 2002), pp. 351–393, and Koutrakos, *supra* n. 52, at pp. 17–129.

[81] See M. Cremona, 'Expanding the Internal Market: An External Regulatory Policy for the EU?' in B. Van Vooren, S. Blockmans and J. Wouters (eds.), *supra* n. 41, pp. 162–177, at pp. 167 *et seq.*

[82] For the decision-making procedures governing the negotiation and conclusion of international agreements by the Union, see Koutrakos, *supra* n. 52, at pp. 133–160.

[83] *Opinion 2/00* [2001] ECR I–9713 (paragraph 5).

to proceed on an incorrect legal basis is ... liable to invalidate the act concluding the agreement and so vitiate the [Union]'s consent to be bound by the agreement it has signed. That is so in particular where the Treaty does not confer on the [Union] sufficient competence to ratify the agreement in its entirety, a situation which entails examining the allocation as between the Community and the Member States of the powers to conclude the agreement that is envisaged with non-member countries, or where the appropriate legal basis for the measure concluding the agreement lays down a legislative procedure different from that which has in fact been followed by the [Union] institutions.[84]

In the case of a treaty deemed to be concluded by the Union in violation of its rules conferring upon its external competence or the procedural rules governing the negotiation and conclusion of international agreements, the Union measure concluding the treaty would be invalidated whilst the Agreement may well be binding on the EU under international law.[85] After all, Article 27 VCLT provides that internal law may not be invoked in order to justify failure to comply with treaty obligations.[86] As this provision lays down customary international law,[87] which is binding on the Union,[88] this rule would render an agreement concluded in violation of the Treaties binding on the EU under international law. Article 46 VCLT provides for an exception to Article 27 VCLT in so far as it refers to a violation of internal rules on competence to conclude treaties which is 'manifest' and concerns 'a rule of ... internal law of fundamental importance'.[89] However, given the complexity of the EU rules on external competence, the relevance of this exception would be difficult to envisage in this context.[90]

Therefore, the choice of legal basis is of profound significance for the Union's legal order. However, it is often fraught with problems. This is due to a number of reasons. First, whilst essential, the Union's competence to negotiate and conclude an international agreement may be deeply contested. The Lisbon Treaty sets out for the first time the circumstances under which the Union is endowed with such

---

[84] *Ibid.* [85] Case C-327/91 *France v. Commission* [1994] ECR I–3641 (paragraph 25).
[86] *Supra* n. 1.
[87] See *Case Concerning Certain Questions of Mutual Assistance in Criminal Matters*: Djibouti v. France (2008) ICJ Rep. 177.
[88] Case C-162/96 *Racke* ECLI:EU:C:1998:293 and Case C-366/10 *Air Transport Association of America* [2011] ECR I–13755.
[89] *Supra* n. 1.
[90] See A. Aust, *Modern Treaty Law and Practice* (Cambridge: Cambridge University Press, 3rd ed., 2013), p. 274.

competence. However, the relevant provision, Article 216(1) TFEU, is drafted in broad terms the interpretation of which is by no means clear.[91] The same applies to Article 3(2) TFEU which sets out the circumstances under which the Union's competence to conclude treaties is exclusive. Both provisions were intended to reflect the case law of the Court of Justice which, over the years and in the absence of detailed primary rules, shaped the existence and exercise of the Union's external competence. However, in doing so, they fail to capture the subtleties of this case law and the specific context within which the Court has articulated the main principles governing the Union's treaty-making activity.[92]

Secondly, in light of the increasing interaction between different policy areas, the scope of a treaty negotiated by the Union may well fall within the scope of a number of TEU/TFEU provisions. Whilst this makes sense in principle, it may give rise to complexities in practice: different legal bases provide for different decision-making procedures, grant EU institutions different powers to participate in the decision-making process and may endow the Union with a different type of competence. For instance, the Union's competence to negotiate and conclude environmental treaties under Article 191(4) TFEU is shared with the Member States, whereas in the area of trade in goods or foreign direct investment (Article 207(1) TFEU) the Union is endowed with exclusive competence under Article 3(1)(e) TFEU. In practical terms, the determination of the preceding issues may have profound legal implications, not least in order to ascertain whether the Union will conclude a treaty on its own or along with the Member States. In the latter case, the treaty is known as a 'mixed agreement', one of the most interesting and complex creatures of the EU's external relations law which raises numerous questions about its negotiation, conclusion, application and interpretation.[93]

---

[91] And which provides: 'The Union may conclude an agreement with one or more third countries or international organizations where the Treaties so provide or where the conclusion of an agreement is necessary in order to achieve, within the framework of the Union's policies, one of the objectives referred to in the Treaties, or is provided for in a legally binding act of the Union or is likely to affect common rules or alter their scope'.

[92] See M. Cremona, 'The Union's External Action: Constitutional Perspectives' in G. Amato, H. Bribosia and B. de Witte (eds.), *Genesis and Destiny of the European Constitution* (Brussels: Bruylant, 2007), pp. 1173–1217, at p. 1184; A. Dashwood, M. Dougan, B. Rodger, E. Spaventa and D. Wyatt, *Wyatt and Dashwood's European Union Law* (Oxford: Hart Publishing, 6th ed., 2011), pp. 918–922, and Koutrakos, *supra* n. 52, at pp. 75–77 and 126–129.

[93] See C. Hillion and P. Koutrakos (ed.), *Mixed Agreements Revisited: The EU and its Member States in the World* (Oxford: Hart Publishing, 2010).

According to the Court of Justice, the choice of legal basis is of an objective nature and 'must rest on objective factors amenable to judicial review'.[94] However, it becomes often a terrain for legal disputes between the Union institutions and the Member States. This manifests itself in different ways at the different stages of the life of treaties for which both the Member States and the EU lay a claim. At the negotiating stage, the European Commission, which may negotiate on behalf of the Union under Article 218(3) TFEU,[95] would have to reach an agreement with the delegations of Member States prior to its negotiation with the delegations of third parties. If the agreement is concluded as mixed, questions are raised as to which of its provisions are subject to the jurisdiction of the Court of Justice and which are subject to the jurisdiction of national courts. As for the application of mixed agreements, questions are raised as to which provision of the treaty incurs the responsibility of the Union or the Member States or both.

It becomes apparent that the exercise of the Union's treaty-making competence often becomes deeply contested. In practical terms, both the EU institutions and the Member States dedicate considerable energy and time in their effort to maintain and develop their role as subjects of international law. And both do so on the ground, that is, in the course of the conduct of the EU's external relations and before the Court of Justice. As far as the latter is concerned, a case in point is the conclusion of treaties with both a trade and environmental dimension. These two policy areas are governed by different rules and procedures in the EU legal order and their legal implications for the international role of the Union and the Member States differ significantly, as the Union is endowed with exclusive competence on trade whereas it shares competence with Member States in the area of environment. In the past, the EU institutions and the Member States have argued before the Court of Justice about the legal basis on which the EU should conclude the 2000 Cartagena Protocol on Biosafety to the Convention on Biological Diversity,[96] the 2000 Energy Star Agreement between the EU and the United States,[97] the 1998 Rotterdam Convention

---

[94] See Case C-300/89 *Commission v. Council (re: Titanium Dioxide)* [1991] ECR I-1689.

[95] The Commission negotiates where the treaty envisaged does not relate exclusively or principally to the common foreign and security policy – where it does, it is the High Representative of the Union for Foreign Affairs and Security Policy who negotiates (Art. 218(3) TFEU: *supra* n. 27).

[96] 226 UNTS 208; see *Opinion 2/00 (re: Cartagena Protocol)* [2001] ECR I-9713.

[97] [2001] OJ L 172/3. See Case C-281/01 *Commission v. Council* [2002] ECR I-12049. The Agreement has been superseded twice, more recently by an agreement concluded in 2013 ([2013] OJ L 63/7).

on the Prior Informed Consent Procedure for Certain Hazardous Chemicals and Pesticides in International Trade[98] and the 1989 Basel Convention on the Control of Transboundary Movements of Hazardous Wastes and Their Disposal.[99] These inter-institutional disputes have given rise to judgments whose consistency and helpfulness are by no means apparent.[100]

Over the years, the Union has developed different techniques for dealing with such questions. For instance, both the EU institutions and the Member States developed practical and often *ad hoc* arrangements which enable them to negotiate treaties on a basis of a mutual understanding of what is expedient in practical terms whilst avoiding the issue of competence until the negotiation of the treaty has been concluded.[101] On the issue of interpretation, the Court has construed its jurisdiction to interpret mixed agreements in broad terms.[102] As for the issue of responsibility, the Union often submits declarations of competence in multilateral treaties which are intended to provide some clarity as to the areas of the treaty over which the Union is responsible,[103] even though it is highly contestable whether their opaque wording achieves this objective.

This brief overview of the various issues to which the Union's treaty-making gives rise illustrates the following three points. First, the negotiation and conclusion of treaties by the Union has a strong internal dimension which is heavily marked by the struggle between Member States and EU institutions to ensure their presence on the international scene. This dimension has given rise to the development of a set of rules and principles of considerable complexity.[104]

---

[98] 2244 UNTS 337; see Case C-94/03 *Commission v. Council* [2006] ECR I–1.

[99] 1673 UNTS 126; see Case C-411/06 *Commission v. Council* [2009] ECR I–7585.

[100] See P. Koutrakos, 'Legal Basis and Delimitation of Competence in EU External Relations' in M. Cremona and B. de Witte (eds.), *EU Foreign Relations Law: Constitutional Foundations* (Oxford: Hart Publishing, 2008), pp. 171–198.

[101] See Koutrakos, *supra* n. 52, at pp. 170–174. For judicial endorsement and enforcement of such arrangements, see Case C-25/94 *Commission v. Council* [re: voting arrangements in FAO] [1996] ECR I–1469.

[102] See Case C-53/96 *Hermès International v. FHT Marketing* [1998] ECR I–3603 and Joined Cases 300/98 and 392/98 *Parfums Christian Dior* [2000] ECR I–11307. See, also, the analysis in P. Koutrakos, 'Interpretation of Mixed Agreements' in Hillion and Koutrakos (eds.), *supra* n. 93, pp. 116–137.

[103] See J. Heliskoski, 'EU Declarations of Competence and International Responsibility' in M. Evans and P. Koutrakos (eds.), *The International Responsibility of the European Union: European and International Perspectives* (Oxford: Hart Publishing, 2013), pp. 189–210, and the criticism in Koutrakos, *supra* n. 52, at pp. 174–177.

[104] A. Aust has written in his previous edition of *Modern Treaty Law and Practice* (Cambridge: Cambridge University Press, 2000), p. 55, that '[a]nything to do with the

Secondly, this internal dimension has considerable practical implications. For instance, the European Commission insists that the continuing presence of Member States in the Union's treaty-making activity slows down decision-making and hampers the Union's negotiating position.[105] Third parties are often baffled by what they view as theological internal disputes which make treaty-making more complex than necessary.[106] On the other hand, Member States are keen to ensure that their international role is not completely subsumed by the European Union and the Court of Justice is loathe to let the practical difficulties of the coexistence between EU and Member States determine the issue of competence.[107]

Thirdly, in the light of the preceding account, the case law of the Court of Justice has a considerable impact on the way in which the Union engages in treaty-making. It is not an exaggeration to point out that the EU's judiciary has shaped the law governing the EU's international conduct. The complexity of this area of law and the high stakes for both the Member States and the EU institutions have given rise to the considerable judicialisation of EU external relations. This is not confined to the different areas of economic activity outlined previously;[108] it also emerges from the increased securitisation of what the Union does on the international scene and the various interactions between the EU's Common Security and Defence Policy and other strands of external action, such as development cooperation.[109] Whilst there is considerable dialogue between the EU legislature and the Court of Justice in the area,[110] this feature of EU external relations does not reduce the complexity of the relevant legal framework.

European Union is complex, and this is particularly so for the law governing its external relations'.

[105] See, for instance, the arguments by the Commission in *Opinion 1/94 (re: WTO Agreements)* [1994] ECR I-5267.

[106] See, for instance, P. Olson, 'Mixity from the Outside: the Perspective of a Treaty Partner' in Hillion and Koutrakos (eds.), *supra* n. 93, pp. 331–348.

[107] See, for instance, *Opinion 1/94 (re: WTO)* [1994] ECR I-5267 (paragraph 107).

[108] At the time of writing, the Court is considering the scope of the Common Commercial Policy and whether the Union has exclusive competence to conclude agreements with provisions on investment protection, sustainable development, environmental protection and transport services: Opinion 2/15 on EU-Singapore Free Trade Agreement.

[109] See P. Koutrakos, *EU Common Security and Defence Policy* (Oxford: Oxford University Press, 2013), pp. 210–247.

[110] See G. De Baere and P. Koutrakos, 'The Interactions between the European Court of Justice and the Legislature in the European Union's External Relations' in P. Syrpis (ed.), *The Relationship between the Judiciary and the Legislature in the Internal Market* (Cambridge: Cambridge University Press, 2012), pp. 243–273.

5 Treaties as the Foundation for EU Law Obligations of Member States

The analysis so far has examined the process of the negotiation and conclusion of treaties by the Union as a deeply contested context within which the different actors of the Union's legal order seek to maintain their prerogatives and increase their influence and visibility. This section will focus on the role of the treaties as the foundation for legal obligations imposed on Member States by EU law. In doing so, it will ascertain the impact of these duties on the position of Member States as sovereign subjects of international law.[111]

The starting point for this analysis is the main principle which governs the conduct of Member States in the context of the EU legal order – that is, the duty of cooperation. Set out in Article 4(3) TEU, this has been an important tool in the Court's armoury which has contributed to the constitutionalisation of the Union legal order over the years. It has also been developed by the Court since the early 1990s on the basis of the requirement of unity in the international representation of the Union and the Member States.[112] Over the years, the duty of cooperation has been applied in different contexts and in different ways.

5.1 'Special Duties of Action and Abstention'

In cases where there appears a concerted EU position, the Court has held that the Member States are under 'special duties of action and abstention'.[113] This raises two questions: how is an EU position construed, and what types of 'special duties' does it entail for Member States? In relation to the latter, it is clear that a Member State may not negotiate and conclude a treaty with a third country. In relation to the former, the

---

[111] This section draws on P. Koutrakos, 'In Search of a Voice: EU Law Constraints on Member States in International Law-Making' in R. Liivoja and J. Petman (eds.), *International Law-Making: Essays in Honour of Jan Klabbers* (Abingdon: Routledge, 2014), pp. 211–224.

[112] See M. Cremona, 'Defending the Community Interest: The Duties of Cooperation and Compliance' in Cremona and de Witte (eds.), *supra* n. 100, pp. 125–170; C. Hillion, 'Mixity and Coherence in EU External Relations: The Significance of the "Duty of Cooperation"' in Hillion and Koutrakos (eds.), *supra* n. 93, pp. 87–115, and E. Neframi, 'The Duty of Loyalty: Rethinking Its Scope through Its Application in the Field of EU External Relations', *Common Market L. Rev.*, 47 (2010), 323–359.

[113] Case C-266/03 *Commission v. Luxembourg* [2005] ECR I–4805 (paragraph 59); Case C-433/03 *Commission v. Germany* [2005] ECR I–6985 (paragraph 65) and Case C-246/07 *Commission v. Sweden* (re: PFOS), [2010] ECR I–3317 (paragraph 74).

limited case law so far suggests a rather broad approach to the scope of what constitutes an EU position.[114] Therefore, the provision of a timetable for the adoption of internal measures by the Union imposed on Member States both negative duties (not to assume any international obligations) and positive duties (to facilitate the Union's participation in an international agreement in which they are already parties).

Similar duties are also imposed where the Union institutions have adopted a decision to initiate negotiations of an international agreement. This was the case in the two *Inland Waterways* judgments,[115] where Luxembourg had signed, ratified and implemented and Germany had ratified and implemented inland waterway transport agreements with Romania, Poland and Ukraine without consulting or cooperating with the Commission.

5.2 The Member States in the Absence of EU Action

The Union legal order imposes duties on Member States even in cases where the EU has not acted on the international plane. In Case C-45/07 *Commission* v. *Greece*, the Court elaborated on the specific implications of this arrangement.[116] Greece had submitted a proposal to the International Maritime Organization (IMO) Maritime Safety Committee in which it asked the Committee to examine the creation of check lists or other appropriate tolls for assisting the contracting States of the 1974 International Convention for the Safety of Life at Sea (SOLAS)[117] in monitoring whether ships and port facilities complied with the requirements of an Annex to that Convention, as well as the International Ship and Port Facility Security Code (ISPS Code).[118] The Commission objected to the submission of this proposal as its subject matter fell within the Union's exclusive competence following the adoption of Regulation 725/2004 on enhancing ship and port facility security.[119] This measure was intended to incorporate in substance both the SOLAS Convention and the ISPS Code in EU law.

---

[114] Joined Cases 3, 4 and 6/76 *Kramer* [1976] ECR 1279.

[115] Case C-266/03 *Commission* v. *Luxembourg, supra* n. 113, and Case C-433/03 *Commission* v. *Germany, supra* n. 113.

[116] Case C-45/07 *Commission* v. *Greece* [2009] ECR I–701.   [117] 1184 UNTS 278.

[118] International Ship and Port Facility Security Code, 12 Dec. 2002, U.N. Doc. SOLAS/ CONF.5/34, Annex 1.

[119] Regulation (EC) No 725/2004 of the European Parliament and of the Council of 31 March 2004 on enhancing ship and port facility security, OJ 2004 L 129/6.

The starting point for and the foundation of the judgment is the duty of cooperation as set out in primary law as well as the setting of a common transport policy as one of the Union's objectives. The Court concludes that the submission of the Greek proposal set in motion a process which could have led to the adoption of new rules that would then have forced the Union to act in order to incorporate them in its legal order.

This judgment is interesting on a number of grounds. First, it confirms the wide construction of the duty of cooperation. The Greek Government argued that, in fact, it was the Commission which had violated the duty of cooperation. Greece had sought to raise the issue at the Maritime Safety Committee (an EU body set up under Regulation 725/2004), but the Commission, responsible for the discussion at the Committee, had failed to submit its proposal. The Court rejected this argument, and, in a thinly disguised slap on the Commission's wrist, pointed out that 'any breach by the Commission of Article 10 EC (now Article 4(3) TEU) cannot entitle a Member State to take initiatives likely to affect Community's rules promulgated for the attainment of the objectives of the Treaty, in breach of that State's obligations'.[120] This conclusion is hardly surprising, given the specific legal context of the procedure pursuant to which the Court rendered its ruling. It is recalled that enforcement actions brought under Article 258 TFEU have been consistently viewed by the Court to be of an objective nature: it is the existence of a violation by a Member State which determines the outcome of the case irrespective of other considerations which might have a bearing on the Commission's decision to bring the action under Article 258 TFEU.[121]

Secondly, this judgment raises the issue of a Member State acting as a medium for the Union in an international context. The Court accepted early on that a Member State may act as the medium through which the Union exercises its competence in the context of an international organization. It held so expressly in the *ILO* Opinion[122] and confirmed it in the *IMO* case.[123] However, the question raised is whether, when the Member States are in such a position, they are under even more onerous duties than those imposed normally by the

---

[120] Case C-45/07 *Commission v. Greece, supra* n. 116 (paragraph 26).
[121] See, for instance, Case 416/85 *Commission v. UK* [1988] ECR 3127.
[122] *Opinion 2/91 (Re: Convention No 170 ILO on Safety in the Use of Chemicals at Work)* [1993] ECR I–1061.
[123] Case C-45/07 *Commission v. Greece, supra* n. 116.

duty of cooperation.[124] This judgment may not provide a definitive answer, as the subject matter of the dispute fell within the exclusive competence of the Union, a fact which was not disputed by either of the parties. However, suffice it to point out that the ruling itself is couched in quite broad terms. In particular, it does not only apply to cases where a Member State is instrumentalised in order to achieve the Union's objectives in circumstances where the Union itself may not do so for objective reasons. Instead, it applies to whatever a Member State might do in the context of an international set of rules and procedures: 'The mere fact that the Community is not a member of an international organization in no way authorises a Member State, acting individually in the context of its participation in an international organization, to assume obligations likely to affect Community rules promulgated for the attainment of the objectives of the Treaty'.[125]

5.3   The Member States Where They Co-exist with the EU in the Context of a Treaty

The preceding section outlined the considerable and constant tension between the EU and the Member States over competence. An interesting aspect of the relationship between the EU and Member States in the context of treaties concluded by both is about the freedom of Member States to act on their own: to what extent does their coexistence with the Union limit the scope for autonomous initiatives as fully sovereign subjects of international law?

In the past few years, this question has been addressed in two important cases. The first is the *Mox Plant* case.[126] As this judgment has been analysed exhaustively elsewhere,[127] suffice it to recall that the Court held that Ireland acted against the duty of cooperation by initiating proceedings against another Member State before an international tribunal for the violation of provisions of the 1982 United Nations Convention on the Law of the Sea (UNCLOS)[128] in areas covered by EU law.

---

[124] See M. Cremona, 'Extending the Reach of the AETR Principle: Comment on Commission v. Greece (C-45/07)', *European L. Rev.*, 34 (2009), 754–768.

[125] Case C-45/07 *Commission v. Greece, supra* n. 116 (paragraph 30).

[126] Case C-459/03 *Commission v. Ireland, supra* n. 32.

[127] See, for instance, N. Lavranos, 'The Scope of the Exclusive Jurisdiction of the Court of Justice', *European L. Rev.*, 32 (2007), 83–94, and E. Neframi, 'La mixité éclairée dans l'arrêt Commission contre Irlande du 30 mai 2006 (affaire Mox): une double infraction, un triple apport', *Revue du Droit de l'Union européenne*, 3 (2007), 687–713.

[128] 1833 UNTS 3.

The legal and policy context of this case was so specific as to caution against any general conclusions about the restrictions on the legal position of Member States. It is recalled that Article 282 UNCLOS enables Member States to rely upon the judicial system set up under the EU Treaties in order to resolve disputes between them in the context of UNCLOS. This justifies the conclusion reached in the judgment as to the appropriate forum for resolving the dispute between Ireland and the United Kingdom.

Furthermore, the line of reasoning followed by the Court is convoluted and somewhat unhelpful. A considerable part of the judgment is about seeking to ascertain whether, 'by becoming a party to the Convention, [the Union] had elected to exercise its external competence in matters of environmental protection'.[129] This process is fraught with problems and heavily dependent upon general criteria and factors difficult to establish. It is also of questionable usefulness. Instead, it is the existence of Union legislation in the area of the dispute, the submission of this legislation by Ireland to the international tribunal, and the right of Ireland under UNCLOS to bring the action before the Court of Justice which determine the outcome of the dispute.

Another layer in the study of the international role of Member States is added by the more recent *PFOS* judgment.[130] It is recalled that Sweden was found to have acted contrary to EU law by having proposed the listing of a substance known as perfluorooctanesulfonic acid (PFOS) in an Annex to the 2001 Stockholm Convention on Persistent Organic Pollutants.[131] What is interesting about this case is that Sweden had sought to get EU agreement on the matter: it had sought to convince the Union to make the proposal the subject matter of a concerted action. The Union institutions had not adopted a decision refusing to propose the listing of the specific substance. Instead, they proposed the listing of two other substances.

This judgment has attracted criticism.[132] In effect, does the Court not expect the Member States to remain silent? Is there anything differentiating the duty imposed on Sweden in the context of this agreement to which it participates from another agreement to which it would not participate because of its rules which would fall within the Union's

---

[129] Case C-459/03 *Commission v. Ireland, supra* n. 32 (paragraph 96).
[130] Case C-246/07 *Commission v. Sweden (re: PFOS), supra* n. 113.   [131] 2256 UNTS 119.
[132] See A. Delgado Casteleiro and J. Larik, 'The Duty to Remain Silent: Limitless Loyalty in EU External Relations?', *European L. Rev.*, 36 (2011), 524–541.

exclusive competence? Has the Court not viewed the Stockholm Convention as if its rules fell within the Union's exclusive competence?

The judgment has a distinct policy focus. This has two dimensions. On the one hand, any proposal to list substances under the Stockholm Convention has financial implications. This is because Article 13 of the Convention provides for financial aid to developing countries or countries with economies in transition. These are mentioned by the Court time and again, as it points out that they had been raised by the Presidency at a meeting of the Council Working Party on International Environmental Issues.[133] On the other hand, there appears to be a choice made by the Union institutions to bring the EU rules on organic pollutants closer to the Stockholm Convention. This is done by prioritising the listing in the latter of those covered by the former. The substance which Sweden proposed to be listed was not amongst these. And therein lay the problem: what Sweden deemed to be 'a decision-making vacuum' the Court characterised as 'a Community strategy'[134] and 'a concerted common strategy'.[135]

A unilateral proposal is viewed as a deviation from this concerted common strategy, and is ruled out because it would have 'consequences' for the Union. This conclusion is substantiated on the basis of three alternative arguments. The first is based on voting: under the Convention, either the Union or Member States would vote. If Member States had voted, given that Sweden had made the proposal, then the effect of the proposal would have been to deprive the Union from its voting rights. If the Union had voted, it would not have had the votes to prevent the adoption of the proposal. Therefore, either way, the Union would have been bound by the listing of PFOS. The second argument is based on the Convention's provisions on opt-out. Whilst these enable a party to opt out, provided that it does so within a year from the date on which the depositary communicated the amended Annex,[136] the Court felt that that was not possible. This was because the Convention did not allow it to exercise voting rights concurrently with its Member States.

Whilst intervening States argued that opting out was possible, the Court did not examine their arguments. Instead, it responded by relying

---

[133] Case C-246/07 *Commission v. Sweden, supra* n. 113 (paragraph 39).
[134] *Ibid.* (paragraph 76).   [135] *Ibid.* (paragraph 91).
[136] Arts. 25(4), 22(3)(b) and 22(4) of the Stockholm Convention: *supra* n. 131.

upon a third argument related to legal uncertainty: the Court held that to opt out from an amendment proposed and voted for by several Member States could give rise to legal uncertainty for the Member States, the Secretariat of the Convention as well as other parties to the Convention. Legal certainty, like effectiveness, appears to be the last refuge of a weak line of reasoning. In this context, the argument is not convincing because there is no explanation as to how the exercise by the Union of a right which is bestowed upon it by the Convention would give rise to legal uncertainty: Would it be the apparent disagreement between its position and that of some of its Member States? Would it be the emergence of questions as to the application of the Convention rules to the product in relation to Sweden and other States which might have voted for it? These are valid questions, and they are far from straightforward to address. And yet they are being ignored by depriving Member States of a freedom which mixity is purported to protect.

There is another question which the reliance upon 'legal certainty' by the Court in *PFOS* raises. This has to do with the wide scope of actors which the Court views as affected by it. In addition to the Member States, it refers to the Secretariat of the Convention and to third parties which are parties to the Convention. This argument is not easy to follow. The whole question here is what the Union's deeply idiosyncratic legal order requires a Member State to do in the context of a mixed agreement. It has been a constant in EU external relations law that this question is internal to the Union and of no interest to third parties,[137] whose interests to know with whom they are dealing are intended to be addressed on the basis of the declarations of competence. And yet the Court appears prepared without substantiating its conclusion sufficiently to protect the interests of third parties by reducing the scope of what Member States may do when they act along with the Union as sovereign subjects of international law.[138]

---

[137] Ruling 1/78 [1978] ECR 2151.

[138] The conclusion reached by the Court is viewed by Heliskoski in the light of the mixed nature of the Stockholm Convention, and is, therefore, interpreted as confined to mixed agreements: 'The Obligation of Member States to Foresee, in the Conclusion and Application of Their International Agreements, Eventual Future Measures of the European Union' in A. Arnull, C. Barnard, M. Dougan and E. Spaventa (eds.), *A Constitutional Order of States? Essays in EU Law in Honour of Alan Dashwood* (Oxford: Hart Publishing, 2011), pp. 545–564, at pp. 561–563. However, it is not entirely clear how this argument is affected by the *IMO* judgment: Case C-45/07 *Commission v. Greece, supra* n. 116.

5.4   The Member States and Their Pre-existing Treaties

An area where the Member States have seen their activities as fully
sovereign subjects of international law being curtailed by the Court of
Justice is where they have concluded agreements prior to their accession
to the European Union. This is covered by Article 351 TFEU which reads
as follows:

> The rights and obligations arising from agreements concluded before
> 1 January 1958 or, for acceding States, before the date of their accession,
> between one or more Member States on the one hand, and one or more
> third countries on the other, shall not be affected by the provisions of the
> Treaties.
>
>   To the extent that such agreements are not compatible with the
> Treaties, the Member State or States concerned shall take all appropriate
> steps to eliminate the incompatibilities established. Member States shall,
> where necessary, assist each other to this end and shall, where appropriate,
> adopt a common attitude.

In applying the agreements referred to in the first paragraph, Member
States shall take into account the fact that the advantages accorded under
the Treaties by each Member State form an integral part of the establishment of the Union and are thereby inseparably linked with the creation of
common institutions, the conferring of powers upon them and the
granting of the same advantages by all the other Member States.

   Therefore, a balance ought to be struck between the obligations which
Member States have assumed pursuant to such agreements, and their
duty to comply with EU law. How is this balance to be struck in practice?
Over the years, the Court of Justice has rendered a number of rulings
which appear to restrict the room for manoeuvre which Member States
have in their effort to eliminate incompatibilities. For instance, they are
required as a matter of EU law to renounce pre-existing agreements if any
political or practical difficulties make their renegotiation impossible.[139]

   The interpretation of Article 351 TFEU by the Court of Justice[140] has
been criticised. Jan Klabbers, for instance, argues that it illustrates
a consistent effort to by-pass international law in favour of EU law.[141]
In fact, he suggests that there is no longer any point for a Member State to

---

[139] See, for instance, Case C-170/98 *Commission v. Belgium (re: Maritime Transport
Agreement with Zaire)* [1999] ECR I–5493 and Case C-62/98 *Commission v. Portugal*
[2000] ECR I–5171.

[140] See, for instance, Koutrakos, *supra* n. 52, at pp. 321–342.

[141] See J. Klabbers, *Treaty Conflict and the European Union* (Cambridge: Cambridge
University Press, 2009), pp. 115–149, and J. Klabbers, 'Moribund on the Fourth

try to squeeze the application of a pre-existing treaty within the scope of application of the first paragraph of Article 351 TFEU: the Court is likely to interpret the second paragraph in such a way as not to allow the Member State to apply the agreement in question.

More criticism against the Court was levelled following the three *BITs* judgments which were rendered in 2009.[142] In these cases against Sweden, Austria and Finland, the Court ruled that certain pre-existing bilateral investment treaties (BITs) were incompatible with EU law. It was the transfer clause of these Agreements, guaranteeing to the investors of each party the free transfer, without undue delay, of payments connected with an investment, that was problematic. The Union's primary rules enable the EU institutions to impose restrictions on the movement of capital from a third country in relation to direct investment, as a safeguard measure or in order to implement economic sanctions decided within the context of Common Foreign and Security Policy.[143] The Court held that the transfer clause in the national BITs was contrary to this power.

What differentiates these cases from the other Article 351 TFEU cases is that the incompatibilities in question had not, in fact, arisen. They were all potential and would arise as and when the Union decided to exercise the right laid down in Articles 64(2), 66 and 75 TFEU. However, the Court held that the effectiveness of any restrictive measures which the Union might be required to impose under the preceding provisions would depend on whether they would be capable of being applied immediately. The transfer clause in the contested BITs would undermine such an objective. The Court also noted that the Agreements provided no other clause which would enable the Member States to apply EU restrictive measures immediately.[144] It also concluded, albeit without further elaboration, that no international law mechanism would allow the Member States to fulfil their EU obligations and deviate from the BITs.

The *BITs* judgments may be viewed as an unwarranted restriction on the ability of the Member States to act as fully sovereign subjects of

---

of July? The Court of Justice on Prior Agreements of the Member States', *European L. Rev.*, 26 (2001), 187–197.

[142] Case C-249/06, *Commission v. Sweden* [2009] ECR I–1335; Case C-205/06, *Commission v. Austria* [2009] ECR I–1301 and Case C-118/07 *Commission v. Finland* [2009] ECR I–10889.

[143] See respectively Arts. 64(2), 66 and 75 TFEU: *supra* n. 27.

[144] The insertion of a regional economic integration organization clause, while mentioned by Austria, had not actually been followed up.

international law: the mere possibility of future EU law action prevents them from maintaining an international agreement which is not inconsistent with current EU law and which was concluded prior to their accession to the Union. However, the temptation to adopt this perspective should be resisted. Two points are worth making. First, the judgments should be understood as being confined to the very specific legal context within which they were rendered: it is the specific nature of the restrictive measures which the Council may be called upon to adopt under the specific TFEU Treaty legal bases which renders the transfer clause problematic. Any transfer of capital could be carried out with a click of a button – literally. Therefore, any time required by a Member State in order to adjust its policy and render it compatible with the EU restrictions would undermine the latter and deprive them of their purpose.

Secondly, the notion of effectiveness is charged in the EU law vocabulary. One hardly needs to be reminded of the central role that it played in the formative years of the Union, when the Court introduced the principles which gradually constitutionalised the EU legal order. This principle of *effet utile* marked the development of a legal order which the Court shaped out of the bare provisions of the Treaties. This is a different notion from the one which emerges in the *BITs* judgments. The latter is construed more narrowly, and emerges from the very specific practical implications of measures designed to restrict the movement of capital.[145] Rather than a general policy imperative which shapes the nature of the Union legal order, effectiveness in the latter case is inextricably linked to the very specific characteristics of the transactions to which the TFEU provisions apply.

6   Conclusion

The European Union is a creature of treaties. And yet the idiosyncrasies of its legal order, the sophistication of its constitutional arrangements and the development of its integration render its definition as an international organization inadequate.

---

[145] See P. Koutrakos, 'Annotation of Case C-205/06 Commission v. Austria and Case C-249/06 Commission v. Sweden (re: Bilateral Investment Treaties)', *Common Market L. Rev.*, 46 (2009), 2059–2076. See, also, E. Denza, 'Bilateral Investment Treaties and EU Rules on Free Transfer: Comment on Commission v. Austria, Commission v. Sweden, and Commission v. Finland', *European L. Rev.*, 35 (2010), 263–274.

This chapter explored what treaties tell us about the EU. Four main functions emerge from this analysis. First, whilst providing the foundation for the very existence of the Union, the founding treaties of the latter, along with their amending treaties, have been constitutionalised and have given rise to the construction of the EU legal order as an autonomous legal system. However, the constitutional character and the autonomy of its legal order do not eliminate the public international law character of the foundations of the EU.[146] Secondly, its enthusiastic treaty-making activity enables the Union not only to become a more assertive international actor but also to instrumentalise treaties in order to achieve internal objectives and export its policies. Thirdly, the negotiation and conclusion of treaties has provided the terrain in which EU institutions and Member States compete in order to increase or maintain their role as subjects of international law. Therefore, whilst treaty-making is about external conduct, namely interactions with third parties, there is also an internal dimension for the management of which EU and national institutions spend considerable energy and time. Fourthly, treaties have emerged as the foundation of considerable EU law duties for Member States which are articulated gradually by the Court of Justice. Such constraints are imposed on the international conduct of Member States even in the case of a treaty which has not been concluded by the Union.

Therefore, and their role for the Union's contested legal nature notwithstanding, treaties have not only become an instrument for influence in the world, but also a tool for the consolidation of EU law and the coherence between EU and international action. Given the radically creative manner in which its founding documents have been construed, it is perhaps not surprising that treaties should assume such a multifaceted role in the EU's legal order.

---

[146] Denza notes that 'the original character' of EU law was 'a treaty-based international legal order, albeit one which displayed a number of intrusive and effective features which when taken cumulatively made it unique': E. Denza, 'Placing the European Union in International Context: Legitimacy of the Case Law' in M. Adams, H. de Waele, J. Meeusen and G. Straetmans (eds.), *Judging Europe's Judges: The Legitimacy of the Case Law of the European Court of Justice* (Oxford: Hart Publishing, 2013), pp. 175–196, at p. 176.

30

The Council of Europe

JEREMY McBRIDE

1 Introduction

The Statute of the Council of Europe – a treaty – established this inter-governmental organization in May 1949 with the aim of achieving 'a greater unity between its members for the purpose of safeguarding and realising the ideals and principles which are their common heritage and facilitating their economic and social progress'.[1] Treaty-making has been a principal tool for the pursuit of this aim[2] and more than two hundred treaties have been concluded since the organization's foundation, with the 1950 European Convention on Human Rights and Fundamental Freedoms (ECHR)[3] and its Protocols being the most well-known.[4] Various terms are used to describe them – notably 'agreement', 'arrange-ment', 'charter', 'code' and 'convention' – but the last is most common.[5] Many have also been designated 'European', but since 2005 'Council of Europe' has been preferred.

Although certain treaties have been the subject of detailed analysis, the organization's treaty-making in general has attracted relatively little attention.[6] There has, however, been growing concern within the

---

[1] CETS No. 001, Art. 1a. It has grown from ten to forty-seven Member States, i.e. all European States other than Belarus and the Holy See. The latter is an Observer State – as are Canada, Israel, Japan, Mexico and the United States.

[2] Unlike under Art. 19 of the Constitution of the International Labour Organization, 15 LNTS 40, they are not acts of the organization: *Opening of Conventions and Agreements to Signature by Member States* (CM(68)239, paragraphs 9–10).

[3] The invariable way of reference despite formally being the Convention for the Protection of Human Rights and Fundamental Freedoms: CETS No. 005.

[4] Available at http://conventions.coe.int.

[5] On the general insignificance of the terminology used, see J. Polakiewicz, *Treaty-Making in the Council of Europe* (Strasbourg: Council of Europe, 1999), pp. 11–13.

[6] Notable exceptions are Polakiewicz, *supra* n. 5, and F. Benoît-Rohmer and H. Klebes, *Council of Europe Law: Towards a Pan-European Legal Area* (Strasbourg: Council of Europe, 2005).

organization about its continued relevance and effectiveness, leading to action by the Parliamentary Assembly of the Council of Europe[7] and a review by the Secretary General.[8] This chapter first analyses the Statute, its significant features, subsequent changes and issues concerning its operation. It then examines certain aspects of the treaty-making activity (volume, subject-matter and characterisation, including what is seen as 'core'), with some consideration also of the use made of other forms of instruments. Thereafter, certain issues bearing on the commitment made to them (level of participation, relationship with other international obligations, treatment of certain provisions as optional, territorial reach and accommodations made for the European Union as well as derogations and denunciation) are reviewed. Consideration will then be given to aspects of implementation and dispute settlement. The chapter concludes by noting the steps being taken to maintain the relevance and effectiveness of the treaties.

2 The Statute of the Council of Europe

The Statute provides for the aims of the organization and its membership, organs, seat, official languages, secretariat, finance and privileges and immunities as well for amendment and final provisions concerning ratifications and entry into force. Since its entry into force, the amendments to the Statute have been minimal,[9] but its application has been affected in fairly significant ways by resolutions of a statutory character adopted by the Committee of Ministers[10] dealing with the need for consultation with the Consultative Assembly (of national parliamentarians) before admitting new members, provision for the conclusions of the Committee of Ministers to take the form of a convention, the establishment of a Joint Committee of the Committee of Ministers and the

---

[7] Resolution 1732 (2010) on 'Reinforcing the Effectiveness of Council of Europe Treaty Law' and Recommendation 1920 (2010) on 'Reinforcing the Effectiveness of Council of Europe Treaty Law'.

[8] Report by the Secretary General on the Review of Council of Europe Conventions (SG/Inf (2012)12 2012).

[9] They concerned the functioning of and representation of Member States in the Consultative Assembly and the submission of expenditure estimates for recommendations to be adopted by the Committee of Ministers.

[10] Pursuant to Arts. 15a and 16 of the Statute: *supra* n. 1. The designation of resolutions as 'statutory' is not governed by the Statute and has only been in use since 1993. Moreover, it has not been used for all resolutions of an institutional nature; E.g. the one creating the Council of Europe Commissioner for Human Rights: *infra* n. 16.

Consultative Assembly, the creation of specialised authorities, relations with intergovernmental organizations and non-governmental international organizations,[11] provision for partial and enlarged agreements,[12] the creation of observer status,[13] the majorities required for decisions of the Committee of Ministers[14] and the establishment of the Congress of Local and Regional Authorities.[15]

In addition, other institutions or mechanisms within the organization have been established by resolutions of the Committee of Ministers that are not termed 'statutory'[16] as well as by treaties.[17] Another change – more symbolic than substantive – was the decision of the Committee of Ministers in February 1994 that the Consultative Assembly should henceforward be referred to as the Parliamentary Assembly (but there has been no amendment made of the Statute). Furthermore, practice in applying the Statute can also evolve in significant ways. Thus, although there are no specific requirements for election as Secretary General other than that it be by the Parliamentary Assembly on the recommendation of the Committee of Ministers, a practice of electing only Assembly members was ended in 2009 when the only candidates proposed were former prime ministers who were not such members.

The elaboration of the organization's aims in Article 3,[18] and its stipulation that their fulfilment is a condition for being a member, is undoubtedly the most significant feature of the Statute. This is particularly so when coupled with the power of the Committee of Ministers

---

[11] All covered by the Resolution adopted by the Committee of Ministers at its Eighth Session in May 1951.

[12] Resolution on Partial Agreements (2 Aug. 1951) and Statutory Resolution (93) 28 on partial and enlarged agreements.

[13] Statutory Resolution (93) 26 on observer status.

[14] Statutory Resolution (93) 27 on majorities required for decisions of the Committee of Ministers.

[15] The current one is Statutory Resolution CM/Rès(2011)2 relating to the Congress of Local and Regional Authorities of the Council of Europe and the revised Charter appended thereto but the first was adopted in 1994.

[16] E.g. Resolution (99) 50 on the Council of Europe Commissioner for Human Rights; Resolution Res(2002)8 on the statute of the European Commission against Racism and Intolerance and Resolution Res(2002)12 establishing the European Commission for the Efficiency of Justice (CEPEJ).

[17] E.g. the European Court of Human Rights and the European Committee for the Prevention of Torture and Inhuman or Degrading Treatment or Punishment.

[18] That '[e]very member of the Council of Europe must accept the principles of the rule of law and of the enjoyment by all persons within its jurisdiction of human rights and fundamental freedoms, and collaborate sincerely and effectively in the realisation of the aim of the Council as specified in Chapter I'.

under Article 8 to suspend the rights of representation of a member which has seriously violated them and to request its withdrawal as well as to decide that it has ceased to be a member if it does not comply with the latter request.[19]

So far, there has only been one instance of a 'voluntary' withdrawal under Article 7 – by Greece by way of a *note verbale* in December 1970 – but this was precipitated by the lodging of an inter-State application against it under the ECHR and the institution of steps to invoke Article 8 following a military *coup d'état*. As the Article 8 power has never been exercised, it has never been conclusively resolved whether suspension is a discrete sanction or merely a prelude to the request for withdrawal but the latter view seems more consistent with the formulation of the provision.[20] However, a lesser sanction has been developed through the Parliamentary Assembly's power to reject the credentials of a delegation, which it has used or threatened where it considers a Member State has committed serious human rights violations or has not honoured commitments made when joining the organization.[21]

The provision for associate membership in Article 5 – invitations to become one may be extended 'in special circumstances' to any European country which is deemed to be able and willing to fulfil the provisions of Article 3[22] – has not been used since the Federal Republic of Germany and the Saar held such membership in 1950s. In view of its limitation to European countries and the extent of the present membership, this is unlikely to be relevant in the future without some amendment. Moreover, it has probably been rendered redundant by the establishment of observer status with respect to both the organization as whole[23] and

---

[19] Art. 9 authorises the Committee of Ministers to suspend the right of representation of a Member State on it and on the Parliamentary Assembly where it has failed to fulfil its financial obligation during such period as that obligation remains unfulfilled. This 'financial obligation' is understood to refer primarily to the contribution to the general budget (set under Art. 38b of the Statute: *supra* n. 1). See, further, Benoît-Rohmer and Klebes, *supra* n. 6, at p. 44.

[20] See Benoît-Rohmer and Klebes, *supra* n. 6, at p. 41.

[21] *Ibid.*, at pp. 41–44. See, e.g., the suspension of the voting and other rights of the Russian delegation following the annexation of Crimea: Resolution 2034 (2015) (28 Jan. 2015).

[22] Allowing representation only in the Parliamentary Assembly.

[23] Since 2006, Observer States have all been authorised to observe regular meetings of the Committee of Ministers in addition to the possibility of participating in various expert bodies, of being invited to conferences of specialised ministers and of appointing permanent observers.

the Parliamentary Assembly[24] as well as the creation in 1989 of special guest status under the Rules of Procedure of the Parliamentary Assembly.[25]

3 Treaty-Making Activity

Treaties may be proposed at the initiative of the Committee of Ministers, the Parliamentary Assembly, the Congress of Local and Regional Authorities of Europe, a conference of specialised ministers or one of the steering committees that have been established. However, their adoption can only be pursued with the approval of the Committee of Ministers, with the drafting generally being entrusted to a steering committee or a committee of experts. The Parliamentary Assembly's opinion on a draft treaty is normally sought before its adoption and opening for signature by the Committee of Ministers, both of which require a two-thirds majority.[26] Although treaties have often been amended by the adoption of separate protocols, some specifically provide for their amendment upon a Party's proposal, which can come into force once accepted by all the other Parties.[27]

This section considers the volume of the treaty-making undertaken, its subject-matter and characterisation and the use made of partial and enlarged agreements that are not treaties.

---

[24] Under Rule 61 of its Rules of Procedure. Currently Canada, Israel and Mexico have this status in the Parliamentary Assembly as opposed to the organization as a whole (on which, see *supra* n. 1).

[25] Rule 60.1 provides that: 'The Bureau may grant special guest status to national parliaments of European nonmember states which have signed the Helsinki Final Act of 1 August 1975 and the Charter of Paris for a New Europe of 21 November 1990; accepted the other instruments adopted at the OSCE conferences; and signed and ratified the two United Nations Covenants of 16 December 1966 on Civil and Political Rights and on Economic, Social and Cultural Rights'. This status has been granted to States in Central and Eastern Europe prior to their becoming Member States, with the exception of Yugoslavia (which ceased to be a State) and Belarus (whose status was suspended in 1997 because the political situation there was considered incompatible with the principles of the organization).

[26] For the process of drafting and adoption of treaties, see Polakiewicz, *supra* n. 5, at pp. 19–28.

[27] E.g. Art. 27 of the 2015 Council of Europe Convention against Trafficking in Human Organs: CETS No. 216. Occasionally, there is provision for amendments to enter into force if less than one-third of the Parties object but only for those Parties accepting them: e.g. Art. 54 of the 1990 Council of Europe Convention on Laundering, Search, Seizure and Confiscation of the Proceeds from Crime and on the Financing of Terrorism: CETS No. 141.

3.1   Volume

The Council of Europe Treaty Series (CETS)[28] comprises 224 treaties.[29] Of these, some 32 are not yet in force,[30] while eleven have ceased to be operative, whether because they have been deleted from the Series,[31] have been repealed,[32] lost their purpose[33] or are no longer open for signature.[34] Sixteen treaties have become integral to the instruments which they amend,[35] and there are five treaties which are revised versions of already existing treaties.[36]

The scale of the treaty-making effort has remained at a fairly constant level. Thus five were concluded in the organization's first nineteen months,[37] and the rate of production in succeeding decades has been broadly similar, namely twenty-eight for 1951–1960, forty-one for 1961–1970, thirty-seven for 1971–1980, thirty-four for 1981–1990, thirty-six for 1991–2000 and thirty-two for 2001–2010, although the figure of seven concluded since the beginning of 2011 points to some slowing down. Nonetheless, this level of activity significantly exceeds that of other comparable regional organizations.[38]

---

[28] Technically this series only begins with number 194 as treaties adopted before that were published in the European Treaty Series, but in practice the two series are treated as one.

[29] Although the last CETS number is 216, numbers 3, 4, 6–8 and 11 have no entry, and eight numbers are supplemented by lettered entries. CETS does not yet include the Additional Protocol to the Council of Europe Convention on the Prevention of Terrorism adopted by the Committee of Ministers on 19 May 2015.

[30] CETS Nos. 56, 57, 60, 61, 61A, 61B, 75, 79, 91, 119, 129, 131, 136, 139, 142, 145, 146, 150, 153, 154, 172, 175, 180, 184, 190, 203, 205, 211 and 213–216.

[31] CETS Nos. 3, 4, 6, 7, 8 and 11.

[32] Protocol No. 9 to the ECHR (CETS No. 140) was repealed following the entry into force of Protocol No. 11 (CETS No. 155).

[33] Protocol Nos. 10 and 14bis to the ECHR (CETS Nos. 146 and 204) lost their purpose following the entry into force respectively of Protocol Nos. 11 (supra n. 32) and 14 (CETS No. 194).

[34] E.g. the Second, Fourth and Fifth Protocols to the General Agreement on Privileges and Immunities of the Council of Europe (CETS Nos. 022, 036 and 137) following the entry into force of Protocol No. 11 (supra n. 32) to the ECHR.

[35] CETS Nos. 44, 45, 55, 81, 103, 109, 110, 111, 113, 118, 134, 151, 152, 155, 170 and 171. These are sixteen of the eighty protocols that amend or supplement treaties. In addition, there is one supplementary agreement (No. 78A).

[36] These are, with the earlier versions in brackets, CETS Nos. 139 (78), 143 (66), 163 (35), 193 (65) and 202 (58). Of these, CETS No. 139 is not yet in force and the parties to Nos. 139, 143 and 163 do not so far include all the parties to the treaties which are being revised.

[37] May 1949–Dec. 1950.

[38] The website of the Organization of American States (www.oas.org/DIL/treaties_signatories_ratifications_year.htm) shows seventy-six treaties concluded up to 2013, and the

3.2   Subject-Matter

The website of the Council of Europe's Treaty Office groups the treaties
into fifty fields, although some are listed under more than one in order to
take account of their mixed subject-matter. However, they can also be
regarded as falling into the following six broad categories: namely, one
concerned with the operation of the Council of Europe itself
('institutional')[39] and five addressed to the Member States and any
other Parties to them, i.e. culture and sport,[40] democracy and human
rights,[41] environmental and social issues,[42] legal process and cooperation[43] and private law.[44] Although the use of the 'human rights'
designation for some treaties is not necessarily what those adopting them
had in mind or indeed reflected in the division of work between the
Council's Directorate-Generals,[45] this is a fair portrayal of their substantive contribution to European standards. The five non-institutional

---

website for the African Union shows forty-nine treaties up to 27 June 2014 (including
those concluded under its predecessor, the Organization of African Unity (www.au.int
/en/treaties)).

[39] Comprising treaties in the field: legal status of the Council of Europe.

[40] Comprising treaties in these fields: audiovisual law, cinema, culture, radio and television
and sport.

[41] Comprising all or some of the treaties in these fields: biomedicine, data protection,
European Social Charter, family law–rights of children, general international law,
human rights, human rights (Convention and Protocols only), local and regional authorities, migrant workers, minorities, movement of persons, mutual assistance in criminal
matters, nationality, prevention of torture, refugees and social law.

[42] Comprising all or some of the treaties in these fields: *au pair* work, environment, higher
education, legal co-operation in criminal matters, migrant workers, movement of persons, protection of animals, public health, social and medical assistance, social law and
social protection of farmers and social security.

[43] Comprising all or some of the treaties in these fields: arbitration, corruption, court
procedure, cybercrime, enforcement of sanctions, extradition, family law–rights of children, general international law, legal co-operation in administrative and fiscal matters,
legal co-operation in civil matters, legal co-operation in criminal matters, local and
regional authorities, mutual assistance in criminal matters, other legal co-operation,
protection of victims, radio and television, terrorism, testaments and transfer of
proceedings.

[44] Comprising all or some of the treaties in these fields: civil law, civil liability, commercial
law, family law–rights of children, financial law, intellectual property and radio and
television.

[45] E.g. the 1995 Framework Convention for the Protection of National Minorities (CETS
No. 157) is within the responsibility of the Directorate General of Human Rights and
Legal Affairs, but the 1992 European Charter for Regional or Minority Languages (CETS
No. 148) is a matter for the Directorate General of Education, Culture and Heritage,
Youth and Sport.

categories all fall firmly within the aims set for the Council of Europe in its Statute.[46]

3.3   Character

The essential character of the non-institutional treaties for which Member States and other Parties are the addressees have previously been described as being either ones that 'seek to achieve harmonisation of national legislation' (harmonisation treaties) or ones which 'aim at facilitating and improving international cooperation between national law enforcement agencies'[47] (cooperation treaties). In making this distinction between them, it was suggested that harmonisation treaties were essentially concerned with aspects of private law and cooperation treaties applied mainly to cooperation in the administrative and penal fields.[48]

Furthermore, it has been suggested that this distinction affected the implementation techniques that were adopted. Thus, the focus in harmonisation treaties is only on preventive measures to forestall divergent practices, namely, the preparation of explanatory reports and the promotion of official translations that correspond with the original text in English and French. On the other hand, the cooperation treaties have tended to employ corrective measures of varying intensity[49] in order to ensure their implementation on the basis that difficulties in applying their provisions could not be anticipated beforehand but were only likely to arise when steps were actually taken to apply them.[50]

---

[46] The Secretary General has classified all the treaties by reference just to the organization's three broad mandates: human rights, rule of law and judicial co-operation and democracy: *supra* n. 8, at pp. 4–8.

[47] H.-J. Bartsch, 'The Implementation of Treaties Concluded within the Council of Europe' in F. G. Jacobs and S. Roberts (eds.), *The Effect of Treaties in Domestic Law* (London: Sweet & Maxwell, 1987), pp. 197–219, at p. 200.

[48] For other approaches to characterisation, see Benoît-Rohmer and Klebes, *supra* n. 6, at pp. 96–104.

[49] Implementation techniques are considered further in Section 5 of this chapter. See, also, J. Polakiewicz, *supra* n. 5, at pp. 119–151. On the discrete role of the Parliamentary Assembly in supervising the implementation of treaty obligations, see F. Benoît-Rohmer, 'Mécanismes de supervision des engagements des états membres et autorité du Conseil de l'Europe' in B. Haller, H. C. Kruger and H. Petzold (eds.), *Law in Greater Europe: Towards a Common Legal Area – Studies in Honour of Heinrich Klebes* (The Hague: Kluwer Law International, 2000), pp. 80–101.

[50] An explanatory report could, of course, address particular difficulties that were anticipated.

While harmonisation treaties remain firmly in the sphere of private law, the use of 'cooperation' – a term used to describe treaties that 'do not seek to reform domestic substantive law but relate to the procedural aspects of national legislation, and to internationally oriented procedures at that'[51] – to designate a significant element of the treaty-making undertaken within the Council of Europe does not really do justice to either their objectives or achievements. Such a term is certainly far from apt to describe many of the treaties in the field of democracy and human rights as well as some dealing with the conservation of wildlife,[52] corruption,[53] cybercrime,[54] money-laundering,[55] the prevention of torture,[56] the protection of archaeological, architectural, audiovisual and cultural heritage and the landscape,[57] sexual exploitation of children,[58] spectator violence,[59] sports manipulation,[60] terrorism,[61] trafficking in human beings[62] and in human organs[63] and violence against women and domestic violence.[64]

Although these treaties are not directed at harmonisation in the sense of seeking identical rules on given matters in the legal systems of Member States and other parties, they do entail both (a) establishing certain minimum standards to be respected by national law and practice and (b) (generally) creating mechanisms to ensure that this actually occurs. Indeed, the implementation mechanism in at least some of them is a primary rationale for their adoption and in one case it is the sole rationale.[65] Although the constraint imposed on parties' freedom of action can be viewed negatively, a more positive view of them is that they not only articulate shared values but also consitute an important means of assisting in their realisation. Such treaties might, therefore, be better regarded as forming a discrete grouping from those concerned with either harmonisation or cooperation.[66]

The significance of the democracy and human rights treaties, in particular, is further underlined by the requirement for many of

---

[51] Bartsch, *supra* n. 47, at p. 205. [52] CETS No. 104. [53] CETS Nos. 173, 174 and 191.
[54] CETS Nos. 185 and 189. [55] CETS Nos. 141 and 198. [56] CETS No. 126.
[57] CETS Nos. 121, 143, 176, 183 and 199. [58] CETS No. 201. [59] CETS No. 120.
[60] CETS No. 215. [61] CETS Nos. 90, 190, 196 and 198. [62] CETS No. 197.
[63] CETS No. 216. [64] CETS No. 210.
[65] See, E.g., the 1987 European Convention for the Prevention of Torture and Inhuman or Degrading Treatment or Punishment: CETS No. 126.
[66] See G. de Vel and T. Markert, 'Importance and Weaknesses of the Council of Europe Conventions and of the Recommendations Addressed by the Committee of Ministers to Member States' in Haller, Kruger and Petzold (eds.), *supra* n. 49, pp. 345–353.

them[67] to be ratified as a condition of becoming a member of the Council of Europe.[68] However, they are not unique in this regard since in addition to them and the institutional treaties,[69] this fundamental status has also been accorded to an increasing number of treaties dealing with criminal matters and combating terrorism that fall into the cooperation grouping.[70] The actual list of 'obligatory' treaties has grown with the enlargement of the membership,[71] undoubtedly

[67] Namely, the ECHR and Protocols Nos. 1, 4, 6, 7, 12, 13 and 14 (CETS Nos. 009, 046, 114, 117, 177, 187 and 194); the 1985 European Charter of Local Self-Government (CETS No. 122); the European Convention for the Prevention of Torture and Inhuman or Degrading Treatment or Punishment (*supra* n. 65), as amended by its protocols (CETS Nos. 151 and 152); the 1992 European Charter for Regional or Minority Languages (*supra* n. 45); the 1996 European Convention on the Exercise of Children's Rights (CETS No. 160); the 1996 European Social Charter (revised) (CETS No. 163); the 1997 European Convention on Nationality (CETS No.166); the 2005 Council of Europe Convention on Action against Trafficking in Human Beings (CETS No. 197) and the 2006 Council of Europe Convention on the Avoidance of Statelessness in Relation to State Succession (CETS No. 200).

[68] Prescribed in the invitation extended by the Committee of Ministers under Art. 4 of the Statute of the Council of Europe: *supra* n. 1.

[69] I.e. the Statute of the Council of Europe (*supra* n. 1) and the 1949 General Agreement on Privileges and Immunities of the Council of Europe and Protocols Nos. 1 and 6 (CETS Nos. 002, 010 and 162).

[70] Namely, the 1957 European Convention on Extradition (CETS No. 024); the 1959 European Convention on Mutual Assistance in Criminal Matters (CETS No. 030); the 1970 European Convention on the International Validity of Criminal Judgments (CETS No. 070); the 1974 European Convention on the Non-Applicability of Statutory Limitation to Crimes against Humanity and War Crimes (CETS No. 082); the 1977 European Convention on the Suppression of Terrorism (CETS No. 090) and its 2003 Protocol amending the European Convention on the Suppression of Terrorism (CETS No. 190); the 1980 European Outline Convention on Transfrontier Co-operation between Territorial Communities or Authorities (CETS No. 106) and the protocols thereto (CETS Nos. 159, 169 and 206); the 1983 Convention on the Transfer of Sentenced Persons (CETS No. 112) and its 1997 Additional Protocol (CETS No. 167); the 1983 Convention on the Compensation of Victims of Violent Crimes (CETS No. 116); the 1999 Criminal Law Convention on Corruption (CETS No. 173) and its 2003 Additional Protocol (CETS No. 191); the 1999 Civil Law Convention on Corruption (CETS No. 174); the 2001 Convention on Cybercrime (CETS No. 185) and its 2003 Additional Protocol (CETS No. 189); the 2005 Council of Europe Convention on the Prevention of Terrorism (CETS No. 196) and the Convention on the Laundering, Search, Seizure and Confiscation of the Proceeds of Crime (*supra* n. 27).

[71] Those referred to in *supra* n. 67 and n. 70 are the requirements imposed on the most recent State to become a member of the Council of Europe – Montenegro – taking into account those that it would have been expected to ratify but for the fact that it had already done so. See *Accession of the Republic of Montenegro to the Council of Europe*, Opinion No. 261 (2007) of the Parliamentary Assembly of the Council of Europe, 17 Apr. 2007, and Letter from the Chairman of the Committee of Ministers to the Authorities of

reflecting not only the development in this body of treaty law but also the growing recognition of the significance of the treaties concerned.

Almost all the treaties just cited have been described as 'key' by the Committee of Ministers and 'core' by the Parliamentary Assembly.[72] However, it is noteworthy that the majority of the treaties for which ratification is now being imposed as a condition of membership have not yet been accepted by all the existing Member States.[73]

3.4 Partial and Enlarged Agreements and Other Instruments

The significance of the treaty-making of the Council of Europe needs to be viewed also in the light of a range of other standard-setting and monitoring arrangements established without recourse to the adoption of a legally binding instrument.[74]

The most treaty-like of them are the agreements concluded as a form of cooperation in respect of an activity within the organization's mandate

---

Montenegro, 3 May 2007 (https://search.coe.int/cm/Pages/result_details.aspx?ObjectID=09000016805ac9db).

[72] The latter – in Resolution 1732 (2010) ('Reinforcing the Effectiveness of the Council of Europe Treaty Law') – listed as 'core' all the ones referred to in *supra* n. 67 and n. 70 with some additions (the protocols to the European Social Charter (CETS No. 035); the 1981 Convention for the Protection of Individuals with regard to Automatic Processing of Personal Data (CETS No. 108); the Framework Convention for the Protection of National Minorities (*supra* n. 45) and the 2007 Council of Europe Convention on the Protection of Children against Sexual Exploitation and Sexual Abuse (CETS Nos. 201); the protocols to the European Convention on Extradition (CETS Nos. 086, 098, 209 and 212)) and exclusions (the European Convention on the Exercise of Children's Rights (*supra* n. 67); the European Convention on Nationality (*supra* n. 67); the Council of Europe Convention on the Avoidance of Statelessness in Relation to State Succession (*supra* n. 67); the European Convention on the International Validity of Criminal Judgments (*supra* n. 70); the European Convention on the Non-Applicability of Statutory Limitation to Crimes against Humanity and War Crimes (*supra* n. 70); the European Outline Convention on Transfrontier Co-operation between Territorial Communities or Authorities and the protocols thereto (*supra* n. 70); the Convention on the Transfer of Sentenced Persons (*supra* n. 70) and its 1997 Additional Protocol (CETS No. 167) and the Convention on the Compensation of Victims of Violent Crimes (*supra* n. 70). In endorsing the listing of the Parliamentary Assembly, the Secretary General used the term 'key': *supra* n. 8 (paragraph 29).

[73] I.e. those referred to in *supra* n. 67 and n. 70. See, further, B. Haller, 'L'Assemblé Parlementaire et les conditions d'adhésion au Conseil de l'Europe' in Haller, Kruger and Petzold (eds.), *supra* n. 49, pp. 27–79.

[74] Relations with other international organizations and the European Union are governed by various co-operation and co-ordination agreements, other texts and, in the case of the European Union, a Memorandum of Understanding: see, further, Benoît-Rohmer and Klebes, *supra* n. 6, pp. 127–140, and www.coe.int/en/web/portal/european-union.

but which involve only some Member States (partial agreements), only some Member States and some non-Member States (enlarged partial agreements) or all Member States and some non-Member States (enlarged agreements).[75] Their object is to establish 'flexible and non-institutionalised arrangements' for those concerned to 'pursue an inter-governmental activity together on an equal footing', but they must still be 'founded on the political priorities as defined by the Committee of Ministers, and must in all events contribute to the achievement of the Organization's priority aims'.[76] The normal minimum membership should be at least a third of the Member States, and this membership should 'reflect a certain geographical balance amongst the different regions covered by the Organization, in order to avoid a drift away from the Organization's core values and an associated lack of coherence, as well as the creation of unduly "restricted" Agreements'.[77] Such agreements are financed by a budget constituted by contributions from those participating in them.

The setting up of any agreement requires authorisation first from the Committee of Ministers – by a two-thirds majority of the representatives casting a vote and a majority of the representatives entitled to sit on it – and then the adoption only by those States that wish to do so of a resolution setting it up, which will contain the agreement's statute. Those Member States adopting the resolution thereby become members of the agreement, but others may accede to it at any time thereafter by means of a declaration addressed to the Secretary General. Accession by non-Member States requires a favourable decision of the Committee of Ministers unless the statute of the agreement confers this right on them, in which case they also accede by means of a declaration addressed to the Secretary General. In all cases, withdrawal is by such a declaration.[78]

The agreements currently in operation concern a wide range of structures that are concerned with audiovisual industries,[79] combating corruption,[80] drug abuse and trafficking,[81] major natural and

---

[75] The European Union may also be invited to participate in any of these agreements.

[76] Statutory Resolution (93)28 on partial and enlarged agreements.

[77] Resolution (96)36 establishing the Criteria for Partial and Enlarged Agreements of the Council of Europe, as amended by Resolution CM/Res(2010)2.

[78] See, further, *Partial and Enlarged Agreements – Practical modalities governing accessions to and withdrawals from partial and enlarged agreements* (CM(2013)58).

[79] European Audiovisual Observatory.

[80] Group of States against Corruption (GRECO).

[81] Pompidou Group: Cooperation Group to Combat Drug Abuse and Illicit Trafficking in Drugs.

technological disasters,[82] quality standards for medicines,[83] financing films,[84] promoting dialogue and cooperation between Europe, the South of the Mediterranean and Africa,[85] promoting sport,[86] providing finance and technical expertise,[87] providing legal advice on compliance with international standards[88] and the teaching and learning of languages.[89] The mechanisms established by these agreements are intimately linked with the treaty obligations of Member States and non-Member States in that they can elaborate standards that are binding pursuant to them[90] and assist with or monitor the implementation of particular ones[91] as well as contribute to their revision and updating.[92]

Standard-setting can also be seen in the many Recommendations of the Committee of Ministers,[93] Resolutions of the Parliamentary Assembly (as well as its various decisions, action plans and guidelines),[94] the normative statements elaborated by monitoring bodies established by treaty or otherwise[95] and the case law of the European Court of Human Rights.[96] Equally, implementation mechanisms

---

[82] European and Mediterranean Major Hazards Agreement.

[83] The European Directorate for the Quality of Medicines and Health Care.

[84] Eurimages: European Cinema Support Fund.

[85] European Centre for Global Interdependence and Solidarity (North-South Centre).

[86] Enlarged Partial Agreement on Sport (EPAS).

[87] Council of Europe Development Bank.

[88] European Commission for Democracy through Law (the Venice Commission).

[89] European Centre for Modern Languages.

[90] The European Directorate for the Quality of Medicines and Health Care pursuant to the 1964 Convention on the Elaboration of a European Pharmacopoeia and its 1989 Protocol (CETS Nos. 050 and 134) and European Union Directives 2001/82/EC, 2001/83/EC and 2003/63/EC, as amended.

[91] E.g. the Venice Commission with respect to the former and GRECO with respect to the latter. GRECO was given the role of monitoring the implementation of all the treaties concerned with corruption by those treaties.

[92] E.g. Eurimages with respect to the 1992 European Convention on Cinematographic Co-production: CETS No. 147.

[93] E.g. Recommendation Rec(2006)2 of the Committee of Ministers to Member States on the European Prison Rules and Guidelines of the Committee of Ministers of the Council of Europe on Human Rights and the Fight against Terrorism (11 July 2002).

[94] E.g. the urgent need to combat so-called 'honour crimes' (Resolution 1681 (26 June 2009)) and human rights of irregular migrants (Resolution 1509 (27 June 2006)).

[95] E.g. *The CPT Standards 'Substantive' Sections of the CPT's General Reports* (CPT/Inf/E (2002) 1 – Rev. 2006) and the General Policy Recommendations of the European Commission against Racism and Intolerance.

[96] On all of these forms of standard-setting, see, further, J. Polakiewicz, 'Alternatives to Treaty-Making and Law-Making by Treaty and Expert Bodies in the Council of Europe' in R. Wolfrum and V. Röben (eds.), *Developments of International Law in Treaty-Making* (Berlin: Springer, 2005), pp. 245–290.

concerned with both treaty and soft law commitments have also been established by Resolutions of the Committee of Ministers.[97]

The attraction of standard-setting outside of a treaty framework can be its looser normative formulation and the readiness to agree on something that is not legally binding when the analysis of problems and their possible solutions may not yet be clear cut. Moreover, despite their informal status, such standards can nonetheless be highly influential within and beyond the membership of the Council of Europe.[98] This is equally true of certain monitoring mechanisms that do not have a treaty basis for their activities, both as regards Member States directly and through the use of their work by bodies that do have a treaty basis.[99]

However, non-legally binding standards and mechanisms are not free-standing and can really only exercise their influence because they come into existence against a background of extensive treaty law. This is true of the rulings of the European Court of Human Rights, which are formally binding only on the respondent States[100] but which in many ways clarify or crystallise the obligations of all parties to the ECHR. It is, however, also the case with all other standards which codify and concretise a whole range of treaty obligations, even if they may go beyond those norms as well.[101] Furthermore, treaty provisions, unlike those in soft law instruments, can be more readily applied by national courts, particularly where they form part of national law. Similarly, the monitoring mechanisms that are not established by a treaty invariably rely at least to some extent on standards that are treaty-based, whether very specific instruments such as the ECHR or the more general commitment made in Article 3 of the Statute. Moreover, non-legally binding standards and mechanisms sometimes act as a useful staging post on the way towards adopting a treaty, particularly where the nature of a problem is not yet fully appreciated. Such non-legally

---

[97] E.g. Resolution (99)50 on the Council of Europe Commissioner for Human Rights and Resolution Res(2002)8 on the Statute of the European Commission against Racism and Intolerance.

[98] E.g. the OSCE has made considerable use of the Fundamental Principles on the Legal Status of Non-governmental Organizations, even though they were only taken note of by the Committee of Ministers at its 861st meeting on 19 Nov. 2003. They have since been developed into. Recommendation CM/Rec(2007)14 of the Committee of Ministers to member states on the legal status of non-governmental organizations in Europe.

[99] Such as the use made by the European Court of Human Rights of reports on individual countries by the Council of Europe Commissioner for Human Rights.

[100] Art. 46 ECHR: *supra* n. 3.

[101] Such as the instruments referred to in *supra* n. 93 and n. 95.

binding instruments should, therefore, be seen as a confirmation of, and complement to, the value that treaties can achieve and not as an alternative to them.[102]

4 Issues of Commitment

The expression of consent to be bound by a treaty generally entails a separate act of ratification, acceptance or approval from that of signature, but some treaties provide for the possibility of signature without reservation as to ratification, acceptance or approval.[103] The level of commitment to all the treaties turns on issues relating not only to formal participation but also to their relationship with other obligations, reservations and other qualifications on acceptance, territorial reach, accommodations made for the European Union and the practice of derogations and denunciation.[104]

4.1 Participation by Member States

Generally low ratification thresholds are set for the entry into force of treaties. Thus, the overwhelming majority of them require between just two and six ratifications (primarily three),[105] with only twenty-one treaties requiring between seven and fourteen ratifications.[106] In addition,

---

[102] See, further, de Vel and Markert, *supra* n. 66.

[103] E.g. Art. 12(1) of the 2001 European Convention on the Legal Protection of Services based on, or consisting of, Conditional Access: CETS No. 178. For the process of expression of consent to be bound, see Polakiewicz, *supra* n. 5, at pp. 29–36. There is no provision for State succession but this has been the basis on which some successor States have been treated as bound by certain Council of Europe treaties: see Polakiewicz, *supra* n. 5, at pp. 173–188. However, whereas the dissolution of the Czech and Slovak Federative Republic was regarded as ending its membership of the organization so that the Czech Republic and Slovakia had to apply anew for this, Serbia remained a member after Montenegro's declaration of independence from the State Union of Serbia and Montenegro, with Montenegro being granted membership just under a year later.

[104] Many of these are issues addressed in the *Model Final Clauses for Conventions and Agreements concluded within the Council of Europe* that were adopted by the Committee of Ministers at its 315th Meeting in Feb. 1980, but they do not determine the approach followed in all treaties. See, further, the contribution to this volume of Bowman at pp. 392–439 (Chapter 13).

[105] Thus, twenty treaties require two ratifications, eighty-four require three, seventeen require four, thirty-five require five and two require six.

[106] Thus, six treaties require seven ratifications, four require eight, eleven require ten, one requires twelve and two require fourteen.

there are twenty-nine treaties which amend existing ones and require ratification by all the Parties to the latter ones.

There does not seem to have been any general raising of the ratification threshold in the light of the considerable enlargement of the Council of Europe. However, a requirement of two or three ratifications now tends to be used just for protocols where the nature of the amendment is not such as to require acceptance by all parties, and the larger thresholds are employed primarily in institutional treaties and ones concerned with human rights.[107] Nevertheless, the size of the threshold does not in practice seem particularly material to the ability to attract ratifications, with the larger thresholds not appearing more difficult in practice to attain than the lower ones. Furthermore, the requirement that a protocol amending a treaty must be ratified by all the parties has not normally been a serious obstacle to its entry into force – the notable exception being Protocol No. 14 to the ECHR, amending the latter's control system.[108] Be this as it may, the extent to which a treaty does attract ratification is an indicator of its impact and low thresholds could encourage the view that the treaty is optional rather than an important part of the standards and procedures being developed within the Council of Europe.

Whatever the explanation, only twenty-one of the treaties have been ratified by all the Member States.[109] Moreover, there is quite a variable level of participation by them in the other treaties. Thus, eight treaties have attracted no ratifications, nine have only one ratification, and there

---

[107] But also treaties concerned with patents (CETS No. 47), Pharmacopoeia (CETS No. 50) (both eight), corruption (CETS Nos. 17 and, 174, both fourteen), landscape (CETS No. 176) and cultural heritage (CETS No. 199) (both ten).

[108] *Supra* n. 33. As a consequence of Russia's failure to ratify this instrument, Protocol No. 14 *bis* (*supra* n. 33) was adopted, allowing those parties who wish to do so to accept some amendments to the mechanism in the ECHR. This required just three ratifications to enter into force but, having done so on 1 Oct. 2009, was soon rendered inoperative by the entry into force of Protocol No. 14 on 1 June 2010.

[109] The main institutional treaties, the ECHR but not its substantive Protocols, i.e. Nos. 1, 4, 6, 7, 12 and 13 (CETS Nos. 009, 046, 114, 117, 177 and 187); the European Convention for the Prevention of Torture and Inhuman or Degrading Treatment or Punishment (*supra* n. 65) and its Protocols (*supra* n. 67); the 1989 Anti-Doping Convention (CETS No. 135); the European Charter of Local Self-Government (*supra* n. 67); the 1954 European Cultural Convention (CETS No. 018); the European Convention on Extradition (*supra* n. 70); the European Convention on Mutual Assistance in Criminal Matters (*supra* n. 70) and the Convention on Laundering, Search, Seizure and Confiscation of the Proceeds from Crime (*supra* n. 27).

are fifteen with between two and five ratifications,[110] twenty-eight with six to ten ratifications,[111] twenty with eleven to fifteen ratifications,[112] twenty-two with sixteen to twenty ratifications,[113] thirty-one with twenty-one to twenty-five ratifications,[114] ten with twenty-six to thirty ratifications, thirteen with thirty-one to thirty-five ratifications, fourteen with thirty-six to forty ratifications and seventeen with forty-one to forty-six ratifications.[115]

Although some of the treaties with no or few ratifications are obviously ones that have only recently been adopted and domestic action to permit ratification can take some time, there are forty-nine treaties adopted ten or more years ago that have yet to attract even ten ratifications and a further forty-five treaties of the same vintage that have not attracted more than twenty ratifications. In respect of the latter it may, of course, be that some matters of significance for 'older' Member States are less important than for the 'newer' ones. Moreover, in some cases the issues addressed in them have undoubtedly been overtaken by events.

Overall, only seventy-seven of the treaties have been ratified by twenty-four or more Member States, i.e. only just over a third of the total treaties adopted have been ratified by at least half of them.[116]

This undoubtedly means that the actual impact of many treaties has been significantly diluted. Furthermore, this lack of support inevitably undermines the extent to which the body of treaties as a whole can properly be regarded as forming part of an *acquis* established within the framework of the Council of Europe or indeed ever expected to become a part of one. Nonetheless, the subject-matter of the forty treaties accepted by forty or more Member States – dealing with issues such as anti-doping, archaeological and architectural heritage, extradition, human rights, local self-government, national minorities and

---

[110] But CETS No. 149 was subsequently denounced by one of the three ratifying States and CETS No. 72 by all four of them.

[111] But there were four denunciations to No. 54, one to CETS No. 68 and three to CETS No. 178.

[112] But CETS No. 17 was subsequently denounced by all thirteen ratifying States and there have been four denunciations in respect of CETS No. 34 and one in respect of CETS No. 43.

[113] But sixteen denunciations in respect of CETS No. 16 and two in respect of CETS No. 58.

[114] But there have been nine denunciations in respect of CETS No 65, twenty in respect of CETS No. 66 and one in respect of CETS No. 103.

[115] All these figures include treaties that are no longer operative or have become an integral part of other treaties.

[116] These figures include ratifications for treaties that are no longer operative.

terrorism – underlines the significant contribution being made to both the setting of standards and their implementation.

4.2 Relationship with Other International Instruments

The potential existence of other obligations relevant to the issues addressed in Council of Europe treaties is recognised in a significant number of the latter.[117] Moreover, the Statute specifically provides that '[p]articipation in the Council of Europe shall not affect the collaboration of its members in the work of the United Nations and of other international organizations or unions to which they are parties'.[118] However, the approach with respect to whether or not such obligations – including those arising from Council of Europe treaties – are accorded any priority has been quite varied.

Thus, certain treaties are specifically designed to implement obligations under other treaties concluded outside the Council of Europe framework,[119] and in others it is clearly stated that a treaty is intended only to supplement other Council of Europe treaties.[120] In still others, there is a specific requirement that they prevail over other international obligations,[121] although this will still not always mean that (a) all obligations incurred under another treaty which contains or may contain clauses governing specific aspects of the treaty's subject-matter are affected[122] and (b) special regimes already established or to be established between certain parties cannot be operative between them[123] or the taking on of supplemental obligations by particular parties is precluded.[124]

Moreover, some treaties state that their provisions do not affect rights or obligations under specified treaties[125] or other unspecified ones that

---

[117] Sixty-three.   [118] Art. 1c: supra n. 1.

[119] E.g. the 1995 Agreement on Illicit Traffic by Sea, implementing Art. 17 of the United Nations Convention against Illicit Traffic in Narcotic Drugs and Psychotropic Substances: CETS No. 156.

[120] Art. 26(1) of the Council of Europe Convention on the Prevention of Terrorism: supra n. 70.

[121] E.g. Art. 28(1) of the European Convention on Extradition: supra n. 70.

[122] E.g. Art. 26(2) of the European Convention on Mutual Assistance in Criminal Matters: supra n. 70.

[123] E.g. Art. 19(3) of the Civil Law Convention on Corruption: supra n. 70.

[124] E.g. Art. 35(2) of the Criminal Law Convention on Corruption: supra n. 70.

[125] E.g. Art. 20(1) of the 2003 Convention on Contact Concerning Children (CETS No. 192) (with respect to, amongst others, the Hague Convention of 25 Oct. 1980 on the Civil Aspects of International Child Abduction: 1343 UNTS 89).

have been (and sometimes have not yet been) concluded[126] or rules of the European Union,[127] which does not actually give any indication as to whether this is to secure a more exacting obligation. In addition, one treaty provides that powers under it are not to be used where a similar role is performed by another international entity.[128] There are still other treaties that stipulate that they are without prejudice to the application of provisions in any international agreement (or in domestic law) that provide for more favourable treatment or greater protection than their own ones.[129] Also, in some cases, there is a requirement that a treaty be applied subject to the same limitations and reservations applicable under other specified treaties.[130]

Only in one instance is there a stipulation that a treaty is not to affect any obligations that a party may have towards a non-party under an international instrument dealing with matters governed by it.[131]

There is no reference in any of the treaties to the stipulation in Article 103 of the 1945 United Nations Charter that obligations under the Charter are, in the event of any conflict, to prevail over the obligations of Members of the United Nations under any other international agreement.[132] Although the European Court of Human Rights considers it appropriate to adopt, if possible, interpretations that avoid a conflict of

---

[126] E.g. Art. 9 of the 1966 European Convention providing a Uniform Law on Arbitration: CETS No. 056. However, in certain instances, those dealing with certain topics may be specifically mentioned as well, e.g. Art. 48 of the 1967 European Convention on Consular Functions (regarding the protection of refugees): CETS No. 061.

[127] E.g. Art. 27(2) of the 1988 Convention on Mutual Administrative Assistance in Tax Matters: CETS No. 127. Such provisions concern only Parties that are Member States of the European Union. See, further, Section 4.6 of this chapter.

[128] Art. 17(3) of the European Convention for the Prevention of Torture and Inhuman or Degrading Treatment or Punishment (*supra* n. 65) with respect to 'places which representatives or delegates of Protecting Powers or the International Committee of the Red Cross effectively visit on a regular basis by virtue of the Geneva Conventions of 12 August 1949 and the Additional Protocols of 8 June 1977 thereto'.

[129] E.g. Art. 53 ECHR (*supra* n. 3) and Art. 12 of the 2000 European Landscape Convention (CETS No. 176).

[130] Art. 13 of the 1980 European Agreement on Transfer of Responsibility for Refugees (CETS No. 107) (referring to the 1951 Convention Relating to the Status of Refugees (189 UNTS 150) or the 1967 Protocol Relating to the Status of Refugees (660 UNTS 267)) and Art. 34(1) of the 2014 Council of Europe Convention on the Manipulation of Sports Competitions (CETS No. 215) (referring to the ECHR (*supra* n. 3) and the 1966 International Covenant on Civil and Political Rights (999 UNTS 171)).

[131] Art. 20(1) of the 1980 European Convention on Recognition and Enforcement of Decisions concerning Custody of Children and on Restoration of Custody of Children: CETS No. 105.

[132] 1 UNTS 16.

obligations arising, it would also seem to accept that obligations under the Charter would prevail over those under the ECHR only where the Security Council uses clear and explicit language to show an intention that States should take particular measures which would conflict with their obligations under international human rights law.[133]

4.3 Reservations and Other Qualifications on Acceptance

The impact of the treaties is also to some extent affected by the fact that, with respect to many of them, States may qualify the extent to which they accept particular provisions through making reservations[134] or declarations which determine either (a) the provisions accepted pursuant to a scheme of opting-in or opting-out specifically authorised by the treaties themselves[135] or (b) whether any of the provisions will apply to non-metropolitan territories.[136]

In addition, two treaties authorise a federal State to reserve the rights to assume obligations under specified chapters 'consistent with its fundamental principles governing the relationship between its central government and constituent States or other similar territorial entities', provided that it is still able to fulfil the obligations of international co-operation and exchange of information established by the treaties.[137] Moreover, they bar such reservations from excluding or substantially diminishing the State's obligations to provide for measures to be taken at the national

---

[133] See *Al-Jedda v. United Kingdom* [GC], No. 27021/08, 7 July 2011 (paragraph 102) and *Nada v. Switzerland* [GC], No. 10593/08, 12 Sept. 2012 (paragraph 172).

[134] Sometimes these are expressed as 'declarations' but they are in substance reservations because they can only be understood as limiting the legal effect of one or more provisions with respect to the State or organization ratifying the treaty concerned.

[135] The former require acceptance of a minimum number of provisions (e.g. the European Social Charter in its original and revised forms: *supra* n. 67). See the Convention on Mutual Administrative Assistance in Tax Matters (*supra* n. 127) for an instance of the latter.

[136] See Section 4.4 of this chapter.

[137] Art. 41 of the Convention on Cybercrime (*supra* n. 70) and Art. 36 of the Council of Europe Convention on the Manipulation of Sports Competitions (*supra* n. 130). In addition, under Art. 25 of the 1985 European Convention on Offences Relating to Cultural Property (CETS No. 119), a federal government is bound to implement those provisions that come within its legislative power but only to give a favourable opinion to constituent entities of provisions coming under their jurisdiction but in respect of which there is no constitutional requirement to take legislative measures. There can also be declarations on ratification to protect the division of competence within federal States: see J. Polakiewicz, *supra* n. 5, at p. 55.

level. Furthermore, there is also a requirement for the federal government to inform – with its favourable opinion – the constituent entities of provisions coming under their jurisdiction (but in respect of which there is no constitutional requirement to take legislative measures), encouraging them to take appropriate action to give them effect.

The making of reservations initially tended to be only allowed in treaties in respect of matters where there was a conflict between their provisions and ones in the law of the ratifying State.[138] However, the practice regarding reservations has since evolved so that several possibilities now exist: (a) the treaty says nothing about reservations;[139] (b) reservations are expressly prohibited;[140] (c) reservations are permitted without qualification;[141] (d) specified reservations and/or ones restricted to certain provisions are permitted[142] and (e) reservations negotiated by a particular State or organization are permitted.[143] Of these, the first and fourth possibilities continue to be the most common ones overall, despite an increasing tendency to prohibit reservations entirely.[144] There is thus considerable scope for making reservations since the effect of the former is generally to authorise reservations, notwithstanding the treaty's silence

---

[138] E.g. Art. 57 ECHR: *supra* n. 3.

[139] E.g. the European Cultural Convention: *supra* n. 109.

[140] E.g. Art. 25 of the Convention on Contact Concerning Children: *supra* n. 125.

[141] E.g. Art. 7 of the 1969 European Agreement Relating to Persons Participating in Proceedings of the European Commission and Court of Human Rights: CETS No. 067. There may, however, be a requirement that reservations be 'established': e.g. Art. 48 of the Council of Europe Convention on the Protection of Children against Sexual Exploitation and Sexual Abuse (*supra* n. 72).

[142] E.g. Art. 4(2) of the Council of Europe Convention on Human Trafficking in Human Organs: *supra* n. 27.

[143] E.g. Art. 7 of the 1972 European Convention on the Place of Payment of Money Liabilities: CETS No. 075. See, further, S. S. Åkermark, 'Reservation Clauses in Treaties Concluded within the Council of Europe', *ICLQ*, 49 (1999), 479–514; Polakiewicz, *supra* n. 5, at pp. 77–117; N. Levrat, 'De quelques particularités du mode d'élaboration des normes conventionnelles, et de leur influence sur la nature des traités conclus au sein du Conseil de l'Europe', *Revue de droit de l'ULB*, 22 (2000), 19–58, and J. Polakiewicz, 'Collective Responsibility and Reservations in a Common European Human Rights Area' in I. Ziemele (ed), *Reservations to Treaties and the Vienna Convention Regime: Conflict, Harmony or Reconciliation* (Leiden: Martinus Nijhoff, 2004), pp. 95–132.

[144] The analysis by Åkermark, *supra* n. 143, shows the former possibility occurring in 43 per cent of treaties adopted between CETS Nos. 38 and 170, with the latter in 35 per cent of treaties, while reservations were only prohibited in 14 per cent of treaties. For the forty-six treaties subsequently adopted, there is a prohibition on reservations in fourteen (i.e. 28 per cent) of them, but categories (a) and (d) taken together remain in the majority, with twelve (26 per cent) and 16 (34 percent) treaties respectively.

on the issue, either because the treaty is a protocol and action in this regard is governed by a reservation clause in the main treaty or because the making of a reservation that is compatible with the treaty's object and purpose is permitted under general international law.[145]

Although possibilities (a) and (d) – as well as the much more infrequent use of opt-ins[146] and opt-outs – are envisaged by the treaties themselves, their existence weakens the extent to which such treaties can be regarded as embodying, in their entirety, a generally applicable set of standards. Moreover, this has been borne out in practice as certainly some advantage has been taken of the various possibilities of qualifying the level of acceptance by those who become parties to them.[147] As a consequence, not only is the body of treaty law not binding on all Member States, but those who are parties are not fully bound by all of the provisions of the treaties concerned. The existence of a possibility of making reservations and declarations is undoubtedly essential to securing the participation of some Member States, but achieving breadth in the extent of commitment at the expense of its depth can also make it harder to establish what are the core values that they share. This has become increasingly problematic with the considerable expansion in membership over the past two and a half decades.

This situation can also be regarded as being exacerbated by the fact that there is no generally available means of determining authoritatively the admissibility of the reservations and declarations that have actually been made. It is only in respect of the ECHR and its Protocols that it is in practice possible for a reservation or declaration to be ruled inadmissible, with the result that a party must fulfil the requirements of the provision concerned without the qualification it had advanced.[148]

Some safeguard against the integrity of a commitment being improperly compromised does exist in the capacity of the Secretary General as depositary to draw problematic reservations or declarations to the attention of other parties, who could then object to them. However, this can only really be helpful where a problem is evident from the text of a reservation or declaration rather than its purported application in a specific situation.

---

[145] Art. 19 of the 1969 Vienna Convention of the Law of Treaties: 1155 UNTS 331.

[146] Which might be subject to reciprocity; see Levrat, *supra* n. 143, at 40–45.

[147] An analysis of the detailed character of the various reservations, opt-ins and opt-ins by States is not addressed in this chapter.

[148] See, e.g., *Belilos v. Switzerland*, No. 10328/23, 29 Apr. 1988, and *Loizidou v. Turkey* (Preliminary Objections) [GC], No. 15318/89, 23 March 1995.

Moreover, other parties may not be prepared to pursue an objection for reasons unconnected with the issue of admissibility.[149] It remains to be seen whether the introduction of a provision for review of reservations seen in the Protocol amending the European Convention on the Suppression of Terrorism,[150] together with a substantial recasting of the provision governing reservations in the principal treaty[151] – which is replicated in the Council of Europe Convention on the Prevention of Terrorism[152] that complements these instruments – will overcome such reluctance to object.[153]

The trend, already noted, for more recent treaties to prohibit the making of reservations entirely must be regarded as welcome insofar as it can be seen as enhancing the essential nature of the obligations being undertaken, thereby strengthening the values that these embody. Similarly worth a welcome is the practice sometimes seen of setting time limits on the life of any reservations made.[154] Even though provision may be made for renewing their operation, such an approach necessitates a reconsideration of the appropriateness of maintaining them.[155]

4.4 Territorial Application

Various approaches have been followed in addressing the potential territorial reach of commitments under the treaties.[156]

---

[149] On the rarity of objections being made, see Polakiewicz, *supra* n. 5, at pp. 99–101.

[150] *Supra* n. 70.

[151] The latter now requires reservations refusing extradition in respect of an offence considered to be a political offence, an offence connected with a political offence or an offence inspired by political motives to be applied 'on a case-by-case basis, through a duly reasoned decision and taking into due consideration, when evaluating the character of the offence, any particularly serious aspects of the offence' and such reservations to be valid only for renewable periods of three years. Furthermore, if within a reasonable time no judicial decision on the merits of a refusal has been taken in the requested State, the requesting State may now communicate this fact to the Secretary General who shall submit the matter to a new Conference of States Parties against Terrorism (COSTER), which must issue an opinion on the conformity of the refusal with the Convention. The Protocol further provides that COSTER is responsible for ensuring the examination of any reservations that have been made.

[152] In Art. 20; the same role in this treaty is given to the Consultation of the Parties.

[153] No relevant practice seems to have occurred so far.

[154] See, e.g., in Art. 79 of the 2011 Council of Europe Convention on Preventing and Combating Violence against Women and Domestic Violence: CETS No. 210.

[155] Particularly when coupled with the review provision discussed in the preceding paragraph.

[156] See, further, Polakiewicz, *supra* n. 5, at pp. 43–47. See, further, the contribution to this volume of Miltner at pp. 468–505 (Chapter 15).

Sometimes, there is no reference to this issue at all,[157] and in twelve treaties no definition of 'territory' is to be found even though there are provisions in which this concept is specifically mentioned. In just one treaty and its amending protocols,[158] the obligation undertaken is expressed as being 'within its jurisdiction', but as it is concerned with transfrontier co-operation between the territorial communities of parties who must be Member States or European non-Member States, this will necessarily be restricted to Europe.

For sixteen treaties (including the ECHR),[159] there is no uncertainty as the commitments are expressly limited to the metropolitan territories of the party,[160] albeit with the option in all but one case[161] for extending them to other territories for whose international relations it is responsible or for which it is empowered to legislate. However, in the case of two treaties, there is a variant on this possibility in that not only must the extension be by direct arrangement between two or more parties but also the Federal Republic of Germany was authorised to extend their application to the *Land* of Berlin; the Netherlands was similarly authorised to do this with respect to the Netherlands Antilles, Suriname and Netherlands New Guinea and they are specified to apply automatically to certain territories.[162]

---

[157] In nineteen treaties (including protocols).

[158] European Outline Convention on Transfrontier Co-operation between Territorial Communities or Authorities and the protocols thereto: *supra* n. 70. However, with respect to the last instrument a Party may designate the categories of territorial communities or authorities which it excludes from its scope.

[159] As well as Protocol Nos. 1 and 4: CETS Nos. 009 and 046.

[160] This is implicit in the Sixth Protocol to the General Agreement on Privileges and Immunities of the Council of Europe (*supra* n. 69) as Art. 9 only provides for the possibility of a Party extending it to all or any of the territories for whose international relations it is responsible and where the ECHR and its Protocols apply.

[161] The 1964 Protocol to the European Convention on the Equivalence of Diplomas leading to Admission to Universities (CETS No. 049); 'territory' is not defined in the principal treaty (CETS No. 015).

[162] Art. 27 of the European Convention on Extradition (*supra* n. 70) (Algeria and overseas Departments in respect of France and the Channel Islands and the Isle of Man in respect of the United Kingdom) and Art. 25(2) of the European Convention on Mutual Assistance in Criminal Matters (*supra* n. 70) (Algeria and overseas Departments in respect of France and the territory of Somaliland under Italian administration).

In a few instances, the territorial applicability of commitments is to be determined by a declaration[163] or notification,[164] but the approach now generally followed is to include a provision authorising a party to specify, at the time of signature or when depositing its instrument of ratification, the territory or territories to which the treaty concerned shall apply and then, at any later date by a declaration addressed to the Secretary General, extend its application to any other territory specified in the declaration and for whose international relations it is responsible or on whose behalf it is authorised to give undertakings.[165] In either case, it is also possible – again by notification to the Secretary General – to withdraw the treaty's applicability in respect of any of the territories specified.[166] A variant on this approach is found in one treaty, in which the only territories that can be specified are those for whose international relations the party is responsible.[167]

In the case of those treaties where there is no reference to 'territory' at all, it is not evident from the nature of their provisions that these are necessarily limited in their scope to the metropolitan territory of the party,[168] but the absence of any such limitation does not seem to have given rise to any problems in practice. Moreover, the nature of the subject-matter of the treaties in which 'territory' is a material consideration but is neither specifically defined nor subject to any limitation regarding its scope also does not generally point to a narrow definition being appropriate.[169]

---

[163] With respect to an updatable Annex or Appendix to the relevant treaty (e.g. the 1972 European Convention on Social Security: CETS No. 078).

[164] The sole example of this is the Fourth Protocol to the General Agreement on Privileges and Immunities of the Council of Europe (*supra* n. 34), which is no longer operative.

[165] This is the approach seen in Protocol Nos. 6, 7, 12 and 13 (*supra* n. 109) to the ECHR, in contrast to that in the latter treaty itself.

[166] It is found in more than half of the treaties adopted. It was first used in 1963 for the Convention on the Unification of Certain Points of Substantive Law on Patents for Invention: CETS No. 47.

[167] The Framework Convention for the Protection of National Minorities: *supra* n. 45.

[168] E.g. the 1959 European Convention on the Academic Recognition of University Qualifications: CETS No. 032.

[169] E.g. the 1957 European Convention for the Peaceful Settlement of Disputes (CETS No. 023) and the 1962 European Agreement on Mutual Assistance in the matter of Special Medical Treatments and Climatic Facilities (CETS No. 038). However, it should be noted that the preamble of the last instrument envisages mutual assistance as helping to 'strengthen European consciousness and solidarity'. Also, a narrow application might be appropriate for the European Cultural Convention (*supra* n. 109), which is concerned with 'the common cultural heritage of Europe'. Furthermore, it seems unavoidable in the case of the European Charter for Regional or Minority Languages (*supra* n. 45) given the preambular reference to the 'the historical regional or minority languages of Europe' and

Indeed, in those concerned with nationality and statelessness this might seem inappropriate.[170]

Parties with non-metropolitan territories have not generally taken advantage of the possibility of extending treaties that are initially limited to metropolitan territory, but such extensions as have been made have been to most of the territories concerned. The ECHR is a significant exception in this regard, but even then it has never been extended to all the non-metropolitan territories of the parties.[171] Similarly, the ability, found in more recent treaties, to specify the territories to which a treaty is applicable has not been exercised in a way that brings non-metropolitan territories of parties generally within the scope of the commitments undertaken.[172]

However, the issue of territorial application of the treaties is not just about non-metropolitan treaties, as some Member States have sought to exclude any obligation in respect of parts of their territory where they do not exercise control and others have been challenged to observe treaty provisions in places that do not form part of the territory of any Member State.[173]

So far, this only seems to be an issue with respect to the ECHR and some conclusions have been reached by the European Court of Human Rights on this issue. Thus, lack of control by a party over its

the definition of such languages as being those 'traditionally used within a given territory of a State by nationals of that State who form a group numerically smaller than the rest of the State's population' (Art. 1).

[170] E.g. the 1963 Convention on the Reduction of Cases of Multiple Nationality and on Military Obligations in Cases of Multiple Nationality (CETS No. 043) and the Council of Europe Convention on the Avoidance of Statelessness in relation to State Succession (*supra* n. 67). Nonetheless, the European Convention on Nationality (*supra* n. 67) is one of the treaties for which Parties are free to specify the territory to which it is applicable.

[171] France currently extends it to all its overseas territories, the Netherlands to the Netherlands Antilles and Aruba and the United Kingdom to the Bailiwick of Guernsey, Isle of Man, the Bailiwick of Jersey and the British Overseas Territories apart from the Pitcairn Islands and those in the Antarctic and the Indian Ocean. It was never extended to Hong Kong.

[172] E.g. the Netherlands has accepted the European Convention for the Prevention of Torture and Inhuman or Degrading Treatment or Punishment (*supra* n. 65) with respect to the Netherlands Antilles and Aruba and the United Kingdom has done so with respect to the Bailiwick of Jersey and the Isle of Man.

[173] See, also, the possibility in Art. 25 of the European Convention on Recognition and Enforcement of Decisions Concerning Custody of Children and on Restoration of Custody of Children (*supra* n. 131) for a Party to determine in which of its metropolitan territorial units a treaty's provisions were to apply on account of those units having different systems of law.

own territory does not mean an end to all of its obligations under this instrument in respect of events taking place there.[174] In addition, the exercise of control over territory – whether or not that of another Member State – and over persons can result in responsibility for violations of the guaranteed rights and freedoms.[175] Although occupation or control of another State's territory could possibly raise issues with respect to the fulfilment of obligations under other treaties – such as those concerned with social rights and the protection of various heritage interests – the absence of a comparable duty in the relevant treaties to that for a party under Article 1 of the ECHR to secure the enumerated rights and freedoms to everyone within its jurisdiction means that these obligations are unlikely to be considered applicable outside any territories to which they have been specifically applied.[176]

4.5   Participation by Non-member States

There are only forty-four treaties for which ratification is restricted to Member States,[177] while 174 are open to other European States,[178] 159 are open to non-European non-Member States,[179] and fifty-five are open to the European Union.[180] Ratification of treaties by non-Member States and the European Union could be an indication of their wider significance, although this would not necessarily mean that the standards in

---

[174] *Ilaşcu and Others v. Moldova and Russia* [GC], No. 48787/99, 8 July 2004.

[175] E.g. *Cyprus v. Turkey* [GC], No. 25781/94, 10 May 2001 (control over territory) and *Medvedyev and Others v. France* [GC], No. 3394/03, 29 March 2010 (control over persons). In the latter case, there will be an obligation to secure to any individual concerned only the rights and freedoms that are relevant to his or her situation: *Jaloud v. Netherlands* [GC], No. 47708/08, 20 Nov. 2014.

[176] The reference to 'jurisdiction' in the European Outline Convention on Transfrontier Cooperation between Territorial Communities or Authorities and the protocols thereto (*supra* n. 70) is exceptional.

[177] Primarily ones that are institutional ones or concerned with democracy and human rights and those dealing with terrorism, with just a few from the fields relating to culture and sport, environmental and social issues and private law.

[178] Covering all fields apart from the institutional one. However, as most European States are now Member States, this is currently only of significance for Belarus and the Holy See.

[179] Covering treaties in all the fields apart from the institutional ones.

[180] Mainly ones concerned with culture and sport, environmental and social issues, legal process and cooperation and private law, but also some relating to democracy and human rights. The entry into force of Protocol No. 14 to the ECHR would enable the European Union to accede to the Convention and its other Protocols.

them do not already apply in other fora in which the entities concerned also participate.

In practice, the level of participation by entities other than Member States is still rather low.[181] Thus, the European Union has ratified only eleven of the fifty-five treaties open to it, and no European non-Member State has ratified more than ten of the 174 treaties open to them.[182] Moreover, while thirty-five non-European States have ratified at least one treaty, only one has ratified ten treaties, and two have ratified eight treaties, with the majority of them having ratified three or fewer treaties.[183]

The extension of the possibility of ratification to non-Member States clearly seems desirable in principle, not least because such ratifications could secure the wider applicability of the standards concerned and facilitate cooperation. However, current practice does not suggest that this opportunity is being taken up to any significant extent by the sixty-two non-European States to whom it has been given, and as a consequence it has not significantly enhanced the impact of the treaties concerned.

4.6   EU Exceptionalism

A number of treaties provide that that those parties which are also members of the European Union shall, in their mutual relations, apply any applicable European Union rules governing the matter in question.[184] Such a 'disconnection clause' is supposed to reflect the fact that implementation of the treaties concerned may involve the

---

[181]   However, requests from and invitations to non-Member States to accede to Council of Europe treaties has more than trebled since 2010, albeit from a low base. Thus, the totals of eighteen and twenty-three respectively for requests and invitations is still modest.

[182]   Belarus has ratified nine and the Holy See has ratified eight but the latter has denounced one of these (CETS No. 66) following the adoption of a revised treaty on the protection of archaeological heritage (CETS No. 143).

[183]   The detailed figures are as follows: Argentina (2); Australia (8 but it has denounced CETS No. 17); the Bahamas (1); Belize (2); Bolivia (1); Burkina Faso (1); Canada (4); Chile (4); Colombia (2); Costa Rica (4); the Dominican Republic (1); Ecuador (1); Ghana (2); Honduras (1); India (2); Indonesia (2); Israel (10 but it has denounced CETS No. 17); Japan (4); Kazakhstan (5); Korea (8); the Kyrgyhz Republic (1); Mauritius (2); Mexico (5); Morocco (6); New Zealand (5); Nigeria (1); Panama (2); Senegal (1); South Africa (6); Sri Lanka (1); Tajikistan (1); Tonga (1); Trinidad and Tobago (1); Tunisia (6); the United States (3); Uruguay (2) and Venezuela (1). Most ratifications by non-European States have concerned treaties in the legal process and cooperation field.

[184]   See, e.g., CETS Nos. 132, 133 and 197.

competence of both the parties and the European Union and thus require the enactment of Union law, which would supersede any treaty provision.[185] The clause does not seek to affect the application of the treaty concerned in relations between the parties who are members of the European Union and those who are not.[186]

It does not, of course, really matter whether the source of the implementing measure is a national or European Union one as long as it is effective, though concern has been raised about such clauses because of the potential for different rules to be applied between European Union Member States to those applied between them and the other parties to the treaty concerned.[187] This is possible as a treaty obligation is no defence to the requirement to fulfil the requirements of European Union measures,[188] and a broad construction of the clause could be seen as authorising this. Indeed, viewed in this way, such a clause would appear effectively to authorise a diminution of obligations as and when the European Union sees fit. This would be incompatible with the specificity generally required for reservations to Council of Europe treaties.[189]

There thus seems to be a need to clarify the actual scope of such disconnection clauses, and if they do go beyond simply establishing the source of the implementing measure and allow for different but lower standards to operate between European Union Member States, it would be more appropriate for what is in reality an opt-out or reservation to be specified in the same way as applies to other parties to Council of Europe treaties.[190]

More specific efforts to accommodate the nature of the European Union can be seen in the efforts to facilitate its accession to the ECHR.

---

[185] Although the competence is supposed to be shared, none of the treaties to which the European Union is actually a party (CETS Nos. 26, 33, 39, 50, 84, 87, 104, 123, 134, 170 and 180) has such a clause.

[186] See, further, J. Polakiewicz, 'The European Union and the Council of Europe – Competition or Coherence in Fundamental Rights Protection in Europe?' Paper Presented at the Jean Monnet Conference, Macau, 27–28 May 2008, pp. 8–9.

[187] See Reinforcing the Effectiveness of Council of Europe Treaty Law, Recommendation 1920(2010) of the Parliamentary Assembly of the Council of Europe.

[188] Case C-222/94 Commission v. United Kingdom [1996] ECR I-4025.

[189] However, the disconnection clause has not been used since the 2007 Council of Europe Convention on the Protection of Children against Sexual Exploitation and Sexual Abuse: CETS No. 201.

[190] It is questionable whether the use of such a clause could be effective in respect of human rights provisions as their *erga omnes* character would preclude different standards applying to any group of parties to the treaty concerned.

Under the draft agreement between its parties and the European Union,[191] provision was made to protect the autonomy of the latter's legal order and of the Court of Justice through a 'co-respondent' mechanism enabling the European Union to become a party to any proceedings involving one of its Member States where the compatibility with Convention rights of a provision of European Union law arose. In addition, there was provision for the European Court of Human Rights to request the Court of Justice to rule on a matter that it had not previously addressed and for determining the distribution of any responsibility for a violation between the respondent and the co-respondent. However, these accommodations were not sufficient to prevent the Court of Justice from concluding that the draft agreement was contrary to European Union law since it was seen as ignoring the intrinsic nature of the Union.[192] In particular, there was concern about the potential adverse effect of the co-respondent mechanism on the division of power between the European Union and its Member States and the insufficiency of the provision for the prior involvement of the Court of Justice in a case as a safeguard for its role under European Union law.[193]

4.7 Derogation and Denunciation

Six treaties provide for the possibility of taking measures in derogation from obligations that have been undertaken in time of war or other emergency threatening the life of the nation. These are the 1950 ECHR,[194] the 1961 European Social Charter in its original and revised forms,[195] the 1978 European Convention on the Control of the Acquisition and Possession of Firearms by Individuals,[196] the 1992 Convention on the Participation of Foreigners in Public Life

---

[191] At www.echr.coe.int/Documents/UE_Report_CDDH_ENG.pdf.

[192] Opinion 2/13 of the Court, 18 Dec. 2014.

[193] Another problem that has emerged from the participation of the European Union in Council of Europe treaty-making concerns the respective competence of the Union and Member States regarding their implementation. Thus, the opening for signature of a protocol to the Council of Europe Convention on the Prevention of Terrorism (*supra* n. 29 and n. 70) was delayed pending the resolution of whether its subject matter fell within the exclusive competence of the European Union or was shared or mixed with that of the Member States.

[194] Art. 15 ECHR: *supra* n. 3.   [195] *Supra* n. 67 and n. 72; Arts. 30 and F respectively.

[196] CETS No. 010, Art. 18. This allows derogations in the event of war 'or other exceptional circumstances'.

at Local Level[197] and, perhaps rather surprisingly, the 1966 European
Convention on the Establishment of Companies.[198] In all but one of
them, this is only authorised to the extent strictly required by the
exigencies of the situation and provided that such measures are not
inconsistent with its other obligations under international law.[199]
A party availing itself of this possibility must notify the Secretary
General about having done so, and generally, reasons for this must
be provided.[200] Any failure to give the notification required is
regarded by the European Court of Human Rights as rendering
ineffective a derogation in respect of the ECHR. Only the latter
instrument excludes the possibility of derogating from certain of
the obligations undertaken.[201]

So far, derogations have related only to the rights and freedoms
guaranteed under the ECHR. Eight parties have made such derogations
on one or more occasions,[202] and they have generally been found to be
effective except where no emergency was established,[203] where the
measures concerned an area of the country not covered by the
derogation[204] or where the measures were found not to be strictly
required by the exigencies of the situation.[205] However, not all situations which might be regarded as constituting an emergency – including armed conflict within parties (such as the Russian operation in
Chechnya between 1999 and 2009 (the 'Second Chechen War')) or
involving other States (as occurred with the United Kingdom's participation in the invasion and occupation of Iraq (2003–2009)) – have been
ones in which it has been considered necessary to seek the protection
afforded by a derogation.

In addition to these derogation provisions, the 1957 European
Agreement on Regulations governing the Movement of Persons between

---

[197] CETS No. 144, Art. 9.
[198] CETS No. 057, Art. 15. However, this has only been ratified by Luxembourg and has not
entered into force.
[199] The European Convention on the Control of the Acquisition and Possession of Firearms
by Individuals (*supra* n. 196) allows a party to 'make rules temporarily derogating from
the provisions of this Convention and having immediate effect'.
[200] This is not required by the European Convention on the Establishment of Companies:
supra n. 198.
[201] These concern Arts. 2, 3, 4(1) and 7 ECHR: *supra* n. 3.
[202] Albania, Armenia, France, Georgia, Ireland, Turkey, Ukraine and the United Kingdom.
[203] *The Greek Case*, No. 3321/67, YbECHR, 12*bis* (1972).
[204] *Sakik and Others v. Turkey*, No. 23878/94, 26 Nov. 1997.
[205] *Aksoy v. Turkey*, No. 21987/93, 18 Dec. 1996, and *A. and Others v. United Kingdom* [GC],
No. 3455/05, 19 Feb. 2009.

Member States of the Council of Europe[206] and the 1959 European Agreement on the Abolition of Visas for Refugees[207] both provide for the possibility of a party, for reasons of *ordre public*, security or public health, to delay its entry into force or to order its temporary suspension in respect of all or some of the other Parties, apart from one of its provisions.[208] Delays in the former Agreement have been just with respect to particular parties[209] but have been more general in the case of the latter one.[210] Several parties have suspended the provisions of the former Agreement with respect to one or more parties,[211] whereas the only suspension of the latter one – by France – has been general in its effect.[212]

The overwhelming majority of treaties – including the Statute – provide for the possibility of denunciation.[213] However, not all protocols do so as either their provisions become an integral part of the principal treaty following entry into force or this is governed by the relevant provision in that treaty.[214] In those protocols which do make separate provision for denunciation, the exercise of this right will not normally have any repercussions for the operation of the principal treaty.[215] Nonetheless, some protocols additionally stipulate that their denunciation is the automatic effect of such an act with respect to the principal treaty.[216] Just a few treaties permit denunciations with respect to individual provisions[217] and/or permit denunciation in respect of territories to which they have been extended by the Party concerned.[218]

---

[206] CETS No. 25.   [207] CETS No. 31.

[208] Art. 7 of both Agreements. The exception concerns the obligation in Art. 5 to re-admit refugees to whom travel documents have been issued.

[209] By Hungary and Slovenia.

[210] By Denmark, Norway and Sweden (for just over a month).

[211] Austria, Belgium, France, Germany, Greece, Italy, Luxembourg, Malta, the Netherlands, Portugal, Spain, Switzerland and Turkey.

[212] With effect from 16 Sept. 1986. See also the unusual power in Art. 10 of the Convention on Insider Trading to suspend the application of provisions on exchange of information in respect of a Party found to be in substantial breach of the confidentiality undertaking

[213] There is no provision in the General Agreement on Privileges and Immunities of the Council of Europe (*supra* n. 34) (which is relevant only to member States), the European Convention on the Equivalence of Diplomas leading to Admission to Universities and the European Convention on the Equivalence of Periods of University Study.

[214] Notably the Protocols to the ECHR.

[215] See, e.g., Art. 27 of the 2008 Additional Protocol to the Convention on Human Rights and Biomedicine, Concerning Genetic Testing for Health Purposes: CETS No. 203.

[216] E.g. Art. 11(4) of the 1988 Additional Protocol to the European Social Charter: CETS No. 128.

[217] E.g. Art. 17(2) of the European Charter of Local Self-Government: *supra* n. 67.

[218] E.g. Art. M(3) of the European Social Charter (revised): *supra* n. 67.

Some treaties stipulate that denunciation will not release a party from obligations arising before this takes effect[219] or affect rights acquired or in the course of being acquired[220] and that their provisions will continue to apply to proceedings already introduced.[221] Just a few provide that denunciation by one party will not affect the validity of the treaty for other ones.[222] However, some treaties stipulate that ceasing to be a member of the Council of Europe will also result in the party ceasing to be a party to them.[223] Moreover, one treaty precludes the possibility of remaining a party once it ceases to be a party to another treaty, albeit not a Council of Europe one.[224]

The exercise of the right to denounce is always conditional on giving notice to the Secretary General[225] – the period ranging from three to fifteen months,[226] but generally six months or one year – before it can take effect. In certain cases, the right is also conditional on the treaty having been in force for a certain period, ranging from one to five years,[227] and in a few cases there is also a bar on denunciation until the elapse of successive periods after the first one has elapsed without a denunciation.[228]

Notwithstanding all these provisions, only fourteen treaties have been denounced. In most cases, this has been by all[229] or a significant

---

[219] E.g. Art. 58(2) ECHR: *supra* n. 3.

[220] Art. 16(2) of the European Agreement on Transfer of Responsibility for Refugees: *supra* n. 130.

[221] E.g. Art. 40(2) of the 1972 European Convention on State Immunity: CETS No. 074.

[222] E.g. Art. 17(2) of the European Charter of Local Self-Government (*supra* n. 67) but this is subject to the number of Parties not falling below four.

[223] E.g. Art. 58(3) ECHR (*supra* n. 3) and Art. 15 of the European Convention on the Suppression of Terrorism (*supra* n. 70).

[224] Art. 13 of the 1960 European Agreement on the Protection of Television Broadcasts, CETS No. 034, with respect to the 1961 International Convention on for the Protection of Performers, Producers of Phonograms and Broadcasting Organizations: 496 UNTS 43.

[225] Except for non-Member States party to the 1954 European Convention on the International Classification of Patents for Invention (CETS No. 017) who must notify the Government of the Swiss Confederation (Art. 8(2)).

[226] Denunciation of the Statute requires notice within nine months of the end of the financial year in which it is to take effect otherwise it will only do so at the end of the following one.

[227] E.g. Art. 58(1) ECHR (five years) (*supra* n. 3) and Art. 24 of the European Convention on Social and Medical Assistance (CETS No. 014) (two years). However, Art. 12 of the 1958 European Convention on Compulsory Insurance against Civil Liability in respect of Motor Vehicles is alone allowing a denunciation earlier than the minimum period 'in case of emergency': CETS No. 029.

[228] E.g. Art. 88(1) of the 1990 European Code of Social Security (Revised): CETS No. 139.

[229] The 1954 European Convention on the International Classification of Patents for Invention (*supra* n. 225) and the 1970 Convention relating to Stops on Bearer Securities in International Circulation (CETS No. 072).

number[230] of the parties and in just a few instances by one[231] or a limited group of them.[232] The former situation reflects the instrument concerned being overtaken by a different approach to its subject-matter that has not necessarily emerged within the Council of Europe, and the latter one points to the existence of more particular concerns for the Parties in question. Apart from one instance – Greece's denunciation of the ECHR and withdrawal from the Council of Europe in 1970 – the practice of denunciation does not indicate any difficulty for the parties concerned to fulfil the fundamental goals of the organization, even if a somewhat different conclusion might be drawn from some judgments of the European Court of Human Rights and findings by other monitoring bodies.

5   Implementation and Dispute Settlement

Treaties devoted to private law issues do not generally include any special implementation measures. This is unsurprising given their harmonisation character and the one exception – which provides only for the holding of multilateral consultations on implementation[233] – is not a significant departure from this approach. However, implementation is generally addressed in treaties concerned with other issues, although

---

[230] The 1953 European Convention relating to the Formalities required for Patent Applications (CETS No. 016) (all but one), the 1968 European Convention for the Protection of Animals during International Transport (CETS No. 065) (nine out of twenty-four) and the 1969 European Convention on the Protection of the Archaeological Heritage (CETS No. 066) (21 out of 25).

[231] The ECHR (Greece); the Convention on the Reduction of Cases of Multiple Nationality and on Military Obligations in Cases of Multiple Nationality (*supra* n. 170) (Germany); the 1979 Additional Protocol to the European Convention for the Protection of Animals during International Transport (CETS No. 103) (Sweden) and the Second Protocol Amending the Convention on the Reduction of Cases of Multiple Nationality and Military Obligations in Cases of Multiple Nationality (CETS No. 149) (France).

[232] The European Agreement on the Protection of Television Broadcasts (*supra* n. 224) (four out of eleven); the 1965 Protocol to the European Agreement on the Protection of Television Broadcasts (CETS No. 054) (four out of ten); the 1967 European Convention on the Adoption of Children (CETS No. 058) (two out of eighteen) and the European Convention on the Legal Protection of Services based on, or consisting of, Conditional Access (*supra* n. 103) (three out of ten).

[233] The 1994 European Convention relating to questions on Copyright Law and Neighbouring Rights in the Framework of Transfrontier Broadcasting by Satellite: CETS No. 153.

there are still some that do not do so.[234] In many instances, the treaties rely on a combination of one or more of the methods outlined later. Although these methods reflect the varying approach to implementation seen in treaties concluded at the international level, it is more usual for the mechanisms in Council of Europe treaties to be obligatory than in the former ones. Moreover, a tendency to use 'stronger' forms of implementation measures can be seen in more recent treaties, which could benefit their impact.[235]

The least exacting forms of implementation are undoubtedly those just requiring steps to enhance public awareness,[236] notification of measures taken by Parties, either just at the outset[237] or also on later request,[238] as well as those requiring a network of information centres,[239] designation of national authorities to cooperate with each other[240] and periodic multilateral consultations on the treaty's application.[241]

Slightly more exacting are requirements for an expert body to consider proposals for the treaty's application and questions relating to its interpretation and then making recommendations to the Committee of Ministers,[242] a consultative committee that can express an opinion on applying the treaty at a Party's request and make proposals to facilitate or improve the treaty's application,[243] a consultation or conference of the Parties to ensure the effective use and operation of the treaty (including the identification of problems)[244] and a committee of the Parties to

---

[234] CETS Nos. 31, 43, 95, 96, 107, 124, 138, 147, 149, 166 and 200 (treaties concerned with cinematic co-production, equivalence of periods of university study, nationality, non-governmental organizations and refugees, matters potentially having a harmonisation character).

[235] See, further, Polakiewicz, *supra* n. 5, at pp. 123–148.

[236] E.g. Art. 4 of the European Convention on Offences Relating to Cultural Property: *supra* n. 137.

[237] E.g. Art. 14 of the European Charter of Local Self-Government: *supra* n. 67.

[238] E.g. Art. 7 of the European Convention on the Academic Recognition of University Qualifications: *supra* n. 168.

[239] E.g., Art. X.3 of the 1997 Convention on the Recognition of Qualifications Concerning Higher Education in the European Region: CETS No. 165.

[240] E.g. Art. 2 of the European Convention on Recognition and Enforcement of Decisions Concerning Custody of Children and on Restoration of Custody of Children: *supra* n. 131.

[241] E.g. Art. 9 of the European Convention on the Legal Protection of Services based on, or consisting of, Conditional Access: *supra* n. 103.

[242] E.g. Art. 6 of the European Cultural Convention: *supra* n. 109.

[243] E.g. Art. 19 of the Convention for the Protection of Individuals with regard to Automatic Processing of Personal Data: *supra* n. 72.

[244] Art. 46 of the Convention on Cybercrime: *supra* n. 70.

facilitate the collection, analysis and exchange of information, experience and good practice and to express an opinion on any question concerning its application.[245]

More substantial still are the requirements for the monitoring by a standing committee of information submitted by Parties with power to make general recommendations for measures to be taken and proposals for reform,[246] or to examine (on request) issues of interpretation,[247] the reporting by a group of specialists on the adequacy of implementation measures as well as the expression by it of an opinion on any issue of application,[248] the examination of periodic reports submitted by Parties by a committee of experts whose recommendations may then be adopted by the Committee of Ministers[249] and a commission charged with the elaboration of standards.[250]

In a number of treaties, there are also provisions concerned with facilitating friendly settlements of any difficulties arising out of their execution[251] or imposing a duty to seek a settlement of the dispute as to its interpretation or application through negotiation and then either to binding arbitration[252] or to any other peaceful means of their choice, including submission of the dispute to the conference of the parties, to an arbitral tribunal whose decisions shall be binding upon the parties or to the International Court of Justice, as agreed upon by the Parties concerned.[253]

---

[245] E.g. Art. 41 of the Council of Europe Convention on the Protection of Children against Sexual Exploitation and Sexual Abuse: *supra* n. 72.

[246] E.g. Art. 9 of the 1985 European Convention on Spectator Violence and Misbehaviour at Sports Events and in particular at Football Matches: CETS No. 120.

[247] E.g. Art. 17 of the 2001 European Convention for the Protection of the Audiovisual Heritage: CETS No. 183.

[248] Art. 11 of the 2009 Council of Europe Convention on Access to Official Documents: CETS No. 205.

[249] E.g. Arts. 15–17 of the European Charter for Regional or Minority Languages: *supra* n. 45. In the case of the 1964 European Code of Social Security (CETS No. 48 and *supra* n. 228) and the European Social Charter (*supra* n. 67 and n. 72), in their original and revised versions, there is also provision for the involvement of the International Labour Organization in the evaluation process.

[250] See Convention on the Elaboration of a European Pharmacopoeia and the Protocol to it: *supra* n. 90.

[251] E.g. Art. 31 of the European Convention on Offences Relating to Cultural Property: *supra* n. 137.

[252] E.g. Art. 15 of the European Agreement on Transfer of Responsibility for Refugees: *supra* n. 130.

[253] E.g. Art. 48 of the Council of Europe Convention on Laundering, Search, Seizure and Confiscation of the Proceeds from Crime and on the Financing of Terrorism: *supra* n. 27.

In some, there is provision for disputes about interpretation or application to be submitted to the International Court of Justice.[254]
Furthermore, a European Tribunal to deal with state immunity disputes
has been created,[255] and one treaty – the European Convention for the
Peaceful Settlement of Disputes[256] – provides for the submission to the
judgment of the International Court of Justice of all international legal
disputes which may arise between the Parties including, in particular,
those concerning the interpretation of a treaty, any question of international law, the existence of any fact which, if established, would
constitute a breach of an international obligation and the nature or
extent of the reparation to be made for the breach of an international
obligation, as well as for conciliation or arbitration in respect of any
other dispute. All these arrangements have the potential to be quite
demanding for the Parties and their simple existence could be enough
to encourage effective implementation. However, the participation rate
in the treaties concerned remains low and the actual use of these
arrangements has been very limited,[257] so that these implementation
mechanisms remain more in the realm of potential than actual
achievement.

In practice, the most significant means of implementation have been
the possibility of examining collective complaints in respect of social
rights by a committee of independent experts, whose views are subject to
adoption by the Committee of Ministers,[258] the production and publication of reports – together with the possibility of public statements – on
conditions of detention and corruption based on visits which Parties are
bound to allow[259] and the adjudication by the European Court of Human
Rights of complaints from individuals and Parties about violations of
civil and political rights followed by supervision of the execution of its

---

[254] E.g. Art. 19 of the European Convention on the Establishment of Companies: *supra*
n. 198.
[255] Pursuant to the 1972 Additional Protocol to the European Convention on State
Immunity: CETS No. 074A. The Tribunal consists of members of the European Court
of Human Rights and members designated by those non-member States who are parties
to the European Convention on State Immunity: *supra* n. 221.
[256] *Supra* n. 169.   [257] See, further, Polakiewicz, *supra* n. 5, at pp. 121–122.
[258] The 1995 Additional Protocol to the European Social Charter Providing for a System of
Collective Complaints: CETS No. 158.
[259] Pursuant to the European Convention on the Prevention on Torture and Inhuman or
Degrading Treatment or Punishment (*supra* n. 65), the Criminal Law Convention on
Corruption (*supra* n. 70) and the Civil Law Convention on Corruption and the
Additional Protocol to the Criminal Law Convention on Corruption (*supra* n. 70).

judgments by the Committee of Ministers.[260] Although problems may exist with respect to these implementation mechanisms – notably the delay arising from the volume of cases before the Court – there is no doubt that these remain the most demanding forms of implementation yet achieved at either the regional or international level, and they have done much to make a reality of the standards that they were designed to protect.[261]

The – as yet unused – general power in Article 8 of the Statute to suspend and require withdrawal where there has been a serious violation of obligations relating to the rule of law and human rights should also not be forgotten. Certainly, although such a prompt to compliance with treaty commitments fundamental to membership ought not normally be necessary, there have been some systemic failings to implement them which might justifiably have prompted resort to it.[262]

6   Conclusion

Council of Europe treaties have been addressing vital and pressing issues, often providing a leadership that extends beyond the region, but they have also concerned just useful, if more mundane, matters. Many of them have also been marked by significant innovations as regards implementation techniques, often exceeding by far what is found in treaties adopted at the international level or in other regions. However, not all treaties have managed to keep pace with societal and technological developments. Moreover, despite many of them supposedly embodying values shared by all Europeans, the actual commitment to them through ratification is still far from comprehensive. As such, the establishment of

---

[260] Pursuant to the ECHR: *supra* n. 3. The European Court also has an advisory jurisdiction under Art. 47 with respect to the interpretation of the ECHR and its Protocols, but this does not extend to questions relating to the content or scope of the rights and freedoms. This has only been exercised twice. A more substantive competence – exercisable at the request the highest courts and tribunals of a State Party – would be conferred by Protocol No. 16, but this has yet to obtain the ten ratifications required for entry into force. In addition, the Court has been empowered to give advisory opinions on legal questions concerning the interpretation of the 1997 Convention on Human Rights and Biomedicine: CETS No. 164.

[261] Also important, however, is the process of post-accession monitoring by the Parliamentary Assembly to which new Member States must submit.

[262] E.g. the consistent failure to remedy systemic problems leading to undue length of proceedings – the largest single source of cases before the European Court of Human Rights and its resulting backlog – might be viewed as approaching, if not constituting, a serious violation of the commitment to the rule of law.

a genuine European *acquis* with specificity and added value remains very much work in progress.

Nonetheless, these shortcomings have been acknowledged by the organization and its Member States. Prompted by the work of the Parliamentary Assembly and the Secretary General's review,[263] the Committee of Ministers has welcomed efforts to promote the treaties in various ways.[264] It also noted the need to develop means to gauge their impact and preserve their relevance and has required this to done, at regular intervals, for all treaties by steering or ad hoc committees dealing with the topics covered. These committees are also to be charged with proposing ways of improving the visibility, impact and efficiency of the treaties, identifying both any operational problems or obstacles to ratification and any reservations which impact substantively on the effectiveness of implementation and advising on the necessity or advisability of drafting amendments or additional protocols. The implementation of these and other steps[265] were then to be evaluated in the course of 2016.[266]

How successful these efforts will ultimately prove remains to be seen. Nonetheless, it is clear that the Council of Europe is seeking to respond to the challenge of ensuring not only that its treaties remain relevant and adequate but also that they attract the full engagement of all its Member States, both formally and with respect to their effective implementation. This may lead to the volume of treaty-making being reduced and its range narrowed but also its impact undoubtedly being enhanced.

---

[263] See *supra* n. 7 and n. 8.

[264] 1168th Meeting, 10 Apr. 2013. The promotion efforts include a focus on particular treaties during each chairmanship of the Committee of Ministers, ceremonies for signature and ratification and dialogue with national authorities.

[265] Including the need to focus on the appropriate regime for reservations in new treaties and to raise the need to retain existing ones.

[266] It is not clear whether this actually occurred and certainly nothing has so far been published.

PART III

Final Reflections

31

Taking Stock: Where the Modern Law
of Treaties Goes from Here

MICHAEL BOWMAN AND DINO KRITSIOTIS

Each of the contributions to this edited volume reaffirms the significance of the treaty instrument to the conduct of present and future international relations and, through the exploration of the controversies within its remit, acknowledges in turn the importance of a law (or set of laws) to govern treaties and treaty relationships. In theory, the treaty presents a sure foundation for the stability and predictability of these relationships, but it cannot realistically entertain this ambition unless it operates within an appropriate normative and institutional matrix that determines how the treaty can claim its own ultimate authority – the modalities that enable a treaty to come into being and which condition the entire course of its life. In this penultimate chapter of our edited volume, we recall the organising vision of the project – namely, its emphasis on the 'conceptual' and 'contextual' perspectives on the modern law of treaties – as we reflect on some of the overarching themes and ideas that come forward from the volume as a whole. The concluding section sets out a series of questions – or, more truthfully, thought-provocations – on where the modern law of treaties could go from here.

1 The Evolution of the Modern Law of Treaties

In an early attempt to establish a normative framework for treaty rela-tions, the 1928 Havana Convention on the Law of Treaties,[1] with its bare twenty provisions, set out rules to govern such matters as when treaties would be 'effective' or applicable,[2] relief from or modification of treaty

---

[1] Adopted by the Sixth International Conference of American States; the Convention is reproduced in *AJIL Supp.*, 29 (1935), 1205–1207.

[2] *Ibid.* (Art. 8).

obligations,[3] impossibility of execution[4] and the cessation of effectiveness.[5] Mindful of the jealousy with which States regarded their own freedom of action, that Convention went on describe both a State's refusal to ratify a treaty that it had signed and any formulation of reservations to treaties as 'acts inherent in national sovereignty' which 'as such constitute the exercise of a right which violates no international stipulation or good form'.[6] As if to demonstrate this attachment to sovereignty, only eight of the original twenty signatories ever became a party to the Convention,[7] a fact that would have significantly curtailed its relevance in practice since the logic of privity was an implicit assumption of the entire Convention.[8] Furthermore, the Convention contemplated the possibility of agreement between two or more States 'that their relations are to be governed by rules other than those established in general conventions celebrated by them with other States'.[9]

The idea of a celebration might seem a wholly apposite word choice in this context,[10] a fitting moment of self-congratulation that certain generalisable rules and principles could be enshrined in written form on so crucial a topic as the law governing treaties. For it can fairly be said that

---

[3] *Ibid.* (Art. 10: 'No state can relieve itself of the obligations of a treaty or modify its stipulations except by the agreement, secured through peaceful means, of the other contracting parties').

[4] *Ibid.* (Arts. 12 and 13).

[5] *Ibid.* (Art. 14). According to Art. 14, treaties cease to be effective (a) when the stipulated obligation has been fulfilled; (b) when the length of time for which it was made has expired; (c) when the resolutory condition has been fulfilled; (d) by agreement between the parties; (e) by renunciation of the party exclusively entitled to a benefit thereunder; (f) by total or partial denunciation, if agreed upon, and (g) when it becomes incapable of execution.

[6] *Ibid.* (Art. 7). For a brief discussion of the Convention's significance, see S. Rosenne, *The Law of Treaties: A Guide to the Legislative History of the Vienna Convention* (Leyden: A.W. Sijthoff, 1970), p. 31.

[7] Writing in Nov. 1962, Lissitzyn dismissed the Havana Convention as 'today of little more than historical interest': O. J. Lissitzyn, 'Efforts to Codify or Restate the Law of Treaties', *Columbia L. Rev.*, 62 (1962), 1166–1205, at 1167.

[8] *Ibid.* (Art. 5; Art. 8 and Art. 9).

[9] *Ibid.* (Art. 18(1) – where '[t]his precept applies not only to future treaties but also to those in effect at the time of concluding this convention' (Art. 18(2)).

[10] Koskenniemi has written of how the preamble 'is a celebration': 'Like a manservant, the preamble clothes the body/text of the one it serves with another body/text, different in nature and genre, more festive and dignified, a statement of the seriousness and position of the one who wears it, a signifier of origin, present status and lofty purpose': M. Koskenniemi, 'The Preamble of the Universal Declaration of Human Rights' in G. S. Alfredsson and A. Eide (eds.), *The Universal Declaration of Human Rights: A Common Standard of Achievement* (The Hague: Kluwer Law International, 1999), pp. 27–39.

the Havana Convention viewed itself as an articulator of certain 'stipulations'[11] or 'precepts' of law,[12] such as its announcement that '[t]reaties are obligatory only after ratification by those contracting States, even though this condition is not stipulated in the full powers of the negotiators or does not appear in the treaty itself'.[13] The objective of certainty – for further stability and predictability – in international legal relations cannot therefore be doubted by this initiative; it clearly also inspired the work of the 1935 Harvard Codification Project on the Law of Treaties, which observed in its introduction that, 'at the threshold of this subject, one encounters the fact that there is no clear and well-defined law of treaties'.[14] This Project was not only moved to draw attention to this 'fact' but also to explain the urgency of its mission: the making of treaties rested 'for the most part in the hands of persons who are not experts and whose habits lead them to seek results with little regard for legal forms'[15] and had been characterised by 'the lack of common standards accepted as such by the various governments'.[16] This perceived 'diversity of practice with reference to the parties to international instruments'[17] was described in terms of an 'anarchy' that:

> may continue to prevail, perhaps without any catastrophic results. Yet the dominant positions in international law and relations which treaties have now come to hold, would seem to impose upon the legal profession a duty to attempt to substitute some measure of order for the existing confusion, and perhaps this may be done without loss of the obvious advantage of elasticity.[18]

***

Notwithstanding the exponential rise of and reliance on treaties through-out the twentieth century,[19] it is perhaps a matter of some surprise that the Vienna Convention on the Law of Treaties (VCLT)[20] was concluded as late – or, from the modern vantage point, as recently – as May 1969

---

[11] *Ibid.* (Art. 17(2)).   [12] *Ibid.* (Art. 18(2)).

[13] *Ibid.* (Art. 5). See, also, Art. 20 ('[t]he present Convention does not affect obligations previously undertaken by contracting parties through international agreements').

[14] *AJIL Supp.*, 29 (1935), 653–1226, at 666.   [15] *Ibid.*   [16] *Ibid.*, at 667.

[17] *Ibid.*, at 668.   [18] *Ibid.*, at 669.

[19] J. E. Alvarez has written, for instance, of the 'dense treaty network' that has accompanied the end of the Second World War: 'The New Treaty Makers', *Boston Coll. Int'l & Comp. L. Rev.*, 25 (2002), 213–234, at 216. In his chapter on the Council of Europe, McBride observes that the level of treaty-making activity 'significantly exceeds that of other comparable regional organizations'.

[20] 1155 UNTS 331.

and that it had to wait until January 1980 before it came into force, upon the deposit of the thirty-fifth instrument of ratification or accession (by Togo).[21] The protracted nature of the process has been explained on the basis that the law of treaties had become 'beset with conceptual complexities and long-standing differences of doctrine among legal scholars',[22] all coming at a time of immense political change for world order when international diplomacy had entered an entirely different phase of its history from the 'gin-bottle' treaties of the colonial period.[23] There was thus a great deal of optimism – of positive aspiration – that the eventual product of these deliberations, the Vienna Convention on the Law of Treaties, would produce 'a new international law' that would meet the needs and challenges of the future.[24]

2 An Outline of the Current Project

Given this background of conceptual uncertainty, the identification and exploration of certain key concepts and phenomena by which the law of treaties continues to be infused seemed to us to be especially worthy of research endeavour, whether or not these have been given explicit recognition in the Vienna Convention.[25] We considered, moreover, that the appropriate platform from which to launch and pursue these enquiries had to be broader than the 1969 Convention itself because, however seminal that Convention might appear to be in the annals of public international law, it represents only a part of the relevant normative paradigm. Indeed, it is possible to detect numerous indications of resemblance between the first set of draft articles presented to the International Law Commission (ILC) on the law of treaties and the contents of the Havana Convention of February 1928.[26] By May 1969, however, this

[21] In accordance with the terms of Art. 84(1) VCLT: *ibid.*

[22] Lissitzyn, *supra* n. 7, at 1168.

[23] A remark attributed to Ghana in the Sixth Committee of the General Assembly, and cited by R. D. Kearney and R. E. Dalton, 'The Treaty on Treaties', *AJIL*, 64 (1970), 495–561, at 501 ('whenever it suited them to do so, [colonial Powers] elevated . . . treaties [concluded with African chiefs] to the status of solemn international agreements or reminded their luckless partners that the agreement which they had thus concluded had no standing in international law').

[24] *Ibid.*, at 501.

[25] For example, the function and practice of preambles; the notion of differentiated obligations; the 'object and purpose' of treaties; the provisional application of treaties etc.

[26] See J. L. Brierly, First Report on the Law of Treaties, Doc. A/CN.4/23 (14 Apr. 1950), pp. 222–248, and J. L. Brierly, Second Report on the Law of Treaties, Doc. A/CN.4/43 (10 Apr. 1951), pp. 70–74.

original corpus of eleven provisions had matured into an instrument of some eighty-five articles or so, with its preamble additionally affirming 'that the rules of customary international law will continue to govern questions not regulated by the provisions of the present Convention'.[27]

The Vienna Convention is thus itself conscious of the fact that it is but one component of *the* law regarding treaties all told,[28] a point re-emphasised in its acknowledgement of the limitations of its own temporal scope, where it was at pains not to call into question the applicability of 'any rules set forth in the present Convention to which treaties would be subject under international law independently of the Convention'.[29] This refrain is repeated elsewhere in the text, in the context of international agreements concluded between States and other subjects of international law or between such subjects,[30]

---

[27] An insertion into the preamble of the Convention that caused some consternation because 'questions not regulated by the Convention would continue to be governed by all general international law, regardless of their source': H. Pazarci, 'Preamble (1969)' in O. Corten and P. Klein (eds.), *The Vienna Conventions on the Law of Treaties: A Commentary* (Vol. I) (Oxford: Oxford University Press, 2011), pp. 1–11, at p. 10. See, however, the final recital of the preamble of the 1986 Convention and that of the 1978 Vienna Convention on the Succession of States in Respect of Treaties ('affirming that the rules of customary international law will continue to govern questions not regulated by the provisions of the present Convention'). And even where the Vienna Convention can be said to *govern*, it is important to appreciate the basis on which it does so: the 'Vienna rules' on interpretation evidently thrive in the context of international criminal law and jurisprudence, even though, as Elizabeth Wilmshurst maintains in her chapter:

> The courts and tribunals have accepted the Vienna rules without much concern about their legal basis. The rules are not applicable *as treaty law* to the Statutes of the *ad hoc* Tribunals or to the [Special Tribunal for Lebanon] Statute, all of which rely on Security Council resolutions. The customary law status of the rules has on occasion been referred to in the Tribunals' case law, as has the fact that they are drawn from or consistent with general principles found in domestic systems. The application of the Vienna rules to the [International Criminal Court] Statute is said to be as treaty law, though without a recognition that as treaty law the Convention can apply only in the relations between the 'parties' to it; indeed in the context of individual criminal responsibility there is a question as to who the relevant 'parties' can be (original emphasis).

[28] Albeit, no doubt, 'the greater part' of the law of treaties as it exists today: R. Y. Jennings and A. Watts (eds.), *Oppenheim's International Law* (Vol. I: Peace) (London: Longman, 9th ed., 1992), p. 1198.

[29] *Supra* n. 20 (Art. 4).

[30] As well as international agreements not in written form: *supra* n. 20 (Art. 3(b)). See, also, Art. 43 VCLT ('[t]he invalidity, termination or denunciation of a treaty, the withdrawal of a party from it, or the suspension of its operation, as a result of the application of the present Convention or of the provisions of the treaty, shall not in any way impair the duty

confirming the ongoing significance of the relevant 'rules' of public international law that pre-existed the Convention. Reference is also made to '[a]ny relevant rules of international law applicable in the relations between the parties' which, the Convention says, shall be taken into account when a treaty is interpreted.[31] In the light of these considerations, the rubric of a 'modern law of treaties', a phrase which had appeared more than once in the deliberations of the ILC itself,[32] secured general acclaim amongst our contributors as apposite for marking out the parameters of our project.[33]

In addition to our interest in investigating the *concepts* upon which this modern law is constructed, we were ever conscious of the critical importance of the circumstances or *contexts* in which these concepts and their associated norms are applied. In this respect, it is interesting to recall that the inaugural Special Rapporteur for the law of treaties in the International Law Commission, J. L. Brierly, remarked in his first report that 'the principal problems which arise in practice in connexion with treaties are due not so much to any degree of doubt or dispute as to what the general rules of law applicable may be, but rather to the infinitely various application of those rules in fact'.[34] To what extent does that 'infinitely various application' of the rules continue after or beyond the Vienna Convention? And at what point, if any, does the diversification of application – the raw practice, if you will – come to affect the authority of the supposed general rule? Such questions generated the desire and underlined the necessity for us to feel the pulse of treaty practice in as many substantive areas of legal activity and institutional fora as possible.

Invitations were accordingly issued to a team of expert practitioners and scholars to explore and explain the particular 'context' of their respective fields of expertise – prioritising the principal developments and challenges concerning the law of treaties which had arisen in their fields of study. The results proved extremely interesting as some of these contributors came to interrogate the very 'rubric' that they had been assigned, most noticeably in the chapters on human rights (Christine M.

---

of any State to fulfil any obligation embodied in the treaty to which it would be subject under international law independently of the treaty').

[31] Art. 31(3)(c) VCLT: *supra* n. 20.

[32] See the discussion in relation to what was to become Art. 29 VCLT, *YbILC* (1966–II), 213, and its observations on the rule concerning coercion of a State by the threat or use of force, *YbILC* (1966–II), 247.

[33] As opposed to making the Vienna Convention the epicentre of its focus.

[34] Brierly, First Report on the Law of Treaties, *supra* n. 26, at p. 224.

Chinkin), the law of war/law of armed conflict/international humanitarian law (Françoise J. Hampson), investment protection (Julian Davis Mortensen)[35] and the World Trade Organization (Joost Pauwelyn and Isabelle Van Damme).[36] The question of how an area of law is to be identified – or, perhaps, identifies itself – is not often shared with a general audience, and our project has undoubtedly been enriched through having the particular historical nuances or technical idiosyncrasies of these contexts teased out for us.

These 'contexts' were of a wholly different, essentially subjective, character from the country-based surveys that helped to shape the early thinking of the ILC.[37] No assumption was made of any necessary uniformity of correlation between these contextual studies and the 'concepts' that had been identified for treatment in the first part of the work. Rather, the brief to contributors to Part II of the volume was for them to be guided by the history and practice of the relevant field in the framing of their contributions, with a view, hopefully, to feeding back into our appreciation of the 'concepts' themselves and of the law of treaties more generally: this 'interaction', as Joost Pauwelyn and Isabelle Van Damme remind us in their chapter on the World Trade Organization, 'is not a one-way street'.[38] That is why the chapters in this set do not all proceed from exactly the same template or cue, a feature which has in

---

[35] Describing investment law's 'signal characteristic of diversity amidst sameness'.

[36] Who express concern at designating a 'homogenous set of treaties': 'these treaties can diverge widely in terms of their content, structure, wording and the process through which they are concluded'.

[37] In July 1949, an invitation was issued by United Nations Secretary-General Trygve Lie for suggestions of topics that needed to be addressed for the purpose of the codification of the law of treaties: LEG 291/01/YLL (11 July 1949). Eleven countries – Canada, Costa Rica, Denmark, France, Israel, the Netherlands, the Philippines, Poland, the Union of South Africa, the United Kingdom and the United States – responded, with varying degrees of enthusiasm and detail. The responses are reproduced at *YbILC* (1950–II), 197–221. For a further example of this approach, see A. D. McNair, *The Law of Treaties: British Practice and Opinion* (New York, NY: Columbia University Press, 1938) (designed 'to state the practice of the United Kingdom in the matter of treaties, their conclusion, their interpretation, the scope of their operation, their termination and modification, and the law which is relevant to these topics so far as it can be gathered from United Kingdom sources' (p. vii)). See, further, D. Hutchinson, 'McNair and the Law of Treaties Revisited', *OJLS*, 9 (1989), 374–382.

[38] Indeed, as they observe, '[t]he documentation available does not show that the provisional application of the GATT 1947 formed part of the practice that was the basis of the International Law Commission's ... codification of the law of treaties on provisional application' – so that the context becomes an important aspect of filling out the historical record on the concept of, in this case, provisional application.

turn produced a most fruitful basis for *intra*-disciplinary comparison and reflection. In particular, light is shed on exactly why each sub-discipline's relationship with the law of treaties has evolved in the way or ways it has and why particular treaty topics have come to dominate certain areas more than others – such as the question of successive treaties for the law of the sea (the chapter of David M. Ong) or third States and third parties (the chapter of Elizabeth Wilmshurst).

***

One of the implications of the ILC's reference to a 'modern law of treaties' was its aspiration to meet contemporary needs, and therefore, its work necessarily involved a combination of pure codification and progressive development,[39] albeit that the line between these two processes (or functions) is inherently difficult to draw.[40] So, it has been said that 'the very act of formulating a rule which is generally thought to reflect State practice, precedent and doctrine may involve the transformation of that rule into progressive development, for example, where it is found necessary or desirable to incorporate a qualification or exception in relation to which the practice of States is ambivalent or conflicting'.[41] What is more, conceptualising the law in terms of a simple binary between codification and progressive development carries with it the risk of insensitivity to the intertemporal vagaries of the customary rules that are being codified. Custom is, after all, not an ensemble of static rules all of which can be traced back to the same point in time immemorial: it is, by its very nature, the product of a process of continuous change and renewal.

That being so, the question arises as to whether a similar element of dynamism is present within the law as codified, in the sense that the Vienna Convention might equally contain the potential for its own subsequent evolutionary development.[42] After all, the Convention was not to be a mere freeze-frame of the *lex lata* as it presented itself in May 1969: the ILC was acting with one eye on the durability of the Convention over the long term, a fact which surely explains the

---

[39] Both of these imperatives find expression in the preamble of the VCLT: *supra* n. 20 (seventh preambular recital).

[40] See I. Sinclair, *The Vienna Convention on the Law of Treaties* (Manchester: Manchester University Press, 2nd ed., 1984), p. 12 ('[i]t is only in rare cases, and then by implication rather than by express pronouncement, that one can determine where the Commission has put forward a proposal by way of progressive development rather than codification').

[41] *Ibid.*, at p. 12.

[42] On the significance of subsequent practice more generally, consider the contribution to this volume of Buga at pp. 363–391 (Chapter 12).

tremendous flexibility and practicality that informs many of its provisions as well as the resolute silence it maintains regarding its own envisaged shelf life.[43]

3 Conceptual and Contextual Dimensions of the Modern Law

The Vienna Convention's presumed aspiration for its own longevity amply demonstrates the advantage to be gained from the adoption of both conceptual and contextual perspectives in the reading of the modern law of treaties. Not only does the Convention remain silent with regard to its duration, but it contains no explicit provision for denunciation or withdrawal by individual parties. Presumably, then, the Convention stands to be governed by the rule in its own Article 56 – although this, in turn, must surely depend on the customary status of that rule given the Convention's formal commitment to its own non-retroactivity.[44] That provision makes clear that denunciation or withdrawal from a treaty are prohibited *unless* '[i]t is established that the parties intended to admit the possibility'[45] *or* '[a] right of denunciation or withdrawal may be implied by the nature of the treaty'.[46] This provision introduces us to two concepts which usefully illustrate the virtues of a conceptually orientated reading of the Vienna Convention – namely, the *nature* of a given treaty and the complex notion of *intention*.

As regards intention, the Vienna Convention makes reference to this concept in a range of provisions in addition to Article 56 – such as its articulation of the arrangements governing full powers (Article 7(1)(b)); consent to be bound (Articles 12 and 14); the obligation of a signatory State not to defeat the object and purpose of a treaty prior to its entry into force (Article 18(a)); the practice of acceptance of and objections to reservations (Article 21(4)(b)); the provisional application (Article 25(2)),

---

[43] A. Aust, *Modern Treaty Law and Practice* (Cambridge: Cambridge University Press, 3rd ed., 2013), p. 255.

[44] As contained in Art. 4 VCLT: *supra* n. 20. This reflects a peculiarity of the Vienna Convention, in the sense that it is – again, presumably – governed by Art. 28 on the non-retroactivity of treaties which would entail no need for a provision of the order of Art. 4 VCLT. Apparently, its insertion in the Convention is explained 'in the interests of legal certainty' where the application of the new rules of the Convention would only be applied to those who were party: P. V. McDade, 'The Effect of Article 3 of the Vienna Convention on the Law of Treaties 1969', *ICLQ*, 35 (1986), 499–511, at 502. Art. 28 VCLT has confidently been argued to represent a codification of custom: F. Dopagne, 'Article 28 (1969)' in Corten and Klein (eds.), *supra* n. 27, pp. 718–728, at p. 719.

[45] Art. 56(1)(a) VCLT: *supra* n. 20.   [46] Art. 56(1)(b) VCLT: *supra* n. 20.

non-retroactivity (Article 28) and territorial scope of treaties (Article 29); the general rule of interpretation (Article 31(4)); the establishment of obligations or rights for third States (Articles 35 and 36 respectively) and their subsequent revocation or modification (Article 37); the amendment (Article 40(5)), modification (Article 41(2)) or suspension (Article 58(2)) of the operation of multilateral treaties and, finally, the termination or suspension of the operation of a treaty implied by the conclusion of a later treaty (Article 59(2)).[47] This catalogue of provisions that itemise the various literary *contexts* in which the concept of intention appears illustrates that those contexts are themselves defined by reference to, and therefore require an understanding of, further *concepts* of a highly complex and technical character.[48]

The many occasions on which the Vienna Convention makes explicit reference to the concept of 'intention',[49] while omitting it from the terms itemised for definition in Article 2 VCLT, might cause one to think that the meaning of intention is self-evident and that its identification in the ordinary course of events is an untroubled affair. Yet we have been alerted to the possibility that the 'intentions of the parties' can only really be claimed 'in a highly specialized, almost figurative sense' – and that 'any quest to discover such intentions comprehended literally would be doomed to failure'.[50] This is because it is confounding to attribute an intention (or set of intentions) to the entity of a State as such, since, as might be expected, 'a considerable divergence of understandings regarding the meaning and objectives of the instrument in question may be apparent, rendering the "intentions" of the delegation as a whole an elusive commodity'.[51] Also, given that the Vienna Convention requires us, on occasion, to decipher the intention not of one single delegation but of *all* delegations present at the creation of a treaty collectively, 'some

[47] See, further, Sinclair, *supra* n. 40, at p. 6.

[48] This explains the selection of topics such as a treaty's object and purpose, provisional application and interpretation included in Part I of the volume.

[49] Including where it is not mentioned in terms: e.g. the International Law Commission considered that 'the element of intention is to be embraced in the phrase "governed by international law"', which appears in the definition of a treaty in Art. 2(1)(a) VCLT: *YbILC* (1966–II), 189. See, however, J. Klabbers, *The Concept of Treaty in International Law* (The Hague: Kluwer Law International, 1996), p. 55. On 'intention' – or lack thereof – behind Memoranda of Understanding, consider Aust, *supra* n. 43, at pp. 15 and 17, and, also, p. 51.

[50] M. Bowman, '"Normalizing" the International Convention for the Regulation of Whaling', *Michigan JIL*, 29 (2008), 293–499, at 317 (writing in the context of treaty interpretation).

[51] *Ibid.*

sense begins to dawn of the extraordinary difficulty involved in the task in hand'.[52] More colourfully, it has been claimed that, for general multi-lateral conventions, many States accede to conventions 'not on the basis of what the original negotiators intended but rather on the basis of what the text actually says and means', so that 'a search for the common intentions of parties' in this context 'can be likened to a search for the pot of gold at the end of a rainbow'.[53]

To elaborate, it is striking how – consistently with the essential thematic of this volume – the context in which *intention* arises in the Vienna Convention helps to inform our understanding of how, more precisely, this concept is meant to work in practice: at times, for example, and as noted previously, the Vienna Convention envisages the intention of the parties as a whole as the relevant metric;[54] on other occasions, it is the intention of a single (e.g. signatory[55] or objecting)[56] State that forms the focus of concern, and at yet other times, it is apparently the intention of the treaty itself that is brought into play.[57] Perhaps more importantly, it is noteworthy that the Vienna Convention does not leave 'intention' to the realm of the abstract or the purely cerebral: the intention must be expressed to others,[58] or 'deliberately expressed' as it is put in the case of those States objecting to

---

[52] *Ibid.* (concluding that 'the emphasis must inevitably be placed on *objective* appearances and *ostensible* intentions, and that the undeclared aims or secret aspirations of the parties cannot be allowed to dictate the instrument's meaning'). To similar effect, see Klabbers, *supra* n. 49, at p. 65 (intention 'imbues those who conclude agreements with a psychological state they may never really have had').

[53] Sinclair, *supra* n. 40, at pp. 130–131.

[54] Art. 31(4) VCLT ('[a] special meaning shall be given to a term if it is established that the parties so intended') and Art. 59(2) VCLT ('[t]he earlier treaty shall be considered as only suspended in operation if it appears from the later treaty or is otherwise established that such was the intention of the parties'): *supra* n. 20.

[55] Art. 18(a) VCLT ('[i]t has signed the treaty or has exchanged instruments constituting the treaty subject to ratification, acceptance or approval, until it shall have made its intention clear not to become a party to the treaty'): *supra* n. 20.

[56] Art. 20(4)(b) VCLT ('[a]n objection by another contracting State to a reservation does not preclude the entry into force of the treaty as between the objecting and reserving States unless a contrary intention is definitely expressed by the objecting State'): *supra* n. 20.

[57] As with non-retroactivity: Art. 28 VCLT ('[u]nless a different intention appears from the treaty or is otherwise established, its provisions do not bind a party in relation to any act or fact which took place or any situation which ceased to exist before the date of the entry into force of the treaty with respect to that party'): *supra* n. 20. See, also, Art. 29 ('[u]nless a different intention appears from the treaty or is otherwise established, a treaty is binding upon each party in respect of its entire territory'): *ibid.* As opposed to intentions that emerge 'from the circumstances': Art. 7(1)(b) VCLT: *ibid.*

[58] Consent to be bound: Arts. 12(1)(c) VCLT and 14(1)(d) VCLT: *supra* n. 20.

reservations;[59] elsewhere, it must make itself apparent or be 'otherwise established'.[60] At still another point, it is said that the intention must be made 'clear',[61] all of which seem to suggest something beyond mere private or presumed intention.[62] A second observation which needs to be made is that reliance on intention may also sometimes involve the allocation of the evidential burden as to who is to marshal the proofs of its existence: regarding denunciation/withdrawal, for example, it would seem that it is the State proposing such action who must demonstrate that 'the parties intended to admit the possibility' that is being seized,[63] though Article 56 VCLT does not spell out any more of the detail.

What, then, is to be said of the 'nature' of a treaty? This concept is itself of an inherently contextual character in that it explicitly focuses our attention upon the subject matter of the treaty in question. It is therefore closely connected with the idea of a treaty's object and purpose, which makes several appearances in the Vienna Convention (as examined in the chapter by Dino Kritsiotis). In contrast, the 'nature' of a treaty – which might be thought to introduce a broader set of considerations – is mentioned only once, though it is a theme which can surely be said to maintain a subliminal presence throughout the text: thus, the Vienna Convention not only categorises treaties according to their bilateral or multilateral character,[64] it also attributes significance to the jural

---

[59] Art. 20(4)(b) VCLT: *supra* n. 20.

[60] Arts. 28 and 29 VCLT: *supra* n. 20. And this approach recurs persistently in the 2011 International Law Commission *Guide to Practice on Reservations to Treaties*, Doc. A/66/10: see, e.g., Guideline 4.5.3 ('[t]he status of the author of an invalid reservation in relation to a treaty depends on the intention expressed by the reserving State or international organization on whether it intends to be bound by the treaty without the benefit of the reservation of whether it considers that it is not bound by the treaty').

[61] Art. 18(a) VCLT: *supra* n. 20.

[62] See, e.g., *YbILC* (1966–II), 214. Also discussed by the ILC in the context of treaties and territory (*ibid.*, at 214) and successive treaties (*ibid.*, at 216). Note, too, the observation that, on conditions for a treaty's entry into force, intention has been evidenced by 'express provisions or by cogent implication': H. Blix, 'The Requirement of Ratification', *BYbIL*, 30 (1953), 352–380, at 380.

[63] *Supra* n. 45. Critically, Art. 56(2) VCLT demonstrates both of these points: it requires that notice be given of the intention to denounce or withdraw a treaty – where a minimum period of twelve months is instituted.

[64] This distinction might result in a dichotomy of rules, e.g. on reservations, the recourse to *travaux préparatoires*, material breach: see, generally, J. Crawford, *Brownlie's Principles of Public International Law* (Oxford: Oxford University Press, 8th ed., 2012), p. 370 – though not 'as a structuring principle of the VCLT itself' (Mortensen). See, also, the provision of plurilateral treaties as an instance of multilateral treaties: Art. 20(2) VCLT.

personality of the particular parties.[65] Furthermore, the Convention makes specific provision for treaties by virtue of their respective subject matter, such as 'any treaty which is the constituent instrument of an international organization and . . . any treaty adopted within an international organization' (Article 5),[66] treaties which establish boundaries (Article 62(2)(a)) and 'treaties of a humanitarian character' (Article 60(5)).

Another aspect of the 'nature' of a convention could be said to relate to its *function*[67] – that is to say, whether or not it conceives itself as an exercise in codification of the law – since this is likely to produce an impact on the provision that it makes for its relationship with the preexisting (customary) law. In that vein, the 1982 United Nations Convention on the Law of the Sea provides for denunciation but confirms that this 'shall not in any way affect the duty of any State Party to fulfil any obligation embodied in this Convention to which it would be subject under international law independently of this Convention'.[68] The Geneva Conventions of August 1949 also all address the 'liberty to denounce' the instrument in question[69] but make clear that denunciation 'shall in no way impair the obligations which the Parties to the conflict shall remain bound to fulfil by virtue of the principles of the law of nations, as they result from the usages established among civilized peoples, from the laws of humanity and the dictates of public conscience'.[70] Clearly, this liberty (or, better, power), which two of our authors describe as 'the ultimate contractual right within the law of

---

See, further, Aust, *supra* n. 43, at p. 125, and, also, D. Azaria, *Treaties on Transit of Energy via Pipelines and Countermeasures* (Oxford: Oxford University Press, 2015), pp. 103–104.

[65] That is, where these include 'other subjects of international law' that are not States. See Art. 3 VCLT: *supra* n. 20.

[66] Indeed, as Trebilcock's chapter reminds us, Art. 5 'is known within the institution as "the ILO clause"'. See, further, Kearney and Dalton, *supra* n. 23, at 505–506, and, also, Art. 20(3) VCLT: *supra* n. 20.

[67] Relatedly, worthy of note here is the distinction often made between contractual treaties and law-making treaties – a distinction that is 'controversial and theoretically faulty' according to *Oppenheim's International Law* because '[i]n principle, all treaties as lawmaking inasmuch as they lay down rules of conduct which the parties are bound to observe as law': *supra* n. 28, at p. 1204. Two of our authors – Pauwelyn and Van Damme – give this distinction the benefit of the doubt in their analysis.

[68] 1833 UNTS 397, Art. 317(3).

[69] 75 UNTS 31, 75 UNTS 85, 75 UNTS 135 and 75 UNTS 287, common Arts. 63/62/142/158.

[70] *Ibid*. A variation, of course, of the famous Martens Clause: T. Meron, 'The Martens Clause, Principles of Humanity, and Dictates of Public Conscience', *AJIL*, 94 (2000), 78–89, at 80.

treaties',[71] might attach to a conventional arrangement whose nature is such that the act of exit might make 'little or no legal difference' in the final analysis.[72]

These various approaches to classification found in the Vienna Convention bring to mind the cross-cutting criteria for categorising animals employed by Jorge Luis Borges, drawing upon the Chinese encyclopaedia titled *Celestial Emporium of Benevolent Knowledge*.[73] And in her chapter, Catherine Brölmann sounds an important note of caution on the hazards of devising classification schemes for treaties: she provides us with three possible typologies based on form, normative effect and content, where '[t]he notion of typology suggests a classification of concepts rather than empirical facts, and it points to a construct built around particular attributes or dimensions to which the actual objects of classification do not necessarily correspond fully, nor exclusively'. And, yet, it is clear from some of the chapters how firm a hold on the legal imagination the desire for classification actually has: it instructs the telling of the historical narrative of treaties (Randall Lesaffer),[74] it helps to bring to life the vivid metaphor of the treaty as a 'living instrument'

---

[71] I.e. 'the right to withdraw from a treaty' (French and Scott) – especially given their recurring presence in multilateral environmental agreements. Note in this respect Art. 54(b) VCLT – that 'termination of a treaty or the withdrawal of a party may take place … [a]t any time by consent of all the parties after consultation with the other contracting States': *supra* n. 20. This provision was drawn to the attention of the Government of the Democratic People's Republic of Korea in an *aide-mémoire* of United Nations Secretary-General Kofi A. Annan of Sept. 1997 in the light of the former's announcement of its intention to withdraw from the 1966 International Covenant on Civil and Political Rights: '[I]t would appear that, except as provided for in VCLT Article 54, the ICCPR is not subject to withdrawal'. See Depositary Notification C.N.467.1997.TREATIES-10 (12 Nov. 1997).

[72] Aust, *supra* n. 43, at p. 256. This is especially since 'a good number of articles [of the VCLT] are now essentially declaratory of existing law; those which are not constitute presumptive evidence of emergent rules': Crawford, *supra* n. 64, at pp. 367–368. Recalling the *North Sea Continental Shelf Cases*, Bowman reminds us that not all norms are 'capable of acquiring customary status' (emphasis removed). See, further, B. H. Oxman, 'The Rule of Law and the United Nations Convention on the Law of the Sea', *EJIL*, 7 (1996), 353–371, at 356.

[73] Which he does in his essay, 'The Analytical Language of John Wilkins', where animals are divided into those: belonging to the Emperor, embalmed, tame, suckling pigs, sirens, fabulous, stray dogs, included in the present classification, frenzied, innumerable, drawn with a very fine camelhair brush, *et cetera*, having just broken the water pitcher, that from a long way off look like flies: E. R. Monegal and A. Reed (eds.), *Borges: A Reader* (trans. A. Read) (New York, NY: E.P. Dutton, 1981), pp. 141–143.

[74] On 'the modern distinction between *traités-contrats* and *traités-lois*' – and 'the function of treaties as 'social contracts' which constitute or reform the legal and political order to

(Daniel Moeckli and Nigel D. White),[75] and it serves to underpin the very idea of privity (Michael Waibel).[76]

In reflecting on these chapters, one is frequently struck by the extent to which the application of the term 'treaty' itself involves an act of generalisation. Indeed, as many of the contributions to this volume attest, treaties are typically divisible into four distinct parts – the preamble, the 'principal provisions' of the treaty, the section on final clauses and, finally, the testimonium[77] – though, invariably, professional preferences and prejudices tend to prioritise the substantive provisions of the treaty over and above these other elements. Jan Klabbers' exegesis on preambles is a cautionary tale in recalibrating this imbalance: he discerns a certain 'ambivalence' within the Vienna Convention toward the 'precise status' of the preamble, an ambivalence that can only be resolved by focusing on the structure of the instrument and the distinct purposes which its component parts are designed to serve.

In particular, the preamble remains squarely within the four corners of the treaty and, far from it being merely a requiem to 'hopeless causes, both large and small',[78] it can provide its own rich seam of evidence as to the intentions of the treaty-makers – on what the treaty is actually *for*.[79] This act of disassembling a treaty into its component parts becomes fertile ground for enquiry, precisely because of the illumination it

---

which they belong. In other words, a third category of *traités-constitutions* needs to be added'.

[75] Where they distinguish 'between different forms of contract, in particular "social contracts", which are more profound than a contractual transaction whereby one party agrees to give up weapons if the other party does'. They go on: 'A social contract at the international level is found in the UN Charter, whereby the five Great Powers agreed to act as the world's police force in exchange for voting rights that no other member would possess. It is no coincidence that those five permanent members are the [nuclear weapons States] at the heart of the [Non-Proliferation Treaty] "grand bargain", thus suggesting that the NPT is something more profound than an ordinary *traité-contrat*; indeed, it may be more constitutional than a *traité-loi* since it develops the "grand bargain" found in the UN Charter by extending the inequality between the P5 and other members of the UN to the possession of nuclear weapons'.

[76] Where the focus is on objective regimes, international investment law and individual rights.

[77] Jennings and Watts (eds.), *supra* n. 28, at pp. 1210–1211.

[78] Aust, *supra* n. 43, at p. 367.

[79] Note the considerable attention paid to the preamble of the 1946 Convention in *Whaling in the Antarctic*: Australia v. France; New Zealand intervening (2014) ICJ Rep. 226, at pp. 251–252 (paragraphs 56 and 58). Note, too, the reliance on the preamble of the 1996 Comprehensive Test Ban Treaty for establishing its 'object and purpose' prior to its entry into force in the chapter of Tabassi and Elias.

provides with respect to the operation of the rules of the Vienna Convention themselves. An example is provided by the separate significance that is accorded to the moment of the adoption of the text of a treaty (Article 9 VCLT) and its entry into force (Article 24 VCLT): 'The provisions of a treaty regulating the authentication of its text, the establishment of the consent of States to be bound by the treaty, the manner or date of its entry into force, reservations, the functions of the depositary and other matters arising necessarily before the entry into force of the treaty apply from the time of the adoption of its text'.[80]

This phased activation of the terms of a treaty is, of course, essential to its normative vitality: in her chapter on the provisional application of treaties, Anneliese Quast Mertsch advises that such application 'can cover all of a treaty's provisions *except* for those covered by Article 24(4) VCLT'.[81] The practical implications in the particular institutional context of the International Maritime Organization are explored in Dorota Lost-Sieminska's discussion of the possible provisional application of the amendment provision of the 2004 International Convention for the Control and Management of Ships' Ballast Water and Sediments. This development calls into question the Vienna Convention's allocation of competences for this task since, she writes, '[t]he proposed interpretation of Article 25 VCLT jeopardises the general rule that only parties can amend a treaty (Article 39 VCLT), and there are no parties until the Convention is in force'.[82]

This reference to interpretation of the Vienna Convention reminds us that the 'treaty on treaties'[83] is itself no less in need of interpretation than any other agreement, and at Richard Gardiner's patient urging, there remains considerable need for 'greater understanding and application of the Vienna rules' in the course of this exercise; for him, those 'rules' are in fact a series of principles that form part of a 'structure' that 'has become virtually indispensable scaffolding for the reasoning on questions of treaty interpretation'.[84] The unity of that structure is a point very much emphasised

---

[80] Art. 24(4) VCLT: *supra* n. 20.

[81] For these – provisions regulating the authentication of its text; the establishment of the consent of States to be bound; the manner or date of its entry into force; reservations; the functions of the depositary and other means arising necessary before the entry into force of the treaty – 'apply from the time of the adoption of the text'.

[82] As she points out, Article 2(1)(g) VCLT defines a 'party' as 'a State which has consented to be bound by the treaty and for which the treaty is in force': *supra* n. 20.

[83] The phrase of Kearney and Dalton, *supra* n. 23.

[84] After H. Thirlway, 'The Law and Procedure of the International Court of Justice 1960–1989, Supplement 2006: Part Three', *BYbIL*, 77 (2006), 1–82, at 19. 'This is because',

by Elizabeth Wilmshurst in her contribution: 'An interpretation which looks over-expansive in the criminal law context may be due not to the use of the Vienna rules but to their abuse: a purely "purposive" approach to interpretation extracts only one of the factors from Article 31 [VCLT] and ignores the others'. Still, even with the benefit of this insight, certain perennial questions will continue to dominate the literature: What counts as an act of legitimate interpretation – and when does that act become a modification of the treaty? How, as Irina Buga asks in her chapter, is one to distinguish between subsequent practice and what she labels 'supervening rule[s] of customary law'? How is interpretation meant to work with respect to successive treaties or normative arrangements?[85] And exactly who 'owns' the treaty once it has left the drafters' table?[86]

These are, of course, all valid questions to pose and to ponder, and the peculiarity of the enterprise of interpretation to the instrument under consideration is driven home by Michael Wood's chapter on the interpretation of Security Council resolutions by comparison with treaties. That chapter lays bare the distinctiveness of the *instrument* of the Security Council resolution,[87] underlining the fact that such instruments are adopted in a fundamentally different consensual environment from that of treaties – consent, in this context, is attenuated since States are not signing up specifically to individual resolutions as and when they are enacted: the 'consent' that furnishes these resolutions with their authority derives from the fact that, in the mists of the recent or distant past, States have chosen to become members of the United Nations Organization

Gardiner writes, 'it conveys the idea of the rules as a structure in some way supporting or ancillary to the substantive reasoning'.

[85] A question posed to cogent effect by Wilmshurst in relation to the contrasting object(s) and purpose(s) of Geneva Convention (IV) Relative to the Protection of Civilian Persons in Time of War and the Statute of the ICTY. It should not be overlooked, however, that 'the consent of the parties relating to the object of a treaty is by no means "petrified" at its adoption: the treaty remains, after all a creation of its parties, subject to their will during the whole period of its operation': B. Simma, 'Consent: Strains in the Treaty System' in R. St. J. Macdonald and D. M. Johnston (eds.), *The Structure and Process of International Law* (Dordrecht: Martinus Nijhoff, 1986), pp. 485–511, at p. 494.

[86] On ownership of treaties – at least of one set of treaties – see K. Anderson, 'Who Owns the Rules of War?', *N.Y. Times (Magazine)*, 13 Apr. 2003, 38.

[87] Cf. the discussion of the status of the Annex to the 1996 Resolution Establishing the Preparatory Commission for the Comprehensive Nuclear-Test-Ban Treaty Organization by Tabassi and Elias (on 'over two decades [of] diverging views' as to whether it constitutes a treaty or not).

and have thereby embraced the terms of its Charter,[88] where '[t]he Members of the United Nations agree to accept and carry out the decisions of the Security Council in accordance with the present Charter'.[89]

Few other treaties, including those of an institutional character, require quite such a willingness on the part of their parties to forgo their future freedom of action. Typically, discretion is retained at least to exclude the effect of measures subsequently adopted within the organization, even those that might be described as being of a 'legislative' character:[90] by way of example, Egle Granziera and Steven A. Solomon draw attention, in their chapter on the World Health Organization (WHO), to the 'opting out' mechanism for regulations contained in Article 22 of the WHO Constitution. The power in question is described as involving the 'rejection' of regulations by member States of WHO, a word that faithfully conveys the continuing potency of consent within the dynamic of the organization, as does the capacity to make reservations to regulations.[91] They contrast this with the notion of active 'consent', necessary, for example, for the act of adopting or of becoming party to a treaty[92] and, in their terms, 'a key overall element of "treaty-ness"'. There are therefore diverse ways in which accommodation can be made for consent in the design of a treaty. And both the complexities and the opportunities involved in this regard are vividly demonstrated in the case of the European Union, which creates a distinct legal order of its own, entailing the capacity to enact laws for all of its Member States. Yet, as Panos Koutrakos goes on to point out in his contribution, the parties have ultimately chosen to return to the consensually based haven of the public international legal order whenever it has become necessary to revise the fundamental basis of their constitutional arrangements.

---

[88] 1 UNTS 16.

[89] *Ibid.* (Art. 25). See, further, K. Doehring, 'Unlawful Resolutions of the Security Council and their Legal Consequences', *Max Planck Yb. UN Law*, 1 (1997), 91–109, at 104.

[90] Though they have of course given their consent to this possibility in advance by becoming a member of the organization. See, further, N. D. White, *The Law of International Organisations* (Manchester: Manchester University Press, 2nd ed., 2005), p. 171 (writing of 'the legislative decision-making capacity of an organization' in discussing the World Health Assembly's power to adopt regulations as well as its practice of deciding by majority on reservations made to regulations).

[91] Which must be notified to the Director-General of the Organization: Art. 22 of the WHO Constitution, 14 UNTS 185.

[92] The Constitution of the WHO 'shall come into force for each Member when accepted by it in accordance with its constitutional processes'. See Art. 19 of the WHO Constitution: *ibid.*

It should therefore come as no surprise that the Vienna Convention appears to venerate 'free consent',[93] its preamble proclaiming it alongside good faith and *pacta sunt servanda* as 'universally recognized' principles in international law.[94] Indeed, it has been said that 'there is as much emotion as logic invested in it, so much so that consent theory in [the law of treaties] has the power of myth'.[95] In his chapter, Matthew Craven contemplates the possibility that its true function may be 'to immunize international legal obligation from a critique of power-politics: instantiating, in the form of the contract, the principle of sovereign equality and the idea of self-rule'. He nonetheless acknowledges that the Vienna Convention is 'overtly rigorous about the necessity of consent for purposes of the assumption of obligations under treaty'. We see this quite clearly in the exceptions – if exceptions they indeed be – developed in relation to the principle *pacta tertiis nec nocent nec prosunt*, although it is noteworthy that the Vienna Convention requires third States to provide *express acceptance* for obligations whereas (presumed) *assent* is sufficient for rights arising from treaties to which they are not party.[96] And in his chapter, Michael Waibel explains the way in which the *pacta tertiis* principle, framed by him in terms of a principle of 'privity', has come to exert such a fundamental impact on international legal relations. The current order may have 'relaxed' its rigours in three areas of activity – so-called 'objective regimes', international investment law and individual rights – but on the evidence presented to us, the privity of treaties is here to stay.[97]

While, however, the notion of privity entails that States are bound only by treaties to which they are party,[98] many treaties have found ways to

---

[93] See, also, S. Talmon, 'Security Council Treaty Action', *Revue hellénique de droit international*, 62 (2009), 65–117 (regarding '[t]he principle of voluntary consent [as] a fundamental principle of international treaty law').

[94] Third preambular recital.

[95] D. Johnston, 'Theory, Consent, and the Law of Treaties: A Cross-Disciplinary Perspective', *Australian YbIL*, 12 (1988–1989), 109–124, at 119.

[96] Art. 36(1) VCLT: *supra* n. 20. 'Assent' is not used elsewhere in the VCLT, though it was used prominently in the Commentary on responses to State's reservations, e.g. *YbILC* (1966–II), 206.

[97] See, further, the treatment by Wilmshurst ('the fact that nationals of a non-party State can be prosecuted in an international court does not bind the State').

[98] Giving rise, for example, to the notion of contractual interactionality of successive treaties, which is made apparent in David M. Ong's chapter on Art. 311(1) of the 1982 United Nations Law of the Sea Convention:

> While this provision clearly establishes that the 1982 Convention supersedes the 1958 Conventions for parties to both of these treaties, it is equally clear

accommodate consent within the internal dynamic of the regime they establish. Against the common impression of 'uniform standards' ushered in by multilateral conventions, Michael Bowman has written in this volume of differentiated obligations within treaties – and of the 'ample capacity within the tool-kit of international law to permit, at least to some degree, the personalised tailoring of the obligations accepted to meet the needs of individual States'. While the spirit of uniformity may not be entirely absent from a treaty, the thrust of a given norm may generate different demands – differentiated obligations – for its parties and, perhaps, markedly so. Further evidence of this particular dynamic can be found in the normative implications that some treaties have for non-State actors,[99] a phenomenon of increasing significance in the international legal order.[100]

***

Any focus upon the obligations of a treaty must inevitably lead to the issue of breach and the limited attention that is given to this matter in the Vienna Convention itself: the relevant provision – Article 60 – has moreover been described by Christian J. Tams as 'incomplete and relatively incoherent', while 'the instance of its regulation is also relatively irrelevant in practice'.[101] This may well be due to the 'cautious approach'

> from this formulation of the rule that non-parties to the 1982 Convention – such as Colombia, Turkey and the United States – are not bound by this treaty, whether or not the 1982 Convention significantly changes the previous position on a particular legal issue under the relevant 1958 Convention.

Supra n. 68.

[99] Most dramatically in Art. 4(1) ('[a]rmed groups that are distinct from the armed forces of a State should not, under any circumstances, recruit or use in hostilities persons under the age of 18 years') and Art. 4(2) ('States Parties shall take all feasible measures to prevent such recruitment and use, including the adoption of legal measures necessary to prohibit and criminalize such practices') of the 2000 Optional Protocol to the Convention on the Rights of the Child on the Involvement of Children in Armed Conflict: G.A. Resolution 54/263, Annex I, 54 U.N. GAOR Supp. (No. 49) at 7, U.N. Doc. A/54/49, Vol. III (2000).

[100] As Tabassi and Elias observe in their chapter:

> Negotiated as State-centric, disarmament treaties have nonetheless survived and adapted to the paradigm shift that occurred globally after the terrorist attacks of 11 September 2001. While the purpose of those treaties is directed at State actors, they are now also being implemented with a special focus on preventing proliferation among non-State actors as well, demonstrating that disarmament treaties, particularly those of unlimited duration, are living instruments.

[101] And which Tams characterises as 'a treaty breach by one party may permit another party to suspend or terminate the treaty in whole or in part'.

of this provision, which confines its attention to 'material' breaches, prompted no doubt by the potential severity of permissible responses entailing 'the temporary or permanent extinction of a norm' and hence of 'the underlying legal bond between the parties to the dispute' (Tams). Even so, a measure as extreme as the 'cancellation'[102] of a treaty and a permanent disruption of treaty relations has undoubtedly been enshrined in the modern law and, in her chapter, Malgosia Fitzmaurice brings to the fore a veritable trove of claims that States have made in litigation practice under the law of treaties as well as under the law of State responsibility, highlighting the fraught relationship that exists between the two regimes. To add to the complexity, account must also be taken of any remedies established in the *lex specialis* of any given treaty, such as the institutional power to suspend representation rights to which Jeremy McBride refers in relation to the Statute of the Council of Europe.[103] Indeed, as Duncan French and Karen Scott observe in their chapter, multilateral environmental agreements in particular 'are developing increasingly innovative and sophisticated mechanisms for responding to issues of breach or, as they are more commonly referred to, non-compliance'. The non-compliance procedures that have been developed in this context, at once more detailed but less forbidding than the concept of material breach, reflect how States Parties have found 'their own ways to preserve the integrity of the treaty, rather than rely on the formal rules on treaty termination'.

4 Future Pathways

The publication of a book is commonly perceived as marking the end of a process, in that it represents the physical testament to a series of intellectual engagements – the reaching of a preordained destination. Given the scale and ambitions of this project, however, that could never realistically have been entertained as one of our goals: rather than

---

[102] The word of Jennings and Watts (eds.), *supra* n. 28, at p. 1301.

[103] Art. 8 of the Statute of the Council of Europe provides: 'Any member of the Council of Europe which has seriously violated Article 3 may be suspended from its rights of representation and requested by the Committee of Ministers to withdraw under Article 7. If such member does not comply with this request, the Committee may decide that it has ceased to be a member of the Council as from such date as the Committee may determine.' And, notably, 'breach' – including 'material breach' – is not used in the law of the World Trade Organization, which, instead, adopts a system of 'the nullification or impairment of benefits accruing under the covered agreements that gives rise to remedies' (Pauwelyn and Van Damme).

presenting a comprehensive account of both the 'conceptual' and the 'contextual' perspectives on the modern law of treaties, it is closer to the truth to say that we simply wished to explore where these leads would take us and what light they might ultimately shed upon the *content* of that law. The project therefore sought to establish a new, additional, methodology for the examination of such questions, one which it is hoped will stimulate further collaborative and interactive research along similar lines. With that in mind, we have identified some of the most prominent and recurring themes to emerge from the many long discussions we have had with our contributors in the course of producing this volume. These have, in turn, given rise to a series of questions for future research on the modern law of treaties:

1. The first part of this work has been concerned with various 'concepts' that pervade the law of treaties, but what determines how these concepts are framed in the first place? How analytically useful are these concepts in the quest to understand the theory and practice of the law of treaties? Can these concepts be inferred, deduced and deciphered without further explication of the scope and meaning of the overarching concept of the law of treaties itself, recently described as one that is 'ripe for reappraisal'?[104] And what might any such reappraisal look like? Would it follow the International Law Commission in confining itself, at least in the first instance, to 'treaties between States'?[105] Or would it bring within its embrace all instruments worthy of that name?[106] Would the resulting regime be more or less prescriptive than the current version, and would it aspire to the same degree of flexibility and pragmatism? What would be, in Berman's words, its 'positive defining principle'?[107]

2. Once these various concepts have been identified, what insights can be gained from projecting them back onto the law of treaties itself and asking, for example: What actually constitutes the 'object and

---

[104] As well as a 'curious phenomenon': A. V. Lowe, 'The Law of Treaties; or, Should This Book Exist?' in C. J. Tams, A. Tzanakopoulos and A. Zimmermann (eds.), *Research Handbook on the Law of Treaties* (Cheltenham: Edward Elgar, 2014), pp. 3–15, at pp. 3–4.

[105] Art. 1 VCLT: *supra* n. 20.   [106] Art. 3 VCLT: *supra* n. 20.

[107] For Berman, 'there does exist a general concept of "the law of treaties" sufficient to validate the use of the term, but it consists of propositions of two kinds: rules of law (though these tend towards the abstract) and rules of practice or conduct (though these can at the extreme tend so far towards the workaday that they hardly qualify as "law")'.

purpose' of the Vienna Conventions themselves?[108] How does the interim obligation not to defeat that object and purpose apply in relation to those conventions? Moreover, what (if anything) would a 'material breach' of these conventions look like? Or does their very nature somehow render them immune from standard tropes of treaty law analysis?[109]

3. In light of the perspectives presented in Part I of this volume, is there a need for a ranking of the concepts identified? Are some – such as consent, for example – more important than others? Or are all of them to be accorded equivalent weight? Does the significance of these concepts change over time or in different contexts? Given their importance and the uncertainties of the relationships between them, to what extent (if any) is there need for a greater theorisation of the law of treaties and a lesser concern with practice?[110]

4. In the original design of our project, the intuitive appeal of the bifurcation between conceptuality and contextuality seemed straightforward enough, but to what extent might its utility be open to challenge? One of our contributors, Barbara Miltner, has written that 'territoriality is notoriously difficult to shoehorn because it defies clear divisions between conceptual and contextual aspects of treaty law', and, in tribute to this fluidity, she observes that 'the amorphism of territoriality serves to bridge the volume's two-part structure'. Delving into the chapter, we become aware of the different ways in which the concept of territory is mobilised within treaty relations – as the geographical location where treaties are to be performed (e.g. human rights treaties); the geopolitical unit or units in respect of which treaty commitments are assumed (e.g. when a State extends its formal acceptance of treaties to dependent territories) or as the very subject matter of the treaty itself (e.g. Antarctica and the Panama Canal).[111] Might there be other topics that defy easy categorisation?

---

[108] The 1978 Vienna Convention on the Succession of States in Respect of Treaties, for example, makes reference to its 'object and purpose' on nineteen occasions!

[109] Perhaps on the grounds that, to employ Kearney and Dalton's graphic phrase, they 'grapple with the fundamentals of constructing a world legal order': *supra* n. 23, at 495.

[110] *Pace* Shushi Hsu (China) who is reported in the debates within the International Law Commission to have said that '[f]undamentally there was little difference between a draft convention and a model code of rules, since the Commission seemed generally to have agreed that academic theories should have no place in either text.' See Summary Record of the 621st Meeting: Doc. A/CN.4/SR.621, p. 254 (paragraph 3).

[111] See, more generally, H. Waldock, Third Report on the Law of Treaties, Doc. A/CN.4/167 and Add.1–3 (3 March, 9 June, 12 June and 7 July 1964).

5. Turning to Part II of the volume and the chapters on contextual perspectives on the modern law of treaties, how in fact should we define and describe the 'contexts' for this purpose? Most obviously, this would be done with respect to substantive areas of public international law, but, in the course of the project, the importance of particular institutional contexts progressively impressed itself on our thinking, prompting the reflection that a focus on jural persons might be as valuable as one on subject-matter. Might, therefore, an alternative approach to contextuality be built around such considerations? In particular, what findings would result from an assessment of the practice of States which are not parties to the Vienna Conventions? Also, given the history of the early achievements in this field,[112] what scope might exist in the future for purely regionalised iterations of the law of treaties?

6. To what extent does an emphasis on contextuality of any kind carry the risk of exacerbating the process of fragmentation which is currently such a matter of concern for the discipline of public international law or can it, by total contrast, actually be pressed into service as a means of overcoming that very problem? In that regard, to what extent do the contextual studies in Part II of this work present a consistent, uniform perception of the modern law of treaties and, thus, a viable foundation for a coherent legal order in the future?

7. Finally, given the fact that, as remarked upon in the Introduction to this work, the complex inter-relationship between concept, context and content has been the subject of more explicitly focused attention in areas of intellectual endeavour far removed from our own, what lessons may be learned by standing back a little from the discipline of law and adopting a perspective upon treaty law that derives its inspiration from just such an alternative body of knowledge and understanding? More specifically, what insights, if any, can be gained with regard to the application, coherence and effectiveness of the modern law of treaties by viewing it through the particular prism of science? It is this approach which forms the basis of the concluding chapter in this collection.

---

[112] Note, in particular, the 1928 Havana Convention on the Law of Treaties and the 'different practice' on reservations recognised by the International Court of Justice in *Reservations to the Convention on the Prevention and Punishment of the Crime of Genocide* (Advisory Opinion) (1951) ICJ Rep. 15, at p. 25.

32

The Interplay of Concept, Context and Content in the Modern Law of Treaties: Final Reflections

MICHAEL BOWMAN

The various chapters of this work – whether those of a conceptual or of a contextual nature or, indeed, those that might seem to sit on the cusp between them – represent an invaluable resource against which to consider the issues raised by Vaughan Lowe in the essay to which reference was made in the Introduction to this work.[1] In particular, they provide considerable food for thought when seeking to answer a question which, while seemingly crucial to his broad concerns, is not explicitly addressed by him in that piece: namely, what is it that we are entitled to expect of the law of treaties in its contemporary manifestation? What functions can it legitimately be expected to perform, and how effectively should it be judged to be performing them? It is interesting in this regard to recall from our introductory chapter that perhaps the most pointed criticism that is made by Lowe himself is that this body of law offers only 'the appearance of solidity and certainty',[2] whereas in reality it is 'creaking under the weight of exceptions', being 'applied only formally and in a manner that sits awkwardly with the realities of the underlying situation'.[3]

The preoccupation here with *solidity* and *certainty* as ostensibly critical indicators of effectiveness, and with the relationship of the application of the relevant body of norms to *underlying reality*, is strongly evocative of what has sometimes been conceived as a properly 'scientific' approach to legal discourse, though Lowe himself does not expressly employ the term or advert to the associated tradition. It was, however, particularly vibrant during the formative period of modern international law, being most

---

[1] A. V. Lowe, 'The Law of Treaties; or, Should This Book Exist?' in C. J. Tams, A. Tzanakopoulos and A. Zimmermann (eds.), *Research Handbook on the Law of Treaties* (Cheltenham: Edward Elgar, 2014), pp. 3–15.
[2] *Ibid.*, at p. 3.   [3] *Ibid.*, at pp. 14–15.

obviously explicit in the writings associated with the German rationalist school of philosophy, such as those of Christian Wolff,[4] who proclaimed that 'certitude is a natural goal of the human mind and a bridge between the common and scientific ways of perceiving the facts of reality'.[5] Yet, clear indications of the same general mode of thinking can surely be found in the works of even earlier jurists such as Hugo Grotius and Samuel von Pufendorf.[6]

Such ideas have, moreover, always retained a significant influence upon international jurisprudence, with the law of treaties – and, indeed, the various sub-topics within that field, such as the principles governing the *interpretation* of such instruments – having proved a particularly common target of exhortations favouring a scientific approach.[7] Needless to say, not all authors have been willing to afford this perspective their unqualified endorsement, generating a lively and ongoing debate as to whether, for example, the process of treaty interpretation should properly be considered an art or a science.[8]

---

[4] Note, in particular, C. Wolff, *Jus Gentium methodo scientifica pertractatum* (1748) (Oxford: Clarendon Press, 1934) (J. H. Drake, trans.). See, also, *Le droit des gens ou principes de la loi naturelle* (1758) (Washington, DC: Carnegie Institution, 1916) (C.G. Fenwick, trans.).

[5] M. Hettche, 'Christian Wolff' in E. N. Zalta (ed.), *Stanford Encyclopedia of Philosophy* (https://plato.stanford.edu/entries/wolff-christian/).

[6] It is in fact a key strand within the natural law tradition generally: see, further, K. Haakonssen, *Natural Law and Moral Philosophy: From Grotius to the Scottish Enlightenment* (Cambridge: Cambridge University Press, 1996), esp. pp. 1–62 1; B. Kingsbury, 'A Grotian Tradition of Theory and Practice: Grotius, Law and Moral Scepticism in the Thought of Hedley Bull', *Quinnipiac L. Rev.*, 17 (1997), 3–33, and E. Pattaro (ed.), *A Treatise of Legal Philosophy and General Jurisprudence* (Vols. 9–10) (Dordrecht: Springer, 2009).

[7] See, e.g., Sir G. Fitzmaurice, 'The Law and Procedure of the International Court of Justice 1951–4: Treaty Interpretation and Other Points', *BYbIL*, 33 (1957), 203–293, at 207, where he calls for a 'sounder and more scientific method of approach' to interpretation than the 'intentions of the parties' approach. For further discussion, see the contribution to this volume of Gardiner at pp. 335–362 (Chapter 11) (and the works there cited); J. Stone, 'Fictional Elements in Treaty Interpretation – A Study in the International Judicial Process', *Sydney L. Rev.*, 1 (1954), 344–368, and M. S. Straubel, 'Textualism, Contextualism, and the Scientific Method in Treaty Interpretation: How Do We Find the Shared Intent of the Parties?' *Wayne L. Rev.*, 40 (1993–94), 1191–1225.

[8] See, e.g., Report of the International Law Commission on the Work of its 16th Session, UN GAOR, 19th Sess. Supp. at 200, U.N. Doc. A/CN.4/173 (11 July 1964); J.-M. Sorel and V. B. Eveno, 'Article 31 (1969)' in O. Corten and P. Klein (eds.), *The Vienna Conventions on the Law of Treaties: A Commentary* (Vol. I) (Oxford, Oxford University Press, 2011), pp. 804–837; P. Merkouris, 'Introduction: Interpretation Is a Science, Is an Art, Is a Science' in M. Fitzmaurice, O. Elias and P. Merkouris (eds.), *Treaty Interpretation and the Vienna Convention on the Law of Treaties: 30 Years On* (Leiden/Boston: Martinus Nijhoff, 2010), pp. 1–13, and U. Linderfalk, 'Is Treaty Interpretation an Art or a Science? International Law and Rational Decision Making', *EJIL*, 26 (2015), 169–189.

1 The Dictates of a Scientific Approach

It goes without saying, however, that the extent to which a specifically *scientific* approach is actually to be judged desirable in the field of jurisprudence must depend substantially upon what is considered for this purpose to represent 'science'.[9] The investigation of this question will entail a rather lengthy digression from the conventional paths of legal discourse, though hopefully the relevance of this detour will become apparent in due course.

1.1 Science as 'Substance': What We Know

To begin, it must be borne in mind that the emergence of the modern international legal order coincided very closely with the era of fundamental philosophical transformation in Europe commonly known as the Enlightenment,[10] when the prevailing perception of science was very much more limited than it is today. Indeed, given that even the most basic principles of chemistry and of thermodynamics were only just beginning to be established towards the latter end of the eighteenth century,[11] 'science' during the Enlightenment era was essentially restricted to the basic laws governing motion and mechanics established by Sir Isaac Newton.[12] His work built upon that of a host of other luminaries, including Francis Bacon, René Descartes, Johannes Kepler, Robert Hooke, Robert Boyle and Gottfried Wilhelm Leibniz, who had (quite correctly) perceived the importance of a mathematical approach to the understanding of reality. So fundamental was the importance that

---

[9] For an instructive introduction to this issue, see A. Orford, 'Scientific Reason and the Discipline of International Law', *EJIL*, 25 (2014), 369–385.

[10] For recent reappraisals, see, e.g., J. Gray, *Enlightenment's Wake* (1995) (reissued with new introduction, London/New York, NY: Routledge Classics, 2007); T. Todorov, *In Defence of Enlightenment* (2006) (London: Atlantic Books, 2009) (English trans. G. Walker) and A. Pagden, *The Enlightenment and Why It Still Matters* (Oxford, Oxford University Press, 2015) (containing extensive bibliography). For a valuable compendium of key writings of the era, see I. Kramnick (ed.), *The Portable Enlightenment Reader* (New York, NY: Penguin Books, 1995).

[11] In particular, through the efforts of people like Count Rumford, Joseph Priestley and Antoine-Laurent de Lavoisier (and later John Dalton and Sadi Carnot): for a full picture, see R. Porter (ed.), *The Cambridge History of Science* (Vol. 4: Eighteenth Century Science) (Cambridge: Cambridge University Press, 2003).

[12] Expounded in his 1687 work *Philosophiae Naturalis Principia Mathematica* (i.e. 'Mathematical Principles of Natural Philosophy'), commonly known simply as the *Principia*. For information regarding Newton himself, see J. Gleick, *Isaac Newton* (London: Harper Perennial, 2004).

was attributed to these principles that the German idealist philosopher Immanuel Kant, for example, believed that the proof of his own objectivity lay in demonstrating the precise accordance of his philosophical theories with the basic Newtonian laws.[13]

This worldview came to be known as the mechanical, or mechanistic, philosophy[14] and depended upon the belief that the entire universe, and everything within it, could be viewed as one enormous machine, which operated in accordance with certain highly predictable causative principles.[15] Accordingly, all manner of phenomena were to be analysed and understood in accordance with a resolutely *reductive* approach that entailed breaking everything down into its component parts and then reassembling it in order to determine exactly how it functioned and fitted together.[16] By securing an understanding of the fundamental laws of motion and mechanics, scientists were able to calculate and predict with considerable precision the movement of all material objects, from the planets which traverse our solar system to the balls which are propelled across a billiard table.[17] This was ultimately because all matter, regardless of the scale at which it was examined, was thought to share the same basic properties of extension, hardness, impenetrability, mobility and inertia.[18] It was, indeed, from these critical manifestations of 'underlying reality' that the essential solidity of matter derived and that the motions of material objects could be determined with such apparent certainty.

There can be no dispute that such thinking proved instrumental to the achievement of considerable progress in the fields both of pure science and of its technological applications, with the Industrial Revolution representing the ultimate manifestation of its impact. Yet such

---

[13] R. Scruton, *Kant: A Very Short Introduction* (Oxford: Oxford University Press, rev. ed., 2001), p. 43.

[14] For a sense of the nature and development of this worldview, see E. J. Dijksterhuis, *The Mechanization of the World Picture* (Oxford: Oxford University Press, 1961) and D. C. Goodman and J. Hedley Brooke (eds.), *Towards a Mechanistic Philosophy* (Milton Keynes: Open University Press, 1974). The term itself appears to have originated from Hooke in his *Micrographia* (1665).

[15] Boyle chose as his paradigm the Great Clock of Strasbourg: see Goodman and Hedley Brooke, *ibid.*, at p. 74.

[16] On the question of 'reversible process' and its converse, see J. Daintith (ed.), *Oxford Dictionary of Physics* (Oxford: Oxford University Press, 6th ed., 2009), pp. 261–262 and 475.

[17] The billiard table provided a particularly rich source of explanatory power: see D. Hume, 'Abstract of a Book Lately Published' (1740) – referring to his own *Treatise of Human Nature* (1739) – extracted in Kramnick (ed.), *supra* n. 10.

[18] From Newton's *Principia, supra* n. 12, Bk. 3, Vol. 2.

developments were undoubtedly secured at a price, and a very significant one at that. In particular, it came to be believed that such rules applied to everything, including living organisms, since these were merely a complex variety of machine, in which the 'instincts' typical of particular life-forms were triggered through the bodily equivalent of the cogs, springs and levers by which ordinary machinery was activated.[19] It was only the uniquely human capacity for rational thinking that distinguished our kind from all other life-forms and liberated us from the tyranny of purely physical mechanistic causation.[20] Yet even here, when attempts were made to describe and explain the operation of the mental processes in question, the mechanistic paradigm tended to reassert itself. As one authoritative account explains it:[21]

> The mind was treated as if it were a box containing mental equivalents of Newtonian particles. These were called 'ideas'. These 'ideas' are distinct and separate entities, 'simple', i.e., possessing no parts into which they can be split, that is, literally atomic, having their origin somewhere in the external world, dropping into the mind like so many grains of sand within an hourglass; there in some way they either continue in isolation, or are compounded to form complexes, in the way in which material objects in the outer world are compounded out of complexes of molecules or atoms.

The whole of mainstream philosophy, not to mention its various disciplinary off-shoots such as economics,[22] came to be dominated by this particular worldview, which served to fix the broad parameters within which a wide array of more specific controversies could be investigated.

Even international law itself could arguably be accommodated within an extended version of this paradigm, with the nation States which emerged from the Westphalian settlement capable of being seen as the

---

[19] See, e.g., Hooke, *supra* n. 14. Note, however, that this perspective was challenged from an early stage, but more intensively during the nineteenth century, by the *vitalists*, who insisted (though without ever providing any convincing explanation) that life was distinguished from ordinary mechanisms by some single, special, superadded force or ingredient: see, further, E. Mayr, *This Is Biology: The Science of the Living World* (Cambridge, MA: Belknap Press, 1997), pp. 1–23, esp. pp. 8–13.

[20] The claim recurs throughout Kant's *Critique of Judgment* (1790), for example. Nevertheless, this special status was seldom granted unequivocally to *all* human beings, since many were assumed to lack the appropriate levels of rationality.

[21] I. Berlin, *The Age of Enlightenment* (New York, NY: Mentor Books, 1956), p. 18. For a sample of original readings which exemplify the approach Berlin describes, see Kramnick (ed.), *supra* n. 10, at pp. 181–222. For an indication of the extent to which this paradigm still subsists, see T. Crane, *The Mechanical Mind* (London: Penguin Books, 2nd ed., 2003).

[22] Of crucial importance here, of course, were works such as Adam Smith's *The Wealth of Nations* (1776).

solid, discrete and impenetrable particles of the new international socio-political order, governed only by certain basic legal norms which were needed to regulate their occasional interactions. Although these rules were to be derived in an essentially empirical fashion, earlier notions of a system of natural law grounded in right reason proved hard to shake off; accordingly, conceptions of a social contract based upon the reciprocated application of reason could also be translated on to the international plane, resulting in the belief that some form of natural equilibrium would eventually emerge whereby States consented to curb their nationalistic excesses through the acceptance of norms designed for their mutual reassurance and collective security.[23] Consistently with this mind-set, treaties might typically be conceived as (or at least as containing) reg-ulatory *mechanisms* through which international controversies might be addressed. This mechanistic way of thinking became entrenched during the nineteenth century era of legal positivism and demonstrably still finds ample reflection in the modern era.[24]

Of itself, this general Enlightenment approach need not have proved unduly problematic, since it is indeed a worthy aspiration that all our thinking be grounded upon, or at least informed by, a reliable grasp of underlying reality as described by the natural sciences. Yet, if this aspira-tion is to be pursued assiduously, it will be vital to ensure that our understanding is constantly updated as scientific knowledge itself evolves.[25] In his later writings,[26] for example, Kant began explicitly to acknowledge some of the more obvious limitations and deficiencies of the mechanistic approach in explaining the behaviour of organic, purpo-sive beings but at the time lacked the scientific wherewithal to propose

---

[23] All of these ideas can be found, for example, in the writings of Kant, most notably his 1784 essay 'Idea of a Universal History on a Cosmopolitan Plan' (see especially the Seventh to Ninth Propositions) and also the later 'Perpetual Peace: A Philosophical Sketch' (1795), both now incorporated in H. S. Reiss (ed.), *Kant: Political Writings* (Cambridge: Cambridge University Press, 2nd ed., 1991), pp. 47–51 and 102–109 respectively.

[24] Thus, Orford reminds us, *supra* n. 9, at 373–376, that the polymath Sir William Whewell, who in 1868 endowed a new chair in international law at the University of Cambridge, was first and foremost an astronomer, physicist and philosopher of science and was motivated by the desire to extend the scientific method into the discipline of international law. See further Section 2.2.2 of this chapter.

[25] This point seems to have been fully acknowledged at the time: see, e.g., F. Quesnay, *General Rules for the Economic Government of an Agricultural Kingdom* (1758), Rule II, extracted in Kramnick (ed.), *supra* n. 10, at p. 497. It was also pervasive in Condorcet's *Sketch for a Historical Picture of the Human Mind* (1794).

[26] Most notably, *Critique of Judgment, supra* n. 20, Part II.

any effective solution, retreating instead behind a barricade of garbled circumlocution.[27] By the time of his death, moreover, the various identifiable strands within the overall skein of intellectual endeavours that had until then been known collectively as 'natural philosophy' had already begun to unravel and drift apart, initially into separate, technically specialised modes of enquiry and ultimately into completely discrete disciplines, with only minimal attempts being made to preserve continuity and coherence between them. Before long, the sheer quantity and diversity of specialist knowledge had rendered the pursuit of Kantian polymathy an unattainable aspiration, and scholars commonly contented themselves with what were at best mere fragmentary fossils of understanding of disciplines beyond their own.[28]

Mainstream philosophers, for the most part, appear progressively to have abandoned any expectation that science could provide answers to the mysteries and complexities of human existence; indeed, the belief that it might do has come to be widely derided within their circles as 'scientism'.[29] Somewhat paradoxically, however, they appear to have clung on to certain assumptions regarding the natural order – and the place of humankind within it – that derive precisely from the (avowedly scientific) Enlightenment worldview, as though *outdated* science could somehow prove a more reliable guide to the essential nature of reality.[30]

---

[27] Kant is never the most easily intelligible of authors but *Critique of Judgment, supra* n. 20, is commonly recognised as one of his most obscure and convoluted works. His ultimate conclusion on the mysteries of life, insofar as it is intelligible at all, is really, however, only a primitive form of vitalism: see Mayr, *supra* n. 19, at pp. 12–15.

[28] The problems have proved especially severe for the discipline of economics, as to which see J. Young, 'Organism and Mechanism', *Universitas*, 2 (1998), No. 1, and *The Natural Economy* (London: Shepheard-Walwyn, 1997). To the extent that its original eighteenth-century scientific assumptions have ever been revisited and enriched, it was largely only by highly questionable applications of Darwinian evolutionary theory: note especially Herbert Spencer's *System of Synthetic Philosophy*, published in ten volumes over several decades, which incorporated writings on biology, psychology, sociology and ethics, and is currently viewable online at http://praxeology.net/HS-SP.htm, and W. Bagehot, *Physics and Politics; or Thoughts on the Application of the Principles of 'Natural Selection' and 'Inheritance' to Political Society* (New York: D. Appleton & Co., 1872).

[29] For a variety of perspectives, see F. A. Hayek, *The Counter Revolution of Science: Studies on the Abuse of Reason* (Indianapolis: Liberty Press, 1980); J. Habermas, *Knowledge and Human Interests* (Cambridge: Polity Press, 2nd ed., 1987); M. Midgley, *Science as Salvation: A Modern Myth and Its Meaning* (London: Routledge, 1992); T. Sorell, *Scientism: Philosophy and the Infatuation with Science* (London/New York, NY: Routledge, 1994) and S. Haack, *Defending Science – within Reason: Between Scientism and Cynicism* (Amherst, NY: Prometheus Books, 2003).

[30] See on this point B. Ellis, *The Philosophy of Nature: A Guide to the New Essentialism* (Abingdon: Routledge, 2014). Regarding the extent to which it may arguably have been updated, see C. Craver and J. Tabery, 'Mechanisms in Science' in E. N. Zalta (ed.),

Accordingly, it is still commonplace to find humans depicted as fundamentally and uniquely rational beings liberated by virtue of this faculty from the dictates of the natural, deterministic causation by which other life-forms are governed.[31] In the modern era, however, a host of research findings have exposed this portrayal as little more than a foolish and futile exercise in anthropocentric self-aggrandisement.[32] It is, moreover, quite unnecessary to accord any specially sanctified status to the formal findings of science in order to repent this conceit, since common sense and everyday experience should surely have led us to this realisation long ago.[33]

It is, needless to say, far beyond the ambitions of this chapter to pursue these matters further, still less to attempt to put those other disciplines to rights.[34] Rather, the aim is the much simpler one of ensuring that, insofar as it might be deemed appropriate to evaluate the international legal order by reference to its 'scientific' credentials, the exercise does not fall victim to the pervasive misconceptions that have been so damagingly evident elsewhere. In particular, serious efforts will have to be made to ensure that the notion of 'science' to be utilised for this purpose should pay some regard at least to what has actually been learned by scientists in the course of the past 250 years! In this connection, three key areas of post-Enlightenment scientific development must in particular be taken

The Stanford Encyclopedia of Philosophy (http://plato.stanford.edu/archives/win2015/entries/science-mechanisms/).

[31] See, e.g., R. Trigg, *Philosophy Matters* (Oxford/Malden, MA: Blackwell, 2002), where such assumptions seem troublingly at odds with the author's avowed aim of demonstrating that 'philosophy is crucial in questioning our own beliefs about the nature of the world'!

[32] For an introduction to the vast literature, see P. Waldau, *Animal Studies: An Introduction* (Oxford: Oxford University Press, 2013); R. Corbey and A. Lanjouw (eds.), *The Politics of Species: Reshaping Our Relationships with Other Animals* (Cambridge: Cambridge University Press, 2013) and, for more extended consideration, R. Wilkie and D. Inglis (eds.), *Animals and Society: Critical Concepts in the Social Sciences* (London: Routledge, 2007). On the possible legal implications, see S. M. Wise, *Unlocking the Cage: Science and the Case for Animal Rights* (Oxford: Perseus Press, 2002).

[33] Indeed, it is evident that pre-Enlightenment thinking was in many respects significantly better informed regarding the essential nature of life, and of other life-forms, than the likes of Descartes, Locke, Smith and Kant, whose relatively cosseted and self-absorbed (sub)urban lifestyles did not require, or seemingly permit, any meaningful understanding of non-human attributes.

[34] On reform of the discipline of economics, however, especially by absorbing some of the lessons taught by the discipline of psychology: see, e.g., D. Ariely, *Predictably Irrational* (London: HarperCollins, 2008); G. A. Akerlof and R. J. Shiller, *Animal Spirits* (Princeton, NJ: Princeton University Press, 2009); D. Kahneman, *Thinking, Fast and Slow* (London: Penguin Books, 2011); S. Keen, *Debunking Economics* (London: Zed Books, 2nd ed., 2011) and R. Layard, *Happiness* (London: Penguin Books, 2nd ed., 2011).

on board. These concern respectively the elaboration of the laws of thermodynamics, the emergence of quantum theory and the very radical developments which have transformed the discipline of biology.

1.1.1 Key Post-Enlightenment Developments in Science

As regards thermodynamics, the crucial concept is arguably that of *entropy*. This may in fact be defined in various ways, but perhaps the most useful for present purposes is that it represents a measure of the unavailability for work of the energy within a physical system.[35] Although the energy within any closed system (that is, one that receives no exogenous energy input) is always conserved,[36] it tends inexorably to disperse and equalise over time, as where boiling water cools down in a cold room and ice melts in a warm one; eventually everything finds itself at a uniform temperature, and there is no more work that the energy within the system can perform. Entropy (or disorder) is at a maximum, equilibrium has been achieved, and the process is irreversible. It is for this reason that our universe must eventually perish, albeit over time-scales that we find difficult to comprehend. In the meantime, however, much else is afoot, and other bodies of scientific principle are required to explain precisely what is going on.

The field of quantum mechanics is especially significant here because, while Newton's laws can still be taken to provide a broadly reliable description of the behaviour of classical objects, it is now known that matter itself is not remotely as he supposed.[37] Indeed, when it is examined at the most minute level, wholly new and unexpected properties are revealed, requiring entirely new principles to explain them. In particular, it has become clear that matter is ultimately neither solid nor impenetrable, since the supposedly 'unsplittable' atoms[38] which represent the smallest units into which an elemental substance can be divided without loss of its chemical identity are themselves the product of interactions amongst a variety of more fundamental, sub-atomic 'particles'. These are, it seems, actually of a *qualitatively uniform* character right across the

---

[35] Daintith, *supra* n. 16, at p. 169.

[36] This constitutes the first law of thermodynamics, *ibid.*, at pp. 546–547.

[37] His key error, it seems, lay not in the laws that he had articulated but in a fundamental assumption on which they were based (sometimes called his 'zeroth' law), namely that matter (or its mass) is always conserved. It is now understood that it is not matter as such that is conserved but rather the energy of which it is merely a transient manifestation: see F. Wilczek, *The Lightness of Being: Mass, Ether, and the Unification of Forces* (London: Allen Lane, 2008), pp. 11–17.

[38] The very word atom derives from the Greek *a-tomos*, meaning uncuttable.

Periodic Table, the manifest differences between the various chemical elements being explicable by reference only to their *quantitative distribution*.[39] Confusingly, the particles themselves exhibit few of the properties of the much larger, classical objects with which our everyday experience has familiarised us:[40] indeed, it seems that their behaviour is ultimately only explicable by viewing them as waves and particles simultaneously.[41] Furthermore, although certain of these particles (known as fermions) may properly be seen as the building blocks of matter, others (bosons) are perhaps better viewed as particles of *relationship*, or as the 'matter' of building, if you will. While fermions always remain in some sense individuals, bosons do not, so that however many may be added, the aggregate number is always one(-ish).[42] Although much of this may seem highly counter-intuitive or implausible, it is always to be remembered that matter itself is merely a transient embodiment of *energy*, which represents the primal substance and underlying reality. Interestingly, many physicists refer to this energy as 'information' or, indeed, as 'ideas' capable of embodiment.[43]

The means by which matter emerges from pure energy appears to depend upon the 'collapse' of the wave function associated with these particles, a process known as *decoherence*. This can be physically observed through experiments in which the behaviour of individual

---

[39] More specifically, the chemical identity of the atom is determined by the number of protons in the nucleus: hydrogen has one, helium two and so on up to livermorium with 116: P. Atkins, *What Is Chemistry?* (Oxford: Oxford University Press, 2013), p. 18. Thus, medieval alchemists were actually correct to suppose that one element could ultimately be turned into another, though only a physical, nuclear reaction is capable of producing such a transformation, and not the purely chemical reactions they were capable of inducing.

[40] Atkins, *ibid.*, at pp. 4–6.

[41] For a basic statement of wave-particle duality, see Daintith, *supra* n. 16, at p. 585, and for a succession of more detailed explanations from different epochs, see W. Heisenberg, *Physics and Philosophy: The Revolution in Modern Science* (1958) (London: Penguin Books, 1989), pp. 30–58; P. Davies and J. Gribbin, *The Matter Myth: Dramatic Discoveries that Challenge Our Understanding of Physical Reality* (London: Penguin Books, 1991), pp. 197–234, and B. Cox and J. Forshaw, *The Quantum Universe: Everything That Can Happen Does Happen* (London: Allen Lane, 2011), pp. 27–44.

[42] For a loose analogy here, consider the building of a house. While it is meaningful to consider the number of bricks involved in the process, it is much less so to ask how many 'cements' there are: ultimately, however many *applications* of cement there may have been, there remains only one, continuous, seam of cement throughout (and, indeed, after the completion of) the entire building process.

[43] See respectively V. Vedral, *Decoding Reality: The Universe as Quantum Information* (Oxford: Oxford University Press, 2012) and Wilczek, *supra* n. 37.

light particles, or photons, is registered on laboratory equipment.[44] As a result, the process itself has often been supposed to require that it be *deliberately* measured in some way, and therefore to entail the involvement of a conscious observer as a necessary element. Yet this view is increasingly falling out of favour – a conscious observer is certainly required to enable us to *perceive* the collapsing of the wave function, but seemingly not in order to enable the process to occur in the first place.[45]

Rather,

> [i]t is taking place all the time inside every single classical object as its quantum constituents – the atoms and molecules – undergo thermal vibrations and get buffeted around by all the surrounding atoms and molecules, so that their wave-like coherence is lost. In this way we can think of decoherence as the means by which all the material surrounding any given atom – what is referred to as its environment – is constantly measuring that atom and forcing it to behave like a classical particle. In fact, decoherence is one of the fastest and most efficient processes in the whole of physics. And it is because of this remarkable efficiency that decoherence evaded discovery for so long. It is only now that physicists are learning to control and study it.[46]

Thus, even at this most basic physical level, *concepts* (i.e. the information or ideas inherent in sub-atomic units of energy) are translated into substantive *content* (i.e. tangible matter) by the precise way in which they are *contextualised* (as reflected in their interactions with other entities).

For a long while, it was believed that quantum effects operated only at the sub-atomic level and had no discernible effects at all at the macroscale, but more recently it has become apparent that this is not the case at all – indeed, a number of significant technological developments have depended upon the harnessing of quantum effects for everyday practical purposes.[47] As two prominent physicists have recently pointed out:

---

[44] This is the famous 'double-slit' experiment, which is discussed in virtually every work which touches upon quantum theory.

[45] See, e.g., M. Nauenberg, 'Does Quantum Mechanics Require a Conscious Observer?' www.journalofcosmology.com, 14 (2011) (citing a host of leading experts including Feynman, Bell and Wheeler). Indeed, Heisenberg had made the same point himself, *supra* n. 41, at p. 89. For a convenient summary of the various theories, see H. C. von Baeyer, 'Four Interpretations of Quantum Mechanics', *Scientific American*, 308 (2013), 46–51.

[46] J. Al-Khalili and J. McFadden, *Life on the Edge: The Coming of Age of Quantum Biology* (London: Bantam Press, 2014), p. 120.

[47] Lasers represent the most obvious example: see, further, S. Strogatz, *Sync: The Emerging Science of Spontaneous Order* (New York: Hyperion Books, 2003).

It is important to realize that the situation is not 'Newton for big things
and quantum for small': it is quantum all the way.[48]

Be that as it may, the crucial point is to understand that two of the key
suppositions of the Newtonian worldview – that is to say, certainty and
solidity – have been unceremoniously displaced from centre-stage within
the modern scientific perspective upon 'underlying reality'. As to the
former, the change is formally encapsulated in the axiom known as
Heisenberg's Uncertainty Principle, which is to the effect that, in relation
to the various complementary properties that fundamental particles
exhibit (such as location and momentum), full scientific certainty is not
merely unachievable in practice but *unattainable in principle*, not least
because the very process of measuring such values entails interference
with the phenomena themselves.[49] As far as solidity is concerned, it
seems that it, too, is largely an illusion. Although we commonly think
of the ground beneath our feet as representing the ultimate solid – *terra
firma*, as we describe it – the truth is that, like every other form of
material substance, it is composed primarily of 'empty space'.[50]
The only thing that in reality prevents us from falling into or through
this substrate is the electrostatic repulsion between the particles in our
bodies and those in the ground itself, which is more than sufficient to
overcome the countervailing force of gravity.[51] This is plainly very
different indeed from anything that we have traditionally conceived as
'solidity'.

The final, and arguably most crucial, area of scientific advance which
must be taken into account concerns the discipline of biology, which was
little more than a descriptive activity during the Enlightenment period
itself. The one major exception, by virtue of its importance to the practice
of medicine, was the field of Anatomy, though that was typically conceived and explained in essentially mechanistic terms.[52] Biology itself (or
'natural history') was not regarded as a genuine science at all by the likes

---

[48] Cox and Forshaw, *supra* n. 41, at p. 16. Explicit recourse to quantum theory at the
macroscopic scale is not usually necessary, however, because its predictions essentially
coincide with those of classical physics: Vedral, *supra* n. 43, at p. 132.

[49] For further explanation, see Daintith, *supra* n. 16, at pp. 570–571.

[50] More accurately, of a cloud of statistical probability of its complement of electrons being
present at any given location: Atkins, *supra* n. 39, at p. 22.

[51] Cox and Forshaw, *supra* n. 41, at pp. 116–135.

[52] This mode of thinking was pervasive, transcending perspectives on whether or not it
implied an ultimate 'creator': for extreme examples, see R. Descartes, *Traité de l'Homme*
(1644); J. O. de la Mettrie, *L'Homme Machine* (1747) and D. Hartley, *Observations on
Man* (1749).

of Kant, and it was only during the nineteenth century that viable governing principles began to emerge through the formulation of Charles Darwin's Theory of Evolution, followed by the rediscovery of Gregor Mendel's earlier work on heredity.[53] Indeed, it was not really until the 1940s that a reasonably clear picture of the evolutionary process came to secure general scientific acceptance, in the form of the modern 'evolutionary synthesis'.[54] Shortly afterwards, the unravelling of the mysteries of DNA led to the emergence of the discipline of genetics, which in turn produced highly significant advances in terms of our understanding of biological processes more generally.[55]

The theory of natural selection was of such substantial moment that its impacts were bound to be felt beyond the confines of formal science, though what actually seeped into public consciousness, unfortunately, was something very much more crude and simplistic than Darwin himself had proposed, being strongly influenced by the general spirit of the Victorian age. Although even Darwin came eventually to embrace it as a synonym for natural selection,[56] the maxim 'Survival of the Fittest' was not originally his but was coined by his contemporary Herbert Spencer,[57] a would-be polymath and ardent champion of competitive entrepreneurialism and the free market. The enduring impression created of evolution was accordingly one of unrelenting combat, as reflected in Tennyson's celebrated poetic conception of nature as 'red in tooth and claw'.[58] This characterisation no doubt captures certain aspects of the natural order, as manifest, *inter alia*, in the direct competition between conspecifics for the resources that nature has to offer and the ongoing

[53] See, generally, Mayr, *supra* n. 19, at pp. 175–206, and C. Darwin, *On the Origin of Species By Means of National Selection, or the Preservation of Favoured Races in the Struggle for Life* (London: John Murray, 1859).

[54] Mayr, *ibid.* In addition to Mayr himself, key contributors to this process included Theodosius Dobzhansky, Julian Huxley and George Gaylord Simpson.

[55] For an introduction, see, e.g., R. Dawkins, *The Blind Watchmaker* (London: Penguin Books, 1986) and *The Selfish Gene* (Oxford: Oxford University Press, rev. ed., 1989); S. Jones, *The Language of the Genes* (London: Flamingo, 1994); R. A. Wilson, *Genes and the Agents of Life* (Cambridge: Cambridge University Press, 2005) and A. Waddingham (ed.), *The Britannica Guide to Genetics* (London: Robinson, 2009).

[56] Specifically, in *The Variation of Animals and Plants under Domestication* (1868) and *On the Origin of Species* (5th ed., 1869); it had not featured in earlier editions of the latter.

[57] H. Spencer, *Principles of Biology* (London: Williams and Norgate, 1864). Spencer is often described as the most influential thinker of his time. Though a strong advocate of evolutionary theory, his own conception of it was actually more Lamarckian than Darwinian. Gradually, his ideas fell from general favour, though some have resurfaced in later philosophical theories and political agendas.

[58] Lord Alfred Tennyson, *In Memoriam AHH* (1849), Canto LVI.

battle of resourcefulness between species that is reflected in the process of predation. The ecological significance of the latter process is, moreover, demonstrated by the fact that apex predators (such as whales and sharks at sea or wolves in certain terrestrial ecosystems)[59] are commonly acknowledged as *keystone species* – that is, life-forms that seem to carry particular significance in the shaping and maintenance of the natural ecosystems in which they are found.[60]

Yet, simple common sense suggests that unbridled conflict and competition would be a hopelessly inefficient and inherently unsustainable way of living, and it has gradually become apparent that nature's actual *modus operandi* depends at least as much upon conciliation, cooperation and cohesion.[61] Such processes are, moreover, evident both within and across species barriers. As to the former, it is likely that multi-cellular life-forms were first created by adventitious agglomerations of unicellular organisms, which found so much advantage in community living that they ultimately opted to surrender their individuality altogether.[62] As to the latter, it is now believed that the 'eukaryotic' cells by which all complex life-forms are characterised[63] first appeared when one form of primitive life ingested another without digesting it, enabling the latter to

---

[59] An apex predator is one that occupies the highest trophic level, predating upon other life-forms but suffering little, if any, natural predation itself: for further discussion, see W. T. Flueck, 'Predators' Effects on Ecosystem Entropy', *Science*, 333 (2011), 1092–1093; W. Stolzenberg, *Where the Wild Things Were: Life, Death and Ecological Wreckage in a Land of Vanishing Predators* (New York, NY: Bloomsbury, 2008) and J. Terborgh and J. A. Estes (eds.), *Trophic Cascades: Predators, Prey and the Changing Dynamics of Nature* (Washington, DC: Island Press, 2010).

[60] For discussion, see R. T. Paine, 'Food Web Complexity and Species Diversity', *American Naturalist*, 100 (1966), 65–75, and 'A Conversation on Refining the Concept of a Keystone Species', *Conservation Biology*, 9 (1995), 962–964; L. S. Mills, M. E. Soulé and D. F. Doak, 'The Keystone-Species Concept in Ecology and Conservation', *Bioscience*, 43 (1993), 219–224, and R. D. Davic, 'Linking Keystone Species and Functional Groups: A New Definition of the Keystone Species Concept', *Conservation Ecology*, 71 (2003), r11.

[61] Thus the molecular geneticist Enrico Coen includes both competition and cooperation amongst his seven key principles that shape life at every level: *Cells to Civilizations: The Principles of Change That Shape Life* (Princeton, NJ: Princeton University Press, 2012).

[62] For a life-form capable of both modes of existence, note the slime moulds, which function either as individual amoebas in the soil or collectively in the form of a large multicellular 'slug', depending upon environmental conditions: B. H. Lipton, *The Biology of Belief* (London: Hay House, rev. ed., 2008), p. 100. The 'slug' form has shown itself to be capable of collective learning, so much so that in the laboratory it can navigate its way through a maze by the most efficient route.

[63] 'Eukaryotes' have been defined as 'organisms with a well-developed nucleus; all organisms above the level of prokaryotes': Glossary in Mayr, *supra* n. 19.

serve as its internal energy source in exchange for receiving greater protection from the hazards of the external environment.[64] Here again, such arrangements ultimately became entrenched through reproduction of the partnership as a unity, rather than as distinct individuals.[65]

In fact, genetic fusions of this kind should properly be seen merely as extreme versions of the collaborative spirit that is evident throughout the natural world. In this vein, various familiar biotic phenomena, such as lichens, are now understood not actually to be unitary life-forms at all but rather highly integrated consortia of very different biological taxa.[66] Furthermore, innumerable other species survive and flourish by virtue of complex exchanges of life-supporting services, albeit not in circumstances of quite such integrated intimacy.[67] Thus, whereas early interpretations of evolution and natural selection were expressed almost exclusively in terms of division, divergence, competition and conflict, modern perspectives are wont to attribute equal emphasis to combination, cooperation, conciliation and even compassion.[68] It should therefore be evident that 'fitness' in the biological sense carries few if any of its popular connotations, and must be understood as

---

[64] This theory of *endosymbiosis* was roundly ridiculed when first proposed by the biologist Lynn Margulis in the 1960s, before eventually becoming more or less established orthodoxy: for an accessible account, see L. Margulis and D. Sagan, *What Is Life?* (London: Weidenfeld & Nicholson, 1995), and for a contemporary assessment of Margulis' overall impact, see M. Brasier, *Secret Chambers: The Inside Story of Cells and Complex Life* (Oxford: Oxford University Press, 2012), esp. pp. 118–144.

[65] Reproduction of this kind is called *symbiogenesis*: Brasier, *ibid.*, at p. 129.

[66] Specifically, they arise from the colonisation of the filaments of a fungus by algae, cyanobacteria or both. These combinations exhibit characteristics that are quite unlike anything found in the component organisms individually: see, generally, Brasier, *ibid.*, at pp. 124–127.

[67] For example, numerous species of 'cleaner' fish obtain immunity from predation by setting up cleaning stations where they remove dead tissue and parasites from larger fish, which themselves employ a series of stylised movements to signal their willingness to enter the compact: K. L. Cheney, 'Interspecific Relationships in Blennies' in R. A. Patzner, E. Goncalves, P. Hastings and B. G. Kapoor (eds.), *Biology of Blennies* (Enfield, NH: Science Publishers, 2009), pp. 379–494.

[68] In addition to the work of Margulis, *supra* n. 64, see R. L. Trivers, 'The Evolution of Reciprocal Altruism', *Q. Rev. Biology*, 46 (1971), 35–57; R. Axelrod, *The Evolution of Cooperation* (New York, NY: Basic Books, 1984); R. D. Alexander, *The Biology of Moral Systems* (Piscataway, NJ: Transaction Publishers, 1987); F. de Waal, *Good Natured* (Cambridge, MA: Harvard University Press, 1996); J. Roughgarden, *The Genial Gene* (Berkeley, CA: University of California Press, 2009) and M. Nowak, with R. Highfield, *Super Cooperators* (Edinburgh: Canongate Books, 2011). Note, also, the addition by Richard Dawkins of two new chapters (one titled 'Nice Guys Finish First') to *The Selfish Gene*, *supra* n. 55, in the revised edition of 1989.

a technical term concerned with comparative reproductive success: it may well be enhanced by an innate or acquired inclination to *avoid* conflict wherever possible, and in many species entails interludes of total inactivity.[69]

It is interesting to note here that Spencer chose explicitly to explain his understanding of the struggle for survival 'in mechanistic terms',[70] since it has become clear from the later developments in biology highlighted previously that, while a certain amount can always be learned from the reductive, mechanistic approach, the level of insight thereby offered is inherently limited: indeed, taken alone, it risks generating misconceptions of the most serious kind.[71] In particular, many of the most crucial properties of living organisms simply cannot be found in their component parts, or even from the purely linear, mechanistic interactions between them, but emerge only from the overall pattern of organization of the life-form in question[72] and from the nature of its interactions with the surrounding environment. As a particular variety of complex system, such entities have to be investigated and understood *holistically* – that is to say, from the top down (i.e. from the whole to the parts) as much as from the bottom up. On one view, indeed, causation itself must be seen to operate in two directions in this context.[73]

It has to be admitted, however, that the notion of 'emergent' properties is not exactly pellucid, a problem exacerbated by the fact that it is seldom explained with great clarity by those that employ or endorse it.[74] Consequently, the suspicion may be created that resort to the idea is little more than a verbal conjuring trick, designed as a distraction from our inability to explain certain processes in genuinely rigorous, reductive fashion. Fortunately, therefore, there have lately been a number of more serious attempts to provide an explanation of the spontaneous

---

[69] Behaviours such as sleep, torpor and hibernation are all, *inter alia*, energy-saving strategies that contribute to evolutionary fitness: for a simple introduction, see E. Grabianowski, 'How Hibernation Works' (viewable at http://animals.howstuffworks.com/animal-facts/hibernation.htm).

[70] Spencer, *supra* n. 57, at p. 444.   [71] Mayr, *supra* n. 19, at pp. 17–18 and *passim*.

[72] As noted previously, Kant himself was one of the first to acknowledge the very considerable problems in this regard, especially in *Critique of Judgment, supra* n. 20, Part II.

[73] See, e.g., G. F. R. Ellis, D. Noble and T. O'Connor (eds.), 'Top-Down Causation', *Interface Focus*, 2 (2012), Issue 1 (theme issue); N. Murphy, G. F. R. Ellis and T. O'Connor (eds.), *Downward Causation and the Neurobiology of Free Will* (Berlin/Heidelberg: Springer Verlag, 2009). Other commentators see systems thinking as distinct from either of these perspectives, however: see Brasier, *supra* n. 64, at pp. 96–98.

[74] In this vein, Mayr's explanation, *supra* n. 19, at pp. 19–20, leaves much to the imagination.

emergence of order,[75] one version of which places the phenomenon of *synchronicity* at its heart.[76] Essentially, it depends upon the inherent propensity of entities called 'oscillators' – that is to say, anything that naturally follows a cycle,[77] repeating itself over and over again at approximately equal intervals – to align or synchronise those cycles as a result of some chemical or physical process of communication,[78] wherever the background circumstances are conducive to this outcome. Typically, moreover, this process of alignment appears to occur not in any gradual, linear fashion but suddenly and not necessarily predictably once a certain critical level of activity is reached, resulting in a 'phase transition'.[79] A prime illustration is provided by the propensity of fireflies to synchronise their rhythmic flashing so as to generate the astonishing natural lightshows by which innumerable travellers have over the centuries been transfixed.[80] Yet this is merely one example of what has been described as 'one of the most pervasive drives in the universe, extending from atoms to animals, from people to planets'.[81]

Indeed, the most fundamental manifestations of this process occur at the quantum level, in the sense that the coherence of the wave function of elementary particles may sometimes be preserved as if through mutual reinforcement, rather than simply collapse as it does in the course of the creation of purely inanimate matter. In such cases, moreover, the oscillators in question do not merely beat as one, as they do at the macro-scale, but actually *become* one, it seems.[82] It has been proposed that the special characteristics of living things may derive in some way from the additional creative potential that is inherent in this process. Such ideas are currently beginning to acquire a degree of traction in the scientific

---

[75] An illuminating discussion, with extensive current bibliography, can be found in T. O'Connor and H. Y. Wong, 'Emergent Properties' in E. N. Zalta (ed.), *The Stanford Encyclopedia of Philosophy* (http://plato.stanford.edu/archives/sum2015/entries/properties-emergent/).

[76] See, especially, Strogatz, *supra* n. 47.

[77] The beating of the heart is perhaps the most familiar and obvious example.

[78] Strogatz, *supra* n. 76, at p. 3.

[79] A useful analogy here concerns the way in which ice forms, at a very specific temperature, transforming the nature of the substance in question. For an accessible explanation of the mathematics of synchronicity, see *ibid.*, at pp. 40–69.

[80] An early account can apparently be found in the log of a voyage by Sir Francis Drake in 1577: *ibid.*, at p. 191.

[81] *Ibid.*, at p. 14.

[82] *Ibid.*, at pp. 127–152, esp. at p. 132. As indicated in *supra* n. 42 and accompanying text, this appears to be one of the key characteristics of the particles known as bosons.

world, through the emerging discipline of quantum biology, which represents a novel and particularly interesting attempt to explain the mysteries of life.[83] The key idea here is that although quantum coherence is very rapidly and easily lost, there may be circumstances in which it is preserved, through the medium of various nano-structural processes, for just sufficient a time for it to produce significant impacts on organisms at the macro-scale. There is already widespread agreement amongst scientists that quantum coherence is implicated in the process of photosynthesis, which is critical to the capacity of living things to harness the energy of the sun. Plants, for example, are known to perform this process at a level of efficiency which approaches 100 per cent, far in excess of anything which has ever been attained by any human machine.[84] The emerging theory proposes that this is merely one example of a much broader phenomenon, through which a host of other special capacities of living things might be effectuated.[85] If this is correct, it suggests that, whereas inanimate matter constitutes a once-and-for-all capitalisation of the potential inherent in ambient energy, living things are entities which embody the capacity to perform the trick on a systematic and recurrent basis, and through a variety of means.

Much of this remains speculative at present, but what is clear is that the process of initial self-generation and subsequent, ongoing self-renewal that is exhibited by organisms is quite unlike anything that can be found in the purely mechanical world. While it cannot be ruled out in principle that a machine might one day be created that could replicate every one, and all collectively, of the functions and features of an organism, we remain far away from any such development at present.[86] Furthermore,

---

[83] Al-Khalili and McFadden, *supra* n. 46.

[84] *Ibid.*, at pp. 127–135; G. S. Engel, T. R. Calhoun, E. L. Read, T.-K. Ahn, T. Mančal, Y.-C. Cheng, R. E. Blankenship and G. R. Fleming, 'Evidence for Wavelike Energy Transfer through Quantum Coherence in Photosynthetic Systems', *Nature*, 446 (2007), 782–786. For a sustained attempt to demonstrate the superior efficiency of natural processes over artificial ones generally, see J. Harman, *The Shark's Paintbrush: Biomimicry and How Nature Is Inspiring Innovation* (London/Boston, MA: Nicholas Brealey Publishing, 2013).

[85] Through an example involving bird migration, such processes have been putatively implicated not merely in photosynthesis, but in flight, navigation, olfaction, reproduction and, indeed, evolution itself: Al-Khalili and McFadden, *supra* n. 46, at pp. 330–331. One recently advanced hypothesis, which still awaits experimental demonstration, implicates quantum effects in brain processes generally: see M. P. A. Fisher, 'Quantum Cognition: The Possibility of Processing with Nuclear Spins in the Brain', *Annals of Physics*, 362 (2015), 593–602, and M. Brooks, 'A Bit in Two Minds', *New Scientist*, 5 Dec. 2015, p. 28.

[86] Recent claims that 'life' has been 'created' in the laboratory cannot yet be taken literally because the experiments involved depend, at least to some extent, on harnessing certain

no machine that was known to the scholars of the eighteenth century came remotely close to emulating the complexity of even the simplest kind of living thing (by general consensus, the bacterium,[87] a life-form the very existence of which they were in any event largely unaware).[88]

One final area of grave deficiency that permeated Enlightenment conceptions of the living world lay in the near-total lack of appreciation of the inherently and relentlessly *transformative* nature of biological entities: this is manifest, of course, both at the individual level (through learning and behavioural modification) and at the collective level (through genetic mutation, natural selection and consequent evolution).[89] Instead, the eighteenth century worldview clung to a perception of other living things as essentially fixed, unchanging, mechanistic and predictable: only occasionally did common sense and everyday experience leak through, and prompt them to doubt whether this could possibly be the case.[90] It has already been noted that some of the many anomalies and inconsistencies in this perspective came gradually to be perceived by Kant, but he was able to make relatively little progress in their resolution – indeed, he seemed ultimately incapable even of freeing himself from his original, instinctive characterisation of the suggestion that all life might have evolved from a single, common source as one which led to 'ideas so monstrous that reason recoils from them'.[91]

It should therefore be apparent that the ignorance of these luminaries with regard to basic biological process was in truth so profound and pervasive that little of what they had to say about living things of any

---

existing organic functions: see, e.g., A. Coghlan, 'Synthetic Life from Scratch', *New Scientist*, 16 March 2013, p. 5, and Al-Khalili and McFadden, *supra* n. 46, at pp. 319–320.

[87] Although they contain genetic material, viruses, by contrast, have generally been considered not to be a form of life as such, since they must hijack the machinery of another organism to reproduce. Nevertheless, the matter remains formally unresolved: see, e.g., G. Rice, 'Are Viruses Alive?' (2015) (http://serc.carleton.edu/microbelife/yellowstone/viruslive.html).

[88] The invention of the microscope led to the detection of 'animalcules' by Antoine van Leeuwenhoek as early as 1673, but little significance was attached to this discovery until the work of Ignaz Semmelweis, Louis Pasteur and Robert Koch almost 200 years later.

[89] See generally S. Rose, *Lifelines: Biology, Freedom, Determinism* (London: Allen Lane, 1997); S. B. Carroll, *Endless Forms Most Beautiful* (London/New York, NY: W.W. Norton & Co., 2005) and A. Minelli, *Forms of Becoming* (Princeton, NJ: Princeton University Press, 2009).

[90] On this point, see Mayr, *supra* n. 19, at p. 175.

[91] Kant, *Reviews of Herder's 'Ideas on the Philosophy of the History of Mankind'* (1785), republished in Reiss, *supra* n. 23, pp. 201–220, at pp. 209–210.

description merits any serious attention today. Regrettably, the main-stream of our contemporary philosophical worldview is still inclined to treat it more or less as unchallengeable truth.[92] Even worse, the reductive standpoint has also continued to generate unfortunate consequences in certain areas of science itself. Thus, it is still relatively common to encounter discussions about 'genes for' such-and-such a trait,[93] creating the risk that genes themselves are seen as no more than simple cogs, springs and triggers, which produce pre-ordained and determinate effects on natural phenotypes.[94] In reality, the genome of any organism represents a massive storehouse of information, and the determination of which of its particular elements happen to be acted upon will depend very much upon the internal inter-relationships between the component 'ideas' themselves, as well as upon the nature of the interactions that the organism as a whole experiences with the external environment (including all other life-forms, whether similar or distinct). Thus, discussions about whether the essential qualities of human (or other biotic) entities are determined primarily by nature or by nurture have now largely been sidelined by the realisation that these are two factors that can scarcely operate as independent forces at all, but only by dint of their continual interplay.[95] To put it another way, the content of any given phenotype will be determined by the interaction of concept (genetic information) with context (environment). As at the sub-atomic level, causation must be expressed in terms not of certainties but of statistical probabilities, and any attempt to secure greater determinacy through more intense investigation can ultimately only have the effect of interfering with the

[92] Consider, for example, the work of Trigg, *supra* n. 31: in the light of his claim in the Preface to be concerned with 'the problem of the nature of the world, and how we obtain knowledge of it, particularly through science', the poverty of reference to modern scientific material, by comparison with the philosophical works of the Enlightenment era, is remarkable.

[93] Dawkins, *supra* n. 55, is particularly inclined to fall into this trap.

[94] The phenotype of an organism has been defined as the 'totality of the characteristics of an individual, resulting from the interaction of the genotype with the environment': Glossary in Mayr, *supra* n. 19. For an advanced exploration of the idea, see R. Dawkins, *The Extended Phenotype* (Oxford: Oxford University Press, rev. ed., 1989).

[95] For a variety of perspectives, see Mayr, *supra* n. 19; L. Moss, *What Genes Can't Do* (Cambridge, MA: MIT Press, 2003); E. Jablonka and M. J. Lamb, *Evolution in Four Dimensions* (Cambridge, MA: MIT Press, 2005); D. Noble, *The Music of Life: Biology beyond Genes* (Oxford: Oxford University Press, 2006); S. Pinker, *The Blank Slate: The Modern Denial of Human Nature* (London: Allen Lane, 2002); P. J. Richerson and R. Boyd, *Not by Genes Alone* (Chicago, IL: University of Chicago Press, 2006) and M. Rutter, *Genes and Behaviour* (Malden, MA/Oxford: Blackwell, 2008).

causative process itself. This observation in turn highlights the crucial link between *what* we know and *how* we may come to know it.

1.2 Science as Process: How We Know

To recapitulate, the question of what exactly is known for scientific purposes is directly connected to that concerning the means by which authoritative scientific knowledge may reliably be obtained. Once again, from the Enlightenment period onwards, the natural corollary of the mechanistic mindset was that the phenomenon under consideration could best be understood by taking control of it, breaking it down into its component parts and then working out how it could be reassembled and recreated. Thus, the laboratory experiment, conducted under carefully conceived and strictly controlled conditions with all potentially confounding variables systematically excluded and key indicators precisely measured in such a way that the results could be readily replicated by anyone else performing the same operation, became the gold standard – and very soon virtually the only acceptable standard – by which scientific knowledge could be acquired and verified.

Yet, while this approach has yielded highly impressive results in the fields for which it was originally devised – namely, chemistry and physics – it should be immediately obvious that it is by no means as likely to offer the same advantages in the area of the life sciences, where experimental subjects can seldom be guaranteed to offer the same levels of cooperative predictability as magnetism and heat or sodium and copper. The chance events of evolutionary and behavioural history cannot simply be replicated in the laboratory, or even necessarily in the precise locations in which they occurred, and the removal of living subjects from their natural environment to a captive one is as likely to *introduce* as to exclude confounding variables. Thus, a number of the behaviours exhibited by animals under controlled conditions and then written up and theorised about by the experimenters have subsequently been revealed to be mere artefacts of confinement and quite untypical of anything that might occur in nature.[96] The extraordinary advances in knowledge and understanding of the living world that have been secured by researchers who were prepared patiently to observe and chronicle events as they occurred naturally in the wild, and over real rather than laboratory-budget-dictated time, have served as

---

[96] A noted example is S. Zuckerman, *The Social Life of Monkeys and Apes* (Abingdon: Routledge, 1932).

a welcome reminder that passive and dispassionate observation must actually be the scientist's first resort.[97]

It is unnecessary for present purposes to explore these matters further except to take note of the important observation of Iain McGilchrist, in the neuroscientific study cited in the Introduction to this work,[98] that the traditional thirst for assuming experimental control is the very clearest of manifestations of the particular mode of thinking that derives from the left hemisphere of the brain rather than the right – controlling, mechanistic and reductive, and seeking always certainty and quantitative precision as opposed to being oriented towards observation, contextualisation, qualitative sensibility and organic holism, and tolerant of indeterminacy and even of paradox.[99] Once this form of cognitive bias has become established, moreover, it tends to feed upon itself, since the left brain has the tendency to spurn the moderating influence of the right, being inherently divisive and exclusionary in inclination, whereas the right brain's sharply contrasting tendencies cause it naturally to seek out the left's analytical input. While it should therefore be apparent that, if anything approaching a complete picture of the world is to be obtained, it is the left brain that must be subservient to the right,[100] the position that has actually tended to prevail, in Western thinking at least, is precisely the converse.

Yet, what McGilchrist's thesis arguably fails to emphasise sufficiently is that, just as it was science that originally encumbered us with this legacy of dogmatic determinism based upon excessive mechanistic reductionism, so too is it science that is currently presenting us with the escape route.[101] As indicated earlier, quantum theory has largely displaced the ideas of certainty and solidity from the realm of physics, while, at a much more general level, scientific knowledge and

[97] J. Goodall, *In the Shadow of Man* (1971) (London: Phoenix Giants, rev. ed., 1996) and *The Chimpanzees of Gombe* (Cambridge, MA: Belknap Press, 1986): C. J. Moss, *Portraits in the Wild* (Chicago, IL: University of Chicago Press, 2nd ed., 1982); D. Fossey, *Gorillas in the Mist* (New York, NY: Houghton Mifflin, 1983); B. M. F. Galdikas, *Reflections of Eden* (London: Victor Gollancz, 1995) and J. Poole, *Coming of Age with Elephants* (London: Hodder & Stoughton, 1996).

[98] I. McGilchrist, *The Master and His Emissary: The Divided Brain and the Making of the Western World* (New Haven: Yale University Press, 2009).

[99] It may be, indeed, that paradox *actually is* the ultimate reality: see A. Wagner, *Paradoxical Life: Meaning, Matter and the Power of Human Choice* (New Haven, CT: Yale University Press, 2009). In that vein, the celebrated Danish physicist Nils Bohr has suggested that whereas the opposite of an ordinary truth is a falsehood, the opposite of a fundamental truth is another fundamental truth: see Wilczek, *supra* n. 37, at p. 11.

[100] McGilchrist, *supra* n. 98, esp. pp. 176–208.

[101] There are certainly fleeting acknowledgments of this possibility: see, e.g., *ibid.*, at p. 460.

understanding are now conventionally accepted to be essentially of only a provisional character,[102] with their established principles and theories representing simply the most plausible explanations currently available in light of the evidence; accordingly, if reliable evidence comes to light which cannot satisfactorily be accommodated within those principles and theories, they will simply have to be refined, modified or abandoned.[103]

Thus, although the reductive, mechanistic paradigm still enjoys extremely wide currency, on account of the admittedly very considerable explanatory and educative power that it continues to import, it has, crucially, now been supplemented by an additional, much more subtle and sophisticated, paradigm deriving from the biological sciences and from interdisciplinary work on complex systems. Studies in the area of ethology and ecology lay emphasis upon a resolutely *holistic* perspective and stress the inherently *inter-relational* nature of biotic entities,[104] leading to the conclusion – paradoxical as it may seem – that true autonomy (of the kind with which the atomistic, reductionist natural philosophers of the Enlightenment were so preoccupied) is actually only possible as a form of inter-dependence.[105] These findings would seem to demonstrate that, where contemporary science is concerned, the right brain perspective is actually very much alive and indeed thriving.

---

[102] Thus, as even its most ardent advocates readily concede, science 'can only ever deliver probabilistic and partial answers': 'Leader: Uncertainty Principles', *New Scientist*, 19/26 Dec. 2015, p. 7.

[103] See, generally, S. McCarthy and M. Sanders, 'Broad Classification and the Provisional Nature of Science', *J. Bio. Ed.*, 41 (2007), 123–130; K. Popper, *Conjectures and Refutations: The Growth of Scientific Knowledge* (London: Harper & Row, 1963); T. S. Kuhn, *The Structure of Scientific Revolutions* (Chicago, IL: University of Chicago Press, 1962) and A. F. Chalmers, *What Is This Thing Called Science?* (Maidenhead: Open University Press, 3rd ed., 1999).

[104] These ideas began to become established from the late 1970s onwards. For a diverse sample of relevant works, see I. Prigogine and G. Nicolis, *Self-Organization in Non-Equilibrium Systems* (Chichester/Oxford: Wiley/Blackwell, 1977); N. B. Davies, J. R. Krebs and S. A. West, *Behavioural Ecology* (1978) (Chichester/Oxford: Wiley/Blackwell, 4th ed., 2012); R. A. Hinde, *Ethology* (Waukegan, IL: Fontana Press, 1982); F. Mathews, *The Ecological Self* (London: Routledge, 1991); C. A. R. Boyd and D. Noble (eds.), *The Logic of Life: The Challenge of Integrative Physiology* (Oxford: Oxford University Press, 1993); A. Drengson and Y. Inoue (eds.), *The Deep Ecology Movement* (Berkeley, CA: North Atlantic Books, 1995); W. Fox, *Towards a Transpersonal Ecology* (Albany, NY: State University of New York Press, 1995) and F. Capra, *The Web of Life* (London: HarperCollins, 1996).

[105] See especially Wagner, *supra* n. 99.

2   From a 'Treatise' on Science to the 'Science' of Treaties

By this stage of the discussion, even the most patient and forbearing of readers will doubtless be demanding to know what glimmer of relevance any of this could possibly hold as far as the modern law of treaties is concerned. The answer is, of course, that the discussion began with a recognition of the many references to the utility of a 'scientific' approach to the exposition and development of treaty law while acknowledging the existence of considerable uncertainty regarding precisely what such an approach should properly entail. If there is indeed a set of fundamental scientific principles that under-pin the whole of physical reality, a basic grasp of their purport may help to shed light upon all forms of natural phenomena, including human behaviour[106] – and even, perhaps, that of treaty-making.

2.1   The Function of a Scientific Approach to Law

The functional relevance of such principles in this context might possibly be explained in various ways, including that (i) they must be regarded as directly applicable and indeed central to a proper understanding, on the grounds that the practice of treaty-making is merely one example (albeit an extremely rarefied and specialised one) of the behaviour of living things, which therefore may ultimately demand a biological (or even quantum biological) explanation;[107] or because (ii) though not necessa-rily definitive in the previous sense, they are nonetheless integral to a broader body of scientific principles, still under elaboration, which will ultimately be shown to govern all forms of complex system, whether mechanical, biological,[108] social, economic or purely theoretical,[109]

---

[106] For explorations of this point, see, e.g., J. Baggott, *A Beginner's Guide to Reality* (London, Penguin Books, 2005); R. P. Crease and A. Scharff Goldhaber, *The Quantum Moment* (New York, NY: W.W. Norton & Co., 2014) and D. Deutsch, *The Fabric of Reality* (London: Penguin Books, 1997).

[107] See, further, Al-Khalili and McFadden, *supra* n. 46; Lipton, *supra* n. 62; Mathews, *supra* n. 104; D. Zohar, *The Quantum Self* (London: Flamingo, 1991) and H. Maturana and F. Varela, *The Tree of Knowledge: Biological Roots of Human Understanding* (Boston, MA: Shambhala Publications, rev. ed., 1992).

[108] Thus Coen, *supra* n. 61, argues that a detailed understanding of the same few basic principles – specifically variation, persistence, reinforcement, competition, cooperation, combinatorial richness and recurrence – is sufficient to explain all biological phenomena from individual cells to entire civilisations.

[109] For recent discussion, see, e.g., Vedral, *supra* n. 43; Strogatz, *supra* n. 76; F. Capra and P. L. Luisi, *The Systems View of Life: A Unifying Vision* (Cambridge: Cambridge University Press, 2014) and C. Hidalgo, *Why Information Grows: The Evolution of Order, from Atoms to Economies* (New York, NY: Basic Books, 2015).

including manifestations of human regulatory behaviour; or because (iii) regardless of their possible formal applicability in either of the previously mentioned senses, they form a most pertinent and instructive analogy which can profitably be deployed in order to help explain such activities.

As intriguing as it might undoubtedly be to explore the first two possibilities, the challenge would be formidable and the utility questionable, for the needs of the present work are amply met by confining attention to the minimalist option, numbered (iii) in the preceding paragraph, since even the deployment of principles derived from the realm of the natural sciences merely as *analogies* for that of normative regulation may serve to provide valuable elucidation regarding the essential nature of the treaty-making process. The ultimate justification for the appropriateness of the analogy lies in the recognition that the process of treaty-making, in common with that which gives rise to the behaviour both of sub-atomic particles and of living organisms, is one where content, or meaning, emerges from the contextualisation of concept.[110] Thus, in order better to understand this process, it may be instructive to examine other paradigms of this kind.

As noted in the Introduction, however, one important qualification to be borne in mind lies in the fact that the ultimate substantive content of treaty law is itself of an essentially abstract, conceptual and normative, rather than concrete and physical, character. In consequence, the process takes on a rather more complex, multi-layered and recursive aspect, whereby the concepts and contexts under consideration may themselves have to be conceptualised and contextualised. Thus, one of the ways in which we typically contextualise treaties and the commitments they generate is by reference to the particular sub-disciplines of international law from which they have emanated: in this vein, we speak of trade treaties, human rights treaties, maritime treaties and so on. This usage seems perfectly natural, since it exactly reflects the way in which we divide up the broader discipline of international law for a host of practical purposes concerning their implementation and administration,[111] not to mention those of teaching and research. It is, moreover, precisely this

---

[110] See, especially, on this point Wagner, *supra* n. 99.

[111] Thus, within national administrative systems, functional responsibility for the negotiation, implementation and oversight of particular treaty commitments may be allocated to 'appropriate' government departments on the basis of general descriptions such as these.

mode of categorisation that has largely been adopted for the purposes this work.

Yet while this may constitute a perfectly rational conceptualisation of context for the purposes of investigating and elucidating the practical application of the law of treaties, it certainly cannot just be taken for granted that this mode of contextualisation should play any definitive role in the process through which the actual contents – i.e. constituent principles – of treaty law itself are formally elaborated and prescribed. Can it really be the case, as some have argued, that specific bodies of treaty obligations categorised in that fashion require their own peculiar *principles of treaty law* if they are to be implemented and administered effectively?[112] Or is this merely a further manifestation of left-brain predilection for abstraction, compartmentalisation and concomitant narrowing of focus, reinforced in this context by an instinctive disinclination to undertake the onerous task of acquainting oneself with principles and illustrative examples derived from outside one's own intellectual stamping ground? The point is an important one, for while a single, unified law of treaties might serve as something of a bulwark against the widely deprecated tendency towards fragmentation within the international legal system, a multiplicity of special regimes could surely only exacerbate it. Accordingly, a key part of the reason for adopting this mode of classification in the present work was to enable some of these contentions to be tested, so as to determine whether a unitary or a fragmented system of treaty law should ultimately be judged preferable. With those general considerations in mind, it is possible to commence our examination of precisely what may be learned from the scientific analogy.

2.2   A Scientific Approach to Treaties

The first lesson to emerge is that modern scientific perspectives provide reason to believe that Lowe's own particular conception of the operation of treaty law, as discussed previously, may indeed have rather too much in common with the (left-brain) mechanistic worldview, which can no longer be regarded as providing a fully adequate foundation for our understanding of things: above all, certainty and solidity of the kind he appears to demand are likely to prove as unattainable in the world of legal normativity as they are in the physical realm. Such qualities are essentially mere illusions of a middle-distance perspective, destined to become

---

[112] This would seem to be the implication of Lowe's essay: *supra* n. 1.

ever more elusive and unascertainable the more closely the phenomena under investigation are examined.

Whenever the treaty-making operation is subjected to scrutiny, the formal conceptualisation of the concerns that have driven the negotiation and conclusion of any particular agreement must be conjured from the raw energy of political motivation, a process which is seldom easy to analyse or even describe with any precision. Thus, the overall object and purpose of the exercise may seem by turns to be both obvious and unfathomable.[113] A crucial aspect of the problem here is that both the foundational concepts by which such instruments are inspired and the normative provisions that are intended to give effect to them have necessarily to be expressed in words, and words seldom exhibit the degree of clarity and certainty that Enlightenment philosophers seemed commonly disposed to assume.[114] Interestingly, Lowe's own essay throws up a particularly illuminating example of their inherent trickiness, which it may be useful to explore briefly.

2.2.1 The Inherent Limitations of Language

It will be recalled from the Introduction to this work that Lowe's principal reservation regarding the viability of a single, uniform law of treaties was that the class of instruments to which it must apply is extremely diverse, or, in his words, 'by no means ... homogenous'.[115] To some writers, however, the expression 'homogeneous' might have been the one which most naturally came to mind for this purpose. For anyone vacillating uncertainly between the two forms, definitively establishing appropriate usage would be unlikely to prove an easy task. Reference to the current plethora of online dictionaries, for example, might variously indicate that the two forms are essentially synonymous, or merely alternative spellings of the same word, or even that one them (most likely 'homogenous' itself) is not actually a recognised word form at all! It would require recourse to a dictionary of some sophistication[116] to discover that while these two words (for two different words they indeed

---

[113] See, further, the contribution to this volume of Kritsiotis at pp. 237–302 (Chapter 9).

[114] For an instructive discussion of this point by a celebrated physicist, see Heisenberg, *supra* n. 41, at pp. 39–52, esp. at p. 51.

[115] Lowe, *supra* n. 1, at p. 12.

[116] To wit, C. Schwartz *et al.*, *Chambers English Dictionary* (Cambridge: Chambers/ Cambridge, 7th ed., 1998). To broadly similar effect, see W. R. Trumble and A. Stevenson (eds.), *Shorter Oxford English Dictionary* (Oxford: Oxford University Press, 5th ed., 2002).

appear to be) are themselves demonstrably *homogenous* – that is to say, *of common descent* (understood here, naturally enough, in an etymological sense),[117] explaining their striking *similarity in appearance*[118] – they unfortunately cannot be considered to be perfectly *homogeneous* – meaning, *of uniform character* (with the emphasis placed, for present purposes, upon their specifically semantic connotations).[119]

An even more specialist reference source would be required, moreover, to shed real light on the matter.[120] Specifically, it appears that the term 'homogeneous' (associated noun, *homogeneity*) first came into usage in the seventeenth century, an era when it would typically have been assumed that closeness of relationship, similarity in appearance and uniformity of character were all of a piece – just as pumps, looms and engines exhibited certain readily recognisable physical and functional attributes, so too must plants and animals of any particular 'kind'.[121] Indeed, these ideas were formally consolidated in the system of biological taxonomy devised by Carl Linnaeus in the century which followed.[122] It has subsequently become apparent, however, that such inter-linkage cannot simply be assumed, the vagaries of evolution being such that morphological or behavioural similarity can serve at best as only a provisional guide to kinship, and at worst as a source of serious misdirection.[123] During the nineteenth century, it began to be appreciated

---

[117] To be specific, both derive from the Greek *homogenes*, a compound of *homos*, meaning 'same' and *genos*, meaning 'race', 'stock' or 'kin'. See, further, T. F. Hoad (ed.), *Concise Dictionary of English Etymology* (Oxford: Oxford University Press, 1996).

[118] *Chambers English Dictionary, supra* n. 116, specifically incorporates this element in its definition, though, as will be seen later, it is questionable whether it is strictly correct to do so.

[119] This is the sense that Lowe presumably intends: *supra* n. 1.

[120] See, e.g., the definitions, illustrations and readers' responses presented in *Grammarist*: 'Homogenous vs. homogeneous', viewable at www.grammarist.com/usage/homomogen ous-homogeneous/.

[121] The long-running philosophical deliberations on the question of 'natural kinds' has indeed been gravely undermined by the fact that they began long before any reliable understanding of biological reality was available, and continued largely unaffected even once it developed: oddly, it seems not to have occurred to most philosophers that the most 'natural' kind of 'natural kind' was the kind of kind that was found in nature!

[122] C. Linnaeus, *Systema Naturae* (1735) (10th ed., 1758). Interestingly, the system included minerals, alongside plants and animals.

[123] It appears, for example, that the closest extant relative of the whales is probably the hippopotamus, a markedly different creature in terms of appearance, habitat and behaviour. Conversely, swallows and swifts – birds which to the untrained eye may appear hard to distinguish – are not at all closely related, representing lineages which diverged millions of years ago, long before modern humans even appeared on the earth.

that such issues should not be pre-judged, and the word 'homogenous' (noun form, *homogeny*) accordingly came into usage amongst scientists as a means of signifying genuine biological kinship, shorn of any unwelcome overtone or assumption of phenotypical similarity. This suggests that *homogeneous* would indeed have been *le mot juste* for Lowe's purposes, though even the online guardians of linguistic propriety acknowledge that attempting to maintain the distinction today is probably 'a lost cause in popular usage'.[124]

This brief etymological foray is instructive for present purposes because it not only demonstrates the inherent slipperiness of words in general but also serves more specifically to confirm McGilchrist's diagnosis of the domineering propensity of the left-brain, where linguistic capacity is primarily located, in its attempts to represent the world, and its inbuilt resistance to achieving an effective synthesis with the input of its more organically oriented right-sided counterpart. First, an expression of manifestly biological nuance was systematically invested with the mechanistic overtones that then dominated human conceptualisation of natural kinds, so as to maintain our skewed perspective of organic reality, and then subsequently a cognate term devised by life scientists precisely in order to counteract or circumvent those misconceptions itself becomes sequestered into popular parlance in such a way as to undermine that very initiative – and all, no doubt, without our even realising it!

These considerations prompt further thoughts regarding the attributes of language as a vehicle for conveying meaningful information about the nature of the world and for marshalling our projects for action. These are, first, that words are commonly coined well before there is any clear understanding of the phenomena to which they relate. As a result, it may well become evident in the longer term that the language selected to describe them is actually highly tendentious or inappropriate or even that the very phenomenon they seek to denote is in reality wholly illusory. Secondly, even where terminology is carefully and aptly selected in the first instance, it may easily be diluted, distorted or misappropriated subsequently in everyday usage. Finally, it is a characteristic of language users generally to slide between literal and metaphorical usage without any clear appreciation of when, or indeed whether, this particular line has been crossed.[125]

---

[124] *Supra* n. 120.

[125] Nowhere, indeed, is this clearer than in relation to the word 'mechanism' itself, where it is now virtually impossible to disentangle one from the other. Both the Greek *mekhane* and Latin *machina* are most commonly translated as 'contrivance', implying something

All of this suggests that there is something inherently unpredictable, and indeed potentially hazardous, in the use of words to achieve any complex or elaborate objective and that the quest for a 'scientific' approach to treaty-making must necessarily take these issues into account. In particular, while it is certainly possible to conceive of words as resembling the solid, discrete and definitively measurable particles of Newtonian physics, it is far from clear that this faithfully captures their essential nature. Rather, it may be more appropriate to think of them as the close equivalents of the elementary particles of the quantum world – i.e. as somewhat blurry surges or pulses of semantic potential, pinned down in particular contexts to produce broadly predictable substantive effects by virtue of their interactions with other such particles. Consider, for example, the difficulties involved in determining the meaning even of such a familiar expression as 'civil law', other than by reference to the particular alternative concept ('criminal Law', 'common law', 'military law', 'international law') with which it is being contrasted. It is therefore unsurprising that the maxim *noscitur a sociis* – 'one is known by the company one keeps' – is a long-established principle of statutory interpretation.[126] *Contextualisation* is accordingly crucial to the emergence of meaning and hence to the very possibility of meaningful content.

In the first instance, the *milieu* in question is essentially a literary/linguistic one, encompassing primarily the text of the treaty itself (that is to say, its provisions, preamble and annexes, if any)[127] but also certain closely associated agreements and instruments.[128] Co-location within this *milieu* is, however, much more than a process of mere juxtaposition because the principles of syntax – the 'bosons' of the linguistic system, if you will – generate vital information of a structural character, specifying the nature of the inter-relationships between the various components and thereby enabling the semantic thrust of the individual verbal 'fermions' to be channelled into some meaningful overall message. In this way, a provisional sense of what the instrument in question is

that is (i) specifically created by someone (ii) for a particular purpose. It is, however, completely unclear whether (or, if so, which of) these implications are to be imported into contemporary discourse. In centuries past, the 'mechanistic' universe seemed profoundly irreligious to some, through being explicable in purely mundane, physical, scientific terms, yet to others (including Newton himself) it merely confirmed the existence of an ultimate creator.

[126] See, e.g., I. Van Damme, 'Treaty Interpretation by the WTO Appellate Body', *EJIL*, 21 (2010), 605–648, esp. at 621.

[127] Art. 31(2) VCLT.   [128] As defined by sub-paragraphs (a) and (b), *ibid.*

seeking to achieve begins to emerge. Yet, although the term 'context' itself is explicitly restricted to this verbal domain for the specific internal purposes of treaty law,[129] it is clear that an interpretational field of this particular kind cannot feasibly be understood or applied in isolation, but must itself be subjected to further modes of contextualisation.

Accordingly, the *travaux préparatoires* to the treaty in question (the historical record of the *deliberative context* of diplomatic negotiations from which the text itself emerged) constitute a further legitimate source of relevant information (also expressed, of course, in verbal form). In addition, both the specific aspirational and the general socio-political 'contexts' in which those negotiations took place also have their part to play in the interpretation process,[130] while normative domains contiguous to that of the treaty in question (i.e. the broader *juridical* context) must also be taken into consideration.[131] It is, indeed, only through this process of structured and progressive contextualisation that these inherently rather fuzzy and elusive conceptual inputs can be combined in such a way as to achieve a legal instrument of at least ostensible normative solidity and tolerably clear substantive content.

As suggested earlier, however, it is for practical reasons very much open to question whether the levels of certainty and solidity attainable can ever even come close to reaching the absolute. Furthermore, it is by no means obvious that any such potential should necessarily be considered an unqualified advantage in principle, for fixity of this degree produces rigidity, and structures of an excessively rigid nature are prone to buckle or fracture under pressure.[132] Treaties have in the very nature of things to be applied over the course of time,[133] and if there is

---

[129] In accordance with the definition established by Art. 31(2) VCLT. It is tempting to describe this as a textual (or better still, perhaps, multi-textual) domain, because that is predominantly its character, but it is doubtless possible that an 'agreement relating to the treaty' of the kind contemplated by sub-paragraph (a) might be purely oral.

[130] These factors are introduced by reference respectively to the 'object and purpose' of the treaty (Art. 31(1) VCLT) and the 'circumstances of its conclusion' (Art. 32 VCLT).

[131] Art. 31(3)(c) VCLT.

[132] See, generally, NDT Resource Centre, 'Tensile Properties', viewable via the 'Materials and Processes Primer' at www.nde-ed.org/SiteNav/TableofContents.htm. To highlight an interesting example, the Wikipedia entry on 'Ultimate Tensile Strength' notes that spiders' silk typically has a UTS that is significantly greater than steel (though the details are still being debated, it seems): https://en.mwikipedia.org/wiki/Ultimate-tensile-strength. See, generally, A. Basu (ed.), *Advances in Silk Science and Technology* (Cambridge: Woodhead Publishing, 2015).

[133] This is actually true even of dispositive treaties, such as boundary treaties. Although Lowe, *supra* n. 1, at p. 5, is in one sense correct to suggest that their 'legal effects are

one thing of which we can be reasonably confident it is that the political and practical circumstances within which they have to operate are unlikely to remain unaffected by change. Unless the normative instrument adopted to tackle the problem in question has an inbuilt capacity to respond to such changes, the risk is that it will progressively become marginalised and eventually discarded as obsolete.[134] Accordingly, it could be contended that, where treaty regimes are concerned, *flexibility* and *adaptability* constitute qualities that are of comparable value, at the very least, to certainty and solidity. Ideally, therefore, treaty negotiators should be looking to strike some kind of acceptable pragmatic balance amongst these various desiderata.

2.2.2   Treaties Conceived as 'Mechanisms'

This observation prompts another, which is that the very conceptualisation of treaties as 'mechanisms' may prove problematic in various respects. It is unsurprising that they should originally have been viewed in that way, since the historical period when they began to be utilised with progressive frequency coincided with that when the mechanistic mindset still held undisputed sway in human affairs. Accordingly, they were seen essentially as self-contained systems of rules designed to tackle particular problems through the reciprocated governmental assumption of obligations that, once performed, would bring about a solution. Yet, while this approach might serve tolerably well in situations where the task in question was small-scale and short-lived, the enterprise would be prone to falter in other circumstances. In particular, in the absence of the continual input of additional energy, the arrangement would, like any closed physical system, be likely to experience a progressive dissipation of operational vigour until it eventually reached maximum entropy and ground to a halt altogether.

Ideally, of course, the strength of commitment of States would sustain itself in perpetuity of its own accord, but experience suggests that such an outcome can seldom be guaranteed in the real world of human affairs.[135]

---

wholly realized immediately upon their conclusion', it is also true that the primary purpose of such a treaty is actually to determine, for jurisdictional or related purposes, the effects or implications of activities that will occur subsequently.

[134] In this context, readers may care to consider, for example, the implications of Hampson's contribution to this volume, at pp. 538–577 (Chapter 17), that the contemporary regime governing the conduct of hostilities has little or no capacity for evolutionary development.

[135] So too in physics, the quest for a perpetual motion machine – one that sustains itself without an external source of energy – has proved fruitless, since it violates the second law of thermodynamics.

Indeed, the moment of conclusion all too often constitutes the high-water mark of enthusiasm for any particular treaty-making project, especially where the interests that the agreement in question seeks to advance or defend are not those of governments or States as such or are not especially close to their hearts.[136] Thereafter, commitment tends to dissipate rather rapidly, leaving the instrument in question little more than a mere historical monument to governmental irresolution. Just occasionally, it might prove possible to 'kick-start' the process again by some means – perhaps through a determined propaganda onslaught on the part of some interested party or the institution of legal proceedings either at the international or the national level – but the impediments strewn in the way of such an initiative are often so numerous and substantial as to negate its feasibility altogether.[137]

These considerations, it should be noted, are applicable even where the treaty has been reasonably well designed initially and can only be magnified where inherent faults and failings have been incorporated in the mechanism from the outset. In such circumstances, as with a machine, there may conceivably be scope to remedy or ameliorate apparent deficiencies through structural modifications of some description, but any such prospect will again require the input of exogenous energy (in the form of renewed political commitment and ingenuity) from beyond the confines of the mechanism itself. In the world of treaties, the principal method by which design flaws can be remedied or emergent operational problems addressed is obviously that of treaty *amendment*, but this is a process the practical implementation of which has proven to be fraught with difficulty in international law.[138]

---

[136] Early conservation treaties (which often resulted from political pressure from non-governmental factions rather than from the enthusiasm of governments themselves) represent an obvious example here.

[137] As regards litigation, on the international plane preliminary hurdles concerning jurisdiction and admissibility must be overcome before any question concerning the merits can even be broached. At the national level, basic questions concerning the status of treaties within the legal order must be considered, along with issues of legal standing and the essential nature (i.e. 'self-executing' or not) of the provisions sought to be enforced: for an instructive example, involving an (ultimately unsuccessful) attempt to breathe life into the 1950 Convention for the Protection of Birds, 638 UNTS 186, through the institution of legal proceedings in the domestic courts, see *Count Lippens v. Etat Belge, Ministre de l'Agriculture*, ILR, 47 (1974), 336–340.

[138] For illustrations of such difficulties, see, e.g., M. J. Bowman, 'The Multilateral Treaty Amendment Process – A Case Study', ICLQ, 44 (1995), 540–559, and M. J. Bowman, 'Towards a Unified Body for Monitoring Compliance with UN Human Rights Conventions? Legal Mechanisms for Treaty Reform', HRLR, 7 (2007), 225–249.

Typically, no provision will originally have been made in the text itself to allow for its own revision, not least because any such possibility is dependent in a practical sense upon the availability of a suitable forum in which such an amendment can be proposed, debated and adopted, whereas in the case of the traditional treaty-instrument, no such forum is likely to exist in permanent form. Consequently, even if the contingency of a possible future need for revision of the treaty occurred to anyone at the time of its conclusion, the only remedy would be to provide for the holding of an entirely new diplomatic conference – much the same process as would be available even if the problem had never been envisaged at all.[139]

2.2.3 Treaties Conceived as 'Organisms'

It is for reasons such as these that the extraordinary capacities for self-maintenance, self-repair and self-modification that are intrinsically characteristic of *biotic* entities have begun to appear so appealing as sources of inspiration for the creation of normative systems of a more resilient kind. It is surely no coincidence that, just as our levels of understanding of the natural world have seemed to soar exponentially in the modern, post-war era, so too has our conception of the international community transformed itself from an essentially mechanistic one, in which a host of solid, unyielding and impenetrable sovereign particles jostle and bump against one another in search of some minimalistic mode of mutual accommodation, to a more ecologically based conception in which the various protagonists progressively adjust and adapt themselves to the realities of life in a shared biotic environment. Competing needs are addressed less by the simple mathematics of physical collision than by the emergence of co-operative processes of an ever more elaborate and systematic character, in which sovereign aspirations may ultimately become harmonised or aligned and independent identities to some extent commingled through the emergence of networks of an altogether more complex and organic character. These processes have been reflected not only in the rapid growth and increasing sophistication of international inter-governmental

---

[139] For an example of a treaty which made express provision for such a contingency, see the 1968 African Convention on the Conservation of Nature and Natural Resources, 1001 UNTS 3, Art. XXIV, and for the product of its eventual activation, see the 2003 Revised Convention, text and commentary in A. Steiner and L. Ravelomanantsoa, 'An Introduction to the African Convention on the Conservation of Nature and Natural Resources' (IUCN Environmental Policy and Law Paper 56) (2006).

organizations *stricto sensu*[140] but in the investment of treaty-based arrangements generally with a far more dynamic, and indeed biotic, quality. Hence the emergence in recent decades of what have come to be known as 'living instruments',[141] the defining characteristic of which is the structural capacity to evolve and develop over time so as to meet emerging challenges on the basis of their own internal resources. This in turn creates a new, inter-temporal, *evolutionary/developmental* context to govern their application and interpretation.[142]

Furthermore, just as life itself exists in 'endless forms most beautiful',[143] there is an enormous range of means by which modern treaty instruments can be, and indeed have been, invested with this organic quality. What they seemingly have in common is the way in which the synchronisation of the pulses of normative aspiration amongst their parties may be carried beyond the formative phase in which the treaty is negotiated and concluded, and into its ongoing application and development. As a result, the treaty becomes capable not merely of basic, minimal self-maintenance but of ongoing self-renewal and even, perhaps, of complete self-recreation if the need arises. This autopoietic[144] dimension may be achieved either through some form of (quasi-)judicial dispute resolution process (whereby States are effectively dragooned into broadly uniform approaches to implementation through judicial determinations) or through a network of institutional arrangements whereby the parties progressively navigate their own way towards collective solutions to on-going or emerging problems.[145]

---

[140] As to which, see, generally, P. Sands and P. Klein (eds.), *Bowett's Law of International Institutions* (London: Sweet & Maxwell, 6th ed., 2009) and H. G. Schermers and N.M. Blokker, *International Institutional Law* (Leiden: Martinus Nijhoff, 5th rev. ed., 2011).

[141] The term has now become so ubiquitous as to merit recognition in general reference sources: see, e.g., the entry in *Encyclopaedia Britannica* (www.britannica.com/topic/living-instrument). See, further, the contribution to this volume of Moeckli and White at pp. 136–171 (Chapter 6).

[142] S. T. Helmersen, 'Evolutive Treaty Interpretation: Legality, Semantics and Distinctions', *EJLS*, 6 (2013), 127–148.

[143] The expression is, of course, a quotation from the closing words of Darwin's *The Origin of the Species, supra* n. 53, and is recapitulated in Carroll, *supra* n. 89.

[144] *Autopoiesis* (meaning self-realisation) is in origin a biological term coined by the Chilean scientists Humberto Maturana and Francisco Varela in their *Autopoiesis and Cognition: The Realization of the Living* (Dordrecht: D. Reidel Publishing, 1980). For accessible discussion, see Margulis and Sagan, *supra* n. 64; Rose, *supra* n. 89, and Mathews, *supra* n. 104.

[145] As to the latter, see R. R. Churchill and G. Ulfstein, 'Autonomous Institutional Arrangements in Multilateral Environmental Agreements: A Little-Noticed Phenomenon in International Law', *AJIL*, 94 (2000), 623–659.

One regularly deployed strategy entails the establishment of a small bureaucracy to administer the treaty in question, the pre-eminent virtue of which is, of course, that it will bring into existence an entity that has no other function or commitment than to dedicate itself to the advancement of the treaty's objectives, while the parallel creation of a network of ancillary committees operating under the purview of a plenary body may very well mean that the particular individuals who represent their States on these groups may also share this special sense of commitment, or at least come to do so in time. Furthermore, the resources of pre-existing autonomous institutions (typically, the inter-governmental organizations under whose aegis the treaties in question have been negotiated) may be drawn upon to provide an alternative or additional means of life-support, while the drive and commitment of organizations from the non-governmental sector may also be harnessed for this purpose. Elaborate combinations of these arrangements may also be possible,[146] as indeed may other patterns of organization entirely. Through these various means, such regimes may be perpetually energised. In this way, the 'living instruments' of recent decades are gradually coming to replace the rusting and obsolescent treaty mechanisms of yesteryear in the normative regulation of international affairs. It may be no coincidence that some of the more imaginative examples of such development have emerged from the network of conventions which directly concern the conservation of living resources, suggesting that the parties may have drawn their institutional inspiration from the very nature of the subject matter they are seeking to regulate and protect.[147]

2.2.4   The Inherent Limitations of Treaties

Needless to say, however, the investment of treaty arrangements with this organic quality is by no means guaranteed of itself to provide the solution to all problems. In particular, there may be instances where it simply proves impossible to coax the various participants into conformity with a single, uniform pulse or beat: their cultural traditions, political

---

[146] See, e.g., the 1972 Convention for the Protection of the World Cultural and Natural Heritage, 1972 UNJYB 89, which not only creates certain organs of its own but also relies for certain purposes on the existing organs of UNESCO, and the 1979 Bern Convention on the Conservation of European Wildlife and Natural Habitats, 1284 UNTS 209, which stands in a similar relation to the Council of Europe. Both also make provision for the extensive participation of NGOs.

[147] See further on this point, M. J. Bowman, 'Beyond the "Keystone" CoPs: The Ecology of Institutional Governance in Conservation Treaty Regimes', ICLR, 15 (2013), 5–43.

perspectives and perceived vested interests, for example, and hence their respective approaches to the implementation and interpretation of the treaty in question, may simply prove too diverse to overcome. It is plain, for example, that the quest for 'proper conservation of whale stocks' and 'orderly development of the whaling industry' was critical to the adoption of the 1946 International Convention for the Regulation of Whaling (ICRW),[148] but the precise meaning and implications of those expressions and the intended relationship between them (especially when considered serially over the course of the intervening decades) depend very much upon how they are to be conceptualised and contextualised.[149] It is clear not only that the various parties to this particular treaty have taken highly divergent views upon these crucial questions but also that neither the contrasting perspectives themselves nor their precise inter-relationship has necessarily remained constant over time.[150] Such considerations indeed represent a standard feature of the difficulties facing not only the drafters of international treaties but also those who are subsequently charged with the task of their practical implementation, whether as contracting parties, as representatives of treaty institutions or as wholly independent arbiters of their meaning.

These points are, of course, amply demonstrated by the jurisprudence of international courts and tribunals. Indeed, the ICRW itself is one of the very treaties to have recently fallen for consideration before the International Court of Justice[151] and in circumstances which placed the fundamental principle of good faith under unusually direct scrutiny.[152] Interestingly, the Court was afforded a direct opportunity in the course of those proceedings to formally determine the meaning of the elusive concept of *science* itself – or, to be more precise, the purport of the phrase 'for purposes of scientific research', which qualified the power established by Article VIII of the Convention for parties to issue whaling permits unilaterally and independently of any harvesting quotas agreed

---

[148] 161 UNTS 72 (see, in particular, the seventh preambular recital).

[149] For discussion, see M. J. Bowman, '"Normalizing" the International Convention for the Regulation of Whaling', *Michigan JIL*, 29 (2008), 293–499.

[150] A significant determinant is, of course, the extent of political and economic commitment to whaling which is evident in any particular country at any particular time: see, further, *infra* n. 157 to n. 165 and accompanying text.

[151] *Whaling in the Antarctic*: Australia v. France; New Zealand intervening (2014) ICJ Rep. 226.

[152] This was doubtless because the dispute revolved primarily around the legitimacy of the exercise of a power; the Court was, however, noticeably coy about invoking this notion explicitly.

collectively.[153] In the event, however, the Court opted to decline the invitation to collapse the wave function associated with this particular manifestation of unresolved semantic moment[154] – partly, perhaps, through fear of creating a particle of unpredictable or inappropriate 'spin'.[155] It preferred to sidestep the problem altogether by concluding, in effect, that, *however* the notion of scientific research might reasonably be understood, the application of the Japanese government's JARPA II programme had not been directed in good faith to the service of its purposes.[156]

This decision clearly came as a considerable shock to the Japanese authorities themselves, but there are grounds for suggesting that any such reaction cannot really have been the result of anything but a failure to come adequately to terms with the realities of the commitment they had entered into.[157] In their eyes, the ICRW represented a simple continuation of the policy of earlier whaling conventions, to be treated as dedicated to the maximisation of industrial profitability and sustainable yield, just like any other 'fisheries' agreement.[158] Yet, this approach pays scant regard either to the very singular political, socio-economic or ecological context in which the convention was adopted or to the highly significant impact which this produced upon the philosophical and practical concepts by which it was inspired;[159] above all, it disregards the fine detail of the actual contents of its preamble and operative

---

[153] See, in particular, Art. VIII ICRW, which establishes a significant potential loophole in the Convention's conservation regime by excluding from the quota system which regulates the taking of whales any permits unilaterally granted by States to its nationals for such purposes.

[154] See *Whaling in the Antarctic, supra* n. 151, at p. 258 (paragraph 86) and, for the antecedent reasoning, paragraphs 73 onwards.

[155] 'Spin' (or intrinsic angular momentum) is, along with charge and mass, a fundamental property of atoms, nuclei and particles: see Daintith, *supra* n. 16, at pp. 515–516.

[156] More particularly, they concluded that, while the JARPA II programme could broadly be characterised as one that involved the performance of scientific research, its application in practice could not be regarded as having been pursued *for those purposes* because its design and implementation could not be deemed reasonable in relation to the achievement of the Japanese government's own stated research objectives: see, generally, *Whaling in the Antarctic, supra* n. 151, at pp. 253–293 (paragraphs 62–227).

[157] It should not be forgotten that the conclusion of the ICRW in the immediate aftermath of World War II meant that neither Japan nor Germany was permitted to play any part in the drafting Conference.

[158] See the Counter-Memorial of Japan (www.icj-cij.org/docket/files/148/17384.pdf), especially Chapter 2. The crucial earlier agreement was the 1937 International Agreement for the Regulation of Whaling, 190 LNTS 79.

[159] See further Bowman, *supra* n. 149, esp. 375–436.

provisions.[160] Thus, references to industrial prosperity and maximum sustainable yield were pointedly omitted from its preambular statement of purposes – and seemingly quite deliberately.[161] The latter principle was transmogrified by Article V(2) ICRW into the very different goal of *'conservation, development and optimum utilization* of the whale resources', while the 'interests of the whaling industry' were relegated by the same provision to the status of a mere factor to be taken into consideration, on a par with those of the 'consumers of whale products', in the fixing of harvesting quotas. These features of the ICRW, alongside its (also quite deliberate) opening of the Convention to participation by non-whaling nations, render it extremely difficult to endorse descriptions of the IWC as a 'cartel' in the normal sense of that word.[162] The Court itself found it unnecessary to pursue these issues in any depth, though it certainly did not offer any explicit support to the notion that ensuring the prosperity or expansion of the industry constituted any part of the Convention's objectives.[163]

What all of this indicates, if confirmation were actually needed, is that the process of making sense of any particular treaty, and getting firmly to grips with its goals, strategy, substance and purport, is by no means a straightforward one. Certainly, the simplistic allocation of a treaty to a particular broad category (in this case, 'fisheries') does not seem to

---

[160] Indeed, it is noticeable that, in quoting the relevant passage of the preamble at paragraph 2.28 of its Counter-Memorial, Japan pointedly omits the wording which crucially undermines its interpretation of complete continuity from earlier agreements: thus, regulation was *not* to be pursued, as it claimed "'on the basis of the principles embodied'" in the previous agreements and protocols' but rather 'on the basis of the *principles embodied in the provisions*' of the 1937 Agreement and its protocols (an extremely unusual formulation for a treaty preamble, italics added here for emphasis, arguably signifying the deliberate abandonment of the 1937 *preambular* commitment to the prosperity of the industry as the key objective. The Memorial of Australia, by contrast, emphasised a significant break in continuity (at paragraphs 2.15–2.20).

[161] Early versions of the preamble had indeed included explicit reference to maximum sustainable yield, but this was ultimately excised at the drafting Conference itself. This calls into question Japanese reliance (at paragraphs 2.30 and 2.31 of its Counter-Memorial) upon statements made about the preamble during the earlier stages of the Conference, though the matter is undeniably a complex one: see further Bowman, *supra* n. 149, at 418–419.

[162] See, e.g., S. R. Harrop, 'From Cartel to Conservation and on to Compassion: Animal Welfare and the International Whaling Commission', *JIWLP*, 6 (2003), 79–104.

[163] It is difficult to disagree with the Court's rather bland observation, *supra* n. 151, at p. 251 (paragraph 56), that the 'preamble of the ICRW indicates that the Convention pursues the purpose of ensuring the conservation of all species of whales while allowing for their sustainable exploitation', though this itself, of course, leaves many crucial questions unanswered.

provide any reliable basis for the drawing of significant conclusions regarding its essential nature and purpose, which may have been entirely unprecedented, mould-breaking or peculiar in some other sense. In this particular case, indeed, the characterisation seems to have proved positively counter-productive.

When seeking to understand the substantive *content* of any given agreement and to extract the meaning of particular terms, it will therefore be crucial to identify with as much specificity and precision as possible the key foundational ideas or *concepts* by which the instrument in question was originally motivated, and to which it seeks to give effect, and especially its underlying object and purpose. Yet, it is unlikely to be possible to secure a reliable grasp of this process without regard to the precise *context* in which these developments have occurred; as indicated previously, moreover, context is itself a highly complex and multi-layered phenomenon. Accordingly, close examination of these various contextual strata may serve to cast those foundational ideas, and the terms which have been employed to give them effect, in a completely different light. Thus, the de-emphasising of concern for industrial prosperity in the ICRW may seem a little less surprising when it is realised that all the preliminary drafting work was undertaken unilaterally by the United States, where (i) the whaling industry was all but defunct in 1946[164] and (ii) a key aim of post-war US policy was the *breaking* of the power of cartels, the activities of which it regarded as having contributed significantly to the eruption of the conflict which had so recently wrought such devastation.[165]

While these considerations may seem to endorse the virtue of commencing the quest for meaning with an examination of the (political and socio-economic) context, the reality is probably that there simply is no ideal starting point for this operation. A key factor here is that the process itself should certainly not be viewed as linear. Rather, it may be more appropriate to see it as best depicted in the form of the conventional symbol for infinity ∞, with the treaty terms themselves located in the narrow neck in the middle and the unrelenting flow of conceptual and contextual input represented by the loops on either side. The search for meaning has no naturally predetermined starting point because the

---

[164] The industry briefly flickered back into life in the United States during the 1950s and '60s, however, producing a discernible change in its position and causing it to oppose certain restrictions on quota. Eventually, however, it decided to forswear commercial whaling entirely through the 1972 Marine Mammal Conservation Act.

[165] On these points generally see Bowman, *supra* n. 149, esp. at 374–436.

journey travelled will in due course inevitably take in all the same way-stations, with true purport, hopefully, emerging gradually with every investigatory 'lap' completed. Accordingly, it may not matter too much where it begins, as long as the interpreter does not become unduly obsessed with first impressions and is prepared to subject them to continuous modification or refinement as additional information and perspective comes to hand.

Furthermore, in view of the greatly increased incidence of 'living instruments' in recent times, this quest can no longer be regarded simply as a once-and-for-all operation notionally performed at the moment of the treaty's conclusion; rather, it is one which must be subjected to continuous, on-going review with the passage of time. Accordingly, it may be unhelpful to imagine the infinity symbol referred to previously as having a single, fixed location and preferable to see it as travelling through temporal space, so that the contexts within which it is situated are subject to continual modification, with potential implications for the foundational concepts by which it is infused and the precise thrust of the substantive provisions which have been designed to give them normative effect.

2.3 A Scientific Approach to the Law of Treaties

Just as the preceding observations are true of individual treaties, so too are they applicable to the *law of treaties* itself, not least because that law itself came ultimately to be encapsulated in treaty form, as manifest pre-eminently in the Vienna Convention of the Law of Treaties (VCLT) of May 1969.[166] In this particular instance, however, the type of conduct which the agreement in question aims to regulate is, of course, that which specifically concerns the creation, application, modification or extinction of treaty instruments themselves, imbuing the subject-matter of the regime with a compoundedly abstract, and at the same time unusually wide-ranging, foundational and meta-normative quality. Indeed, the successful implementation of the codification process was of such fundamental importance to the development of the international legal system generally that it must be regarded as a prime example of what Lowe himself describes as 'hammering into place the ... great beams of [the] legal order'.[167]

---

[166] 1155 UNTS 331. For access to the entire product of the Commission's work on the law of treaties, see the *Analytical Guide to Work of the ILC* at http://legal.un.org/ilc/guide/gfra .htm (Topic 1).

[167] *Supra* n. 1, at p. 6 (though the reference there is actually to EU law).

Such a description plainly demands that the regime be capable of bearing a very considerable load, but it pays to remember here that much structural support can be offered by materials which may seem from some perspectives to be lacking in absolute solidity or substantiality. Beams themselves, after all, are traditionally fashioned from wood, and wood itself grows if not exactly *on* trees then *in the form* of trees, by which it is, almost literally, simply conjured out of thin air.[168] Assuredly, the process requires the existence of a broad instructional programme that has evolved from situational trial and testing over time, but happily this has long been available in the form of arboreal genomes;[169] thus, provided only that they are firmly anchored in a suitable substrate and supplied continuously with nutrients and energy, great oaks may indeed from little acorns (and thin air) grow. Here again, moreover, flexibility contributes considerably to vigour, as the ability to yield a little to the ravages of climatic contingency is crucial to the flourishing of trees, as it also is, indeed, to that of treaty law itself.

As to the latter specifically, given that the ultimate purposes to be served by the Vienna regime are so broad and generalised, and the substantive contexts in which the rules are to be applied so diverse, it is no accident that the vast majority of the norms which the Convention establishes are of an essentially *residual* character, permitting those that are parties to the multifarious instruments it regulates to determine the specifics of their own legal relationship if they choose to do so. Indeed, the parties are given almost unlimited freedom to stipulate the nature of their relationship down to the very last detail, if they so desire. It is only relatively rarely that the draft departs from this standard pattern of rules of generalised application expressed in broad terms, the most obvious exceptions being the rules concerning *ius cogens*.[170]

Another provision worth noting in this regard, however, is Article 62(2)(a) VCLT, which provides that a 'fundamental change of circumstances may not be invoked as a ground for terminating or withdrawing from a treaty if the treaty establishes a boundary'. The policy justification for the inclusion of this provision in this form is explained in the accompanying Commentary of the International Law Commission

---

[168] The chemical composition of wood is by weight more than 90 per cent carbon and oxygen, obtained from carbon dioxide in the atmosphere. During the eighteenth century, this gas was known as 'fixed air'.

[169] In the case of treaty law, of course, it derives from the customary antecedents of the VCLT.

[170] See Arts. 53 and 64 VCLT: *supra* n. 166.

(ILC)[171] as residing in the overriding imperative, long recognised in international law, for certainty and permanence wherever territorial boundaries are concerned.[172] In this particular context, it is asserted, the *rebus sic stantibus* principle has the potential to become 'a source of dangerous frictions', instead of the 'instrument of peaceful change' that it would typically be, and it was therefore deemed essential to eliminate that risk.[173] Yet, the extent to which the fixity of existing boundaries is genuinely a source of security, rather than of conflict, in international affairs might actually prove to be a rather tricky empirical question,[174] and stronger justification might therefore be found for the VCLT rule if only there were a well established and widely accessible political procedure for addressing cases where established boundaries had come to represent a major source of social disruption or unrest. In the absence of any permanent institution dedicated to that task, the question remains whether the untypically categorical drafting of Article 62(2)(a) VCLT leaves something to be desired.[175]

It is useful for present purposes to note that the thrust of this provision is 'categorical' in the twin senses of (i) making explicit provision for a particular type of treaty and (ii) being expressed in calculatedly definitive and ostensibly inflexible terms, whereby the mechanical application of a simple verbal formula produces a readily predictable outcome. It might therefore seem to represent one of those exceptions which are designed to create certainty but under the weight of which, according to Lowe's essay mentioned earlier, the law of treaties is currently 'creaking'. While acknowledging in passing the 'almost fetishistic respect for boundaries' that international law exhibits, Lowe himself sees the explanation for the incorporation of Article 62(2)(a) VCLT as lying less in this attitude of unquestioning reverence for delimitational fixity than in the fact that

---

[171] For the Draft Articles and Commentary, see *YbILC* (1966–II), 177–274, and for treatment of the *rebus sic stantibus* principle specifically at 256–260 (Draft Art. 59).

[172] In terms of prior legal authority, this exception was explicitly substantiated by reference only to its common acknowledgment by both parties in the *Free Zones of Upper Savoy and District of Gex Case*: France v. Switzerland, 1932 PCIJ, Series A/B, No. 46, together with its recognition by that most influential but shadowy of focus groups, namely 'most jurists': see Commentary, *ibid.* (paragraph 11).

[173] *Ibid.*

[174] Such considerations doubtless underpinned the concerns of certain members of the Commission, also noted in the Commentary, that a framing of the exception in absolute terms might undermine the principle of self-determination.

[175] Actually, the ILC's own proposed wording referred simply to 'a treaty establishing a boundary', but the slight modification in the final draft does not affect the present argument.

boundary treaties constitute an example of *executed* rather than *executory* agreements:[176] they 'are dispositive in the sense that their legal effects are wholly realized immediately upon their conclusion'.[177] Such instruments are apparently to be distinguished from '"relationship" treaties that create new legal regimes'.[178]

Yet, it is debatable just how useful (or, indeed, meaningful) such distinctions really are, since the fixing of a boundary is surely less a matter of resolving once and for all a disputed historical fact than of prescribing for the future the outcome of a whole series of jurisdictional issues that will inevitably arise in relation to the territory in question. Consequently, it does in a sense create a 'new legal regime' which will be of vital importance in determining the on-going 'relationship' between the parties regarding the distribution of sovereign authority. Indeed, given the many vagaries and uncertainties that are associated with boundaries, and especially such well-established practices as the utilisation of rivers to mark them, the parties to treaties that adopt such techniques have sometimes actually found it necessary to establish institutional arrangements to oversee and manage the on-going implications. In this vein, the tribunal in the *Chamizal* arbitration[179] noted that the United States and Mexico, having adopted a treaty of 1884 which reaffirmed the Rio Grande as marking the border between them for part of its length,[180] had subsequently decided to establish a boundary commission 'for the purpose of carrying out the principles contained in the convention of 1884 and to avoid the difficulties occasioned by the changes which take place in the bed of the Rio Grande'.[181] This does not really support the notion that the legal effects of the boundary treaty were 'wholly realized' immediately upon its conclusion. Indeed, it rather suggests that the precise boundary between 'executed' and 'executory' agreements may be as fluid and elusive as that between the respective territories of Mexico and the United States proved to be.

This leads on to doubts regarding the coherence and utility in principle of such modes of treaty categorisation – including that of 'boundary treaty' itself – especially when it is remembered that international agreements very commonly aspire to fulfil several functions at once.[182] It is

---

[176] Lowe, *supra* n. 1, at p. 9.   [177] *Ibid.*, at p. 5.   [178] *Ibid.*, at p. 8.

[179] *Chamizal Case* (Mexico, United States), RIAA, Vol. XI, 309–347.

[180] The text of the convention is set out in full, *ibid.*, at pp. 323–324.

[181] *Ibid.*, at pp. 317–318. The Commission was established by treaty signed on 1 March 1889 (www.ibwc.gov/Files/TREATY_OF_1889.pdf).

[182] Lowe himself explicitly acknowledges this point, *supra* n. 1, at p. 5.

easy to imagine scenarios where the establishment or confirmation of a section of boundary is merely a minor and incidental aspect of a treaty concerning other matters and is not at all clear why – as a strictly literal reading of Article 62(2)(a) VCLT would seem to demand – the operation of the *rebus sic stantibus* principle should be excluded in such cases, especially where the boundary itself is not actually being called into question. Any undesired consequences might, of course, have been avoided by a relatively minor redraft of the provision (for example, replacing 'if' by 'insofar as' 'the treaty establishes a boundary'),[183] and it is doubtless possible that a sympathetic adjudicator might simply choose to read it in that way in any event.[184] Yet this is not the only unhelpfully prescriptive aspect of this article of the VCLT,[185] and the clear impression left is that the formulation of rules in unhelpfully definitive terms seems just as likely to generate operational problems, if not more so, as the expression of principles in more flexible and indicative language; such difficulties seem only to be intensified, moreover, where provisions of the former kind are made applicable only to particular sub-genres of treaty instrument.

Accordingly, the drafters of the VCLT are to be applauded for their reliance, for the most part at least, on provisions of a more semantically generalised and functionally residual character. If there is any matter upon which the parties to a particular agreement require specificity or certainty, they can always ensure that is established through tailor-made stipulations in the text. This plainly does not, moreover, relegate the VCLT itself to a purely contingent, 'fall-back' role, since it continues to mould the entire process through which individual treaties are negotiated. Thus, the very itemisation through its provisions of the issues routinely to be addressed in treaty-making lends shape and structure to

---

[183] Though this would still presumably leave the issue of severability to be resolved in accordance with Art. 44 VCLT: *supra* n. 166.

[184] Indeed, the ILC itself noted, *supra* n. 171 (paragraph 4), that even in the very authority it had invoked in support of the boundary treaty exemption, the *Free Zones Case*, France had explicitly sought to draw a distinction between the upsetting of territorial rights as such and the mere displacement of '"personal" rights created on the occasion of a territorial settlement'. For the argument in question (which was not ultimately addressed by the PCIJ), see Documents of the Written Proceedings, PCIJ Rep., Ser. C, No. 58, pp. 136–143. See, also, the comments of the International Court in *Case Concerning the Territorial Dispute*: Libyan Arab Jamahiriya v. Chad (1994) ICJ Rep. 6, at p. 37 (paragraphs 72 and 73).

[185] Another derives from Art. 62(1)(b) VCLT, which demands that the 'effect of the change' be 'radically to transform the extent of the obligation still to be performed': the appropriateness of this precondition is questionable, however, since the principle might arguably be judged equally applicable where the propriety, necessity or justification for the obligation has radically altered, even though its *extent* has not.

all such negotiations, making it much less likely that important matters will be overlooked in the drafting, as they often were in the past. In addition, the definitions section in the Convention,[186] although declared to serve specifically for its own internal purposes, has established an invaluable lexicon which has achieved a considerable degree of currency across the entire spectrum of treaties generally,[187] cutting down the uncertainties inherent in language. Finally, it does establish certain boundaries of tolerable fixity to constrain the entire process, such as the rules concerning *ius cogens* mentioned previously.

In addition, it is noteworthy that any *apparently unwarranted* vagueness or uncertainty that may become evident from the generally residual nature of the substantive rules that collectively comprise the modern law of treaties may often be significantly mitigated or dispelled for practical purposes by the rigour, richness and intensity of the particular *deliberative context* from which those norms themselves emerged. Most notably, the *travaux préparatoires* for the various Vienna Conventions are of an altogether different, and markedly superior, character from those associated with many other treaties. This is because they represent a meticulous record of the formal collaborative endeavours of the ILC, comprising leading experts on public international law from across the globe; further, the commentaries which represent the culmination of this process are designed specifically for the dispassionate technical elucidation of their subject matter rather than simply to advance or preserve the entrenched political positions of particular governments.[188] For that reason, they are likely to shed much more light upon the formal *content* of those rules, and upon the fundamental *concepts* upon which they are grounded, than is the case with treaties generally. Even where the *travaux* fail to resolve particular uncertainties, they may serve to foster an understanding of the reason such indeterminacy has been tolerated or approved or at least shed light upon why they have gone undetected. In addition, the rarefied nature of the process through which the regime was elaborated has clearly facilitated a degree of coherence in its overall

---

[186] See Art. 2 VCLT: *supra* n. 166.

[187] Thus, much greater consistency is evident within post-VCLT treaty-making practice in the deployment of terms such as 'party' and 'contracting state'.

[188] That is not to suggest that such considerations exert no impact upon the discussions whatsoever; indeed, the responses of governments to draft ILC proposals are recorded in its documentation and taken into consideration during later rounds of drafting. In some areas of treaty law, moreover, political considerations are likely to loom especially large: the entire subject matter of the 1978 Vienna Convention on Succession of States in Respect of Treaties, 1946 UNTS 3, renders it an obvious example.

literary structure (i.e. the 'context' for the specialised, internal purposes of treaty law itself).[189] These undoubtedly represent major strengths of the established treaty law regime.

2.3.1 The Vienna Regime and the Evolving Regulatory Landscape

This is not to suggest, of course, that any guarantee of plain sailing through these normative waters can be expected because the protracted process through which the Vienna regime was established itself occurred within a broader political and legal environment that was characterised by change of a radical and relentless kind. In particular, and as already explained previously, the members of the international community long ago began to perceive that the regulatory challenges which are continually generated within the global political order are commonly such as to exclude the possibility of definitive, cut-and-dried legislative treatment in advance and that normative systems of considerably greater flexibility and sophistication would be needed for the achievement of its more complex and ambitious political objectives. Thus, from the late nineteenth century onwards, and more particularly after World War II, it became increasingly common for States to create international organizations of an essentially permanent character, charged on an on-going basis with an array of tasks of a technically specialised kind. Typically, these organizations would themselves be created by treaty,[190] with the consequence that their basic constitutions would fall to be governed by the general law of treaties in the same way as any other legally binding arrangement applicable amongst States. To commentators such as Shabtai Rosenne, the subjection of such instruments to standard treaty law seemed to threaten serious, if not potentially insuperable, problems,[191] which were in his view only overcome (at least to a tolerable degree) by the insertion into the Vienna Convention of a specific saving provision to cover their case.[192] This was Article 5 VCLT, which provided that, in the case of a treaty which was the constituent instrument of an international organization, the Vienna regime

---

[189] As described in the previous sub-section.

[190] This is not universally the case, however: bodies such as the Organization of American States and the World Tourism Organization are now constituted on a treaty basis but were preceded by institutions established by other means.

[191] For a trenchant statement of this position, see S. Rosenne, *Developments in the Law of Treaties 1945–1986* (Cambridge: Cambridge University Press, 1989), p. 252.

[192] Note the continuation of his discussion, *ibid.*, to p. 258.

was to be applied without prejudice to any relevant rules of the organization itself.

Looking back on this discussion, however, it now seems slightly overwrought, for the effect of Article 5 is surely no more than to reaffirm in one particular respect the characteristically residual nature of the Vienna regime as well as the pervasive need for *sensitivity to context* in the application of the detailed rules it contains: indeed, this constitutes a requirement which might in any event be judged to be mandated by the universally recognised principle of good faith. Certainly, little indication emerges from the various institutional chapters within the present work that any significant difficulty has been occasioned by the subjection of constituent instruments to the dictates of general treaty law. Indeed, far from confirming the peculiar and distinct status of constituent instruments, it might even be argued that this provision actually rather undermines the idea of any sharp and unbridgeable discontinuity between such agreements and other – what might for this purpose be regarded as 'ordinary' – treaties: this is because it is expressed to apply *not merely to constituent instruments themselves* but also to 'any treaty adopted *within* an organization',[193] a description which, if attention is restricted to multilateral agreements, must in the modern era surely embrace a sizeable proportion, if not a clear numerical majority, of the 'ordinary' treaties as well![194]

What is more, any ontological gulf which might once have been supposed to exist between constitutive instruments and other treaties is no longer as easy to discern as it might once have been. The reason is, of course, that, as noted earlier, a considerable proportion of modern multilateral treaties (whether concluded within existing international organizations or not) display as one of their key features the establishment of supporting institutional arrangements of their own, though without going so far as to create an intergovernmental organization with independent legal personality in a formal sense. Typically, these systems are centred upon a regular meeting of a plenary body designated as the 'Conference of the Parties' or CoP, and quite commonly incorporate also a permanent secretariat as well as additional standing committees

---

[193] Emphasis added. This may, indeed, have constituted the most important aspect of Art. 5 VCLT as far as certain organizations, such as the ILO, were concerned: see, further, the contribution to this volume of Trebilcock at pp. 848–880 (Chapter 26).

[194] One need think only of the enormous number of treaties concluded within the UN, the ILO and the Council of Europe, to take just three examples, to get a sense of the numbers involved.

and other supporting organs.[195] Plainly, arrangements of this kind have the effect of bridging the categorical divide originally postulated by Rosenne (i.e. between IGO constitutions and ordinary treaties) through the creation of a form of hybrid entity which exhibits some of the legal characteristics of each type. Indeed, since governments negotiating international treaty regimes have an almost completely free hand regarding the substantive and implementational provisions they incorporate, any attempt to establish a rigid and definitive system for the categorisation of treaty instruments seems likely to be rapidly undermined by the emergence of intermediate and hybrid forms. It is perhaps for this reason that in her chapter in the present work Catherine Brölmann prefers to speak in terms of a (potentially multi-dimensional) *typology* of treaties rather than of any more categorically rigid and strictly compartmentalised *taxonomic* system.[196]

Yet, whatever confidence might be entertained that the radical changes in treaty-making practice outlined earlier can effectively be accommodated within an overarching contemporary law of treaties, it certainly does not seem plausible to suppose that they could be entirely without significance for the specific nature and content of that regime. Accordingly, it would seem highly desirable, to say the least, that the process through which the Vienna regime was elaborated should have taken full account of that developing practice and all its attendant implications. That being so, it must be acknowledged that the actual timing of the codification effort – and above all its completion – fell some way short of the ideal. For, even if it were to be assumed that the final draft of the 1969 Vienna Convention was concluded in a form that took full cognisance of every advance in treaty-making practice that had occurred right up to that moment, the value of that knowledge would have been limited for its purposes, since the majority of the more significant developments had yet to occur at that time.

Indeed, it was arguably the sub-discipline of environmental law which generated many of the most interesting innovations, and in that particular field the passing of the 1960s proved something of a watershed, with

---

[195] For discussion, see Churchill and Ulfstein, *supra* n. 145; J. Brunnée, 'COPing with Consent: Law-Making under Multilateral Environmental Agreements', *Leiden JIL*, 15 (2002), 1–52, and M. Fitzmaurice and D. French (eds.), *International Environmental Law and Governance* (Leiden: Brill/Nijhoff, 2015).

[196] See the contribution to this volume of Brölmann at pp. 79–102 (Chapter 4). In point of fact, the barriers established by biological speciation are not completely impermeable, but they may be treated as such for most practical purposes.

the 1971 Ramsar Convention on Wetlands of International Importance, especially as Waterfowl Habitat[197] serving as the 'tentative herald of a new dawn' for treaty-making,[198] and other drafting operations rapidly surging beyond its relatively cautious forays into previously unexplored organizational territory.[199] Consequently, even on the most favourable assumptions, there was little or no experience of the existence, let alone the operation, of the new style of living instrument for the drafters of the Vienna Convention to draw upon. In reality, of course, the circumstances were even less auspicious than this, since the ILC had effectively completed its work by the mid-1960s, which also therefore excluded from consideration most of the invaluable experience acquired in the other key area of substantive law to have breathed life into the living instrument concept – that of human rights. Here, although the European regional agreement in this field had been adopted back in 1950,[200] the Court that it established did not dispose of its first case until a decade later, with only a handful of decisions following over the next few years.[201] Through another unfortunate quirk of timing, the counterpart agreement for the Americas was not concluded until shortly after the Vienna Convention itself.[202] The key global instruments in the area, moreover, were not formally adopted until the very year in which the ILC originally submitted its report,[203] and none of them was actually in force,[204] effectively precluding them from exerting any significant influence on the treaty law codification process.

In any event, the basic foundations of this legal reform operation had effectively been laid during the previous decade (the 1950s), and the bulk

---

[197] 996 UNTS 245.   [198] Bowman, *supra* n. 147, at 9–12.

[199] Compare, for example, the 1973 Convention on International Trade in Endangered Species, 993 UNTS 243, concluded only two years later (especially Arts. IX, XI-XIII, XV-XVIII).

[200] 1950 European Convention for the Protection of Human Rights and Fundamental Freedoms, 213 UNTS 221.

[201] It must be acknowledged, however, that the other key organ under this treaty, the European Commission on Human Rights, had been established a little earlier, in 1954, and had begun to generate jurisprudence of its own which possessed at least provisional authority for the purposes of the regime.

[202] 1969 American Convention on Human Rights, 1144 UNTS 123.

[203] *Viz.*, 1966 International Convention on the Elimination of All Forms of Racial Discrimination (CERD), 660 UNTS 195; 1966 International Covenant on Economic, Social and Cultural Rights (ICESCR), 993 UNTS 3, and 1966 International Covenant on Civil and Political Rights (ICCPR), 999 UNTS 171.

[204] Relevant dates were 4 Jan. 1969, 3 Jan. 1976 and 23 March 1976, respectively, meaning that only CERD was in force even by the time the VCLT was actually adopted.

of the practice by which the Commission's work was centrally informed derived from an even earlier period than that. Indeed, Rosenne himself expressed the opinion that the 'mould' in which the resulting regime was truly cast was essentially that of the nineteenth century.[205] This serves only to underline the point that precious little, if any, experience of the new style of treaty-making was available for the ILC to draw upon, creating an obvious risk that the regime designed specifically to govern that process for the future might prove damagingly out of kilter with contemporary requirements. Yet, in evaluating the seriousness of this risk, it is surely reasonable to query whether it is helpful to think of the Vienna Convention regime as having been 'cast in a mould' at all, let alone one of the nineteenth century, for this would imply that it had itself been conceived and created in accordance with an essentially mechanistic paradigm, and was on that account characterised by fixity, rigidity and an inbuilt tendency towards obsolescence.

2.3.2   Organic Treaties and the Vienna Regime

At first sight, admittedly, it displays scant sign of having been designed to cater specifically for the multitude of 'living instruments' that it now has perforce to regulate (in company, no doubt, with a great many other agreements of a more traditional and conservative ilk). Apart from the explicit reference to international organizations in Article 5 VCLT, there is little indication that the treaties for which it is making provision might exhibit an element of institutionalised dynamism, still less any attempt to cater for it explicitly in the rules established. Indeed, most of the provisions which specifically address the eventuality of adventitious challenges to the original operational assumptions of treaty regimes (e.g., supervening impossibility, fundamental change of circumstances, emerging incompatible peremptory norms) do so under the specific rubric of contingencies that might potentially trigger the treaty's demise.[206]

On a more positive note, Articles 39 and 40 VCLT do at least provide for the possibility of amendment, but it is noteworthy that they envisage that this will typically be achieved through the rather cumbersome method of creating a wholly new agreement;[207] unfortunately, experience

---

[205] Rosenne, *supra* n. 191, at pp. 1–84, and 'Afterthoughts', esp. at p. 83.

[206] Arts. 61, 62 and 64 VCLT, all located in Part V, Section 3, headed 'Termination and Suspension of the Operation of Treaties': *supra* n. 166.

[207] For discussion, see A. Aust, *Modern Treaty Law and Practice* (Cambridge: Cambridge University Press, 3rd ed., 2013), pp. 232–244, and J. Brunnée, 'Treaty Amendments' in

suggests that this approach is not one which is particularly easy to implement successfully in practice.[208] Since the provisions in question are only residual, they clearly do not preclude the possibility of any more streamlined arrangements being established by the original instrument itself or by its internal institutions,[209] but they certainly do not explicitly address this eventuality either.[210] Furthermore, an additional proposed provision allowing for the possibility of amending treaties through the *practice* of the parties was ultimately deleted at Vienna in the face of objections in principle by a number of States.[211]

For all that, however, any initial impression of die-cast rigidity in the Vienna regime (a 'Procrustean bed', as Lowe terms it)[212] is by no means all-pervasive or unshakeable, as various considerations will affirm. First, any thought that it might be premised upon an expectation that treaties should simply collapse in the face of unanticipated supervening contingencies is firmly dispelled by the language of the relevant provisions, which impose a series of formidable barriers, both substantive and procedural, in the way of the extinction of treaty commitments by such means.[213] These provisions surely confirm that the objective is actually to maintain treaty arrangements in existence wherever possible. In pursuit of this aim, it would plainly be counter-productive to deny or discount whatever opportunities might reasonably be available to adapt those

---

D. Hollis (ed.) *The Oxford Guide to Treaties* (Oxford: Oxford University Press, 2012), pp. 347–366.

[208] See Aust, *ibid.*, at pp. 232–233, and Bowman, *supra* n. 138. These difficulties have persisted despite (or, perhaps, have even been exacerbated by) the abandonment of the traditional customary rule requiring unanimity for treaty amendment.

[209] Accordingly, the original and the amending instruments are viewed essentially as successive treaties relating to the same subject matter, as addressed by Art. 30 VCLT: *supra* n. 166. The distinction between this approach and that involving internal institutional procedures for amendment should not be overstated, however, because the latter not infrequently call for the convening of an *extraordinary* meeting, rather than simply processing amendments at a regular meeting of the CoP, presumably because full powers, rather than mere credentials, will be required for voting.

[210] Though Aust, *supra* n. 207, at p. 233, may well be justified in commending the ILC's wisdom in not embarking on any more elaborate exercise than that adopted in the Convention.

[211] For the flavour of those discussions (which saw, *inter alia*, China, the United Kingdom, the United States and the USSR united in opposition to draft Art. 38): see UN Conference on the Law of Treaties, First Session, 38th Meeting of the Committee of the Whole: U.N. Doc. A/CONF.39/C.1/SR.38, pp. 210–215.

[212] Lowe, *supra* n. 1, at p. 4.

[213] One factor here is the negative cast of certain provisions: thus, under Art. 62 VCLT, fundamental change of circumstances 'may not be invoked . . . unless' certain stringent conditions are satisfied: *supra* n. 166.

arrangements to on-going need.[214] Thus, the rather cautious and conservative nature of the 'fall-back' provisions on amendment in the VCLT certainly has not prevented the adoption of various progressive arrangements in individual treaty regimes, some of which allow even for amendments to which particular States have not specifically consented to become binding upon them – provided, of course, that they have given generic agreement to that possibility in advance.[215]

Furthermore, the absence of any formal provision for amendment by means of practice has proved to be less significant than might have been supposed in the light of Article 31(3)(a–b) VCLT, which requires that any manifestations of practice or agreement relating to the treaty that have emerged amongst the parties subsequent to its adoption be taken into account for the purposes of its interpretation. It seems clear that the relevance of such material was seen initially as lying in its capacity to shed light back upon the *original* intentions of the parties at the time of the treaty's adoption,[216] but there is little doubt that it has come to be viewed additionally as a means of elucidating the way in which that intent may have evolved and modified itself over the course of time, confirming that this is a perfectly legitimate factor to take into consideration in the on-going interpretation of a treaty.[217] It might also be observed that, while this process is in theory quite distinct from the possibility of amending a treaty by practice, the precise boundary line between the two is likely to prove extremely difficult to draw for any practical purpose.[218] In view of

---

[214] *Case Concerning the Gabčikovo-Nagymaros Project (Hungary/Slovakia)* (1997) ICJ Rep. 7 demonstrates just how strongly the International Court will strive to uphold existing agreements.

[215] This approach was pioneered within certain of the United Nations Specialised Agencies: see, further, Brunnée, *supra* n. 207, at 356–360.

[216] This certainly seems to have been true of the principal authority cited in the Commentary, the advisory opinion concerning the *Competence of the ILO in regard to International Regulation of the Conditions of Labour of Persons Employed in Agriculture*, 1922 PCIJ, Series B, No. 2.

[217] See, e.g., *Dispute Regarding Navigational and Related Rights*: Costa Rica v. Nicaragua (2009) ICJ Rep. 213, at p. 242 (paragraphs 63–64), and R. Gardiner, 'The Vienna Convention Rules on Treaty Interpretation' in Hollis (ed.), *supra* n. 207, pp. 475–506, at pp. 497–498. Needless to say, the detail remains controversial, and the matter is still under consideration by the ILC itself: see, further, the contribution to this volume of Buga at pp. 363–391 (Chapter 12).

[218] See Gardiner, *ibid.* Indeed, part of the reason why certain delegations opposed the inclusion of provision for amendment by subsequent practice was not that they were opposed to it in principle, but because they believed it to be superfluous in the light of Art. 31(3) VCLT: see, e.g., the observations of Rosenne (Israel), *supra* n. 211 (paragraph 48).

these developments, it seems reasonable to conclude not only that the VCLT regime has demonstrated a certain capacity for accommodating the living instrument model of treaty but that it has arguably manoeuvred itself into that same category as part of the process.

2.3.3   The Organic Potential of the Vienna Regime Itself

This last observation highlights a point of more general relevance, for it would seem plausible to entertain far more confidence in the capacity of the Vienna regime to meet the ongoing needs of contemporary international society if it could itself be shown to be imbued with attributes of a sufficiently organic character to permit or facilitate *its own* continuous evolutionary development. Despite the one example already given, the VCLT does not at first sight convey that impression, for it establishes no institutional machinery for its own implementation and does not even contain any general dispute settlement provision of the traditional kind. While it does, as noted previously, impose certain procedural requirements regarding the resolution of disputes arising out of the purported termination or nullification of treaties generally,[219] this particular section of the Convention is one which does not seem to have commanded the enthusiastic support of States.[220] As a result, it appears to represent the least securely established of all the various elements of modern treaty law, whether judged in terms of formal acceptability to the contracting parties, actual application in practice or effective absorption into customary law.[221]

It would, however, constitute a serious error to judge the organic potential of the Vienna regime in these terms alone for two distinct reasons. The first is that, although the VCLT created no formal institutions of its own, its inherently meta-normative character naturally provides it with *indirect* access to institutional sustenance and life support from across the entire range of treaty-making systems – thus, whenever a treaty body of any description (whether policy-making, administrative or judicial) formulates principles or develops practice for the implementation, interpretation, revision, reorientation or even termination of the

---

[219] Part V, Section 4 (Arts. 65–68 VCLT): *supra* n. 166.

[220] See on this point B. Simma and C. J. Tams, 'Reacting against Treaty Breaches' in Hollis (ed.), *supra* n. 207, pp. 576–604, at pp. 592–594 (and the cases there cited).

[221] Note especially the number of reservations to the provisions in question (and especially to Art. 66 VCLT) that have been formulated by parties to the Vienna Convention, listed in *Multilateral Treaties Deposited with the Secretary-General* (2015), viewable at https://treaties.un.org/pages/participationstatus.aspx, Chapter XXIII.

particular instrument which established it, it also makes a potential substantive contribution to the application and evolutionary development of treaty law itself. Thus, the unfolding practice of organizations like the International Labour Organization and the Council of Europe has over the course of time generated a series of interesting alternatives to the employment of reservations as the means of imparting a desired degree of differentiation to the obligations of States and standard-setting agreements,[222] experience which could be of considerable utility elsewhere. Equally, the development within certain of the Specialised Agencies of the tacit amendment procedure for particular categories of provision has long been recognised as an innovation that might profitably be adopted more widely as a means of circumventing the pervasive practical problems by which the amendment process has traditionally been beset across the entire gamut of international treaty regimes.[223] In particular, it enables the strong proclivity of States towards inertia in treaty-related matters to be enlisted in the cause of reform, rather than stagnation.

Needless to say, this organic potential, being reflected in processes which are essentially iterative and experimental, offers no guarantee of untrammelled progress, but merely serves as a potential source of innovative practice and re-conceptualised perspective in the application of treaty law which will be available for subsequent testing within other substantive contexts and institutional arenas. While certain of these developments may offer obvious and immediate advantages, some may prove to be effectively neutral in impact and others outright aberrations. In such circumstances, the better ideas will tend to catch on and the less good to be called into question and possibly abandoned. This, after all, is essentially the way that evolution works:[224] by its very nature, it tends to maximise the opportunity for beneficial adaptations to spread across the population as a whole.[225]

---

[222] See the contribution to this volume of Bowman at pp. 392–439 (Chapter 13).

[223] See *supra* n. 138 and n. 208 (and accompanying text).

[224] For accessible accounts, see, e.g., R. Dawkins, *The Blind Watchmaker* (London: Penguin Books, 1986); B. Goodwin, *How the Leopard Changed Its Spots* (London: Weidenfeld & Nicholson, 1994); S.J. Gould, *Life's Grandeur* (London: Jonathan Cape, 1996); S. B. Carroll, *The Making of the Fittest* (London: Quercus, 2008) and N. Lane, *Life Ascending* (London: Profile Books, 2010).

[225] The *literal* application of the principles of natural selection to the cultural world of ideas, where 'memes' take the place of genes, is well explored in the literature: see, e.g., R. Dawkins, *The Selfish Gene* (Oxford: Oxford University Press, rev. ed., 1989), pp. 245–260; S. J. Blackmore, *The Meme Machine* (Oxford: Oxford University Press, 1999);

   At this point, however, it might possibly be objected that the population upon which natural selection effectively operates in the realm of
biology is one that represents a common gene pool (i.e. a single species),
whereas the very criticism that has been levelled against the establishment of a uniform law of treaties is that it must necessarily operate
across a range of very different treaty types. This may raise doubts
regarding the transferability of innovatory treaty practice from one
category to another. Yet, it remains open to question whether these
various legal genres are truly so very divergent or whether their differences are merely indicative of the diversity that is typically to be found
within any particular natural kind and which indeed serves as a major
determinant of its evolutionary resilience and strength.[226] In any event,
even should they properly be regarded as distinct 'species', it is always to
be remembered that some of the most important evolutionary developments in natural history have actually resulted from horizontal
exchanges or fusions of genetic information *across* the species barrier,
as explained earlier.[227] It may therefore be the case that, in like fashion,
these different treaty bodies, and bodies of treaty law, have everything to
gain from closer co-ordination and mutual exchanges of perspectives
and ideas.

   Consideration of a concrete example may prove instructive here. In the
chapter in this work concerning the International Maritime
Organization, Dorota Lost-Sieminska discusses the considerable practical difficulty that has been encountered with regard to the 'amendment'
of a treaty that is not yet in force but has already been shown to be
unsatisfactory in some respect; to be precise, the slow rate of ratification
of the International Convention for the Control and Management of
Ships' Ballast and Water Sediments[228] rendered unfeasible certain dates
that were originally stipulated in the text for the performance of

---

R. Aunger (ed.), *Darwinizing Culture: The Status of Memetics as a Science* (Oxford:
Oxford University Press, 2000) and K. Distin, *The Selfish Meme: A Critical Reassessment*
(Cambridge: Cambridge University Press, 2005). Although the validity of this approach
remains extremely controversial, resort to the principles of biology in this chapter is
purely by way of analogy.

[226] It is this principle, of course, which underpins the Biodiversity Convention's concern for
genetic diversity within species.

[227] See Margulis and Sagan, Brazier, *supra* n. 64; C. R. Woese, 'On the Evolution of Cells',
Proc. Nat. Acad. Sci., 99 (2002), 8742–8747; G. Lawton, 'Why Darwin Was Wrong about
the Tree of Life', *New Scientist*, 21 Jan. 2009, pp. 34–39, and M. P. Francino (ed.),
Horizontal Gene Transfer in Microorganisms (Norfolk: Caister Academic Press, 2012).

[228] IMO Doc. BWM/CONF/36, Annex, now in force as from 8 Sept. 2017.

particular functions.[229] Given the controversy that must inevitably attend any attempt to apply amendment procedures on a 'provisional' basis – that is, prior even to the actual entry into force of the convention concerned – the question naturally arises whether any alternative remedies might usefully have been considered.

On the assumption that the difficulty related not to the securing of substantive agreement upon revised dates,[230] but only to the precise legal means by which this could be effectuated, it is worthy of consideration whether a possible method for affecting the change in question might be the process of *rectification* under Article 79 VCLT, which appears to have been widely used in IMO practice generally. Admittedly, the instant situation differs somewhat from the typical scenario where this procedure is applied, which concerns cases where the intention of the parties has been *wrongly recorded* in the instrument adopted. Here the dates in question were presumably recorded perfectly correctly – it is simply that, for reasons not anticipated, those originally agreed have become unfeasible. Nevertheless, the only requirement actually stipulated by Article 79 is that 'the contracting states are agreed that [the text of the treaty] contains an error', and there is arguably nothing in the VCLT or the accompanying Commentary which explicitly confines the remedy to errors of transcription. Indeed, the Commentary merely suggests, in surprisingly general terms, that 'the error or inconsistency may be due to a typographical mistake or to a misdescription or mis-statement due to a misunderstanding'.[231] It also allows that 'the correction may affect the substantive meaning of the text as authenticated'.[232] Accordingly, it might be argued that there is indeed an error in this treaty – albeit one of *expectation* on the part of the negotiating States as to how quickly the process of ratification would proceed. It should therefore be possible to substitute an alternative formulation of the time-schedule which captures the spirit of the original while adjusting it to take account of the fact situation as currently known. This might even entail the substitution of expressly stipulated dates by a simple formula through which they might easily be calculated.

Although it might be responded that there is no precedent for the application of the rectification procedure in this way, there is in fact such a wealth of practice on such matters that this objection might prove

---

[229] See in particular the Annex to the Convention, Regulation B3.

[230] Needless to say, if such a supposition was inappropriate, the solution proposed in the text following would be rendered unworkable.

[231] See the Commentary, *supra* n. 171, to draft Art. 74, paragraph 1.   [232] *Ibid.*

difficult to substantiate. Indeed, it appears from the chapter in this work by Lisa Tabassi and Olufemi Elias that the Preparatory Commission for the Comprehensive Nuclear-Test-Ban Treaty Organization[233] is proposing to employ it in a broadly similar fashion. The problem encountered in this instance is apparently that the Commission 'has found that certain geographical coordinates for monitoring station locations' specified in the Convention were 'not feasible'.[234] The proposal is therefore that once the CTBT enters into force, the list of coordinates will be communicated to the first CoP, with the proposal that Article 79 be used 'to substitute corrected coordinates to reflect the actual coordinates of the stations established during the preparatory phase'. In point of general principle, indeed, it is actually not even necessary to wait for entry into force in order to initiate the rectification process, if it is feasible and desirable to act sooner.[235]

It would certainly be interesting to discover if there are other precedents for utilisation of the rectification process in this way. Its great advantages would seem to be that, (i) as indicated previously, it can be applied at any moment after authentication of the text; (ii) the *procès-verbal* procedure through which it is effectuated is both straightforward and familiar and (iii) its availability depends only upon the absence of objection.[236] Consequently, it seems to be the optimum process for making the necessary adjustments to the text, one where tacit acceptance is already the established rule. We have seen earlier how Article 31(3)(a–b) VCLT, albeit a rather slender reed for the considerable weight it is being asked to bear, can be viewed as having invested the process through which treaties are interpreted with a certain dynamism and flexibility that might otherwise have been lacking. The suggestion here, in effect, is that this autopoietic potential might be directed reflexively upon the VCLT itself, with the result that concepts such as 'rectification' might come to be understood and applied in ways which may not have been specifically envisaged by those who originally drafted the Convention itself. From a purely formalistic perspective, such transformations may appear problematic, but the overriding contemporaneous need in international affairs is surely not for unrelenting

---

[233] For details concerning the Commission, the Organization and the Treaty itself, see www.ctbto.org.

[234] See Section 8 of the chapter of Tabassi and Elias, at p. 608 of this volume. The location references in question may be found in Annex 1 to the Protocol to the Convention.

[235] Art. 79(1) VCLT suggests that the procedure may be applied at any time after authentication of the text: *supra* n. 166.

[236] See Art. 79(2) VCLT: *ibid.*

mechanistic formalism but for well-directed organic dynamism, so that the constantly changing demands of global political intercourse can more effectively be addressed. A further virtue of such exegesis is that it is typically conducted on a relatively informal, pragmatic, trial-and-error basis, with the result that experiments in practice which seem to be proving unsuccessful may be modified, reformulated or abandoned entirely without undue technical or bureaucratic formality.

A key message to be derived from this experience of evolutionary development in treaty law is that there may be valuable lessons and instructive practice to be found in areas very far removed from those with which any particular specialist practitioner is likely to be familiar, placing a premium on the maintenance within the overall discipline of cross-fertilisation and coherence to the greatest extent possible. To resort to the biological analogy once again, it is now increasingly recognised that cooperation and coordination, whether within or across species barriers, have proved at least as important as competition and compartmentalisation to evolutionary change and ecological process generally. Consequently, the tendency towards sub-categorisation and fragmentation within the public international legal system generally must be counted a major impediment to progress, and as a further unfortunate manifestation of left-brain predominance in our thought-processes generally.

It must, of course, be recognised that the process envisaged is not altogether free of hazard, and it would certainly be understandable if there were those that feared the development of some kind of unconstrained 'free-for-all' in the contextual, and indeed trans-contextual, application and evolutionary development of the fundamental concepts and principles of treaty law. By way of reassurance, it might be noted that there are in fact a number of institutional safeguards within the international legal order that help to mitigate the absence of permanent institutions created by the VCLT for its own internal purposes, and above all to serve as the guardian of its own inspirational and operational flame. The first concerns the availability of the International Court of Justice to correct any major departures from the path of normative rectitude that might emerge from the many manifestations of its day-to-day application. Yet, here, it might fairly be observed that the vagaries and infrequency of litigation are such as to render this a rather unreliable source of security. At the same time, it should not be overlooked that the VCLT is itself the creation of a permanent organ of the United Nations which enjoys considerable authority and capacity, namely the ILC, and that its establishment under that hand should not be seen as merely a self-contained, once-and-for-all exercise in official codification but rather as an individual staging-post along a much more complex and protracted journey of legal reform.

Thus, the 1969 Vienna Convention was followed in due course by the later treaties of 1978 and 1986, which covered matters that had been deliberately omitted from its own purview, as well as an additional set of provisions in 2001, this time not cast in treaty form,[237] which addressed a topic situated at the interface between treaty law and that governing other forms of obligation, to wit State responsibility.[238] A more important point for present purposes is that the nature of the ILC's engagement with these issues is such that its formal interest is never completely relinquished: rather, it remains an integral element of the institutional ecology of the Vienna regime. Accordingly, one aspect of the 1969 codification which has generated particular difficulty – namely, the rules concerning reservations – has already been substantively revisited, while others are currently on the agenda.[239] Consequently, the legal regime for treaties can legitimately be regarded as being imbued with a permanent institutional dynamic, and hence systemic organic dimension, of its own; this is, moreover, of a rather singular, and singularly authoritative, character within the international legal order as a whole.

It is pertinent to recall here the trenchant response offered by the ILC, at the outset of their revisitation of the vexed issue of reservations to treaties, to the suggestion of the Human Rights Committee in 1994 that the relevant provisions of the VCLT were 'inappropriate to address the problem of reservations to human rights treaties'.[240] To the contrary, the ILC observed, the VCLT regime was no less applicable to such treaties than to any other type, and any shortcomings in its provision were better addressed by its own expanded clarification of that regime than by human rights bodies exceeding the powers afforded to them.[241] To an

---

[237] Official Records of the General Assembly, Fifty-Sixth Session, Supp. No. 10 (A/56/10).

[238] For exposition of this relationship, see in particular the contributions to this volume of Tams and Fitzmaurice at pp. 440–467 (Chapter 14) and 748–789 (Chapter 23) respectively.

[239] For details, see the *Analytical Guide* to the work of the ILC: *supra* n. 166.

[240] Human Rights Committee, General Comment No. 24: Issues Relating to Reservations made upon Ratification or Accession to the Covenant or the Optional Protocols thereto, or in Relation to Declarations under Article 41 of the Covenant, U.N. Doc. CCPR/C/21/Rev.1/Add.6, 11 Apr. 1994.

[241] See 'Preliminary Conclusions on Reservations to Normative Multilateral Treaties including Human Rights Treaties', Report of the ILC on the Work of its 49th Session, *YbILC* (1997–II), Part Two, 57 (especially paragraphs 2 and 8).

impartial observer, it may seem difficult to disagree. What this exchange therefore tends to demonstrate is that, while substantive context is undoubtedly vital to the application of any regulatory process, the international community's fundamental, long-term interests are almost certainly less well-served by a multiplicity of treaty law regimes each *constructed in an essentially context-specific fashion* than by a single law of treaties that is simply *construed and applied in an appropriately context-sensitive manner*. The ILC, moreover, seems particularly well-equipped to oversee this operation and keep it on track, especially since both the capacity and the propensity to keep abreast of legal scholarship and of national juridical developments are enshrined within its very DNA. In that sense, it fulfils a role akin to that of a biological keystone species, helping to maintain an overall homeodynamic balance within the regulatory ecosystem as a whole – if not exactly an apex predator, then an apex predicator at least! As indicated previously, such creatures are critical to the way in which natural selection operates and evolution plays out.

3   Some Tentative Conclusions

Although the 'complex triangulation' which exists amongst the notions of concept, context and content has been long appreciated in disciplines such as architecture and the fine arts, it appears to have attracted much less overt attention within the realm of jurisprudence. Yet, this oversight represents a considerable impediment to our understanding of the operations of law, since the relationship can be shown to be as significant to the realisation of our normative structures as it is to their edificial and aesthetic counterparts. It may very well, indeed, underpin the process of creation in all its manifestations, since the means by which matter emerges from raw energy and living things from heredity are equally amenable to explanation in such terms. Furthermore, since these particular instantiations of creativity are of a very much more primal and foundational character than those by which paintings or buildings are brought into existence, they may have even more to teach us about the principles by which creation itself is governed.

The lessons, in fact, turn out to be rather sobering, especially for those who lament the uncertainties inherent in the contemporary law of treaties. For expert scrutiny of these other forms of creative process have revealed them to be not merely *fraught with* uncertainty but actually *wrought from* it. In the realm of biology, for example, it is the random mutations which occur in the genomes of living things in the course of the reproductive process that provide the source material for the strength, resilience and adaptability that will be required if organisms of that kind are to survive at all in the longer term. Similarly, it is the apparent capability of elementary particles to be in several places – and hence to explore several different pathways – at once that give rise to the extraordinary efficiency of processes such as photosynthesis, upon which all life is ultimately dependent. Whereas in the seventeenth and eighteenth centuries the pronouncement by Sir Isaac Newton of the basic laws of motion and mechanics offered promise of a world of absolute scientific predictability – and unrelenting human progress based upon it – science itself has subsequently confounded these expectations. Causation is now understood to be essentially probabilistic rather than definitive in character, and all attempts to achieve absolute certainty or definition must ultimately risk interfering with the causal process itself and thereby transform the very subject matter which is being investigated.

Yet, the vagaries of language are such that old expectations linger on in popular consciousness, where 'science' is still widely taken to be indicative of certain, incontrovertible knowledge or the process by which it is secured. Indeed, this misconception occurs even in formal deliberations and documentation – for example, in connection with the so-called 'precautionary' principle in environmental law, which preaches that the absence of 'full scientific certainty' should not be treated as a reason to postpone or preclude the adoption of measures for environmental protection.[242] This formulation is grounded upon the entirely false assumption (and may accordingly only serve to perpetuate the expectation) that the achievement of such certainty is only a matter of time, whereas in reality it is all but unattainable both in practice and in principle. Therefore, it should never have been treated even as a potential impediment to protective action in the first place, the only genuinely relevant issue being the precise level of risk at which a regulatory response should be deemed appropriate. Clearly, the very term 'science' is yet another example of a word being coined long before there was any genuine understanding of the phenomenon to which it relates:[243] ideally, the word selected to describe generically the pursuit of disciplines such as physics, chemistry and biology would never have been

---

[242] See, e.g., Principle 15 of the Rio Declaration on Environment and Development.
[243] Intriguingly, it was apparently none other than Whewell himself who was responsible: S. Ross, 'Scientist: The Story of a Word', *Annals of Science*, 18 (1962), 65–85.

grounded in the Latin root *sciens* (meaning 'knowing') at all but rather in the more appropriate alternative *cognoscens* (meaning 'becoming acquainted' or 'getting to know'). While that boat has doubtless sailed, we can at least strive to acknowledge the incongruity involved in our established lexicon and of the concomitant misconceptions into which we are prone to be drawn.

In particular, the craving for certainty in our understanding of the world may very well be the product of the left hemisphere of the human brain, as indeed is the conviction that such perfect grasp can actually be delivered by means of the reductive, mechanistic processes of mastery and control and the categorical, language-mediated abstractions in which the left-brain itself is disposed to specialise. Yet, although this mode of thinking has contrived to achieve predominance in the philosophical perspectives associated with certain regions and epochs – and most notably the European Enlightenment – the evidence suggests that this triumph has been secured at great cost and that the need remains for this mode of cognition to be balanced by and integrated with the more holistic intuitions and organic awareness of the right brain. Making sense of the world is, it seems, a little like handling an exceedingly hot potato, which must be rapidly transferred back and forth from one cerebral hand to the other if tolerable management of the troublesome item is to be secured without incurring undue injury. And just as it was science, in its narrowly focused manifestation of times gone by, that brought the reductive, mechanistic mode of thinking to the fore, so too it has been science, in its more recent, expansive and holistic form, that has provided the much-needed balance of perspective.

Yet, appreciation of this transformation has been extremely patchy and inconsistent across the broader spectrum of human intellectual endeavour. Where the discipline of law is concerned, much of the explicit discourse has seemed to remain becalmed in the past, with the result that explicit references to 'science' tend usually to reflect the Newtonian conception rather than the post-Darwinian. On that basis, the processes entailed in the creation, application and interpretation of legal norms will doubtless not seem very 'scientific', since, as the law of treaties amply demonstrates, absolute precision, certainty and predictability are scarcely evident. In response, certain commentators have called for fundamental reform of the principles of treaty law, with a view to the introduction of greater certainty, solidity and particularity through an entirely new regulatory mechanism or series of mechanisms to govern different treaty types.

It is difficult to deny that certain aspects of the Vienna codification process, and especially its timing, left a certain amount to be desired and that if the entire exercise were to be repeated now, the end result might look rather different. In particular, it is likely that a few particular anomalies, incongruities and uncertainties might profitably be removed. Yet, at the same time, the vagaries of formal language and the limitations of human perspicacity would almost certainly be such that novel deficiencies and causes of uncertainty or concern would be introduced. During this process, moreover, the security born of familiarity would be jeopardised or lost entirely and established continuities of understanding exposed to disruption. Worst of all, if a series of sub-regimes or separate streams of treaty law were envisaged for different categories of treaty, a new dimension of complexity and potential internal tension would be introduced. Much of this would relate to the process for addressing the issue of categorisation itself, since real treaties resist allocation into neat compartments in the way that this proposal envisages. In addition, rules of reconciliation would inevitably be required not only for determining the legal relationship between individual treaties themselves but also for that which pertained between the diverse variants of treaty law that would come into being. In the event, considerable time, energy and resources would have to be expended on creating a highly complex legal regime that might ultimately prove no better (or, indeed, considerably worse) than what is already available.

Even if the actual aim were to introduce a regime of the more modern, 'living instrument' style, the question which would naturally then arise would concern the respects in which it would actually differ in substance from what we have already have, since, as demonstrated in the foregoing sections, treaty law in general appears to have assumed a far more organic hue over recent years and, indeed, almost from the moment of conception of the VCLT itself. A host of operationalising institutions stand ready at its beck and call, with the ILC itself occupying pride of place, so that the rougher edges of the regime can be (and in some cases already have been) smoothed off by dint of formal, substantive clarification or adaptive, evolutionary interpretation. The need to tolerate an occasional shortfall in certainty and solidity may be a price worth paying if greater flexibility and enhanced fitness constitute the prize, a realisation which seems to have been grasped, if a little tentatively as yet, by the international community across the spectrum of its treaty-making functions generally. Along the way, the international law of treaties seems gradually to be assuming both the general ethos and the specific trappings of a *genuinely* scientific perspective (as it must currently be understood), even if not explicitly under that rubric. It is therefore surely time that lawyers began explicitly to recognise that 'science' is no longer what it was once supposed to be, being much the better for the change, and that there is accordingly no incongruity at all in labelling the modern approach to the creation and implementation of treaties and treaty law as 'scientific' in that revised sense.

In support of this proposal, our preliminary review of the operation of treaty-making and the application of treaty law across a wide range of substantive areas does not seem to have exposed a host of significant problems that are genuinely attributable to its unitary nature, as the threads which bind the subject together seem significantly stronger than the forces that would pull it apart. In that respect, it might be compared to a spider's web, the ostensible flimsiness of which is belied by its actual tensile strength, often claimed to be proportionally greater than that of steel.[244] Naturally enough, that has made spiders' silk a subject of great interest to the technological community, since its potential for all sorts of mechanistic applications promises to be very considerable. Yet in order fully to understand the web the spider spins, one must first secure an understanding of 'the web that spins the spider':[245] that is to say, the network of ecological relationships through which spiders have come to be as they are, and contrived to maintain themselves, over the course of evolutionary time.[246] It is also now beginning to be understood (especially in light of the latest global economic crash) that the study of such networks may have much of value to tell us about the operations of complex systems generally, whether natural or man-made.[247]

Identification of the specific characteristics that impart strength and resilience to natural ecosystems remains a work in progress, but there is a growing consensus that one crucial consideration concerns the precise balance to be struck between connectivity and modularity. In particular, ecological networks tend to organize themselves into smaller hubs or

---

[244] *Supra* n. 132.

[245] Unfortunately, the original source of this memorable aphorism defining evolutionary process now escapes me.

[246] As to which, see, e.g., L. Brunetta and C. L. Craig, *Spider Silk: Evolution and 400 Million Years of Spinning, Waiting, Snagging and Mating* (New Haven, CT: Yale University Press, 2010) and D. Penney and P. A. Selden, *Fossil Spiders: The Evolutionary History of a Mega-Diverse Order* (Manchester: Siri Scientific Press, 2011).

[247] See Capra and Luisi, *supra* n. 109, and R. M. May, S. A. Levin and G. Sugihara, 'Complex Systems: Ecology for Bankers', *Nature*, 451 (2008), 893–895.

clusters of relationships, at the heart of which are typically to be found the keystone species, and these clusters are themselves interlinked by a looser series of connections.[248] This arrangement is such that breaches of individual connections can usually be tolerated without causing the entire network to collapse, giving time for them to be repaired wherever possible. By virtue of these features, the spider's web has come to be regarded not merely as a micro-scale manifestation of ecological activity in its own right but as a potent metaphor for the nature of the biosphere as a whole,[249] of which it arguably represents a form of fractal. Yet, however strong such webs may be, they are demonstrably not indestructible,[250] especially if key anchoring points at the periphery of the web or the focal points at the heart of the clusters come under sustained attack, and it is, of course, precisely through such assaults that human activities are coming to impose an intolerable strain upon the planet's ecological life-support system.

In broadly analogous fashion, the coherence and continued viability of the international legal order is currently being placed under strain by a range of factors, with the proliferation of treaty-making activity, the enhanced complexity of individual arrangements and the corresponding growth of sub-disciplinary expertise producing a well-recognised fragmentation within the system and threatening to cause it to unravel. It is natural that treaty-making activities will evolve in the form of subject-based clusters, which may even represent a source of its strength, but the ultimate viability of the process of norm creation will surely depend on the threads of *interconnectivity* which hold the entire system together. In such circumstances, the prospect of a series of sub-disciplines of treaty law, each tailored to the supposed needs of particular treaty types, seems one to be viewed with grave concern: the maintenance of unifying, pervasive norms of treaty law (including that of State responsibility, in so far as is relevant) would seem to be much more in keeping with the needs of the international community as a whole. Undoubtedly, each individual area of international law is likely to be affected by certain considerations that are peculiar to itself, and these may well demand

---

[248] See, generally, R. V. Solé and J. Bascompte, *Self-Organisation in Complex Systems* (Princeton, NJ: Princeton University Press, 2006).

[249] Thus, the original linear metaphor of 'food chains' has now been superseded in technical discourse by that of 'food webs', as to which see C. Park, *Oxford Dictionary of Environment and Conservation* (Oxford: Oxford University Press, 2007), p. 175.

[250] See, e.g., J. M. Montoya, S. L. Pimm and R. V. Solé, 'Ecological Networks and Their Fragility', *Nature*, 442 (2006), 259–264.

formal recognition in the law of treaties as a whole; as indicated earlier, however, there is reason to suppose that this recognition is best afforded not through a multiplicity of treaty law regimes constructed in an essentially context-specific fashion but through a single, all-embracing regime that is construed and applied in an appropriately context-sensitive manner, as is broadly the case at present.

This conclusion naturally depends upon the existence of certain unifying concepts of sufficient cogency, flexibility and universal valency to provide the connectivity which any system requires. It is difficult to deny that the key concepts by which the established law of treaties is underpinned – consent, intention, good faith, privity, object and purpose, obligation, breach, interpretation and the like – are somewhat uncertain and that the more intense and abstracted the scrutiny to which they are subjected, the more elusive they are likely to appear. Yet, that is really only to be expected, since it is in the very nature of matter, whether in its physical or purely conceptual manifestation: as explained previously, it is only through the specific contextualisation of such material that meaningful content can emerge. Where this emergent meaning is concerned, moreover, absolute certainty and solidity must be recognised as inherently unattainable, and should in any event be considered as readily tradable against the rival considerations of flexibility and adaptability. At present, there is little to indicate that the system is seriously out of kilter, though that is certainly not to suggest that it is altogether free from risk.

Indeed, if there is currently a major cause for concern, it must surely be the aforementioned fragmentation which is evident within the international legal order as a whole and threatens to undermine its most cherished aspirations. One aspect of the risk lies in the different fragments drifting progressively apart, though here, as noted earlier, the existence of a uniform law of treaties is one of the factors which offer a degree of cohesive force. Potentially more serious, however, is the converse threat, namely of the abrasion or outright collision of their substantive masses, whereby different bodies of treaty-based norms come into actual conflict. Here the most appropriate analogies are drawn less from the world of ecology than from that of geology and plate tectonics: the havoc wrought by the grinding together of the earth's lithospheric plates is all too well known[251] and has obvious and

---

[251] For details, see, e.g., N. Oreskes (ed.), *Plate Tectonics: An Insider's History of the Modern Theory of the Earth* (Boulder, CO: Westview, 2003) and D. L. Turcotte and G. Schubert, *Geodynamics* (Cambridge: Cambridge University Press, 3rd ed., 2014), esp. pp. 1–91.

immediate parallels in the world of treaty law. This is something with which the Vienna regime seems rather less well equipped to deal, offering only a few spindly bargepoles to stave off whole-scale inter-continental impaction.

Foremost amongst these, perhaps, is Article 31(3)(c) VCLT, a vaguely stated and long-neglected provision,[252] which certainly allows for an accommodation between different bodies of rules to be attempted but provides little by way of positive guidance or assistance through which it might be actually accomplished.[253] Rather more definition is provided by the provisions of Articles 53 and 64 VCLT, concerning the overriding nature of peremptory norms, though the substantive scope of these provisions is plainly limited, in the sense that few treaty conflicts are likely to bring them into play. There is doubtless room for greater clarification concerning the precise reach of *ius cogens*, and possibly for some expansion of that category, but rather than seeking to increase the chances for freely negotiated norms to be nullified entirely, it seems preferable that emphasis be placed upon their more effective and systematic harmonisation and prioritisation. Here the Vienna Convention offers explicitly only the dubiously framed rules of temporal priority found in Article 30, as supplemented by whatever canons may be derived from customary law, such as the *lex generalis/lex specialis* principle.[254] Yet, where two broadly comparable and largely distinct bodies of treaty norms chance to overlap in a particular small field in such a way as to produce a potential conflict of obligations, the task of determining which, if any, should be deemed *specialis* may well prove impossible. Furthermore, the relationship between this principle and that of Article 30 VCLT itself is by no means clear, suggesting that new rules of reconciliation may be required to harmonise or prioritise the rules of reconciliation themselves. Nor is this really a situation where matters can safely be left to the parties to make express provision to avoid such conflicts, for here it has become standard practice (indeed, almost a standing joke) for clauses to be

---

[252] It has been justly described as 'rather unrevealing of its intentions': Gardiner, *supra* n. 217, at p. 485.

[253] See, further, D. French, 'Treaty Interpretation and the Incorporation of Extraneous Legal Rules', *ICLQ*, 55 (2006), 281–314, and C. McLachlan, 'The Principle of Systemic Integration and Article 31(3)(c) of the Vienna Convention', *ICLQ*, 54 (2005), 279–320.

[254] For discussion, see C. J. Borgen, 'Treaty Conflicts and Normative Fragmentation' in Hollis (ed.), *supra* n. 207, pp. 448–471.

inserted within treaties forswearing any intent to impact upon other such instruments, even where it is evident that serious incompatibilities may exist.[255]

It seems that we may once again have succumbed here to the insistent and atomistically oriented demands of the left brain for abstraction, analytical division, compartmentalisation and competition to the detriment of the more holistic and integrative perspectives of the right, creating another instance of need for this imbalance to be addressed. It is, however, perhaps unrealistic to expect that clashes of commitment of the kind highlighted previously can be avoided by the mere development of general rules of treaty law, since everything will depend upon the precise nature and consequences of the incompatibility in question, the strength and seriousness of the political imperatives that underlie the respective sets of obligations and the identity of the parties bound by them. Nor is it necessarily feasible, given the sheer scale and intensity of treaty-making activity, simply to demand higher levels of awareness of potential clashes from particular sets of negotiating States. More useful will be the development beyond the law of treaties of specially crafted substantive principles of reconciliation of particular bodies of norms, such as the principle of sustainable development, though the risk remains that these will simply prove too vague and generalised to facilitate a satisfactory accommodation of competing concerns in any particular case.

What really seems to be required, therefore, is a new tectonics of coherence and conciliation to govern the normative activities of the international community, which may very well require the creation of dedicated institutions to oversee its implementation and development in a suitably organic fashion. Perhaps a process should be established whereby proposed treaties are scrutinised in advance by some suitably qualified inter-sub-disciplinary team to assess their potential for 'transboundary' disruption of cognate areas of law – a form of impact assessment for the international normative environment, if you will. Any such regime would doubtless require the development of its own specialised principles, practices and procedures, which may in turn demand that attention be given to the formulation of novel concepts, and to the ways in which they can best be contextualised to create normative content of the most effective, integrated and harmonic kind.

But that will have to be a task for another day and another work.

---

[255] Note especially the studiously Delphic preamble to the 2000 Cartagena Protocol on Biosafety, 2226 UNTS 208.

INDEX

CPSIA information can be obtained
at www.ICGtesting.com
Printed in the USA
LVHW080347141220
674108LV00017B/781

9 781108 978521